A Day in the Life of an American Worker

1

A Day in the Life of an American Worker

200 Trades and Professions through History

VOLUME 1: 1607–1914

Nancy Quam-Wickham and
Ben Tyler Elliott, Editors

ABC-CLIO®

An Imprint of ABC-CLIO, LLC
Santa Barbara, California • Denver, Colorado

Library of Congress Cataloging-in-Publication Data

Names: Quam-Wickham, Nancy, editor. | Elliott, Ben Tyler, editor.
Title: A day in the life of an American worker / Nancy Quam-Wickham and Ben Tyler Elliott, editors.
Description: Santa Barbara, California : ABC-CLIO, [2020] | Includes bibliographical references and index. |
Identifiers: LCCN 2019015045 (print) | LCCN 2019017984 (ebook) | ISBN 9781440845017 (eBook) | ISBN 9781440845000 (set : alk. paper) | ISBN 9781440845024 (volume 1) | ISBN 9781440845031 (volume 2)
Subjects: LCSH: Labor—United States—History. | Occupations—United States—History. | Employees—United States—History. | United States—Social conditions. | United States—Economic conditions.
Classification: LCC HD8066 (ebook) | LCC HD8066 .D39 2020 (print) | DDC 331.700973—dc23
LC record available at https://lccn.loc.gov/2019015045

ISBN: 978-1-4408-4500-0 (set)
978-1-4408-4502-4 (vol. 1)
978-1-4408-4503-1 (vol. 2)
978-1-4408-4501-7 (ebook)

24 23 22 21 20 1 2 3 4 5

This book is also available as an eBook.

ABC-CLIO
An Imprint of ABC-CLIO, LLC

ABC-CLIO, LLC
147 Castilian Drive
Santa Barbara, California 93117
www.abc-clio.com

This book is printed on acid-free paper ∞

Manufactured in the United States of America

Contents

Preface

This book focuses on the daily experiences of workers in distinct occupations and trades throughout American history. These are the generations of working people who built our nation as we know it today. Workers as varied as watchmen during the American Revolution, pharmacists during the post–World War II period, and Antebellum-era hucksters are covered equally as each are representatives of the American workforce. Thus, this text cannot be considered only working-class history, nor is it a study of the struggles and successes of organized labor. Instead, this work takes an expansive view of the American worker, one more extensive than that of Chicago's twentieth-century journalist and oral historian Studs Terkel, who wrote in the introduction to his 1974 classic book, *Working*, about the ambiguity of The Job: "A search . . . for daily meaning as well as daily bread, for recognition as well as cash, for astonishment rather than torpor" (Terkel 1974, xiii). While informed by Terkel's observations, this book is based on the premise that all work has value and should be honored. The waste collector and the farrier are every bit as important to their contemporary societies as the social worker, IT architect, and social media coordinator are today.

In this book, we present an introduction to the variety of jobs that Americans performed. Some workers may have detested their roles, while others found satisfaction—even joy—in doing their jobs day after day. Entries outline the typical daily responsibilities of a worker in an occupation or a profession. However, the occupations and professions covered within this volume are not at all inclusive; it would have been impossible to address the many different jobs Americans held during our over four hundred years of history. Instead, this book comprises representative selections.

Two additional principles inform the choices of the occupations included in this volume. The working people who held these professions were an incredibly diverse lot: indigenous and immigrant, white and black, men and women, the elderly and children. Our choice of occupations was in part to highlight the diversity of our nation. Additionally, we recognize that occupations change over time, sometimes remarkably, sometimes relatively little. While a pharmacist might also have been an entrepreneur running their own drug store in the mid-1950s, by the twenty-first century, they may be an employee filling prescriptions in a large drug warehouse for a corporation providing mail-order prescription services. In that sense, a pharmacist's social status and attitude toward "The Job" may in fact have changed dramatically over time. Similarly, a machinist today may create many of the products previously made by a patternmaker in the late nineteenth century, but rather than using tools, paper, pen, and muscle, they now use sophisticated computer software to create a design and then program computer-operated machining tools to create everything from trinkets to sell at a local craft fair to parts for rocket engines. Today, machinists and pharmacists are equally likely to wear a laboratory coat while working; this certainly has not always been the case. Furthermore, we assert that the nature of occupations is fluid, not static. Industrialization processes, advances in material and technologies, and computers have driven many of these occupational changes.

This book is divided into six primary sections that are sorted by era, and each section is prefaced with an introduction that provides context to the entries contained within. While there are many vocations that have been around for millennia—like bakers, for instance—many jobs only existed for a short time. The slave driver's occupation no longer exists in America, but examining the daily life of a slave driver informs the era in which they lived, what came before, and why things needed to change. Examining major eras of American history through the lens of their relevant occupations provides an opportunity to see how broader historical contexts were reflected in the lives of the average American. The steelworker's life, for example, changed drastically once the United States entered World War II and the federal government needed an incredible amount of steel as quickly as possible; their hours and pay increased substantially, and those changes had a profound effect on the economy, the workers' neighborhoods, and American society.

It is true that this book could have been organized differently, or its chapters could have been sorted into different eras. But we have chosen to parse this cross section of American labor at watershed moments in U.S. history: the end of the colonial era, the start of the Civil War, the end of Reconstruction, the start of World War I, the start of World War II, and the rise of the internet. American life is always evolving, but these few moments have, in many ways, been the most pivotal in U.S. history—both broadly and as effectuated in the daily lives of its citizens.

This is not to say that these moments are elevated above all others in importance. Rather, they serve the same function as an intermission—a sensible break from the action. But that these breaks are foregrounded herein should not distract from the other divisions, struggles, and revelations that existed and persisted during, between, and across these eras. The industrial revolutions of the late eighteenth and nineteenth centuries, for example, had a profound impact on every sector of the economy and society, and they were in many ways apolitical, ubiquitous developments that were agnostic toward most of the legislative, societal, or international challenges that the United States faced. Likewise, changes in the organization of production in the late nineteenth and twentieth centuries, and the invention of computers and the internet in the late twentieth and early twenty-first centuries, have enjoyed similar sovereign progressions and certainly affected American life in persistent, evolving ways—not all of them positive. But those layers notwithstanding, we believe that this book benefits greatly from its presented structure. Each watershed moment had an immediate and demonstrable impact on every industry, and, branching out, such moments are common touchstones in countless other books and avenues of study.

Many entries have also been appended with primary documents, which provide a "boots-on-the-ground" snapshot of singular voices and lived experiences that have been directly involved with the performance of the associated job. After you read an entry, you may be able to read an oral history of someone who labored as this book describes, or a historical newspaper advertisement for a job posting, or an excerpt from a transcription of a famous speech.

The vast majority of people have to work for a living. This has always been true. The prevalence of this shared experience forms a common bond that brings society together and fosters understanding. It is our hope that this book helps to further that understanding, illuminate unfamiliar histories, and cultivate empathy for the workers who have been—and the workers we are.

FURTHER READING

Terkel, Studs. 1974. *Working: People Talk About What They Do All Day and How They Feel About What They Do.* New York: Pantheon/Random House.

Chronology

ca. 1540s	Spanish whalers reach North America and sail throughout the Gulf of Maine.
1607	English colonists settle at Jamestown in Chesapeake, Virginia.
1612	Englishman John Rolfe imports tobacco seeds to Chesapeake from the West Indies, leading to the growth of the colonies' first significant export crop.
1619	The first African slaves arrive in colonial Virginia.
1620	Pilgrims arrive in present-day Massachusetts at Plymouth.
1622	Native American fighters kill 347 English settlers at Jamestown in colonial Virginia.
1624	The Netherlands establishes a permanent settlement on Manhattan Island to serve as a fur-trading post.
1662	Virginia establishes a law specifying that a child's status rests on the mother's status, defining chattel slavery.
1676	Nathaniel Bacon leads a rebellion of farmers, indentured servants, and slaves against the colonial policies of Governor William Berkeley.
1681	William Penn receives the Pennsylvania charter.
1701	The oldest-surviving sales records of silversmith Francis Richardson are made, marking the beginning of a revolutionary American silversmithing dynasty.
1715	War between English colonists and Indians in South Carolina leads to the deaths of ninety colonists.
1739	In the largest colonial slave uprising to date, African-born slaves in South Carolina revolt in attempt to flee to Spanish Florida, where they would be emancipated.
1750	After arriving in Boston a year earlier, shopkeeper Elizabeth Murray opens a business selling imported goods from England.

1767	England adopts a new tax on all imported goods in American colonies; in response, colonists organize a boycott of English-made goods, which encourages domestic production.
1773	A group of colonists throw shipment of imported tea off vessels in Boston Harbor in an act of protest against British taxation in an event that will become known as The Boston Tea Party.
1774	Delegates from twelve colonies join to organize opposition to the Intolerable Acts.
1775	April: The Second Continental Congress authorizes the formation of a continental army after open warfare begins between local American militias and British troops in Massachusetts.
July 4, 1776	Congress issues the Declaration of Independence, forming the United States.
1780	Nantucket native William Rotch moves his whaling operations to Bedford, Massachusetts, which will become the center of the American whaling industry by the early 1800s.
1785	Martha Ballard begins keeping a detailed diary recording her work as a midwife in Massachusetts, providing one of the best sources of the daily life of a woman worker.
1791	U.S. Secretary of the Treasury Alexander Hamilton releases his Report on the Subject of Manufactures to Congress, detailing a plan to impose heavy tariffs on British imports to stimulate American manufacturing.
October 28, 1793	Eli Whitney applies for a patent for his cotton gin, facilitating the spread of long fiber cotton culture throughout the Deep South.
1793	The first fully mechanized cotton mill opens at Pawtucket, Rhode Island.
1804–1806	Meriwether Lewis and William Clark lead the Corps of Discovery from St. Charles, Missouri, to the Pacific Coast (and back) to explore and map lands of the recent Louisiana Purchase.
1808	The U.S. government bans importation of slaves.
1808	A negative assessment of the nation's transportation infrastructure leads to major internal improvements, which will be financed by the federal government rather than local communities.
1812–1815	The U.S. declares war on Britain, sparking the War of 1812, in response to a naval blockade, impressment of American sailors, and other long-standing resentments.

1817	The Erie Canal Company is organized, leading to construction of a canal through New York state.
1820	A group of American missionaries arrives in Hawaii in an effort to convert native Hawaiians to Christianity.
September 27, 1821	Mexico declares independence from Spain, opening California and much of the Southwest's cattle ranching.
1831	The first indigenous nation of the Five Civilized tribes is removed from their ancestral lands in what will become known as the Trail of Tears, which will contribute to the expansion of cotton culture in Georgia, parts of Alabama, Mississippi, and Louisiana.
1834	Lowell mill workers organize the first of two strikes (second in 1836) to protest company paternalism and cuts in wages.
1835	Carpenters and masons in Boston wage a seven-month-long strike for a ten-hour day.
September 4, 1841	The Preemption Act allows squatters to purchase up to 160 acres of public land for $1.25 per acre before the land they're living on goes up for public sale, which facilitates a land speculation boom.
1844	In Wisconsin, iron ore production begins in the Marquette mountain range, stimulating production of metal goods.
1847	New Hampshire adopts a mandatory ten-hour workday.
January 24, 1848	John Sutter's employee, carpenter James Marshall, discovers gold in the American River at Coloma in the foothills of the Sierra Nevada, sparking the California Gold Rush.
May 30, 1848	The Treaty of Guadalupe Hidalgo ends the war with Mexico, which cedes extensive lands in Texas, the Southwest, and California to the United States and leads to the expansion of slavery.
1856	In *Dred Scott v. Stanford*, the U.S. Supreme Court rules that the United States has no rights to prohibit slavery in its territories.
1859	Edwin Drake discovers commercial quantities of oil in Titusville, Pennsylvania.
1861–1865	The Civil War is responsible for more than 1.6 million casualties—or roughly 5 percent of the 1865 U.S. population.
June 18, 1861	The private U.S. Sanitary Commission is founded to provide support to injured and ill Union soldiers.
1862	The Homestead Act provides for distribution of free land in the West, which opened western lands to farmers and provided for the funding of public schools.

July 1, 1862	President Abraham Lincoln signs the first of the Pacific Railway Acts, authorizing construction of the transcontinental railroad on a northerly route.
1863	The Union's largest prisoner of war camp is established at Point Lookout, Maryland, housing up to twenty-two thousand Confederate prisoners on forty acres; the camp employs African Americans as guards.
January 1, 1863	President Abraham Lincoln signs an executive order to abolish slavery in the United States.
1864	The first industrial-scale production of steel in the United States begins at Wyandotte Iron works near Detroit, Michigan, revolutionizing steel production in the country.
March 3, 1865	Congress establishes the Bureau of Refugees, Freedmen, and Abandoned Lands to protect African Americans in the former Confederacy and assist in their recovery.
December 6, 1865	The Thirteenth Amendment to the U.S. Constitution, which abolishes slavery and involuntary servitude, except as punishment for a crime, is ratified by twenty-seven of the thirty-six states and becomes law.
1869	The nation's first national labor union was founded by Uriah Stephens as a secret organization to protect workers against employer intimidation.
1873–1877	A prolonged economic recession, brought on by the Panic of 1873, leads to wage cuts in many manufacturing industries and widespread suffering among the American working class.
1877	In the Compromise of 1877, the last of the U.S. army troops are withdrawn from the South, ending Reconstruction and leading to violence and discrimination against African Americans.
July 14–September 4, 1877	A Baltimore and Ohio railroad workers strike spreads across the country in the first Great Upheaval.
1982	In the Homestead Strike, steel and iron workers are locked out of the giant steel mills in Homestead, Pennsylvania.
May 6, 1882	President Chester Arthur signs legislation prohibiting most Chinese from immigrating to the United States, substantially impacting farming and rail labor forces in California and elsewhere.
September 2, 1885	White workers in Rock Springs, Wyoming, riot against employment of Chinese coal miners working for the Union

	Pacific Coal Company, killing at least twenty-eight miners and destroying the town's Chinese neighborhood.
May 4, 1886	Eight labor radicals are tried and convicted for the Chicago Haymarket Square bombing, although little evidence pointed to their involvement.
1886	In the second Great Upheaval, hundreds of thousands of railway and industrial workers strike throughout the nation.
December 8, 1886	The American Federation of Labor (AFL) is formed in response to industrial labor action in the 1880s, providing national structure and political influence for those trade unions.
1892	Workers begin mining iron ore at Minnesota's Mesabi Iron Range, which is the richest deposit discovered to date.
1893–1897	The Panic of 1893, brought on by a series of railroad company closings, instigates a serious economic depression that affects the entire American economy.
1894	The Pullman Strike, in which members of the American Railway Union protest against paternalism and wage cuts in the company town of Pullman, near Chicago, spreads to most rail companies west of the Great Lakes region, eventually involving nearly 250,000 workers, prompting President Grover Cleveland to order the U.S. Marshals and Army to intervene to stop the strike.
April 1904	The National Child Labor Committee forms in response to results from the 1900 U.S. census, which showed that one in six children between the ages of five and ten were gainfully employed.
June 30, 1906	In likely response to the 1905 publication of Upton Sinclair's novel *The Jungle*, which exposed systemic, hazardous meat processing practices, President Theodore Roosevelt signs legislation regulating drugs and prohibiting the manufacture of foods that contain "deleterious ingredients."
December 6, 1907	An explosion deep in the mines of the Fairmont Mine Company in Monongah, West Virginia, kills hundreds of mostly immigrant workers.
February 12, 1909	The National Association for the Advancement of Colored People (NAACP), a major civil rights organization working to dismantle Jim Crow and fight for racial equality, is founded in New York City.
November 1909	Members of the Women's National Trade Union League of America, who are employed in the New York City shirtwaist

	industry, strike to demand better wages and improved working conditions.
March 25, 1911	A garment factory catches fire in New York City, killing 146 young, mostly immigrant workers.
1912–1918	The first of two coal wars begins in southern West Virginia, leading to armed skirmishes between miners and their allies on one side and armed security guards, coal companies, local police, state militias, and federal troops on the other.
1913	Congress passes legislation creating the Department of Labor.
1915–1970	Nearly six million African Americans migrate to the North and West, seeking better jobs, housing, and schools.
April 15, 1916	The first national labor organization representing school teachers, early childhood educators, college professors, and other paraprofessionals is founded in Chicago.
1919–1921	The Second Coal Wars in southern West Virginia feature open warfare between coal miners and their allies and employers, private security firms, and others.
August 18, 1920	Women's suffrage is ratified, granting women the right to vote.
October 1929	The U.S. stock market crashes and signals the beginning of a twelve-year-long Great Depression, which will impact every Western industrialized country.
November 8, 1932	Franklin D. Roosevelt wins the U.S. presidency in a landslide against incumbent Herbert Hoover and directs the founding of the first New Deal.
June 16, 1933	President Roosevelt signs legislation that allows workers in most industries to organize into unions.
1933	Thousands of mostly Mexican American agricultural workers strike against cotton growers, who retaliate by evicting workers from company housing, which leads to violence and subsequent government intervention.
May 9–July 31, 1934	A coastwide strike of longshoremen escalates in July when San Francisco police kill two workers at a planned protest, which inspires a four-day strike in which 150,000 workers bring the city of San Francisco to a standstill.
May 16–August 21, 1934	When warehouse workers are left out of a Teamsters strike agreement, the Teamsters call for a general strike; Governor Olson calls in the National Guard to bring an end to the walkout.

1935	The U.S. Department of the Interior establishes a Board of Indian Arts and Crafts to encourage tribal people to engage in traditional arts and crafts to attain economic self-sufficiency.
July 5, 1935	The Wagner Act establishes the National Labor Relations Board, authorizes workers to strike against their employers, stipulates that employers must bargain collectively when a majority of workers join a union, and prevents intimidation by employers.
August 14, 1935	President Franklin D. Roosevelt signs the Social Security system into law, creating a basic right to a simple pension in a citizen's old age and a federal system of unemployment insurance for workers.
November 9, 1935	The Committee for Industrial Organization (later known as the Congress of Industrial Organizations) is founded as an alternative for workers in industrial jobs whose interests were not represented by trade unions.
1936–1937	Autoworkers strike against General Motors in Flint, Michigan, which will lead to the formation of the United Autoworkers' Union (UAW).
May 26, 1937	Workers at several small steel companies, including Republic Steel and Youngstown Sheet and Tube, strike for union recognition as well as better wages and working conditions.
1938	Congress passes legislation establishing a minimum wage and overtime pay and prohibiting the employment of minors in difficult work environments.
1941	President Franklin D. Roosevelt issues Executive Order 8802, prohibiting racial discrimination in defense employment after a mass march on Washington, D.C. is planned to protest such discriminatory practices.
1941–1945	The United States enters World War II after the Japanese attack on Pearl Harbor in December 1941. Sixteen million Americans join the military.
1942–1945	After the United States enters the Second World War, 110,000 people of Japanese descent—60 percent of whom were native-born citizens—are forcibly removed from their homes in Washington, Oregon, and California and placed in internment camps.
1942–1964	The U.S. and Mexican governments coordinate a guest worker program in which Mexican workers migrate to fill jobs in manufacturing and agricultural industries in the United States.

May 29, 1943	Norman Rockwell's illustration of a woman defense worker, "Rosie the Riveter," appears on the cover of the *Saturday Evening Post*, becoming both a wartime propaganda icon as well as a symbol of women's empowerment on the job in post–World War II society.
June 22, 1944	In what will become known as the G.I. Bill, President Franklin D. Roosevelt signs the Serviceman's Readjustment Act, which provides a comprehensive package of benefits for returning veterans and leads to postwar booms in housing construction, small business growth, and education.
1946	The Great Strike Wave sweeps across the country, involving more than five million workers in key industries.
June 23, 1947	Congress overrides President Harry Truman's veto of the Taft-Hartley Act (later known as the Slave Labor Bill), which restricts the rights of labor unions to enforce boycotts, outlaws the "closed shop," requires unions to notify employers of impending strikes, and prohibits federal workers from striking without first resorting to arbitration.
1947	Jackie Robinson becomes modern Major League Baseball's first black player.
1948	Bell Labs introduces transistor technology, which allows for drastically smaller and more powerful electronic components and devices.
December 5, 1955	The federations of trade and industrial unions merge, creating a major organization representing the economic and political interests of most unionized American workers.
September 25, 1957	The AFL-CIO expels the International Brotherhood of Teamsters for corruption.
1958	The American Library Association holds the first annual event advocating for expansion of libraries into underserved communities and promotion of free public libraries for all.
1960	Members of the Writers Guild of America and the Screen Actors Guild strike against seven major Hollywood studios, demanding pension and welfare funds and residual payments for films rebroadcasted on television.
1960	Edward R. Murrow narrates a shocking television documentary that highlights the plight of America's migrant agricultural workers.
June 10, 1963	President John F. Kennedy signs the Equal Pay Act, which amends the Fair Labor Standards Act to prohibit gender-based wage discrimination.

August 28, 1963	Martin Luther King Jr.'s March for Jobs and Freedom brings hundreds of thousands of Americans to the nation's capital; King gives his "I Have a Dream" speech.
July 2, 1964	President Lyndon Johnson signs the landmark Civil Rights Act, which outlaws discrimination based on race, color, religion, sex, or nationality.
1964	President Johnson introduces his federal War on Poverty program, which is a comprehensive effort to reduce the nation's staggering 19 percent poverty rate.
1965	Cesar Chavez organizes the United Farm Workers Organizing Committee (later known as the United Farm Workers Union), which represents farm workers in California and the Southwest, most of whom are Mexican-American and Filipino.
December 29, 1970	President Richard Nixon signs the Occupational Safety and Health Act to ensure that employers provide employees with a sanitary work environment that is free from known hazards.
1973	The armed forces adopt a plan for a Modern Volunteer Army (MVA), leading to the professionalization of some military occupational categories and the emergence of the military as a major vocational training institution.
1976	Steve Jobs and Steve Wozniak introduce a consumer-friendly computer, the Apple I, which forms the basis of the home computer industry. The pair uses microprocessors developed in the early 1970s and incorporates software to run the computer.
August 3, 1981	The Professional Air Traffic Controllers Organization strikes; within two days, President Ronald Reagan orders striking workers to be fired, breaking the union and casting a pall on public union organizing.
1983	In an event that is widely viewed as originating the modern internet, Advanced Research Projects Agency Network adopts a computer communication model using the Transmission Control Protocol and Internet Protocol, developing a process by which connected computers could communicate with each other.
1988	The first modern Wal-Mart superstore opens in Bentonville, Arkansas, and offers tremendous discounts, which are subsidized by a majority workforce to whom Wal-Mart offers no benefits and minimum-wage pay.
1990	The Service Employees International Union develops an organizing campaign for janitors and cleaning staff in several

	major U.S. cities, including Los Angeles, Washington, D.C., Boston, Miami, and Houston.
September 3, 1991	A factory fire at the Imperial Chicken Processing plant in Hamlet, North Carolina, kills twenty-five workers, who had been locked into the factory.
1993	The 1989 invention of the World Wide Web is advanced further by the global adoption of URLs, which standardize the hosting procedure for internet addresses.
January 1, 1994	NAFTA, an agreement among Mexico, the United States, and Canada, seeks to facilitate movement of manufacturing and trade of goods by removing tariffs and other controls in three primary industries: agriculture, textiles, and auto-making.
1995	Amazon begins selling books online at discount prices; brick-and-mortar bookstores close as competition for customers intensifies
2007–2012	A subprime mortgage scandal leads to a worldwide recession; unemployment rises to high levels, and incomes decline.
2011	A broad coalition of students, the unemployed, and others emerge in New York to protest economic inequality.
2012	Nevada issues the first licenses for driverless cars on public roads as most major car manufacturers announce plans for fully autonomous vehicles to become common within fifteen years.
January 1, 2014	The Affordable Care Act goes into effect, making health insurance accessible to millions of Americans and creating the largest expansion of the social welfare state in a generation.
December 22, 2017	President Donald Trump signs legislation that changes the U.S. Tax Code for the first time in more than thirty years, reducing tax rates for most Americans and drastically increasing the national deficit.
July 6, 2018	Thirty-four billion dollars in new tariffs against Chinese imports go into position, to which China responds with retaliatory tariffs against American products across every major industry, threatening the start of the largest trade war in history.
2019	Some studies suggest that more than a quarter of Americans participate in the "gig economy," earning income through app-based service jobs like driving passengers or delivering food, with around 10 percent of laborers listing such work as their primary source of income.

1607–1775: THE COLONIAL PERIOD

INTRODUCTION

Some of the first English colonists, those who arrived at Jamestown in 1607, had high hopes of establishing a vibrant colony in the Chesapeake Bay region. Within months, though, expedition chronicler George Percy began documenting the problems attending this colonization venture. Surrounded by the indigenous Powhatan tribes, left without sufficient food and entrenched in their small fort, the 104 colonists suffered greatly. Percy's initial optimism about finding fat sturgeons swimming aimlessly in the rivers and seeing forest floors covered in strawberries gave way to a grim accounting of the dead, as eighteen men died during just twenty-two days in August. Two more men died in early September, as Percy wrote, "destroyed with cruell diseases, as Swellings, Flixes, Burning Fevers, and by warres, and some departed suddenly, but for the most part they died of mere famine . . . . Our food was but a small Can of Barlie sod in water, to five men a day, our drinke cold water taken out of the River, which was at a floude verie Salt, at a low tide full of slime and filth, which was the destruction of many of our men" (Tyler 1907, 22). A turn of events kept the company of explorers and would-be colonists alive, an episode that would be repeated among the earliest European colonists in the Americas: the "mortall enemies," members of the Paspahegh and Chickahominy tribes, rescued the men, bringing gifts of bread, fish, corn, and meat.

The members of this first group failed to understand the critical importance of labor to England's colonization efforts. Unlike the indigenous people who had saved them and the European arrivals who had come after them, the first colonists at Jamestown did not work to break the land, grow crops, build shelter, fish, or hunt deer for food and hides that would provide them with the necessary subsistence to survive in this New World. Such basic labor of subsistence—farming, fishing, hunting, tending to livestock, and building houses—made it possible for later colonists to establish a viable presence on the North American continent. Engaging in subsistence work and, later, growing tobacco for export were the primary economic activities of successful colonists in North America. However, those who relied on the generosity of local tribespeople or expected that a resupply ship would arrive on time often failed, leading to their deaths from starvation, sickness, and other causes.

On the other hand, those colonists who did not shrink from the immense physical demands of working the land, fishing in the local waters, and caring for livestock—or who found or coerced others to work for them in these occupations—created the foundation for England's successful colonies. While Americans have long thought of their nation as representing freedom, in the colonial period, nearly three-quarters of those who arrived in the colonies that would become the United States were not free. The largest group consisted of slaves (47 percent), brought there against their will from Africa and colonies in the Caribbean. The next largest group of laborers comprised indentured servants primarily, though not exclusively, from England, Scotland, Wales, and Northern Ireland, some of whom, like the slaves, had previously served on plantations in England's Atlantic and West Indian colonies: Bermuda, Jamaica, and Barbados. The third group was made up of convicts and common criminals sentenced by courts in England to be transported to "some of the Plantations across the Seas," as is recorded in the 1674 case of "Mall. Floyd," a habitual thief, formerly "a distressed Lady," who had frequented the "Inchanted Castle" of Newgate Prison (Old Bailey, July 17, 1674). In some colonies, settlers enslaved Indian tribespeople or bound them into servitude for a period of years.

There were both geographic and chronological distinctions among those bonded and enslaved laborers who came to North America. Indentured servants were the most numerous of the unfree workers early in the period, recruited by enterprising residents of the Chesapeake Bay colony who used the head-right system to enlarge their personal land holdings; anyone who recruited a worker was entitled to an extra fifty acres of land from the Virginia Company. Africans came to the Chesapeake as well, beginning in 1619; by the end of the seventeenth century, about 5,500 people of African descent, most of them slaves, lived in the colony of Virginia. Historians estimate the white population of early Virginia in 1700 to be ten times more numerous—at 56,100, consisting of descendants of those gentlemen, artisans, and others who arrived early in the colony, as well as a much larger group of indentured servants, transported criminals, some voluntary settlers, and their descendants. In seventeenth-century Maryland, a higher proportion of residents consisted of indentured servants; again, the need for laborers to work on tobacco plantations and to provide food and shelter was extreme, leading to the recruitment of bonded workers, both male and female.

In other colonies such as Massachusetts Bay, free workers emigrated from England and other countries. The free exercise of religion was but one of the attractions for prospective immigrants. Land for their families and, with it, wealth brought many colonists across the Atlantic. Endeavoring to attract more colonists to West New Jersey in the late seventeenth century, Quaker Gabriel Thomas wrote to authorities in London in "encouragement to persuade the Poor, the Idle, the Lazy, and the Vagabonds of these Kingdoms and Wales to hasten thither, that they may live plentifully and happily" in a land where there was such great need for labor that workers could expect to make three or four times what they earned at home (Myers 1912, 338). Adventurous souls from Sweden and Germany migrated to secure their futures through hard work, largely coming to the middle colonies. The Dutch settled in Manhattan Island, where they concentrated their trading operations, though they also cleared land along the Hudson River for farms to support their commercial establishments in the village of New Amsterdam. In historian Donna Merwick's words, the Dutch were "alongshore people," colonists who, like their countrymen back home, settled along the coastline and river valleys. Most Dutch colonists dedicated themselves to the fur and timber trade with sovereign indigenous nations (Merwick 2006, 53).

In the decades after those harshest years of early colonial settlement, the population of Massachusetts, first, and then Virginia and other colonies grew substantially. Between 1660 and 1680, most colonies had nearly doubled their populations, much of it through immigration from Europe but, increasingly after 1660, also by childbirth. In 1681, the colony of Pennsylvania was founded, thus creating what would go on to be one of the most important colonies in economic and political terms. Philadelphia expanded its spheres of influence, with cities such as Boston, Massachusetts; Charles Town, South Carolina; and Richmond, Virginia, following. With a population rapidly expanding from an estimated 155,000 in 1680 to 2,205,000 by 1770, the colonies became a thriving region, requiring workers to engage in many more trades and occupations than in the lean subsistence years.

In the maritime colonies of Massachusetts, Rhode Island, and elsewhere, the colonists needed shipwrights and riggers to build and maintain both coastal and oceangoing vessels. England still supplied the colonists with a majority of their consumer goods, so much so that weekly arrivals of ships carrying combs, bedding, tools, and even used clothing were widely advertised in colonial broadsides and newspapers; once a ship arrived dockside, colonists flocked to the ports to purchase items just unloaded. Goods that could not easily be imported due to their bulk or other factors but could be made domestically were, in fact, crafted in the colonies: barrels by coopers, rough fabric by weavers and spinners, wagons and carriages by cartwrights. Other craftsmen—blacksmiths, harness makers, gunsmiths—often worked to repair items previously imported from Europe. In a region that had no banks, wealthy colonists who had accumulated significant amounts of silver needed silversmiths to create identifiable items out of their coins to prevent theft.

In other cases, specialized services that colonists had to purchase domestically provided a robust job market for colonial workers such as millers, shopkeepers, apothecaries, farriers, scriveners, and others. Some workers, like basket makers and translators, were likely to be indigenous tribespeople, not Anglo American colonists, demonstrating the key role that native people played in the colonial American economy. Slaves, too, learned trades; in the South, they commonly worked as blacksmiths and farriers as well as potters and basket makers. In this way, the American workforce has always been very diverse.

Economic diversification created a wealth of occupations for colonists and slaves, as well as those who lived on the North American continent before them. By the middle of the eighteenth century, Americans could provide for their own needs and those of their neighbors. Commerce within individual colonies, between different colonies, and throughout the Atlantic basin led to even more opportunities. This largely self-supporting and diffuse internal economy did much to prove to colonists that they could survive as their own nation, even as England began to impose laws that regulated trade on the colonies after 1765. American colonists had begun to see themselves as distinctly American, separate from England in political and economic ways that contributed to the unrest leading to the revolution.

Nancy Quam-Wickham

FURTHER READING

Merwick, Donna. 2006. *The Shame and the Sorrow: Dutch-Amerindian Encounters in New Netherland.* Philadelphia: University of Pennsylvania.

Myers, Albert Cook. 1912. *Narratives of Pennsylvania, West New Jersey and Delaware, 1630–1701.* New York: C. Scribner's Sons.

The Proceedings of the Old Bailey: London's Central Criminal Court, 1674 to 1913. https://www.oldbaileyonline.org/.

Tyler, Lyon Gardiner. 1907. *Narratives of Early Virginia, 1606–1625.* New York: C. Scribner's Sons.

APOTHECARY

In colonial America, apothecaries were men and women who worked as healers, primarily modern-day pharmacists who also served as folk doctors; most lacked any formal medical training. Apothecaries commonly created, mixed, and dispensed medicines based largely on herbal remedies. By the early 1700s, many were essentially druggists, creating proprietary medicines that they advertised widely in colonial newspapers and broadsides. Some visited the sick in their homes, while others treated patients directly in their apothecary shops. Apothecaries were valued members of the colonial merchant elite as colonists frequently experienced illness and injuries. Sometimes referred to as "practical physicians," apothecaries might, on any given day, dispense advice on nutrition and provide a concoction of herbs to improve digestion; prepare a poultice designed to loosen phlegm by warming the chests of those suffering from lung congestion; or wash, disinfect, and bandage a wound caused by snakebite or careless use of knives while dressing game. With its untreated water, numerous parasites, rural character, and many rudimentary practices that posed danger to residents, the environment of colonial America created great demand for these professionals.

Since the nation's first medical school, the Medical School of the College of Philadelphia, did not open until the eve of the American Revolution in the 1760s, apothecaries generally learned their trade as apprentices until the end of the eighteenth century. Occasionally, an apothecary might also work as a midwife or a "surgeon," especially if he or she had obtained formal training as an apprentice under a more highly skilled practitioner who had pursued a formal course of study in medicine at a college in England or elsewhere in Europe. Most practitioners of this ancient art, however, learned their trades as apprentices. Medical knowledge was elementary as most colonial apothecaries still adhered to a belief in the vapors or "humours" theory of the body—an idea that harmful gasses and liquids lead to illness. Believers in these theories likewise reasoned that ridding the body of such substances, by means of purging and bloodletting or replacing toxic vapors by inhaling beneficial ones, resulted in more healthful physiological states. Such practices today might seem outrageous. For example, one 1708 pharmaceutical text advised apothecaries that chronic nosebleeds, which we now know are sometimes a symptom of hypertension or other cardiovascular disease, could be cured by application of a compress of "Hogs Dung very hot, done up in fine Taffeta, and put into the nose" (Rance 2014, 10). Contemporaneous texts instructed apothecaries to extract a quart of blood from a patient's veins to cure "melancholy" and administer strong emetics to induce vomiting to cure a range of ailments from diarrhea and irregular menstrual periods to cancer. Some apothecaries prescribed antimony, arsenic, mercury, and bismuth—all deadly, heavy metallic elements—in small doses as both primary treatments and adjunctive therapies (to allegedly increase the efficacy of the primary treatment, usually an herbal remedy or physical intervention like blistering or bloodletting).

Other treatments were less outlandish. Many herbal remedies did have a basis in experimentation and were at least partly effective. The New World provided colonial apothecaries with many new botanical species not known to Europeans;

indigenous people had long used many of these plants as medicinal agents. Apothecaries shared their herbal knowledge broadly; they wrote about their successes and published them in newspapers, broadsides, and books as they learned about New World botanical remedies, what we might today call "folk medicine," and customarily tested their effectiveness on patients. Apothecaries collected useful plants in the field, grew them in their shop gardens, and traded botanical substances with other practitioners.

By the early 1700s, practitioners regularly shared their knowledge with other practitioners through professional knowledge networks, including apprenticeship training, local medical societies, and other associations of educated elites. One such network was London's Royal Philosophical Society, which produced and disseminated pharmacopeia from the late seventeenth century onward. The Royal Society routinely published notes about American botanical "discoveries," such as a 1698 publication that contained lists of New World plants and animals from Maryland, some of which were used as medicinal agents. Colonial apothecaries used the root of a plant commonly known as monkshood or wolfsbane, a member of the Ranunculae family, for treating scurvy, a systemic disorder caused by nutritional deficiencies of vitamin C. Apothecaries harvested the root of the plant along Maryland's Patuxent River, dried and grated it, and then steeped a pound of it in a gallon of cider until evaporation reduced the substance by half; then they strained the liquid and prescribed a pint a day for treating and preventing scurvy (Petiver 1698, 403–404). As this plant's root has no vitamin content, its alleged usefulness was likely because, as a highly toxic poison, it provided some neuralgic properties that lessened the debilitating pain caused by the disease. Roots that were not carefully processed (to leach out the poisonous alkaloids) or given as an improper dose, however, could prove deadly.

The American environment was responsible for causing many diseases and maladies. In one of the first medical texts published in the colonies in 1727, apothecary and physician John Tennent noted, "Our Country is unhappily subject to several very sharp Distempers. The Multitude of Marshes, Swamps, and great Waters, send forth so many Fogs, and Exhalations, that the Air is continually damp with them: This, in Spight of our Precautions, is apt to shut up the Pores all at once, and hinder insensible Perspiration. From hence proceed FEVERS, COUGHS, QUINSIES, PLEURISIES, and CONSUMPTIONS, with a dismal Train of other Diseases, which make as fatal Havock here, in Proportion to our Population as PLAGUE does in the *Eastern* Parts of the World" (Tennent 1727, 4–5).

While "fogs . . ., exhalations," and dampness were not responsible for the "Distempers" that Tennent wrote about, colonists did routinely suffer from digestive disorders, many of which were caused by poor nutrition, lack of fiber in the diet, fresh water contaminated with amoeba, and common parasites like pinworm and roundworm. Like many colonial apothecaries of his time, Tennent prescribed to those suffering from dysentery a concoction of "Indian Physick" (the root of the native plant *Gillenia trifoliate*, a member of the Rose family), "new Milk" boiled with oat or wheat flour, grated nutmeg, and finely ground deer horn, as well as wormwood tea, followed by a diet that included tea, chicken broth, and poached eggs. Tennent also advised patients to refrain from eating unripe fruit and "windy Meats" and drinking large quantities of "Cold Water" and "fermented Drinks" (Tennent 1727, 16–18). Such herbal concoctions could be successful in treating dysenteric diarrhea, as Indian physick induced vomiting and also had a rapid purgative effect, leading a patient to violently empty his or her bowels, thus partially expelling worms and parasites like Giardia. Nutmeg and wormwood both have antibacterial properties. Tea and broth rehydrated ill patients, while boiled milk thickened with oat flour was essentially a mixture of insoluble fiber to bulk up bowel contents. Avoiding unripe fruits, poorly preserved meats (those that caused intestinal distress such as flatulence), and "Cold Water" (water not boiled for purification) ensured that a patient's tender digestive system had a chance to heal. Experimenting with different botanicals, adopting indigenous use of medicinal plants, and sharing successful techniques with others led practitioners like Tennent to combinations of plants and agents that actually helped colonists.

By the start of the Revolutionary War, though, apothecaries in rapidly growing colonial cities began to specialize in selling proprietary cures, seeking ever-expanding markets for herbs and chemicals combined and bottled as elixirs, tinctures, drops, and pills, which they advertised as cures for dropsy, pleurisy, and even rabies. Some of colonial America's best-known merchants included Benjamin Franklin and Benedict Arnold, both of whom sold these proprietary cures in their shops in Philadelphia and New Haven, respectively.

Nancy Quam-Wickham

See also: Midwife; *1776–1860:* Physician; *1861–1914:* Surgeon; *1946–1991:* Pharmacist

FURTHER READING

Breslaw, Elaine G. 2012. *Lotions, Potions, Pills, and Magic: Health Care in Early America.* New York: New York University Press.

Helfand, William H. 1998. "Advertising Health to the People." In *"Everyman His Own Doctor": Popular Medicine in Early America.* Philadelphia: Library Company.

Henckel, George, and C. M. Spalding. 1891. *The Practical Physician and Home Apothecary.* Chicago: Smucker & Co. https://archive.org/details/63580190R.nlm.nih.gov.

Kipps, Robin. n.d. *The Art and Mystery of the Apothecary.* Colonial Williamsburg Foundation. http://www.history.org/foundation/journal/autumn06/apothecary.cfm.

Petiver, James. 1698. *Remarks by Mr. James Petiver, Apothecary, and Fellow of the Royal Society, on Some Plants, Animals, etc. Sent to Him from Maryland, by the Reverend Mr. Hugh Jones.* London: Philosophical Society.

Rance, Caroline. 2014. *What the Apothecary Ordered: Questionable Cures through the Ages.* London: Oldhouse Books.

Sonnedecker, Glenn. 1976. *Kremers and Urdang's History of Pharmacy.* 4 ed. New York: J. B. Lippincott.

Tennent, John. 1734. *Every Man His Own Doctor: Or, The Poor Planter's Physician. Prescribing plain and easy means for persons to cure themselves of all, or most of the distempers, incident to this climate, and with very little charge, the medicines being chiefly of the growth and production of this country.* Williamsburg: William Parks, 2e. https://quod.lib.umich.edu/e/evans/N03178.0001.001/1:2?rgn=div1;view=fulltext.

PRIMARY DOCUMENT

In this document, John Tennant, an early eighteenth-century apothecary and physician, describes a treatment for dropsy, or edema, the retention of fluid in the body, including legs, ankles, and feet. Normally caused by systemic diseases like heart and kidney problems, liver failure, or cancer, edema is treated by medical doctors by addressing the systemic diseases that cause it. In his advice to patients, Tennant makes a clear connection between jaundice (caused by liver diseases like cirrhosis or cancer) and dropsy. His prescription for curing the disorder, however, is interesting as he suggests that patients limit their alcohol consumption, eat light meals, and undertake the following cures, including fasting throughout the day while chewing on a piece of sassafras bark.

[T]he most fatal Consequence of keeping an *Ague,* or *Jaundice* too long, is, a DROPSY. This dire Calamity befalls ancient People sometimes, by Means of natural Decay; and sometimes, those that are young, when they have made too bold with their Constitution. 'Tis also apt to follow too great a Loss of Blood, or too long a Familiarity with Opiates.

A DROPSY first shews it self, by the Swelling of the Legs about the Ankles, in such a Manner as to retain the Impression of your Finger. The Swelling appears most at Night, and is usually attended with a Shortness and Difficulty of Breath, ever most troublesome when the Patient lies down.

HE must therefore resolve upon proper Remedies, before the Waters rise high enough to drown him: And, if he have but the Gift of Self-denial, he may, by God's Help, get the better of this mortal Enemy; provided there be no universal Decay, no Depravation of the Liver, or other Organs, necessary for Blood-making . . .

[I]nstead of *Sassafras,* you may hold the *Seeds* of *Pellitary of Spain* in your Mouth, which will salivate still more powerfully.

THE rest of the Cure must be compleated with restorative Meats, and a very short Allowance of Drink. For your *Diet,* I would recommend *Poach'd Eggs, Thin Hominy, Hoggs Feet, Cow Heel,* and *Jelly Broth:* all which will renew, and enrich the Blood, without provoking too much Thirst: And for Drink, use none, but *Sorrel Beer,* or sound *Cider,* wherein a *hot Iron* has been quench'd several Times.

TO guard your self against this wretched Distemper, be cautious of scorching your Liver, with Spirits, or Excess of other strong Drink. In Case you be troubled with *Bleeding,* stop it as soon as you can. By no means accustom your self to *Opiates,* or suffer an *Ague,* the *Jaundice,* or lingering *Fevers,* to dwell long upon you.

BECAUSE I mentioned Loss of Blood to be one Cause of the *Dropsy,* I will hint at some Means to stanch those BLEEDINGS that threaten the most Danger.

IN Men, the excessive FLUX OF THE BLEEDING PILES sometimes ends in a *Dropsy,* if not stop'd in Time. In that Case, *purge* with *Indian Physick* 2 or 3 Times; and the Mornings you don't do that, drink the *Expressed Liquor* of *fresh Ass-dung,* sweetened with *Syrup* of *Quinces,* to be repeated 3 Times. In the mean while, take an Ounce of *Conserve* of *Roses,* twice or thrice a Day; and after every Stool, wash your Fundament clean with *Decoction* of *Comfrey Leaves,* made very warm.

LIVE all the Time upon a cooling *Diet,* without Meat; and only drink *Burnet,* or *Yarrow Tea,* sweetened with *Syrup* of *Quinces.*

THOSE that are liable to this, or the like Infirmities, should avoid heating themselves with strong Drink, or too boisterous Motion; nor must they fall into violent Passions, either of Love or Anger.

Source: John Tennant. 1734. *Every Man His Own Doctor: or, The Poor Planter's Physician. Prescribing plain and easy means for persons to cure themselves of all, or most of the distempers, incident to this climate, and with very little charge, the medicines being chiefly of the growth and production of this country.* Williamsburg: William Parks, 2e, 35–39, passim. https://quod.lib.umich.edu/e/evans/N03178.0001.001/1:2?rgn=div1;view=fulltext.

BAKER

Bakers are food producers who combine flours, fats, salt, sugar, water, yeast, and other specialty ingredients with a concentrated heat source to make cakes, breads, pastries, pies, and other edible items, especially commercially. Typically, bakers are responsible for acquiring and preparing the ingredients and equipment necessary for baking, measuring, and weighing a recipe's ingredients; combining them in the right quantity and order; kneading, rolling, and cutting the recipe's dough mixture and placing it in a baking pan or mold or on a baking sheet; setting and maintaining the correct oven temperature; observing the baking process; and applying finishing icings, toppings, or glazes. Many bakers sell their baked goods directly out of the bakery, but it is common for a baker to sell the goods at a market. Until the advent of natural gas and electric ovens, most bakers used wood-burning stoves. As baked goods have been a staple in the human diet for millennia, the baker's vocation is an exceptionally old one.

When Great Britain established its North American colonies in the early seventeenth century, the British emigrants who sailed west across the Atlantic brought much of their culture and many of their habits and social practices with them to the New World; fewer than two hundred years later, those colonists' descendants would establish the United States of America. While that decision was politically complicated, methodical, and slow to develop, some of the earliest bits of resentment toward British rule started showing up almost as soon as the colonies' first buildings were constructed.

For hundreds of years, real estate has been at a premium in London; there isn't much room to build out, and so many buildings have to be built up—or down. Since seventeenth-century kitchens were greasy, smoky, generally undesirable places to work or spend time in, many kitchens were built into buildings' basements. Since many building owners also had underpaid or slave labor, these basement kitchens became associated with society's lowest classes.

There was plenty of room to build in the New World, though, and since single-level buildings are almost always less expensive to build and maintain than multilevel ones—and also because many of the people who came to the New World weren't wealthy—kitchens started to be built on the same level as the rest of a building. Such a detail might seem small or unimportant, but little decisions like this often served both as responses to the old lives that colonists left behind in England and as small gestures in support of the ideas that would later become distinctly American.

In the colonies, most people had to be able to do a little bit of every kind of job. One of these roles that became very popular and necessary was that of the baker. The British-colonial diet included wild game and seafood, seasonal vegetables, and almost always a coarse, simple bread made from whatever kind of grain was available. Bread was inexpensive and relatively easy to produce, could be made year round, and created useful byproducts that could be repurposed around the town. Most importantly, it helped the average colonist's diet become more predictable; a hunter or a fisherman might come home empty-handed on some days, but having a baker around meant that there'd always be something to eat.

Just like their modern counterparts, colonial bakers would get up very early in the morning, often hours before sunrise. Though this was a common schedule for any working person in the years before the Industrial Revolution, the early schedule was especially practical for the colonial baker. Before home refrigeration became common in the first half of the twentieth century, most cooked food was eaten on the same day it was prepared. Because bread was one of the few prepared foods that would take days or weeks to spoil, bakers would often try to get all of their baked goods prepared as early as possible during the day so the oven would be available to prepare other meals that were more difficult or impossible to store.

Because bread was easy to store and would stay fresh for at least a few days, colonial bakers would often bake bread only once or twice a week, and bakers would spend many of their mornings baking cakes, tarts, and pies with whatever ingredients were handy. A lot of experimentation was necessary, though; because colonial ovens and ingredients weren't always refined or predictable, many baking efforts would turn out as failures. Some of those failures would turn into feed for livestock. Because leftover or unusable grain or dough could also be turned into beer or other alcohol, colonial bakers were often the village's self-appointed brew-masters and distillers.

Several challenges faced the colonial baker. Before Oliver Evans invented the automatic flour mill at the end of the eighteenth century, bakers had to mill flour by hand. This was very time-consuming and difficult work for any baker who needed to produce baked goods for more than just a few people. Sort of like the modern baker, the colonial baker was never completely sure how a given baking effort would turn out, but the colonial baker's difficulties were nothing like today's. Yet another problem facing colonial bakers was the burden of the job's routine. The schedule was difficult, and the work was very repetitive. Unlike for famers or fishermen, where every day might be different, the baker's life was often very mundane.

The Industrial Revolution changed just about every aspect of urban and rural life, and bakers were affected perhaps most drastically. Industrial flour mills could grind flour hundreds of times faster than it could be milled by hand. The invention of the microscope allowed scientists and bakers to understand the yeasts that had been used in bread production for thousands of years. Margarine was invented in the late nineteenth century, and its function as a spoil-resistant butter substitute allowed an even wider variety of baked goods to last even longer in pantries and on shelves.

Bakers were especially important during World War I, both on the home front and out in the field. At home, factory bakers produced crackers, biscuits, and simple loaves of bread by the millions and shipped them to soldiers fighting all around the world. However, because even the best wartime plans would sometimes go awry, soldiers who had baking experience would improvise simple bread and biscuit recipes with whatever ingredients they could forage or steal.

After the end of World War II, the postwar economy and continued advancements in the manufacturing industry meant that for the country's bakers, there was a lot more money to be made and spent. Later in the twentieth century, once every store in the country was well-stocked with inexpensive bread, industrious bakers continued to hone their craft, and a wave of artisanal bakeries began to open. Modern bakers produce baked goods made from almost any ingredient imaginable.

Ben Tyler Elliott

See also: Farmer; Fisherman; Miller; Potter

FURTHER READING

Glasse, Hannah, Jennifer Stead, and Priscilla Bain. 2012. *First Catch Your Hare: The Art of Cookery Made Plain and Easy (1747).* Totnes, United Kingdom: Prospect Books.

Iannone, Olivia. "Bread-baking Was not Easy in Colonial Times." Daily Record. Last modified July 2, 2014. www.dailyrecord.com/story/life/food/2014/07/02/bread-baking-easy-colonial-times/11963373/.

Nelson, Paul E. 1957. "Baking in America, Vol. I: Economic Development." *Journal of Political Economy* 65, no. 5 (October), 450–451.

Olmert, Michael. "Kitchens: Places Apart." The Colonial Williamsburg Foundation. Last modified July 2007. http://www.history.org/Foundation/journal/Summer07/kitchens.cfm.

Snodgrass, Mary Ellen. 2005. *Encyclopedia of Kitchen History.* London: Fitzroy Dearborn.

United States. 1917. *Manual for Army Bakers, 1916: Corrected to October 15, 1917 (Changes No. 1).* Washington: Govt. Print. Off.

Welky, David. 2008. *Everything Was Better in America Print Culture in the Great Depression.* Urbana: University of Illinois Press.

Whitten, David O., and Bessie E. Whitten. 1990. *Handbook of American Business History.* New York: Greenwood Press.

BASKET MAKER

A basket maker is a person who makes and sells baskets. Before the advent of plastic containers in the twentieth century, most Americans carried items in baskets. Loose bulk goods, such as wheat and grains, were shipped in burlap sacks, while tobacco was transported in wooden barrels. Liquids, like milk, were carried in small wooden tubs and pails, and butter was churned from cream in a wooden butter churn and then stored in butter crocks made of wood or pottery. For many other goods, colonists used baskets to carry and store them. Baskets were essential.

Children collected eggs from family chickens and carried them to the house in baskets, while women collected garden vegetables, wild berries, and other fresh foods in baskets. Fishermen stored their gear in baskets. Farmers shook their grain in wide, shallow baskets to separate the grain from its chaff. Even poor families were likely to own at least one basket due to its universal utility for collecting all kinds of goods. Baskets were affordable containers for most colonists, and many made their own baskets for home use. In the period before the Revolutionary War, some colonial families specialized in making baskets; a small group of people living in upstate New York, known locally as the "bushwhackers," made Taconic baskets—splint baskets—that were considered to be of the highest quality available at that time.

Basketmaking had long been a traditional craft in North America prior to the arrival of European colonists and explorers. Nearly every indigenous American tribe practiced some form of basketmaking before the seventeenth century; so important were baskets to tribal culture that many groups believed that knowledge of basketmaking was originally given to a tribe by a beneficial spirit or god. As such, basketmaking is one of the oldest artistic practices in North America.

Unlike most European basketmaking, North American tribal basketmaking was a well-respected, functional art form. Whereas Euro American colonists created baskets from strips of willow wood or other malleable tree barks through a process known as open work, many indigenous groups utilized a variety of vegetation to make their baskets. Native Americans used dye to color the vegetation and carefully interwove the colored material into the basket to make elaborate designs. They adorned their baskets with beads made from tiny bones, shells, and mother of pearl (abalone). They interwove brightly colored bird feathers to create even more beautiful baskets for particular ceremonial and family uses. They also made highly functional baskets that could carry water, ones in which acorn or seed porridge could be cooked by submerging hot rocks into the basket's contents, and baskets that were used to trap rabbits and fish. While many colonists made their own baskets, they also clearly recognized the superior basketmaking abilities of their tribal neighbors as they routinely purchased or traded goods for native-made baskets.

As slaves were imported into the American colonies, they brought African basketmaking along with them, which included creating baskets made of fine weaves with grass fibers. Particularly in the southern lowlands of Georgia and South Carolina, slave-made baskets were used for many purposes. Even today, Gullah baskets from this region are highly prized art forms.

Whether Euro American, African American, or tribal, one of the first duties of the basket maker was to determine the basket's intended use. Farmers often needed tray-like baskets to sift wheat from its chaff. Many housewives needed baskets to carry loaves of hot bread to market. Some people used ceremonial baskets for their cultural or family traditions. Regardless, the baskets' intended uses and forms determined their materials of construction. For handled baskets designed to hold items with some bulk, such as just-harvested potatoes or freshly laid eggs, colonists might choose to use white oak or black ash strips as such materials were strong and the basket did not need to have a tight weave. For baskets holding water or gruel, tribal people generally chose fibers of plants that could be twisted tightly, and then tight baskets would be "woven" with these twines of fiber. Large baskets with tight weaves needed "stems," or a strong internal frame-like structure, made of stiffer material like dried willow or hazel shoots.

Once a basket maker determined the size, purpose, and shape of the baskets to be made, she had to travel to areas and harvest the materials to make them. Most tribal basket makers were women, as were most, but not all, Euro American colonists who made baskets. Basketmaking was generally an activity associated with subsistence, not a single occupation, though there were opportunities for accomplished basket makers to sell their wares to colonists and others.

Groups of women and girls searched for the proper basketmaking materials in well-known areas. The Pomo of northern California, who were perhaps the most skillful of all American indigenous basket makers, searched creek and river banks for young shoots of willow and hazel bushes to serve as the stems. They removed the shoots, carefully placing them in their collecting baskets; willow and hazel were used as the stems and as the material for the warp, which was the collective name for the stationary structures through which other fibers—known as the woof or the weft—would be woven. For the woven fibers, Pomo basket makers chose sedge or bulrush, both plants native to precontact California. Sedge and bulrush grow along streams and in marshes along lakes and ponds. Using digging sticks to uproot the sedges and bulrushes, basket makers harvested the plants and then split them open to reveal the inner tough fibers, which could be carefully extracted in long string-like pieces as thin as cotton thread. Basket makers then coiled the fibers and put them aside, much like a skein of wool today. Should a Pomo basket maker want to dye some fibers deep black for a ceremonial basket, she buried a coil of fiber with ash and mud along the shore of a lake, where it stayed for a time until the fibers took the dye. Pomo basket makers used other materials as well: bracken ferns, the roots of a small conifer known as digger pine, bark of the native redbud tree, juniper roots, wild grape sapwood, and even tule reeds, among others. Once the basket maker gathered and prepared her raw materials, she brought them back to her village for further preparation.

All baskets are woven, generally starting with the base. The basket maker wove the warp material together, flattening them to make the base, while the ends of the warp material extended to the basket's desired height. Basket makers then began to interweave the weft materials back and forth between the warp, continuously tightening or loosening these fibers to give the basket its shape; this element of a basket is known as the wall. For intricately woven ceremonial baskets, Pomo basket makers took fine fibers and twisted them together to create a twine-like weft fiber, which gave the basket wall exceptional strength and beauty. These basket makers also sometimes decorated the exterior of their basket walls by interweaving small colorful feathers from the topknot of the California quail or the top feathers of the redheaded woodpecker. Some basket makers covered their baskets with these feathers, giving the exterior a velvet-like decorative texture. Other materials used include yellow feathers from meadowlarks, blue feathers from bluebirds or California jays, and orange tufts from orioles. Sometimes basket makers interwove beads made of abalone or tiny white clam shells, hard rock known as magnesite, or even mesquite seeds. Once the basket maker completed the basket walls, she had to finish the lip, carefully tying off and interweaving the warp and weft materials, often weaving into the lip a thicker border piece and then knotting the warp and weft fibers underneath it on the inside of the basket.

Basket makers practiced a craft that had worldwide, ancient origins. They produced both art and functional pieces for many different uses. Some baskets were created to last generations, while others were cheaply woven for specific purposes like catching rabbits or birds and then discarded. Throughout the country—even in the late nineteenth century—Americans were still purchasing baskets made by their contemporary tribal neighbors. In New England, impoverished tribal people traveled about the region as itinerant basket makers, selling their baskets for what the market would allow. In southern Louisiana, the Coushatta tribe sold baskets made of river cane to their white neighbors, as did the Ojibwe of northern Michigan. In Yosemite National Park, Pauite-Miwok basket maker Lucy Telles and other accomplished tribal artists demonstrated native basketmaking techniques to visitors throughout the mid-twentieth century. By this time, too, anthropologists, artists, and museum collectors began to purchase baskets made by tribal people, the bushwhackers, and descendants of African slaves. All recognized the quality and uniqueness of basketmaking as an art form.

Nancy Quam-Wickham

See also: Potter; Weaver and Spinner; *1776–1860:* Milliner

FURTHER READING

Barrett, S. A., and Sherrie Smith-Ferri. 1996. *Pomo Indian Basketry*. Berkeley: Phoebe Hearst Museum of Anthropology, University of California, Berkeley.

Scott, Amy. 2006. *Yosemite: Art of an American Icon*. Los Angeles: Autry National Center.

Turnbaugh, William A., and Sarah Peabody Turnbaugh. 1999. *Basket Tales of the Grandmothers: American Indian Baskets in Myth and Legend*. Peace Dale: Thornbrook Publishers.

Wetherbee, Martha, Nathan Taylor, and Mary Lyn Ray. 1986. *Legend of the Bushwhacker Basket*. Sanbornton: M. Wetherbee Basket Shop.

BLACKSMITH

Blacksmiths are workers who make tools and other metal products like nails, hinges, chains, cowbells, locks, gears, weathervanes, pots, and kettles out of iron and, beginning late in the colonial period, out of steel. Blacksmiths performed their work by hand and also commonly repaired broken items. Some blacksmiths specialized in making or repairing certain types of metal goods and, consequently, were known by different names: those who worked on wagon hardware and wheels were known as cartwrights or wainwrights; gunsmiths made gun components and barrels; farriers made and applied horseshoes. Nailers, or blacksmiths who specialized in making nails, were general workmen who transformed metal rod into nails, and this was perhaps the easiest metal item for a blacksmith to create. These more specialized smiths tended to live and work in towns and cities, while general blacksmiths worked in the countryside as well as more populous areas of the colonies. Blacksmiths' work was essential for the colonies' economic success: without axes, farmers could not clear forests; without horseshoes, residents could not easily bring their goods to market; without nails, carpenters could not construct buildings. Given their importance to colonial society and economy, blacksmiths and their shops were ubiquitous, and their work was in high demand. Owners of large plantations even routinely trained some of their slaves in the trade to ensure self-sufficient estates.

Blacksmiths worked in enclosed workshops as well as open-air settings. Their most important piece of equipment was a forge, which was a brick or stone hearth or oven-like structure, complete with chimney, in which the blacksmiths heated the metal bars that they transformed into products. The furnace-like forge had a large central pit where burning coal or charcoal created the heat required to induce basic metallurgic changes, like making the metal malleable enough to be formed into other products. Blacksmiths—or, more commonly, their apprentices and helpers—kept the fires hot by using a bellows to push air into the pit. A bellows was a large leather device shaped something like a hollow, three-dimensional triangle with wooden handles on two sides; as the smith forcefully moved the handles back and forth, the bellows inflated and then deflated, forcing air out of the canister, much like a lung inflates when one inhales and deflates when exhaling. A bellows was a large device, and it took considerable strength to work the bellows while leaning over a hot hearth in a dirty workshop.

It also took muscle, skill, and good hand-eye coordination to mold malleable metal using little more than tongs, an anvil, and a hammer. Blacksmiths manually shaped heated metal by pounding it with a smithy hammer that was designed to pound metal on an anvil; most blacksmiths owned several such hammers of different sizes, weights, and shapes. Some workshops, however, had trip hammers, mechanical devices, driven by cam action and sometimes powered by water, that automatically pounded on a piece of metal in replication of a handheld hammer's action. Another essential tool was the anvil, a heavy metal tool with a flattened and steel-hardened top and shaped sides that a blacksmith used to shape the heated metal. Blacksmiths hammered the metal mass on the anvil, giving it the desired form. The blacksmith held the hot metal with his tongs. As the blacksmith worked with the metal, he "drew it out" by lengthening and reshaping the bar, removing any impurities in the material. To join two pieces of iron together, they used "snowball" heat (or white-hot heat) in the forge to weld the item's pieces together, and then they would hammer the weld together to achieve a seamless look.

Blacksmiths distinguished themselves in their communities in part by their appearance. They wore the distinctive blacksmiths' apron, made of heavy leather and extending below their knees, to protect against burns. Smithies were hot, smoky, and very loud workshops; many older blacksmiths became deaf because of the constant loud hammering. The blacksmith had to use both his strength and skill to hand-shape metal goods. Colonial newspapers were full of advertisements offering rewards for runaway servants who had worked as blacksmith apprentices.

As artisans, blacksmiths were knowledgeable about the properties of forge fuels, metals, and the mechanics of tools and items they might be asked to make or repair. Master blacksmiths took pride in their work and in their physical strength and ability to withstand the heat and smoke of smithy forges. Some evidence exists that suggests that a few colonial women also worked as blacksmiths or owned the forge and tools, but as a whole, colonial blacksmiths overwhelmingly were men. In Europe, blacksmiths had long been members of craft guilds, but there is little evidence today that guilds were widespread in the colonial era. Most workers entered the occupation through the apprenticeship system or family connections. In reprinting an earlier Welsh tombstone epigraph, an 1818 Pennsylvania almanac alludes to this blacksmiths' craft in a poem, "An Epitaph on a Blacksmith":

My sledge and hammer lie reclin'd
My bellows too have lost their wind;
My fire's extinct, my forge decay'd,

And in the dust my vice is laid;
My coal is spent, my iron's gone,
My nails are drove, my work is done.
(Collum 1818)

Blacksmithing remained a vital craft well into the nineteenth century until new, more modern tool factories encroached on the work of the blacksmith. Today, public interest in blacksmithing and new artistic sensibilities that privilege handmade over factory-built have encouraged young artisans to renew interest and pursue ways to shape metal, if only for handmade wrought iron and fancy consumer products.

Nancy Quam-Wickham

See also: Gunsmith; Silversmith; *1861–1914:* Puddler; *1915–1945:* Ironworker; Steelworker

FURTHER READING

Collum, William. 1818. *The Pennsylvania and New-Jersey Almanac for the Year of Our Lord 1819.* Doylestown: Asher Miner.
Fisher, Verna. 2010. *Colonial Jobs.* White River Junction: Nomad Press.
Hiller, Sandra J. 2014. *The Life of a Colonial Blacksmith.* New York: PowerKids Press.
Pursell, Carroll W., and Lemelson Center. 2005. *A Hammer in Their Hands: A Documentary History of Technology and the African-American Experience.* Cambridge: MIT Press.
Wilds, Mary. 2005. *A Colonial Craftsman.* Detroit: Thomson/Gale.

CABINETMAKER

In colonial America, cabinetmakers designed and crafted fine furniture and hand-built ornate furnishings using mostly European stylings. Unlike the common forms of furniture that the majority of colonists owned, which utilized rough-hewn lumber, nails, and rudimentary construction techniques, fine furniture was constructed using specially selected wood species that were appropriate to that piece's intended task. A cabinetmaker's work required attention to clean and square joints; it incorporated elaborate joinery techniques, and its surfaces were normally lacquered or finished to a fine shine. Furniture built by cabinetmakers was designed to last for generations. Like works of art, most pieces also clearly communicated their owner's social and economic status. Upholstered sofas, bureaus adorned with hand-carved elements and inlays of mother of pearl, and chairs with elegantly turned legs neither served the needs of nor were affordable to the average colonist. Factory-built furniture did not emerge until after the Revolutionary War (1775–1783).

Most colonists in America lived simple and spare lives, unburdened by the consumer goods that so define life in modern America. Analysis of probate records, which are a sort of public inventory of deceased people's possessions, provides an understanding of what property a typical colonist most valued. Often when individuals were near death, they'd write a "last will and testament" that outlined what should happen to their assets and possessions, and they would have this document filed with colonial legal officials.

For landholders, their land was often their most valuable possession, and in many colonies, landholders stipulated that their heirs were to receive particular parcels of the estate's land. Southern white slaveholders commonly allocated their slaves to heirs; most did not hesitate to break up slave families. A deceased person's livestock, business inventory, or fine tools were carefully and specifically assigned to individual heirs, as were silver goods, jewelry, coats, boots, and feather beds. Furniture was rarely assigned to particular inheritors but instead was lumped into the catch-all category of "household goods." An exception to this rule, however, was often made in the case of fine, specially crafted furniture pieces, each of which was normally built by cabinetmakers. Throughout the colonial period, well-to-do citizens such as business or plantation owners, merchants, esteemed artisans, and politicians owned fine furniture built by cabinetmakers. In life, as well as in death, owners ensured that these prized pieces were treasured.

As with many other artisans who created fine goods, cabinetmaking was largely bespoke—or custom—work, with most artisan workshops located in larger towns and cities. Cabinetmakers catered to the fashion senses of their customers, who often sought to imitate fanciful and ornate styles then popular in Europe; the most sought-after designs were baroque, Queen Anne, and, by the middle of the eighteenth century, Chippendale. Many of these design elements incorporated thin, finely carved legs, sometimes with ornate "feet" that looked much like the foot of a lion. Casegoods—or heavy bureaus, desks, sideboards, and chests—often featured drawers or fronts curved outwardly. Some casegood fronts incorporated veneers, or thin sheets of decorative wood, like birdseye maple or fine-grained mahogany, which gave the furniture a distinctive look. Chairs, sofas, and benches might be upholstered with fine, heavily embroidered, or otherwise intricately patterned cloth.

Cabinetmakers' goods were distinguishable by their personal styles but also by the methods and techniques that artisan cabinetmakers used; most eschewed nails or screws when assembling a piece of furniture's constituent parts. Only rough work—ordinary, everyday furniture created by carpenters and joiners, known as "wood butchers"—utilized nails and screws to join wood for furniture.

Typical cabinetmakers worked in workshops and were normally assisted by apprentices and also journeymen, burgeoning cabinetmakers who had already completed apprenticeships that comprised several years of formal training. With their helpers, the cabinetmakers used two-handled saws with small, fine teeth to saw eighth-inch-thick veneers. Early lathes, which used a wheel to turn a piece of wood while a cabinetmaker applied a chisel to the rotating wood stock, required several workers to operate; one apprentice constantly operated a series of gears and belts to spin the lathe at high speed, while the cabinetmaker or journeyman precisely used an assortment of chisels and edged tools on the rapidly spinning material. The cabinetmaker carefully carved ornate legs for chairs and casegoods and also turned and carved baluster spindles, ornamental handles for spoons and kitchen utensils along with other fine goods. Cabinetmakers used heavy stock of hardwood (maple, American walnut, cherry, and magnolia) sometimes greater than three inches thick to create elaborate casegoods with curved fronts. For such pieces, cabinetmakers and their assistants had to carve the shape of the drawer fronts with chisels to shape the wood. All furniture was handmade in this period.

Once the cabinetmaker designed and cut the elements of a piece of furniture, he used special tools to cut mortise and tenon joints that held individual pieces together. Mortise and tenon joints hold wood together without using nails or screws; the tenon is a projecting section of the end of a piece of wood, which is carved or shaped and is then inserted into a mortise, which is a precisely recessed hole built into another of the design's constituent parts. This method is still used in fine furniture-making today. Other artisan wood joints are dovetails, blind mortises, and wedges. These types of joints are largely imperceptible to the eye, which is why cabinetmakers used them as often as possible.

Cabinetmakers glued pieces together; an expertly constructed glued mortise and tenon joint was normally stronger than the original piece of wood. Once the item was assembled and glued, cabinetmakers directed apprentices in the finishing process, which involved sanding or rubbing the piece and then repeatedly applying linseed oil, shellac, or wax to the product to bring out the grain of wood and make it shine. Once this laborious and monotonous step was complete, cabinetmakers installed any of the piece's hardware, like brass drawer pulls or hinges. Most cabinetmakers also marked the item with a distinctive symbol. Many also offered refinishing services to remove scratches and other superficial wear and restore the finish to its original luster.

As with other artisanal products, colonial cabinetmakers benefited from the move to buy home products as the conflict between England and the colonies increased prior to the revolution. Consumers took great pride in colonial-made goods, and cabinetmakers responded with elegantly constructed and highly durable pieces. So enduring and expertly crafted was fine furniture that, today, museums like the Metropolitan Museum of Art in New York feature items made by colonial cabinetmakers. While not every colonial cabinetmaker was a master craftsman who created functional yet beautiful furniture, the preference for handcrafted goods persisted well into the modern period. For example, an 1895 article in *The Decorator and Furnisher*, a monthly magazine devoted to interior design, bemoaned the "Passing of the Cabinetmaker" as machine processes replaced their expert skills.

Nancy Quam-Wickham

See also: Basket Maker; Silversmith; *1776–1860:* Joiner; *1946–1991:* Interior and Industrial Designer

FURTHER READING

Brown, Mills, and Thomas K. Ford. 1969. *The Cabinetmaker in Eighteenth Century Williamsburg, Giving Attention to the City's Chief Craftsmen in the Furniture Way; and to Their Tools and Methods of Working.* Colonial Williamsburg Foundation.

Greene, Jeffrey P. 1996. *American Furniture of the 18th Century.* Newtown: Taunton Press.

Heckscher, Morrison H., with the assistance of Laurie H. Zabar. 2005. *John Townsend: Newport Cabinetmaker.* The Metropolitan Museum of Art and Yale University Press.

Tunis, Edward. 1965. *Colonial Craftsmen and the Beginnings of American Industry.* Baltimore: Johns Hopkins University Press.

CARTWRIGHT AND WAINWRIGHT

Cartwrights and wainwrights were people who built carts and wagons, respectively. Wagons and carts were critical items for farmers, who typically used them to transport goods to market, move stones from fields to construction sites, and haul firewood from forests to their home hearths. During the colonial period, families also used carts to transport household goods and children when moving to new quarters, usually in the springtime. Despite the absence of well-maintained roads, these vehicles were essential to colonial life. Those who made these vehicles were equally essential to colonists as building a functional wagon required several sets of skills, including blacksmithing, carpentry, and constructing complicated wheels, normally the duty of a wheelwright. Design and elementary engineering skills were also important, especially as roads developed from rough trails. As colonial roads expanded, cartwrights began to design heavier, more efficient wagons, like the Conestoga of early eighteenth-century Pennsylvania, as well as lighter, two-wheeled carts, called chaises, for carrying passengers on rough city streets.

In a typical colonial workshop, a cartwright or wainwright was a master artisan; he employed apprentices (often indentured servants) as well as blacksmiths and wheelwrights. Sometimes the cartwright and wheelwright were synonymous, though not always. Wheelwrights also had to have blacksmithing skills. In making a wagon, the wheelwright first consulted with a prospective wagon purchaser to determine his or her needs.

A common cart was essentially a large, open wooden box mounted on a frame onto which the axletrees and hitch were attached. The axletree was a wooden frame that held the axles in place; the wheels turned around both ends of the axles. Most carts and wagons had large wheels that tilted inward at the bottom to maintain the wagon's smooth motion over bumpy roads. Wainwrights built the running gear (axles and axletrees) of wagons and carts while supervising the wheelwrights as they built the wheels. Heavy lumber was used for the hitch—a long piece running perpendicular to the axles—to which the draft animals (oxen, mules, and horses) were attached. The wainwright used axes and adzes, much like a joiner, to construct the axles with a geared hub at each end. The wainwright also constructed the body of the cart or wagon. In the middle of the eighteenth century, Germans, known as "Pennsylvania Dutch," created the large-wheeled, high-sided Conestoga wagons based on European designs. A century later, migrants heading west on the Oregon trail nicknamed these distinctive wagons "prairie schooners."

Wheelwrights constructed the wheels, each made of several pieces of wood shaped or steam-bent to form an arc. The wheelwright then attached each arc, or felly, to the others using wooden dowels until creating a full circle. Blacksmiths constructed the iron "tire" attached to the wheel felly. There were two methods for making tires. Most wheel tires in the early period were constructed of several individual pieces of iron, called strakes, which the wheelwright set over the wooden wheel felly joints to strengthen the wheel. Wheelwrights and their helpers set the strakes when they were hot, nailed them on, and then hammered them until they were "welded" together. This process created a tight-fitting tire that covered the weaker wooden wheel. In later periods, a full iron hoop was used for the tire; it had to be heated to expand to fit over the wooden wheel and hammered into place by workers using sledgehammers. Then to cool the iron and draw the wheel fellies together, the wheelwrights and their assistants soaked the tire and wheel in water. Once the wheels were completed, the wainwright, wheelwright, and apprentices assembled the entire wagon.

Since blacksmithing was a requisite skill for wheelwrights, many started out as blacksmith's apprentices. Some enterprising wagon and cart makers built crude vehicles without completing full training as wheelwrights and wainwrights. While early colonial farmers found these rough-built wagons to be serviceable, by the end of the period, the wainwright and wheelwright came to dominate the trade. Colonial governments funded the improvement of horse and foot trails in the early 1700s, creating "post-roads," or reliable roads on which mail, goods, and people could travel. Additionally, farmers moved westward into the hinterlands surrounding Philadelphia, New Haven, and other colonial cities. These farmers needed to get their produce to market. In Pennsylvania, German immigrants grew wheat and other grains; the weight of grain and the need to transport it to distant seaports for export to the Caribbean, for instance, required heavier wagons and better roads.

In cities, urban residents demanded lighter carriages that were small enough to maneuver through the narrow streets that characterized many towns, as well as stable enough to provide a smooth ride over cobblestone, wooden, or rutted lanes. Urban consumers, in particular, wanted carriages with built-in springs to cushion their rides. After the revolution, states authorized the construction of "turnpikes," a late-eighteenth-century version of a modern highway. To meet the demand for vehicles, new wagon and carriage companies emerged in the early republic. With their access to capital, modern manufacturing techniques, and attention to consumer preferences, carriage companies—rather than the individual workshops of the wainwright—came to dominate the carriage- and wagon-making industry by the first decades of the nineteenth century.

Nancy Quam-Wickham

See also: Blacksmith; Cooper; Harness Maker and Saddler

FURTHER READING

Hegel, Richard. 1974. *Carriages from New Haven.* Hamden: Archon Books.

Jenkins, J. Geraint. 1981. *The English Farm Wagon: Origins and Structure.* Newton Abbot, Devon: David & Charles.

Mather, Increase. 1684. "An Essay for the recording of illustrious providences: wherein, an account is given of many remarkable and very memorable events, which have happened in this last age; especially in New-England," 401–403.

Sherman, James E., Edward F. Ronstadt, and Fred Ronstadt. 1975. *Wagon Making in Southern Arizona.* Tucson: Tucson Corral of the Westerners.

COOPER

Coopers were craftsmen who made wooden containers to store and ship virtually all products for market. They made large casks called hogsheads for storing and shipping tobacco in the Antebellum South; they made pails and piggins (a small pail shaped like a wooden ladle, with one extended stave to be used as a handle) for carrying and drinking water. Coopers made barrels for dry goods: grains; apples, turnips, and other produce that would bruise if shipped in bags; salt; refined sugar; gunpowder; and iron nails. Skilled coopers crafted "wet" barrels for liquid goods—molasses, rum, wine, cider, turpentine, and whale and seal oils. Wet barrels were also used for goods like salted meats and fish, which could leak small amounts of liquid as they cured. Without the cooper, neither farmers nor other producers could have taken their goods to market, so essential was this occupation to the development of American agriculture and industry.

The job of a cooper was a common one in colonial America. Those who engaged in coopering work usually learned the trade as apprentices or, in the case of slaves, as children. Many coopers specialized in making particular types of wooden containers. The casks called hogsheads, for instance, were constructed of rough wood; hogshead dimensions were set by colonial governments as tobacco functioned as currency in a cash-poor colonial economy. In North Carolina, hogsheads were usually circular in shape, four feet deep, thirty inches in diameter, with straight sides, and held about half a ton of pressed tobacco. Colonial regulations normally required coopers to affix their mark onto the hogsheads they crafted; Virginia fined coopers whose hogsheads did not meet very specific criteria for size. Slaves often learned to craft hogsheads as they worked as coopers' helpers, rolling these massive barrels around the workshop and onto wagons, boats, and ships for transport. Hogsheads, though customarily made with rough-hewn oak staves (the lengthwise wooden boards that created the cask's shell), also had to be made well enough to withstand rough handling and long sea voyages. To help finance the costs of the Revolutionary War, Philadelphia resident Robert Morris, the superintendent of finances (a position later called the U.S. Treasury secretary), contracted with American growers to deliver twenty thousand hogsheads of tobacco to French ports annually between 1785 and 1787 (Morris 1785). This represented just a part of the export and none of the domestic trade during those years.

Other coopers labored in cooperages, workshops where they used specialized tools to cut, shape, and trim the wood from which they made barrels and casks. The wood used depended largely on the types of barrels that coopers made. Softer wood like cedar, birch, and even some pinewood could be used for barrels holding relatively lightweight products, like apples or flour, while cedar or oak was typically used for barrels holding heavier goods. Coopers normally made wet barrels only of red or white oak staves, with thicknesses as much as an inch for valuable products like oils, turpentine, and rum. While coopers normally cut the wood with axes and saws and shaped the staves using a special tool called a froe, sometimes others brought readymade staves to cooperages. This was a practice common among farmers, who contracted with local coopers to make barrels for shipping grain; a farmer and his son might spend their winters and other downtime during the seasons to saw wood and then shape the staves.

Most types of storage and shipping barrels had a slightly rounded shape, making the cask both stronger and more easily rolled about and stacked. Coopers used the froe, a wedged cutting tool, to give the wooden staves their rounded shapes.

Coopers then used jointer planes—a cutting tool with a raised sharp blade—mounted atop long tables to slide the edges of the stave to the desired angle, much like a cook uses a mandolin to slice and make julienned and ribbon vegetables. Each stave edge had to be beveled properly so that it fit together with its neighboring staves without allowing seepage.

Once a full set of shaped staves fit together well, the cooper then slipped a truss hoop over them, which held the staves roughly in place for the workmen. Coopers then fashioned the hoops to hold the staves together; each cask had multiple hoops. Barrels and casks in the colonial period had hoops primarily made of hickory or other hardwood with a notch, or nib, that clicked the two ends of the wooden hoops together. Like each stave, each wooden hoop had to be meticulously crafted with close-fitting pieces that joined together seamlessly. To make a rope hoop, the cooper wound a length of hemp or cotton rope around the cask, drew it tight using a small windlass, and then braided the rope ends together tightly. Only when the barrel or cask had been formed did the cooper add the heads, or the flat wooden ends of each container. Again, the cooper had to carefully bevel the edges of the heads to fit tightly within the staves. He then hammered the heads into place, trimmed the extra lengths of each stave using a hand adze, and completed the container.

Other types of barrels might involve more work or slightly different processing. For whiskey barrels, for instance, coopers often had to use a torch to char the interior of their casks to provide particular flavoring. "White" coopers made pails, butter churners, open containers, and other kinds of products, often to be sold in their own shops to town dwellers. Coopers who worked aboard whaling and trading vessels often had to construct liquid-tight casks while at sea—a special danger for those working with razor-sharp tools and knives while a ship was tossing about on the waves.

As craftsmen in England and, later, America, coopers often passed their skills, knowledge, and tools from one generation to another within the same family—thus, the common surname Cooper. Other children—and some young indentured servants—were apprenticed to coopers. The period any apprentice served might depend upon the types of casks his master and journeymen made; coopers who specialized in one type of container, such as charred white oak whiskey barrels, could maximize their production, and their profits, as they created only one product. Apprentices who worked under coopers who made a variety of casks and containers would likely have a much longer apprentice period. So skilled were master coopers that they generally rejected the use of any measuring equipment; they gauged length, size, shape, and fit solely by the eye.

Coopers also needed to be physically capable as forcing a hardwood hoop onto a sleeve of loose staves required strength as well as skill. Colonial coopers took great pride in their skilled trades, part of the practice of "wrights," or men who crafted items primarily of wood. They brought their guilds—or associations of workers that set apprentice standards and determined work processes—with them from England. While guild membership diminished in the late nineteenth century as mechanized production of casks, barrels, and other containers eclipsed handcrafted products, even today at places like Colonial Williamsburg and other living history museums, traditional coopers create their products using the same techniques, skills, and tools as their colonial counterparts.

Nancy Quam-Wickham

See also: Cartwright and Wainwright; Shipwright

FURTHER READING

Crews, Ed. 2003. "Making Circles." *The Colonial Williamsburg Journal* 25, no. 3 (fall).

Holcomb, Alison. 2009. "Tobacco Barrels: Hogsheads." Raleigh: NCPedia, North Carolina Museum of History. https://www.ncpedia.org/tobacco/barrels.

Morris, Robert. 1785. "Contract between Robert Morris and the Farmers-General of Tobacco in France concerning the tobacco trade between the United States and France." Chapel Hill: University of North Carolina. http://docsouth.unc.edu/csr/index.html/document/csr18-0124.

Tolpin, Jim. 1998. *The Toolbox Book.* Newtown: Taunton Press.

Tunis, Edward. 1965. *Colonial Craftsmen and the Beginnings of American Industry.* Baltimore: Johns Hopkins University Press.

FARMER

Farming was the primary economic activity of America's early English colonies. In the Chesapeake region in Virginia, after colonists determined that rumors of great gold deposits were baseless, they turned to another way to make cash: growing tobacco for export to England. Maryland followed the Virginia example. The Puritans who came to Massachusetts expected to recreate the English countryside, where mixed farming and animal husbandry predominated. The colonists who populated southern New England, the Jerseys, New York, and, to a lesser extent, the Albermarle Sound area of Carolina also sought abundant land and pursued farming, both for subsistence and market production. In the southernmost English colony on the North American continent, the lowlands around Charleston in southern Carolina, a small group of planters also exploited the land to produce wealth through agriculture. The Dutch settlers of New Amsterdam had as their priority the protection of the fur trade, but they did establish farms in the Hudson Valley to supply food to settlers in their Manhattan settlements. What America offered to settlers was abundant land, and though native people lived on that land, European colonists had few scruples about taking it from them, whether by purchase or force.

In the years between 1607 and 1680, when William Penn (1644–1718) received a patent to what later became Pennsylvania, one of the "breadbasket" colonies, farming and agriculture looked much different than it did later in the 1700s. The Puritans who settled Massachusetts Bay may have immigrated for religious freedom, but they were also lured by the prospect of establishing an idealized English farming, or yeoman, society. Remarkably, most Puritans were not themselves English farmers but instead were primarily urban residents: tradespeople and merchants whose families may have been at least a generation or two removed from the land. The elites who governed and organized settlement in the Chesapeake, in Maryland, and the area around Charleston (or Charles Town), Carolina, may have been more familiar with the responsibilities of managing agricultural estates in England (or Barbados for those who settled Charles Town), but they were not themselves men who got their hands dirty working the soil. The most vexing problem of all the colonies was the problem of labor: who was to do the work?

Early colonists solved some of their labor problems by relying on indentured servants, as was the case in the Chesapeake. There, indentured servants did much of the work of clearing the land to prepare to plant tobacco. In New England, families relied on each other, and sometimes their neighbors or a servant, for the tasks of farming: clearing and fencing land, building barns for livestock, plowing the fields, and harvesting crops. In New England, the land may have been abundant, but it tended to be rocky and marginally fertile, and it eroded easily when marshlands and bogs were drained and native pasturelands trampled by livestock. The Charles Town planters brought slaves with them from their sugar plantations in Barbados. Elsewhere, as in the Pueblos of present-day New Mexico, Spanish missionaries and the few settlers they brought with them relied mostly on natives to work the land, where tribal people like the Hopi and Zuni had long traditions of successful horticulture.

One way that English colonists resolved the labor problem was to adapt English farming techniques to New World environments. To clear fields, colonists girdled native trees, cutting a thick ring through the bark and underlying layers (phloem and xylem) critical for nutrient transportation between roots and branches. Girdling a tree will cause it to die; colonists then burned the tree, leaving it to rot and provide soil nutrients, or felled it for fuel wood. Cutting trees down and removing stumps and root balls required much greater effort, so girdling and burning were efficient alternative techniques. Early colonists tended not to use draft animals, instead using handheld implements to prepare fields for planting. Early New England settlers seldom bothered to remove the stones from fields as that act, too, required more labor power than was available. The immigrants who chose the site of Plymouth, for instance, chose it largely because of the proximity to abandoned Indian cornfields.

Corn, the primary agricultural staple of both early New England and early Virginia and Maryland, grew well in haphazard fashion, not in carefully groomed rows but planted on hillocks in complementary manner with legumes and squash (a tribal practice). Tobacco, likewise, did not need to be planted in rows as it was a tender crop cared for by hand tools. Subsistence vegetable gardens tended to be just large enough to satisfy the needs of the householder, while most colonists planted only small fields of wheat, barley, or peas and beans as the effort required to clear land for crops grown "under the plow" was considerable. European grains required lands to be worked through to fine soil for the seeds to sprout. Growing tree fruit was also a common practice as orchards required little effort other than pruning and harvesting once the trees were established. Orchards did not require the wholesale clearing of land either.

These adaptations gave pause to commenters of the time, who often assumed that early colonial farmers were "lazy" as they failed to properly protect their fields, were sometimes content to use natural landmarks like creeks as fencing, let livestock roam freely, and did not adhere to early modern techniques of English agriculture. Court proceedings from the Massachusetts Bay colony are full of accounts of disputes between neighbors over inadequate fencing or fields and vegetable plots trampled by cattle or swine. Even tribal people were subject to the colony's laws: in September 1632, the Pawtucket leader Wonohauquaham, known to the colonists as Sagamore John, was admonished in court for failing to fence his cornfields and then demanding remuneration from colonists whose livestock overran his fields (Massachusetts, Court of Assistants, Vol. II, 26). Less than a year later, Wonohauquaham and most of his people died of smallpox in the 1633 epidemic.

Animal husbandry could provide greater economic rewards than farming; on the eastern shore of Virginia, a small group of free Africans made enough money from raising livestock and selling animals to tidewater planters to purchase land for their community settlement in the area of Northampton, Virginia, during the mid-1600s.

In the Chesapeake region, by the 1660s, colonists seeking liberty from the laws of the colony began to move southward, into the Albermarle Sound area of present-day North Carolina, where they settled on homesteads. Farming here was a sometime occupation, according to Virginian William Byrd, who surveyed the area a few decades later. Throughout an account of his travels, Byrd noted with dismay the conditions of the farms of these Carolinian homesteaders, with untended vineyards and orchards of unpicked fruit, presided over by languid, drunken men. Of one such homestead, Byrd wrote,

> . . . the distemper of laziness seizes the men oftener much than the women. These last spin, weave and knit, all with their own hands, while their husbands, depending on the bounty of the climate, are slothful in every thing but getting of children, and in that only instance make themselves useful members of an infant colony. There is but little wool in that province, though cotton grows very kindly, and, so far south, is seldom nipped by the frost. The good women mix this with their wool for their outer garments; though, for want of fulling, that kind of manufacture is open and sleazy. Flax likewise thrives there extremely, being perhaps as fine as any in the world, and I question not might, with a little care, be brought to rival that of Egypt; and yet the men are here so intolerably lazy, they seldom take the trouble to propagate it. (Byrd 2001, 20–21)

Such accounts do not reveal the real labor of farming in early colonial America. Homesteaders who worked the land did so gradually, perhaps only fully clearing an acre or two of land per year. Breaking the soil and planting was seasonal work, beginning in early spring or, in the northern colonies, as soon as the ground was unfrozen. Only once fields were planted with corn (or tobacco and corn) did farmers take on other agricultural duties: beginning to prepare orchard land for planting young trees, plowing a small field for barley or wheat, or putting in a household vegetable garden. The last was generally women's work. Sheep were also sheared at this time, before the heat of the summer.

During the summer, farmers and their sons (and sometimes servants) used scythes to cut meadow grasses for hay, which had to be dried and bundled to store as livestock feed for use in winter. While crops grew and hay dried, farmers built and mended fences, sharpened and repaired farm implements, and prepared corncribs and other storage areas to receive the yearly harvest. When harvest came, farming families worked feverishly to bring in the corn and other grains, while servants in the Chesapeake area carefully cut large tobacco stalks, splitting them to allow the plant to hang upside down on racks. Both crops needed preparation—corn husked, tobacco leaves cleaned and deveined—and both required drying for storage. Apples and pumpkins ripened in the autumn; onions, parsnips, turnips, and other root vegetables were also harvested at that time of year. Surplus produce was carted to local markets to be sold. Once the harvest was brought in and crops processed and stored, then animals needed to be slaughtered, ham brined and smoked, and the barn and other outbuildings readied for winter. In the colder climates, farm households spent the winter months mostly indoors, where they continued their work—women spinning and weaving, men making hand tools, and children shelling beans and peas and sorting seeds for next year's planting.

Farming was never-ending work—though by adapting agricultural practices, they could conserve energy and slowly improve their holdings. It was not until well into the 1700s that American farms took on the character of productive establishments producing bountiful harvests for market. By this time, the population of colonial America had multiplied, providing the labor necessary to truly transform frontier lands into modern farms.

Nancy Quam-Wickham

See also: Indentured Servant; *1776–1860:* Field Hand; Planter; *1915–1945:* Farmworker

FURTHER READING

Breen, T. H., and Stephen Innes. 2004. *"Myne Owne Ground:" Race and Freedom on Virginia's Eastern Shore, 1640–1676.* Second Edition. New York: Oxford University Press.

Byrd, William. 2001. *The Westover Manuscripts: Containing the History of the Dividing Line Betwixt Virginia and North Carolina; A Journey to the Land of Eden, A.D. 1733; and A Progress to the Mines. Written from 1728 to 1736, and Now First Published.* Electronic Edition, transcription of the 1841 publication by Edmund and Julian Ruffin. Academic Affairs Library, University of North Carolina at Chapel Hill. http://docsouth.unc.edu/nc/byrd/byrd.html.

Colonial Williamsburg Foundation. "Experience the Life: Trades—Historic Farming." http://www.history.org/Almanack/life/index.cfm.

Massachusetts, Court of Assistants. 1901. *Records of the Court of Assistants of the Colony of Massachusetts Bay, 1630–1692.* Edited by John Noble and John Cronin. Boston: County of Suffolk, Massachusetts.

Rutman, Darrett B. 1967. *Husbandmen of Plymouth: Farms and Villages in the Old Colony, 1620–1692.* Boston: Beacon Press.

Vickers, Daniel. 1994. *Farmers and Fishermen: Two Centuries of Work in Essex County, Massachusetts, 1630–1850.* Chapel Hill: University of North Carolina Press.

FARRIER

A farrier was a worker who attended to the feet of horses, donkeys, mules, and oxen that pulled the plows of early American farmers. Part veterinarian, part blacksmith, the farrier's job was to care for these animals' feet, inspecting them for wear, cleaning and shaving down uneven growths, and creating iron shoes to fit each individual hoof. In the wild, horses seldom needed shoeing, but as domesticated work animals, it was crucial that their feet be kept clean, well cared for, and shod to protect them from splitting on stone roads and other hard surfaces.

The farrier was skilled in livestock care in the colonial period and afterward. To keep healthy for farm and transportation work, draft animals needed regular care and shoeing. Before the mid-nineteenth century, animal care was generally restricted to work animals. Draft animals—those that pulled wagons, plows, and other implements—were essential to pre-industrial society. Colonial residents used oxen and mules to pull plows and wagons and horses to pull plows, wagons, and buggies. Colonists also rode horses as means of individual transport, as did the British Army and local militia. Due to their size, build, and stresses exerted by pulling implements and buggies or carrying a rider (or heavy goods), horses and other draft animals often developed injuries or health problems with their lower limbs and feet. These animals all had hooves that required regular cleaning, filing and trimming, and fitting with protective iron "shoes." Without regular care, draft animals' hooves would chip, split, and sometimes become overgrown, all causing an animal pain and lameness. Some of these injuries, like overgrowth of the hoof, could be debilitating, requiring emergency care or, in the worst cases, euthanasia. As an early horse-care textbook, *The American Farrier*, noted in its first line, "No animal is so useful as the horse, and yet there is none so liable to disease" (Haynes 1865, i).

The first guild (or professional organization) of farriers, the Worshipful Company of Farriers, was organized in England in 1356. By the beginning of the eighteenth century, despite the period's labor shortages, American farriers had gained a measure of status in the colonies afforded to their English counterparts. One of the first books Benjamin Franklin published at his own press was the 1735 volume *The Gentleman's Farrier*. Later texts even linked veterinary care performed by farriers with medical care for humans. Farriers were knowledgeable about hoof conditions, of course, but also provided regular care for livestock. Among the most common illnesses treated by farriers was inflammation, which colonists believed was caused by "fullness of blood" and thus required bloodletting (or puncturing a vein and extracting two or more quarts of blood), followed by administration of a laxative. Respiratory conditions in draft animals required administration of "smoke" from caustic or stringent elements like burning sulfur. Farriers administered a mixture of ammonia and ale, to which they added certain seeds, to worm animals. Sprains, boils, and abscesses were treated with liniments and often wrapped tightly to heal. Farriers treated cattle and oxen that had "lost their cud," or had a blockage in their rumen (the first of a cow's four-compartment stomach system), with a mixture of warmed bran gruel, "Barbadoes" aloe, brandy, salt, and red pepper. When animals became injured and ill or turned lame, many farmers would call on the local farrier to determine and direct best treatments.

Most farriers owned a blacksmithing forge as horseshoes and the nails that held them to an animal's hoof were not machine made until well into the mid-1800s. In smaller villages and farming communities, a colonial farrier might also double as the local blacksmith. A forge consisted of a brick oven-like crucible in which charcoal or coal was burned at high heat and into which an iron bar was placed for heating to a high temperature, at which it became pliable. Using tongs, the farrier would then extract the hot iron, place it on an anvil (a large metal block flattened on the top), and then hammer it into the preferred shape. Often, the farrier would have to reheat the iron as he shaped it into a horseshoe. Horseshoes were handmade, fitted to each animal's hooves.

Once the farrier had inspected the animal's hooves, determined the shoe sizes and shapes needed, and fabricated the shoes and nails to fit, he then cleaned the hoof. A horse's hoof is essentially a vestigial toe, covered by a hard surface, called the horny laminae, which is like a toenail. Under the laminae sits a cartilage-like piece of tissue that acts as a cushion between the horse's foot (bones, muscles, blood vessels) and its hoof. The hoof must be cleaned (removing debris with brushes and picks), trimmed, and filed to balance it for shoeing. Then the farrier attaches the iron shoe he has fabricated, hammering short nails, which he then bends and trims, onto the hoof. While horses and mules were shod with the typical semicircular single horseshoe, a farrier would have to fabricate special two-piece shoes for oxen as they have split hooves, or a hoof that is essentially two vestigial toes.

Most horses and other draft animals need their hooves cleaned and inspected daily by a farmer or owner to detect serious injury or infections like thrush, a bacterial infection frequently caused by long exposure to wet ground, mud, and dirty barnyards with wet manure. Animal owners called on the farriers when home remedies did not work or serious problems were detected. Farriers shod horses and other draft animals every few months, though, today, a horse may be re-shod as often as every four to six weeks. While colonial farriers learned the trade most commonly by serving an apprenticeship or working for their father, today, most farriers attend a technical college to learn the trade. A two-year program of study is now the most common form of training and includes college-level classes in anatomy, physiology, metal working, animal care, and business operations.

Nancy Quam-Wickham

See also: Blacksmith; Husbander; *1861–1914:* Cowboy; *1946–1991:* Veterinarian

FURTHER READING

American Farrier's Association. https://americanfarriers.org/.

Boorstin, Daniel J. 1958. *The Americans: The Colonial Experience.* New York: Vintage Books.

Haynes, S. R. 1865. *The American Farrier and Horsemen's Companion.* Philadelphia: The Author.

PRIMARY DOCUMENT

In this document, British author Francis Clater offers veterinary advice to those who worked as farriers, many of whom would have called themselves "horse doctors." His book, Everyman His Own Farrier, *was widely read on both sides of the*

Atlantic; it was republished at least thirty times during the nineteenth century. In this selection, Clater advises farriers to treat horses with the same rigor and tools of the apothecary—using firm diagnostic techniques and tinctures and drugs to heal horse injuries and illnesses. Such practical guides were common in early America and were used to treat livestock as well as humans.

Directions for the Management of Horses

The best method of treating horses, is never to bleed or purge them, except in cases which evidently require such operations. A horse's food chiefly consists of grain and herbage, which, if good in quality, and dispersed with judgment (not omitting proper exercise and dressing) will secure him from those complicated disorders he is subject to, by improper treatment . . . [1]

Of bruises: A Horse that is much bruised with falls or blows, should first be bled, and then treated as follows:

Recipe: Verjuice, four ounces; oil of turpentine, one ounce; bole Armenian, half an ounce: mix them all together, and rub well the bruised parts with it, once or twice a day.

If the horse appears heavy, dull, stiff and sore, and his appetite fails, give him the following comfortable sweating drink:

Recipe: Peruvian bark, half an ounce; gentian root, in powder, half an ounce; mithridates, half an ounce; cream of tartar, one ounce; give these in a pint of warm ale.

This drink may be repeated every morning, or every other morning, fasting, till his appetite is recovered, and the soreness and stiffness be abated, and give him warm water and mashes, twice a day, until his recovery . . . [45]

Of Hoof-bound:

A horse is hoof-bound, when the hoof is very tight around the instep, between the hair and hoof, and wide at the bottom, resembling the shape of a bell. It is often occasioned by setting on broad and hollow shoes; though, sometimes, by a fever falling down in the horse's feet. In this case, the farrier generally falls to work, in paring and drawing the horse's foot, in order to find out the lameness, and afterwards puts on a broad shoe, very much hollowed. By this fatal practice, in a week, or a fortnight's time, the horse's coffin drops, and all cure is rendered ineffectual.—This is owing to the chief support of the foot being taken away, and bad shoeing. But if the above complaint be taken in time, it may be cured by easing the shoe, and stopping the foot with the [following preparation]: [124]

Recipe: Tar, four ounces; hog's lard, four ounces; common turpentine, one ounce: melted together in an iron ladle . . . [121]

[A]nd then rubbing the blistering ointment . . . all around the instep, just above the hoof. [124]

Recipe: Bee's wax, four ounces; hog's lard, two ounces; common turpentine, six ounces; simmer them over a slow fire until dissolved; then add oil of turpentine, four ounces; corrosive sublimate, in powder, half an ounce; euphorbium and cantharedis, each an ounce; train oil, half a pint, stir them all gently together over a slow fire, then take it off, and let it stand till almost cold, and add a half an ounce of oil of vitriol, stirring the ingredients well together. [80]

In a few days after, let the horse be turned out to grass [for] two to three months. [124]

Source: Francis Clater. 1806. *Everyman his own Farrier, or the whole art of farriery laid open: containing cures for every disorder a horse is incident to . . . To which is added an appendix; including several excellent recipes, and preparation of many valuable medicines.* London: A. Tomlinson for B. Crosby. https://archive.org/details/b22038619.

Medicine ingredients:

Verjuice is an acidic juice made from unripe grapes.

Bole Armenian is a red medicinal clay, high in iron oxide content, from Armenia.

Turpentine oil is a concentrated oil made from the resin of certain pine trees; distillation produces camphor and other chemicals used for medicinal and antiseptic purposes.

Peruvian bark is also known as cinchona bark, the bark of the flowering cinchona plant, *Cinchona succirubra*, and has astringent and anti-malarial properties. It was commonly sold in London and elsewhere by the end of the seventeenth century.

Gentian root is a bitter herbal remedy created from dried roots of flowering plants of the *Gentiana* genus. Plants from this genus are found in the wild throughout the world. In North America, they were sometimes known as "mountain roses."

Mithridates (also mithridatum) was an ancient antidote to poison, composed of a variety of herbs, seeds, and roots. It was used for numerous ailments, though it is unknown if it was effective against any poison. During the Middle Ages, some people took mithridatum to protect themselves against the plague.

Corrosive sublimate is an archaic term for mercury chloride; it was used as an antiseptic, but toxic exposure (mercury poisoning) was common.

Euphorbium is a medicinal resin from succulent plants of the genus *Euphorbia*. It was used for a wide variety of disorders, from stomach ulcers to bone cancer.

Cantharedis was a poisonous substance made from dried blister beetles.
Cantharedis poisoning was common in North America.
Train oil is another name for certain kinds of whale oil.

FISHERMAN

Evidence suggests that the first English colonists survived primarily on a diet of fish, not poultry or wild turkeys, during their first years on the North American continent. Traditionally, tribal people living in American coastal regions relied on fish for much of their protein needs, while even before the English and French arrived as colonists, European fishermen had long worked along the northern coasts of North America. In the mid-1500s, 60 percent of the fish eaten in Europe was salted cod, or *bacalao*, caught and processed primarily by thousands of Portuguese, French, and Basque fishermen working in the cod fishery off Newfoundland, where it was reported that the "sea there is swarming with fish" (Kurlansky 1997, 50–51). When colonists arrived, they tried to replicate these earlier patterns of resource exploitation by fishing to provide dietary protein. The abundance of fish, shellfish, and mollusks in the seventeenth century made fishing a logical choice for hungry colonists, though it was not an easy task to harvest those fish to provide needed food.

As Europeans colonized North America, explorers were among the first to note the abundance of fish; John Smith wrote that on his trip to Chesapeake in 1607, he and his crew "lived for ten weeks on oisters [sic]" while they caught dozens of sturgeon, some nine or ten feet in length, in the bay. In his *Description of Virginia*, Smith describes the Chesapeake region as being alive with many species of fish "more divers [sic] than elsewhere" and oysters so thick in the rivers that they seemed like stones (Tyler 1907, 84–85). So plentiful and well established were these oyster beds that Smith's vessel had even grounded on a bank of oysters while leaving the Potomac River. Likewise, in New England, early explorers noted the abundance of fish. While anchored near the Georges Islands of southern Maine in 1605, George Waymouth described how in just a "small time with two or three hooks," a small party from his ship caught enough cod, haddock, and skate to supply the crew for three days. Later that evening, the crew cast a small net, bringing up "thirty very good and great Lobsters, many Rockfishes, some Plaice [flounder], and other small fishes, and other fishes called Lumpes, very pleasant to the taste: and we generally observed that what kind soever we took were well fed, fat, and sweet in taste" (Burrage 1884, 104–105).

It was difficult for early colonists, however, to harvest this amazing abundance of fish, shellfish, and mollusks. The problem was one of labor: too few of the original colonists knew how to harvest the riches of the sea, bay, and rivers. Most

English colonists in both New England and the Chesapeake area were land-bound residents from towns and villages in southern and eastern England, or they were Londoners, like many of the indentured servants sentenced to transport. As farmers or urban residents, they lacked knowledge of sailing and seamanship, fishing technologies, or methods of processing their catch. This shortage of skilled fishermen led early colonists to rely on local tribal people to supply them with fish in a flourishing trade.

Colonists also copied native fishing techniques, erecting fish weirs across rivers to trap migrating species, as did early residents of Watertown, Massachusetts—who, in one day in the early 1630s, harvested a reported 100,000 shad and alewives from a weir built across the Charles River near Boston (Roberts 2007, 51). Unlike the larger stone weirs common to English beaches, native fish weirs were wooden fence-like structures, built in a V-shape across a river, with a small opening leading to another temporary entrapment where fish migrating upstream could easily be scooped from the enclosure. Building fish weirs of this type was a community enterprise for early colonists, as was processing the great numbers of fish captured in such a manner. Fish needed to be gutted, salted, and either put into barrels or dried. Sometimes brined fish was smoked for days until the moisture was eliminated, creating a kind of fish jerky.

To catch oceangoing fish, early colonial "companies" were formed to import young men as fishermen; they hailed from the western coasts of England, where they had learned the trade. These fishermen generally signed one-year indentures, arriving in New England in the early spring, and fished the bays and banks of the region while living in thatched huts for the season before returning to England in the fall. It was back-breaking work: going to sea in small sailing vessels every morning, tending to nets and traps, and processing the fish upon return in the evenings. There were nets to construct and repair and buoys to replace. Some worked in row- or sail-powered skiffs, bringing their catches to a larger vessel after hauling the nets. This work paid little; most fishermen employed in these early joint-merchant ventures did not renew their indentures the following year. While in New England, they lived in largely insular communities of other indentured fishermen, apart from local townspeople. The lifestyles of these fishermen were like those of other maritime workers: in their predominantly male communities, they drank, swore, smoke, and were regarded as "disorderly" in part because they were adherents to the Church of England, rejecting membership in the Puritan churches of the region.

The colonial New England fishing industry changed because of the disruption of the English Civil War, which began in 1642. Prices for dried cod rose in continental Europe as migration of fishermen from western England was largely cut off by war. At the same time, England's West Indies plantations devoted land and labor primarily to sugar, creating a need for food for the slaves and servants who worked those plantations. The industry became financially viable—one that produced fish for a relatively small number of colonists on the American frontier but also could produce sizable profits for investors by selling dried, salted, or smoked fish abroad. Seeing these profit-making possibilities, by the 1640s, American and English merchants developed a client system that allowed fishermen to work independently, not as indentured servants. Merchants extended supplies (a small vessel, rope and twine, other gear, salt, bait, timber, tools, food, and rum) to fishermen in exchange for agreement to sell that merchant all of their catch at the end of the season at current prices. In 1660, a team of fishermen could make as much as £9 sterling in a season, an enormous sum for the day, equivalent to about five hundred U.S. dollars in 2015. This system of credit encouraged enterprising young men to pursue fishing; among these fishermen were some of those indentured servants from western England who had run away from their obligations to settle along the coasts of present-day Maine and Massachusetts. In earlier years, runaway indentured servants were seldom pursued as frontier conditions made it unlikely for a captain to capture a fugitive fisherman.

While fishing for food for the local population was generally a local endeavor, with greater opportunities to export their catch, colonial fishermen began to head northward to the Gulf of Maine, where enormous cod runs occurred. Exports were shipped from Boston and other New England ports in April and November, so fishermen often left in winter on small sailing vessels, called shallops, of about thirty feet in length. A group of fishermen loaded the shallop and set out for the Gulf, where once they had arrived, they built small docks (stages) and large drying racks (flakes) on local beaches. Fishing in outlying waters has always been a dangerous job with accidental mortality rates approaching 50 percent as fishermen often contended with bad weather and storms, overloading, leaky vessels, and other hazards. Fishing nets and lines could become entangled on the bottom. Cod fishing was generally done with baited hooks, dropped to the bottom with lead weights. Fishermen "soaked" the lines for short time and then brought the line up, pulling it hand over hand, coiling the line into a barrel, and then removing the fish on the hooks. When the cod were running thick, a single fisherman might drop and pull multiple lines a hundred times or more per day, working eighteen to twenty hours at a stretch before returning to the stages to unload. Some fishermen employed others as fish processors, known as shoremen, so that once they got a meal and a nap, they'd head out to sea again. Those fish processors on the beach worked hurriedly as failing to gut, salt, and dry the cod properly, or leaving it in the rain, could result in "refuse" fish—cod that could only be sold to West Indian plantations, where it was used as food for slaves and livestock. Once a crew had a full load of processed cod, they would set sail for Massachusetts ports, hoping to make the April or November export shipping deadlines. Once they arrived in port, most fishermen took a few weeks to rest and recuperate from their hectic voyages.

As the colonial towns of New England matured, fishermen increasingly settled down in coastal fishing ports. Many married, set up households, and fathered children, with sons later following their fathers into the trade. By the 1670s and '80s, fishing towns like Marblehead had established fishing families. In other places, like on Nantucket, seafaring families employed both their sons and nephews, as well as young tribal men, many indentured to serve in the cod and whale fisheries. These families established a fishing industry that lasted centuries.

Nancy Quam-Wickham

See also: Rigger; Shipwright; *1776–1860:* Sailor

FURTHER READING

Burrage, Henry. 1884. *Rosier's Relation of Waymouth's Voyage to the Coast of Maine, 1605.* Portland: The Gorges Society.

Kurlansky, Mark. 1997. *Cod.* New York: Penguin.

Roberts, Callum. 2007. *The Unnatural History of the Sea.* Washington, DC: Island Press.

Tyler, Lyon Gardiner, ed. 1907. *Narratives of Early Virginia, 1606–1625.* New York: C. Scribner's Sons.

Vickers, Daniel. 1994. *Farmers and Fishermen: Two Centuries of Work in Essex County, Massachusetts, 1630–1850.* Chapel Hill: University of North Carolina Press.

GOVERNOR

The role of a governor in colonial America was twofold: to enforce English policies in the colonies and to represent the English Crown (and, often, to administer royal policies on behalf of the Crown). These two central responsibilities were at the heart of the tension between colonists and their governors; from early in the colonial period, English policies established local assemblies and councils on which colonists sat. Additionally, local governance structures were usually staffed by colonists, many of whom had left England to establish new self-governing communities in the Americas. The religious strife and insatiable desire for wealth that drove so many Europeans to the Americas was replicated here, on the continent, as settler colonists sought to create—or recreate—the communities they had left. Governors also had to enforce English trade policies, interpret English laws as they might apply in a colonial environment, and negotiate with colonial councils and assemblies to accede to royal policies.

Hostilities with tribal people led to demands for greater services: protection, boundary setting, and the suppression of indigenous people through warfare. Petty jealousies and sectarian divisions created often fractious communities, leading some settlers to set off to organize their own colonies. Elsewhere, as in the Chesapeake area, social stratification was enforced by laws passed by assemblies, often imposing harsh penalties on those who committed even relatively minor infractions. In Carolina, King Charles II issued a charter to seven noblemen to organize an entirely different colonial government, one that attempted to recreate older patterns of the English gentry, with large landowners, known as "lord proprietors," who wielded most governmental and political power—but only for a short time.

Colonial governors were typically appointed by the Crown. They were usually men with significant military and political experience. Thomas Dongan, for instance, had spent many years in the service of the French Army before returning to England after the restoration of Charles II. Fluent in French, Dutch, and English, Dongan was appointed by Charles II to an English diplomatic post in Tangier, where he spent two years before once again returning to England. In 1682, Dongan was appointed vice admiral in the English Navy and governor of New York. Ties to the royals—Dongan was a descendant of the Earl of Limerick—created opportunities for him that other gifted politicians might not have been granted. Like James II, Dongan was also friendly to the French and practiced Catholicism. James II sent Dongan to New York to restructure the colony, fend off Canadian claims on the region, and organize law enforcement (sheriffs) to suppress colonists' discontent.

Although appointed by the Crown, governors were often paid by the local colonial assemblies (legislatures), giving local politicians significant leverage over them. To be effective, governors had to empower locals, often organizing colonial assemblies elected by all male freeholders of a certain age. In New York, for instance, immediately upon arrival in 1683, Dongan ordered colonists to elect representatives to a new colonial assembly; he also proclaimed a policy of religious tolerance and organized the colony into several counties. The assembly subsequently created the first provincial constitution in all of the American colonies, a critical step toward self-rule later in the colonial period. As governor, Dongan led diplomatic efforts to normalize colonial relations with the Iroquois Confederacy, known to the English as the Five Nations, in conjunction with the governor of Virginia, Lord Howard of Effingham. But Dongan's appointment as governor did not last long; within five years, he was succeeded by Edmund Andros, who was overthrown by rebellious colonists soon after James II was deposed.

The sources of colonists' displeasure with colonial governors were many. Governors issued land, grants of large estates, often to colonists with political clout or to those who had served the governor in a military or other significant capacity. These land grants could both overlap and supersede the headright system, in which any colonist who survived (for a period of years) in the colonies would receive a land grant. Royal trade policies were also a point of contention as England prohibited commerce with foreigners, while in the eighteenth century, England flooded the colonies with so many cheap goods that it suppressed domestic production and led to hardship among those merchants and tradespeople who could not compete with inexpensive imports. Colonists resented requirements to serve in colonial militias; they also resented imposition of fees and taxes to support the English military, especially during and after the French and Indian War. Frontiersmen and settlers in rural Georgia also resented Governor Henry Ellis's success in making peace with the Creek Nation in the late 1750s, though stiff fines on those who illegally purchased Indian lands seem to have quelled some dissent, at least temporarily.

The resentment of elected colonial assembly members and local officials to governors was more troublesome. In the early 1700s, members of the Virginia assembly complained that Governor Francis Nicholson was arbitrary and abusive, that he limited debates within Virginia's colonial legislature (assembly and council), and that he often favored officials who fell in line with royal policies. In 1711, Thomas Cary led a rebellion in northern Carolina that overthrew royal authority and then installed himself as governor, though Carolina's lord proprietors had appointed a different governor, Edward Hyde, leading to a short period of political chaos until English troops arrived to settle the conflict. In 1719, colonists in South Carolina rebelled against royal officials after the disastrous Yemassee War in 1715 and organized their own government on a model of self-rule.

Two years later, the Crown attempted to restore royal policies by appointing Nicholson as governor, but he soon left for England. A series of governors followed his departure, but most were either ineffectual or inflamed colonists' resentment by trying to enforce unpopular policies on them. Governors' success was also dependent upon their relationships with local elites. In eighteenth-century Virginia, William Byrd II, a local elite, served Alexander Spotswood, the local governor; he organized militia campaigns against local tribal people and surveyed the Virginia-Carolina border, but they later disagreed about Spotswood's imposition of land taxes. Byrd considered himself a representative of Virginians and was in fact a member of the House of Burgesses; as such, he complained bitterly about the issue. It was years before the two men reconciled.

The authority of colonial governors was eventually undercut by colonists' sense of being Americans, not English subjects, by the 1750s, much as Byrd had seen himself decades earlier. English attempts to enforce royal policies on rancorous Americans led to revolution, a development that governors contributed to in their service to the Crown.

Nancy Quam-Wickham

See also: *1776–1860:* Customs Collector; Diplomat; Politician; *1861–1914:* Pension Bureau Clerk

FURTHER READING

Cashin, Edward J. 1994. *Governor Henry Ellis and the Transformation of British North America.* Athens: University of Georgia Press.
Wilson, Thomas D. 2016. *The Ashley Cooper Plan: The Founding of Carolina and the Origins of Southern Political Culture.* Chapel Hill: University of North Carolina Press.
Wright, Louis B., and Marion Tinling, eds. 1941. *The Secret Diary of William Byrd of Westover, 1709–1712.* Petersburg: The Dietz Press.

GUNSMITH

Gunsmiths were blacksmiths who specialized in the intricate art of making firearms, particularly muskets, pistols, and rifles in colonial America. Among the colonial artisans, few were as necessary to a community's survival as the gunsmith. Muskets were common: colonists used guns to wage war against Indian tribespeople, to protect themselves against attack from imperial powers as well as their own neighbors, and to hunt the game that provided a significant part of the colonial diet.

Until the 1720s, gunsmiths did not make so many muskets or pistols as much as they repaired them. English laws prohibited the manufacture of most guns in America. Thus, most early gunsmiths spent their days straightening barrels, reboring the barrels of old guns, or repairing broken stocks or firing mechanisms. With the immigration of Germans into colonial Pennsylvania, however, American gunmaking expanded. Immigrants around present-day Lancaster and Bucks Counties in Pennsylvania made improvements to traditional German hunting rifles they had brought with them from Europe. By lengthening the barrel and making other adjustments, these immigrants, their neighbors, and apprentices created the Kentucky rifle, a long-barreled rifle that was easier (but slower) to load than the musket but considerably more accurate.

While later American gunmakers engineered vast improvements in pistols in the mid-nineteenth century, American gunsmiths were known for their innovations in rifle design. Every skilled gunsmith had to be knowledgeable about the blacksmithing trade: how to fire and tend a forge, heat iron or steel properly, wield a hammer correctly to create the desired shape, and "weld" or join two pieces of metal. Gunsmiths also had to be proficient in working brass as the trigger mechanism and guards were brass, as were elaborate inlays in many high-quality early rifles.

Gunsmiths created these long barrels from rods of iron that they heated over the forge. For the finest rifles, the gunsmith took two or more hot bars, locked one end of them into a vice grip, and used tongs to twist the rod slowly into an elongated, ribbon-like shape. This created a circular rod that could be flattened by forging with a hammer and then wrapped around a circular form. Twisting the metal before flattening it both strengthened it and formed beautiful markings in the barrel, which were revealed when polished. For common rifles, the barrel was created from bars of wrought iron. Whether twisted and flattened or regular bar, the iron was then molded around a long rod, requiring hundreds of passes in the forge and then hammering to "weld" it together. Most long rifle barrels were actually created in two pieces welded at the center joint by heating the barrels and forging the joint.

Gunsmiths forged barrels on a mold called a swage, which left the exteriors multisided—usually octagonal. The gunsmith then smoothed the barrel by heating and hammering its exterior to make it round. Once a gunsmith created a rounded barrel, he then bored out the barrel using a hand-cranked boring tool. Gunsmiths used successively thicker boring bits, one after another, to enlarge the hole to its desired circumference. This tedious process required both strength and patience as the bore needed to be as straight as possible; any imperfections were reduced by heating and hammering the barrel at spots where the bore was not straight. A gunsmith's trained eye could determine the straightness of the barrel, though they also used tools to help them gauge the barrel's alignment. Once the barrel was bored to the appropriate diameter, the gunsmith finished this first process using a square bit called a reamer. Ideally, the reamer left the bore uniformly circular in shape.

Working at a long table onto which the barrel was secured, the gunsmith then cleaned out the bore—polished it and then created internal grooves inside the barrel to enable the bullet to make a rotating movement as it was propelled through the barrel by the powder. Bullets fired from rifles with grooved barrels were more accurate than the shots fired from muskets, which typically had smooth barrel bores. To create the bore, a gunsmith used a special tool, the rifle broach, which was slowly rotated and pulled through the barrel bore; one historian estimated that a gunsmith had to run the broach through a rifle barrel a hundred times to create an accurate finished gun barrel with eight to ten grooves (Tunis 1965, 64). The gunsmith then shaped a threaded breech stop to protect the shooter.

Once the barrel was near finished, the gunsmith crafted the firing mechanism using wrought iron into which a "pan" of powder was placed; the flintlock consisted of a piece of flint against which a metal pin was scraped, creating sparks that lighted the gunpowder and propelled the bullet through the barrel. Gunsmiths often used English-made springs that triggered the flintlocks. These firing mechanisms required precision work as each one had multiple moving parts, and they were often slightly different, made to fit with a specific barrel and gunstock. Once the firing mechanism was completed, the entire assembly and the barrel were filed down and polished to perfection. Then the gunsmith marked the lock with his specific design, many of which were quite ornate, featuring flowers, shells, and other scroll marks.

To create the brass patchbox and butt cover, the side, trigger, and tang plates, as well as any inset brass pieces, the gunsmith heated and annealed (or strengthened) scrap brass in a forge and then poured it into a mold created using sand and charcoal set within a wooden mold box. To finish the brass plates, the gunsmith filed off any burrs and polished the visible brass.

Gunsmiths were also skilled woodworkers: They selected curly maple, walnut, and sometimes persimmon wood for the gun stocks, on occasion shaping it carefully to fit a customer's shoulder. They measured the stock—early rifles had not only the customary butt—and also surfaced the underside of the barrel for nearly its entire four-foot length. The lock assembly had to be inset into the stock, which required the gunsmith to utilize chisels and wood-carving tools. He had to attach the ramrod, which shooters used to push the bullet, cloth, and powder into the barrel at the muzzle end. Hunters and soldiers wrapped the bullet in greased paper, leather, and cloth, so the gunsmith had to carve a patchbox into the stock end that held the patches of bullet wrapping as well as any cleaning materials. The gunsmith then carved any decorative pieces into the stock, normally including scrollwork that helped to focus the shooter's eye down the barrel. He then sanded the stock repeatedly until it attained a polished patina.

While some gunsmiths expertly made fine rifles, others made rough utilitarian firearms meant for use on the frontier or, as the revolution approached, in the ranks of local militia. Some prominent and ambitious gunsmiths, like William Henry of Lancaster, Pennsylvania, went on to become armorers for the Americans during the war, though to do so, they had to give up their artisan careers to serve the interests of the young nation. Named in 1778 as superintendent of arms for the Continental Army, Henry relied on business networks that he created in previous decades to contract out for services of other gunsmiths, some of whom ran factories. Importantly, these gunsmiths repaired firearms more often than made them as the time required to produce good rifles was significant; a lesser musket could be hastily repaired and placed back into service. The need for weaponry during the Revolutionary War led some gunsmiths to become public servants and others to enlarge their own shops, creating factories employing a dozen or more men to repair (and make) cannons, muskets, and rifles—the last to supply the hundreds of men who served as snipers during the war, to the frustration of British officers. The industry of making firearms continued to expand in the 1800s.

Nancy Quam-Wickham

See also: Blacksmith; *1776–1860:* Fur Trapper; Militiaman

FURTHER READING

Colonial Williamsburg Foundation. 1969. "The Gunsmith of Williamsburg." Video.

Gordon, Scott Paul. 2012. "The Ambitions of William Henry," *Pennsylvania Magazine of History and Biography* 136: 253–284.

Halsey, Ashley, Jr. November 26, 1955. "All American Weapon." *Saturday Evening Post.*

"The most fatal widow and orphan makers in the world." *Life Magazine*, May 30, 1955.

Tunis, Edwin. 1965. *Colonial Craftsmen and the Beginnings of American Industry.* Baltimore: Johns Hopkins.

HARNESS MAKER AND SADDLER

Harness makers and saddlers built horse harnesses, horse saddles, and other tack (accessories and equipment put onto horses in the course of their domestic use). In the eighteenth century, these were indispensable trades in a growing commercial center like Philadelphia and that likely provided a comfortable living. Harnesses and saddles were generally bespoke work, completed under contract for a particular customer and to the customer's designations.

Those who "make harness," as it is known even today, were skilled craftsmen. As leather workers, they were often tanners themselves or at least had a keen sense of that trade as good harness requires leather to be tanned with waxes or oils to preserve its quality and strength. So important was the tanning process that in 1737, Virginia passed laws that required harness makers to forfeit any work and "the value thereof" if leather had not been properly tanned. Harness makers also had to be familiar with the work of farmers and teamsters and the draft animals with which they worked. Farmers seldom used harnesses on oxen; a draft horse or mule required a different harness than a horse pulling a coach as the harness itself is the complicated gear that helps the driver maneuver the plow, cart, or coach and makes it possible for the animal to pull the load. The harness has elements that allow pulling (the tugs attached to the leather harness) and braking power (the breechings or crupper), as well as allowing the driver to steer the rig. Familiarity with horses, the physics of locomotion, and the structure of carts, farm implements, and coaches or wagons was also required knowledge for harness makers. The harness maker needed basic sewing skills as well, which he may have learned as an apprentice worker or even as a common sailor or sail maker.

Some harness makers also produced their own metalwork and so had the skills of blacksmiths (and, sometimes, farriers). These multiple skills and that extensive knowledge allowed expert harness makers to also make saddles and other leather work, work as upholsterers, and make bags and trunks for travelers. Some, like Edward Sedgwick of Philadelphia, also made wagons and coaches or worked as farriers. Saddle maker Alex Craig of Williamsburg, Virginia, also sold tanned leather for shoes, boots, and other leather goods, becoming quite successful; in the 1760s, Craig employed several workers in his shops—servants, three apprentices, and at a number of journeymen harness makers—and he owned slaves who labored there too (Gill 1966, 66–68).

A well-made harness that is cared for properly can last one hundred years or more, so it represented a significant investment for farmers and others as it could be used over several generations. A 1792 guide for "gentlemen farmers" in fact warned those unfamiliar with farming work and technology to keep harnesses "in thorough repair . . . [as] in the common course of business, work of importance frequently stands still, [so] that something or other may be mended" (*Rural Economy* 1792, 122). Colonial harness makers not only made harness but also spent a significant amount of their workdays repairing them. Breechings often broke and needed to be repaired as this part of a harness was set on the horse's rump, under the tail, and allowed the animal to essentially "sit" on the breeching to act as a brake for the wagon, plow, or coach—especially when going downhill too rapidly. Straps and lines also broke with use, while buckles and other gear attaching the heavy collar to pull straps needed occasional replacement. Harness makers also adjusted old harnesses for new draft animals, such as fashioning a collar pad and new strap lines for a smaller animal.

To make a harness or saddle, the worker started with good leather (cowhide) and then cut straps and other harness elements by hand by pulling a drawknife through the hide. Some used patterns for parts of the harness like the collar, and they always cut to preserve as much of the hide as possible. They used a skiving, too, which functioned like a leather plane, to pare leather to a desired thickness. Using a collar-measuring tool, some harness makers constructed fitted collars for animals. They then stitched parts of the harness together, using an awl and leather sewing tools. Some elements of a harness were not sewed together but attached to each other using brass loops and fasteners. The complex structure of the harness required different fasteners: hame fasteners, breast straps, trace holders, and more.

A saddler used many of the same tools, though some of the cutting tools are different—rather than a drawknife, saddlers used rounded half-knives, shaped like a half-circle, which they pressed into the hide to make curved parts of the saddle. Similarly, saddlers preferred different types of tanned leather as many saddle pieces called for leather not as stiff as that of the harness maker. Saddlers sometimes decorated saddles, using leather chisels and hammers to create embossed patterns on some saddle parts as a way for owners to identify their saddles. Saddlers also customarily made bridles for horses as well, though harness makers also had these skills.

The work of saddlers and harness makers was important to colonists. Without effective harnesses, draft animals could not have pulled the implements needed to clear and plow the land. Once farmland was cleared, animals pulled tillers over plowed land to prepare for planting. Good harnesses permitted farmers to carry their produce to markets as well. These technologies—and the workers who made them possible—facilitated the rapid settlement of colonial America.

Nancy Quam-Wickham

See also: Cartwright and Wainwright; Farrier; *1861–1914:* Cowboy; Teamster

FURTHER READING

Gill, Harold B. 1966. "Leather Workers in Colonial Virginia." *Colonial Williamsburg Research Papers.* http://research.history.org/DigitalLibrary/view/index.cfm?doc=ResearchReports%5CRR0107.xml&highlight.

Keegan, Terry. 1974. *The Heavy Horse; Its Harness and Harness Decoration.* South Brunswick: A. S. Barnes.

N. A. 1792. *Rural economy, or Essays on the practical parts of husbandry: designed to explain several of the most important methods of conducting farms of various kinds; including many useful hints to gentlemen farmers, relative to the economical management of their business. To which is added, The rural Socrates, being memoirs of a country philosopher. By the author of The farmer's letters.*

HUSBANDER

In the American colonies, environmental conditions created new opportunities for husbanders and herders, workers who cared for domesticated farm animals of all kinds: oxen and cattle, pigs, sheep, goats, horses, mules and donkeys, and chickens. Husbandry refers to the act of tending to such animals by ensuring that they are stabled or fenced, fed properly and provided with fresh water, bred at the right time, cared for if injured or ill, milked (for cattle, sheep, and goats), sheep shorn for wool, horses trained to ride and mules and oxen trained for the yoke, eggs collected from the henhouse, and cattle, sheep, hogs, and goats slaughtered when leather and meat were necessary. A herder also transferred grazing animals from one pasture to another, mended fences broken by his herd, and traded animals with other colonists.

The lives of early colonial husbanders varied by region. In New England, colonists generally practiced mixed husbandry, or a mixture of agriculture and livestock-owning geared primarily to subsistence and small-scale market production. The predominant social institution was the family, and here, farm families worked together as a unit to care for their animals. Women and girls collected eggs, youngsters milked cows and goats, women made butter and cheese for family consumption and to sell to townspeople, and adolescents herded livestock, moving them from pasture to fenced enclosures on the family farm. In the earliest period, New England colonial towns featured "commons," communal plots of land to which each household head was granted a section for care of his livestock. Farmers used draft animals—oxen, horses, and mules—to power plows to clear the land and till fields.

In contrast, in Maryland and Virginia, much of the region consisted of vast meadows of grassland interspersed with rivers, marshlands, and forests. Agriculture was oriented not toward subsistence but to production for export of tobacco. Colonists received land from the authorities—the Virginia Company and then the Crown—to create vast plantations of tobacco. They expanded their holdings under the headright system, which provided landowners with an additional fifty acres for each laborer—indentured servants, family members, or slaves—they brought to the region. Their market orientation mandated that they clear as much land as possible, especially near rivers for ease of transporting the bulky tobacco, for this singular crop. While some land was set aside for corn, which formed the basis of the colonial Chesapeake diet, few farmers devoted much land to growing hay, oats, or other fodder that domestic farm animals required. Additionally, most tobacco growers used handheld hoes to plant and tend the tobacco fields as the stems of this plant are especially fragile. Unlike their counterparts in England and New England, they seldom used draft animals to pull plows for reasons other than to break in new fields.

At the same time, the unique environment of the largest estuary on the continent shaped how colonists practiced agriculture and animal husbandry. Nearly 200 miles in length, the Chesapeake Bay region is fed by several major rivers, including the Susquehanna, James, Potomac, and Rappahannock, as well as about 100,000 smaller tributary streams and creeks. At the time of the arrival of English colonists, the coastal plain contained great swamps, marshlands, and vast meadows, as well as thick forests of pine and spruce. Deciduous forests were interspersed throughout much of the region.

The abundance of large open meadows encouraged many Chesapeake husbanders and herders to allow their animals to graze freely; farmers reasoned that in this way, they could turn their animals out to pasture while they labored in the tobacco fields. To prevent hungry cattle from trampling tobacco fields, husbanders often relocated their herds to some of the many islands where the rivers formed a natural barrier. Others set their hogs loose in the pinewoods, where they bred freely and were called "swine of the forest" (Anderson 2002, 400). In this region colonized mostly by men, few male settlers milked their cows as churning butter and making cheese was considered "women's work," so a typical chore of animal husbandry—milking—was infrequently performed unless wives, women servants, or children comprised part of one's household. Herders routinely left small piles of corn out for their loose livestock as a way to entice or train them to return home periodically.

Historians have estimated that colonial livestock, subject to malnutrition, predators, and inconsistent care in the Chesapeake and southern colonies, produced perhaps only one half the number of offspring as animals on English farms (Carr, Menard, & Walsh 1991, 46–50). Despite what outsiders said about the health of early colonists' livestock, though, farmers did assert their rights of ownership. Under the law, livestock was considered personal property, no matter where animals roamed, so herders marked theirs, cutting certain marks in the ears of young animals and registering those marks with the local authorities.

This seemingly indifferent attitude toward livestock contrasts to that of England, where livestock was generally stabled or kept within fenced areas. In early Virginia and Maryland, fences were built to keep livestock out of tobacco fields rather than keeping the animals contained within a specific area like a barnyard. Such unrestrained herding and husbandry practices had serious consequences, however. Open-range cattle became victims of the region's swamps, where they drowned in brackish water or were mired in mud and starved to death or died of thirst. Natural forage provided fewer nutrients than hay and oats, leading to stunted growth; by the mid-1600s, European observers remarked on the small stature of Chesapeake cattle, hogs, and horses. Stray animals bred with other strays, leading to generations of feral livestock that created havoc on plantations. During cold winters, few colonists sheltered their herds, so livestock froze in some years. Hungry colonists and tribespeople stole livestock, while wolf predation was a significant danger to untended sheep and goats.

As the colony grew and settlement on the western frontier opened, cattle rustling increased as westward-moving colonists stole cattle to start their own herds. Those convicted of stealing cattle were whipped, marked (or cut) on their ears, and, for recidivists, executed. The hilly regions of western Virginia and the northern edges of the Carolinas allowed herders to hide stolen stock with relative ease, so despite severe punishment if caught, cattle rustlers conducted raids with little restraint and posed significant burdens to colonial husbanders and herders.

Despite the many challenges, however, herders—often servants or children—provided much-needed products to early colonists: meat, milk, leather, and wool. Early colonists ate significantly more meat than their counterparts in England. Cows, ewes, sows, and other female stock past their breeding prime or that had become barren (infertile) were routinely slaughtered for meat or sold at market, as were gelded male livestock. Feral livestock of all kinds posed threats to farms and their occupants; wild hogs regularly charged at colonists who disturbed them, so colonists hunted them seasonally to thin their numbers and provide food. In the northern and middle colonies, butter and cheese provided much-needed calories to colonists, especially during harsh winters, when nutritional needs are greater. Wool from sheep, rabbit fur, and leather also provided poverty-stricken early colonists with the goods to make home-manufactured articles and clothing.

Nancy Quam-Wickham

See also: Farmer; Farrier; Indentured Servant

FURTHER READING

Anderson, Virginia DeJohn. 2002. "Animals into the Wilderness: The Development of Livestock Husbandry in the Seventeenth-Century Chesapeake," *William and Mary Quarterly* 59: 377–408.

Carr, Lois, Russell Menard, and Lorena Walsh. 1991. *Robert Cole's World: Agriculture and Society in Early Maryland.* Chapel Hill: University of North Carolina Press.

PRIMARY DOCUMENT

The lackadaisical manner in which colonists in early Virginia cared for their livestock is recounted with scorn by Robert Beverley in the following document. The son of an early settler, Major Robert Beverley, the younger Beverley was born in Virginia, sent to England for education, and then returned to the Chesapeake area, where he worked in Jamestown, apparently as a clerk, a position that required him to have knowledge of the colony's politics, legislative operations, and legal procedures. He inherited a large plantation, to which he added more land, and later became a burgess and member of the colonial court. As a member of Virginia's gentry, he found much to dislike about the common colonist. The book from which this document is taken, The History and Present State of Virginia in Four Parts, *is the first account of an English colony in North America written by an author born in that colony; it was published in London in 1705.*

The Families being altogether on Country-Seats, they have their Graziers, Seedsmen, Gardiners, Brewers, Bakers, Butchers, and Cooks within themselves: they have a great Plenty and Variety of Provisions for their Table; and as for Spicery, and other things that the Country don't produce, they have constant supplies of 'em from *England.* The Gentry pretend to have their Victuals drest, and serv'd up as Nicely, as at the best Tables in *London.*

When I come to speak of their Cattle, I can't forbear charging my Countrymen with exceeding Ill-Husbandry, in not providing sufficiently for them all Winter, by which means they starve their young Cattle, or at least stint their Growth; so that they seldom or never grow so large as they would do, if they were well manag'd; for the humour is there, if People can but save the lives of their Cattle, tho' they suffer them to be never so poor in the Winter, yet they will presently grow fat again in the Spring, which they esteem sufficient for their purpose. And this is the occasion, that their Beef, and Mutton are seldom or never so large, or so fat as in *England:* And yet with the least feeding imaginable, they are put into as good case, as can be desired.

But the Pork, Bacon, and Fowls of all sorts, both Dunghil-Fowl, and Water-Fowl, Tame and Wild, must be allowed to have very much the advantage in their several kinds, of those in *England* . . .

There is yet another kind of Sport, which the young People take great Delight in, and that is, the Hunting of wild Horses; which they pursue sometimes with Dogs, and sometimes without. You must know they have many Horses foaled in the Woods of the Uplands, that never were in hand, and are as shy as any Savage Creature. These having no mark upon them, belong to him, that first takes them. However, the Captor commonly purchases these Horses very dear, by spoiling better in the pursuit; in which case, he has little to make himself amends, besides the pleasure of the Chace. And very often this is all he has for it, for the wild Horses are so swift, that 'tis difficult to catch them; and when they are taken, tis odds but their Grease is melted, or else being old, they are so sullen, that they can't be tamed.

The Fruit-Trees are wonderfully quick of growth, so that in six or seven years time from the Planting, a Man may bring an Orchard to bear in great plenty, from which he may make store of good Cider, or distill great quantities of Brandy; for the Cider is very strong, and yields abundance of in Spirit. Yet they have very few, that take any care at all for an Orchard; nay, many that have good Orchards, are so negligent of them, as to let them go to ruin, and expose the Trees to be torn, and barked by the cattle . . .

The Sheep increase well, and bear good Fleeces, but they generally are suffer'd to be torn off their Backs by Briers, and Bushes, instead of being shorn, or else are left rotting upon the Dunghil with their Skins.

Bees thrive there abundantly, and will very easily yield to the careful Housewife, two Crops of Honey in a Year, and besides lay up a Winter store sufficient to preserve their Stocks.

The Beeves [beef], when any Care is taken of them in the Winter, come to great Perfection. They have noble Marshes there, which, with the Charge of draining only, would make as fine Pastures as any in the World; and yet there is not an hundred Acres of Marsh drained throughout the whole Country.

Hogs swarm like Vermine upon the Earth, and are often accounted such, insomuch that when an Inventory of any considerable Man's Estate is taken by the Executors, the Hogs are left out, and not listed in the Appraisement. The Hogs run where they list, and find their own Support in the Woods, without any Care of the Owner; and in many Plantations it is well, if the Proprietor can find and catch the Pigs, or any part of a Farrow, when they are young, to mark them; for if there be any market in a Gang of Hogs, they determine the Property of the rest, because they seldom miss their Gangs; but as they are bred in Company, so they continue to the End . . .

Thus they depend altogether upon the Liberality of Nature, without endeavouring to improve its Gifts, by Art or Industry. They spunge upon the Blessings of a warm Sun, and a fruitful Soil, and almost grutch the Pains of gathering in the Bounties of the Earth. I should be asham'd to publish this slothful Indolence of my Countrymen, but that I hope it will rouse them out of their Lethargy, and excite them to make the most of all those happy Advantages which Nature has given them; and if it does this, I am sure they will have the Goodness to forgive me.

Source: Robert Beverley. 1705. *On the History and Present State of Virginia, in Four Parts. Book IV, On the Present State of Virginia.* London: R. Parker, 54–55, 75–78, 81–83.

INDENTURED SERVANT

Indentured servitude was a form of bonded labor widely used by European immigrants and residents of English North America throughout the colonial period. Historians now estimate that as many as two-thirds of all white residents of colonial North America served an indenture at one time in their lives. Indentured servants included field hands, common laborers, farmers, herders, sailors, maids, and those apprenticed to tradesmen. Indentured servants performed much of the work in early colonial America, often working ten- to fourteen-hour days, six days per week, for much of the year. Indentured servitude was ubiquitous in the Chesapeake region of colonial Virginia and Maryland, places where the market was devoted to tobacco cultivation. Here, the natural environment influenced the duties of many indentured servants as field hands worked long hours—generally from dawn to dusk—during planting and harvesting time in the Chesapeake, though during cold winters and inclement weather, the hours of their labor could be shorter as they were put to work burning trash, chopping wood, and attending to chores inside.

An indenture is a period of time, generally four to seven years but sometimes shorter or longer, often agreed to by a person who works under a contract in exchange for the cost of the voyage to North America, clothes, housing, and food during the indenture and, in some areas, a small parcel of land or payment in goods (tobacco, for instance) at the conclusion of the indenture if a servant performed his or her tasks to the satisfaction of the contract's owner.

Indentured servitude is distinguished from chattel slavery, the forced labor of generations of Africans in America, as slaves were the property of their owners; they could be bought, sold without their permission, transported to other areas, punished mercilessly, and separated from loved ones. Furthermore, the descendants of slaves were considered property too. In contrast, indentured servants sold their labor to their "owners," they were promised freedom after a certain period of time, and they had recourse to courts and the law if they felt they were being abused, though there are few examples of servants taking advantage of colonial court systems. Unlike most slaves, indentured servants could accumulate wealth and purchase their freedom before the end of their indentures.

Indentured servants were "bonded labor," so they were subject to many of the same kinds of exploitation—punishment, abuse, and cruelty—that slaves faced. Countless servants ran away from those to whom they were bound. Some were beaten to death for insolence or refusal to work. By 1642, however, the Virginia general assembly enacted laws governing relationships between servants and their masters. In contrast, just twenty years later, the same governing body passed laws defining the inferior status of African slaves relative to "English" (or white) servants and determining that a child's status as free or slave was determined by the mother's status: if the mother was a slave, so was the child—for life. Both indentured servitude and slavery were ways in which the English sought to solve the problem of labor shortages in the colonies.

Individuals became indentured servants in a myriad of ways. Many became indentured voluntarily, choosing to leave England for the colonies to find work and opportunity. Generally, Europe's population grew rapidly in the early modern period, particularly between 1500 and 1650. Demographers estimate that the population of England, in particular, more than doubled in this period, resulting in great pressures on the land; food shortages followed. People displaced from the countryside migrated to cities like London and Bristol, where they found few opportunities for work but instead encountered strict legal codes—so-called vagrancy laws—against unemployment and homelessness. The English Civil Wars during the middle of the seventeenth century (1638–1651) led to widespread suffering. Religious persecution throughout the continent also resulted in anguish. At the same time, England's imperial projects in the Caribbean and North America needed colonists to occupy the lands. All of these factors led great numbers of young people, particularly men between the ages of fourteen and twenty-five, to leave England voluntarily as indentured servants, hopeful that at the end of their service, they would be granted land and enjoy prosperity. For some, indentured servitude and transportation offered economic opportunities unavailable to them in their homeland.

Very early in the colonial period, however, the need for labor in England's overseas colonies was so great that both English and colonial officials explored ways to increase the flow of indentured servants to America. The need for labor was exacerbated by early mortality rates, which were as high as 30 percent in the first year of colonial residence due to death from malaria, typhoid, salt poisoning, and dysentery, among other diseases. Residents of the Chesapeake region in the 1620s recognized that newly arrived servants needed a "seasoning" period, time to recover from the voyage and survive their first hot and humid summer, during which many contracted malaria. During the seasoning year, illness and malnourishment often left new servants unable to work full time, if at all. Such conditions led to the growth in what historian John Wareing has called the "servant trade" in England: the brisk business of enticing poverty-stricken people to agree, nominally voluntarily, to be transported to the colonies, primarily the Chesapeake area, where their contracts were then sold. This was the case for seventy-four servants who arrived in 1637 on the vessels *Tristram* and *Jeane*. Wareing tracked the fate of those individuals; twenty-eight of the indentured servants were sent by one merchant, who simply saw them as "goods for sale." Forty-four different buyers, most of them tobacco farmers, bought the contracts of these seventy-four servants; of these, twenty-eight buyers purchased just one servant each. The servants were spread across a wide expanse of the Chesapeake region, where most labored alongside their masters on tobacco farms, known as plantations despite their size (Wareing 2017, 95–96).

The servant trade, rather than voluntary migration, made it possible for English officials to forcibly move significant numbers of the lower classes to the colonies. Those found guilty of petty crimes—stealing a spoon or a piece of lace—were routinely sentenced to "transportation" to the colonies as bound laborers, especially if they were repeat offenders. Many criminals begged for transportation rather than face the gallows; criminal punishments in early modern England were extraordinarily severe. Such was the case of Londoner Elizabeth Longman, described in court records as "an old offender, having been above a Dozen times in Newgate [Prison] . . . she was convicted and obtained the benefit and favor of Transportation, and was carried into Virginia," having been sentenced to forced labor and banishment in October 1673. She arrived in Maryland on the vessel *Charles* in May of the following year. Within two years, though, Longman purchased her freedom and returned to London, despite her banishment. Once there, noted the court, she "returned to her old Trade" (larceny), stole several pieces of silk, and for that crime and surely because she had been found "incorrigible," she was executed in 1676 (Proceedings of Old Bailey, May 17, 1676).

Misfortune led others to indentured servitude, and the courts routinely sent "vagrants" to the colonies. Parish churches normally cared for indigent people in England. Weary of the cost of their care, however, churches in England sometimes sent orphans and children born out of wedlock to North America as indentured servants; after 1660, they could do so without permission from a child's mother. This was the case for at least one of the illegitimate children of Rose Finche, who refused to reveal the names of their fathers, though most parish members suspected local men. All three children were supported by the parish until their early teenage years, when one was old enough to be sent to the Caribbean and another, a trouble-prone boy, to Virginia as indentured servants. Later, Finche married the father of another child, her son Thomas, eight years after he was born; Thomas's children later left for the Chesapeake to pursue opportunities they did not have in London.

Unexpected life changes as well as poverty led others to indenture themselves and their children. Desperately poor parents sold children as young as infants into servitude for reasons that historians can only speculate: perhaps they were too poor to care for a child or hoped that she or he would have a better life abroad. Delinquent youth were frequently indentured and transported. Individuals indentured stepchildren with whom they quarreled. Kidnapping was common enough that in 1645, the English parliament passed an "Ordinance against Stealing Children" (Wareing 2017, 172). Children orphaned by the death of their parents could find themselves on vessels bound for the Americas, victims of "spirits"—merchants who brokered labor contracts and then arranged for trans-Atlantic passage. These merchants were part of a thriving trade in "spiriting away" the poor, desperate, helpless, and too often unwilling English left vulnerable to economic, social, and political upheaval both at home and in the colonies.

Once they arrived in the colonies, servants were put to work. In the northern colonies like Massachusetts Bay, young male servants were often tasked with the hardest work of subsistence agriculture: clearing timber, breaking fields and readying them for planting, and building fences and paths. Some were put to work caring for farm animals. Others worked at shore whaling stations, where they butchered whales and other sea mammals, or went to sea on coastal traders or near-shore fishing vessels. In the tobacco-growing regions, however, male servants were nearly universally field hands, at least in the early years of the colony before the 1680s. Tobacco was a labor-intensive crop. Land had to be cleared of trees and fields broken in, tilled, and planted, and then young plants had to be tended until maturity. When mature, the plants had to be harvested carefully by hand, leaves spread to dry and cure and then bundled carefully for export. It was back-breaking, tedious labor. Young women servants performed household duties in the overwhelmingly male colony of Virginia.

In all regions, indentured servants were often housed separately from those who owned their contracts, usually in inferior outbuildings (barns and sheds) and fed poorly (unless allowed to till a small plot of their own). Indentured servitude even took hold among native-born children in the Americas as parents in northern cities sought opportunities for sons, in particular, who were apprenticed to tradesmen under "indenture" contracts.

Early colonial laws focused on ensuring that indentured servants would be held to the requirements of their contracts. In Virginia, servants had to register upon arrival and carry their indenture certificates with them. Owners of indentures could discipline their servants at they saw fit, though occasionally servants did protest to colonial governments that a master had been unusually vicious in their discipline, as Jane Dickenson testified to the Virginia governor about her treatment by Dr. John Pott, her master, in 1624 (Wolfe & McCartney 2015). Disciplining labor, however, was of great concern. Early Virginia laws stipulated punishments for refusal to work, drunkenness, lying, and other behavioral offenses. Of greatest concern to owners, however, was what to do if a servant could not work and thus not meet the requirements of his or her contract.

Laws against sexual activity became commonplace. The colonial government provided that indentured women who became pregnant would have their terms of service extended—usually two years to compensate for the expected loss of production during a woman's pregnancy and the early years of childrearing or until the toddler could be left alone without constant supervision. If the father of the child was also a servant, his indenture was extended as well; if he was the servant's master, he was fined.

Strict regulations also governed the responsibilities of those who owned the contracts of indentured servants as a servant not under the control or guidance of an employer could easily present a challenge to small, insular communities like those of early colonial America. In the Plymouth, Massachusetts, Bay Colony, as early as 1638, the local court ordered Stephen Hawkins to take control over his servant Dorothy Temple. Temple had given birth to a child out of wedlock while in Hawkins's service; the baby's father had been executed in the colony for highway robbery, leaving her without a way to provide for her child. Hawkins soon contracted with another resident to take over the responsibility of Temple and her child. For £3 sterling "and other considerations to him paid," Hawkins transferred Temple to Holmes, where the "said Dorothy is to serve all the residue of her time [about two years] with the said John Holmes, according to her indenture" in exchange for food and clothing for herself and her infant (Shurtleff 1855, 190). Other court documents record the efforts of colonial officials to mediate community disputes in which the contracts of indentured servants were transferred to resolve debts or other legal obligations.

Early colonial records contain abundance evidence of growing social tensions between indentured servants and their owners and between community members, in which indentured servants played some role. These tensions eventually contributed to political crises in late seventeenth-century Virginia, where demands for land and a series of Indian wars encouraged the gentry to adopt a system of plantation labor that relied on slaves, who were denied rights by law, instead of more unruly servants who increasingly demanded equality as white men. By 1700, a majority of elite Virginia plantation owners relied on a slave labor force. Only owners of small plantations, often those farmed by a single proprietor and one or two servants, still relied on indentured servants arriving from England to grow their tobacco.

Although indentured servitude continued until the early twentieth century, after 1700, it became more common for indentured servants to serve as common labor for farm families and as skilled tradesmen and unskilled workers in urban areas than simply as field hands on the plantations of the South. Furthermore, in the period after 1700, a shift occurred in the origin of indentured immigrants as Irish, German, and other Europeans displaced the poor of England as the majority of indentured servants in America.

Nancy Quam-Wickham

See also: Blacksmith; Farmer; Fisherman; *1776–1860:* Laborer; Laundress; *1861–1914:* Sharecropper; *1915–1945:* Farmworker

FURTHER READING

Alderman, Clifford. 1975. *Colonists for Sale: The Story of Indentured Servants in America.* New York: Macmillan.

Bly, Antonio, and Tania Haygood. 2016. *Escaping Servitude: A Documentary History of Runaway Servants in Eighteenth Century Virginia.* Lanham: Lexington Books.

Isenberg, Nancy. 2016. *White Trash: The 400-Year Untold History of Class in America.* New York: Viking.

Proceedings of the Old Bailey. https://www.oldbaileyonline.org/.

Salinger, Sharon. 1987. *"To Serve Well and Faithfully": Labor and Indentured Servitude in Pennsylvania, 1682–1800.* UK: Cambridge University Press.

Shurtleff, Nathaniel, ed. 1855. *Records of the Colony of New Plymouth in New England: printed by order of the legislature of the Commonwealth of Massachusetts.* Volume 1: Court Orders, 1633–1640. Tucson: AMS Press.

Wareing, John. 2017. *Indentured Migration and the Servant Trade from London to America, 1618–1718.* New York: Oxford University Press.

Wolfe, Brendan, and Martha McCartney. 2015. "Indentured Servitude in Colonial Virginia," *Encyclopedia of Virginia.* https://www.encyclopediavirginia.org/Indentured_Servants_in_Colonial_Virginia.

PRIMARY DOCUMENT

In this unusual document, indentured servant Richard Frethorne writes to his parents in London, begging for assistance. Frethorne had only been in Virginia for a few months when he appealed to them for help.

1623

LOVING AND KIND FATHER AND MOTHER:

My most humble duty remembered to you, hoping in god of your good health, as I myself am at the making hereof. This is to let you understand that I your child am in a most heavy case by reason of the country, [which] is such that it causeth much sickness, [such] as the scurvy and the bloody flux and diverse other diseases, which maketh the body very poor and weak. And when we are sick there is nothing to comfort us; for since I came out of the ship I never ate anything but peas, and loblollie (that is, water gruel). As for deer or venison I never saw any since I came into this land. There is indeed some fowl, but we are not allowed to go and get it, but must work hard both early and late for a mess of water gruel and a mouthful of bread and beef. A mouthful of bread for a penny loaf must serve for four men which is most pitiful. [You would be grieved] if you did know as much as I [do], when people cry out day and night—Oh! That they were in England without their limbs and would not care to lose any limb to be in England again, yea, though they beg from door to door. For we live in fear of the enemy every hour, yet we have had a combat with them . . . and we took two alive and made slaves of them.

But it was by policy, for we are in great danger; for our plantation is very weak by reason of the death and sickness of our company. For we came but twenty for the merchants, and they are half dead just; and we look every hour when two more should go. Yet there came some four other men yet to live with us, of which there is but one alive; and our Lieutenant is dead, and [also] his father and his brother. And there was some five or six of the last year's twenty, of which there is but three left, so that we are fain to get other men to plant with us; and yet we are but 32 to fight against 3000 if they should come. And the nighest help that we have is ten mile of us, and when the rogues overcame this place [the] last [time] they slew 80 persons. How then shall we do, for we lie even in their teeth? They may easily take us, but [for the fact] that God is merciful and can save with few as well as with many, as he showed to Gilead. And like Gilead's soldiers, if they lapped water, we drink water which is but weak.

And I have nothing to comfort me, nor is there nothing to be gotten here but sickness and death, except [in the event] that one had money to lay out in some things for profit. But I have nothing at all no, not a shirt to my back but two rags (2), nor clothes but one poor suit, nor but one pair of shoes, but one pair of stockings, but one cap, [and] but two bands [collars]. My cloak is stolen by one of my fellows, and to his dying hour [he] would not tell me what he did with it; but some of my fellows saw him have butter and beef out of a ship, which my cloak, I doubt [not], paid for. So that I have not a penny, nor a penny worth, to help me too either spice or sugar or strong waters, without the which one cannot live here. For as strong beer in England doth fatten and strengthen them, so water here doth wash and weaken these here [and] only keeps [their] life and soul together. But I am not half [of] a quarter so strong as I was in England, and all is for want of victuals; for I do protest unto you that I have eaten more in [one] day at home than I have allowed me here for a week. You have given more than my day's allowance to a beggar at the door; and if Mr. Jackson had not relieved me, I should be in a poor case. But he like a father and she like a loving mother doth still help me.

For when we go to Jamestown (that is 10 miles of us) there lie all the ships that come to land, and there they must deliver their goods. And when we went up to town [we would go], as it may be, on Monday at noon, and come there by night, [and] then load the next day by noon, and go home in the afternoon, and unload, and then away again in the night, and [we would] be up about midnight. Then if it rained or blowed never so hard, we must lie in the boat on the water and have nothing but a little bread. For when we go into the boat we [would] have a loaf allowed to two men, and it is all [we would get] if we stayed there two days, which is hard; and [we] must lie all that while in the boat. But that Goodman Jackson pitied me and made me a cabin to lie in always when I [would] come up, and he would give me some poor jacks [fish] [to take] home with me, which comforted me more than peas or water gruel. Oh, they be very godly folks, and love me very well, and will do anything for me. And he much marvelled that you would send me a servant to the Company; he saith I had been better knocked on the head. And indeed so I find it now, to my great grief and misery; and [I] saith that if you love me you will redeem me suddenly, for which I do entreat and beg. And if you cannot get the merchants to redeem me for some little money, then for God's sake get a gathering or entreat some good folks to lay out some little sum of money in meal and cheese and butter and beef. Any eating meat will yield great profit. Oil and vinegar is very good; but, father, there is great loss in leaking. But for God's sake send beef and cheese and butter, or the more of one sort and none of another. But if you send cheese, it must be very old cheese; and at the cheesemonger's you may buy very good cheese for twopence farthing or halfpenny, that will be liked very well. But if you send cheese, you must have a care how you pack it in barrels; and you must put cooper's chips between every cheese, or else the heat of the hold will rot them.

And look whatsoever you send me be in never so much look, what[ever] I make of it, I will deal truly with you. I will send it over and beg the profit to redeem me; and if I die before it come, I have entreated Goodman Jackson to send you the worth of it, who hath promised he will. If you send, you must direct your letters to Goodman Jackson, at Jamestown, a gunsmith. (You must set down his freight, because there be more of his name there.) Good father, do not forget me, but have mercy and pity my miserable case. I know if you did but see me, you would weep to see me; for I have but one suit. (But [though] it is a strange one, it is very well guarded.) Wherefore, for God's sake, pity me. I pray you to remember my love to all my friends and kindred. I hope all my brothers and sisters are in good health, and as for my part I have set down my resolution that certainly will be; that is, that the answer of this letter will be life or death to me. Therefore, good father, send as soon as you can; and if you send me any thing let this be the mark.

ROT

RICHARD FRETHORNE, MARTIN'S HUNDRED

Source: Richard Frethorne. 1935. Letter to his father and mother, March 20, April 2 and 3, 1623. In *The Records of the Virginia Company of London*, edited by Susan Kingsbury. Washington, DC: Government Printing Office, 4:58–62.

MIDWIFE

The practice of midwifery is almost as old as human history, but its role as a profession and its place in society, the economy, and medicine has changed greatly over time. By definition, a midwife assists a woman through childbirth. While some men acted as midwives, this occupation remained the primary realm of women. For most of history, childbirth took place in the home, and midwives were one of the most important community members involved in the birth of a new baby.

Particularly in Western Europe, the exclusive use of midwives to aid childbirth changed from the Dark Ages into the early modern era with the growth of science and professionalization of medicine. However, by the seventeenth and eighteenth centuries, midwives faced new professional challenges as more men formally trained and practiced medicine and obstetrics. One of the most important tools that separated medical methods of midwives from male physicians was the forceps. Forceps consisted of pincers designed to grab a baby's head to help it down the birth canal during a difficult delivery. Designed by Peter Chamberlain in the early 1600s, they remained a proprietary tool for the select few until the early eighteenth century, when more physicians gained access to them. The utilization of forceps epitomized the difference between obstetrician and midwife as a job as doctors increased their use as part of their professional training. While some wealthy families increasingly opted for the physician, most families continued to rely on the midwife's services for the birth of a baby.

In seventeenth- and eighteenth-century America, midwives delivered the vast majority of babies. Midwife Martha Ballard practiced in Hallowell, Maine, from the late 1770s until her death in May 1812. Like many midwives, she received training informally and most likely began to assist in childbirths from observation and participation in births while living in Oxford, Massachusetts, in the 1750s and 1760s. Ballard also gained practical knowledge about childbirth from giving birth to nine children. Ballard was a valued member of her community in Maine, and neighbors and family turned to her for medical and obstetric care. Her carefully prepared diary reveals just how valuable a midwife proved to community life. Yet as her diary demonstrates, the work of a midwife was episodic at best. Page after page of Ballard's diary address only the weather or other mundane events like knitting, making soap, or writing letters. Most of her ten thousand entries end with "I was at home all day."

In the late eighteenth century, Hallowell, Maine, represented the American frontier. The community was always growing, and new families arrived and spread out into the countryside along the Kennebec River. Ballard delivered at least 816 babies during her time in Maine. The ceremony of childbirth remained very similar to the practice for women in other Western societies. Delivering a new baby was a community event among women in the area. Ballard would often consult with pregnant women in the weeks before their babies were born as her diary notes frequently that such women were "unwell." Once a woman was in labor, a male family member usually sent for Ballard, who would come to aid the birth, regardless of the hour. She traveled in all sorts of weather; on some occasions, she fell from her horse or had to be ferried across the partly frozen Kennebec River.

Once she arrived at the woman's home, she often had assistance from "attendants." Female neighbors and relatives gathered to participate in childbirth activities including preparing the mother for birth, assisting through the delivery, and administering postnatal care of child and mother. On other occasions, Ballard found the woman in "false labor," or experiencing preterm contractions, so she would stay with the expectant mother until she was certain that delivery was not imminent—or until she was called away to another birth. In the 1790s, Ballard spent a full week comforting a Mrs. Parker in her home until called to another delivery. Once that other baby was born, she hurried back to Mrs. Parker and delivered her child. On the rare occasions when a woman experienced complications in delivery, such as hemorrhaging, Ballard sent for the local doctor, Dr. Colman. Very rarely, only a handful of times during her twenty-seven years of work as a midwife, did a woman die in childbirth. In those cases, Ballard was invited to attend the autopsy to ascertain cause of death.

Martha Ballard was particularly skilled as a midwife because she had extensive knowledge about herbs and holistic treatments for a variety of ailments. This medicinal expertise was useful if any mothers she treated took ill during any part of the childbirth process. Ballard used a variety of "herbs and roots" to treat women she described as unwell. Undoubtedly, she treated young mothers' infected breasts, a condition known as mastitis, with hot poultices infused with the herb sorrel, which has anti-inflammation properties and was used as a crude antibiotic before modern penicillin was developed.

Ballard was trusted in her community for the overall success rate of the births she assisted. Of the over eight hundred live babies she delivered, the vast majority lived past infancy. Likewise, the herbal and homeopathic treatments Martha prescribed were often effective, and most of her patients survived illness. The majority of Ballard's patient deaths usually clustered around disease epidemics like diphtheria or fever that periodically coursed through the community.

As a midwife, Ballard had a role that connected her to a variety of social and even legal aspects of American life at that time. For example, the mid-eighteenth century remained a time of high premarital birth rate among American couples. For the most part, this status of men and women unmarried at the time of their child's birth was not considered too controversial as long as the couple wed after the birth. Midwives were called upon to ask a mother at the height of labor to identify their child's father, which was considered a legally binding admission. Part of a midwife's job was to report the "true" father on the birth certificate, important if a mother needed to legally demand financial obligation of the father to the child. In July 1791, Ballard assisted the childbirth of Sally Pierce, who identified Ballard's own son Jonathan as the father of her baby. Ballard dutifully noted the paternity of the child as her new grandson to the local court, and Jonathan Ballard and Sally Pierce were married four months later in February 1792.

Reflecting the dynamic of doctors and midwives in this era, Martha Ballard's midwifery practice existed along with the medical practice of Dr. Daniel Cony, who also moved to Hallowell in 1778. Town residents valued Dr. Cony and his membership in the Massachusetts Medical Society and knew he delivered one baby in Hallowell—his son. But while Dr. Cony and other regional doctors were respected and served their communities well, their work in assisting childbirth stood as supplementary to midwives. For many ailments and the vast majority of childbirths, most community members continued to rely on Ballard not only for her care and expertise but also because she charged less for her services than physicians. As with other frontier communities, economic exchange or trade for services was common. Martha Ballard accepted hard currency or informal exchange of labor, food, or other goods for her work.

Among professions in early America, few remain as significant and enduring as midwives. As colonial America gave way to a new constitutional republic, the population rate grew to four million people by 1790, primarily due to natural increase. At the forefront of this population boom was the midwife, who provided essential care for mother and baby in the birth process. The life and work of women like Martha Ballard exemplified the value of midwives in communities large and small and remained cornerstone fixtures of American society long into the nineteenth and twentieth centuries.

Jennifer Metz Foster

See also: Apothecary; *1776–1860:* Physician; *1861–1914:* Nurse; Surgeon; *1992–2019:* Home Health Aide

FURTHER READING

Black, Jeremy, and Roy Porter, eds. 1996. *A Dictionary of Eighteenth-Century History*. London: Penguin Books.

"RCOG Heritage: The Chamberlain Family." 2018. Royal College of Obstetricians and Gynecologists. https://www.rcog.org.uk/en/guidelines-research-services/library-services/archives-and-heritage/archives/rcog-heritage-the-chamberlen-family/.

Towler, Jean, and Joan Bramall. 1986. *Midwives in History and Society*. Dover, New Hampshire: Croom Helm.

Ulrich, Laurel Thatcher. 1990. *A Midwife's Tale: The Life of Martha Ballard, Based on Her Diary, 1785–1812*. New York: Alfred Knopf.

MILLER

Millers were people who owned or worked in grain mills. Most American colonists consumed maize, or "Indian corn," (now simply known as corn) as their primary grain during the seventeenth century, and colonists consumed corn in prodigious amounts throughout much of the colonial period. Compared to wheat, millet, and oats, which were widely consumed in Europe, corn kernels were softer and more easily harvested from the corn cob and could be prepared in many ways. Corn was nutritious and tasty, and, as a New World plant that tribal people taught European colonists to grow, corn was ideally suited to the American environment. To process both corn and these tougher-kernelled grains, colonists built grist mills, powered by water or wind, to grind the grain into flour. There were many more varieties of corn mills, however, than there were grist mills. Millers operated these grist mills, and they were integral to expanding the wheat industry and the colonial diet. Eighteenth-century farmers exported wheat and wheat flours to southern colonies and to the West Indies and even Brazil, where it was used to feed gentry who owned slaves laboring on sugar plantations. In the 1700s, colonial farmers, especially in parts of inland New England, Pennsylvania, and the Chesapeake region also turned to growing European wheat and other grains for both domestic consumption and export.

Corn was so central a staple to the colonial diet that many colonists consumed it two or three times daily. Colonists might eat a corn pudding sweetened with cream for breakfast, a bean and hominy (cracked corn) stew or a succotash mixed with fish for dinner at midday, and corn pone (flat cornmeal biscuits baked directly in hot ashes) and dried apples for dinner. Only in New York did early colonists consume large amounts of wheat bread, pancakes, and other wheat- and barley-based foods. Elsewhere, colonists made corn and egg muffins, sweet potato cakes, and potato and oat breads.

Many colonial towns had grist mills, even if there was little wheat to grind. In much of English North America, the earliest of colonial grist mills were built alongside streams, whose running water provided a constant power source that could turn the millstones. A miller would construct a primitive waterwheel, sometimes using wooden blades to propel a shaft that, in turn, would rotate the millstone. Some millstones were powered by windmills, though wind was far less reliable than water for powering the grindstones. But even with water-driven mills, a dry spell left the mill without power, requiring farmers to cart their grain to other towns often at a significant distance. Alternatively, farmers could wait for rain to resupply the streams with water, or they could pound their own corn.

When milling, a miller shoveled grain into a hopper that funneled it into an enclosed vat wherein two millstones were stacked together. The top stone, or runner, sat atop the bedder stone. The rotating shaft slowly turned the millstones; the miller previously chiseled grooves into the large granite millstones so that as they turned, they drew in grain between the stones as they rotated, where the grain was then crushed, or milled. The grain's bran, chaff, and flour were pushed out toward the edges of the grinding stones and fell into a chute, where they then fell into large meal bins.

Millers generally milled wheat and other grains on request: farmers brought in sacks of grain and expected to receive flour made from their own grain, not simply exchanged for other, pre-milled flour. Before the 1800s, millers generally produced whole-grain or minimally processed flour. Most millers received payment as a percentage of the grain, usually 12 to 20 percent of the product, rather than in sterling (silver) or other money. Some colonies regulated the percentage of flour that millers could demand as pay, thus preventing them from demanding excessive fees at busy times of the year. Some millers even constructed their mills so that small amounts of flour would fall into crevices within the housing holding the grinding stones, which they then salvaged once the farmer left the premises. Commonly, millers then exchanged their "profit" of the grain they received or flour they ground for other goods or sold it in town or urban markets, often to bakers. Millers could expect to work only part of the year; many were also farmers or engaged in other economic activities.

Colonists often devised strategies to mill their own grains—especially corn—which complicated the millers' work. Colonists constructed mortars in bedrock, as Native Americans had done, and used pestles (hand-grinding tools made of rock or hardwood) to grind their corn. Colonists also devised an ingenious way to pound corn into meal: they located a large tree near a stand of younger saplings, cut the larger tree down, and left a stump at waist height, which they hollowed out partway. They then attached a short log to a nearby sapling tree, which could be bent without breaking; this caused the sapling to function much like a spring. The colonists then placed corn into the hollow that they'd carved into the stump, repeatedly lowered the log by a rope into that hollow, and then sprung the log upward with the action of the saplings. The pounding action of the log crushed the corn kernels. These homemade "sweep mills" allowed farmers to entirely bypass a miller's fees. Often, families simply scraped dried corn from the cob and then soaked the kernels in milk or water overnight, which eliminated the need for milling.

As they were essential labor-eliminating machines, grist mills could be the site of much local conflict in the early colonial era. Many country towns exempted millers from having to pay fees or taxes, which angered ordinary residents, who were not similarly exempted. Furthermore, millers did not have a reputation for being inscrutably honest, and the typical miller did not work regularly. An early mill in Roger Williams' colony of Providence near Narragansett Bay provides one such example of how millers and their mills could embroil colonists in conflict. Sometime in the 1640s, the town's proprietors provided ten acres of land to the miller John Smith and his son, John Smith, Jr., in exchange for constructing a rudimentary corn mill for the fledgling community of about a hundred families. Between that time and the 1760s, when the issue was brought before the town's courts, community conflict revolved around the state of the mill. Smith had indeed built the mill. In return, he obtained his ten acres. But he did not maintain the mill in working order—a provision that had not been part of the original land grant.

Smith, Sr. died not long after completing the mill's construction. In 1649, community members demanded that his widow keep the mill in working order, but they did not follow through with crafting a legal agreement that would have mandated she do so. Smith, Jr. also absolved himself of any responsibility for maintaining the mill. Community members who complained about the nonfunctional mill were commonly called *gristemillites.* Sometime later, likely after the land had changed ownership several times, it was sold to Elisha Brown, and the original town's descendants brought suit against Brown in the early 1760s. For decades before and thereafter, the mill sat unused, in disrepair, as the town council, community members, and attorneys wrestled with the legal issues concerning the maintenance of the mill. As late as 1829, lawsuits pertaining to John Smith's land patent for the original mill were still occupying the calendar of local courts.

As wheat cultivation spread during the 1700s, the need for grist mills intensified. Millers constructed larger, more powerful grist mills, a process that required building a dam to create a millpond that fed a small canal dug by hand; millers then constructed a waterwheel and mill housing atop the canal. As in the earlier corn mills, a waterwheel powered a shaft that turned the grinding stones, but in these larger mills, the miller could control the water flow by releasing water from the dam, thereby speeding up the milling process. These larger flour mills were sometimes four stories tall and generally employed a miller and several helpers. As farmers planted wheat for the domestic market and for export, millers could depend on regular wages, even if they still took a percentage of the flour or grain as their pay. An expanding commercial class and landed gentry later in the eighteenth century also drove the market for wheat production, as the well-to-do developed a more sophisticated and varied diet. Bread—not corn pone or the pudding-like corn spoonbread—now occupied the centerpiece of diets among the elite and middling classes. Pies, cakes, crumpets, cookies, cinnamon rolls, and other pastries helped these people differentiate themselves from those impoverished and working colonists.

By 1785, the inventor Oliver Evans designed a semi-automated flour mill that could operate around the clock, with continuous feeder and grinding rollers that took the place of rotating grinding stones. Wheat could be efficiently and rapidly ground and processed, yielding more of the highly processed white flour that so many antebellum Americans preferred. As wheat cultivation spread across the nation, the center of milling was no longer the eastern seaboard—the cities of Baltimore, New York, or Philadelphia—but, instead, large automated flour mills were built in the western cities of Minneapolis and St. Louis along the great Mississippi River and its tributaries. Industrialization had overtaken the milling trade for the next century and more, until the whole-grain movement of the 1960s and 1970s encouraged a return to stone-ground flour.

Nancy Quam-Wickham

See also: Baker; Farmer; *1776–1860:* Ginner

FURTHER READING

Bishop, J. Leander. 1861. *A History of American Manufactures from 1608 to 1860, Volume 1*. Philadelphia: Edward Young and Company.

Bullock, Helen. 1972. *The Williamsburg Art of Cookery, or Accomplish'd Gentlewoman's Companion*. Dietz Press.

Chandonnet, Ann. 2013. *Colonial Food*. London: Shire Publications.

Cowell, Benjamin. 1829. *Ancient Documents Relative to the old Grist-mill, With Some Remarks on the Opinions of Messrs. Hunter and Greene, Counsel Employed by the Town to Examine the Same*. Providence: The Herald Office.

Hodge, Christina. 2014. *Consumerism and the Emergence of the Middle Class in Colonial America*. Cambridge: Cambridge University Press.

Jones, Capers. 2006. *The History and Future of Narragansett Bay*. Irvine: Universal Publishers.

MINISTER

Among the earliest European settlers to the Americas, ministers were central to the colonizing project. In the Southwest, Franciscan priests were instrumental in converting thousands of indigenous Pueblo people to Catholicism in the 1500s and 1600s in service of the Spanish. In the mid-1600s, missionaries of the Society of Jesus and other apostolic orders operated throughout the Great Lakes region as frontline representatives of the French colonial enterprise. In British North America, ministers accompanied Puritan and other nonconforming Protestant colonists as they journeyed to New England, while in the Chesapeake region, clergymen affiliated with the Church of England were essential partners of governors and others allied with the Crown. In all cases, ministers were tasked, to one degree or another, with nurturing the spiritual needs of early European settlers, proselytizing Christianity among indigenous people so that, as Christian converts, they might serve as colonists in their own lands, and representing the interests of both colonists and imperial governments in the New World.

From its earliest colonial origins, the United States has been defined by its affirmation of religious freedom. Ministers accompanied church dissenters—Pilgrims in 1620 and Puritans in 1630—to Massachusetts, where each group organized houses of worship and congregations of the faithful. For the Pilgrims at Plymouth, who rejected outward displays of religiosity, which they considered a form of idolatry, the first church doubled as a community meetinghouse and military fort. A simple planked building, this first church had no steeple or cross signifying its purpose. The church elder, William Brewster, organized weekly worship. Brewster led Bible readings, preached sermons, prophesied (explained Biblical passages), openly addressed his personal sins, and conducted prayers, which the Pilgrims believed should be spontaneous and inspirational, not written and read by a clergyman. Because he was not an ordained minister, he did not baptize babies.

At Plymouth, the church services were marathon affairs, consisting of three-hour-long services in the morning and afternoon each Sunday; many congregants came to both services. Before seeking refuge in Leiden, Holland, for his religious beliefs, Brewster had studied at Cambridge for a short time; he was uncommonly well educated among those who first arrived on the *Mayflower* in the autumn of 1620. As such, he became a trusted leader of the small colony, a position that occupied a great deal of his time; he helped the first governors draft reports to the Crown, mediated disputes among colonists, and negotiated agreements with local tribespeople, including Massasoit, the Great Sachem (or chief) of the Wampanoag.

Religious life in Plymouth, however, was not peaceful for long. Within two years of the colony's founding, a series of Anglican ministers and representatives arrived in the colony. Some were reportedly sent to observe and report on the community of separatists, those Pilgrims who had broken from the Church of England (Anglicans). Others attempted to start competing plantations, or colonies, meant to bolster the official Church's presence in New England. The case of Rev. John Lyford, an Anglican minister who arrived in Plymouth in early 1624, illustrates the suspicions with which the Pilgrims received a formally ordained minister of the Established Church, the Church of England, whose leader was the king.

Lyford arrived with his wife and children; nearly immediately, he professed his loyalty to the Pilgrims. At the same time, however, the Pilgrims carefully watched his movements throughout the colony, noting that he began to preach sermons and conduct the sacraments observed by the Anglicans: formal confessions, baptisms, communion, marriages, and observations of religious holidays like Easter and Christmas. The Pilgrims soon accused Lyford of "private meetings and whisperings," brought charges against him in the local court, and proclaimed him to "bee a spotted beast," or one who refused to renounce his allegiance to the Church of England. He was sentenced to banishment in England, though he and his family later moved to Virginia, where the colonists were largely adherents of the official Church (Pennington 1941, 252–253).

In the Chesapeake region, ministers with the Church of England established fledgling parishes and did much of the policing of behavior among the earliest colonists. In Virginia, ministers held Sunday services that, in liturgy, resembled a Sunday service in England; they conducted the sacraments but also participated actively in civil affairs. The Anglican Church of Jamestown, for instance, was also the meeting place for the Grand Assembly of 1619, the first representative legislature in Virginia. Ministers were required to report on and police moral violations, primarily swearing and drunkenness but also other crimes against the social order.

Colonists in the early Chesapeake region were expected to attend church services regularly; they were fined if they did not do so. These fines were determined by law; a regulation in 1631 set a fine of one shilling for "every time of a person's absence from the church having no lawful or reasonable excuse to be absent" (Goodwin 1927, 38). All colonial families in Virginia were also subject to a hefty tithe, or tax, for the building, upkeep, and maintenance of the individual parishes to which they belonged, an act that was inconceivable to New England's separatists, for whom profession of their faith and membership in a congregation were voluntary and deeply personal. Complaints of excessive tithing, as well as distant parishes and unresponsive Anglican ministers, appear often in colonial Virginia records. Yet parishioners who criticized ministers without foundation could be fined up to five hundred pounds of tobacco and ordered to apologize publicly to the minister during a Sunday service.

In these tidewater communities, the House of Burgesses, the colonial government, ordered ministers to keep vestry books that documented all vital records in the parish, so ministers had to note every birth, marriage, and death among their parishioners. Besides recording parish vital statistics and delivering sermons on Sundays, Virginia's ministers had to hold catechism for the youth, perform frequent funerals in this dangerously unhealthful colony, and conduct marriages, unlike their separatist counterparts in New England, who viewed marriage as a civil, not religious, contract.

In the first decades of European colonial settlement, frontier towns and communities were often riven with conflict. Ministers engaged in and at times fostered this conflict as they sought to temper the influence of rival churches and other Christian denominations. Puritan ministers in New England had enormous civil authority within early colonial communities. Like Pilgrims, Puritans did not follow the strict teachings of the Church of England but instead broke sharply with the Anglicans. Fellow colonists often accused the Puritans of being a quarrelsome bunch. Colonial governments reinforced church authority and religious expression. Ministers and parishioners alike sought redress from the Massachusetts Bay's Court of Assistants for defiance of social conventions and endorsement of radical separatist Christian beliefs. In 1630, for instance, the Rev. William Braxton, a nonpracticing Anglican minister, was bought out of his home and forced to move from Boston when local residents imposed fees upon themselves to finance his relocation. The following year, William Ratcliffe was whipped, fined, and had his ears cut off before he was ordered banished—all for questioning a relationship that was developing between the Salem Church and local government. This relationship reflected a practice then spreading among the New England colonies wherein ministers provided advice and direction to colonial government officials.

This close relationship between local governments and the Puritans led to further expulsions, and by the early 1630s, the requirement that only church members who had signed a covenant agreeing to abide by church policies could vote. Not long afterward, Mary Oliver was convicted of "disturbing the Salem Church" and imprisoned until someone posted bond to ensure her "good behavior." Rev. Roger Williams, the lay religious teacher Anne Hutchinson, and her husband, William, and son, Francis Hutchinson, were all banished for preaching that only true believers, as measured individually by a person's spirituality, not one's outward behavior as determined by a minister, could achieve salvation. Religious differences within the separatist communities of Massachusetts contributed to the formation of new settlements throughout New England as colonists at odds with Puritans and their descendants, the Congregationalists, fled to find greater freedoms in religion and secular life.

As the Puritans solidified their religious views in the 1640s with the founding of Congregationalism, religious strife subsided within the colonies. Ministers and laypeople sought to extend the faith to local tribespeople. Empowered by a Massachusetts law of 1646 that called for the Christianization of Indians, Rev. John Eliot published an Algonquian-language Bible between 1660 and 1663 so that he could more easily spread the faith to Indians in the region. He was already a successful missionary, having helped to establish several "Praying Towns" of converted Algonquian-speaking tribespeople along Massachusetts Bay. Colonists believed that these towns might form a barrier between Euro American settlements and Indians in the interior who had rejected Christianity. Other Congregational missionaries worked among tribespeople as far away as Maine, where they sought to limit the spread of Catholicism brought by the French.

After Metacom's War (1675–1678), some of New England's most celebrated ministers turned away from converting Indians and instead implored colonists to take up arms as their Christian duty to protect the colonies against them. In 1678, Rev. Samuel Nowell preached a sermon, "Abraham in Arms," that typified this new genre of religious literature—the artillery election sermon—delivered on the occasion of forming a local militia to protect colonists against their religious and political enemies: Indians, French, Spanish, and, later, the English themselves. These new Christian soldiers, inspired by hundreds of sermons penned by ministers of many denominations, protected the settlements of the colonies after 1675 and were essential to motivating colonists to fight against the British during the French and Indian and Revolutionary Wars of the following century.

Nancy Quam-Wickham

See also: Sexton; *1776–1860:* Missionary; *1992–2019:* Clergyperson

FURTHER READING

Goodwin, Edward Lewis. 1927. *The Colonial Church in Virginia: with Biographical Sketches of the First Six Bishops of the Diocese of Virginia, and Other Historical Papers, Together with Brief Biographical Sketches of the Colonial Clergy of Virginia.* Milwaukee: Morehouse Pub. Company.

Little, Ann M. 2007. *Abraham in Arms: War and Gender in Colonial New England.* Philadelphia: University of Pennsylvania Press.

Manseau, Peter. 2015. *One Nation, Under Gods: A New American History.* Boston: Little, Brown.

Morgan, Edmund. 2007. *Roger Williams: The Church and the State.* New York: W. W. Norton.

Pennington, Edgar Legare. 1941. "Anglican Beginnings in Massachusetts." *Historical Magazine of the Protestant Episcopal Church* 10 (3): 242–289.

Rasor, Paul, and Richard E. Bond, eds. 2011. *From Jamestown to Jefferson: The Evolution of Religious Freedom in Virginia.* Charlottesville: University of Virginia Press.

POTTER

Potters are craftspeople who create various forms of pottery, art and utilitarian items from clay, through a process of collecting the raw materials, mixing them with water and other minerals, shaping the item, and then firing the item to eliminate the water content and make it more durable. Pottery is an ancient craft. In ancient Greece, the Hellenic period (ca. 500–323 BCE) was a time of great artistry in pottery. But in later times, including early colonial America, potters generally produced what are called utility ware: jugs, jars, and large crocks for holding liquids, mugs for drinking both hot and cold beverages, tobacco pipes, and, less frequently, bowls, plates, and decorative pieces. Labor shortages, cultural traditions, and environmental conditions in North America all had deep influences on the work of the potter in this period.

The wealthiest of the English colonists brought with them some stoneware mugs, generally manufactured in Germany but often later embellished with silver—as was the case with a mug that Governor John Winthrop brought to the Massachusetts Bay colony in 1630. These kinds of imported stoneware mugs were status symbols and so highly prized that this same mug appears in legal documents as it was specifically gifted to descendants for several generations. English regulations required colonists to purchase durable goods, like jars and mugs, from English manufactories, so for most of the colonial period, most pottery—stoneware, creamware, and porcelain—was imported. The initial market for such goods was small. Among the poorer colonists, pottery was far less prized as it was crudely constructed, usually from local clay with higher moisture content than the harder German stoneware. Throughout the colonies, potters produced local utility ware known as red-ware for the high levels of iron oxide in American clay. This red-ware was more easily broken than imported stoneware, which was made from gray-colored clays that had lower moisture content, and thus could be fired at higher temperatures without breakage and be made more durable. Most early colonists at this time also used wooden plates and bowls, with families eating communally from one large bowl or plate. This cultural tradition, born from necessity, had been practiced by medieval and early modern Europeans, thus coming with the colonists to the New World.

Historians know relatively little about specific potters during this early period of American colonial history. Archeology has provided most of our knowledge of the potter's work and life as digs at old kilns and garbage dumps at both colonial and Native American sites have provided most information we have about early potters. Pottery was widely practiced throughout continental North America, particularly along the Atlantic coast, among the tribal people of the Mississippi River basin, and in the Southwest, particularly by the Pueblo peoples. There are some historical records of early colonial potters; Phillip Drinker arrived in Charlestown, Massachusetts, in 1635 and set up a pottery manufactory, eventually employing his sons. In nearby Salem, Richard Vinson worked with a partner. A woman potter apparently worked near Boston. In the Chesapeake area and the southern colonies, a number of early colonists constructed kilns to fire bricks, which were made of the same red clay, and crude pots.

By 1800, however, there are records of only about a few hundred potters in the new United States, although the population had reached over 2.5 million. With independence from Britain, Americans were no longer bound to purchase imported pottery, so American manufacturing of finer ware increased dramatically. Among the most famous of nineteenth-century potters was David Drake, known as Dave the Potter (or Potter Dave), a slave who worked in an Edgefield, South Carolina, pottery factory. Unlike most individual potters of the day, Drake signed his works ("Dave") and often inscribed them with scripture, poetry, or other short verses. Today, art collectors value Drake's pots very highly, and they command extraordinary prices as examples of early American folkware and as museum pieces.

The work life of an individual potter was remarkably similar throughout early America, be they Pueblo potters from the fifteenth century, early New England potters in the mid-1600s, or enslaved potters like Drake, who worked in Edgefield, a center of early pottery manufacturing in the South. First, the individual potter or his helpers had to dig the clay out of the ground. This was no easy process as clay soils dry very hard, leading many potters to dig their clay for the year during rainy weather, when it could more easily be extracted by hand using spades or shovels.

Most clays had to be washed repeatedly to remove any impurities—pebbles, bone and wood chips, and other detritus like decomposing leaves or pine needles—using manpowered or horse-powered clay mills and heavy iron sieves. Potters mixed the raw clay with great amounts of water in large wooden tubs and suspended the clay, allowing for it to be effectively strained using a laborious decanting process. As the suspended clay settled on the bottom of the tub, the potter spooned out the water on top using a heavy ladle, often made of wood or iron. Clay could be stored for long periods in this manner.

Eventually, the suspended clay became a soup-like mixture. To this clay soup, the potter then mixed tempering agents that allowed the clay to be fired at higher temperatures without cracking. Cracked jars were useless for holding liquids, of course, but also butter, cheese, grains, and other goods since bacteria, insects, and rodents could access them through the cracks. Tempering agents varied but generally included silicates like sand and ground quartz, as well as calcium compounds such as finely ground shell, bone, and limestone. Although the original clay varied, along with individual practices, most potters' final product included about 15 to 20 percent tempering agents.

Once the clay was ready for manufacturing, practices again differed. Indigenous artisans throughout the Atlantic coastal woodlands tended to make pots and jars using coiled techniques: creating long, yarn-like pieces of wet clay and then coiling layers of clay on top of each other to the desired dimensions. Indigenous potters often then scraped coiled works with bone or impressed them with rough fabric to eliminate obvious coil markings. Potters of European and African ancestry tended to use the more common potter's wheel—a tablelike round slab of wood that would revolve using a foot-powered mechanism—in a process called "throwing" a pot. Here, the potter placed a chunk of wet clay onto the wheel and then spun the wheel while slowly working a hole into the clay and pulling the spinning clay up to form walls, or the sides of a pot. Once the item was formed, it was removed from the wheel and placed to dry. At this point, some early potters might paint a small design like a sunflower on the item, like eighteenth-century German immigrant potters did in Pennsylvania. Others might dip the item in a slip, or glaze, to improve its hardness and make it more water-tight. Later, potters glazed stoneware with salt. Then the vessels were fired in wood- or charcoal-powered kilns for hours before they were ready for use.

The work of potters was episodic as the market for goods dictated their work lives. In this period, few colonists worked full time as potters. Most were likely men (and some women) of limited skill who had learned the techniques of making pottery by watching others, or perhaps they had been indentured to potters in Europe. Others surely experimented with local clays before finding the proper techniques to create utility ware. Many were likely young as strength was needed to dig and clean the clay. Necessity required innovation but not excellence. Pottery made in the colonies during the earliest years was not durable. The great numbers of pot shards found in colonial "dumps" and the lack of mention in probate documents demonstrate to modern historians that early American pots were used for specific purposes, but they broke often, were routinely discarded, and, although necessary for food storage, were not highly valued.

Nancy Quam-Wickham

See also: Basket Maker; *1861–1914:* Mason

FURTHER READING

Hill, Laban Carrick. 2010. *Dave the Potter: Artist, Poet, Slave.* New York: Little Brown.
Maryland Department of Planning, Jefferson Patterson Park and Museum, State Museum of Archeology. http://www.jefpat.org/.
Skerry, Janine E., and Suzanne Findlen Hood. 2009. *Salt-Glazed Stoneware in Early America.* Williamsburg: Colonial Williamsburg Foundation.
Todd, Leonard. 2008. *Carolina Clay: The Life and Legend of the Slave Potter Dave.* New York: W. W. Norton.
Tunis, Edward. 1965. *Colonial Craftsmen and the Beginnings of American Industry.* Baltimore: Johns Hopkins University Press.

RIGGER

A rigger's job began after a shipwright launched a vessel. Once that happened, the vessel was brought to a quay, where a rigger stepped, or attached, the masts to the deck, fastened the standing rigging, and attached the running rigging to it. The masts were upright timbers used as the foundation for the sails and rigging; each mast on a vessel had a particular name. Riggers frequently worked alongside sailmakers in the same loft. During the colonial period of American history, a rigger needed to know how to rig commonly used vessels. Sailing vessels were classified by their rigs in the mid-eighteenth century. Similar designations were nonexistent prior to that date. The ship (a particular type of sailing vessel) was the most identifiable vessel and was commonly used for transatlantic voyages. It carried a rig with square sails on the main and fore masts and lateen sails on the mizzen mast. Pinnaces could be used for both transatlantic and coasting voyages. This vessel's rig varied from a single mast with a main and stay sails to something that was very similar to a full-rigged ship. Barks and ketch were single-decked vessels used in the coasting trade and on fishing voyages. While both vessels had two masts, they were distinguished by their rigs. Barks carried square sails, and ketches had fore and aft sails. The smallest type of coasting vessel used in the seventeenth century was the shallop, which carried a single mast with main and stay sails.

Although ketches and barks were popular in the early seventeenth century, ship owners began to order sloops and brigs starting in midcentury. Ship owners also requested fewer shallops and pinnaces. Once advances in hull design and rigs were made, ketches, barks, shallops, and pinnaces were replaced by newer and more functional vessels. Sloops were single-masted vessels developed in the Netherlands that later came to New Netherlands and from England to New England. Sailors preferred the sloop because it carried a fore and mainsail from a short gaff. It was more easily operated than a ketch, which carried an awkward spirit sail. Brigantines, which carried a combination rig with square sails on the foremast and a fore and aft sail on the mainmast, replaced barks. Sometimes these vessels, which were also called brigs, carried square sails on their mainmasts as well. While brigantines and barks were similar, the brigantine's rig was more complex but easily adaptable. By the eighteenth century, brigantines became characterized by rigs that carried two or more square sails on the foremast and a fore and aft sail on the mainmast. The mainmast frequently carried a square topsail as well. Another square-rigged vessel that became popular during the eighteenth century was the snow, which carried square sails on both masts but had a fore and aft sail on a pole behind the mainmast.

Riggers needed to be aware of the advances in naval architecture that changed the way vessels were classified beginning in the eighteenth century. By the mid-eighteenth century, vessels were classified solely by the way they were rigged; hull design ceased to be used for vessel classification. Along with the sloop and the brigantine, the schooner and the snow began to replace the ketches, barks, and shallops. Not only did a rigger need to know how to rig these vessels, but he also needed to know how to rig different variations of each type of vessel. For example, two types of sloops were used in the eighteenth century. A rigger needed to be able to rig both small sloops used in the coasting trade as well as the large sloops used in the West Indian trade. Coasting sloops carried a fore and aft rig with a main sail, a stay sail, and a jib. On the other hand, the larger sloops involved in the West Indian trade carried square main and topsails. Since large masted vessels were difficult to handle, many ship owners began to adopt schooners. Sailors preferred schooners because they redistributed the sails between two masts, which made them more manageable. Although the schooner descended from the ketch and carried a two-masted fore and aft rig, it had gaffs instead of spirits. It also carried a headsail on a bow sprit.

After the owner decided what type of rig he wanted, the rigger started at the bow of the vessel and began working toward the stern. Shears or crane-like apparatus with blocks were set up on the wharf and used to hoist the masts and yards (cross-pieces attached to the masts on square-sailed rigs) onto the vessel. When a rigger selected timber for masts, he chose pieces that lacked knots or other imperfections. Occasionally, a rigger constructed masts from composites if suitable timber was not available. A rigger also partially rigged the running rigging before he attached the masts to the hull. The running rigging consists of the ropes and lines sailors used to help control the vessel. Next, he stepped the bowsprit, or the front-facing timbers at the bow of the vessel. The bow sprit was followed by the lower masts. This could begin with the foremast or the mainmast and would end with mainmast or the mizzen, depending on the type of vessel he was rigging. After the lower masts were in place, the rigger attached the top masts and topgallant masts.

Once the masts were in place, it was time to attach the standing rigging to the vessel. The standing rigging held the mast in place and made it possible for a sailing vessel and its mast to function as a single unit. Attaching the standing rigging to a vessel made it possible to put the other components of the vessel's propulsion system into place. This process began when the rigger attached the mast to the vessel's sides with shrouds. After the shrouds were in place, the rigger fastened stays and stout ropes to the fore and aft of the vessel. Next, ratlines were attached to the shrouds to create rope ladders, which the rigger used to ascend the masts and attach the yards. With the yards in place, the rigger could complete the running rigging, which he began prior to stepping the masts. Then sails were placed on the yards, and the running rigging—the lines used to operate them—was finished.

Edward J. Martin

See also: Shipwright; *1776–1860:* Sailor

FURTHER READING

Goldenberg, Joseph A. 1976. *Shipbuilding in Colonial America.* Charlottesville: University of Virginia Press.

Horsley, John E. 1978. *Tools of the Maritime Trades.* London: David & Charles.

Smith, Roger C. 1993. *Vanguard of Empire: Ships of Exploration in the Age of Columbus.* New York: Oxford University Press.

SADDLER, *see* HARNESS MAKER AND SADDLER

SCRIVENER

Before the printing press became broadly accessible and popular in the late seventeenth century, a person who was able to read and write could make a respectable living as a scrivener, a tradesman who would write official documents, take dictation, or copy written material by hand.

A scrivener often performed a variety of writing jobs, depending on the availability of the work. If a scrivener's business was good, he might write a deed to a house in the morning, transcribe a brief court session after lunch, take dictation for a letter to the governor in the afternoon, and work on copying a textbook in the evening. Some scriveners became exceptionally good at one type of job or another and found salaried work as a clerk or a secretary, but most operated as freelancers and took whatever jobs were available.

Scriveners rarely had a hard time finding work, in part because they were able to produce legible documents in a time when even the most literate people had difficulty reading text that wasn't typeset. While probably 70 percent of colonists were somewhat literate by 1700, most people had poor handwriting, could only write very slowly, and were not great spellers. A good scrivener, on the other hand, could write quickly and clearly and rarely made errors when writing, so was often hired whenever there was important writing that needed to be done.

Paper was rare and extremely expensive until after the Revolutionary War (1775–1783), creating a high demand for scriveners. For hundreds of years, any paper used in North America had to be shipped across the Atlantic from paper mills in England and other places in Western Europe. The first paper mill wasn't built in the colonies until 1690, but paper production did not meet colonial demand until around 1800. Scriveners remained essential in part because most people could not afford clean sheets of paper unless it was for something essential like an official document or a letter to someone important, and they couldn't afford to buy extra paper in the event that they misspelled a word or didn't write legibly.

The paper shortage also affected a young scrivener who was learning his trade. Because paper was so scarce, writing practice often had to be done in the margins of books or on used paper that had been found or bought. (Paper was so scarce, in fact, that a person could sell odd scraps of it or paper that had already been written on, and it would sell quickly.) The young scrivener would persevere in his practice, though, because that career path was a viable way for people to lift themselves out of poverty.

If a family was impoverished, a child could expect to be working full time by the age of seven or eight to help support them. For many people, the vocation that they began at that young age would end up being their career unless they could find a way to become proficient at some other trade. Because typesetting text was difficult, time consuming, and expensive, and because there was sufficient demand for handwritten documents, an intelligent person looking to move up in the world might practice to become a scrivener. The work wasn't viewed as glamorous—which, in turn, was part of its broad appeal as a vocation for someone from the lower class since the wealthy didn't want to write when they could afford to hire people to do it for them—but it was often far preferable to working the land, the mines, or the docks.

Steel-tipped pens didn't become popular until the 1820s, and the earliest mention of such instruments are from around 1725, so historians know that scriveners working before that time wrote with quill and ink. Quill pens had to be replaced every week or so, but they were relatively simple to make. A scrivener would take a large wing feather from a goose or a turkey, remove the small feathers and barbs from the end of the shaft with a sharp knife, cut and shape the tip to a sharp point, and clear the inside of the cut shaft with a bit of straw or a thin piece of metal. Alternatively, ready-to-use quills could be bought for the equivalent of a dollar or less in today's money.

The scrivener's vocation waned in popularity as the nineteenth century progressed, in part because the Industrial Revolution gave birth to quicker, easier methods of printing and also because society became more literate as a whole. Working scriveners found their responsibilities shifting more toward what might be considered today to be those of a clerk: organizing archives, balancing finances, or creating, maintaining, and filling out forms for the government, accountants, or large businesses. While it is difficult to say when the practical aspect of the vocation finally became irrelevant, few could argue against the notion that the first commercially successful typewriter (1868) contributed greatly to the end of the scrivener's era.

Ben Tyler Elliott

See also: *1776–1860:* Pamphleteer; Printer; *1861–1914:* Bookkeeper; *1946–1991:* Office Clerk

FURTHER READING

Bidwell, J. 2012. *American Paper Mills, 1690–1832: A Directory of the Paper Trade with Notes on Products, Watermarks, Distribution Methods, and Manufacturing Techniques.* Hanover: Dartmouth College Press.

Child, H. 1986. *The Calligrapher's Handbook.* New York: Taplinger Pub.

Current, Richard N. 1954. *The Typewriter and the Men Who Made It.* Urbana: The University of Illinois Press.

Defoe, D., and G. D. Cole. 1962. *A Tour through the Whole Island of Great Britain.* London: Dent.

Lockridge, K. A. 1974. *Literacy in Colonial New England: An Enquiry into the Social Context of Literacy in the Early Modern West.* New York: Norton.

Wroth, L. C. 1964. *The Colonial Printer.* Charlottesville: Dominion Books.

SEXTON

In the seventeenth and eighteenth centuries, religion played a significant role in the lives of Americans. Churches provided physical and spiritual space for colonists to gather, and they served as centerpieces of community life. In addition to holding religious services, churches often acted as meeting places for town government and provided space to hold social activities. Although there were many predominately Protestant religious denominations throughout colonial America, almost all maintained a parish pastor and varying staff members. One common and important church staff position was the sexton. Sextons served as employees of a church, and their responsibilities included maintenance of church buildings and grounds. Sextons cleaned the sanctuary and prepared many aspects of the religious service, from maintaining a minister's vestments to preparing the altar for worship. Sextons polished silver chalices and other items used in worship services, baptisms, funerals, and other religious functions.

Early colonial churches tended to be modest structures, often temporary buildings like the one at James City, Virginia, which had to be rebuilt four times in the first few years of its existence. By the 1660s, however, colonial churches emerged in their more modern brick form, with bell towers and ornate steeples. In these newer buildings, sextons were the primary people who rang the church bells for services or other important events in town life. As maintainers of the parish, sextons also would have been involved in determining which parish members had not attended services; colonial governments routinely fined congregants who failed to attend them on Sunday.

Many church sextons also maintained the parish graveyard, and the distinct and at times eerie aspect of this profession has been described in the literature of the era. For example, sextons acting specifically as gravediggers appear in William Shakespeare's *Hamlet*. In this play, Hamlet and Horatio encounter sextons preparing a space to bury Ophelia. Hamlet talks with these busy sextons about the bodies that lay in the graveyard. Literary scholars note that other Shakespearean works were inspired by the often difficult social conditions in England's New World colonies. In early colonial Virginia, so many people died of starvation and disease that tending to the deceased, preparing the graves, and maintaining the church graveyard could become a position that demanded a person work long hours tending to just these chores, besides caring for the parish and minister. Like most early colonists, though, sextons also worked in the fields or held other jobs as well.

Colonists brought their religious customs with them when they migrated from western Europe to colonial America in the seventeenth and eighteenth centuries. These customs included a set of practices and beliefs that reinforced the patriarchal nature of colonial society. Aside from a few religious denominations like

Quakers, who included female participation in worship services, ministers and most church staff members were men. As for economic status, sextons themselves were not wealthy, but most maintained a stable living. Other community positions like selectmen, clerks, and surveyors were appointed by town governments, and local taxation paid for these jobs. By comparison, local churches hired sextons, and salaries for the post generally came from tithing and donations from individual congregations. In many parishes, a sexton's salary could be augmented by fees charged for organizing a funeral service, preparing the body of the deceased for viewing, and other such duties besides tending to the graveyard.

The diverse and important role of the sexton remains essential in American religious life. Long after the revolutionary era, sextons actively served communities and denominations throughout the United States. Although the role and importance of the church as a centerpiece of town life has waned over the course of American history, many religious groups and congregations continue to employ sextons to maintain their churches and grounds today.

Jennifer Metz Foster

See also: Minister; *1776–1860:* Missionary; *1992–2019:* Clergyperson

FURTHER READING

Cook, Edward M., Jr. 1976. *The Fathers of the Towns: Leadership and Community Structure in Eighteenth-Century New England.* Baltimore: Johns Hopkins University Press.

Speth, Linda E., and Alison Duncan Hirsch. 1983. *Women, Family, and Community in Colonial America: Two Perspectives.* New York: Haworth Press, Inc.

SHIPWRIGHT

The colonial shipwright worked without many of the restrictions experienced by his English counterparts in the Royal Dockyards and private shipyards of England. Unlike his English counterpart, the colonial shipwright rarely worked from a written plan. When a client approached a colonial shipwright, this master craftsman began by assessing his customer's needs. Most of a shipwright's clients were English or colonial merchants. Once the shipwright determined the type of vessel, its purpose, its size, and sail qualities, he carved a model. The shipwright used the model to learn more about his client's needs. He altered the model to ensure that the vessel he constructed had the lift, the ability to heel, and the capability to ground without listing. Although shipwrights frequently designed the vessels they constructed, some merchants sent plans to them describing the type of vessel they desired.

Once the shipwright and a merchant agreed on the type of vessel the merchant needed, they entered into a contract. While most shipwrights preferred to be paid in cash, merchants frequently desired to compensate the shipwright with goods. Most contracts combined payments in cash with payments in goods. On some occasions, a merchant assumed some of the shipwright's debts in exchange for the construction of a vessel. Regardless of the means of payment a shipwright and a merchant agreed upon for the construction of a vessel, merchants frequently distributed payments in thirds. Merchants disbursed one-third at the beginning of construction, another third halfway through the vessel's construction, and the final payment upon its completion. Contracts also discussed the materials that the merchant wanted the shipwright to use to build his ship. Although shipwrights used local timber to construct vessels, other materials such as iron, cordage, and sail cloth could come from England.

Construction began when the shipwright took the lines from the model and translated them to full-size wooden patterns that were used to cut the frame of the vessel. The colonial shipwright and the sawyers he employed selected white oak timbers that corresponded to the shape of these patterns. After the timber was cut in a sawpit, it was shaped with axes and adzes (a tool with arched blades used for cutting large pieces of wood). Once the timber was shaped, it was time to lay the keel, raise the stem and stern post, and attach the futtocks (curved parts of timber) to create the vessel's frame. Shipwrights attached these timbers together by drilling holes in them with augers and hammering wooden pegs (called trunnels) made from black locust into them. Having assembled the frame, the shipwright and his workers planked the vessel and lay the decks. Finally, the vessel was caulked with cotton and a tarred hemp known as oakum and sealed with pitch to ensure that it was watertight. When the shipwright launched the vessel, the oak timbers and planks swelled, sealing the trunnels and caulking in place. The hulls of whaling vessels were encased in sheets of copper for protection from collisions and for durability. Copper also inhibited the growth of marine worms and other organisms that could destroy a wooden hull. Shipwrights preferred to launch a vessel upon completion. They were reluctant to let a vessel season on the stocks for a year because they had to compensate the merchant for any damage to the vessel while it sat in the shipyard.

Before a shipwright could operate a shipyard, he needed to learn how to construct a vessel. Although colonial shipwrights learned their trade through an apprenticeship, it was not as vigorous as the one served by his English counterpart. There were no guilds in the American colonies, and skilled labor was in demand. Therefore, master shipwrights never charged an apprentice a premium. Under these circumstances, the training of a shipwright in the colonies was more flexible than that in England. An apprenticeship lasted between four to seven years. Towns frequently indentured poor boys to a shipwright until his twenty-first birthday. In exchange for his service, an apprentice received instruction in the art and mastery of ship construction. Since a shipwright needed to maintain an account book that recorded transactions made on credit, the shipwright was also expected to give his apprentice instruction in reading, writing, and arithmetic. Most shipwrights only trained two or three apprentices at a time.

After an apprentice completed his training, he might receive two sets of clothes or a set of tools to start his career as a journeyman. Apprentices rarely violated the terms of their indenture or ran away, nor did masters send them to sea. Although most apprentices completed their indentures, it was still possible for a master shipwright to lose the time and money he invested in an apprentice. Death or accident could deprive a master shipwright of his investment. Likewise, the death of a master could deprive an apprentice of his education. When a master shipwright died, his heirs were expected to sell the apprentice's indenture to another master shipwright so he could complete his training. Apprentices who lacked a responsible parent or guardian might find themselves exploited by his master's heirs, who could sell his indenture to someone who was not a shipwright.

Shipwrights benefited from the shortage of skilled labor that plagued the colonies. High wages and the absence of guilds provided powerful incentives for journeymen to set up shipyards of their own. Furthermore, land was considerably cheaper than in England. In some instances, towns would provide a shipwright land to relocate to their community. A shipwright only needed a waterfront lot with a gentle slope for a shipyard. Some shipwrights would construct a wharf after they purchased a lot. Possession of a wharf made it possible for a shipwright and his workers to complete a vessel after its launching. Once a shipwright had a lot, he could start constructing vessels with his tools. Even if a shipwright located his shipyard in an isolated area, he could build coasting vessels with a couple of apprentices or bonded laborers. Most shipwrights preferred to establish their shipyards in communities where they could take advantage of skilled tradesmen who helped to finish a vessel.

Edward J. Martin

See also: Cartwright and Wainwright; Rigger; *1776–1860.* Sailor

FURTHER READING

Goldenberg, Joseph A. 1976. *Shipbuilding in Colonial America*. Charlottesville: University of Virginia Press.
Horsley, John E. 1978. *Tools of the Maritime Trades*. London: David & Charles.

SHOPKEEPER

Although tradition and law restricted women's ability to participate in economic activities in the colonies, the realities of colonial life as well as the close relationship between work and home meant that women played significant roles in the economy. Even women who fell under coverture laws were allowed, on occasion, to conduct business on behalf of their husbands or other male relatives. A woman might help order supplies, keep the books, or maintain her husband's shop. In this way, many women, especially in the larger cities of colonial America, learned the skills necessary to run businesses. Women who proved successful under the tutelage of their husbands or fathers might even be permitted to conduct business independently. This practice was not technically legal in most colonies and could be challenged in court, making women's economic freedom tenuous at best.

Women who engaged in keeping shop were often widows, usually carrying on professions begun by their husbands using resources they inherited. But there were other paths to business. Because cash was rare in the colonies, a barter economy developed where men's and women's work was often paid for in goods. Wives might become shopkeepers by selling surplus bartered goods or home-manufactured products. This unofficial commerce was a fundamental part of the colonial economy dominated by widowed and married women. The streets of most urban areas in colonial America were full of shopkeepers selling all kinds of items: household goods, homemade beer, cider and spirits, and foodstuffs. Independent single women shopkeepers were rarer but not unknown, and large ports like Boston offered women of means the opportunity to open shops of their own.

Running a shop required a set of skills that both women and men found difficult to attain. Successful shopkeepers had to be literate and have basic mathematics skills. Carefully recording payments and debts in detailed ledger books was essential for merchants, and early ledger books contain entries for items like a small length of ribbon or a handful of nails, goods that cost less than the equivalent of a few cents today. Shopkeepers diligently recorded the dates, names of buyers, items purchased, cost of items, and whether credit was extended (most commonly) or cash paid for goods while noting the same information for their suppliers. Shopkeepers developed networks of craftspeople and traders who sold them goods for resale. Shopkeepers had to be trustworthy as most bought their supply on credit, so protecting their good names was critical. They learned of shiploads of fine goods arriving from England or elsewhere from members of their trading networks. They had to be shrewd arbiters of local fashion and keep abreast of changing styles arriving from abroad. Out-of-season stock arriving from abroad put great strain on a shopkeeper's tenuous finances. In the shop, customers haggled for goods, demanding more favorable prices by threatening to withhold their purchases and take their business elsewhere. Shopkeepers also had to advertise their goods, attract customers, and maintain the shop itself. Many shops had living quarters within but separate from the shop, though other shopkeepers, particularly the more successful ones, lived in homes apart from their shops. Shopkeepers often employed assistants, usually family members or distant kin.

Single women who went into shop keeping usually did so with familial support. The Boston shopkeeper Elizabeth Murray got her start with help from her older brothers. The eldest, James, contracted the sale of several slaves who Elizabeth Murray owned in North Carolina, sent her the proceeds, and also loaned her £100. In addition, he encouraged their brother John (still in England) to send her letters of credit equaling more than £100. James also used his own good credit, reputation, and network of connections to ensure that merchants in London would extend her credit for the merchandise they provided her. Furthermore, he helped Elizabeth decide what kinds of merchandise to buy and from whom. In many ways, this example reveals the difficulties that women had in running a business. Given social and legal customs of the colonies, many merchants and creditors did not trust a woman, especially a single one, in business. Putting a male face on a women's business activity eased that tension and comforted many colonial and European merchants.

While Elizabeth Murray's story offers a unique businesswoman's experience, Abigail Whitney, another Boston shopkeeper, presents a more typical case. She inherited her mother's business after years of working at her side in the family's shop. In fact, many young women got their start this way, often leading to great success. Another New England shopkeeper, Hannah Newman, left only insignificant property to both her sons and instead bequeathed her business to her daughter, Susannah, preferring to set her up in a business that would survive well into Susannah's old age. Southern shopkeepers Mary Cooper and Anne Matthews both inherited their husbands' shops and continued their success, with Matthews expanding her stock and contracts with English merchants.

Outside of family support or inheritance, the personal and professional networks that developed between shop keeping women, those who worked for them, and the merchants who supplied them created a self-support system that provided many women with the means, skills, and education necessary to open shops of their own. As historian Patricia Cleary notes of Elizabeth Murray, "Over the course of the 1760s Elizabeth actively directed the education of her nieces . . .; sponsored the mercantile career of the Cumming sisters; and continued to help her friend [and fellow shopkeeper] Jannette Day" (Cleary 2000, 92–93).

No matter how women gained their business, whether through their own initiative or outside support, they were becoming more prevalent throughout the eighteenth century. Between 1750 and 1760, there was a dramatic increase in the number of female shopkeepers: New York boasted 170, Philadelphia more than

160, and, in Boston, 90 women kept shop between 1740 and the 1770s (Cleary 1995, 183). While southern colonies offered women fewer opportunities, the number of women shopkeepers was still impressive. Advertisements in Annapolis, Williamsburg, and Charleston reveal a rather large number of active female shopkeepers (Spruill 1972, 278–284).

Like their male counterparts, women shopkeepers solicited business and attracted customers through newspaper advertisements and broadsides, both promoting their wares and becoming arbiters of taste. Again, Elizabeth Murray's broadside, printed around 1750, offers an interesting case study as it served several important functions for her new business. As a newcomer to Boston, Elizabeth used her detailed broadside to introduce herself and her business to consumers. Listing a lengthy variety of high-end goods, she let literate consumers know that she was a woman of good taste and comportment who maintained a shop filled with only the best goods in the current fashion. Her location, noted on the broadside, was also a hint at the quality of goods and her character, being near some of the most important economic and cultural structures in the city. While this broadside is unique in its size and detail, it is representative of the thousands of smaller advertisements posted in colonial newspapers by other women shopkeepers throughout the eighteenth century. From the 1720s on, colonial newspapers carried increasing numbers of advertisements from women shopkeepers. In this way, women were expanding their economic success and independence while also using their shops to promote the consumer fashions of the day.

In taking up shop, women actively participated in both the local and Atlantic economies, carving out a niche that allowed them an opportunity to find economic independence or at the very least contribute to their own families' well-being and financial security.

Sean Smith

See also: Scrivener; *1776–1860:* Tobacconist; *1861–1914:* Bookkeeper; Haberdasher; *1915–1945:* Grocer

FURTHER READING

Berkin, Carol, and Leslie Horowitz, eds. 1998. *Women's Lives, Women's Voices: Documents in Early American History*. Boston: Northeastern University Press.

Breen, T. H. 2004. *Marketplace of Revolution: How Consumer Politics Shaped American Independence*. New York: Oxford University Press.

Cleary, Patricia. 1995. "'She Will Be in the Shop': Women's Sphere of Trade in Eighteenth-Century Philadelphia and New York." *The Pennsylvania Magazine of History and Biography* 119, no. 3: 181–202.

Cleary, Patricia. 2000. *Elizabeth Murray: A Woman's Pursuit of Independence in Eighteenth-Century America*. Amherst: University of Massachusetts Press.

Salmon, Marylynn. 1986. *Women and the Law of Property in Early America*. Chapel Hill: University of North Carolina Press.

Spruill, Julia Cherry. 1972. *Women's Life and Work in the Southern Colonies*. New York: W. W. Norton and Company.

Ulrich, Laurel Thatcher. 1982. *Good Wives: Image and Reality in the Lives of Women in Northern New England, 1650–1750*. New York: Knopf.

PRIMARY DOCUMENT

Like other women who kept shop in colonial Boston, Jane Eustis sold a variety of local and imported British goods. Below is the oldest known trade card belonging to a female trader, and it provides an interesting glimpse at the imported wares maintained by a woman shopkeeper in 1769. It also hints at the fashion of the day and the way that shopkeepers became arbiters of colonial tastes.

Transcription:

Imported from LONDON and sold by
JANE EUSTIS

At her shop near the Town-House BOSTON
NEW ENGLAND
English and India Goods, Vizt. Brocades,
Damasks, Padusoys, Sattens, Persians,
Ducapes, Mantuas, Brolios, Irish Linnen,
Silk and Worsted Hose, Silk & Worsted Shoes,
with a Variety of Millinary & Haberdashery
All cheap for cash.

Source: Courtesy of the American Antiquarian Society. Catalog Record 384361.

SILVERSMITH

A silversmith is a person who makes and sells silver articles. Among most colonial Americans, the surname Smith (or Smythe, Schmidt, Smit, and others) denoted a family occupational heritage of working in the metal trades. Silversmiths were workers who created products like cups and plates out of silver. Colonists highly valued silversmiths' work in part because they created identifiable products, which, unlike silver coins, were easier to recover should that item ever be stolen; theft, embezzlement, and larceny were common problems both in England and in colonial towns and cities.

Expanding urban economies encouraged migration into the cities as people sought more opportunities than in agricultural regions. Unlike in rural areas and small towns, where residents tended to know each other, cities provided anonymity—neighbors could be strangers to each other, creating ideal conditions for crime. Growing wealth, especially in northern cities, offered many opportunities for silversmiths. So silversmiths worked not just as artisans but as creators of goods that could be banked or insured against loss in rapidly transforming America. Silversmiths marked their creations with recognizable symbols, known as maker's marks; customers sometimes ordered silver goods inscribed with particular family marks like coats of arms that made items much easier to identify—and much harder for a thief to sell illicitly, or fence. Over time, creating identifiable products led silversmiths to produce ever-more elaborate artistic pieces for their clients.

Silversmiths labored in workshops, using time-tested techniques that many had learned from family members or as apprentices to master smiths. Most silversmithing was bespoke work: a silversmith made a product only after it had been ordered by an individual and designed to that client's specifications. A client desiring to protect his or her wealth in silver products brought silver coins to the workshop, where the silversmith first melted the coins into ingots, or skillets, which could then be shaped into platework—thin sheets of silver that a silversmith shaped into silver products. Silver is a relatively soft metal, not requiring extensive heat or pressure to melt, mold, or shape.

Most smiths then cut these sheets of metal into constituent shapes of the silver vessel, like a teapot or vase, as specified by the client. He shaped these constituent pieces by using a smithing hammer, carefully tapping the piece over a wooden mold to form a design or over a wooden block to flatten an area of the work. Using silver soldering techniques, silversmiths bonded the pieces together; a number of techniques were used to hide this bond, or seam. The most skilled silversmiths planished their work, which involved holding the seams of a work over a small flame and applying borax and acids to them, which fused the seam and eliminated any evidence that it was there. Colonists especially prized these fine planished works because they were difficult—and expensive—to produce.

Silversmiths added distinguishing marks to their work by stamping, engraving, chasing, and embossing it. These methods required expert fine motor skills as smiths used hand instruments, like a burin (a small pen-shaped instrument), to engrave the products. Similar to engraving, chasing required a silversmith to carefully apply dents to a piece; for example, making lines in silverware required silversmiths to use chisel-like instruments to impress a series of precise, shallow grooves along a silver spoon handle. Stamping silver products simply required the smith to tap a design into the work using a stamp and hammer.

As customers desired more fanciful works, silversmiths used embossing techniques later in the colonial period. To emboss a work, the smith outlined a design on a piece and then applied tar or pine pitch over the lines, which he then removed with heat. The heat temporarily discolored the silver where the pitch or tar had been applied. Working from the inside of the vessel, the silversmith then used a particular tool, the snarling iron, to create what were essentially outward-facing dents, which were the substance of the embossed design. He then had to clean the piece carefully, removing any discoloration from it.

Silversmithing work could pay very well, especially for those with exceptional skill. Antique collectors today consider some colonial silversmiths, like the Richardsons of Philadelphia and John Coney (1655–1722) of Massachusetts, to be among the best in the world at that time. Paul Revere (1734–1818), an accomplished silversmith who is as famous for his political activism as he is his silverwork, was a descendant of one of John Coney's apprentices. Because silversmithing was a lucrative occupation, many skilled men passed knowledge of their trade down through the family, hiring sons and nephews as apprentices. The Richardsons of Philadelphia are an example of this family-based occupational activity. Francis Richardson, Jr. (1681–1729) was the first of the family to pursue work as a silversmith, although he may not have had much of a choice in his pursuit of this occupation. His father, a prominent New York Quaker merchant and mariner, had died in 1688, when Francis, Jr. was a young child. His mother remarried soon afterward, and the blended family moved to Philadelphia, where Francis, Jr. was apprenticed to a master goldsmith. There was little gold in these early colonies, however, so most goldsmiths worked with silver as silversmiths, though they may have retained their master goldsmith titles earned before they migrated to the New World.

Colonial Philadelphia was a center of commerce in the eighteenth century. Francis, Jr. likely learned the craft of silversmithing in Philadelphia, where he opened his own silversmithing workshop in 1701, when he was just twenty years old. One of his first clients was William Penn (1644–1718), the founder of the colony, who had ordered a pair of silver shoe buckles from him. By the 1730s, Richardson's sons Frank and Joseph were also practicing silversmiths. It was Joseph Richardson who became one of the most accomplished silversmiths in the colonies; his works today are owned by collectors and museums. Joseph's two sons, Joseph, Jr. and Nathaniel, also worked as silversmiths after serving long apprenticeships under their father. Joseph, Jr. continued to practice the family trade into the early 1800s.

Several factors contributed to the status and occupational gains of colonial silversmiths. There were few repositories in which colonial elites could store their wealth in coinage or bank deposits. Colonial merchants participated actively in the trade of the Atlantic world, financing slaving expeditions, participating in the sugar and rum trade, and transshipping American agricultural goods (wheat, salted fish, and meat) to offshore plantations. Participating in these lucrative businesses created great wealth, bringing more silver into the colonies, especially bustling port cities and urban centers of commerce like New York and Boston. Furthermore, there was no assaying office in the colonies—no place where the well-to-do could take their coins to be measured for weight and assayed, or tested, for impurities.

In England, counterfeiters had long participated in a trade that melted silver coins, mixed in other elements to dilute their value, and then recast them as the Queen's coinage. "Offenses against the Queen" (or King) was a euphemism for counterfeiting coins; other criminal acts under this statute included the practice of shaving silver from the edges of coinage, also with the goal of reducing their value. This coinage then circulated throughout the Atlantic world and often ended up in the coffers of colonial elites. Melting these coins down, then, and creating silver products was a way to preserve and store the value of money in the colonies.

By the eighteenth century, colonists also increasingly argued for home-manufactured goods, or those goods made in America. Here, silversmiths' reputation for honesty and skill enhanced these sentiments; when ordering from a colonial silversmith of good standing in the community, a client could be sure that what he supplied to the smith in value was returned to him. A silversmith's reputation as an honest craftsman was as important to his clients as his artistic skill.

Nancy Quam-Wickham

See also: Blacksmith; Indentured Servant

FURTHER READING

Fales, Martha G. 2000. "Richardson, Joseph (1711–1784), Silversmith." *American National Biography Online*.

Merriman, Philippa. 2009. *Silver*. Cambridge: Harvard University Press.

Smith, Andrea P. 2012. *A Day in the Life of Colonial Silversmith Paul Revere*. New York: PowerKids Press.

SPINNER, *see* WEAVER AND SPINNER

TRANSLATOR

Translator-guides were Native Americans who made a living translating between English and other European languages and Native American dialects while also operating as cultural guides for traders and colonists who needed to navigate and traverse unfamiliar Native American lands and regions. Historians broadly apply the term "cultural broker" to describe the diverse men and women who moved among and facilitated exchanges between various European, Creole, and indigenous societies during the early contact and colonial period in North America. European colonies depended on entangled networks of trade and diplomacy for their survival, and these complex relationships required interpreters and envoys to bridge the cultural and linguistic divides between European and Native American worlds.

Because native peoples regarded diplomacy as a sacred process—often requiring strict ceremonial and gift-giving protocols—European cultural brokers not only had to understand complex native languages but also the dances, songs, rituals, and manners required to effectively conduct councils with indigenous communities. Children of European colonizers learned indigenous languages and customs by living in indigenous villages. Some children even grew up as war captives who were abducted and adopted into Native American families at an early age. Often, European leaders intentionally left orphaned European children in indigenous villages so that they could grow up to become cultural brokers. Colonial and native leaders alike saw the value in exchanging children so that both societies could learn about the other's culture.

Conversely, Native Americans proved more adept at mastering European languages because most indigenous peoples were accustomed to living in culturally rich and linguistically diverse communities. Before European colonialism, native children learned to speak two to three other languages as extensive family ties made villages into multicultural spaces. Beginning in the sixteenth century, European explorers often captured children and brought them back to Europe to teach them to be language interpreters. Some children were sold as slaves, learning whichever language their enslaver possessed in the process.

Those indigenous children who survived childhood in colonial communities often acquired several European languages before returning to their native communities as adults. These survivors' experience played a key role in helping their indigenous communities understand the strange European customs that were so ill-suited to the American environment. One of these early native culture brokers who returned home from captivity was a young Patuxet man named Tisquantum, who learned English during his enslavement and facilitated peaceful diplomacy between the Patuxet chief and the first English settlers at Plimoth (now Plymouth) Colony in 1621.

European empires developed formal and informal strategies for negotiating with the myriad indigenous nations they encountered. As Europeans established colonies on the American mainland and in the Caribbean, worldly individuals—like rum merchants, slave traders, Catholic priests, Protestant clergy, healers, fur trappers, land speculators, sugar planters, military officers, and enslaved women—became culture brokers based on their unique economic, social, or political circumstance and facilitated relations between the indigenous and colonial worlds. Sometimes the empires paid these individuals for their services as official interpreters to negotiate peace settlements. At other times, these culture brokers used their influence and kinship with Native American societies for illegal activities, such as smuggling, human trafficking, and illicit land sales.

Since the linguistic and cultural expertise required to be an interpreter or negotiator was so rare, working as a cultural broker could be very lucrative. They often enjoyed privileged trading relationships within extensive kinship networks that connected European, African, and indigenous peoples across the Atlantic world. But cultural brokers' work on the margins of these societies also came with lethal occupational hazards. Their work on the frontier meant enduring harsh environmental hazards like starvation, dehydration, or hypothermia. Culture brokers often had fluid national and imperial loyalties, and in times of conflict they became suspicious to both sides of the intercultural divide. As such, when imperial wars or endemic settler violence erupted, cultural brokers were often the first ones killed or jailed. This was especially unfortunate because frontier violence had a tendency to escalate into unremitting cycles of vengeance without experienced mediators to negotiate peaceful settlements.

Women played a critical yet often overlooked role as culture brokers. Women wielded considerable power within indigenous communities, particularly matrilineal societies like the Iroquois Confederacy, where status and property descended through the mother rather than the father. For example, Degonwadonti, also known as Molly Brant, was a clan mother and the widow of a British superintendent of Indian affairs. During the American Revolution, the British Army depended on her goodwill and support to prevent Britain's Haudenosaunee allies from abandoning the war effort. The war forced Degonwadonti to flee her homelands, but the British Army built her a private stone house and granted her unrestricted access to the army's supplies to compensate her for her losses. No other civilians—and few British officers—received such wartime perks.

After the American War for Independence, cultural brokers became incorporated into the machinery of several governments. Both the British Empire and the young United States organized centralized bureaucracies to manage their relationships with native nations. Officially sanctioned interpreters and missionaries were paid by the government to move indigenous peoples to reservation lands and keep them there.

By the mid-nineteenth century, the United States made a national policy of Native American assimilation into American culture. Culture brokers now became charged with eradicating native traditions as Indian agents enforced harsh policies on reservations. Practicing indigenous religions and customs became crimes punishable by prison. Each year, the Bureau of Indian Affairs rounded up native children and sent them to boarding schools far from their families. Cultural brokers—now teachers—routinely beat Native American children for speaking their language or for singing traditional songs. These policies remained in place until the Indian Self-Determination and Education Assistance Act of 1975, which finally recognized First Amendment protection of Native American religious freedom and cultural sovereignty.

Loren Michael Mortimer

See also: *1776–1860:* Fur Trader; Fur Trapper; *1861–1914*: Tribal Representative

FURTHER READING

Barr, Juliana. 2007. *Peace Came in the Form of a Woman: Indians and Spaniards in the Texas Borderlands.* Chapel Hill: University of North Carolina Press.

Cayton, Andrew, and Teute J. Fredrika, eds. 1998. *Contact Points: American Frontiers from the Mohawk Valley to the Mississippi, 1750–1830.* Chapel Hill: University of North Carolina Press.

Erdrich, Louise, ed. 1994. *The Falcon: A Narrative of the Captivity and Adventures of John Tanner*. New York: Penguin Books.
Fitz, Caitlin A. 2008. "'Suspected on Both Sides': Little Abraham, Iroquois Neutrality, and the American Revolution." *Journal of the Early Republic* 28, no. 3: 299–335.
Hackel, Steven W. 2005. *Children of Coyote, Missionaries of Saint Francis: Indian-Spanish Relations in Colonial California, 1769–1850*. Chapel Hill: University of North Carolina Press.
Merrell, James H. 2000. *Into the American Woods: Negotiators on the Pennsylvania Frontier*. New York: W. W. Norton & Company.
Taylor, Alan. 2007. *The Divided Ground: Indians, Settlers and the Northern Borderland of the American Revolution*. New York: Vintage Books.

WAINWRIGHT, *see* CARTWRIGHT AND WAINWRIGHT

WATCHMAN

Watchmen were generally men who were familiar with community members and could quickly spot an outsider. Although male colonists typically volunteered for revolving duty, Boston and New York both employed full-time watchmen to patrol their towns at night by 1660. Watchmen were a form of local law enforcement. They stopped and interrogated outsiders and sometimes alerted the community to the presence of thieves and drunkards. They routinely chastised youngsters out after curfew, sending them home or to their masters' workshops. They rounded up tipsy locals leaving public houses, helping them find their way home. They roused unaccompanied young couples, taking them back to their respective parents. Later, they lit the town's oil lamps that served as streetlights. Watchmen had a simple, albeit important, job; their daily responsibilities and routines were few in number, but their presence was impactful. Most colonial towns had a night watchman, though "watchman" was a term that was more commonly used when describing ministers—who "watched over" their parishioners' souls. The use of this term, "watchman," in religious writings suggests the importance of the duties of a worker known as a watchman: to safeguard the community.

On the eve of the Revolutionary War (1775–1783), though, watchmen performed a variety of new duties, as well as their traditional ones. As the population of the colonies increased by the middle of the eighteenth century, more people traveled into and out of communities, making the work of the watchman more dangerous. In 1766, a watchman patrolling Boston's North End was seriously wounded by a newly arrived immigrant from Scotland, by way of Halifax, Nova Scotia, who operated a "House of Ill Fame." The paper noted that, increasingly, the city's watchmen "had been called often upon to prevent disturbances in the night by a Parcel of Renegadoes" (*Boston News-Letter*). Watchmen carried long spears to protect themselves and customarily had guard dogs with them as well.

In the years leading up to the American Revolution, colonial watchmen found themselves increasingly involved in conflict with British Army sentries. These conflicts between American colonial watchmen and British Army soldiers certainly intensified after the Quartering Act of 1765, in which the British authorities ordered colonial officials to house a British standing army in peacetime, after the end of the Seven Years' War (1754–1763). The billeting of British troops in colonial towns was a major grievance of colonists leading to the Revolutionary War and caused tensions throughout the colonies. In several instances in the winter of 1770, the "King's Troops" prevented Boston's watchmen from responding to and stopping burglaries, public disturbances, robberies, and assaults on women and children. Some of the perpetrators were reportedly British soldiers, who, in one case, assaulted a watchman who had tried to stop a bayonet assault on a woman who had rejected an officer's advances (*New York Journal*, 1770).

The importance of watchmen on the eve of the revolutionary period quickly became clear: they could alert the local populace to the movement of British troops, or, if a town was a Loyalist one, the watchman could alert residents to the presence of Patriots or Continental soldiers. The watchman as vigilant protector of the community grew in stature during this period, as William Livingston, a New Yorker, wrote and published a series of broadsides entitled "The Watchman." Published in full in both New York and Boston newspapers in the spring of 1770, these broadsides politicized the role of the watchman in their withering attacks on the Loyalist De Lancey family—who later supported the British occupation of Staten Island in 1776.

Other revolutionary authors penned columns in local newspapers under the pseudonym "The Watchman" (or "The Watch-man"), including one in a Connecticut paper advising "the fairer sex" to weave greater amounts of woolen and linen cloth to satisfy American demands for domestically manufactured goods—thus performing their patriotic acts to assist colonial consumers in their efforts to boycott English goods. In October 1774, one New York paper published yet another tract from "A Watchman," purportedly a "hand-bill delivered by Mr. [Paul] Rivere" [sic]. Here, the "watchman" reports on conditions facing revolutionaries and colonists alike in Boston: "The poor devoted town of Boston has suffered, and is still suffering, all the unmerited malice of men and devils could invent for her destruction; but although impoverished and distressed, she is not yet subjugated and enslaved; though immured within the fortresses of their enemies, the free and generous bosoms of the inhabitants beat strongly in the cause of liberty" (*New York Journal*, 1774).

The rhetorical use of revolutionary language reported by "A Watchman" increased once open warfare broke out across the country. Columns appeared regularly in the Massachusetts newspaper *The Massachusetts Spy Or, AMERICAN ORACLE OF LIBERTY,* entreating colonists to support American independence and openly reporting on British encampments and troop movements. Paradoxically, however, during the war itself, the job of watchman turned from that of a civilian duty to a military one. Radical revolutionary columns by "A Watchman" continued to appear in newspapers in New England and other regions until the summer of 1783, the end of the war. After the war, newly independent state and local governments reinstituted and formalized the role of the watchman. The post-revolutionary watchman, long a civilian position not formerly associated with law enforcement, increasingly became a paid member of local police forces, authorized to make arrests, hunt runaway slaves, and refer cases to local courts.

Nancy Quam-Wickham

See also: Militiaman; *1861–1914:* Police Officer

FURTHER READING

Boston News-Letter. October 16, 1766.

Gilje, Paul A. 1987. *The Road to Mobocracy: Popular Disorder in New York City, 1763–1834*. Chapel Hill: University of North Carolina Press.

Jones, Thomas. 1879. *History of New York During the Revolutionary War, and of the Leading Events of the Other Colonies at That Period*, no. 2. Edited by Edward Floyd De Lancey. New York: New York Historical Society.

New York Journal; or, the *General Advertiser*. April 6, 1770.

New York Journal; or, the *General Advertiser*. October 6, 1774.

Tiedemann, Joseph S. 2018. *Reluctant Revolutionaries: New York City and the Road to Independence, 1773–1776*. Ithaca: Cornell University Press.

PRIMARY DOCUMENT

The following document, published in a 1768 newspaper report, highlights some of the tensions between British soldiers and Americans in Boston shortly before the American Revolution. Such reports were fairly common at the time. In this case from November of that year, a town watchman fell victim to British aggression, in what many colonial readers may have seen as a parallel to their own treatment.

The troops still occupy the Town-House, and the Main Guard is fixed in a house on the South-Side of the Same, and two Pieces of Cannon planted before the door . . .

Nov 2. Two men and a Lad coming over the Neck into the Town, were hailed by one Guard [soldier] and passed them; soon after they were challenged by another, they replied they had just answered one, but they hoped they were all Friends;

upon which a Soldier made a pass or two with his Bayonet at one of them, who parried the Bayonet at first, but was afterward badly cut on the Head and grievously wounded in diverse parts of his Body. One passing the South Town Watch was challenged but not stopped, he drew his Sword and flourished it at the Watch, using very insulting language; he was then discovered to be an Officer a little disguised, another soon joined him, full as abusive, both declared that if they had been challenged in the Street and no Orders shewn [sic], they would have deprived the Watchman of his Life. A Country man also coming into Town, was thought to have approached nearer the Guards that he should have done, for which Offense he was knocked off his horse with a Musket.

Source: "Boston, Journal of Occurrences." *New York Journal*. November 17, 1768.

WEAVER AND SPINNER

Until 1790, all fabrics made in America were produced entirely by hand. Making fabrics, also called textiles, required multiple steps, from acquiring the raw fiber to finishing the cloth for clothing, household furnishings, or industrial use. Textile production then, as now, had four main stages: acquiring the fiber, spinning the fiber into yarn, weaving or knitting the yarn into fabric, and finishing the cloth using various mechanical and/or chemical treatments. Spinners and weavers were important occupations in the production cycle.

The fibers available to American colonists included flax (linen), hemp, cotton, wool, and silk. Colonists mainly used wool and linen. Although the English encouraged cultivation of silkworms in the colonies, silk production was ultimately not successful. Likewise, cotton—a fiber that now constitutes a substantial percentage of almost every American's wardrobe—was not grown in the colonies in the seventeenth century. It was first cultivated in Barbados and traded to the colonists. By the eighteenth century, cotton farming, and the slave trade that supported the cotton plantation system, had migrated to the American South, where the climate allowed enough frost-free days to grow the fiber.

Growing flax for linen and raising sheep for wool involved hard work. Converting the fiber to usable cloth first required spinning the raw fiber into yarn. Spinning was a time-consuming process that varied depending on the fiber. Wool fleeces had to be sorted and cleaned and then the fibers straightened to produce yarns. If the fibers were straightened once (carding), the yarn was termed "woolen." Straightening a second time (combing) produced a smooth worsted yarn. Wool is a relatively easy fiber to spin since it has crimp, which allows fibers to twist together easily without coming apart. Colonists used a special wheel called a great wheel, wool wheel, or walking wheel, whereby the spinner drew out the fibers and then rotated the wheel while twisting the fibers into a yarn. This was a discontinuous process that required walking back and forth, and spinners could often walk several miles a day.

Unlike wool, flax comes from a plant that grows well in cool, damp climates. New England's weather was ideal, and the colonies of New Hampshire and Connecticut soon developed regions that grew flax for fiber, seed, and linseed oil. To prepare flax fiber for spinning into yarn demanded several steps: pulling the plants, retting (soaking) the stalks to loosen the fibers, breaking the stalks to separate the inner fiber from the outer stem, and straightening the fibers. Short flax fibers produced heavy tow cloth, while long fibers produced linen. Spinning took place with a different type of wheel called a flax wheel. The spinner sat on a stool and worked a foot pedal that powered the wheel in a continuous process. Cotton spinning was similar to flax spinning, although cotton fibers had to be separated from the cotton seed before carding. Sometimes cotton and linen fibers were blended before spinning.

Spinning was monotonous work often assigned to women and children. The constant demand for yarn to supply weavers meant that hands should never be idle. Older, unmarried women who did not have childcare responsibilities often spun yarn, thus becoming known as spinsters.

Most spinning took place in private homes as part of the household economy. However, because of high demand for yarns, spinning was considered suitable employment for the indigent. In Boston, authorities established spinning schools and factories where women and children who had no means of support were sent. Such factories did not last long, however.

Inventories show that while most families owned spinning wheels, only a third to a half of colonial households possessed looms. A typical barn-frame loom was a large object that took up space in a small colonial home. If a household did not have a loom, a professional weaver might be employed. Although both men and women wove, as a profession, weavers were more often men. In urban areas, they worked in small shops. In rural areas, professional weavers worked out of their homes. Some weavers were itinerant, meaning they temporarily set up their looms in a client's home.

The colonists who arrived on American shores from England and other parts of Europe included experienced weavers, fullers, and dyers as well as tailors and dressmakers. But Europe, India, and China produced much more sophisticated textiles than what Americans could produce. In the years before the Revolutionary War (1775–1783), merchants enjoyed a lively trade with England that brought fabrics from all over the world to colonial doorsteps. The colonists who dressed most fashionably and had the finest furnishings in their homes bought imported fabrics. It was mostly the country people who used homespun cloth for their clothes and household furnishings. Whenever possible, they bartered (exchanged) yarn and woven cloth for imported goods at local general stores. Shops regularly advertised "Fresh and Fashionable Goods" from abroad.

When the first rumblings of conflict with the English arose after the Stamp Acts, colonists embraced spinning and weaving as a form of resistance. Wealthy ladies held spinning parties, learned to weave, and attended balls wearing homespun gowns. Men proudly wore suits of made-in-America fabrics. But truth be told, they did not like those fabrics. They were rough, scratchy, and only available in a limited range of colors. Thomas Jefferson described the home-produced fabrics of wool, hemp, and flax that he saw in Virginia as "very coarse, unsightly, and unpleasant" (Tryon 1966, 60). For women especially, giving up the beautiful and economical calicoes and chintzes from India made wearing homespun a real sacrifice.

As soon as the Revolutionary War was over, many Americans went back to buying imported fabrics. By that time, the Industrial Revolution was well under way in England. In 1790, Samuel Slater spun cotton by machine at his mill in Pawtucket, Rhode Island. Weaving with water power soon followed. The transition from hand production to machine production for textiles had begun, and the occupation of spinner and weaver shifted from farm to factory.

Linda Welters

See also: *1776–1860:* Ginner; Milliner; *1915–1945:* Garment Worker

FURTHER READING

Bogdonoff, Nancy Dick. 1975. *Handwoven Textiles of Early New England.* Harrisburg: Stackpole Books.

Hood, Adrienne D. 2003. *The Weaver's Craft: Cloth, Commerce, and Industry in Early Pennsylvania.* Philadelphia: University of Pennsylvania Press.

Miller, Marla R. 2006. *The Needle's Eye: Women and Work in the Age of Revolution.* Amherst: University of Massachusetts Press.

Tryon, Rolla Milton. (1917) 1966. *Household Manufactures in the United States, 1640–1860.* New York: Augustus M. Kelley Publishers.

Ulrich, Laurel Thatcher. 2001. *The Age of Homespun.* New York: Alfred A. Knopf.

PRIMARY DOCUMENT

The following passages provide clues about the work and status of weavers and spinners in the American colonies. Unlike their counterparts in England and Holland, weavers' work was largely domestic work, essential but largely unnoticed by outsiders. It was not until the later colonial period that weavers began to work in shops and factories.

In the following passage, John Wily provides instructions for how to make worsted wool from domestic sheep that had long-fibered fleece wool. Like many promotional tract authors, Wily takes an entirely positive view of the prospects for wool production in America, comparing the domestic products here with the finest of the German serge cloth in central Europe, where wool manufacturing had been well organized for decades. Europe, particularly Germany and the low countries, produced the finest wool fabric in the world, while worsted wool was a type of thin stranded yarn made from long fibers of wool that was washed, combed, and spun into yarn to make fine fabric, primarily for suits and dresses. Wiley details how domestic worsted wool production in colonial America was still largely a handmade product. In this passage, he explains the tedious process of producing worsted wool.

It requires the longest and finest wool to make good Worsted, and to prepare it for spinning you should have a Pair of Worsted Combs (which will cost about 35 Sterling) but I look upon the coming of Worsted to be so great a Difficulty that I believe no Person can do it to Perfection unless they have served an Apprenticeship to it, or could a person acquainted with it stand by and direct them, therefore have omitted how the Operation or Process is performed. But if you can light on a Person acquainted with the Business, and will comb your Wool fit for spinning, you may spin it on a Flax Wheel, as hereafter directed, or on a large Wheel, as Cotton or Wool; only with this Difference, the Worsted when combed is made into a large Bat, Fleece, or Sliver, and not into Rolls. And to spin it you are to take for the Bat about as much as would make a Roll, and give it a Turn round the fourth Finger of your left Hand; then join it to a Thread on the Spindle, and, turning the Wheel with your right Hand, draw out the Worsted to what Size you think proper. A good Spinner of Worsted will spin Half a Pound a Day, that will warp between 6 and 7 Yards to the Pound, and in 10 Days a good Spinner will spin sufficient to warp 30 Yards suitable for Shalloon, Taminies, Duroys, or any Worsted Stuffs that are but three Quarters of a Yard wide. The German Serge requires more Warp, because of its Width; and Camelot, on Account of its being doubled and twisted.

The Method to make with Wool what is called Camelot (though it often hath Silk or Hair in it) is to have the Wool combed, and take the longest of it and spin it into Worsted, then double and twist two Threads hard together for both Warp and Filling. It is in common wove in the plain Way, but should be stayed as thick as possible , and drove as close together as it can be with the Slay, &c. These plain Camelots after they are wove[n] are put in a hot Press, to give them a glossy Stiffening, and close the Thread. The watered Camelots are those which after weaving receive a certain Preparation with Water, and are after passed under a hot Press which gives them a Smoothness and Lustre.

Duroys, Taminies, and many other Worsted Stuffs, are wove in the plain Way; and after weaving are passed under a hot Press, to give them a Gloss and Lustre.

Shalloon, Sagathy, Calimanco, Plaids, and many other Worsted Stuffs, are made of raw Worsted, but are double wove; and the Difference in them is performed by the different Methods the Weavers have of putting the Warp in the Harness, and by working it with a larger Number of Treadles than they make Use of in the weaving of plain Cloth.

Source: John Wiley. 1765. *A Treatise on the propagation of sheep, the manufacture of wool, and the cultivation and manufacture of flax, with directions for making several utensils for the business.* Williamsburg: J. Royle, 16–17.

In the second document, teenager Abagail Foote recounts her duties as a young unmarried woman working for her family and for her neighbors.

Fix'd Gown for Prude Just to clear my teeth,—Mend Mother's Riding hood—Ague in my face—Ellen was spark'd last night—Mother spun short thread—Fix'd two Gowns for Welch's girls—Carded tow—spun linen—worked on Cheese Basket—Hatchel'd flax with Hannah and we did 51 lb a piece—Pleated and ironed—Read a sermon of Dodridges—Spooled a piece—milked the cows—spun linen and did 50 knots—made a broom of Guinea wheat straw—Spun thread to whiten—Went to Mr. Otis's and made them a swinging visit—Israel said I might ride his jade (horse)—Set a red Dye—Prude stay'd at home and learned Eve's Dream by heart—Had two scholars form Mrs Taylor's—I carded two pounds of whole wool and felt Nationaly—Spun harness twine—Scoured the Pewter.

Source: Abagail Foote. 1897. "Selections from the Diary of Abagail Foote, 1773." In *Men, Women, and Manners in Colonial Times*, edited by Sydney George Fisher. Philadelphia: J. J. Lippincott, 275.

WIGMAKER

Wigmakers are people who made and sold wigs, which are head coverings made from human or animal hair or synthetic fiber. A common image of George Washington features a stately figure with a dignified, attentive facial expression, who is wearing a skillfully coiffed wig. George Washington's "wig," however, was just his own heavily powdered and dressed natural hair. Wigmakers were commonplace in colonial American society, although few people could afford the expensive wigs that often distinguished wealthy gentlemen and gentlewomen from the colonies' working class. Wigs were fashion accessories worn primarily as a status symbol rather than as a garment to hide a balding head. Furthermore, wig wearing mostly ended after the 1700s; the fad of wig-wearing gentry was in imitation of European elites, and as colonists strove to break with England and establish themselves as citizens of an independent nation, they increasingly rejected such imitative forms of fashion.

Throughout most of the seventeenth century, colonists were largely oriented toward survival. Most colonists worked as farmers, livestock raisers, or fishermen, and they worked toward securing a future for themselves and their families, both in the near term and the long term. While many colonists desired European goods like shoes, fine china, and expensive clothing, few English colonists outside tobacco-growing regions of Maryland and Virginia ever secured enough essential goods to be able to trade for luxuries like wigs. But wigmakers did find a substantial amount of related work in the colonial world.

In colonial America, wigmakers did much more than make wigs—they offered haircuts and shaves to businessmen and elites; they styled, curled, and dyed the long locks of natural hair on women and men alike; they sold hairbrushes and curlers made of ceramic or clay, and they sold ribbons and other decorations; they sold fragrant powders to apply to both natural hair and wigs. Additionally, they offered a treatment for lice, in which they patiently used fine-toothed combs to remove the pests from a customer's hair. Wigmakers also sold perfumes and scented waters to mask the colonists' body odor since most colonists rarely bathed.

Wigmakers made various types of wigs: toupees, perukes, periwigs, as well as strings of curls, braids, and other headpieces to extend or add to a colonist's natural hair. Colonists who wore wigs generally did so only in public—they were removed in the home. Those who labored in the fields and as militiamen, in hot workshops, or on the docks and on ships tended not to wear wigs at all.

To make a wig, a wigmaker had to procure hair or fibers resembling hair, which often were finely combed flax or silk threads. The wigmaker measured a customer's head carefully and then stitched a wig base, which is a fitted cap known as a caul. Next, the wigmaker prepared the hair or fiber by wetting it and curling it onto small clay curlers; he dried the hair in an oven on the hearth, taking care not to burn the wig, though this happened regularly. Working with a wooden model head, the wigmaker then carefully knotted together several pieces of hair or fiber and stitched those tiny bundles onto the caul, starting at the bottom. The wigmaker completed this process over and over again until he had assembled a full line of hair across the caul's bottom. Working upward, the wigmaker repeated this process, spacing the lines of hair or fiber about a quarter-inch above each previous, lower line of hair.

The wigmaker was not done with his work once the caul was covered with hair or fiber; wigs needed dressing, or styling—the curls needed to be adjusted, and powder needed to be applied. While white hair and fiber were used for many wigs, wigmakers also made wigs from a great variety of colored materials because wigs could often be dyed or powdered to a customer's taste. Wigs made of light-colored hair, for instance, could be powdered different colors; some colonial men even preferred their wigs to be powdered pink. Wigmakers also periodically dressed—or cared for—wigs for their customers. They sold storage boxes for wigs, nets to keep the wig's hair out of its wearer's face, and ribbons and bows to hold the wig's hair back.

English gentry began to wear wigs after the end of the English Civil War (1642–1651), when the monarchy was restored, and Charles II (1630–1685) returned from continental Europe to take the throne. Royal fashion at this time tended to be ornate—deep purple robes, billowy blouses, and red garments adorned with gold embroidery. Charles II also shunned the nonconformist's plain appearance and dour manners by making popular the peruke or periwig, which was a type of headpiece that featured an exaggerated mound of curls on top of the head, with more curls flowing down to below the shoulders. By the 1670s, even more elaborate perukes were popular among the English gentry; the cost of a peruke made of human hair was prohibitive except for those with the greatest wealth. In England, lesser gentry, businessmen, and lawyers, judges, and other officers of the court wore imitation periwigs made of horsehair, goat hair, or even fine threads of flax. Those who wore wigs in seventeenth-century America seem to have been recently arrived gentry, governors, and others with high status.

By the 1700s, however, more colonists sought ways to denote their higher social status by wearing wigs and fine clothing, purchasing china and fine furniture, and indulging in imported wines and food. The eighteenth-century colonial wigmaker was likely a recent migrant to the colonies. But evidence of their arrival is elusive. By 1721, the market for wigs was apparently good enough in Philadelphia that the wigmaker Oliver Galtery sought to purchase "any light [colored] hair" from any person who wanted to sell it. An advertisement in a Boston newspaper in May 1730 lauded the wares of Robert Jenkins, peruke maker, who offered ribbons, hairbrushes, and other "things belonging to the peruke-makers trade" at his shop near the Boston town center. A September 1733 notice in a Philadelphia newspaper noted that peruke maker George Sheed had offered a £3 reward for the return of his runaway Irish servant, Stephen Roe, who was a wigmaker. The market for wigs expanded with the economy; by the 1740s, colonial wigmakers routinely advertised their goods and services in newspapers along the eastern seaboard.

For a time, many colonists' demand for wigs was so great that they were willing to purchase imported, used wigs just as soon as they could be unloaded from the ship. Sons of businessmen wore wigs made of flax, goat hair, cow tails, and other materials less expensive than human hair. Even as the wig-wearing fashion of the mid-eighteenth century flourished, American tastes also favored the practical. The length of hair on wigs was significantly shorter, cut in bobs and curled to look as if it were longer. Some wigs featured removable hair extensions like braids, ponytails, and pigtails; some extensions were made of ribbon only. As in other areas of consumption of nonessential goods, Americans on the eve of the revolution largely distanced themselves from those who sought to rule over them and embraced new styles distinctively American. This transformation in taste led to the decline in wigs and wig making by the 1770s and 1780s. Even Benjamin Franklin traded his white powdered wig for a fur cap in 1776, when he returned to France as ambassador; his choice to don a heavy cap made of beaver fur and wear it everywhere was clearly a conscious one meant to signify the youth, sensibility, and ruggedness of these new Americans.

Nancy Quam-Wickham

See also: *1776–1860:* Barber; *1946–1991:* Beautician

FURTHER READING

Georgini, Sara. 2017. "Ambassador in a Fur Hat: The Sartorial Power of Benjamin Franklin's Fur Cap." *The Junto.* February 3, 2017. https://earlyamericanists.com/2017/02/15/roundtable-ambassador-in-a-hat-the-sartorial-power-of-benjamin-franklins-fur-cap/.

Hodge, Christina J. 2014. *Consumerism and the Emergence of the Middle Class in Colonial America.* Cambridge: Cambridge University Press.

Staples, Kathleen A., and Elizabeth Shaw. 2013. *Clothing through American History: The British Colonial Era.* Santa Barbara: Greenwood.

1776–1860: THE REVOLUTIONARY PERIOD TO THE ANTEBELLUM ERA

INTRODUCTION

As Captain Seth Clark sailed his vessel into its home port of Newburyport, Massachusetts, on September 17, 1776, he may have thought his voyage was ending—but in fact, it was just beginning. An English warship was docked in Newburyport, and upon docking his boat, Clark was taken prisoner and forced into the service of King George III. He was put to labor as a common sailor on an English warship bound for Jamaica and then transferred there to the *Squirrel*, another English vessel under arms. Aboard the *Squirrel*, Clark soon found himself bound to South Carolina and, from there, on to England. In England, Clark was taken before a judge, who ordered him to sail as an ordinary seaman again, not as a captain. Clark refused. The English naval officer warned Clark that his refusal would lead to him being "brought to the gangway, [and there] severely flogged" (*Evening Post*, August 5, 1777). After this threat, Clark acquiesced.

Clark was then put aboard another ship, where he observed many other indentured Americans, "closely confined" and in irons, with only quarter rations of food and water. These other workers informed Clark that many similarly impressed American seamen—sailors who had been forced into military service by threat of violence—had been posted to English vessels that were engaged in Indian Ocean and African coastal trades. Clark eventually took ill and was removed to an English hospital, where he provided testimony about the fate of yet more American sailors—testimony that was later published widely in American newspapers by order of the Continental Congress.

As published in American newspapers, Clark's testimony served as a cautionary tale for not only sailors but also all American workers; he related how the English did not respect American workers—and, in fact, chained, bound, and essentially kidnapped them. Americans of the time understood the plight of sailors to be their own, regardless of their occupation. The metaphor of a rapacious England holding its colony hostage resonated with citizens who supported American independence: England was holding America back, not just politically but economically as well. The workers of revolutionary America—the authors and politicians, members of the militia and sailors, those who provided intelligence and town watchmen—all labored to create the independent and free nation they had imagined.

In the era of the early republic, Americans engaged in work that would prove central to the formation of their new nation. Custom officials collected import duties to support the young government. Diplomats negotiated agreements of import with other nations, particularly internally with tribal nations. Judges oversaw the functioning of local, state, and federal courts, borrowing common law practices from England to interpret laws in a distinct American environment. Explorers traveled to the Pacific and beyond, throughout the new states and western frontiers, to report about people and resources that became critical to national expansion in subsequent decades. Inventors toiled in workshops and used the newly established U.S. Patent Office to secure ownership and the authority to distribute licensing and use rights, even when the operational systems of inventions—like the cotton gin—were well known and easily modified. Ordinary men and women tilled the land, harvested crops, operated stores, and, most importantly, succeeded remarkably in creating domestically made goods that, under the yoke of England, had been formally prohibited from manufacture within the colonies.

These years—from 1789 through 1815, which saw the end of the War of 1812—set a momentum for American development, despite the common worker's struggle with changing ideas and attitudes about their work. Diplomatic efforts to secure tribal lands, for instance, could be undercut by the actions of Americans on the edges of the frontiers, who believed their rights as Americans—coupled with racial antagonism against Indians—entitled them to expel tribal people whose lands they desired.

The great "market revolution," as historian Charles Sellers framed it in his monograph of the same name, swept through the nation with the end of the War of 1812 (1812–1815). Americans turned their energies and attention from home production and subsistence activities to production for market. Even as most Americans remained attached to the land, living and working on farms, the work of commerce also required men to build canals and roadways to move bulky wheat, cotton, and other goods to market. Surveyors and cartographers assisted these efforts—marking the land, setting boundary lines (at least on paper), and determining the most efficient routes for new roads and canals. Land speculators both preceded and followed the mapmakers. Missionaries moved swiftly into new territories, dedicated to helping indigenous people assume the habits of "civilization." At the same time, shipping, commercial, and manufacturing centers arose on the eastern seaboard in places like Charleston, South Carolina; Philadelphia, Pennsylvania; and Lowell, Massachusetts. New technologies that mechanized hand production of textiles, for instance, were crucial to the reorientation of the American economy toward market and industrial production in what became known as the "American system of manufacture" (Cowan 1997, 82).

Population growth, improvement in transportation networks, and an abundance of available land gave American workers advantages but only for those who were free and (for the most part) of Euro American descent. Governments and laws provided even more advantages to those Americans who turned their eyes toward commerce and the market.

As cotton became the primary agricultural export of antebellum America, planters in Virginia and elsewhere shackled their slaves into gangs and marched them to the Deep South to areas opened for settlement by slave owners and their human property. Here, enslaved men and women worked as field hands, in the homes of their owners, and in other occupations as slave owners maximized their "investments" by hiring out unneeded labor. In some areas, such as Alabama, many in the planter class arose from the ranks of common farmers who, as a class, "increased by 70 percent between 1830 and 1860" in the South (Sellers 1991, 280). Tensions between farmers who owned slaves and those who did not led a great exodus of free white southerners to the old Northwest (Indiana and Ohio), the western frontier, and the old Southwest. In these states and regions, non-slave-owning southerners engaged in a host of other trades: providing tobacco and liquor to townspeople and farmers alike as well as other services and goods to residents of their new communities. Some moved westward, joining companies of fur trappers and traders.

More than any single law, congressional act, or religious precept, the labor of these American workers, black and white, immigrant and native born, free and enslaved, created a nation that was aggressively oriented to the market and to the ideas of profit—too often at the expense of national unity. In so doing, they created a nation on the verge of disintegration.

FURTHER READING

Beckert, Sven. 2014. *Empire of Cotton: A Global History*. New York: Vantage.

Cowan, Ruth Schwartz. 1997. *A Social History of American Technology*. New York: Oxford University Press.

Johnson, Rashauna. 2016. *Slavery's Metropolis: Unfree Labor in New Orleans during the Age of Revolutions.* Cambridge, UK: Cambridge University Press.
Maris-Wolf, Ted. 2015. *Family Bonds: Free Blacks and Re-enslavement Law in Antebellum Virginia.* Chapel Hill: University of North Carolina Press.
Sellers, Charles. 1991. *The Market Revolution: Jacksonian America, 1815–1846.* Oxford, UK: Oxford University Press.

ACTOR/ACTRESS (STAGE)

Actors and actresses who were well trained in the dramatic arts performed for antebellum audiences, as did those with little formal training but with skills in oratory or comedy. Some were hucksters—those who simply found money to be made in entertainment when sales of products were slow. Others were imitators, or performers who could somewhat aptly impersonate others, thereby contributing to the cultural creation of stereotypes of "happy slaves" or bossy Irish women. Actors and actresses made their livings by entertaining audiences in many types of venues and performing all kinds of acts, from drama and comedy to singing, dancing, and magic. Others combined work on the stage with playwriting, operating theaters, or promoting plays. Much as it is today, acting in antebellum America was an occupation that could provide substantial wealth or, for most, only a financially precarious living.

The theater in antebellum America was a remarkably democratic space. As the late historian Lawrence Levine wrote, the theater was not only "one of the earliest and most important cultural institutions" of antebellum America but also a "kaleidoscopic, democratic institution presenting a widely varying bill of fare to all socioeconomic groups" (Levine 1986, 18, 21). Audiences interacted with actors and actresses on the stage, singing along with the chorus, goading actors to break out into popular songs in the middle of a serious Shakespearean production, and demanding long evenings of performances and encores of comedic farces. Plays, readings, and other dramatic performances were held not only in theaters but in saloons, at open markets and fairs, in political halls, and even in mining camps.

For most men and women who worked in the theater, performing for others' enjoyment was a job with few rewards other than an audience's applause. The career of actor Harry Watkins is a case in point. Watkins was born in 1825 in New York, and at the age of thirteen he enlisted in the U.S. Army, serving with Company I at Fort Snelling, Iowa Territory (now Minnesota). During his three years of military service, he spent a great deal of time in the fort's library, reading plays and memorizing lines. He and some of his fellow soldiers formed a theater company, producing plays for the entertainment of others, both military and civilian audiences. As he noted in his journal in 1846, his study of Shakespeare's plays at the fort allowed him to play almost every part in *Othello*.

After his military service, Watkins pursued an acting career, appearing with the legendary actor Edwin Forrest (1806–1872) in New York. But in 1853, Watkins was out of work. Aspiring to continue in the theater, he almost single-handedly organized a new theater company in Brooklyn, which closed down within months. He attempted to reorganize that theater, renaming it the Odean Gardens, but that effort, too, failed quickly thereafter. Watkins continued his career as an actor, often volunteering to act in benefits, or productions organized for the monetary support of actors and actresses. Watkins never became famous or widely revered by audiences; we know of his experiences because he conscientiously detailed his daily activities in a journal covering the years 1845 to 1860.

Other actresses and actors surely shared Watkins's career trajectory. Antebellum newspapers are full of notices for appearances of traveling theater troupes, usually without noting the names of any of the actors or actresses. Many focused instead on audience's behavior—the raucous exchanges among performers, audiences, and theater operators. Especially common in frontier towns and in the Midwest by the 1840s were minstrel performances. In the colonial period, minstrels were regarded as restless, itinerant poets and musicians who gave a performance and then moved on to the next town. But by the mid-nineteenth century, minstrelsy took on vulgar racist connotations—a minstrel show consisted of songs, dances, and comedic acts that depicted outrageous stereotypes of deformed and foolish slaves and free African Americans. Many of these minstrel performers were of Irish descent, performing in blackface; in Frederick Douglass's words, these actors and actresses were the "filthy scum of white society" (Douglass 1848) for their exaggerated portrayals of African Americans' supposed debauchery.

Actors in these minstrel troupes traveled from town to town, offering several performances on successive evenings, even on the Sabbath, some observers disapprovingly noted. While some actors might have rehearsed their lines and acts, it was also common for minstrel actors and actresses to skip rehearsals. Sometimes new lines were written before a performance; others were improvised on the stage. Until the 1840s, most well-to-do Americans regarded minstrel shows as a form of lowbrow entertainment.

Some actors and actresses in the antebellum era were in fact well-known experts in their profession. Some of the century's most famous stage actors included Edwin Forrest, the Shakespearean actor who performed many leading roles in New York as well as giving public dramatic readings in which he read a character's lines from a play as if he were in a production. A star performer like Forrest also provided private readings for wealthy patrons. Forrest was at the center of the Astor Place riots in 1849 New York, when audiences fought violently over stars, resulting in almost two dozen deaths. Other prominent stage performers were members of theater families, those in which generations of family members worked in one capacity or another in American—and European—theater. The Booth family was widely known. Entry into the profession often required not only talent but also connections with people who introduced aspiring actors and actresses to wealthy theater owners and arts patrons.

Regardless of talent, not all actors and actresses were able to maintain a career on the stage. Much of respectable society, for instance, frowned upon women who maintained a public presence, so many major roles, especially Shakespearean characters, were performed by men. Anna Cora Mowatt (1819–1870) was unusual, though not unique, in that she was an American woman who gained fame as an actress. She had performed in productions in Europe, though when she and her husband returned to America, she declined to resume her acting career, instead writing a play called "Gulzara, or the Persian Slave" for a women's theater troupe, the *corps dramatique*, in which all the characters were women; she wrote the central figure, the "Sultan," as a man whose presence was felt on the stage, yet he never appeared as he had gone to war. When Mowatt's husband lost his sight, she decided to begin to offer private readings, earning income in the comfort of a patron's home or at such venues as the Rutgers Institute for Young Ladies, where she could avoid taking the stage with a male actor.

Mowatt understood that contemporary American audiences did not respect women on the stage. Eventually, she took acting roles in theaters, though she concluded her autobiography with a warning to other women to avoid acting as a career. It was not, though, just women who found it difficult to pursue a career on the American stage because of audience prejudices. The Shakespearean actor Ira Aldridge, an African American born in 1807 in New York, had to immigrate to Britain, where he became quite famous—though he had to perform most of his roles in whiteface (heavy white cosmetics). Such was the world of antebellum theater.

Nancy Quam-Wickham

See also: *1915–1945:* Radio Announcer; *1946–1991:* Actor/Actress (Film and Television)

FURTHER READING

Butsch, Richard. 2007. *The Making of American Audiences: From Stage to Television, 1750–1990.* Cambridge: Cambridge University Press.

Douglass, Frederick. 1848. "The Hutchinson Family.—Hunkerism." *The North Star* (Rochester). October 2. http://utc.iath.virginia.edu/minstrel/miar03bt.html.

Keetley, Dawn. 1996. "The Power of 'Personation': Actress Anna Cora Mowatt and the Literature of Women's Public Performance in Nineteenth Century America." *American Theater Quarterly* 10: 187–201.

Levine, Lawrence. 1986. *Highbrow/Lowbrow: The Emergence of Cultural Hierarchy in America.* Cambridge: Harvard University Press.

Lindfors, Bernth. 2017. "'Mislike Me Not for My Complexion . . .' Ira Aldridge in Whiteface." *African American Review* 50: 1005–1012.

Ritchie, Anna Cora Mowatt. 1854. *Autobiography of an Actress, or Eight Years on the Stage.* Boston: Ticknor, Fields, and Reed.

BARBER

Barbers were workers who provided personal grooming services primarily to men but sometimes also to women during the antebellum period. Using a handheld razor sharpened with a strop (a leather sharpening tool), the barber shaved men as well as sharpened the razors of those men who shaved themselves. Barbers also cut men's hair. In both northern and southern regions, as service workers, barbers were primarily African American. Among antebellum America's most famous barbers was the abolitionist Frederick Douglass. Douglass was famous in the decades before the Civil War (1861–1865) for being America's most ferocious critic of slavery. But among the country's barbers, he was known for something else: his unkind words about their profession.

The problem with barbering, according to Douglass, was that it encouraged laziness and debased the African American men who dominated the profession. "To shave a half dozen faces in the morning and sleep or play guitar in the afternoon—all this may be easy," Douglass wrote in his newspaper. "But is it noble, is it manly, and does it improve and elevate us?" (Thomas 1984, 83–84) Particularly upsetting to Douglass was the fact that most barbershops, including those owned by African Americans, were segregated establishments that only served white men.

Barbers themselves, however, did not choose to segregate their shops; white customers demanded it, normally by social pressure but sometimes by law as well. Their jobs were anything but easy. Most barbers arrived at work early and left late. William Johnson, who was a barber in Natchez, Mississippi, shaved an average of sixteen customers per day and cut the hair of three. He visited customers at their homes and hotels, shaved corpses at the local morgue, and, on his busiest days, served upward of 120 patrons.

Tending to customers' needs was no easy task. Barbers' work required enormous training and skill. Shaving in particular—which represented 80 percent of Johnson's services—was a more complicated task than it is today. Barbers had to wrap their customers' heads in hot towels to open their pores, whip hard cakes of soap into frothy shaving cream using badger-bristle brushes, and shave their customers' faces with sharp blades that were both fragile and difficult to maintain. They did all this quickly, without causing their customers pain and without the aid of mechanical chairs in which they could easily raise or lower the customer.

Shop owners like Johnson, moreover, had a variety of responsibilities beyond shaving and cutting hair. They had to manage their shop's finances; keep it stocked with razors, scissors, and countless other necessities; supervise and train less experienced workers; and, in the case of African American barbers, navigate a society that frowned on black business ownership. While a handful of barbers, both black and white, became wealthy, influential members of their communities, they worked exceptionally hard for these rewards. Admittedly, Johnson's occupation was less physically demanding than those of many friends and neighbors. Barbers spent long hours on their feet, but even the most tiring day for a barber was less draining than the daily grind of cooks, cleaners, artisans, and day laborers.

Still, barbers endured other kinds of hardships. Nearly all served customers who were wealthier and more powerful than themselves. Because of these customers' wealth and status, they could get away with treating their barbers rudely. These problems were even worse for African Americans, who also had to contend with their customers' racism. On one occasion, for instance, African American barber James Thomas made the mistake of asking a customer about politics, a topic that people of color were supposed to avoid. "The set back I got from him for asking such a question," Thomas wrote, "caused me to be careful as to who I plied questions to with regard to politics" (Thomas 1984, 83–84).

Despite these insults, barbers were expected to keep calm. In fact, they were expected to entertain their customers and maintain a friendly, inviting atmosphere in their shops. Frequently, they created this atmosphere by telling memorable stories and tall tales. A Massachusetts paper noted that a customer described his barber as "the essence of good-nature" (*Salem Gazette*, 1832). St. Louis barber Frank Robinson could "rattle out more nonsense in ten minutes than any sensible man would believe in a week" (Clamorgan 1858, 59).

Barbers, however, were not simply entertainers. They also kept secrets for the men who visited their shops. William Johnson, for instance, frequently saw or heard things that his customers preferred he kept secret. On one occasion, Johnson confided to his diary that he had seen a customer wet his pants after drinking too much alcohol. On several other occasions, he secretly jotted down gossip about his customers' sexual affairs.

More frequently, Johnson and his fellow barbers had to referee their customers' rowdy behavior. While patrons typically passed time by chatting and reading newspapers, they also used the shop as a makeshift saloon. When drunken customers started arguing, insulting one another, or, on at least one occasion, lighting each other's hair on fire, barbers had to keep the peace: no small task given customers' lack of respect for their barbers' authority.

Worse yet, barbers saw their fortunes decline in the decades leading up to the Civil War. While barbering had once been a reliable pathway for poor men—particularly African Americans—to attain a decent life, by the 1840s and 1850s, the profession was in a state of crisis. During those decades, thousands of immigrant barbers arrived from Ireland and Germany; the story of Sweeney Todd, which depicts a barber who murders his customers, became a cultural sensation, and many men either started shaving themselves or growing beards. The net result was increased competition among barbers for a shrinking number of customers. Reflecting on this crisis, Alabama barber John Rapier, Sr. confessed, "I hate the name of a barber" (Rapier 1856). Instead, he advised his son to take up farming.

The barbering profession never fully recovered from this crisis. While the Civil War–era beard fashion eventually passed, shaving—which had once represented 80 percent of barbers' income—remained a secondary source of revenue. In fact, by the time the beard trend had ended, businessman King Gillette had popularized cheap, disposable razor blades that enabled even the most uncoordinated men to shave themselves safely at home. Deprived of income from shaving, barbers increasingly relied on hair cutting alone. Thus concluded America's golden age of barbering, when customers visited their local barbershop three or more times per week and relaxed as skilled professionals "peel[ed] off the beard," in the words of barber Cyprian Clamorgan, "like a dairy-maid skimming cream" (Clamorgan 1858, 53).

Sean Trainor

See also: *1607–1775:* Wigmaker; *1946–1991:* Beautician

FURTHER READING

Bristol, Douglas W., Jr. 2009. *Knights of the Razor: Black Barbers in Slavery and Freedom*. Baltimore: The Johns Hopkins University Press.

Clamorgan, Cyprian. [1858] 1999. *The Colored Aristocracy of St. Louis*. Reprint edited by Julie Winch. Columbia: University of Missouri Press.

Davis, Edwin Adams, and William Ransom Hogan. 1954. *The Barber of Natchez*. Baton Rouge: Louisiana State University Press.

Herzig, Rebecca M. 2015. *Plucked: A History of Hair Removal*. New York: New York University Press.

Lee, Hannah Farnham Sawyer. 1854. *Memoir of Pierre Toussaint, Born a Slave in St. Domingo*. Boston: Crosby, Nichols, and Company.

"Meditations in a Barber's Shop." *Salem Gazette* (Salem), Nov. 6, 1832.

Mills, Quincy T. 2013. *Cutting Along the Color Lines: Black Barbers and Barber Shops in America*. Philadelphia: University of Pennsylvania Press.

Rapier, John H., Sr. to John H. Rapier, Jr. Dec. 13, 1856. Letter. Florence, Washington, DC: Rapier Family Papers. Howard University, Moorland-Spingard Research Center, 84–1, 30.

Thomas, James. 1984. *From Tennessee Slave to St. Louis Entrepreneur: The Autobiography of James Thomas*. Edited by Loren Schweninger. Columbia: University of Missouri Press.

BARGEMAN

Bargemen, or boatmen, in the nineteenth century were city scow (a flat-bottomed boat) operators whose boats were generally used as floating incinerators; they were an earlier version of the twentieth century's garbage barge. In 1858, David McLyman, a bargeman who operated a scow on which clothing and bedding of the diseased were burned in New York harbor, gave testimony in court that provides a window into the daily work of these bargemen. In addition to incinerating clothing and bedding of sick patients, McLyman also captained a small vessel that ferried sick patients and the deceased from ships to Staten Island and the mainland shores.

On September 1 and 2, 1858, arsonists burned down the several quarantine hospitals on Staten Island in what observers at the time considered a community act of protest. Residents of the hamlet of Tompkinsville on the island had resented the presence of sick and dying patients, infected with diseases like smallpox, yellow fever, cholera, and typhus. The U.S. Revenue Service inspected all passengers and crew arriving on ships in New York harbor, quarantining some at anchor before clearance while removing others to the hospitals. Most residents of Tompkinsville knew that the arsonists were led by two local men, who were quickly arrested. Within a few weeks, however, both defendants were acquitted by a local judge, who was reportedly allied with Tompkinsville residents. Although the quarantine hospitals had been located on the island since 1799, a dramatic increase in immigration through the 1840s and 1850s, as well as a concomitant increase in commerce, fueled the concerns of locals about their exposure to these deadly infectious diseases, even though they did not understand mechanisms of disease transmission.

As McLyman testified to the court, he lived on Staten Island at what was called Bargemen's Row, a set of ramshackle cabins near the docks. The location of workers' housing was critical: it allowed the medical staff to call upon the bargemen at all hours of the day and night, as needed. When a vessel came into the harbor, McLyman towed the iron scow out to it; if sick (or dead) passengers were aboard, he loaded them into his small vessel, which he called the "sick boat," placed the clothing, bedding, and other materials used by the infected on the scow, and brought them to the quarantine hospitals' docks. Even though stevedores were assigned to help the sick off the vessel and transport them to the hospitals, McLyman and his two bargemen assistants often found themselves doing this work.

Remarkably, McLyman insisted that he was not particularly concerned about disease exposure, stating at one point, "I might have had a slight attack of yellow fever, but I don't think it was; I called it a cold" (Staten Island 1858). He intimated that the stevedores were often fearful of engaging with seriously ill passengers by noting that he was "not afraid to handle a sick person and have taken them in my arms to place them on board my boat; afterward I have gone among the villagers [of Thompkinsville] as usual" (Staten Island 1858). He boasted that he didn't even routinely change his clothing unless he found them particularly dirty. Once the passengers were transferred, McLyman took the scow back out to the harbor about six hundred yards from the island and burned the items, even though sometimes there was "good clothing" that might have been scavenged onboard the scow. Another bargeman's duty in the harbor was fumigating the vessels that arrived in the harbor at the point known as Upper Quarantine, an anchorage. Ships were fumigated using lime or sulfuric acid, whether passengers or crew were infected with any diseases. McLyman reported that he sometimes fumigated as many as eight vessels a day. By the late 1850s, some five thousand ill passengers were treated at the island's quarantine hospitals complex.

By the mid-1850s, most bargemen labored in these kinds of environments as scow operators or garbage barge operators or operating lighters. The last job required bargemen to take shallow draft vessels out to anchorages in harbors, like at Los Angeles, where there was insufficient depth for vessels to dock. A lighter operator then transferred cargo, crew, and passengers from the ship to the shore or shore to ship. Lightering a vessel is a labor-intensive operation, requiring sailors to move the cargo, using cranes and nets, into the smaller vessel for transfer. Once the bargeman piloted the vessel to the harbor docks, stevedores, later known as longshore workers, transferred the cargo from the barge to the ship. Bargemen had to be knowledgeable about weather, seamanship, and wind and ocean current patterns. McLyman, for instance, testified that he had to gauge the wind direction and current when he took his scow out to incinerate infected passengers' possessions, lest the smoke blow toward inhabited areas. Bargemen also had to understand how to reckon current actions and how they might shift sandbars leading into a small port to ensure they didn't ground their vessels. In his four years of work as the senior bargeman at Staten Island, McLyman had never grounded his vessel, though once it broke from its moorings and drifted toward Robin's Reef before he was able to corral it and return it to its anchorage.

Earlier generations of bargemen operated the shallow river boats, called keel boats, that plied the waters of the Ohio and Mississippi Rivers, though by the 1820s, most river boats were steam powered, eliminating the bargemen's monopoly on operating vessels on navigable rivers. Before the arrival of steam vessels, the bargemen of the 1810s operated their keel boats using long oars, though the principle motive power for keel boats was the river current. These bargemen were characterized by their reputation as "a race of men of hardy and peculiar habits," in the words of one contemporary observer (Bennett 1853, 9). These were men who drank heavily and swore and engaged in "rough and tumbles," or vicious hand-to-hand fights with rivals to prove their manhood, that could leave the loser with an eye gouged out or an ear bitten off. By the time McLyman testified about his daily work, the river bargemen of the past were mostly men of myths and legends, the Mike Fink character who was victorious in all of his endeavors. The folklore of the older bargemen masked the real work of the men who operated barges at mid-century.

Nancy Quam-Wickham

See also: *1861–1914:* Waste Collector; 1946–1991: Industrial Hygienist

FURTHER READING

Baldwin, Leland D. 1980. *The Keelboat Age on Western Waters*. Pittsburgh: University of Pittsburgh Press.

Bennett, Emerson. 1853. *Mike Fink, a Legend of the Ohio*. Cincinnati: J. A. & U. P. James.

"The Quarantine Arson." *The New York Times*. September 18, 1853, 1.

Staten Island Executive Committee. 1858. *Facts and Documents Bearing upon the Legal and Moral Questions: Connected with the Recent Destruction of the Quarantine Buildings on Staten Island.* New York: Wm. C. Bryant & Co., printers.

Stephenson, Kathryn. 2004. "The Quarantine War: The Burning of the New York Marine Hospital in 1858." *Public Health Reports* 119: 79–92.

CARTOGRAPHER

Cartographers are people who draw and make maps, and the nineteenth century was a busy time for them in North America. Land cessions resulting from events such as the Louisiana Purchase of 1803, U.S. President Andrew Jackson's Indian Removal Act of 1830, and the Mexican-American War of 1846–1848 multiplied the area controlled by the new United States. Manifest Destiny, the idea that the continent had been opened by providence to extensive Anglo American settlement and resource extraction, became popular in the 1840s, encouraged by eastern newspapers. Yet the population, government, and businesspeople of the incipient United States knew little about much of the vast landmass between the Appalachian Mountains and the Pacific coast. The intensive U.S. settlement and economic development of the trans-Appalachian and trans-Mississippi regions required many, many maps, but few in 1815 were qualified to do this sort of work.

In 1803, President Thomas Jefferson sent army officers Meriwether Lewis and William Clark to scout some of these lands and produce a map for government use. Like those of their Euro American predecessors, a varied lot including fur traders and Jesuit priests, their travels largely followed rivers, and their maps and, indeed, their lives depended heavily on the knowledge of indigenous North Americans with whom they interacted along the way. Subsequent decades saw a transition from such river-journey maps to systematic gridding of the land. Many more trained cartographers would be required, and these cartographers came from all walks of life.

In 1812, the General Land Office of the United States was established, sending surveyors and cartographers into the field to produce local surveys that could be used for such diverse endeavors as delineating territorial and farm boundaries to arbitrating mining claims. These mapping expeditions moved slowly across the continent, attracting crews willing to leave towns and farms in pursuit of new skills and economic opportunities. Among those was the largely self-trained William Austin Burt, who had gone from surveying his father's farm in Upstate New York to becoming a deputy surveyor for the U.S. General Land Survey in 1833. Burt's work took him to the rocky, forested country of Michigan's Upper Peninsula, a land frozen in ice and snow for several months of each year, where even his magnetic compass proved unreliable due to the local geology. The resourceful Burt devised a solar compass, allowing his crew to fill field books with rough sketch maps that formed the basis of grander maps drawn in the relative comfort of cities like Washington, D.C. and Philadelphia. In these cities, cartographers performed their duties in print shops, where skilled urban workers trained in copper-plate engraving and lithography were responsible for the products that, at this time, saw early stages of mass production and distribution, initially for government and military purposes but increasingly commercially as well, as commercial publishers rose to meet the demand of growing numbers of immigrants.

Charles Brotherton, a member of Burt's crew in the 1840s, was the first of several generations of men from the local Brotherton family to survey and map this challenging landscape on contract. When government contracts expired, cartographers took their skills to the private sector, scouting and mapping for logging and mining companies when such work was available. When it was not, such field cartographers sometimes took other jobs in those industries. The drawing of maps was perhaps the easiest part of the work of mapping in the field, which often involved slogging through swamps with swarms of mosquitos and blackflies in the heat of the summer, as well as drawing maps in freezing conditions while traveling on snowshoes in winter, towing supplies on sleds that easily capsized in drifting snow. Crews worked in the field for weeks on end, and a shopping list written on the back of a sketch map by Charles's son Frank Brotherton in the 1870s suggests they regularly carried large amounts of dried beans, salt pork, coffee, and other staples into the field with them. If mapping and surveying tools (to say nothing of food or clothing) were broken or lost in boat or sled accidents, field crews often had to return to resupply points, sometimes in rough conditions.

Like Burt, commercial cartographers such as John Melish in Philadelphia, Henry Schenck Tanner in New York City, and John Farmer in Detroit came to employ growing crews in their respective print shops, as did government printers in Washington. This work was fairly well compensated for the time as it involved considerable training, which often took the form of apprenticeships. Many of the men who took such jobs had some level of education, and Melish himself had both formal education and, from other ventures, the means to invest in his own publishing house, which opened in 1816. Yet formal training in topographic survey, which involved disciplined courses in such subjects as trigonometry, was for the most part exclusive to institutions like the U.S. Military Academy at West Point, which trained its cadets, who were most often from prominent, wealthy families, in increasingly technologically sophisticated military skills.

After 1838, West Point graduates such as George Gordon Meade and Gouverneur Keble Warren put their systematic mapmaking and surveying skills to work in the field before those same skills contributed to the Union victory in the American Civil War (1861–1865). While Meade charted and built lighthouses on the Atlantic Coast and across the Great Lakes, Warren's meticulously detailed topographical maps played a key role in the bridging of the Mississippi River and in route selection for the Transcontinental Railroad. Their notes and journals describe the military equivalents of Burt's and various Brothertons' accounts of life and work in sometimes challenging field conditions.

In the case of Warren and Burt, both of whom took great interest in the then-rough earth sciences, their maps and notes set the stage for another era in the history of cartography and of the nature of cartographic work, namely the vast and productive scientific expeditions and geological surveys that would begin in earnest later in the century. That period would see the true industrialization of the printing, hence the mapping, industry, as well as many other industries. With newfound consumer spending power, public schools and land-grant universities, and new travel options, the period after the Civil War would offer many opportunities for cartographers.

Peter Nekola

See also: Explorer; Land Speculator; Surveyor

FURTHER READING

American Congress on Surveying Mapping. 1974. *The American Cartographer: An Official Semiannual Journal of ACSM, American Congress on Surveying and Mapping*. Washington, DC: ACSM.

Bricker, Charles, and R. V. Tooley. 1969. *A History of Cartography: 2500 Years of Maps and Mapmakers*. London: Thames and Hudson.

Ehrenberg, Ralph E. 2006. *Mapping the World: An Illustrated History of Cartography*. Washington, DC: National Geographic.

CUSTOMS COLLECTOR

Customs collectors were government employees charged with overseeing the collection of custom duties, which were a kind of tax on imported goods, in a particular region or city. Customs duties on goods imported into the new nation's ports were a significant source of revenue for the U.S. government in the years after the revolution. In 1807, for instance, customs revenue had grown to $15,840,000—nearly twice what it had been in 1800—and helped to reduce the national debt remaining from the war. Customs collectors were employees of the federal government's Customs Service, a federal agency established by an act of Congress in 1789.

Customs collectors met vessels when they arrived in the harbor or at docks and wharves along rivers, evaluated arriving passengers, assessed the value of goods, and imposed duties, or import taxes, on imported items. Their work was critical to government operations as the revenue that customs inspectors collected represented more than 80 percent of all federal revenue, including the sale of western lands. Customs collectors, appointed by the president, were typically men who had gone to sea and understood the structure of cargo holds and maritime documents; they could quickly determine whether a ship captain was trying to hide assets and evade imposition of import duties. Others were political appointments, well connected to local and national political elites. Each customs station also had a naval officer. The nation's busiest ports, like New York, Boston, Baltimore, Philadelphia, Charleston, and New Orleans, also employed other workers who weighed goods, inspected cargo and passengers, and surveyed vessels for seaworthiness.

Customs officials also inspected and licensed American vessels, determined whether sailors had the proper documents to enter and clear port, and checked to see that all crewmembers had signed onto a vessel's Articles of Agreement before departing port. Another responsibility of the customs worker was to ensure that maritime and navigation laws were followed. Customs workers performed a wide variety of duties falling under five general headings: tax collection, local and national security, marine inspection, enforcing trade laws, and labor regulation. In any one day, a customs officer might meet a vessel engaged in domestic trade on the wharf, inspect the vessel and its paperwork, clear it to offload goods at a public warehouse, check the captain's crew list for an outbound vessel leaving to engage in the West Indies trade, meet an incoming passenger vessel and inspect passengers for communicable diseases as well as their luggage for dutiable goods hidden to evade import duties, order removal of a leaking vessel from a navigable channel and order it to a shipyard for repair, and issue certificates of inspection for new vessels leaving for their first voyages. Customs officers and inspectors had to fill out a dizzying number of forms and reports for each port within their customs' district: certificates of cargo inbound and receipts for duties paid, certificates of inspection for cargo on ships transiting from one domestic port to another (and for which duties had not yet been paid), certificates of cargo discharged, certificates of passengers and baggage checked, permits to land cargo and passengers and to leave quarantine stations, and certificates attesting to volume and type of cargo as signed off by inspectors. Completed forms were filed in the customs house; customs collectors filed quarterly statements with the Treasury Department.

Newspaper notices of ships arrived and sailed in American and foreign ports helped customs officers anticipate their workloads in advance of a vessel's arrival. A Boston newspaper in May 1793, for instance, noted that five vessels had arrived in the small harbor of Newburyport, most of them coming from Caribbean ports (Tobago, Port-au-Prince). The issue also published reports of other vessels from New England arriving in Calcutta, leaving Bengal for Ostend (Belgium), rounding the Cape of Good Hope bound for Salem with freight, arriving at the south Atlantic island of St. Helena, trading in Siam (Thailand) and Burma, and at least ten vessels engaged in the China trade, including where they were last sighted. These kinds of information networks, gleaned from ships' captains and mates who had "spoke" (communicated with) or observed the movement of other American vessels, helped customs officers keep track of maritime commerce into and out of U.S. ports. Other shipping news included notice of British, French ,and Spanish privateering and the wreck of an American ship off the Malabar Coast, as well as notice of cargo space available in the holds of American vessels bound for England and coastal domestic ports and the pending sale of four other ships.

Tensions between France and England and their respective allies leading to the Napoleonic Wars (1803–1815) of the early nineteenth century tested the resolve of America's customs and elected officials. The British Royal Navy openly impressed American sailors—stopping U.S. flagged vessels at sea or in foreign ports, kidnapping their crewmen, and forcing them to work for foreign navies to satisfy their manpower requirements unmet after a century of warfare. Customs officers had to reconcile departing ships' crew lists with that of the arriving vessels, carefully documenting crewmen's status. So troublesome had the harassment of Americans become that in December 1807, President Thomas Jefferson ordered a complete embargo of all foreign goods coming into American ports, lasting until March 1809. The embargo prohibited American ships from sailing for foreign ports but allowed them to engage in coastal domestic trade and instructed customs officers to order foreign vessels to depart from American ports without taking on any cargo. As historian Glenn Gordinier documented in a study of the New London, Connecticut, customs district, some ship captains brazenly made attempts to evade the embargo: vessels stood off the port of New London in Long Island Sound, waiting to surreptitiously transfer cargo, or captains left smaller ports like Stonington without appropriate documents.

Among the American merchant class, the embargo was quite unpopular as hundreds had their fortunes tied up in cargos at foreign ports, while their debts were being called in by creditors. In response, Congress passed an amendment to the embargo act that instructed customs collectors to receive and evaluate exceptions petitions, requests from merchants and captains to allow them to retrieve cargoes previously purchased but stranded in foreign ports. As a result, customs officers were besieged with requests and had to make decisions about the validity of each request for exception, issue certificates to those approved for exception, and report them as "permission ships" to the Treasury Secretary. Later, the president ordered customs collectors to intercept smugglers and seize suspicious or contraband cargoes. Jefferson's embargo eventually failed due in large part to its unpopularity among merchants, shipping companies, shipbuilders and sailors, and farmers, all affected by the prohibition on maritime commerce. The act was succeeded by the Non-Intercourse Acts, however, which lessened restrictions on trade as well as the responsibilities of customs collectors to enforce these laws.

Nancy Quam-Wickham

See also: Bargeman; Fur Trader; Wharfinger; *1992–2019:* Supply Chain Logistician

FURTHER READING

Gordinier, Glenn S. 2010. "Enterprise and Authority: Southeastern Connecticut Responds to the Jeffersonian Embargo." *Connecticut History Review* 49: 33–55.

Stein, Douglas L. 1804. "American Maritime Documents: Customs Certificates and Forms." Mystic Seaport Museum. https://research.mysticseaport.org/item/l006405/l006405-c018/.

United States. 1814. *Report of the Committee of Commerce and Manufactures, on the Petition of Joshua Sands, Late Collector of the Customs for the Port of New York.* Washington, DC: Roger Weightman.

DIPLOMAT

A diplomat is a person who represents a country abroad. The process of negotiating with other nations, diplomacy holds a critical role in government and political development for all nations. American diplomats are those individuals tasked with the enormous responsibility of representing U.S. interests and negotiating and managing interactions with other countries. Some of the United States' most important men served as diplomats during and after the Revolutionary War (1775–1783), including such luminaries as Benjamin Franklin, Thomas Jefferson, John Adams, John Jay, Robert Livingston, and James Monroe.

Even before the new United States emerged from a long and costly Revolutionary War, its leaders had long advocated engagement with foreign powers to bolster the cause of independence. Americans in Massachusetts Bay negotiated the first foreign alliance, the Treaty of Watertown, with tribes of the Wabanaki in July 1776. The next year, Benjamin Franklin negotiated French recognition of an independent American nation, followed by a formal treaty of alliance. Spain and, later, other nations joined the French in allying with an independent United States, and their military and diplomatic support was essential to the American war effort.

Those Americans who served as diplomats during the period between 1789 and 1815 were entrusted with great responsibility; as such, they tended to be patriotic luminaries like Franklin, Jefferson, and Adams, and former military men who had served their nation in the Continental Army during the revolution. Robert Livingston had been a prominent New York politician and judge and was one of the original drafters of the Declaration of Independence. These men were well known to leaders of other nations and thus had the social standing and credibility to engage in high-level conversations about military, political, and governmental matters. Their work was not easy: after the end of the revolution, American foreign policies favored neutrality with major European nations, especially France and Great Britain, while maintaining open commerce with both. Two treaties in the 1790s, the Jay Treaty and the Pinckney Treaty, encapsulated these twin policy goals even as war broke out among France, Great Britain, and Spain in this decade (Wars of the French Revolution) and in the early 1800s (Napoleonic Wars).

Internal politics also shaped early American foreign policies: Federalists, under Secretary of the Treasury Alexander Hamilton, argued for a strong central government that protected international commerce, while the Anti-Federalists (later known as the Democratic-Republicans), allied with Secretary of State Thomas Jefferson, sought internal expansion and smaller government aligned with his visions of a classless agrarian nation. These political tensions manifested in foreign policies that sought commercial alliances with European nations, as well as treaties with tribal nations in the interior. The Democratic-Republicans' great diplomatic triumph was the Louisiana Purchase of 1803, in which the young nation purchased a vast area encompassing much of the Mississippi and Missouri River Valleys from France for $15 million. Both political parties, however, shared one central idea, in the words of historian George Herring, "of a providential mission . . . to do good in the world" by spreading American values of freedom and liberty (Herring 2008, 4).

Diplomats working in this period had many responsibilities, whether oriented toward negotiations with tribal people or European government ministers. Senior diplomats held a variety of titles during this time but were often referred to as ambassadors and consuls. In their work on both the North American continent and abroad, the job of a senior diplomat often revolved around social engagements and meetings with senior representatives with whom they were engaged in policy negotiations. Based in France during the war, Benjamin Franklin kept a diary of his social engagements: On Friday, January 26, 1781, in Paris, Franklin called on Princess Katerina Dashkova, an associate of Russia's Catherine II the Great, and visited with Prince and Princess Masserano (of Italy) as well as the Duke of Rouchefoucault-Liancourt and his wife. As he continued to make his social calls, he found that neither the American ambassador to Russia, Francis Dana, nor member of the Continental Congress James Searle, who had been sent to Europe to obtain a hefty loan to help prosecute the war, was home, though Franklin left both his calling card and a request to join him for dinner. In the evening, Franklin called on French Admiral Hector Comte D'Estaing and former French minister Anne Robert Turgot, Baron de l'Aulne, though he also found both men absent. After a long day of calling on important foreign representatives, Franklin returned to his office to "accept bills" that his country could not pay.

In later years, Napoleon Bonaparte unexpectedly offered the American diplomat Robert Livingston an opportunity to purchase the Louisiana territory in spring 1803, even as James Monroe, who President Thomas Jefferson had dispatched to try to negotiate the sale of the port of New Orleans and the territory of Florida, was still at sea. Once Monroe reached Paris, he and Livingston had a series of conversations and dinners with Bonaparte before the deal was settled—causing both American diplomats some anxiety about Bonaparte's stated willingness to part with Louisiana.

Senior diplomats also gathered and exchanged intelligence about their allies as well as enemies during time of war. In their lengthy correspondence in 1781, for instance, diplomats Franklin and Jay describe the difficulty of obtaining reliable information about the war in America even as they tried to broker a peace between several foreign governments and America. As Jay wrote to Franklin, however, the Spanish "want Jamaica, they want Gibraltar, and Mahon [part of the Balearic Islands] would be a trump card in their hands" (Hale 1887, 431). Likewise, the diplomat Thomas Jefferson wrote regularly to John Jay during the French revolutionary summer of 1789, reporting on how crowds in Paris had murdered members of the former French government, including "Monsieur Foulon, one of the obnoxious Ministry," who had been captured, hanged, and then decapitated before his body was drawn through the streets of the city (Department of State 1833, 310). Jefferson later provided information to Jay about the health of Britain's King George III, who was recovering from illness, as well as reporting on bread riots in Paris, a brief naval engagement between Russia and Sweden in the Baltic Sea, and conflict between the clergy and French revolutionary sympathizers in Liege. Diplomats' correspondence—reports, personal letters, and financial statements—comprised the bulk of the record of their activities in the service of the United States.

Consuls met with Americans abroad, usually merchants and seamen, to represent their interests with foreign governments or facilitate their repatriation home. Staff members accompanied senior diplomats during their appointments, helping to draft letters, arrange meetings, and attend to other duties as required. During negotiations with the Ottoman states of Algiers, Tunis, and Tripoli during the Barbary Wars (1801–1815), for instance, the American consul in Tunis, Mordechai Noah, was instructed to offer the Tunisians ransom for imprisoned American sailors. To prevent the Tunisians from discovering the Americans' plans, Noah contracted with an American businessman who was successful in attaining the release of only a few of the sailors. Travel, delicate negotiations spread over days, secret correspondence, and hours spent each day composing letters and reports were the work of early American diplomats.

Nancy Quam-Wickham

See also: *1607–1775:* Governor; *1946–1991:* Foreign Service Officer

FURTHER READING

Hale, Edward E., and Edward E. Hale, Jr., eds. 1887. *Franklin in France.* s.l.: Roberts Brothers.

Herring, George C. 2008. *From Colony to Superpower: U.S. Foreign Relations since 1776.* London: Oxford University Press.

U.S. Department of State. 1833. *The Diplomatic Correspondence of the United States of America, 1783–1789.* Washington, DC: U.S. Department of State.

DOMESTIC WORKER, *see* LAUNDRESS

EXPLORER

Explorers traveled into unknown, often unmapped territory to claim land for themselves, their company, or their country. Throughout the antebellum period, hundreds of American explorers sought to place their nation's flag upon distant and "undiscovered" sites. Most famous of the terrestrial—or overland—journeys was Louis and Clark's "voyage of discovery" (1804–1806), but Americans like John L. Stephens trekked through Guatemala to find traces of a lost Mayan civilization in 1839, and William F. Lynch traveled to the Mediterranean's Jordan River to explore the Holy Land in 1847.

However, it was pelagic and littoral (open sea and coastal) exploration that opened the world to Americans through "voyages of commerce and discovery." After the revolution, Yankee mariners were freed from Britain's Navigation Acts, which had prevented colonists from sailing beyond the Atlantic basin. This allowed them to search for new coastal markets throughout the Pacific and Indian Oceans. Adventuring voyages to distant lands opened Americans not only to uncharted sources of goods but also introduced them to unfamiliar places, peoples, and experiences.

The most notable maritime expedition was the government-sponsored U.S. Exploring Expedition (1838–1842). Cruising through 87,000 miles of ocean, the expedition's surveyors drew 180 charts that plotted navigational routes around 280 Pacific atolls and archipelagoes, located hazardous reefs and shoals, marked depths, and identified previously unknown islands. Charles Wilkes and his men explored 800 miles along the Northwest Coast, filling in the map of what would become the states of Oregon and Washington. The expedition's "scientificks" contributed to the library of botanical knowledge by collecting 2,000 specimens of flora and fauna previously unrecorded in European academies and 40 tons of ethnographic specimens and artifacts.

Most antebellum voyagers were interested in rediscovery; in finding routes to well-established Asian ports such as Canton, Bombay, and Calcutta, where they could exchange goods for teas, silks, porcelain, and spices; locating islands that produced the sandalwood, birds' nests, and bêche-de-mer that fetched high prices in Asian markets; and probing coasts where indigenous peoples would trade otter pelts or pepper to fill a ship's hold. Even "discoveries" of uncharted Pacific islands recorded sites that were inhabited by indigenous peoples or had been previously reported by Europeans, sometimes centuries earlier. In April 1791, Joseph Ingraham encountered a set of islands unmarked on any of the nautical maps he carried. They were the Marquesas, inhabited by several tribes and marked by the Spanish, but Ingraham dubbed them the Washington Islands.

The American mariner of Pacific waters was something of an amateur anthropologist and a discoverer of novel products, tools, and inventions. Long days of tedious routine at sea were punctuated by encounters with cultures that had only been heard of in rumors. For the typical explorer, every day began with an observation of the weather and location. At sea, a typical ship's log began with the date and then "commenced with light breezes" or "commenced with gale." The mariner then recorded latitude and longitude, the latter difficult to measure until the chronometer became widespread in the nineteenth century.

Antebellum explorers often imagined their journals and logs as guides for later travelers. Their "narratives of voyages and travels" took early American readers through the Revenge Straits and Endeavor Straits off Timor and New Guinea, through the Storm Bay passage off Tasmania, and around Inaccessible Island in the South Seas. At any moment, a tranquil evening could be broken by shrill cries from the crow's nest after spotting "one continued sheet of white foam" breaking over the reefs of yet another uncharted reef, bringing the vessel perilously close to shipwreck.

Dane A. Morrison

See also: Cartographer; Fur Trader; Fur Trapper; Land Speculator; Surveyor; *1915–1945:* Geologist

FURTHER READING

Blum, Hester. 2008. *The View from the Masthead: Maritime Imagination and Antebellum American Sea Narratives*. Durham: University of North Carolina Press.

Delano, Amasa. 1817. *A Narrative of Voyages and Travels in the Northern and Southern Hemispheres: Comprising Three Voyages Round the World; Together with a Voyage of Survey and Discovery, in the Pacific Ocean and Oriental Islands*. Boston: E. G. House.

Ingraham, Joseph. n.d., ca 1791. *Journal of the Brigantine Hope on a Voyage to the Northwest Coast of North America, 1790–92*. Barre: Imprint Society.

Morrison, Dane A. 2014. *True Yankees: The South Seas and the Discovery of American Identity*. Baltimore: Johns Hopkins University Press.

Viola, Herman J., and Carolyn Margolis. 1985. *Magnificent Voyagers: The U.S. Exploring Expedition, 1838–1842*. Washington, DC: Smithsonian Institution Press.

PRIMARY DOCUMENT

The following passages are taken from William Clark's official journal of the Lewis and Clark Expedition. In 1803, President Thomas Jefferson commissioned the expedition, known as the Corps of Discovery, to explore, map, and record their observations on a journey from the Missouri River near St. Louis to the Pacific Ocean. Jefferson had hoped that the explorers would discover a navigable water passage from St. Louis to the Pacific. Headed by Meriwether Lewis and Clark, the group included a number of U.S. Army enlisted men of various backgrounds (including men from Virginia, Pennsylvania, and New England), several men of French and French and native ancestry, one German immigrant, a Metís boatman (of French and Omaha parentage) who served as the expedition's pilot, and the slave York. During the first winter at Fort Mandan, three others joined the Expedition: French trapper Toussaint Charbonneau and his Shoshone wife, Sacajawea, who Charbonneau bought from the Hidatsa, who in turn had kidnapped and enslaved her when she was a child. Their child, Jean Baptiste Charbonneau, was born in February 1805 at Fort Mandan and accompanied his parents on the expedition.

These passages describe the group's experiences at a camp near the mouth of the Columbia River in late 1805, when, on November 7, 1805, they think they've finally caught a glimpse of the Pacific Ocean. What Clark observed, however, was the Columbia River estuary; it would be almost two more weeks before Clark and a small party of his men reached a vantage point near present-day Cape Disappointment that allowed them an unobstructed view of the Pacific. The expedition over-wintered upstream from this point, at Fort Clatsop on the south side of the Columbia River near Astoria, Oregon. These passages describe how bad weather, tides, hunger, sickness, and interactions with local tribal people shaped the experiences of these explorers.

November 7 Thursday 1805

A cloudy foggey morning Some rain. we Set out early proceeded under the Star. [starboard] Side under a high rugid hills with Steep assent the shore boalt and rockey, the fog so thick we could not See across the river, two cano[e]s of Indians met and returned with us to their village which is Situated on the Star. side behind a cluster of Marshey Islands, on a narrow chan[nel] of the river through which we passed to the *village* of 4 houses, they gave us to eate Some fish, and Sold us, fish, *wap pa to* roots [arrowroot, or "Indian potato"], three *dogs,* and 2 otter skins for which we gave fish hooks principally of which they were very fond.

Those people call themselves *War-ci-â-cum* and Speake a language different from the nativs above with whome they trade for the *Wapato* roots of which they make great use of as food. their houses differently built, raised entirely above ground . . . Supported and covered in the same way of those above, [doors] about the Same size but in the Side of the house in one corner, one fire place and that near the opposit end, around which they have their beds raised about 4 feet from the flore which is of earth, under their beds they Store away baskets of dried fish, berries & *Wappato,* over the fire they hang the flesh as they take them and which they do not make immediate use. Their Canoes are of the Same form . . . The Dress of the men differ verry little from [other natives nearby]. The womin altogether different, their robes are Smaller only covering their Sholders & falling down to near the hip . . . The garment which occupies the Waist and thence as low as the knee before and mid leg behind, cannot properly be called a petticoat . . . it is a *Tissue* formed of white cedar bark bruised or broken into small stran[d]s, which are interwoven in their center by means of Several cords of the same Materials . . . This tissue is Sometims formed of little Strings of the Silk grass twisted and knoted at their ends &c. . . .

[A]fter delaying at this village one hour and a half we Set out piloted by an Indian dressed in a Sa[i]lor's dress, to the Main Chanel of the river, the tide being in we should have found much difficulty in passing into the main Chanel from behind those islands without a pilot, a large marshey Island near the middle of the river near which several Canoes came allong Side with Skins, roots fish &c. to Sell, and had a temporary residence on this Island . . . [We] continue[d] on the Star. Side, about 14 miles below the last village and 18 miles of this day we landed at a village of the same nation. This village . . . contains 7 indifferent houses built in the same . . . here we purchased a Dog, some fish, *wap pa to* roots, and I purchased 2 beaver skins for the purpose of makeing me a *roab,* as the robe I have is rotten and good for nothing . . . We proceeded on about 12 miles below the Village under a high mountaneous Countrey . . . shore boald and rockey and Encamped under a high hill . . . with difficuelty [we] found a place clear of the tide and Sufficiently large to lie on, and the only place we could get was on round stones on which we lay our mats. Rain continued moderately all day & Two Indians accompanied us from the last village . . . the river being too wide to See either the form, Shape or Size of the Islands on the [other] side.

Great joy in camp we are in *View* of the *Ocian [as the fog lifted],* this great Pacific Octean which we been so long anxious to See. and the roreing or noise made by the waves brakeing on the rockey Shores (as I suppose) may be heard disti[n]ctly.

We made 34 miles to day as computed.

November 8 Friday 1805

a cloudy morning Some rain, we did not set out until 9 oClock, haveing changed our Clothing. proceeded on close under the Star. side, the hills high . . . Several low Islands in a Deep bend or Bay . . . river about 5 or 7 miles wide, three Indians in a canoe overtook us, with salmon to Sell, passed 2 old villages on the Star. Side and at 3 miles entered a nitch [bay] of about 6 miles wide and 5 miles deep . . . we found verry Shallow water and call it the Shallow [Bay]. We came too at the remains of an old village at the bottom of this nitch and dined, here we Saw great numbers of fowl, Sent out 2 men and they killed a Goose and two *canves back* Ducks here we found great numbers of flees which we treated with the greatest caution and distance; after Diner the Indians left us and we took the advantage of a returning tide and proceeded on . . . [where] we found the Swells or Waves so high that we thought it imprudent to proceed; we landed unloaded and drew up our Canoes. Some rain all day at intervals, we are all wet and disagreeable, as we have been for Several days past, and our present Situation a verry disagreeable one in as much, as we have not leavel land Sufficient for an encampment and for our baggage to lie cleare of the tide, the High hills jutting in so close and steep that we cannot retreat back, and the water of the river too Salt to be used, added to this the waves are increasing to Such a hight that we cannot move from this place, in this

Situation we are compelled to form our camp between the hite of the Ebb and flood tides, and rase our baggage on logs. We are not certain as yet if the white people who trade with those people or from whome they procure their goods are Stationary at the mouth [of the Columbia River], or visit this quarter at stated times for the purpose of trafik &c. I believe the latter to be the most probable conjecture. The Seas roled and tossed the Canoes in such a manner this evening that several of our party were Sea sick.

Source: *Original Journals of the Lewis and Clark Expedition 1804–1806. Volume 3.* 1905. Edited by Reuben Gold Thwaites. New York: Dodd, Mead & Company, 208–212.

FACTORY OPERATIVE

Factory operatives were the earliest modern factory workers. In the early nineteenth century, industrialists in New England reorganized production, creating the modern American factory system in which men and women alike labored for long hours on water- or steam-powered machines, primarily in the textile trades. Factory operatives tended the spinning machines (sometimes called jennies) and power looms in these textile factories.

While domestic, household manufacturing dominated the making of most textiles—linen, wool, and some cotton—in the colonial period, by the early 1800s, American factory owners began to emulate their British counterparts and introduce machinery into the process of making cloth and other textiles, like rugs. This revolution in production did not arrive uniformly throughout the United States. Rather, factory production in textiles was largely limited to New England and a few other areas on the east coast. In 1790, the Rhode Island inventor Samuel Slater developed machinery to spin cotton yarn; the first machine-powered spinning mills were built in Rhode Island and Connecticut. In the 1810s, new power looms further revolutionized textile production by introducing mechanized processes not only to the spinning of yarn but also the weaving of textiles. Within a few years, textile mills dominated the New England industrial landscape at places like Waltham, Lowell, and Lawrence (Massachusetts), Manchester, Portsmouth, and Dover (New Hampshire), Biddleford, Lewiston, and Saco (Maine), Providence (Rhode Island), and Centerville and Willimantic (Connecticut).

In the spinning mills, factory operatives often tended machines operating many spindles and spools (or bobbins) at once and had to quickly replace bobbins once the spinning yarn had filled them; this required nimble fingers and great manual dexterity to remove the full spools and replace them with new ones before the yarn, which was drawn from the cleaned raw cotton, twisted and then wound simultaneously into yarn or thread, on a spindle and fed onto the bobbins from above, became loose or tangled or overfilled the bobbin capacity. The factory operative stood at the large cast-iron machine, called a frame, with whirring spindles and bobbins, operating a set of foot pedals to speed up or stop the twisting and winding of cotton into yarn or thread. Marks on the frame indicated yarn width; to create thinner thread, the operative continued the twisting and winding process until the desired thickness was achieved. The operative also oversaw the winding of yarn or thread onto the bobbins. Once a set of bobbins was full, the factory operative stopped the machine, removed a set of bobbins, and replaced them with a new set.

Factory operatives working in spinning and weaving mills also operated power looms, while others operated spinning machines. The workers who operated the power looms set the weaving frames in which the warp yarns were threaded under tension; another part of the machine wove the weft through the warp yarns. These power-loom workers operated the weft mechanism and fed threads from the bobbins into this mechanism, all while constantly monitoring the weaving process to ensure that the textiles were woven properly. Monitoring the machines meant that factory operators had to move steadily from loom to loom, temporarily stopping the machines to refill bobbins and check for imperfections in the cloth; some machines had foot-operated brakes, while others required turning a hand wheel.

Working conditions within these early factories were difficult: Loose cotton fibers filled the air, and there was no lighting as candles and lamps could spark disastrous industrial fires. Factory operatives typically worked six-day weeks, for twelve or more hours a day, with only three or four holidays per year. Having some weaving or spinning skills could be an advantage for factory operatives, but most of these in the great mills required little real skill as the machinery accomplished most of the work. Factory owners tended to recruit unskilled but eager workers, and early in the years of industrial growth, young women from New England's agricultural areas flocked to the great mill towns as factory employment offered some independence and better wages than women generally found in domestic labor. Factory owners had built these mill towns intentionally to attract young women; boardinghouses promised meals and safe places to live under the watchful eye of the matron, an older woman who supervised women workers during their off-work hours. Many mill owners required women factory operatives to live in these boardinghouses, where they were expected to attend church services on Sundays, obey curfews, and refrain from pursuing relationships with young men. While a factory operative might earn two dollars per week, based on her total production of yarn or cloth, living costs in factory boardinghouses took up the lion's share of her weekly earnings.

Factory operatives also suffered from the speed-up, in which managers ordered machinery adjusted to produce more textiles in shorter time periods, thus requiring workers to move more quickly and maintain their attentiveness to the machinery at all times. If a factory operative slipped and fell while rushing from loom to loom, she could be caught in the machinery and injured. Bales of cotton and wool sometimes fell onto operatives in the spinning rooms, crushing them to death. As increasing competition affected the entire nation's textile industry, factory managers slashed pay, leading many workers to protest their conditions. The first union, the Factory Girls Association of Lowell, Massachusetts, was formed in 1836, and in that year, some 1,500 women factory operatives struck for better wages, marching in the streets for their cause. Their identity as factory operatives also led many to write for the *Lowell Offering*, a monthly newspaper that featured stories, poetry, and other writings by factory operatives.

Over time, the workforce in New England's industrial textile mills changed dramatically as owners began to recruit Irish immigrants during the 1840s; these immigrants generally earned even lower pay than those factory girls. By 1860, nearly 60 percent of all workers in Lowell's great mills were immigrants, men and women who accepted lower wages as young native-born women began to leave the factories for other opportunities.

Nancy Quam-Wickham

See also: *1861–1914:* Meat Packinghouse Worker; *1915–1945:* Autoworker; Cannery Worker; Garment Worker; Warehouse Worker; *1992–2019:* Package Handler

FURTHER READING

Cameron, Ardis. 1993. *Radicals of the Worst Sort: Laboring Women in Lawrence, Massachusetts, 1860–1912.* Champaign: Illinois University Press.

Candee, Richard M. 1982. "New Towns of the Early New England Textile Mills." *Perspectives in Vernacular Architecture* 1: 31–50.

Cohen, Norm. 2005. "Where Is the Lowell Factory Girl? A Tangled Yarn from the Textile Mills." *Fund for Labor Culture and History*, Occasional Paper No. 5.

FIELD HAND

By the beginning of the nineteenth century, most agricultural workers, or field hands, who did not labor on their own small farms were bonded laborers, mostly slaves. Enslaved individuals during the antebellum era were assigned to many different tasks. Some enslaved persons were taught skills such as blacksmith work, carpentry, and masonry, while others would be tasked with domestic servitude or childcare. The majority of slaves, however, were field hands who toiled from sunup to sundown in the vast fields of the American South.

Cotton was the most prominent agricultural product of the antebellum South; it was also the most profitable. With the beginning of the Industrial Revolution in England during the 1700s, the mass production of textiles demanded large sums of cotton. During the eighteenth and nineteenth centuries, Britain was the most powerful nation in the world with the largest economy. English factories relied on slave-produced American cotton for over 80 percent of their raw materials, while textile (cloth) mills accounted for 40 percent of Britain's exports. These English products were shipped to every corner of the world. Prior to the Industrial Revolution, a normal, middle-class American might have possessed only three to five outfits and two pairs of shoes. This average more than tripled in fifty years, and that booming industrial field began with slaves who worked in America's cotton fields.

Field hands who toiled in the cotton fields faced extreme conditions. The demand for cotton, and the corresponding wealth that came with its supply, created a situation in which plantation owners pushed their workers to extreme production. During peak harvest time, which was typically late summer or fall, enslaved workers were expected to pick cotton from sunup to sundown. This involved staying in a bent-over position (as cotton plants are not very tall) and walking through the fields, rapidly snatching the cotton from the sticky plants. Additionally, before the invention of the cotton gin in the late 1700s, the prickly cotton seeds found in every bulb had to be hand-removed from the white fluffy cotton fibers. The seeds' spines were so sharp that often a workers' hands would be bloody within the first hour of picking. Documents of the time refer to how much blood was visible within a bale of cotton as traders examined it before setting a price. All workers would be assigned a very high goal to pick and process, with some records indicating that adult men and women should be able to harvest two hundred pounds of cotton every day; cotton is exceptionally lightweight, so this would amount to several bags of cotton. If the goal was not met, field hands were routinely punished. Common punishments included lashings or whippings, having food rations withheld, having one's deficit poundage placed on a loved one to increase his or her workload, and more.

Harvest season was not the only busy time on cotton plantations. During the 1930s, the federal government, under the auspices of the Works Progress Administration (WPA), sent workers out to interview hundreds of elderly former slave men and women. As field hands accounted for the most enslaved individuals, many WPA narratives recount harsh days of labor in fields throughout the year. Ambus Gray was enslaved in Alabama, and when interviewed, he stated, "Bout all I remembers bout slavery was how hard the hands had to work . . . when we wasn't clearin new ground and rollin pine logs and burnin brush, we was buildin fences and shuckin and shellin corn . . . We clear new ground all day den burn brush and pile logs at night. We build fences all day and kill hogs and shuck corn dat night. No use to say a word bout bein tired" (Federal Writers' Project Part 2 1936, 78).

Tom Douglas, who was enslaved in Louisiana, also relayed stories of long hours and hard work. He recalled, "If we acted like we didn't want to work, our hands was crossed and tied and we was tied to a tree or bush and whipped until we bled" (Federal Writers' Project Part 3 1936, 193). Even cotton plantation owners who did not incorporate whippings as punishment pushed their captive labor forces to unhealthy and inhumane levels.

Another byproduct of the demand for cotton was the vast movement of enslaved individuals from the Upper South to the Deep South. Although some illegal shipments of slaves landed in the United States after the trans-Atlantic slave trade was outlawed in 1807, by the nineteenth century, most slaves were the American-born descendants of those Africans who had been enslaved and transported across the Atlantic. As "King Cotton"—the external market for cotton—expanded, the majority of slaves who worked in the Deep South were those African Americans who had been relocated from Virginia or North Carolina. Tobacco, one of the leading crops of the Upper South, required fewer hands to harvest than cotton, so the tobacco farmers in the Upper South made money by selling enslaved individuals to other owners in Georgia, Alabama, or Mississippi. Often this meant that families were separated; many would never again be reunited. The relocated slaves were chained together and had to walk hundreds of miles to the Deep South in groups called coffles.

While cotton was "king" of the American economic system of the South, it was not the only agricultural product that employed field hands. Climate and geographic location determined the cash crop of the region. Tobacco was an early cash crop and remained important to the agrarian economies of North Carolina and Virginia. The coastal, swampy region of South Carolina was ideal for growing rice. Rice requires flooded farm land and less hands-on time, so those slaves belonging to owners of rice plantations were often hired out to do work such as light carpentry, brick work, or other tasks during times when they were not required to be in the field. Many homes in Charleston, South Carolina, were built by slaves being hired out from rice fields. Indigo was another product grown in South Carolina, and it was used in dyes for clothing; it also permanently dyed the hands of its laborers.

There was no off-season for field hands. Whether a worker was on a large cotton plantation in Mississippi or a small tobacco farm in the piedmont of North Carolina, he or she was kept busy repairing fences, growing other subsistence crops, preparing food to sell (such as shucking corn), doing butcher work, or being hired out to assist non-slave holders with tasks that needed completion. Field hands were the largest percentage of enslaved individuals, and their lives were exceptionally difficult.

Christy Davenport

See also: *1607–1775:* Farmer; Indentured Servant; *1775–1860:* Slave Driver; *1915–1945:* Farmworker

FURTHER READING

Blassingame, James. 1974. *The Slave Community*. New York: Oxford University Press.

Dusinberre, William. 1996. *Them Dark Days: Slavery in the American Rice Swamps*. Athens: University of Georgia Press.

Faust, Drew Gilpin. 1985. *James Henry Hammond and the Old South: A Design for Mastery*. Baton Rouge: Louisiana State University Press.

Federal Writers' Project. 1936a. *Slave Narrative Project, Vol. 2, Arkansas Part 2, Cannon-Evans*. Manuscript/mixed material. Retrieved from the Library of Congress. https://www.loc.gov/item/mesn022/.

Federal Writers' Project. 1936b. *Slave Narrative Project, Vol. 2, Arkansas, Part 3, Gadson-Isom*. Manuscript/mixed material. Retrieved from the Library of Congress. https://www.loc.gov/item/mesn023/.

Johnson, Walter. 1999. *Soul by Soul: Life Inside the Antebellum Slave Market*. Cambridge: Harvard University Press.

Johnson, Walter. 2013. *River of Dark Dreams: Slavery and Empire in the Cotton Kingdom*. Cambridge: Harvard University Press.

Rothman, Adam. 2007. *Slave Country: American Expansion and the Origins of the Deep South*. Cambridge: Harvard University Press.

PRIMARY DOCUMENT

In the following document, the northern writer Joseph Holt Ingraham describes life on a southern plantation and the work done there. This description, formatted as a letter to a friend from a pseudonymous woman, "Kate," offers some insight into the place of field hands and cotton gin operators on a large southern plantation in the years before the Civil War.

Mr. -----------------:

Dear Sir,--A residence on a large plantation is to a Northerner rich with subjects of interest. Every thing is so different from what he has been accustomed to, his curiosity is continually excited by the novelties which are brought before him, or which he is running his face against. First, there is the slave himself, his condition, his cabin, his dress, his manners, his labors, his amusements, his religion, his domestic relations; then there is the plantation, with fences a mile apart, presenting in one broad enclosure land enough to make a score of Yankee pastures; then there is the cotton-plant, with its rich, pure, white, fleecy treasures, hanging to the gathering hand; then there is the cotton-gin, with the negroes at work in it, the snowy cotton flying from the wind-fans in fleecy showers that mock a December snowstorm! [T]hen there is the baling and screwing, the roping and marking with planter's name, all objects of interest to witness; then there is the planter himself, so different in his manners, tastes, education, prejudices, notions, bearing, feelings, and associations, from the New England man . . .

Source: J. H. Ingraham. 1860. *The Sunny South; Or, The Southerner at Home, embracing five years' experience of a northern governess in the land of the sugar and cotton.* Letter XXVII. Philadelphia: G. G. Evans, 222.

FUR TRADER

Fur traders' commercial interests dealt primarily with the acquisition, trade, and sale of animal fur and pelts. In modern times, the fur trade has been greatly diminished, but it was once a thriving, worldwide industry. In the late eighteenth and early nineteenth centuries, fur traders worked throughout what was then considered the western frontier, from upper New York westward through the Great Lakes region, to Detroit and its environs, as well as in the upper Mississippi and Missouri River valleys. Other fur traders worked in the Southwest, at the edge of the southern Rocky Mountains, along the Pacific Coast, and in what are now British Columbia, Alaska, and the Aleutian Islands. In all of these areas, fur traders had one goal: to obtain furs, primarily from indigenous hunters. While many fur traders were contracted to work for large commercial firms—including the Russian-American Company, Hudson's Bay Company, American Fur Company—others worked for smaller firms and sometimes as independent traders.

Outfitting for a trader's voyage required access to substantial amounts of capital, or funds, to outfit the boats, purchase the horses or pack animals, and obtain the goods (muskets and musket balls, black powder, knives, textiles, tobacco, alcohol) needed to exchange for furs, as well as to supply the trading crews with clothing, food, knives, tools, personal weapons, and other items. In exchange for these resources, fur traders organized crews of workers, planned and executed wilderness travel, and learned about the geography of an assigned region, as well as about a region's indigenous residents and their political alliances and enemies. Traders had to have basic land and water navigation skills and be familiar with local weather patterns. Many traders were fluent in English and French but were also conversant in indigenous languages. Fur traders also needed to be knowledgeable about fur and pelt preservation techniques: how to dry pelts to prevent spoilage, package them well to protect from damage during the return trip, and transport them back to the company's warehouses.

A fur trader began his annual work by meeting with the company agents to obtain the goods he needed and his instructions for purchasing furs or pelts. While colonial fur companies had aggressively pursued trading monopolies with individual tribes, thus securing territorial monopolies in the Northeast and Great Lakes regions, by the end of the Revolutionary War (1775–1783), the fur, pelt, and deerskin trade had moved westward, where companies were hard pressed to enforce trade restrictions. Complicating any effort to secure trading monopolies were traders' own practices of engaging in sexual relationships with tribal women, thereby tying these traders into familial and tribal networks, especially after the birth of mixed-race children, called Metís. The traders negotiated with company agents and prepared travel plans for the trading crew, with designated stops at some tribal settlements along the way and often terminating at a company's interior trading post. Traders then assembled their gear and crews and began their journeys into the interior of the nation, normally by watercraft, though in the Southwest, some traders traveled on horseback with wagons drawn by oxen or mules. The journeys from interior ports like St. Louis usually began in spring after floodwaters had subsided; Indian hunters had worked through the winter to capture beaver, otter, and foxes when their pelts had the thickest and most luxurious fur.

One famous fur trader, Jean-Baptiste Trudeau, kept a detailed diary while he worked. In one sequence of entries, he recounted struggling to guide his uncommonly large boat, which was powered by eight oarsmen, up the Missouri River to trade with members of the Arikara tribe in the summer of 1794, and he fretted about whether or not he would reach his goal before rival tribes detained him. Trudeau worried that if these other people found him, they would seize his trade items—primarily light muskets known as fusils—without his having gotten any of the large beaver and otter pelts he desired. Instead, noted Trudeau, "The policy of the Indians of this river is such that they are absolutely determined to prevent communication between us and the nations of the upper Missouri, depriving the latter of munitions of war" as they were terrified about what would happen to their tribal homeland if other nations (tribal groups) obtained guns (Trudeau 2017, 87).

Trudeau's concerns reflect the role of the fur trader in the larger history of North America: how traders connected rival nations of hunters with "munitions of war," thereby shaping geopolitical rivalries among tribal people, Americans, French, British, Spanish, and Russians in the western frontier. The work of the fur trader, however, was not to serve as unofficial diplomats but to travel into the wilderness to obtain the furs and pelts in demand in markets as near as St. Louis and as distant as China and Paris.

As a trading crew rowed or paddled up the region's rivers and across large lakes, they often encountered tribal settlements in the river valleys, as Trudeau did when he first came upon the Kansas and Pawnees, who he described as "good warriors and good hunters" (Trudeau 2017, 83). Traders also met with other traders, exchanging goods, letters, and gifts for tribes in other territories with whom a trader had formerly had business. The work of transporting their trading goods and gear on water was often difficult as traders routinely had to portage, or carry, their boats around rapids or waterfalls. In 1802, teenager George Nelson complained about "portages over rocks, hills & Swamps, mostly covered with dense forests. Not a few of them the themes of legends, stories, & tales of adventure, accidents & miracles &c" (Nelson 2002, 38).

Weather, however, presented the most challenges to traders on their journeys. Trudeau, for instance, spent several days rowing up the lower Missouri River from St. Charles but made little progress because of the rain. Floodwaters could upset the boats, emptying their contents into the river, while heavy rain soaked boat contents and crews, requiring traders to stop frequently and dry their boats' contents over a fire. Writing about the famous eighteenth-century fur trader Peter Pond, historian David Chapin explains that successful traders needed "toughness" and often displayed a "risk-taking nature" (Chapin 2014, 59).

Violence, too, was often a feature in the life of traders as they interacted with tribal people, each group jostling for superiority in the terms of exchange. Intercultural violence—between traders and their Indian "wives," between traders and tribal hunters, and between different tribal groups—was common and often exacerbated by alcohol. Regardless of their backgrounds, drunken men initiated brawls and fought violently with each other; some traders, like Peter Pond's brother Phineas, were infamous within the fur trading industry for the numbers of people they had killed. The isolation of a trader's life sometimes took a toll, when individual members of a crew wandered off into the wilderness. Traders also adopted native beliefs and superstitions, including shaking a newly pitched tent to remove harmful forest spirits.

Once arrived in the interior, fur traders parlayed with favored hunters; a parley was a form of verbal transaction (based on the French "parler," or to speak or converse with) between the trader and his tribal contacts. Some tribal people specialized in becoming the intermediaries between hunters and traders, so traders had to operate within strict guidelines set by their Indian hosts. Traders generally had a route they would travel, parlaying with tribal representatives and hunters at Indian settlements. Once they completed their trading there, they moved to the next stop. By the 1820s, though, with the influx of white professional trappers into the Rocky Mountain regions, an annual trading fair, the rendezvous, became an institution where white trappers, Indian hunters, intermediaries, and traders would gather in a single location (announced the previous season) for a summer-long meeting, during which company traders purchased furs, skins, and pelts without having to travel long distances from settlement to settlement.

At an interior post or camp, the trader processed the pelts—cleaning, drying, and packaging them for transport—a labor-intensive endeavor that typically took several weeks. Once the trader had filled his boats with furs, he then transported the goods back to the company's warehouses, usually in the autumn or early winter. Some traders, such as those attached to the Russian American Company's Fort Ross settlement on the California coast, worked at formal outposts in the wilderness; after 1812, the company's native Aleut hunters brought furs to the fort, while other workers tried to farm to provide food for the company's outposts in Alaska.

Fur traders were critical actors in the discovery, exploration, and resettlement of North America. Their activities disrupted native patterns of trade, brought European and American technologies and goods into the interior, and fathered a class of intercultural experts, the Metís, whose roles as cultural arbiters became increasingly important to fur companies. Fur traders represented not only their employers but also their nations, sometimes reporting back to political leaders on "intelligence" about changes in intertribal relationships and alliances on the frontiers. However, the traders, hunters, trappers, and, especially, those who so sought the furs that these men procured were also instrumental in the environmental destruction of wildlife across the nation.

Nancy Quam-Wickham

See also: Explorer; Fur Trapper

FURTHER READING

Chapin, David. 2014. *Freshwater Passages: The Trade and Travels of Peter Pond.* Lincoln: University of Nebraska Press.

Nelson, George. 2014. *My First Years in the Fur Trade: The Journals of 1802–1804.* Edited by Laura Peers and Theresa M. Schenck. Montréal: McGill-Queen's University Press.

Trudeau, Jean-Baptiste. 2017. *A Fur Trader on the Upper Missouri: The Journal and Description of Jean-Baptiste Trudeau, 1794–1796.* Edited and translated by Raymond J. DeMallie, Douglas R. Parks, Robert Vézina, and Mildred Mott Wedel. Lincoln: University of Nebraska Press.

FUR TRAPPER

At the turn of the nineteenth century, the fur trade extended across North America, Europe, and Asia. The industry was dominated by two large companies that employed hundreds of fur trappers: the Hudson's Bay Company (HBC), which was founded in 1670 and headquartered at York Factory on Hudson Bay in Manitoba, Canada; and the North West Company (NWC), the major competitor of HBC, founded in 1789 in the Canadian city of Montreal. The fur trappers that were employed by these or other companies, or were self-employed, spent their days hunting and killing furry mammals and processing their skins and pelts for sale. Fur trapping required a variety of skills related to hunting, tracking, boating, bartering, and trading. Also important was wayfinding—navigating one's way across the land and waters of North America.

John Jacob Astor, a German immigrant, established the first major American company, the American Fur Company, based in New York City. Astor established a trading post called Astoria in 1811 near the mouth of the Columbia River in northwestern Oregon, but NWC officials took over the post in 1813 during the War of 1812 (1812–1815). After the demise of Astoria, several American companies were founded in St. Louis—a city itself founded fifty years before the Louisiana Purchase to exploit the market for animal furs. The St. Louis-based companies had greater success than the American Fur Company in part because they focused on the one region of North America not dominated by the great British firms: the Missouri River region and Rocky Mountains. The fur trade in St. Louis was dominated by René-Auguste and Jean-Pierre Chouteau (two brothers from the founding family of St. Louis) and Chouteau family's main competitor, Manuel Lisa, who established the Missouri Fur Company in 1809. Famous explorer and guide Hugh Glass's employer, the Rocky Mountain Fur Company, was founded in St. Louis in 1822 by William Henry Ashley and Andrew Henry.

The fur trade can be broken into three main phases: hunting and killing furry mammals, processing animal skins, and trading and shipping the processed animal products. Fur trappers engaged in all three activities but spent most of their time hunting and killing mammals, including deer, bears, mink, ermines, arctic foxes, skunks, beavers, sea otters, and others. However, the foundation of the fur trade in North America was the beaver. Beaver pelts were highly prized in Europe and elsewhere due to the great density of the animal's fur—in some places, tens of thousands of hairs per square inch—which made them an ideal material for fashioning hats, coats, and robes.

By the nineteenth century, fur trappers used a variety of well-established tools and techniques to kill beavers. There were three main tools: rifle; axe or hoe; and trap. Most of the hunting practices of fur trappers were based on Indian techniques. Native American labor and knowledge was central to the establishment of the fur trade in the early 1600s and remained centrally important throughout the eighteenth and nineteenth centuries.

Beavers are mostly nocturnal, which meant that beaver hunting usually took place at night. In his memoir of his travels among the Ojibwa Indians of the Great Lakes region, Alexander Henry, one of the founders of NWC, explained one of the main methods of hunting beavers: "To kill beaver, we used to go several miles up the rivers . . . and after dusk came on, suffer the canoe to drift gently down the current, without noise. The beaver, in this part of the evening, come abroad to procure food, or materials for repairing their habitations; and as they are not alarmed by the canoe, they often pass it within gun-shot" (Henry 1809, 127). As Henry indicates, beavers were sometimes shot with a rifle or bow and arrow. Another method of harvesting beavers involved destroying their lodges using an axe, hoe, or similar tool. As the trappers started to break apart the lodge, the beavers would escape into the river through one of the lodge's holes or washes. In the winter—the preferred season to hunt beaver since the animal's fur was most dense—trappers would then locate the washes by breaking the ice below the riverbank and pull each beaver out of the ice with a net or by hand. Finally, fur trappers earned the title of fur trapper by also using a variety of traps. Deadfall traps (made of heavy logs) using different wood as bait were sometimes used. Using castoreum (the scent or musk created by beavers to mark their territory) as bait, steel traps that locked around the legs of the animal were also used.

The work of trading—but also of processing the pelts of beavers and other animals—was often completed at a trading post or factory. Trading was often done by managers of the company. Processing was usually done by women, usually native women. At the time of their merger in 1821, HBC and NWC operated dozens of hunting and trading forts across Canada and the United States. At Fort Vancouver, the major HBC fort located along the Columbia River near the modern city of Portland, Oregon, HBC employed hundreds of Native American, Métis (i.e., mixed race, or Native Euro Americans), French, and British workers divided into one of two main groups of employees: gentlemen and servants. Fur trappers were among the servants or *engages*, and thus some of the lowest-paid employees of the company. Hunting was conducted in a large group known as a brigade. Fifty to a hundred men—along with wives and children of all the trappers—would leave the fort to hunt. Women (usually Indian or Métis women) played key roles in all phases of the fur trade. In the brigade, women not only cooked and looked after the men and children but also acted as interpreters and used their connections with other native peoples to help conduct trade. Back at the factory, women were heavily involved in processing the pelts for shipment, a process that included skinning and fleshing each beaver and then stretching and drying each individual pelt. In the words of historian Anne F. Hyde, "To get furs . . . men needed women—specifically women from Native nations" (Hyde 2011, 91–92).

William Henry Ashley (1778–1838) innovated a new system of trapping and trading in the 1820s—one that did not require establishing permanent forts. Setting his brigades into the field in the fall and winter, he met up with them in the summer at a specific rendezvous site in the mountains. All trade would be conducted at the rendezvous, after which time the trappers would go back to the field and return to the next rendezvous the following year. The rendezvous system of the Rocky Mountain Fur Company began in 1824 and continued for fifteen years. Many of the rendezvous were held in Wyoming, and the system proved highly successful because Ashley opened the rendezvous not just to his employees but all fur trappers and traders in the region. The rendezvous not only helped created a new form of trapper, the "free trapper" (as opposed the company servant or *engage* of HBC), it also drew in hundreds of American, Native American, Métis, French, and British trappers to the Rocky Mountain borderlands. The rendezvous also changed fur trapping in one other respect. Hunting parties attached to American companies like the Rocky Mountain Fur Company tended to hunt in much smaller numbers and without women. Consequently, in the United States, the fur trapper—or mountain man, as he came to be known—was associated with men and men alone.

Fur trappers were some of the earliest explorers of North America. Alexander Mackenzie, the first Euro American to reach the Pacific Ocean after traveling overland across the continent, did so in the 1790s while working for the North West Company. Other fur trappers like Jedidiah Smith of the Rocky Mountain Fur Company located many of the routes thousands of agricultural settlers would later take to places like Oregon and California during the 1840s and 1850s. The year 1840 brought the final rendezvous and the beginning of the end of the fur trade. After more than two centuries of extensive hunting, not only had fashion trends in Europe moved away from beaver pelts, but beaver populations were in steep decline all throughout North America. The fur trade, thus, went into steep decline after the final Rocky Mountain rendezvous but not before leaving a deep mark on the both the natural and human history of North America.

Erik Altenbernd

See also: Explorer; Fur Trader; Land Speculator; *1607–1775:* Translator

FURTHER READING

Dolin, Eric Jay. 2010. *Fur, Fortune, and Empire: The Epic History of the Fur Trade in America*. New York: W. W. Norton & Company.

Hall, J. E. 1825. "The Missouri Trapper." *The Port Folio* 19 (March): 214.
Henry, Alexander. 1809. *Travels and Adventures in Canada and the Indian Territories between the Years 1760 to 1776*. New York: I. Riley.
Hyde, Anne F. 2011. *Empires, Nations, and Families: A New History of the North American West, 1800–1860*. Lincoln: University of Nebraska Press.
Juen, Rachel B., and Michael S. Nassaney. 2012. "The Fur Trade." Western Michigan University, Fort St. Joseph Archaeological Project. https://scholarworks.wmich.edu/cgi/viewcontent.cgi?article=1009&context=fortstjoseph.
Webber, David, J. 1971. *The Taos Trappers: The Fur Trade in the Far Southwest, 1540–1846*. Norman: University of Oklahoma Press.
Wishart, David J. 1979. *The Fur Trade of the American West, 1807–1840: A Geographical Synthesis*. Lincoln: University of Nebraska Press.

PRIMARY DOCUMENT

Osborne Russell was born in Maine in 1814, and as a young man of twenty, he joined Nathaniel Wyeth's fur trapping and trading company in the Rocky Mountains. Between 1834 and 1843, Russell traveled throughout the Rocky Mountains and Western America, from Oregon through the inland Northwest, and into the central Rockies. During this time, Russell kept a journal of his travels and experiences. In these selections, he outlines the typical seasonal cycle of work for fur trappers and traders during this time period. One of the most interesting of Russell's observations is the diversity of individuals who participated in this trade on the frontier, including Americans, tribal people, Hawaiians, Spaniards, Mexicans, the French, and the English.

[After several days of travel, the group] stopped for the night. Here some of the trappers knew the country. This stream is called Stinking River, a branch of the Bighorn which after running about 40 miles through the big plain enters the above river about 15 miles above the lower Bighorn Mountain. It takes its name from several hot Springs about 5 miles below the forks producing a sulphurous stench which is often carried by the wind to the distance of 5 or 6 miles. Here are also large quarries of gypsum almost transparent of the finest quality and also appearances of Lead with large rich beds of Iron and bituminous coal. We stopped at this place and rested our animals until the 23d. By this time our wounded comrade had recovered so far as to be able to hobble about on crutches.

[After several more days of traveling, averaging 12 to 15 miles per day] We crossed the mountain in a West direction through the thick pines and fallen timber, about 12 miles and encamped in a small prairie about a mile in circumference. Through this valley ran a small stream in a North direction which all agreed in believing to be a branch of the Yellow Stone. 28th We descended the stream about 15 miles . . . at length came to a beautiful valley . . . surrounded by dark and lofty mountains . . .

Here we found a few Snake Indians comprising 6 men, 7 women, and 8 or 10 children who were the only Inhabitants of this lonely and secluded spot. They were all neatly clothed in dressed deer and Sheep skins of the best quality and seemed to be perfectly contented and happy. They were rather surprised at our approach and retreated to the heights where they might have a view of us without apprehending any danger, but having persuaded them of our pacific intentions we then succeeded getting them to encamp with us. Their personal property consisted of one old butcher Knife nearly worn to the back, two old shattered fusees which had long since become useless for want of ammunition, a Small Stone pot, and about 30 dogs on which they carried their skins, clothing, provisions etc. on their hunting excursions. They were well armed with bows and arrows pointed with obsidian. The bows were beautifully wrought from Sheep, Buffalo and Elk horns secured with Deer and Elk sinews and ornamented with porcupine quills and generally about 3 feet long. We obtained a large number of Elk, Deer, and Sheep skins from them of the finest quality and three large neatly dressed Panther Skins in return for awls, axes, kettles, tobacco, ammunition etc. They would threw the skins at our feet and say "give us whatever you please for them and we are satisfied. We can get plenty of Skins but we do not often see the Tibuboes" (or People of the Sun). They said there had been a great many beaver on the branches of this stream but they had killed nearly all of them and being ignorant of the value of fur had singed it off with fire in order to drip the meat more conveniently. They had seen some whites some years previous who had passed through the valley and left a horse behind but he had died during the first winter . . . We stopped at this place and for my own part I almost wished I could spend the remainder of my days in a place like this where happiness and contentment seemed to reign in wild romantic splendor surrounded by majestic battlements which seemed to support the heavens and shut out all hostile intruders.

Source: Osborne Russell. 1921. *Journal of a Trapper: Or, Nine Years in the Rocky Mountains, 1834–1843.* Boise: Syms-York Company, 30–32, passim.

GINNER

Cotton gin operators, or ginners, ran the machines that separated cotton lint from the boll, seeds, and other plant materials. Cotton is central to the history of antebellum America. Cotton was the South's primary export crop on the eve of the Civil War (1861–1865), and cotton production led directly to the vast expansion of slavery into the Deep South and the southwestern states of Texas and Arkansas. But less than a century earlier, cotton was rarely grown in America, grown primarily in small quantities in Georgia's Sea Islands. On plantations in the antebellum South, ginners were mostly slaves, but freed slaves and poor whites also found work as ginners there.

Cotton is a member of the mallow family; the plant flowers and then goes to seed within the boll, a seed shell. Inside this hard boll, cotton fibers develop to protect the sticky seeds and help disburse them in the wind. Removing cotton fibers from the seeds, boll, and other plant material was a difficult and time-intensive job when done by hand. That changed with the development of Eli Whitney's cotton gin machine in 1793, which mechanized the separation of cotton seeds and other plant material from the cotton fibers and then combed to separate and untangle them into fine lint. The cotton gin made cotton production profitable in the antebellum United States. Word of Whitney's invention of a mechanical gin swept throughout the South. It was not a particularly difficult concept to replicate, so planters and mechanics adapted the mechanical process without respecting Whitney's patent or paying him the requisite fees. Different types of cotton gins appeared, with slight modifications on Whitney's design; they were relatively inexpensive to build. Whitney's patented cotton gin—and all its successors, however modified—cemented the place of single-crop (monocrop) export agriculture in the South.

The cotton gin itself consisted of a chute into which a ginner fed the raw cotton, a gear mechanism that spun a roller with metal teeth or small hooks to separate the fibers while letting the other material fall onto a screen, and a set of brush rollers that lengthened and combed the fibers and pushed them through to a bin for cleaned cotton fiber. A gin could be as big as a wagon or even larger, taking up a full room. Slaves usually operated small gins with hand cranks. Larger gins were powered by livestock (mules or horses) or by water power from streams. Once the cleaned cotton fibers were deposited into a bin (or even a room below the gin, called the lint room), the fiber was then checked for impurities. Once that process was complete, cleaned cotton fibers were moved out to the cotton press machine; using hand- or horse-powered cranks, this machine compressed the cotton into bales weighing 450 to 500 pounds. These bales were then shipped by railroad or riverboat to coastal towns, where it was transshipped, normally to northern U.S. ports for export to England.

Once cotton growing was established in the Deep South and Southwest, most of the larger plantations had their own cotton gins, usually operated by slaves. Only smaller cotton growers lacked gins on their properties. In these cases, planters took their unprocessed cotton to a local cotton gin. Ginners in these community facilities were both white and African American. But like millers, town ginners had to be trustworthy individuals as they were paid a percentage of the cotton ginned (usually one-fifth). Planters kept rough track of how many bales they could expect from their crop by examining the overseer's records of production to calculate the number of "hundred weights" of cotton that had been picked by each slave during harvest season. Thus, if a ginner was off on the number of bales a planter expected, the planter would accuse him of being dishonest and disreputable—a cheat or scoundrel. Many southern states enacted laws that required ginners and compress operators to stamp their mark on cotton bales to counteract dishonesty, much as the Virginia colonial government did with tobacco hogsheads in the seventeenth century.

The process of running a gin was fairly straightforward. Slaves or ginners' helpers fed unprocessed cotton into the feed chute, while others provided the power. South Carolina native Joseph Le Conte, the son of a planter, recalls that on his father's property, the cotton gin was powered by foot pedals, operated by "great numbers [of slaves] working together . . . always singing and shouting and keeping time with the work" (Le Conte 2016, 23). At larger gins, slave children often rode the horses or mules that powered the gin. Born into slavery and raised on a cotton plantation, Levi Branham remembered how, as a boy, he rode a horse that powered the "lever that pulled the gin," or powered the brush rollers that pulled the cotton fibers from the metal teeth and then packed it (into a partly compacted length of cotton batting) using a wooden screw mechanism. This batting was then pushed through to the lint room below the gin (Branham 2000, 54). Other slaves inspected the processed cotton in the lint room and then packed it into large baskets and carried them to the cotton press machine, also powered by a horse. All of the ginning work on that plantation was completed by slaves.

Ginners also had to keep an eye on the cotton being fed into the chute, making sure to prevent rocks and other material from entering it. Slave overseers assigned "tasks," or certain weights, to each slave during cotton-picking season, but not all slaves could make their assigned tasks. As a child, Israel Campbell had worked as a house slave, tending to the needs of his owners on a plantation in Kentucky. His owner, however, endeavored to go into the cotton business, so he moved his household and slaves to a new plantation near Vicksburg, Mississippi. Once there, the young Campbell was hired out to another planter for the year, whose overseer assigned him the task of picking one hundred pounds of cotton per day. Having never worked in the fields, let alone in the hot and humid August in the Deep South, Campbell was unable to meet his task on his first day as a picker in the cotton fields. He ran away rather than being whipped for underperforming. When he continued to be unable to make his task, he discovered that he could weigh his cotton-picking basket down with a large melon from a nearby field, covering it carefully with cotton. At the nightly weigh-in, the overseer did not detect Campbell's deception. Campbell shared his means for making his task with other young boys unaccustomed to picking cotton; the penalty for detection was a serious whipping, yet the overseer whipped anyone who did not make his or her task.

When he transferred the content of his basket into the ginning room, Campbell was careful to hide the heavy items—melons, pumpkins, rocks—that helped him make his task. Slaves elsewhere weighed their baskets and bags down with rocks, dirt, wood, and other heavy items to make their assigned weights. The ginner had to be on guard for such material since rocks could break the teeth that separated the fibers, bringing the gin to a halt. Ginners also had to repair any damage to the gin, as much as they were able to do. Ginning was seasonal work, occurring only in late summer and early fall after the harvest. Planters transported their ginned and pressed cotton to market for export as soon as possible after the raw cotton was harvested.

In the years after the Civil War, steam and electric plants became the primary power for cotton gins. Given the more reliable power sources, gins and compress machines also became bigger and more powerful, processing raw cotton at a fast pace. Gin operators now had to ensure that they did not fall into the feed chute, get entangled in the gear mechanisms, or become injured by the motion of the gin itself. Ginning and cotton compressing was now very dangerous work; one slip and an operator could be killed. Ginning was now its own occupation, performed by machine operators, and beginning in 1902, the Census Bureau collected data about cotton production, processed cotton, and gin operatives at every one of the nation's approximately thirty thousand ginneries. In subsequent decades, gin and compress operators formed unions to protect their interests, achieve wage increases, and enforce occupational safety requirements. But these developments were far in the future from the perspective of a ginner in antebellum America.

Nancy Quam-Wickham

See also: Field Hand; Planter; Slave Driver

FURTHER READING

Branham, Levi. 2000. *My Life and Travels*. Atlanta: Whitfield-Murray Historical Society.

Campbell, Israel. 1861. *An Autobiography: Bond and Free: Or, Yearnings for Freedom, from My Green Brier House; Being the Story of My Life in Bondage, and My Life in Freedom*. Chapel Hill: Ibiblio.

Hovland, Michael. 1994. "The Cotton Ginnings Reports Program at the Bureau of the Census." *Agricultural History* 68: 146–156.

Le Conte, Joseph. 2016. *Autobiography of Joseph Le Conte (Classic Reprint)*. London: Forgotten Books.

GOLD MINER

Gold miners were workers who extracted this valuable metal using a variety of methods that depended on the state in which the gold was embedded in the earth. In the United States, gold mining was a relatively new occupation; only very small deposits of gold, primarily in the southern states of North Carolina and Georgia, were found before 1848. In the years between 1848 and the Civil War, however, gold mining became a popular occupation pursued by thousands of young men, first in California and then in Nevada, Colorado, Idaho, British Columbia, and elsewhere.

The discovery of gold along the middle fork of the American River on January 24, 1848, by a sawmill worker named James Marshall did not generate immediate interest in California or even elsewhere in the nation. Marshall had been hard at work on the river at Coloma when, as the legend goes, a ray of sunshine reflected off a small nugget of gold, creating a glint that caught his eye. He stooped to pick up the gold fleck but was not yet sure that this was, indeed, gold. Spanish and Mexican settlers in Old California had searched for decades for gold deposits, without any real success.

Within months of Marshall's discovery, however, the news of his find became widespread throughout California and the eastern Pacific basin. Local farmers in the Central Valley dropped their tools to participate in the frenzied rush to the gold fields in the Sierra foothills. The jailer at Monterey rounded up his inmates, chained them together, and took off for the gold regions. Shipowners in California could not keep their crews onboard once vessels entered the San Francisco Bay; sailors abandoned their posts and raced to the hills, all hoping to find that elusive yet enormous deposit of gold.

In that first year, 1848, several thousand men—along with some women and children—left their homes, farms, and businesses to try their hand at mining for gold. The gold deposits that Marshall had stumbled upon are known as placer deposits. The valuable mineral had its origins in the twisting and heaving of the geological processes of granite mountain building in the creation of the Sierra Nevada range. Rain and melting snow dislodged gold deposits high in the mountains, carrying flecks and nuggets downstream. In the northern Sierras and the Trinity Mountains, gold deposits washed down rapidly flowing rivers, becoming trapped in still waters along the stream edges, in bars created by the action of rushing waters.

In the more southern section of the Sierras where the region was more geologically active as well as more prone to spells of drought, the old placer gold deposits had settled in areas that would later dry out or in old stream beds that had been altered by tectonic action of earthquakes. These deposits were called dry diggings.

In this first year, prospectors used implements of all kinds to unearth and capture deposits of gold: shovels, pickaxes, spoons, the backs of claw hammers, and even pocket knives. Miners utilized the action of flowing water to separate gold deposits from the alluvia—pebbles, sand, rocks, and organic debris like sticks and leaves—in which gold was embedded. When using a shovel or other similar tool, a placer miner dug into the riverbed, tossed some shovelfuls of unwashed dirt onto the bank, and then used a pan or other similar shallow container to repeatedly wash the gold free from the dirt, using a repetitive shaking motion to separate it from other material. Standing in frigid mountain water for hours at a time, leaning bent over the riverbank to inspect the washing process, and laboring in all kinds of weather made for incredibly hard work, as many miners soon found out. In the dry diggings, gold was more often found embedded in quartz rocks, requiring that these hard rocks be crushed to free the gold cemented into veins of quartz. In these areas, miners similarly dug up gold deposits, but rather than using water power to separate the gold, they crushed the gold in quartz mills, normally using animal power to drag the heavy grindstone in a circle over and over to pulverize the rock. Then miners used quicksilver—a heavy metal now known as liquid mercury—to bind the gold to the mercury, which could be heated in a small furnace and then separated into their constituent elements, mercury and gold. Like placer mining, working in a dry diggings was dirty, hot work, where one was subject to changes in weather. Furthermore, mercury is a toxic metal, and in the process of binding quicksilver to gold, trace amounts of quicksilver were spilled on the ground and on miners' bodies and clothing, where its harmful heated vapors were often inhaled, leading many miners to experience the symptoms of heavy metal poisoning.

In 1848, most Americans did not hear of the California gold rush until late in the year, when, on December 5, President Polk announced the discovery to the nation. The '48ers, as they called themselves, were mostly local residents of California, Oregon, Mexico, Hawaii, and Latin America, where news of the massive discovery of gold had already arrived before Polk's announcement. This first group of prospectors in 1848 benefited from the slow pace at which news traveled. Fewer miners meant less competition from other workers for the coveted resource. Men from throughout the region dug, washed, crushed rock, and built new tools to capture more of the desired metal. In this first year, historians estimate that the average California gold miner could make twenty dollars a day if he worked hard. Prospectors could increase their daily wages by drafting others to work for them in their "companies," crews of men (and sometimes women) who performed the heavy work of digging, washing, and crushing rock. Indigenous people, Latinos, youth, and even African American slaves who had been brought to the territory before gold was discovered found themselves working, often unwillingly, for enterprising prospectors who had little concern about exploiting vulnerable workers.

Once President Polk publicized the discovery of enormous gold deposits in California's foothills, however, the "rush" was on. Between 1849 and 1852, an estimated 300,000 Americans traveled to California to participate in the gold rush, eager to quickly find their own stash of gold, remove it, and return home wealthy to enjoy their futures—or so most thought. In reality, the great numbers of men who arrived in search of gold had no experience as miners. They were unfamiliar with the California landscape of mountains, steep canyons, rushing cold-water streams, and hot, dry weather in the summer. Many were unprepared to work for hours at a time in cold, dangerous water, returning to their tents for a cold meal at night, and then repeat the same again the next day. Moreover, miners seemed to arrive in ever greater numbers each month, creating more competition among prospectors for a rapidly diminishing resource. The arrival of more miners increased labor competition, drove down the average daily wage, and led to innovation in work processes.

By 1849, these '49ers found it necessary to build more elaborate gold-catching machinery to find enough of the metal to make a living. Men now had to construct new, longer washing containers called cradles or rockers—wooden receptacles four to eight feet long, or longer, into which miners shoveled dirt they hoped would bear gold. More invasive and environmentally damaging techniques followed as prospectors built temporary dams across streams and rivers to divert the water flow away from its original channel in the hopes that they could uncover previously undiscovered gold. Miners built enormous water wheels and elaborate aqueduct systems to carry a river's flow away from its original channel. Even then, gold was becoming harder to find in great quantities.

By 1850, just two years after Marshall's discovery at Coloma, prospectors who had arrived from across the world found it difficult to make a living working traditional methods of mining. In that year, the Empire Mine was established near Grass Valley, California—an underground mine where miners were lowered by basket into deep caverns to extract gold from veins in the earth. The Empire Mine, which only closed in 1956, had over 350 miles of underground tunnels, where miners used dynamite to free gold-bearing rock and pushcarts to remove the debris from the mine. Later, the Empire Mining Company introduced mules to this process, sending these draft animals deep underground to pull cars of ore to the surface. Once there, miners transported the rock to stamp mills, where it was pulverized, and then on to a refinery, where mercury was used to create the amalgamate. Only later were cleaner methods introduced to separate gold from the pulverized debris, when, after 1900, the mining industry adopted the practice of using cyanide to leach gold out of quartz ore.

By this time, placer mining had also become largely obsolete. Heavily financed companies transported machinery—narrow-gauge railroad cars, huge steam-driven pumps, elaborate pipe systems—to utilize a technique called hydraulic mining. In this process, a pump engine fed water through pressurized pipes, where miners held nozzles that released incredibly powerful streams of water onto hillsides and dry riverbeds, blasting away gold ore and debris into basins, like small lakes, where miners operated dredges and other mechanical means to wash the gold flakes from the wet muck that flowed down the mountains.

In both of these cases—hydraulic mining and underground hard-rock mining—prospectors became wage workers, no longer working for themselves with hopes of discovering a significant deposit that was all their own. Instead, the gold they freed from California's mountainsides belonged to the companies for which they worked. Men labored for ten- or twelve-hour shifts each day, six or seven days a week. They often took their meals in company dining rooms and slept in company bunkhouses. They might spend their wages at the company store, where prices were inflated to the advantage of the owners. This fall from the ideal of a hopeful independent entrepreneur—the miner in boots, jeans, and a red flannel shirt, bent over a pan, swishing water around to separate the gold—to that of a simple wage worker, earning two to three dollars per day in difficult conditions, happened rapidly in California. The miners who had rushed there intending to strike it rich became disillusioned, and many traveled home only after parents, in-laws, and friends financed their return.

For those workers who did not return home, many followed subsequent rushes to other places, primarily in the western states, where gold was discovered in the 1850s and early 1860s. Others pursued jobs underground as silver miners in places like Virginia City, Nevada, where colossal deposits of silver were discovered in 1859. The lure of getting rich by mining precious metals like gold and silver had inspired many adventurous young men to travel thousands of miles to make their fortunes in the decades before the Civil War. Those few who continued to work as miners after the California gold rush became itinerant workers, following new discoveries from place to place, working for others, and yet, for many, still dreaming of easy riches.

Nancy Quam-Wickham

See also: Laborer; *1861–1914:* Coal Miner

FURTHER READING

Brands, H. W. 2003. *The Age of Gold: The California Gold Rush and the New American Dream.* Portsmouth: William Heinemann.

Eifler, Mark A. 2016. *The California Gold Rush: The Stampede That Changed the World.* London: Routledge.

Johnson, Susan Lee. 2000. *Roaring Camp: The Social World of the California Gold Rush.* New York: W. W. Norton.

Levy, JoAnn. 2014. *They Saw the Elephant: Women and the California Gold Rush.* Norman: Oklahoma University Press.
Paul, Rodman. 1947. *California Gold: The Beginning of Mining in the Far West.* Cambridge: Harvard University Press.

HARPOONER

The harpooner, known by the technical name boatsteerer, played an integral role for the United States between 1815 and 1860, "the Golden Age of American Whaling," for it was he who caught whales. Whaling proved to be a viable and substantial component of antebellum American life. Harpooners who risked their lives hunting these upward of sixty-ton leviathans did so for oil (derived from a whale's fat) and whalebone. Among the many uses for whale oil were illuminates, lubricants, soap, grease, stearine, and a base for other oils such as machine and clock oil. When heated, baleen, referred to as whalebone, could be molded into a desired shape and remained durable yet flexible (comparable to today's plastic). Shapes included corset stays, umbrella ribs, whips, hooks, bristle for brushes, and canes. Returning whale ships set off a chain reaction through the nation. Factories refined or manufactured the whale oil and bone, others transported these goods to markets, and merchants distributed the goods to the public. Whale goods contributed anywhere from 20 to 40 percent of America's industrial production and overall economy (Dolin 2007, 12, 206).

The requisites for being one of the three to four boatsteerers on a whaleship included being a man (standard for all other whaling roles), having served on at least one previous whaling voyage, and obvious physical might. While a perilous occupation for all involved, a boatsteerer, in particular, faced grave danger during hunting. Rowing with all his might at distances of up to a couple of miles, nearing exhaustion, he would then have to prove his value to the entire expedition by employing his unique responsibility aboard the whaleship: "his muscles taut and his heart racing, he would raise the harpoon, draw back his body like a bow, and, waiting for the best time to strike, hurl the harpoon into the whale's back or flank" (Dolin 2007, 95). Novice boatsteerers "had been known to faint dead away when first presented with the terrifying prospect of attaching themselves to an infuriated whale" (Philbrick 2000, 52).

When not hunting whales, all members of a whaleship's crew worked every day. While on a voyage, the boatsteerer generally worked common labor like other experienced sailors on a whaleship. Most days, like others, the boatsteerer would stand a watch at the helm of the ship, taking orders from the mate or master (captain) of the vessel. When not on helm duty, the crew was responsible for maintaining the vessel in good shape: cleaning and scrubbing the decks, attending to the sails up in the rigging when the master ordered a change in speed or direction, mending sails, and splicing ropes and rigging. The boatsteerer had the additional duty of ensuring that the ship's blacksmith kept his harpoons (or irons) sharp. When in port, the crew had to cut wood (for firing the boilers to reduce whale blubber into oil) and trade for fresh water and food. In this period, a voyage might be as long as two to three years. Regardless of weather or day of week, whaleship crews took turns attending to the work of the vessel around the clock.

When not at work, whalers and harpooners alike lived a life of monotony, having to fend off boredom by reading, playing games, or scrimshawing. Boatsteerers would assuredly practice the art of hastily grabbing and thrusting a harpoon, as failure to procure a whale meant no whale, which meant no oil, no whalebone, no grease, no illuminates, no whalebone products. Thus, a boatsteerer played a substantially critical role not only for the whaleship but also for the broader American economy. Given the crucial nature of a harpooner, tradition situated his billet in the middle of the ship, just before that of the mates. Typically, after several successful voyages as a boatsteerer, one could be promoted to mate. Their critical role also dictated that they be paid better (often twice or three times more) than common sailors, though all crew members on a whaleship were paid in shares, or a share of the profit. An unsuccessful voyage could mean a very meager paycheck at the end of a long voyage.

As with the whaling industry in general, harpooning was an occupation of experience, meaning merit during the hunt provided promotion and job security. This meant any antebellum American male could be a boatsteerer, for race or creed mattered nothing when a person was one of six men in a tiny, wooden rowboat attempting to subdue a sixty-ton whale in the vast ocean. This is exemplified by the character of Queequeg, a heavily tattooed cannibal native of some Pacific Island in Herman Melville's *Moby Dick* (1851). John Thompson, a fugitive slave from Maryland, detailed his exploits as a harpooner in his notable autobiography, *The Life of John Thompson, A Fugitive Slave*, first published in 1856. In fact, the whaling industry proved attractive for runaway slaves as an expedition typically lasted two to three years, in other words, several years away from America, avoiding apprehension from slave catchers and the constitutional requirement for fugitive slaves to be returned. Another fugitive slave, Lewis Temple, living in New Bedford, Massachusetts (the industry's epicenter), invented the Temple toggle harpoon, an improved harpoon still in use today (as a testament to his contribution to whaling, the city erected a statue of Temple).

The development of oil drilling and kerosene during the 1850s brought an end to the once-consequential whaling industry in America and, with that, the American harpooner. Crude oil and kerosene performed every function whale oil did with the added element of being cheaper and easier to produce, never mind the seeming abundance of the natural resource. By 1860, having deprived the oceans of many whales, a whaling voyage now took up to four years. Yet for the previous half century, there is no question of the benefit whaling had on the national landscape. The boatsteerer was a critical cog in that industry as it was he who caught the whale, allowing it to be processed for its oil and bone. He risked his life to stab an animal of immense size and power so that people could read late into the evenings in their parlors, so that the Industrial Revolution could not only operate but also function late into the night, so that people could remain dry during a storm—and those are but a few of the many contributions a harpooner provided. While no longer an occupation today, before the Civil War, an entire nation relied on the singular efforts of the harpooner for the country to function.

Benjamin Van Dyk

See also: Sailor

FURTHER READING

Dolin, Eric Jay. 2007. *Leviathan: The History of Whaling in America*. New York: W. W. Norton and Co.

Moment, David. 1988. "The Business of Whaling in America in the 1850s." *The Business History Review* 31, no. 3: 264–265.

Philbrick, Nathaniel. 2000. *In the Heart of the Sea*. New York: Penguin Books.

Thompson, John. 2011. *The Life of John Thompson, a Fugitive Slave*, edited by William Andrews and Henry Louis Gates, Jr. New York: Penguin Books.

PRIMARY DOCUMENT

In 1849, seventeen-year-old Nelson Cole Haley of Maine, already a veteran of one whaling voyage, convinced his mother to allow him to again leave school to go to sea on a whaling ship. When he arrived in New Bedford, Captain John D. Sampson of the Charles W. Morgan, *bound for the Pacific whaling grounds on its second voyage, seemed to believe reports that young Nelson, barely five feet in height, could indeed handle the critical job of harpooner on the* Morgan, *even though Nelson admitted that his only experience was spearing sharks and dolphins. Nelson Cole Haley kept a journal of this nearly four-year-long voyage, one of the very few original accounts of a harpooner on a nineteenth-century American whaling ship.*

In this passage, Nelson recounts the taking of a whale in the south Atlantic Ocean as the ship sailed south, bound for the Cape of Good Hope and the Pacific by way of the Indian Ocean. Young crewmen like Haley, new to seafaring life, were commonly called "greenhands" until they had proven their worth.

Whales like cattle, which they resemble in some respect, seem to have favorite spots to feed in (and although may be seen in any parts of the oceans . . .), seem to not be at rest only when in them.

The Capt had been perched aloft in foretop-gallant crosstrees with glass in hand, for fifteen or twenty minutes, [when he] suddenly sang out, "There she blows, four points on the lee bow, mile and a half off. Clear away the boats! The whales are still, heading aft on the ship, use great care so not to sally [frighten] them."

All was bustle and excitement, every man sprang to his boat . . . As soon as the boats got away from the ship's side and oars out, the sails of each boat were set . . .

Shortly after, we could see the low bushey spouts of fifteen or twenty whales right ahead, as the whales lazily blew them out, showing to us that they had seen nothing to alarm them, little thinking four greedy little monsters were pointing straight at them armed by twenty-four stalwart men who thirsted for their oily hides.

After covering two thirds of the distance between the whales and ship, the whales went down.

The boats stopped paddling, and sailed toward the spot where last seen, stop[p] ing with the sails shaking in the wind . . .

After fifteen or twenty minutes the whales broke water, some so near us we could hear them spout, and see every motion of their massive frames that showed above water when they raised to spout. The position of our boat was such that we were on their eye, (a sperm whale can hardly be approached directly at right angles to his body, they see better that way a boat in that position is called on their eye.) The mate's boat however being farther to leeward and astern of us was directly ahead of the school and in about the middle, so he took them head on . . . [H]e had hardly set his boat under good headway when he was up to them, the boat-steerer had his first iron in his hand, ready to dart, when the whale's head had passed him enough to reach his body with the iron. (It is almost impossible to dart an iron into a whale's head.) It was but a few seconds before up went his hands grasping firmly the iron, arms extended, body bent back, one foot firmly braced against a cleat, right thigh set hard into a right circle (cut for that purpose into a two-inch pine plank fitted to each gunwale . . .), the iron was sent with force enough to drive the shank out of sight into the whale's body. Like a flash, the second iron followed the first. The whale in his pain threw his body half out of the water; with a terrific blow of his flukes he sent a volume of snowy water twenty feet into the air, then disappeared, taking the line so fast out of the boat it burnt the loggerhead and caused smoke to arise from the friction.

After sounding about half the line—say 100 fathoms—he rose to the surface, rolled, tumbled, run his head out of water, snapped his jaws together making them sound like pistols report [gunshots]. Now dropping his head under water until his tail reared aloft ten or fifteen feet, it thrashing the water into foam that would spread over half an acre on the surface. As the other whales went off without our having a chance to strike again, we turned our attention to help kill the mate's captured monster.

We soon had him fin 'out, set the signal for ship to come and take him alongside. The wind was fair so the ship soon run down and soon had him tied up by the flukes, got up cutting tackles, and commenced to cut him in. It took about four hours as everything was new to most of the men. The green hands acquited themselves well, and seemed not afraid of the whale.

Source: "Journal of the voyage of the *Charles W. Morgan,* 1849–1853." Log 145. Manuscripts Collection, G. W. Blunt Library, Mystic Seaport Museum, Inc., Mystic, 46–48. https://research.mysticseaport.org/item/l030775/.

HUCKSTER

In the antebellum period, the tumultuous environment of American cities became an ideal space for hucksters, independent entrepreneurial workers who peddled goods from carts, street corners, stalls, valises, and even from packs on their backs. Hucksters, sometimes called peddlers, had long been a feature of the American urban environment, where there were concentrations of prospective customers; beginning in the 1700s, Boston and New York passed ordinances against selling goods openly, except at certain locations, at certain times of the day, and on certain days of the week—all in an effort to stymie the hucksters.

As a general occupational classification, hucksters include any person who worked selling goods to others outside of a formal retail establishment. By the early 1800s, newspapers defined most hucksters as those who sold small goods, like bolts of calico cloth or "pins and needles," and distinguished those individuals from the "country people" who brought their farm-produced fruits, vegetables, cheeses, butter, eggs, fowl, meat, and fish to open-air public markets. Cities required public markets to install scales and calibrated them to ensure that buyers received what they had ordered and were not cheated by the seller. Increasingly, cities mandated that butchers, retailers, and "country people" obtain licenses to sell their goods.

Because they largely operated on the edges of the formal economy, hucksters were able to evade much legal regulation. They also had a reputation for being boisterous in that they often remonstrated passersby to stop and examine their goods, hawked their wares assertively, approached city residents loudly, and sometimes even followed a disinterested person and pleaded with him or her to purchase something. Moreover, hucksters often advertised marked-up goods, stale food, and broken items that they may have scavenged from refuse heaps. Hucksters had a public reputation for dishonesty. The American press referred to them in uncharitable ways: thieves, cheaters, frauds, swindlers, or disreputable individuals who could turn violent if angered. During the credit crisis of the Banking Panic of 1819–1821, newspapers derisively equated bankers, land speculators, and advocates of paper money with hucksters who had perpetrated mass fraud on ordinary Americans.

Like retailers, hucksters worked as merchants; by the 1800s, most did not own physical stores, though these boundaries were not always absolute. Some proprietors of early resale shops were called hucksters, perhaps because they sold used goods or items pilfered from others. Hucksters often congregated on the docks, where they bought firewood, fish, or other goods directly from vessels, and then walked the streets, calling out their wares to residents who could purchase the items on their own doorsteps. Locals referred to these hucksters as go-betweens, who provided consumers with convenient shopping experiences while "taxing the citizens' pockets for his officious service," according to a protest letter published in the *Washington Gazette* on August 15, 1821. Throughout the first half of the nineteenth century, the market revolution—in which production was geared toward sale rather than subsistence—and the rise of an industrializing economy offered hucksters great opportunities to peddle their wares. The "country people" who brought loads of eggs and vegetables into town to sell directly to the consumer were replaced by specialized middle men, who bought goods directly from the producer and sold to the consumer at a profit.

As the nation produced more goods, as well as a greater variety of items, hucksters increasingly offered a greater variety of novel wares. This abundance of new goods offered American consumers a kind of fantasy world where personal fulfillment was found not in work and righteous behavior but in things that gave a person a sense of uniqueness and status. As historian Jackson Lears notes, "Peddlers promised seductive enchantments to people who purchased their silks and elixirs" (Lears 1994, 38). American consumers sought novelty in their lives, and some hucksters delivered.

During the antebellum period, most hucksters simply sold consumer goods and food to customers. Some carried their goods on their person, while others invested in movable stalls, tables, or handcarts. The more successful hucksters who dealt in novelty goods bought wagons and teams of draft animals to pull them. Hucksters sold not just products but entertainment, medical care (much of it quackery), and new experiences to consumers. In the 1830s, a form of touch healing arrived in America; this practice, known as mesmerism, involved a practitioner laying hands on a patient to channel the healing power of "magnetic fluids." Enterprising hucksters claimed to be mesmerism practitioners and quickly found audiences willing to pay for these services, even though scientists at the time had debunked the theory of magnetic fluids in the human body.

Other hucksters peddled different treatments: hydropathy (drenching patients in cold water and ice), homeopathy (tinctures to cure the sick, using minute amounts of substances that induced the same symptoms in healthy people), phrenology (determining a person's character and potential by "reading" the shape of his or her skull), and other unusual methods. Hucksters also provided entertainment to American audiences—they charged admission to see shows featuring malformed and disabled people, automatons (lifelike animated machines that performed certain actions such as playing a drum), exotic species (like monkeys), and wild animals that had been trained to perform tricks. With the transition to entertainment, hucksters became hustlers—men and women on the make to earn money and who willingly duped naïve and unsuspecting customers and audiences to purchase ineffective products and patronize shows that required audiences to suspend rational belief. These were the hustlers, the "confidence men," as novelist Herman Melville entitled his fantastical 1857 novel about the devil who swindles Americans' hard-earned money.

The greatest huckster was the showman Phineas T. Barnum (1810–1891), who, in the 1830s, purchased an elderly slave woman, Joice Heth (c. 1756–1856), and took her on tour; Barnum advertised her as the nurse of a young George Washington. Audiences in New York and Boston paid to attend the exhibition. After Heth died, he continued his hoax, exhibiting Heth's teeth and fingernails and claiming that she had been 161 years of age when she passed away. Barnum later exhibited a variety of odd characters to credulous audiences: a "Feejee mermaid" borrowed from a Boston museum collection, Tom Thumb (a young boy who suffered from dwarfism), and the "Swedish nightingale" Jenny Lind (an opera singer of extraordinary talent) at his American Museum in New York City. In each case, Barnum manipulated his audiences into believing the fraud he had committed against them: Tom Thumb was not an adolescent but in fact a boy of four years old. The "Feejee mermaid" was likely a creation of an imaginative taxidermist who sewed a primate's head and torso to the tail of a large fish. Eventually, Barnum was convicted of fraud.

Barnum sold "humbug"—deception—to a willing public, who consumed it voraciously. In the process of doing so, he helped to tarnish the reputations of hucksters with that of conmen and others. By the end of the nineteenth century, the association of hucksters with swindlers and confidence men took on new, negative connotations as hucksters and peddlers in most American cities began being denounced with anti-Semitism and anti-immigrant sentiment.

Nancy Quam-Wickham

See also: *1946–1991:* Salesperson

FURTHER READING

Armstrong, David, and Elizabeth Metzger Armstrong. 1991. *The Great American Medicine Show: Being an Illustrated History of Hucksters, Healers, Health Evangelists, and Heroes from Plymouth Rock to the Present.* New York: Prentice Hall.

Barnum, P. T. 2000. *The Life of P.T. Barnum, Written by Himself.* Introduction by Terence Whalen. Urbana-Champaign: University of Illinois Press.

Lears, Jackson. 1994. *Fables of Abundance: The Cultural History of Advertising in America.* New York: Basic.

"Protest Letter." 1821. *The Washington Gazette.* August 15, 1821.

INTELLIGENCER

Intelligencers were covert operatives tasked with secretly collecting and reporting information on the movements, plans, or activities of an enemy. During the Revolutionary War (1775–1783), both the British and the colonial resistance employed intelligencers to gather information to help subvert the other side's efforts, often through grooming and leveraging loyalists who were already operating as citizens or soldiers for the other side. The information that those intelligencers provided—to both sides—was pivotal in shaping the war.

In December 1773, the Boston Tea Party sparked colonial protests and catalyzed the Revolutionary War, but the relationship between American colonists and the British government had been deteriorating since the end of the French and Indian War in 1763. Colonists protested British imposition of a variety of revenue-raising taxes on the colonies, including the Stamp Act (1765). In Massachusetts, New York, Virginia, and other colonies, groups of intellectuals and artisans formed a secret group, the Sons of Liberty, which led many of the protests and riots against the Stamp Act, eventually resulting in its repeal barely a year later. At times, Americans and British fought openly in small skirmishes, especially in colonial port cities and larger towns; these hostilities often took on the character of brawls between British troops and American colonists.

While Britain needed to raise revenue to support the thousands of British soldiers stationed in North America, colonists also had begun to see themselves increasingly not as subjects of the King but as Americans. Many families had been settled in the colonies for generations, as was the case of future president John Adams, who was a third-generation American whose father and grandfather had been born in North America. Colonists increasingly dreamed of independence. By the summer of 1774, in part as a response to increasing tensions after Britain closed Boston's port as a consequence of the Tea Party and ensuing violence, colonists had organized the First Continental Congress to bring these dreams to fruition.

War seemed inevitable to many colonists in the spring of 1775. To keep track of the other side's preparation for war—troop movements among the British, militia drills among the colonists—each side used intelligencers, now known as spies. The colonists first organized a Committee of Secret Correspondence by act of the Second Continental Congress in November 1775; the committee's purpose was to coordinate intelligence-gathering for the American revolutionary forces. It employed intelligence agents abroad, developed various codes and methods of transferring intelligence, secured the assistance of trustworthy locals to provide information to the revolutionaries, and planned covert actions. Intelligence agents communicating between American forces and their sympathizers in Bermuda successfully traded food for gunpowder in the war's first covert action in July 1775, an action that even surprised commanding general George Washington.

Most intelligencers were officers in the Continental Army or in sympathetic colonial militias. Military officers served as intelligence agents for the British. Both sides had commissioned intelligence units to collect information, deposit spies behind enemy lines, and report on troop movements. As the military conflict moved to New York in the summer of 1776 after the Second Continental Congress issued the Declaration of Independence in July, intelligence-gathering grew exponentially. Unlike Massachusetts, where most of the population supported American Independence, New York had a significant number of Loyalists among its residents. British General William Howe created Rogers Rangers, an intelligence unit whose namesake, Robert Rogers, unmasked American spy Nathan Hale on Long Island. The British subsequently executed Hale for espionage. General George Washington had organized the Knowlton Rangers, to which Hale belonged.

Hale's orders indicate some of the duties of an American intelligencer: He was to be transported across Long Island Sound from Norwalk, Connecticut, slip behind enemy lines on Long Island, proceed westward to a point near Brooklyn, and observe and document British troop movements and fortifications. To do so required that he integrate himself into local communities without raising suspicions; he was also instructed to travel about the region without being detected. Once he had made his observations, he was to draw accurate maps of fortifications and troop masses; an intelligencer or spy normally did so using special code, but Hale did not do so. He was then to report on his findings to his superiors once he was able to cross to American lines. Hale was to pose as a schoolteacher looking for work, his cover for this intelligence operation. Hale followed his orders, arrived in Brooklyn, took a boat ride across to Manhattan to survey conditions there, and then returned to Brooklyn and began making his way back to his rendezvous point.

At the time, Howe's fifteen thousand troops had arrived on Long Island from Staten Island, while the Americans under Washington were stationed on Manhattan and at Harlem Heights. Howe's forces were in the process of routing local militia and Continental Army forces as Hale collected intelligence, a fact about which he was apparently not fully aware. British intelligence officers, including Robert Rogers, had learned that Hale had been inquiring about Loyalist sympathizers, which raised suspicions. In his own act of spying, Rogers trailed Hale's movements, surmised his role, and then befriended him in a local tavern, where Hale confided his orders to Rogers, apparently after Rogers bought him several rounds of alcohol. The next day, Rogers and Hale met, purportedly for breakfast but actually for Hale's arrest.

Not all intelligence agents were as unlucky and unprepared for covert operations as Hale. George Washington's most accomplished intelligence unit was the Culper Ring, organized by senior commander Major Benjamin Tallmadge. The group gained its name from the aliases assigned to its leaders: Samuel Culper, Sr. (Abraham Woodhull) and his "son," Samuel Culper, Jr. (Robert Townsend). Established in New York in 1778, the ring provided valuable intelligence to General Washington and Major Tallmadge. While much of the work of intelligencers remains uncovered due to the demands of their surreptitious information-gathering techniques, historians have documented that the ring included both military officers and civilians, some of whom reported on British troop strength and movement of men and materiel while acting as committed Loyalists. Members used an elaborate codebook to prepare their reports and even used a special stain (a type of invisible ink) to write messages in between lines of letters; the words were uncovered with application of another chemical, causing a reaction that revealed the intelligence reports.

Some members of the ring were women, including Robert Townsend's sister Sally, a beautiful young woman who charmed several important British Army officers, who unwittingly revealed important information that she later passed on to her brother. In a departure from the methods Hale employed, ring members communicated by transferring messages by couriers, who traveled through the region undercover as businessmen or farmers. Ring courier Austin Roe, for instance, pretended to graze cattle in a field, where communications were left in a secure drop. Other informants operated boardinghouses in which British Army officers resided; these boardinghouses served as safehouses where intelligencers could stay as well, further concealing the activities of ring members who mingled easily with resident Tories. The Culper Ring even used slaves as intelligence collectors and couriers. Not even George Washington knew the identities of all of its members.

While the Culper Ring was operational between 1778 and the end of the War for Independence in 1783, other individuals acting as intelligence gatherers worked elsewhere in the colonies—the Carolinas, Philadelphia, and New Jersey. All of them contributed enormously to George Washington's efforts to obtain the strategic advantages that allowed the smaller Continental Army and its local militiamen to secure victory over the much larger and better-funded forces of Great Britain.

Nancy Quam-Wickham

See also: Militiaman; *1946–1991:* Foreign Service Officer; Spy

FURTHER READING

Daigler, Kenneth A. 2014. *Spies, Patriots, and Traitors: American Intelligence in the Revolutionary War.* Washington, DC: Georgetown University Press.

Kilmeade, Brian, and Don Yaeger. 2013. *George Washington's Secret Six: The Spy Ring That Saved the American Revolution.* New York: Sentinel.

Morgan, Edmund S. 2004. *The Genuine Article: A Historian Looks at Early America.* New York: W. W. Norton.

Phelps, M. William. 2014. *Nathan Hale: The Life and Death of America's First Spy.* Lebanon: University Press of New England.

PRIMARY DOCUMENT

This selection from a book based on the memoirs of New Yorker Enoch Crosby, an American intelligencer, or spy, details the methods that these men used to infiltrate local networks of Loyalists and uncover their activities. Throughout the first years of the Revolutionary War, New York was contested space, with General Washington's forces centered north of New York City and Long Island, while the British Army, under Lord Howe, and their Loyalist supporters generally inhabited Long Island, Staten Island, and other southern, or "lower," regions of the state. Enoch Crosby assumed the persona of a traveling shoemaker, gathering information from colonists. The Committee of Safety, to whom he reported the Loyalists that night in September 1776, was a local governmental body whose leaders included John Jay, who, after the war, became one of the greatest statesmen of the new United States.

In one of Crosby's reconnoitering excursions, the approach of the evening and some fatigue of body, reminded him that it was time to look out for comfortable quarters for the night. There was no public house of entertainment within several miles, and only a few poor farm-houses, thinly scattered, within the whole circumference of his vision. To one of these, therefor, he determined to apply, for supper and lodgings. He accordingly struck off into a footpath which led to the nearest; and, bending beneath the weight of his pack, advanced to the door, and knocked for admittance.

A rosy-cheeked girl, of about fifteen, just budding into maturity, of rustic appearance and bashful demeanour, at length appeared, with visible reluctance, to answer to his summons. On being made acquainted with his wishes, the timid maiden hesitated, stammered, and then suddenly retreating; saying, as she closed the door, "I will ask mother, sir."

In a few minutes, however, she again made her appearance, and bade him to walk in. He did not wait for a second invitation; but followed his fair conductor into an apartment that served at once the two-fold purpose of parlour and kitchen. Here he repeated his request to a middle-aged female, who sat in a corner of the capacious fire-place, very busily employed with her knitting-work.

"Lodging, did you say?" exclaimed the good woman, surveying her weary guest over the top of her spectacles. "We don't keep lodgings, sir."

"I am very much fatigued madam; and would be very grateful for permission to stay in your house till morning."

"O well, I don't know," returned the old woman, rising from her seat and approaching the stranger to examine him more particularly. "There's some strange works, now-a-days, and I don't like to keep anybody for fear of something. What, in mercy's name, is that great bag there?"

"That, Madam, is my shop. I am a shoemaker, by trade, and am in search of work, with my shop upon my back. Will you give leave to dismount it?"

"Well, I don't care if you stay long enough to make our John a pair of shoes, for he is going over east, to see some men that are going down to the army next week."

"Are they going to *our* army?" asked Crosby, as he disencumbered himself from his ponderous pack.

"I 'spose you mean the lower army; don't you, sir?"

"O, yes, madam; certainly," answered Crosby, helping himself to a chair. "I mean the royal army, a large detachment of which is now at Throg's Neck. The rebel army has run away from York Island, and is now moving toward White Plains. But How will soon overhaul them, and give a good account of them, too, or I miss my guess . . ."

As a good loyalist, Crosby was now made welcome to the best the house afforded. While he was thus refreshing himself, and chatting with his loquacious landlady, the good man of the house himself came home, to whom she eagerly introduced her guest as a warm adherent of his Majesty, and a sworn enemy to the rebels. This assertion was abundantly confirmed by the remarks of Crosby himself, during a long and interesting conversation on the subject of that wicked rebellion against the mother country . . .

[O]ur adventurer arose the next morning completely refreshed and invigorated; and, after partaking of a hearty breakfast, he accompanied his host to the residence of the tory Captain . . . Crosby was most cordially received, and politely invited to stay to dinner, and to spend the remained of the day and the coming night at the Captain's house.

This invitation was readily accepted; and, in the course of the evening, Crosby was made acquainted with many interesting particulars relative to the plans and intentions of the Captain and his confederates . . .

Night soon returned, and Crosby was still the Captain's guest. At the usual hour, he retired to his bed, where he lay, listening attentively to every movement in the house, until he felt perfectly assured that the family were safely locked in the arms of sleep. When "every sound was hushed, and all was still," he cautiously arose, dressed himself, and stole out of the house without giving any alarm. Before midnight he was consulting with his employers at White Plains.

Such arrangements were immediately adopted by the Committee of Safety as were considered, by all parties, appropriate to the emergency. Their informant then took his leave; and, before daylight, was again snoring in his bed, at the house of the loyal Captain.

Source: H. L. Barnum. 1828 (1886). *Enoch Crosby, or the Spy Unmasked.* New York: J. & J. Harper, 41–43, passim.

INVENTOR

In early America, inventors were people who invented a particular device or process or who made a living by inventing things. They were often known as tinkerers—primarily men who tinkered in their workshops, day in and day out, engineering solutions to practical problems that perplexed early Americans. Their work propelled the British colonies down the path of industrialization, even before the revolutionary period. Benjamin Franklin (1705–1790), statesman, printer, and writer, and perhaps America's most well-known inventor of the time, began his tinkering when he was still a young man but never sought a patent for his inventions. As the new nation organized its government, though, inventors looked to capitalize on their tinkering by securing patents for the things they created. A patent allowed an inventor to license the invention in order to generate income from those who utilized it. Among the first inventions in the early United States were Samuel Mullikan's machines for threshing corn and grain, a pile-driving machine patented in 1791 by Massachusetts inventor John Stone, and Philadelphian John Fitch's steamboat, patented the same year. While tinkerers, mechanics, and artisans had, for millennia, created new processes and machines for doing things, the founding of the United States made inventions something that could be registered nationally, or patented, by action of Congress and, after 1836, the U.S. Patent Office.

Some of America's most famed inventors were gentlemen of the revolutionary era, like Benjamin Franklin and Thomas Jefferson. One of the most prolific inventors in early America, Franklin is recognized for creating bifocals, the lightning rod, and the Franklin stove (which produced less smoke than ordinary brick fireplaces). Jefferson perfected the swivel chair and invented a new mechanism for a plow that made it easier for farmers to break and till soil. These gentleman inventors had the financial means to own tool-filled workshops, to which they could retire during the day to work on innovative projects. Other American inventors were simply workers trying to make labor-saving improvements to processes and machines they used on a daily basis, like the farmer George Stroud, who complained to Congress that he, not the prominent inventor Oliver Evans, had invented the first mechanical grain elevator that used buckets and a long circular leather belt to move grain from ships to shore. Gunsmiths, blacksmiths, and farmers often tinkered, developing new mechanical ways to improve efficiency. Other inventors created innovative machines when encountering vexing issues but would not be considered inveterate tinkerers. Eli Whitney, for instance, was a Yale-educated young man who had traveled to the South to take a position as a private teacher for a planter's children but had worked to create a machine that could separate cotton from its boll and seeds, the cotton gin, which he then patented. His employer had encouraged Whitney's efforts.

Those individuals who worked as inventors were often artisans who used scientific knowledge and engineering talents to create new machines. Oliver Evans had been a wheelwright's apprentice, but as he testified to Congress, he had been fascinated by the actions of fellow apprentices who made "Christmas crackers," in which some "blacksmith's boys [apprentices] in their sport . . . put water into the breech of a musket barrel, rammed down a wad tight, stop the touch hole, and place the breech in the fire," creating a loud bang. Watching his fellow apprentices play, Evans "discovered that great fundamental principle in nature, the increase of the elasticity of steam . . . [which] could be applied to work very light and powerful engines, to propel land carriages and boats" (Evans 1817, 4). Evans and his brothers later worked in a shop, designing innovative machinery on contract for manufacturers.

Evans described his work process: First, he obtained preliminary financing and a building contract, often for construction of a major work like that of a large flour mill. Then he studied all of the labor processes of the constituent trades; in the case of the Delaware flour mill, he "being neither millwright nor miller . . . had first to ascertain what operations were to be performed by manual labor." He then designed a way to reduce those labor requirements by using water power to turn giant millstones. Like many inventors, Evans described much of his work as imagining or conceiving of more efficient ways to accomplish certain tasks.

Evans described his labor as decidedly intellectual work, animated by an unshakable belief that he could achieve his goals—a way of thinking that he referred to as "a zeal and indefatigability peculiar only to *inventors*" (Evans 1817, 5). Once he determined he had invented a new machine, he constructed a model to test it. Once he had perfected the working model, he created detailed drawings illustrating his plans for the construction of an innovative machine and went about recruiting investors for his elaborate projects.

Like Evans, the New York inventor Christopher Colles was also a dreamer, one who imagined a great interconnected transportation network in the United States, a man whose "mind was teeming with plans of western canals, steam-boats, rail-roads, and other public enterprises" (Verplanck, quoted in Popper 2005, 178). Colles had designed a freshwater reservoir system and underground plumbing to provide for New York City's drinking water needs in the 1770s but, like many ambitious inventors, did not ever find sufficient private capital to finance it or some of his other greatest projects, including a system of canals that connected Albany with Oswego, New York. Author of the first U.S. road atlas, Colles didn't even find sufficient funding to support that important venture, despite congressional encouragement. In 1791, Colles obtained a patent for a new process for manufacturing bricks.

A crucial element of an inventor's work was obtaining the support of influential politicians. Those who failed to raise capital for their inventions may have held patents for their work, but they did not labor exclusively as inventors. Like Evans and Colles, inventor John Fitch, a clockmaker by training, also struggled to excite patrons to invest in his plans to build steamboats to ply the waters of the Mississippi River, but George Washington instead supported the plans of inventor James Rumsey to build a network of canals in the Potomac Valley, including a patent Rumsey shared with his rival, Fitch, for an improved steamboat. Like Colles, Fitch worked as a surveyor; he also owned his own workshop, where he worked as a gunsmith and silversmith, and made maps of the western frontier—all while his working steamboat, aptly named the *Perseverance*, operated on the Delaware River.

Inventors in the early United States gained notoriety as industrious artisans, continually reimagining ways to improve upon machinery and processes in ways that prefigured the industrial growth of the young nation in subsequent decades. Artisans in metal shops across New England and the mid-Atlantic states developed new processes to mechanize butter churning, mill flour, run sawmills, grind tanners' bark, cut nails, and roll iron rods. As patriotic artisans, these inventors saw themselves as representatives of the Jeffersonian ideal of a nation of farmers and artisan-entrepreneurs, yet they also confronted restrictions on their ambitions as they unsuccessfully sought the patronage of powerful politicians with access to the capital necessary to bring their plans to reality. Independent artisans and engineering geniuses, in the words of historian Laura Rigal, these inventors experienced firsthand the "shifting social hierarchy where class difference was slowly and often painfully emerging" (Rigal 1998, 185).

Nancy Quam-Wickham

See also: *1607–1775:* Blacksmith; *1946–1991:* Artist; Scientist; *1992–2019:* Machinist

FURTHER READING

Cowan, Ruth Schwartz. 1997. *A Social History of American Technology.* London: Oxford University Press.

Evans, Oliver. 1817. *Oliver Evans to His Counsel, who are engaged in the defense of his patent rights for the improvements he has invented: Containing a short account of two out of eighty of his inventions, their rise and progress in despite of all opposition and difficulties.* Early American Imprints, Series 2, no. 40778 (microfilmed).

Popper, Deborah Epstein. 2005. "Poor Christopher Colles: An Innovator's Obstacles in Early America." *Journal of American Culture* 28: 178–190.

Rigal, Laura. 1998. *The American Manufactory: Art, Labor, and the World of Things in the Early Republic.* Princeton: Princeton University Press.

JOINER

A joiner is a person who constructs the wooden components of a building, such as doors and doorframes, window frames, and stairs. Like carpenters, joiners were essential American artisans and tradesmen during British colonial rule and during the years between the Revolutionary War (1775–1783) and the Civil War (1861–1865). Joiners were specialists in connecting wood at any angle in all kinds of structures; they also worked with cabinetmakers and other artisans who made fine goods for furnishing interiors. Joiners often worked alongside carpenters, helping to join together two or more pieces of lumber to create a solid and secure joint. During the colonial and revolutionary periods, joiners were sometimes also called "rough carpenters," cabinetmakers, or housewrights. Like other artisans, most joiners learned their trade through apprenticeships. Once an apprentice joiner completed his (joiners at this time were exclusively male) apprenticeship, he often set out on his own to work, unencumbered by ties to his former master. Before the revolution, many apprentice joiners were indentured servants, but as Americans moved westward and into the upland areas of the South, many entrepreneurs followed the building boom by becoming joiners who worked as independent contractors.

As specialists in the construction of wooden frames for structures and other kinds of items, joiners had to be knowledgeable about the properties of a variety of woods and the kinds of tools needed to work them. Joiners had to have a good understanding of geometry and mechanics as early houses and cabins were often erected without the use of nails or bolts. Joiners finished rough lumber, shaving it down with a tool known as a plane until the lumber was smooth, true, and square; then he cut the mortise and tenon so that the boards could be fitted together, often at a ninety-degree angle. The tongue-like tenon was cut into the end of one board, while the mortise was cut into the other board where the angled joint was to be created. The tenon was then assembled into the matching mortise, creating the joint. Each joint consisted of a pair of boards with matching tenon and mortise. The joiner used a square—a tool that measured ninety-degree angles—though most early houses had few truly perfectly squared joints. Then, using a hand drill, joiners drilled a hole through the joint and hammered in a wooden fastener to act much like a nail. In houses and cabins, these fasteners were called trunnels, and a joiner's apprentice cut them from trees. In furniture and other fine work, joiners used finished dowels to secure the connection. In well-built furniture, only the angles and corners of the item distinguished a joiner's work as the fit of the pieces were so tight as to be indistinguishable.

The beginnings of industrialization and the use of machines changed the work of the joiner. Throughout the eighteenth century, Americans increasingly favored sash window frames, which is a two-part frame that holds the top half of the window's glass stationary while the bottom half can be raised and lowered to open or close a room to the outside air. Prior to the advent of the sash window design, windows generally were smaller and opened outward on hinges.

A new kind of joint, the dovetail joint, also changed joiners' work as it required less lumber than a mortise and tenon joint; the dovetail joint was such that it worked much like interlocking fingers, with "pins" on one end of a board interlocking with tails on the end of another board. The joint was then glued, eliminating the need to drill holes for trunnels or dowels. A dovetailed joint is very strong. Jigs on foot- or water-powered saws could cut multiple pins and tails in a board at once. By the middle of the nineteenth century, many joiners lost their artisanal status, instead laboring in shops, creating machined dovetail joints for furniture and mortise and tenon joints for sash windows.

Machines drove the changes in joiners' work. Even as early as the late 1810s, Boston manufactories advertised "various kinds of machinery and mechanical work" that could be used "in turning of metals and wood, screw cutting, pattern making, joiner work" to create what consumers needed "in short order" (*Boston Patriot and Daily Chronicle*, June 10, 1819). Air-driven lathes replaced older lathes that joiners powered by foot, speeding up the process of turning spindles for furniture and balusters for stairways. Enterprising joiners with access to capital opened shops across the eastern seaboard, where they installed machinery that made a joiner's carefully handcrafted joints costly and unnecessary. Throughout the 1820s and 1830s, joiners worked raising houses on the frontier, in the countryside, and elsewhere but in urban areas tended to move into working not for themselves but for others in shops and primitive factories, running machinery and assembling factory-made furniture like chests and tables.

Boxes of balusters, sets of window frames, and other items formerly crafted by the joiner's hand were shipped to carpenters, who simply installed them in the new houses, many of them created in the new balloon-frame method. Balloon-framed houses were built using multiple studs to create a framework on which the exterior and interior could be set; thus, carpenters and their helpers could construct a balloon-framed house by themselves. Older architectural methods required joiners to create a heavy timbered frame that was assembled using joinery techniques. Balloon-frame houses were cheaper and faster to build; they were especially popular on the frontier, where the traditional rectangular farmhouse was built using these techniques.

While some joiners continued advertising their services in local newspapers, taking care to note that they were trained in recent architectural skills, many others found work as ships' carpenters on America's burgeoning merchant and whaling fleets. In the age of sail, every ship carried a "carpenter" (often a joiner) who could shape masts from large trees and then step (anchor) them to the ship. Some ship carpenters were joiners who also had skills in coopering. On ships, joiners could practice their craft using handheld tools—planes, adzes, saws—to shape the masts and spars. Joiners who went to sea traveled the world, though they also succumbed to illnesses like consumption (tuberculosis) and accidents at sea.

On the eve of the Civil War, joiners were less likely to be specialists than they had been during the colonial era. Instead, they worked as machine operators, carpenters, coopers, ships' carpenters—all of whom worked with wood to make the buildings, furniture, masts, and other goods needed to build America.

Nancy Quam-Wickham

See also: *1607–1775:* Cabinetmaker; *1915–1945:* Glazier; *1946–1991:* Architect

FURTHER READING

American Technical Society. 1917. *Cyclopedia of Architecture, Carpentry and Building: A General Reference Work on Architecture, Carpentry, Building*. Chicago: American Technical Society.

Fitzgerald, Oscar P. 1995. *Four Centuries of American Furniture*. Radnor: Wallace-Homestead Book Co.

Howard, Thomas Osbert, and Frederick Oughton. 1975. *Joinery*. London: Hodder & Stoughton.

JOURNALIST

Newspapers and printing played an important role in the early history of the United States. Early newspapers were often written, edited, and printed by the same person. However, early in the nineteenth century, these jobs began to diverge, and the professional journalist, a writer for a newspaper, magazine, or other publication, became an increasingly important job in the United States.

In 1810, the venerable printer Isaiah Thomas of Massachusetts published *The History of Printing in America, and an account of newspapers*, a "concise view" of the relationship among printers, newspapers, and the press in America. Thomas detailed the history of every newspaper of note published in the colonies and, subsequently, in the United States. Unsurprisingly, he wrote approvingly of his own newspaper, the *Massachusetts Spy*, a publication that supported the Patriots during the revolutionary period, and of the *Pennsylvania Gazette*, a newspaper that Benjamin Franklin once printed, which was, at that time, the oldest newspaper in the nation.

While the newspapers of the colonial period featured patriotic verse, editorials, and local and international news (as well as plentiful advertising), the printers and editors were often one and the same—as well as being the primary writers, or journalists, for their newspapers. Many early newspapers sought to present all sides of a political controversy. Most early newspapers were only a page or two, often printed on half sheets or, during the revolution, as large handbills. After the Revolutionary War (1775–1783), however, the roles of printers (or publishers), editors, and journalists became more distinct. The freedom of the press, as enshrined in the Bill of Rights, is critical to understanding the central role of newspapers in both reporting on and shaping political beliefs in the United States. After the War of 1812 (1812–1815), as Americans chose sides along political and sectional lines, newspapers began to publish articles written by professional writers (journalists), who not only reported on the news of the day but also penned editorials that captured subscribers' interests. The new newspapers of the Jacksonian period were liberated from the political party ties that had characterized earlier versions of the American newspaper.

Unlike their predecessors, the printer-editors, the emergence of the role of journalist in the 1820s and afterward was made possible by several factors, as media historian Christopher Daly notes: steam-powered printing presses that made it possible to print thousands of copies of newspapers a day, significant urban growth that provided a ready market for news consumers, and declining prices of paper, particularly cheap paper. In 1833, the publisher Benjamin Day began to produce the *New York Sun*, a daily—rather than weekly—newspaper that cost just a penny (rather than the usual six cents per copy). To produce a daily paper, Day hired writers who could fill it with business and political doings as well as local "interest" news, like lurid crime stories or tales of fallen women (Daly 2011, 59–60). Writers for the *Sun* were dispatched to local courtrooms, police precinct houses, and even the morgue to find stories that would sell Day's newspapers.

Once a journalist gathered information, he returned to the newspaper office to write the story. Day's formula for producing news that readers wanted spread quickly throughout the newspaper world. Within a year, journalists at the Boston *Morning Post* produced their own local version of the seedy New York Police Court proceedings, as this article from May 8, 1834, crafted in the style of the *Sun*, shows: "Mistress *Lydia Simpson*, an elderly, wind-dried, jaundiced-looking woman—with a 'disposition like a cross-cut saw,' but blessed with a peculiarly sanctimonious, camp-meeting twang of voice—ascended the stand to swear that her 'own darter *Abigail*, and her fellow *Ephraim,* warn't conducting credible, in the face of heaven and arth, and they had broken her doors in and threatened her life . . .'" (*Boston Morning Post* 1834). The journalist who crafted this unflattering report went on to note that the case was dismissed after mother and daughter traded accusations that each had been a prostitute and from Abigail that her mother had stolen her grandchild's gown to pawn for a bottle of gin. Readers in impersonal antebellum cities full of strangers gobbled up these kinds of local interest articles.

Day's competitors soon hired reporters to gather information and write about not just local but also national and international news. James Bennett's *New York Herald* went beyond the local interest stories of the *Sun* and its imitators as he hired journalists to write about business and financial issues (and he himself wrote a column about Wall Street, "Money Matters"), as well as paying writers to file stories about national issues, drawn in part from observations of Congress and the courts. Both Day and Bennett, though, still tended toward publishing sensational stories about the "news of the day," or items of intense local interest, like the murder of New York prostitute Helen Jewett in 1836. Both also claimed independence from political parties; these were not the printer-editor-journalist publications of the past, when a newspaper was clearly partisan (Daly 2011, 62). These new daily newspapers, the "penny press," certainly featured articles about politics, but they were not simply an arm of one or another political party.

In the 1840s, the invention of the telegraph further markedly changed the daily work of the journalist. A writer could gather news of events and issues that happened at great distance without having to personally attend the event. Writers could send a telegraph message to a newspaper, but given the pricing structure of the service, journalists learned to write concisely, offering a brief summary of the event or issue in the first paragraph, which became known as the lede. So critical was the telegraph to immediately reporting on news stories that the newspapers proved to be the biggest investors in Samuel Morse's new company, leading eventually to the formation of a shared news organization, the Associated Press, for which journalists produced articles that were then shared, and later sold, to various national and regional newspapers (Daly 2011, 77–78).

While colonial and early national period newspapers were often aligned with political factions and the "news" published in them was often simply repurposed and previously published items of interest, the newer newspapers helped to create the occupation of journalist, whose daily responsibilities included gathering information and writing stories for readers' consumption. The business of operating a newspaper that printed thousands of copies daily, rather than a few hundred copies per week, required editors and publishers to hire journalists to find newsworthy stories.

Nancy Quam-Wickham

See also: Pamphleteer; Printer; *1946–1991:* Broadcast Journalist

FURTHER READING

Boston Morning Post. 1834. "Police Court." May 8.

Daly, Christopher B. 2011. *Covering America: A Narrative History of a Nation's Journalism*. Amherst: Massachusetts University Press.

Henkin, David. 1998. *City Reading: Written Words and Public Spaces in Antebellum New York*. New York: Columbia University Press.

Payne, George Henry. 2011. *History of Journalism in the United States*. Breinigsville: Nabu Press.

JUDGE

The US Constitution had three primary functions: First, it established a federalist system of government with one central government (federal) and multiple smaller, regional governments (state). Second, it helped impose limitations on the powers that federal and state governments were allowed to exercise. Third, it created the three branches of the federal government: legislature, executive, and judiciary. The judiciary was composed of judges, whose main roles were to interpret and apply the laws written by the legislative and executive branches in accordance with the individual sets of facts and circumstances presented by the cases that went before them. When a dispute about the law arose or when an individual or group was accused of breaking a law, judges were the people who ultimately decided how the law should be applied and whether the accused had broken it.

While the Constitution only determined the composition of the federal government, the state governments ultimately adopted the same basic structure, comprised of the three branches. In both the federal government and the state governments, the legislative and executive branches were the primary lawmakers, while judges were the primary interpreters of the law. By necessity, most laws were written vaguely to account for all of the situations that might arise under that particular law's jurisdiction. Due to the ambiguity of laws, judges were essential for studying, analyzing, and interpreting them to make sure that the laws were being applied justly. Analyzing and interpreting the law was hard work, and it came with big consequences—not only did a decision about how the law should be applied affect the individuals personally involved in the case, but it also had the potential to set precedent. In the American legal system, precedent is when an earlier decision is considering to be binding. If a decision is binding, it means that the decision and legal interpretation used in the case must be used in all other subsequent legal disputes except for the most extreme cases. With the concepts of binding decisions and precedents, the framers of the Constitution wanted to ensure that judges did not make laws themselves; the separation of powers was maintained.

Much like today, at the founding of the United States, all judges were required to have extensive legal training. Many judges had been lawyers before becoming judges, which meant that they had practiced law and were familiar with many of the subject matters before presiding over cases. At the time, lawyers generally learned the law not through formal university training but individual study and a kind of professional apprenticeship to practicing lawyers. In the federal government, judges had to be appointed by elected government officials. While most states also opted for the appointment of judges by government official, some states, such as Georgia in 1812, wrote or rewrote their constitutions to allow for judges to be elected by popular vote.

Except for the subject matter of the laws that they studied, the day-to-day lives of federal and state judges were largely the same. However, their daily tasks varied drastically based on what level of court an individual judge worked in. The federal government and most state governments at the time had three levels of courts: supreme courts, courts of appeals, and trial courts. Trial courts were the first courts where a legal dispute would be examined. The judges who worked in these were fact-finders, which means that they were the ones who would, after both sides presented evidence and argued their cases, ultimately determine what had really happened and whether the accused party had broken a law. They presided over trials, listened to witness testimony, and made initial decisions in pretrial hearings, which shaped how the parties could introduce evidence during trials. Trial judges were also responsible for presiding over settlements for cases, which meant that the parties came to an agreement instead of participating in a formal trial, and for deciding what punishment to hand down to criminal defendants who had been convicted during the trial. In some cases, especially at the local and state levels, juries might decide on a defendant's culpability or a civil case remedy, but, ultimately, judges managed the courtroom proceedings even when juries were empaneled.

Unlike trial judges, judges who worked in courts of appeals did not preside over trials or listen to witness testimony. Instead, court of appeals judges were typically more senior than their trial judge counterparts and only reviewed decisions that trial judges had made. While trial judges were fact-finders, court of appeals judges mainly ensured that trial judges had made the correct decisions. Court of appeals judges were not allowed to examine new evidence that had not been introduced in the trial court and instead only evaluated choices and interpretations of laws that had been decided by trial judges. Court of appeals judges also worked in panels, or groups of multiple judges, unlike trial judges, who worked on their own. If a panel of court of appeals judges decided by a majority vote that the trial judge had wrongly decided something in the case, they could overturn the ruling and send the case back to the trial judge with guidance about how the error should be corrected.

The supreme courts, like the courts of appeals, were also appellate courts, which meant that the judges who worked there were responsible for reviewing decisions made by judges who worked in a court that was lower in the judicial hierarchy. These judges were typically the most qualified and had the most expertise. They were the ones who had the final decision in the outcome of a case. The Supreme Court of the United States, a federal court that decides issues of federal and constitutional law, was established in Article 3 of the Constitution in 1789. While today the Supreme Court is well-known for being composed of nine justices in Washington, D.C., the Supreme Court in 1790 looked much different. Then, there were only six justices, and the court was required to travel to each judicial circuit—three in total—to decide cases. The Supreme Court in 1790 also held more limited power than it does today. Rather, much of the Supreme Court's power was determined during John Marshall's tenure as Chief Justice, which began in 1801. In 1803, he wrote the majority opinion in *Marbury v. Madison*, an important case that scholars typically cite as the landmark that began to shape the court into the institution that it is today.

There remain many disagreements among both experts and laypeople regarding the proper role of judges and how they should exercise their power. Everything from how judges become judges to what methods they should use to decide cases is up for dispute. For example, John Jay (1745–1829), the first Chief Justice of the U.S. Supreme Court between 1789 and 1795, urged juries to weigh the law alongside the facts when deciding cases—ostensibly advocating for the law's ability to evolve through failures of application or the presentation of cases where the facts show the law in question to be inadequate or unjust (Abramson 2003). Oliver Ellsworth (1745–1807), the third U.S. Supreme Court Justice, voted for the Three-Fifths Compromise, which established each slave as "worth" three-fifths of a non-slave for the purpose of calculating congressional representation, because he saw it as a necessary, albeit distasteful, stepping stone to abolition (Solberg 1958). Judges' difficult decisions and challenging positions like these are some of the forces that continue to shape the law—and the role of judges—in American society.

Rosalia Quam-Wickham

See also: *1776–1860:* Politician; *1946–1991:* Attorney

FURTHER READING

Abramson, Jeffrey B. 2003. *We, the Jury: The Jury System and the Ideal of Democracy*. Cambridge: Harvard University Press.

Barkson, Larry C., Rachel Caufield, and Malia Reddick. n.d. *Judicial Selection in the United States: A Special Report*. American Judicature Society. http://judicialselection.us/uploads/documents/Berkson_1196091951709.pdf

Federal Reports, Inc. 1997. *The ALJ Handbook: An Insider's Guide to Becoming a Federal Administrative Law Judge*. Washington, DC: Federal Reports.

Solberg, Winton U., and James Madison. 1958. *The Federal Convention and the Formation of the Union of the American States*. New York: Liberal Arts Press.

LABORER

In the antebellum years, laborers were unskilled common workers, or hands, who did much of the heavy work in the rapidly expanding United States. Laborers built roads, dug ditches and canals, created railroad beds and laid tracks, cleared land, constructed tunnels, and built the transportation and, in some cases, urban infrastructures of the country, projects that were known as public works. These workers had not been displaced from the artisanal workshops of the colonial period, nor were they generally indentured servants, as had been the case with white common laborers before the revolution. Instead, historian Peter Way noted the men, women, and children who worked as common laborers were "more fully exploited, worse off economically, socially fragmented, and, as a result, with a culture (or, more accurately, cultures) that reflected their alienation as much as a sense of community" (Way 1993, 6). In general, laborers were the "rough," not "respectable," members of an emerging American industrial working class. They found work when and where they could get it, often as itinerant workers who traveled from job site to job site. Contractors hired laborers for their brawn and stamina, not their brains.

In the South, slaves performed most of this work, and slave owners hired out their slaves, profiting from their labors.

In the years after the War of 1812 (1812–1815), states resumed an aggressive period of canal building and construction of other public works, which coincided with improvements to Fulton's steamboats and to changes in river navigation. Canals linked bodies of water to ease transport of goods and people; New York's Erie Canal (1825), for instance, linked the Hudson River (near Albany) to Lake Erie (near Buffalo) in an artificial inland waterway that stretched over 350 miles. Similarly, the Chesapeake and Ohio Canals (1831) connected the Potomac River near nation's capital to the Allegheny mountain town of Cumberland, Maryland. Canals also facilitated the movement of Americans into the West. Canal building provided common laborers with work digging the ditches and building dams and locks, docks, and loading facilities at their junctures and terminuses.

The process of creating a cut (canal channel) was complex: After the engineers determined the location, laborers cleared the land of trees and other vegetation. Workers dug by hand or, in rock, used black powder explosives to blast through the earth to create a rough channel, and then laborers used shovels and wheelbarrows to extract the loosened debris from the cut. Some workers tended to horses that powered drill bits, boring into rock, or worked as team drivers, leading mules that drew cartload after cartload of debris out of the cut, and some operated the rudimentary cranes that lifted large boulders during excavation. Other laborers built scaffolding, shored up the canal's sides, or created the embankments lining the sides of the cut. They used pickaxes, saws, hammers, shovels, carts, and wheelbarrows.

Most public works projects employed workforces of between a few hundred and several thousand laborers. Most common laborers on large public works projects like building canals, roads, or railroads worked outside, in rain or sun, and were exposed to snakes, mosquitos, and other insects and wildlife. On some canals, work in the cut was mostly dry, but in others, such as the drainage cuts in New Orleans, the projects traversed swampy lands where laborers worked constantly in mud. Large construction projects in the northern states usually shut down only during the hard winter snows, though some projects continued despite the adverse weather. Laborers worked from dawn to dusk, sometimes more than fourteen hours per day, depending on the location and season. The work was hard, dirty, relentless, and often unsafe as, in this period, governments paid contractors by the excavated ton; contractors increased workers' pace to maximize their own payments even while they did not raise wages. Workers who could not keep up due to illness, age, injury, or other reasons were discharged. Those injured on the job—from falling debris or premature blasting—might successfully argue for a small pension from the canal construction company. Others died of injuries, some in catastrophic accidents like that on the Oswego Canal near Syracuse in August 1841: More than thirty workers and local residents were killed and many more injured when a fire spread from a carpenter's shop to the building in which the canal's black powder was stored. The explosion left body parts in fragments scattered across the landscape.

Throughout this period, laborers increasingly resisted managerial attempts to speed up the work pace. In autumn 1829, a group of English immigrants claimed that they had not agreed to work as common laborers in exchange for their passage across the Atlantic and refused to go to work on the Chesapeake and Ohio Canal; they were imprisoned. Sparked in part by concerns about nonpayment of wages, in January 1834, gangs of one thousand canal laborers rioted in Maryland, leading the federal government and the state militia to send in troops to quell the disturbances. After the Panic of 1837 led to declining investments in public works, a prolonged economic depression led to more strikes and riots in the late 1830s and early 1840s. On Indiana's Wabash and Erie Canal, contractors paid workers in scrip that devalued rapidly, to the point that some laborers were earning the equivalent of just three dollars monthly, a 70 to 80 percent decrease in wages.

Adding to these difficult work environments were the living conditions most laborers experienced on these massive construction projects. Work sites were often located in isolated areas away from workers' homes. Many contractors often preferred young, single men whom they housed in barracks with dozens of other men. These workers seldom had more than a hard plank for a bunk and ate meager meals provided by the contractor's cooks, some of whom might be the wives or daughters of laborers. On other work sites, workers themselves hastily built huts and cabins made of materials they scavenged. These temporary, worker-built camps were called shantytowns for their impermanence and rough conditions.

Shantytowns also arose outside of contractors' barracks as some men traveled with wives and children. The shantytowns also had cafés, laundresses, bars, gambling houses, prostitutes, music halls, and other services that young laborers sought out. On sites like rail bed construction areas, where the work progressed quickly, tent cities replaced wooden shantytowns, and camp followers (professional gamblers, prostitutes, liquor dealers) moved along with the tent cities—giving rail camps a particularly disreputable reputation as "hells on wheels." Additionally, the close living quarters and poor living conditions in shantytowns led to disease, as was the case among canal laborers in New Jersey in 1832 during a nationwide cholera epidemic, when cholera and other diseases spread rapidly because of filthy working conditions and the great numbers of workers crowded together.

The country's early and mid-nineteenth-century common laborers' workforce was mostly made up of slaves and immigrants. Among immigrants, the Irish predominated, with some Germans doing the work as well. Native-born white

Americans viewed the Irish with disdain: not only were most Catholic, unskilled, and illiterate, but, at the time, the Irish were not even considered "white." The public works projects of these years brought Irish common laborers to this country, even before the famine of the late 1840s. The harsh working and living conditions on these projects only reinforced American attitudes about the Irish as rough and unsophisticated.

Nancy Quam-Wickham

See also: Factory Operative; Ginner; Gold Miner

FURTHER READING

Stone, William L., George W. Clinton, and Frank H. Severance. 1910. *The Holland Land Co., and Canal Construction, in Western New York: Buffalo-Black Rock Harbor Papers, Journals and Documents.* Buffalo: Buffalo Historical Society.

Tower, Elizabeth A. 1999. *Anchorage: From Its Humble Origins As a Railroad Construction Camp.* Fairbanks: Epicenter Press.

Way, Peter. 1993. *Common Labour: Workers and the Digging of North American Canals, 1780–1860.* Cambridge, UK: Cambridge University Press.

LAND SPECULATOR

Land speculators were surveyors who employed their expert knowledge to seek out, describe, mark, map, and then claim high-quality tracts of land with the intention of selling them at a high price to settlers and fellow speculators. Land speculation accompanied the conquest of Native American land from the earliest times of European settlement in North America. In the thirteen British Colonies and in the United States, market forces, not ancient laws and the whims of kings and nobles, determined land acquisition. In America, land was a commodity that could freely be purchased and sold.

In colonial times, land speculation had been the realm of extremely well-to-do colonists who formed large joint-stock companies and petitioned colonial legislatures to grant them huge tracts of land, which they intended to sell to groups of settlers. These companies were largely unsuccessful, especially because British authorities tried to curb settlement in the American West.

The American Revolution democratized and individualized land speculation, and from then on, land speculators came in many shapes and forms. There were petty speculators on the peripheries of Euro American settlement who purchased a few hundred acres, sometimes with the intention of using part of it for their own farms, subsequently selling the remainder to fellow settlers. Yet those speculators who became most infamous in American history were the so-called absentee land speculators: rich men from the East Coast, who disposed of the funds necessary to purchase land amounting to tens of thousands of acres in the American West.

Absentee speculators gained the wrath of their contemporaries. Their business behavior seemed to stand in complete contradiction to the Puritan work ethic and the American agrarian myth. Many of them had never even traveled to the American West—they purchased land they had never seen. Not intending to settle or improve his land, the absentee speculator's sole aim was to hold on to it until he could sell it for a maximum return on his initial investment. Americans in the late eighteenth and early nineteenth centuries believed these men were slothful gamblers who inflated land prices at the expense of the single-family farmer, who tilled the land with his own hands and gained his subsistence through hard work.

Even with a more objective and less critical view, land speculation can hardly be defined as an occupation in the narrow sense of the term. Absentee land speculators were usually traders and planters from the East who speculated in land to diversify their businesses. For example, one speculator from Richmond, Virginia, who owned more than thirty-five thousand acres of land in Ohio in the early nineteenth century, also traded in tobacco as well as owning three plantations in Goochland and Henrico Counties, a coal pit operated by one hundred slaves, and a freestone quarry whose stone had been used to build Virginia's State Capitol. To such rich gentlemen, undeveloped land in the American West was simply another asset in their portfolio of investments. As a congressman from South Carolina pointed out in session on February 19, 1796, "I consider land as fair an object of speculation as coffee or any other article of commerce."

Absentee land speculators typically ran their business from their homes. Their main concern was to find the right time to purchase and sell. Thus, gathering information that could affect land prices was extremely important to them. Newspapers were a significant source of information, but probably more important was word-of-mouth news. Absentee land speculators were well-connected in East Coast society: they frequently talked to other traders or planters and exchanged information on land quality and prices. Rumors about, for example, land sales at a high price spread quickly, and it was the speculator's task to evaluate this information and act accordingly.

Handling correspondence was another main task of absentee land speculators. They wrote to land holders or fellow speculators to affect land purchase or sales, sometimes assisted by clerks who kept their accounts, sorted their letters, and copied outgoing mail into letter books. Speculators' most important correspondents were agents who handled their land business in the West—men who had expert knowledge of the land, regularly frequented the land offices, paid the speculators' taxes, and purchased and sold land on their accounts. Sometimes, these agents were land surveyors, who were typically paid for their services with a share of the speculators' land.

Land speculation in North America often occurred in boom-and-bust cycles. One such cycle happened shortly after the American Revolution, in the 1780s and 1790s; after the end of the Revolutionary War, settlers rushed to the rich lands west of the Appalachian Mountains. At that time, many American traders had reestablished their ties with Great Britain. Trade was strong, and many traders and planters sought ways to invest their surplus capital. Western land, Americans in the late eighteenth century believed, was the most promising property in the country.

Since many people purchased during these boom times, prices inflated quickly, fueling the speculators' assumption that enormous profits could be realized. However, these boom times were often followed by busts that were related to larger economic issues. The 1790s boom, for example, came to an abrupt halt as early as 1797, when British traders tried to collect outstanding debts from their American partners because of a cash shortage originating in bank closures in England. In the United States, a panic quickly erupted as everybody was looking to turn assets into cash to pay debts, but buyers could not be found. Land prices fell, and land speculators either had to sell at a great discount and on credit or were stuck with their property for long periods of time. The speculator from Richmond, for example, complained as late as 1809 that he had unsuccessfully tried to turn his Ohio lands into "active capital"—or cash—for ten years.

A key problem for land speculators was that, with the exception of gold and silver, there existed in the early nineteenth century no reliable medium of exchange in the United States that connected the East Coast and the West. When the Panic of 1797 struck, many speculators tried, with the aid of their frontier agents, to sell their land in small parcels to actual settlers rather than *en bloc* (in one large collection) to fellow speculators or investors on the East Coast, as they had originally intended. Many settlers were willing to buy, but they usually lacked cash and purchased on credit. It was difficult for absentee speculators and their frontier agents to collect these debts as farmers in the West lived in barter trade economies and generated little cash income from their farming activities. The Appalachian Mountains divided the East Coast and the West, and farmers in states where slavery had been outlawed lacked a staple crop that could profitably be exported. Thus, absentee land speculators in the late eighteenth and early nineteenth centuries frequently failed to turn a profit. Not everybody fared as terribly as Philadelphian Robert Morris, who owned more than six million acres of land and was sent to debtors' prison in 1798, but land speculation at that time was rarely profitable.

The nature of land speculation changed considerably during the nineteenth century, when, from the 1820s on, canals and, ultimately, the railroad connected the West and the East Coast, and the United States became a much better integrated market. Commercial farming could be established much quicker, and land speculators could reap cash profits more easily on their investments, meaning that business became more profitable.

Historians differ widely in their assessment of land speculators. For a long time, they have followed the view of eighteenth- and nineteenth-century contemporaries and pictured speculators as diametrical to frontier development. Beginning in the 1950s, however, some historians have challenged this view, arguing from a quantitative analysis of land records that speculators served an important role by subdividing land into small parcels for distribution to settlers and by offering credits. Today, historians dismiss the static view of an unequal distribution of power between land speculators and settlers, instead pointing to the collective bargaining power of settlers in relation to speculators.

Hanno Scheerer

See also: Cartographer; Explorer; Fur Trader; Fur Trapper; Surveyor

FURTHER READING

Aron, Stephen. 1992. "Pioneers and Profiteers: Land Speculation and the Homestead Ethic in Frontier Kentucky." *The Western Historical Quarterly* 23, no. 2: 179–198.

Clarke, John. 2001. *Land, Power, and Economics on the Frontier of Upper Canada.* Montreal: McGill-Queen's University Press.

Gates, Paul Wallace. 1987. *History of Public Land Law Development.* Washington, DC: Wm. W. Gaunt & Sons.

Swierenga, Robert P. 1968. *Pioneers and Profits, Land Speculation on the Iowa Frontier.* Ames: Iowa State University Press.

PRIMARY DOCUMENT

In this document, the Quaker abolitionist Benjamin Lundy attempts to explain the role of land speculators in the extension of slavery throughout the South, as well as their involvement in the formation of the Republic of Texas in the 1830s. As monied professionals who made their living by investing in land made available for purchase by the federal government and then selling it to settlers, land speculators were both important to the re-peopling of the western and southern frontiers as well as serving as emblems of rampant and unrestrained exploitation of ordinary Americans.

The land-speculations . . . have extended to most of the cities and villages of the United States, the British colonies in America, and the settlements of foreigners in all the eastern parts of Mexico. All concerned in them are aware that a change in the government of the country *must* take place, if their claims shall ever be legalized . . .

The breeders of slaves, in those parts of the United States where slave labour has become unprofitable,—and also the traffickers in human flesh, whether American or foreign, desire an extended market, which Texas would afford if revolutionized, and governed as well as inhabited by those who are in favour of re-establishing the system of slavery in the section of the country. The northern land speculators most cheerfully cooperate with the southern slave-holders in the grand scheme of aggression, with the hope of immense gain and the slave-merchants play into the hands of both, with the same heartless, avaricious feelings and views. The principal seat of the operations for the first, is New York—though some active and regular agencies are established at New Orleans and Nashville . . .

Such are the motives for action—such the combination of Interests—such the organization, sources of influence, and foundation or authority, upon which the present *Texas Insurrection* rests. The resident colonists compose but a small fraction of the party concerned in it. The standard of revolt was raised as soon as it was clearly ascertained the slavery could not be perpetuated, nor the illegal speculations in land continued, under the *government* of the Mexican Republic. The Mexican authorities were charged with acts of oppression, while the true causes of the revolt—the motives and designs of the insurgents—were studiously concealed from the public view. Influential slave-holders are contribution money, equipping troops, and marching to the scene of conflict. The land speculators are fitting out expeditions from New York and New Orleans, with me, munitions of war, provisions &c., to promote the object. The Independence of Texas is declared, and the system of slavery, as well as the slave trade (with the United States) is fully recognized by the government they have set up . . .

I cannot now bring to my recollection, in the history of the world, so foul and abominable a conspiracy against the laws of nations, of civil society, and the rights of man, as this nefarious combination of land speculation, land-pirates, and man stealers . . .

Source: Benjamin Lundy. 1836. *The war in Texas; a review of facts and circumstances, showing that this contest in the result of a long premeditated crusade against the government, set on foot by slaveholders, land speculators, &c. with the view of re-establishing, extending, and perpetuating the system of slavery and the slave trade in the republic of Mexico.* Philadelphia: Merrihew & Gunn, 39–40, 55, passim.

LAUNDRESS

During the antebellum period, laundresses and domestic workers were those who washed and cleaned clothing, bedding, diapers, and other personal items, while domestic workers generally cleaned the homes of families other than their own. Some domestic workers cleaned, did laundry, and cooked, though usually only in smaller households. Almost all of these workers were women; many were slaves, though after 1850, Irish immigrant women and Chinese men moved into these jobs, particularly in urban areas in the North and West, respectively. A relatively small number of white women worked in U.S. Army camps on the frontier washing uniforms, but these were generally wives of enlisted men. In the South, the vast majority of antebellum laundresses and domestic workers were African American women. Before the advent of machinery, laundresses washed everything by hand. Domestic workers swept and scrubbed floors, washed dishes, cleaned rugs by beating the dirt out of them, and washed windows, walls, and furniture. Both jobs involved hard, hot, dirty menial labor.

Within the institution of slavery, there were many people who viewed domestic help, or enslaved individuals assigned to care for the house, and laundresses as being recipients of better lots in life than field hands who were forced to toil outdoors. While, arguably, there was less physical labor involved in the domestic tasks of enslavement, there were additional hardships and perils inherent to domestic help due to slaves' closer proximity to their owners. In many antebellum plantations, duties assigned to and individual treatment of slave men and women often corresponded with skin tone. For example, after Francis Wolle invented a machine to produce paper bags in 1852, many plantations employed a "brown bag test": if an African American's skin tone was lighter than a brown paper bag, he or she was considered more civilized and was thus often trained to work in the house. This was based on unscientific beliefs during the antebellum era that linked skin color to purported intellectual and moral characteristics. These beliefs were so ingrained that in 1861, Mississippi's declaration of secession stated that individuals of African descent were naturally suited for enslavement and for working under the harsh sun of the Deep South due to their darker skins.

Whatever their skin tone, laundresses and domestic slaves did not have easy or pampered lives. If field hands began their workday at sunup, those tasked with meal preparation began even earlier. The same held true for late evening meals as clean-up was necessary before the "house slaves" could retire to their own homes within the slave quarters. In between meals was certainly not downtime as domestic help, including cooks, maids, laundresses, and seamstresses, would have busy days assigned to them as their primary duties were to ensure the cleanliness, attractiveness, and presentation of their white owners, who identified themselves strongly with their appearance, clothing, manners, and home. Domestic workers also were very involved in the raising, feeding, and nursing of the owner's children, while their own children were often neglected, raised by the elderly slaves, or went without sustenance in order to provide for the owner's family.

The daily lives of laundresses, or washerwomen, were very important to running the plantation house. The women who performed washing and mending duties labored both inside and outside of the slave owner's home. Water had to be procured to wash clothes, often from a well that supplied drinking water to the plantation. Then the laundress heated the water on a wood-fired stove or, more commonly, in a large pot over an open flame. The laundress used soap that she had made, scrubbing dirty clothes and linens over a washboard, and then rinsing and hanging the items to dry. Once dry, many clothes needed to be starched and ironed. Any small tear or lost button had to be fixed before an item could be returned to the owner. Not only did laundresses need to ensure the dress and cleanliness of the owner and his family, but they were required to do the best they could for their enslaved brothers and sisters. However, the repairs to work clothes for the field hands would often have to be done at night after tasks assigned for the "big house" were completed; this would mean attempting to darn clothing and thread needles in poor lighting after a sixteen-hour workday.

Additionally, the proximity of washerwomen, maids, and house servants often resulted in additional dangers and, naturally, very complex relationships between the white and black women and other members of the family. By being in the house, domestic workers were under constant scrutiny, had no privacy, and were often resented by the field hands. Also, the light-skin offspring so desired for domestic workers was often a result of the white owner raping his enslaved females. Of course, enslaved field hands also faced the possibility of sexual violence, but it was increased for the women with daily interactions with their masters. In fact, the selling of attractive women for the purposes of domestic help was recognized, and many slave markets had a "fancy trade" alongside field hands. If a man boasted an attractive maid who did not appear to have the harshness of field experiences on her body, such as scars from whipping or calloused hands, he was seen as rich enough to be able to afford "fancy" slaves, and these women often became long-term concubines. The fate of these women included sexual exploitation as their value as individuals corresponded to their sexuality. Likewise, darker-skinned African or African American women had their value assigned to their ability to reproduce and were often exploited sexually and their children sold.

During the antebellum era, free white and black washerwomen, and some enslaved black women, worked for slave traders who participated in slave auctions. For example, in Richmond, Virginia, there was an exceptionally lucrative slave trade business presence. Often, seamstresses, washer-women, and maids in Richmond created clothing for the enslaved individuals facing the auction pens;

attractive, well-clothed, well-groomed slaves with the appearance of strength fetched a higher price in auctions.

While enslaved domestic helpers may not have had the same physical demands as their field-hand relations, their lives were still exploited and difficult. Additionally, the stigma of black women sacrificing their own homes and families to assist with the betterment of wealthy white families would become a social aspect that would remain well past emancipation and the end of slavery. In 1910, nearly 400,000 women, both black and white, worked as laundresses in the United States. The 1870 census showed that 52 percent of employed African American women worked in "domestic and personal service" to white families. This trend continued up through the 1950s.

Christy Davenport

See also: Field Hand; Slave Driver; *1607–1775:* Indentured Servant; *1992–2019:* Housekeeper

FURTHER READING

Baptist, Edward. 2013. *The Half Has Never Been Told: Slavery and the Making of American Capitalism.* New York: Basic Books.

Berry, Dania Ramey. 2017. *The Price for Their Pound of Flesh: The Value of the Enslaved, from Womb to Grave, in the Building of a Nation.* New York: Beacon Press.

Camp, Stephanie. 2004. *Closer to Freedom: Enslaved Women and Everyday Resistance in the Plantation South.* Chapel Hill: The University of North Carolina Press.

Finley, Alexandra. 2017. "'Cash to Corinna': Domestic Labor and Sexual Economy in the 'Fancy Trade.'" *Journal of American History* 104, no. 2 (September 1, 2017): 410–430.

Fox-Genovese, Elisabeth. 1988. *Within the Plantation Household: Black and White Women in the Old South.* Chapel Hill: The University of North Carolina Press.

Glymph, Thavolia. 2008. *Out of the House of Bondage: The Transformation of the Plantation Household.* New York: Cambridge University Press.

Johnson, Walter. 1999. *Soul by Soul: Life Inside the Antebellum Slave Market.* Cambridge: Harvard University Press.

Morgan, Jennifer L. 2004. *Laboring Women: Reproduction and Gender in New World Slavery.* Philadelphia: University of Pennsylvania Press.

PRIMARY DOCUMENT

In this document, Harriet Ann Jacobs, a former slave of both African and Euro American heritage, describes the maltreatment she and other house slaves endured during their working lives. A domestic slave worked in close proximity to slave owners, providing them with an intimate look into the latter's family dynamics.

Tensions between husband and wife or parents and children, whether grown or not, could erupt in ways that imperiled the safety of slaves. Women, in particular, were subject to sexual assault and physical violence in their daily lives, as Jacobs notes. Later in her life, Jacobs escaped slavery and became a noted abolitionist and writer. This account of her life was first published in 1861 under a pseudonym, Linda Brent. Although she also used pseudonyms for her owners, the general contours of her story are accurate.

Mrs. Flint, like many southern women, was totally deficient in energy. She had not strength to superintend her household affairs; but her nerves were so strong, that she could sit in her easy chair and see a woman whipped, till the blood trickled from every stroke of the lash . . . If dinner was not served at the exact time on that particular Sunday, she would station herself in the kitchen, and wait till it was dished, and then spit in all the kettles and pans that had been used for cooking. She did this to prevent the cook and her children from eking out their meagre fare with the remains of the gravy and other scrapings. The slaves could get nothing to eat except what she chose to give them. Provisions were weighed out by the pound and ounce, three times a day. I can assure you she gave them no chance to eat wheat bread from her flour barrel. She knew how many biscuits a quart of flour would make, and exactly what size they ought to be.

Dr. Flint was an epicure. The cook never sent a dinner to his table without fear and trembling; for if there happened to be a dish not to his liking, he would either order her to be whipped, or compel her to eat every mouthful of it in his presence. The poor, hungry creature might not have objected to eating it; but she did object to having her master cram it down her throat till she choked . . .

I now entered on my fifteenth year—a sad epoch in the life of a slave girl. My master began to whisper foul words in my ear. Young as I was, I could not remain ignorant of their import. I tried to treat them with indifference or contempt. The master's age, my extreme youth, and the fear that his conduct would be reported to my grandmother, made him bear this treatment for many months. He was a crafty man, and resorted to many means to accomplish his purposes. Sometimes he had stormy, terrific ways, that made his victims tremble; sometimes he assumed a gentleness that he thought must surely subdue. Of the two, I preferred his stormy moods, although they left me trembling. He tried his utmost to corrupt the pure principles my grandmother had instilled. He peopled my young mind with unclean images, such as only a vile monster could think of. I turned from him with disgust and hatred. But he was my master. I was compelled to live under the same roof with him—where I saw a man forty years my senior daily violating the most sacred commandments of nature. He told me I was his property; that I must be subject to his will in all things. My soul revolted against the mean tyranny. But where could I turn for protection? No matter whether the slave girl be as black as ebony or as fair as her mistress. In either case, there is no shadow of law to protect her from insult, from violence, or even from death; all these are inflicted by fiends who bear the shape of men. The mistress, who ought to protect the helpless victim, has no other feelings towards her but those of jealousy and rage. The degradation, the wrongs, the vices, that grow out of slavery, are more than I can describe. They are greater than you would willingly believe. Surely, if you credited one half the truths that are told you concerning the helpless millions suffering in this cruel bondage, you at the north would not help to tighten the yoke. You surely would refuse to do for the master, on your own soil, the mean and cruel work which trained bloodhounds and the lowest class of whites do for him at the south . . .

I would ten thousand times rather that my children should be the half-starved paupers of Ireland than to be the most pampered among the slaves of America. I would rather drudge out my life on a cotton plantation, till the grave opened to give me rest, than to live with an unprincipled master and a jealous mistress. The felon's home in a penitentiary is preferable. He may repent, and turn from the error of his ways, and so find peace; but it is not so with a favorite slave. She is not allowed to have any pride of character. It is deemed a crime in her to wish to be virtuous.

Mrs. Flint possessed the key to her husband's character before I was born. She might have used this knowledge to counsel and to screen the young and the innocent among her slaves; but for them she had no sympathy. They were the objects of her constant suspicion and malevolence. She watched her husband with unceasing vigilance; but he was well practiced in means to evade it. What he could not find opportunity to say in words he manifested in signs. He invented more than were ever thought of in a deaf and dumb asylum. I let them pass, as if I did not understand what he meant; and many were the curses and threats bestowed on me for my stupidity. One day he caught me teaching myself to write. He frowned, as if he was not well pleased, but I suppose he came to the conclusion that such an accomplishment might help to advance his favorite scheme. Before long, notes were often slipped into my hand. I would return them, saying, "I can't read them, sir." "Can't you?" he replied; "then I must read them to you." He always finished the reading by asking, "Do you understand?" Sometimes he would complain of the heat of the tea room, and order his supper to be placed on a small table in the piazza. He would seat himself there with a well-satisfied smile, and tell me to stand by and brush away the flies. He would eat very slowly, pausing between the mouthfuls. These intervals were employed in describing the happiness I was so foolishly throwing away, and in threatening me with the penalty that finally awaited my stubborn disobedience. He boasted much of the forbearance he had exercised towards me, and reminded me that there was a limit to his patience.

When I succeeded in avoiding opportunities for him to talk to me at home, I was ordered to come to his office, to do some errand. When there, I was obliged to stand and listen to such language as he saw fit to address to me. Sometimes I so openly expressed my contempt for him that he would become violently enraged, and I wondered why he did not strike me. Circumstanced as he was, he probably thought it was better policy to be forbearing. But the state of things grew worse and worse daily.

I had entered my sixteenth year, and every day it became more apparent that my presence was intolerable to Mrs. Flint. Angry words frequently passed between her and her husband. He had never punished me himself, and he would not allow any body else to punish me. In that respect, she was never satisfied; but, in her angry moods, no terms were too vile for her to bestow upon me. Yet I, whom she detested so bitterly, had far more pity for her than he had, whose duty it was to make her life happy. I never wronged her, or wished to wrong her; and one word of kindness from her would have brought me to her feet.

After repeated quarrels between the doctor and his wife, he announced his intention to take his youngest daughter, then four years old, to sleep in his apartment. It was necessary that a servant should sleep in the same room, to be on hand if the child stirred. I was selected for that office, and informed for what purpose that arrangement had been made. By managing to keep within sight of people, as much as possible during the day time, I had hitherto succeeded in eluding my master, though a razor was often held to my throat to force me to change this line of policy. At night I slept by the side of my great aunt, where I felt safe. He was too prudent to come into her room. She was an old woman, and had been in the family many years. Moreover, as a married man, and a professional man, he deemed it necessary to save appearances in some degree. But he resolved to remove the obstacle in the way of his scheme; and he thought he had planned it so that he should evade suspicion. He was well aware how much I prized my refuge by the side of my old aunt, and he determined to dispossess me of it The first night the doctor had the little child in his room alone. The next morning, I was ordered to take my station as nurse the following night. A kind Providence interposed in my favor. During the day Mrs. Flint heard of this new arrangement, and a storm followed. I rejoiced to hear it rage.

After a while my mistress sent for me to come to her room. Her first question was, "Did you know you were to sleep in the doctor's room?"

"Yes, ma'am."

"Who told you?"

"My master."

"Will you answer truly all the questions I ask?"

"Yes, ma'am."

"Tell me, then, as you hope to be forgiven, are you innocent of what I have accused you?"

"I am."

She handed me a Bible, and said, "Lay your hand on your heart, kiss this holy book, and swear before God that you tell me the truth."

I took the oath she required, and I did it with a clear conscience.

"You have taken God's holy word to testify your innocence," said she. "If you have deceived me, beware! Now take this stool, sit down, look me directly in the face, and tell me all that has passed between your master and you . . ."

The secrets of slavery are concealed like those of the Inquisition. My master was, to my knowledge, the father of eleven slaves. But did the mothers dare to tell who was the father of their children? Did the other slaves dare to allude to it, except in whispers among themselves? No, indeed! They knew too well the terrible consequences . . .

Southern women often marry a man knowing that he is the father of many little slaves. They do not trouble themselves about it. They regard such children as property, as marketable as the pigs on the plantation; and it is seldom that they do not make them aware of this by passing them into the slave-trader's hands as soon as possible, and thus getting them out of their sight. I am glad to say there are some honorable exceptions.

Source: Harriet Jacobs. 1861. *Incidents in the Life of a Slave Girl*, 22, 44–45, 49–52, 55, 57.

MILITIAMAN

Militiamen were members of a military force that were raised from the civil population to supplement regular military forces in an emergency. Local militias served as the backbone of security for colonial American societies for nearly two centuries, from the establishment of Jamestown in 1607 through the end of the eighteenth century. Like many other cultural and societal norms during the era, American military customs were inherited from Great Britain. Rather than rely on a body of professional soldiers kept during times of peace—more commonly known as a standing army—colonial Americans depended on local citizen-soldiers to muster (or assemble) for the purpose of defending individual communities, colonies, and, later, states. A standing army during peacetime existed as a foreign concept in England until the mid-seventeenth century, and after its introduction, British citizens witnessed numerous leaders utilize standing armies to enforce their policies and will by using the threat of violence to stoke fear in both British and

American populations. With much deeper roots and history of utilization, the militia system existed as a time-honored English tradition with its origins linked in documentation to the reign of Henry II (r. 1154–1189). Operating and managed at the local level, soldiers in the militia maintained an impermanence that cast them in stark contrast to standing, professional soldiers like British Regulars or soldiers in America's Continental Army.

Both British citizens and American colonists widely believed that although a local militia may not have been as effective as an organization of professional soldiers in combat or in thwarting insurrection, the militiamen's ties to local communities, spirit of volunteerism, and willingness to fight to maintain liberty guaranteed their loyalty, virtuousness, and incorruptibility. In other words, Americans believed militias could only be utilized to stop dangerous and tyrannical actions, never to support them.

In every colony (and, later, state), local American militiamen periodically mustered and trained during the year to perform soldierly duties. Rarely donning matching uniforms, the citizen-soldiers provided their own weapons, ammunition, and other equipment. After marshalling, militiamen practiced various tasks such as how to assemble, march, and deploy into battle formations, how to understand verbal commands and signals, how to properly carry, maintain, and fire a musket or rifle, and, in some cases, how to perform basic first aid for injured compatriots. These skills proved absolutely essential for local militias to effectively respond to local crises and threats. While few militiamen had extensive experience as soldiers, most were skilled in other professions. Ranging in age from teenagers to grandparents, American militiamen came from many walks of life including farmers, laborers, artisans, blacksmiths, clergy, and even local officials.

They distinguished themselves from British Regulars and Continental soldiers in other ways as well. One important distinction between professional soldiers and American militiamen is that the latter elected their officers rather than served under appointed commanders. Additionally, American militiamen frequently signed short-term contracts that protected them from service outside the colony (or state). Conversely, some professional British soldiers enlisted for life, suffered harsh disciplinary punishments, and received very low wages. Likewise, in 1776, the American Continental Congress authorized the creation of eighty-eight battalions of Continental soldiers to serve wherever needed for the duration of the war—an undefined location for an indeterminate amount of time.

Perhaps most famously, American militiamen gained distinction and notoriety for their actions at the Battle of Lexington and Concord, Massachusetts, the location of the first openly hostile actions between American colonists and British Regulars that sparked the American Revolution. On April 19, 1775, American militiamen known as Minutemen—due to their prowess for rapid readiness in response to emergencies—gathered and engaged a numerically superior British force in the countryside west of Boston. Though not as well armed or trained in military tactics, American militiamen defended their local communities and were later memorialized by poet Ralph Waldo Emerson, who credited the Americans for firing "the shot heard round the world."

American militiamen continued to serve a prominent role in the American Revolution after the Battle of Lexington and Concord. Citizen-soldiers took the offensive following the opening battle and began the Siege of Boston, which lasted more than ten months, until March 1776. During that campaign, the Continental Congress authorized the creation of the Continental Army, a national military force, distinct from state-controlled militia units, under the auspices of the governing body and command of General George Washington. Washington and the Continental Army arrived in Boston during the siege shortly after the inaccurately named Battle of Bunker Hill (the fighting actually took place on Breed's Hill), where, until overwhelming numbers of enemy forces and shortages of ammunition, American militiamen repeatedly prevented British advances from taking a piece of key terrain on the heights overlooking the city. Militiamen continued to serve in combat alongside Continental soldiers throughout the American Revolution and participated in notable actions in both northern states such as New Jersey and in the southern theater, particularly South Carolina.

American militiamen often performed duties beyond the battlefield. Many citizen-soldiers worked as sentries and guards in American camps as well as performed fatigue duties, those that did not require the use of any weapons. Examples of these responsibilities included felling trees, improving roads, cooking and cleaning in camps, and building earthworks. With roots extending back to Jamestown and earlier English history, the American Militiaman gained distinction and historical prominence during the American Revolution, and the concept and role of the American citizen-soldier continued well into the nineteenth and twentieth centuries.

Nicholas Browning

See also: *1861–1914:* Soldier; *1915–1945:* Infantryman; *1992–2019:* Combat Engineer

FURTHER READING

Shea, William L. 1983. *The Virginia Militia in the Seventeenth Century*. Baton Rouge: Louisiana State University Press.

Stubbs, William. 1921. *Select Charters and Other Illustrations of English Constitutional History from the Earliest Times to the Reign of Edward the First*. Edited by H. W. C. Davis, 9th ed. Cambridge: Cambridge University Press.

United States. 1792. *An Act More Effectually to Provide for the National Defence, by Establishing an Uniform Militia Throughout the United States*. Philadelphia: Printed by John Fenno.

MILLINER

Milliners were workers who created women's clothing, especially fancy dresses, hats, and gowns for wearing outside of the home. They also sold textiles, most of it imported from England, to home seamstresses. Milliners, and women's fashion generally, flourished in the years prior to the American Revolution (1775–1783). Fashion played an important role in society, especially in the association between consumption and liberty, which greatly increased in the colonies prior to the war. Milliners transformed English goods, primarily textiles, into fashionable garb. While most women and girls sewed their "house clothes" (loose-fitting linen dresses, aprons, skirts, and undergarments) at home, for going out, whether to just to stroll in public or for shopping, courtship, or to a ball, women with the money to do so retained the duties of a milliner to design and construct a flattering and fashionable dress or mantua (a long-robed, formal dress for special occasions).

"I know their very foibles . . . are amicable," wrote the pseudonymous Censor on the eve of the American Revolution, in reference to fashionable women; in an indictment of fashion, he called on women of the "Art Millenary" to produce only the most useful clothing, like bonnets "to defend against the severity of the sun and Season." Writing at the time of immense political tensions and calling for patriotic residents to consider the terms of the non-importation agreements as passed by the Continental Congress in 1774, Censor then addressed consumers, urging women to ask themselves this question before making any clothing purchase: "Can you subsist in civilized life without them?" (*Connecticut Gazette*, 1775)

Like many patriotic editorialists just before the revolution, Censor called his readers' attention to the great amount of money that colonists had been spending on imported goods, advising consumers to refrain from purchasing the imported "superfluities, unnecessary Frippery, which Fashion introduces" and instead exercise economy and frugality. While Censor did implicate the honest farmer in his polemic, his was a gendered attack. It was women's fashion—"the lace, the flimsy silks"—that were at the root of the problem. Indeed, American Revolutionary writers connected their political goals of independence with consumer boycotts against the purchase of English goods, in part to support "home manufactures" and partly to enforce an economic boycott of English goods. Not many years later, another editorialist noted how, in Tory-occupied Philadelphia, young "ladies who were in the city with the enemy, and wear the present fashionable dresses, have purchased them at the extent of their virtue." A woman's virtue, thus, rested not on her respectable behavior but on her consumption patterns and her preference for "fashionable dresses" (*Continental Journal*, 1777).

English textile companies produced all kinds of fabrics that were exported to the colonies: silks, gauze crapes, chintzes, lawns, printed cottons from India, calicos, lace, and fine linens, as well as decorative silk flowers, feathers, and ribbons of every color and size. Some silk was embroidered with ostentatious floral designs in warm colors. For nearly the entire eighteenth century, women's fashion had been evolving, becoming less plain and more a reflection of the individual wearing the clothing. Women sought to distinguish their social class by adopting fashionable dress, as did men—and men and women of all classes sought to better their reputations by embracing fashionable styles. A rapid increase in available consumer goods from England after midcentury had made it possible for greater numbers of colonial women to have access to these goods and for milliners to both sell them and create clothing for their customers.

Many milliners had shops in which they offered these textiles and other goods for sale before the revolution. A customer sought a milliner's services for purchase of the fabric for a dress or gown. The milliner who sold the fabric customarily measured the customer and then cut the garment, normally not from a specific uniform pattern, as seamstresses do today, but partly according to a customer's specifications and particular body type; as a milliner measured a woman, she also suggested appropriate fashions for different women to ensure a flattering fit and look. Dresses with tightly stitched fronts and pleated backs emphasized a thin woman's bosom and narrow waistline but would prove less flattering on an older or more matronly figure. Milliners were experts in fitting women of all types; they also had to possess good communication skills to ensure that customers were not offended by their fitting and fashion advice. At times, milliners deconstructed dresses that girls had outgrown to use as the pattern for new garments in larger sizes. Many milliners created paper patterns reflecting the particular measurements of a woman's or girl's frame and the style of the garment.

Often, customers ordered "basted" or "in part" garments, or those that had been cut and tacked together with long basting stitches but which a customer (or her servant or slave) might complete at home. Assembling a dress or gown required good spatial skills and expert dexterity in the use of needles, as all garment were handsewn. Those who sewed together the garment used different stitches, including backstitching, whipstitching and topstitching, employed for different purposes: to bind linings to the garment, provide a tough seam permitting the washing of garments, and allow the seamstress to economize her efforts. A milliner provided ribbons, robing, and other accessories to add to the garment to complete its look. Other milliners had apprentices or seamstresses who stitched garments together by hand, or she did it herself. Once a customer had been measured, the garment cut and basted together, the milliner fitted it to the customer, who then left the item at the milliner's shop until it was complete. A customer then returned to the shop for a final fitting and the addition of accessories such as silk flowers or ribbon adornments.

The tools of the milliner included parchment or other paper for measuring and making patterns, scissors, pinking tools (which worked like embossers to produce patterns on ribbon or fabric), shears, needles of different kinds (sewing, basting, embroidery, quilting), pins, thimbles, an iron, ironing sleeves and hams, and an ironing board, as well as pencil or chalk. Milliners used long strips of parchment or muslin as makeshift measuring tapes to determine a woman's fit. She carried in her inventory assortments of textiles and accessories, including buttons.

Milliners also altered and repaired women's clothing, one primary area of work for those milliners who observed non-importation agreements during the revolutionary period. Others produced plain homespun dresses and gowns made of domestic linen for women who wished to demonstrate their patriotism. In Philadelphia, though, despite the non-importation agreements, milliners continued to do a good business as wealthy and middle-class women flouted fashionable styles, even at the height of the city's occupation by British troops from the fall of 1777 to the spring of 1778. As a result, notes historian Kate Haulman, Philadelphia was the "locus of a series of culture wars" that at times pitted fashionable women and their milliners against the values of "republican simplicity" during this period (Haulman 2005, 625). Less than a year later, Philadelphia papers carried regular advertisements of milliners' shops readying for spring fashions—noting, for instance, in January 1779 the arrival of a milliner who had moved her shop from New York City, offering Philadelphia's women "a very elegant assortment of gauzes, etc." Elsewhere, newspapers carried notices of the opening of millineries only later in the war, becoming common again in New York after 1780, New England in 1781, and in southern cities after 1782. In 1783, in Charleston, South Carolina, for instance, the Bowers—William, a watchmaker, and Katherine, a milliner—opened a shop on Broad Street, having just received a shipment of luxury goods from London on the vessel *Friendship*. The copy for Katherine's notice was twice the size of William's. It offered an "assortment of Millinary" including feathers, hoops, textiles, handkerchiefs, children's caps, fans, hat pins, gloves, fringe, ribbons, and "other articles too tedious to enumerate" for sale at the "most reasonable terms." Normalcy returned to the milliner's trade at the end of the war.

Yet, even then, newspaper editorialists observed that fashionable women threatened the republican values of our nascent nation. Not unique among the editorialists of the time, one Bostonian waxed on about the need for education in self-sufficiency and suggested that both the barber and the milliner "did no good in society." He concluded his lengthy denunciation of fashion wistfully, noting that he hoped one day the bookseller's shop would compete for women's business on an equal basis with that of the milliner and suggested to "gain the taste and discernment of Female customers," publishers should print more poetry and less news of politics and business.

Nancy Quam-Wickham

See also: *1607–1775:* Shopkeeper; Wigmaker; *1861–1914:* Haberdasher; *1915–1945:* Garment Worker

FURTHER READING

Breen, T. H. 2004. *Marketplace of Revolution: How Consumer Politics Shaped American Independence.* London: Oxford University Press.

Connecticut Gazette (New London). April 7, 1775.

Continental Journal and Weekly Advertiser (Boston). July 30, 1777.

Haulman, Kate. 2005. "Fashion and the Culture Wars of Revolutionary Philadelphia." *William and Mary Quarterly.* Third Series. 62: 625–662.

Miller, Marla R. 2006. *The Needle's Eye: Women and Work in the Age of Revolution.* Amherst: Massachusetts University Press.

Staples, Kathleen A., and Madelyn Shaw. 2013. *Clothing through American History.* Westport: Greenwood.

PRIMARY DOCUMENT

While many milliners specialized in designing and making women's hats, more generally, milliners designed and crafted women's wear of all kinds. Milliners crafted the fashions of the revolutionary era, but in the public mind, fashionable women were of a certain class and temperament: the vain, arrogant, vacuous well-to-do women who cared more about their personal appearances than they did about the spirit of an oppressed people fighting for their freedom from tyranny. In American culture of the time, fashionable women—and the milliners who dressed them—were often the subjects of jokes, rhymes, songs, and stories. Some examples follow.

1. Report from Philadelphia

[The] morals of the inhabitants have suffered vastly [under the British occupiers]. The enemy introduced new fashions and made old vices more common . . . The females who staid in the city while it was in the possession of the enemy cut a curious figure: their hats, which are of the flat round kind, are of the size of a large japonned tea waiter; their caps exceed any of the sarcastic prints you have seen, and their hair is dressed, with the assistance of wool, & c. in such a manner as to appear too heavy to be supported by their necks: If the caps would not blow off, a north-wester would certainly throw these belles off their center . . . Last Saturday . . . a noted strumpet was paraded in the modern *British* taste, to the no small amusement of a vast crowd of spectators . . .

Source: *Continental Journal and Weekly Advertiser.* July 30, 1778. Boston.

2. Necessary for all Families

Q: What is fashion?

A: An agreeable tyrant.

Q: What is its progress?

A: It begins with the vain, is improved by the silly, and stops with the wife.

Q: What does it regulate?

A: The dresses of the ladies, the philosophical, religious, and political tenets of the men; the hours of meals, and the value of toys; it determines which is the best stage-dancer, the best physician, the best milliner, and most heavenly opera, the soundest lawyer, and the finest woman of pleasure.

Source: *Continental Journal and Weekly Advertiser.* October 23, 1783. Boston.

3. AIR

Zounds, sir! then I'll tell you without any jest,
The things of all things, which I hate and detest,
  A coxcomb, a fop,
  A dainty milk sop;
Who, essene'd and dizen'd from bottom to top,
Looks just like a doll from a milliner's shop.
  A thing full of prate,
  And pride and conceit;
  All fashion, no weight;
  Who shrugs and takes snuff,
  And carries a muff;
    A manikin,
    Fimking,
French powder puff;
And now, sir, I fancy, I've told you enough.

Source: Isaac Bickerstaff. 1818. *Lionel and Clarissa; or, A school for fathers. A comic opera:* 11. New York: Longworth.

4. *Par Example*

Fair praise is sterling gold—all should desire it—
Flatt'ry, base coin—a cheat upon the nation;

And yet, our vanity doth admire it,
And really gives it all its circulation . . .

Praise is a modest, unassuming maid,
As simply as a Quaker-beauty drest:—
No ostentation hers—no vain parade:
Sweet nymph! and of few word possest;
Yet, heard with rev'rence when she silence breaks.
And dignifies the man of whom she speaks.

Flatt'ry's a pert French milliner—a jade
Covered with *rouge*, and flauntingly array'd—
Makes saucy love to ev'ry man she meets,
And offers ev'n her favours in the streets . . .

Source: *The Works of Peter Pindar.* 1811. Vol. 1, 289. Boston: Charles Williams.

5. Jaw-Bone of An Ass Examined

Breathless and faint, leaning upon my sword,
Came there a certain lord; neat; trimly dress'd;
Fresh as a bridegroom; and his chin, new reap'd,
Show'd like a stubble-land at harvest-home.
He was perfumed like a milliner;
And 'twixt his finger and his thumb, he held
A pouncet box, which ever and anon
He gave his nose, and took'd away again.
And still smil'd and talk'd:
And, as the soldiers bare dead bodies by,
He call'd them 'untaught knaves, unmannerly,
To bring a slovenly unhandsome corpse
Betwixt the wind and his nobility.'

Source: Price Armstrong. 1811. *The Jaw-Bone of an Ass Examined, being a dialogue between Mr. Sneerhim Speakplain and Mr. Surface Shallow Brain* . . ., 36. New York: Southwick and Pelsue.

6. Joke Upon Joke

A gentleman who had been desired by his wife to make a purchase for her at a milliner's, being accosted by a friend on his return, to call in, begged to be excused from stopping, as he had bought a bonnet for his wife, and was afraid *the fashion would change before he got home.*

Source: Sam Splicem. 1818. *Broad grins, or A new remedy for the heart-ache; being a new and choice collection of anecdotes, bon mots, puns, oddities, and most approved witty sayings, by Phil. Fudge, A.S.S.* New Haven: Maltby, Goldsmith & Co., 12.

MINER, *see* GOLD MINER

MISSIONARY

Christian missionaries were individuals who combined religious proselytization with social reform in an attempt to create utopian societies that reflected both Christian religion and American culture. The missionaries' goals of imparting Christianity and "civilization," meaning white Christian American culture, were separate yet connected objectives as they worked both in the United States and overseas. In addition to theological instruction, missionaries created schools, educated locals, delivered medical care, taught useful trade skills, and participated in social activities within their new communities. While the primary duty of a missionary was to preach the gospel, most missionaries—whether single men or married couples—also performed other duties. They supervised the construction of the mission. They opened primitive hospitals. They planted crops and sometimes raised poultry or livestock. Women often spent their days teaching children in mission schools and training indigenous women to work as nurses and cooks. Missionaries sometimes mediated disputes between natives. Their work was varied, though, on Sundays, missionaries tended to the religious needs of their congregations.

Missionaries, however, have been criticized for destroying indigenous culture and interfering with native political systems as they acted as unofficial ambassadors of a growing nineteenth-century American colonial empire. The growing missionary movement in the nineteenth century was impacted by the rise of the idea of a "benevolent empire," a unification of Christian denominations around a common religious plan based upon charity, religious conversion, moral reform, and nation building. Missionary organizations were created to locate, examine, support, and send out vetted volunteers who would preach the gospel of both Jesus Christ and America's national greatness during the formative years of the early American republic.

Founded in 1810 as the earliest and largest U.S. missionary board of its kind, the American Board of Commissioners for Foreign Missions (ABCFM) was a Congregationalist organization established to spread Christianity in what they called heathen lands. In partnership with the London Missionary Society (LMS), which was founded in England in 1795, the ABCFM oversaw the majority of American

Protestant missionary efforts in the nineteenth century. The board's missionary legacy began when it sent out three couples and two single men as missionaries to Calcutta, India, in 1812. The ABCFM embarked on its first solo missionary effort when it sent the first Protestant missionaries to Hawai'i, also known as the Sandwich Islands, in October 1819. Arriving in Kailua, Hawai'i, in March 1820, the pioneer company was comprised of seven married couples, one couple's five children, and three Hawaiian "helpers" from the Foreign Mission School in Cornwall, Connecticut. Between 1819 and 1863, the ABCFM sent twelve companies that founded seventeen missionary stations and two schools throughout Kaua'i, O'ahu, Moloka'i, Maui, and the Island of Hawai'i.

Arriving in 1820, Asa Thurston (1787–1868) and Lucy Goodale Thurston (1795–1876) were some of the longest-serving Sandwich Islands missionaries, with Asa serving forty-eight years and Lucy serving fifty-six. Like nineteenth-century missionaries in many foreign locations, the Thurstons permanently moved to their "mission field" until their deaths. As was customary with missionary organizations until the late nineteenth century, Lucy Thurston was her husband's assistant and biblical helpmeet like Eve from the Book of Genesis, but the ABCFM did not consider her an official or fully appointed missionary. Yet missionary women challenged the boundaries of proper female behavior as they grappled with living in a foreign frontier. Early Sandwich Islands missionary women, for example, were instrumental in negotiating with Hawaiian royalty for safe living conditions.

During the nineteenth century, most missionary organizations allowed only married women with their husbands to serve abroad. This limitation was primarily for the moral safety of missionary men, not the physical safety of women, as it was believed that wives were a protection against temptation in exotic locations with "savage" women who were often scarcely clothed. Female missionaries on foreign missions were expected to teach children and help with other tasks of the mission when their schedules permitted. Nevertheless, missionary women as a whole, whether married or unmarried, had earned their place in the mission field as they often were well educated, had worked as teachers, and had the reputation of being respectable Christian women in their communities.

Unmarried Christian women who desired to serve in foreign missions faced additional barriers to becoming commissioned for service. Until the late nineteenth century, the few single American female missionaries sent to foreign locations were expected to marry one of the eligible or newly widowed bachelors in the mission. In an act of defiance against this pattern, forty women created the Woman's Board of Missions in Boston's Old South Church in 1868. This foundational step allowed Christian women to commission and fund their own female missionaries while sharing organizational duties with the male-led ABCFM. Other Christian denominations followed suit, and the second half of the nineteenth century saw many single Christian women, primarily widows, serving as fully commissioned missionaries in places such as India without the expectation of missionary marriage. Nevertheless, for the majority of nineteenth-century women missionaries, marriage remained a ticket to foreign missionary service.

The race of those the missionaries sought to convert was often a focal point of missionary endeavors. Prior to foreign missionary work, the American Protestant missionary movement had only sent missionaries on home missions, meaning in the United States, among American Indians during the nation's westward expansion. Missionary work in itself was a continuation of America's fascination with the closing frontier, and missionaries became unofficial ambassadors of the U.S. federal government as they settled new areas on the frontier in the name of American Christianization.

Beginning in 1817, Cyrus Kingsbury (1786–1870) served the Cherokee and the Choctaw as he preached, led churches, and ran missionary schools for over fifty years. The first Methodist mission in Oregon was founded in 1834. Missionary outreach in the Pacific Northwest continued when Presbyterian missionary sisters Susan Law McBeth (1830–1893) and Kate Christine McBeth (1833–1915) arrived in the Clearwater River valley in Idaho among the Nez Percé during the 1870s. The McBeth sisters were missionary teachers and transmitters of Anglo American culture, as seen with Sue McBeth's creation of a Nez Percé/English dictionary and Kate McBeth's teaching of Euro American domestic skills. Missionaries introduced Christianity and American culture into Native American communities, but indigenous peoples' experiences were often rife with competing notions of acceptance of the missionaries' offerings and anger at the decimation of natives' population, culture, and ancestral traditions.

The nineteenth century witnessed the birth of a new American-born religion and its early emphasis on missionary work. Joseph Smith founded this new Christian religion, known as the Church of Jesus Christ of the Latter-day Saints, in Fayette, New York, on April 6, 1830, and its members were referred to as Mormons for their belief in the Book of Mormon. The first four LDS missionaries, which included Oliver Cowdery (1806–1850), headed west in October 1830 to proselytize American Indians in Ohio and Missouri. Known as the Lamanite mission, this first LDS mission doubled the church's size a mere six months after its founding while simultaneously placing an early emphasis on the importance of all older men partaking in missionary work. In 1850, the LDS followed in the steps of the ABCFM and sent missionaries to Hawai'i, such as George Q. Cannon (1827–1901), who served as a governing church leader and five-time Utah territorial delegate. Church president Brigham Young, who had asked Cannon to serve in Hawai'i, later organized the Southern States Mission in 1875 with an initial eight-man missionary group based in Rome, Georgia. When this mission ended in 1898, 1,760 Mormon missionaries had served in the South. The official Southern States Mission ended due to violence toward missionaries ranging from harassment and threats to forced expulsion and murder, which was the case with twenty-four-year-old missionary Joseph Standing (1854–1879), who was mobbed in Varnell, Georgia.

Nineteenth-century missionary work interrupted a long intermingled history of race, chattel slavery, and Christianity in the South. Not all nineteenth-century Christian missionaries were white, a fact that divided lay Christians, missionaries, and missionary boards alike. Historically, Christianity had been used by both slave owners and missionaries to subdue enslaved Africans and African Americans as they were taught from Christian scripture to obey their earthly masters. Enslaved African Americans had appropriated Christian teachings to use them as tools of resistance as they memorized stories about emancipated Jewish slaves and God's view of equality. Nineteenth-century American Christians and missionaries were split on the issue of slavery even as the Civil War loomed on the horizon. Some Christian missionaries believed that the Bible sanctioned inequality and racial hierarchy on earth, while others believed in a God who sided with Moses as he demanded "let my people go." Black and white missionaries alike poured into the South during the federal Reconstruction era to bring about full equality by educating newly emancipated slaves. Amanda Berry Smith (1837–1915), a former slave and widowed evangelist, became a self-appointed missionary in Africa in 1882. Most African Americans who served in the early to mid-nineteenth century, however, were commissioned and sponsored by white congregations with white patrons since African American churches and missionary boards had not been founded yet.

Missionary work has remained an important role of religious organizations in the twenty-first century. Some of the missionaries' legacy is tainted with unintended consequences, such as Lorrin A. Thurston (1858–1931) and other grandchildren of early Sandwich Islands missionary families overthrowing the sovereign Hawaiian government and forcing the annexation of Hawai'i to the United States in 1898. The impact, however, of the missionaries' spread of literacy and emphasis on education is significant. The nineteenth-century American missionary lives on today as Protestant missionary work focuses on humanitarian concerns, such as providing medical care, building wells for access to clean water, or educating others about human trafficking. While missionary work still carries a religious and social agenda component, most contemporary missionaries make positive contributions as they function with a strong understanding of racial equality, social justice, and a desire to alleviate suffering in the world.

Michelle Stonis

See also: *1607–1775:* Minister; Sexton; *1992–2019:* Clergyperson

FURTHER READING

Bays, Daniel H., and Grant Wacker, eds. 2010. *The Foreign Missionary Enterprise at Home: Explorations in North American Cultural History*. Tuscaloosa: University of Alabama Press.

Grimshaw, Patricia. 1989. *Paths of Duty: American Missionary Wives in Nineteenth-Century Hawaii*. Honolulu: University of Hawaii Press.

Martin, Joel W., and Mark A. Nicholas, eds. 2010. *Native Americans, Christianity, and the Reshaping of the American Religious Landscape*. Chapel Hill: The University of North Carolina Press.

Richardson, Joe M. 2009. *Christian Reconstruction: The American Missionary Association and Southern Blacks, 1861–1890*. Tuscaloosa: University of Alabama Press.

Thigpen, Jennifer. 2014. *Island Queens and Mission Wives: How Gender and Empire Remade Hawai'i's Pacific World*. Chapel Hill: The University of North Carolina Press.

Yohn, Susan M. 1995. *A Contest of Faiths: Missionary Women and Pluralism in the American Southwest*. Ithaca: Cornell University Press.

PRIMARY DOCUMENT

The first organization of American missionaries came to the Hawaiian Islands in 1820, sent by the American Board of Commissioners for Foreign Missions (ABCFM), a group consisting mostly of Presbyterians and Congregationalists founded just a decade earlier in 1810. The ABCFM established "missionary stations" in India, Hawaii, south China, Micronesia, Syria, and parts of Africa. In the summer of 1820, a group of ABCFM missionaries arrived at Hawaii to establish missionary stations in the chain of islands. Among the missionaries who traveled from New England on the ship Thaddeus *was Dr. Thomas Holman and his wife, Lucia. Lucia's brother, Reverend Samuel Ruggles, also arrived on the* Thaddeus. *The Holmans lived in the islands, primarily on Maui, for only two years before they returned to their native Connecticut.*

In these passages from her journal and book of letters, Mrs. Lucia Ruggles Holman recounts some of her first impressions of the Hawaiian people and the conditions of her work as a missionary.

July 1 [1820]. We receive daily supplies of provisions from the King such as the country offers, hogs, fowls, fish, taro [sic] and potatoes—but they are all of an inferior quality. The hogs & fowls are ill-flavored, having but little sweetness of them. Of the fruits of Owhyhee [Hawai'i], the Bannana & melon is all that I am fond of. The breadfruit has been quite overrated by narrators. It has an insipid taste, not much like gingerbread to which it has by some been likened.

We have had a few fine apples and oranges, but they are scarce upon this Island. At Attooi where we hope to go soon, they grow in abundance. Raspberries and strawberries, I am told grow upon some parts of these Islands, but they bear no resemblance to those of America. They are raised by the natives, only for painting their tapper.

In short, the fruits and vegetables, and everything else that these Islands produce, taste heathenish.

I believe that if the pleasant sunshine of the Gospel should beam upon this land, it would have no small tendency to sweeten its fruits. And I cannot but hope the period is not far distant, when the Son of righteousness will arise with healing in his beams, and shine upon this nation, till it shall bud and blossom as the rose.

But deplorable, beyond description is the present situation of this people, sunk to the lowest depths of sin and depravity—they appear to glory in what should be their greatest shame. There is no sin, the commission of which, disgraces them—drunkenness is an honor, theft a virtue, and murder a mark of valour, if it can be done slyly. Such my dear sister is the wretched condition of this people, and such the society among whom the Lord has cast our lot.

The trials and tribulations of a missionary life can be easily talked of at home, but cannot be known and felt. Think not then to imagine what would be your feelings, situated more than 18,000 miles from friends and home amidst a savage race of people—a people whose very appearance must shock the delicacy of an American beholder—where the Sabbath and sanctuary privileges cannot be enjoyed without molestation—and where not only the comforts and conveniences of life are denied, but the necessaries also.

Think not, my dear sister, that I am complaining or repining at the allotments of providence, or, that I mention these things to pain you—far from it—but only that you should know the truth of my situation according to my engagement and likewise that I may have your sympathy and prayers, which is all I ask, and all that you can give me.

I could say much that would interest a dear sister but shall be obliged to abridge many circumstances, and things, which, for want of time I should otherwise notice, and I purpose to be always talking to some of you every day, or at least every week, until I meet you.

Farewell, my dear sister—remember my love and the Drs.to Brother B and the children, and not forget, your sister Lucia.

September 18, 1820—Oahoo, Hannaroorah . . .

I am fully convinced that females may be useful, eminently useful to a foreign Mission; that their influence and example are everything to a Missionary establishment. Yet where it can possibly be, that men can go first onto the ground, and begin and prepare the rough way a little, before he brings her who after all he has done, is capable of suffering enough—I think it would not be inconsistent with reason, humanity, or revelation. But this cannot always be the case; it could not have here, conveniently.

I believe the females of this Mission have done more, much more towards the prosperity of it thus far, than the men—on account of the jealousy existing toward the white people. It has been thought by some, that they would not have got permission to land had it not been for the females. I will further add that could any female know before she left her home, all the trials and afflictions through which she must inevitably pass, she would not of herself have strength or grace to enlist in so great an enterprize. I think I may say the same of man.

In this we may see the wisdom of God manifest, that we, weak and timid mortals should not foresee future events, how unhappy should we be, and how illy calculated, to prosecute the work allotted to us.

Source: Lucia Ruggles Holman. 1931. *Journal of Lucia Ruggles Holman.* Honolulu: Bernice P. Bishop Museum, 32–33; 37–38.

OVERSEER, *see* SLAVE DRIVER

PAMPHLETEER

In the Revolutionary War period (1775–1783), pamphleteers were literary laborers who worked tirelessly to produce leaflets and pamphlets that could be used to promote political, economic, and social causes. Pamphleteers came from many diverse backgrounds and places. The American Revolution, and the years before and after it, was a moment of military and also cultural conflict. Written media, from maps to newspapers, shaped and were shaped by the tensions within the British Empire. Pamphlets, however, were a particularly powerful medium. Authors like Thomas Paine, who wrote the pamphlet *Common Sense* in 1776, labored in opposition to, or defense of, American independence.

There were many types of media in the eighteenth century. Newspapers were widely read, as were other forms of nonfiction books such as encyclopedias and almanacs. Novels, although not as widely read as they are today, were gaining more readers. Legal documents, from government minutes to changes in the law, were also of interest. Authors took their work seriously and devoted considerable energy to what they believed was civic duty. Fitting with values of the Enlightenment,

American authors believed that their work elevated society and prepared their readers to be active participants in a democratic, educated culture.

While people read and processed printed words in a variety of ways, pamphlets were a central site of information in colonial America and the early United States. Unlike more expensive types of print, however, pamphlets were often widely circulated. Because they were relatively easy to manufacture and not too expensive, pamphlets were easier for nonelite people to acquire, and because they were so accessible to readers, they were, in turn, a more accessible forum for writers. Pamphleteering was considered a type of labor that anyone who knew a printer and had a little bit of money could do.

Pamphleteers were a type of writer who published their work in this format. Authors like Thomas Paine were frequently inspired by anything from a very specific issue, i.e., a given tax or a dispute between two individuals, to broad social commentary. *Common Sense* was a bit of both, a call to revolution in the broadest sense but also focused on specific examples and grievances. While its circulation numbers are a subject of debate to historians today, it is clear that *Common Sense* was widely read and discussed. Given the nature of literary labor in colonial America—copyright and literary property claims were almost impossible to enforce—and the challenges of compensation between writers and printers, Paine made little to no income from his text. Certain authors, like Benjamin Franklin and William Billings, were able to make a profit off of their work. However, literary labor in this period was a difficult profession to enter into. The idea of an author as a professional category, rather than a printer or a specific category writer—mapmakers, hymnodists, ministers and their sermons—was not typical. Often, pamphleteers wrote and did something else. For example, prolific writer Alexander Hamilton was also a soldier and, later, a lawyer and government official while writing his pamphlets. Poet Phyllis Wheatley was enslaved when she published her works.

There were several characteristics of pamphlets in the revolutionary period that stand out. First, they were very frequently published anonymously. This was in large part done to protect the author from persecution, either by those in power or, more informally, in one's social circle. Second, if pamphlets were not printed anonymously or with the person's given name, they were often written with a pseudonym or nom de plume, a fictitious pen name used to protect the identity of the author. Often, these pseudonyms were selected to echo or reinforce the message of the pamphlet. For example, *Common Sense* was credited originally to "An Englishman." Third, pamphlets frequently relied upon historical and biblical references to make their contemporary points clear. Specifically, pamphleteers used examples from Ancient Greek and Roman history or more recent English history to contextualize their arguments. Fourth, they were not designed to be new stories or always objective. While pamphlets were often written on scientific topics and to promote knowledge, they were more often than not about debated issues that took a specific stance. Like the pamphleteers John Trenchard and Thomas Gordan, authors of the English essays *Cato's Letters*, American writers often wrote with deliberate goals.

Pamphleteers like Paine were one of many vocal writers in the late eighteenth century whose work shaped American lives. Like the digital world today, pamphlets were a type of media that was absorbed quickly and then talked about in people's homes, on the streets, in the taverns, and in their churches. Some types of journalists, bloggers, and social media influencers of today are in some respects the heirs of the pamphleteers' legacy.

Nora Slonimsky

See also: Journalist; Printer

FURTHER READING

Amory, Hugh, and David D. Hall, eds. 2007. *A History of the Book in America, Volume I: The Colonial Book in the Atlantic World.* Chapel Hill: University of North Carolina Press.

Cotlar, Seth. 2010. *Tom Paine's America: The Rise and Fall of Transatlantic Radicalism in the Early Republic.* Charlottesville: University of Virginia Press.

Hackel, Heidi Brayman, and Catherine E. Kelly. 2008. *Reading Women: Literacy, Authorship, and Culture in the Atlantic World, 1500–1800.* Philadelphia: University of Pennsylvania Press.

O'Donnell, Catherine. 2008. *Men of Letters in the Early Republic: Cultivating Forums of Citizenship.* Chapel Hill: Publishing for the Omohundro Institute by the University of North Carolina Press.

PHYSICIAN

From the colonial era to the late nineteenth century, there were many kinds of doctors providing healthcare—most of whom had little formal education. Physicians are people qualified to practice medicine and are typically tasked with diagnosing a broad variety of medical ailments and treatments but do not usually perform complicated, dangerous, or specialized surgeries. Some were university educated, and others learned through apprenticeships under more senior physicians. Midwives, who were apprentice-trained women, offered many of the same services as physicians, though their primary duties were to preside over childbirth—a skill that few men acquired until the nineteenth century. Contemporary physicians understood disease to be the result of an imbalance of "humors" in the body or of a "miasma" (bad air) brought on by offensive odors; germs and pests were not understood to be vectors for disease until later in the nineteenth century.

One Maryland doctor, Alexander Hamilton (no relation to the Founding Father and first secretary of the U.S. Treasury), a graduate of the University of Edinburgh in Scotland, depended on his horse to visit patients located far from his home in Annapolis. During a series of visits to a patient's rural household, Hamilton treated every member of the family—along with any of the patient's slaves. If a person was sick, the doctor might "blister" the patient, a process in which the doctor heated metal cups to burn the patient's skin and cause a blister; the contemporary theory was that the pus from the blister would carry forth the morbid matter that was causing the illness and to allow the pus to escape would eliminate the problem and thus relieve the patient.

Hamilton himself was once treated with a combination of nutmeg and cinnamon and another time with a cathartic called julep cardamom to "purge" his body of his ailment. He once gave a slave an unspecified "antidysenteric" powder that may have been used for treatment of either a serious case of dysentery, called "bloody flux," or some other digestive upset. Dr. Hamilton also administered a "worming powder," and he treated the child's mother with an "antiphlonsic" tincture for an inflammation—possibly a fever—and an "antihysteric" powder for a menstrual problem. Contemporary medical remedies were usually a collection of herbs and ingredients that today are used for seasoning food, such as marjoram, sage, thyme, nutmeg, and cinnamon.

Hamilton was not paid immediately for his medical care, which was a typical practice of the time. After several years, he began suing his patients for those unpaid medical fees. Those lawsuits required that he keep diligent records of his visits and itemized lists of his remedies; such lists have been invaluable to colonial and medical historians.

After treating his patients, Hamilton—who was called Sandie by his family and friends—returned to his Annapolis home, where he kept an apothecary shop. There, he sold pills and powders that he concocted from ingredients in his own garden, as well as imported chemical remedies such as animal dung, opium, mercury (used to treat venereal diseases), and "the bark." This particular bark was from the South American cinchona tree and contained quinine, a remedy that could cure malaria and, as such, was one of the era's few demonstrably effective therapies.

Martha Ballard, midwife of Hallowell, Maine, had a different type of practice, but many of her remedies were similar to those used by Hamilton. She had very little education and no formal medical training, but she was literate and kept a diary describing the care she gave, which included delivering 816 infants between 1785 and her death in 1812. She, too, used a horse to visit patients but also depended on canoes to cross the river or walked through ice and snow. She had a much colder and more demanding climate with which to contend, but her patients lived closer to her.

Ballard reported few difficulties in tending women in birth. Of the over eight hundred deliveries, five mothers died; this survival rate was extraordinary for the time. The most typical case was that of Martha Malloy. On a stormy and cold night in November 1793, Ballard arrived in time to deliver the daughter in the presence of several women. Two days later, she checked on her patient and found her "Tolerable Comfortable." There is no further reference to Malloy until two years later, when Ballard again assisted in the successful delivery of a child with no complications.

There were occasional crises. After a successful delivery of Mrs. Craig's child, Martha Ballard was called back a few days later. Mrs. Craig was not well, feverish and in pain. The midwife gave the woman a clyster (an enema) and applied an ointment of various herbs: tansy, mugwort, chamomile, and hyssop. A week later, Ballard was called again because the patient was no better. Craig had prescribed "the bark" for herself in the mistaken belief that it would cure all fevers, but what is now known as puerperal fever, a bacterial infection, took her life the next day.

Like Hamilton, Ballard used a variety of herbal remedies as well as strong laxatives to cause purges. Unlike Hamilton, she dealt mainly with women and children and only very occasionally the man of the household. She, too, understood disease to be something to be removed from the body and discomfort to be eased with remedies supported by tradition. Unlike him, Ballard called on other women to assist, what is called social childbirth. The presence of other women was essential to take care of the cleaning up, to help comfort the woman giving birth, and to join in a celebration afterward. Hamilton always worked alone, and if he was treated to a meal, it is not mentioned in his court cases. Ballard did not have the same difficulty collecting her fees and did not need to resort to the legal system. However, both Hamilton's and Ballard's experiences were typical for physicians of their era.

Elaine G. Breslaw

See also: *1607–1775:* Apothecary; Midwife; *1861–1914:* Nurse; Surgeon; *1946–1991:* Dentist; Pharmacist; Radiologist and Radiology Technician; Veterinarian; *1992–2019:* Home Health Aide; Physical Therapist

FURTHER READING

Breslaw, Elaine G. 2008. *Dr. Alexander Hamilton and Provincial America: Expanding the Orbit of Scottish Culture*. Baton Rouge: Louisiana State University Press.

Breslaw, Elaine G. 2016. *Lotions, Potions, Pills, and Magic: Health Care in Early America*. New York: New York University Press.
Duffy, John. 1976. *The Healers: The Rise of the Medical Establishment*. New York: McGraw-Hill.
Ulrich, Laura T. 1990. *A Midwife's Tale: Life of Martha Ballard Based on Her Diary, 1785–1812*. New York: Random House.

PLANTER

By the eve of the Civil War (1861–1865), there were around 400,000 slave owners in the American South. That number represents the total number of southern slaveholders, a diverse group of which the majority owned five slaves or fewer. "Planters," however, refers to an even smaller, more homogenous group, seen as the traditional southern ruling elite. These planters, as described by U.S. census officials in 1860, comprised forty-three thousand slaveholders who owned twenty or more slaves. Alternatively, in *Masters of the Big House*, historian William Kauffman Scarborough focuses on the wealthiest individuals, who owned at least 250 slaves by the beginning of the Civil War. Broadly, antebellum planters are a class of southern slaveholders and landowners who maintained a distinct culture with specific customs and who had disproportionate influence on the events leading up to 1860 because their wealth was dependent on the continuation of a labor system that was increasingly being challenged.

Prior to the Civil War, the planter class dominated agricultural markets by enslaving Africans. Their business of planting was one characterized by a uniform type of unskilled labor. Because mechanical methods did not exist or were uneconomical, there was an active, unrelenting demand for cheap agricultural labor. The first planters in the Americas initially relied on indentured servants. However, that demand transformed into a demand for African slaves. In the process, racial slavery came to displace white servitude. It was also accompanied by a shift from class and religion to race as the fundamental basis of enslavement.

The single most important characteristic of planters was that their wealth was intertwined with the brutal and oppressive system of slavery. The expansion of the Atlantic Slave Trade in the late seventeenth and eighteenth centuries gave planters access to inexpensive labor for planting and harvesting in the South. After the Missouri Compromise of 1820, planters began amassing even greater wealth through the expansion of their plantations and labor system throughout the West.

Historian Bertram Wyatt-Brown explains the defining characteristics of planters: an allegiance to families, kinsmen, and immediate neighbors and states; an emphasis on the rituals and values of rustic living; and the belief in the subordination of blacks (Wyatt-Brown 1973). In his study, Scarborough notes that most were born in slave states to large families, had been educated by northern institutions, and were devout Christians. He continues that they were "well-bred, cosmopolitan in background and outlook, intellectually curious, broadly educated, trained for leadership, and gifted with exceptional entrepreneurial skills" (Scarborough 2003, 1).

The wealthiest of this group owned slaves on multiple plantations across the South. For instance, in 1838, Edward Lloyd VI established two new plantations in Mississippi and Louisiana. Cotton, of course, was king as it was the most popular crop among the wealthiest slaveholders. Growers of sugar (grown in southern Louisiana) and rice (grown in coastal Carolina and Georgia) made up a disproportionately large percentage of the antebellum aristocracy. Because of the vastness of their agricultural empires, planters traveled frequently throughout the year but not only for work. Many planters took long vacations, often leaving their day-to-day business operations for weeks at a time in the summer and winter.

Planters worked in collaboration with overseers, drivers, and factors to run their businesses. They relied on two types of managers—overseers, or white supervisors, and drivers, who were enslaved foremen—to run their large plantations. From sunrise to sunset, overseers and drivers worked to maximize production and profit, often using coercion and punishment to motivate slaves. Factors, or commission merchants, assisted planters by financing and marketing their crops. They also routinely took responsibility for a range of informal requests including furnishing household goods, personal items, and plantation supplies; fielding orders of European imports; making transportation and lodging arrangements for planters and their families; and even checking on planters' children who were enrolled in distant northern schools.

In addition to their agricultural empires, many planters were involved in banking, real estate, securities, manufacturing, mercantile activities, railroads, and land speculation. Ultimately, they were businessmen who viewed their plantations and workforce as investments, managing them with an eye on national and international markets. They often did no manual labor, instead monitoring conditions that might impact the supply and demand of their harvests. They remained aware of the impact of economic depressions and a range of natural disasters from infestations and rains to droughts and windstorms. As the sectional crisis escalated, planters also tracked changes in national politics and culture, especially as it threatened business. By remaining informed of external and internal threats to business, they determined the most profitable time to sell their products. Much would change with the Civil War.

The Civil War devastated the planter class. The Union confiscated their lands and freed their slaves. In the wake of its destruction, some were compelled, for the first time in their lives, to do physical labor. Over time, however, they devised another labor system to replace the old one. Former slaves worked for their former masters as sharecroppers and kept one third to one half of the crop for themselves with the remainder going to the landowner. This system kept blacks in poverty and ensured a continual supply of cheap labor to the planter class. Thus, after Reconstruction, many planters regained their wealth and local prestige.

Lauren Ayers

See also: Field Hand; Laborer; Ranchero; Slave Driver; *1607–1775:* Farmer; *1861–1914:* Sharecropper

FURTHER READING

Green, Fletcher M., ed. 1961. *Ferry Hill Plantation Journal: January 4, 1838–January 15, 1839*. Chapel Hill: The University of North Carolina Press. https://docsouth.unc.edu/fpn/blackford/blackford.html.

Kemble, Frances Anne. 1863. *Journal of a Residence on a Georgian Plantation, 1838–1839*. New York: Harper & Brothers, Publishers. https://www.gutenberg.org/files/12422/12422-h/12422-h.htm.

Oakes, James. 1982. *The Ruling Race: A History of American Slaveholders*. New York: Alfred A. Knopf.

Roark, James L. 1977. *Masters Without Slaves: Southern Planters in the Civil War and Reconstruction*. New York: W. W. Norton & Co.

Scarborough, William Kauffman. 2003. *Masters of the Big House: Elite Slaveholders of the Mid-Nineteenth Century South*. Baton Rouge: Louisiana State University Press.

Wyatt-Brown, Bertram, ed. 1973. *The American People in the Antebellum South*. West Haven: Pendulum Press.

PRIMARY DOCUMENT

During the antebellum period, among the most important responsibilities of southern planters was to set the terms upon which their labor force—nearly all slaves or other forms of bound labor—was governed. This document, condensed from the journal Southern Planter, *which provided advice and helpful tips on such matters as field drainage, varieties of corn, and new forms of "scientific agriculture" to planters across the South, may seem to illustrate planters' benevolence toward their slaves, a public stance that planters wished to project. Yet slavery was an extraordinarily brutal practice, as some of this document demonstrates.*

Management of Negroes.

Mr. Editor:

As the proper management of our negroes is a subject not second in importance to any discussed in your columns, I hope it will not be deemed amiss if, in giving my views, I enter somewhat into detail . . .

Our first obligation is undoubtedly to provide them with suitable food and clothing . . . The most common practice is to allow each hand that labors, whether man woman or child (for a boy girl ten years old or over, who is healthy and growing rapidly will eat quite as much as a full grown man or woman,) 3-1/2 lbs. bacon, if middling, or 4 lbs., if shoulder, per week, and bread at will . . . With plenty of vegetables, this allowance is quite sufficient . . . With very little trouble we can always during spring and summer, have plenty of cabbage, kale or mustard for greens, also squashes, Irish potatoes and beans. In fall and winter sweet potatoes, turnips, pumpkins and peas . . . As there is no vegetable of which negroes are more fond than of the common field pea, it is well to save enough of them in the fall to have them frequently during the spring and summer . . . If occasionally a little molasses be added to the allowance, the cost will be but a trifle, while the negro will esteem it as a great luxury . . . [T]he negroes, during the spring and summer, usually get plenty of milk once a day. During fall and winter the quantity of milk is more limited, and what molasses they get, they are made to win by picking cotton . . .

The negroes should be required to keep their houses and yards clean; and in case of neglect should receive such punishment as will be likely to insure more cleanly habits in future . . .

The master should never establish any regulation among his slaves until he is fully convinced of its propriety and equity. Being thus convinced, and having issued his orders, implicit obedience should be required and rigidly enforced. Firmness of manner, and promptness to enforce obedience, will save much trouble, and be the means of avoiding the necessity for much whipping. The negro should feel that his master is his law-giver and judge; and yet his protector and friend, but so far above him, as never to be approached save in the most respectful manner . . . While at work they should be brisk. If one is called to you, or sent from you, and he does not move briskly, chastise him at once.—If this does not answer, repeat the dose and double the quantity. When at work I have no objection to their whistling or singing some lively tune, but no *drawling* tunes are allowed in the field, for their motion is almost certain to keep time with the music . . .

One of the most important regulation on a farm is to see that the hands get plenty of sleep. They are thoughtless, and if allowed to do so, will set up late of nights. Some of them will be up at all hours, and others instead of going to bed will set on a stool or chair and nod or sleep till morning . . . If any one is caught out of bed after [10:00 p.m.], they should be punished . . .

In the infliction of punishment it should ever be borne in mind that the object is *correction.* If the negro is humble and appears duly sensible of the impropriety of his conduct, a very moderate chastisement will answer better than a sever one. If, however, he is stubborn or impertinent or persevere in what you *know* to be a falsehood, a slight punishment will only make bad worse. The negro however should see from your cool, yet determined manner, that it is not in consequence of your excited temper, but of his fault, and for his correction that he is punished.

Source: "Tattler." 1860. "Management of Negroes." *The Southern Planter,* 11, 39–42, passim.

POLITICIAN

Politicians are those who are professionally involved in politics, often as holders or candidates for elected office. In the late eighteenth century, political occupations were held exclusively by white men. Most politicians came from British or western European descent and practiced some sect of Protestant Christianity. They represented constituencies that shared these demographics, but the concerns of enslaved or free African Americans, Native Americans, women, and children were largely excluded from political consideration.

Serving as a politician offered minimal prospects for financial gain. Salaries were quite low and rarely covered a politician's living expenses, let alone those of his family. Furthermore, other opportunities to make money from a prominent position were limited. Eighteenth-century politicians rarely published books or gave speeches to raise additional funds. As a result, most politicians came from middling or elite families and depended on another source of wealth to maintain their lifestyles. Many were married with children and had worked in another profession prior to entering public service. Politicians were often lawyers, doctors, plantation owners, farmers, or merchants. At the very least, they could read and write basic English, but many completed higher education to pursue careers in law, finance, or science. As part of their education, elites and professionals studied foreign languages, including French, Greek, Latin, and Hebrew, and were well versed in ancient Roman and Greek histories.

Because of the poor financial benefits, many politicians served out of a sense of duty or honor. They believed the best men in society were obligated to lead and set an example for their fellow citizens. Others were motivated by a specific cause, like American independence, or they worked toward a particular outcome. As a result, politicians rarely stayed in public service for more than a few years. Most served a term or two before returning home to care for their families, farms, or businesses. Others grew disheartened by their inability to effect change and abandoned public life. After the Treaty of Paris (1783) ended the Revolutionary War, delegates often neglected to attend sessions of the Confederation Congress. Frustrated by Congress's lack of power, some delegates never showed up, and others went home in disgust. At several points, attendance was so low that Congress could not convene a quorum to start a session.

Unlike modern state and federal governments, eighteenth-century legislatures did not meet year round. Instead, they usually met in one or two sessions in the winter and spring months. They adjourned during the summer and early fall so members could return home to participate in or oversee the harvest on their farms and plantations. In the late summer and early fall, delegates also hoped to avoid cities, where legislatures typically met, because of disease. Transmitted by mosquitoes that thrived in hot, swampy weather, yellow fever and malaria epidemics terrorized eighteenth-century cities.

When in session, whether at the state or federal level, legislatures convened six days a week. Legislatures usually met officially for a few hours per day, gathering to vote on motions, debate proposed legislation, or introduce new issues for consideration. After each session, delegates turned to committee meetings, where the lion's share of work was accomplished. Legislatures created committees to deal with every task, including corresponding with other states, raising revenue, drafting legislation, organizing the militia, and advising the governor or president. Later in the evening, politicians continued their work at home. They drafted proposals, corresponded with colleagues or business associates across the world, and wrote letters to family members. They exchanged bits of news, checked on their family's health, managed their business interests, and coordinated efforts behind the scenes with politicians in other cities or states.

Starting in the early evening, most politicians enjoyed a robust social life. After committee meetings, many delegates shared a meal or tea with friends or colleagues. Some delegates rented houses in capital cities, like Williamsburg, Boston, and Philadelphia, and brought their families with them when government was in session. Wives of prominent politicians and local elites hosted tea, dinners, dances, and balls for friends, colleagues, and visiting dignitaries. Most politicians, however, left their families at home and resided in boarding houses, which served as a hub of social activity. Politicians would gather to eat and strategize over a meal in the shared dining room. Boarding houses also served as a valuable way to shore up alliances between state delegations.

In 1774, when the delegates arrived in Philadelphia for the first Continental Congress, more delegates had visited London than Philadelphia. They often did not know anyone outside their own delegation and had more emotional and commercial ties to Europe than the other states. Because boarding houses catered to visiting politicians, they fostered new relationships between delegates and helped politicians build support for their proposals. The relationships forged in boarding houses, dining rooms, and private meetings also shaped the development of the state and federal governments for decades to come, even as political occupations expanded to include white men from all classes in the years following the revolution.

Lindsay M. Chervinsky

See also: Diplomat; *1607–1775:* Governor; *1992–2019:* Campaign Manager

FURTHER READING

Burnett, Edmund Cody. 1941. *The Continental Congress*. New York: The Macmillan Company.

Locke, Joseph, and Ben Wright, eds. 2014. "Pursuing Political, Religious and Individual Freedom." In *The American Yawp: A Free and Online, Collaboratively Built American History Textbook*. Stanford: Stanford University Press.

Van Cleve, George William. 2017. *We Have Not a Government: The Articles of Confederation and the Road to the Constitution*. Chicago: University of Chicago Press.

PRIMARY DOCUMENT

In this oratory given before the House of Burgesses (Virginia) shortly before the beginning of the Revolutionary War, the lawyer and politician Patrick Henry offered a stark dichotomy for those who sought independence from the British. In his "Give Me Liberty or Give Me Death" speech, Henry outlined the significant consequences associated with pursuing independence. He noted that the British possessed the most powerful military in the world—and its full attention was directed toward the American revolutionaries. In likening the Americans' relationship with the British as similar to that of a slave and an abusive master, Henry's speech galvanized opposition to the British as war loomed.

Mr. President, no man thinks more highly than I do of the patriotism, as well as abilities, of the very worthy gentlemen who have just addressed the House. But different men often see the same subject in different lights; and, therefore, I hope it will not be thought disrespectful to those gentlemen if, entertaining as I do, opinions of a character very opposite to theirs, I shall speak forth my sentiments freely, and without reserve. This is no time for ceremony. The question before the House is one of awful moment to this country. For my own part, I consider it as nothing less than a question of freedom or slavery; and in proportion to the magnitude of the subject ought to be the freedom of the debate. It is only in this way that we can hope to arrive at truth, and fulfil the great responsibility which we hold to God and our country. Should I keep back my opinions at such a time, through fear of giving offence, I should consider myself as guilty of treason towards my country, and of an act of disloyalty toward the majesty of heaven, which I revere above all earthly kings.

Mr. President, it is natural to man to indulge in the illusions of hope. We are apt to shut our eyes against a painful truth, and listen to the song of that siren till she transforms us into beasts. Is this the part of wise men, engaged in a great and arduous struggle for liberty? Are we disposed to be of the number of those who, having eyes, see not, and, having ears, hear not, the things which so nearly concern their temporal salvation? For my part, whatever anguish of spirit it may cost, I am willing to know the whole truth; to know the worst, and to provide for it.

I have but one lamp by which my feet are guided; and that is the lamp of experience. I know of no way of judging of the future but by the past. And judging by the past, I wish to know what there has been in the conduct of the British ministry for the last ten years, to justify those hopes with which gentlemen have been pleased to solace themselves, and the House? Is it that insidious smile with which our petition has been lately received? Trust it not, sir; it will prove a snare to your feet. Suffer not yourselves to be betrayed with a kiss. Ask yourselves how this gracious reception of our petition comports with these war-like preparations which cover our waters and darken our land. Are fleets and armies necessary to a work of love and reconciliation? Have we shown ourselves so unwilling to be reconciled, that force must be called in to win back our love? Let us not deceive ourselves, sir. These are the implements of war and subjugation; the last arguments to which kings resort. I ask, gentlemen, sir, what means this martial array, if its purpose be not to force us to submission? Can gentlemen assign any other possible motive for it? Has Great Britain any enemy, in this quarter of the world, to call for all this accumulation of navies and armies? No, sir, she has none. They are meant for us; they can be meant for no other. They are sent over to bind and rivet upon us those chains which the British ministry have been so long forging. And what have we to oppose to them? Shall we try argument? Sir, we have been trying that for the last ten years. Have we anything new to offer upon the subject? Nothing. We have held the subject up in every light of which it is capable; but it has been all in vain. Shall we resort to entreaty and humble supplication? What terms shall we find which have not been already exhausted? Let us not, I beseech you, sir, deceive ourselves. Sir, we have done everything that could be done, to avert the storm which is now coming on. We have petitioned; we have remonstrated; we have supplicated; we have prostrated ourselves before the throne, and have implored its interposition to arrest the tyrannical hands of the ministry and Parliament. Our petitions have been slighted; our remonstrances have produced additional violence and insult; our supplications have been disregarded; and we have been spurned, with contempt, from the foot of the throne. In vain, after these things, may we indulge the fond hope of peace and reconciliation. There is no longer any room for hope. If we wish to be free if we mean to preserve inviolate those inestimable privileges for which we have been so long contending if we mean not basely to abandon the noble struggle in which we have been so long engaged, and which we have pledged ourselves never to abandon until the glorious object of our contest shall be obtained, we must fight! I repeat it, sir, we must fight! An appeal to arms and to the God of Hosts is all that is left us!

They tell us, sir, that we are weak; unable to cope with so formidable an adversary. But when shall we be stronger? Will it be the next week, or the next year? Will it be when we are totally disarmed, and when a British guard shall be stationed in every house? Shall we gather strength by irresolution and inaction? Shall we acquire the means of effectual resistance, by lying supinely on our backs, and hugging the delusive phantom of hope, until our enemies shall have bound us hand and foot? Sir, we are not weak if we make a proper use of those means which the God of nature hath placed in our power. Three millions of people, armed in the holy cause of liberty, and in such a country as that which we possess, are invincible by any force which our enemy can send against us. Besides, sir, we shall not fight our battles alone. There is a just God who presides over the destinies of nations; and who will raise up friends to fight our battles for us. The battle, sir, is not to the strong alone; it is to the vigilant, the active, the brave. Besides, sir, we have no election. If we were base enough to desire it, it is now too late to retire from the contest. There is no retreat but in submission and slavery! Our chains are forged! Their clanking may be heard on the plains of Boston! The war is inevitable[2]and let it come! I repeat it, sir, let it come.

It is in vain, sir, to extenuate the matter. Gentlemen may cry, Peace, Peace but there is no peace. The war is actually begun! The next gale that sweeps from the north will bring to our ears the clash of resounding arms! Our brethren are already in the field! Why stand we here idle? What is it that gentlemen wish? What would they have? Is life so dear, or peace so sweet, as to be purchased at the price of chains and slavery? Forbid it, Almighty God! I know not what course others may take; but as for me, give me liberty or give me death!

Source: Selim H. Peabody. 1880. *American Patriotism: Speeches, Letters and Other Papers Which Illustrate the Foundation, the Development, the Preservation of the United States of America.* New York: American Book Exchange, 108–110.

PRINTER

A printer's job or business concerns commercial printing. Americans have long held dear the idea of the free press—a concept so fundamental and important that it was enshrined in the very first amendment to the U.S. Constitution. A free press in a democracy functions to bring knowledge to the nation's citizenry. But without printers, there would be no press—and certainly no free press. The trade of the printer in colonial America was one of great importance, not just because it required a certain set of skills but also because of the social and political roles that printers played in the nation-to-be. For that reason, many historians refer to printers as the "aristocrats" of colonial American workers.

In this period, a printer's career likely began as a lowly apprentice, often when a young boy—or girl—was in his—or her—early teens. The printer's apprentice performed much of the janitorial work of the printing company (a large printing company might have three or more printing presses). Apprentices lived under the watchful eyes of the master for as long as seven years. An apprentice's daily work consisted of sweeping and cleaning the work area and assisting the compositor, who placed the individual letters of typeface into a type case, into which letters and punctuation were arranged to create words and sentences. An apprentice also accomplished various small tasks and fetched ink for the pressmen, who operated the hand presses that printed works on paper. Apprentices worked long hours six days per week; they were often expected to be first in the shop and the last to leave. Because printers had to be literate to do their work, masters customarily sent undereducated apprentices to night schools after the long workday. Most apprentices took these educational opportunities seriously as failing to obtain aptitude in reading and writing prevented an apprentice from ever achieving journeyman's status. Apprentices who ignored their responsibilities, talked back to their masters or journeymen, or snuck out at night to drink with their peers were routinely punished with beatings from their masters. These beatings could be severe and led many apprentices to run away even though employment prospects for a printer's apprentice without great talent were limited; in many cities, master printers refused to hire runaway apprentices who had escaped other printing shops.

Journeymen printers and apprentices with experience and talent worked as compositors. Compositors set the blocks of individual typeface into the type case, using a compositor's rod to horizontally align each line of type. Many printers developed their own particular letter fonts. To do so required a caster to manually carve and chisel an entire alphabet (including upper- and lowercase letters), numerals, and punctuation marks into a hardened steel block no more than one inch tall and often much smaller. Once the type font was completed, the caster set a single steel letter block into a type mold and then poured hot metal into it, which made the typeface with each raised letter clearly distinguished. Even a small but busy printer with just one press needed an extensive set of typeface to print out just a weekly newspaper. Many colonial printers instead bought their type from English manufacturers, though the quality was often poor. These English typeface makers produced letters that often needed repair or that were not of uniform font.

However, the font Caslon is, in fact, a typeface created by an English manufacturer that printers praised for its design and quality. Printers also imported paper from England as the first North American papermaker to begin producing paper, made from old rags, did not open until 1690 in Philadelphia.

Once the compositor set the typeface in the cast for work, the press workers placed an individual sheet of paper on the inked letters set in type casts, hand pulled a press onto it, and then lifted the machine to produce a printed page. All printed works in the colonial period were handprinted on a letterpress machine; automated machines that fed paper into the press were not created until after the invention of the steam engine in the early nineteenth century. Once a sheet was printed, an apprentice took it off the press and prepared it for shipment. Apprentices also folded newspapers, assisted the bookbinders in making books, and saw to other menial duties.

Early colonial printers produced religious texts, sermons, and Bibles in various indigenous languages for the instruction of nearby Native Americans, as well as other useful books such as apothecary manuals, medical or anatomical texts, and grammars. Almanacs that provided weather forecasts, tide tables, and other information to farmers were particularly popular. Because England's printing trades were far more advanced than American presses, especially before the late colonial period, colonists mostly read books imported from England or the European continent. More popular in America were newspapers, broadsheets (often one-page political commentary), and other informational and political tracts. Colonists looked to printers to produce reading material that could be read repeatedly, shared with family members and friends, and circulated widely among themselves. A single issue of any newspaper was often read by so many colonists that it eventually disintegrated from being handled so many times.

American printers benefited from professional networks they carefully fostered with other printers. Printers not only produced printed goods but also customarily wrote material for the newspapers, broadsheets, pamphlets, and other materials they printed. Master printers created thin volumes of collected works or wrote copy for the newspapers they printed themselves. Commonly, printers not only set type, managed the press, and distributed reading material, but they also worked as editors, journalists, and opinion writers. Many printers saw their work as a way to help mold colonists' religious, moral, and political views. Because printers were highly esteemed and often earned moderately high incomes, printing family "dynasties" emerged early. The (Samuel) Green family included several generations of printers, while the Franklins, of whom Benjamin was the most notable, might be the most famous of colonial printers. Both the Green and Franklin families included women who owned print shops as well as worked as compositors and printers. These networks of printers provided moral and financial support to each other. Since printing orders were often materials ordered by colonial governments, a printer whose presses were occupied referred orders to another printer within his network. Additionally, colonists who objected to a printer's work often protested vigorously—and sometimes in error—while other printers provided safety and financial support from angry mobs.

Printers' networks also encouraged the spread of the printing trade into the South and onto the western frontier, as in the case with several printers associated with Benjamin Franklin's network. In South Carolina, Franklin had supported several printers who published the *South-Carolina Gazette*, a newspaper established in Charles Town (now Charleston) that traded news items with Franklin's own *Pennsylvania Gazette*. In the years before the revolution, Peter Timothy, who had taken over the newspaper from his mother, Elizabeth, a widow, and Franklin, was sanctioned by the royal authorities for his reporting on their handling of sensitive affairs within the colony, including its relationship with members of the Choctaw tribe. Franklin and Timothy corresponded often about business and political matters. Building upon both family ties and business networks, printers throughout the colonies contributed enormously to the expansion of newspapers as by 1740, most newspapers were published by printers. These professional networks helped facilitate not only the growth of American newspapers but shaped how colonists increasingly grew to understand their identity as independent Americans.

Nancy Quam-Wickham

See also: Inventor; Pamphleteer

FURTHER READING

Clark, Charles E. 1994. *Public Prints: The Newspaper in Anglo-American Culture, 1665–1740.* London: Oxford University Press.

Frasca, Ralph. 2006. *Benjamin Franklin's Printing Network: Disseminating Virtue in Early America.* Columbia: University Press of Missouri.

Tunis, Edwin. 1965. *Colonial Craftsmen and the Beginnings of American Industry.* Baltimore: Johns Hopkins University Press.

PRIMARY DOCUMENT

In this document, Benjamin Franklin describes how he became a printer. His father apprenticed him at the age of twelve to his older brother James in Boston. Central to Franklin's training was literacy—developing and refining his reading and writing skills to improve his abilities as a printer. In a time when many citizens were only marginally literate, to become a printer, a young man had to be able to read and write well. Because of these skills, printers like Franklin often became influential writers as well.

From a child, I was fond of reading, and all the little money that came into my hands was ever laid out in books. Pleased with the *Pilgrim's Progress*, my first collection was of John Bunyan's works in separate little volumes. I afterward sold them to enable me to buy R. Burton's *Historical Collections*; they were small chapmen's books, and cheap, 40 or 50 in all.

This bookish inclination at length determined my father to make me a printer, though he had already one son (James) of that profession. In 1717 my brother James returned from England with a press and letters to set up his business in Boston. I liked it much better than that of my father, but still had a hankering for the sea. To prevent the apprehended effect of such an inclination, my father was impatient to have me bound to my brother. I stood out some time, but at last was persuaded, and signed the indentures when I was yet but twelve years old. I was to serve as an apprentice till I was twenty-one years of age, only I was to be allowed journeyman's wages during the last year. In a little time, I made great proficiency in the business, and became a useful hand to my brother. I now had access to better books. An acquaintance with the apprentices of booksellers enabled me sometimes to borrow a small one, which I was careful to return soon and clean. Often I sat up in my room reading the greatest part of the night, when the book was borrowed in the evening and to be returned early in the morning, lest it should be missed or wanted.

And after some time an ingenious tradesman, Mr. Matthew Adams, who had a pretty collection of books, and who frequented our printing-house, took notice of me, invited me to his library, and very kindly lent me such books as I chose to read. I now took a fancy to poetry, and made some little pieces; my brother, thinking it might turn to account, encouraged me, and put me on composing occasional ballads. One was called *The Lighthouse Tragedy*, and contained an account of the drowning of Captain Worthilake, with his two daughters: the other was a sailor's song, on the taking of *Teach* (or Blackbeard) the pirate. They were wretched stuff, in the Grub-street-ballad style; and when they were printed he sent me about the town to sell them. The first sold wonderfully, the event being recent, having made a great noise. This flattered my vanity; but my father discouraged me by ridiculing my performances, and telling me verse-makers were generally beggars. So I escaped being a poet, most probably a very bad one; but as prose writing has been of great use to me in the course of my life, and was a principal means of my advancement, I shall tell you how, in such a situation, I acquired what little ability I have in that way.

When about 16 years of age I happened to meet with a book, written by one Tryon, recommending a vegetable diet. I determined to go into it. My brother, being yet unmarried, did not keep house, but boarded himself and his apprentices in another family. My refusing to eat flesh occasioned an inconveniency, and I was frequently chided for my singularity. I made myself acquainted with Tryon's manner of preparing some of his dishes, such as boiling potatoes or rice, making hasty pudding, and a few others, and then proposed to my brother, that if he would give me, weekly, half the money he paid for my board, I would board myself. He instantly agreed to it, and I presently found that I could save half what he paid me. This was an additional fund for buying books. But I had another advantage in it. My brother and the rest going from the printing-house to their meals, I remained there alone, and, dispatching presently my light repast, which often was no more than a biscuit or a slice of bread, a handful of raisins or a tart from the pastry-cook's, and a glass of water, had the rest of the time till their return for study, in which I made the greater progress, from that greater clearness of head and quicker apprehension which usually attend temperance in eating and drinking . . .

My brother had, in 1720 or 1721, begun to print a newspaper. It was the second that appeared in America, and was called the *New England Courant*. The only one before it was the *Boston News-Letter*. I remember his being dissuaded by some of his friends from the undertaking, as not likely to succeed, one newspaper being, in their judgment, enough for America. At this time (1771) there are not less than five-and-twenty. He went on, however, with the undertaking, and after having worked in composing the types and printing off the sheets, I was employed to carry the papers thro' the streets to the customers.

He had some ingenious men among his friends, who amused themselves by writing little pieces for this paper, which gained it credit and made it more in demand, and these gentlemen often visited us. Hearing their conversations, and their accounts of the approbation their papers were received with, I was excited to try my hand among them; but, being still a boy, and suspecting that my brother would object to printing anything of mine in his paper if he knew it to be mine, I contrived to disguise my hand, and, writing an anonymous paper, I put it in at night under the door of the printing-house. It was found in the morning, and communicated to his writing friends when they called in as usual. They read it, commented on it in my hearing, and I had the exquisite pleasure of finding it met with their approbation, and that, in their different guesses at the author, none were named but men of some character among us for learning and ingenuity. I suppose now that I was rather lucky in my judges, and that perhaps they were not really so very good ones as I then esteemed them.

Encouraged, however, by this, I wrote and conveyed in the same way to the press several more papers which were equally approved; and I kept my secret till my small fund of sense for such performances was pretty well exhausted, and then I discovered it, when I began to be considered a little more by my brother's acquaintance, and in a manner that did not quite please him, as he thought, probably with reason, that it tended to make me too vain. And, perhaps, this might be one occasion of the differences that we began to have about this time. Though a brother, he considered himself as my master, and me as his apprentice, and, accordingly, expected the same services from me as he would from another, while I thought he demeaned me too much in some he required of me, who from a brother expected more indulgence. Our disputes were often brought before our father, and I fancy I was either generally in the right, or else a better pleader, because the judgment was generally in my favor. But my brother was passionate, and had often beaten me, which I took extremely amiss; and, thinking my apprenticeship very tedious, I was continually wishing for some opportunity of shortening it . . .

Source: Benjamin Franklin. 1922. *The Autobiography of Benjamin Franklin.* Garden City: Doubleday and Page Company, 14–16, 19–20.

RANCHERO

Rancheros were cattle ranch (*rancho*) owners during the nineteenth century, primarily in California and other western territories. Andrés Pico was one of the most famous rancheros in California before the U.S. Civil War, a period in which large-scale cattle ranching was common only in California and parts of the Southwest. California, with its abundant natural resources and access to Pacific trade, was the biggest prize for the United States as a result of the Mexican-American War (1846–1848). Despite assurances that property rights would be respected, many Americans squatted (settled without permission) on Mexican ranchos following the war. Rancheros like Pico fought these squatters in the courts while simultaneously trying to confirm their land titles. Although most rancho titles were ultimately confirmed, many rancheros had to sell off the bulk of their land to pay legal fees, new taxes, and debts they acquired while trying to adapt to a more cash-based American economy. They also had to contend with a rising tide of American racism and racial violence. Most rancheros had African or Native American heritage. Rancheros used a variety of strategies to deal with these challenges. Many, including Pico, drew upon their expertise leading, controlling, and sometimes harming people, as well as animals, from horseback.

Like most rancheros, Pico owned property as a result of his military service, his personal and political connections, and the service and connections of his relatives. Pico's grandfather arrived in California in the eighteenth century as a soldier for the Spanish missions. As the frontier institutions of both the Spanish Empire and Catholic Church, the missions were ranching and farming communities led by Spanish priests and built and maintained by local Native Americans who received no pay and lived under harsh discipline. Native American *vaqueros* (cowboys) tended the cattle and horses on mission lands and, later, on the ranchos, which increased in number and importance after the missions were secularized (removed from Church control) following Mexico's independence from Spain. The conditions of vaqueros and other Native American workers were not improved on the ranchos, and their willingness to continue working without pay speaks to their continued vulnerability amidst social and environmental upheaval. The animals, plants, and diseases that arrived along with the missions greatly disrupted the hunter-gatherer lifestyles of local Native Americans. One of the most visible changes was the sudden appearance of "cattle on a thousand hills," in the words of one historian. Horses, also non-native, spread quickly as well and were treated as expendable by the rancheros. When riding long distances, rancheros would typically be accompanied by a mounted vaquero who tended eight extra horses. Every two dozen miles or so, the men would change horses, and the used-up animals would be abandoned to either recover on their own or perish.

The style of riding Pico's grandfather and the other mission soldiers brought to California was suitable for both fighting and ranching. The most noticeable modification on the traditional Spanish military style was the backward movement of the stirrups toward the center of the horse's belly. This ensured that the pull of a lassoed animal would be more evenly distributed between the horse's front and hind legs. The *riata* (lasso) was the most important tool of rancheros and vaqueros. According to one firsthand account, boys who grew up on a rancho would learn to rope kittens and other small animals before ever mounting a horse. Experienced rancheros and vaqueros could use a riata to take down cows for branding or slaughter, young horses for breaking, and even grizzly bears, which were sometimes captured by teams of riders for use in bear and bull fights.

In addition to riatas, rancheros and vaqueros could also skillfully wield the horseman's spear—the lance. In what may have been the largest battle in California history and the biggest American setback in the Mexican-American War, Pico commanded a group of about one hundred lance-wielding rancheros and vaqueros against a larger body of American soldiers whose firearms had been rendered useless by wet gunpowder. After the Americans regrouped and renewed the offensive, Pico negotiated California's surrender to U.S. forces, but he found other ways to display his skills as a horseman. A week after U.S. soldiers conducted Los Angeles's first Fourth of July celebration in 1847, local rancheros invited the soldiers to come down from their hilltop fortress to watch a bullfight in the main plaza. One soldier recalled that they instead watched from the hill, fearing that the invitation might be a trick. "General Pico," the soldier recollected, "took an active part" in the bullfight, a violent spectacle that amazed the American servicemen. Pico also impressed the Americans by striking out at common enemies.

Native livestock raiders, some of whom had escaped from the missions and ranchos, stole horses in droves to ride, eat, or sell them to Native American horse traders in the interior. Rancheros sometimes responded to these raids by calling on their vaqueros, relatives, and the men of neighboring ranchos to join them on punitive counterraids. Livestock raiding increased amidst the chaos of the Mexican-American War, and Pico led a series of retaliatory strikes against Native Americans in the aftermath of the conflict. These actions made a positive impression on the newly arrived Americans, as did his pivotal role leading a company of lancers in 1857 in pursuit of a band of Hispanic men implicated in the death of a Los Angeles County sheriff. For these efforts, the governor of California made Pico a general in the state militia.

Pico also launched a successful American political career, repeatedly winning election to the state legislature. Rancheros did much of their politicking, and spent many of their waking hours, on horseback. It was not uncommon for a man to mount up when visited by a ranchero so that the two men could talk at the same level without forcing the ranchero to dismount. Pico's occupation may have influenced his political style in other ways as well. One newspaper claimed that his voters were typically "herded and driven" to the polls. While this was an exaggeration, rancheros did exert considerable political influence by corralling the votes of relatives, workers, and other men enmeshed in their social networks. To a great extent, these networks grew out of the hide and tallow trade, which flourished in the decades before the Mexican-American War. While most California beef was consumed locally, hides and tallow (processed fat) were frequently shipped to the industrializing U.S. Northeast, where they were transformed into manufactured goods such as shoes, belts, candles, and soap. In return, rancheros received factory-made tools and weapons as well as clothing, furniture, and luxury items like fine liquor and cigars. These imports could then be used as status symbols by the rancheros or given to others to strengthen the bonds of obligation that held their social networks together.

Despite efforts by Pico and other rancheros to keep their vast lands and maintain their positions atop large social networks, the forces arrayed against them ultimately proved too strong. In addition to having to contend with a military invasion and a relentless stream of settlers, rancheros also suffered a string of bad luck. Demand for beef from gold rush emigrants was strong in the early 1850s, spurring massive cattle drives across the state, but boom turned to bust when California's tough, stringy beef lost favor to superior meat shipped in from elsewhere. Then came environmental catastrophe in the 1860s with a massive flood followed by several years of drought. When rain returned, many rancheros had little in the way of cattle and much in the way of debt. Pico died in 1876, the same year that brought the railroad to Los Angeles. His son continued to operate a small ranch at the former San Fernando Mission, but the era of the big ranchos came to a close as the growing and increasingly U.S.-born population implemented more land-intensive methods of farming and livestock raising throughout the state.

Daniel Lynch

See also: Planter; *1861–1914:* Cowboy; Sharecropper

FURTHER READING

Cleland, Robert Glass. 1951. *The Cattle on a Thousand Hills, Southern California, 1850–1880.* San Marino: Huntington Library.

Gray, Paul Bryan. 1998. *Forster vs. Pico: The Struggle for Rancho Santa Margarita.* Spokane: The Arthur H. Clark Co.

Haas, Lisbeth. 2014. *Saints and Citizens: Indigenous Histories of Colonial Missions and Mexican California.* Berkeley: University of California Press.

Monroy, Douglas. 1990. *Thrown among Strangers: The Making of Mexican Culture in Frontier California.* Berkeley: University of California Press.

Phillips, George Harwood. 2010. *Vineyards and Vaqueros: Indian Labor and the Economic Expansion of Southern California, 1771–1781.* Norman: The Arthur H. Clark Co.

Pubols, Louise. 2009. *The Father of All: The de La Guerra Family, Power, and Patriarchy in Mexican California.* Berkeley: University of California Press.

SAILOR

Sailors worked on boats and ships of all sorts—fishing vessels, sailing ships, and coastal barges—that carried goods and people throughout the Atlantic world, from England to New York, Charleston, and other Atlantic seaboard ports and to the Caribbean, South America, Southern Europe, and Africa. They worked long hours on ships that often leaked, in both good and bad weather, for weeks or months at a time. Sailors also played a seminal role in every aspect of the American Revolution.

Although mariners, or sailors, were among the most poorly paid labors in colonial America—probate records demonstrate that they were considerably poorer than other white workers—they took an active role in the prewar protests leading to the American Revolution and the combat that followed them. Many sailors acquired substantial experience resisting British aggression through impressment riots. Sailors saw impressment, the act of removing sailors from a merchant or fishing vessel and forcing them to serve on a British warship, as a form of slavery. They frequently justified their resistance to impressment with words like "freedom" and "liberty." Resistance to impressment could take many forms including fleeing, fighting, rioting, and murdering. Mariners took control of the town of Boston during the Knowles Riot in 1747 to protest impressment. One Marblehead fisherman struck and killed a Royal Navy officer from HMS *Rose* with a harpoon in 1769 to resist impressment. Since sailors experienced harsh discipline such as being lashed with a cat-o-nine tails and contracted infectious diseases like typhus on board the King's ships, there was good reason to avoid them at all costs.

Many sailors in the colonies found taxation especially obnoxious British policy. Coastal fishermen objected to being taxed to support a mariner's hospital in Greenwich, England. They thought it was absurd that the British government would force them to pay for a hospital on the opposite side of the Atlantic Ocean. When they heard the cries of patriot organizers against the Sugar Act, the Stamp Act, the Townsend Act, and the tax on tea, sailors identified with these arguments against oppression. Two of the victims killed at the Boston Massacre were sailors. Several others also participated in the Boston Tea Party. Furthermore, the practice of tarring and feathering British officials had its origins in maritime culture.

When hostilities broke out between Great Britain and the colonies on April 19, 1775, trade with Britain also ceased. Having worked on both merchantmen and fishing vessels, sailors were familiar with ship board discipline. Hence, the shift from civilian life to military and naval pursuits was far less dramatic than the transition experienced by farmers and tradesmen. Coastal communities such as Marblehead, Massachusetts, sent 50 percent of their adult male populations to war. The Continental Navy, state navies, and privateers all needed sailors to man their vessels. Approximately 200,000 men fought in the American Revolution at sea in different capacities. Naval actions during the American Revolution began when George Washington fitted out a fleet of schooners during the Siege of Boston and continued as both individual states and the Continental Congress created naval forces and commissioned privateers. Privateers were privately armed vessels that were authorized to seize enemy vessels and carry them into port, where their fate would be decided by prize courts. When privateers and naval vessels seized enemy vessels, those seized ships became prizes. The captain of a naval vessel or a privateer put a crew on the prize and sent it into the nearest friendly port. Both privateers and naval vessels carried considerably larger crews than merchant vessels, and sailors frequently signed up for another cruise after they carried a prize into port.

Normally, a sailor began his career as a boy and advanced to the rank of seaman. Once a sailor learned the important skill of reefing, sheeting, and steering, he became an able-bodied seaman. If a seaman was fortunate, he might advance to a mate or a master of a vessel. The American Revolution accelerated this process of advancement. Some sailors served on both privateers and naval vessels during the war. As a sailor completed each cruise, it became easier to advance through the ranks of the maritime world. He could even acquire command experience as prize master that would not be available in peacetime. The lure of prize money convinced many fishermen to sign on to privateers rather than reenlist in the regiment commanded by the Marblehead merchant Jonathan Glover.

Although a sailor's opportunities for advancement increased substantially with the American Revolution, his possibility of being wounded, killed, or captured did as well. Eighteenth-century naval warfare was a brutal business. Sailors were given a double ration of grog, watered-down rum, to make them indifferent to the bloodshed. Operating the guns on a man-of-war could result in temporary deafness. Blinding smoke added to the confusion brought on by combat. While battles where men-of-war exchanged broadsides and hand-to-hand combat with boarders were rare, the sailors who survived them described them in terrifying detail. Sailors recalled seeing mangled corpses in heaps on the decks of both vessels after the American vessel *Bon Homme Richard* defeated the HMS *Serapis*, an English warship, in the North Sea in 1779. During the battle with the HMS *Serapis*, the *Bon Homme Richard's* officers forced several sailors who retreated below decks back to their stations at gunpoint.

While some sailors experienced death or crippling injury, capture was more common experience. Captured sailors had a variety of experiences when the enemy seized their vessels. Some signed the articles (a sort of labor contract) of the enemy vessel and joined its crew. Hence, there were sailors who fought on both sides of the American Revolution. On the other hand, capture might result in incarceration in a prison or prison ship. Sailors who were sent to Forten Prison or the Mill prison in England fared better than their comrades on prison hulks. Prison hulks such as the *Jersey*, which was moored in New York Harbor, were overcrowded and filled with disease. Many captured sailors on board the *Jersey* suffered from smallpox, dysentery, or typhoid. One sailor went as far as to inoculate himself for smallpox. Obviously, he thought he had a better chance of surviving the mild infection contracted through inoculation than the deadlier infection that was killing his countrymen.

Edward J. Martin

See also: Bargeman; Harpooner; *1607–1775:* Rigger; Shipwright; *1992–2019:* Navigator

FURTHER READING

Gilje, Paul A. 2004. *Liberty on the Waterfront: American Maritime Culture in the Age of Revolution*. Philadelphia: University of Pennsylvania.

Magra, Christopher. 2004. "Bred to the Sea, Maritime Marblehead, Massachusetts and the Origins and Progress of the American Revolution." *New England Quarterly* 77, no. 4: 531–562.

Roland, Alex, W. Jeffery Bolster, and Alexander Keyssar. 2008. *The Way of the Ship: America's Maritime History Revisioned, 1600–2000.* Hoboken: John Wiley & Sons Inc.

PRIMARY DOCUMENT

One of the primary causes, or outrages, that had long inflamed international tensions after the revolution was the British practice of impressing American sailors. Impressment was the forced capture of a sailor and his subsequent service on a British naval vessel. The account of sailor James M'Lane of Hartford, Connecticut, tells in vivid detail how an American vessel, bound (presumably on a slaving voyage) from the coast of west Africa to Grenada, was stopped at Grenada and some of its crewmembers, including M'Lane, impressed, or "pressed." As an impressed sailor, M'Lane served on British naval vessels for seventeen years in many seas and oceans—the Baltic, Mediterranean, Atlantic, Indian, and western Pacific—before he was finally able to make his escape in Portugal and then make his way back to Newport, Rhode Island, and from there to Hartford to see his astonished parents.

We had no sooner let go our anchor, than an English Man of War's boat, came on board and pressed me and two more of the Seamen, and carried us on board the Madrass, 50 gun Ship, commanded by John Dilks, who immediately asked me for my protection [certificate, a document that certified the citizenship of a sailor]. I immediately shewed [sic] him one from a Notary Public in New York, by the name of Keyes; he replied, 'I could get one, if I was in America, for half a crown, as good as that.' He further said, 'it is of no use for you to pretend that you are an American, for you was born in Scotland.' The first Lieutenant, then stepped up and said, 'yes, that he was, for I knew his friends in Greenock.' The Capt. then made answer, 'he shall then do his duty in the main-top.' I then went off the quarter deck, down below. The day following I went to the Capt and told him, I hoped he would send me aboard of my own ship, as I was an American citizen; to which he replied, 'You *Scotch Rascal,* if you do not go to your duty, I'll punish you.' I then went to my station. Several days after, while we were letting a reef out of the main top sail, the sail got tore; he immediately said, it was my fault 'for I was a sulky rascal.' He ordered me to be seized, and the boatswain's mate to punish me; which he did, by giving me twelve lashes on my bare back with cat o nine tails; he then ordered me to be cast off and sent to my duty . . .

Source: James M'Lean. 1814. *Seventeen Years' History, of the Life and Sufferings of James M'Lean. An Impressed American Citizen & Seaman, embracing but a summary of what he endured, while detained in the British Service, during that Long and Painful Period. Written by Himself.* Hartford: B. & J. Russell.

SLAVE DRIVER

Slave drivers—also called overseers—worked for antebellum plantation owners and were tasked with supervising, organizing, and motivating the plantation owner's slaves as they went about their jobs and duties. Overseers often used corporal punishment as a means of chastising slaves who were being indignant or were not performing up to expectation.

Prior to the ratification of the Thirteenth Amendment, slavery was the predominant labor system in the agrarian-focused southern states. The enslavement of African Americans was common and a profitable and integrated component of the United States' economic system. Most slaveowners did not operate on large-scale plantations; in 1860, approximately 88 percent of slave holders owned twenty slaves or fewer (MacKay n.d.), and these smaller plantations were often managed directly by the plantation owner. However, for those who owned twenty or more slaves, it was necessary to hire overseers to manage this captive workforce.

Overseers were under great pressure from the plantation owner, or master, to produce as much product at the lowest possible price. Just like in factories today, peak efficiency and low overhead costs were the goals. And while many workers today may disagree with or resent their managers in American workplaces, we now have laws that protect workers, which was not the case during the antebellum era. Instead, productivity was achieved by any means necessary. Therefore, overseers often used incredibly harsh practices, including whipping underachieving workers and threats of violence against the loved ones of workers who did not achieve goals. There are reports of overseers whipping, beating, or denying food to the children of enslaved individuals who did not meet the day's work goals or quota.

Overseers would typically be career managers on large plantations. Occasionally, the overseer may be a poor relative of the plantation owner, but this was not typical. Also, at times, the overseer himself may have owned a slave or two. However, one aspect that was constant was that the overseer always reported to the plantation owner. On large plantations, or those with more than fifty enslaved individuals, there was often an additional hierarchal position—that of a slave driver. Quite often, the driver was himself a slave, but this was seen as a position entrusted to very few individuals. On very rare occasions, an enslaved driver was promoted to an overseer, or there would be a free African American overseer. This was an exceptionally rare occurrence, but two notable examples were brothers, Moses and Henry Pettigrew, who were overseers in northeast North Carolina.

Though they worked on separate farms, both brothers reported to the same owner: William Pettigrew. Mr. Pettigrew was often out of town on either business or personal vacations, and there are several letters preserved in archives that were written by either Moses or Henry to Mr. Pettigrew to relay the daily business of the plantations. The letters written by Henry and Moses are not only telling of daily operations on an antebellum plantation but also provide insight to how the two men identified themselves as they had power over enslaved individuals—while, simultaneously, the United States considered them to be Mr. Pettigrew's property.

The topic of overseers is very important to many aspects of the historical studies of southern enslavement, including culture, identity, and the connection between slavery and the American capitalistic system. Capitalism, in its most basic elements, promotes individuals making as much profit as possible, with distribution of wealth and power being a subsequent concern. This focus on production and profit, combined with a hierarchal social and cultural system that reinforced racial chattel slavery, allowed the innately exploitative nature of chattel slavery to flourish. The results of this perfect storm are seen in the harsh treatments, bullying, whippings, and torture that many overseers inflicted on the individuals for whom they were responsible.

Christy Davenport

See also: Field Hand; Planter; Turpentiner

FURTHER READING

Baptist, Edward. 2014. *The Half Has Never Been Told: Slavery and the Making of American Capitalism*. New York: Basic Books.

Berry, Daina Ramey. 2017. *The Price for Their Pound of Flesh: The Value of the Enslaved, from Womb to Grave, in the Building of a Nation*. Boston: Beacon Press.

Johnson, Walter. 2014. *River of Dark Dreams: Slavery and Empire in the Cotton Kingdom*. Cambridge: Harvard University Press.

Kolchin, Peter. *American Slavery: 1619–1877*. New York: Hill and Wang Publishing, 1993.

MacKay, Catherine. n.d. "Selected Statistics on Slavery in the United States." Ogden: Weber State University. https://faculty.weber.edu/kmackay/selected_statistics_on_slavery_i.htm.

PRIMARY DOCUMENT

In this document, the former slave Austin Steward, who was raised on a Virginia plantation but fled to Canada when he was twenty-two years old, describes the work of an overseer from the view of an enslaved person. An overseer was generally the first disciplinarian on any plantation; he could exact punishment for the most minor infraction of a plantation's rules. Rules were almost never written but were widely understood: report to duty on time, work hard despite weather or health, follow orders without openly resisting, and submit to demands of all white people, even young children. Overseers could also punish a slave as an example to others, a powerful way to terrorize enslaved people as one knew that he or she could become a victim of a capricious overseer.

It was usual for men and women to work side by side on our plantation; and in many kinds of work, the women were compelled to do as much as the men. Capt. H. employed an overseer, whose business it was to look after each slave in the field, and see that he performed his task. The overseer always went around with a whip, about nine feet long, made of the toughest kind of cowhide, the but-end of which was loaded with lead, and was about four or five inches in circumference, running to a point at the opposite extremity. This made a dreadful instrument of torture, and, when in the hands of a cruel overseer, it was truly fearful. With it, the skin of an ox or a horse could be cut through. Hence, it was no uncommon thing to see the poor slaves with their backs mangled in a most horrible manner. Our overseer, thus armed with his cowhide, and with a large bull-dog behind him, followed the slaves all day; and, if one of them fell in the rear from any cause, this cruel weapon was plied with terrible force. He would strike the dog one blow and the slave another, in order to keep the former from tearing the delinquent slave in pieces,—such was the ferocity of his canine attendant.

It was the rule for the slaves to rise and be ready for their task by sun-rise, on the blowing of a horn or conch-shell; and woe be to the unfortunate, who was not in the field at the time appointed, which was in thirty minutes from the first sounding of the horn. I have heard the poor creatures beg as for their lives, of the inhuman overseer, to desist from his cruel punishment. Hence, they were usually found in the field 'betimes in the morning,' (to use an old Virginia phrase), where they worked until nine o'clock. They were then allowed thirty minutes to eat their morning meal, which consisted of a little bread. At a given signal, all hands were compelled to return to their work. They toiled until noon, when they were permitted to take their breakfast, which corresponds to our dinner [lunch hour].

On our plantation, it was the usual practice to have one of the old slaves set apart to do the cooking. All the field hands were required to give into the hands of the cook a certain portion of their weekly allowance, either in dough or meal, which was prepared in the following manner. The cook made a hot fire and rolled up each person's portion in some cabbage leaves, when they could be obtained, and placed it in a hole in the ashes, carefully covered with the same, where it remained until done. Bread baked in this way is very sweet and good. But cabbage leaves could not always be obtained. When this was the case, the bread was little better than a mixture of dough and ashes, which was not very palatable. The time allowed for breakfast, was one hour. At the signal, all hands were obliged to resume their toil. The overseer was always on hand to attend to all delinquents, who never failed to feel the blows of his heavy whip.

The usual mode of punishing the poor slaves was to make them take off their clothes to the bare back, and then tie their hands before them with a rope, pass the end of the rope over a beam, and draw them up till they stood on the tips of their toes. Sometimes they tied their legs together and placed a rail between. Thus prepared, the overseer proceeded to punish the poor, helpless victim. Thirty-nine was the number of lashes ordinarily inflicted for the most trifling offence.

Who can imagine a position more painful? Oh, who, with feelings of common humanity, could look quietly on such torture? Who could remain unmoved, to see a fellow-creature thus tied, unable to move or to raise a hand in his own defense; scourged on his bare back, with a cowhide, until the blood flows in streams from his quivering flesh? And for what? Often for the most trifling fault; and, as sometimes occurs, because a mere whim or caprice of his brutal overseer demands it. Pale with passion, his eyes flashing and his stalwart frame trembling with rage, like some volcano, just ready to belch forth its fiery contents, and, in all its might and fury, spread death and destruction all around, he continues to wield the bloody lash on the broken flesh of the poor, pleading slave, until his arm grows weary, or he sinks down, utterly exhausted, on the very spot where already stand the pools of blood which his cruelty has drawn from the mangled body of his helpless victim, and within the hearing of those agonized groans and feeble cries of 'Oh do, Massa! Oh do, Massa! Do, Lord, have mercy! Oh, Lord, have mercy!' &c.

Nor is this cruel punishment inflicted on the bare backs of the male portion of slaves only. Oh no! The slave husband must submit without a murmur, to see the form of his cherished, but wretched wife, not only exposed to the rude gaze of a beastly tyrant he must unresistingly see the heavy cowhide descend upon her shrinking flesh, and her manacled limbs writhe in inexpressible torture, while her piteous cries for help ring through his ears unanswered. The wild throbbing of his heart must be suppressed, and his righteous indignation find no voice, in the presence of the human monster who holds dominion over him.

After the infuriated and heartless overseer had satiated his thirst for vengeance, on the disobedient or delinquent slave, he was untied, and left to crawl away as best he could; sometimes on his hands and knees, to his lonely and dilapidated cabin, where, stretched upon the cold earth, he lay weak and bleeding and often faint from the loss of blood, without a friend who dare administer to his necessities, and groaning in the agony of his crushed spirit. In his cabin, which was not as good as many of our stables at the North, he might lie for weeks before recovering sufficient strength to resume the labor imposed upon him, and all this time without a bed or bed clothing, or any of the necessaries considered so essential to the sick.

Perhaps some of his fellow-slaves might come and. bathe his wounds in warm water, to prevent his clothing from tearing open his flesh anew, and thus make the second suffering well nigh equal to the first; or they might from their scanty store bring him such food as they could spare, to keep him from suffering hunger, and offer their sympathy, and then drag their own weary bodies to their place of rest, after their daily task was finished.

Oh, you who have hearts to feel; you who have kind friends around you, in sickness and in sorrow, think of the sufferings of the helpless, destitute, and downtrodden slave. Has sickness laid its withering hand upon you, or disappointment blasted your fairest earthly prospects, still, the outgushings of an affectionate heart are not denied you, and you may look forward with hope to a bright future. Such a hope seldom animates the heart of the poor slave. He toils on, in his unrequited labor, looking only to the grave to find a quiet resting place, where he will be free from the oppressor.

Source: Austin Steward. 1857. *Twenty-two Years a Slave, and Forty Years a Freeman; Embracing a Correspondence of Several Years, While President of the Wilberforce Colony, London, Canada West [Ontario]*. Rochester: William Alling, 14–19. https://docsouth.unc.edu/fpn/steward/menu.html

SURVEYOR

Antebellum surveyors created neighborhoods, city plans, and state and international borders by marking and measuring lines on the ground. With silver compasses, wooden stakes, stone monuments, and measuring chains, they parceled and plotted lands for sale, settlement, and mapping. Their job required knowledge of arithmetic, geometry, trigonometry, and astronomy, as well as survival skills. In their everyday activities, surveyors faced environmental challenges ranging from the nuisance of poison ivy to dangerous confrontations with herds of animals and exposure to the harsh elements. Not only did they have to know how to navigate rivers, lakes, and steep terrain, but they had to be able to measure them accurately. Their missions often took them to unmapped places, so they had to use the position of the sun and stars in the sky as guides. More than most other professions, surveyors' work helped shaped the nation's geographical division, road systems, expansion, and settlement.

Most surveyors were soldiers, planters, or budding scholars who worked for large-scale government projects such as the surveys of the West. Immigrants often worked on surveyor teams as assistants, carrying chains and equipment. By a system of apprenticeship, many assistants became surveyors on their own. The government frequently employed surveyors, and the bulk of a county-certified surveyor's work consisted of measuring plots for private sale. Because of their role in the sale of land, surveyors often advertised their services in newspapers.

Surveying was a painstaking process that required precision and patience, as well as teamwork and endurance over long distances and difficult conditions. A surveyor's responsibilities included preparing a rough sketch of the surveyed track; measuring the land's borders, terrain, and elevation; and calculating its acreage. Most surveyors kept field books identifying topographical elements in the environment, particularly when the survey included land to be developed for settlers.

To prepare a survey, a surveyor went into the field with a team of three or four assistants. The chief surveyor first used a compass on a long wooden pole planted in the ground to identify the magnetic meridian. Next, the crew measured the perimeter of the area with chains. The chains had to be straight and parallel to the horizon, and workers used instruments like compasses, telescopes, mirrors, and rulers to check their work.

After finishing a survey, surveyors prepared a map of the measured field. This map was a full representation of the plot, and it included any structures, bodies of water, or significant markers such as trees, walls, stones, and roads. The scale of the map varied according to the type of survey, as well as the complexity of the assignment. Internal improvement projects such as bridges, roads, canals, and railroads all required complex survey work, making surveyors integral to the development of the country.

Survey work was foundational for the country's land division system. Using government regulations, surveyors carved unmapped and unowned territories into ranges and lots to prepare them for sale. Surveyor activities were also integral to the establishment of state and international borders. Their work survives in the rectangular borders of the western states and the gridded city plans across the country. Famous surveyors include George Washington, who became a professional surveyor with the county of Culpepper, Virginia, at the age of seventeen and assisted in surveys of the Shenandoah Valley; Abraham Lincoln, who mapped Sangamon county roads, schools, and farm plots to make ends meet; and Henry David Thoreau, who surveyed areas including Walden Pond, site of his famous work *Walden*.

One of the most well-known large-scale surveys was done by Charles Mason and Jeremiah Dixon, who settled the boundary dispute of Maryland, Pennsylvania, and Delaware by marking a line at latitude 39° 43' north. The British surveyors marked the extent of their line with stone markers every five miles, some of which still stand to this day. The product of their work, which is still known as the Mason-Dixon line, was a grand achievement at the time. Their four-year survey solved the boundary line controversy by measuring latitude and longitude with the stars. The line also left a permanent mark on the history of the nation as it helped mark a cultural and political division between the North and South of the country during the nineteenth century.

Other surveys with significant consequences for the country were Lewis and Clark's survey of the West after the Louisiana Purchase of 1803 and the surveys to settle the boundary with Mexico from 1848 to 1854. These last surveys entailed traveling through inhospitable deserts and mountain passes in projects that lasted years.

Some of the most relevant regulations that guided a surveyor's work were the land ordinances of 1785 and 1787, which created the Public Land Survey System. Besides establishing borders, surveys also connected different parts of the nation. For example, the transcontinental railroad was only possible after the Pacific Railroad Surveys of 1853–1855, which plotted roads and trails of the western states and located a suitable route for a railroad to connect the nation. The city plots of our neighborhoods as well as the maps of our states are the products of a surveyors' work. Their everyday surveys parceled public lands that became part of government projects. And their painstaking work revealed new lands, new profits, and new prosperity for an expanding nation that would triple its size in less than one hundred years. However, their work also enabled the destruction and resettlement of Indian nations and ushered drastic changes to the landscape and the environment. Survey work was tedious, arduous, exacting, and scientific, but it was not neutral. Instead, it influenced American narratives both inspiring and unsettling.

Elsa Barraza Mendoza

See also: Cartographer; Explorer; Land Speculator

FURTHER READING

Chura, Patrick. 2011. *Thoreau the Land Surveyor*. Gainesville: University Press of Florida.

Love, John. 1796. *Geodaesia: or, The Art of Surveying, and Measuring Land Made Easy : Shewing, by Plain and Practical Rules, to Survey, Protract, Cast Up, Reduce or Divide Any Piece of Land Whatsoever ; with New Tables for the Ease of the Surveyor in Reducing the Measure of Land : Moreover, a More Facile and Sure Way of Surveying by the Chain, Than Has Hitherto Been Taught : As Also, to Lay Out New Lands in America, or Elsewhere : and How to Make a Perfect Map of a River's Mouth or Harbour ; with Several Other Things Never Before Published in the English Language.* New York: Printed and sold by Samuel Campbell, 124 Pearl-Street.

Taylor, William. 1800. *A Complete System of Practical Arithmetic: With Various Branches in the Mathematics. The Second Edition. By William Taylor, Teacher of the Mathematics, and Land Surveyor, Author of a Collection of Tables for the Use of His Majesty's Officers of Excise; the Arithmetician's Guide; Key to the Arithmetician's Guide; the Measurer's Assistant; the Tradesman's Correct Ready Reckoner; a Treatise of Chronology; Correct Tables of Discount, &C. &C.* Birmingham: Printed and sold by the author, No. 15, Spiceal-Street, T.A. Pearson and the other Booksellers.

PRIMARY DOCUMENT

Surveyors routinely traveled through what they usually described as "the wilderness," using their tools to measure the continent, map landforms like mountains and rivers, and prepare lands for American settlement. These great areas of wilderness, however, were not uninhabited—as surveyors themselves clearly understood. These documents describe the work of surveyors in the "Old Northwest," the current states of Ohio, Indiana, Illinois, Michigan, and Wisconsin. The last document is a surveyor's report on the suitability of lands for settlement in Iowa, dated 1840. It illustrates that once a surveyor had measured and mapped land, his work was still not yet done: surveyors had to provide voluminous reports to local, state, and federal governments, as well as to businesses, transportation companies (such as the Central Pacific Railroad Company), and other entities who had keen interests in the surveyor's work.

January 1794. Continued on at Canadarque [now Canandaigua, New York] during the winter for the first time. Much talk of Indian war with the Six Nations, and the inhabitants of this new settlement are under some serious apprehensions of an invasion in the spring if measures are not taken by the General Government to quite them. Early in the Spring news was brought to Israel Chapin Esquire, Superintendent of Indian Affairs, that Capt. Brant had assembled with his warriors at Buffalo Creek and was proceeding on to Presque Isle [now Erie], State of Pennsylvania, to prevent the surveyors from surveying that part of the country called the Triangle. To prevent serious consequences Mr. Chapin repaired to Buffalo Creek. My brother Samuel Colt accompanied him as secretary and Horatio Jones as interpreter. The Indians were assembled. After some consultation part of the young men were dismissed and a few of the chiefs took passage by water, along with the Superintendent, secretary and interpreter, to Presque Isle, and from thence went on foot to Le Boeuf, where were stationed a small command of State troops, commanded by a Capt. Ebenezer Denny.

On the Indians making their business known, viz, to see the surveyors and to forbid them running lines, etc., they were informed they had shortly before left the country and had gone down the river. They agreed to return home upon assurances being given that the matter should be laid before the President of the U.S., which was done by the Superintendent. It was agreed with them to hold a treaty with them the ensuing fall . . . [I]n the month of October, . . . all matters of difference were amicably settled to the full satisfaction of all parties.

Source: Charles Robinson. 1904. "Journal of Judah Colt." *Papers Relating to Pioneer Surveyors*. Buffalo: Buffalo Historical Society, 395–396.

In making this traverse of the south shore of Lake Erie, . . . its object was to ascertain the entire area of the Western Reserve. To do this, it was necessary for use to penetrate some fifty miles into the Indian country, the Cuyahoga River being at that time its eastern boundary. In proceeding west, therefore, from the mouth of that river, the traversing party under my direction and lead, was accompanied coastwise by our boat, which contained our provisions, etc., and which would always afford us the means of escape in case we should be attacked by hostile Indians. We passed on however without any such interruption. Indeed we saw no Indians until we reached the western point at the mouth of Sandusky Bay. Here, near the site of an immense burial place we encountered a party of some twenty or thirty. Of their disposition toward us we could only judge from their manner, which appeared to us anything but friendly and conciliating. They examined our instruments very closely and minutely, and with apparently gloomy jealousy and disapprobation.

Source: Charles Robinson. 1904. "Augustus Porter's Own Narrative." *Papers Relating to Pioneer Surveyors.* Buffalo: Buffalo Historical Society, 311.

Township 73—Range 2, W.—Is handsomely situated, embracing every variety of soil and timber; there is prairie and timber sufficiently intermixed to make the whole one of the most valuable townships in the territory. It is handsomely situated on the Iowa river, which passes through it, dividing in nearly into equal parts. The whole well watered by numerous small streams which empty themselves into the Iowa; numerous springs of pure water issue from the Iowa bluffs.

This township is one of the most noted in the territory. Here the celebrated Indian chief Blackhawk resided, until the Indian hostilities of 1832—and it is here where the bones of his ancestors have rested in place for centuries—and it was for this spot, this sacred spot, that he gave the warwhoop and rallied forth his countrymen to the last deadly struggle in defence of this, the home of their ancestors; but there were conquered, and this celebrated chief doomed to wander as a stranger in the land of his forefathers. His house was still standing at the time when the surveys were made; it stood on the south bank of the Iowa river, in sec. 20.—Growth on upland, white and black oak, and hickory; on the bottoms, cottonwood, maple, sugar, and some ash.

The N. fraction . . . middle part E. and W. of river . . . embrace all the 1st rate timber land. The S. fraction . . . embrace all the 1st rate prairie; residue 2nd rate timber and prairie land. This township is rapidly settling. The village of Florence is located on the S. fraction sec. 20; the village of Blackhawk on the NE. qr. Sec. 10.

Source: Jesse Williams. 1840. *A Description of the United States Lands in Iowa: Being a Minute Description of Every Section and Quarter Section, Quality of Soil, Groves of Timber, Prairies, Ledges of Rock, Coal Banks, Iron and Lead Ores, Water-Falls, Mill-Seats, Etc., Etc., Etc.*, 47–48.

TALLOW CHANDLER

During the colonial period, tallow chandlers turned animal fats and waste products into usable goods, primarily soaps and candles but also lubricating greases and other products. Like curriers, butchers, and brewers, tallow chandlers in colonial times were considered workers in the nuisance trades—those whose work processes polluted the waters and fouled the air, so much so that they were required to practice their "trades and mysteries" away from colonial populations, on the edges of and downwind from towns. The work of tallow chandlers, like that of curriers, however, was valuable, and despite being consigned to work spaces at the periphery of colonial towns, many colonies also banned the export of their products.

On farms and plantations throughout the colonies, housewives and their daughters, indentured servants and slaves made homemade soap and candles. But by the end of the Revolutionary War (1775–1783), Americans began turning to factory-made candles, soaps, and other products. Those who lived in towns and cities did not have access to the raw materials to make these products, while the rise of the whaling industry and hide and tallow trade brought new fats to market. Sperm whaling off the coast of New England provided a new material, spermaceti, a waxy, smelly substance extracted from the heads of sperm whales that, when made into candles, provided excellent light—brighter and longer-lasting candles than those made from fats from cattle, oxen, and goats. Common whale oil, called "brown oil" because it was not clear and transparent like that from the sperm whale, was extracted from other whales, porpoises, seals and sea lions, and, later, even walruses to make soap, candle, and industrial greases. The hide and tallow trade, which began in the 1820s and accelerated thereafter, brought raw hides and tallow from California's ranches to New England on ships traveling around Cape Horn. With these new sources of raw materials, as well as population growth in the young nation's cities, the work of the tallow chandler changed significantly.

Tallow chandlers typically took animal fats, chopped them into pieces, and then rendered it by boiling the fat into liquid form in large pots, usually made of copper. Once the fat began to render, chandlers then removed impurities with a skimming ladle. After the tallow was rendered and purified, they emptied the contents of the boiling pot into a cooling receptacle, normally a rectangular, relatively shallow vat. They then turned the raw materials into candles or soap using different processes. The earliest of the chandlers, as they were called, simply dipped lengths of twisted linen (made of flax) or cotton into the partially cooled liquid; as the wicks were removed from the vat, the cooling fat congealed. The chandler repeated this process over and over, building up layers of fat to create a candle, which typically was tapered at one end—the end into which the wick was dipped. Chandlers devised new and faster methods, however, to speed the process of making candles. By the mid-eighteenth century, they used both frames onto which dozens of wicks were hung, which allowed them to dip many candles at once, as well as candle molds, into which wicks were placed, followed by pouring the cooling fat into the molds.

Those early chandlers who also made soap added lye to the boiling rendered fat, which released putrid, smoky fumes. Later, chandlers used potash, an alkaline compound extracted from the residue of wood ash (scraped from the inside of a fireplace, pot, or burn pit), as a substitute for lye, though the smell was just as bad as that of boiling tallow with lye. "Manufacturies," or small soap-making factories, used potash to make higher-quality soaps than that made with lye. Most soaps were designated as white or yellow soaps, based on the color of the product. Yellow soaps were made of animal fats or whale oil, while white soaps were higher quality and generally made of plant oils, like olive oil. Beeswax was used for both candles and soaps. Different solutions of potash and water were made, and then the chandlers carefully poured these solutions—starting with the weakest—into the boiling pots of fats or oils. The addition of water and potash created a chemical reaction that released more fumes. As the solution of water, potash, and fats began to solidify, chandlers let it rest overnight. The mixture was then reheated, salt was added, and they then poured the substance into soap molds, generally large wooden or metal trays. Once the material cooled, chandlers used wire to cut soaps into blocks.

The work of a chandler was a noxious process, creating smells that no colonist or, later, American wanted to experience. Tallow chandlers were among the most highly regulated trades in both colonial and later early republic periods. In 1787, for instance, the Pennsylvania legislature passed laws prohibiting the dumping of "any foul or nauseous liquors from . . . their workshops" into town streets or waterways and warned chandlers not to "keep, collect, or use . . . any stale, putrid, or stinking fat or other matter" (Pennsylvania 1787, 355–356)—both under threat of severe fines. Likewise, South Carolina passed similar legislation the next year, prohibiting chandlers from creating a public nuisance by boiling "noisome, offensive, and stinking liquors" near populated areas. In 1794, Massachusetts passed laws further regulating the tallow chandler's trade that allowed any town constable to seize one half of the raw or processed materials of a chandler found to be using his own house or yard to make candles or soap. The seized materials were then to be sold to support town government. New York determined that chandlers who carried on their trades near towns and in cities carried on "business too noxious as to be endured." The effect of these laws were to push tallow chandler's workshops and manufacturies to the periphery of towns and cities—acts that created conditions for further industrialization of the trades. Chandlers understood the consequences of these regulations: they were to give up their businesses or be consigned to less desired spaces. In New York, a trade organization of chandlers protested these regulations, arguing that their work—despite the fumes it generated—was no more offensive than the rest of New York's common, ubiquitous smells.

By 1800, most states, cities, and towns had passed laws regulating the siting of chandlers' workshops and factories. While townspeople benefited from these regulations, chandlers and soap makers organized into trade associations, unions, and other protective organizations to argue for their trades. At the same time, however, larger workshops and small factories produced a greater share of the candles and soap used in the nation. In some areas, whale oil lamps replaced candles as the primary form of illumination. And in the early nineteenth century, industrial soap makers began to specialize in making their product, advertising the healthful benefits of bathing; these soap makers also began to market scented products, appealing to female consumers. By 1879, two soap makers, Proctor and Gamble, invented a floating soap bar, Ivory, a product that appealed to consumers tired of searching for sunken soap bars in their baths or losing bars in the creeks, streams, and lakes in which they bathed.

Nancy Quam-Wickham

See also: *1607–1775:* Shopkeeper; *1861–1914:* Currier

FURTHER READING

Dana, Richard Henry. 2012. *Two Years Before the Mast: A Personal Narrative.* Mineola: Dover Publications.

Faraday, Michael. 2005. *The Chemical History of a Candle.* New York: Barnes & Noble Books.

Mitchell, Samuel L. 1797. *The Case of the Manufactures of Soap and Candles, Stated and Examined.* New York: Association of Tallow Chandlers and Soap Makers, 45.

Tunis, Edwin. 1965. *Colonial Craftsmen and the Beginnings of American Industry.* Baltimore: Johns Hopkins.

TOBACCONIST

The tobacconist—an individual who sells cigars, tobacco, pipes, snuff, and smoking supplies—was an important cultural figure in virtually every city, town, and burg in America and elsewhere through the nineteenth century. It was not at all unusual to find tobacconists in so-called "dying" towns. Most U.S. men used tobacco in some form: taking "dips" of snuff, enjoying cigars, or smoking pipes. The tobacconist provided a space where men could purchase their tobacco and then meet with other men to visit, share stories of work and family, and gossip about items of interest.

The tobacconist's shop was a distinctly male space in the antebellum United States as men and boys typically indulged in tobacco use and most Americans disparaged women who smoked in public—though much evidence suggests that in colonial times, the wives and daughters of farmers and artisans smoked pipes and used snuff. By the nineteenth century, though, women's use of tobacco seems to have declined, at least among those respectable women of the middle class.

Like most small shopkeepers in this period, tobacconists had multiple responsibilities. They had to stay abreast of new consumer tastes, keep their shelves stocked, and manage the paperwork associated with operating a business. They had to advertise their products as well—especially if their shop faced competition from other tobacconists. Most tobacconists likely obtained their raw, dried tobacco leaves from a tobacco dealer from Kentucky, which was a western center of tobacco production at this time, or another major tobacco-producing state, like North Carolina. Depending on their business needs, a tobacconist might have bought dried tobacco in lots of fifty pounds or more; some urban tobacconists purchased tobacco by the full hogshead, which was around five hundred pounds. Most tobacconist shops had a back room for processing tobacco and a front room for sales, smoking, and customer conversation. In the back room, a tobacconist and his helpers, if he had them, untied the bundles of tobacco leaves and then wet them lightly and stacked them to cure, or ferment. Most tobacco consumers rejected raw dried leaves as tobacco of this sort was harsh to smoke. Customers preferred flavored or sweetened tobacco for most uses, so tobacconists often added honey, molasses, or sweet herbs like licorice or vanilla bean to the curing tobacco. After curing, some tobacconists heated the product over a fire to impart some light smoke flavoring, like apple wood, to the tobacco.

Tobacconists normally sold different flavors of tobacco. Different mixes of tobacco were also common, so much so that early school texts for "mechanical arithmetics" routinely featured mathematical word problems that required students to calculate the costs of a pound of mixed tobacco. No fewer than nine school texts published in 1808 included mathematics word problems using tobacco as an example—a clear nod to the substance's ubiquity in America.

Once the tobacconists cured and mixed the product, they further processed it for the different ways customers used it. For pipe tobacco, the tobacconist cut the processed leaves into strips and then sold either the strips, chopped finely, or further prepared ropes or plugs. A rope was a thin twist of tobacco, much like a thin rope, while plugs were created by pressing moist tobacco into a hollow vessel and then compressing it until it became a solid piece, from which smaller pieces, or plugs, could be cut off. Tobacco ropes (or threads) were commonly used in pipes. Plug tobacco could be used in pipes but was also favored for chewing or dipping—pressing a bit between the gums and teeth and sucking on it. Those who dipped tobacco normally spat out the accumulated tobacco juices rather than swallowing them as the active stimulants in tobacco were easily absorbed into the bloodstream through tissues in a user's mouth.

Not all tobacco was cured in just this manner, however. Like tobacco processed for other uses, snuff was flavored typically with mint or oil of roses. Most snuff was slightly moistened as well. For snuff, the tobacconist finely ground the product in a mortar and pestle or, in larger shops, a mill, creating a powder-like substance. Customers bought the snuff, packaged in paper envelopes; transferred it to their snuff boxes; and when they were ready to use it, pinched a small bit and, using either their fingers or spreading it on the back of a hand, snorted the product.

The role of the tobacconist in American culture is secure, even as tobacco use has declined in modern America. Plays, novels, and poetry about the tobacconist proliferated during the colonial period and afterward. Just before the American Revolution, some enterprising tobacconists began advertising their shops by using carved statues of traditionally dressed Native Americans to promote their sales of "Indian tobacco." These carvings were universal for tobacconists throughout the nineteenth century. In addition, tobacconists and early tobacco companies appropriated imagery of "traditional" tribal people—sometimes presented in cartoonish forms—to sell their products. Tobacco companies used western imagery of cowboys and Indians to sell cigarettes and other tobacco products well into the 1980s. One company even called tobacco the American Indians' "gift to grateful humanity" (D'Silva, et al. 2018). While scientists and the public now understand the harmful effects of smoking, for some, tobacco use remains a positive feature of American consumer society.

Nancy Quam-Wickham

See also: *1607–1775:* Shopkeeper; *1861–1914:* Cigarmaker; Haberdasher

FURTHER READING

American Tobacco Company. 1900. *Annual Report.* Jersey City: American Tobacco Company.

D'Silva, Joanne, Erin O'Gara, and Nicole T. Villaluz. 2018. "Tobacco Industry Misappropriation of American Indian Culture and Traditional Tobacco." *Tobacco Control.* https://tobaccocontrol.bmj.com/content/early/2018/03/01/tobaccocontrol-2017-053950.

Noyes, James. 1808. *The Federal Arithmetic, or A Compendium of the Most Useful Rules of That Science Adapted to the Currency of the United States, for the Use of Schools and Private Persons.* Concord: Printed by George Hough.

TURPENTINER

Turpentine workers—or turpentiners—were often slaves, and their labor was difficult and dangerous. Groups of laborers worked together to gouge grooves into living coniferous trees so that the trees' resin could be collected and distilled to produce turpentine, along with byproducts that could be used in soap, lamp black, and ink production. Turpentine is a volatile oil that is still used as a common solvent and wood preservative; before the advent of kerosene, it was also used as an inexpensive alternative to lamp oil.

Turpentine collection in the United States began during the colonial era as England used its North American territories to provide turpentine for the Royal Navy, which used it to maintain and waterproof its ships. In the colonies, this commodification caused turpentine, tar, and pitch from pine trees to come to be known as "naval stores."

The turpentine industry boomed in the late eighteenth century, and by the 1830s, the forests in the northern colonies were greatly depleted. This depletion, along with improvements to the distillation process, made turpentine distillation attractive to large plantation owners. Soon, turpentine plantations began popping up in North Carolina, South Carolina, Georgia, Alabama, and Florida due to their expansive longleaf pine forests. By 1850, North Carolina alone supplied over 96 percent of the nation's turpentine, surpassed only by Georgia in the early 1870s when North Carolina's tree supply became exhausted and the business owners moved further south. By the 1850s, naval stores were the third largest export in the South after cotton and tobacco.

Enslaved African Americans performed almost all of the antebellum turpentine extraction and distillation. Most turpentiners were male, though female turpentiners were sometimes tasked with preparing harvested resin for distillation. The labor became so heavily associated with African Americans that those slaves who were working in the industry came to be called "Turpentine Negros." One turpentine plantation owner in North Carolina developed a grading system for resin, which was based upon his slaves' skin tones. The clearest and lightest—and, therefore, highest-quality resin—was named after the lightest-skinned turpentiner, and the darker, less valuable resin was named after the darkest skinned.

Enslaved turpentiners worked according to a task system, which differed from a gang system wherein groups of enslaved people labored all day under the surveillance of an overseer. In a task system, individual slaves were given a specific task to complete, and once that task was finished, they were free to do as they wished until their next task was assigned.

Many turpentine industries owned their own slaves, but other plantation owners also leased their slaves to assist during the busy turpentine season, which stretched from November to July, or hired task laborers who were temporarily unassigned. These task laborers could often earn additional money by performing extra chores such as cutting wood or clearing forests and roads, but these extra wages were often withheld until December to disincentivize a slave from running away. Turpentine work was grueling and unpleasant. Summers in the pine forests were hot and rife with snakes, mosquitos, ticks, and poison ivy, and wet, boggy ground made deliveries difficult, if not impossible, for mule-driven carts.

The task system of the turpentine industry required several types of specialized laborers, called boxers, chippers, dippers, distillers, and coopers. Boxers cut holes in the base of the pine as a container for the resin that would drip from the tree. Some longleaf pines needed up to four boxes, each of which could hold one to two quarts of resin. The process required a great amount of strength, and an experienced worker could cut between fifty and eighty boxes a day.

After the boxes were constructed, chippers made cuts into the tree above the box to increase the turpentine flow. Cutters continued to slice upward as the tree's earlier wounds dried up; this process would continue until the tree ran out of resin, which might take three to six years from the first cutting. This process was dangerous, and many cutters injured themselves with their own tools.

Dippers removed the resin from the boxes and sent them to the distillery. The distilling process was very dangerous as the flammable turpentine caused many accidental fires at the still. Though many distillers were enslaved, some turpentine producers hired white men for this specialized task, and their salary was often double that of a white overseer. Each barrel of crude dip produced six to seven gallons of turpentine spirits, and the remaining resin at the bottom of the kettle was drained and separated into its own barrel. This leftover material could be sold to ink or soap manufacturers, who used such byproducts in their manufacturing processes.

Coopers made barrels for the turpentine, and enslaved workers would also be responsible for transporting those barrels to the markets. In addition, enslaved men and even some enslaved women also worked as scrapers, who removed the hardened gum from the tree boxes or from equipment in the distilling process. Even this dried turpentine scrape was salable.

The Civil War (1861–1865) damaged the turpentine industry, but it regained strength during the postbellum period as turpentine camps moved from the exhausted North Carolina forests to the Deep South, particularly Georgia. The labor continued to be extremely strenuous and relied upon the African American workforce and immigrant laborers, who were often exploited via the system of debt peonage, which forced indebted workers to work until their debt was paid. Debt peonage was outlawed in 1867, but exploitative practices persisted in turpentine camps throughout the early twentieth century.

Melissa DeVelvis

See also: Field Hand; Slave Driver

FURTHER READING

Butler, Carroll B. 1998. *Treasures of the Longleaf Pines: Naval Stores*. Shalimar: Tarkel Publishing.

Glave, Dianne D. 2014. *To Love the Wind and the Rain: African Americans and Environmental History*. Pittsburgh: University of Pittsburgh Press.

Outland, Robert B. III. 2004. *Tapping the Pines: The Naval Stores Industry in the American South*. Baton Rouge: Louisiana State University Press.

Vollmers, Gloria. 2003. "Industrial Slavery in the United States: The North Carolina Turpentine Industry, 1849–1861." *Accounting, Business and Financial History* 13.3 (November): 369–92.

PRIMARY DOCUMENT

In the 1800s, extracting turpentine from pine trees was largely done by slave labor as it was hard, dirty, physical work. In this document, journalist Frederick Law Olmsted describes his travels through the "turpentine orchards" of North Carolina shortly before the Civil War. Olmsted had extraordinary observational talents and a keen eye for detail, as is clear from his description. Like white men and women of his time, he refers to slave men simply as nameless "Negroes," though he also opposed slavery. Later, Olmsted became well known for his work as a landscape architect, co-designing several significant public spaces, including San Francisco's Golden Gate Park, New York City's Central Park, and the Niagara Falls parkways, as well as director of the precursor of the American Red Cross, the U.S. Sanitary Commission, during the early years of the Civil War.

Turpentine is the crude sap of pine-trees. It varies somewhat, in character and in freedom of flow, with the different varieties; the long-leafed pine (*Pinus Palustris*) yielding it more freely than any other.

There are very large forests of this tree in North and South Carolina, Georgia, and Alabama; and the turpentine business is carried on, to some extent, in all these States. In North Carolina, however, much more largely than in the others; because, in it, cotton is rather less productive than in the others, in an average of years. Negroes are, therefore, in rather less demand; and their owners oftener see their profit in employing them in turpentine orchards than in the cotton-fields . . .

If we enter, in the winter, a part of a forest that is about to be converted into a "turpentine orchard," we come upon negroes engaged in making boxes, in which the sap is to be collected the following spring. They continue at this work from November to March, or until, as the warm weather approaches, the sap flows freely, and they are needed to remove it from the boxes into barrels. These "boxes" are not made of boards, nailed together in a cubical form, as might be supposed; nor are they log-troughs, such as, at the North, maple-sap is collected in. They are cavities dug in the trunk of the tree itself. A long, narrow ax, made in Connecticut, especially for this purpose, is used for this wood-pecking operation; and some skill is required to use it properly . . . The boxes are made at from six inches to a foot above the roots, and are shaped like a distended waistcoat-pocket. The lower lip is horizontal—the upper, arched; the bottom of the box is about four inches below the lower lip, and eight or ten below the upper. On a tree of medium size, a box should be made to hold a quart. The less the ax approaches towards the centre of the tree, to obtain the proper capacity in the box, the better, as the vitality of the tree is less endangered; but this is little thought about.

An expert hand will make a box in less than ten minutes; and seventy-five to a hundred—according to the size and proximity of the trees—is considered a day's work.

The boxes being made, the bark, and a few of the outer rings of the wood of the tree, are cut off ("hacked") along the edge of the upper lip. From this excoriation, the sap begins to flow about the fifteenth of March, and gradually fills the boxes, from which it is taken by a spoon or ladle, of a peculiar form, and collected into barrels.

In from seven to ten days after the first hacking, the trees are again scarified. This is done with a hatchet, or with an instrument made for the purpose. A very slight chip, or shave, above the former, is all that is needed to be removed; the object being merely to expose a new surface of the cellular tissue—the flow from the former being clogged by congelations of the sap. These hackings being made three or four times a month, the excoriation is constantly advancing higher up the trunk. The slighter the cut, the less the tree is injured, and the slower the advance, and the longer and the more conveniently may the process be carried on . . .

By the middle of March, the turpentine is flowing abundantly, and the negroes must be employed in hacking, as each tree requires to be freshly scarified once in a week, or ten days. Soon afterwards, it is necessary to commence dipping, or the removal of the turpentine from the boxes to barrels. There are two ways of arranging the labor for this purpose used by the larger proprietors. In one, all the negroes employed are divided into two classes—"hackers" and "dippers." The hackers are wholly employed in scarifying the trees. A task, of a certain number of trees, is given to each, which he is required to go over, hacking each tree, once in seven or eight days. The dippers are constantly employed in emptying the boxes, as they fill with turpentine. The other way—and this is more common—is to give each hand a task of trees, each of which he is required to both hack and dip steadily. Twenty-five hundred trees give a man five days' employment hacking, and one day dipping, in a week.

From one to four boxes are made in each tree, according to its size; a few inches of bark being left between them. The greater number of trees, from which turpentine is now obtained, are from a foot to eighteen inches in diameter, and have three boxes each. The hacking is carried on year after year, until, in the oldest orchards, it is extended twelve or fifteen feet, and ladders have to be used to carry it further up the trunks of the trees. The turpentine flows from the most recent hack, down over the previously scarified wood of the tree, towards the box, a considerable proportion of it congealing by the way, and remaining attached to the wood. From this adhering portion, a part of the spirits or oil has evaporated in the process of drying; it is, therefore, of less value than that which is taken, in a more liquid condition, from the box. It is occasionally—perhaps but once a year—scraped off, and barreled by itself. It is, therefore, known in market as "scrape;" while that which is dipped from the box, and which is of considerably higher value, is termed "dip."

Source: Frederick Law Olmsted. 1856. *A Journey in the Seaboard Slave States, with remarks on their economy.* London: Sampson Low & Sons, 338–343.

WHARFINGER

Wharfingers were owners and keepers of a wharf and were responsible for overseeing the wharf's day-to-day activities, resolving disputes, keeping tide tables, and receiving and maintaining custody of goods delivered to the wharf. Throughout the colonial period, American harbors were often busy and chaotic places. Harbors and bays were not charted well as there was no federal cartographic service: Boston Harbor, for instance, essentially was an estuary with a ragged, rocky shoreline and shoals that shifted with the tides and seasons. A 1775 map of Boston's harbor shows no fewer than thirty-seven islands located at the mouth and within the estuary. The wharves, which were privately owned, were clustered on the north side of the estuary, some on the mainland, while others were on small islands connected to the mainland by drawbridges. Vessels of all kinds plied the waters—rowboats, fishing vessels, and larger ships engaged in coastal and oceanic trade.

Many other harbors were similarly situated in estuaries and up local rivers, away from larger bodies of water. Given the poor state of roads in early America, water transportation was the cheapest and most efficient way to move goods and people throughout the colonies. With the founding of the nation, the federal government assumed the responsibility for safe navigation within harbors and ports, but that jurisdiction ended at the high tide line. To move goods from land to water required that shippers navigate a maze of private ownership of a patchwork of wharves, docks, and other port facilities in American harbors. Wharfingers managed these individual private facilities; one harbor might have a dozen or more docks, wharves, and loading facilities, each managed by a different wharfinger.

In early colonial America, a wharfinger usually owned his own wharf, but as seaports and maritime commerce expanded, by the end of the colonial period, wharfingers often only managed a dock, wharf, or single harbor facility. Wharfingers arranged for dockage for vessels, helped to coordinate the storage of goods awaiting transshipment—from ship to shore or shore to ship—on the wharf, and often operated small chandleries, or shops that sold items that sailors needed, like cordage, special tools, or clothing. Some cities tried to regulate the actions of wharfingers even in the colonial period, particularly prohibiting them from storing and selling firewood and loose lumber at dockside. Virtually all American cities experienced devastating urban fires; these regulations were designed to prevent the stockpiling of wood that could fuel a conflagration on a wooden pier or wharf where it could spread to other waterside (and interior) areas. Similarly, cities prohibited the storage of oils and other flammable goods, as well as gunpowder, by wharfingers.

In the early nineteenth century, cities also began to task wharfingers with administrative duties, particularly the collection of dues or taxes for use of publicly constructed facilities. In these cases, private wharfingers took on a role more like that of a modern harbormaster. For instance, in 1816, the city council of New Orleans passed an ordinance that specified where in the port certain cargoes could be landed, prohibiting the offloading of livestock, rotting produce, or goods with an offensive smell anywhere but along the upper harbor, away from the city itself. The council also appointed a wharfinger to collect the duty (or tax) levied by the city for moorage along the city levees and supervise the landing of barges, steamboats, and other vessels along the city's levees. The city wharfinger was also required to ensure that loading and unloading of cargo needed to be completed in such a way as to provide safe passage for pedestrians along the Mississippi River's embankments. Likewise, other cities passed ordinances that set certain "wharfage" (fees) that vessels had to pay to use docks and wharves that were privately owned. The city of Charleston, South Carolina, published a detailed guide to wharfage costs based on types of cargo in 1819. Landing a thousand feet of finished lumber had a wharfage fee of 47.5 cents, while wharfage fees for a hundred barrels of potatoes, corn, or other grain were 31.5 cents. Charleston established wharfage fees for every imaginable item, from soap to paving stones, chocolate to prunes. Additionally, Charleston set storage fees and cartage fees, based on product, where it was stored in the harbor, and destination of the cargo within and outside of the city. Importantly, the city established these fees not to raise city revenue but, instead, to regulate the business practices of wharfingers and teamsters, ordering them to charge uniform rates that were published in local guides. Local ordinances prevented wharfingers from overcharging customers, a practice long associated with those who operated and managed the nation's critical maritime commerce facilities.

The first harbor to municipalize all of its dockside facilities—piers, wharves, storage sheds and warehouses, and docks—was San Francisco. The California State legislature authorized the construction of municipal wharves, allowing the city to lease them out to private businesses. Like the earlier case of New Orleans, San Francisco employed city wharfingers to manage these facilities. San Francisco's history of shipping was one reason for making wharves publicly owned. During the California gold rush only a few years earlier, sailors and captains were so frenzied to reach the gold regions inland that they had abandoned hundreds of ships along San Francisco's waterfront, where they eventually rotted or were cut up for their lumber. Some of early San Francisco's businesses were constructed from pieces of salvaged vessels hauled ashore and dragged to their resting places along the city's Market Street. These abandoned ships impeded maritime commerce and trade in the city along the bay. Other cities followed San Francisco's model of managing wharves and dockside facilities, using wharfingers to supervise commercial maritime operations: Galveston, Texas, in 1854 and New York in 1870. In doing so, cities transformed the role of the wharfinger from a manager of a single privately owned dock or wharf to the manager of urban complexes of marine facilities. These new harbormasters, as they became known, increasingly supervised many employees, oversaw construction and renovation, determined commercial needs of growing cities, managed municipal budgets, and took on many other professional duties.

Nancy Quam-Wickham

See also: Customs Collector; Sailor; *1607–1775:* Shipwright

FURTHER READING

American Association of Port Authorities. http://www.aapa-ports.org/files/pdfs/governance_uscan.pdf.

The Directory and strangers guide to the City of Charleston. 1819.

Sherman, Rexford B. 2000. *Seaport Governance in the United States and Canada.* Alexandria: American Association of Port Authorities.

1861–1914: THE CIVIL WAR, RECONSTRUCTION, AND THE GILDED AGE

INTRODUCTION

In the decades before the Civil War (1861–1865), American manufacturing grew rapidly as inventors and entrepreneurs created new machinery and employed different production schemes to expand factories and increase the production of goods. In the mid-1850s, around twelve thousand mostly immigrant workers toiled in highly mechanized Massachusetts factories under a scheme called the Lowell System, which turned raw cotton into finished textiles. Other products were also made using machines and factory models: shoes and boots, small arms and rifles, clocks, sewing machines, and paper. Eli Whitney's (1765–1825) conception of an "American system of manufacture," in which tools and machines made goods rapidly and with precision, accelerated during and after the Civil War. The demands of war—for textiles, clothing, boots, armaments, cannons, and other goods—drove this rapid industrialization. In 1864, the Wyandotte Iron Works in Michigan produced the first factory-made steel from pig iron; by the end of the war, investor Andrew Carnegie (1835–1919) pursued opportunities in railroad, bridge, and, shortly thereafter, steel production. While millions of young men joined the armies of the United States and the Confederate States of America, other Americans participated in industrial and agricultural expansion to serve both the military and the divided nation.

In the first year of the Civil War, many northerners put their normal lives on hold to join state militias, in what many thought would be nothing more than a three-month enlistment. The first significant military engagements, especially the Union's disastrous performance at the first Bull Run (Virginia) and the subsequent prolonged warfare in late 1861 and early 1862, eventually led Congress to pass the first conscription bill in July 1862. While men from farming and rural communities enrolled in the military with varying degrees of enthusiasm, working-class men in Pennsylvania's coal regions, for instance, opposed the draft, primarily by evading it. A year later, after passage of the Enrollment Act, white workingmen in New York City again protested against the draft, transforming their opposition into a deadly riot against African Americans throughout Manhattan in July 1863.

For soldiers and workers during the war, these conflicts highlighted growing differences between native-born whites, many of whom were proprietors or owned farms and had middle-class aspirations, and wage workers of immigrant backgrounds who built the railroads, worked on the docks, worked in factories producing arms, boots, and clothing, and mined the coal and iron ore that the Union needed to secure victory. During the war, soldiers, surgeons, and guards served both the Confederate and Union forces. Union regiments of men of African descent, recruited within the South, served as effective soldiers as well as guards at prison camps. Women worked as nurses, administering comfort more often than medical aid, to wounded or ill soldiers. Former slaves flocked to cities behind the Union line, like Washington, D.C., where they found paid employment as laborers with the U.S. Army's Quartermaster Corps.

The war also necessitated a substantial federal bureaucracy, creating roles for thousands of people who tended paper: tax registers and draft forms, records of enrollees, and reports of the injured, dead, and ill. Among these workers were a force of mostly men who processed pension requests on the behalf of Union soldiers and sailors disabled by their service in the war, as well as their widows; their jobs grew even more significant after the war. Telegraph operators relayed news of battles won and lost throughout the nation's communities. In the West, rural communities formed before the war required teachers for their children; after the war, teachers also went to the South to staff schools established for free African Americans by the Freedman's Bureau.

The social, political, and economic hostilities that led to war were hardly resolved by the Confederate defeat at Appomattox Court House, Virginia, in April 1865. Racial antagonism, discrimination against immigrants (often by other immigrants), and class tensions persisted after the war. Southern whites forced newly freed slaves who worked as sharecroppers into new forms of bonded labor: debt peonage and the crop-lien system. Generations of black farmers throughout the South, as well as many poor whites, fell victim to these vicious labor practices. Meanwhile, American Indians fought to preserve their lands and freedom, serving as representatives to federal and local governments on behalf of their nations, believing that government officials would treat them as equals. Elsewhere, Chinese railroad workers, merchants, and miners endured violent riots against them: first in Los Angeles (1871) and then in San Francisco (1877), Rock Springs, Wyoming territory, and Tacoma (1885), Seattle (1886), and Oregon (1887). Racism, cast as labor competition between Chinese and whites, was at the heart of these deadly riots and forceful expulsions.

The years of the Gilded Age (1870s–1890s) and the Progressive era (1890s–World War I era) were similarly characterized by class conflict brought on by a rapidly expanding industrial system that reoriented almost all goods production in the United States to the factory. Industrial growth brought both more immigrants from abroad, as American companies could not fill all the jobs they created, and fostered spectacular urban development. More than thirty thousand miles of railroad track were laid between the end of the Civil War and 1873, when an economic boom spread from Europe and engulfed the nation. Railroad companies cut wages sharply in the aftermath, as did other industries—coal, steel, and iron production. The ripple effects of the 1870s depression affected workers in most industries as new building construction and real estate investments plunged. Factories cut wages as well. On the great plains and in the West, subsistence farming became more commercial as farmers sought to mortgage their farms to finance the expansion of their holdings and purchases of new machines, thus becoming indebted to creditors. Coupled with cyclical periods of drought, this brought farmers to express their discontent in political activism that resulted in more government intervention in the agricultural economy.

Workers protested wage cuts in the 1870s; the 1877 Great Upheaval—a mass strike affecting communities in the East and Midwest—drew rail workers and labor sympathizers in related industries (coal mining, iron production, logging) to the protests after the Baltimore and Ohio Railroad cut wages for brakemen and rail firemen for the third time in a year. Strikers marched in streets, manned picket lines, and committed acts of vandalism against the rail companies, often in conjunction with local unemployed citizens. Rail companies hired armed private guards who fired on demonstrators, heeding the advice of the owners of the Pennsylvania Railroad, who had suggested that a "rifle diet" would put an end to any labor unrest. In Cincinnati, a reporter for the *New York Times* observed a "crowd of thieves and ruffians" forced workers throughout the city to join the strike, assisted by the local police force, who were in a "state of masterly inactivity and did not make any attempt to prevent this lawlessness" (*New York Times*, July 25, 1877). Violence escalated on both sides as governors called in their respective state militias; some regiments refused to fire on strikers. President Rutherford B. Hayes (1822–1893) then called in the U.S. Army to suppress the strike. In the end, at least one hundred people, workers and onlookers alike, were killed in the violence.

In the wake of the depression of the 1870s, companies sought to mechanize work even further, speeding production and cutting labor costs. Mechanical engineers like Frederick Winslow Taylor (1856–1915) studied production processes, pioneering so-called scientific management principles to further subdivide the work of skilled craftsmen into constituent tasks—a process that came to be known as "deskilling." In turn, companies replaced skilled craftsmen with lower-paid unskilled workers, often immigrants who eagerly sought out work that paid far more than they could make at home in eastern and southern Europe, Asia, or Latin America. Those workers, like puddlers, whose jobs had been eliminated or changed by deskilling, mechanization, and new factory regimes, resented their loss of status in the workplace. Some workers and farmers organized into unions (Knights of Labor, Workingman's Party), which became powerful for a time, while others expressed their frustrations through protest movements and political action, like the march of Jacob Coxey's Army of the Commonwealth of Christ on Washington (1894) and the People's Party (1892–1896).

Impressive economic growth—and horrific economic retractions in the recessions and depressions of the late nineteenth century (1882–1885, 1893–1897)—overwhelmed workers in many occupations. The second Great Upheaval (1886), a series of mass strikes in the rail and metal manufacturing industries, spread across the country and involved nearly half a million workers. Those in the building trades, like masons and painters, often resorted to tramping, or following the work from site to site to remain fully employed. Burgeoning urban areas needed new workers as factories transformed the goods of the rural hinterlands into products for consumption by city dwellers. In this way, cowboys drove cattle to rail centers to be transported to the great stockyards and packinghouses of Chicago and other cities. Furthermore, as the decade closed, middle-class reformers sought to reform urban spaces through the City Beautiful Movement. Armies of waste collectors and sanitation workers cleaned the streets, while police fought crime and endeavored to clean up immigrant communities in many cities.

The discontent of ordinary Americans from many walks of life encouraged political and social reformers during the late nineteenth and early twentieth centuries to pursue limited government intervention into the economy. The National Committee to Abolish Child Labor, formed in 1904, used the works of talented photographer Lewis Hines (1874–1940) to put a spotlight on the abuses of children in the workplace. Children as young as six or seven worked in hazardous environments like coal mines and textile mills. The committee and its political supporters lobbied successfully for prohibitions on child labor in hazardous industries in many states but did not succeed in their goals to have Congress enact a national prohibition. Protectionist labor laws also found adherents in other states, which sought to impose hours and wage controls on some women workers—those who worked in factories but not in domestic work, where there was no male competition for jobs. Extraordinarily tragic events, such as the 1911 Triangle Shirtwaist Fire in New York's Greenwich Village neighborhood, in which 143 workers, mostly young immigrant women, died of smoke inhalation and burns after a fire broke out inside the factory where they were locked in (to prevent theft), did lead to other industrial health and safety reforms in some states.

For American working people, the period between the start of the Civil War and the beginning of World War I (1914–1918) was one of great paradox: enormous opportunity and great economic instability. Those trades unions affiliated with the American Federation of Labor exercised considerable power in the workplace, channeling conflict largely into the labor-management realm within an industry, a city, or a local shop. Although reforms of the Progressive era and the growth of respectable trades unions representing skilled craftsmen in building, mechanical, and metal trades had contained radical working-class unrest for a time, the period during and after World War I saw a renewal of the great conflicts between workers and industry to an extent that few could have imagined in earlier years.

FURTHER READING

Arnold, Andrew B. 2014. *Fueling the Gilded Age: Railroads, Miners, and Disorder in Pennsylvania Coal Country.* New York: New York University Press.

Byrkit, James W. 2016. *Forging the Copper Collar: Arizona's Labor-Management War of 1901–1921*, 2nd ed. Tucson: University of Arizona Press.

Currarino, Rosanne. 2010. *The Labor Question in America: Economic Democracy in the Gilded Age.* Champaign-Urbana: University of Illinois Press.

Fink, Leon. 2015. *The Long Gilded Age: American Capitalism and the Lessons of a New World Order.* Philadelphia: University of Pennsylvania Press.

Green, James. 2007. *Death in the Haymarket: A Story of Chicago, the First Labor Movement, and the Bombing That Divided Gilded Age America.* New York: Anchor.

Lause, Mark. 2015. *Free Labor: The Civil War and the Making of an American Working Class.* Champaign-Urbana: University of Illinois Press.

Montgomery, David. 1987. *The Fall of the House of Labor: The Workplace, the State, and American Labor Activism, 1865–1925.* Cambridge: Cambridge University Press.

Prout, Jerry. 2016. *Coxey's Crusade for Jobs: Unemployment in the Gilded Age.* DeKalb: Northern Illinois University Press.

BANKER

Bankers owned and operated local and regional banks and were in charge of providing customer service, processing deposits and withdrawals, safeguarding the bank's vaults, and designing and approving customer loans. The banking profession in postbellum America was far from diverse. The work environment was hierarchical, interpersonal, and limited primarily to white middle-class men. Part of this is understandable: business culture did not have the public appeal it has either today or by the time President Calvin Coolidge could assure newspaper editors that business was the chief business of the American people. In the midst of the chaos and instability of the Civil War (1861–1865), the greenback controversy, the Panic of 1873, the Silver Question, and the Panic of 1893, banks needed their bankers to be dependable, loyal, smart, and artful in their ability to catch and instill confidence in men; bankers were thus drawn from an elite demographic.

Moreover, because banking—and, in some ways, finance—was as much about personal relationships as it was about monetary policies and principles, the hiring of African Americans, women, or even foreign bankers would have been seen as unappealing. This meant that the transformative events and macro developments expanding active citizenship in the late nineteenth century did not substantially influence how bankers judged the character of the broad public or, more specifically, potential customers: the banking clientele usually looked like the personnel who worked at commercial and private banks insofar as bankers were usually white, male, and middle-class.

Immigrants and African Americans were forced to create alternate, parallel economic institutions. Immigrants, for example, set up informal unlicensed, unregulated banks that performed such financial services as procuring jobs for immigrants, financing a trip to America, and extending credit to fellow immigrants. African Americans patronized some banks and created a colorful palette of fraternal, benevolence, and mutual aid organizations designed to help widows, orphans, or the sick, and by the twentieth century, blacks across the country opened their own private banks.

Other people who worked in banks—cashiers, tellers, clerks, messengers, and bookkeepers—were sometimes referred to as bankers too. Each banking position required a bevy of exceptional personal qualities and skills. Discernment of character, appreciation for time, clarity on appropriate mores, accounting skills, and strong memories were invaluable for making a normal day at a bank flow smoothly. These various positions with their specialized banking tasks worked like a system of checks and balances to protect against human error.

Bank customers entered a world of numbers, character inspection, and specificity. Depositors would have given different forms of currency to receiving tellers, who would weed out phony bills and other counterfeit deposits. These tellers needed to make assessments at a fast pace. Receiving tellers would also evaluate both the character of the depositor and his signature. Paying tellers, able and honest accountants, monitored the tasks of the other banking officials and had to memorize the signature of every depositor. Discount clerks were often responsible for keeping track of the bank loans and, thus, like all bank personnel, had to judge character, a process which discriminated against and controlled who utilized a bank's resources. In addition, there was usually more than one individual bookkeeper because they were responsible for every open account. They also needed good handwriting for writing customer information in account books. Individual bookkeepers also needed to be good, discreet listeners as they frequently discussed concerns related to bank accounts.

Banks reinforced the demographics found within the business community—white, male, and middle-class space. The Wharton School of the University of Pennsylvania, America's first business school, only opened in 1881, and bankers would soon be the product of an elite college—an elite demographic. Years of schooling developed skills like impeccable handwriting and other accounting practices. Although immigrants established informal banking institutions, these were much more rudimentary than commercial banks. Middle-class white women could have potentially worked at banks, respectable institutions, but a woman's sphere was still the home, and the world of business was viewed as cold, hard, taxing, male space.

African Americans, despite social, legal, and economic constraints, were able to open their own banks and gain experience in banking. The Freedman's Savings and Trust banks provided the first opportunity that African Americans had to work as banking officials, and these helped African American soldiers during the Civil War save money and develop a sense of thrift. African American depositors would eventually lose their savings as the bank was used as an investment bank. However, a number of African Americans worked as tellers and in other positions before its demise. Blacks gained further experience in banking by opening their own banking institutions. The first black bank in America was The Savings Bank of the Grand Fountain United Order of True Reformers in Richmond, Virginia. Founded in 1888, True Reformers Bank became a beacon of hope for the black community in Richmond. Although the bank was able to survive the Panic of 1893, it was closed by 1910. The most successful black bank during this period was owned by a black woman, Maggie Lena Walker. Walker organized the St. Luke's Penny Savings Bank and created a culture of savings, thrift, and uplift in Richmond's black community. These early banking experiences gave African Americans hope and experience as banking officials, but they were also important in providing financial aid and relief during an era of transition.

After the Civil War, the banking profession played a central role in financing the industrial growth that helped establish America as a global power. Local bankers fueled civic pride and helped give business a progressive image. In addition, commercial banks were places that reinforced white, male, middle-class identity. In response to being excluded from these banks, Italians, Poles, Greeks, Serbs, and Hungarians created informal banking institutions that allowed them to make the transition into America.

Marcus Anthony Allen

See also: Bookkeeper; *1946–1991:* Accountant; Economist

FURTHER READING

Anthony, David. 2009. *Paper Money Men: Commerce, Manhood, and the Sensational Public Sphere in Antebellum America.* Columbus: Ohio State University Press.

Bodenhorn, Howard. 2000. *A History of Banking in Antebellum America: Financial Markets and Economic Development in an Era of Nation-Building.* Cambridge: Cambridge University Press.

Willis, Henry Parker. 1980. *American Banking.* New York: Arno Press.

BOOKKEEPER

A bookkeeper is responsible for keeping records of the financial transactions and affairs of a business. Keeping records of sales and expenditures is an occupation that goes back to ancient times, when scribes and clerks kept track of monies collected and spent by governments and armies. Early merchants and moneylenders also kept track of credit extended and receipts. The double entry system of bookkeeping, in which receipts and expenditures are noted, dates to medieval times. The bookkeeper enters records of a business's sales and expenses for each item, regardless of value, in a register or special accounts book. In America, many artisans and small merchants kept their own books or hired clerks who they then trained to enter these data. At regular intervals, the bookkeeper then totaled all items by category (sales and expenses) and then deducted expenses from sales to determine profit. The job of bookkeeper required patience, attention to minute details, and some mathematical ability.

In the mid-nineteenth century, young men with some schooling could become clerks and bookkeepers. The industrialist John D. Rockefeller, for instance, got his start in business as a bookkeeper at a firm in Cleveland, Ohio, in 1855. Rockefeller dropped out of school at age sixteen, before he completed secondary school. But his conscientiousness and careful record-keeping of the mercantile store's books led him to go into business for himself after several years of working as a bookkeeper. While Rockefeller's case is atypical in that he became one of the world's richest businessmen after organizing Standard Oil Company, other business owners similarly got their start as bookkeepers. The former Confederate soldier Thomas Wragg worked as a bookkeeper for some time during the 1870s, a position that required long work hours—Wragg often toiled over the books until midnight. Entering numbers for sixteen hours a day took its toll on Wragg, and he became morose and sullen, eventually sending his wife and children to her mother's house. Wragg the bookkeeper dreamed of moving to Florida, where fishing was exceptionally good, he told his father. Wragg did resign from his mind-numbing work, but he began dealing in land throughout Georgia and later opened a store; he didn't move to Florida until later in his life, when he passed examinations that qualified him as a physician and took a job as the surgeon for the Florida Railway and Navigation Company.

Most bookkeepers, however, did not become rich industrialists or doctors. The job required that they enter numbers into columns all day, copied from sales and expense receipts. Each kind of receipt needed to be categorized, an organizational scheme determined by business owners and managers with the input of their bookkeepers. Unlike the later-day accountants, bookkeepers seldom analyzed business patterns as that was the responsibility of the owner. Instead, bookkeepers entered data into the book in the proper categories. Expenses, for instance, might include categories such as wages, office rent, purchase of inventory for sales, supplies, shipping and travel costs, and legal fees. At the end of each term (week, month, quarter), the bookkeeper prepared a report for the business manager and owner, listing the sales and expenditures. Sometimes, bookkeepers might note seasonal differences in sales, for instance, but in small businesses, that work was normally the purview of the owner.

This occupation was one that required little ambition or initiative from the worker. Businessmen and -women, however, did desire another quality in their bookkeepers: honesty. Dishonest bookkeepers could embezzle company funds, underreport sales, or in other ways undermine the financial foundations of a business. Among the most notoriously dishonest bookkeepers was William Miller, a New Yorker who devised the first Ponzi-like scheme in 1899, in which he guaranteed returns of 10 percent annually on investments but used others' funds to pay off those who invested their money first. Miller's scheme was eventually uncovered; he was arrested, tried, convicted, and spent years in prison for this financial fraud.

Inattentive and disinterested bookkeepers, however, were of equal concern as a misreported amount could seriously impact sales and profitability. Business owners often closely supervised bookkeepers for this reason. In the late nineteenth century, most bookkeepers were young men, who often rebelled at this surveillance. The imagery of the bookkeeper focused intently on his work, with supervisorial oversight, helped to create in the public mind an image of soft young men, without ambition, who labored inside offices for long workdays. A bookkeeper was a lower-middle-class employee, an office worker. A poem in the American humor magazine *Puck* embodied the daydreaming, inattentive young bookkeeper who, while entering numbers into columns, wondered, "Oh! I wish I'd make my 'bundle,' my 'roll,' and eke my 'bunch,'/Like the Old Man a-taking his two-hour lunch. The cruel spite of fortune and gross Inequality/he thought on for one instance, quite grievedly . . . " Like untold numbers of office workers, however, the owner returned to the office, prompting the bookkeeper to "instantly [discard] his Wandering Willy Mien/To assume a deep laboriousness quite painful to be seen" (Fish 1893, 70).

Nancy Quam-Wickham

See also: *1776–1860:* Customs Collector; *1861–1914:* Pension Bureau Clerk; *1946–1991:* Office Clerk

FURTHER READING

Banville, Scott D. 2011. "'A Bookkeeper, Not an Accountant': Representing the Lower Middle Class from Victorian Novels and Music-Hall Songs to Television Sitcoms." *Journal of Popular Culture* 44, no. 1: 16–36.

Fish, Williston. 1893. "The Bookkeeper." *Puck* 35, no. 863 (September 20, 1893): 70.

Hain, Pamela Chase. 2005. *Confederate Chronicle: The Life of a Civil War Survivor.* Columbia: University of Missouri Press.

Segall, Grant. 2000. *John D. Rockefeller: Anointed with Oil.* Oxford: Oxford University Press.

PRIMARY DOCUMENT

In her short story "The Bookkeeper's Wife," novelist Willa Cather tells of a young bookkeeper, Percy Bixby, who embezzled one thousand dollars from his employer, Mr. Remsen of Remsen Paper Company, to provide for the luxuries that his soon-to-be wife, Stella Brown, so desired. Bixby had intended to pay back the money he had stolen before his employer discovered it, but five years later, now married to Stella, he had been unable to do so. He confessed his crime to Mr. Remsen, who, though shocked, did not prosecute Bixby but instead kept him in his employ, deducting ten dollars from each week's paycheck until the remaining seven hundred dollars was repaid. Cather's description of the bookkeeper at work resonates with contemporary accounts of office workers in New York City in the mid-1910s.

Nobody but the janitor was stirring about the offices of the Remsen Paper Company, and still Percy Bixby sat at his desk, crouched on his high stool and staring out at the tops of the tall buildings flushed with the winter sunset, at the hundreds of windows, so many rectangles of white electric light, flashing against the broad waves of violet that ebbed across the sky. His ledgers were all in their places, his desk was in order, his office coat on its peg, and yet Percy's smooth, thin face wore the look of anxiety and strain which usually meant that he was behind in his work. He was trying to persuade himself to accept a loan from the company without the company's knowledge. As a matter of fact, he had already accepted it. His books were fixed, the money, in a black-leather bill-book, was already inside his waistcoat pocket.

He had still time to change his mind, to rectify the false figures in his ledger, and to tell Stella Brown that they couldn't possibly get married next month. There he always halted in his reasoning, and went back to the beginning.

The Remsen Paper Company was a very wealthy concern, with easy, old-fashioned working methods. They did a long-time credit business with safe customers, who never thought of paying up very close on their large indebtedness. From the payments on these large accounts Percy had taken a hundred dollars here and two hundred there until he had made up the thousand he needed. So long as he stayed by the books himself and attended to the mail-orders he couldn't possibly be found out. He could move these little shortages about from account to account indefinitely. He could have all the time he needed to pay back the deficit, and more time than he needed.

Although he was so far along in one course of action, his mind still clung resolutely to the other. He did not believe he was going to do it. He was the least of a sharper in the world. Being scrupulously honest even in the most trifling matters was a pleasure to him . . . He loved his desk, he loved his books, which had no handwriting in them but his own . . . He would have hated to let any one else put so much as a pen-scratch in them. He liked all the boys about the office; his desk, worn smooth by the sleeves of his alpaca coat; his rulers and inks and pens and calendars. He had a great pride in working economics, and he always got so far ahead when supplies were distributed that he had drawers full of pencils and pens and rubber bands against a rainy day.

Percy liked regularity: to get his work done on time, to have his half-day off every Saturday, to go to the theater Saturday night, to buy a new necktie twice a month, to appear in a new straw hat on the right day in May, and to know what was going on in New York. He read the morning and evening papers coming and going on the elevated, and preferred journals of approximate reliability. He got excited about ball-games and elections and business failures, was not above an interest in murders and divorce scandals, and he checked the news off as neatly as he checked his mail-orders. In short, Percy Bixby was like the model pupil who is satisfied with his lessons and his teachers and his holidays, and who would gladly go to school all his life. He had never wanted anything outside his routine until he wanted Stella Brown to marry him, and that had upset everything . . .

These were the factors in Percy's present situation. He went over them again and again as he sat stooping on his tall stool. He had quite lost track of time when he heard the janitor call good night to the watchman. Without thinking what he was doing, he slid into his overcoat, caught his hat, and rushed out to the elevator, which was waiting for the janitor. The moment the car dropped, it occurred to him that the thing was decided without his having made up his mind at all. The familiar floors passed him, ten, nine, eight, seven. By the time he reached the fifth, there was no possibility of going back; the click of the drop-lever seemed to settle that. The money was in his pocket. Now, he told himself as he hurried out into the exciting clamor of the street, he was not going to worry about it any more.

Source: Willa Cather. "The Bookkeeper's Wife." *The Century Illustrated Monthly Magazine* 92 (May 1916), 51–59.

CIGARMAKER

Cigarmakers sorted and ranked tobacco and then rolled it, usually by hand, into cigars. Many cigarmakers were immigrant men: Germans and other central Europeans, Cubans and other immigrants from the Caribbean, and Chinese, particularly in California. In the 1870s, cigarmaking was a new industry in the United States as before the American Civil War (1861–1865), Cuba dominated the cigar industry through the perceived quality of its tobacco. The island's influence diminished in the late 1800s due to rebellions, trade restrictions of the Spanish empire, and U.S. tariffs on imported cigars. Those factors convinced many Cuban cigar producers to relocate to the United States. While Florida hosted many of the relocated cigar factories, so did New York and other large cities such as New Orleans, Chicago, and San Francisco. This migration provided a welcome boost to the domestic industry of the United States.

By the 1880s, much of the cigar industry was based in factories rather than the small, local workshops prevalent in the 1860s. Those who actually made the cigars bunched together the cigar's filler by hand, wrapped it in a binder leaf, and finally rolled it in the wrapper leaf. Since most factories produced cigars of various sizes, workers also had to produce consistent output that matched the products' specifications. The demands upon the manual skill of the workers were extremely high. Under the handmade model, it took a three-year apprenticeship (at a fraction of the pay) to cultivate the skills needed for a typical job. As a result, cigarmakers were difficult to replace.

The status of pre-mechanized cigar makers was embodied by their unions. Samuel Gompers (1850–1924) worked in London's cigar industry before working in the Cigar Maker's International Union and forming the American Federation of Labor between 1881 and 1886. The male-only CMIU recognized the international nature of the employees and employers in the industry and became important in the United States because of its relatively moderate political approach. Radicalized workers from Europe and Cuba often formed more militant unions that reflected their political views.

Less-skilled workers received training in the workplace, while cigarmakers received their apprenticeships and training through the labor unions. Once they became journeymen, cigarmakers built careers in the profession and showed little loyalty to any firm, oscillating between locales and employers as convenience dictated. Because the industry demanded skilled workers who were often scarce on the U.S. mainland, foreign-born workers filled in the gaps, mostly notably those from Cuba and Europe. The steamship and relatively open borders made it possible for workers to follow the demands of the market. Because wages were slow to rise, workers always kept their options open.

The typical factory contained five departments: tobacco preparation, leaf stripping/stemming, cigar manufacturing, packing, and shipping. Teams of workers in casing rooms unpacked bales of tobacco and moistened the leaves for use the following day. Unskilled women usually served as strippers, removing the stems from tobacco leaves to be used as wrappers and filler. Filler men briefly cured special blends for cigars. Wrapper selectors chose the best of the destemmed leaves and sorted them into fifty grades of various qualities. The cigarmakers received the ingredients for the specific styles of cigar they were expected to produce. They then combined the wrappers and filler into specific sizes. Pickers and packers sorted the cigars and boxed them. Each cigar was banded with its brand's logo by the workers of the boxing department, who were typically female.

Although women were initially excluded from the skilled jobs in the industry, this changed over time. Between 1890 and 1920, the female proportion of cigar workers doubled to 59 percent. While the lesser-skilled workers were paid by the hour, the cigarmakers earned their pay through piece work, or being paid a fixed amount for every finished cigar.

Beginning in about 1900, large tobacco trusts acquired many of the most important cigar firms. As investors tried to raise profits, they sought to replace skilled, unionized, male workers with unskilled, unorganized women. Various devices came into use to make production more efficient. The process began with the mold in 1869, allowing unskilled workers to accurately bunch tobacco. This meant the cigarmakers only had to roll the finished product. Wages were notoriously slow to increase because the industry constantly used labor-saving devices to undermine the need for skilled workers.

In the late 1890s, new technology allowed machines to automatically bunch and roll cigars, and in 1917, the automatic long-filler machine turned out higher-quality products. Between 1900 and 1940, the industry aggressively added cigarmaking machines to their facilities, which dramatically changed the industry. Workers could be trained to work the machines in a week. To run the machines, factory owners tended to seek out workers new to the cigar industry with no expectations to attain a skilled position. The new workforce was female, young, and native born, and men claimed the new mechanic positions to maintain the machines.

In 1921, only 11 factories produced more than 40 million cigars, or about 15.7 percent of the whole. In 1939, 32 factories produced that amount, or 67.4 percent of the nation's whole. Conversely, small factories (producing under half a million cigars annually) decreased from 4,121 in 1921 to 132 in 1939.

Cigar production peaked in 1920 at more than eight billion individual cigars, but the industry soon found itself in steep decline. The proliferation of cheaper products undermined the entire industry. Many smokers favored the five-cent cigar because it was more affordable than handmade varieties, which were often ten cents or more. In 1921, less than a third of cigars produced in the United States sold for five cents, but in 1940, 90 percent sold for that price. Cheap mass-produced cigarettes gained in popularity during the 1930s, especially in Hollywood films, so many smokers simply discarded one mass-produced product for another. Production of cigars fell from 8 billion in 1921 to 4.3 billion in 1933, while employees dwindled from 112,000 in 1921 to 51,000 in 1939. In the meantime, cigars lost their mass appeal, and the decline of the industry had just begun.

Andrew T. Huse

See also: *1607–1775:* Apothecary; *1776–1860:* Tobacconist

FURTHER READING

Cooper, Patricia A. 1987. *Once a Cigar Maker: Men, Women and Work Culture in American Cigar Factories, 1900–1919.* Urbana-Champaign: University of Illinois Press.

Livesay, Harold. 1978. *Samuel Gompers and Organized Labor in America.* Boston: Little, Brown.

Perez, Louis A. 1978. "Cubans in Tampa: From Exiles to Immigrants, 1892–1901." *Florida Historical Quarterly* 57 no. 2: 129–140.

Thomas, Lorrin. 2010. *Puerto Rican Citizen History and Political Identity in Twentieth Century New York City.* Chicago: University of Chicago Press.

PRIMARY DOCUMENT

Cigarmakers in America worked in two settings at the turn of the century, c. 1900. Workers belonging to the International Cigar Maker's Union tended to work in factories and small shops paying relatively good wages. In this setting, workers had specific tasks: Strippers stripped whole tobacco leaves from their stems to be used as the wrapper that formed the outer layer of hand-rolled cigars. Rollers hand-rolled the cigars to specifications, using different mixes of tobacco (filler) for different flavors of cigars. Readers were usually youngsters who read the daily news—including the union newspaper—as well as books, magazines, and other reading material to other workers as a form of entertainment and edification in an era before radios were invented. In the second setting, the non-union shops, cigarmakers routinely labored in harsh conditions in poorly lit workspaces that often doubled as living spaces. In this document, social reformer and journalist Jacob Riis describes the working conditions of Czech (Bohemian) immigrants in tenements in New York City.

Probably more than half of all the Bohemians in this city are cigarmakers, and it is the herding of these in great numbers in the so-called tenement factories, where the cheapest grade of work is done at the lowest wages, that constitutes at once their greatest hardship and the chief grudge of other workmen against them. The manufacturer who owns, say, from three or four, to a dozen or more tenements contiguous to his shop, fills them up with these people, charging them outrageous rents, and demanding often even a preliminary deposit of five dollars "key money;" deals them out tobacco by the week, and devotes the rest of his energies to the paring down of wages to within a peg or two of the point where the tenant rebels in desperation. When he does rebel, he is given the alternative of submission, or eviction with entire loss of employment. His needs determine the issue. Usually he is not in a position to hesitate long . . . .

Men, women and children work together seven days in the week in these cheerless tenements to make a living for the family, from the break of day till far into the night. Often the wife is the original cigarmaker from the old home, the husband having adopted her trade here as a matter of necessity, because, knowing no word of English, he could get no other work. As they state the cause of the bitter hostility of the trades unions, she was the primary bone of contention in the day of the early Bohemian immigration. The unions refused to admit the women, and, as the support of the family depended upon her to a large extent, such terms as were offered had to be accepted . . . Doubtless the people are poor, in many cases very poor; but they are not uncleanly, rather the reverse; they live much better than the clothing-makers in the Tenth Ward, and in spite of their sallow look, that may be due to the all-pervading smell of tobacco, they do not appear to be less healthy than other indoor workers. I found on my tours of investigation several cases of consumption, of which one at least was said by the doctor to be due to the constant inhalation of tobacco fumes. But an examination of the death records in the Health Department does not support the claim that the Bohemian cigarmakers are peculiarly prone to that disease. On the contrary, the Bohemian percentage of deaths from consumption appears quite low . . . The sore grievances I found were the miserable wages and the enormous rents exacted for the minimum of accommodation. And surely these stand for enough of suffering.

Take a row of houses in East Tenth Street as an instance. They contained thirty-five families of cigarmakers, with probably not half a dozen persons in the whole lot of them, outside of the children, who could speak a word of English, though many had been in the country half a lifetime. This room with two windows giving on the street, and a rear attachment without windows, called a bedroom by courtesy, is rented at $12.25 a month. In the front room man and wife work at the bench from six in the morning till nine at night. They make a team, stripping the tobacco leaves together; then he makes the filler, and she rolls the wrapper on and finishes the cigar. For a thousand [cigars] they receive $3.75, and can turn out together three thousand cigars a week. The point has been reached where the rebellion comes in, and the workers in these tenements are just now on a strike, demanding $5.00 and $5.50 for their work. The manufacturer having refused, they are expecting hourly to be served with notice to quit their homes, and the going of a stranger among them excites their resentment, until his errand is explained. While we are in the house, the ultimatum of the "boss" is received. He will give $3.75 a thousand, not another cent. Our host is a man of seeming intelligence, yet he has been nine years in New York and knows neither English nor German. Three bright little children play about the floor.

His neighbor on the same floor has been here fifteen years, but shakes his head when asked if he can speak English. He answers in a few broken syllables when addressed in German. With $11.75 rent to pay for like accommodation, he has the advantage of his oldest boy's work besides his wife's at the bench. Three properly make a team, and these three can turn out four thousand cigars a week, at $3.75. This Bohemian has a large family; there are four children, too small to work, to be cared for . . . Here is a suit of three rooms, two dark, three flights up. The ceiling is partly down in one of the rooms. "It is three months since we asked the landlord to fix it," says the oldest son, a very intelligent lad who has learned English in the evening school. His father has not had that advantage, and has sat at his bench, deaf and dumb to the world about him except his own, for six years. He has improved his time and become an expert at his trade. Father, mother, and son together, a full team, make from fifteen to sixteen dollars a week.

A man with venerable beard and keen eyes answers our questions through an interpreter, in the next house. Very few brighter faces would be met in a day's walk among American mechanics, yet he has in nine years learned no syllable of English. German he probably does not want to learn. His story supplies the explanation, as did the stories of the others. In all that time he has been at work grubbing to earn bread. Wife and he by constant labor make three thousand cigars a week, earning $11.25 when there is no lack of material; when in winter they receive from the manufacturer tobacco for only two thousand, the rent of $10 for two rooms, practically one with a dark alcove, has nevertheless to be paid in full, and six mouths to be fed. He was a blacksmith in the old country, but cannot work at his trade here because he does not understand "Engliska." If he could, he says, with a bright look, he could do better work than he sees done here. It would seem happiness to him to knock off at 6 o'clock instead of working, as he now often has to do, till midnight. But how? He knows of no Bohemian blacksmith who can understand him; he should starve. Here, with his wife, he can make a living at least. "Aye," says she, turning, from listening, to her household duties, "it would be nice for sure to have father work at his trade." Then what a home she could make for them, and how happy they would be. Here is an unattainable ideal, indeed, of a workman in the most prosperous city in the world! There is genuine, if unspoken, pathos in the soft tap she gives her husband's hand as she goes about her work with a half-suppressed little sigh.

Source: Jacob Riis. 1890. *How the Other Half Lives.* New York: Charles Scribner's and Sons, 138–142.

COAL MINER

Coal miners are workers who labor in mines to extract coal for their company or refinery to process for sale. While many immigrants labored in America's largest cities in thunderous factories, a large number also migrated to the rural coalfields. Whether it was the Anthracite mines of eastern Pennsylvania, the smokeless, bituminous coalfields of southern Western Virginia, the Midwest, or in the foothills of the Rocky Mountains in southern Colorado, immigrant miners cut, blasted, and hauled the coal that fueled America's industrial expansion in the late nineteenth and early twentieth centuries. Immigrants constituted almost half of the workforce in the 1870s. Welsh, Irish, and Scandinavian immigrants used mining as a way to supplement their farming income, with each different geographic region attracting clusters of particular immigrant groups. In the 1880s, Finns began laboring in the iron ore mines of Michigan and Minnesota. New arrivals from southern and Eastern Europe soon replaced them.

Polish, Italian, Serbian, Hungarian, Greek, and Czech miners were often paid by the ton, while some unskilled labor was paid by the hour. Pick miners, on average, earned about ninety cents per ton, and on a good day loading three tons, they could expect to earn $2.70 a day. Coal companies hired a diverse labor force to play off Old World tensions between certain groups. The French disliked German miners; the Germans often viewed the Poles as beneath them; the Poles looked down on Lithuanians and Ukrainians. As a coal operator in West Virginia noted, this "judicious mixture" of differing ethnicities and races helped undermine solidarity and the ability of the United Mine Workers of America (UMWA) to organize (Bailey 1973, 141–161).

The living conditions and overall experience of living and working in a coal company town were similar for both Americans and foreign-born miners. Frank Lencek arrived in the country in 1911 at the age of nineteen, after growing up in the village of Unec, which is located in present-day Slovenia. Enticed by a neighbor who found success in mountainous Tucker County in northern West Virginia, Lencek arrived in the town of Thomas and began work as a coal loader for the Davis Coal & Coke Company. On a good day underground in the early 1910s, Frank earned about $2.50 per coal car.

Miners like Lencek had physically exhausting jobs. They went underground at the start of their workday and then did not emerge until the end of their shift. They ate, drank, and tried to maneuver in very tight and dangerous quarters. Upon entering a mine shaft, they descended to a depth of several hundred or a thousand feet, with some using a rickety elevator or shaft, and went to work in their "room." Others arrived by walking a considerable distance to the coalface. Sometimes there was space for men, mules, and railcars to enter and exit the mine; otherwise, miners had to make a tight squeeze past disgruntled mules and dodge runaway rail cars.

Most labored under the room-and-pillar system, in which they extracted coal from horizontal layers in small sections (rooms), moving ever deeper along a horizontal plane into a mountain as more coal was retrieved. When they got to the face, miners had to be wary of the overhead, watching for chunks of rock (known as slate) that could fall and crush them. Most immigrant miners utilized hand picks, shovels, and drills to bore holes into the wall, filled them with blasting powder, and then broke off a huge chunk of the coal face. Unskilled coal loaders discarded slate and loaded the black rock into cars pulled by mules to the surface. Often the children of the male immigrants worked as drivers, managing the horses and mules needed to move the heavy coal cars out of the mines. This system created a web of tunnels, literally streets and alleyways through the underground coal seams, that needed to be watched and properly supported with timbers to prevent collapses.

Their labor at the coal face exposed them to far more dangers. Cracks and fissures often formed, weakening the mountain above their heads. Miners had to be on watch for slate falls, loose electrical cables, and also high concentrations of methane gas. Large numbers of miners also died in violent explosions resulting from an accumulation of methane gas. On the morning of February 4, 1907, twenty-five men perished in an explosion at the Davis Coal & Coke Company No. 25 mine near Thomas, West Virginia. Twelve were Italians, six Lithuanians, and five were Croatians or Slovenians. The worst mine disaster occurred in Monongah, West Virginia, when an explosion at the Fairmont Coal Company's No. 6 and No. 8 mines exploded on December 6, 1907, killing an estimated 362 miners, who were mostly immigrant men and boys.

Unwilling to accept the harsh dangers underground, the lack of freedoms in coal company towns, and the depressed wages, immigrant coal miners were at the forefront of the organizing efforts led by the UMWA. When Kanawha Valley operators insisted on paying miners by the long ton of 2,240 pounds, nearly 1,500

Calabrian miners from Italy went on strike in the spring of 1909. Rocco Spinelli, another Calabrian immigrant, came to America in 1905 and found work in the mines near Eskdale on Cabin Creek, just south of the state capital in Charleston. When a strike broke out in the spring of 1912, Rocco and his wife, Nellie, joined with vigor, going throughout the coal camps and urging other Italian miners to join. During the height of the Colorado Coalfield War of 1913–1914, Louis Tikas, leader of the Greek strikers, died along with a number of women and children after being shot by Colorado state militiamen. They, together with thousands of other foreign-born miners, joined in the various strikes and organizing campaigns to bring true democracy to the coalfield communities across America.

William Hal Gorby

See also: *1776–1860:* Gold Miner; Laborer

FURTHER READING

Alexander, June Granatir. 2007. *Daily Life in Immigrant America, 1870–1920: How the Second Great Wave of Immigrants Made Their Way in America*. Chicago: Ivan R. Dee.

Andrews, Thomas G. 2010. *Killing for Coal: America's Deadliest Labor War*. Cambridge: Harvard University Press.

Bailey, Kenneth R. 1985. "A Judicious Mixture: Negroes and Immigrants in the West Virginia Mines, 1880–1917." In *Blacks in Appalachia*, edited by William H. Turner and Edward J. Cabbell, 117–132. Lexington: University Press of Kentucky.

Leneck, Frank. May 19, 1967. Interview by John E. Stealey III. West Virginia & Regional History Center: Oral History Collection.

West Virginia. 1916. *Annual Report of the Department of Mines, For the Fiscal Year Ending June 30, 1916*. Charleston: Tribune Printing Co.

COOK

Cooks are people who prepare and cook food, often in restaurants or commercial eating establishments. In most nineteenth-century families, women did the cooking—whether as wives and housewives or as domestic workers who cared for children, cleaned, washed, and prepared meals. Middle-class Americans, single as well as married, took occasional meals at tavern inns, something of an anachronism by the end of Prohibition in 1933; tavern inns were places that provided beer and other alcoholic drinks but also meals and often lodging. In some places, like California, tavern inns were just called inns, and most offered basic meals for lodgers and travelers. In many of these establishments, women cooked for the clientele. Robert Louis Stevenson described one such inn, the Frisby House in South Vallejo, as he encountered it in the late 1870s: "At dinner there was the ordinary display of what is called in the West a two-bit house; the table-cloth checked red and white, the plague of flies, the wire hen-coops over the dishes, the great variety and invariable vileness of the food, and the rough, coatless men devouring it in silence" (Stevenson 1888). Also popular during this period were boardinghouses that provided lodging and meals, usually breakfast and supper, to young men and women and families. As ambitious young people left the countryside to find work in cities, running a boardinghouse became a stable, if not lucrative, means for older women to earn a living.

In this period, however, the work of cooking transformed for many as restaurants—stand-alone dining houses unattached to taverns and inns—became popular among the growing middle class. Restaurant work provided men with jobs as cooks: in fine dining establishments like Delmonico's in New York City or Antoine's in New Orleans, both black and white men worked as chefs and line cooks, though, for a time, after Antoine Alciatore returned to Europe in 1875, his wife, Julie Freyss Alciatore, ran the restaurant as executive chef until their son, Jules, returned from his European culinary training in the 1880s and took over control of Antoine's. In Chinatowns throughout the nation, discrimination and segregation also drove Chinese men into working as cooks as American immigration laws had prohibited most immigration of Chinese women after the 1860s while limiting employment of Chinese men by imposing heavy occupational taxes; Chinese domestic workers were, consequently, overwhelmingly male in western cities like San Francisco, Sacramento, and Seattle.

In other cases, male cooks worked in railroad, logging, oil, and mining camps, on ranches, in jails and prisons, and on the new ocean liners as well as steamboats—all distinctly male spaces where employers generally preferred male workers in order to limit interpersonal conflict between men. Especially on ships, gay men and men of color found employment in the steward's departments working as cooks, bakers, servers, and wine stewards and doing other "women's work." In later years, among those who worked in steward's departments on vessels as young men were Langston Hughes, Revels Cayton (grandson of the first black U.S. senator, Hiram Revels), Cisco Houston, and Ralph Ellison.

The job of cooking in such diverse environments makes it difficult to generalize about cooks in this period, though there are some similarities between all men and women who did this work. Technology made the work of cooking more efficient and less taxing, though kitchen work was always heavy labor. As historian Tera Hunter noted in her study of southern domestic workers after the Civil War, the cast-iron stoves that replaced open fireplaces "required less fuel, worked more efficiently and safely, and were built high enough off the ground to prevent constant bending by the cook" (Hunter 1997, 55). A cook in a camp, an inn, or a hotel had to light the stove—carry in wood, coal, or oil—in the morning, usually well before sunrise. Cast-iron stoves had no thermostat, so cooks had to judge the temperature of the oven by experience. Yeast was put to rise for bread as the stove was lit, and then the cook mixed the dough and set the bread loaves to leaven near the stovetop.

Cooks then began food preparation for breakfast, commonly bread, potatoes, meat, eggs, and pancakes, though in the South, cornbread, molasses, and bacon were the most common fare. The cook at one inn in Indiana customarily served fried squirrel and wild turkey as well as the standard fare for breakfast. Fresh milk and buttermilk were also standard, though most inns and camps also offered tea and coffee. Coffee beans may have been purchased before roasting, and if this was the case, the cook had to roast the beans in the oven or in a frying pan on the stovetop before grinding them and making coffee. While a cook kept his or her stove fired all day, this process of food preparation was repeated at each subsequent meal: chopping ingredients, adding seasonings, baking, roasting, and frying food. Before refrigeration was common, most meat was cured, especially pork (ham and bacon), or there was fresh poultry that a cook's helper might slaughter in the back of the inn. Outside of cities, many inns and hotels had chicken coops on the premises, as well as a milk cow. At smaller establishments, cooks served diners as well, though in the rough logging camps and other such worksites, men lined up cafeteria style as the cooks dished out their plates of food. Except for in the finest dining restaurants, most diners ate to their content as meals were served family or cafeteria style.

In most environments, those who became cooks learned their trades on the job, often as helpers to the cook or as children in their parents' workplaces. In inn and camp kitchens, cooks did not follow recipes but used their experience and taste to craft dishes. Cooking was a job that required innovation, intelligence, and a good palate. Cooking was also a creative endeavor, as the case of Chinese cooks illustrates. White hostility to Chinese immigrants characterized the second half of the nineteenth century; seeking to overcome prejudice, some enterprising Chinese workers promoted Chinese restaurants because, as Erica Peters writes of the traditional proverb, "After eating other people's food, you cannot criticize them" (Peters 2015, 6). To appeal to the American palate, Chinese cooks altered a traditional stir-fried dish that incorporated "a mixture of chicken livers and gizzards, fungi, bamboo buds, pig's tripe, and bean sprouts stewed together with spices, stewed and served over rice" (Freedmen 2016, 218). Aware that Americans of this period balked at eating organ meat, Chinese cooks working in Chinese restaurants created a new version of chop suey, combining vegetables, chunks of pork meat, and brown gravy. Even as early-twentieth-century middle-class Americans continued to discriminate against Chinese and support anti-Asian immigration laws, they also flocked to Chinese restaurants to enjoy this new Americanized Chinese dish, with hundreds of chop suey restaurants spread throughout the country's cities and towns.

High-end restaurants serving tourists and well-to-do locals generally employed male cooks. These establishments were distinguished by enormous menus and specific dishes, so in these workspaces, cooks used specific, and sometimes proprietary, recipes. New York's Delmonico's, the first of the *haute cuisine* houses, had separate kitchens for basic food preparation like washing and chopping vegetables and fruit, preparing pastries, and stove and oven work—bringing dishes together over the cast-iron appliances. Here, a head cook, or chef, prepared menus well in advance of a day's offerings, shopped for the freshest ingredients, and supervised a large staff of cooks, bakers, busboys, dishwashers, and waiters. A typical Delmonico's menu offered diners a choice of beefsteak prepared ten or twelve ways, as well many other main course entrées. At Antoine's in New Orleans, members of the Alciatore family supervised cooks who popularized Louisiana *creole* cuisine, a combination of French, Acadian, and African dishes. Creole cooks used sauces made of roux and aromatic vegetables (onions, garlic, celery, and peppers) rather than plain brown gravy favored more by American cooks. They incorporated spices, tomatoes, and Caribbean and African vegetables like chayote (squash) and okra and liberally added cultured creams and shellfish—the latter possible in the days before refrigeration was common because of New Orleans's proximity to the Gulf Coast's then-plentiful fishing grounds.

At the end of the nineteenth century, though, cooking became a more popular and professionalized occupation outside of America's fine restaurants. Accomplished chefs, like Delmonico's Charles Ranhofer, and cooks formally trained in culinary arts institutes, like Fannie Farmer of Massachusetts, published hefty cookbooks that provided home cooks with recipes for new dishes while standardizing old favorites. The authors of many of these new cookbooks also had training in nutrition (or asserted that they did). Cookbooks advised women how to prepare healthy food for their families and offered advice about saving money by replacing costly ingredients with inexpensive alternatives and making weekly menus. Those written by advocates of the domestic sciences—or modern home economics—movement also provided cooks with ways to keep their kitchens sanitary to avoid food-borne illnesses, a serious concern for nineteenth- and early-twentieth-century cooks. Cookbooks, advances in technology, and new interests in sanitation, diet, and health—along with the rise of chain restaurants in the post-World War I period—continued to transform the cook's profession.

Nancy Quam-Wickham

See also: Cowboy; *1915–1945:* Waiter/Waitress; *1946–1991:* Dietitian

FURTHER READING

Berube, Allan. 2011. *My Desire for History: Essays in Gay, Community, and Labor History.* Chapel Hill: University of North Carolina Press.
Freedman, Paul. 2016. *Ten Restaurants That Changed America.* New York: W. W. Norton.
Hunter, Tera W. 1997. *To Joy My Freedom: Southern Black Women's Lives and Labors After the Civil War.* Cambridge: Harvard University Press.
Peters, Erica J. 2015. "A Path to Acceptance: Promoting Chinese Restaurants in San Francisco, 1849–1919." *Southern California Quarterly* 97: 5–28.
Ross, Alice. 1993. "Health and Diet in Nineteenth Century America: A Food Historian's Point of View." *Historical Archeology* 27: 42–56.
Stevenson, Robert Louis. 1888. *The Silverado Squatters.* https://cdn.loc.gov//service/gdc/calbk/132.pdf.

COWBOY

Cowboys are workers who commonly work on horseback and tend to and herd cattle, especially in the western United States. Though their primary responsibility is to drive cattle from one location to another—often toward better grazing pastures, a cattle sale, or a slaughterhouse—cowboys are responsible for a host of other ranch-type duties like building and mending fences, hunting wild predators, protecting the livestock from theft, and making sure that the livestock does not disturb private property.

Historically, cowboys were laborers who participated in one of the greatest economic booms in the period after the Civil War. The Transcontinental Railroad was finished on May 10, 1869, and its completion heralded a new era of connectedness and trade. The American economy's invigoration wasn't limited only to the cities and towns along the rail corridor, though, and growing demand for goods and trade of all kind meant that almost every industry enjoyed major growth.

As the American economy surged near the end of the nineteenth century, demand for cattle grew immensely. Consumers across the country needed beef, dairy, and leather—and Texas, having an already established and vibrant cattle industry, became the source of much of the country's cows. But the biggest rail corridors didn't run through Texas; they cut through Nebraska and Wyoming, hundreds of miles to the north. So cattle ranchers hired cowboys to drive herds of cattle from their properties in Texas up to railways so that their cows could be shipped all over the country.

The life of an average cowboy was idyllic, but it was certainly not easy. Most cowboys were small- or medium-sized men since men with large frames would eventually cause their horses to tire after weeks and weeks of riding for twelve or fifteen hours each day. For these long hours, the average monthly wage was about twenty-five dollars and "found," or room and board when at the ranch. A typical cowboy's wardrobe might include a vest, a bandana, gloves, leather chaps (leggings worn over pants to provide additional protection and warmth), boots, spurs, and the iconic cowboy hat. A cowboy could usually be found with a knife, a revolver, a rifle, and a lasso. Ammunition was expensive, and so a cowboy would discharge a firearm only if it was absolutely necessary.

The cowboy would often need to be up with the sun to begin his day. They'd start a fire, prepare breakfast and coffee, roll up their sleeping mats, feed and tend to their horses, and collect the water that they'd need for the day. If the cattle drive happened to pass near a town, a cowboy might be able to purchase dairy or fruit, but the typical cowboy's diet consisted mostly of beans, jerky, bread, and other nonperishable food.

On the trail, the cowboy's time was mostly spent watching out for threats; the cattle themselves—and especially the cowboy's horse—did much of the work involved with driving the herd once it had started moving. A cowboy would spend his day looking out for wolves, watching the horizon for fires, and finding the best place for the herd to cross a river.

After the Civil War, the cowboy's vocation was one of the most accessible and lucrative jobs for newly freed black men. Regardless of their skin color, a first-season cowboy could earn twenty-five dollars per month, and many cowboys earned around forty dollars per month. Trail bosses—or senior cowboys who led teams of other cowboys—could earn $125 per month ("Cowboy Pay"). Slaves had originally been taken from African countries such as Gambia and Ghana, where cattle had been herded for hundreds of years, and so many ex-slaves had been exposed to cattle ranching from a very young age. Also, when the Civil War broke out, cattle ranchers would often go off to battle and would leave their ranches to be run by their slaves under the supervision of the rancher's wife or other family members. By the time the Civil War ended, there was a newly enfranchised generation of able-bodied workers who had plenty of experience driving cattle. And since racial and sociopolitical tensions were still running high in the East, freed slaves needed little excuse to move westward to search for work.

One of the most famous black cowboys was Bill Pickett, who first became a ranch hand around 1880, when he was about ten years old. He invented a technique called bulldogging, which is used for capturing a stray steer. To bulldog a steer, Bill would ride his horse hard up alongside the running steer, and he'd leap from his horse, grab the steer by the horns, and twist its head around as he fell to the ground. A version of this technique is still used today.

Blacks weren't the only minority to find great success while working as cowboys. Latinos, too, were able to leverage their cultural heritage—which, for centuries, had been linked closely with the horse and the cow—and build careers and businesses out of America's surging desire for cattle. *Vaqueros*, as they were called, were often of mestizo descent, and while many of them worked as traditional cowboys who were hired to drive cattle, many others made their livings by catching, breaking, and selling wild horses or retrieving cattle that had somehow become separated from a rancher's herd.

The life of the cowboy was hard, but it was rewarding. Perhaps most importantly, the role of the cowboy was integral to a rapidly growing America at the end of the nineteenth century, and it provided good, honest work opportunities for minorities and newly freed slaves at a time when good, honest work was difficult to find. As the rail system continued to grow, and especially once the automobile was invented, the large need for cowboys to drive cattle died down but never went away entirely. Even today, there are cowboys driving cattle much in the same way as was done in the late 1800s.

Ben Tyler Elliott

See also: Teamster; *1776–1860:* Ranchero

FURTHER READING

Acosta, Teresa Paloma. 2010. "Black Cowboys." Texas State History Association. http://www.tshaonline.org/handbook/online/articles/arb01.

Burton, Arthur T. 1991. *Black, Red, and Deadly: Black and Indian Gunfighters of the Indian Territory, 1870–1907.* Austin: Eakin Press.

"Cowboy Pay & Cowboy Rope." n.d. The Wild West. http://www.thewildwest.org/cowboys/wildwestcowboyfacts/225-cowboy-pay-cowboy-rope.

Dary, David. 1981. *Cowboy Culture: A Saga of Five Centuries.* New York: Knopf.

Durham, Philip, and Everett L. Jones. 1965. *The Negro Cowboys.* New York: Dodd, Mead.

Fishlow, Albert. 1965. *American Railroads and the Transformation of the Ante-Bellum Economy.* Cambridge, MA: Harvard University Press.

Watkins, Thayer. n.d. "The Origins of the Cowboy Culture of Western America." San Jose State University, Faculty Page. http://www.sjsu.edu/faculty/watkins/cowboyculture.htm.

"The Ways of the Cowboy." n.d. U.S. History. http://www.ushistory.org/us/41b.asp.

CURRIER

Curriers were specialized workers who produced finished, salable leather from raw animal hides. The work of preparing animal hides for use as leather is an ancient craft, though the process through which leather was produced in America changed remarkably with the introduction of industrial processes to leather manufacturing. In the colonial period, most farmers tanned and processed their own animal hides, but by the revolutionary period, an increasing number of farmers opted to pay specialized workers to do this noxious job. By the middle of the nineteenth century, leather manufacturing firms produced much of the leather used in making consumer goods, from gloves to saddles to shoes. Consumer demand for particular fashions—beaver hats, buffalo coats, and mink stoles, among others—helped to expand the processing of animal hides on an industrial scale.

While tanners, those who process the rough hide, and curriers, those who finished the partially processed hides for particular products, coexisted with industrial leather manufacturing firms in some areas after the Civil War (1861–1865), workers in small shop environments tended to satisfy the markets at two extremes: very rough work, which was often performed in isolated and rural areas, or high-end luxury production, which typically took place in urban centers for upper-class consumers. Workers formerly known as tanners and curriers produced most other leather goods in factories. These factories subdivided the work of tanners and curriers into many additional jobs, known by different occupational titles: splitters, shavers, glazers, cutters, stretchers, finishers, wet cellar workers, gelatin workers, shearers, buffers, trimmers, and operators of machines that stripped off hair, sucked parts of small animal bodies (like muskrats) out of their skins, and pressed skins flat. By the 1880s, the currier in the modern factory might perform many of these individual jobs.

Workers prepared the skins and hides of all sorts of animals to be turned into useful items. The modern factory processed hides from cattle, oxen, pigs, sheep, and goats after animals were slaughtered for their meat. Workers also processed skins harvested from horses, mules, buffalo, moose, elk, wolves, coyotes, and deer, as well as hides of smaller fur-bearing animals like otters, minks, muskrats, rabbits, foxes, ermines, seals, raccoons, and even skunks and possums. In the nineteenth century, leather for boots was created from alligator skins, a fashion trend that, by the early 1900s, designers seized upon when they began to use alligator, crocodile, snake, iguana, and lizard skins—thus creating a market for those who were processing those skins as well.

The work of turning the hide or skin of an animal into leather or fur suitable for clothing, shoes, and other goods was dirty and smelly. Slaughterhouses sent raw hides to the leather factories; these raw hides were normally covered in filth (dirt, urine and feces, harmful bacteria, and sometimes maggots) and normally had a small amount of flesh that adhered to the inside of the hide. Sometimes, fur-bearing animals like muskrats arrived only partly butchered and had to be stripped of their fur, with workers disposing of the carcasses or sending them to other factories to be further processed into fertilizer or other goods. Workers then scraped the hides, using either hand tools or machines, to strip unwanted hair from the external sides and then scrape the remaining flesh from the insides of the hides. Wool was generally stripped by hand from sheep and then sent to textile mills for processing into fabric. Workers in the tanning trades then treated the hides and skins by soaking them to hasten the process of curing the hides; these baths included a mixture of chromium chloride or sulfates, or other chemicals, into which hides and pelts were immersed or placed into an agitating drum. These methods cured the leather, removing keratin and other gelatinous material (such as scent ducts and mammary glands) from the dermis, the mid-layer of skin. Cured hides were then washed to remove the tanning liquids and any leftover waste deposits. Industrial tanneries usually employed a chemist to treat the tanning liquids for reuse.

Tanned or cured leather was then sent to members of the currier team, while skins for fur were sent to the furriers. Each of these workers treated the processed leather for different products. Workers in the currier classifications finished leather hides: they had to make the cured and stiff leather supple and water resistant. Workers in the currier rooms worked the leather, replacing the natural keratin that had been removed from the dermis with other softening agents, including "tallow, stearines, mineral greases, etc., together with a mixture of cod or other fish oil," according to one turn-of-the-century manual (Standage 1920, 63). For shoe soles, curriers also treated leather with paraffin and other waxes. This work was done either by hand or, more commonly, by machine for cheaper leather products. The leather then had to be spread out and dried, allowing the greases to fill the pores in the skins or hides. Other finishers, known as curriers' dyers and glazers, then dyed leathers different colors and added external treatments such as patenting, glossing, and coating with rubber. Polishers provided a final sheen to some treated leather goods. While individual artisanal curriers usually had their own "recipes" for each dye or treatment, by 1900, most industrial leather-processing plants had regularized those individual treatments, often securing patents on their own processes or zealously guarding their proprietary treatments, whose components were mixed by factory chemists. Once the leather was fully treated, it was sent on to be manufactured into leather products of all kinds.

This process of creating leather and fur from raw animal skin was laborious: workers labored in stinking "wet cellars" containing the tanning pits, were exposed to acids and salts and chromium (which led to elevated levels of kidney diseases), and were subjected to demands for faster work even though a single mistake—like a poorly executed cut—could ruin a pelt or hide. By the end of the nineteenth century, German immigrants and German Americans dominated the leather trades; Jewish immigrants from Eastern Europe increasingly dominated the fur trades. Their common cultural and linguistic backgrounds, along with the difficulty of the work, led many to organize into unions, some of which procured the ten-hour workday before workers in other trades. However, these victories did not last long as employers subdivided the labor tasks of leather and fur workers into many classifications; the trade-centric American Federation of Labor encouraged the formation of individual union locals of specific workers, sometimes even by gender, ethnicity, and religion. For instance, in 1896, the United Brotherhood of Leather Workers on Horse Goods was organized to "ameliorate the conditions of all leather workers" but limited its membership to those "journeymen working on harness, saddles, collars, horse-boots, gig-saddles, machine operators and skilled workmen directly employed in the manufacture of saddlery or anything made of leather or other fabric which a horse wears" (UB 1910, 13). The Ladies Fur Workers Union formed in Minneapolis near the turn of the century, while local branches of the German Leather Workers' Union formed in major cities across the Midwest.

Unlike in England, where a curriers' guild formed early in the fifteenth century, in the United States, the organization of workers into distinct unions prevented cooperation between workers in different trades within the leather and fur industries. Thus, in 1907, when the Jewish Fur Workers union struck for better wages and conditions in New York City, fur and leather workers elsewhere organized into separate locals of trimmers, cutters, polishers, and others, continued to work, crippling the ability of a single trade union to successfully carry out a strike. It was not until 1913 that activists organized the International Fur and Leather Workers' Union on an industrial basis, including all classifications of workers within the plants. In industry and in unions, the role of the traditional currier was largely nonexistent.

Nancy Quam-Wickham

See also: Haberdasher; *1607–1775:* Harness Maker and Saddler

FURTHER READING

Foner, Philip S. 1950. *The Fur and Leather Workers Union: A Story of Dramatic Struggles and Achievements.* Newark: Nordan Press.

Standage, H. C. 1920. *The Leather Workers' Manual.* London: Scott, Greenwood & Son.

United Brotherhood of Leather Workers on Horse Goods. 1910. *Constitution of the United Brotherhood Leather Workers on Horse Goods.* United States: United Brotherhood Leather Workers on Horse Goods.

HABERDASHER

A haberdasher owned and operated one of the fine men's clothing stores that emerged in large cities in the mid-nineteenth century. A 1920 article in the *New York Times* attempted to explain the difference between a haberdashery and a department store that offered many different products to consumers. Stylish men purchased their shirts and ties from haberdasheries as these were prominent items of clothing that distinguished them from other, less stylish men, whose wives or mothers bought their clothes at department stores.

Having started in large cities like New York, Boston, and Philadelphia in the mid-nineteenth century, department stores gained a greater share of the market for clothing only late in the 1800s and principally by consolidating the sale of dry goods, workmen's wear, and ladies' and children's clothing and accessories. In most large cities, specialized men's furnishing stores continued to do brisk business at the turn of the century, especially among the middle class and businessmen. In a haberdashery, a banker or attorney could select from a range of shirts, collars, ties and tie clips, cufflinks, handkerchiefs, vests, shoes, suspenders, belts, outerwear, toiletries, hats, and other accessories. Many haberdashers also sold suits, though the most stylish men patronized tailors' shops for these articles of clothing. Some haberdashers in New York sold men's "lingerie," particularly male corsets, to dandies (or men who carefully cultivated their physical appearance, some of whom were gay) as well as West Point students who needed to have waistlines. Those haberdashers who sold these items were discrete about their customers' needs, though one haberdasher did reveal that one customer was nearly six feet tall, but the corset gave him a waistline that was less than twenty-two inches in circumference.

While the haberdasher was the owner, clerks also worked in haberdasheries. Most haberdashers were men as male consumers preferred to interact with male workers, especially when it came to fashioning the male body. The late nineteenth century was a period in which middle-class men became acutely aware of their appearance; advertisers touted the benefits of exercising, bodybuilding, outdoors activities, and the use of dubious tonics and other products that purported to make middle-class men more muscular and virile. Hair tonics promised to cure baldness. Men's anxiety about their place in a rapidly changing business world was complicated by the economic upheavals of the 1880s and 1890s. By the turn of the century, new service clubs, like Chicago's Rotary Club and Kiwanis International, provided middle-class and professional men with fellowship in a respectable environment—not in the saloons or dance halls frequented by many working-class men. Dressing well to impress other men was part of this larger-scale men's improvement movement. One historian estimates that men in 1890 spent two-and-a-half times as much on clothing as women did (Swiencicki 1998). Middle-class and professional men dressed for work and social occasions.

As business owners, haberdashers had to stay informed about new trends in male fashion. They read about the newest fashions, some of which emerged in particular cities. In Chicago, for instance, the bowtie became a popular men's accessory rather than the tie; as cultural studies scholar Rob Shields notes, the bowtie "sometimes presides over a massive gut," which, among older male professionals, "became the embodiment of authority . . . a form of conspicuous expression of class power to over-consume" (Shields 1998, 171). Haberdashers anticipated demand for new styles—examining new fabrics and ordering ties, bowties, waistcoats (vests) and fabric from clothing contractors. Haberdashers cultivated their networks with producers of men's wear: tailors, ready-made clothing wholesalers, and independent jobbers. Sometimes, haberdashers miscalculated consumer demand, as was the case when dress shirts incorporated soft cuffs and collars rather than stiff collars and cuffs that a wearer attached to the shirt. Sizing adjustments had to be made for these new shirts as soft collars and cuffs hung differently; haberdashers were slow to acknowledge the need for shorter sleeves, but department stores offered ready-made shirts that fit men better, so for a time in the late 1910s and early 1920s, haberdashers experienced a decline in their collective revenues. Haberdashers had to manage inventory, keeping close track of stock and sales. They performed other tasks common to business owners: ensuring cleanliness of the store, hiring and supervising clerks, and keeping the books (or hiring bookkeepers to manage finances).

Many haberdasheries had windows that permitted customers to see inside the store. Some displayed goods in the storefront windows, though customers preferred unadorned windows so that they could see the inventory from the street. A haberdasher welcomed his customers into his store by name and customarily kept notebooks with customers' names and clothing preferences. He suggested items to customers in a process that is popularly known today as upselling. A haberdasher often had some training in clothes fitting, or they sometimes employed tailors to fit and alter any item a customer wanted prior to purchase. A haberdasher or his clerk helped men pick out suitable items based on their preferences and body types to ensure that they achieved the fashionable look they desired. Among middle-class men, clothing signified their class status. The exercise craze of this period required men to purchase additional clothing specific to a sport, such as lightweight sweaters suitable for wearing while playing tennis.

Haberdasheries are still part of the retail hierarchy today, though the word "haberdashery" is not common and refers to a men's store that specializes in hats, gloves, and other accessories, not the entire range of men's business attire. Today, many haberdasheries are simply known as "men's stores," a gendered retail space in modern America.

Nancy Quam-Wickham

See also: Currier; *1607–1775:* Shopkeeper; *1915–1945:* Garment Worker; Retail Clerk

FURTHER READING

Chauncey, George. 1994. *Gay New York: Gender, Urban Culture, and the Makings of the Gay Male World, 1890–1940*. New York: Basic Books.

Kimmel, Michael S. 2018. *Manhood in America: A Cultural History*. Oxford: Oxford University Press.

Shields, Rob. 1998. "A Tale of Three Louis." In *Consuming Fashion: Adorning the Transnational Body*, edited by Anne Brydon and Sandra Niessen, 163–175. Oxford: Berg.

Swiencicki, Mark A. 1998. "Consuming Brotherhood: Men's Culture, Style and Recreation as Consumption, 1880–1930." *Journal of Social History* 31: 773–808.

"Where Haberdashers Lose Out." *The New York Times*. September 10, 1920.

LOGGER

Loggers—known colloquially as lumberjacks—are people who fell trees for timber. Between 1870 and World War I (1914–1918), the Pacific Northwest forests supplanted the southern states and the Great Lakes region as the nexus of American logging. During the late nineteenth century, an American logger's daily routine and duties depended upon several factors, such as the region in which he logger worked, whether his job was in the forests or in the timber mills, and each logger's race and ethnicity. Loggers who operated in Michigan's frozen forests lived a very different life than those who worked in Floridian or Louisianan swamps, of course—but logging work was exhausting and dangerous no matter where it took place. Loggers often worked in filthy, isolated logging camps, and the almost entirely male logging workforce had to survive their employers' utter indifference to workplace safety.

When a working logger woke up in the morning, he was most likely deep in a forest; good logging forests were often far in the wilderness, and so commuting back to town at the end of a shift was impractical. The logger was surrounded by his fellow workers, all crammed together. Records show that one camp provided a floor space of merely 3,586 square feet—roughly sixty feet per side—in which 108 men had to live and sleep, which works out to around 33 square feet of floor space available for each logger; for comparison, the average, modern American prison cell is around 48 square feet.

Loggers who worked in one of the nation's wettest environments hung their soaked socks on the bunkhouse heater to dry, which made the dwelling smell very bad. Even washing their faces could be dangerous; a 1917 report from a Red Cross doctor told the story of eighty men sharing the only towel in a bunkhouse, and when one new worker used it to wipe an area of his body infected with venereal disease, the disease spread through the bunkhouse like wildfire.

Before work, the logger went to breakfast. Logging camps became famous for the sheer amount of food served. Loggers at least ate huge meals three times a day, which set them apart from large parts of the working class at this time. A 1915 study of Maine loggers estimated that they ate almost 6,500 calories every day, of which around 3,400 came from meat. Decades later, retired loggers often remembered the great quality of the food, but evidence from the time suggests that the typical ration's quality was mediocre at best. Too often, employers also placed the outhouse next to the kitchen, which led to foul smells and contributed to the overall lack of sanitation. If there were any women in the camp, they were usually in the kitchen, but employers often stopped hiring women because they would marry the loggers and then quit.

In the nineteenth century, much logging work was accomplished with animal labor, but in 1882, the donkey engine was invented, which was a machine that dragged fallen trees by cables to a central location. This eliminated most animal labor, and growing innovations meant the workplace now consisted of logs flying through the air on cables without safety precautions, falling tree limbs constantly threatening unsuspecting workers, and catastrophic rates of death and injury. In 1914, 63,000 people worked in Washington's logging industry. That year, there were 4,928 reported accidents that injured or killed timber workers. The entire day was a cacophony of booming machinery, falling timber, and orders shouted in different languages as everyone tried to get through the day alive.

When the loggers returned to camp after the workday, they had very little to do. Camps provided no recreational facilities. Some loggers built stills to make alcohol, which everyone would share after dark. They might also talk to their fellow workers about joining a union, especially the radical Industrial Workers of the World (IWW); founded in 1905, this union sought to create a revolutionary movement to overthrow capitalism, and it found a great deal of support in the logging camps of both the southern states and the Northwest. By the 1910s, the IWW increasingly challenged employers' control over workplace safety and the logging camps' terrible living conditions. Before the 1920s, some logging companies began efforts to improve the camps and working conditions.

When it came time to go to sleep, loggers faced further discomfort. During the day, they carried their own blankets around on their backs, which meant that a logger's blanket might be soaking wet if it had rained that day. Blankets also became infested with fleas, which then took over the bunkhouses, and many employers provided only hay for bedding. Winds and rain would blow through the bunkhouses, which typically were poorly constructed and were often located close to filthy outhouses.

The next day, the logger would get up and start the same routine. The working life of a logger would not meaningfully change until nationwide strikes during World War I forced the federal government to intercede and mandate revisions.

Erik Loomis

See also: Coal Miner; Railroad Construction Worker; *1776–1860:* Gold Miner; Laborer; *1915–1945:* Ironworker

FURTHER READING

Felt, Margaret Elley. 1978. *The Enterprising Mister Murray: Pacific Northwest Logger.* Caldwell: Caxton Printers.

United States. 1984. *Injuries in the Logging Industry.* Washington, DC: U.S. Department of Labor, Bureau of Labor Statistics.

United States. 1995. *Black Lake Trail: A Logging History of Black Lake.* Washington, DC: U.S. Department of Agriculture, Forest Service, Eastern Region.

MASON

Masons were builders and workers who worked with brick and stone. In the late nineteenth century, masons were in high demand. In February 1883, the El Paso newspaper *Lone Star* published an advertisement for workers, as was typical for the day: "One hundred Stone Masons and Fifty Laborers to work in quarry on Mexican Central Railroad." A few months later, Las Vegas newspapers reported on favorable employment for masons; later still, masons in Albuquerque were in short supply and earning wages up to five dollars per day—the highest wages of all skilled building tradesmen. All across America, the demand was high for highly skilled masons and other building trades workers. In the 1870s and for decades later, as the nation's industrial growth and urban development advanced, new glistening modern buildings were erected to signify a corporation's status or replace old wooden structures prone to fire, as had been the case in 1871 with the conflagration in Chicago. Other cities burned too: Boston, Seattle, Baltimore, Jacksonville, and, the biggest of all, the 1906 San Francisco earthquake and fire. New construction technologies, especially the use of reinforced cement, created even greater employment options for masons. Those who followed the work, the "tramping artisans," may have been employed steadily, without the common interruptions in employment that most members of the American working class faced in this period, but it came at the cost of nearly constant geographical mobility. These itinerant tradesmen traveled from job site to job site, city to towns, and domestically within the United States and often abroad.

As members of the "trowel trades," masons were building tradesmen who cut stone in quarries (stone masons) or who specialized in building with stone, brick, or cement. Stone masons worked in quarries and directed the extraction of large blocks of granite, limestone, slate, and similar raw materials. As quarry workers, they examined the stones that were to be cut and paid special attention to any imperfections, striations, cracks, or other factors that might interfere with the extraction of the large stone blocks. The methods stone masons used to extract blocks or slabs from the rock face differed according to the density and character of the rock. For relatively soft rock like limestone, which was used extensively in buildings in Chicago and other Midwestern cities, stone masons used hand saws to cut a solid block from the rock face. First, though, they used a large square or rectangular pattern to mark the top of the stone, ensuring that the corners were squared. They then drew their saws down two sides of the block to cut the limestone block from its face, or exposed section at the quarry. Large quarries employed laborers, rather than stone masons, to do the tough job of sawing, under the supervision of stone masons. Once the block of limestone was cut, stone masons lowered it to the ground with help from laborers, ropes, and pulleys and then carefully measured the block to square off any edges, inspect for defects, and cut off rough ends. These limestone blocks could also be cut into smaller building pieces. The blocks were then transported to a building site. Stone masons also finished stone pieces, such as headstones, lintels, projecting stones, or other decorative stonework.

In the building trades, masons used these stone blocks, as well as brick, to construct office buildings, courthouses, churches, hotels, and other buildings. During the late nineteenth century, among the trowel trades, masons specialized in stone construction techniques, while bricklayers laid brick, though these two terms were often used synonymously. In Chicago, engineers experimented with building fireproof (really, fire resistant) buildings, employing iron or steel frames that were then clad with stone or reinforced cement with stone facings. These taller buildings—skyscrapers—allowed for smaller footprints and sleeker architectural lines than the earlier heavy brick or wooden buildings, which generally were limited to just a few floors. Masons were key to the construction of skyscrapers. Architects and city officials sought to beautify their cities, imposing strict building codes and mandating certain kinds of construction in urban cores. Masons set the stone much as bricklayers did with their materials: lay a line of stone on the bottom, followed by another row, offset by thirds or halves to increase the strength of the wall; between each brick or stone was a line of mortar. Anchor stones helped to guide the pattern of stone placement, while staggered joints accommodated irregularly shaped stones, such as field or river stone. Stones cut to set solidly on each other needed little mortar; some of the world's oldest buildings, in fact, feature stones hewed to set tightly on each other, creating walls, bridges, and archways without the use of mortar.

Dramatic improvements in construction technology changed the work of masons. After the great earthquake and fire of 1906, architects, contractors, and builders favored the use of lighter cement, reinforced with steel bars, over other materials. Increasingly, masons learned how to build with this concrete material: set its forms, ensured that others properly reinforced the interior of a wall or slab, and then directed the pouring of cement into the molds. Once the cement dried, the wooden molds were removed. Then masons went to work to face these new cement buildings with veneers of stone "bricks" so that buildings had the appearance of stone but were not as heavy (and, thus, less likely to subside) and were cheaper and faster to build. Masons attached steel anchors to the cement; the anchors strengthen the veneer wall. For large buildings, veneer stones are six inches or more in thickness. Masons spread "mud," or an adhering compound, between the cement wall and set the stone into it, carefully measuring each stone to ensure that it is level and square with those it sets on and those adjacent to it. Masons thus helped to transform the cityscape of American urban areas, creating handsome buildings, often using polished stone veneers that glistened in the sunlight. These new cities appeared modern and clean, unlike the haphazard building practices of earlier times.

By 1880, most masons worked for building contractors, companies that took contracts to complete an entire building. Contractors directly hired masons, carpenters, electricians, and other tradespeople. Building trades unions—including the Bricklayers and Allied Craftworkers—secured union contracts with contractors or, more often, pressured city officials to require that public works projects be accomplished only with union workers. A significant percentage of new buildings in the 1880s to 1910s were public works: construction of courthouses, city halls, libraries, schools, and government office complexes. Masons took great pride in their roles building these monuments to civic importance; the union's code of conduct requires that masons show up and work an honest eight hours, monitor their behavior on the job, and, most importantly, take responsibility for the quality of their work.

Nancy Quam-Wickham

See also: Logger; *1915–1945:* Steelworker

FURTHER READING

Fitchen, John. 1986. *Building Construction before Mechanization.* Cambridge: MIT Press.

Lone Star (El Paso). 1883. Advertisement. February 3.

Tygiel, Jules. 1992. *Workingmen in San Francisco, 1880–1891.* Shrewsbury: Garland.

Wylde, James. 1878. *The Book of Trades: A Circle of the Arts and Manufactures, Adapted for Schools, Colleges, and Families.* London: Gall & Inglis, 1878.

MEAT PACKINGHOUSE WORKER

Meat packinghouse workers processed and packed meat for sale at the markets, and theirs was a dirty, bloody, greasy job. In slaughterhouses and packinghouses across the country, thousands of workers prepared the meat that fed this new consumer nation in the early twentieth century. Large meat processing factories of this period were possible only after the invention of the refrigerated railroad car in 1881; before that time, the majority of urban Americans obtained their meat from local butchers, although regional slaughterhouses served some cities, like Boston and New York. Many impoverished city dwellers only occasionally ate meat. Most farm families butchered their own meat and game and then salted, smoked, and preserved it for later consumption.

Turning animals—primarily cattle, sheep, and pigs—into market-salable meat involved the same processes whether it was done on a farm or in a slaughterhouse. Animals were killed, dressed (removing the viscera and internal organs to limit spoilage from bacteria) and bled, and then cut. The scale of the enterprise in the factory setting distinguished the work of a packinghouse or slaughterhouse worker. The two types of factories are essentially synonymous, though some packinghouses did not have a killing floor—a designated space for stunning and bleeding out an animal—but instead received dressed and cooled animal carcasses packed in railroad cars from distant slaughterhouses. In a factory, the disassembly of an animal in a packinghouse was done in such an organized way that the meatpackers created "one of the earliest mass-production industries" (Barrett 1987, 14). A job that a farmer or hunter might have accomplished on his own was now accomplished on a grand scale by hundreds of workers, each performing just one task in the extensive process of disassembling animals and repacking them as meat. In 1900, in Chicago alone, at their peak, some 25,000 workers in the city's packinghouses processed 75,000 cattle, 80,000 sheep, and 300,000 hogs daily in a "continuous flow" of activity.

Workers on the killing floor did perhaps the harshest work in the entire slaughterhouse. Here, when slaughtering cattle, a worker stunned an animal, most often with the swing of a heavy sledgehammer. Hogs and sheep were seldom stunned. Another worker then attached shackle and chains to the animal's back legs, and a conveyor belt moved the animal upside down to another worker, who, in one motion, slit the animal's throat. As the animal bled out, the chain system then moved it further. Hogs were dropped into a vat of boiling water and then lifted mechanically onto another belt, where workers with large scraping tools removed the hair from the pigskin. Since cowhide and sheepskin were valuable byproducts, these animals were skinned by workers skilled in the use of knives. As the partly processed animal was pushed or propelled along a type of conveyor, another worker slit its abdomen completely open, while other workers cut off the head or pulled out the entrails, organs, or offal. Debris fell onto the floor, where workers used squeegees to push the heads, offal, and other byproducts into holes through which they would fall, landing in large bins below, where these materials were further processed into meat products, gelatin, and fertilizer. Strong men specialized in splitting a cow's spine as this job required special strength and skill. Once dressed, the flayed carcass was washed and sent onto the processing and packing floors.

Because freshly killed animals are often contaminated by the dirt and bacteria on and in the body, meat is highly perishable and must be kept cool. By the early 1900s, most factories had refrigerated rooms to keep the carcasses cooled as they moved along to the processing floors. Many factories seasoned their beef in coolers; carcasses were suspended from the ceiling on meat hooks. Workers in the refrigerated rooms had to dress warmly, even in the middle of the summer, and keep their hands flexible and fingers nimble enough to grasp a knife and position it properly to make the correct cuts. On the processing floors, workers carved the carcass into specific cuts (roasts, flank steak, and so forth)—each worker repeatedly making the same cuts hundreds of times per day. For example, a worker assigned to cut the bacon strip from a hog (along the belly) worked on just one side of the hog carcass; another worker cut the bacon strip from the opposite side. The bacon strip was then dropped in a bin and sent to another worker, who trimmed it and then sent it along to the salting house for a cure and then along to the smokehouse to finish the process of making a side of bacon. Other workers sliced the hams from the rear legs and sent them along to the trimming station and then to the pickling room, where they were cured and readied for packaging or canning. Workers sent other inferior cuts of meat to the pickling room to make, for instance, canned chipped beef or potted meats. In the cellars, the lower floors of the factory where products like offal or heads were sent (via holes in the killing room floor), other workers removed partly digested material from the intestines to make tripe, split open cow skulls to extract the brains, and trimmed whatever meat or fat could be used to make ground meat, sausages, lard, or tallow. Bones were turned into gelatin or sent to fertilizer plants.

Before the mid-twentieth century, meat packinghouses generally were not highly mechanized. Most cutting work was done by hand; electric saws were decades in the future. Nonetheless, packinghouse workers were often hurt on the job, and the injuries could be catastrophic. Workers shoving hogs into the vats of boiling water could fall in, too, and cook to death before being rescued. Other workers suffered terrible burns, some by handling cleaning or disinfecting acids, while others cut themselves trying to handle the pace of work. By the turn of the century, in most of the larger packinghouses, employers had replaced butchers and other skilled workers with unskilled laborers, mostly immigrants (many of whom spoke little English) or African Americans. By subdividing the "disassembly" process into so many distinct tasks—the right-side bacon strip cutter, for instance—the work process no longer required more than a single skill, something that could be taught in a few hours. Factory managers customarily sped up the work process, often pitting the workers of one room against another in the drive to reduce production costs and increase profits. Workers were largely interchangeable, and the packinghouse workers adopted employment processes that relied on casual labor. Workers might be employed for only a day, or a week, or as long as the factory needed them and were then laid off for long periods. Consumer taste also dictated packinghouse worker employment as factories focused on providing hams for Christmas or lamb for the spring holidays. The military placed large orders for canned meat during wartime. However, work in the packinghouses was never secure.

While most packinghouses focused on meats, some also specialized in the preparation and canning of fish, particularly salmon. As with meat, immigrants largely worked on the fish-packing lines—Filipinos, Hawaiians, and some tribal people in the Alaskan fish-canning industry, and Japanese, Serbians, Italians, and Portuguese in the fish-canning houses of Monterey, San Pedro, and San Diego, California. The clustering of different immigrant ethnic groups was not primarily determined by management preference but instead was a product of the smelly, hazardous conditions, operating at all times of the day and night for low wages. While American-born white workers had other opportunities, immigrants and African Americans accepted work in the packinghouses at the wages offered.

In his 1906 novel *The Jungle*, writer and activist Upton Sinclair shocked the nation with his discussion of the filthy circumstances and working conditions in the slaughterhouses and meatpacking factories in Chicago. American consumers were revolted by Sinclair's vivid discussion of making sausages of spoiled meat, floor sweepings, and sawdust. While Sinclair hoped to illustrate the plights of poor immigrants, *The Jungle* actually spurred Congress to pass the Pure Food and Drug Act of 1906, the first of several consumer protection laws in the early twentieth century, which also established the Food and Drug Administration.

Nancy Quam-Wickham

See also: *1915–1945:* Cannery Worker

FURTHER READING

Barrett, James R. 1987. *Work and Community in the Jungle: Chicago's Packinghouse Workers, 1904–1922.* Urbana: University of Illinois Press.

Chiang, Connie Y. 2009. *Shaping the Shoreline: Fisheries and Tourism on the Monterey Coast.* Seattle: University of Washington Press.

Fink, Deborah. 1998. *Cutting into the Meatpacking Line: Workers and Change in the Rural Midwest.* Chapel Hill: University of North Carolina Press.

Friday, Chris. 1994. *Organizing Asian American Labor: The Pacific Coast Canned Salmon Industry, 1870–1942.* Philadelphia: Temple University Press.

Warren, Wilson J. 2007. *Tied to the Great Packing Machine: The Midwest and Meatpacking.* Iowa City: University of Iowa Press.

MECHANIC

Before World War I (1914–1918), mechanics were "operating engineers" responsible for making sure that the machinery in larger factories and shops was assembled correctly and maintained to a high standard. These mechanics might repair a locomotive in a railroad yard on one day and assemble gearworks in a foundry on the next. They had broad experience across a variety of engineering disciplines but typically were not renowned experts in one specific area. As the United States industrialized in the late nineteenth century, mechanics were workmen in railroad shops, factories, mines, and other heavy industries who helped build, operate, and repair heavy machinery. A turn-of-the-century mechanic worked in a shop or industrial site. Mechanics maintained and repaired locomotive engines, operated cranes lifting heavy machinery in mines, fixed ring spinners and other machines in textile mills, kept the steam processing units in fish and fruit canneries operational—wherever there was machinery powering American industry, there was usually a mechanic keeping those machines humming.

In early America, skilled artisans of master or journeyman status—blacksmiths, carpenters, cabinetmakers, and wainwrights, to name a few—were sometimes called "mechanics." These workers generally owned their own tools and negotiated their terms of labor, often setting prices for their work products. Early-American mechanics organized libraries, benefit associations, banks, theater clubs, institutes, and other kinds of groups and institutions that operated as social support systems, educational and training offices, working-class cultural centers, and even places where working-class people met to discuss union formation, coordinate political action, and unite artisans to support candidates friendly to workers' issues.

The definition of "mechanic" changed with industrialization. By the beginning of the 1880s, mechanics were no longer independent artisans—instead, they were employees who served the interests of their employers. Rather than specialists in a particular trade, by the end of the nineteenth century, a mechanic was a generalist who understood how machines of all sorts worked.

The daily life of a mechanic varied enormously by industry. Mechanics working in railroad shops worked on regular shifts, tending to locomotives, railcars, and the array of parts—the running gear—that kept them moving. In a rail roundhouse, for instance, a mechanic spent time in the pits, a space under which a railroad car or locomotive engine was brought to a stop. After skimming through the train engineer's report, a mechanic determined which repairs were needed to ensure that a locomotive was ready for its next run. Delays cost the railway money in lost income. In conjunction with shop engineers, a mechanic ordered repairs and supervised the shop laborers, junior mechanics, and machinists who made them. The repair log for just one locomotive engine, as it entered the Elkhart, Indiana, shop of the Lake Shore and Southern Michigan Railway in 1907, included repairs that were completed within five days: install "new shoes and wedges; two new driving box brasses and remaining driving box brasses rebored; one new driving box; valve chambers rebored; new packing rings in valves; valve stems turned; new pistons and piston packing applied; guides closed; cross head shoes rebabbitted and planed; eccentric straps closed and refitted; full set of tires applied to driving wheel centers; new bushings for all side rods; front and back end main rod brasses renewed; all valve motion work repaired" (Elkhart 1907). In less than a week, the main pistons of this engine and the valves that closed and opened to allow combustion within the piston chambers were replaced, as were the main wheels (tires and shoes) and brakes; all mechanisms (driving boxes) that transferred energy from the engine to the wheels were overhauled and re-machined, and the rods that connected the driving wheels (those that the engine powered) to other wheels were replaced.

For those mechanics who worked in factories and kept the machinery of production operating, a typical workday was different, requiring mechanics to troubleshoot and repair all kinds of machinery. Mechanics inspected boilers and steam plants, adjusted loose bolts, ensured that bushings and bearings were set properly to avoid damaging moving parts, and checked for proper clearances in and around every moving part. In a textile mill, for instance, mechanics had to check spinning machines—those that automatically carded (the process of untangling and combing cotton fibers) and then twisted and spun fiber into thread and spooled the thread onto bobbins for use in weaving. In a large textile mill, spinning machines had multiple bobbins; in the early twentieth century, child workers, who were smaller and were believed to be quicker, had to snatch the full bobbin and replace it as the machine parts passed.

Those mechanics who worked in packinghouses had to keep the steam plant running, the conveyor belts operating continuously, and, like their counterparts in other factories and mills, the machinery running, or production would stop. Mechanics who worked for logging companies, lumber mills, and mining companies often had to travel to the production site—in the forest or down in a mineshaft—to assess a broken piece of machinery. In the field, these mechanics repaired machinery on the fly, often jerry-rigging repairs, or repairing a machine with whatever parts were immediately on hand to keep it operating.

Many mechanics were journeymen who worked for master mechanics; the master mechanics occupied a position comparable to shop foremen, not independent master artisans. Mechanics were experienced in basic mechanical and power plant operations. They could disassemble and reassemble engines, machines, and those parts that connected power sources to machines, like a locomotive's driving boxes and rods. Master mechanics often had superior mechanical and spatial reasoning skills and were also adept machinists. Although companies began to supply spare parts to railways and factories, many repair processes required use of metal lathes, spindles, cutters, and boring tools to create replacement parts. Because tool parts required close tolerances, mechanics had to be proficient in using calipers and micrometers; these tools measure the fit between machined parts down to microns.

Although they did jobs far different than their forebears with the same title, mechanics held a special place in the panorama of tradespeople for the industrial working class. New mechanics institutes were founded to provide adult education—basic literacy, mathematics, and machine processes—for prospective workers. Mechanics and other workers posed proudly on large machinery for photographs—gangs of men crowding atop locomotives, cranes in steel mills, oil rigs, and steam donkeys (steam-powered winches)—and in doing so, they put themselves, as workers, in front of the machines that often replaced humans in the production process. Labor iconography in the late nineteenth and early twentieth century celebrated the raw muscular and hyper-masculine image of the mechanic; statues, prints and artwork, and murals featured "mechanics" (workers)—usually shirtless—operating machines, pulling levers, and taming the iron and steel beasts of industrial America.

In the twentieth century, mechanics were increasingly defined as those who kept automobiles operating. In the shops and factories of the nation, new occupational titles redefined the role of turn-of-the-century mechanics: mechanical engineers, steam plant operators, operating engineers, crane operators, machine operators, and maintenance engineers took the place of the multifaceted mechanic. But the imagery of the nineteenth-century generalist has persisted in contemporary America.

Nancy Quam-Wickham

See also: *1915–1945:* Autoworker; *1992–2019:* Machinist

FURTHER READING

The Colonial Advocate, or, The Farmer, Manufacturer, Mechanic, and Fisherman's Journal. 1845. Halifax: Public Archives of Nova Scotia.

Elkhart Shops. 1907. "Record in Locomotive General Repairs." *Railway Master Mechanic* 31 (February): 41.

Jones, Alvin Lincoln, and C. B. Webster. 1894. *Under Colonial Roofs.* Boston: C. B. Webster.

NURSE

The outbreak of the Civil War (1861–1865) was accompanied by a sudden increase in the numbers of malnourished, ill, and injured young men who were often far from home and the kinfolk (sisters, mothers) who would normally care for them.

Those who needed care were, by and large, previously healthy young men. They were treated in primitive makeshift facilities near battlefields, in recital halls, schools, and other public buildings commandeered for use as asylums (or rehabilitation centers), as well as in proper hospitals. The war created opportunities for thousands of women to work as nurses, assisting the sick and wounded.

Prior to the war, nursing was not an established profession. There were few well-equipped nursing schools where women and men trained to treat patients. Those men and women who volunteered to work as war nurses largely learned as they took on their jobs. Most nurses started off as volunteers: bathing the wounds of the injured, comforting the dying, and simply waiting on the men by bringing them food and water or writing letters home to families. Many served under the auspices of the United States Sanitary Commission, a private organization created to help provide medical equipment and care for those in the war. But within months, as the fighting intensified, an influx of soldiers overpopulated the hospitals, overwhelming those who cared for them. Early in the war, Kate Cumming, a nurse who worked in Confederate hospitals, wrote that soldiers appeared worn out, and some doctors claimed they had "scarcely slept since the start of the war" (Cumming 1998, 15).

After a disastrous defeat at the first battle of Manassas (also known as Bull Run) in July 1861, General William Hammond appointed prominent social reformer Dorothea Dix as superintendent of Union Army nurses. Dix had been a teacher and author early in her life but, in the decades before war began, had also led several successful campaigns to provide more humane treatment to indigent people, primarily those with developmental delays and mental illnesses. A year later, in July 1862, while desperately trying to coordinate medical care, Dix and Hammond issued Circular Number 8, which outlined the requirements for prospective nurses. This document was one of the first to attempt to impose professional standards on those who wished to work as nurses. According to Dix, applicants for nursing positions had to meet certain restrictions: They were not to be under thirty-five or above fifty years of age, as Dix worried that young nurses could become attached to soldiers they treated. They were to be "plain" in appearance and dress, obedient to authority, sober, industrious, healthy, and strong. Those who had some training in caring for others or in medical arts had priority. All prospective nurses who endeavored to work in military hospitals had to agree to a six-month term of service; those who volunteered for longer periods were preferred. In particular, noted Dix, "matronly persons of experience, good conduct, and superior education and serious disposition will always have preference" (Dix 1862).

Many prominent women kept records of their experiences during this period of time, giving readers insight into the daily lives of a nurse during the Civil War. In her diary, Confederate nurse Kate Cumming recounted her active hours on the job at a hospital in Tennessee. The men lay in crowded rooms, filling the air with a repugnant smell caused by decaying flesh, vomit and other body fluids, and dirt. She claimed that the smell made her feel sick, but she quickly got over the feeling once she got busy. On some nights, patients she cared for suffered horribly, praying or groaning all night long. When one patient with a shoulder wound who had "suffered awfully" passed away, Cumming wrote, "I trust that he is now at rest from this dreary world of strife and bloodshed" (Cumming 1998, 16). Nurses like Cumming did basic chores, seldom assisting in actual medical treatment; instead, they found themselves changing dressings, emptying bedpans, or spooning soup or water to men prostate with fever.

Northerner Louisa May Alcott shared some of the same perspectives as Cumming. She, too, saw the men looking gloomy and the nurses exhausted by their work. Alcott's "Hospital Sketches" detail her experience as a nurse and were published in 1863 in the abolitionist newspaper the *Boston Commonwealth.* During her daytime hours, Alcott invested her time in the usual duties of a nurse: washing, serving, and giving medicine to the patients. She was surrounded by the sick, "pneumonia on one side . . . five typhoids on the opposite, and a dozen dilapidated patriots, hopping, lying, and lounging about, all staring more or less at the new 'nuss,' [nurse] who suffered untold agonies, but concealed them under as matronly an aspect as a spinster could assume, and blundered through her trying labors with a Spartan firmness, which I hope they appreciated, but am afraid they didn't" (Alcott 1863, 31). She hustled from man to man, wishing only for their survival but often only seeing the most tragic impacts of the war as men died regularly from disease and infection. She spent her evenings reading to and comforting her patients.

In her hospital, Alcott managed to sort the patients by placing them in different rooms: a "pathetic room," a "duty room," and a "pleasure room." She would bring different materials to each, such as books, teapots, games, or gossip and lullabies. Even in her most organized setting, Alcott recalls hearing patients' cries from upstairs and surgeons rushing to them. Since nurses spent so much time in the hospitals, they quickly adjusted to the men and their needs. Alcott wrote that she was able to tell which men were which solely based on the sound of their snoring. Patients seemed their most vulnerable at night, growing "infinitely sad and pathetic," as Alcott explained. For this reason, nurses routinely sang lullabies or recited biblical stories that might comfort young men far from their homes. Soon, though, Alcott longed for the most "unpatriotic wish" to be back home in safety (Alcott 1863, 31–33). After six weeks working as a nurse, she contracted pneumonia, undoubtedly from some of the men she cared for, and spent months recovering at home. She did not return to nursing. "Hospital Sketches" established Alcott as a writer, for which she later became famous when her semi-autobiographical novel, *Little Women*, was published in 1868. Other famous Civil War nurses include the evangelist ex-slave Sojourner Truth, Clara Barton, Helen Gilson, and, for a short time, Harriet Tubman.

Whether they wrote about their experiences at the time—as Alcott and Cumming did— after the war, or not at all, nurses who served in the Civil War received meager wages, food, and housing. They had to provide their own clothing; uniforms were not universal. Nurses also had to scrounge for medical and other supplies. Young women often wrote home to ask townspeople in their home communities to send clean fabric for dressings, packs of cards, soap, combs, hymnbooks, newspapers, and writing paper and pencils. They endured trying conditions. The U.S. government did not provide nurses with pensions, regardless of their length of service, until 1895.

Overall, many women became nurses to honor their patriotic beliefs and to help the war effort in one of the few ways available to women of the time. Thousands of women and hundreds of men served as nurses to soldiers on both sides. Those who wrote about their experiences in letters and diaries or spoke to audiences after the conflict shared some of the most intimate moments of a ghastly war.

Stephanie Cornejo

See also: Surgeon; *1607–1775:* Apothecary; Midwife; *1776–1860:* Physician; *1992–2019:* Emergency Medical Technician; Home Health Aide

FURTHER READING

Alcott, Louisa May. 1863. *Hospital Sketches.* Boston. http://digital.library.upenn.edu/women/alcott/sketches/sketches.html.

Cumming, Kate. 1998. *Kate: The Diary of a Civil War Nurse.* Baton Rouge: Louisiana State University.

Dix, Dorothea. 1862. "United States Army, Circular No. 8." July 14. https://www.docsteach.org/documents/document/circular-no-8-regarding-requirements-for-female-nursing-applicants.

PRIMARY DOCUMENT

In this document, Clara Barton, a Civil War–era nurse and one of the founders of the American Red Cross, offers a host of reasons American women volunteered to work as nurses during the Civil War. Barton was nearly forty years old and working as a government clerk in the U.S. Patent Office when the war began in 1861, and she made an abrupt decision to become a nurse for Union soldiers. Barton had not attended nursing school, but she served with honor and came to be known as the "angel of the battlefield." Barton describes the enthusiasm and sense of duty that nurses—many of whom were not paid for their service—prided themselves on during the Civil War.

The women who went to the field, you say,
The women who went to the field; and pray,
What did they go for?—just to be in the way?—They'd not know the difference
betwixt work and play,
What did they know about war, anyway?

What could they do?—of what use could they be?
They would scream at the sight of a gun, don't you see?
Just fancy them round where the bugle notes play,
And the long roll is bidding us on to the fray.
Imagine their skirts 'mong artillery wheels,
And watch for their flutter as they flee 'cross the fields

When the charge is rammed home and the fire belches hot:—
They never will wait for the answering shot.
They would faint at the first drop of blood, in their sight.
What fun for us boys,—(ere we enter the fight;)
They might pick some lint, and tear up some sheets,
And make us some jellies, and send on their sweets,
And knit some soft socks for Uncle Sam's shoes,
And write us some letters, and tell us the news.

And thus it was settled by common consent,
That husbands, or brothers, or whoever went,
That the place for the women was in their own homes,
There to patiently wait until victory comes.

But later, it chanced, just how no one knew,
That the lines slipped a bit, and some 'gan to crowd through;
And they went,—where did they go?—Ah; where did they not?
Show us the battle,—the field,—or the spot
Where the groans of the wounded rang out on the air
That her ear caught it not, and her hand was not there,
Who wiped the death sweat from the cold, clammy brow.
And sent home the message;—"'T is well with him now"?

Who watched in the tents, whilst the fever fires burned,
And the pain-tossing limbs in agony turned,
And wet the parched tongue, calmed delirium's strife
Till the dying lips murmured, "My Mother," "My Wife"!

And who were they all?—They were many, my men:
Their record was kept by no tabular pen:
They exist in traditions from father to son.

Who recalls, in dim memory, now here and there one.—
A few names where writ, and by chance live to-day;
But's a perishing record fast fading away.

Of those we recall, there are scarcely a score,
Dix, Dame, Bickerdyke,—Edson, Harvey and Moore,
Fales, Wittenmeyer, Gilson, Safford and Lee,
And poor Cutter dead in the sands of the sea;
And Frances D. Gage, our "Aunt Fanny" of old,
Whose voice rang for freedom when freedom was sold.

And Husband, and Etheridge, and Harlan and Case,
Livermore, Alcott, Hancock and Chase,
And Turner, and Hawley, and Potter and Hall,
Ah! the list grows apace, as they come at the call:
Did these women quail at the sight of a gun?
Will some soldier tell us of one he saw run?

Will he glance at the boats on the great western flood,
At Pittsburg and Shiloh, did they faint at the blood?
And the brave wife of Grant stood there with them then,
And her calm, stately presence gave strength to his men.

And Marie of Logan; she went with them too;
A bride, scarcely more than a sweetheart, 't is true.
Her young cheek grows pale when the bold troopers ride.
Where the "Black Eagle" soars, she is close at his side,
She staunches his blood, cools the fever-burnt breath,
And the wave of her hand stays the Angle of Death;
She nurses him back, and restores once again
To both army and state the brave leader of men.

She has smoothed his black plumes and laid them to sleep,
Whilst the angels above them their high vigils keep:
And she sits here alone, with the snow on her brow—
Your cheers for her comrades! Three cheers for her now.

And these were the women who went to the war:
The women of question; what did they go for?
Because in their hearts God had planted the seed
Of pity for woe, and help for its need;
They saw, in high purpose, a duty to do,
And the armor of right broke the barriers through.

Uninvited, unaided, unsanctioned ofttimes,
With pass, or without it, they pressed on the lines;
They pressed, they implored, till they ran the lines through,
And this was the "running" the men saw them do.
'T was a hampered work, its worth largely lost;
'T was hindrance, and pain, and effort, and cost:
But through these came knowledge,—knowledge is power.-
And never again in the deadliest hour
Of war or of peace shall we be so beset
To accomplish the purpose our spirits have met.

And what would they do if war came again?
The scarlet cross floats where all was blank then.
They would bind on their "brassards" and march to the fray,
And the man liveth not who could say to them nay;
They would stand with you now, as they stood with you then,
The nurses, consolers, and saviours of men.

Source: Clara Barton. *The Women Who Went to the Field.* 1892 In *The Red Cross: A History of This Remarkable International Movement in the Interest of Humanity* (1898). Washington, DC: American National Red Cross, 509–513.

PAINTER, COMMERCIAL

A commercial painter paints buildings, ceilings, and walls. During the late nineteenth and early twentieth centuries, commercial painters labored painting both the exteriors and interiors of houses and commercial buildings as well as roadways and signs for businesses, elevated railways, shipyards, factories, and other structures.

In the spring of 1907, some ten thousand painters in the New York City metropolitan area threatened to go on strike for higher wages—$4 a day for general house painters, $4.50 per day for painters who specialized in fancy work and sign painting. This was not the first walkout among painters in the region. New York's painters, in fact, had gone on strike regularly. In 1875, 1880, 1886, 1887, and 1906, members of the painters' unions, of which there were three competing ones, had walked off the job for higher wages. For decades, painters' wages had depended on the strength of their unions.

During this time, smaller disputes between painters and painting contractors had also characterized the painters' workplaces. In 1885, journeymen painters complained that contractors were employing "country" painters at very low wages to work in the city's hotels, resulting in inferior-quality work and, consequently, impugning the reputation of skilled union painters. Painters also protested retailers who sold wallpaper, which had formerly only been available to contractors through wholesalers. As a result, noted the painters in 1886, dealers then "hired irresponsible workmen and so-called decorators" to hang wallpaper, "to the injury of industrious artists" ("Painters and Decorators," 1886). In 1896, members of the varnishers' union struck against the painters' union for usurping their work. In 1902, a wildcat strike of journeymen painters—joined by masons, carpenters, and ironworkers—led a contractor to discharge the master painters he had hired to finish a job on time. In 1909, a union local composed of Jewish painters refused to merge into another union local—pitting that local against the New York District Council of the Brotherhood of Painters and other building trades organizations. Journeymen painters' unions successfully limited apprenticeships to one for every five or six journeymen, controlling entry into the trade and, thus, competition for work and wages—to the objections of painting contractors. Such fractious divisions within the painting trade characterized the jurisdictional and other disputes among many of the building trades unions not only in New York but in most northern, midwestern, and western cities where unions were present.

Painters learned their trades by apprenticing to journeymen for three to four years. During this time, apprentices learned how to mix the components of paints—usually white lead, linseed oil, and turpentine, along with pigments—to meet the requirements of the job. Before the First World War (1914–1918), painters were routinely exposed to high levels of lead; in the early 1900s, corporations like the National Lead Company began to advertise their premixed paint products, like National Lead's Dutch Boy brand paints, as preferable to paints mixed by painters. Many of these new products proclaimed the durability of lead and its superior quality, allowing housewives to scrub their walls clean, unlike previous products. Drawing on the home-efficiency movement of the Progressive era, these paint companies extolled the cleanliness of walls painted with white lead products.

A painter's daily work varied: preparing walls by sanding them by hand, having the apprentice prepare the interior or exterior by masking windows and varnished surfaces, constructing scaffolding to allow painters to paint difficult-to-reach surfaces, mixing paints containing these volatile chemical compounds, and then using paintbrushes or rollers to apply the paint to surfaces. Skilled painters had superior color senses; contractors and homeowners often consulted painters about planned color schemes and routinely permitted them to make minor alterations to them. Once painters completed a job, they cleaned up their workspaces. For housepainters working outside, painting exterior buildings, exposure to harmful chemicals was lower than for those working inside, painting interiors. Compressed air spray guns were not widely used in the painting trades until after 1910; spray cans were only introduced in 1949.

Sign painters had different daily duties. Their work was more skilled than that of house painters, requiring close attention to minute detail. First, the sign painter prepared the material, normally straight pine lumber without knots or cracks. Some sign painters glued linen or cotton canvas onto the lumber and then smoothed it over, using fillers much as an artist would prepare a canvas. In most cities, businesses preferred signs with black background and gold lettering, using expensive gold leaf paints. Most sign painters had the skills of an artist, or, as one newspaper noted, "to become a first-class sign painter, it is absolutely essential to possess a natural ability for free-hand drawing, and also a quick eye" ("The Sign Painters of Old New York," 1900). Aside from blocking out the work's parallel lines, sign painters seldom sketched out their work before beginning to paint; they simply had a well-practiced sense of letter shape, size, and spacing.

The first handbook of letter fonts was introduced to the New York sign painters in 1830, though different cities were known for distinct font styles, with Boston's sign painters preferring a font based on Roman lettering, New York having its own "perfect style," and Philadelphia and Baltimore sign painters using less artistic "heavier" fonts. Many sign painters also illustrated their signs, painting the tools of the business onto them to facilitate immediate recognition by customers who were illiterate or who spoke other languages. An apothecary or early pharmacy, for instance, was designated by a small icon of the mortar and pestle. Sign painters had to respond to business demands and design more complex illustrations of businesses for their signage. Once the sign painter completed the sign, he assisted in hanging it outside the business. Sign painters also painted lettering on glass windows and doorways. The heyday of sign painters was the nineteenth century, before electric neon signs became popular in the 1920s.

Industrial exposure to harmful poisons contained in paint compounds was of great concern to early industrial hygienists like Alice Hamilton, who reported on some of the first studies linking occupational exposure to lead to health problems. Her studies demonstrated that painting contractors seldom supplied painters with safety gear—overalls, masks, safety glasses—and often didn't even provide washtubs, water, or soap so that painters could clean up before going home at the end of the workday. Thus, painters who had spent the day prepping interior walls by sanding them would be covered with minute particles of lead, which acted on the central nervous system, liver, and kidneys. Interior painters customarily mixed their paints with turpentine, petroleum naphtha, and pigments that contained benzenes, all now known to be carcinogenic.

Hamilton's pioneering study, published by the U.S. Department of Labor in 1913, found that painters accounted for 40 percent of New York's industrial lead-poisoning cases and 65 percent of the fatal cases of lead poisoning due to their relatively greater exposure. In Chicago, a union local of the Brotherhood of Painters, composed primarily of German and Scandinavian immigrants, undertook its own study of industrial poisoning and found that 70 percent of the painters had experienced temporary paralysis, nausea, "nervousness," headaches, abdominal pain, tremors, and even loss of consciousness—all symptoms of industrial exposure to the chemicals used in painting. In time, unions, health officials, and the federal government began to regulate painters' workplaces and the components used in paint, making the trade safer in subsequent decades. But for those painters who worked in this period in history, chronic lead poisoning was understood to be an occupational hazard, one worth the higher wages paid to them and worth fighting vigorously for the right to employment as union members.

Nancy Quam-Wickham

See also: *1946–1991:* Artist

FURTHER READING

Hamilton, Alice, MD. 1913. *Hygiene of the Painters' Trade*. Washington DC: U.S. Government Printing Office.

"Painters and Decorators." *New York Times*. January 26, 1886.

"The Sign Painters of Old New York." *New York Times*. April 8, 1900.

Tichi, Cecilia. 2009. *Civic Passions: Seven Who Launched Progressive America (And What They Teach Us)*. Chapel Hill: University of North Carolina Press.

PRIMARY DOCUMENT

In this pioneering industrial toxicology report, the physician Alice Hamilton reports on some of the occupational hazards that painters faced in their everyday jobs. Among the most prominent of the negative health outcomes painters experienced was various forms of industrial poisoning. As Hamilton noted elsewhere in the report, about 15 to 20 percent of all painters experienced symptoms of chronic lead poisoning, as many paints for exterior buildings, ships and railroads, and other commercial applications contained lead. But lead was hardly the only industrial toxin painters used. In this selection from her health study of painters, Dr. Hamilton describes the health effects of using newer types of interior paints.

Flat-Finish Paints

At present three are on the market numbers of quick-drying "dull-coat" or "flat-finish" paints which are comparatively cheap, easily applied, and require no rubbing. As a usual thing these paints are leadless, the pigment consisting of zinc white or lithopone or the cheaper inert pigments. There is, however, a quick-drying white lead paint made for carriages and railway cars. The Germans have already called attention to the dangers of these new paints and point out the fact that rapid drying means a large quantity of volatile substance in the paint, and this substance is always one of the petroleum products, with a varying proportion of turpentine . . .

In December 1912, Dr. John H. Landis, health officer of the city of Cincinnati, reported to the Bureau of Labor Statistics that a number of painters had complained to him of various distressing symptoms which were caused by the use of certain brands of flat-finish dull surface paints in interior work when the ventilations was very faulty. Dr. Landis requested that an inquiry be made by the Bureau to ascertain the substance or substances in these paints which were responsible for the disorders complained of, and in pursuance of this an investigation was made in Cincinnati in the course of which nine painters were interviewed, all of whom had had much experience with this kind of paint. These men were members of the Brotherhood of Painters and Decorators and were very intelligent men, able to give a clear and detailed history of their experience to the examining physicians. Their histories may be condensed as follows:

After a longer or shorter period of employment with the paint in question, a period usually of two or three days, dependent on the closeness of the room in which the work was done, the man would begin to suffer from dizziness, headache, spots before the eyes, dryness and choking feeling in the throat, burning of the eyelids. Appetite was always interfered with and six of the nine complained of nausea, four of frequent vomiting. Pain of a colicky character was felt in the region of the navel in five cases, along the margin of the ribs in three, and in the lumbar region in three. One man suffered from ulcers on the lips and gums. In the morning there would be a feeling of "dopiness," sleep had brought no refreshment, and the man felt as if he had worked all night. Constipation was not common, but more or less strangury and painful urination was complained of by five men. One man who had used the paint for two years had suffered severely from bladder trouble, resulting in a chronic cystitis. Three years before he had been accepted by a life insurance company, but at this time he had just been rejected for a second policy because he was found to have albuminuria. A cystoscopic examination showed catarrhal cystitis.

Disturbances of sight (transient always) occurred in six of the nine men. Usually the man described it as a veil or cloud before the eyes, sometimes as floating spots.

Some of the men said that toward the end of the day they could no longer do the finer work, partly because of dizziness, partly because of impaired sight. One man fell from the scaffold because "everything went black before his eyes," another began to stagger and had to be half carried out into the open air, while another was blinded and had to be led out of the room. In some cases, curiously enough, the weakness, nausea, and dizziness were felt when the man first got out into the fresh air. One man said that he always would stagger then, though he could walk steadily inside.

It was evident that the substance which gave rise to these symptoms was not any compound of lead, or indeed any part of the pigment content of the paint, but a volatile constituent, with a special affinity for the central nervous system. This was shown not only by the character of the symptoms, but by the rapidity of their development and the fact that they subsided to a large extent in the fresh air. The men stated that the paints dried very rapidly, and that air must be excluded from the room as much as possible lest the drying take place so quickly that by the time the painter had reached the bottom of the wall he would find that the edge of the paint at the top had begun to dry, and a streak would show between it and the fresh paint applied next to it. Any draft of air would turn streaky the fresh paint. The worst trouble was experienced by some men who were employed on a big cheap apartment house. Each apartment had a tiny kitchen with no outside windows and the walls were painted with this dull-finish paint. The men could only work two hours at a time; then they were obliged to go out on the fire escape for an hour to get rid of the headache, dizziness and choking, and the smarting and watering of the eyes. On a damp, heavy day the evils of the work were all accentuated.

Source: Alice Hamilton. 1913. *Hygiene of the Painters' Trade.* Bulletin of the United States Bureau of Labor Statistics, Industrial Accidents and Hygiene Series, Number 2. Washington, DC: Government Printing Office, 14–16.

PATTERNMAKER

Patternmakers were specialized engineers and designers who built templates that could be used to produce tools, machines, and products that could, in turn, be used to mass produce industrial and consumer goods. In the metalworking and construction trades of the nineteenth century, patternmakers were held in high regard. Patternmakers had the skills of machinists: they could cut tools and die from metal, using lathes, cutting tools, drills, shapers, and other machinery. Patternmakers had the skills of draftsmen and construction workers as well—they could both make and read blueprints, visualize three-dimensional structures from their representation on paper, and construct prototypes or models from those designs. They made some prototypes from raw lumber, using the saw, drill, and conceptual skills of a carpenter. They had metal-casting skills, too, as they customarily cast molten metal into sand molds to create rough objects to be turned later into tools, gears, tools, and other special items. Patternmakers also had advanced mathematical skills—not only did they need to know basic arithmetic but also had significant skills in algebra and geometry to translate complicated plans into unique objects. They distinguished themselves from the common machinist, also a highly skilled worker in the 1870s, by the title "patternmaker." By the twentieth century, the patternmakers' union joined forces with the machinists to form a powerful metal trades union, the International Association of Machinists and Patternmakers (IAM), one of the largest of U.S. trade unions by the mid-twentieth century.

As the United States experienced industrialization, not only did more artisans become factory workers, but also the need for patternmakers, typically called "engineers" in early nineteenth century Britain (and, to a lesser degree, America), expanded. Patternmakers helped to create the new machines that made industrial production possible. Every machine invented needed a prototype to ensure that it functioned as intended. In Scotland, where many engineers first developed their skills before emigrating to the United States or Canada, apprentices learned their trade in the great machine shops of the day. Apprentices learned to draw first—this was an essential element of a patternmaker's work—and practiced their mathematical skills as well: calculating the size of a prototype, finely sketching out the planes of a three-dimensional object, and noting the degrees, in geometric calculations, of the prototype. An apprentice might assist a master craftsman, a patternmaker, in sketching out the structure for a railway bridge over a particularly deep canyon or draw a plan for a small piston for a steam engine to power a saw and feed belt in a lumber mill. Apprentices enthusiastically pursued education in mathematics and the arts, as well as critical thinking and problem solving, at mechanics institutes and in workers' reading rooms and libraries. They also assisted patternmakers in the work required to build a prototype. They built the wooden boxes that held the "green," or fine, sand into which wooden molds were pressed and then removed to create the shape of a metal casting. Apprentices spent long hours filing down rough work under the watchful eyes of the master patternmaker. Apprentices might work for a time as a machinist before gaining employment as a highly skilled patternmaker.

As journeymen and master craftsmen in late-nineteenth-century America, patternmakers were often known as "inventors" or, like their Scottish peers, machinists. One union official of the time, in fact, estimated that perhaps half of American machinists and patternmakers were immigrants from England and Scotland, where they had learned their trade. They worked in railroad shops, foundries, and machine shops. Even as American machine-shop owners subdivided the tasks of common machinists into ever-more discrete occupations, patternmakers exercised a great deal of control over their daily work lives. In their introduction to the publication of the diary of Andrew McIllwraith, an accomplished patternmaker, historians Andrew Holman and Robert Kristofferson note that even in the 1860s, McIllwraith sometimes worked from his own home—a practice more akin to that of the earlier artisans than to modern foundry workers. Because of their skills, patternmakers could slow production down, though it was seldom to their benefit to do so. Competition from European patternmakers characterized the labor market of the 1860s and 1870s in the United States as skilled workers like McIllwraith immigrated to America for greater economic opportunities.

Once a patternmaker had created a design for a prototype, he created a wooden model first—at a smaller scale for larger projects but in full dimensions for smaller tasks. A patternmaker created the constituent parts of a prototype using saws and various planes, including block, router, rabbet, and jointer planes most commonly used by carpenters and cabinetmakers. He utilized chisels and drills to create the intricate pieces of a wooden prototype. Like a machinist, he also used calipers, gauges, and micrometers to measure the item. Some models were created only of wooden items, but most were eventually used to cast or shape the metal prototype. To do this, the patternmaker built simple boxes and then filled them with green and dried sand. He used a wooden, plaster, or ceramic model to create the mold to press into the sand to create the casting shape. The tops and bottoms of the sand casting boxes were then carefully joined so that a three-dimensional part could be produced. Pouring the molten metal into the sand mold through a hole in the box assembly, the patternmaker created a rough metal prototype. A patternmaker then took the cooled metal prototype and finished it using files and other machinist and foundry tools. Items that had not been cleaned and polished well could introduce catastrophic damage into a machine's operations by cavitation or vibration, wrecking both the prototype and the mechanism in which it was a part. Each prototype created by a patternmaker might require different metal compositions, including copper, iron, steel, aluminum, and other metals. Patternmakers had to determine the correct metal composition for each prototype and so had to possess the skills of a foundry expert.

The patternmaker did what has been characterized as "respectable brainwork." As modern machine shops specializing in certain products began to dominate the landscape of industrializing America in the last decades of the nineteenth century, many patternmakers became "engineers" who supervised gangs of lesser-skilled machinists and mechanics who worked on contract for a few months or as long as a year at a time. Patternmakers thus became contractors, paid on the basis of a shop's production. One machine-shop owner, James See, advised his counterparts to pay the highest-skilled of workmen, which would have included patternmakers, the highest wages and to adopt a collaborative shop culture in which the "engineers" and employers solved the most perplexing and difficult machine problems. As workers, patternmakers enjoyed their privileged status, and as machinists and others unionized in the great shops like those of the Pullman Company, the unions they formed in this period remained centered on craft divisions, not collectivism. They called themselves the "aristocrats of labor" and demanded the pay and conditions of labor that allowed them to maintain their dignity and relatively high status.

Nancy Quam-Wickham

See also: *1915–1945:* Draftsman; Mechanical Engineer

FURTHER READING

Dabakis, Melissa. 1995. "Douglas Tilden and the Mechanics Fountain: Labor and the 'Crisis of Masculinity' in the 1890s." *American Quarterly* 47: 204–235.

Holman, Andrew C., and Robert B. Kristofferson. 2013. *More of a Man: Diaries of a Scottish Craftsman in Nineteenth-Century North America.* Toronto: University of Toronto Press.

Montgomery, David. 1987. *The Fall of the House of Labor: The Workplace, the State, and American Labor Activism, 1865–1925.* Cambridge: Cambridge University Press.

PENSION BUREAU CLERK

During the Civil War (1861–1865) and afterward, clerks of the U.S. Pension Bureau examined the service records of hundreds of thousands of military veterans who served in the Union Army. They worked in the Pension Bureau government offices in Washington, D.C., under the auspices of the secretary of the interior. Pension clerks reviewed applicants' files, corroborated claims with military service records and medical doctors, and made determinations about benefit payments. They also arranged for appropriate payments for both veterans and widows, based on applicants' eligibility for benefits. Working as a pension clerk required spending long hours at a desk evaluating paperwork; the number of pension clerks grew significantly in the decades after the Civil War and into the early 1900s as veterans aged and made claim to benefits.

On the eve of the Civil War in 1861, the U.S. Army had only about 18,000 officers and enlisted men, some of whom were not even on active duty. Defending the Union against the rebels of the South required a massive effort, increasing military forces exponentially to more than 2,200,000 officers and soldiers who served in the Union during the war. To conduct warfare, however, required an enormous effort far beyond what took place among soldiers in training camps and battlegrounds. Armies need supplies; to procure these supplies, governments need civilian officials to serve as procurement workers, planners, transportation officials, and in other capacities. Government officials enacted tariffs and new taxes to pay for the war. While the U.S. Army Quartermaster Corps was responsible for military procurement for the Union Army, providing clothing, arms, and food to soldiers, the immense demands of warfare on society as a whole led to an expansion of workers—both paid and volunteer—at the federal, state, and local levels during wartime and the Reconstruction of the South. Volunteer regiments organized at the state level were sometimes outfitted by state or local governments. Throughout the war, both the Union and Confederate governments maintained diplomatic envoys in foreign countries. Teachers flocked to the South, albeit briefly, to help African

Americans organize schools under the Freedmen's Bureau. The nature of government employment changed during this time period.

As it became clear to federal officials that the war would not be a short one as first anticipated, the Union government prepared for the inevitable: in 1862, Congress enacted pension legislation to support the families of fallen soldiers as well as disabled veterans whose injuries could be traced to their wartime service. The Civil War Pension system formed the basis of the U.S. public retirement and pension systems, which took a more modern form in the passage of the Social Security Act in 1935. Pensions for service veterans was nothing new as the federal government had provided some forms of these to those most impoverished of the Revolutionary War veterans. The Civil War pension system and the government agencies created to administer it, however, were of a different scale: over 3 percent of all Union soldiers died or were seriously injured during the war, a staggering number when considering the total of those who served. By 1900, the Bureau of Pensions had granted more than 741,000 applications for assistance to veterans and their dependents.

As government workers, those who worked in the Bureau of Pensions had to follow the instructions of Congress to determine a veteran's eligibility for pension payments. Pension personnel developed the government forms that each former service member or survivor had to complete; these forms were revised frequently as Congress changed eligibility requirements several times between 1862 and 1878. Clerks evaluated completed forms and the requisite supplementary documents; by the 1870s, many applicants used the services of attorneys to help file this extensive paperwork. If claiming a pension for himself and his family, an applicant had to demonstrate that he had held prewar employment sufficient to support his family; similarly, a widow had to provide documents: marriage documents, evidence that her deceased husband had indeed been the family breadwinner before the war, and testimony, often from neighbors, that she had both lived with the decedent and not divorced him before his death. Applicants had to provide statements from medical doctors testifying to the degree of their disability. Once the application was received within the pension offices, a clerk had to request statements from the headquarters of two military agencies—the Adjutant General's and the Surgeon General's Offices—to verify an applicant's service and disability records. Once the military provided substantiation of an applicant's service record, Pension Bureau clerks then had to assess the veracity of other supporting documents. Clerks in the Pension Bureau were commonly veterans themselves as the U.S. Sanitary Commission, a civilian organization providing medical aid and war relief, had lobbied for the employment of disabled veterans in government; veteran clerks were "favorably disposed toward applicants," though contemporary observers reported no systematic fraud within the Bureau (Skocpol 2009, 118). Clerks had no ability to interview applicants who submitted claims from across the country, though there were special examiners who evaluated partial or particularly suspect claims.

The decisions of Pension Bureau clerks reflected the social and political milieu and values of the time in which they worked. The original legislation required that an applicant be disabled for manual labor. Although many civil war nurses were immigrant women or women of color, generally only middle-class white women who had served as nurses were approved for pensions. Evaluating African Americans' claims that required a statement of prewar employment disadvantaged thousands of black men who had been enslaved but joined U.S. Colored Troops battalions once they were emancipated in occupied regions. Working-class men generally had more difficulty proving their disabilities than did officers, some of whom obtained pensions but continued to work in their chosen professions. In some cases, political affinities determined how an evaluator determined an applicant's claims. Congressional aides also spent untold hours lobbying Pension Bureau personnel for benefits for constituents who had submitted claims. The 1879 Arrears Act allowed veterans, survivors, or dependents whose claims had previously been denied to reapply with new supporting documents, requiring clerks to reevaluate claimants' original and updated applications. Adding to the confusion was the lack of supervision of Pension Bureau personnel—prior to civil service reforms instituted in the 1880s, the federal government lacked basic-training manuals and organizational charts for most non-military agencies. Clerks were often empowered to make decisions on a veteran's claim based on their instincts about the truthfulness and accuracy of any individual's application.

During the 1860s and 1870s, most Pension Bureau personnel seem to have evaluated cases of white male applicants on the basis of their eligibility. There was fraud, though historians disagree about its extent. In the 1880s, however, the political patronage system corrupted the bureau. Observers at the time noted the importance of political patronage, as 40 percent of those receiving pension benefits came from just five states—and one director ordered bureau clerks to approve every application prior to the 1884 presidential election in the hopes that approved applications would translate into votes for the Republican Party. Applicants whose claims were denied could petition their congressional representative for private pension bills that were universally adopted by Congress, establishing the right of a rejected applicant to a pension, which bureau personnel would then be required to process. So entrenched was this system of political patronage that Congress designated a special pension office within it during this time, just to draft legislation approving pensions for individual claimants.

Political considerations during the presidential election of 1890 altered the duties of the Pension Bureau, as Republicans regained office. President Harrison and his director of the Bureau of Pensions, James Tanner, pushed through legislation that once again altered the eligibility for pensions: removing the wartime disability requirement, which made it possible for any veteran or survivor to claim benefits based on service, and subsequent disability such as old age. Under this new law, the Dependent and Disability Act of 1890, the Pension Bureau expanded again, moving into a new federal building in Washington, D.C., and with civil service reforms, it became a professional government organization staffed by trained workers.

Nancy Quam-Wickham

See also: *1861–1914:* Bookkeeper; *1946–1991:* Office Clerk

FURTHER READING

Johnson, Russell L. 2011. "'Great Injustice': Social Status and the Distribution of Military Pensions after the Civil War." *The Journal of the Gilded Age and Progressive Era* 10: 137–160.

Lippman, Ellen, and Martin McMahon. 2017. "Professionalization and Politics in the Procurement Process: United States Civil War Early Years." *Accounting Historians Journal* 44: 63–76.

Schultz, Jane E. 1994. "Gender, Race, and Bureaucracy: Civil War Army Nurses and the Pension Bureau." *Journal of Women's History* 6: 45–69.

Skocpol, Theda. 2009. *Protecting Soldiers and Mothers: The Political Origins of Social Policy in the United States.* Cambridge: Harvard University Press.

PHOTOGRAPHER

A photographer is a person who takes photographs and is often involved with the chemical (or, in modern times, digital) processes necessary to convert the captured image into a photograph that can be archived, displayed, given, or sold. Early photographers worked in portrait studios and at carnivals and fairs, and their work was often seen as little more than a novelty. Early photographers made tintypes, which were photographs whereby the targeted image was projected onto a thin sheet of iron that was lacquered with light-sensitive chemicals that reacted to form a permanent image that could be handed to a customer just a few minutes later. Modern American photography emerged as a form of communication in the two decades before the Civil War (1861–1865), when, in the late 1830s, the French inventor and artist Louis Daguerre developed a process for capturing light and shadows on a silver-plated piece of copper using a mix of iodine, mercury, salt, and water that produced a record of the captured light and shadow as a permanent image. The daguerreotype, as its inventor christened it, made it possible for artists to purchase an expensive device—the early camera—and, using some basic chemistry, capture images for archival display, or sale. Since exposure time was generally measured in minutes, not fractions of a second as with cameras today, most daguerreotypes were of stationary objects: still life, landscapes, famous architectural monuments, and other artistic works.

By the late 1840s, improvements in lens technology, chemical processes, and plate coatings reduced exposure time dramatically and facilitated the creation of new cameras. By the 1850s, American photographers were using glass plates—rather than metallic—that were wetted with a silver colloidal solution and exposed to light through the camera lens and then developed using an acid wash. Soon after, photographers began using emulsions, which are a fine dispersion of minute droplets of one liquid in another, to produce tintype images through the use of a camera with multiple lenses that captured multiple images onto thin sheets of iron. This process further reduced exposure times, making tintype photography suitable for inexpensive portraiture. Tens of thousands of Americans sat for portraits, creating memorials in photography for future generations. They often took aspirational poses in an effort to portray themselves as living a life that they wanted rather than the life that they actually had: a teenager, posing solemnly, with a belt of ammunition strung across his chest and holding a large six-shooter that dwarfed his left hand; a matronly woman, sitting on a chaise, gazing out a large window, turned away from the lens, perhaps out of vanity—or modesty.

For two decades after the 1850s, most photographers used glass or tin plates, emulsions, and chemical washes to create portraits as well as artistic photographs. Across the nation, photographers opened studios where they specialized in tintype portraiture. Individuals as well as groups—lovers, friends, families, baseball clubs, marching bands, classes of schoolchildren—all posed for portrait photographers. Immigrants posed in traditional garb. Tradesmen demonstrated their craft. African American photographers sought to portray fellow African Americans with the dignity usually denied to men and women of their race in postbellum society. Some portraitists traveled, setting up temporary studios along beach boardwalks or at carnivals, county fairs, and popular resorts during the summer season or in small towns and hamlets across the country. Whereas in the 1850s, an individual might be able to afford only one or two portraits during his or her lifetime, by the 1870s and early 1880s, the cost of tintypes and the competition among photographers drove prices for a portrait down to pennies apiece. Respectable working-class families could afford a group portrait of the family, as well as individual portraits of each of their children at two or three different ages.

In some studios, photographers offered their customers different backdrops and props (clothing, guns, furniture, fans, and even taxidermy animals) for stylized and unconventional portraits. Subjects had to sit still for several seconds while the photographer exposed the wet plate to light by opening the lens. Once the photographer had judged the plate exposed, he or she then took the wet plate and developed it in a chemical bath, rinsed it, and then dried it before varnishing it and cutting the multiple sets of the same image into several smaller tintypes. Some photographers touched up their images if a customer desired pink cheeks or a colored outfit. Since anyone could call herself or himself a photographer, the quality of tintype portraits varied immensely. A child might move during exposure, or a temporary setup might lack sufficient light, requiring long exposures, both of which could create a significantly blurred image. Some photographers worked within customers' homes, practicing postmortem photography, or capturing the image of recently deceased individuals, often children—though this was never a profitable specialty.

Other late enterprising photographers in this period specialized in stereographs, in which the photographer simultaneously took two negative images on glass plates and then printed the positive images (in which the light patterns are reversed, similar to what the human eye sees) on heavy paper. Extracted from egg whites, when applied to paper, albumen made it possible for the photographer to print an image from a glass negative directly onto paper, the technique commonly used by stereograph photographers. Viewers then looked through a stereoscope to see a three-dimensional representation of the image. The Goodridge brothers, who were grandsons of slaves, opened a studio in Saginaw, Michigan, in the mid-1860s; in subsequent decades, their specialties included stereographs documenting the development of that region—the Saginaw Valley to Saginaw Bay on Lake Huron in central Michigan. Viewers could appreciate critical events—like the annual float of logs downriver to Saginaw Bay or the great fires of 1873—in three dimensions, even if they had not witnessed these events themselves. The successes of these early stereographs led the Goodridge brothers, Glenalvin, William, and Wallace, to expand their work in the 1880s, when they toured the state, taking stereographs of "Picturesque Michigan" for a serial publication of the same name. Wildly popular among consumers, such stereographs provided these men with a steady living and regional acclaim.

Yet other photographers in this period produced more artistic images, often of grand vistas—the Yosemite Valley, the Grand Canyon of the Yellowstone River, or Canyon de Chelly—to showcase America's national treasures. Landscape photographers traveled on expeditions with the United States Geographic Survey, as William Henry Jackson and John Hillers had done. Using mules to transport heavy glass-plate cameras on rough trails, and with the assistance of helpers, these two photographers produced stunning images. Situating men of the survey in the background (and on rock outcroppings and mountain summits), these photographers posed humans in dramatic nature, creating for the viewer a sense of the sublime in which amazing natural landscapes dwarfed humans. Other large-format photographers specialized in industrial images, in which workers often sat atop huge redwood stumps, on partly constructed bridges, or on large industrial machines—creating a sense of the industrial sublime. Both kinds of photography required photographers to use large-format cameras that utilized heavy negative plates, some twenty by twenty-four inches in size. The photographer then transferred the image by placing the negative onto albumen paper in light and then fixing the image by bathing it in one or more chemical washes.

Technological advancements defined the development of photography as practice and occupation. The use of gelatin on celluloid for dry photography facilitated the development of modern camera film. In the 1880s, George Eastman of Rochester, New York, patented the Kodak camera, an easy-to-use camera marketed to the world and advertised as "the only camera that anybody can use without instructions." At the turn of the century, more Americans purchased the Kodak camera and took portraits and photographs of their everyday lives and of their travels, thereby cutting into the work of ambrotype and tintype portraitists. Gelatin prints produced sharper and more defined images; the more exacting work required to produce artistic images remained the work of the professional photographer. Film photography also made possible the mass production of photographs in magazines and newspapers, creating new specializations of the press and documentary photographers. These professionals told stories with their photographs, using them, as did Jacob Riis, to draw public attention to the plight of immigrants and the poor. Other photographers produced images for postcards; Americans avidly collected these new items, fueling tourism as a twentieth-century industry. As a medium of communication, photography advanced rapidly in this period.

Nancy Quam-Wickham

See also: *1946–1991:* Artist

FURTHER READING

Davis, Keith F. 2007. *The Origins of American Photography, 1839–1885: From Daguerreotype to Dry-Plate.* Kansas City and New Haven: Nelson-Atkins Museum of Art and Yale University Press.

Jezierski, John Vincent. 2000. *Enterprising Images: The Goodridge Brothers, African American Photographers, 1847–1922.* Detroit: Wayne State University Press.

Newhall, Beaumont. *The History of Photography from 1839 to the Present.* New York: Museum of Modern Art, New York and Little, Brown and Company.

Willis, Deborah. 2000. *Reflections in Black: A History of Black Photographers 1840 to the Present.* New York: W. W. Norton.

PRIMARY DOCUMENT

Among Americans' many collective industrial and artistic interests, photography was one of the most popular. Local photography clubs formed to provide education in the craft, disseminate new techniques, and host talks by famous photographers. This document describes a late-nineteenth-century meeting of a photography club, as published in one of many magazines, The Philadelphia Photographer, *catering to both professional photographers and amateur enthusiasts. This report describes the difficulties that photographers faced in the American West at the time.*

NEW YORK CORRESPONDENCE,

The photographic section of the American Institute met Feb. 1st, V. P. Bogardus in the chair. A large presentation of prints was made by Messrs. Kurtz, Mason, Captain Russell, photographer of the U. P. R.R. [Union Pacific Railroad], Bierstadt, and Bogardus.

Captain Russell, at the request of the gentlemen present, "gave his experience." It might well be called photographing under difficulties.

Owing to the generally alkaline nature of the water in large sections of our "big great West," he had been forced to carry good water a distance of seventy miles; he had often travelled fifty miles upon foot for certain views; was often absent four and five weeks, and forced to subsist upon game. Many of his situations and of his companions as well, were unpleasant and not uncommonly ludicrous. Upon one occasion in descending a mountain almost as steep as the side of a house, the horse of one of the party, either from uncontrollable gravitation or a desire to go faster, started, the result being that he left his rider, but no longer master, pendant in a tree, an astonished and dissatisfied mass of helpless humanity. Upon another occasion the Captain was astride his mule descending some upright mass or another of nature, when he found himself moving faster than his faithful servant; they both moved downwards together, but the Captain beat the mule, and declares that had it not been for the ears of said mule he would have gone overboard; they proved his salvation and kept him aboard. The Captain is not responsible for my words; I only report facts, not exact language.

This reminds me of the mule Josh Billings tells about: how he spells it is more than I know, but he says: "The mule is a bird of larger growth than the turkey, he has two legs to walk with and two to kick with, and he wears his wings on the side of his head." This, I judge, to be the kind of a mule Russell had.

The Captain exhibited his camera-box; it was of novel and ingenious construction, but without drawings, I cannot explain it. Mr. H. T. Anthony volunteered to have a drawing made of it, so that by your next I trust it will be in shape to publish . . .

Yours, &c., C. W. H.

Source: N. A. 1870. "New York Correspondence." *The Philadelphia Photographer* 7, no. 75 (March), 82–83.

POLICE OFFICER

The United States' first police departments were formed in the mid-nineteenth century as rapid growth in many cities helped to expose the inadequacies of earlier systems of law enforcement. Cities grew as immigrants from abroad and migrants from the countryside moved in search of jobs and a better life. New York City's population increased from roughly 33,000 residents in 1790 to over 500,000 in 1850; 45 percent of the metropolis's population was foreign born. Competition for both skilled and unskilled jobs was stiff. This often resulted in ethnic and racial tensions that boiled over into violence, riots, and disorder as native and foreign-born workers clashed. So many riots occurred in New York in 1834 that it was designated the "Year of the Riot." In 1837, a riot in Philadelphia involved over 15,000 residents.

During this period, there was also a growing fear of crime among many city residents. Homicide, robbery, theft, and vandalism, they feared, were on the rise. The large, sprawling cities provided criminals with the ability to escape detection and avoid apprehension. The cities were crowded. Criminals could blend in and disappear. The new wealth created in the manufacturing and commercial districts meant an abundance of potential targets for criminals to victimize.

City leaders, with the support and urging of wealthy businessowners, began to search for a new system to maintain law and order and adopted the example of the Metropolitan Police Department in London. In the early nineteenth century, London had faced problems similar to those in American cities and, in 1829, the British Parliament passed the Metropolitan Police Act, written by Sir Robert Peele. The act became the foundation for police departments in England and the United States, and the principles it established remain the cornerstone of American policing today. These principles included the idea that the mission for which the police exist is to prevent crime and disorder; that the ability of the police to perform their duties is dependent upon public approval of police actions, and that police use physical force to the extent necessary to secure observance of the law or restore order only when the exercise of persuasion, advice, and warning is found to be insufficient (Lyman 1964, 141).

Early police departments in the United States often proved ineffective at preventing crime and disorder. Chief among the problems faced, especially for those who worked as police officers, was the lack of a clearly defined job description. Depending on the jurisdiction they worked in, police officers could be expected to enforce sanitation regulations; inspect commercial licenses; house and feed the indigent, homeless, and intoxicated; clean and maintain the streets; remove dead animals; collect trash; guard trash that was deemed salable; pick weeds; and enforce disease and health regulations. With such a variety of tasks to perform, preventing crime often became secondary or was not pursued at all.

Police officers were also frequently called upon to break up strikes and arrest striking workers, especially in the years after the Civil War. This activity increasingly brought police officers into open conflict with the public and resulted in arrests, injuries, and deaths. One of the most significant events occurred in 1887 when Chicago police officers opened fire on a group of striking workers, killing one and injuring five others. The following day, at a rally held to protest police brutality in Haymarket Square, a bomb was thrown into the ranks of the 180 police officers who had shown up to disperse the crowd. Seven police officers were killed, and 70 were injured, many by friendly fire. The number killed and injured among the crowd remains unknown.

Further complicating the life of the early police officer was their control by urban political machines that oversaw appointments to city jobs. Positions on the police department, from the lowliest patrol officer to the chief of police, were distributed to faithful political party members as patronage for their support of the ruling party. When political power changed hands and the governing party was removed from power, police officers often found themselves looking for new jobs as the incoming party replaced them. In Cincinnati, for instance, 219 of the 295 members of the police department were fired when a new political party won the local election. In Los Angeles, there was a standing agreement between the political parties that whoever had a majority on the city council was entitled to distribute 75 percent of the police department jobs. Similar arrangements existed in many other cities.

There were no hiring standards and no training for police officers. Jobs were often given out to the roughest and toughest individuals. Police brutality was common, and law and order were often maintained with the end of a nightstick. Police officers could expect to work twelve hours a day, six or seven days a week. At least half of their shift was spent walking a beat. The other half was often spent in the station house as a reserve in case of riot. Officers were often called upon to get out the vote on election day, ensuring that people got to the voting booths and voted for the right candidates.

Although working as a police officer could be dangerous and uncertain work in the nineteenth century, it could also be lucrative. By the turn of the twentieth century, police officers were making between $600 and $1200 a year, "more than laborers, weavers, miners, factory workers and about as much as painters, carpenters, teamsters, blacksmiths, and railway conductors" (Johnson, 101). In addition, police officers often received free medical treatment and at least a modest pension. As early as 1857, New York established a Police Life and Health Insurance Fund, which provided a disabled police officer with a $150 annual payment. By the 1880s, many cities were offering retirement pensions to police officers. St. Louis police officers, for instance, could retire with a $450-a-year pension, while New York police officers could retire with half their pay annually.

In addition to their salary and benefits, police officers also made money through bribes, payoffs, and kickbacks. Corruption among the rank and file was commonplace. It was so normal in Chicago in the 1870s that owners of gambling halls formed an association to provide for the smooth and consistent payment of monies to the police for protection. Some officers were able to more than double their salaries by blackmailing arrestees, being paid by criminals to arrest their rivals, or selling property stolen from arrestees.

As complaints about police corruption and brutality grew, so did calls for reform. In 1894, the State of New York convened the Lexow Committee to investigate charges of police corruption. The committee's findings were shocking to many. It reported, "The police secured appointments and won promotions through political influence and cash payments. In return for regular payoffs they protected gambling, prostitution, and other illicit enterprises. Officers extorted money from peddlers, storekeeps, and other legitimate businessmen who were hard pressed to abide by municipal ordinances. Detectives allowed con men, pickpockets, and thieves to go about their business in return for a share of the proceeds. Officers also assaulted ordinary citizens with impunity" (New York State Senate Committee on Police Department of the City of New York 1971).

Spurred by the Lexow Committee's findings, police departments and social reformers in the Progressive era began to revise the police. One of the most important changes for police officers came in the form of the civil service system, which required applicants to meet predetermined hiring standards and pass a competitive examination before they were hired. These reforms freed police officers and police departments from the control of corrupt politicians and allowed them a degree of professionalism that had not previously existed.

The police officer in this era, reformers believed, should be male and white. While the first female police officer was appointed in 1891 and the first African American officer was appointed in 1889, women and minorities on police departments remained an anomaly until late in the twentieth century. They were expected to be able-bodied, physically fit, intelligent enough to pass a civil service exam, and of good character with no history of arrest or trouble. They sought to wipe away the image of the overweight, intoxicated, dimwitted police officer that dominated nineteenth-century characterizations of the police. Furthermore, police officers should, "weigh 150 pounds, measure 5 feet 9 inches tall, and be between 21 and 31 years of age" (Vollmer 1932). Reformers recommended that police officers be paid a wage that would ensure a decent standard of living. They also recommended an eight-hour workday with one day off weekly, annual vacation leave, sick leave with pay, accident and death benefits, and reasonable pensions. These benefits, they argued, would help attract the best-qualified applicants and make them immune from bribery and corruption.

The police officer's mission also began to change in the early twentieth century. The social services they had once performed were stripped away in favor of a new model of policing: crime control. Police officers, many believed, could be more effective as crime fighters. Arrest statistics became the standard by which police effectiveness was judged. Technological advances were introduced to aid the police in their new mission, including the adoption of standardized police training programs, motorized patrol, and two-way radio communication systems. Many agencies also implemented scientific approaches to law enforcement, such as the use of fingerprint evidence, lie detectors, police record-keeping systems, and science-based crime labs.

Police officers in the early twentieth century were in a far better position than their predecessors of the previous century. They had succeeded in establishing themselves as an independent agency devoted to the observance of law and order. But the goal of professionalizing the police and rooting out corruption would continue throughout the twentieth and into the twentieth century.

Scott McClellan

See also: *1607–1775:* Militiaman; Watchman; *1915–1945:* Firefighter

FURTHER READING

Adler, Herbert M. 1904. "The Police System of London." *American Academy of Political and Social Science* 24: 126–129.

Fogelson, Robert M. 1979. *Big City Police*. Cambridge: Harvard University Press.

Johnson, David R. 1979. *Policing the Urban Underworld: The Impact of Crime on the Development of the American Police, 1800–1887.* Philadelphia: Temple University Press.

Lyman, J. L. 1964. "The Metropolitan Police Act of 1829: An Analysis of Certain Events Influencing the Passage and Character of the Metropolitan Police Act in England." *Journal of Criminal Law and Criminology* 55: 141–153.

New York State Senate Committee on Police Department of the City of New York. 1971. *Report and Proceedings of the Investigation of the New York City Police*. New York: Arno Press.

Richardson, James F. 1970. *New York Police: Colonial Times to 1901*. New York: Oxford University Press.

Vollmer, August. 1932. "Abstract of the Wickersham Police Report." *Journal of Criminal Law and Criminology* 22: 716–723.

PRISON GUARD

Prison guards are responsible for the operation and oversight of buildings and institutions that house prisoners. The Civil War (1861–1865) created an immense need for soldiers but also for guards who policed them and the communities from which they came, especially in the South. Antebellum prisons had generally been small, housing both those convicted of crimes and the mentally ill. Local constables and jailers had to provide for the needs of early prisoners; in many smaller towns, the jailer's wife cooked meals for them. Only the largest institutions had guards. The new mental hospitals, colloquially known as "lunatic asylums," that arose in America around the time of the American Revolution and grew in numbers, albeit slowly, during the early nineteenth century generally housed the severely mentally ill and severely disabled. To compensate for the lack of guards, asylum operators routinely chained unruly "inmates" to walls or the floor or confined them in tiny cells. Orphanages, almshouses, and work farms in America were also similarly small, usually operated by local officials or private interests with little oversight over operations or guarding of residents. In the 1840s and 1850s, social reformer Dorothea Dix wrote and lectured extensively about the conditions in asylums and jails, drawing public attention to the matter.

Americans' ideas about imprisonment of soldiers who had fled battle in fear or been captured by the enemy evolved during the war. During the early war years (1862–1863), both sides agreed to exchange captured soldiers on an equal-rank, man-for-man basis. Captured troops were exchanged regularly; some soldiers were captured and exchanged more than once. Under this system, neither side had much need for extensive prisoner of war (POW) camps—such as Point Lookout, Elmira, Andersonville, Castle Thunder, and Fort Lawton—which would come to dominate the later years of the war. But the Confederate leader Jefferson Davis refused to exchange captured African American soldiers (and the white officers who led those troops), so the POW exchanges stopped; Abraham Lincoln refused to allow only white soldiers to be exchanged, while his commanding general, Ulysses S. Grant, favored imprisoning captured Confederates as doing so kept them out of battle. Additionally, in southern and northern communities, town officials arrested and imprisoned local residents or outsiders who interfered with the war effort; political prisoners and dissenters including women, POWs, and common criminals were sent to North Carolina's Castle Thunder prison complex. After the Civil War, Union troops occupied much of the South for years as the U.S. military sought to reconstruct the region. All of these efforts during and after the Civil War required more manpower—guards to oversee prisons, protect communities, and prevent the nation from descending into war again.

Those men—and a small number of women—who worked as guards during the Civil War and Reconstruction were primarily soldiers: They were the guards of

POW camps and the occupying military forces. As guards, their primary directive was to prevent escape. They patrolled the perimeters of POW camps with orders to shoot any who attempted to flee. Guards also maintained artillery positions, which were designed to deter any attempt at rescue, and they attended to guard dogs, who chased anyone who tried to run.

Guards in POW camps also oversaw the centralized distribution of meager rations. These would be given to prisoners' representatives—generally imprisoned officers—who then arranged for the equitable distribution of food to individual prisoners. Unlike jailers, guards in most POW camps did not prepare meals or provide clothing, shelter, or other items; that was the responsibility of prisoners themselves. Prisoners also were mostly responsible for self-policing within POW camps: implementing sanitation measures, refereeing disputes between themselves, and providing rudimentary medical care.

The conditions at Andersonville, a Confederate POW camp in southwest Georgia that, in mid-1864, housed more than thirty-three thousand prisoners on a tract of land just over five hundred acres, illustrate the limited duties of civil war POW camp guards. Andersonville was situated on the banks of Sweetwater Creek, but the guards' housing unit was upstream of the camp. Guards and, later, patients at the camp hospital discharged their waste into the creek; downstream, prisoners had to utilize this creek for drinking water. The prison was so overcrowded that it ran out of space to dig pit latrines. When it rained, the polluted creek overflowed its banks, mixing with open latrines and mud to create a mucky mess. Prisoners suffered from dysentery, exposure, gangrene, pneumonia and other bacterial and viral diseases, scurvy, and starvation. Nearly 30 percent of all Union POWs imprisoned at Andersonville died, and the prison ran out of burial space. Guards supervised imprisoned men, who simply stacked the bodies of their dead compatriots outside the stockade fences.

Confederate guards did little to alleviate the suffering; after the war, Captain Heinrich "Henry" Wirz, a camp commandant, was tried and executed by the U.S. government for murder and other war crimes. The guards who Wirz commanded were untrained in policing; most were boys too young to serve in the Confederate Army, old men, or those considered unfit for military service. Few guards performed their jobs with professionalism; many Confederate guards singled out African American prisoners for particularly brutal treatment, while African American military guards in northern POW camps sometimes shot disobedient Confederate POWs who refused to take orders from their captors, some of whom had been formerly enslaved by those they now guarded.

The Union military occupiers who were garrisoned in southern towns during the war also performed guard duties. Historian Andrew Lang wrote that the duties of military occupiers included "regulating both passive and hostile civilian enemies, administering conquered territory through martial law and fortified garrisons, and transforming society through emancipation." Although these guards were more formally trained members of the U.S. military, few were trained specifically for the tasks of domestic policing that effectively guarding communities required. Americans' long-held suspicions of standing armies led many men working as occupying guards to devalue their work, or as one Massachusetts soldier wrote despairingly of his duties, occupying soldiers were reduced to picking up "the naughty ladies who stick their tongues out at the soldiers."

Throughout the war years, and especially as martial law was imposed on defeated southern territories, the Union's fighting forces performed extensive guard duties. They protected emancipated slaves and whites who opposed secession. In some regions, guards assisted freed people in negotiating labor contracts with landowners, and military guards helped to reunite black families separated by slavery. They guarded farms in Louisiana, Texas, and other areas and protected workers and families from guerilla warfare enacted by Confederate rebels.

Military occupation provided those guards who tried to keep the peace with a sense of the challenges they would face in the immediate postwar years, before Congress mandated stricter eligibility requirements for readmission to the Union. In 1865 and 1866, white southerners committed widespread extralegal violence—rape, physical assault, robbery, and murder—against African Americans; they also enacted the brutal Black Codes (1865–1866) that regulated virtually all black life throughout the South. Former confederates and their supporters formed the Ku Klux Klan during these years as well. A southern race war threatened the stability of the nation and alarmed many among the occupying forces, with deadly white riots that left dozens of African Americans dead in Memphis and New Orleans in 1866.

In many areas, military occupation forces were themselves the targets of roving gangs of white men; southern resistance to the idea that African Americans and Union supporters needed protection was manifest in the pervasive violence committed by these organized gangs. At greatest peril were those African American troops who had been deployed to protect southern communities as many former rebels were enraged at the sight of armed blacks guarding their communities. Paradoxically, after Congress passed the Reconstruction Acts (1867), which organized the South into five military occupation districts, the numbers of troops deployed to guard southern communities declined. Once former rebellious states had rewritten their constitutions to conform to federal mandates for readmission, federal officials approved the withdrawal of many occupying forces, leaving guard and policing duties to local communities.

Nancy Quam-Wickham

See also: Police Officer; Soldier; *1992–2019:* Correctional Officer

FURTHER READING

Foner, Eric. 1988. *Reconstruction: America's Unfinished Revolution, 1863–1877.* New York: Harper & Row.

Lang, Andrew F. 2017. *In the Wake of War: Military Occupation, Emancipation, and Civil War America.* Baton Rouge: Louisiana State University Press.

Litwack, Leon. 1979. *Been in the Storm So Long: The Aftermath of Slavery.* New York: Alfred Knopf.

Zombek, Angela M. 2018. *Penitentiaries, Punishment and Military Prisons: Familiar Responses to an Extraordinary Crisis during the American Civil War.* Kent: Kent State University Press.

PRIMARY DOCUMENT

In these passages, Lessel Long, a young Union soldier of the 13th Indiana Regiment, Volunteer Infantry, writes about the conditions inside the Confederate Army's prison at Andersonville, Georgia. Long survived a year-long confinement there. Like many Union prisoners, he was often taken out of the camp on the pretense of an exchange of prisoners between the Union and Confederate Armies, but no exchange ever came. He describes horrendous conditions that haunted him even twenty years after the Civil War ended.

The stockade was crowded to its utmost capacity, there being over 20,000 men confined in a space of less than seventeen acres. We were perfectly amazed at the horrible sight that met our eyes. At every step we saw men prostrated by disease, men dying from neglect, men almost naked, men blackened by smoke, men begrimed by dirt. All the horrible sights of suffering humanity could here be seen in a few minutes' time . . .

The sun would come out and the heat would be fearful. The skin on the men's bare backs would raise up in great blisters and make running sores. These sores would be covered with great big green flies. Soon you could see those sores full of maggots, then the gangrene would set in, and death soon followed. In this manner hundreds died. Men soon got the scurvy, and then it soon run to the dropsy. I have seen hundreds of men with their ankles swelled to three or four times their nature size . . . Thirty thousand men, all of them having the diarrhea, and all must go to attend the calls of nature, and that on as limited a space as one acre of ground. What condition do you think it would be in the course of two or three months? Do you think you would like to be compelled to breathe this kind of an atmosphere? . . .

How would you like to take your breakfast in this pleasant parlor where you could look in any direction from you and see dead men and dying men?

Source: Lessel Long. 1886. *Twelve Months in Andersonville. On the march—in the battle—in the rebel prison pens, and at last in God's country.* Huntington: T. and B. Butler, 43, 56–57.

PUDDLER

Puddlers worked in iron manufacturing and were responsible for converting "pig" iron—a colloquial name for crude, high-carbon iron ore—into wrought iron, which is a finished iron alloy with very low carbon content, through the use of specialized furnaces. At the heart of an industrializing America were the great iron and steel mills of the nineteenth and twentieth centuries, where workers transformed minimally processed raw materials into all of the finished metal goods that then transformed America: iron and steel rails for the nation's great railroads and giant structural beams used in all sorts of construction projects, as well as sewer, water, and gas pipes for municipal utilities. At the center of these great mills were the puddlers, men who heated batches of semi-processed material called pig iron with other materials in blast furnaces to create a molten mass of metal that later became wrought iron, an exceptionally strong and widely used type of metal. Puddlers created molten metal that was then sent to other workers, who produced iron, or muck, bar. Other workers called the puddlers "boilers." They called themselves the Sons of Vulcan, in reverence of the ancient Roman god of fire.

For a few decades between the 1860s and the 1890s, iron mills—huge industrial plants that produced wrought iron—dominated the landscape of many industrial areas in the East and Midwest. Towns in western Pennsylvania, Ohio, Indiana, and Illinois sprung up around those plants. The iron manufactories of Jones and Laughlin Company, later Jones and Laughlin Steel, were centered near along the Monongahela River outside of Pittsburgh, while the Lackawanna Iron and Coal Company was located near Scranton, in northeastern Pennsylvania. Before the adoption of the Bessemer converter—a mechanical way to process iron ore more efficiently to convert it into steel—the Jones and Laughlin Company simultaneously operated over a hundred iron furnaces. Demand for iron rails, pipe, beams, and armaments increased rapidly after 1840, though the market for iron products proved wildly erratic in these decades, while competition among companies for business was often ruthless. These market forces led businesses to consolidate their holdings in iron ore and coal fields; iron ore and coal (as coke, a processed form of coal) were the primary constituents of wrought iron. This vertical integration of the iron and steel industry was first realized by Andrew Carnegie's (1835–1919) many corporations, though other iron-producing companies also attempted to implement this innovation. Before iron furnaces converted to steel plants, some thirty thousand puddlers worked in American iron manufactories at any one time in the late 1870s and early 1880s.

During the nineteenth century, the process of producing iron from its constituent materials was difficult. The work of puddling required skill, knowledge of metallurgical processes (often gained on the job as apprentices or helpers), and strength. Each puddler controlled his own furnace, where the iron and coke were mixed, sometimes with other elements, depending on the quality of the iron ore. Most early puddling furnaces had sand bottoms. Working with a helper, the puddler consistently stirred the molten mass—called the charge—to create a pliable molten iron, free of most impurities, known as slag. Once each charge had been suitably processed, puddlers then extracted parts of the charge, known as balls, from the furnace. Each ball generally weighed 200 to 250 pounds. As a puddler extracted a ball, he had to continually manipulate it with rods and sets of tongs to keep it pliable. He then sent the balls to the rolling mills, where the hot mixture was run or rolled to create iron bars. Other workers, known as rollers and roughers, then reheated these iron bars, forcing them into mill machines that produced the finished iron product.

Essentially a refining process that generated great amounts of heat, noxious fumes, and smoke, puddling often created a poor working environment. Workers also had to contend with adverse weather, especially during the summer, when the heat outside the open-air manufacturing spaces amplified heat from the furnaces. In 1868, one journalist noted that conditions in the iron furnaces were so extreme that in the summer, puddlers had to remove their boots periodically during the workday to pour out the sweat that had accumulated in them. Two shifts, or stints, of puddlers and their helpers worked each furnace in most plants, with work ceasing in the early afternoons and then resuming in the evenings after the summer heat subsided.

Puddlers were highly skilled industrial workers who learned the craft on the job. There were no training facilities that provided instruction in the iron-refining process; for example, only through experience and knowledge of how iron behaved under heat did puddlers learn when a charge had matured, or come to nature, and was ready for extraction. Learning to manipulate a hefty set of tongs to extract the molten balls and avoid burns required practice. Puddlers were among those craftsmen who some historians refer to as the nineteenth-century "labor aristocracy," as workers themselves—not plant managers—set the pace of work. Puddlers also controlled the labor supply by controlling access to helper positions; before the 1880s, most puddlers were of English or Anglo American heritage, and many puddlers employed their own sons as their helpers. This way, access into the trade was controlled through family and ethnic ties. Iron foundries usually paid a group of workers—puddlers and their helpers, or rollers and roughers and their helpers—by a per-piece rate, which was based on a certain price per ton of iron bar produced. Until the 1880s, groups of men in each work unit collaboratively determined how those piece rates would be divided among all workers. Puddlers received the most generous distribution of the rate for each ton produced because all of the other foundry workers depended on them to produce high-quality materials; without the puddlers' work, other ironworkers would be unable to do their jobs. The role of the puddler, then, was largely as an internal subcontractor, not simply an employee. Puddlers and others in the work unit also disciplined their own and others' behavior on the job: they ostracized workers who drank too much, worked too fast, or performed the duties of a fellow worker in the unit.

The extraordinary autonomy that puddlers had over their working environment and conditions was reflected in their power outside of the workplace. Their unions, the Amalgamated Association of Iron and Steel Workers and the Sons of Vulcan, were extraordinarily successful in securing favorable contracts for workers, even after the severe economic depression of the 1870s. But their power began to wane late in the century as steel production increased markedly. The adoption of cost-cutting measures and innovative technologies led the steel industry to eclipse iron production by 1900.

Nancy Quam-Wickham

See also: *1915–1945:* Ironworker; Steelworker

FURTHER READING

Davis, James John. 1922. *The Iron Puddler. My Life in the Rolling Mills and What Came of It . . . Introduction by Joseph G. Cannon.* Indianapolis: Bobbs-Merrill Co.

Heron, Craig, and Charles Docherty. 1985. "Steel and Steelworkers: The Sons of Vulcan." *Labour/Le Travail* 16: 319.

Walker, Charles Rumford. 2012. *Steel: The Diary of a Furnace Worker.* Project Gutenberg.

PRIMARY DOCUMENT

In the following passage, James J. Davis relates his early experience as a helper to his father, who worked as an iron puddler in a rolling mill in Sharon, Pennsylvania. Although Davis apprenticed as a boy and would likely have assumed a position as a puddler had he stayed in the trade, he left the mills to pursue a career in politics and public service. In 1921, he became secretary of the Labor Department under President Warren G. Harding.

The rolling mill where father worked was Life's Big Circus tent to me, and like a kid escaped from school, eager to get past the tent flap and mingle with the clowns and elephants, I chucked my job sorting nails when I found an opening for a youngster in the rolling mill. Every puddler has a helper. Old men have both a helper and a boy. I got a place with an old man, and so at the age of twelve I was part of the Big Show whose performance is continuous, whose fire-eaters have real flame to contend with, and whose snake-charmers risk their lives in handling great hissing, twisting red-hot serpents of angry iron.

In this mill there is a constant din by day and night. Patches of white heat glare from the opened furnace doors like the teeth of some great dark, dingy devil grinning across the smoky vapors of the Pit. Half naked, soot-smeared fellows fight the furnace hearths with hooks, rabbles and paddles. Their scowling faces are lit with fire, like sailors manning their guns in a night fight when a blazing fire ship is bearing down upon them. The sweat runs down their backs and arms and glistens in the changing lights. Brilliant blues and rays of green and bronze come from the coruscating metal, molten yet crystallizing into white-hot frost within the furnace puddle. Flaming balls of woolly iron are pulled from the oven doors, flung on a two-wheeled serving tray, and rushed sputtering and flamboyant to the hungry mouth of a machine, which rolls them upon its tongue and squeezes them in its jaw like a cow mulling over her cud. The molten slag runs down red-hot from the jaws of this squeezer and makes a luminous rivulet on the floor like the water from the rubber rollers when a washer-woman wrings out the saturated clothes. Squeezed dry of its luminous lava, the white-hot sponge is drawn with tongs to the waiting rollers—whirling anvils that beat it into the shape they will. Everywhere are hurrying men, whirring flywheels, moving levers of steam engines and the drum-like roar of the rolling machines, while here and there the fruits of this toil are seen as three or four fiery serpents shoot forth from different trains of rollers, and are carried away, wrought iron fit for bridging the creek, shoeing the mule and hooping the barrel that brings the farmer's apples into town.

An iron puddler is a "pig boiler." The pig boiling must be done at a certain temperature (the pig is iron) . . . [T]he metal "pig boiler" ages ago learned by experience how to make the proper "heat" to boil the impurities out of pig-iron, or forge iron, and change it into that finer product, wrought iron. Pig-iron contains silicon, sulphur and phosphorus, and these impurities make it brittle so that a cast iron teakettle will break at a blow, like a china cup . . . So those early iron workers learned to puddle forge iron and make it into wrought iron which is tough and leathery and can not be broken by a blow. This process was handed down from father to son, and in the course of time came to my father and so to me. None of us ever went to school and learned the chemistry of it from books. We learned the trick by doing it, standing with our faces in the scorching heat while our hands puddled the metal in its glaring bath . . .

[T]he metallurgists have written down the chemical formula for puddling iron. But the man who learns it from a book can not do it. The mental knowledge is not enough; it requires great muscular skill like that of the heavyweight wrestler, besides great physical endurance to withstand the terrific heat. The worker's body is in perfect physical shape and the work does not injure him but only exhilarates him . . .

The old man that I worked with when I first entered the rolling mill was gray with his sixty years of toil. Yet his eye was clear and his back was straight and when he went to the table he ate like a sixteen-year-old and his sleep was dreamless. A man so old must conserve his strength, and he made use of his husky helper whenever he could to save his own muscles and lengthen his endurance. My business was to do the little chores and save time for the helper. I teased up the furnace, I leveled the fire, I dished the cinders in to thicken the heat, and I watched the cobbles. During the melting of the pig-iron the furnace had to be kept as hot as coal could make it . . .

When I became my father's helper he began teaching me to handle the machinery of the trade. The puddling furnace has a working door on a level with a man's stomach . . . [T]he working door of a puddling furnace is the door through which the puddler does his work. It is a porthole opening upon a sea of flame. The heat of these flames would wither a man's body, and so they are enclosed in a shell of steel. Through this working door I put in the charge of "pigs" that were to be boiled. These short pieces of "mill iron" had been smelted from iron ore; they had taken the first step on their journey from wild iron to civilized iron. There isn't much use for pig-iron in this world. You've got to be better iron than that. Pig-iron has no fiber; it breaks instead of bending. Build a bridge of it and a gale will break it and it will fall into the river . . .

Six hundred pounds was the weight of pig-iron we used to put into a single hearth. Much wider than the hearth was the fire grate, for we needed a heat that was intense. The flame was made by burning bituminous coal. Vigorously I stoked that fire for thirty minutes with dampers open and the draft roaring while that pig-iron melted down like ice-cream under an electric fan. You have seen a housewife sweating over her oven to get it hot enough to bake a batch of biscuits. Her face gets pink and a drop of sweat dampens her curls. Quite a horrid job she finds it. But I had iron biscuits to bake; my forge fire must be hot as a volcano. There were five bakings every day and this meant the shoveling in of nearly two tons of coal. In summer I was stripped to the waist and panting while the sweat poured down across my heaving muscles. My palms and fingers, scorched by the heat, became hardened like goat hoofs, while my skin took on a coat of tan that it will wear forever.

What time I was not stoking the fire, I was stirring the charge with a long iron rabble that weighed some twenty-five pounds. Strap an Oregon boot of that weight to your arm and then do calisthenics ten hours in a room so hot it melts your eyebrows and you will know what it is like to be a puddler. But we puddlers did not complain. There is men's work to be done in this world, and we were the men to do it. We had come into a country built of wood; we should change it to a country built of steel and stone.

Source: James J. Davis. 1922. *The Iron Puddler: My Life in the Rolling Mills and What Came of It.* Indianapolis: The Bobbs-Merrill Company, 85–99.

RAILROAD CONDUCTOR

Railroad conductors were in charge of all aspects of a passenger train's client interactions and mechanical operations. The railroads operated very much in a military fashion for most of their history, and the conductor was at the top of the train's chain of command. A conductor set the train's orders and saw that they were implemented. They were responsible for the safe and timely passage of the train's cargo and passengers and directed and checked the work of brakemen and porters. A conductor had authority even over a locomotive engineer—although an engineer, who commanded the locomotive car, might complain when a conductor exercised this control. Women were not allowed to be conductors, even though they labored in other industries.

Train conductors were either freight conductors, who focused on carrying cargo, or passenger conductors, who accommodated travelers. Every conductor had to be literate and have some aptitude with numbers to keep track of accounts and manage the train. Passenger conductors also had to be both courteous and authoritative with customers to please patrons and keep charge of the train. Conductors kept a small, makeshift office inside the caboose where they could process paperwork. Cabooses usually had a high seat with windows so that the conductor could attend to his record keeping and tallying and also oversee the train and its brakemen, who set and released the train's handbrakes.

Conductors were part of the running trades, which also included brakemen, engineers, and firemen; these workers were also called trainmen. Trainmen traveled between destinations, unlike railway shopmen and yardmen, who were stationed at one trainyard.

Conductors did not engage much in heavy manual labor in the way that other trainmen did, and they often took pride in their distance from manual labor and did not want to be associated with the dirty, hard work of other trainmen. They dressed in stately uniforms and wore top hats. In turn, engineers, firemen, and brakemen often considered conductors to be soft paper pushers and junior railroad officials. They did not see conductors as members of a manly working class that braved firsthand the dangers of railroad work and actually made the train's wheels turn.

Many conductors belonged to the Order of Railway Conductors (ORC), a union that sought to improve its members' lives through mutual aid and the cultivation of friendly relations with railroad companies. The railway brotherhoods represented men in the running trades during the industrial era. The engineers organized the Brotherhood of Locomotive Engineers, and the firemen organized the Brotherhood of Locomotive Firemen, for example. These unions were established in the 1860s and 1870s. The ORC was by far the most conservative of the railway brotherhoods. For much of its history, it refused to associate its members with strikes. Yet sometimes individual conductors, in times of crisis, joined in work stoppages with other railroaders. In the 1890s, a terrible economic depression brought wage cuts and a faster pace of labor despite the dangerous nature of most railroad occupations. This convinced the ORC to consider the use of strikes. However, the ORC was more often a no-strike organization. It rejected labor protest during the Great Strike of 1877, and in the Burlington Strike of 1888–1889, ORC members took the place of striking engineers. In the early twentieth century, after a series of violent and tumultuous railroad labor conflicts, railroad companies began to negotiate directly with railway brotherhoods—including the ORC—over wages, working conditions, and rules.

Like the other unions of skilled workers, the ORC wanted to protect its members from job competition with less-skilled and non-members. Conductors were also attracted to the ORC because members contributed to insurance programs that aided wives and children of conductors injured or killed on the job. With the ORC, conductors participated in rituals and ceremonies that recognized members for their competence and gave them a sense of belonging. ORC members were part of a secret world of men who identified strongly with their occupation and with whiteness.

Conductors were almost exclusively native-born white men whose ancestors had migrated to the United States several generations prior, and they enjoyed protection from competition with African Americans and immigrants; the ORC barred black railroad workers from promotion to the prestigious and commanding position of conductor. This was the case until the late 1960s and early 1970s. For over one hundred years, a black conductor was an absolute rarity; Henry Vanness

(1841–1926) of New Haven is perhaps the only example of a black conductor in the United States before World War I (1914–1918).

Almost all conductors and engineers were married. A conductor was paid well enough that he was the sole breadwinner for the household, while the wives of fireman and brakemen often had to work to make ends meet. Although conductors' wives stayed at home to raise the children, the family life of conductors was not entirely traditional due to conductors often being away from home on an irregular schedule. Wives of conductors—like wives of fishermen and sailors—tended to exercise greater independence, initiative, and authority within the home because the husband was absent.

Railway conductors lived at the top of the "labor aristocracy" in that they earned much better wages than many other workers. They also possessed status and authority, both at work and in their communities. Still, conductors struggled with some of the same issues as their fellow railroaders. Railroad companies were often hit hard by economic busts and unscrupulous business dealings and were always under pressure to deliver profits to stockholders.

Theresa Case

See also: Railroad Construction Worker; Railroad Station Agent

FURTHER READING

Arnesen, Eric. 2001. *Brotherhoods of Color: Black Railroad Workers and the Struggle for Equality*. Cambridge: Harvard University Press.

Case, Theresa A. 2010. *The Great Southwest Railroad Strike and Free Labor*. College Station: Texas A&M University Press.

Kornweibel, Theodore, Jr. 2010. *Railroads in the African American Experience: A Photographic Journey*. Baltimore: Johns Hopkins University Press.

Stowed, David O. 2008. *The Great Strikes of 1877*. Urbana: University of Illinois Press.

Taillon, Paul Michel, ed. 2009. *Good, Reliable, White Men: Railroad. Brotherhoods, 1877–1917*. Urbana: University of Illinois Press.

RAILROAD CONSTRUCTION WORKER

Nineteenth-century railroad construction workers were ordinary men—often immigrants from Europe and Asia as well as some native-born migrants—who swung hammers and laid rails to build the railroads. Railroads were one of the most profound and influential technologies of the nineteenth century because they actualized the triumph of American ingenuity over wilderness, distance, and time. Nothing better symbolized this march toward the future than the jubilant May 1869 Golden Spike celebration at Promontory Summit, Utah Territory, which marked the linking of the Union Pacific and Central Pacific railroads. When other transportation projects reified these dreams of progress, Americans interpreted them as the "blessings of liberty" writ large. But the railroad construction workers who built this revolutionary infrastructure were largely hidden from view; they left virtually no paper trail and lived on the economic fringes of society.

Despite leaving few records, however, historians do know the general outline of railroad workers' daily lives, drawn largely from the records of their employers. Early supporters of American railroad and canal projects praised a labor force of virtuous, American-born small farmers who worked overtime to build internal improvements during lulls in the agricultural cycle. But such part-time digging and track laying had everywhere proven woefully insufficient. To complete the transcontinental railroads, however, contractors needed a more permanent, dependent labor force that could be set apart. Those men who constructed the great transcontinental railroads in the mid-nineteenth century generally lived in company camps, which moved as the tracks were extended. Each morning, six or seven days a week, depending on the terrain and the season, men would begin their ten- to twelve-hour (or longer) workdays.

The work was typically heavy physical labor. On flat territory, some skilled mule drivers worked on grading crews to prepare the roadbed, while men with picks, shovels, and hand-drawn carts moved the earth. In the Sierra Nevada, where mountains had to have tunnels, gangs of Chinese immigrant laborers were sometimes lowered in baskets down the rock face to set the blast fuse. In these mountains, Chinese railroad workers labored in all weather, including blizzards that caused snow slides, burying construction operations. By 1866, most workers on the Central Pacific construction project earned thirty-five dollars a month; white workers received board as well, while the Chinese had to purchase their own food from company storehouses. When Chinese workers struck for shorter hours in June 1867, contractors made provisions to replace them with several thousand recently freed slaves from the South, though the strike failed quickly because corporations refused to provide food in the remote Sierras, essentially ensuring that the strike would end when strikers wanted to eat.

The history of railroad construction labor has unique ties not only to the worst types of "common" or unskilled wage labor but to the labor of enslaved peoples and convicts. It is linked, as well, to the nation's canal construction labor. Charles Dickens, writing to a U.S. audience in 1842, noted that without Irish immigrants, "It would be hard to keep your model republics going . . . for who else would dig, delve, and drudge . . . and make canals and railroads, and execute great lines of internal improvement" (Dickens 1842, 96). Progress—one of the most influential yet problematic bywords of the nineteenth century—demanded hard labor that was filthy, dangerous, painful, disease-ridden, unfair, degrading, and underpaid.

Workers moved earth but were also subject to its unrelenting forces. They were exposed to cycles of blistering hot and bone-chilling cold weather as they toiled in knee-deep muck, braved water-borne illnesses, chipped away at solid granite, and endured hard rock blasts and cave-ins. Workers also faced the constant pressure of their section bosses to finish the job—in an occupation where blunt force, rapidity, and technology didn't always harmonize. Railroads were praised as a novel technology that would annihilate the space and civilize the wilderness of the West, but they too often annihilated the men building them instead. Nevertheless, thanks to another source of hard work, the narratives crafted by canal and railroad promoters, politicians, and historians, the brutal labor of transportation workers came to seem natural, inevitable, and strangely bloodless.

A menial occupation in this period contributed directly to a person's social dislocation. Wielding pickaxes and shovels to clear swamps, dig ditches, move rocks, and build roadways thus came to be seen as the work of the desperate "laboring poor," not of free and independent American men. Early canals and railroads relied almost exclusively on slave labor, and several states sanctioned convict labor to haul stones and perform grading work. Race and labor put the newest of nineteenth-century immigrants, the Irish, in a double bind, and for most of the century, they reacted with hostility to narratives comparing them to African Americans—slave and free. "The poor Irishman," wrote Ralph Waldo Emerson, "the wheelbarrow is his country" (Dearinger 2016, 34). The editor of the *Boston Pilot*, which was the official newspaper of that city's Archdiocese, implored the Irish to avoid the exploitative nature of canals and railroad work, stating that it was "the ruin of thousands of our poor people," who were treated "like slaves" on "massive transportation projects" (Duff 1971, 19). Their work was the filth of progress. Immigrants and outcasts increased America's canal mileage from around 100 in 1810 to over 3,500 by 1840 and were equally responsible for the dramatic growth in railroad track from 10,000 miles in 1850 to over 165,000 miles by 1890.

The ongoing search for able-bodied men who could move earth and build transportation networks flung American capitalists all over North America and overseas. America needed workers willing to relocate to the periphery of the nineteenth-century industrial world, to unforgiving western railroad frontiers. Company officials from Maryland to Illinois and from Iowa to California complained endlessly about a deficiency of hands while also noting that they were deluged with applicants for highly coveted positions of engineers, machinists, conductors, telegraph operators, and clerks. Dishonest milk-and-honey stories were thus crafted to lure immigrant construction workers, and companies everywhere sought to inflate the labor pool, thereby driving down wages. Contractors, the quintessential middlemen, routinely violated company policies when it came to wages, provisions, and boarding. Railroad workers could make as much as forty dollars per month, but many were paid in scrip, a kind of currency that was only valid at stores and establishments owned or operated by the company that issued it.

Workers devised many ways to combat the harsh realities of railroad capitalism. They created firsthand information networks to identify and then boycott the worst bosses along the line, petitioned state and private commissioners, struck for improved wages and conditions, destroyed work for which they had not been paid, used violence and intimidation to stack work crews with familiar faces, and rigged the selection of new section bosses who were more amenable to their plight. Uninvited immigrant workers were even known to physically disrupt celebrations of projects that only their backbreaking labor had made possible.

With the hiring of Chinese immigrants in the 1860s and 1870s, capitalist innovations in race management unfolded in processes linked ever more directly to settler colonial expansion and the growth of empire. The political economy of the West and the nation was forever transformed by the pitting of Irish (the UPRR employed around eight thousand Irish, German, and Italian immigrants) and Chinese (the CPRR employed well over ten thousand) workers against each other in the great "race" to build the transcontinental railroad. Mormons, yet another outcast group seen as neither white nor American in the late nineteenth century, were absolutely crucial to the joining of the Union Pacific and Central Pacific in 1869, performing grading and tracklaying work in the formidable Wasatch Mountains. These groups, each of whom were held in some degree of contempt by free and white (native-born) Americans, greased the skids of progress with their sweat and blood. They did it, as well, without union representation for most of the century.

Still, railroad construction workers continued—against inconceivable odds—to demonstrate their worth to the grand American empire-building project, often reminding their employers of the dangers of distancing and dehumanizing a labor force. In 1867, when hundreds of the CPRR's Chinese workers, most of them playing up employment offers from local mining companies, threw down their picks and shovels and struck for higher wages and ten-hour days in the Sierra Nevada, Central Pacific officials panicked. The CPRR was ultimately able to squash the strike with threats of violence and a stoppage of food deliveries to the camps. More extreme measures were occasionally taken by workers, such as in the days leading up to the May 10, 1869, Golden Spike ceremony, when a group of Irish tracklayers near Piedmont, Wyoming, kidnapped Dr. Thomas Durant, vice president of the Union Pacific Railroad, over back wages.

Once the final railroad spikes were driven, transient and immigrant construction workers collected whatever remained of their meager pay and took their skills elsewhere, often to other transportation frontiers, where they continued to transform the nation's landscape, build progress, usher in civilization, and fill in seemingly empty spaces on the national map. Regrettably, the popular writers, artists, and statesmen who performed the important work of celebrating progress contested and rewrote history, distancing perceived outsiders from the fruits of their labor and from any scrap of credit or dignity.

Ryan Dearinger

See also: *1776–1860:* Laborer; Railroad Station Agent

FURTHER READING

Bain, David Haward. 2000. *Empire Express: Building the First Transcontinental Railroad.* New York: Penguin.

Dearinger, Ryan. 2016. *The Filth of Progress: Immigrants, Americans, and the Building of Canals and Railroads in the West.* Berkeley: University of California Press.

Dickens, Charles. 1842. *American Notes for General Circulation, Volume 1.* Leipzig: Bernard Tauchnitz.

Duff, John B. 1971. *The Irish in the United States.* Boston: Wadsworth Publishing Company.

Fiege, Mark. 2012. *The Republic of Nature: An Environmental History of the United States.* Seattle: University of Washington Press.

Way, Peter. 1993. *Common Labour: Workers and the Digging of North American Canals, 1780–1860.* New York: Cambridge University Press.

White, Richard. 2012. *Railroaded: The Transcontinentals and the Making of Modern America.* New York: W. W. Norton.

RAILROAD STATION AGENT

Railroad station agents worked in railroad waystations—or small stopping points—along railroad routes, and they provided transport information and sold tickets to passengers, carried their luggage (as well as moved freight), dispatched trains and kept records of arrivals and departures, and maintained the station itself. At some stations, agents also operated telegraph communication devices, hired cooks to staff cafés, and arranged for travelers' comfort.

The railroad industry began in the nineteenth century, and by 1900, American railway stations numbered in the thousands. In larger cities, depots were often immense structures built of stone or brick, sometimes designed by America's most prominent architects; even Ottumwa, Iowa, had a substantial depot designed by the noted architectural firm of [John] Burnham and [Daniel] Root of Chicago. The size of a station determined the many responsibilities of depot clerks. Ottumwa's station, opened in 1887, had the usual ticket office and baggage room of most stations but also separate waiting rooms for men and women, an express room, toilets and washrooms, laundry, lunch counter, dining room, and a full kitchen and bakery; the station was operated by the Chicago, Burlington and Quincy Railroad

Company. As only a few railway companies offered transcontinental service, the fractured nature of rail companies led to different station sizes and operating rules. About thirty miles north of New York City, for instance, the Hawthorne station on the New York Central Railway was a small but beautifully designed stone building with just four rooms, only one of which passengers could access—a single waiting room; the others were the office, baggage room, and a small room that housed the station's heater. All across the country, stations varied in their structure, size, and company ownership, but all station workers had critical responsibilities.

Station agents were the face of the railroad company, which required them to be fluent with the Rail Rulebooks, a set of corporate regulations and requirements for employee behavior to which every rail company demanded its employees adhere. Station agents were also customer-facing, so they were required to be polite and courteous, serious, and efficient. All railway companies had personal behavior regulations prohibiting drinking alcohol, gambling, and smoking or using tobacco on the job. Railway companies required station employees to wear their uniforms. For men, this meant pants, button-down long-sleeved shirt, tie, suspenders or belt, a badge, and a visor or cap. Station agents also had to understand safety regulations to ensure safe operations of the station: keep passengers at a safe distance from the tracks, ensure that water and coal were available for engines stopping to refuel, and assess freight (for weight, prohibited items, and tracking information), as well as to collect charges for freight and forward that revenue to the central rail offices.

At large stations, the stationmaster supervised many agents, porters, signalmen, and other workers who kept the operations flowing smoothly. At a small one- or two-room station, the agent sold tickets, worked as the porter handling baggage and freight, kept the station's stove heater going, chopped wood and carried water, and operated the telegraph machine (Richards 1986, 232). In many stations, the agent had to supervise the switching of trains from one set of tracks to another and then make a record of that track switch.

By the end of the 1880s, most U.S. railway companies had published extensive rule books that outlined workers' duties and behavior. Any employee caught violating these rules and regulations were issued demerits, which most railway employees colloquially called "Brownies," after George Brown, the originator of one of the first Book of Rules (of the Fall Brook Railway company). An employee who received too many demerits was dismissed. Large stations as well as railyards also employed railroad policemen, known as bulls by the 1910s, who kept drifters, hobos, and other unauthorized passengers off the trains.

Railroad transportation involved thousands of trains operating on nearly 200,000 miles of track by 1900; station agents thus filled out a mountain of paperwork each day. Trains were—and still are—powerful pieces of equipment that are heavy and difficult to stop quickly. To keep the trains running smoothly, station agents had to fill out multiple forms each day, especially after the 1880s, when companies began to run their trains on foreign roads—the tracks of other rail companies. To manage the train traffic, station agents had to keep track of train operations: origins and destinations of trains, freight carried and weight, and other information communicated down the lines to other stations. An early study of station paperwork noted that agents had to file the following daily reports:

> A train book, showing initials and number of cars received and forwarded in trains, together with the impression of seals attached to cars; a daily yard check, showing the car situation in the yard each day of the year; a general record of cars received, forwarded and remaining on hand; records of cars ordered by shippers; daily (telegraphic) report of cars loaded, loading, unloading, empty, wanted to load, etc.; special report of "foreign cars . . . ." on hand; special report of bad-order cars; daily reports of cars received and forwarded; daily reports of cars interchanged; special reports . . . as may be required by officials; various incidental and special reports made, mostly by wire, to the dispatcher. (Burt 1911, 93–94)

Station agents also had to report on accidents, usually just brief two- or three-sentence reports detailing a grisly scene. Accidents in which workers or pedestrians were seriously injured, maimed, or killed by trains were incredibly common. The Report of Accidents of the New Jersey Railroad and Transportation Company, which operated trains running along a sixty-mile section of track between Jersey City and Trenton, is instructive. In 1869, for example, it had no fewer than thirty-five reports of accidents—mostly detailing fatal ones in which pedestrians, many of them deaf or apparently intoxicated, were run over by trains, sometimes just outside of the company's stations. In a particularly tragic accident near Plainsboro, a five-year-old boy stepped off the tracks to let a train pass but, in doing so, stepped onto the tracks in front of a train bound in the other direction.

The station agent was an essential occupation in industrializing America. Train transportation allowed manufacturers and farmers to get their products to market. Passengers rode trains to commute to their jobs in the city, as well as to reach vacation destinations (often part of a railway company's package tours). Station agents can be compared to the cogs in a complicated system as, without their labor, the systems would have collapsed.

Nancy Quam-Wickham

See also: Railroad Conductor; Railroad Construction Worker; *1776–1860:* Wharfinger

FURTHER READING

Alexander, Edwin P. 1970. *Down at the Depot: American Railway Stations from 1831 to 1920.* New York: Clarkson N. Potter.
Burt, Benjamin Chapman. 1911. *The Railway Station Service.* United Kingdom: Stanhope Press.
Grand Rapids and Indiana Railway. 1910. *Book of Rules.* Grand Rapids: The Company.
Richards, Jeffrey, and John M. MacKenzie. 1986. *The Railway Station: A Social History.* London: Oxford.

PRIMARY DOCUMENT

In this document, author Bret Harte describes the lonely life that a typical rural stationmaster likely had. As is characteristic with much of Harte's work, he provides a twist to the story at the end of this poem.

The Station-Master of the Lone Prairie

An empty bench, a sky of grayest etching,
A bare, bleak shed in blackest silhouette,
Twelve years of platform, and before them stretching
Twelve miles of prairie glimmering through the wet.

North, south, east, west,—the same dull gray persistence,
The tattered vapors of a vanished train,
The narrowing rails that meet to pierce the distance,
Or break the columns of the far-off rain.

Naught but myself; nor form nor figure breaking
The long hushed level and stark shining waste;
Nothing that moves to fill the vision aching,
When the last shadow fled in sullen haste.

Nothing beyond. Ah yes! From out the station
A stiff, gaunt figure thrown against the sky,
Beckoning me with some wooden salutation
Caught from his signals as the train flashed by;

Yielding me place beside him with dumb gesture
Born of that reticence of sky and air.
We sit apart, yet wrapped in that one vesture
Of silence, sadness, and unspoken care:

Each following his own thought,—around us darkening
The rain-washed boundaries and stretching track,—
Each following those dim parallels and hearkening
For long-lost voices that will not come back.

Until, unasked,—I knew not why or wherefore,—
He yielded, bit by bit, his dreary past,
Like gathered clouds that seemed to thicken there for
Some dull down-dropping of their care at last.

Long had he lived there. As a boy had started
From the stacked corn the Indian's painted face;
Heard the wolves' howl the wearying waste that parted
His father's hut from the last camping-place.

Nature had mocked him: thrice had claimed the reaping,
With scythe of fire, of lands she once had sown;
Sent the tornado, round his hearthstone heaping
Rafters, dead faces that were like his own.

Then came the War Time. When its shadow beckoned
He had walked dumbly where the flag had led
Through swamp and fen,—unknown, unpraised, unreckoned,—To famine, fever,
and a prison bed.

Till the storm passed, and the slow tide returning
Cast him, a wreck, beneath his native sky;
Here, at his watch, gave him the chance of earning
Scant means to live—who won the right to die.

All this I heard—or seemed to hear—half blending
With the low murmur of the coming breeze,
The call of some lost bird, and the unending
And tireless sobbing of those grassy seas.

Until at last the spell of desolation
Broke with a trembling star and far-off cry.
The coming train! I glanced around the station,
All was as empty as the upper sky!

Naught but myself; nor form nor figure waking
The long hushed level and stark shining waste;

Naught but myself, that cry, and the dull shaking
Of wheel and axle, stopped in breathless haste!

"Now, then—look sharp! Eh, what? The Station-Master?
THAR'S NONE! We stopped here of our own accord.
The man got killed in that down-train disaster
This time last evening. Right there! All aboard!"

Source: Bret Harte. 1896. *The Writings of Bret Harte: Poems and Two Men of Sandy Bar*. Boston: Houghton, Mifflin and Company, 261–263.

SEAMSTRESS

Seamstresses and tailors make a living by making or repairing clothing. Seamstresses and tailors perform the same work, but only women were referred to as seamstresses. In the nineteenth century, seamstresses and tailors were considered part of the "needle trades," which included vocations directly involved with clothing production.

Like most work, the needle trades experienced vast changes in the daily tasks of workers during America's industrial development. While early factories in New England and elsewhere began to produce boots, shoes, and textiles on an industrial basis during the early nineteenth century, most Americans in 1850 still lived on farms, in rural areas, and in small towns, and most wore clothing made at home by mothers, wives, sisters, and daughters, though men's ready-made clothing had appeared. In the nation's largest cities, ready-made clothing become popular, with New York the center of the industry; later, retail firms such as Hart, Schaffner and Marx in Chicago also grew remarkably in the period after the Civil War.

Many factors contributed to the industrialization of garment making. The industry standardized clothing sizes, making the work of individual dressmakers and tailors, who measured, made, and fitted clothing to the buyer's body, largely obsolete, except for those in the luxury bespoke shops and who sewed for family members at home. Some manufacturers adopted economies of scale, specializing in one or two types of ready-made clothing, such as the San Francisco firm of Levi Strauss, which exclusively made denim pants; Strauss and his partner, Jacob Davis, patented the use of copper rivets to reinforce the pants, called blue jeans, at key seams. Other garment manufacturing firms set fashion trends, particularly for men's suits, by dominating the import of fine wool fabric as well as cheaper cotton-wool blends from Europe, while others used extensive credit and capital networks to establish companies that sold ready-made men's clothing at wholesale prices to distributors and retailers across the continent. The greatest innovations, however, were in labor: the development of subcontracting and piecework pay scales.

In the nineteenth century, seamstresses and tailors often worked long hours for little pay. Their workday would often begin near dawn and continue until the evening. Workers might get one short break for a meal in the middle of their shift, but they were almost always paid by quantity of the work that they produced, so their breaks were usually brief—if they occurred at all. Seamstresses in particular often lived in dormitories that were near—or sometimes attached to—the shops in which they worked.

By the 1870s and 1880s, the typical American seamstress worked for a subcontractor: labor agents who specialized in the completion of one or two tasks in the entire process of making clothing. These labor agents subcontracted with manufacturers for delivery of the products; subcontractors then picked up the partly finished garments and distributed them to the seamstresses who worked for them. Seamstresses had mostly learned to sew at home. The work that they completed was determined by the subcontractor. Some seamstresses worked in subcontractor's shops, on the new sewing machines introduced in the 1850s, while others took the garments home and had children help them with the assigned task using thread and needles by hand, though this was less common after the Progressive era, when reformers helped to pass legislation banning child labor and home manufacturing. Some seamstresses worked for clothing manufacturers directly, though, like others bound in the subcontracting system, they might work on only one task—such as basting the belt lining inside of men's trousers—while others attached leg pieces together, sewed pockets in, or hemmed the finished garment.

The method of making a pair of trousers was essentially the same as it had been earlier: pieces of fabric were sewed together to make a garment, but rather than one worker completing the entire garment, now a dozen or more workers might have a hand in its construction. During this time, seamstresses also worked for steam laundries, repairing garments and other cloth goods. Many seamstresses worked simultaneously at several jobs: operating a sewing machine in a garment factory, taking jobs from subcontractors to work at home during the evenings and Sabbath, and advertising their services directly to customers, especially men, who needed clothing repaired.

On the other hand, tailors earned considerably more than women seamstresses, yet their work processes also underwent major transformations during this period. But as men, they generally had more access to capital than women merchants and dressmakers; even by the 1830s, the distinctions between the tailor of old, who measured, cut, made, and fitted men's clothing (suits, coats, vests, and shirts), and clothier grew narrower. As historian Michael Zakim has shown, the clothier was more often a businessowner who "still personally measured for a specific customer" but also contracted with others (journeymen tailors) to make the garment and then sold it to the customer. The clothier was, in Zakim's words, simply a "middleman" (Zakim, 73). The work of creating men's clothing was still the work of a tailor, but like seamstresses, their work process was also subdivided into discrete tasks, particularly cutting and marking. By the 1880s and 1890s, most tailors worked either as cutters and markers—using power shears to cut fabric into the constituent parts of garments or marking the pieces for assembly by others—or as subcontractors, operating their own small workshops of a dozen or more seamstresses and sewers or "putting out" pieces for assembly to other shops or those working from home. Some tailors worked as pressers, operating the steam irons that pressed finished garments. Wholesale clothing houses continually cut piece rates; tailors had no choice but to accept lower rates and thus pressed their subcontracted workers for higher production to compensate. Tailors also participated in the domestic or putting-out system, employing their families and relatives.

The movement to the United States of thousands of immigrants who had experience as tailors and seamstresses, particularly Italians like Carmen Messina or Eastern European Jews, sustained this highly exploitative labor system. Ethnic divisions between these new immigrants and others, too, drove competition and kept payments low. A long history of segregation and discrimination against Jews in Europe had created a demand for tailors in Jewish communities as the guild system prohibited Jews from pursuing most trades. European Jews, though, dominated the "rag picking" trade: the collection and repair of used clothing for resale. Tailors were thus essential workers in these segregated communities, and when Jews immigrated to America, they put their experience to work. Strikes by seamstresses and tailors against manufacturers were common by 1900, but manufacturers responded by moving their production to inside shops within the factory walls, where managers could more easily speed up production rates and enforce worker discipline. Early attempts to establish worker organizations were largely unsuccessful until industry-specific unions of workers, often first organized along ethnic and occupational lines, united in the 1910s. Chicago's Hebrew Trades Council, Italian locals of the United Garment Workers, and women's locals within the International Ladies' Garment Workers Union (ILGWU) overcame traditional divisions to organize effectively, now that most seamstresses and tailors were effectively just machine operators in garment-making factories.

Nancy Quam-Wickham

See also: Haberdasher; *1607–1775:* Weaver and Spinner; *1915–1945:* Garment Worker; *1946–1991:* Fashion Designer and Model

FURTHER READING

Edelstein, T. J. 1980. "They Sang 'The Song of the Shirt': The Visual Iconology of the Seamstress." *Victorian Studies* 23, no. 2: 183–210.

Ferrari, Mary. 2005. "'Obliged to Earn Subsistence for Themselves': Women Artisans in Charleston, South Carolina, 1763–1808." *The South Carolina Historical Magazine* 106, no. 4: 235–255.

Zakim, Michael. 1999. "A Ready-Made Business: The Birth of the Clothing Industry in America." *Business History Review* 73: 61–90.

SHARECROPPER

Sharecroppers were tenant farmers who gave part of their crop as rent and whose work and lives revolved around the seasons. The nature of a sharecropper's day depended on his location, the crop he was presently growing, and the expectations of the landowner on whose land he was working. Whether it was winter, spring, summer, or fall, sharecroppers worked long hours for little pay.

Most sharecroppers lived in the southern United States. Sharecropping developed in the years following the Civil War (1861–1865) as a way of replacing the slave labor that southern planters had exploited to grow cotton and tobacco. Sharecropping was a form of tenancy in which sharecroppers worked all year for a landlord in exchange for a place to live and a percentage (or share) of the crop. Most sharecroppers worked for half of their crop. In the years immediately following the abolition of slavery in 1865, most sharecroppers were African Americans, but by the early twentieth century, when the sharecropper population reached its peak, the numbers of white and black sharecroppers were nearly even.

Sharecroppers often worked as families. Fathers, mothers, and children worked side by side in the fields. Most grew cotton, but many grew tobacco. On cotton farms, sharecroppers usually grew forty to eighty acres; on tobacco farms, the acreage was often much less because tobacco was a difficult and time-consuming crop to cultivate, harvest, and process.

The demands of the agricultural calendar shaped sharecroppers' lives. On January 1, they signed contracts for the coming year. Winter weather usually delayed crop planting until March or April, but a sharecropper might spend January and February fixing fences, clearing ditches, preparing new fields, chopping firewood, or doing other work around the farm. On tobacco farms, sharecroppers had the extra task of clearing ground for seedbeds for the small tobacco seeds.

Early spring brought plowing time. Sharecroppers hitched a plow to a mule or team of mules and broke ground for planting all day. Planting followed plowing. On cotton farms, this meant planting seeds in the freshly plowed fields. Tobacco sharecroppers transplanted seedlings from the seedbeds to the fields.

Once the planting was complete, sharecroppers spent the late spring and early summer weeding their fields, using hoes to chop up weeds that could harm or stunt their crops. This meant long days in the hot sun for adults and children alike. As the plants grew, they shaded the ground enough to bring weeding to an end. Cotton sharecroppers called this the "lay by" period, but on tobacco farms, the work continued. Sharecroppers still had to remove insects from the leaves by hand and do other tasks to cultivate the leaves of the plants.

In early summer, sharecroppers also turned their attention to growing corn. They grew it primarily for home consumption, but most also owed the landowner half of the corn crop. Some sharecroppers also grew gardens, but not all landowners allowed them to use the land this way. Sharecroppers might also own a few chickens or pigs, but most did not.

August through October was harvest time for both cotton and tobacco sharecroppers. This was the hardest part of the year. On tobacco farms, they worked long hours harvesting individual leaves from the tobacco plants as they ripened. This required them to bend over for hours on end. Because the leaves did not ripen all at once, they would have to go over the same fields multiple times. They then dried the leaves in a process called curing. Women and girls tied groups of leaves together, while young men carried these bunches high into the curing barns. Entire families might spend the night around the barn to make sure the fires used to cure the leaves did not burn out or set the barns on fire. Once the leaves finished curing, sharecroppers and their families spent several days sorting the leaves based on their quality to prepare them for market.

Cotton harvesting involved fewer steps but was equally strenuous. Sharecroppers tied long sacks around their shoulders and pulled the ripe bunches of cotton, called bolls, from the plant by hand. Because the bolls were surrounded by sharp spikes, the work was often painful. They filled the sacks with cotton as they walked down the rows. A full cotton sack could weigh as much as 150 pounds. Men, women, and children all picked cotton. Many times, sharecroppers picked cotton not only on the land they rented but also on the landowner's other properties.

Most sharecroppers handed over control of the crop to the landowner once it was picked. Some tobacco sharecroppers might sell the crop themselves, but most landowners preferred to control the sale. This left sharecroppers at the mercy of the landowner to determine how much they might get paid. It was not uncommon for sharecroppers to earn almost nothing for their year's work. Since landowners often provided food and other goods on credit during the year, some sharecroppers ended the year in debt despite their hard labor.

By the 1950s, new tools like mechanized cotton harvesters and chemical weed killers had begun to do the work sharecroppers had once done. Landowners increasingly hired former sharecroppers as wage workers to run the machines.

Other sharecroppers, unable to find work around the farms, moved to cities to find work in factories or other jobs. By the 1960s, postwar industrialized farming continued to flourish, and there were very few sharecroppers left.

Evan P. Bennett

See also: *1776–1860:* Field Hand; Planter; *1915–1945:* Farmworker

FURTHER READING

Asch, Chris Myers. 2008. "'No One Can Honestly Say Negroes Are Satisfied': The Sharecropper Embraces the Movement." In *The Senator and the Sharecropper: The Freedom Struggles of James O. Eastland and Fannie Lou Hamer*, 167–197. Chapel Hill: University of North Carolina Press.

Braverman, Avishay, and Joseph E. Stiglitz. 1982. "Sharecropping and the Interlinking of Agrarian Markets." *The American Economic Review* 72, no. 4 (September): 695–715.

Volanto, Keith J. 1996. "Leaving the Land: Tenant and Sharecropper Displacement in Texas During the New Deal." *Social Science History* 20, no. 4: 533–51.

PRIMARY DOCUMENT

This 1882 contract stipulates the laborer-landowner relationship of a sharecropper. Note that the sharecropper not only had to provide a "share" of the crop to the landowner but also had to improve the land he "cropped" and provide other goods to the owner.

To every one applying to rent land upon shares, the following conditions must be read, and agreed to. To every 30 and 35 acres, I agree to furnish the team, plow, and farming implements, except cotton planters, and I do not agree to furnish a cart to every cropper. The croppers are to have half of the cotton, corn, and fodder (and peas and pumpkins and potatoes if any are planted) if the following conditions are complied with, but-if not-they are to have only two-fifths (2/5). Croppers are to have no part or interest in the cotton seed raised from the crop planted and worked by them. No vine crops of any description, that is, no watermelons, muskmelons . . . squashes or anything of that kind, except peas and pumpkins, and potatoes, are to be planted in the cotton or corn. All must work under my direction. All plantation work to be done by the croppers. My part of the crop to be housed by them, and the fodder and oats to be hauled and put in the house. All the cotton must be topped about 1st August. If any cropper fails from any cause to save all the fodder from his crop, I am to have enough fodder to make it equal to one-half of the whole if the whole amount of fodder had been saved.

For every mule or horse furnished by me there must be 1000 good sized rails . . . hauled, and the fence repaired as far as they will go, the fence to be torn down and put up from the bottom if I so direct. All croppers to haul rails and work on fence whenever I may order. Rails to be split when I may say. Each cropper to clean out every ditch in his crop, and where a ditch runs between two croppers, the cleaning out of that ditch is to be divided equally between them. Every ditch bank in the crop must be shrubbed down and cleaned off before the crop is planted and must be cut down every time the land is worked with his hoe and when the crop is "laid by," the ditch banks must be left clean of bushes, weeds, and seeds. The cleaning out of all ditches must be done by the first of October. The rails must be split and the fence repaired before corn is planted.

Each cropper must keep in good repair all bridges in his crop or over ditches that he has to clean out and when a bridge needs repairing that is outside of all their crops, then any one that I call on must repair it.

Fence jams to be done as ditch banks. If any cotton is planted on the land outside of the plantation fence, I am to have three-fourths of all the cotton made in those patches, that is to say, no cotton must be planted by croppers in their home patches.

All croppers must clean out stable and fill them with straw, and haul straw in front of stable whenever I direct. All the cotton must be manured, and enough fertilizer must be brought to manure each crop highly, the croppers to pay for one-half of all manure bought, the quantity to be purchased for each crop must be left to me.

No cropper is to work off the plantation when there is any work to be done on the land he has rented, or when his work is needed by me or other croppers. Trees to be cut down on Orchard, house field, & Evanson fences, leaving such as I may designate.

Road field is to be planted from the very edge of the ditch to the fence, and all the land to be planted close up to the ditches and fences. No stock of any kind belonging to croppers to run in the plantation after crops are gathered.

If the fence should be blown down, or if trees should fall on the fence outside of the land planted by any of the croppers, any one or all that I may call upon must put it up and repair it.

Every cropper must feed or have fed, the team he works, Saturday nights, Sundays, and every morning before going to work, beginning to feed his team (morning, noon, and night every day in the week) on the day he rents and feeding it to including the 31st day of December. If any cropper shall from any cause fail to repair his fence as far as 1000 rails will go, or shall fail to clean out any part of his ditches, or shall fail to leave his ditch banks, any part of them, well shrubbed and clean when his crop is laid by, or shall fail to clean out stables, fill them up and haul straw in front of them whenever he is told, he shall have only two-fifths (2/5) of the cotton, corn, fodder, peas, and pumpkins made on the land he cultivates.

If any cropper shall fail to feed his team Saturday nights, all day Sunday and all the rest of the week, morning/noon, and night, for every time he so fails he must pay me five cents.

No corn or cotton stalks must be burned, but must be cut down, cut up and plowed in. Nothing must be burned off the land except when it is impossible to plow it in.

Every cropper must be responsible for all gear and farming implements placed in his hands, and if not returned must be paid for unless it is worn out by use.

Croppers must sow & plow in oats and haul them to the crib, but must have no part of them. Nothing to be sold from their crops, nor fodder nor corn to be carried out of the fields until my rent is all paid, and all amounts they owe me and for which I am responsible are paid in full.

I am to gin & pack all the cotton and charge every cropper an eighteenth of his part, the cropper to furnish his part of the bagging, ties, & twine.

The sale of every cropper's part of the cotton to be made by me when and where I choose to sell, and after deducting all they owe me and all sums that I may be responsible for on their accounts, to pay them their half of the net proceeds. Work of every description, particularly the work on fences and ditches, to be done to my satisfaction, and must be done over until I am satisfied that it is done as it should be.

No wood to burn, nor light wood, nor poles, nor timber for boards, nor wood for any purpose whatever must be gotten above the house occupied by Henry Beasley—nor must any trees be cut down nor any wood used for any purpose, except for firewood, without my permission.

Source: Grimes Family Papers (#3357). 1882. Southern Historical Collection, The Louis Round Wilson Special Collections Library. Chapel Hill: University of North Carolina.

SOLDIER

Over three million soldiers served in the American Civil War, which began in April of 1861 and ended in May of 1865. A little over two million of these soldiers fought for the Union Army in the North, and around one million served the Confederate Army in the South. Regardless of whether a person fought for the North or the South, the lives, duties, and routines of the Civil War's common soldier were largely similar, dangerous, and difficult.

The average solider in the American Civil War was slim, a little over five and a half feet tall, brown-haired, blue-eyed, white, probably Christian, and most likely worked as a farmer before the fighting began. About two-thirds of the soldiers were under twenty-one when they joined an army, and fewer than 10 percent of soldiers were over the age of thirty ("Who Fought?"). Much older men certainly participated in the conflict, though they often served as officers. Those deemed too young for traditional infantry roles were either tasked to be musicians or lied about their age in order to make their way into combat. Nearly all of the soldiers were men—though a small number of women disguised themselves as men and joined the fight.

It is difficult to determine just how many soldiers died as a result of the conflict, but some scholars think the number could be higher than 900,000. Far more records from the Union side of the conflict survived the war, and from those we can determine that only about 200,000 Union soldiers succumbed to wounds inflicted on the battlefield. About 60,000 soldiers died in prison after being captured by either the Union or the Confederate Armies. Almost 300,000 soldiers were wounded but survived. Perhaps most shockingly, it is likely that more than 500,000 deaths were caused by accident, disease, or malnutrition—not bullets, bombs, or mortars ("Civil War Facts").

Disease ran rampant through encampments, killing hundreds of people every day. Common diseases included whooping cough, measles, mumps, malaria, typhoid fever, tuberculosis, smallpox and chicken pox, malaria, pneumonia, and scarlet fever. These diseases are serious threats even with today's modern medicine; on the battlefield, they were more often more dangerous than the opposing army.

Civil War camps were large, cramped, and muddy. Sanitation was not very well understood at the time, and so camps quickly became disgusting. Almost everyone had to deal with lice and rotting clothes. Dysentery, which is usually caused by drinking water that has been contaminated by sewage, killed more men than were killed by bullets. Nearly everybody was sick with some illness or was recovering from sickness.

Life in camp was stressful and structured. If a soldier was still able to walk, then he was expected to participate in drills throughout the entire day. A typical schedule might be: wake up; eat; drill; inspect and clean equipment; drill; contribute to the camp by hauling firewood, digging trenches or wells, or building structures; drill again; eat; drill yet again; sleep. This routine would continue daily for weeks or months on end until the army would need to move or fight. Some battles would last for days or weeks, but most were over within a few hours. And then the same routine of drills and waiting would begin again. For this, the average white Union soldier earned thirteen dollars a month; African American soldiers earned about half of that. Common soldiers in the Confederate Army were supposed to earn eleven dollars a month, but most went months without any payment at all.

When the fighting would eventually start, the battlefield would be incredibly loud, smoky, and disorienting. While some of the Civil War's most famous battles were fought on a wide-open battlefield, nearly all of the smaller fights and skirmishes took place in forests, in swamps, across valleys, or on other difficult terrain. Communication was difficult, and orders to maneuver or attack or retreat were often given by blasts from a whistle or a trumpet. Most hostilities occurred at distances shorter than one hundred yards. Soldiers, in many cases, were encouraged to wound their enemies rather than kill them outright if at all possible—the thought being that a wounded soldier, screaming in the middle of a confusing battlefield, might cause some of his comrades to lose focus and try to find and help him, and if that happened, then the shooter might be able to wound or kill several other enemies. Also, because the terrain was often so difficult, an injured soldier might require help from two or three healthy men to be removed from the battlefield, and because the risk of and danger from infection was so high, the injured soldier would probably die anyway. Both sides of the conflict used these tactics, and both armies' soldiers suffered equally as a result.

Some Civil War soldiers were killed on the battlefield within their first days of warfare, while others suffered no harm after many years of army service. Others might be drafted and then released a few months after training, only to be called up for a few months' duty, time after time. Some soldiers on both sides were captured as prisoners of war (POWs); some were released in prisoner trades between the two sides, while others were sent to infamous POW camps—like the Confederate Army's Andersonville Prison in Georgia, where nearly a third of the Union prisoners died of disease before the war ended. Many soldiers died of disease or injury, sometimes well after the conflict ended. Some soldiers left home and did not see their families until the conflict ended. Regardless of the color of their uniform, the typical Civil War soldier's life was mired by the same difficulties, dangers, and personal hardships.

Ben Tyler Elliott

See also: *1776–1860:* Militiaman; Sailor; Watchman; *1915–1945:* Infantryman; *1992–2019:* Combat Engineer

FURTHER READING

Alexander, Edward. 2013. "Life of the Civil War Soldier in Battle: . . . And Then We Kill." *Hallowed Ground Magazine.* https://www.battlefields.org/learn/articles/life-civil-war-soldier-battle

"Civil War Facts." American Battlefield Trust. Last modified April 23, 2018. http://www.civilwar.org/education/history/faq/.

Denmark, Sharon. 2013. "Life of the Civil War Soldier in the Army: Drill Drill Drill." *Hallowed Ground Magazine.* https://www.battlefields.org/learn/articles/life-civil-war-soldier-army

Foote, Shelby. 1974. *The Civil War*. New York: Random House.
Helm, Gary. 2013. "Life of the Civil War Soldier in Camp: Disease, Hunger, Death & Boredom." *Hallowed Ground Magazine*. https://www.battlefields.org/learn/articles/life-civil-war-soldier-camp
"Who Fought?" American Battlefield Trust. Last modified June 12, 2018. http://www.civilwar.org/education/history/warfare-and-logistics/warfare/who-fought.html.

PRIMARY DOCUMENT

The following letter describes the enthusiasm of an African American soldier at the end of the Civil War. Joseph Christy was a Pennsylvanian and a member of the Massachusetts 54th Infantry Regiment, a highly decorated volunteer unit of black soldiers commanded by white officers. In this letter, Joseph Christy writes his sister, Mary Jane Demus, about the last days of the Civil War. This letter is part of the compilation of letters from residents of two counties, one in Virginia and one in Pennsylvania, that comprise a remarkable collection of digitized Civil War–era documents, In the Valley of the Shadow: Two Communities in the American Civil War.

Aprile the 27th
1865
George town, S.C.

My Dear sister

i take my pen in hand to in form you that We ar All Well at present and I hope thes fue lins may find you all Well When i gut your letter i Was on Bord of the steem boat Coming from savannah to georgetown and When i gut thear i set my self down to Ancer it and the nix thing i heard Was fall in Company J in *[unclear: lite]* marcing orders and the nix thing i hard Was forword March and a Way We went to hunt the Johneys and We found them too and kild a grate meney of them We fot for six days

We didin lose verry meney We took all old mare meet and every thing he had to eat And burnt down thear houses We Went a but one hundred And fifty nils a bouve george town and We hard that peace Was decleard and then We Cam back to george town a gane think that We Will be home in too months We ar giting a long verry Well We had quite a nice time on the rode We Didin lost enny out of our Companey give my love to all the rest and all the rest of the boys sends thear love to you all David is Well and george We Captered A but two hundred Cars and twenty thee lokemotives and burnt them up and We brot for thousand slaves With us to george town *[unclear: O J T]* Was one of the grates sits that i ever seen We started on the 4th of Aprile and gut back on the 26 and We march every Day this is all i have to tell you this time so i think i must Com to a Close this time nothen mor at present but still remane

your Brother

Joseph L. Christey

Derrect your letter to George town South Carolina Company J 54th Mass

pleas to Write soon good by

Modern English:

April the 27th 1865

Georgetown, S.C.

My Dear Sister,

I take my pen in hand to inform you that we are all well at present and I hope these few lines find you well. When I got your letter, I was aboard the steamboat coming from Savannah to Georgetown and I set myself down to answer it. The next thing I heard was "Fall in, Company J in marching orders!" And the next thing I heard was "Forward March" and away we went to hunt the Johnnies [Confederate soldiers]. We found them, too. We killed a great many. We fought for six days.

We didn't lose very many [of our own men]. We took an old mare, meat and everything else [they] had to eat, and burnt down their houses. We went about 150 miles above Georgetown [when] we heard that peace was declared. Then we came back to Georgetown again. [I] think that we will be home in two months. We are getting along very well. We had quite a nice time on our ride. We didn't lose any [members] out of our Company.

Give my love to all of the rest. All of rest of the boys send their love to you all. David is well and George [is too]. We captured about 200 [railroad] cars and 23 locomotives and burnt them up. We brought 4000 slaves with us to Georgetown [to freedom]. It was one of the greatest sights I've ever seen. We started on the 4th of April and got back on the 26th. We march every day. This is all I have to tell you this time so I think I must come to a close. Nothing more at present. But still [I] remain,

Your brother,

Joseph L [Christy]

Direct your letter to Georgetown, S.C., Company J, 54th Mass.

Please to write soon, too. Goodbye.

Source: Original letter, Franklin County, Joseph Christy to Mary Jane Demus. April 27, 1865. Case File of Wesley Krunkleton, Approved Pension Applications of Veterans Who Served in the Army and Navy Mainly in the Civil War and the War with Spain, Record Group 15, National Archives and Records Administration, Washington, D.C. From *Valley of the Shadow: Two Communities in the American Civil War.* University of Virginia Library. http://valley.lib.virginia.edu/papers/F3023.

SURGEON

During the American Civil War (1861–1865), surgeons were physicians serving with the army or navy. It was a military title and did not designate a medical specialty as it does today. Medical training in this country began in the colonial period as an apprenticeship because there were no schools. A man signed articles of apprenticeship with a doctor in practice. He spent three years working with the doctor, reading his books, seeing his patients, and doing whatever else the doctor wanted him to do. At the end of that time, he opened his own medical practice. Initially, those who wanted to learn more about medicine went to Europe if they could afford to do so, particularly to the medical schools in England and Scotland. Most could not afford the trip to Europe, so eventually medical schools were started in America to supplement the learning of the apprenticeship. This consisted of a series of lectures, five days a week for about sixteen weeks for each of two years. More of the apprenticeships moved to the doctors at the medical school. Some still went to Europe to study. This now included Paris, France, and occasionally Germany. By 1860, about two-thirds of the doctors in practice had attended medical school. Some of the schools were very good, but many were little better than a book off the shelf. The biggest shortcoming of most American medical schools was the lack of practical training in anatomy because of the shortage of bodies on which to learn.

Very little real surgery was done in America prior to the war. Most surgery was only setting broken bones, lancing boils, or letting blood. More surgery was being done in Europe but still usually only by a few doctors. The French were doing postmortem examination, so more anatomy was learned there. Anesthesia was first used in 1846 in the United States, and ether and chloroform were both in use at that time. Doctors also used the stethoscope and microscope. The ophthalmoscope had been invented in the 1850s, as was the hypodermic syringe. The list of medicines available for the doctor to use was long, but few had any real effect on the course of the disease. Quinine for the treatment of malaria was known, as was morphine for pain relief. Unfortunately, little was known about the cause of most disease, and the role of bacteria and viruses was not yet understood.

At the time the Civil War started, the army was small, with only a few doctors. Large numbers of volunteers were called into the army, but most of these were people who had no idea of the needs of the military. This was also true of the doctors. The army was organized into regiments, and the regiments were grouped into larger forces. A regiment was about one thousand men, and each regiment had a surgeon in charge and one or two assistant surgeons. Initial care was given to soldiers at the regimental level, but more severe cases were sent on to larger hospitals organized for the care of the severely ill and wounded. The major goal of the army was always to try to return as many men to combat units as possible.

The doctors in the army were called surgeon or assistant surgeon with a rank of lieutenant, captain, or major, depending on experience and time in service. The highest rank was major, and doctors could not give orders outside the hospitals. Actually, most of the time, the doctor worked as a physician rather than a surgeon as the term is understood today. The major problem for the army was disease, particularly what is now known as infectious disease. The army was in combat only a small portion of the total time of the war, and surgery (caring for injured soldiers) took only a small portion of their total time except when a battle occurred.

The first role of the surgeon in the regiment was as public health officer. This was at a time when this was not usually understood. When the army chose a location for the regiment camp, the surgeon inspected it and decided whether it was healthy. This included checking that the water supply was clean and that latrines (toilet trenches) were dug and managed. When the surgeon felt the army poorly chose the site, he went to the colonel in charge of the regiment, but he could only advise, and the colonel often did not listen. Eventually, the surgeon would also be responsible for the diet of the troops, but diets were never adequate, and the importance of vitamins and minerals in the diet was not known. Scurvy, now known to be vitamin C deficiency, was recognized, as was the role of citrus fruit and some other raw fruits and vegetables in its treatment and prevention.

The surgeons also provided medical care for the troops in the regiment. Disease not related to battle casualties was ultimately responsible for the deaths of two-thirds of the men who died during the war. The surgeon was also responsible for sending reports to his superiors and the Surgeon General's Office. He had to report the health of the troops, diagnoses and number of cases of diseased patients, treatment of these cases, and disposition (returned to duty, in hospital, or transferred to larger hospital). He also recorded the weather and the temperature for each day for what would become the weather service.

Other than accidents and injuries, the surgical part of military medicine came into play when a battle occurred. An assistant surgeon and a private set up an aid station at the edge of the battlefield, where they examined the wounded. For minimal injuries, the surgeon dressed the wound, and the soldier returned to the battle. If a soldier suffered a wound to the head, chest, or abdomen, and it was unlikely that the man could be saved, the surgeon gave him water and pain medication and put the case aside until later. For arm or leg injuries or wounds in another site but judged treatable, the man was sent to the field hospital, where another surgeon further classified the injury and determined appropriate treatment.. This sorting of casualties later became known as triage, from the French verb *trier*, meaning "to sort."

Surgeons at the field hospitals treated soldiers as well. When a soldier received a wound in the arm or leg, this often meant removal of the injured part, an amputation. At the beginning of the war, few doctors had any experience with surgery, but with time, they learned. By 1863, teams had been created so that only the best operators did the actual surgery. The surgeons also had to clean and dress wounds and at times had to reoperate to clean wounds.

From the field hospitals, the injured men were sent to the general hospitals, usually in larger cities and often closer to home. Here, the surgeons cared for the severely ill and the wounded until they recovered enough to return to their units or, if this was not possible, to go home either on furlough or discharged from the army.

About 20 percent of the doctors in the country served with the armies in some capacity during the war, and this had a major impact on medicine. There were many changes in medicine in the United States because of the war. General hospitals had been uncommon prior to the war, but the need that had created them continued, and they remain today. The large number of surgeons who served during the war vastly increased their experience and interest. They had seen many more different diseases and surgical procedures than before the war. This was no longer just book knowledge but extensive personal experience. They took home this vast increase in clinical knowledge and used it to move medicine forward. Interest in public health increased and advanced. The fields of neurology, neurosurgery, orthopedic surgery, and plastic and reconstructive surgery developed. Specialization into the different medical fields of today began and has lasted.

Robert G. Slawson

See also: Nurse; *1607–1775:* Midwife; *1776–1860:* Physician; *1915–1945:* Actuary; *1946–1991:* Anesthesiologist

FURTHER READING

Barnes, Joseph K. 1875. *The Medical and Surgical History of the War of the Rebellion.* Washington, DC: U.S. Government Printing Office.

Bollet, Alfred Jay. 2002. *Civil War Medicine. Challenges and Triumphs.* Tucson: Galen Press Ltd.

Child, William. 2001. *Letters from a Civil War Surgeon.* Solon: Polar-Bear & Company.

Dowart, Bonnie Brice. 2009. *Death in the Breeze. Disease during the American Civil War.* Frederick: The National Museum of Civil War Medicine (NCMCWM) Press.

Slawson, R. G. 2012. "Medical Training in the United States prior to the Civil War." *JEBCAM* 17, no. 1: 11–27.

PRIMARY DOCUMENT

Jonathan Letterman, a surgeon and the director of the medical corps of the Army of the Potomac, recounts the experiences of surgeons and medical personnel at the Battle of Gettysburg in early July 1863 in this report to his commanding general.

Over 650 medical officers are reported as present for duty at that battle. These officers were engaged assiduously, day and night, with little rest, until the 6th, and in the Second Corps until July 7, in attendance upon the wounded. The labor performed by these officers was immense. Some of them fainted from exhaustion, induced by over-exertion, and others became ill from the same cause. The skill and devotion shown by the medical officers of this army were worthy of all commendation; they could not be surpassed. Their conduct as officers and as professional men was admirable. Thirteen of them were wounded, one of whom (Asst. Surg. W. S. Moore, Sixty-first Ohio Volunteers, Eleventh Corps) died on July 6 from the effects of his wounds, received on the 3d. The idea, very prevalent, that medical officers are not exposed to fire, is thus shown to be wholly erroneous. The greater portion of the surgical labor was performed before the army left. The time for primary operations had passed, and what remained to be done was to attend to making the men comfortable, dress their wounds, and perform such secondary operations as from time to time might be necessary. One hundred and six medical officers were left behind when the army left; no more could be left, as it was expected that another battle would within three or four days take place, and in all probability as many wounded thrown upon our hands as at the battle of the 2d and 3d, which had just occurred. No reliance can be placed on surgeons from civil life during or after a battle. They cannot or will not submit to the privations and discomforts which are necessary, and the great majority think more of their own personal comfort than they do of the wounded. Little more can be said of those officers who have for a long period been in hospitals. I regret to make such a statement, but it is a fact and often a practical one. Dr. [Henry] Janes, who was left in charge of the hospitals at Gettysburg, reports that quite a number of surgeons came and volunteered their services, but "they were of little use." This fact is so well known in this army that medical officers prefer to do the work rather than have them present, and the wounded men, too, are much better satisfied to be attended by their own surgeons. I, however, asked the Surgeon-General, July 7, to send 20 medical officers to report to Dr. Janes, hoping they might prove of some benefit, under the direction of the medical officers of this army who had been left behind. I cannot learn that they were ever sent.

Dr. Janes was left in general charge of the hospitals, and, to provide against contingencies, was directed, if he could not communicate with me, to do so directly with the Surgeon-General, so that he had full power to call directly upon the Surgeon-General to supply any want that might arise.

The ambulance corps throughout the army acted in the most commendable manner during those days of severe labor. Notwithstanding the great number of wounded, amounting to 14,193, I have it from the most reliable authority and from my own observation that not one wounded man of all that number was left on the field within our lines early on the morning of July 4. A few were found after daylight beyond our farthest pickets, and these were brought in, although the ambulance men were fired upon when engaged in this duty by the enemy, who were within easy range. In addition to this duty, the line of battle was of such a character, resembling somewhat that of a horseshoe, that it became necessary to remove most of the hospitals farther to the rear as the enemy's fire drew nearer.

This corps did not escape unhurt; 1 officer and 4 privates were killed and 17 wounded while in the discharge of their duties. A number of horses were killed and wounded, and some ambulances injured. These facts will show the commendable and efficient manner in which the duties devolving upon this corps were performed, and great credit is deservedly due to the officers and men for their praiseworthy conduct. I know of no battle-field from which wounded men have been so speedily and so carefully removed, and I have every reason to feel satisfied that their duties could not have been performed better or more fearlessly.

Before the army left Gettysburg, and knowing that the wounded had been brought in from the field, six ambulances and four wagons were ordered to be left from each corps, to convey the wounded from their hospitals to the railroad depot, for transportation to the other hospitals. From the Cavalry Corps but four ambulances were ordered, as this corps had a number captured by the enemy at or near Hanover a few days previous. I was informed by General Ingalls that the railroad to Gettysburg would be in operation on the 6th, and upon this based my action. Had such been the case, this number would have been sufficient. As it proved that this was not in good running order for some time after that date, it would have been better to have left more ambulances. I acted on the best information that could be obtained.

The number of our wounded, from the most reliable information at my command, amounted to 14,193. The number of Confederate wounded who fell into our hands was 6,802, making the total number of wounded thrown by that battle upon this department 20,995. The wounded of July 1 fell into the hands of the enemy, and came under our control on the 4th of that month. Instruments and medical supplies belonging to the First and Eleventh Corps were in some instances taken from the medical officers of those corps by the enemy.

Previous to leaving Gettysburg, I, on July 5 and 6, ordered supplies to be sent to Frederick from Washington and Philadelphia, to meet the wants of the department in the event of another battle, which there was every reason to suppose would occur shortly after the army left Gettysburg. While at the latter place, I asked the Surgeon-General to have 50 medical officers ready to meet me at such a point as I should thereafter indicate.

Source: Reports of the U.S. Army, Jonathan A. Letterman to the Medical Director's Office, Headquarters, Army of the Potomac, October 23, 1863. In *The War of the Rebellion* (1889), series 1, volume 27, part I (Reports). Washington, DC: Government Printing Office, 197–198.

TAILOR, *see* SEAMSTRESS

TEACHER

In 1783, the Treaty of Paris ended the Revolutionary War between the United States and Great Britain—granting, in the process, a great deal of territory (commonly called the Northwest Territory) to the newly established U.S. government. The United States did not have mechanisms for settling this new land at the time, however, and thus created the Public Land Survey System with the passing of the Land Ordinance Act in 1785. This system established a means by which new territories of the United States could be mapped using a rectangular survey system and then parceled out into six-mile squares of land called townships along a series of principal meridians and base lines. In each of these townships, there were 36 sections of 640 acres each—and, from the very beginning, section 16 of each of these townships was set aside for the establishment of schools. Later, another section was also set aside for education, further increasing community access to schools. In this way, as the nation expanded westward, the education of the country's young was assured. And, because of this, all across the frontier, there was a demand for schoolteachers.

By the 1860s, most of the territory we associate with the modern-day contiguous United States had been established. Not all of this land had been shaped into states, however, and much of it was still being settled. One incentive for Americans to move west, and for immigrants to move to America and become American citizens, was the promise of free land under the Homestead Act of 1862. This law gave away 270 million acres of free land across the nation over the 123 years that it was in effect and went a long way in encouraging the settlement of the West. Where the settlers went, they brought their children, and where there were children, teachers were needed to teach them. As Catherine A. Pellarin notes in an issue of the *Museum Gazette* published by the Jefferson National Expansion Memorial, a "fledgling frontier community was well on its way to civilization when it included a teacher and a school" (Pellarin 1992). Yet education on the Great Plains saw several significant changes between the 1860s, when settlement in this part of the country was still quite new, and the 1880s, when the newly founded states of this region were growing into their statehood.

At the start of the 1860s, communities preferred male rather than female teachers. The prevailing belief at the time was that male teachers were able to maintain discipline in the classroom. However, with the beginning of the American Civil War, many men entered the army. After the war, homesteading and factories across the United States drew men away from lower-paying teaching jobs. With more of the country settled in the 1860s, it was clear that there would not be enough male teachers to fill all of the new schools being built, so more women were hired. Many superintendents and school boards reassessed their previously less favorable opinions of women teachers, with one county superintendent of schools writing that the female teachers' "superior cleanliness and arrangement of their rooms, [and] the effect of their natural gentleness and goodness on the scholars . . . amply compensated for their want of physical force" (Volo and Volo 2007, 289). School boards also favored female teachers because they believed they could pay them less money than male teachers. Male teachers at the Freeman School—a one-room schoolhouse outside of Beatrice, Nebraska—were paid about $42.50 per month during the 1860s, whereas female teachers at the same school were paid between $30 and $35 per month ("Freeman School," n.d.). By the 1870s, and certainly by the 1880s, female teachers outnumbered male. Men did still continue to teach, though, often as a way to put themselves through college. U.S. Senator George W. Norris, for example, sometimes took entire semesters off college, teaching at country schools or earning money by farming to pay for his education.

Teaching on the Great Plains in these days usually meant teaching alone. Schools were not big buildings with multiple teachers and classrooms. Most communities could only employ a single teacher in a one-room school building; these one-room schools required that the teacher instruct a range of students from as young as kindergarten age to as old as eighth grade—and all at the same time. Teachers often changed from year to year or even semester to semester. Because teaching requirements were much different then, many men and women began teaching as young as fifteen or sixteen years old—sometimes teaching students who were older than they were. This practice continued for many years on the Great Plains, even beyond the 1860s, 1870s, and 1880s As late as 1936, one former one-room schoolteacher, Alice L. Soffa, described her duties: "As a teacher I was also the school nurse, disciplinarian, psychologist, janitor, arbitrator, and more, besides teaching, and I was only a couple years older than some of my pupils" (Pellarin 1992).

Another challenge a teacher faced was that he or she often had to travel for work when posted to a new school in a community where housing was scarce. Thus, a teacher had to live with a local family, usually staying in the home of one of the children he or she was teaching, where there was very little privacy. Sometimes they would even have to share beds with the children or sleep in an outbuilding because houses were usually not large. Teachers were also expected to follow many strict rules, which dictated how they'd live their lives both in and out of school. One set of rules for teachers, published in Kansas in 1872, stated:

1. Teachers each day will fill lamps, clean chimneys.
2. Each teacher will bring a bucket of water and a scuttle of coal for the day's session.
3. Make your pens carefully. You may whittle nibs to the individual taste of the pupil.
4. Men teachers may take one evening each week for courting purposes, or two evenings a week if they go to church regularly.
5. After ten hours in school, the teachers may spend the remaining time reading the Bible or other good books.
6. Women teachers who marry or engage in unseemly conduct will be dismissed.
7. Every teacher should lay aside from each pay a goodly sum of his earnings for his benefit during his declining years so that he will not become a burden on society.
8. Any teacher who smokes, uses liquor in any form, frequents pool or public baths, or gets shaved in a barber shop will give good reason to suspect his worth, intention, integrity, and honesty.
9. The teacher who performs his labor fruitfully and without fault for five years will be given an increase of twenty-five cents per week in his pay, providing the Board of Education approves. (Volo and Volo 2007, 288)

For lessons, all teachers were expected to teach the "Three Rs": Reading, wRiting, and aRithmetic. Additional lessons included penmanship, spelling, geography, history, elocution, recitation, and music. Most lessons were learned through rote memorization and recitation. Because the teacher had to juggle groups of children of different ages, he or she might give lessons to one group while the others worked on an assignment and then check that assignment while the first group worked on their desk work. Frequently, the older students would help the younger students with their lessons, as well as help out with classroom chores. A wide variety of school textbooks was published by the 1860s, but rural schools could not always afford them, and lessons might be taken from the Bible or from assorted books donated by the community. Perhaps the most popular schoolbooks of the age were William H. McGuffey's *Readers*. It is estimated that more than 120 million copies of *McGuffey's Readers* were sold between 1836 and 1920, making it one of the most popular textbooks ever sold (Hoppe 1993).

In addition to frequently lacking basic school supplies on the rural plains, teachers themselves might not always be well trained. There were not teaching credentials like there are today. During the 1870s, "normal schools" offered three- or four-year teacher training programs, but rural schools and frontier schools could not often find a teacher who attended a normal school and "had to settle for whatever reasonably well-educated person they could find" (Volo and Volo 2007, 286–288). Nevertheless, teachers were expected to oversee everything from injuries to discipline. Sometimes it *was* the discipline that caused injuries. Teachers in the 1860s, '70s, and '80s could hit their students with rulers, switches, books, and so on and enacted other punishments that in these days would be illegal or at least very inappropriate.

The school term averaged about five months in 1860, with children in rural communities generally attending school for shorter periods of the year than did children in urban communities. The course of a school day for most teachers would begin with their arriving early to start the fire or open the windows, depending on the season. They'd fill the water pail or have early-arriving students do so and then get class started. The school day began around 9:00 a.m. with the recitation of a religious verse, patriotic saying, or a similarly natured song, and then lessons would start. School days did not start much earlier than 9:00 a.m. because students were still expected to help with morning chores at their farm homes, and then they usually had to walk to school after that. Lessons lasted until lunchtime around noon, when everyone would eat and have a short recess, and then picked up again from about 1:00 p.m. until about 4:00 p.m., when school was dismissed. For classes that had students of different ages and ability levels, a teacher "might need to prepare as many as 40 daily lessons for 20 scholars" (Pellarin 1992).

As the teachers' rules suggest, it was considered inappropriate for a female teacher to be married, so most female teachers only taught for a few years until they were wed, and then their career in education was over. Male teachers, too, frequently stopped teaching after marriage to pursue a higher-paying job with which they might support their family. As a result, most teachers during this period were young, inexperienced, and ill equipped—but they nevertheless made do, teaching thousands of children all across the rural plains. It was through their efforts that these communities were able to educate their children.

Robert Marcell

See also: *1946–1991:* Registrar; *1992–2019:* Early Childhood Educator

FURTHER READING

"Freeman School." Homestead National Monument of America. Accessed October 16, 2017. https://www.nps.gov/home/planyourvisit/freemanschool.htm.

Hoppe, Nancy Marie. 1993. "William Holmes McGuffey and His Readers." *The Museum Gazette*. Jefferson National Expansion Memorial (January 1993). Accessed October 16, 2017. https://www.nps.gov/jeff/learn/historyculture/upload/mcguffey.pdf.

"The Late Nineteenth-Century One-Room School." n.d. *Oak Hill School Teacher's Resource and Curriculum Guide*. Accessed October 16, 2017. http://www.heritageall.org/wp-content/uploads/2013/03/Americas-One-Room-Schools-of-the-1890s.pdf.

Pellarin, Catherine A. 1992. "One-Teacher Schools on the Western Frontier." *The Museum Gazette*. Jefferson National Expansion Memorial (December 1992).

Volo, James M., and Dorothy Denneen Volo. 2007. *Family Life in 19th-Century America*. Westport: Greenwood Press.

Zimmerman, Jonathan. 2014. *Small Wonder: The Little Red Schoolhouse in History and Memory*. New Haven: Yale University Press.

PRIMARY DOCUMENT

In this document, Oberlin College graduate Fannie Jackson-Coppin writes about the critical importance of elementary education for American children, specifically for recently freed African American children. Born a slave in 1837, Jackson-Coppin had an aunt who purchased her freedom when she was just twelve years old. She went on to become a teacher, high school principal, and, as the wife of Reverend Levi Jenkins Coppin, a missionary to South Africa. Coppin State University in Maryland, a Historically Black College (HBCU) near Baltimore, is named for her.

MY DEEP interest centers in elementary education for several reasons; first, because it is at this period of the child's life that habits are formed and tastes cultivated which may guide him in the pursuit of knowledge and happiness in after life, and which by the alchemy of experience are to change the elements of what he has learned into wisdom for his highest happiness. All higher learning is but a combination of a few simple elements, and when these are well taught, it clears away the difficulty of future acquisitions, and nature can spread her beauty before eyes that can see and teach the marvelous precision of her laws, to ears that can hear. I call this opening the doors upward and outward, whereas a different way of instruction is like going out of a room backward.

Again, we want to lift education out of the slough of the passive voice. Little Mary goes to school to be educated, and her brother John goes to the high school for the same purpose. It is too often the case that the passive voice has the right of way, whereas in the very beginning we should call into active service all the faculties of mind and body. Unfortunately book learning is so respectable, and there is so much of it all about us, that it is apt to crowd out the prosy process of thinking, comparing, reasoning, to which our wisest efforts should be directed.

Now, when we consider how much is lost by those who lose the benefit of the elementary development, and are therefore unable to pursue the higher branches with any degree of success or comfort to themselves or others, it is evident that this subject is worthy of a wise investigation and we must ask ourselves, how far are we responsible for this condition of affairs? I fear that the reason that so many are unable to keep up when they begin the higher studies is because they never mastered the elementary principles.

Source: Fannie Jackson-Coppin. 1913. *Reminiscences of School Life and Hints on Teaching.* Philadelphia: A. M. E. Press, 39–40.

TEAMSTER

Teamsters are laborers whose work primarily involves driving goods from factories and ports to their distribution centers and loading and unloading of cargo from transportation vehicles. In the past, teamsters were also responsible for the hitching of horses and oxen to carts and feeding their working animals. Prior to the formation of the International Brotherhood of Teamsters in 1903, individuals or small cohorts and companies of teamsters would work with local businesses that needed their goods delivered to another location—often from the point of production, like a factory or a farm, to a market. Teamsters would draw up and give to the producer a "bill of lading," which is a receipt that outlines the goods that the teamster was transporting, and would then load their vehicles with the producer's goods. On the road, teamsters would have to deal with mechanical or animal problems and complete the journey safely. At the destination, the teamster would unload the goods and obtain a receipt of delivery. Although they might have transported different goods or relied on different modes of transportation, teamsters across the country performed the same important task: they transported goods from production sources to markets. They were the connective tissue for America's industrial muscle.

The term "teamster" comes from early America, when teams of horses and oxen pulled wooden carts driven by small groups of laborers. By the start of the Civil War (1861–1865), the term was used across North America. The life of a teamster was fraught with difficulties. The job required considerable physical strength and extreme mental endurance, but it was dangerous and did not pay well. Early American teamsters worked long hours and received low pay: in 1900, the average teamster workday lasted twelve to eighteen hours, seven days a week, and paid around about two dollars per day. Additionally, workers often bore the responsibility for lost or damaged merchandise; if a teamster stopped to rest and someone made off with cargo, then that teamster had to pay for the lost goods. Despite working long and hard hours, many teamsters lived in poverty, and automobiles were not widely used for transporting goods locally until after World War I.

America's early teamsters did not have a union, and this was partly responsible for the harsh conditions that they endured. Teamsters operated at local levels and were divided by industries—beer drivers grouped with other beer drivers, and dairy drivers banded together. This separation among groups of workers presented challenges for collective action to improve working conditions. In 1903, the Team Drivers International Union and the Teamsters National Union merged to form the International Brotherhood of Teamsters (IBT). The IBT immediately joined the already powerful American Federation of Labor (AFL). Following the merger, membership in the IBT grew to around fifty thousand by 1904.

For much of American history, jobs were segregated by race, ethnicity, class, and gender. The early teamsters were no exception as most of the jobs were open only to white men. This standard persisted until the election of a new union president, Daniel J. Tobin (1875–1955), in 1907. Under his leadership, the IBT dramatically overhauled the organization and composition of its membership. The IBT consolidated local unions into regional districts, which created a balance between local interests and the IBT's national polices. The IBT was one of the first major American unions to understand the importance of organizing women. They took this a step further when they sought to address racial inequality, boasting, "Teamsters know no color line." In an era of pronounced gendered and racialized workplaces, the IBT publicly touted the merits of a diversified workforce. However, despite its public support for diversity, women and workers of color did not regularly work alongside their white male counterparts.

In the early twentieth century, changes to American society and the economy forced workers to adjust to their new world. As the automobile industry grew, traditional horse-drawn carts and wagons were slowly phased out. The IBT helped normalize this transition through the use of automobiles and trucks. In 1912, a group of Philadelphia teamsters delivered three tons of soap to Petaluma, California, as a testament to the reliability and power of automobile technology; the trip took ninety-one days. It was the first transcontinental delivery by a motor vehicle and a significant moment for the union, proving that unionized workers could perform great tasks. Despite its newfound embrace of the automobile, the IBT vowed in 1919 to keep the horse as its icon as a nod toward its equestrian past.

The teamsters' growth and modernization meant that they held a position of power in American organized labor. If a teamster local supported and joined a strike—even if they were not directly involved with the matter in question—they could accelerate the progression of that strike and resolve the issue faster and more favorably. This action was called a sympathy strike, and it became a powerful tool for organized labor; if a large portion of the labor pool participated in a sympathy strike, then corporations would be unable to fill the positions that were being vacated by the original strikers. Because of this, a strike that was supported by the local teamsters often had a greater chance of achieving some success.

Unfortunately, this power to establish solidarity with other workers also opened the door for corruption. Local teamsters frequently took bribes to join or abstain from strikes, often depending on who could pay more. Additionally, some workers sought to make money by illegally transporting contraband for organized crime.

Under the banner and guidance of the IBT, teamsters were responsible for transporting important everyday goods, such as bread, milk, ice, soap, newspapers, and lumber. With locals in dozens of cities across the country, the IBT represented one of the loudest and most influential voices in American organized labor. As the country continued to industrialize in the postwar years, its influence and membership continued to expand.

Bradley Sommer

See also: *1915–1945:* Truck Driver

FURTHER READING

Brill, Steven. 1978. *The Teamsters*. New York: Simon and Schuster.

Dobbs, Farrell. 2008. *Teamster Power*. New York: Pathfinder Press.

Tobin, Daniel J. 1932. *Labor and International Relations*. Chicago: Published for the Workers Education Bureau Press by the University of Chicago Press.

PRIMARY DOCUMENT

This short poem is typical of poetry written by and about workers in the American press during the nineteenth and early twentieth centuries. The tradition of labor troubadours, working-class poets, and poets who wrote about workers transcends time and place, though in the United States, local newspapers published their work routinely only through about the 1940s. Today, the Smithsonian Institution, D.C.-Labor Fest, and other universities and poetry collectives sponsor worker poetry readings. "The Teamster" appeared on the editorial page of a San Francisco newspaper in early 1907, not quite a year after the catastrophic earthquake of April 18, 1906. During the city's recovery, teamsters were absolutely essential to the debris-moving process. Some teamsters worked their teams so hard as to work them to death and then left their carcasses in the street to be dragged away by city workers. This poem also addresses the role of the teamster in a world where machines are increasingly taking the place of his horses and mules.

The Teamster

The teamster is a wayward man.
    It's very plain to see
He has to have the right of way
    In hauling out debris;
And toting goods from shop to shop
He hasn't got the time to stop—
    He's out for quick delivery.

The teamster is a fearless lad
    Who grips his steady reins
Upon a team that blocks the way
    Of trolley cars and trains.
Pedestrians and auto men
Can curse the teamster yes—, and then
    Get laughed at for their pains.

A teamster has a deep guffaw
    And swear words too. Content he
Is to plod his given way.
    The odds are ten to twenty
That if he pilots up the street
A team of dapple grays he'll beat
    A street car good and plenty.

But not because his team is fast,
    His wagon is so strong
That no one has the strength to cast
    To shove the thing along.
So everybody stops and smiles
To cheer the teamster's weary miles
    (With epithet—not song).

Source: N. A. "The Teamster." San Francisco *Call.* February 18, 1907, 18.

TELEGRAPH OPERATOR

The telegraph system required transmitting and receiving machines, wires that connected the two offices, and telegraph operators who inputted the message on one end and received it on the other. Prior to the invention of the electric telegraph, information rarely moved faster than a human could travel. It was only in the 1830s and 1840s that the combination of discoveries regarding electricity, magnetism, and other sciences allowed messages to be transmitted over wires. In 1838, Samuel

Morse patented his version of the electromagnetic telegraph, and in 1844, with the help of a government grant, he transmitted his first long-distance message, "What hath God wrought?," over a telegraph line between Baltimore and Washington. Over the next few decades, the telegraph became an integral part of newspaper, business, railroad, and military operations. The telegraph sped up the world. Newspapers sold extra copies when they were the first to report breaking news. Commodity traders made fortunes by knowing the movement of prices before their competitors. Railroads scheduled trains and avoided accidents. Generals outmaneuvered their opponents and directed their troops. Big business ultimately dominated the telegraph industry. While early telegraph companies connected just a few cities, by the end of the Civil War (1861–1865), Western Union dominated the industry.

The Morse Code was the language of telegraphy, with combinations of shorter dots and longer dashes indicating the letters. For instance, the SOS signal of three dots, three dashes, and three dots is still a well-recognized call for help. Some technologies allowed the message to be automatically recorded, but it was soon discovered that the fastest way to transmit and receive messages was to have the operator at one end tap in the message using Morse Code, while the operator at the other end listened to the combinations of dots and dashes, translated them into letters, and recorded the message by hand.

Because speed was essential, telegraph operators created abbreviations for many words. For example, the question "Here is a combination special, three copies, one city and two boroughs, about 300 words, shall I report it?" was sent as "Hrs a combn spl 3 cys 1 city & 2 trus abt 3 hnd wds, shall I rept it?" The answer, "Yes, you better" was sent as "Es u btr" (Dodge 1901, 61). Sending and interpreting these messages was like learning another language, a skill that was in high demand as the telegraph spread across the country. A first-class operator could send or receive thirty to forty words per minute error free. A second-class operator could do about half that.

Becoming a telegraph operator was a way for young people to secure employment in a town or city. Telegraph operators were usually in their late teens and early twenties, but a career as a telegraph operator became more common over time. Initially, operators learned by listening in on messages sent between experienced operators. Later, schools arose that taught telegraph operating as a trade. Many illustrious people started their careers as telegraph operators. Andrew Carnegie, the steel magnate and one of the richest men in the world, began his career as a telegraph messenger boy delivering messages from the telegraph office to customers' homes and offices. He was then promoted to telegraph operator and finally to the assistant and personal telegrapher to the superintendent of the Pennsylvania Railroad. The inventor Thomas Edison also began his career as a telegraph operator.

On one occasion, he requested the night shift, hoping to have some time to experiment and explore town. But his supervisor required that he check in with the main station every half hour. To avoid this work, Edison invented a mechanism that automatically sent a message every half hour to his supervisor. On another occasion, he used the electricity from the telegraph batteries to electrocute cockroaches that were trying to eat his lunch. Many of Edison's inventions, such as the stock ticker and improvements in the telegraph and telephone, were based on the knowledge of electricity that he learned as a telegraph operator.

Both men and women worked as telegraph operators, with the number of women growing over time. In telegraph offices located in cities, telegraph operators focused on sending and receiving messages. The more strenuous of the two jobs was receiving a message as it required interpreting the dots and dashes and transcribing them into text. First-class operators were assigned to large jobs, such as newspaper accounts, which were transmitted simultaneously to several stations. Operators in smaller towns often worked for the railroad. Since there was less telegraph business, these operators spent only some of their time sending and receiving messages. They spent the rest of their time repairing the line, tending to incoming and outgoing trains, and managing other aspects of the train station. The operators in smaller towns were often second-class operators, so they had a hard time keeping up with the rapid rate at which the city operators could send messages.

Friendships, and sometimes romances, between operators often bloomed as they learned their counterparts' styles and tendencies. Downtime might be spent exchanging jokes or playing checkers with an operator in a distant city. Communication across the lines made organizing telegraph operators relatively easy. An early organization, the National Telegraphic Union, founded in 1863, provided insurance to telegraph operators, helping them with medical and funeral expenses. The Brotherhood of Telegraphers, founded in 1882, fought for increased pay, better working conditions, and equal pay between men and women. They went on strike over these demands, but their strike had little effect. The number of people willing to learn the skills needed to become a telegraph operator continued to grow, making the supply exceed the demand and giving Western Union a strong bargaining position over its workers. Nevertheless, a career as a telegraph operator remained a step into the lower middle class, giving many young Americans a foothold into a professional world and the possibility for upward mobility.

Tomas Nonnenmacher

See also: Railroad Station Agent; *1915–1945:* Radio Announcer; Telephone Exchange Operator

FURTHER READING

Baldwin, Neil. 1995. *Edison: Inventing the Century*. New York: Hyperion.

Blondheim, M. 1994. *News over the Wires: The Telegraph and the Flow of Public Information in America, 1844–1897*. Cambridge: Harvard University Press.

Dodge, George. 1901. *The Telegraph Instructor.* Valpariaso: N.P.

Gabler, Edwin. 1988. *The American Telegrapher: A Social History*. New Brunswick: Rutgers University Press.

Hochfelder, David. 2012. *The Telegraph in America: 1832–1920*. Baltimore: Johns Hopkins University Press.

Jepson, Tom. 2000. *My Sisters Telegraphic: Women in the Telegraph Office, 1846–1950*. Athens: Ohio University Press.

TRIBAL REPRESENTATIVE

After European colonialism began in North America, and especially after the United States was founded and began its relentless westward expansion, Native American tribes began to train and employ tribal representatives tasked with negotiating for concessions, reparations, and fair treatment on behalf of the native population. These representatives often spoke English, traveled into American cities, and eventually began to wear a combination of native and western clothing. Through processes of gift giving and culture sharing, these representatives tried to humanize the native population in the eyes of Americans and European colonizers, which, in turn, allowed them to negotiate for fairer treatment for their people. And while American expansionism eventually overwhelmed and subjugated the Native American population, the efforts of the native representatives helped to offset the United States' selfishness and systemic disregard for indigenous nations' rights and needs.

Though Native American representatives had been interacting with European colonists since before the formation of the United States, the period after the American Civil War (1861–1865) was particularly important. The 1862 Morrill Land Grant Act made the plains a place of white settlement and not merely a place to pass through on a journey to the west coast. One source of conflict lay in the native culture that predominated in the plains; most tribes associated manhood with a person's ability as a warrior. Before American settlement, young Native American warriors might seek to prove themselves by attacking dangerous animals or members of hostile tribes; the presence of American settlers served as a convenient, meaningful foil for the young warriors' activities, which would have taken place regardless of an American presence. But, of course, such violence raised tensions on all sides. The U.S. government, attempting to address these issues, negotiated with many of the plains tribes to form the Treaty of Fort Laramie in 1851, which sought to establish the boundaries of tribal territories and promise government enforcement of good behavior by traveling whites. Native American representatives were instrumental in drafting this treaty, and many Native Americans believed they were negotiating from a position of parity. Unfortunately, this was not the case.

Americans did not share the white vision of individual property ownership. Native Americans eventually learned that this would be a major source of conflict. They did see specific territories as being controlled by particular tribes, and territorial conflict could arise if one tribe expanded into territory claimed by another—much in the same way as white settlers had been unilaterally doing to all Native American tribes. In the wake of the Civil War, and with many Americans desiring to move onto the plains and ensure what they viewed as "proper" use of the land rather than the inefficient and nomadic use made by the Indians, the U.S. government turned to a new, superseding policy.

The U.S. government decided to confine Indian tribes to specific, out-of-the-way locations called reservations. These locations often had little relation to territory that Native Americans considered theirs and on which many of their tribal practices and beliefs were based. This problem was exacerbated by systemic racism on behalf of most Americans, who saw the Native Americans as uncultured savages who were undeserving of anything but minimal consideration. This meant that Native American representatives began the postwar period believing they were engaging in negotiations about territory, and they ended the century negotiating to protect their way of life. Mutual differences in cultural understanding exacerbated this task.

A native representative delegation seeking to negotiate a treaty traveled to Washington, D.C., and once the members arrived, they'd be housed in a hotel—often crowded in a single room in which the furniture was replaced with cots. Representatives spent much of their day in meetings. If a meeting was especially important, they might hold a ceremony the night before with singing and dancing to ensure that it went well. Representative delegations typically included both diplomatic agents and translators. Upon arrival, Native Americans were given gifts—in the latter part of the century, this tended to be a new suit of clothes with all the accoutrements, referred to as "citizen clothing." Representatives learned that wearing a combination of native and American clothes helped humanize them during negotiations. Diplomats often gave gifts as well, though these were rarely considered valuable by the whites who received them. Most meetings began with the smoking of the calumet, which was supposed to ensure truthfulness by the speakers. Native American societies valued face-to-face meetings, but Americans tended to view these as annoyances; after the 1870s, the American military defeated most of the native tribes, and they increasingly saw Indian relations as a waste of time. These differences, combined with language and translation difficulties, meant that Americans and Indians often left encounters with very different views of what had transpired.

Many Native Americans believed that a compromise could be struck with the government—or at least with the president—and so they formed unauthorized delegations that traveled to Washington, D.C. to petition politicians on behalf of all Native American peoples. Whether they viewed the president as an equal or as a mighty leader who might help solve their problems, Native Americans still wanted to meet with the "chief" of the American people. When this became increasingly difficult in the late 1870s, they often turned their attention to other officials, especially the secretary of the interior and the head of the Bureau of Indian Affairs. These were viewed as people who might address problems they were having—issues with land, intra- or intertribal disputes, or countless other problems caused by American annexation of native lands. Advances in transportation, an increasing number of Native Americans who had encountered modern amenities, and access to tribal funds meant that groups of Indians still came to Washington without official invitation.

It remains difficult to generalize the experience of the Native American representative. Every individual represented tribes and issues that were both disparate and unique, and their concerns evolved greatly over time. In the immediate aftermath of the Civil War, Native American representatives often had little to no experience with white society—they found trains to be terrifying, cities to be large and overwhelming, and the everyday cultural differences to be daunting. As the century proceeded, Native American representatives grew familiar with aspects of white society and became less overwhelmed, and they were less likely to let themselves be treated poorly by individuals and businesses. After the turn of the century, a new generation of leaders emerged—many with a command of English and an understanding of American culture—and circumstances began to shift again. Native American representatives began earning law degrees and, much to the consternation of the Bureau of Indian Affairs, came to negotiations ready and able to take legal action on behalf of their people.

Anne Paulet

See also: *1607–1775:* Translator; *1776–1860:* Diplomat

FURTHER READING

Buckley, Jay H. 2008. *William Clark: Indian Diplomat*. Norman: University of Oklahoma Press.

Hatt, Christine. 2000. *The American West: Native Americans, Pioneers, and Settlers*. New York: Scholastic, Inc.

Inskeep, Steve. 2015. *Jacksonland: President Andrew Jackson, Cherokee Chief John Ross, and a Great American Land Grab*. New York: Penguin Books.

PRIMARY DOCUMENT

Sarah Winemucca was the daughter and granddaughter of noted leaders of the Northern Piute Tribe in Nevada. As a young woman, she was often approached to interpret for her people as they were moved from reservation to reservation throughout the region after the 1860s. While we may think of such noted tribal ambassadors as the Winnebago Red Bird and Cheyenne Two Moons and American Horse, who traveled to Washington, D.C., to confer with federal representatives, for most tribal people, the role of tribal representative was less nationally prominent and more like the position that Winemucca took on, episodically but repeatedly, as her tribe was relocated by federal Indian agents. In this passage, she writes about some of the duties she performed as the representative for her people.

While Batemann was agent, I was asked to act as interpreter to the Shoshones by a man called Captain Dodge, agent for the Shoshone Indians. He was going to issue clothing to them at a place called Battle Mountain. My brother Natchez went all about to summon the people there. I told Colonel Dodge all about our agent at Pyramid Lake Reservation. He said he would go to see him, which he did. It took three days for the people to come up. Oh, such an issue! It was enough to make a doll laugh. A family numbering eight persons got two blankets, three shirts, no dress-goods. Some got a fishhook and line; some got one and a half yards of flannel, blue and red; the largest issue was to families that camped together, numbering twenty-three persons: four blankets, three pieces of red flannel, and some of blue, three shirts, three hooks and lines, two kettles. It was the saddest affair I ever saw. There were ready-made clothes of all kinds, hats, shoes, and shawls, and farming utensils of all kinds. Bales upon bales of clothing were sent away to Salt Lake City. After the issue, the things were all to be put into one place. Holy songs were offered up to the Great Spirit Father. The things were blessed before they were to be worn, and all the young men put the blankets round them and danced. In the morning some of the men went round with only one leg dressed in flannel, which made all the white people laugh. At this issue our agent, Mr. Batemann, gave the Shoshones one ton of flour before this new agent, which made me very angry, and I talked to him before Colonel Dodge. I said, "You come up here to show off before this man. Go and bring some flour to my people on Humboldt River, who are starving, the people over whom you are agent. For shame that you who talk three times a day to the Great Father in Spirit-land should act so to my people." This man called himself a Christian, too. . .

I must tell a little more about my poor people, and what we suffer at the hands of our white brothers. Since the war of 1860 there have been one hundred and three (103) of my people murdered, and our reservations taken from us; and yet we, who are called blood-seeking savages, are keeping our promises to the government. Oh, my dear good Christian people, how long are you going to stand by and see us suffer at your hands? Oh, dear friends, you are wrong when you say it will take two or three generations to civilize my people. No! I say it will not take that long if you will only take interest in teaching us; and, on the other hand, we shall never be civilized in the way you wish us to be if you keep on sending us such agents as have been sent to us year after year, who do nothing but fill their pockets, and the pockets of their wives and sisters, who are always put in as teachers, and paid from fifty to sixty dollars per month, and yet they do not teach. The farmer is generally his cousin, his pay is nine hundred dollars ($900) a year, and his brother is a clerk. I do not know his name. The blacksmith and carpenter have from five hundred to eleven hundred dollars per year. I got this from their own statements. I saw a discharged agent while I was on my way here, who told me all the agents had to pay so much to the Secretary of the Interior, who had to make up what he paid to the agents. This I know to be a true confession, or the Secretary of the Interior and all the government officers would see into the doings of these Christian agents. Year after year they have been told of their wrong-doings by different tribes of Indians. Yet it goes on, just the same as if they did not know it.

When I went to Carson City in 1870, to see about my people's affairs, I was sent by the officials from one to another. At last we went to San Francisco to see General Schofield, and he sent me back to see Senator Jones. So brother and I went to where he was living in Gold Hill. I told him how my people were treated by the agents. He said, "I will see to it." He then put into my hands twenty dollars, which I took gratefully, for we were always poor, and brother and I went away. I have never seen or heard from him since. . .

There were now nine hundred in all at Camp McDermitt. Every head of a family was furnished with a good tent of the requisite size for his family, such tents as are used by the soldiers; and every morning, at five o'clock, rations for the day were issued. A pound and a half of meat was given to every grown person, and good bread,—for they actually baked good bread for them,—and once a month coffee, rice, sugar, salt, pepper, and beans were issued. Each woman came to me every day with her basket, and her number on a tag, fastened to a leather thong tied round her neck, and told the size of her family and took what she needed from me; and everything was recorded, for that is the way things are done in soldiers' camps.

Every one had enough. My father was with us at that time. He told my people in council one day that he thought it was an imposition to be living entirely on the soldier-fathers, when we could do something to support ourselves. He wanted them to go on hunting excursions in the summer, and bring in dried venison, rabbits, and what other game they could find; and the women to go out and gather grass-seed, and dig roots and do what they could toward the supplies of the next winter. I told Col. McElroy what my father had said to his people, and he told them to go to the sutler's store and get what ammunition they wanted and bring him the record of it, and he would see that it was paid for. My father knew that the army gave this support for the Indians as prisoners out of its own supplies. My people had enough, I said; they had more than enough, and by being prudent about their rations they could save and sell enough to get calicoes and other necessary things for the women and children; for these things are not found in army supplies. It is this generosity and this kind care and order and discipline that make me like the care of the army for my people.

Source: Sarah Winnemucca Hopkins. 1883. *Life Among the Piutes: Their Wrongs and Claims*. Edited by Mrs. Horace Mann and Printed for the Author. New York: G. P. Putnam's Sons, 86–87, 89–90, 91–92.

WASTE COLLECTOR

During the late nineteenth and early twentieth centuries, a waste collector was an individual who swept city streets, collected garbage from households and businesses, removed dead animals, and in other ways cleaned cities and towns of their overwhelming filth. Throughout much of the nineteenth century, Americans tolerated dirt. At mid-century, European travelers remarked about how frontier families lived in one- or two-room houses, often with dirt floors, on properties surrounded by animals and their waste, broken items, and other detritus of their lives, located far from reliable sources of fresh water. American cities were filthy. Raw sewage often just made its way to local waterways and then to the oceans, which at the time were wrongly imagined to be great cleansing basins. Manure piled up in empty lots and on streets. Urban residents simply discarded any spoiled food, soiled clothes, and garbage onto the streets. Pigs roamed city streets, scavenging anything they found edible and running in herds that terrorized residents. Apartment buildings had outhouses, centrally located in the interior court, for use of all building residents. Draft animals who died under harness were often left in the streets to rot.

After the 1870s, doctors and nurses began to notice correlations between filth and epidemic diseases, such as the 1866 cholera epidemic and New York's typhoid epidemic in 1906–1907. During the Progressive era (ca.1890s–1920), reformers and public health officials lobbied for the creation of city sanitation agencies, not only as part of the City Beautiful movement but also to reduce the spread of diseases. As a result of these efforts, waste collector, also known as sanitation worker, became a legitimate occupation within the United States.

While scrap collectors and rag pickers had been part of the American urban experience since colonial times, these earlier individuals were entrepreneurs who scavenged items to sell for money—not employees of cities or collection firms that contracted their services to municipalities. New York City was among the most innovative of municipal governments, organizing a board of public health in 1866, a sanitation department in 1881, and a bacteriological laboratory in the 1890s, all of which were headed by physicians. One of the first activities of these new boards and departments was to organize a Bureau of Street Cleaning. The bureau employed street cleaners who spent their days removing garbage and solid waste from the city's streets and parks; street cleaners worked in pairs, pushing the cart of garbage along and using brooms, rakes, shovels, and dustbins to fill it and then dumped it at transfer stations. This small army of street cleaners was known as the White Wings as, for forty years after 1895, their uniform consisted of all white pants and shirts and white caps or helmets. The white uniforms were designed to impress residents with the idea of cleanliness.

Sanitation departments also tasked waste collectors with removal of manure piles and dead animals and the cleaning and sanitation of tenement outhouses. Each morning, waste collectors were dispatched to their duty stations to complete their daily tasks. In many cities, including New York, waste collectors took the garbage and waste to transfer stations, where other waste collectors and teamsters then moved that waste to large incineration facilities, which burned trash. Other cities had municipal dumps outside of their city limits, where urban garbage and trash was taken and buried. Washington, D.C.'s waste collectors put the city's garbage on barges that were floated down the Potomac River to be dumped in the Chesapeake Bay, while some of Chicago's garbage—and its raw sewage and industrial wastes—was dumped and discharged directly into Lake Michigan. In 1896, New York City required its residents to separate their wet garbage from ashes and to place them in different cans for pickup, while many Boston residents refused to pay for city garbage pickup so took to surreptitiously disposing of household wastes in public places, increasing the workload of waste collectors.

Waste collectors understandably resisted increasing workloads and, by the 1910s, had formed associations and unions to protect their interests. In New York in 1909, for instance, they went on strike in the middle of summer, demanding not only higher wages but also the freedom to begin their workday early in the morning, before the summer heat made their loads more noxious and their days more physically taxing.

Urban growth complicated the work of waste collectors, as a 1911 newspaper report demonstrates: "With the constantly added population, new apartments, new hotels, dwelling houses and tenements spring up, with their extra output of ashes, garbage, and light refuse. The mileage of the streets in increasing. Pavements are torn up, and the work of cleaning the thoroughfares becomes more difficult." Furthermore, new immigrants "have a habit of throwing their garbage into the streets," which required one hundred more night sweepers (*New York Times*, October 1911). At the same time, city dwellers complained about the new night shifts that waste collectors had received as a result of the earlier strike, noting that this "pampered lot" of waste collectors not only had an eight-hour workday, but they also wanted vacation time at the city's expense, even though their night work "manifests itself in the making the night hideous with shouts, the wanton rattling of cans, the smashing of bottles in courts and alleyways" (*New York Times*, July 1911). Like that of their counterparts in later decades, the work of waste collectors in the Progressive era was critical to the removal of filth in cities and the control of disease, but their work conditions—lifting heavy ash cans, separating wet garbage from ashes and dry refuse, and sweeping streets—was hardly appreciated by their fellow citizens.

Nancy Quam-Wickham

See also: *1776–1860:* Bargeman; *1946–1991:* Industrial Hygienist

FURTHER READING

Benidickson, Jamie. 2007. *Culture of Flushing: A Social and Legal History of Sewage.* Vancouver: UBC Press.

Hoy, Suellen. 1996. *Chasing Dirt: The American Pursuit of Cleanliness.* London: Oxford University Press.

The New York Times. 1911a. "The Street Cleaners." October 6.

The New York Times. 1911b. "The Street Cleaners." July 11.

Steinberg, Ted. 2002. *Down to Earth: Nature's Role in American History.* London: Oxford University Press.

Zimring, Carl. 2005. *Cash for Your Trash: Scrap Recycling in America.* New Brunswick: Rutgers University Press.

A Day in the Life of an American Worker

2

A Day in the Life of an American Worker

200 Trades and Professions through History

VOLUME 2: 1915–2019

Nancy Quam-Wickham and
Ben Tyler Elliott, Editors

ABC-CLIO®

An Imprint of ABC-CLIO, LLC
Santa Barbara, California • Denver, Colorado

Library of Congress Cataloging-in-Publication Data

Names: Quam-Wickham, Nancy, editor. | Elliott, Ben Tyler, editor.
Title: A day in the life of an American worker / Nancy Quam-Wickham and Ben Tyler Elliott, editors.
Description: Santa Barbara, California : ABC-CLIO, [2020] | Includes bibliographical references and index. |
Identifiers: LCCN 2019015045 (print) | LCCN 2019017984 (ebook) | ISBN 9781440845017 (eBook) | ISBN 9781440845000 (set : alk. paper) | ISBN 9781440845024 (volume 1) | ISBN 9781440845031 (volume 2)
Subjects: LCSH: Labor—United States—History. | Occupations—United States—History. | Employees—United States—History. | United States—Social conditions. | United States—Economic conditions.
Classification: LCC HD8066 (ebook) | LCC HD8066 .D39 2020 (print) | DDC 331.700973—dc23
LC record available at https://lccn.loc.gov/2019015045

ISBN: 978-1-4408-4500-0 (set)
978-1-4408-4502-4 (vol. 1)
978-1-4408-4503-1 (vol. 2)
978-1-4408-4501-7 (ebook)

24 23 22 21 20 1 2 3 4 5

This book is also available as an eBook.

ABC-CLIO
An Imprint of ABC-CLIO, LLC

ABC-CLIO, LLC
147 Castilian Drive
Santa Barbara, California 93117
www.abc-clio.com

This book is printed on acid-free paper ∞

Manufactured in the United States of America

Contents

1915–1945: WORLD WAR I TO WORLD WAR II

INTRODUCTION

In the years before World War I (1914–1918), workers in many American industries enjoyed rising wages, better sanitation, expanding public school systems, and improved health and safety systems and considerations both on the job and in their communities. While this pattern of developments was generally true for most workers, coal industry laborers did not see similar advancements at work or in their neighborhoods. In the first decades of the twentieth century, coal miners and their union, the United Mine Workers, engaged in intense conflict with their employers over wages and working conditions. Mining was one of the nation's most dangerous occupations: nearly two thousand miners lost their lives yearly between 1910 and 1940; in 1907, over thirty-two hundred miners were killed in mine collapses, fires, explosions, and other mining accidents. The "coal wars" of West Virginia (1912–1918; 1919–1921) pitted miners against companies and, sometimes, against one another.

The spatial organization of coal production in West Virginia's mountains was such that most companies maintained camps (housing for miners and their families); sometimes they paid wages in company scrip, which was a proprietary currency that was only redeemable for goods at the company's store. The coal wars were typified by miners' strikes, often in response to an accident, a wage cut, or a speed-up (requirements to work harder for the same pay), followed by the company's eviction of mining families and their replacement by foreign-born workers. These brutal wars in Appalachian coal camps presaged much of the hardship that was to affect other workers later, in the 1920s and especially 1930s. For many

American workers, the period from 1914–1945 was one of short-term economic stability followed by episodes of economic catastrophe and class strife.

Many Americans enjoyed prosperity during the years of the first war, but it came at a cost. In most industries besides coal, average weekly wages for male workers increased 60 to 100 percent between 1914 and 1919 (National Industrial Conference Board 1919, 3). Women workers generally saw smaller wage gains. Prices rose as well; workers earned more money because of war demands in manufacturing and production. Employment rates for male and female workers both rose as well, with the increase of women workers outpacing that of men after the war. An economic downturn in 1919 led to wage cuts—and more strikes, including in the steel industry (1919), which idled half the nation's steelworkers, who sought recognition of their union, and in textiles and coal. Even Boston's police officers went on strike that year. Tensions increased as workers competed for jobs; race riots in Chicago, Illinois; Elaine, Arkansas; and Omaha, Nebraska (all in 1919), and in Tulsa, Oklahoma (1921), all involved some significant elements of labor competition at their heart.

Throughout the early 1920s, labor discontent manifested in more strikes in which workers demanded union recognition, collective bargaining rights, and better wages and working conditions. Factory and farm workers, railroad workers, longshoremen, sailors, and workers in other industries went on strike without any lasting successes. Even the 1922 Appalachian coal strike, in which ten thousand armed miners held off several thousand strikebreakers and policemen in nearly a week of running gun battles, failed when U.S. Army troops and the West Virginia National Guard were called in to end the violence. The show of force crushed the miners' union.

Although some characterize the decade known as the "Roaring Twenties" as a period of increased social mobility and changing cultural mores, for many American workers, the 1920s was a time in which industry expanded, though wages did not. Farmworkers, for instance, were generally impoverished as agricultural prices tumbled due to overproduction. In the 1920s, overproduction, brought on by the discovery of rich new fields in California and Texas, also affected the oil industry, driving down wages for even the most accomplished and skilled workers, the drillers. Automobile plants were organized on the assembly-line model, which limited opportunities for skilled metal workers. Mill workers in the great textile-producing cities of Passaic, New Jersey; New Bedford, Massachusetts; and Gastonia, North Carolina, also suffered their own labor defeats. New technologies like the radio and motion pictures offered millions of workers and their families inexpensive entertainment in the 1920s, even though they could not afford the automobiles or appliances they built. Many workers in rural areas relied on home gardens, fishing and hunting, and raising chickens and livestock to provide enough food for their families. Business expansion in the 1920s opened up new employment fields—telephone operator, stenographer, and retail clerks—and women often filled these positions.

Economic stagnation and retraction were evident in some industries and areas of the country well before the October 1929 stock market crash. For instance, construction tradesmen—glaziers and ironworkers—primarily found work in commercial building, not in residential construction. With the 1929 crash and accompanying bank failures came widespread suffering as millions had their hours cut or lost their jobs entirely. When there were opportunities, workers competed against each other for day jobs, often paying off a labor contractor for a few days' work, as was the case with warehouse workers on the West Coast. Workers in factories and canneries grew desperate in the Great Depression of the 1930s, especially before Franklin D. Roosevelt's (1882–1945) election to the presidency. The first months of Roosevelt's New Deal provided government relief jobs for some workers, but others took to the streets in waves of massive strikes in the mid-1930s. Autoworkers, longshoremen, and truck drivers (teamsters) organized into new industrial unions now that the New Deal's National Industrial Recovery Act (1933), Section 7a, protected union organizing and allowed authorized unions to bargain collectively with employers in contract talks in an attempt to promote economic recovery and stabilize business. Workers in some of these same unions led impressive citywide "general strikes" that ultimately brought about union recognition and better wages. When the NIRA was ruled unconstitutional, Congress passed the National Labor Relations Act, also known as the Wagner Act (1935), which clearly established workers' rights to organize into unions and protest their wages and working conditions.

In the 1930s, hard-won union-organizing drives and, too often, costly and bloody strikes resulted in higher wages, better working conditions, job security based on seniority, and, overall, real improvements in working environments on the "shop floor." Industrial unions, such as the Steelworkers and the Autoworkers, were unlike older trades unions. Instead, workers in an entire auto plant were members of the United Auto Workers' union (UAW) rather than workers in a factory being organized into separate trades unions. These powerful unions, the "Big Labor" element of the New Deal trilogy (of which Big Business and Big Government were the others), affiliated with a new organization, the Congress of Industrial Organizations (CIO), and exercised their political muscles, too, while the American working class consistently voting for Democratic Party candidates throughout the World War II (1939–1945) years.

World War II brought other challenges to American workers. Some sixteen million Americans served in the wartime military, and industries expanded to meet the needs of the United States and its allies, creating serious labor shortages throughout the war. African Americans, Latinos, and women flocked to work in shipyards and aircraft factories, as well as into other fields to which they had previously been denied access. A U.S. government agency, the War Labor Board, was organized to ensure the flow of workers into industries that needed them; the board also certified military draft exemptions for some "highly skilled" and "essential" workers in the steel and transportation industries. Americans migrated to northern and western industrial centers, where they worked long hours, saved their money, and set down roots for themselves and their families. At the end of the war, as servicemen returned to their home communities, many of these workers found themselves displaced by returning workers (military veterans) and by plant closures. Although at the war's end, many Americans were concerned that depression-era conditions would return, government investment in industry and in returning veterans buoyed the postwar economy, creating, for many, a sustained period of prosperity with its foundation of social supports and significant rates of union membership.

FURTHER READING

Brody, David. 1993. *In Labor's Cause: Main Themes on the History of the American Worker.* New York: Oxford.

Cowie, Jefferson. 2016. *The Great Exception: The New Deal and the Limits of American Politics.* Princeton: Princeton University Press.

Faue, Elizabeth. 1991. *Community of Suffering and Struggle: Men, Women, and the Labor Movement in Minneapolis.* Chapel Hill: University of North Carolina Press.

Gluck, Sherna Berger. 1983. *Rosie the Riveter Revisited: Women, the War, and Social Change.* Boston: Twayne Publishers.

Green, James. *The Devil Is Here in These Hills: West Virginia's Coal Miners and Their Battle for Freedom.* New York: Atlantic Monthly Books.

National Industrial Conference Board. 1919. *Wartime Changes in Wages: September 1914 to March 1919.* Boston: The Board.

Stoll, Steven. 2017. *Ramp Hollow: The Ordeal of Appalachia.* New York: Hill and Wang.

White, Ahmed. 2016. *The Last Great Strike: Little Steel, the CIO, and the Struggle for Labor Rights in New Deal America.* Berkeley: University of California Press.

ACTUARY

Actuaries calculate the cost-benefit ratio of insurance and other benefit programs, generate revenue models based on demographic data, and assist in the creation of taxation tables. Modern actuarial science originated in America between World War I and World War II, during a period known as the "interwar" years. These years also comprised the Great Depression and the federal government's response to that worldwide economic crisis through a sprawling program called the New Deal. Prior to this, actuaries recorded early church records in Europe; they served essentially as clerks of ecclesiastical courts. In the seventeenth and eighteenth centuries, however, they started to take on new responsibilities. Actuaries began finding work as computational specialists, who used mathematics to calculate risk and financial reward for insurance companies. That is, they determined rates for policyholders based on statistical models of risk to the insurer: actuaries determined what rates an insurance company needed to charge to remain solvent enough to cover any liability payouts while remaining profitable enough to continue operation; they also calculated what kinds of provisions against loss an insurance company needed to hold.

During the nineteenth century, many working- and middle-class Americans purchased shares in mutual aid or "friendly" societies. These subscription-based programs, which were primarily organized around occupational, religious, or ethnic affiliations, offered a basic payout to subscribers in the event of that subscriber's sickness or death. Some benefit societies simply provided funds to finance the funeral of a deceased subscriber. Members of these organizations paid either a lump sum or an affordable monthly subscription fee to the society. The fiscal health of an organization was thus borne entirely by its subscribers. During the Progressive era, which was a widespread period of social justice and political reform between the 1890s and 1920s, some companies began providing a form of insurance against occupational injury or illness, often by combining their resources into industry-based pools. But in the early twentieth century, mutual aid societies and corporate self-insurance programs increasingly found themselves insolvent, which meant that they lacked the financial resources to provide for the needs of all their subscribers and their insured. Furthermore, employers resisted payments to injured workers, arguing instead that a worker was at fault for his or her own injury or that an injured worker was malingering to collect insurance payments in lieu of work.

As calculators of revenue and risk, actuaries collect, analyze, and provide the basic information that insurance companies and government agencies, like a state disability insurer or the Social Security Administration, need to determine benefits to participants to create relatively equitable payments to all those insured. Two factors—the rise of welfare capitalism in the 1920s and the growing role of government in social life—led to a vast growth in actuarial sciences.

Welfare capitalism was a set of strategies corporations used to keep workers healthy and content during the 1920s and included such provisions as group health insurance, modest retirement accounts, and vacation and sick leave. Corporate managers understood that providing workers with low- or no-cost benefits helped to quell unionization and labor strife. Likewise, the expansion of government into insurance provision and the growth of the occupation of actuaries cannot be underestimated.

The federal government employed actuaries to predict tax revenues based on the new federal income tax laws that took effect in the 1910s. New state laws, like California's Workers' Compensation Act of 1913, provided that all employers pay into a state fund from which injured workers could draw money. Thirty-two states passed workers' compensation programs during the Progressive era. New state laws in the 1920s and 1930s also prohibited so-called "cancelability clauses," with which insurers could cancel individual coverage for virtually any reason, often right after a worker claimed illness or injury. But in general, widespread health and life insurance, old age pensions, and retirement programs did not emerge until the 1930s.

The Actuarial Society of America, an association of actuarial scientists and actuaries, first sponsored research in the 1910s to develop more systematic ways to predict risk and determine benefits. Using early computational machinery that employed punch cards, actuaries began to process large amounts of demographic data to develop actuarial "tables"—or matrices of factors like age, gender, and occupation—which predicted the likelihood of an adverse event, like an accident or death, at any given stage in an insured person's life. Actuaries also calculated claim behavior such as the likelihood that length of incapacity or disability would be extended based on whether a worker returned to work within a certain number of days. By creating these large-scale databases, actuaries provided the data and created mathematical models that could predict both costs and revenues for governments, insurance companies, and other entities. During the 1920s, researchers in the actuarial sciences completed several in-depth studies of worker health, thereby creating new sickness, disability, and death tables based on actual records of insurance companies. In 1937, twenty-six-year-old Gilbert Fitzhugh, who went on to become the CEO of the Metropolitan Life Insurance Company and the head of New York City's Chamber of Commerce, published a predictive table that provided detailed information about costs, risks, and worker behavior; this table was used in American actuarial sciences until well into the post-World War II era.

The two major fields of actuarial practice are insurance product development and pension compensation consulting. Using early computer technology and predictive tables, actuaries compiled and analyzed data to determine new products and evaluate existing products for insurance companies in accident, health, and life insurance. Actuaries then set rates for insurance products to ensure financial solvency of the insurer. In the insurance industry, actuaries worked in offices, often in teams.

In pension consulting, actuaries also worked in offices but often for specialized consulting firms that designed pension products to suit their clients' needs based on the type of industry they operated in, their union contracts, and their workforce characteristics. In this setting, an actuary often directly interacted with clients. Actuaries needed a strong affinity for mathematics and statistics, research and computing skills, and the ability to communicate complex mathematical-based models to beneficiaries, as well as to union, pension plan, and insurance company representatives. Actuaries also needed to be knowledgeable about taxation law as insurers and pension funds must still pay taxes.

Innovation in actuarial sciences—particularly the compilation of enormous amounts of insurance and demographic data and their analyses—made it possible for private insurance companies (both for-profit and not-for-profit) to become financially viable corporations in the 1920s and 1930s. By the 1950s and 1960s, new computation methods, greater data collection, and expansion of private and public pension plans created even more employment possibilities for actuaries. Today, actuaries must complete a college degree and pass a series of rigorous examinations to advance in the field.

Nancy Quam-Wickham

See also: *1861–1914:* Pension Bureau Clerk; *1946–1991:* Accountant; Economist

FURTHER READING

Haberman, Steven. 1996. "Landmarks in the History of Actuarial Science (up to 1919)." *Insurance: Mathematics and Economics* 18, no. 2 (March): 153–154.

Hickman, James. 2004. "History of Actuarial Science." In *Encyclopedia of Actuarial Science*. New York: Wiley.

Lewin, Christopher, and Margaret De Valois. 2003. "History of Actuarial Tables." In *The History of Mathematical Tables: From Sumer to Spreadsheets*, edited by Campbell-Kelly, Martin, Mary Croarken, Raymond Flood, and Eleanor Robson, 79–99. New York: Oxford.

ANIMATOR

Animators are responsible for creating a series of images, either by hand or on a computer, that, when viewed in quick succession, presents the viewer with the illusion of motion. The world's earliest surviving silent film debuted in 1888, and the first attempts at animation occurred in Britain and France during the 1890s. But on November 16, 1900, an American named James Stewart Blackton released a ninety-second film called *The Enchanted Drawing*, and its debut brought the new medium of animation to broad attention and set an entire industry in motion.

Blackton and his team (which included Thomas Edison) produced *The Enchanted Drawing* using stop motion—a technique in which an object being filmed is moved or altered while the camera is temporarily stopped, which creates the illusion of movement when the film is played back at regular speed. The process is simple, but it was revolutionary in the earliest years of cinema. Filmmakers and artists saw Blackton's pioneering effort and realized that the same stop-motion technique could be used without any live action at all.

During the first two decades of the twentieth century, artists tinkered with Blackton's technique in an effort to develop and master the medium of the standalone animated cartoon. By around 1920, the industry had evolved and developed a workflow that remained mostly the same until the advent and broad adoption of computer animation in the 1990s—though the same practices are still used today.

To begin, an animator created a storyboard for the entire script, which is like a blueprint for the entire project. For every significant line, action, or description that the story required, the animator created a rough sketch that could be displayed in sequence alongside the script. Just like today, animation was very expensive to produce, so storyboards were necessary to avoid budget overages and production delays further along in production. Storyboarding took an artist between one and three eight-hour working days per minute of finished film, and the finished product looked like a long, complicated comic strip.

Next, an animator created an animatic, which is sort of like an extremely rough draft of the whole animation. If, for example, a finished animated scene needed a character to walk from left to right across a room, an animatic might consist of a sequence of three images: the character standing on the left, walking in the middle, and then standing on the right side of a room. The animatic would usually take an animator about twice as long as the amount of time the project took to storyboard.

After the animatic, the director worked with the animator to finalize the character design and establish the overall timing of every scene. Hundreds of small questions were asked and answered before the animator had a detailed, finalized plan. This phase could take up to twice as long as just the animatic took to finish.

With the script, storyboards, animatic, finalized character design, and timing in hand, the animator began animating the action. On sheets of tracing paper, an animator began drawing detailed frames while using the finalized animatic and timing drawings as a guide. Once those were done, the animator continued to fill in the drawings that fit between those drawings and then repeated this process several more times by using the most recent drawings as a guide. In this way, the animator completed the overall scene while making sure that the animation's timing fit with the director's vision. After this, the animator redrew and then painted the animation onto a transparent material, like celluloid. This process might take two to five times as long as the timing phase took to complete.

In a separate effort, which could be done before or after the action's animation was finished, the animator drew the background of a scene. Any character or object that moved was almost always animated separately and then composited onto a background scene—sometimes called a backplate—at the very end; this saved an enormous amount of time and ensured that the scene's background stayed perfectly still. Once the backplates and the celluloid animation frames were finished, each frame was layered together by hand and transferred to film via camera, and then each frame was played rapidly in sequence to create the finished animation.

The earliest cartoons required between four and eighteen frames per second, with the majority requiring twelve. For context, Disney's 1951 animated classic *Alice in Wonderland*, which is about seventy-five minutes long, required around 54,000 hand-drawn frames of animation and, accounting for inflation, had a production budget of around $29 million in 2017 dollars—or more than $530 per frame.

In 1923, Walt and Roy Disney founded the Disney Brothers Cartoon Studio and, over the next half a century, grew the company into one of the most prosperous businesses in American history. Their first major success was an animated short called *Steamboat Willie*, which featured the popular debut of Mickey Mouse and was also the first major cartoon release that included audio. Owing to the company's dedication to quality, Walt Disney decided to hire only the best animators in the country, pay them the highest wages in the industry, and share the profits with them to keep them happy. In the 1930s, a senior Disney animator might make two or three hundred dollars per week. For comparison, unskilled and semiskilled American laborers were making around fifty cents per hour in 1935.

During World War II, animators found a great deal of work producing training and instructional videos, which were used to support American troops and interests all around the world. On the home front, the well-paid animation industry worked tirelessly to produce a vast amount of topical news and political cartoons, which proved instrumental in disseminating up-to-date information and commentary to the American public in an entertaining way.

After the war ended in 1945, animators all around the country pivoted in response to the still-growing American appetite for animation. More and more households owned television sets, but without the catalyst of the war effort, a void in animation programming began to develop. Savvy producers and directors noticed this and began developing regular animated programming. By the late 1950s, Hanna-Barbera had been founded, and over the next decades, their thousands of animators began churning out cartoon series like *The Flintstones*, *The Jetsons*, *Yogi Bear*, *Scooby-Doo*, and *The Smurfs*, along with countless other smaller-budget weekday afternoon, nightly primetime, and Saturday morning cartoons for every major television network in the United States

In the 1990s, the exponential growths of computing power and affordability saw a rapid increase in computer-generated animation. This renaissance both revolutionized and fragmented the industry. Animators at specialty visual effects companies, like Industrial Light and Magic, ushered in a new era of filmmaking, where anything a director could imagine could be created on the screen. Other companies, like Pixar and DreamWorks, began releasing full-length feature films that were animated entirely with computer software.

In contrast to the modern, computer-driven industry, many animators have dedicated their careers to traditional animation projects that are directed more toward adults or to stories that demand longer attention spans than a typical Saturday morning cartoon. *South Park*, for example, is a syndicated, adult-oriented, stop-motion cartoon that has had hundreds of episodes produced and has been nominated for dozens of awards over the span of more than twenty years. Laika, an American animation studio that specializes in stop-motion feature films and commercials, has had every single one of its films nominated for an Academy Award.

Animation has been evolving from the day it was invented, and it will continue to do so. But perhaps what's most refreshing about the medium is that its many hardworking, talented animators are always learning and trying to push the limits of the art form, while they're also always relying upon the same concepts and breathing new life into many of the same processes and techniques that were used by animation's pioneers.

Ben Tyler Elliott

See also: Screenwriter; *1861–1914:* Photographer; *1946–1991:* Artist

FURTHER READING

Channell, David F. 1984. "Before Mickey: The Animated Film 1898–1928." *Technology and Culture* 25, no. 1: 123.

The Enchanted Drawing. 1900. Directed by J. S. Blackton. New York: Edison Manufacturing Co., Film.

Fleischer, Richard. *Out of the Inkwell: Max Fleischer and the Animation Revolution*. Lexington: University Press of Kentucky, 2006.

Maltin, Leonard, and Jerry Beck. 1987. *Of Mice and Magic: A History of American Animated Cartoons*. New York: New American Library.

Solomon, Charles. 1989. *Enchanted Drawings: The History of Animation*. New York: Knopf.

PRIMARY DOCUMENT

In this document, Richard Huemer, who was born in New York in 1898, discusses his first encounter with animated motion pictures, his fascination with cartoons and animation, and the ways in which the early animation industry operated. Huemer would go on to become one of America's most notable animators in the 1920s, working for a series of studios and directors, including Dave and Max Fleischer.

In the 1930s, he agreed to come to work for the Walt Disney Company, first as an animator and then directing two later films, The Whalers *(1938) and* Goofy and Wilbur *(1939), before going on to make propaganda films for the United States during World War II. Huemer also worked as an artist, drawing a number of cartoon strips and editorial cartoons.*

The first film I ever saw was the Nelson-Ganz fight, which was at Coney Island. It was a film of the fight, of course. They had signs outside of these little restaurants, which said, "Basket Parties Welcome." Which meant that you could go into these places, which were filled with tables, and my father would order a glass of beer or coffee, and hot dogs for us kids, and we would open our sandwiches and eat them, and they would project these strange movies. One of which was the Nelson-Ganz fight, and I'm sure we saw some of Lumiere's and other French producer's pictures then. In shocking pink color, some of them were. Animated cartoon movies were done then by somebody nobody ever mentions: Wallace Carlson. He did something called "Dreamy Dud." And I saw those about 1914 at the local theaters in the Bronx . . .

I really was sold on animated cartoons. Involvement with live-action films seemed out of reach. Especially as I liked to draw. I spent about a year at art school: Art Students' League, in New York City. I studied under Bridgeman, the famous anatomy teacher. Really was famous. Didn't rub off much on me though . . . I always wanted to be a cartoonist. Up in Fordham, where I lived, almost every day I passed a sign on the door of the building opposite the university, which said, "Raoul Barre: Cartoonist." And this intrigued me to no end, and I walked up the stairs, and walked into the animating business. When Raoul Barre Looked up from his desk and said, "what can I do for you?" in his strange Canadian brogue, I said, "I would like a job." He said, "You would like a job?" I said, "Yes." He said, "Go to the next room and sit down, they'll put you to work." It was as simple as that. And they put me to work at something that was called tracing.

This was about 1916 and they were doing Mutt and Jeff cartoons. I had to quit high school to go to the League, that's how much I wanted to be an artist, and now I was quitting the League to go into cartooning. I was abandoning the fine arts. They already had the cell system, but it was not the way it's done today, which is the cells opaqued, to fit over the background. Our cells were used to contain the background and whatever lines on a scene were not "disturbed" by the character. All the action was carried on the paper. We inked on paper, with very flashy techniques, in the imitation of Heinrich Kley, once in a while. And I would take a series of cells that fitted over the paper to complete the picture. If the character walked in front of an object, the drawings that it took for him to pass that object had to have whatever he "disturbed" drawn on that drawing. That's where the tracing came in, we traced that thing in the background onto those five or six drawings while he was passing the object. And then that went on celluloid and stayed there, because he wasn't disturbing it any more. But he was walking in front of something else now, and then that had to be traced. In other words, we broke the scene down into little groups of areas that were disturbed, so that we could trace those onto paper. The foreground stuff was on celluloid, and the ceiling would be on celluloid—which was never disturbed. So it took about three celluloids. I think that's the most we used. And then with the paper, you had your complete frame. I was doing the tracing, from the background that somebody laid out. I didn't do it very long; in three weeks, I was animating. That's how easy it was in those days.

The staff consisted of about five animators, and about five or six tracers. Actually, there weren't more than fifteen people at the studio. Barre made one film a week, that never ran over 450 feet. And, believe it or not, it cost about a thousand dollars. And that's what he got for it, about a thousand dollars. The most he ever got was 1500 dollars . . . Animation in those days was not a difficult art. If it moved, it was good. Actually, the novelty carried it. The business got into trouble when the novelty wore off, and the people expected to see gags, and better animation and better ideas. Which, of course, Disney eventually succeeded in doing . . .

The next thing that really was a tremendous improvement was the opaque cell, which [Paul] Terry [of Terrytown Cartoon Studios] was a great devotee of, when he did his Aesop's fables. Terry's cartoons were already a little better. At least, the characters were cute. And at the end of each picture he'd have a little funny moral: Aesop said, " . . . " The reason he could make slightly better pictures was because he had a great deal with RKO, who had bought into his studio, which assured that each one of his pictures would play all their houses, for a good price. So Terry was the first one to really make money, in this business. Pat Sullivan made money too, but in a different way: his pictures were so popular in England, that they got all sorts of objects and artifacts, handkerchiefs with Felix the Cat on them, and this, similar to what happened to Disney, defrayed the cost of his pictures and gave him a nice profit. Felix the Cat was bigger in England than it ever was here . . .

Animators actually were a very jolly bunch. It used to be a lot of fun, working in the studios, a lot of horseplay. A lot of kidding. No time-clocks or anything like that. We did a lot of things like sending new people for a box of vanishing points, you know, that old gag. When a new guy would come in, they'd send him out for a film stretcher.

Source: Interview of Richard Huemer. 1968. Interviewed by Joe Adamson. UCLA Center for Oral History, Tape No. 1. Transcript July 24, 1968. http://oralhistory.library.ucla.edu/viewItem.do?ark=21198/zz0008ztp4&title=Interview%20of%20Richard%20Huemer. Courtesy of Center for Oral History Research, Charles E. Young Research Library, UCLA.

AUTOWORKER

Henry Ford introduced the concept of the assembly line in the 1910s at his Detroit-area car factory. On assembly lines, autoworkers stood in one spot all day while a moving belt brought individual pieces or sections of a car for them to complete. The autoworker's job was to make one adjustment—like tightening a screw or torqueing a bolt—over and over again, as quickly as possible, all day long, while motorized belts moved parts between workstations. Some autoworkers, for instance, worked at a station where they attached axles to an auto frame, while other workers down the line then fitted wheels and tires onto the axles. On an assembly line, workers labored on specific constituent tasks required to build a complete automobile, such as setting an engine block onto its mounts; bolting a radiator onto the engine; properly installing the springs and transmissions; attaching doors, hoods, and bumpers; and even fitting upholstered seats, pedals, and steering wheels into the automobile body—and many more. Speed was the name of the game, and workers were under intense pressure to make their adjustment as quickly as possible; they might make the same motion thousands of times in a single day.

The autoworker's work was grueling, but by speeding production, an assembly line factory could make far more cars, which meant that they could be sold for much lower prices. Ford's invention revolutionized transportation in America; suddenly, Americans didn't have to be rich to afford a car. Other automakers emulated Ford's assembly line method, as did those companies who made component parts. Working on a Ford assembly line was little different than working on an assembly line at Buick, Studebaker, or even Briggs Motors. Sales skyrocketed, and cars were everywhere by the 1930s—thanks in no small part to the common autoworker.

Most people who worked in automobile factories worked on the assembly line, and they hated it. Autoworkers performed boring tasks at a brutal pace and resented managers who used stopwatches to time workers' speed, urging them to work faster. Conditions inside early auto factories adversely affected autoworkers, with dust, noise, and unregulated temperatures, making the factory hot in the summer and cold in the winter; the focus on speed and the adverse working conditions made autoworkers' jobs dangerous. Workers informally resisted the demands of assembly line work in many ways: they took frequent bathroom and smoke breaks, heckled and teased fellow workers, sang songs and offered oratories in an attempt to slow production on the line, carved out private areas where they played craps and other gambling activities, and, at the Briggs Plant, even challenged corporate officers by yodeling loudly at work since the company had an obscure prohibition against yodeling (Meyer 1999, 123).

When Erskine Caldwell, a famous novelist, visited Detroit in the 1930s, he said that workers were known by their hands and called Detroit the "eight-fingered city" (Peterson 1987, 66). Most workers at these brand-new factories moved to urban areas from rural places like the Midwest and Appalachia and from foreign countries like Poland, Russia, Hungary, Italy, and Mexico. They were mostly lower-class people and were often startled by the breakneck pace of machine-driven work.

Some highly skilled machinists avoided the assembly line. Known as "tool-and-die" makers, these workers were good with mathematics and engineering. They created the molds used for casting the frames and axles of the car, along with making needed tools and parts. In the 1920s and 1930s, many skilled workers came from Britain or Wales. Politically savvy and well-versed in the history of the British labor movement, they were also among the first autoworkers to create labor unions.

Not surprisingly, employee turnover at assembly line factories was high; many workers quit within a few months. In 1914, Henry Ford responded to this problem by raising wages to five dollars a day—more than twice what a blue-collar worker could make at other factories. Ford's "five-dollar day" attracted a new flood of workers from across the country and around the world and made Detroit the nation's fourth-largest city by 1920.

When they moved to America from Poland or Italy, autoworkers brought their cultures with them. Most European immigrants were Roman Catholics, who built churches and schools. Ethnic holidays were often raucous and fun. On the Feast of St. Joseph, huge brass bands would march down the streets of Detroit's Italian neighborhood, while, on the Day of the Dead, Mexican Catholics would host parades featuring the Virgin of Guadalupe. While they assimilated into American society, autoworkers also kept cultural ties to their native countries through ethnic social, political, and sport clubs as well as music, radio stations, newspapers, and grocery stores.

During World War I, African Americans arrived from the South seeking factory jobs, and they faced harsher conditions than other migrants. Most factories refused to hire them. The handful that did—most notably Henry Ford's huge River Rouge plant—offered them only foundry jobs. The foundry was the hottest, grimiest part of the plant, where glass and steel melted in enormous coal-fired ovens and were then molded into auto parts. Charles Denby, a black autoworker, remembered, "The heat from the [furnaces] was so hot that in five minutes my clothes would stick with dirt and grease. We'd walk through on our lunch period to talk with a friend. We couldn't recognize him by his clothes or looks. The men working in his section would tell us where he was . . . by his voice" (Denby 1978, 30). They built churches, founded newspapers, and joined sport leagues, just like European immigrants.

During the 1930s, autoworkers fought hard to form unions. Having a union meant better pay, safer working conditions, and a voice in the running of a factory. However, union organizing could be dangerous. Sometimes, employers hired gangsters or former boxers to beat up workers who dared to strike for better pay and safer work. But autoworkers were clever and resilient. In a famous strike at a Chrysler plant in 1936, workers invented a tactic called the sit-down strike: they stayed *in* the factory after it closed and refused to leave until they were able to form a union. By the time the United States entered World War II, most workers in big auto plants belonged to unions, and by the late 1940s, the United Automobile Workers was one of the most powerful unions in American history.

Matthew Pehl

See also: *1861–1914:* Mechanic; *1946–1991:* Machine Operator

FURTHER READING

Barnard, John. 2004. *American Vanguard: The United Auto Workers During the Reuther Years, 1935–1970*. Detroit: Wayne State University Press.

Caldwell, Erskine. 1935. *Some American People*. New York R. M. McBride & Company.

Denby, Charles. 1978. *Indignant Heart, a Black Worker's Journal*. Boston: South End Press.

Lichtenstein, Nelson, and Stephen Meyer, eds. 1983. *On the Line: Essays in the History of Auto-Work*. Urbana: University of Illinois Press.

Marquart, Frank. 1975. *An Auto Worker's Journal: The UAW from Crusade to One-Party System*. University Park: Pennsylvania State University Press.

Meyer, Stephen. 1999. "Work, Play, and Power: Masculine Culture on the Automotive Shop Floor, 1930–1960." In *Men and Masculinities* 2, no. 2: 115–134.

Peterson, Joyce Shaw. 1987. *American Automobile Workers, 1900–1933*. Albany: State University of New York Press.

BUS DRIVER, *see* STREETCAR OPERATOR

CANNERY WORKER

Cannery workers worked in factories that processed and canned raw fruits and vegetables and prepared them for shipping to market. They worked long hours in difficult conditions for low pay. From 1939 to 1950, California produced more canned fruits and vegetables than any other state, and in 1946, the state accounted for one half of all fruit packed and canned in the United States. The typical cannery was divided into task-defined departments. For example, a load of peaches arrived in the receiving area and then went to a preparation section, where they were washed, graded, and pitted; then they proceeded to the canning department. After canning, a fourth division cooked the syrups and sealed the cans, and finally the warehouse readied the cans for shipping, and the maintenance crew kept the machines humming.

From the depths of the Great Depression until the end of World War II, Carmen Bernal Escobar, a young Mexican immigrant, worked at the California Sanitary Canning Company (Cal San), one of the largest food-processing firms in Los Angeles. Men and women did not work together on the line. Although women comprised around 75 percent of plant employees, departments were segregated by gender with women doing the prep and canning work, while men received the fruit, sealed the cans, and handled the shipping. Canneries ran on a seasonal schedule, following the rhythms of the harvest, with workers conversing in an insider's language. The phrase "We met in spinach, fell in love in peaches, and married in tomatoes" meant that the couple met in March, fell in love in August, and married in October.

Paid by the piece, a woman had to secure a favorable position on the line, which was always a spot near the chutes where the produce first entered a department. In Carmen's words:

> There were two long tables with sinks that you find in old-fashioned houses and fruit would come down out of the chutes and we would wash them and put them on a belt. I had the first place so I could work for as long as I wanted. Women in the middle hoarded fruit because the work wouldn't last forever and the women at the end really suffered. Sometimes they would stand there for hours before any fruit would come down for them to wash. They just got the leftovers. Those at the end of the line hardly made nothing. (Carmen Bernal Escobar, interview with the author, February 11, 1979)

A quick employee standing in a preferred spot could earn as much $1.00 an hour, but the majority earned from 30 to 35 cents. As salaried workers, men earned up to $6.25 a day.

Women also depended on their checkers (all men) to accurately record their production level, and as one can imagine, disputes between workers and checkers ran rampant, with claims of cheating or favoritism. As Carmen remembered, "When I caught the foreman cheating me, he said: 'I love you like a daughter, Carmen, but who's the foreman, you or me?'" (Carmen Bernal Escobar, interview with the author, February 11, 1979). Checkers were not the only challenges workers faced. They routinely encountered slippery floors, itchy peach fuzz, production speed-ups, work-related injuries, tyrannical foreman and floor ladies, and sexual harassment (to name a few less-than-desirable conditions).

Though the piece-rate scale created competition, feelings of solidarity developed, an atmosphere fostered by work conditions and by family and friend networks. Seasoned employees trained new hires on the line. For example, on a worker's first day at Cal San, she took her place on the conveyor belt grading peaches, a job that required speed and precision. Fairly quickly, they had to learn how to recognize which peaches were "fancies" that went into one bin, those considered "choice" into another, those destined for fruit cocktail in a third, and, finally, the "rots" (for which they earned no credit) had to be thrown into a discard bin. All the while, they had to remember not to stare at the belt to prevent feeling nauseous.

Family networks proved integral to the cannery culture, at times spanning several generations. As Carmen recalled, "And to keep the family going . . . in order to bring in a little money . . . my mother, my grandmother, . . . my brother, my sister and I all worked together at Cal San" (Carmen Bernal Escobar, interview with the author, February 11, 1979). Friendships were forged among young women across ethnicities. Standing in the same spot week after week, month after month, they chatted with their neighbors, sharing interests common to American teenagers: movie stars, gossip magazines, music, dances, and fashion. At Cal San, Russian Jewish and Mexican workers also shared the neighborhood of Boyle Heights. Though these women rode the Red Car to work and chatted on the line, most work-buddy friendships existed only at the plant.

In July 1939, Dorothy Healey, an organizer with the United Cannery, Agricultural, Packing and Allied Workers of American (UCAPAWA-CIO), began to distribute union leaflets outside the Cal San gates. Within three weeks, 400 out of 430 employees had joined UCAPAWA. Such success speaks to the strength of the cannery culture as membership cards traveled from one kin or friend network to the next. One can only imagine the hushed tones along the line as workers passed along union news. Cal San's owners, the Shapiro brothers, refused to recognize the union or negotiate with workers.

On August 31, 1939, during a record-breaking heat wave and at the height of the profitable peach season, 400 out of 430 workers at Cal San walked out. The next day, sixteen stragglers joined them on the picket line. In addition to the twenty-four-hour picket line outside the plant, the workers set up boycott teams to picket local grocery stories that refused to take Cal San products off their shelves. After a two-and-a-half-month standoff, the workers came up with an innovative tactic: their children would picket the front lawns of the owners' homes. Within days of the child pickets, who carried signs such as "I'm underfed because my Mama is underpaid" (Dorothy Ray Healey, interview with the author, January 29, 1979), a settlement was reached.

Wages and conditions improved at Cal San as workers took pride in their union. Their contracts provided benefits that few industrial unions could match:

free legal advice and a hospitalization plan. A fierce loyalty developed as the result of rank-and-file leadership. Four decades after the strike, Carmen Bernal Escobar declared, "UCAPAWA was the greatest thing that ever happened to the workers at Cal San. It changed everything and everybody" (Dorothy Ray Healey, interview with the author, January 29, 1979).

Vicki L. Ruiz

See also: *1861–1914:* Meat Packinghouse Worker

FURTHER READING

Escobar, Carmen Bernal. Interview by Vicki L. Ruiz. February 11, 1979.

Healy, Dorothy Ray. Interview by Vicki L. Ruiz. January 29, 1979.

Ruíz, Vicki. 1992. *Cannery Women, Cannery Lives: Mexican Women, Unionization, and the California Food Processing Industry, 1930–1950*. Albuquerque: University of New Mexico Press.

Sidorick, Daniel. 2009. *Condensed Capitalism: Campbell Soup and the Pursuit of Cheap Production in the Twentieth Century*. Ithaca: Cornell University Press.

Zavella, Patricia. 2018. *Women's Work and Chicano Families: Cannery Workers of the Santa Clara Valley*. Ithaca: Cornell University Press.

PRIMARY DOCUMENT

In the 1930s, farm and cannery workers' unions undertook a series of union-organizing drives; workers waged many strikes against their employers over low wages, long hours, and dangerous working conditions. These three newspaper reports from the small-town Healdsburg (California) Tribune *describe some of the conditions that striking cannery workers faced on the West Coast.*

STRIKES OF FARM WORKERS SPREAD NO TROOPS BUT POLICE ARE SENT:

Farmers of Yakima Organize As Vigilantes

Strikes resulting from wage disputes between ranchers and workers assumed coast-wide proportions today as authorities took strong measures to prevent violence. At Sacramento, state officers refused to act on the Teague, Tulare county ranch appeal for national guardsmen for protection, against aroused picketers, but Raymond Cato rushed 26 additional state highway patrolmen to a point near Tulare to prevent potential disorders. With these reinforcements, 39 officers are patrolling the district. Ranch officials at Tulare moved to break up a strike which has halted the peach harvest of virtually the entire San Joaquin valley. H. C. Merritt, Teague's ranch manager, recruited new crews from the ranks of the unemployed, and filed an injunction proceeding to restrain picketers from interference with workers. Strikers asked 35 cents an hour. They have been receiving 17 cents. California Packing company officials threatened to abandon peach harvesting in the Merced district and to charge the loss to acreage reduced under the N.R.A peach canning code. Meanwhile, the labor troubles spread to new fields, union leaders reporting 500 pear pickers on strike in the Santa Clara district. Alert ranchers near Yakima, Washington, organized as vigilantes and drove out agitators who had attempted to induce packers there to strike for higher wages. These disputes boomeranged to throw more than 1100 cannery employees out of work at Hanford and Armona. Lack of peaches forced plants to close.

SAN FRANCISCO, August 15.—A. J. Elliott, chairman of the board of supervisors of Tulare county, requested Governor Rolph late Monday night to send national guard troops to protect the Teague peach ranch, north of Tulare, where practically the entire crew of peach strikers of 700 men were striking for higher wages and shorter hours. Sheriff C. W. Toland of Butte county said Monday night he would ask the Chico national guard unit be called out to maintain peace if there is any further disturbance or outbreak in Butte county's farm labor insurrection. The sheriff said authorities have placed a heavy guard about the Gridley cannery, where 10,000 spinach crates were destroyed after a meeting of workers. Five alleged agitators were arrested near Chico, three of whom were charged with attacking a worker in a peach cutting shed. Other reports of unrest came in from Merced and Salinas. The request for troops was being held in abeyance by Adjutant General Seth Howard on the ground that the sheriff's office should be able to handle the situation as it now stands. Authorities in the San Joaquin valley fruit section said they were holding down a veritable powder keg with more than 5700 workers striking in the southern section. Both orchard and produce workers are involved.

Source: *Healdsburg Tribune.* August 15, 1933. Courtesy of *The Healdsburg Tribune.* CA: Sonoma West Publishers.

Cannery Workers' Strike Is Nearing Crisis, Labor Council Calls for General Walkout

Zero Hour Fixed For Wednesday Morning

Stockton, April 20.—While a "pick handle army" of 1100 deputized men and 150 women, reported armed with paring- knives, awaited the call of Sheriff Harvey M. Odell, to intervene in a cannery workers strike crisis, the San Joaquin county center labor council called a meeting to consider a general strike of all workers. Battle lines were drawn sharply in the rich agricultural city, awaiting the "zero hour" 8 a.m. tomorrow, when cannery operators will attempt to re-open plants with the aid of Sheriff Odell's citizen troops. Vance Ambrose, agricultural workers' union head, said: "Union workers are mobilizing to resist and take action against Sheriff Odell's attempt to break the strike." "We won't use pick handles, tear gas or guns, but watch out!" Walter McHaffey, president of the labor council said: "If they fill this town with vigilantes tomorrow, every worker in Stockton, will stop work and run them out of town. We will meet pick handles with pick handles." Sheriff Odell, ordered all hardware stores to cease selling pick handles and baseball bats, after he received a report that the strikers were laying in a supply of both articles, in preparing for the "zero hour" tomorrow. Shortly afterwards, guards were ordered out to protect a truck which drove up to the court house carrying 1,000 pick handles for use in the citizen army. The pick handles were chosen as weapons by Sheriff Odell, because they are easy to swing. They were convoyed to the court house, where they will be distributed to the deputies tonight. McHaffey said 4,000 Filipino asparagus field workers will be ordered to stop work tomorrow morning if trouble develops. A proposal will be introduced today to call a general labor strike at 6 a.m. tomorrow to crystalize opposition against efforts to resume work in the four strike-bound canneries.

Source: *Healdsburg Tribune.* April 20, 1937. Courtesy of *The Healdsburg Tribune*: Sonoma West Publishers.

DRAFTSMAN

A draftsman is skilled at making detailed technical drawings. These individuals assist the process of building by creating architectural drawings, usually under the supervision or an architect or engineer, that are used as the planning documents for construction. All other building tradespeople consult the building plans created by draftsmen to determine the work they do to build the structure. The role of draftsmen was critical in the building trades but also in many other fields where two-dimensional drawings were required for construction of three-dimensional objects, both big and small. Patternmakers, for instance, relied on drafting skills often obtained as draftsmen to create plans for machine prototypes. Engineers also had drafting skills, as did architects.

Large American corporations expanded dramatically in the first decades of the twentieth century. With that expansion came an upsurge in construction, especially of large corporate headquarters buildings in American cities. This building boom created opportunities for ironworkers, carpenters, masons, bricklayers, glaziers, electricians, and all sorts of building tradespeople. It also created enormous work opportunities for those who worked as draftsmen.

In construction and architecture, draftsmen use their drawing skills to create building plans. But artistic talent itself does not define a draftsman's work. Instead, draftsmen use very precise techniques to draw a two-dimensional plan for structures. They were highly trained in mathematics; most also were familiar with construction techniques. Architectural draftsmen were also knowledgeable about municipal building codes, which required that all buildings followed mandates for fire safety, structural integrity, and preparation of building sites. A draftsman must also have superior spatial intelligence skills to make perspective drawings and flat drawings that indicate the three-dimensional planes of a structure.

Draftsmen used many tools in their work, particularly specialized drafting tables: large tables that accommodate a drawing of a large building, to scale. Draftsmen also used drafting board of various sizes for portability and smaller drawings. Both drafting tables and boards must have squared edges to permit the correct use of a T-square—a tool that allows draftsmen to make perfectly square renderings of a structure. An architectural drawing that incorporates "out-of-square" elements could create serious problems for building tradespeople since they must precisely follow the plans. Among other tools that draftsmen use are various drawing instruments for rendering specific elements (such as a toilet or sink), rulers, protractors, pencils, and both drafting paper and tracing paper for copying their plans.

Although "draftsman" was the census bureau occupational term in 1940, both men and women performed this job, with a significant growth in women's employment between World War I and World War II. The percentage of women draftsmen increased from less than 1 percent of all individuals in 1910 and to over 10 percent in 1940—a ratio that has remained similar ever since. This growth in women employed as draftsmen in this period can be attributed to increasing numbers of women pursuing college education, growth in the building industry, and growing numbers of women trained in engineering and architecture.

In their daily routines, draftsmen and draftswomen worked closely with engineers and architects. After receiving instructions and building specification from them, draftsmen carefully created detailed plans for structures (or other objects). This task required a draftsman to read a surveyor's report, note particular geological challenges to a building site, and then use an architect's perspective drawing, or representation of the building on site, to create an immensely detailed rendering. The draftsman used the perspective drawing to create an orthographic drawing that showed all elements of a structure in three planes: height, width, and depth. The architectural plans include such things as grading of the site, footing depth, and foundation dimensions. Each part—like the footing—had detailed drawings of the depth to which a foundation footing had to be dug, construction materials (concrete, steel pilings, or other), orientation (to compass points), and location of connections to framing and walls. Draftsmen designate the size, material, and placement of bolts that connect the foundation to the frame of a house, for instance. In this way, an architectural drawing provides a set of detailed instructions for the building tradespeople to follow.

Draftsmen create these architectural drawings using paper, pencils, and drawing tools to make detailed plans for every part of the structure: from the location and site to the finished building. Windows, doors, walls, electrical circuits, plumbing schemes, insulation specifications, the roof, installed components and permanent fixtures, and even the driveway and walkway to the building (and sometimes even landscaping) are rendered. Draftsmen used carefully written block lettering to identify certain parts of the plan, but they also employed certain symbols to denote construction materials and elements (even the kind of light switch) as a way to speed the drawing process. Over time, these shortcuts have been incorporated into the common conventions for various construction elements. Once a plan was complete, the draftsman had multiple copies made, either by tracing or by mechanical reproduction in the later years.

The numbers of employed drafters in 1940 numbered about 100,000, the same numbers of individuals employed in the field in 2016. Unlike their earlier counterparts, drafters today use computer-assisted design software to create their plans, eliminating the need for large numbers of highly trained professionals of the past to create more elaborate and numerous buildings than previously done.

Nancy Quam-Wickham

See also: Mechanical Engineer; *1861–1914:* Patternmaker; *1946–1991:* Aeronautical and Aerospace Engineer; Architect

FURTHER READING

Bellis, Herbert F., and Walter A. Schmidt. 1961. *Architectural Drafting.* New York: McGraw Hill.

Bies, John D. 1983. *Architectural Drafting: Structure and Environment.* Indianapolis: Bobbs Merrill.

National Learning Corporation. 1900. *Draftsman.* Syosset: National Learning Corp.

FARMWORKER

Farmworkers plant, cultivate, and pick the produce that is sold at markets and in stores, and their labor has been instrumental in shaping the modern American standard of living. Despite their important contributions to society, farmworkers have historically suffered from low wages, environmentally hazardous work conditions, an absence of strong civil rights, and a low quality of life; transformations within the American agricultural industry, shifts in U.S. immigration policy, and farmworkers' exclusion from New Deal labor protections contributed to a highly exploitative agricultural labor system. As a result of these sets of circumstances, American farmworkers were largely foreign born during the first five decades of the twentieth century, and they were viewed as a racially inferior laboring class that was obligated to endure backbreaking work for low pay. Farmworkers were often met with physical violence when they demanded better living and working conditions. Despite these challenges, farmworkers came up with myriad ways to rectify their difficult situation. They formed mutual aid and religious societies to assist each other during times of personal and collective hardship, organized strikes and work stoppages to demand higher wages, and participated in labor unions. Their work to feed a growing nation during two world wars, and their struggles to attain better working and living conditions, is a true testament to their contributions to U.S. history and society.

Beginning in the late nineteenth century and intensifying throughout the first half of the twentieth century, the American agricultural industry shifted away from the family farm model and became a large-scale, specialized corporate sector. The industrialization of the agricultural industry—what writer-farmworker advocate Carey McWilliams famously coined "Factories in the Field"—had profound implications for agricultural laborers. This new era of American agriculture required a large reserve army of low-paid farmworkers who arrived during the picking season and migrated to other agricultural regions or were deported when their labor was no longer needed. To cut labor costs and have a readily available supply of workers, large growers relied on immigrants and the most marginalized members of society to fill their labor needs. In California, Chinese and Japanese nationals were instrumental in jumpstarting the state's agricultural industry, but with the passing of the Chinese Exclusion Act of 1882 and the 1907 Gentlemen's Agreement with Japan, growers began to heavily recruit Mexican immigrants to labor in the fields. Promises of better pay and social unrest in their homeland during the Mexican Revolution of 1910–1920 helped ensure that by the early 1920s, Mexican nationals were the single largest ethnic group in the southwestern agricultural industry. While American farmworkers are until this present day primarily of Mexican origin, European immigrants, poor white and black Americans, Mexican Americans, Filipino nationals, child laborers, and imported workers from the Caribbean also contributed to the development of the agricultural industry. The rise of the modern American food system, and the growing fortunes of powerful agricultural corporations, was built on the backs of the disenfranchised men, women, and children who followed the crops.

While growers traditionally sought out cheap, deportable, and tractable sources of agricultural labor, the federal government also helped institutionalize an unethical agricultural labor system. During the Depression era, to appease large growers, Congress outright excluded farmworkers from New Deal labor protections that guaranteed other American workers the right to bargain collectively, a fair minimum wage, and federal unemployment benefits. Additionally, during World War II (1939–1945), the federal government launched major contract labor programs that imported Caribbean and Mexican nationals into the United States to work in agricultural fields. Through the H2 Guestworker Program and the Mexico-U.S. agricultural labor agreement (known colloquially as the Bracero Program), hundreds of thousands of primarily Jamaican men and nearly two million Mexican men were contracted to work in the United States as farm laborers. As one contemporary of the Bracero Program noted, "For the growers the program was a dream: a seemingly endless army of cheap, unorganized workers brought to their doorstep by the government" (Kalavita 1992, 3). Despite certain provisions that secured contract laborers' rights to decent living and working conditions, these guest workers regularly lived in dilapidated housing, had no enforceable labor or civil rights, were often coerced into breaking farmworker strikes, and could be easily deported if they demanded better treatment.

Both these programs, but especially the Bracero Program, also lowered wages in agricultural regions and directly contributed to an increase in undocumented immigration because many eager guest worker applicants who did not receive labor contracts began migrating to the United States at unprecedented rates. The H2 Guestworker and Bracero Programs were initially conceived as wartime labor measures but continued well after WWII due to ongoing grower lobbying efforts. In California, the presence of *braceros*, ex-*braceros*, undocumented immigrants, Mexican Americans, poor whites, child laborers, and Filipino nationals in the fields created a diverse pool of easily exploitable agricultural laborers. Farmworkers' exclusion from major New Deal labor legislation, and the establishment of federally sponsored contract labor programs, legitimized and strengthened an agricultural labor system that was beneficial to growers and detrimental to all American farmworkers—both foreign and native born.

Due to the lack of federal labor protections, immigration policies and practices, and grower economic and political dominance, farmworkers lived and worked under some of the harshest conditions in the United States. In California's San Joaquin Valley, agricultural laborers faced an especially perilous existence. One 1960 government survey of one hundred farmworking families in Fresno County found that less than half had water taps installed in their living quarters, two-thirds had no private flush toilets, and the majority lived in overcrowded living accommodations. By midcentury, the average life expectancy of a farmworker was forty-nine, and a quarter of all farmworkers were children.

While farmworkers spent their days picking fruits and vegatables for American consumers at piece-rate wages, they faced constant hunger. The working conditions in the fields further magnified the severity of farmworker life. There were no bathroom facilities in the fields, workers often did not receive rest breaks, work-related accidents were quite common, agricultural laborers suffered from chronic back pain due to the continued use of the short-handle hoe to harvest crops, and access to water was limited in agricultural regions where temperatures during the picking season were regularly over one hundred degrees. The agriculture industry's increasing reliance on pesticides to ensure higher crop yields also had detrimental effects on farmworkers' health, with several reported incidents of farmworkers dying in sprayed fields. Furthermore, farmworkers often had to deal with labor contractors who charged them exorbitant rates to transport them to the fields, robbed them of wages, and burdened them with additional fees for basic essentials.

Although working conditions for all farmworkers were atrocious, women farmworkers often dealt with additional hardships. It was not unheard of for farmworking women to face sexual harassment and assault in the fields, and the absence of bathrooms required many women to regularly go eight to ten hours without relieving themselves. Low wages also necessitated that even heavily pregnant women work in the fields to support their families. Women were also charged with the double burden of working full time during the day and carrying out a second shift at home to feed and care for their families.

Despite lacking basic labor protections and strong citizenship rights during much of the twentieth century, farmworkers have a long tradition of organizing to demand better living and working conditions. In 1913, farmworkers in Wheatland, California, waged one of the first major agricultural labor strikes in the country after a farm labor advertisement overpromoted the needed number of workers and a grower took advantage of the worker surplus in the region to implement wage holdbacks, lower wages, and force farmworkers to live in overcrowded and unsanitary housing. Under the direction of farmworkers affiliated with the Industrial Workers of the World, agricultural laborers joined together to demand higher wages, improved bathroom facilities, access to clean drinking water in the fields, and special accommodations for female and child laborers. Similarly, during the Great Depression, over eighteen thousand mostly undocumented Mexican cotton pickers associated with the Cannery and Agricultural Workers Industrial Union led one of the largest agricultural labor strikes in U.S. history. The 1933 Cotton Strike was primarily led and organized by Mexican farmworkers who relied on family and community networks to demand an increase in wages, an abolition of the contract-labor system, and union hiring.

After WWII, farmworkers in California also repeatedly joined together to urge the federal government to terminate the Bracero Program due to its damaging effect on both foreign and domestic agricultural laborers. During the DiGiorgio Strike of 1947–1950, farmworker organizers publicly called on the non-strikebreaking clause of the Bracero Program to be properly enforced, and throughout the 1950s, anti-Bracero Program activism was central to most farmworker-organizing movements in the Southwest. Without exception, during each of these mobilization attempts, agricultural laborers were violently beaten, murdered, or deported by growers and often with the assistance or tacit approval of local law enforcement officials. These acts of violence, and the inherent inequalities within the agricultural labor system, made it difficult for farmworkers in the first half of the twentieth century to make real strides in advancing their labor and civil rights. Nonetheless, this early period of farmworker organizing reveals that various generations of agricultural laborers faced immense bloodshed, repression, and sorrow all in the hopes of improving their shared plight.

Farmworkers' long struggle to create a better future for themselves and their families culminated in the rise of the United Farm Workers (UFW) Movement in 1965, which was one of the most innovative and viable labor movements in U.S. history and resulted in farmworkers' gaining unprecedented labor protections, an increase in wages, and making everyday Americans aware of the conditions that farmworkers faced in the fields. Despite some major victories during the UFW's heyday in the late 1960s and early 1970s, the movement eventually endured catastrophic setbacks, and farmworkers today still struggle to attain an equitable piece of the American pie. Like American farmworkers of the past, today's farmworkers are disproportionately undocumented immigrants, suffer from wages that have not kept pace with the rising cost of living, labor in environmentally hazardous agricultural fields, and are still some of the most vulnerable workers in American society.

Christina Flores

See also: *1607–1775:* Farmer; *1776–1860:* Field Hand; *1861–1914:* Sharecropper

FURTHER READING

Calavita, Kitty. 1992. *Inside the State: The Bracero Program, Immigration, and the I.N.S.* New York: Routledge.

Galarza, Ernesto. 1977. *Farm Workers and Agri-business in California, 1947–1960*. London: University of Notre Dame Press.

Hahamovitch, Cindy. 2011. *No Man's Land: Jamaican Guestworkers in America and the Global History of Deportable Labor*. Princeton: Princeton University Press.

McWilliams, Carey. 1939. *Factories in the Field: The Story of Migratory Farm Labor in California*. Boston: Little, Brown and Company.

Shaw, Randy. 2008. *Beyond the Fields: Cesar Chavez, the UFW, and the Struggle for Justice in the 21st Century*. Berkeley: University of California Press.

PRIMARY DOCUMENT

In an oral history, John Sanchez, who was raised by his "fruit tramp" parents in the great central valley of California, recalls some of his earliest memories of their way of life as farmworkers. Even some sixty years after these events, he speaks with clear bewilderment about the many ways his family found to survive its crushing poverty.

I was born in Pixley County, California, May the sixth, 1920, in Tulare county. [My parents] were migrant workers, they picked cotton, they picked grapes, they picked potatoes, and worked in the melons, cantaloupes, watermelons, and stuff like that . . . It was a way of life . . . We traveled to Shafter, California, and worked at the Hoover farm in the onions, and as soon as the harvest of the onions was over, we came back to Pixley and picked cotton.

I remember as a kid, little child, four or five years old, I used to walk beside my mother and dad, and I'd carry a little sugar sack and pick at the cotton and when my sugar sack got full, I'd put it in my mother's or Dad's sack. I grew up picking cotton. I got real good at picking cotton. At one time when I was about 18 or 20, I could pick 618 pounds in one day, at $3 per hundred. That was good money then. The cotton harvest would last from September until about March. In February and March, we would pick the bolls . . . The cotton wasn't as good when it was in the bolls as it was when you picked it off the cotton vines . . .

We built little shacks out of cardboard or what we could find, to knock off the wind and cold. We didn't have mattresses, we had these big grape sweatboxes, a raisin sweatbox, my mother would put two of these together, then we would put straw on those boxes and put gunnysacks on them. We covered ourselves with gunny sacks against the cold . . . We took one of those big milk cans and cut the top off of it, and we'd use it as a stove. We'd put wood in it and started a fire in it and put a piece of metal on top of it. That's where my mother cooked our food. I lived [liked this] until I graduated from grammar school in 1935.

At that time, a farmer let us use a little house out in a field . . . John Pavlovich was the owner of the little [one-room] house in his vineyard, and he let us live in there, free of rent, for many, many years. That was the first time we lived in a house. That was in the '30s . . . At that time, there was a lot of eucalyptus groves out there; people used to make their living cutting it down and selling it for firewood. But now it's all just cotton fields . . .

In those days in the thirties, the white people were real cruel. They didn't like the Mexican people. I don't know why. They would treat us bad, they would talk to us bad, they . . . wouldn't tolerate us . . . I remember when we didn't have to go to school, we'd walk three or four miles to the Pixley Refuse Dump, where people would throw stuff that they didn't want. And we'd go there and most of the wealthy people would throw [out] good clothes—good shirts, good pants, good shoes—and my mother and I and my sister, we'd go there and pick them up and bring them home. My mother would fix them up, she'd sew them. My mother got to be a good sewer. She'd sew them up real nice. I'd wear the good clothes to school, you see, and the white kids would see clothes with the patches on, and they'd make fun of me. A lot of times I'd cry because they'd make fun of me. I'd go home that night, and my mother would say, "Well, don't cry, they don't know what they're doing. They don't know what they're saying. Some day their time will come. Some day they're going to regret it." There was one good thing about [school]. I was a little Mexican barefooted kid, but I could sure beat those white kids in class. I could out-read them, I could out-write them. In those days, I guess the white people outnumbered the Mexicans . . . Not very many Black people, I can remember there was four or five Black [families]. They were treated like us, they were treated bad . . . They were mistreated by the white people just like we were, the Mexican kids . . .

[In grape picking season] we used to cut the grapes, put them into canisters, then we would spread them out on paper trays . . . That was for the sun hit the grapes to dry them out and that would make raisins. They'd dry them for a certain amount of time, and then we'd have to go back and turn the trays. We got to where we could turn 1,000 or 1500 trays in a day's time . . . We got used to doing that. First we'd pick the grapes, then let them dry, then we'd come back and turn the trays. I think it was one cent a day for spreading them out on the trays, and then a quarter of a cent to turn the trays. A good person could turn 2000 trays a day. Later on, when the raisins were dried up on both sides, we'd roll up the trays, just like rolling a cigarette, and we'd stack them up under the vines. I can remember rolling so many of them in a day's time . . .

Herbert Hoover, the President of the United States, [had] a ranch, that was in Shafter, we'd go over there and work in the onions. I was real small then, I didn't work . . . We worked there until the onion harvest was over with, then we went back to Pixley . . . We'd always come back to Pixley, because we were in school then . . . During those months [of summer vacation] we would travel to different places in California and work. Sometimes we went to San Jose and work the apricots. One time, I don't recall where it was, we picked prunes. We'd work there and then come back to Pixley [when summer vacation was over] . . .

In those days, if people had a sack of beans they'd share it with you, had a sack of rice, they'd share it with you . . . You know, it gets 115 out there sometimes [in the cotton fields] . . . My dad and mother would take these gallon glass jugs and . . . sew a gunny sack around it . . . I remember my mother would fill up the gallon of water, and she'd do this at night. Then she'd put a little water on the outside of the gunny sack, and this would keep it cold. In the mornings, we'd go to work and that water would be cold till about 10, 11 o'clock until the sun started beating down and then it got hot. I've often wondered how we survived.

Source: John Sanchez Oral History. 1998. Interviewed by Harvey Schwartz. Courtesy of the Labor Archives and Research Center, San Francisco State University. Transcribed from Parts 1 and 2. https://archive.org/details/csfst_000027/csfst_000027_t1_b_access.mp3.

FIREFIGHTER

Firefighters work to fight fires with water and chemical retardants in an effort to put them out, but they also undertake preventive work that attempts to keep fires from starting or spreading. Events of the late nineteenth century—particularly a series of disastrous urban fires that could have been prevented—transformed the work of firefighters in the years between the two world wars. The National Fire Safety Bureau organized National Fire Safety Week in 1922, after the nation's insurance industry advocated for outreach efforts to better educate Americans about the many causes of structural fires. These efforts coincided with the increasing professionalization of urban fire departments, in which more training, civil service exams, and other activities were provided to firefighters in cities across the country. From the colonial period through much of the nineteenth century, firefighting forces had been primarily volunteers—community members who were alerted to fires and rushed to extinguish them. In large urban areas, during the Gilded Age, many firefighters had been awarded their jobs as a result of political and familiar alliances, though Progressive era reforms led many city fire departments to professionalize. Smaller communities had volunteer firefighters even well into the twentieth century, though now, most coordinate with professional forces as well.

Beginning during the early twentieth century, firefighters also took fire prevention work—assisting fire underwriters who determined insurers' risks for insuring buildings and also engaging in public education efforts. Firefighters' unions, particularly the International Association of Fire Engineers (IAFE), had helped firefighters broaden their role beyond that of responding to fire alarms and extinguishing fires. The IAFE, as historian Mark Tebeau has written, "established formal firefighting work procedures and rules," leading toward more professional firefighting forces, in "departments [that] emphasized technology, efficiency of action and procedure, and sober work discipline" (Tebeau 2012, 286–287). Firefighters now worked in regular units (engine houses), attached to departments, with individuals assigned to specialized roles within the unit: rescue squads, technicians, ladder truck drivers, and fire inspectors. Firefighters, especially in urban areas, had regular hours of labor, often assigned to shifts of twenty-four to thirty-six hours, and earned better pay. More importantly, the firefighters in professionalizing units were expected to practice their jobs during regular drills. Fire departments developed training facilities where firefighters could practice using hoses, learning how to climb the new fire ladders, rescuing individuals caught in the flames, and assessing fires for toxic smoke fumes. New chemicals used in all sorts of innovative technologies presented particular danger to firefighters as they responded to structure fires.

A typical firefighter's daily work schedule varied with the calls their unit received. Those members of an engine house on duty waited for emergency calls. When the engine house (or company) was called to fight a fire or investigate a source of smoke, the firefighters reported to their duty stations within the engine house, dressed in their protective gear, and then boarded the assigned truck to attend to the emergency. Once upon the scene, a firefighter had to assess the nature of the emergency: whether a structure was involved, what purpose the structure served, if the structure was in danger of collapse, if individuals were trapped inside the structure, and if so, whether a rescue squad could extract those trapped persons safely and without further endangering others. Firefighters made these assessments rapidly but in an organized fashion, even as they prepared to extinguish the fire and rescue anyone who might be trapped. If a ladder truck had been dispatched, then those firefighters prepared to lift the ladder into place, often to the roof if they had determined it was safe for firefighters to extinguish a fire from that location. Hoses were strung from the truck to a hydrant, tank, or, in newer buildings, fire suppression water pipes within the building that had been part of its design. As hoses were readied, firefighters would direct the water's flow onto what they had determined was the optimal area for fire suppression or to support the efforts of rescue teams. Other firefighters directed water onto the building to cool it in an effort to slow flames' spread.

Firefighters arriving at a fire or for a smoke investigation, however, had to make a number of determinations on the spot, not all of which they could do reliably. For instance, a situation that firefighters encountered on the evening of May 15, 1929, involved three companies that had arrived to investigate an acrid yellow smoke exuding from the basement of the Cleveland Clinic after two explosions. At first, there seemed to be no fire. But the irritating yellow smoke began to exude out of windows in the building—and patients were crowded about the windows, frantically awaiting rescue. As they unfurled their rescue nets and tried to find the source of the smoke (a small fire following the explosions in the basement), they realized that many of the patients and staff could not be rescued as the first firefighter to enter the building exited moments later, barely able to breathe even though he was wearing a full face mask.

The yellow smoke was caused by the burning of large stores of nitrate celluloid film, then used for x-rays, which, when it combusted, produced nitrogen dioxide and other poisonous gases. Firefighters realized then that they could not enter the building because of the smoke's toxicity, so they were only able to rescue those patients and staff who had quickly gotten to windows and doors, but even then so many had tried to exit at once that bodies were jammed into the windows and doorways, and they had to be extracted by untangling them one by one. Another firefighter, a ladder expert, quickly climbed to the roof, where he was able to cut through the building's skylight; he was joined by three others, including the company commander, who lowered themselves to the third floor, where they were able to set up a triage station and, using a new resuscitation technology, the Pulmotor, were able to revive dozens and then remove them to the roof for rescue.

Although 125 people died as a result of the fire, primarily from toxic smoke inhalation, perhaps as many were also saved by the firefighting crews. The 1929 Cleveland Clinic fire alerted firefighters to the dangers that chemicals presented to both themselves and the general public; additionally, because no fire investigators were ever able to determine the cause of the explosion, firefighters understood that even the most diligent examination of a fire's cause might not yield actionable data for future fire prevention when the fire involved such chemicals.

Throughout this period, firefighters developed greater skills, relied on better technology, and became a professional occupation for both internal and external reasons. Technology had both positive and negative influences on the work of firefighters. A tool like the Pulmotor—a heavy air tank and breathing apparatus that forced air into the lungs of unconscious nonbreathing patients—allowed firefighters to rescue those affected by some of the most dangerous fire and smoke conditions known at the time. Motorized ladders that could be operated by one firefighter allowed him to quickly get access to the roof of a building. But other technologies—especially newer substances used in industry, healthcare, and construction—presented greater challenges to the firefighters of this era.

Nancy Quam-Wickham

See also: *1861–1914:* Police Officer; *1992–2019:* Emergency Medical Technician

FURTHER READING

Smith, Dennis. 1972. *Report from Engine Co.* New York: McCall Books.

Smith, Dennis. 1978. *History of Firefighting in America: 300 Years of Courage.* New York: Dial Press.

Tebeau, Mark. 2012. *Eating Smoke: Fire in Urban America, 1800–1950.* Baltimore: Johns Hopkins.

GARMENT WORKER

Garment workers were manual laborers and members of the needle trades who were tasked with fastening or attaching an article of clothing's constituent pieces with a needle and thread or, later, with a sewing machine. Hunched over their work in sweatshops or their homes, early twentieth-century garment workers measured fabric and used patterns to cut fabric into component pieces of a garment (such as a coat) that other workers then stitched together by hand or machine. Buttonholes were sewn and buttons attached by hand; garments, too, were often hemmed by hand—or, rarely, a machine—and then pressed for distribution to wholesalers. In many sweatshops, different workers completed only one of these tasks; child workers, for instance, often sewed buttons, earning perhaps a few cents per hundred sewn. These jobs were often unskilled labor, requiring little education and only the ability to handle a needle and the patience for repetitive tasks.

In 1890, Danish immigrant Jacob Riis published an exposé about the living and working conditions of impoverished New Yorkers. Riis's book, *How the Other Half Lives*, shocked the nation in its gritty depictions of conditions in New York's tenement houses. Riis also drew attention to the work of the city's poor garment workers: largely immigrants who worked at home on a piece-work basis, in which they were paid an amount for each unit they produced. In the garment district, the Lower East Side of Manhattan, and across other impoverished neighborhoods, "sweaters," or middlemen, delivered materials to and took finished work from tenement residents. In the sweatshops and in individual rooms, families worked on a contract basis—typically in their own homes, where tuberculosis and other infectious diseases were often present. Consider one mother, who "had just brought home four pairs of pants to finish, at seven cents a pair. She was required to put the canvas in the bottom, basting and sewing three times around; to put the linings in the waist-bands; to tack three pockets, three corners to each; to put on two stays and eight buttons, and make six button-holes; to put the buckle on the back strap and sew on the ticket, all for seven cents" (Riis 1890, 173).

The garment industry of the late nineteenth and early twentieth centuries was a brutal business for most workers. What a worker earned often depended on how many pieces he or she could finish each day. The work itself was intermittent, following the seasonal changes in fashion and consumer tastes. By 1910, most garment workers could expect to work eight or nine months per year at most and face under- or unemployment during slack periods between seasonal transitions. While Riis's work led to reforms, after the turn of the twentieth century, sweatshops and factories proliferated across New York City, the center of America's garment industry. Many of these factories produced inexpensive clothing, and competition for jobs in the industry was intense. In the shirtwaist (high-collared women's blouses) sector, some forty thousand primarily Jewish and Italian immigrant women and girls worked in five hundred shops. Only those shops producing expensive clothing, mostly men's suits, employed skilled male tailors. Women and girls made most ready-to-wear garments.

Several factors dramatically changed the garment industry and workers' experiences in the years between 1910 and 1940. Trade unions, including the International Ladies Garment Workers Union (ILGWU) and the Women's Trade Union League, began organizing among women workers—pressing shop owners to end the sweating system and raise wages for garment workers. In December 1909, during the Great Uprising, twenty thousand mostly women garment workers demonstrated in the streets of New York, some carrying picket signs reading "We Are Not Slaves." The New York City police department arrested top leadership, while strikers were beaten on the picket lines. In Chicago, forty thousand garment workers walked off the job in September 1910 in a strike against men's clothing maker Hart, Schaffner and Marx. Although the strikers won concessions on piece rates, the strike was characterized by disorganization, strike breaking, and some violence.

Then, in late March 1911, a disastrous fire at a Lower East Side garment factory that had been the focus of the 1909 strike, the Triangle Waist Company, killed 146 workers, most of them young immigrant women who burned to death or leapt to their deaths from the ninth floor of the factory where they labored. As historian Jo Ann Argersinger has written, many workers joined hands and leapt to their deaths, "their hair on fire," in a last embrace of friendship; the public nature of this industrial accident, occurring on the streets of New York on a Saturday—a payday—just before 5:00 p.m., led to intense coverage in local newspapers, a day that would later be known as "the day that it rained children" (Argersinger 1991, 21). In response, New York State passed a comprehensive set of laws that established factory safety regulations and labor protection for child workers and set minimum wages and maximum hours for women workers. While some manufacturers disguised their shops to evade enforcement of these regulations, the legislation did provide some relief to garment workers in New York factories.

Low wages and dangerous working conditions led to a national outrage, especially after one of the Triangle Company's owners was fined just twenty dollars for locking the doors to escape routes, which resulted in the high death toll. Unions and social reformers united to press for improvements in conditions in both the menswear and ladies' garment sectors of the industry. In 1914, Sidney Hillman, a Lithuanian immigrant, organized the Amalgamated Clothing Workers Union (ACWU) on an industrial basis, covering all workers in the menswear sector, regardless of task or title. Simultaneously, the ILGWU led an organizing drive among workers in New York and other eastern cities during the 1910s. The ILGWU led short work stoppages in 1925 and a disastrous strike in 1926. Despite the success of union organizations, most garment workers during the 1910s and 1920s continued to labor in small factories or sweatshops. On a day-to-day basis, cutters, seamstresses, and pressers worked in much the same ways that they had two decades earlier—though they used more machines than handwork.

The Great Depression brought dramatic changes to the industry. As Americans struggled financially, they bought fewer clothes, leading to deep cuts in the garment industry; some estimate that 90 percent of all garment workers employed in the industry in the mid-1920s were unemployed by the early 1930s. Manufacturers' attempts to wring more profits out of those workers who remained employed, by reducing piece rates, led workers to join the ACWU and ILGWU in significant numbers. A Labor Department regulatory change in the early New Deal years, however, transformed the nature of garment work. After the Triangle Fire, Franklin Roosevelt's future secretary of labor, Frances Perkins, had served as an investigator on New York's Factory Investigating Committee and had witnessed the aftermath of the fire. More than twenty years later, Perkins was influential in federal regulation that prohibited sweaters, or middlemen, and contracted labor practices.

As garment workers moved into factories and out of sweatshops, they joined the new industrial unions—the ACWU and ILGWU—and helped to lead the great labor activism during the late 1930s. Garment workers supported organizing drives of steelworkers, autoworkers, electrical workers, and others. They generally enjoyed better working conditions and higher wages through the World War II years, when most clothes sold in the United States were American made. It was not until the 1950s, when factory owners seeking lower, nonunion wages and greater profits, began moving their factories offshore. Taking their factories overseas devastated the American garment-making workforce.

Nancy Quam-Wickham

See also: Textile Worker; *1607–1775:* Weaver and Spinner; *1861–1914:* Seamstress; *1946–1991:* Fashion Designer and Model

FURTHER READING

Argersinger, Jo Ann E. 1991. *Making the Amalgamated: Gender, Ethnicity and Class in the Baltimore Clothing Industry, 1899–1939*. Baltimore: Johns Hopkins University Press.

Argersinger, Jo Ann E. 2009. *The Triangle Fire: A Brief History with Documents*. Boston: Bedford/St. Martin's.

Fraser, Steven. 1993. *Labor Will Rule: Sidney Hillman and the Rise of American Labor*. Ithaca: Cornell University Press.

Riis, Jacob A. 1891. *How the Other Half Lives: Studies Among the Poor*. London: Sampson, Low, Marston, Searle & Rivington.

GEOLOGIST

Geologists are scientists who observe, investigate, and analyze the earth and its many processes. During the Golden Age of geology in the 1800s, natural historians and geologists made numerous discoveries about the planet. They collected fossils and categorized them for display in museums, tested the chemical property of rocks, observed volcanic eruptions' environmental impact on the earth's atmosphere, and opined about the causes of earthquakes. Geologists accompanied parties of explorers and surveyors and filled notebooks with observations about the lands they encountered. Nineteenth-century geologists traveled extensively to expand society's understanding of the earth. They were often intrepid adventurers who willingly lowered themselves into unknown caves or scrambled up steep rock faces to chart new areas and contribute to the field.

American geologists during the twentieth century's interwar years may have shared some traits of their earlier counterparts. Like their professional forerunners, they worked in laboratories and out in the field. Most, however, worked in just three sectors: education, civil service, and natural resource development. New scientific knowledge about earth's processes and industrial needs were some of the generative forces that created specialties within the field of geology. As specialists in a particular industry such as mining, geologists often grew familiar with the industry's business practices; many geologists owned businesses or became business leaders later in their careers. President Herbert Hoover started as a mining engineer and worked across the globe prior to becoming president in 1928.

Important scientific and resource developments of the early twentieth century shaped the field of geology. In 1912, the German geologist Alfred Wegener proposed a theory of continental drift, a precursor to the study of plate tectonics that, in turn, contributed to the scientific study of earthquakes. Seismologists are geologists who map fault lines, and from that subspecialty's outset, it has been demonstrative in any field geologist's basic practices. Like other field geologists, seismologists worked outdoors; they surveyed and mapped faults to help governments and cities assess risk to human life using surveying and engineering tools like alidades, transits, stadia rods, compasses, and plane tables.

Geologists tentatively mapped fault lines by first examining the landscape from a distance or, once airplanes were broadly available for use, by studying aerial photographs. A geologist looked for morphological evidence of fault zones by seeking out new groundwater springs or changes in the course of stream beds, or uplifted and folded sedimentary layers of earth, or discolored surface areas, landslides, and unusual patterns of erosion. They then created basic, hand-drawn overview maps, called reconnaissance maps, which described the studied land's geological features.

Seismologists use specialized instruments called seismographs, or seismometers, to quantify earthquakes' intensity. These instruments capture sudden, significant ground vibrations and convert that information into charts or other discrete data. The earliest seismometers appeared during the third century, but nineteenth-century European and Japanese scientists made enormous improvements to the instrument's overall design and accuracy. Seismologists strategically stationed instruments throughout the western American coast between 1870 and 1890, and those instruments greatly contributed to a large increase in geological knowledge. But even after World War I (1914–1918), seismologists could not reliably measure the intensity of an earthquake; to make a determination about that, a seismologist had to rely on eyewitness accounts from people who were near the earthquake's epicenter.

Seismometers have always been useful when locating the source of an earthquake, but early seismologists often needed to triangulate the point on the earth's surface vertically above the focus of an earthquake—or its epicenter— by combining several seismographic readings, transferring these data onto physical maps, and then charting isoseismic lines that denote different degrees of intensity; modern geologists and seismologists use computers to handle these data, but the process for collecting and using the data remains mostly unchanged.

Once fault zones were identified, geologists measured the fault lines' destructive capacity by digging trenches across the fault lines and examining the trench walls for shifting patterns in the visible layers of sedimentary rock. Much of this work took place in the field, but it would be followed by hours in the office or laboratory spent reading instruments, performing mathematical calculations by hand, checking and rechecking data sources, and creating and revising maps. Once these duties were complete, a seismologist had to complete and file a geological report that assessed the seismic event, its destructive potential, and known or possible risks to construction and development projects such as roadwork, canals and dams, and housing tracts. Typically, seismologists filed their reports with the U.S. Geological Survey (USGS); many also published their findings in scientific and industry journals.

Seismologists, geochemists, glaciologists, geophysicists, paleontologists, and other specialized geologists often worked in colleges and universities that supported their research and widely distributed their findings. Soil specialists, geomorphologists, and hydrologists often worked for the government—principally with the USGS, which is a federal agency that was founded in 1879, and with the Bureau of Reclamation, which Congress created in 1902 and then redefined as an independent agency in 1907. The USGS was tasked with making topographical maps of the nation, while the Bureau of Reclamation's responsibility was to evaluate and make recommendations on western water developments for purposes of irrigation and hydroelectric power generation. In 1928, for example, Congress designated the Bureau of Reclamation as the federal agency to supervise the construction of the Boulder Canyon Dam in Nevada, which was an enormous project that was completed in 1935 and still stands today. Federal economic stimulus funding during the New Deal in the 1930s created many more jobs for geologists in civil service. The federal Soil Conservation Service was created in 1935 to advise farmers and ranchers about the relationship between agriculture and soils and to prevent another Dust Bowl-like event on the southwestern Great Plains. Geologists worked in all these agencies, making science-based recommendations for the conservation and appropriate use of our nation's land, water, and natural resources.

Geologists also worked in industry, primarily in mining and petroleum geology. These workers surveyed a company's holdings and created geological maps of the subsurface based on observation and collection of rock samples, usually by digging; later in the period, geologists used core drilling sample techniques that allowed a lengthy cylinder of rock to be removed from below the earth's surface, which could then be analyzed in a laboratory for telltale signs of mineral deposits associated with coal, gems, mineral, or petroleum. In the subsurface mining industry, geologists often ventured underground to locate new seams of coal or to assess the geological stability of a section of land after it had been subjected to drilling.

Some geologists served as mine safety experts who made recommendations about a site's ongoing excavation and ventilation requirements in an effort to keep miners safe and minimize fire dangers. Geologists also accompanied and often supervised oil drillers, especially in so-called wildcat operations, where new drilling operations began in unproven areas.

During the interwar years, most young geologists began their careers in the mining and petroleum industries because most large companies had operations all around the world. A petroleum geologist might be trained in a domestic field, like east Texas, and then sent to Venezuela, and then to the Middle East, and then back to Texas, and then to Alaska—all within a decade. Living conditions could be rough: remote oil camps in the United States and abroad might feature bunkhouses for workers and only basic medical care, and geologists were expected to work very long hours, often six or seven days per week.

Increasingly throughout the 1920s and 1930s, those geologists who worked in the mining industry began to open their own consulting firms, working as independent contractors for the mining industry, whereby they could be free to reject an appointment that took them away from loved ones and their established communities.

The period between the two world wars offered considerable opportunities for employment of college-trained geologists. The need for a better scientific understanding of our earth was fostered in part by new oil discoveries and geological problems caused by industrial production; the Dust Bowl; catastrophic dam failures resulting in hundreds of fatalities, such as the St. Francis Dam collapse of 1928; major deadly earthquakes in 1925 (Santa Barbara), 1933 (Long Beach), and 1940 (El Centro); and deadly floods in 1927 (Mississippi River and Vermont), 1937 (Ohio River), and 1938 (Los Angeles).

Nancy Quam-Wickham

See also: Oil Driller; *1776–1860:* Cartographer; Gold Miner; Surveyor; *1861–1914:* Coal Miner; *1946–1991:* Scientist

FURTHER READING

Compton, Robert R. 1962. *Manual of Field Geology.* New York: John Wiley and Sons.

Eaton, J. E. 1933. "Long Beach, California, Earthquake of March 10, 1933." *American Association of Petroleum Geologists Bulletin* 17: 732–738.

Steinberg, Ted. 2000. *Acts of God: The Unnatural History of Natural Disasters in America.* New York: Oxford University Press.

PRIMARY DOCUMENT

In this interview, Anaconda geologist Vincent Perry discusses how geologists assisted mining companies to find and extract ore-bearing rock from the earth. Born in San Francisco, California, in 1901, Perry' recalls that his first childhood memory was of the Great San Francisco Earthquake on April 18, 1906, an event that no doubt contributed to his early interest in geology. After earning undergraduate and master's degrees in geology at Berkeley and Columbia, respectively, Perry went to work for Anaconda at its flagship location in Butte, Montana. He spent his entire career with Anaconda, beginning in June 1924 as a geologist and continuing to his retirement from the company in May 1970 as a director and member of the corporation's board in New York, a position he held for four years. During those years, Perry was assigned to mines throughout the western hemisphere.

One of the advantages of working as a Butte geologist was the opportunity it offered to learn the fundamentals of applied mine geology. Butte practiced a special style of mapping and using geology in mine operations . . . The Butte Geological Department was considered an excellent postgraduate school in mining geology.

The field mapping system was simple and practical. Red lines for mineralization and blue lines for faulting here carefully and skillfully weighted using sharp pencils to emphasize proportionate widths and strength of mineralization and faulting. Disseminated mineralization was shown by red dots, and brecciation by appropriate symbols. The resulting portrayal had both qualities of engineering accuracy and artistic expression.

A simple innovation was to get away from the use of bound notebooks, which engineers and geologists had used almost exclusively in the past, and go to a flexible looseleaf system in which each sheet upon which geological notes had been recorded could be filed properly, indexed and thus made available for use by the geologist who had originated the sheet, as well as by successors who followed and continued mapping the same area.

Underground mapping was done during the early part of the day and office work in the afternoon. Notes were transcribed and plotted by hand on plan maps and sections, thus creating the basic geological record. The system included copying of additional maps for the mine superintendent's and foreman's offices. That way, the information gained from the geologists' observations could be graphically displayed so mine operators could use it. It was an effective way to coordinate geological and mining activity.

In addition, there was an excellent system of written recommendations. Driving of each development heading was based upon the recommendation of the mine geologist which then required the approval of the mine superintendent. Starting and stopping of each exploration and development heading was the responsibility of the geologist.

So it was a system based not on any high technology, but rather on good, hard-headed common sense and the development of a team approach so that mine geologists and operators worked together . . . Generally there was close rapport not only with the bosses but with the miners. In my opinion it was typified in the by-word between miner and geologist passing in a crosscut or drift: "How's she going? Did you find any ore today?"

. . . [One] of my first underground experiences . . . was to map a newly discovered ore body on the 500 level of the Diamond Mine. Upon my arrival in Butte I was assigned to be a geologist for the Diamond Mine. My first day underground, I had the opportunity to see this beautiful face of high-grade chalcocite mineralization averaging between 30 and 40 percent copper across a width of about ten feet. It's hard to believe that anything like that existed. Yet in perspective, this was the type of ore that was found by the early-day prospectors when they had mined out the first silver showings and had gone down into the copper zone, finding abundant secondarily enriched chalcocite along the Anaconda lode. Those ore bodies were restricted in vertical range and occurred in a zone of strong enrichment usually several hundred feet in vertical extent. Below the chalcocite enrichment there was primary ore which generally averaged in the order of 4 up to 10 percent copper. But in mapping that high-grade chalcocite ore body on the Diamond 500 level, I was lucky enough to observe the last of the secondarily enriched high-grade ore bodies found in the Butte district.

Source: Vincent D. Perry. 1991. *A Half Century as Mining and Exploration Geologist with the Anaconda Company*. Interviews conducted by Eleanor Swent in 1990. Oral History Center, Bancroft Library, University of California. Berkeley: Bancroft Library, University of California, 18–19.

GLAZIER

In the early twentieth century, glaziers were construction workers who prepared and installed glass windows and doors. At this time, large construction booms in American cities meant the construction of more commercial buildings, especially the new skyscrapers that were lighter in construction and appearance than the older brick and masonry buildings. Department stores, office buildings, and corporate headquarters were all built utilizing these new construction techniques. This building boom dramatically increased the demand for skilled glaziers as well.

Before the late nineteenth and early twentieth centuries, the work of the glazier was radically different than it was in later years. In the twelfth century, a monk named Theophilus wrote admiringly about the work of the glazier, the artist and craftsman who meticulously created stained-glass windows for medieval churches. Glaziers blew their own glass, mixed pigments for coloring, and then cooled and cut the pieces for placement into a pattern, using strips of lead into which the glass was set. Later artistically trained glaziers, like Louis Comfort Tiffany, created elaborate, stained-glass objects for interior decorations. Before the 1850s, most windows consisted of multiple small panes of glass set into a frame in a grid pattern, much like a medieval stained-glass window with the exception that most windows were clear, not colored, and set into wooden frames using glaziers' putty, not lead beads. The manufacture of glass, however, changed with technological and chemical improvements in the process: industrial pouring and rolling glass facilitated the production of larger dimensions of window glass, while new heating and chemical treatment processes created tougher glass suitable for use in large buildings. These production improvements made it possible for architects to use larger and larger plates of glass in their building designs. By the turn of the century, new modern commercial buildings featured large glass windows as a common design feature, allowing natural light into the interiors while emphasizing a more modern building aesthetic.

Glaziers benefited from these changes in architecture and glassmaking. Glaziers worked in several environments: in small glass shops specializing in installation and repair of windows and mirrors, on commercial construction sites, in automobile and other industrial plants where a product includes glass components, and in glassmaking plants. If required to repair a broken window in a small shop, for instance, a glazier traveled to the site to take precise measurements of the frame. He then took a glass panel and, using hand tools (metal T-square, rule, and glass cutters), cut the glass to size. Patience, precision, and a steady hand are some of the glaziers' skills and temperament since one minor miscalculation in measurement or rush to make a cut could break the glass pane. A glazier then set the glass into an L-shaped rabbeted groove in the wooden frame, using glazier's points or sprigs (small headless nails or brads) to set the glass pane in the frame; then he used glazier's putty (a sticky compound containing lead) to secure the pane in the frame. In a common sash window, the elements of a window frame include the stiles (vertical parts) and rails (horizontal parts); if multiple panes constitute a full window, this also includes the astragals that create the grid-like look. Glaziers also cut bevels into glass panes, etched designs and made inscriptions on glass, and did other artistic work on glass and mirrors.

Glaziers also worked on large construction sites, installing framing and glass for windows and doors. In commercial work, glaziers install glass into steel or aluminum mullions. They work both inside and outside, on the exterior of a building, high up on the job site, such as during the construction of the Empire State Building in the early 1930s. Designed by the architectural firm of Shreve, Lamb and Harmon, at a height of 1,250 feet (not including the 200-foot antenna atop it), the Empire State Building was designed to tower over the New York skyline. The building contractors, Starrett Brothers and Eken, had designed the building process to resemble that of an assembly line: Steel beams and girders were brought in batches, enough for several stories, to the site, where then the ironworkers and engineers lifted them into place, riveting them together. An impressive system of high-speed elevators and railway-like tracks on every floor delivered building materials to workers, including the glaziers. Glaziers installed the two window panels—exterior and then interior, separated by steel spacers—into the rails and stiles of the frame. The majority of the building's 6,500 windows were double-hung sash windows. As glaziers inside installed the window panels into their frames, on the exterior of the building, other glaziers stood atop scaffolding ready to receive the panels to set inside the framing. Each week, the thousands of construction workers built three or more floors at a controlled yet frenetic pace. The entire exterior of the building was completed in just over six months, setting records for building construction. At the opening of the building, 32 construction workers were given craftsmanship awards and had their names inscribed on a bronze Art Deco plate in the lobby of the building; among them was Samuel Laginsky, glazier. In New York, it was tradition to name a member of each construction trade for these Craftsmen Awards for all large commercial buildings in this period, with dozens of other glaziers awarded for their labor.

Periodic labor shortages coupled with building booms pushed workers to their limits as contractors rushed to finish the work. In 1936, striking glaziers in New York City destroyed the product of their own labor. Using rubber-banded slingshots to propel stove bolts high in the air, "flying squadrons" of strikers shattered plate glass windows in buildings large and small throughout Manhattan, Brooklyn, Queens, the Bronx, White Plains, and New Rochelle. These campaigns of sabotage had long been a tactic among unionized glaziers as strikers in 1910, 1920, and 1932 had also used this tactic to force contractors to accede to their demands. The destruction in 1920 was so extensive that a New York court issued an injunction in the effort to prevent striking glaziers from committing "acts of violence" against New York's buildings.

The completion of the United Nations Secretariat building in New York in 1952, designed by notable architects Oscar Neimeyer and Le Corbusier (Charles-Edouard Jeanneret), signaled a new era for glaziers. Architectural glass one and two inches thick was now used as the exterior "skins" for buildings, creating an even more modernist look. In the years after World War II, glaziers' work was even more important, and they worked alongside operating engineers and crane men, lifting the heavy tempered glass panels and securing them into the exterior framing using bolts and other means to attach them to the structure. The work of glaziers became indispensable, and it remains today one of the most high-paying of the construction trades, with many opportunities for employment.

Nancy Quam-Wickham

See also: *1946–1991:* Architect; Construction Worker

FURTHER READING

Aaseng, Nathan. 2000. *Construction: Building the Impossible*. Minneapolis: Oliver Press.
Harris, Cyril M. 2012. *Dictionary of Architecture & Construction*. New York: McGraw-Hill.
National Learning Corporation. 1900. *Glazier*. Syosset: National Learning Corporation.

GROCER

In the first half of the twentieth century, grocery clerks in independent shops and chain stores were responsible for weighing and measuring bulk products, selling items at the register, offering product information to customers, wrapping up purchases, consulting with traveling salesmen who worked for food manufacturers and wholesalers, and assembling customer orders for pickup or delivery. The grocery business changed dramatically during the interwar years as the economy grew and technology improved. In the 1910s and 1920s, grocery stores were small and numerous, located throughout residential neighborhoods and commercial districts in small towns and cities. People shopped for food daily because of storage limitations in home kitchens and the perishability of food in an era before refrigeration. During the 1920s, the spread of chain stores and a trend toward larger stores presented strong competition to small family businesses. During the 1930s, huge supermarkets, which sold inexpensive, brand-name products, began to appear in suburban areas and served a customer base that primarily arrived by car.

Grocery clerks worked long hours, though the rhythm of a day varied tremendously; the busiest hours were often early in the morning and at midday, and off-peak hours could be very slow. Warren Desepte remembered working up to twelve hours a day as a grocery clerk in San Francisco in 1909 for twelve dollars a week. "As far as I can remember," he said, "we went to work at seven o'clock in the morning and worked to six or seven p.m." (Desepte 1958). On Saturdays, often the busiest day of the week, stores might stay open late into the night. Besides working behind counters, Desepte explained that grocery work involved heavy lifting of boxes in the stockroom. And clerks needed to be able to read, write, and know how to figure sales and accounts. "You had to know your merchandise, the price of your merchandise and everything about them," Desepte recalled (Desepte 1958). Desepte worked as a union organizer during the 1920s and 1930s to fight for better pay and working hours for grocery clerks.

Because they did not cost much to open before the 1930s, grocery stores offered business opportunity for working-class entrepreneurs. Many immigrants ran neighborhood stores that offered familiar products, and they spoke the various languages of their surrounding neighbors. A survey by the National Negro Business League found that African American businessmen were more likely to operate grocery stores than any other small business. The Colored Merchants Association organized independent African American grocers into a voluntary chain to lower the costs of buying from wholesalers and to share the costs of advertising.

Store owners or managers faced complicated economic decisions when trying to figure out how to make a profit. A typical owner had to monitor the store's financial accounts and inventories, negotiated credit accounts with regular neighborhood customers, and made product-by-product decisions about how best to set prices so that expenses would be covered. Grocery stores weathered a series of economic and labor crises during the interwar years that increased the challenges for store managers. Grocery workers faced increasing responsibilities in administering new sales taxes and labor rules established by state and federal governments during the Great Depression and food rationing policies during World War II. Thousands of small grocery stores went out of business, and chains closed stores that were not profitable as new supermarkets began to present strong competition.

The self-service supermarket changed the nature of work in the grocery store. Instead of working behind a counter filling customer orders, clerks restocked shelves and checked customers out at the cashier's desk, while customers served themselves from open shelves. William Marnell, a grocery clerk during the 1920s, described the grocery store where he worked in Dorchester, Massachusetts, as "in almost all respects a man's work and a boy's" because the vast majority of clerks were male. During World War II, women took the clerking jobs that had previously belonged to men, and by the 1950s, the majority of cashiers operating supermarket lines were women.

Lisa C. Tolbert

See also: Retail Clerk; *1607–1775:* Shopkeeper; *1861–1914:* Haberdasher

FURTHER READING

Desepte, Warren G. 1958. "The Early Days of Grocery Clerk Unionism." An interview conducted by Corinne L. Gilb and David F. Selvin for the Institute of Industrial Relations Oral History Project of the University of California on February 25, 1958, in San Francisco.

Holsey, Albon, L. 1929. "The C.M.A. Stores Face the Chains." *Opportunity* (July): 210–213.

Marnell, William H. 1971. *Once Upon a Store: A Biography of the World's First Supermarket*. New York: Herder and Herder, Inc.

Mayo, James M. 1993. *The American Grocery Store: The Business Evolution of an Architectural Space.* Westport: Greenwood.

Spellman, Susan. 2016. *Cornering the Market: Independent Grocers and Innovation in American Small Business*. New York: Oxford University Press.

PRIMARY DOCUMENT

These two documents from two small-town California newspapers provide a view of the grocer and his clientele. The first document provides advice about how customers should choose their grocer, based on a set of attributes. The second document gives us a poetic view of what the grocer wants most from his customers.

1. "Points on Picking Your Grocer"

It was a hard matter to decide which grocer should have our orders. Not that it would make much difference to the grocers in a money way—our little orders—but because most of them were friends that we met in church or in social circles, and choosing one from the lot when we liked all of them was hard for us. It seemed that some folk decided this momentous question by what the grocer gave when they paid their bill at the end of some period of waiting. Paying as we go, we couldn't expect anything in the line of such favors. Of course, a grocer can't afford to show his gratitude by giving you a box of candy unless you've made him wait for his money a month or a year, or some such trifling bit of time. Some others decide on where they'll trade by what the grocer throws in extra with each dollar's worth purchased. That didn't help us out, either, because we so often bought less than a dollar's worth. There was nothing for it but just to try all around until we had found the right place. Some of them didn't seem to care for small orders, so finally it narrowed down to only a few, and at last we are settled after all by what one grocer threw in. It was thrown in with each purchase, too, and it made you feel that after all you were worth something to him in a business way. He didn't eye you disapprovingly and ask: "What else?" in a tone that seemed to imply; "Surely you wouldn't stop on so small an order as that!" No, sir! Our grocer takes any sort of order, little or big, and throws in a cheery, hearty "Thank you!" He always makes the last word sound as if it were spelled with capitals. His way of taking an order has been copied by his clerks, and every one of them says: "Thank you!" Even little slips of paper upon which they take down telephone orders have this message on the back: "We take pleasure in thanking you for your patronage." We had already guessed as much, by the way he said it. He continues: "We believe that everything you buy of us will please you." Sure, we believe it, too! And he adds, "We want your trade." Well, bless his soul, he shall have it, just as long as he takes the time and the thoughtful care to add to every package, large or small that bright, convincing "Thank you."

Source: "Points on Picking Your Grocer." 1916. Grass Valley and Nevada City (CA) *Morning Union.*' September 19, 4.

The Grocerman's Pleasure Comes At Last

Last evening, I was talking
With a grocer aged and grey.
Who told me of a dream he had,
I think 'twas Christmas day.
While snoozing in his office,
The vision came to view,
For he saw an Angel enter,
Dressed in garments white and new.
Said the Angel, "I'm from heaven.
And the lord sent me down
To bring you up to glory
And put on your golden crown.

You've been a friend to everyone,
And worked hard night and day;
You've supported many thousands,
And from few received your pay.
So we want you up in Glory,
For you have labored hard,
And the good Lord is preparing
Your eternal just reward."

Then the Angel and the grocer
Started upward toward Glory's Gate;
But when passing, close to hades,
The Angel murmured "Wait!
I've a place to show you—
It's the hottest place in hell—
Where the ones who never paid you
In torment always dwell."
And behold, the grocer saw there
his old customers by the score.
And grabbing up his chair and fan,
He wished for nothing more;
But was bound to sit and watch them
As they sizzled, singed and burned,
And his eyes would rest on debtors,
Whichever way they'd turn.
Said the Angel "Come on grocer.
There's the Pearly Gates to see."
But the grocer only murmured,
"This is Heaven enough for me."

Source: Anonymous. 1914. "The Grocerman's Pleasure Comes at Last." Truckee *Republican*. April 30, 1.

INFANTRYMAN

Infantrymen are the foot soldiers of any army or marine forces. During the First and Second World Wars, the infantry was made up of the men with rifles, stationed in the foxholes or storming beachheads in Europe or Pacific Islands. The movement of large fighting forces required coordination with transportation and support units, thousands of men moving on foot, in trucks, and on trains. Supported by the artillery (heavy guns and cannons) and air and naval forces, infantrymen are trained to engage in hand-to-hand combat, work as snipers, conduct reconnaissance missions, and patrol occupied areas during war.

One person who would become an infantryman, Samuel Schmidt, was the son of Romanian Jewish immigrants and arrived in America as a child in 1922. Like many young men, he was in no hurry to enlist in the military after graduating from high school in 1941. But in early 1944, his draft number was called, and he reported for duty—training first in Tennessee to become a military policeman, though the army soon disbanded that camp and sent all the soldiers to Fort Bragg, North Carolina, where Schmidt and his fellow trainees prepared for the infantry.

Despite Schmidt's initial misgivings about military service, his reality was quite different than those infantrymen who, on D-Day, landed at Normandy, where as an infantryman, Schmidt first set foot on French soil—but not until August 1944. His battalion of eight hundred men were then bivouacked in Normandy for a few weeks.

As part of a reserve force of infantrymen, Schmidt's unit saw so little action during the waning months of World War II, even at the Battle of the Bulge, that, years later, he could recall very little of what had happened during his time as an infantryman, until that one day in mid-April 1945, when he was shot; it was also the day that President Franklin Delano Roosevelt died across the Atlantic. Schmidt's wartime service as an infantryman was over; he was transported to a mobile surgical unit, then to a hospital in England, then to a rehabilitation facility on Staten Island, from which he was discharged from the army in November 1945.

While Schmidt's service may have been brief, it was not atypical. While many inductees prepared for the infantry in basic training camps, learning how to handle small arms, toss grenades, and repair their equipment in the field, service in the infantry was not guaranteed. Infantry training camps also prepared men for the physical rigors of work as infantrymen: running, marching with field packs and rifles, climbing, and navigating both natural and manmade barriers. Trainees performed hours of calisthenics every day. They learned how to dig foxholes and take cover from snipers in abandoned buildings. Once trainees graduated from training camp, men were transferred to other camps like Fort Dix, New Jersey, where Schmidt embarked for Europe. Frank Ruffo, another infantryman, was ultimately assigned to work as a medic, not a frontline infantryman. Sent to Europe after D-Day, Ruffo was stationed at an army depot outside of Paris, preparing supplies for transport to the frontlines at the Battle of the Bulge. When his unit was sent to Germany, he recalled that the Germans had abandoned their posts in the countryside so quickly that his unit was sent to collect German medical supplies for use later. While Nazis and Nazi sympathizers were apprehended, the Americans set defeated Italians free; Ruffo recalled seeing the Italians "trying to get home . . .

They were walking by, one who had rags on his feet, tied around his feet because his feet were bleeding, and they'd take a bicycle or motorcycle [until it] will run out of gas" and then abandon that at the roadside and start walking toward Italy again.

During this period, millions of men served as infantrymen, and tens of thousands died in battle. Those who served in combat first were largely members of the regular army, not the later divisions to which Ruffo and Schmidt were assigned. Approximately fifteen thousand men comprised a division in the army in World War II; there were nearly one hundred divisions within the army during these years, but only about twenty-five were regular army. Infantrymen who were regular army members may have served for years before the war; some officers were veterans of World War I. Others were volunteers, men who joined the military soon after Pearl Harbor and then volunteered for battle as infantrymen. These units saw some of the most intense fighting of the war and suffered some of the greatest casualties, like the members of the Third Division, who fought under General Patton first in North Africa and then in Italy, France, and Germany. At Anzio, members of the Third Division were pinned on the beachheads under German fire for almost four months in 1943; later, infantrymen assigned to the Third Division captured Hitler's headquarters outside Munich. Other divisions, like the 34th, saw more days of battle but had far fewer casualties; this division was part of the National Guard, and after participating in the North African campaign, it trained for months for the invasion of Sicily. Long training periods interspersed with heavy fighting typified the experience of most infantrymen during the war.

Nancy Quam-Wickham

See also: *1776–1860:* Militiaman; *1861–1914:* Soldier; *1992–2019:* Combat Engineer

FURTHER READING

George, John B. 1981. *Shots Fired in Anger: A Rifleman's View of the War in the Pacific, 1942–1945, Including the Campaign on Guadalcanal and Fighting with Merrill's Marauders in the Jungles of Burma*. Washington, DC: National Rifle Association of America.

Heller, Joseph, and Robert M. Scotto. 1973. *Joseph Heller's Catch-22: A Critical Edition*. New York: Dell.

O'Donnell, Patrick K. 2013. *Dog Company: The Boys of Pointe Du Hoc: The Rangers Who Accomplished D-Day's Toughest Mission and Led the Way Across Europe*. s.l.: Patrick O'Donnell.

Ruffo, Frank. 2005. "Interview of Frank Ruffo." By Stephanie Ruffo. Rutgers Oral History Archives. Last modified October 7, 2005. https://oralhistory.rutgers.edu/interviewees/30-interview-html-text/267-ruffo-frank.

Schmidt, Samuel. 2004. "Interview of Samuel Schmidt." By Nicholas Molnar. Rutgers Oral History Project. Last modified September 3, 2004. https://oralhistory.rutgers.edu/interviewees/30-interview-html-text/238-schmidt-samuel.

PRIMARY DOCUMENT

A native of Jersey City, New Jersey, Louis Trezza enlisted in the Marine Corps shortly after the attack on Pearl Harbor, December 7, 1941. In a lengthy oral interview, Trezza explains that he was playing pool in a poolhall when he learned of the attack. Just eighteen years old, he had been working in a steel mill but decided that he needed to join the fight against fascism. He choose the marines for their reputation of "being the best"—of creating elite and highly disciplined fighting forces. After basic training at Parris Island, South Carolina, he was assigned to the Fourth Marines Division; he was trained as a mortar man, who carried a collapsible tube that could be assembled to propel sixty-millimeter mortar shells a great distance. As a mortar man, Trezza was also responsible for shooting up flares to light the battlefield during night warfare. As a mortar man and trained rifleman, at times Trezza was positioned forward of the frontlines. Some sixty years after the war, when asked about what it was to experience battle, he replied simply, "Fear."

Trezza's unit was then assigned to Camp Pendleton, California, before embarking for the advance base in Maui, Hawaiian Islands. From there, Trezza was sent to fight at Kwajalein Atoll in the Marshall Islands, a relatively short battle. From that victory, Trezza's unit returned to Maui for several months for training prior to the invasion of the Northern Marianas Islands of Saipan and Tinian in June 1944. He participated in the invasions of both islands, which were extraordinarily costly in lives of both Americans and Japanese. After victory there, Trezza and his unit began training for the Battle of Iwo Jima, one of the bloodiest skirmishes of World War II. In this account, Trezza describes the terror of battle and being wounded during the invasion. He was evacuated from Iwo Jima, hospitalized for months, and ultimately received a medical discharge from the Marines.

Well, like I say, we knew we were in trouble and [the Japanese military] had Mt. Suribachi there, which was one big artillery position. They had all kinds of caves and no straight out caves. All [of them] had angles and they could fire up and down the beach. They had every inch of the beach covered and, when we hit, the first three waves, there was no bombardment until the first three waves [landed], and then, all hell broke loose. It took us three days to get off the beach and a lot of guys never did. In fact, I had a shell fall right in the hole with me and, unbelievably, none of us, there were about ten of us in that hole, that shell hole, and nobody got hurt and that was just one incident, but so many guys got killed and wounded on the beach, it was unbelievable.

These, what we call LCVPs, landing craft, come in and take the guys out. It was just unbelievable the amount of people they had on. After the third day, we were able to get off the beach and, of course, there were plenty of Marines coming in behind us. We had two other divisions on that little island. It was unbelievable, sixty thousand men on eight square miles. It was just unbelievable and we crossed over the airport. We thought we were going to get help keeping the airport, because we didn't shell the airport. We wanted that in as good a shape as possible and we figured, "Well, this is it." We went across that airport; we didn't draw a shot. They were concentrating all their fire on the Navy and on the beach and they hit a couple of ships, you know.

. . . As a matter-of-fact, the third day on Mt. Suribachi, that's when the flag went up and the first flag was small. We didn't realize what was going on at the time, but we saw the flag go up, then, it came down. We said, "Oh, my God, we lost it already? We just got up there," but, then, we saw the other flag, a much bigger flag, go up. We had no idea what was going on, but that's when that famous picture was taken and they had no idea that would be so famous, you know. It's just one of those things. There, the [Japanese] fought smart. There were no *banzai* attacks. The whole island was tunnels and they'd be right under us and we wouldn't know it and, every night, they would come up in groups, small groups, shoot around and disappear.

This one night, it just so happened that we were in a situation where, behind us, it was like a hill and we were up against it and we had a mound of dirt right in front of us, like a barrier, and we were shooting flares up and, all of a sudden, the [Japanese] come out of nowhere. We were mowing them down, and then, they just disappeared. That's how I got hit. It was the eighth day and what we would do in the morning was, we would mop up. That morning, we were out mopping up, my two buddies and me, and I was the lead man. There was a Marine helmet bobbing around and they were great for that, too, for taking our uniforms and acting like Marines. We were pretty sure it wasn't a Marine, but we couldn't take that chance, you know. We wouldn't kill him until we were positive and, sure as hell, it was a [Japanese soldier]. So, he popped his grenade and he held it and we said, "Well, he's going to commit *hari-kari*," but he didn't. He held it for two seconds and out it came. My two buddies took off and I was close to it, so, I just hit the deck and, of course, I got hit. I had quite a few pieces in me and they also got hit, too, but they were running and they didn't get it that seriously. They got it in the back and their legs, but I first thought I was dead. Of course, it blew my helmet off, broke my jaws and I'm thinking to myself, I can't hear anything now . . . and I'm like,

"Oh, my God, I'm dead." When I saw the blood on my hands, I thought, "I'm not dead. I'm alive."

So, I call for a corpsman and he wrapped me up as best as he could, you know, around my neck, my hands. My hands were wounded and he got up and I saw I could walk. So, I had got hit from the waist up and I'm walking through the command post and I'm all wrapped up in these bandages. I always called him an asshole, our commanding officer, a captain, he said, "Where the hell are you going, Trez?" I said, "I'm getting off this goddamn island. Where the hell do you think I'm going?" and I just kept walking. I went down to the beach, got on one of those LCVPs and they took me to a hospital ship . . . They took care of me as much as they could there. One guy; I had to stop, because I had shrapnel in my spine and I didn't know it at the time. So, he's digging around in there and I grabbed his hand and I said, "Wait until they take x-rays." I mean, I don't know where I got that thought from, but I stopped them, because they had no facilities to do that with on these ships. Then, we went to a hospital on Saipan, which I only stayed a day or two in, and then, from there, they sent me back to the hospital in Pearl Harbor. That's where I found out how everything was, you know, especially the shrapnel. In fact, when I was waiting to see a doctor, he's whistling and he said, "Hey, Trez, get in here." I'm sitting outside, waiting to see him, and he had real fancy equipment in those days; he's got my x-rays against the window. He said, "Look at this." He shows me the shrapnel. The vertebra is like that and the shrapnel is right in there. He said, "Why you're walking, I'll never know." He said I should just thank God. It's amazing, because I was partially paralyzed for a while, but that wore off, on the left side. I couldn't move it and I asked him about that. I said, "What's going to happen?" He said, "That's going to take care of itself. Don't worry about it."

Source: Louis Trezza Oral History 2004. Rutgers University Oral History Project, February 29. http://oralhistory.rutgers.edu/interviewees/30-interview-html-text/108-trezza-louis. Used by permission of the Rutgers University Oral History Project.

IRONWORKER

Unlike steelworkers, who make steel, ironworkers do not work in factories making iron. Instead, ironworkers are a classification within the construction trades who are specialists in assembling iron and steel bridges, office buildings, roadways, and other structures. Ironworkers arose as a distinct occupation largely in the late nineteenth and early twentieth centuries as new construction methods emerged. Before this period, most bridges were constructed of wood or, sometimes, stone; wooden and masonry (brick or stone) buildings dominated the American urban scene, but the heavy footings needed for masonry buildings limited their height to about nine or ten stories. There were no skyscrapers, no soaring bridges—not until the 1880s and 1890s, when structural engineers in the United States, Canada, and Europe started to experiment with building iron bridges and steel-framed buildings. An American architectural firm, Burnham and Root, similarly experimented with these new structural materials and, in doing so, changed the skylines of Chicago (Fisher Building), Detroit (Ford Building), and elsewhere by incorporating steel as a building's main structure and then encasing it in glass and granite or other stone and, in the process, creating taller and more elegant buildings, known as skyscrapers. The construction workers who built these tall buildings, massive bridges, and other structures were the ironworkers. These men worked in "high steel" as "skywalkers," as many called themselves.

Immigration and consequent population growth, as well as migration from farms into American cities, propelled the nation's engineers, architects, and construction firms to design better buildings. Business expansion also drove the need for taller and stronger structures in the first half of the twentieth century: corporations needed big buildings as headquarters, where hundreds of office workers kept the company's work going; rising production of all kinds of goods and the growth of markets for those goods, both domestically and abroad, required better transportation systems—bigger locomotives with longer streams of rail cars, carrying increasingly heavy loads. These newer and heavier railroads needed bridges and railway trusses that could support their weight, not the wooden structures of earlier days. Furthermore, wooden structures of all kinds—houses, tenements, bridges—were susceptible to destruction by fire. All of these factors drove innovation in architecture and engineering, in which builders increasingly used and favored iron and steel. To build structures of these metals, construction companies needed ironworkers.

Ironworkers specialized in the assembly of steel and iron structures—primarily bridges and skyscrapers but also railway trusses (high, bridge-like structures that allow trains to cross geographic barriers like canyons), silos, dams, and, later, larger roadways and interstates. Ironworkers generally worked in gangs of a few men, with each man having a particular duty. As a gang, they worked together to connect structural steel together using rivets. Ironworkers known as platers positioned giant steel beams weighing several tons each into place, using cranes, cantilevers, and a traveler (devices that incrementally move materials out onto a horizontal platform to lengthen it) or just heavy blocks and tackle gear. There were predrilled holes in each beam where they were to be connected to each other. To hold the beams into place temporarily, the platers inserted bolts into some of the holes.

While the steel beams were held into place temporarily with bolts, ironworkers precisely lined up these holes and then inserted a hot rivet (a metal rod with a rounded enlarged head on one end) into each hole, hammering the other end to a button-like finish. As the hot metal rivets cooled, they contracted, tightening the connection between the beams and creating a well-assembled structure. Ironworkers who hammered in the rivets were riveters, those who had the greatest skill. In the days before pneumatic riveting drills, riveters had to judge the heat of the rivet by color (deep red), quickly insert the long rivet into the hole, and then hammer the rivet until it set. Riveters judged the set by the sound of the hammer hitting the rivet—rivets that didn't set made a dull, not metallic, sound when hit by the hammer, and the rivet heads could loosen. When manually driving rivets into place, two riveters worked in concert hammering a hot rivet that had been manually inserted into the hole by another member of the work gang, the holder-on. Two other members of an ironworker's crew were needed: the carrier, who delivered hot rivets to the holder-on and riveters, and the forge boy, who prepared the rivets by heating the metal bars in a makeshift charcoal forge.

Every steel skyscraper or large bridge required millions of rivets. And as the structure rose up from the ground, ironworkers had to navigate the "high steel" by walking along the beams to the next set of holes to be riveted as the structure was assembled. As the century progressed and large structures like the Empire State Building in New York City and the Golden Gate Bridge in San Francisco were built, ironworkers found themselves working at great heights—sometimes hundreds of feet above the ground or water surface. Ironworkers had to be comfortable working at these heights; some of the earliest construction companies hired sailors off seagoing vessels because they had work experience at heights in all weather, having had to climb aloft to bring in or let out sails. Even though pay was high, recruitment of ironworkers was often difficult as many workers found themselves uncomfortable working so high off the ground. Ironworkers had to move quickly when carrying rivets or plating and had to be agile on steel beams, sure-footed, and unafraid of heights.

Early construction crews did not use hard hats and seldom utilized safety lines, so ironworkers were often injured by falling debris from others working above them. Some fell to their deaths. Nearly thirty workers died building the Bay Bridge—which connected San Francisco and Oakland, California—during its construction in the 1930s.

One group of willing skywalkers was the Kanien'kéhaka (Mohawk) men who first gained experience working high steel in the 1890s and early 1900s during the construction of steel bridges over the St. Lawrence River. Many Mohawk men worked in other construction trades and transportation; they crewed barges and ships that navigated inland waterways. Already familiar with industrial employment, these tribal members sought employment as ironworkers, and construction firms willingly employed them. Early on, Mohawk ironworkers gained a reputation as fearless—they navigated high steel expertly, worked well in gangs (as cooperative labor in small groups was a cultural tradition), and willingly traveled to faraway worksites, leaving their families at home, known as "booming out." This, too, was a culturally accepted practice; Kanien'kéhaka women had long participated as full members of this matriarchal society and tended to family and community needs when their men were away at work in cities like New York, Buffalo, Chicago, Philadelphia, Detroit, and Pittsburgh. Sons followed their fathers into the trade, and then their sons followed them. Occupational segregation of certain groups, like the Mohawk, was voluntary and common in this period. Since many early Mohawk ironworkers did not speak English, recruiting other workers who spoke the same language was essential to maintaining the efficiency of the gang.

Other groups of ironworkers at this time also maintained ethnically homogenous work groups and recruited new workers from within families from Newfoundland, Scandinavia, and elsewhere. By the 1930s, though, members of the Ironworkers' Union—formally known as the International Association of Bridge, Structural, Ornamental and Reinforcing Iron Workers—spread the word throughout the country about job opportunities on major federally funded construction projects like the Golden Gate and San Francisco Bay Bridges, the Grand Coulee Dam, and other major public works.

As highly skilled craftsmen, ironworkers were generally fiercely pro-union as the union supervised apprenticeship programs and certified a worker's skill. Construction supervisors preferred these trained and certified workers, and while many employers fought unions during the Depression years, most construction companies welcomed members of the iron workers' union onto their jobs. Even today, the union, whose motto is "The Sky's the Limit," offers apprenticeship training to courageous young men and women seeking a good career.

Nancy Quam-Wickham

See also: Glazier; *1861–1914:* Railroad Construction Worker; *1946–1991:* Architect; Construction Worker

FURTHER READING

Rasenberger, Jim. 2009. *High Steel: The Daring Men Who Built the World's Greatest Skyline 1881 to the Present.* New York: HarperCollins.

Schwartz, Harvey. 2015. *Building the Golden Gate Bridge: A Workers' Oral History.* Seattle: University of Washington Press.

Weitzman, David. 2010. *Skywalkers: Mohawk Ironworkers Build the City.* New York: Roaring Book Press.

LONGSHOREMAN

During the middle decades of the twentieth century, seaborne cargo was stowed and unloaded mostly by hand; this work of loading and unloading cargo onto ships was the work of a longshoreman. Longshoremen worked on the docks, where they transferred cargo, and on the decks and in the holds of cargo ships, where cargo was secured. Securing cargo was critical to a vessel's safety as shifting cargoes at sea could cause a ship to list and possibly sink. Most longshoremen who did this work used handheld longshore hooks to grapple sacks, crates, and other types of cargo. Probably the most odious cargo consisted of raw hides: they smelled putrid and were slimy and infested with maggots. All cargo was loaded onto suspended slings controlled by steam-driven winches and then hoisted into or out of the hold of the ship.

This whole process was called break-bulk cargo handling. Only men performed this work until World War II (1939–1945), when a waterfront labor shortage, as many men were serving in the military, drew a few women to the waterfront. African American and other nonwhite men labored as longshoremen in the break-bulk years but typically in segregated groups. They began to achieve a measure of equality in most major West Coast ports beginning in the mid-1930s. In the break-bulk era, this arduous work required strength, stamina, agility, and skill. In loading a ship, longshoremen had to build a proper stow so that cargo would not shift dangerously at sea. They were often aided by a wood butcher, a worker who constructed a wooden line down the middle of a ship to help keep stowed cargo from moving. Huge, unwieldy bags of rice, heavy packing crates and boxes, 160-pound sacks of coffee, 500-pound bales of cotton—such products had to be hand stowed or offloaded efficiently and safely with just a handheld hook. Working cargo with a reliable partner often made the difference between a good day and a bad one on the job.

Before the 1930s on the West Coast and even longer on the East and Gulf Coast ports of the United States, longshore work was characterized by corrupt hiring practices, dangerous job conditions, and inconsistent hours and earnings. In the 1920s, a typical day in the Port of San Francisco began when a longshoreman arrived on the waterfront for an early-morning shape-up, gathering with dozens of other job seekers in the hope of landing work for a few hours for a day, or for a week, depending on the shipowners' needs. Just to get a job, workers were frequently forced to pay a bribe, called a kickback, surrendering part of their pay to the hiring boss or giving him a jug of wine or other incentive. Harry Bridges, a San Francisco longshoreman who, in 1934, would lead the Pacific Coast dock workers in a labor strike, said of this degrading shape-up, "We were hired off the streets like a bunch of sheep standing there from six o'clock in the morning in all kinds of weather."

In other ports along the West Coast in the 1920s, employer-run hiring halls, which dispatched the coveted jobs, practiced variations on this shape-up. At the Los Angeles/Long Beach waterfront, an employer-run "fink hall," as the workers called it, sometimes forced longshoremen to fight each other for a few work-assignment cards thrown onto the floor. Tacoma, Washington, was the only major port with a worker-run longshore hiring hall in these years. Only Tacoma had survived when, just after World War I, strikes and confrontations with the shipping companies had destroyed the waterfront unions in the rest of the big Pacific Coast ports.

If a worker was lucky enough to get a job, he labored in degrading and dangerous conditions. The boss often made groups of men, called "gangs," compete. The result was high productivity but also numerous accidents as men moved heavy cargo too quickly. Workers called this the "speedup." Sometimes shifts extended well beyond eight hours. Along the San Francisco waterfront, shifts of twelve, sixteen, and even more hours were not rare. Fatigue, combined with the grueling work and reckless pace, increased the danger of accidents. At the end of a shift, San Francisco longshoremen were paid off in brass checks that could only be redeemed conveniently in bars, where (in a system created through collusion between bar owners and waterfront employers) the workers had to buy liquor to collect their pay whether they wanted to drink or not.

Conditions like these persisted along the East and Gulf Coasts from the 1920s through the 1950s. There, Joseph P. Ryan, who headed the International Longshoremen's Association (ILA), which was ostensibly a workers' organization, long colluded with the employers to profit from the shape-up. Ryan, dubbed "King Joe" by his critics, became president of the ILA in 1927 and retained that post for twenty-six years by using criminals to enforce his rule and his collusion with the shipping magnates.

On the West Coast, in contrast, things changed during the Great Depression of the 1930s. There, Harry Bridges organized his co-workers and led them in what became known as the Big Strike of 1934. When San Francisco police killed two strike supporters and injured scores more on July 5, 1934, Bloody Thursday, all of the city's unionized workers walked off their jobs for four days in protest. This San Francisco General Strike of July 16–19 was one of the few successful general strikes in American history. Ultimately, the West Coast longshoremen won their strike demands through arbitration. Their gains included a worker-controlled hiring hall, which ended the hated shape-up on the Pacific Coast and allowed the longshoremen to equally share the available work without kickbacks or favoritism. They were awarded a coastwide contract as well, which guaranteed uniform conditions so the shipowners could not play one set of port workers against another. The longshoremen also won a modest hourly pay raise and a six-hour day to spread around the scarce work of the Great Depression.

During the second half of the twentieth century, work conditions on the waterfront began to change. Motorized vehicles called jitneys were increasingly used to move palletized cargo around on the docks and in the holds of ships. In the 1960s, too, containerization began to replace traditional break-bulk cargo handling. On the East Coast, the ILA initially resisted the introduction of what the workers called "cans" and enjoyed some short-term success. But on the West Coast, Bridges recognized the inevitability of automation and in 1960 concluded a Mechanization and Modernization Agreement with the shipowners' Pacific Maritime Association.

Under the M and M Agreement, the shipowners established a fund to encourage early retirement and guaranteed job security for workers who remained in the longshore industry. In exchange, the ILWU allowed the peaceful introduction of the new labor-saving containers and the elimination of noncontract "hip-pocket" work rules that ILWU members had introduced over time to address grievances like the speedup. As containerization took over the waterfront toward the end of the twentieth century, many longshore workers on both coasts became container crane operators; these jobs demanded skill and precision but were less physical. Still, some waterfront jobs, like lashing and unlashing containers tied to ships with heavy metal cables, remained physically challenging and dangerous. In the same years, too, an increasing number of women began to enter the longshore workforce along the Pacific Coast waterfront. As a gesture toward gender equality, the ILWU changed its name again in 1997, becoming the International Longshore and Warehouse Union.

Containerization has dramatically increased productivity in American ports but has significantly reduced the number of longshore jobs. Workers who remain in the longshore industry, however, enjoy decently paid unionized jobs on both the West and East Coast waterfronts to this day.

Harvey Schwartz

See also: Warehouse Worker; *1776–1860:* Wharfinger

FURTHER READING

Afrasiabi, Peter. 2016. *Burning Bridges: America's 20-Year Crusade to Deport Labor Leader Harry Bridges.* Brooklyn: Thirlmere Books.

Cherny, Robert W. 2000. "Longshoremen of San Francisco Bay, 1849–1960." In *Dock Workers: International Explorations in Comparative Labour History, 1790–1970,* vol. 1, edited by Sam Davies et al., 102–140. Aldershot, England: Ashgate Publishing.

Cole, Peter. 2007. *Wobblies on the Waterfront: Interracial Unionism in Progressive-Era Philadelphia.* Urbana: University of Illinois Press.

Davis, Colin. 1998. "'All I Got's a Hook': New York Longshoremen and the 1948 Dock Strike." In *Waterfront Workers: New Perspectives on Race and Class*, edited by Calvin Winslow, 131–54. Urbana: University of Illinois Press.

Fisher, James. 2009. *On the Irish Waterfront: The Crusader, the Movie, and the Soul of the Port of New York.* Ithaca: Cornell University Press.

Kimeldorf, Howard. 1988. *Reds or Rackets? The Making of Radical and Conservative Unions on the Waterfront.* Berkeley: University of California Press.

Larrowe, Charles P. 1977. *Harry Bridges: The Rise and Fall of Radical Labor in the United States.* 2nd ed. rev. Westport: Lawrene Hill.

Levinson, Marc. 2006. *The Box: How the Shipping Container Made the World Smaller and the World Economy Bigger.* Princeton: Princeton University Press.

Magden, Ronald E. 1991. *The Working Longshoreman.* Tacoma: ILWU Local 23.

Nelson, Bruce. 1988. *Workers on the Waterfront: Seamen, Longshoremen, and Unionism in the 1930s.* Urbana: University of Illinois Press.

Nelson, Bruce. 1998. "The 'Lords of the Docks' Reconsidered: Race Relations among West Coast Longshoremen, 1933–1961." In *Waterfront Workers: New Perspectives on Race and Class*, edited by Calvin Winslow, 155–92. Urbana: University of Illinois Press.

Quam-Wickham, Nancy. 1992. "Who Controls the Hiring Hall? The Struggle for Job Control in the ILWU during World War II." In *The CIO's Left-Led Unions*, edited by Steve Rosswurm, 47–67. New Brunswick: Rutgers University Press.

Quin, Mike. 1949. *The Big Strike.* Olema: Olema Publishing.

Schwartz, Harvey. 1980. "Harry Bridges and the Scholars: Looking at History's Verdict." *California History: The Magazine of the California Historical Society* 59, no. 1 (Spring): 66–79.

Schwartz, Harvey. 2000. *The March Inland: Origins of the ILWU Warehouse Division, 1934–1938.* Los Angeles: Institute of Industrial Relations, University of California, 1978; reprint San Francisco: ILWU.

Schwartz, Harvey. 2009. *Solidarity Stories: An Oral History of the ILWU.* Seattle: University of Washington Press.

Selvin, David. 1996. *A Terrible Anger: The 1934 Waterfront and General Strikes in San Francisco.* Detroit: Wayne State University Press.

Stallone, Steve, Harvey Schwartz, and Gene Dennis Vrana. 1997. *The ILWU Story: Six Decades of Militant Unionism.* San Francisco: ILWU.

MECHANICAL ENGINEER

Mechanical engineers are responsible for designing machines. Mechanical engineering in the first half of the twentieth century was the broadest engineering discipline, encompassing the design of automobiles, aircraft, industrial machinery, and consumer products. If something could be picked up, operated, or traveled in, it had been imagined and designed by a mechanical engineer. Not only that, but the method and tools to make it had to be imagined by mechanical engineers as well.

Some mechanical engineers had backgrounds working in workshops and fabrication plants and rose through the ranks to earn their position. More of them, however, attended one of about 150 colleges in the United States that offered comprehensive mechanical engineering degrees. But a university education was just the beginning. Companies like General Electric, Westinghouse Electric, Ford Motor Company, Boeing Aircraft, Caterpillar, and Alcoa each developed their own method of completing the education of a freshly minted graduate mechanical engineer, usually involving a mixture of shop floor experience and engineering responsibility but always under the watchful supervision of a senior engineer. Some companies created specialized in-house schools and course work that were offered to young engineers on a competitive basis with the promise of accelerated advancement (Doherty 1947).

Whether they rose through the ranks of an engineering shop or attended an academic program, every mechanical engineer's workday was largely similar. The working hours were almost the same as those of an office job but with some additional caveats. Most mechanical engineers worked at drafting tables and on chalkboards during regular weekday business hours, but it was often the case that mechanical engineer would need to spend time in the factory or shop in which their designs would be built, installed, or used. Certain aspects of their designs required spatial context and observations of how they would be used by the average worker or consumer—as is often the case, some designs that might look great on paper do not necessarily translate as favorably in the real world.

The job of being a mechanical engineer was both structured and creative. Certain technical rules had to be followed, and costs had to be controlled, but within those constraints, the mechanical engineer was expected to innovate and problem solve. So it was in 1941 when Leroy Grumman, a 1916 graduate of the Cornell mechanical engineering program, was tasked with the urgent need to squeeze more fighter planes onto existing aircraft carrier decks in World War II. He knew folding wings could allow more planes to go to sea with each task force, but various designs up to that time had proven impractical. Grumman's innovation came from toying with a drafting eraser, representing the body of the plane, and two paper clips for the wings. He intuited that if the paper clip ends were inserted into the eraser at just the right angle, they could be pivoted from being in the flight position to being tucked almost parallel to the body (Thruelsen 1976). Grumman's idea worked, and American aircraft carriers were able to carry about 50 percent more aircraft after his' plan was fully developed and executed; in 2006, the American Society of Mechanical Engineers named Grumman's design a Historic Mechanical Engineering Landmark.

Building the arsenal of democracy for World War II was not the only challenge mechanical engineers faced during this period. Safety at home and at work had become primary issues after worker's' compensation laws swept the country in 1911, and some saw engineers as part of the problem. About the time that Leroy Grumman was getting his degree from Cornell, another engineer, Carl M. Hansen, submitted an abstract to the *Journal of the American Society of Mechanical Engineers* expressing his opinion that engineers were culpable in the vast numbers of injuries their machinery had been causing to his fellow citizens working in American industry. It was an entirely new notion.

Up to that time, employers and mechanical design engineers alike had felt no responsibility for the protection of workers. Dangers such as exposed gears and belts regularly pulled men, women, and children into unguarded equipment, claiming 35,000 lives and 2,000,000 injuries every year (Witt 2004). Hansen pointedly asked, "Who is responsible for the hazards in these industries?" to which he answered "We—the engineers. We have created the machines used and it is up to us to eliminate any unnecessary hazard which these machines have introduced" (Hansen 1916). Hansen proposed to expand the job description of the engineer beyond merely making a machine to do a task to imagining how the user might be hurt in the process and making the machine in such a way as to passively prevent the injury if possible, regardless of whether the user adhered to every safety rule.

If gears were exposed, they should be located away from worker platforms. If that wasn't possible, guards should be placed around the hazard. Guards and electrical boxes should be interlocked with the motors running the machine so that if they were left off the machine, it wouldn't run at all. There were hundreds of ways to make cutting, stamping, printing, and crushing operations safer, and a growing number of safety-minded engineers welcomed the responsibility. By 1955, the editors of the third edition of the National Safety Council's *Accident Prevention Manual for Industrial Operations* no longer minced words: "Failure to take necessary precautions against predictable accidents involves moral responsibility for those accidents" and "If an engineer, whether he be a design engineer, a methods engineer, a production engineer, or other, has processed a job and has left an avoidable hazard in it, he has not met his responsibility" (National Safety Council, 1955). In the decades that followed, this became the basis of safe design principles that mechanical engineers are still called on to observe today, whether they are designing electric cars, oil rig platforms, amusement park rides, or medical implants.

W. P. Munsell

See also: Draftsman; *1946–1991:* Aeronautical and Aerospace Engineer

FURTHER READING

Accident Prevention Manual for Industrial Operations, 3rd ed. 1955. Chicago: National Safety Council.

Aldrich, Mark. 1997. *Safety First: Technology, Labor, and Business in the Building of American Work Safety 1870–1939*. Baltimore: Johns Hopkins University Press.

Clarke, Sally H. 2007. *Trust and Power: Consumers, the Modern Corporation, and the Making of the United States Automobile Market*. New York: Cambridge University Press.

Doherty, R. E. 1947. "Education and Practical Training of Mechanical Engineers in the United States." Proceedings of the Institution of Mechanical Engineers 157: 289–293.

Hansen, Carl M. 1916. "Standardization of Safety Principles." *Journal of the American Society of Mechanical Engineers* 38, no. 4 (April): 277–284.

Thruelsen, Richard. 1976. *The Grumman Story*. New York: Praeger Publishers, Inc.

Witt, John Fabian. 2004. *The Accidental Republic: Crippled Workingmen, Destitute Widows, and the Remaking of American Law*. Cambridge: Harvard University Press.

NEWSPAPER SELLER

Newspaper hawkers and carriers of all ages and sexes swarmed American cities in the industrial age and became near-mythic figures, subjects of juvenile novels and genre paintings, popular songs and stage shows, advertising campaigns and reform movements. Such attention generated much information about their daily lives and a fair bit of nonsense about their ability to pull themselves up by their bootstraps—that is, to overcome their humble origins and achieve the American dream. But whether they earned fortunes or barely subsisted from day to day, newsboys and newsgirls strove to cash in on the endless changes that shaped their world.

Newspaper peddlers emerged in the 1830s with the penny press—cheap daily newspapers for the masses. Some worked for wages. Others bought their papers at a discount—usually half price—and sought to earn profits and avoid losses. They developed routes to serve subscribers at their homes or offices or laid claim to busy corners that promised brisk sales. Many boys combined these methods. A few became brokers who recruited other children to work for them.

Like most of their successors, this first generation of newsboys were children of the poor, often immigrants or children of immigrants whose meager earnings helped their families make ends meet. During the recurring depressions of the nineteenth and early twentieth centuries, flocks of children slept as well as worked on the streets, making their beds on unsold newspapers laid out on steps or in doorways. When publishers converted their presses to steam power, many boys huddled over the grates to keep warm and ensure an early start. Being first on the streets with fresh papers increased the odds of not getting "stuck."

Newsboys' earnings ranged from a few cents to a few dollars a day, depending on the weather and the quality of the news. Hawkers usually paid for their papers up front, although suppliers would gladly advance a boy a bundle on credit. Tips accounted for up to half of a boy's earnings, and they became expert at securing them. Savvy newsboys were always slow to make change. Some perfected sad stories or expressions. Tipping a ragged, barefoot newsboy or a loyal carrier on New Year's Day became common forms of charity that distributors counted on, as did publishers, who would otherwise have had to pay them more.

In 1854, Rev. Charles Loring Brace, founder of the Children's Aid Society, opened the first (of several) Newsboys' Lodging House for orphaned or abandoned children. He charged them six cents for dinner, bath, and a bed. They could also use the gymnasium and reading room. Those who wished to quit the city were "placed out" on farms. Scores of such homes sponsored by the Catholic Church and other institutions sprang up in the second half of the century in Chicago; Philadelphia; Washington, D.C.; Baltimore; Detroit; New Orleans; and elsewhere.

Some cities licensed their newsboys and required them to attend school and wear badges. The boys often welcomed these regulations as a way to reduce competition from small fries or out-of-towners. Enforcement was usually lax, however, as police resented this "newsboy duty," and truant officers were severely outnumbered. Fourteen was the typical school-leaving age at the turn of the twentieth century. Many boys left the news trade around then if they could find better jobs. Those who had lucrative routes and corners stayed longer, as did African Americans, who were barred from many skilled trades.

The newsboy usually started his day as early as 3:00 a.m. if he delivered morning papers and could end as late as 2:00 a.m. if he peddled "midnight extras," early "bulldog" editions, or Sunday papers that came off the presses while Saturday-night amusement-seekers were still on the streets. A newsboy's day alternated between periods of rushing and waiting. When the papers were ready, they worked fast to sell or deliver as many copies as they could in the shortest amount of time. They ran rather than walked and shouted out headlines to create excitement about the news. On slow news days, some boys would cry out false headlines about battles or assassinations that never took place. Other boys would invent ridiculous stories to attract buyers: "Extra! Extra! Shipwreck in the subway. All survivors dead!" Between editions, newsboys bided their time in news alleys, playing craps, mora, "pile o' maggots," or other popular street games.

Beginning in the 1880s, some newspapers established summer baseball teams and leagues for their newsboys. Others set up boxing rings to attract potential hawkers and enhance their ability to defend their turf against interlopers. Publishers and philanthropists also organized holiday banquets for the boys. They gave out coats at Christmastime and, between morning and evening editions, treated them to ball games, circuses, and plays. With more spending money than many of their peers, newsies considered themselves aficionados of the theater; they would sit in the pit or balcony and loudly proclaim their delight or disgust with the performance.

Most newsboys sold a variety of papers, but some publishers pressured them to exclusively handle their papers. Circulation managers also imposed fines and price hikes or otherwise tried to trim their incomes and independence. The most common response was to quit. Turnover was great in the trade. Some boys lasted only a few days or weeks when they realized there was "nothin' in it." Others toiled for years. Another response to worsening conditions was to organize a union and strike. Newsboys from New York to San Francisco waged scores of noisy strikes between the 1870s and 1930s, sometimes affiliating with the Knights of Labor, the American Federation of Labor, or the Industrial Workers of the World.

The arrival of streetcars and bicycles in the nineteenth century, and subways and automobiles in the early twentieth century, increased the speed with which newsboys disseminated their papers. However, each mode of transportation presented new hazards. Thousands of newsboys were killed or injured while jumping off trolleys or crossing busy streets. Few received compensation as newspapers and streetcar companies rarely accepted liability.

In the early 1900s, progressive reformers secured laws in many cities and some states that regulated the hours and ages of newsboys and required regular school attendance. Still their numbers grew as the demand for news of war, crime, and scandal burgeoned during the late 'teens and '20s. The mass joblessness of the 1930s brought more adults into the trade than ever and forced boys to stay in it longer than they would have liked. With the spread of suburbs in the 1950s, 1960s, and 1970s, the typical paperboy delivered newspapers by bike after school, but these adolescents increasingly gave way to adults with automobiles. The high-profile kidnapping and murder of several young carriers in the 1980s and '90s further diminished children's place in the trade. Today, with the industry in decline due to the internet, vendors and carriers are primarily grown-ups, including immigrants and senior citizens. They are independent contractors rather than employees and, thus, have to pay for their own vehicles, gas, insurance, and repairs. As in the past, many of them rise early and work late, exploiting themselves in pursuit of the American dream and the next month's rent.

Vincent DiGirolamo

See also: *1776–1860:* Huckster; Journalist; Printer; *1946–1991:* Salesperson

FURTHER READING

Bekken, Jon. 1995. "Newsboys: The Exploitation of 'Little Merchants' by the Newspaper Industry." In *Newsworkers: Toward a History of the Rank and File*, edited by Hanno Hardt and Bonnie Brennen. Minneapolis: University of Minnesota Press, 190–225.

Brace, Charles Loring. 1872. *The Dangerous Classes of New York and Twenty Years' Work among Them.* New York: Wynkook & Hallenbeck.

Clopper, Edward N. 1912. *Child Labor in City Streets*. Norwood: Macmillan.

Davis, Philip. 1915. *Streetland: Its Little People and Big Problems*, with Grace Kroll. Boston: Small, Maynard.

DiGirolamo, Vincent. 2002. "Newsboy Funerals: Tales of Sorrow and Solidarity in Urban America." *Journal of Social History* 36, no. 1 (September): 5–30.

Kildare, Owen Frawley. 1903. *My Mamie Rose; The Story of My Regeneration*. New York: Baker & Taylor.

Linder, Marc. 1997. "What's Black and White and Red All Over? The Blood Tax on Newspapers—or, How Publishers Exclude Newscarriers from Workers' Compensation." *Loyola Poverty Law Journal* 3: 57–111.

McGill, Nettie P. 1928. *Child Workers on City Streets*. Washington, DC: U.S. Department of Labor, Children's Bureau. Pub. No. 188.

Nasaw, David. 1985. *Children of the City: At Work and at Play*. New York: Oxford University Press.

Postol, Todd Alexander. 1997. "Creating the American Newspaper Boy: Middle-Class Route Service and Juvenile Salesmanship in the Great Depression." *Journal of Social History* 31, no. 2 (Winter): 327–45.

Reed, Anna Y. 1917. *Newsboy Service: A Study in Educational and Vocational Guidance*. Yonkers-on-Hudson: World Book Company.

Riis, Jabob. 2010. *How the Other Half Live* (1890), *A Norton Critical Edition*. Edited by Hasia R. Diner. New York: W. W. Norton.

Simpson, Roger. 1992. "Seattle Newsboys: How Hustler Democracy Lost to the Power of Property." *Journalism History* 18: 18–25.

PRIMARY DOCUMENT

At the beginning of the twentieth century, middle-class Americans became increasingly focused on the lives of children, who, social scientists and educators argued, should be able to attend school without worry and enjoy play and friendships when outside of the classroom. Newsboys were one of the targets of these new Progressive-era social reformers. In this document, Edward N. Clopper, a leading proponent of eliminating child labor, addresses the lifestyle and work environment of the nation's newspaper sellers.

By far the majority of the children in street occupations are engaged in the sale or delivery of newspapers. The newsboy predominates to such an extent that he is taken as a matter of course. As Mrs. Florence Kelley says, "For more than one generation, it has been almost invariably assumed that there must be little newsboys." Ever since he became an institution of our city life, the public has been pleased to regard him admiringly as an energetic salesman of penetrating mind and keen sense of humor. There seems to be a tacit indorsement of the newsboy as such.

Ordinarily there are five classes of newsboys to be found in all large cities—(1) the corner boys, (2) those who sell for corner boys on salary, (3) others who sell for them on commission, (4) those who sell for themselves, and (5) those with delivery routes. The bulk of the business is handled by the first three of these classes, which are always associated together and found on the busy corners of the downtown sections of all our cities. The choice localities for the sale of newspapers, namely, the corners in the downtown sections where thousands of pedestrians are daily passing, come under the control of individuals by virtue of long tenure or by purchase, and their title to these corners is not disputed largely on account of the support they receive from the circulation managers of the newspapers . . .

The following individual cases will serve to illustrate the various forms this business takes. One nineteen-year-old boy paid $65 for his corner in Cincinnati about five years ago; he now earns from $4 to $5 a day clear and would not sell the location for many times its cost. He works there from 11 a.m. to 6.30 p.m. on week days, starting an hour earlier on Saturdays, while on Sundays he delivers the morning newspapers over a route to regular customers. Two boys of about twelve years of age work for him, to one of whom he pays 25 cents a day and to the other 30 cents a day; their duties are to hawk the different editions and to dispose of as many copies as possible by hopping the street cars and offering the papers to pedestrians from 3.45 to 6.30 p.m. daily on week days. If they do not hustle and make a large number of sales, they lose their job.

A corner in another part of the city is "owned" by a thirteen-year-old boy who earns about 80 cents a day clear for himself in eight hours, and on Saturdays in nine hours. He has two boys working for him on commission, to whom he pays one cent for every four papers sold; they average about 15 cents a day apiece for three hours' work. When questioned, these commission boys admitted that they could make more money if working for themselves, but in that case would have to work until all the copies they had bought were sold, while on the commission plan they did not have to shoulder so much responsibility . . .

The occupation is characterized by "rush hours," during which the boy will work himself into exhaustion trying to keep pace with his trade, and long hours in which there is little or nothing to do, during which the boy has unlimited opportunities to make such use of the street freedom as he sees fit. During these [day-]light hours newsboys congregate in the streets and commit many acts of vandalism. They learn all forms of petty theft and usually are accomplished in most of the vices of the street. In building up their routes, the boys often include places of the most degrading and detrimental character . . .

The irregularity of newsboys' meals and the questionable character of their food form one of the worst features of street work and are a real menace to health. Many newsboys are in the habit of eating hurriedly at lunch counters at intervals during the day and night, while some snatch free lunches in saloons . . . The use of stimulants is common, and the demand for them is to be expected because of the nervous strain of the work. Liquor is not consumed to any appreciable extent by street-trading children, but coffee is a favorite beverage. In the largest cities, where "night gangs" are found, from four to six bowls of coffee are usually taken every evening. Tobacco is used in great quantities and in all its forms; many boys even appease their hunger for the time by smoking cigarettes, and the smallest "newsies" are addicted to the habit . . .

There are tricks in newspaper selling as well as in other trades, and children are not slow to learn them. A careful observer cannot fail to note that certain newsboys seem always to be without change. Their patrons are generally in a hurry and willingly sacrifice the change from a nickel, even priding themselves on their unselfishness in thus helping to relieve the supposed poverty of the newsboys. As a matter of fact, such an act does real harm, for it arouses the cupidity of boys and leads them to believe that honesty is not the best policy. The temptation for newsboys to develop into "short change artists" is an ever present one, for the bustle of the street creates a most favorable condition for the practice of such frauds. Yet in spite of the many temptations which assail them, numbers of newsboys are scrupulously exact in the matter of making change, even under the most trying circumstances. Another common form of deceit, used to play upon the sympathy of passers-by, is practiced after nightfall by boys of all ages in offering a solitary newspaper for sale and crying in plaintive tone, "Please, mister, buy my last paper?" A kind-hearted person readily falls a victim to this ruse, and as soon as he has passed by, the newsboy draws another copy from his hidden supply and repeats his importuning.

Source: Edward N. Clopper. 1912. *Child Labor in City Streets.* New York: Macmillan, 52–55, 61–64, passim.

OIL DRILLER

An oil driller was part of a team, or crew, of workers who operated a drilling rig in the search for petroleum. The driller was the highest-ranking worker on a crew—the worker with the most experience and talent who, upon consultation with a petroleum geologist, determined where to locate the rig, or the structure that comprises the mechanical drilling apparatus and derrick that supports the drill. As the most experienced worker on a crew, an oil driller usually directed the placement of the derrick on land, determined what kind of rig and power would be optimal for the subsurface conditions, and supervised the start of drilling operations, also known as "spudding in." Although they were very involved in all operations of a drilling rig, drillers generally did not participate in the building of the derrick—that was the work of oil field carpenters and rig builders. Instead, the labor of running the drill as it bore into the earth in search of oil and gas was the job of the driller.

In the late-nineteenth-century United States, oil was produced by a variety of methods. Some of the earliest derricks were simple structures with a single mast and boom, much like on a small sailboat, from which a cable was lifted and lowered rhythmically; at the end was a sharp bit, or drill, that gradually created a hole in the earth from which oil could be extracted, sometimes even by bucket, as with shallow water wells. In the coastal southern California mountains during the 1870s, where tar deposits were similarly located at a shallow subsurface depth, early petroleum workers "dug" for tar in oil "mines" under the surface, where the heat was so great that some workers stripped off their clothes to tolerate the high temperatures. Other workers carried the tar out of these oil mines by bucket. Elsewhere, oil discoveries accelerated as new oil-burning engines (especially in railroad and ship transportation) created new markets for petroleum. From the first commercial production of oil at Titusville, Pennsylvania, in 1859, until the early 1970s, the United States produced most of the petroleum used in the nation. Between 1900 and the 1930s, the United States exported great quantities of oil. It was produced commercially in Pennsylvania and Indiana, in Appalachia, in the great mid-continent fields of Kansas, Oklahoma, and Texas, in Louisiana and the Texas Gulf Coast, Montana, Colorado, and Wyoming, and in California and Alaska by the late 1940s. At the forefront of all of these profitable discoveries was the oil driller.

Once the rig builders had completed the construction of the derrick, the driller began work. In most of the United States before the 1910s, a well was drilled using the cable-tool method. This method involved hammering a hole into the earth by the percussive action of a sharp drill bit that was raised and lowered by the drilling cable. The steel drill bit was often four feet long or larger, attached to a drill stem that was in turn attached to a sinker bar (a heavy steel weight) and the jars, a set of telescoping metal links that acted like a spring to jerk the bit up sharply, thereby ensuring that the drill did not become stuck in the formation at the bottom of the drill hole. The total length of a string of drilling tools varied from thirty to seventy-two feet or longer, weighed two or more tons, and was typically dropped two to five feet each time the cable was lowered. The driller controlled the entire operation of the drilling tools, adjusting the force with which the tools bore into the earth. In this manner, a drill could penetrate sixty or so feet of substrate a day, depending on the geological characteristics of the subsurface. A good cable-tool driller was able to ascertain the features of the subsurface geology just by feeling the vibrations of the cable. The driller's assistant, the tool dresser, changed the drill bit when it became dull, repaired cable, sharpened dull bits, and in other ways helped the driller operate the rig. The tool dresser was essentially an apprentice driller, skilled in blacksmithing and mechanics, and many eventually became drillers in their own right. Inexperienced drillers and tool dressers could ruin a well, break the cable, and foul the hole with broken or stuck drilling tools; in California, poorly skilled drillers were popularly and derisively called “Sears-Roebuck drillers.”

As oil was discovered at deeper depths, companies pioneered a new method of drilling by the 1910s. The rotary drill consisted of a very large steel augur, driven by a rotating steel pipe. The pipe was suspended by a tall derrick, usually built of very heavy timber (often twelve feet by twelve feet stock) or steel. The rotary bit (the augur) weighed as much as five hundred pounds and was attached to the pipe by a rotary tool joint (also called a drill collar). The drill pipe was connected to a drum-like device on the derrick floor, which constantly turned and at different speeds, thereby rotating the pipe. At the top of the derrick was a derrickman, who guided twenty-foot-long sections of pipe to the two or three roughnecks on the derrick floor; the roughnecks connected each new section of pipe. The driller operated a clutch-like device that sped up or slowed down the rate at which the pipe and bit rotated. To keep the well lubricated and reduce friction that might have slowed the progression of the bit, drilling “mud” was pumped into the drill hole. Drillers judged the speed in which the hole was drilled in part by keeping watch on the amount of drilling mud that had been used. A rotary drill could penetrate up to five hundred or more feet per day and be used in all kinds of subsurface formations (sand, hard rock, gravel) and over water as well. Each well had two alternating crews to keep the rig working around the clock.

Regardless of type of rig, the machinery was heavy, and work was dangerous. Cables routinely separated from wear: a flying one-inch-diameter steel cable could easily amputate a worker’s leg. Drill bits became stuck in the formation, requiring expensive and tricky fishing jobs to retrieve the drill tools. A driller who pushed the drill tools too hard could cause the entire derrick to collapse, burying workers under tons of machinery and structure. Drillers who accelerated the rotary tools or carelessly ran a cable drill while nearing the oil sands could cause a well blowout or, worse, a blowout accompanied by fire when the crude oil rained down on steam engines powering the rig. An inexperienced driller caused one such blowout, the Spindletop gusher, in Texas in 1901. Another drilling disaster occurred in 1910 near Taft, California, when a rotary drill punctured a pressurized oil deposit, causing the Lakeview gusher, an uncontrolled geyser-like well that spewed as much as ninety thousand barrels of oil per day for over eighteen months before it was controlled. Most of that oil was not recovered.

Oil drillers were instrumental in the transition from a coal- to an oil-based economy during the first half of the twentieth century. Skilled drillers opened up new fields in the United States and abroad as many U.S. oil companies sent crews to pioneer foreign fields. American oil drillers could be found in such far-flung areas as Azerbaijan, Burma, and Venezuela in the 1910s and 1920s. Expert oil drillers also invented new tools and methods for drilling petroleum; many drillers—not petroleum engineers—obtained patents on new tools and machinery through the 1930s. Oil drillers built an industry that propelled the United States into global economic prominence in the twentieth century.

Nancy Quam-Wickham

See also: Geologist; *1776–1860:* Gold Miner; Surveyor; *1861–1914:* Coal Miner

FURTHER READING

Lynch, Gerald. 1991. *Roughnecks, Drillers, and Tool Pushers: Thirty-Three Years in the Oil Fields.* Austin: University of Texas Press.

Olien, Roger, and Diana Davids Olien. 1982. *Oil Booms: Social Change in Five Texas Towns.* Lincoln: University of Nebraska Press.

Weaver, Bobby. 2013. *Oil Field Trash: Life and Labor in the Oil Patch.* College Station: Texas A&M University Press.

RADIO ANNOUNCER

Radio announcers work at radio stations, and they are responsible for speaking into a microphone and having their speech broadcast through the radio station's antenna for live events or scheduled programming that is received by consumer radios tuned in to the station's broadcast. Radio announcers hosted radio shows, served as news reporters, sold products through on-air advertising, provided special-interest programming, and called sporting events for listeners throughout the nation.

Modern radio gained popularity after World War I. Stations all around the country broadcast programming into American homes, where people of all ages crowded around small receivers to hear the latest news, be entertained by live musicians and storytellers, and listen in on sports broadcasts. The effectiveness of this new form of media and communication rested on the metaphorical shoulders of the radio announcer. A good radio announcer, with a rich and resonant voice, could even become the "face" of a local station and then, later, be recruited to work at a station hosting shows that were regionally or nationally syndicated. Radio announcers were expert communicators but also faceless actors who used their voices to convey emotion to their listeners. As radio stations were licensed across the nation, radio announcers of all ages found work in the field. A few became well-known announcers, applauded for their talent, but most, especially in the 1920s, were local people who worked on air at stations within their communities.

In the early 1920s, all radio stations were assigned the same wavelength, so interference was common. Additionally, most radio receiving sets were at least partly homemade, requiring a degree of technical knowledge to assemble a set of wires, a tuner, vacuum tubes, and the sockets that held them in a wooden box. The radio craze of the early 1920s was driven by young men, in particular, who sought the technical knowhow to build a receiving box; popular magazines, book series for young readers (like *The Wireless Man*), and competitions that challenged listeners to find and tune in to distant stations helped to provide the knowledge needed to participate in this activity. Correspondingly, radio announcing at its start was a young person's occupation, a job that teenagers and high school graduates sought, and a choice for part-time work for college graduates trained in theater arts, communication, and journalism while they sought jobs in their fields of study. Early radio announcers often came from these ranks of youthful enthusiasts. In Fort Smith, Arkansas, in 1922, a fifteen-year-old announcer, Jimmie Barry, began broadcasting at WGAR radio. Young men and women in their twenties, often with acting or singing experience, were hired on the spot, as was the case with a young singer in New York, Joe Barnett, who wanted to audition for a singing job but found himself in the proverbial right place at the right time when the regular songster-announcer didn't show up for his shift. The radio studio, set up in a corner of a New York City department store, asked Barnett to fill in until the regular singer arrived, but after several hours, he had the job.

In the earliest years of radio in the 1920s, many radio stations did not have regular programming, so an announcer might be asked to read the news one shift, introduce a traveling band the next shift, or read children's stories to young listeners on a third day. Sometimes, radio stations asked an announcer to cover a sporting event—a prizefight, college football contest between two rival teams, or World Series game—but would pay the announcer a set fee of a few dollars each broadcast. Radio broadcasting studios were crude offices with rugs or heavy velvet fabric covering the walls to improve sound quality. Some announcers had trouble enunciating words, leading listeners to complain about their performance or accent; Midwesterners, for instance, often criticized the New York City accents of announcers on national broadcasts. Announcers generally stood on their feet throughout the live broadcast session, with a microphone on a stand in front of them. Women announcers often specialized in reading books or stories for children's hours or providing advice to housewives. Some also worked as announcers for symphony and operatic performances. In Boston, an all-women station, WASN, primarily offered broadcasting about shopping and consumer interests. Other local announcers read farm prices, provided livestock reports from local auctions, and talked about farming improvements like crop rotation to listeners in agricultural communities, while local businessmen provided commentary about Chamber of Commerce or local service club activities. Many local stations didn't even go on the air until the end of the workday at 5:00 p.m. and didn't broadcast anything other than a church service on Sunday.

Over time, however, radio stations began to offer regular programming to listeners, interspersed with advertising. By the end of the 1920s and into the 1930s, radio shows had largely transformed from an often impromptu and loose collection of broadcasts at different times of the day to a regular schedule of shows, news, sporting events, and music; large stations published their scheduled broadcasts in publications like *Radio Digest* and *Radio News*. With the formation of these regular schedules, announcing became a steadier occupation, allowing young men like Ronald Reagan to pursue full-time careers as announcers. Upon his graduation from tiny Eureka College in Illinois in 1932, Reagan went to Chicago to find work as an announcer but was rebuffed because of his lack of experience; he later returned to his hometown and sought work at a nearby station as a part-time sportscaster. His resonant voice and enthusiasm for sports, however, soon earned him notice, and he moved into a full-time position providing play-by-play analysis for the station WHO in Des Moines, Iowa.

With regular programming, announcers began to specialize in certain types of programming. Those with newspaper experience went into writing and announcing news on the radio. Singers and musicians announced musical and dance programs of many kinds, from opera and symphonic broadcasts in New York to popular music across the nation and western swing dance hall music in California and the western South. Some announcers branched out into radio dramatic shows, playing parts like that of *The Lone Ranger* (Brace Breemer of Indianapolis) or Myrtle Spear (Myrtle Vail), a fictional former Vaudeville performer in the radio soap opera *Myrtle and Marge*. By the 1930s, national networks had also organized regular programming, propelling some radio announcers into the ranks of popular stars. NBC, for instance, had an entire slate of musical and variety programming with such performers as the South Sea Islanders, the Dixie Circus, Raybestos Twins, and the Dutch Masters Minstrels, the latter two named for sponsors. Announcers introduced these acts, read advertising copy, and sometimes ad-libbed with performers. The field of announcing was such that post-secondary institutions, like the Los Angeles School of Radio Broadcasting and programs in radio at the University of Southern California, opened to train new announcers in the craft of being on air.

Radio was a major new and exciting technology in the early twentieth century. Even with the advent of television, the internet, and streaming devices, radio is today still an important medium of communicating information.

Nancy Quam-Wickham

See also: *1776–1860:* Journalist; *1861–1914:* Telegraph Operator; *1946–1991:* Broadcast Journalist

FURTHER READING

Douglas, George H. 1987. *The Early Days of Radio Broadcasting.* Jefferson: McFarland and Company.

Douglas, Susan J. 1999. *Listening In: Radio and the American Imagination.* New York: Random House.

Halper, Donna L. 2001. *Invisible Stars: A Social History of Women in American Broadcasting.* Armonk: M. E. Sharpe.

Poindexter, Ray. 1978. *Golden Throats and Silver Tongues: The Radio Announcers.* New Orleans: River Road Press.

RETAIL CLERK

Retail clerks work in department stores and outlets, and they stock shelves, service customers, and process transactions. With the growth of the middle class and the emergence of large department stores between 1900 and 1950, the role of retail clerks grew proportionately—the number of Americans employed as retail clerks more than doubled. Although its origins date to the mid-nineteenth century, department stores and chain groceries came into their own in the twentieth century, and as they did so, the number of smaller proprietor-run shops declined dramatically. Retail clerks took the place of the former small proprietor as the worker with whom the customer interacted in this more impersonal environment of the department and chain stores. Since the business model of these larger stores depended on the volume of sales of all goods rather than specialization in one kind of item, managers depended less on workers knowledgeable about the products and more on those who had friendly demeanors.

The modern department store had electric lighting, large floors of goods open to customers, and courteous workers ready to attend to a customer's needs but in a restrained way that welcomed customers and encouraged browsing. These vast stores recast shopping as an enjoyable leisure activity, one of the cornerstones of a new consumer economy. Retail clerks helped customers determine which items to purchase and then wrote up the sales receipts.

Retail clerks were the public face of the modern store owners, and, as such, they were required by managers to dress nicely to appeal to largely middle-class customers. Male clerks wore dress shirts and ties, while female clerks wore neat dresses or modest skirts and blouses. Both men and women had to be clean and well groomed. Retail clerks were also expected to be educated—to read, write, and speak English. As historian Jerome Bjelopera notes, management "showed great concern about the ways that sales personnel presented themselves to customers, how they talked about products, and how they represented the store to the public" (Bjelopera 2010, 43). Managers trained their clerks to professionally interact with customers in ways that some regard as ritualized communication: "May I help you, sir [or madam]?" "Did you find everything you needed today?" "Would this be all for you?" Retail clerks may have been the public faces of their employers, but they generally had only limited interaction with customers.

Despite their white-collar-worker status, retail clerks were generally low paid: in the early twentieth century, the average wage for a retail clerk was about twelve hundred dollars per year—about the same as unskilled manufacturing workers but half of what masons and bricklayers earned annually. Nonetheless, most retail clerks were native-born white men and, increasingly, young white women who had migrated to cities from rural areas or small towns. In large cities like New York, significant numbers of Jewish men and women were employed as retail clerks. Most managers in the retail trade, however, were men.

Retail clerks were often required to stand attentively for long periods of each day, interact graciously with customers, and monitor the workspace—rehanging clothes, tidying up display tables, moving items to the sale shelves, and polishing mirrors and display cases. Before 1910, most department stores lacked the kind of organizational efficiency that many factories had recently adopted, so retail clerks spent more time restacking, re-shelving, and reordering inventory than they did in direct sales. But in the 1910s and early 1920s, managers adopted scientific management and efficiency studies to reorder the modern department store: using clothes hangers and racks to display clothing, grouping products by rooms (kitchen, bath, bed), and dividing apparel into sections by type (women's lingerie, men's outerwear). This reorganization of the retail space led to greater sales as retail clerks engaged in more direct contact with customers.

Personal communication skills were essential for both male and female workers. But women clerks routinely deflected unwanted sexual advances from customers and especially, from managers; a 1914 report noted that "many girls in many department stores have got to give in to the demands in that respect of certain members, buyers, managers, and floor walkers who take advantage of girls working under them and need the jobs very badly" (Kessler-Harris 1982, 103). Managers enforced codes of workplace behavior with complicated systems of fines, though saleswomen often worked together to blunt the impact of an arrogant, demanding customer. As historian Susan Porter-Benson wrote of department store clerks, a group of women clerks effectively ignored a disapproving customer, chatting among themselves, "continuing their conversation while waiting on her" (Porter-Benson 1986, 26).

The retail store environment, however, encouraged both cooperation and competition between employees. Clerks competed with each other for sales to impress management and gain better positions in other departments. Still, clerks routinely gossiped among themselves, revealed intimate details of their personal lives, and used slang in conversations between each other—even in the presence of customers. One Philadelphia department store changed its policy to allow clerks to use the public elevator rather than stairs or freight elevators but soon had to warn clerks against forming "flying wedges" that crowed customers out of the elevator at the store's daily opening (Bjelopera 2010, 125). Furthermore, racial competition arose with the migration of African Americans to northern cities as activists in the black communities organized "Don't Buy Where You Can't Work" campaigns that forced some stores to integrate their workforces, though employment of African American retail clerks was relatively small until after World War II, when the very nature of retail employment itself changed from predominantly full-time work to a mix of full-time and part-time employees, supplemented by casual workers in high seasons like the winter holidays. Unionization, too, was only partly successful before the 1950s, with the grocery sector of retail stores experiencing the most union growth. Department stores, however, primarily remained nonunion enterprises well into the postwar period.

Nancy Quam-Wickham

See also: Grocer; *1607–1775:* Shopkeeper; *1861–1914:* Haberdasher

FURTHER READING

Bjelopera, Jerome P. 2010. *City of Clerks: Office and Sales Workers in Philadelphia, 1870–1920.* Champaign: University of Illinois Press.

Kessler-Harris, Alice. 1982. *Out to Work: A History of Wage-Earning Women in the United States.* London: Oxford University Press.

Phillips, Lisa Ann Wunderlich. 2012. *A Renegade Union: Interracial Organizing and Labor Radicalism.* Champaign: University of Illinois Press.

Porter-Benson, Susan. 1986. *Counter Cultures: Saleswomen, Managers, and Customers in American Department Stores, 1890–1940.* Champaign: University of Illinois Press.

Williams, Christine L. 2006. *Inside Toyland: Working, Shopping and Social Inequality.* Berkeley: University of California Press.

SCREENWRITER

Screenwriters write screenplays for film and television, which provide the movie or television program's dialogue, acting instructions, and scene directions. As Hollywood movies evolved from short spectacles to feature-length stories, so, too, did the role of the screenwriter. The early films had a scenario written out by the filmmaker, but by the 1920s, the movie studios had adopted a factory-like mentality that allowed them to film and distribute hundreds of movies. For economic reasons, the studios required a detailed screenplay that not only told the film's story but also laid out a blueprint for the production.

Under the Hollywood Studio system, writers were on staff and paid a weekly wage rather than per screenplay. They were tasked with writing the script under the supervision of a producer, who controlled the production. The writers would not own the script or have any say in how the story was told. Their job was to please the producer.

The producer assigned one of the studio's staff writers to work on a script based on a concept that the producer had developed or a property the studio owned the rights to, like a book or a play. It was normal for several screenwriters to work on a project until the producer approved the final script. If a screenwriter didn't provide the producer with precisely what he wanted, the producer replaced the screenwriter with another that would meet his demands. Usually, writers were known for having a particular talent, such as romance, comedy, or dialogue, and producers tasked the writers to add their skill to a screenplay. For example, the writer-director Frank Capra, known for *It's a Wonderful Life* (1946), started as a salaried gag writer.

Before the advent of sound, the screenwriter wrote out the dialogue as an inter-title, printed text filmed and cut into the picture. Then in 1927, the first feature-length talking picture, *The Jazz Singer*, was released. Now technology allowed the audio to be synced to the picture, and audiences loved it. The studios quickly transitioned to films with sound, referred to as talkies. This allowed screenwriters to rely on dialogue in their scripts, and many playwrights transitioned to film production.

Usually, writers worked on the studio lot in an office. They'd be assigned the project and submit their work to the producer. A producer wanted a continuity script, which featured a breakdown of the entire production. The locations, characters, details on camera shots, and even the budget were included in this document, allowing little room for creativity from the director or actors. The screenplay for *King Kong* (1933) even went into detail on how the special effects would be filmed.

Despite the constraints, there were still star writers who managed to make a name for themselves and command high wages. Frances Marion was the most renowned female screenwriter of the twentieth century and was the highest-paid writer—male or female—throughout the 1920s and 1930s. She earned fifty thousand dollars a year, an unheard-of amount at the time. Marion was also the first writer to win two Academy Awards (for *The Big House* in 1930 and *The Champ* in 1931).

Other writers managed to transition from writing to directing and gain control of their stories. Preston Sturges was a well-paid writer within the studio system, earning twenty-five hundred dollars a week. Some of his scripts were filmed, but others were shelved, or he was denied a screen credit. He was unhappy with how directors shot his scripts and wanted to take control. He offered to sell his script *The Great McGinty* (1939) to Paramount Pictures for one dollar in exchange for allowing him to direct the picture; Paramount agreed. At the 13th Academy Awards in 1940, the first ceremony featuring the Best Original Screenplay category, Sturges won the award for *The Great McGinty*. The deal paved the way for other writer-directors like Billy Wilder.

In the late 1940s, screenwriters stopped writing a continuity script filled with technical details and instead wrote screenplays that described the action and dialogue. Their only job was to tell the creative story. This was partly because the Hollywood System ended. In 1948, the Supreme Court decision in the case of *U.S. v. Paramount* decided the studios were breaking antitrust laws by owning all aspects of filmmaking from production to distribution. The Court required the studios to sell off the theaters, which allowed more independent movies to be shown. This meant that talent like writers, directors, and actors were no longer bound to studio contacts, and directors had more input in turning the screenwriter's script into the shooting script with technical detail.

Although the end of the studio system allowed screenwriters to work independently, the power was now in the hands of the director. If the writers wanted full control of their story, they would need to become directors themselves.

Sean Cameron

See also: Animator; *1946–1991:* Actor/Actress (Film and Television)

FURTHER READING

Chandler, Raymond. 1945. "Writers in Hollywood." *The Atlantic*. November. https://www.theatlantic.com/magazine/archive/1945/11/writers-in-hollywood/306454/.

Field, Syd. 2007. *Screenplay: The Foundations of Screenwriting*. New York: Random House.

Froug, William. 1992. *The New Screenwriter Looks at the New Screenwriter*. Los Angeles: Silman-James Press.

PRIMARY DOCUMENT

In his oral history, award-winning screenwriter Edmund Hall North describes how he got his break into the Hollywood screenwriting industry. As a teenager, he had attended Stanford University; then, like many well-to-do young men, North went to Europe for a post-college tour. In October 1929, his father summoned him home because of the stock market crash. The elder North had lost some significant money in the crash.

I got a job at the old Fox Company, which was then still on Western Avenue (Fox Hills was building, but not yet built). I got a job in the reading department . . . Each of the big studios, in those days, had a department of readers, who would read whatever material came into the studio as submissions; from agents, usually. It might be a novel, it might be a play, it might be a short story; or an original story that a screenwriter had written. The first filtration of that material was to give it to a reader. He or she would sit down, read the material and make a brief synopsis; sometimes four or five pages, up to fifteen or twenty pages if it warranted it. Along with that, the reader was expected to give a comment on the suitability of this material for picture production. The purpose of this, obviously, was to weed out the totally useless material. Anything that was even half-heartedly recommended would be read, then, by a story editor and passed on to the higher-ups in the studio. I did that for about a year, which was, I think, very good training in terms of story analysis, because you were forced to say why did this one work, and this one not, and give reasons . . . so that there was a kind of discipline there, that forced you to analyze material. I think it was good experience, useful experience. It got terribly tiresome . . .

While I was there—one of the other readers in the department was a man named James Gow, who had been a newspaper man on the New York *World*. We got friendly and decided to write a play together. And we did. The play, by the way, was done out of town of New York and never came in, but it got into the hands, somehow or other, of Harry Cohn, who was then the head of Columbia Pictures. I never could figure out whether he read it, or somebody read it and told him that he ought to like it, or whatever, but on the strength of that he hired us, as staff writers . . .

The play was a thing called *The Drums Professor*, kind of an antiwar satire. I haven't reread it in a long time; at this stage I'm afraid to! That really was—that was the jumping-off place for, you know, a writing career; that point we certainly hadn't made it, we hadn't done anything, but we had access to, to being screenwriters . . . We were hired and they looked around for an assignment for us, and they gave us some kind of an assignment that had been kicking around—I forget what it was now.

We had only been on that a couple of weeks, when Harry Cohn called us in and said that he was going to give us a chance, a really big chance: "You boys think that you can write; well, I'm going to give you the chance to write. We've got a story that we've been working on for Grace Moore, opera singer, very important star in the Metropolitan Opera." She wasn't all that great, but he thought she was, so that was good enough. There was a long three-day New Year's weekend coming up and he said, "We've got to have the story straightened out [and] nobody has been able to do it. You guys think you're hot-shots, if you can come in with a story after this holiday, I'll let you do the screenplay." We were bowled over by this man's generosity! We said, "Of course we can get you a story by Tuesday." We holed up for the three days, and [we] did emerge with a story—I couldn't do it now to save my life, I'm sure! We came back, and we told him the story that we had developed and he said, "That's not bad, that shows some promise." He said, "Put it down on paper," which we did. It was passed around to the upper echelon of the studio there, and they all agreed that now they had a picture; so we went on to the screenplay. It was the first time that Columbia had ever done anything of a musical nature. They had done either the Frank Capra pictures, which were big, expensive action pictures at that time—this is really before the Capra-Riskin pictures, *It Happened One Night*, and that whole group. They were not used to anything delicate, or certainly not musical, and the picture had a rocky road . . .

The film was called *One Night of Love*. The only reason, finally, that it was made, I was told, was that Grace Moore had very shrewdly borrowed $25,000 against her contract, and Harry Cohn knew that if she didn't get this picture made, he would never get his twenty-five thousand back. So they made the picture. The picture, by the way, in those days it was a big picture for them; it cost $300,000, which was a lot of money, a lot of money. They looked at the picture and hated it, they just said, you know, "This is a disaster." But Jim [James Gow] and I felt that we had done a good job—and after all, they had made the picture—and we felt we were entitled to a raise. We were getting—I forgot to tell you—we were getting $125 a week apiece for writing the screenplay. We said, "We got to get more money," and we sent word through the secretary that we wanted to see Mr. Cohn. And, God, he kept us waiting until about nine o'clock at night. By the time we got into see him, we were perspiring freely. We made the long walk up to this desk of his; there was a man sitting along side of him, who was sort of the "grey eminence" of the studio at the time, Sam Jaffe (whom I came to know later as a very nice man). He was always, at that period, sitting with Cohn, advising. We went up to this massive desk and Cohn looked up and he said, "What the hell do you want?" And we said, "Mr. Cohn we, we, you know, did the script on *One Night of Love*—." He said, "Yeah, the picture stinks." We said, "Well, you know, we—we only got a hundred and a quarter apiece for writing this and—we want a raise." He said, "How much do you want?" We said, "We want two-fifty apiece." He turned to Sam Jaffe and [he] said, "Do my ears deceive me?" [laughter] I've never forgotten that line and I must say, as scared as we were, we both burst out laughing. We couldn't, we just couldn't contain ourselves. And, of course, that infuriated him. He said, "You get the hell out of here. Go back to work on what you've been assigned to work on, and I don't want to hear any more talk about this raise." And we said, "No, we're not going to do that." He said, "Then get out." So we said, "Fine." We got out. As it turned out, the picture was previewed in Pasadena and it was a big, big success and subsequently made a great deal of money for the company. As a result of that we got a job at RKO, got a contract at RKO as a matter of fact. The first picture we did there was [a] Lily Pons picture, called *I Dream Too Much*, with Henry Fonda. From then on, we were writers. Jim and I worked together for, I think, about three years and then we split up, very amicably. We decided that arithmetically it didn't work so well, [that] separately we could do better than working as a team.

Source: Edmund Hall North. 1986. Interviewed by Joel Gardner. UCLA Center for Oral History Research (unpaginated). Courtesy of Center for Oral History Research, Charles E. Young Research Library, UCLA.

SLEEPING CAR PORTER

Sleeping car porters worked on railroads across the United States during the late nineteenth and early twentieth centuries. These employees, almost all of them African American men, attended to passengers' comfort. Porters worked long hours under difficult conditions. Although it could be a demeaning position, many sleeping car porters were proud of their job, using it to propel themselves into the middle class. Porters also played a vital role in the labor and civil rights movements.

The rapid expansion of the United States' rail network around the time of the Civil War (1861–1865) made long-distance train travel a reality for the middle and upper classes. Train travel was slow by modern standards; a cross-country trip might take four days. Affluent passengers demanded comfortable, private places to rest during their long journey. Although several companies built sleeping cars, by the 1870s, the Pullman Palace Car Company, formed in 1867 by George Pullman (1831–1897), established a near-monopoly over the business. Pullman train cars represented the height of luxury, featuring noise-reducing wheels, fine linens, polished-wood interiors, and high-end fixtures. Each car featured fold-down beds that recessed into the walls during daylight hours. The Pullman car transformed a bare-bones method of transportation into a rolling hotel for those who could afford it.

A sleeping car porter's work began hours before the train departed. They scrubbed their car to a high shine, checked stocks of shaving cream and other supplies, made beds, and performed a hundred other tasks to ensure that everything was perfect. Once passengers started arriving, porters greeted them, hauled their luggage, and ushered them to their seats.

Once the train was underway, the porters did whatever the passengers wanted. They shined shoes and babysat toddlers, swept cigar ashes and mailed letters, brought ice and emptied spittoons. At night, a porter folded down the beds from the walls, raised the privacy curtains, and bade travelers a good night. Even then his work continued. Porters were on constant call. If a rider needed a hot-water bottle, or a cigarette, or a late-night snack, or just wanted to chat because he couldn't sleep, it was the porter's job to satisfy the request regardless of the time. Porters slept only three or four hours a night. Besides endurance, the job also required discretion. Passengers who got drunk or blabbed personal secrets expected porters to keep their indiscretions a secret.

Beginning in 1867, when the company employed its first sleeping car porters, Pullman exclusively hired African Americans, most of them dark skinned, for the position. The first porters were emancipated southern slaves. The company made the porter a "black job" because it allowed them to pay lower wages and because it fit into contemporary white notions of black servility and the belief that African Americans belonged in service roles. Company executives thought passengers would be more comfortable with African Americans, rather than whites, waiting on them. Pullman hired only a handful of African Americans for other positions throughout the firm.

Porters often harbored mixed feelings about their jobs. The work exhausted them. Every train carried rude or racist travelers. Pullman paid porters so little—about $10 a month in 1879, rising to $81.75 in 1924, far below what was considered a living wage—that they relied on tips to get by. This meant adopting a servile, happy-go-lucky attitude regardless of how poorly passengers treated them. Many riders called every porter "George" (a reference to George Pullman) rather than their actual names. The notion of a faceless army of 10,000 Georges dehumanized the porters, denying them an individual identity.

But many porters were proud of their work. It was one of the best-paying jobs a black man could hope to find. Many considered it superior to fieldwork and other dirty or dangerous jobs available to African Americans. Porters got to see the country and could gain an informal education by reading books and newspapers that passengers left behind. They looked snappy in their crisp caps and dark-blue jackets, and they always had stories to entertain at social gatherings. Some saved enough money to buy homes and nurture dreams of a better life for their children.

Porters' grievances with Pullman mounted throughout the early twentieth century. On average, a porter worked around one hundred hours a week. He paid for his uniform, meals, and shoeshine equipment from his own salary. He did not get paid for the hours spent preparing his car before a trip. If a rider stole a towel, blanket, or other company property, Pullman deducted the cost from his paycheck. The company assigned double shifts at the last second, without paying overtime.

Pullman tried to silence grumblings with incremental improvements to wages and benefits and by using spies to squelch talk of collective action. Nevertheless, in 1925, a committee of porters recruited the black journalist and civil rights activist

A. Philip Randolph (1899–1979) to lead a risky unionization campaign. Randolph, who had never ridden on a Pullman car, fought for twelve years before the company recognized the Brotherhood of Sleeping Car Porters (BSCP) on August 25, 1937. Wages immediately increased, and working weeks shortened. With around twelve thousand members, it was the largest black union in the country.

With Randolph at the helm, the BSCP became an important part of the broader civil rights movement. Porters smuggled African American newspapers into southern states. They spread awareness of lynchings and discrimination that might otherwise have gone unreported outside where they occurred. They contributed money and manpower to various racial-equality crusades. They volunteered their meeting halls for civil rights gatherings.

Train travel grew less popular after World War II (1939–1945) as Americans drove cars and rode buses around the nation's growing highway system. The spread of commercial air travel furthered the railroads' decline. The BSCP became a remnant of a bygone era. There were only around two thousand porters left by the mid-1960s. Pullman discontinued its sleeping car service in 1969, ending the era of the sleeping car porter.

David Welky

See also: *1946–1991:* Flight Attendant

FURTHER READING

Anderson, Jervis. 1972. *A. Philip Randolph: A Biographical Portrait*. New York: Harcourt Brace Jovanovich.

Arnesen, Eric. 2001. *Brotherhoods of Color: Black Railroad Workers and the Struggle for Equality*. Cambridge: Harvard University Press.

Bates, Beth Tompkins. 2001. *Pullman Porters and the Rise of Protest Politics in Black America, 1925–1945*. Chapel Hill: University of North Carolina Press.

Harris, William H. 1977. *Keeping the Faith: A. Philip Randolph, Milton P. Webster, and the Brotherhood of Sleeping Car Porters, 1925–37*. Urbana: University of Illinois Press.

Santino, Jack. 1989. *Miles of Smiles, Years of Struggle: Stories of Black Pullman Porters*. Urbana: University of Illinois Press.

Tye, Larry. 2004. *Rising from the Rails: Pullman Porters and the Making of the Black Middle Class*. New York: Henry Holt.

STEELWORKER

Steelworkers work in steel foundries, operating the machines and processes that are used to create steel out of iron, carbon, and other elements. Starting in the 1880s, the American steel industry went through a technological transformation.

While most mills had been designed around the Bessemer process—a system that dated from the late 1850s—steelmakers built new mills (and revamped older ones) around a new process known as open-hearth steelmaking.

Many steel manufacturers worked hard to eradicate the trade unions in their facilities to keep most of the profits from the productivity increases that came with this new process. Both these changes had a significant effect upon the daily lives of steelworkers, who worked in the mills and operated the machines and furnaces that turned raw ore into salable steel.

Under the Bessemer process, skilled labor had a lot of control over how hard and how long they worked. Puddlers were skilled workers who manipulated pig iron to create steel out of it. Their ability to perform this hot, physically demanding, highly skilled work let them control the pace of the entire mill and command a substantial salary. They were the leaders of the Amalgamated Association of Iron and Steel Workers, the trade union that worked to improve the situation that many steelworkers faced in many mills across the United States.

The advent of the open-hearth process severely undercut the power of steelworkers in general and puddlers in particular because it automated many parts of the steelmaking process and took the judgments that they had once made under the Bessemer steelmaking process out of their hands. Moreover, the quality of open-hearth steel was better than it had been under the Bessemer process. Because unionized workers impeded the transition from Bessemer to open-hearth production, steel manufacturers were willing to accept strikes and lockouts in order to facilitate that change. The best known of those disputes came at Andrew Carnegie's mill in Homestead Mill in 1892, when ten people died in a gunfight between Pinkerton guards and townspeople fighting to keep Carnegie's mill from reopening the temporarily shuttered mill with nonunion labor. However, it took almost twenty more years for other American steelmakers to eradicate the last vestiges of the Amalgamated Association and modernize all of their mills.

The effects of this transformation on the steelworkers were immediate. Wages dropped. The length of the working day increased. Many of the steelworkers hired to work in these new mills were southern and Eastern European immigrants who were willing to work at demanding jobs that native-born Americans refused. Working in an open-hearth mill required a surprising amount of communication between workers at every part of the process. Those who did not speak English relied upon hand signals to coordinate their activities. Because the work remained hot and brutal, it was difficult for steelworkers to keep their mental state sharp over their long working days. That meant that serious accidents were commonplace. Colds were prevalent in winter months, when steelworkers went from one extreme temperature to another whenever they left the mill.

Of all the issues associated with working in this environment, long hours got the most public attention. A campaign to shorten the hours of all American workers began during the 1880s but did not reach the American steel industry until the era of World War I. Most steelworkers worked twelve-hour days, and many of those worked seven days a week. Every two weeks, when the shift changed, some steelworkers would work for twenty-four hours in a row. While there were long periods of idleness while workers waited for the next heat of steel to be prepared to go through the machinery, without a union to protect steelworkers, idle time decreased significantly after the turn of the twentieth century. Moreover, the conditions in the mill were unpleasant, and every hour spent at work meant less time that steelworkers could spend with their families.

The U.S. government encouraged many steelmakers to shorten the hours of their workers during World War I (1914–1918) as a way to guarantee labor peace. To the surprise of many observers, productivity at those mills with shorter hours actually increased. In 1923, under pressure from President Warren Harding, Judge Elbert Gary of United States Steel announced that the rest of the industry had changed its mind and began to phase out the twelve-hour day. Steel was the last major industry in the United States to implement that change.

Steelworkers had once been among the most powerful members of the entire American working class, but technological change made them expendable. Whole classes of less-skilled workers were left without jobs during downtime at the mills during this era. Even the positions of the most well-off steelworkers depended on their willingness to accept the dictates of management without question. It would take the pro-labor legislation of Franklin Roosevelt's New Deal to inspire steelworkers to organize again and take back some of the advantages they had once had in the early days of this vital American industry.

Jonathan Rees

See also: Ironworker; *1861–1914:* Puddler; Railroad Construction Worker; *1946–1991:* Construction Worker

FURTHER READING

Brody, David. 1998 (1960). *Steelworkers in America: The Nonunion Era.* Urbana: University of Illinois Press.

Fitch, John A. 1989 (1911). *The Steel Workers.* Pittsburgh: University of Pittsburgh Press.

Rees, Jonathan. 2004. *Managing the Mills: Labor Policy in the American Steel Industry during the Nonunion Era.* Lanham: University Press of America.

PRIMARY DOCUMENT

On May 30, 1937, workers and labor sympathizers held a rally at the Republic Steel plant in South Chicago to protest owner Tom Girdler's efforts to prevent them

from joining a new union, the Steelworkers Organizing Committee (SWOC), affiliated with the Congress of Industrial Organizations (CIO). As protesters marched across a field toward the plant, a line of Chicago Police Department officers opened fire on the unarmed workers, killing ten and injuring nearly forty more, leaving some permanently disabled. The police shot many of those protesters in the back as they were running away. Other officers beat retreating protesters with clubs. The songwriter Earl Robinson penned this song in response to the "Memorial Day Massacre."

Memorial Day Massacre

On the dark Republic's bloody ground
On the 30th of May.
Oh, workers, lift your voices high
For them that died that day.
The men who make our country's steel
The workers in the mills,
Said in union is our strength
In justice is our will.

We will not be Tom Girdler's slaves
But free men we will be.
Hear the voices from their graves,
"We died to set you free."
In ordered ranks they all marched on
To picket at the mill
They did not know that the boys in blue
Had orders shoot to kill.

As they marched on peacefully,
Old Glory waving high,
The gunmen cops took their aim
And let their bullets fly.
The deep, deep red will never fade
From Republic's bloody ground.
The workers, they should not forget
To always sing this song.

Do not forget Republic's name
Or Girdler's bloody hands,
He'll be a sign of tyranny
Throughout the world's broad land.

Men and women of the working class
You little children too,
Remember on that fateful day (Memorial Day)
The men who died for you.

Source: "Songs of Steel and Struggle." 1975. Smithsonian Institution, Folkways Records. Collection Number COLL01930.

STENOGRAPHER

A stenographer's job is to transcribe speech in shorthand. An author writing in the late-nineteenth-century professional journal *The Stenographer* advised stenographers that becoming better at their craft required much work and more: "Speed in shorthand is the fruit of patient, earnest effort, sown in hope, pruned by mistakes, watered sometimes by tears, nourished by the midnight oil, and after a long period of sickly growth, it is harvested and we enjoy the rewards of our labor" (Laise 1898, 1). Unlike other clerical workers, stenographers are highly trained in a specific skill—the use of shorthand, which is a form of speed writing in which various symbols replace common words. Stenographers may have other clerical skills as well, especially in secretarial work and as typists. But the ability to rapidly take down a speaker's words at the rate spoken, or dictated, is the sole domain of the skilled stenographer. Taking dictation required a stenographer to take shorthand notes from a speaker, sometimes at more than 160 words per minute, by hand. The system of symbols and replacement words was part of the Gregg system of stenography, created in 1888 by John Robert Gregg. Until the widespread adoption of dictation recording and stenotype machines in the mid-twentieth century, Gregg shorthand was widely used in American business and legal environments.

Stenography required extensive training and practice in Gregg shorthand techniques. After the turn of the century, many vocational institutions, called business colleges, offered courses in stenography. Many clerical workers worked as secretaries, typists, and file clerks while they studied stenography in night courses in these business colleges; in 1918, for instance, skilled male stenographers earned nearly as much per year as plumbers, carpenters, and other tradesmen. Stenography was one of the most lucrative careers for women as well, despite wage differentials, even in office work, that meant that women stenographers doing the same job as men earned significantly less. In both cases, unlike tradesmen whose jobs might be affected by seasonal factors and weather, stenographers generally had steady work throughout the year. Rapid expansion of big businesses in the late nineteenth and early twentieth centuries gave stenographers many opportunities for employment.

A stenographer generally arrived in the office at 7:30 or 8:00 a.m. every day and began work. A stenographer's duties were determined by the working environment and size of the office in which he or she was employed, as well as the nature of the work. Large insurance and banking corporations in Chicago, New York, San Francisco, and other major cities had full complements of employees who did only stenographer work: take dictation; transcribe the symbols into a written document, normally using a typewriter; and return this to the person who had spoken (usually a supervisor, manager, or partner in a firm) for approval and signature. In smaller offices, a stenographer was responsible for these same activities, as well as answering phones, scheduling meetings and appointments, filing documents, sorting mail, and performing other clerical duties. While male stenographers often pursued advancement by becoming experts in certain technical fields such as police, engineering, legal, and medical stenography, women often found it difficult to become stenographers in these fields as employers often preferred "serious" employees. Occupational discrimination against women was often reproduced in lighthearted ways in American culture; the eponymous stenographer Tillie of the popular comic "Tillie the Toiler" (1921–1959) was a good-looking, fashionable clerical worker/part-time model who seldom took her job seriously as she stayed out late at parties, took long lunches, and routinely flirted with men.

During the interwar period, stenographers increasingly found employment as court stenographers, those workers who took down every word uttered in civil and criminal cases heard in courtrooms, from the local municipal court all the way to the U.S. Supreme Court. Court stenography became a professional occupation only in the twentieth century, with two developments: professional organization and standards, and improvements in technology. The National Court Reporters Association was founded in 1899, but the organization did not issue certifications based on competency tests until 1937. NCRA Certification required court stenographers to take accurate shorthand or machine notes for three types of spoken words at a high percentage of accuracy at certain rates: literary (160 words per minute, or WPM), jury charge (180 WPM), and testimony (200 WPM)—all rates that only increased over the rest of the century. Additionally, machines known as stenotypes markedly improved after World War I.

Although rudimentary stenotypes had been invented decades earlier, they were clumsy and often unreliable. The first modern stenotype, the Ireland Stenotype, came into use in 1913 but was significantly improved in the 1920s. Stenographers took shorthand dictation on these machines by depressing combinations of keys (chords) to replicate the symbols they took by hand. Unlike typewriters, stenotype machines did not have marked keys, so stenographers had to memorize the combinations of keys that created certain symbols; additionally, stenotypes had far fewer keys than a typewriter. With the introduction of stenotype machines and certification processes, the court stenographer (or court reporter) achieved significant status among clerical workers. During these years, for instance, several U.S.

Supreme Court justices hired as their law clerks only young male attorneys who had worked as stenographers within the federal government.

The occupation of office stenography declined in the post-World War II years as tape recorders, the personal computer, and other technologies eliminated the need for office stenographers, even as the percentage of clerical workers among all American workers increased from 5 percent (1910) to 17 percent (2000). As a separate occupation, the number of stenographers peaked in about 1970, declining every year thereafter. Some stenographers became key operators for the new computer punch cards, while others pursued court reporting. Excluding court reporters, the stenographer was a specialized occupation for only a short period in American history.

Nancy Quam-Wickham

See also: *1607–1775:* Scrivener; *1776–1860:* Judge; *1946–1991:* Attorney

FURTHER READING

Cushman, Claire. 2016. "Fountain Pens and Typewriters: Supreme Court Stenographers and Law Clerks, 1910–1940. *Journal of Supreme Court History* 41, no. 1: 39–71.

Laise, Anna M. 1898. "Six Speed Requisites." *The Stenographer* 8, no. 1: 1.

Mavor, William Fordyce. 1984. *Universal Stenography, or, a Practical System of Short Hand*. London: Printed for Longman, Hurst, Rees, Orme & Brown.

PRIMARY DOCUMENT

In this document, Lois Bernhardt discusses her experiences as a stenographer in Washington, D.C., during World War II. Born and raised in the small town of Schaller, Iowa, Bernhardt had attended a business school in Des Moines, Iowa, where upon graduation, she obtained a secretarial position in that location. After she had been working in Des Moines for a while, her mother encouraged her to take the U.S. Civil Service exam. Although she scored well on the test, Bernhardt was reluctant to leave Iowa, but in the summer of 1941, she moved to the nation's capital to take a position in the War Department. Her experiences during World War II demonstrate how critical a stenographer's job could be to such weighty matters as war.

[A]t that time, if you worked for the Government and war was just starting, you were not permitted to change jobs unless you acquired a skill that you were not using, and then you could apply for another job. So, I went back to the Washington School for Secretaries to be able to use the stenotype fluently. So then I could say,

"I can use a stenotype now; I'd like to have another job." So then they assigned me to the Price Adjustment Board. This was still in connection with the War Department. The Price Adjustment Board was in the new Pentagon. Now, that Pentagon was the largest office building in the world, and was built in one year . . . However, the roof was not finished, and every time it rained, water just came down the walls. You might be working at a desk, and when you came to it you might be surrounded by water . . .

I was a clerk, clerk-typist. [And then a] clerk-stenographer. They had this big, long corridor and I was assigned to be a secretary to Donald Russell. He had never dictated to a stenotypist before. This was my first experience at taking dictation, so all these people in this long corridor stopped their work and watched us. I didn't do very well on that first letter, I'm sure. Mr. Russell and I talked about it a year later when I had worked for him a while, and he said, "Now that was pretty bad, wasn't it?"

But anyway, they didn't have the partitions in yet. We were only in there a short time though, because Mr. [James F.] Byrnes was on the Supreme Court, as Justice of the Supreme Court, and Roosevelt needed him as his assistant. So, he asked him to leave the Supreme Court and come to the East Wing of the White House; that was where our office was. And in turn, Mr. Byrnes asked Mr. Russell if he would come because Mr. Russell had been a law partner of Byrnes in South Carolina. They were good friends, for a lifetime. So, Mr. Russell therefore went to the White House . . .

I was pretty anxious to see if I couldn't get there too. So, Mr. Russell gave me the nod and I got there [in the Office of Economic Stabilization]. They created that office for Mr. Byrnes to be in the White House so that he could be an assistant to Roosevelt. Also, they had this myriad of ABC offices. There was a lot of bickering between the agencies, each one striving to be the most important agency. And Roosevelt had, oh, you could call it a failing or what, but he did not want to put anybody out of office and so he just created another office over them. You know how that's pyramided . . .

I came to the White House [and] Jimmy Byrnes needed somebody to take his conference reporting, and also to take his official dictation. So my stenotype really served me well to do that. Now, Jimmy Byrnes had been a court reporter. He had a very interesting past . . . He was born after his father had passed away. He worked for a judge and passed his bar. Of course, Truman didn't have a college degree either . . .

He was very much on top of things. One day he was dictating to me and he made the remark about some rumor being "all over the lot." I looked puzzled at him and he said, "Lois, you don't know what I mean do you?" I said, "No," and he changed it because he said, "Well, if you don't know what that terms means, then maybe the people that are going to read this won't know it either." Well, it meant that all over Government circles that . . . people that were going to read or hear what he had to say . . .

[W]e had the Manhattan Project file in our office in the East Wing and whenever this was under discussion at the Oval Office, I was the one that carried it over there. Well, of course, at that time, I was not aware what I was carrying. If I had known it was the atom bomb file, I still wouldn't have understood what it was because at that time I didn't know what an atom was . . . It was kept secret; it was in an office in an unlocked file, in an ordinary file. So there was nothing to call attention to it. I never opened it because I thought this was none of my business . . . We just forgot what was in our office when we left it. Even when we'd type a letter, they took the carbons and burned them, in case someone would see that carbon.

Source: Oral History Interview with Lois Bernhardt: Stenographer to James F. Byrnes, Office of War Mobilization, during World War II and from July to November 1945, when Mr. Byrnes was Secretary of State. (1989). Interviewed by Niel M. Johnson. Truman Library, 7–13 passim, 15. https://www.trumanlibrary.org/oralhist/bernhrdt.htm.

STREETCAR OPERATOR

Bus drivers and streetcar operators are government employees—usually hired by cities—to operate buses and streetcars, accept fares or validate tickets, and interact with passengers. Public transportation boomed in the early twentieth century. Some 140,000 young men worked in transit jobs, mostly as trolley drivers, with the bulk of the employment located in the cities of the North between the Atlantic Ocean and the Mississippi River. Approximately one in five of these drivers worked in New York, especially New York City, and nearly one in ten worked in Philadelphia. Almost all of the drivers were young men, usually under thirty years old when they began the job. They were typically recent arrivals from the countryside or members of European immigrant groups such as the Irish. They joined the workforce to get a sharp uniform and regular—if not highly paid—employment. They also vigorously protested the employment of women and African Americans in driving jobs, often with the support of company management. Not until World War II did women and minorities begin to find significant employment as transit vehicle operators—and then only in limited numbers.

In the early years, transit jobs were plentiful and in high demand. Until the late 1910s, every city endeavored to expand its system, and every town wanted to build a trolley network to showcase its growth and modernity. The increasing popularity of the automobile in the 1920s, however, pushed public transportation into a decline from which it did not recover. Under pressure from the spread of car ownership at first and then the financial devastation of the Great Depression, transit company management slashed jobs at every turn in the 1930s and 1940s. Companies removed trolley lines, substituted buses for streetcars, and scrimped on maintenance and upkeep. These efforts eroded the quality of public transportation and made it less attractive for a population that was moving in vast numbers to the suburbs by the end of the 1940s. By 1950, opportunities for men seeking work as bus drivers and streetcar operators were sparse.

The work of operating buses and streetcars was seemingly simple enough. Trolley operators had to learn the mechanics of operating a powerful electric vehicle that could weigh twenty tons and had limited maneuverability because it was on rails and connected to a wire for power. Buses were smaller and lighter than streetcars and required drivers to learn how to operate a diesel-powered engine that many considered underpowered for the load of passengers it had to haul. In addition to driving, operators also collected fares and made change for riders if they did not have a ticket. This work became increasingly dangerous by midcentury as drivers handled significant amounts of cash and often complained of rowdy nighttime passengers. A number of cities in the mid-twentieth century witnessed protests by transit workers concerned about their safety.

Throughout the first half of the twentieth century, transit work was a difficult job. Men worked as many as eighteen hours, often standing unprotected in the harsh elements during winter in northern cities. Many drivers complained that their jobs barely paid enough to support their families and management showed them no respect. Companies balked at providing windscreens or vestibules, provided little time for lunch or rest breaks, and looked for reasons to dock men's pay. It only took a few years of work under these conditions for drivers to develop a number of common diseases, ranging from poor circulation to nervous breakdowns resulting from driving in crowded, sometimes chaotic, urban conditions.

From the earliest days of the industry, workers tried to improve their situation by organizing in unions, and they encountered hostile management at every turn. The Knights of Labor launched the first organizing campaign in New York City in the 1880s. That movement spread to Philadelphia, Baltimore, and elsewhere but soon faltered. The Amalgamated Association of Street and Electric Railway Employees, affiliated with the American Federation of Labor and usually called the Amalgamated, began in Detroit in 1891 and was much longer lasting. It is the forerunner of the Amalgamated Transit Union, which has over two hundred local chapters today. Despite management's opposition, the Amalgamated reached a high point of 100,000 members in the 1920s and increased workers' annual wages from $615 to $1,737 over that span.

The Amalgamated brought about real change in transit workers' lives, but some employees thought it lacked sufficient impact in that it failed to demand enough from management. These workers supported the Transport Workers Union (TWU), a more leftist labor organization affiliated with the Congress of Industrial Organizations that was born during the hard times of the Great Depression and practiced a more militant unionism. The TWU had its greatest strength in New York City but spread to Philadelphia and eventually to other cities such as Miami, Houston, and San Francisco. The TWU generally drove a harder bargain than the Amalgamated at the negotiating table, but, true to its CIO heritage, it also developed broader social campaigns that sought to build working-class coalitions around issues of housing, taxation, and workers' legal rights.

Although TWU members supported these social justice campaigns, the industry still faced significant tensions over the employment of women and minorities. The most explosive manifestation of these tensions occurred in Philadelphia in 1944 when white workers launched a hate strike to prevent the promotion of African Americans to the position of driver and shut down the nation's third-largest war production center just two months after D-Day, during World War II. The strike was only settled when President Franklin Roosevelt sent five thousand heavily armed troops into the city.

Driving a bus or operating a trolley has always been a difficult job. The work was grueling and the pay low. However, drivers in 1910 or 1950 knew that despite these drawbacks, the work was generally steady and could provide for a family, especially after unions helped raise wages and improve working conditions.

James Wolfinger

See also: Truck Driver; *1946–1991:* Pilot

FURTHER READING

Freeman, Joshua. 1989. *In Transit: The Transport Workers Union in New York City, 1933–1966*. New York: Oxford University Press.

Hood, Clifton. 1993. *722 Miles: The Building of the Subways and How They Transformed New York*. Baltimore: Johns Hopkins University Press.

Molloy, Scott. 1996. *Trolley Wars: Streetcar Workers on the Line*. Durham: University of New Hampshire Press.

Post, Robert C. 2007. *Urban Mass Transit: The Life Story of a Technology*. Westport: Greenwood Press.

Wolfinger, James. 2007. *Philadelphia Divided: Race and Politics in the City of Brotherly Love*. Chapel Hill: University of North Carolina Press.

Wolfinger, James. 2016. *Running the Rails: Capital and Labor in the Philadelphia Transit Industry*. Ithaca: Cornell University Press.

PRIMARY DOCUMENT

During the Great Depression, the U.S. government, through the Federal Writers Project of the Works Projects Administration, funded multiple interviews, oral histories, and music and folklore collection efforts throughout the nation. In this selection, the editor of the New York Transit Workers' Union, Maurice Forge, provided this story to the two WPA interviewers. As an item of workers' folklore, or laborlore, *as the late folklorist Archie Green termed it, this piece elicits workers' union pride and their disdain for strikebreakers as they await an apocryphal meeting with St. Peter, leading to heaven. Workers in many trades had stories of St. Peter's guarding the gates of heaven against strikebreakers; among the most famous was the story-song "Casey Jones: The Union Scab," as recorded by folksinger Pete Seeger with Joe Hill's lyrics.*

Last Saturday night I had a dream. I dreamt I was dead. When I landed at the gates of heaven a man outside the gates asked where I came from. I told him. He then asked me where I worked. When I explained that I was a tower-man on the BMT he directed me to the arena across the way.

I walked across as he instructed me and entered the arena. It was about as big as Madison Square Garden. The place was filled with transit workers of New York and it was explained that St. Peter was coming to find out what good deeds each one of us had done on earth.

There was a stage at the front of the arena and I made my way to a seat close to it. I recognized many faces. Right next to me, upon my word, who do you think were sitting, but Al Beers and Charley Landon. Beers never looked better alive. He wore a new suit, his trousers creased, shined shoes and a clean shirt on. And Landon was rarely without his perpetual smile. Beers would not forget his old habits and kept bumming the price of a cup of coffee and a cigarette from other fellows.

Tom O'Shea, McMahon and Quill were seated on the stage. In the back of the stage, McCarthy and Hogan were sitting near the gate leading to heaven. O'Shea then rose and announced the arrival of St. Peter. A silence I never experienced set in. After a short introduction St. Peter addressed the assembly. He closed his remarks by announcing that all the members of the TWU please stand up and walk through the gate. Everyone in the room rose. St. Peter then said that admission would be by membership book. About 10 percent fainted and slumped in their seats. St. Peter continued the address.

"You members of the TWU have performed noble work in New York. Your fight was a hard one. Enemies you had many. You had to fight the transit trust, the Company Beakies, the bankers, the anti-labor papers and a host of others. You have done a good job. Form the line and walk through the gate at my right. Have your books ready."

As I came near the gate I asked permission to remain in the arena for a while. This request was granted. I took a walk around the arena. Way back in a corner I noticed a small group of men. In the center of the group there was a man who seemed to be in terrible agony. When I asked what was the matter, this man appealed to me to help him by using my influence as a TWU member. "My name is Patrick Joseph Connolly," he said. "See what you can do to get me through these gates." "Oh, so you are the Scab . . . from the IRT?" I exclaimed in surprise. "And your mother named you after Ireland's Patron Saint. What a disgrace to St. Patrick and the Irish people you are. And who are these mugs surrounding you, may I ask?"

"These are my delegates, my thugs and stool-pigeons who served me on earth," was his answer.

As I was walking away I felt somewhat sorry for Pat. "Well you would not have to worry about snow storms where you are headed for, anyhow, Pat. So long."

When I reached the stage again I met another surprise. There was Pete Coons pleading with St. Peter. As I got closer I heard St. Peter ask him what action had he taken when the BMT made the towers automatic and did away with the Towermen. "Well," he pleaded "I have only 250 in our union and what could I do about it?"

"What could you do?" Saint Peter was losing his patience. "Why did you not make common cause with the TWU?" His excuse was that he thought they were superior and better than the other crafts, "And moreover, Mr. Menden and Mr. Egan would be extremely displeased if he worked together with TWU, of course, we are all for the principles of the TWU."

"Well," St. Peter admonished him, "If George Washington had done as you did you would still be paying the Tea Tax to the British Crown. All brave and honest men displease their oppressors and make enemies. Good deeds are what count, not good excuses."

Source: S. S. A. C. A. Levitt, H. S. A. C. A. Spector, and M. Forge. 1939. *Transport Workers*. New York City, New York. [Pdf] Retrieved from the Library of Congress. https://www.loc.gov/resource/wpalh2.23010911.

TELEPHONE EXCHANGE OPERATOR

In the late nineteenth and early twentieth centuries, telephone switchboards required that workers—telephone exchange operators—sit at a desk in front of an elaborate hardboard set of dozens of switches, with each switch directing a call to a different location. Alexander Graham Bell's invention of the telephone in

1876 was just the first in a series of innovations that revolutionized how Americans communicated with each other across space. By 1902, the "telephony" industry employed over seventy thousand workers who built the central plants, established telephone substations, installed lines into homes and businesses, and operated the switchboards that routed calls from its originator to the receiver of the call on the other end. Early telephone systems did not use automated systems that allowed for one caller to directly dial another; instead, callers initiated a call to a switchboard operator, who then directed the call to the caller's intended receiver. While early telephony engineering textbooks referred to the central station as the "brains" of a telephony system, the workers at the switchboard operators were the "hands" who ensured that the system functioned properly.

Because the switchboards had multiple switches and required exceptional small motor dexterity, telephone companies believed that women workers, especially young women, were ideal employees: their fingers were smaller, their attention focused, and their dexterity honed by years of doing other precision work requiring quickly moving fingers, like embroidering, sewing, and playing the piano. Young women—primarily white, native born, and middle class—operated these switchboards. A caller picked up his or her telephone receiver, dialed the switchboard, and asked for the number. After a brief greeting, the switchboard operator simply connected the caller to the intended recipient of the call. While other countries quickly adapted their telephony to automated switching systems, in the United States, the major companies maintained human-operated switchboards for decades. As historian Kenneth Lipartito has argued, telephone company managers in the United States sought to distinguish telephony from telegraphy, so they sought out a way to humanize the new communication method, using young, polite women who could put users at ease: "When dealing with cranky and irritable customers, women's purportedly more patient nature—formed, no doubt, from their maternal instincts—was seen to be especially valuable" (Lipartito 1994, 1085).

While women workers dominated the telephone switchboard field, telephone companies soon found out that even women needed training to become personable, helpful, and diligent employees. Telephone companies required new switchboard operators to complete a course in diction and pronunciation to ensure that workers exuded a "tone of eager friendliness" (Carmi 2015, 316). Workers had to comply with company regulations on "deportment:" they had to sit in their chairs, back straight, legs uncrossed, and ask permission to use a handkerchief to wipe their noses. Management noted any deviations from these policies. Additionally, workers were required to connect the lines within three and a half seconds each; fines were assessed and workers punished if their connection rates were too slow (sometimes caused by a chatty caller), if they sat in their chairs improperly (slouching, for instance), or if operators were caught briefly chatting among themselves. Bell Telephone Company even used the services of a German psychologist who tested women's movements to determine best how they could speed their work process during the 1920s.

Operators complained about overzealous supervisors who, rather than gently correct an operator's small mistake, chastised her and noted the infraction on her employment record. As telephones grew more popular in the first decades of the twentieth century, companies expected operators to speed up their services as the human-operated switchboard was the bottleneck in telephony. Fatigue, stress from increasing demands on her work, and illness could negatively affect a worker's performance, leading to punishment. Even as some smaller companies adopted automated switchboards, eliminating the need for human workers, Bell Telephone Company, the nation's largest, relied on women switchboard operators until the 1940s, when labor shortages as a result of World War II led them to adopt automation. With automation, however, Bell also developed a new product, information services, that still relied on women switchboard operators to provide callers with telephone numbers for individuals and businesses. Additionally, in many large corporations, centralized company switchboards persisted well into the twenty-first century. Male workers were employed as telephone switchboard operators only after passage of the 1964 Civil Rights Act, which banned gender discrimination in employment.

The world of a telephone switchboard operator may have been circumscribed by the offices in which she worked, but their work was extraordinarily important, especially during World War I. The U.S. Army recruited several hundred experienced women switchboard operators to join the Signal Corps. The "Hello Girls," as they were called, served near the front lines in France, helping to operate the telephone and radio services required by General John Pershing's fighting forces. Although men had been members of the army's Signal Corps before the war, most were experienced only in telegraphy, not telephony. The army, drawing on the advice of telephone industry executives, sought out women operators for this service. The women who volunteered for service were examined for fitness and tested on their dexterity and their knowledge of both English and French languages. But despite the formal recruitment, all operators signed on as civilian contract workers, though they had to pass military inspections and address their superiors with the requisite deference. Once in Europe, the many female companies attached to the U.S. Army Signal Corps served with excellence, leading President Woodrow Wilson to recommend to the nation that the reward for these women should be the passage of national suffrage legislation. After the war, some of these civilian "veterans" lobbied for official status, while others took up the cause of unionizing the switchboard labor force. Most, though not all, returned to work for the telephone company, where callers requesting a number were unaware of the important role an operator may have played in the war.

Nancy Quam-Wickham

See also: *1861–1914:* Telegraph Operator

FURTHER READING

Carmi, Elinor. 2015. "Taming Noisy Women: Bell Telephone's Switchboard Operators as a Noise Source." *Media History* 21: 313–327.

Cobbs, Elizabeth. 2017. *The Hello Girls: America's First Women Soldiers.* Cambridge: Harvard University Press.

Lipartito, Kenneth. 1994. "When Women Were Switches: Technology, Work, and Gender in the Telephone Industry, 1890–1920." *American Historical Review* 99: 1074–1111.

TEXTILE WORKER

Textile workers labored in factories that produced fabric, mostly cotton textiles by the twentieth century. Brought over from England in the 1790s as an almost exclusively Northern-based industry, the American textile industry broadened to the South between the 1910s and 1940s. During this time, businessmen started and grew the textile industry in the southern states, where post-Civil War businessmen were eager to industrialize the economy. In the first half of the twentieth century, textile mills and their workers were not only common in places like Massachusetts and New York but also across a sweeping southern piedmont crescent that included Virginia, North Carolina, South Carolina, and Georgia.

In the complex processes of shaping raw cotton into fine cloth for bedding, clothing, and even products like tire fiber, textile mill workers had a variety of jobs at the mill. The common work of a textile mill worker in the interwar period included that of pickers, carders, doffers, spinners, spoolers, draw-in hands, and weavers, in addition to supervisors and janitorial positions. To make any kind of cotton fabric, pickers would first clean the raw cotton and then carders would run that cotton through machines that turned it into a loose rope. This cotton rope would be tightened into strands on spools, with doffers and spoolers overseeing the process. At the last stage, draw-in hands and weavers would finish the cloth on a loom, turning out the cloth based on a set pattern. Supervisors were employed to ensure that these other workers kept on track with production quotas.

The workers undertaking these jobs were almost exclusively white. At northern mills, the racial makeup of textile workers in the early twentieth century was more due to demographics and immigration than intentional discrimination. In the

South, however, textile companies almost exclusively hired white workers. Black Americans, if they were hired, were often placed in janitorial and labor-intensive jobs.

Racial homogeny among textile workers was further amplified in the South as southern textile industries adopted the practice of relying on the family labor system. To encourage a more permanent workforce in the face of harsh working conditions, the family labor system relied on the labor of every member of the family—including women and children as young as eight. Mills depended upon this family labor system and built their industry by creating other conditions for a steady, reliable, and cheap labor force.

Textile companies in the South, just as in the North, created mill villages to stabilize their workforce and discourage workers' unionization. Mill villages were towns that textile companies designed, built, and operated for their workers. In these mill villages, textile workers lived among fellow workers, paid rent to their employer, bought groceries from a company-run store, and, in some villages, would even receive weekly allowances of coal and toilet paper delivered to their rented homes. In places like Schoolfield, Virginia, which boasted nearly eight hundred homes, mill villages were often truly independent communities of textile workers who enjoyed their own movie theaters, YMCAs, doctor's offices, and grocery stores. These tightknit communities encouraged workers' development of a common culture that some workers described as being "like a family."

Not all mill workers experienced life in textiles as familial and convenient, however. While unions had advocated for an eight-hour workday for decades, until the passage of federal protections for workers, most textile workers labored over their looms and carding machines for ten- to twelve-hour shifts, six days a week.

Under these difficult working conditions, many textile workers took to instruments to critique their experience in the industry through music. Southern textile workers turned musicians, such as Charlie Poole and David McCarn, made themselves and the culture of the mills famous by voicing problems with mill life through popular songs such as "Cotton Mill Colic" and "Weave Room Blues." These songs helped to fuel a sense of commonality among mill workers, who would have heard the songs on the radio and would have identified with the critiques of mill life.

Music supported the sentiment of many workers who banded together across the nation to improve working conditions. While they peaked in 1934, labor strikes were common in the beginning of the twentieth century. Strikes were part of organizing efforts of workers, who would walk out of work until their demands for better pay or shorter hours were met by mill executives. Labor shortages during World War I (1914–1918) especially helped workers join unions, which gave their workplace grievances a collective voice. In the summer of 1918, for instance, loom fixers from Rhode Island to New Hampshire stopped working at their mills to protest their low pay. In ongoing strikes from 1918 to 1921, many textile workers allied under the American Federation of Labor's United Textile Workers of America union to organize for shorter hours and higher pay. In 1929, the Great Depression, which resulted in a near collapse of the global economy, also exacerbated workers' unrest.

In the 1920s and throughout the Great Depression, the textile industry struggled to stay profitable as raw cotton became increasingly expensive to purchase and demand for finished cotton products waned with the global economy. Textile workers organized again into the '30s as they were "stretched out." A stretch-out meant that workers were required to work longer hours without receiving an increase in pay. In opposition of these stretch-outs and to better their economic condition during the Depression, workers again took to organizing for better pay and job security. Their strikes in the late 1920s through the 1930s garnered national attention for the violence that ensued. Some were even killed during these organizing efforts such as in the 1929 Loray Mill strike in Gastonia, North Carolina, where a young textile worker, Ella May Wiggins, and Gastonia police chief Orville Frank Aderholt were killed. While many of these strikes did not succeed in their goals, textile workers who protested set a foundation for federal government regulations, such as the National Industrial Recovery Act (1933), under the Roosevelt administration.

As workers gained independence through expanding federal oversight of companies and their own organizing efforts in the 1930s and 1940s, textile companies loosened their control on the mill village and family labor system. Companies began to sell the homes they once rented to workers and started to draw back on the welfare programs they had initiated for their employees earlier in the century. Textile workers themselves began to seek greater economic opportunity in other industries. By World War II, the mill village and the communities of textile workers that felt "like a family" had begun their gradual decline.

Ina Dixon

See also: Garment Worker; *1607–1775:* Weaver and Spinner; *1776–1860:* Milliner; *1861–1914:* Seamstress

FURTHER READING

Andrews, Mildred Gwin. 1987. *The Men and the Mills: A History of the Southern Textile Industry.* Macon: Mercer University Press.

Cash, Wiley. 2018. *The Last Ballad.* New York: HarperCollins.

Galenson, Alice. 1985. *The Migration of the Cotton Textile Industry from New England to the South, 1880–1930.* New York: Garland Publishing.

Hall, Jacquelyn Dowd, ed. 2000. *Like a Family: The Making of a Southern Cotton Mill World.* The Fred W. Morrison Series in Southern Studies. Chapel Hill: University of North Carolina Press.

Herring, Harriet L. 2011. *Passing of the Mill Village: Revolution in a Southern Institution.* Chapel Hill: The University of North Carolina Press.

Huber, Patrick. 2014. *Linthead Stomp: The Creation of Country Music in the Piedmont South.* Chapel Hill: University of North Carolina Press.

Kessler-Harris, Alice. 2003. *Out to Work: A History of Wage-Earning Women in the United States.* New York: Oxford University Press.

Roediger, David R., and Elizabeth D. Esch. 2014. *Production of Difference: Race and the Management of Labor in U.S. History.* Oxford, UK: Oxford University Press.

Salmond, John A. 2002. *The General Textile Strike of 1934: From Maine to Alabama.* Columbia: University of Missouri Press.

Zieger, Robert H., Timothy J. Minchin, and Gilbert J. Gall. 2014. *American Workers, American Unions: The Twentieth and Early Twenty-First Centuries.* Baltimore: Johns Hopkins University Press.

PRIMARY DOCUMENT

Life in the textile mill region of the South was difficult. In the days before laws restricting child labor, young people in the regions often began their careers before they became teenagers. Generations of families worked in some mills, where conditions were hazardous: Whirring machines could entrap a person's fingers or hand, leading to serious injuries and even amputation. Air was laden with cotton particles in factories that lacked adequate ventilation, leading many to develop a long-term chronic respiratory disease, byssinosis, or "brown lung disease." Skin rashes were common, as was tuberculosis. Until the successful sanitation campaigns of the first half of the twentieth century, poor sanitation in local mill towns and in factories led to epidemic levels of hookworm infection among those impoverished millworkers who could not afford to wear shoes.

In this document, forty-seven-year-old grandmother Alice Caudle relates her experiences working in a Cannon Cotton Company mill in Concord, North Carolina, where she moved with her family when she was four years old. She never attended school but instead went to work as soon as she was able. In this interview, recorded by a writer with the Federal Writer's Project in 1938, Caudle speaks about her experiences and the sense of wonder she had when she was invited to an awards dinner for long-time employees of the mill. At the time of this interview, Caudle was still working in the knitting mill, where she earned $15.50 per forty-hour work week.

I reckon I was born to work in a mill. I started when I was ten year old and I aim to keep right on jest as long as I'm able. I'd a-heap rather do it then housework . . . When I started down here to plant No. 1, I was so little I had to stand on a box to reach my work. I was a spinner at first, then I learned to spool. When they put in them new winding machines, I asked them to learn me how to work 'em and they did. If I'd a-been a man no telling how far I'd-a gone. It was mighty convenient for 'em—having a hand that could do all three, but I got mad and quit. In them days there was an agreement here in the mills that if a hand was to quit one, then the other mills in town wouldn't hire him, so I went over to Albemarle and I got me a job in the knitting mills. One day the boss man told me the hand that worked the machine that knit stockings was quittin', and he told me to go watch her to see if I couldn't learn it. Well, I stood right close by that hand all day and I watched her, so that the next day when she didn't come I was able to work the machine by myself . . .

I've worked for the Cannon Mills now for over thirty years . . . I have one of them pins they gave at that big supper last spring. One day someone come around asking all the hands how long they had worked for the Cannon Mills. Course nobody knew why such a question was being asked and some of the hands was afeared to tell how long they had worked. Well, I wasn't; when they asked me I said "thirty year" and was proud of it. Several days after that they sent for me to go to the office; "boys," I said to myself, they're a-going to fire me now. When I went in the office Mr. there says "Miss Caudle?, you've worked for the Cannon Company for thirty year, ain't you?" and I said "Yes Sir, Mr., that's right." Then he said "We're a-having a big supper up at Kannapolis on Friday night for them that's worked twenty-five year or more for the company and here's your ticket."

"Well Sir," I said to him, "in all these thirty years this is the first time the Cannon Mill ever offered me anything—are you right sure they're not a-going to take hit off my pay?"

When the day come for the supper Rose Panell come down here to go with me because they was sending a car for us two. It was held up in the Mary Ella Hall in Kannapolis. You went into a great big room, furnished jest as nice as you'd want, and they had a man there who didn't do nothing but take your hat and coat when you come in and hang 'em up fer you. I thought we would kill ourselves laughing and Rose kept a-wondering if we'd get the right coats and hats back. The other room where we was to eat looked as pretty as anything you ever saw. Such a sight of tables—and every one was covered all over and down at the sides with some of that white cloth that was finished down at the Bleachery; and there was flower pots set about on them. I didn't think they'd have much to eat for such a crowd, but the tables was covered. They had turkey and everything; hit was real good.

Yes, they had speeches. Charles Cannon made a fine speech and give out the pins to us. He told about the way young'uns used to stand on boxes to work—the way I done.

Source: Muriel L. Wolf and Alice Caudle (*Aline Caudle*). North Carolina, September 2, 1938, manuscript/mixed material. Retrieved from the Library of Congress. https://www.loc.gov/item/wplh001917/.

TRUCK DRIVER

A truck driver earns a living as the driver of a truck—usually a box truck or a semi-truck. The trucking industry in the period between the First and Second World Wars was largely local and regional in scope, characterized by small companies, called cartage companies, which transported goods over comparatively short distances—from docks in port cities to warehouses, from farming centers to regional marketplaces, and from warehouses to stores and shops. During this period, truck drivers were workers, almost always men, who piloted these short-haul vehicles. Truck drivers worked shifts, often early in the morning until late afternoon, while others worked overnight, moving goods. Since freeways and expressways were largely developments of the 1950s, long-haul combination truck-and-trailer rigs were uncommon in this earlier period. Unlike their counterparts later, most truck drivers went home at night—not spending days on the road, away from home and family. During this time, truck drivers also organized into a trucking union, the International Brotherhood of Teamsters, first formed to represent team drivers, those who carted goods on wagons powered by horse and mule. In the 1930s and 1940s, however, some trucking companies and their drivers offered regional transportation services—extending the reach of railroads into communities across the South or West, for example. Trucks (and their drivers) did not replace trains, which remained the principle means of transporting most goods over long distances in this period.

Trucks hit the American roadways later than automobiles in the early twentieth century. During World War I (1914–1918), however, industry realized the efficiencies that motor trucks, rather than teams, brought to local and regional shipping. Many of earliest trucks were built by Ford and General Motors; they had hard rubber tires and gas engines and were typically of the box or flatbed style. They lacked heat, and drivers often compared their seats to hard benches. Clutch pedals, manual transmission, and manual steering required strength to operate. These trucks delivered ice, coal, groceries, and other goods directly to consumers. Some states limited the size of trucks (by weight) to protect roads, which could be easily damaged by heavy vehicles. By the 1920s, several specialized trucking companies began to produce commercial trucks to transport and deliver goods for consumers: Freuhof, Mack, White, Sterling, and Harvester. These larger cab trucks were generally powered by the more economical diesel engine. Many had trailers, and they were specialized haulers: tank trucks, dump trucks, car haulers, construction equipment (like bulldozers), and trucks to transport logs, produce, and packaged goods. Truck drivers operated these larger vehicles and had to perform basic maintenance on them.

Delivery truck drivers picked up their loads at central locations and then delivered the goods to consumers along a specified route. The "ice man" was a regular figure in urban life, delivering ice for iceboxes in the 1910s through the early 1930s, using large tongs to remove blocks of ice from the back of the truck and take into the customer's house. Drivers and loaders had to pack ice in sawdust to prevent melting on hot days. Milkmen delivered bottles of milk, cream, and other goods directly to households early in the morning, taking individual orders from the truck to the doorstep over and over, hundreds of times per day. Truck drivers delivered all kinds of consumer goods, as well as mail. They also collected goods from consumers: early sanitation trucks required drivers and loaders to lift refuse containers over the side of open-bin trucks. Thus, drivers were goods handlers as well as vehicle operators.

After 1920, the trucking industry grew to accommodate farmers who needed to move their produce and agricultural goods into the nation's expanding urban markets. Tank truck drivers drove routes from dairy cooperatives in upstate New York to New York City. Truck drivers in farming regions specialized in hauling produce, grains, or live animals (hogs, cattle, chickens) to processing plants. These workers were often owner-operators or employees of small trucking firms familiar with the rhythms of agricultural work; their routes were flexible, based on a farmer's immediate need to quickly get goods to processors and markets to prevent spoilage. Consumers of this period demanded cheap food, while farmers sought better prices, leading truck drivers in this subsector to work long hours, often on short notice. Because the federal government exempted most agricultural loads from regulation within the trucking industry, drivers who operated vehicles carrying agricultural goods were largely nonunion, given the splintered industrial and work environments of these firms.

By the 1930s, the trucking industry and its drivers experienced cutthroat conditions. In some cities, especially in the Northeast, mobsters dominated trucking, requiring companies and drivers to pay "fees" to haul some goods. To make money, companies pushed their drivers to work longer hours, serve more customers, and drive more miles each day. By this time, the Teamsters' Union had started to organize truck drivers to demand better conditions and pay. In 1934, truck drivers who had to shovel and deliver coal in Minneapolis went on strike. They blocked the coal yards, prevented strikebreakers from driving any trucks (sometimes using violence), and forced local trucking companies to accept the union's demand for higher wages and shorter work hours; undoubtedly, the timing of this strike—in February in Minnesota—helped workers win. Their success in the coal truck strike led truck drivers to organize with the city's other drivers, resulting in a citywide and general strike in the summer of 1934 that also ended in victory; within a few years, the Teamsters' Union had grown to represent truck drivers and workers at more than five hundred trucking firms in the Midwest.

The trucking industry had grown so rapidly in the 1920s and 1930s that, during the New Deal, the federal government established hours of service (HOS) for truck drivers—or a limit on the number of hours a truck driver could drive (ten hours) before a mandatory period of rest (eight hours), primarily to make trucking safer for all motorists, not just truck drivers. Other regulations established regional routes and prohibited coast-to-coast hauling. The image of a long-haul truck driver, or "asphalt cowboy," was distinctly a post-World War II icon.

Nancy Quam-Wickham

See also: Longshoreman; Warehouse Worker; *1861–1914:* Teamster; *1992–2019:* Supply Chain Logistician

FURTHER READING

Faue, Elizabeth. 1991. *Community of Suffering and Struggle: Women, Men, and the Labor Movement in Minneapolis, 1915–1945.* Charlotte: University of North Carolina.

Hamilton, Shane. 2008. *Trucking Country: The Road to Walmart's America.* Princeton: Princeton University Press.

PRIMARY DOCUMENT

During the Great Depression, putting workers back to work was one important recovery effort. Sometimes this meant that federal programs were created or funded to pay workers to produce work that was not immediately or directly practical but produced a great deal of subjective value. This short interview from Federal Writers' Project's Folklore Project, Life Histories collection was the result of such funding. The interviewer is identified only as L. R., who spoke with a truck driver whose experience was representative of the struggles that many truck drivers faced during the Great Depression.

Durham, N. C.

September 19, 1938

L. R.

JOHN ROGERS, PRODUCE TRUCKER

John Rogers had had seven hours sleep in the past two nights. He would get about four more hours when he got to Durham after midnight. Then he would get up early to deliver his vegetables and fruits to the Durham grocers. This done he would start the hundred and sixty miles back to Richmond where he would arrive early in the afternoon, buy another load, and get back to Durham in time for four or five hours sleep—if everything went right.

When driving like this John Rogers sometimes pulls to the side of the road and lies flat on the warm concrete under his truck, completely relaxed. Five minutes of this and he can drive on as if he had slept. He drinks coffee and Coca-Colas to stay awake but doesn't use or trust such aids as No-Doz. When he started driving four years ago he weighed 165 pounds and has since gained fifteen pounds. He has never had a wreck.

John Rogers owns, or owns with his three brothers-in-law, four trucks, three of them half-ton pickups and one a ton-and-a-half job, all Fords and all but one thirty-five V-8s. Every day but Saturday and Sunday he takes one of the pickups to Richmond. Doing this five days a week makes him feel all wore down sometimes, he admits, but it's a competitive business and the Durham grocers know his stuff is fresh. The Richmond trips net about fifteen or twenty dollars each. The big truck, driven by one of his brothers-in-law, runs to Norfolk and nets more. The big truck requires a helper, whom they hire. It gets ten miles to the gallon, loaded or unloaded; the lighter trucks get twice that unloaded and about eighteen loaded. His first truck was a '26 T model and he has traded in for a succession of newer models ever since. Fords, he thinks, are as good as you want for your money.

Two of the brothers-in-law stay in Durham and get advance orders and deliver with one of the pickups. Their market is Durham though they sometimes help supply Duke University and the University of North Carolina at Chapel Hill. They are all younger than John Rogers, who is thirty-three.

His load on a mid-September night consists of tomatoes, roasting-ears, black-eyed peas, stringbeans, and peaches. He also carries two dozen eggs for his own home. Most of this stuff, he says, is raised close around Richmond. The other truck gets vegetables and fruits grown in the back country around Norfolk and on the Eastern Shore or even brought in on ships. He follows the markets and has hauled about everything that grows.

Last winter he hauled fruit and vegetables from Florida. This winter he is going to do it again, but as a driver for a Durham fruit dealer instead of as an independent. At least he thinks he will get the job which will pay him twenty-five, maybe thirty dollars and expenses. He says last winter was the toughest he ever saw. He was paying on three trucks, his baby was born and his wife wasn't working. The competition was bad, too many trucking. He knows the Florida markets and is a close buyer and he will be able to save his employer money on the stuff. He will start about December first and will store his own trucks. He rarely goes further into Florida than Jacksonville. There he can get anything he wants.

John Rogers likes the uncertainty and chance of trucking but he is getting tired of it. The life of a truck driver, he says, is six years. He thinks this winter may be his last on the highway. He can always get something to do around Durham or he may go back and stay on the farm with his mother and father and take care of the place.

Source: John Rogers and L. R. *John Rodgers*. 1938. North Carolina. Manuscript/Mixed Material. https://www.loc.gov/item/wpalh001883/.

WAITER/WAITRESS

Waiters (male) and waitresses (female) are workers who serve food and beverages to those customers who take meals in dining establishments such as bars, restaurants, cafés, tea rooms, diners, and boarding houses. This occupation transformed during the interwar years (between World War I and World War II) as the workforce became increasingly "feminized": waitresses comprised both an increasing number and a growing percentage of the total workforce. In other words, there were more workers who served food in dining establishments in the United States in 1970, and they were far more likely to be women. This marked occupational segregation among restaurant servers occurred for several reasons during the interwar period: expansion of dining establishments in number and in kind, population and urban growth, employer and customer preference for women workers, and changes in occupational opportunities for men and women alike.

While public houses, or pubs, offered basic homestyle food to colonial travelers, the form of the modern American restaurant first emerged in the 1820s and 1830s as American cities rapidly grew in wealth and population. Large new hotels incorporated formal dining rooms, where male servers carried heavy loads of food to hungry diners, most of whom were also men. Soon, "French restaurants" began to cater to the tastes of a growing middle class and urban elites. These eating establishments were explicitly modeled after French, and particularly Parisian, institutions: they advertised chefs trained in the most recent culinary trends of France, elegant dining halls, and elaborate menus that offered diners a dizzying number of choices for dinner—appetizers, soups, vegetable and fruit plates, cheeses, main entrees, and desserts.

By the 1890s, New York City's Delmonico's was perhaps America's best-known fine restaurant. Delmonico's occupied an eight-story building and employed dozens of waiters who took orders and shuttled dishes back and forth between the kitchen and patrons. At Delmonico's, one menu from 1899 featured no fewer than eleven soups, a host of appetizers and side dishes (including celery, olives, caviar, and tuna), sixteen types of roasts (including "reed-birds," plover, and spring lamb), dozens of salads, vegetables (including new potatoes cooked six different ways), fruits, fish and fowl dishes, cold meats and cheeses, and a choice of eight entrées, including the sumptuous sweetbreads Neapolitan—an entrée of beef thymus cooked in sherry and fine herbs combined with diced chicken, smoked beef tongue, mushrooms, and tomatoes and served on a bed of heavily buttered macaroni—a dish that took at least two days to prepare. In an establishment like Delmonico's, waiters wore gloves and stylish uniforms and immediately attended to the needs of patrons; they stood at the dining rooms' perimeter with pitchers of water or bottles of chilled wine, ready to top off any patron's glass before it became empty. Most patrons were male, though women were allowed to patronize Delmonico's if accompanied by a male chaperone; otherwise, women ate separately in the women's-only dining rooms. Delmonico's closed in the early 1920s due to Prohibition and changes in the American palate.

Aside from these elegant establishments, both men and women worked in more modest cafeterias, saloons, bars, and diners. Prior to World War I, many male waiters were African American as most Americans accepted blacks—particularly southern blacks—in roles of servitude. Some male waiters were immigrants. But by World War I, a shortage of male workers encouraged restaurateurs to experiment with hiring women as waitresses. During the 1920s, cities grew as Americans migrated to them from farms and rural areas, suburbs multiplied, and, during Prohibition, owners converted their bars and saloons into restaurants. Americans also traveled more. Both working-class and middle-class Americans began dining out more often, attracted by new restaurant chains like Fred Harvey's and Thompson's, which offered meals of consistent quality at a modest price.

As American restaurants modernized, the nature of work and who did that work also changed. High-end fine-dining establishments still preferred male waiters, but the newer businesses often sought out waitresses as employers argued that women could make do with lower wages while providing friendly service. Busboys, who were then paid a weekly wage rather than by a share of waiters' pooled tips, helped women carry heavy loads of soiled dishes back to the kitchen. Additionally, during Prohibition, alcohol was not openly served in restaurants, eliminating one justification for hiring only male waiters: most Americans believed that women should not be expected to serve alcohol as doing so might corrupt their morals.

While employers and patrons alike expected waiters to be pleasant but professional in demeanor, attentive but reserved, and impeccably dressed, waitresses had greater latitude in their interactions with customers. Historian Dorothy Sue Cobble describes part of a waitress's job as "emotional labor"—providing a friendly ear and a ready smile as they interacted with patrons on the job, even as restaurants increasingly provided job training and instruction in personal hygiene and proper communication styles to new workers (Cobble 1991, 2). In turn, patrons often reported that women food servers were more approachable than the often-distant waiters. To their credit, waitresses also used these new expectations to their—and their employers'—benefit by encouraging customers to order a dessert or stay a bit longer to finish a cup of coffee. Selling more products and making a customer feel comfortable led to greater profits for both the restaurant owner and the waitress, who found customer gratitude in tips.

In this period, working conditions for both men and women food servers were characterized by long hours, fast-paced work, and heavy physical demands. Through the 1950s, most waiters and waitresses were full-time workers, many with families who depended on their income. Most worked ten hours or more per day in split shifts, which meant that they needed to report to work by 6:00 a.m. for the breakfast shift, working through lunch and then taking a few hours off before returning to serve dinner. The six-day work week was nearly universal; the majority of waiters and waitresses in hotel restaurants worked seven days per week as late as 1939. While wages were low, tips supplemented earnings. Employers routinely deducted fines from wages for "breakage" of dishes and glassware, whether it was the fault of the worker or patrons. Part of a food server's wages was also supplied in kind—most employers provided meals, though waiters and waitresses often complained that their employers gave them only food of such poor quality (spoiled or leftover, without accompanying sauces or seasoning) that they would not otherwise serve to patrons. The work of serving was also physically demanding, requiring constant attention while on one's feet for hours at a time. Large trays of food were heavy, kitchen floors often wet or greasy. Other servers might fly by, loaded with trays of food, not noticing their fellow workers.

Food servers also had to contend with demanding managers and customers. Sexual harassment was rife within the food-serving industry. Sometimes, male managers demanded sexual favors from waitresses to keep their jobs or be assigned the best shifts (Cobble 2001, 94), but just as problematic were male customers who expected waitresses to tolerate a "slap on the fanny" or laugh at an off-color joke to get a good tip. Lonely patrons routinely expected waiters and waitresses to provide constant conversation, which distracted workers from their other customers. Inebriated patrons could become dangerous if agitated. The anonymity of a restaurant also presented particular interpersonal challenges to food servers: a waiter or waitress could never be sure of a demanding or fickle patron's intent.

In response, waiters and waitresses devised strategies to negotiate these potentially hazardous conditions. More experienced wait staff routinely mentored new workers by advising them about managers' expectations and how to handle problematic customers' behavior. A food server might intervene with a customer, stopping by a table and chatting with him or her to allow a fellow server to escape to the kitchen. Food servers developed slang to describe particular customers—those who skipped out on a check, acted capriciously and sent back food, were poor tippers, or tried to monopolize a server's time.

In the 1930s and 1940s, waiters and waitresses sought to unionize as a way to protect themselves on the job and to protect their economic interests. In some cities, like San Francisco, New York, and Detroit, more than half of all food servers were members of unions, primarily AFL-affiliated crafts union locals. Collective action promised better conditions, and in some cases, employers accepted unionization as unions supplied establishments with more experienced and better-trained workers. Even Woolworth's lunch counter servers struck for union recognition during the union drives of 1937. Additionally, in some areas, waitresses in particular sought legislative relief: they supported state-level restrictions on hours of labor for women workers, leading to cuts in their average work weeks. But in the long term, endorsing unions paradoxically worked to the advantage of male waiters over female workers. Better wages and benefits and provisions for maximum weekly hours elevated the status of waiters in an otherwise low-paying industry, which led more men to pursue food-serving jobs in union establishments. After World War II, locals of waiters and locals of waitresses fought over jurisdiction and representation; this gendered internecine strife was highlighted in several midwestern states in the 1940s and 1950s, where women were prohibited from working as bartenders. And it led to differential rates of occupational feminization: women increasingly tended to work in nonunion establishments, sometimes as part-time workers, while men worked full time as wait staff in union houses. As rates of unionization declined in private industry during the late 1950s, women waitresses became the norm, not the exception.

Nancy Quam-Wickham

See also: Sleeping Car Porter; *1946–1991:* Flight Attendant

FURTHER READING

Briscoe, John. 2002. *Tadich Grill: The History of San Francisco's Oldest Restaurant, with Recipes*. Berkeley: Ten Speed Press.

Cobble, Dorothy Sue. 1991. *Dishing It Out: Waitresses and Their Unions in the Twentieth Century.* Champaign: University of Illinois Press.

Cobble, Dorothy Sue. 2001. "Lost Ways of Unionism." In *Rekindling the Movement: Labor's Quest for Relevance in the Twenty-First Century*. Ithaca: Cornell University Press.

Dahl, J. O. 1945. *The Efficient Waitress Manual*. Stamford: The Dahls.

WAREHOUSE WORKER

Warehouses are storage buildings that house items for later use or shipment, and they have been used in America for as long as humans have been present. In the early twentieth century, as the nation's transportation network expanded, the size of warehouses increased, and these new large warehouses required workers to track shipments, divide goods, and, if necessary, repackage the items for distribution. These workers were known simply as warehousemen or warehouse workers. Then, as today, warehouse workers handled the freight, or goods, that arrive to and depart from warehouses. In the early decades of the twentieth century, freight handlers were typically casual workers—those hired for a day or longer, based on the need of the employer, the warehouse manager.

Farmers in the colonial and early republic eras often took their own produce, eggs, and other items to market and sold them directly to consumers. But with new national transportation networks of the nineteenth and twentieth century, a citrus farmer in southern California could sell his entire crop to wholesalers, who could then transport the produce to centralized fruit warehouses and arrange for their shipment to multiple markets across the nation. Once shipments arrived in Kansas City, Cleveland, or Minneapolis, these lots of oranges were subdivided into smaller quantities and taken to groceries or produce markets, where workers sold the oranges to consumers. The warehouse was a critical institution in the emergence of effective transportation networks. In San Francisco, for instance, more than thirty new warehouses were built between 1900 and 1924 just to handle transshipment of goods.

Each morning, men lined up outside of warehouses, often as early as 2:00 or 3:00 a.m., to inquire about work for the day. The manager or his representative looked over the crowd of unemployed men and chose those he preferred, leaving others without work; this was the "shape-up" system so common to other occupations, like sleeping car porters and longshoremen. Those who slipped the manager a bribe—payment in cash or goods, like a bottle of liquor—often received preferential treatment and were regularly given work.

In the early decades of the twentieth century, warehouse workdays could be extraordinarily long: sixteen-hour workdays were not uncommon if a gang of warehouse workers had to finish a certain job. Warehouse workers were usually men due to the heavy weights they commonly had to lift, the quick pace of work that they had to maintain, and the open discrimination against women regardless of whether they were capable of doing the job. Some warehouses located far from larger transshipment facilities, however, employed women warehouse workers on a regular, full-time, hourly basis, not using the shape-up or casual day labor, because shipments were frequent, and women were broadly available to perform the work.

Warehouse workers commonly worked inside the warehouse and on its loading docks. The nature of the work depended on the items stored. Grain, sugar, canned goods, and fresh produce all required different methods of handling. In this period, bulk goods like refined sugar arrived in large hundred-pound sacks; each warehouse worker had to load five or six sacks onto a handcart, which they then moved to a waiting railroad boxcar that would transport the load of sugar to an industrial bakery for use in making pastries or bread. Canned goods were shipped in boxes and were similarly loaded onto handcarts. Fresh produce might arrive in burlap bags or in large, open, wooden boxes, which also had to be moved around on handcarts before the advent of the mechanized forklift.

Workers worked alone or in teams of two to toss bags of rice onto their handcarts, but fresh produce needed more careful handling to avoid damage. Most workers of the time remember the pace of work as being intense, with some employers requiring that men request bathroom breaks. Workers typically received an hour for lunch, the only break of the workday. Warehouse work was largely unskilled labor, requiring that a worker have physical strength, a strong back, and stamina. Workers who could not keep up with the pace were normally discharged. For this work, before union growth in the mid-1930s, workers might receive as little as thirty cents per hour. At such low wages, some workers tried to maximize their incomes by working seven days a week.

Throughout the country, warehouse workers began to organize into unions in the 1930s. One of the first demands of many warehouse workers was the end to the shape-up and the provision of regular employment instead. Warehouse workers often sought to organize into unions as they experienced the great union drives of those whose jobs intersected with their own: teamsters, longshoremen, and retail workers. Warehouse workers fell into the large group of mostly unskilled and semi-skilled workers who joined unions as the strikes of 1934–1937 swept across the nation. In 1934 alone, major strikes in Toledo, Minneapolis, on the West Coast, and in the textile regions of the South affected hundreds of thousands of workers. Warehouse workers on the West Coast benefited when the International Longshoremen's Association (ILA) won contracts against major shippers; the warehouse union locals that were affiliated with the ILA soon followed with their own organizing and bargaining victories. In the Twin Cities region, warehouse workers' union successes followed on the heels of the Teamster's Local 574 strike victory in August of that year.

Warehouse workers also benefited from federal court rulings, including a case involving warehousemen employed by the Santa Cruz Packing Fruit Company that ultimately reached the U.S. Supreme Court and was decided in favor of the workers in 1938. The Santa Cruz case proved important, establishing not only that the warehouse's managers had endorsed unfair labor practices against warehouse union advocates, but, indeed, the jurists noted that the place of warehouses was squarely within the purview of the federal government, in this case the National Labor Relations Board, as warehouses were fully an integral part of the interstate commerce in goods. Warehouse workers might have labored in local plants, but they contributed to the growth of a national trade in goods that changed forever Americans' consumption patterns.

Nancy Quam-Wickham

See also: Truck Driver; *1992–2019:* Package Handler; Supply Chain Logistician

FURTHER READING

Faue, Elizabeth. 1991. *Community of Suffering & Struggle: Women, Men, and the Labor Movement in Minneapolis, 1915–1945*. Chapel Hill: University of North Carolina Press.

Schwartz, Harvey. 1975. *The March Inland: The Warehouse Organizing Drive of the Pacific Coast Longshore Union, 1934–1938.* Los Angeles: Institute of Industrial Relations.

United States. 1986. *Injuries to Warehouse Workers*. Washington, DC: U.S. Dept. of Labor, Bureau of Labor Statistics.

1946–1991: POST–WORLD WAR II AMERICA

INTRODUCTION

At the end of World War II, American workers and their unions lobbied for "jobs for all," a political position that endeavored to ensure that every American who wanted to work had a job, even if he or she had been made jobless through mechanization or technological improvements. The government, they argued, should provide employment when private corporations did not. As part of the post–World War II labor landscape, the "jobs for all" movement proved to be more of a response to past concerns about economic growth than to any particular current threat. Some of the most generous social welfare benefit schemes in the history of the nation, such as the Serviceman's Readjustment Act, also known as the G.I. Bill (passed in 1944), bolstered the postwar economy. Nearly one half of all WWII veterans took advantage of the benefits, which included payment of tuition and living costs for pursuing a high school diploma, college degree, or vocational or technical education; very low-interest loans for the purchase of homes; funds for starting small businesses; and unemployment benefits for returning veterans who could not find jobs. Between 1945 and 1955, benefits paid to veterans helped promote economic growth in home construction and education. Better-educated veterans invested in small businesses and pursued jobs in Cold War defense complexes. Millions of American workers either benefited directly or shared in its benefits.

Shortly after the war, however, American workers also suffered setbacks, especially with the passage of the National Management Relations Act, also known as the Taft-Hartley Act (1947), which limited federal intervention into labor-management affairs, abolished the closed shop (in which only union members were eligible for employment), and allowed state laws to restrict unions in ways the federal government did not. Although Taft-Hartley had a negative impact on organized labor, particularly on union organizing in the South, it did not prevent strikes in the postwar era. In the 1950s and 1960s, for instance, workers continued their history of striking for better wages and benefits, and strike participation was high. But no labor disputes reached the height of violence seen in West Virginia's Coal Wars (1912–1918, 1919–1921). Instead, organized workers fought for cost-of-living increases, employer-provided health insurance, seniority protection, and basic wage increases—which tended to lead to economic security and social mobility. In turn, employment in health professions grew as millions of workers with health benefits could afford routine care for themselves and their families. Well-paid union workers and veterans using the G.I. Bill stimulated suburban growth as they could afford to purchase single-family homes outside of the urban core, propelling the construction industry into a lengthy economic boom. Government expansion in education, public health, and social services opened up new jobs to white-collar workers, many of whom were people of color and/or women. Public employment union membership expanded in tandem.

American workers have always been a diverse group of people. In the 1960s and early 1970s, these people united to protest and fight for the passage of the Civil Rights (1964) and Voting Rights (1965) Acts. The Delano Grape Strike (1965–1970) was one such organized effort by members of the fledgling United Farmworkers Union not just to obtain better wages for farmworkers but also to expand the rights of immigrant farm workers. The Memphis Sanitation Workers' strike (1968) was another example of the merger of worker and civil rights as the predominantly African American strikers' organizing slogan was "I Am a Man." Community organizers partnered with working people to organize the Montgomery Bus Boycott (1955–1956) and the voting rights campaign of Mississippi Freedom Summer (1964). Workers in many occupations, including librarians, organized for racial equality and social justice. The passage of the Civil Rights Act, in turn, facilitated workers' organizing and union campaigns, as was the case for flight attendants, who used the provisions of the act's ban on sexual harassment and discrimination to leverage more favorable response from their employers.

At the same time, however, economic and political transformations across the world emerged to threaten this temporary stability enjoyed by many American workers. Successful independence movements around the globe and the postwar reconstruction of Japan and Europe created opportunities for people of these nations to pursue education and their governments to embrace investment in new manufacturing plants. American companies, particularly in steel but also in other manufacturing industries like garment making, did not reinvest in modernizing their own plants. In the 1970s, a series of international oil crises rocked American consumers and threatened to devastate the American automobile industry that had not until that time prioritized the production of fuel-efficient cars. In response, American manufacturing deindustrialized, or moved production overseas, leaving a wide swath of the industrial Northeast—communities from Connecticut and Rhode Island to Illinois and Iowa—to be renamed the Rust Belt. Massive economic transformations reshaped work in America, eviscerating relatively well-paid (and often union) jobs in the manufacturing sector and replacing them with low-paid, mostly nonunion employment in the service sector. As historian Randi Storch notes, in the decades after 1973, "by almost every measure, working people throughout all sectors of society lost economic ground and power at work and in society" (Storch 2013, 123).

Antiworker political actions accompanied these structural transformations, as was the case when President Ronald Reagan (1911–2004) ordered the firing of 11,000 striking members of the Professional Air Traffic Controllers' Organization (PATCO) during a brief 1981 strike; Reagan's rationale was that the Taft-Hartley Act prohibited strikes by public employees. Private businesses employed labor management professionals who specialized in destroying unions; self-described "union buster" Martin Levitt used police and medical records, personnel files, and other tactics to spread distrust of union officials and members at more than 250 firms across the country in the 1970s and 1980s.

In the 1980s, unemployment increased sharply as plant closings left workers in heavy manufacturing industries without steady jobs. Recurring recessions and recoveries were reestablished as the dominant pattern in the American economy. White-collar workers—advertising executives, dentists, pharmacists, social workers, and others—were less affected by these changes than were machine operators, construction workers, and janitors. Yet in coming decades, nearly all American workers would experience even further structural transformations, brought on by technological change.

FURTHER READING

Albrecht, Sandra. 2016. *The Assault on Labor: The 1986 TWA Strike and the Decline of Workers' Rights in America.* Lanham: Lexington Books.

Dubovsky, Melvin. 2004. *The State and Labor in Modern America.* Chapel Hill: University of North Carolina Press.

Katznelson, Ira. 2005. *When Affirmative Action Was White: An Untold Story of Racial Inequality in Twentieth-Century America.* New York: W. W. Norton.

Leavitt, Martin Jay. 1993. *Confessions of a Union Buster.* New York: Crown Publishers.

Mettler, Suzanne. 2005. *Soldiers to Citizens: The G.I. Bill and the Making of the Greatest Generation.* Oxford: Oxford University Press.

Meyer, Stephen. 2016. *Manhood on the Line: Working-Class Masculinities in the American Heartland.* Urbana: University of Illinois Press.

Storch, Randi. 2013. *Working Hard for the American Dream: Workers and Their Unions, World War I to the Present.* Malden: John Wiley and Sons.

ACCOUNTANT

Accountants are tasked with creating, maintaining, or inspecting formal financial records and other documents. While the stereotype of an American accountant was one of a very shy person wearing glasses and sitting at a desk lit by a green lamp while typing away at a ten-key calculator with pencil in hand noting calculations, the life of an accountant in the postwar period was truly something much different. Accounting careers included all kinds of positions with different job titles: accounts receivable/accounts payable clerk, controller, financial officer, treasurer, financial secretary, auditor, financial analysis, forensic accountant, payroll manager, and strategic analyst. Legally, however, the title "accountant" could only be used by people licensed as a Certified Public Accountant (CPA). In most states, to become a CPA required an individual to hold a college degree in accounting, have work experience, and take a series of exams to demonstrate competency in the many fields of accountancy. The American Institute of Accountants became the American Institute of Certified Public Accountants (AICPA) in 1957 and was the primary professional organization advocating for CPAs, including recommending examination, licensure, and continuing professional education requirements to meet uniform standards for all CPAs working in all U.S. states and possessions.

Accountants gathered financial information (all records of incoming and outgoing financial transactions) and organized this data into reports for their clients, which include businesses, individuals, nonprofit organizations, clubs and groups, and governmental agencies. Unlike the work of a bookkeeper, accountants provided analysis of financial information in their client reports, which then helped clients make better financial decisions. Facility with mathematics and the foundations of business and ethics was important. Additionally, accountants also had to knowledgeably and accurately communicate with their clients. As with any form of communication, accountants must tailor their messages and reports to their audiences. On any day, an accountant might speak with individual clients, report to federal and state tax agents, and confer with bankers and lawyers.

An accountant's day typically started in an office. Before the invention of the personal computer and writing and spreadsheet programs, accounting software, and specialty software for accountants in certain industries (such as tax, government, or cost accounting), accountants used calculators, pens, pencils, and paper to make their financial calculations and typewriters to prepare their reports. Accountants organized revenue and payments and calculated basic profit-and-loss reports for business owners, but there were many issues that accountants also had to take into consideration as they prepared their reports. An accounting balance sheet may incorporate a business's yet-to-be-sold inventory, investments in machinery, production spaces and offices, surplus capital reserves, and, if a business is a publicly traded company, capital stock. Accountants must also consider any alterations in a business's practice of generating revenue (sales), such as discounts for high-volume or preferred buyers. An accounting report was based on fiscal periods, generally on a monthly, quarterly, and yearly basis. This report usually included advice on how to improve revenues, reduce operating costs, and make a business more efficient.

Accountancy had different specialties. Unlike a public accountant, who may serve any client, a private accountant worked for a particular business or agency, performing the work of an accountant internally for just one client such as the Ford Motor Company and providing financial reports for Ford management. Tax specialists worked to advise clients on taxation matters, preparing reports to determine tax liability and filing tax returns. Accountants also worked for the federal Internal Revenue Service (IRS); in 1953, Thomas Coleman Andrews became the first accountant to head the IRS. Accountants worked in other federal agencies, including the General Accounting Office, the Securities Exchange Commission, both legislative branches (House of Representatives and the Senate), as well as for other governmental agencies at the state and local levels. Forensic accounting required accountants to analyze business and other records for fraudulent practices, often for use in court cases; forensic accountants worked in close cooperation with attorneys. On the other hand, auditors examined the work of accountants and bookkeepers for accuracy and to ensure that a business's financial responsibilities are met, including paying taxes on time, making payroll, and investing in the business. Management accountants helped clients manage their money; sometimes, these accountants are called financial advisors. They evaluated a client's expected income and financial responsibilities and then made investment recommendations, such as purchasing income-generating stock to boost an individual's net worth.

Although the AICPA had recommended uniform examinations (which was adopted nationally only in 1997) and uniform requirements for licensure, becoming a CPA varied from state to state. The uniform CPA exam consisted of several parts in various areas: audit and attestation, financial accounting and reporting, regulation, and business environment and concepts. The exams were based on sets of accounting rules founded on the Generally Accepted Accounting Principles (GAAP); these agreed-upon principles and policies allowed all businesses to use the same accounting methods. Despite the AICPA's advocacy throughout the postwar period, uneven and sometimes unethical accounting practices in the 1970s and 1980s led to the adoption of these uniform exams. After passing these exams and accumulating the required experience, accountants may be licensed, which required periodic renewal and the completion of continuing education units—usually in person-to-person classes. It was important to all CPA organizations that those certified in their state were held to the utmost standards of respect, trustworthiness, and ethics. The information that accountants provided was used in many decision-making processes; it was therefore important that the data they gathered and organized was accurate, useful, and dependable.

Most accountants enjoyed making sense out of financial complexities and chaos. Many also found it rewarding to provide peace of mind to their clients when it came to their finances, business or taxes. An accountant's special skills allowed clients to focus on issues of personal interests or business management, not the highly detailed work of accountants.

Rosalba Campbell

See also: Economist; Statistician; *1915–1945:* Actuary

FURTHER READING

Damodaran, Aswath. 2017. *Narrative and Numbers: The Value of Stories in Business.* New York: Columbia Business School Publishing.

Mullis, Darrell, and Judith Orloff. 2008. *The Accounting Game: Basic Accounting Fresh from the Lemonade Stand*, 2nd ed. Naperville: Sourcebooks.

Shim, Jae K., Joel G. Siegel, Nick Dauber, and Anique A. Qureshi. 2014. *Barron's Accounting Handbook*, 6th ed. Hauppage: Barron's Educational Series.

ACTOR/ACTRESS (FILM AND TELEVISION)

In the post–World War II era, Hollywood, California, was the center of the American film industry. Later, while some films were shot on location and television shows aired from studios in other cities, Hollywood was synonymous with success for both film and television actors and actresses. Yet Hollywood's status as a highly competitive work environment for aspiring actors is underpinned by a basic truth: throughout its history, there have always been more actors than available roles. From 1950 to 1999, the number of Screen Actors Guild (SAG) members (one metric of professional actors) jumped from 7,338 to 97,000. Changes to the film industry and the arrival of television in the postwar period only increased the oversupply of talent relative to the demand from producers, making it harder for actors to make a living from onscreen performances. All the while, however, aspiring performers sought employment through talent agencies, onsite calls, and, in later years, by pursuing postsecondary education in the acting and performance professions in specialty schools, like Julliard, or at colleges and universities with strong performing arts programs, like Yale, the University of Southern California, and the University of California, Los Angeles.

Although star actors, such as John Wayne, Audrey Hepburn, Julia Roberts, and Denzel Washington, garner most popular attention, stars are vastly outnumbered by the other actors seen onscreen. Screen performers can be divided into three broad categories that have remained consistent throughout film and television history: extras (also called background actors), character actors (or journeyman actors), and stars. Extras do not have lines of dialogue but instead populate the backgrounds of scenes to make the world onscreen appear more realistic. As workers, background actors do not receive screen credit are paid a day rate, and many struggle to work over twenty days in a year.

Character actors support the main characters in a film and contribute to the story; however, even those who make a living from their roles are less well-known enough and thus less likely to be used in a film's marketing. One such actor is Curtis Armstrong, who played small and iconic roles in films such as *Risky Business* (1983), *Revenge of the Nerds* (1984), and the television show *Moonlighting* (1985–1989). As Armstrong writes in his autobiography, a character actor's career might be marked by breaks between jobs, which they fill with stage work, acting classes, and other short-term work that allows them to keep up their craft. Stars are hired precisely because they are familiar to audiences: they are marketable and generate (somewhat) predictable box-office success. This hierarchy of actors explains the differences in levels of fame and experience of acting as a career, but it should not be mistaken for a career ladder. There is no singular or guaranteed path to stardom, but very few stars begin as extras (Bruce Willis is a notable exception), and many character actors have stable careers but are only recognizable to a few audience members.

Acting has always been an uncertain and competitive career path, and it has only become more unstable throughout the decades. In the immediate post–World War II period, the television industry had not yet solidified, and screen acting was limited to movies. During this period, most actors had long-term contracts with film studios. The Big Five film studios (Warner Bros., MGM, Paramount, RKO, and Fox) were vertically integrated, meaning they produced, distributed, and exhibited their films in their own theaters, thus allowing studios to function as an oligopoly and control the film industry. The immense profits from vertical integration allowed the studios to keep many actors under contract. With respect to actors, contracts benefited studios because they retained exclusive rights to hire and fire stars and had a stable of performers for all their projects.

In 1948, in the landmark *United States v. Paramount Pictures Inc.* decision, the Supreme Court declared that the vertically integrated studios held monopolies that violated fair competition. Studios had to sell off their theater chains and figure out how to reduce their operating costs. One solution was to fire studio employees, including non-star actors. The number of contract employees rapidly declined; prior to the ruling, there were 742 actors under contract, and by 1956, the number had fallen to 229. The actors dropped by the studios were left trying to piece work together in an industry that would increasingly be defined by sporadic rather than continuous employment.

The decline of steady employment for non-star actors in film coincided with the rise of television in U.S. homes. In the early years of television production, most of the new shows were shot in New York using actors trained on the stage or those who had previously worked in radio. Beginning in the late 1940s and continuing to the present day, it was not uncommon for actors to perform on stage, radio, television, and in film. While television was just another way for some to piece together a living, other actors dropped from their film contracts, such as Lucille Ball, found immense success on television. By contrast, the stars who remained bound by contracts to specific studios were barred from working on television.

Many elements of the film and television industries have evolved since the late-1940s, but some core elements of screen acting as a career have remained consistent. Film and television productions are project based, meaning that workers come together for short periods of time to produce films or episodes of television. This means that actors rarely work conventional forty-hour work weeks throughout the entire year. For long-running television shows, actors typically return to set every year, but they have a period of the year when they are not working (typically in the summer, when networks air reruns). Screen acting, for much of its history, has been a freelance job in which actors string together a series of gigs to make a living.

Actors are protected from the inherent insecurity of their profession by the three screen performers unions: SAG, founded in 1933; the American Federation of Television and Radio Actors (AFTRA), founded in 1952 and later merged with SAG in 2012; and the Screen Extras Guild (SEG), founded in 1947 and absorbed by SAG in 1992. These unions engage in collective bargaining for actors, which means that representatives meet with the Association of Motion Picture and Television Producers (AMPTP) to negotiate benefits, pensions, minimum payments, rest periods, travel per diems, and screen credits and eventually to determine residuals for work on film, television, commercials, etc. The performers unions are important for all actors but especially actors below the level of star who have less power than bankable stars. One of the major bargaining victories for actors was residuals, or payments for reuse of material. While actors do their jobs once, films and television shows can be replayed to continually generate profit for studios. As a result of this imbalance, the unions bargained for a share of this revenue, and since 1952, actors have received a small payment each time a film or television program is replayed. These small payments often accumulate to help offset periods of unemployment.

Unlike stage performers, film and television actors and actresses perform on contained sets where the only audiences are normally other performers and members of the crew responsible for lighting, scenery, sound, and camera operation. Film and television performers spend much of their time on the set, waiting as lighting is changed, camera angles reset, and scenes filmed over and over until the director is satisfied with the performance. For most film and television actors and actresses, a day's work starts well before filming—usually days before—as the performer must audition for a role and then, if awarded, prepare for filming by memorizing lines and rehearsing with other actors. On the day of a shoot on a set, actors and actresses must arrive early for makeup and costume fitting; some elaborate roles may take two hours or more of makeup and costuming preparation before an actor is ready for the shoot. Actors and actresses then arrive on the set, block out the scene (ensuring that the actor knows his or her position on the set), and then rehearse lines with other actors. Sometimes, a director has changed the lines of performers, who must then relearn them. Scenes may be filmed in nonsequential order as well, requiring actors and actresses to be constantly ready to adapt. Retakes, or re-filming scenes, are common in film and television.

Even though the odds of aspiring actors achieving fame and success are notoriously slim, this has never stopped talent from moving to Los Angeles to break into "the biz." Acting is a high-risk career with relatively few barriers to entry: there is no necessary training, degrees, certificates, or technical skills required for actors seeking work in the film industry. The combination of few barriers with the wealth, fame, glamor, and promise of creative fulfillment associated with success has inspired many to pursue this line of work. Unions made inroads to improving the working conditions for actors, but throughout the twentieth century, acting only became more competitive and unattainable as a career.

Kate Fortmueller

See also: *1776–1860:* Actor/Actress (Stage); *1915–1945:* Radio Announcer; Screenwriter

FURTHER READING

Armstrong, Curtis. 2017. *Revenge of the Nerd.* New York: Thomas Dunne Books.

Becker, Christine. 2009. *It's the Pictures That Got Small: Hollywood Film Stars on 1950s Television.* Middletown: Wesleyan University Press.

Fortmueller, Kate. 2016. "Pay to Play: Booking Roles in the Post-Network Era." In *Journal of Film and Video* 68, nos. 3–4 (Fall/Winter): 115–128.

Harvey, Rita Morley. 1996. *Those Wonderful, Terrible Years: George Heller and the American Federation of Television and Radio Artists.* Carbondale: Southern Illinois University Press.

Prindle, David. 1988. *The Politics of Glamour: Ideology and Democracy in the Screen Actors Guild.* Madison: University of Wisconsin Press

Slide, Anthony. 2012. *Hollywood Unknowns: A History of Extras, Bit Players, and Stand-Ins.* Jackson: University of Mississippi Press.

Yuen, Nancy Wang. 2016. *Reel Inequity: Hollywood Actors and Racism.* New Brunswick: Rutgers University Press.

PRIMARY DOCUMENT

In the following interview, successful stage actor Ed Asner discusses why he moved into television in the early 1960s and his subsequent experiences on the Mary Tyler Moore *and* Lou Grant *shows. Many of his contemporaries at this time looked down on "TV work" as the medium required a different sort of work: looking for jobs, auditioning, learning new scripts, and playing roles on many different shows every season, quite unlike the work of a stage actor, who might have been engaged in one role during one theatrical season in New York City. The differences of and possibilities for work are clear in his interview.*

[I was interested in television] Just to be able to support my wife and myself and a couple of kids, send them to college, that's what I was hoping for. I think there was an inner being that said I want to be a name up at the title, but I don't know that I talked it up that often . . . Well, in '63, I was busy. They got me into, as they bargained for it and got it, as first co-star on *Slattery's People*, starring Richard Crenna. I was looking for importance. The pay was certainly not great. I'd been zooming along as a freelance actor and was feeling very good about it. Well, in the meantime, my wife was busily looking at houses all over the place for us to settle in, and we got a wonderful house in '62, a cantilevered house right off Mulholland, and the money was higher than what we thought we'd be going for. We were looking at a house with an empty lot across from where we rented. I came across this house. She wanted to show me what kind of house I was looking for, and, by god, it was almost within reach. So I contacted all the members of my family who could come up with any money, and most all of them did, and we put down a down payment, and I was in seventh heaven. We had a view with an eighteen-foot deck that looked out over the whole valley and it was marvelous . . .

Then in '68 I got the *Slattery's People*, and Richard Crenna was the star of the movie, and he was also the conscience, state legislator, so that almost all the stances he took on whatever problems were attacked I had very little or nothing to do or say. I was seemingly an unnecessary appendage. So I did the first thirteen. I saw show after show coming along with more of the same, so I thought I would have been happier continuing to do guest shots . . .

I complained to [my agent] Jack, and he said, "Well, yeah," and he tried to stall me out of it, but I guess I seemed determined. Finally, he showed me how much money I'd be sneering at. The series ran its course. I didn't care. I wanted to act. So, god bless him, Sid Gold finally said, "Okay, we got you out of the contract." Gene Cooper was also in the show. "We got you out of the contract. What we have to do is guarantee—they want you to agree to come back and do whatever show they want you for at the same price, solo price." So I said, "Yeah." Sid said to me at the time, he said, "Don't worry about it. You worked before. You'll work again." So I took that as a blessing and freed myself from the show. As it turned out, they had a script written for me, heavily starring me, and I would have paid to do it. Leo Penn directed it, a wonderful man, wonderful director, and Sean Penn's father, and I benefited from Leo's direction, and it came off well. I began my march again, doing *Route 66*s, *FBI*, *Gunsmoke*s . . . four *Untouchables*, two of which were spinoffs with Barbara Stanwyck. They went nowhere. An *Eleventh Hour*, with Wendell Corey. Maybe a *Please Don't Eat the Daisies* in there. That was about the only comedy I did . . .

In the meantime, we had twin babies, boy, girl, in '63, and in '67 we had another girl. I'd do the TV or whatever movies I happen to be in at the time, I can't remember what they were, and everything seemed fine. Then in '67, '68, '69, the well all of a sudden dried up, '67 to '68, I think it was, and it got to such a point where I began to think we'd lose the house. My son says he can remember how I'd get the Sunday Times early Saturday night and go through the want-ads looking for work to supplement.

[I was looking for] Whatever I could do. But almost everywhere it seemed like—I was approaching forty, and I was untrained to do most of the work. It was more depressing than not working. I never found something that I could really jump up and hope to achieve, hope to get . . .

In the meantime, I was going under financially. Then '69 came along and, wonder of wonders, I had the best year I had of all the times in California. I did two TV movies for [Walter] Wally Grauman directing. One was a spinoff starring Jim Hutton to replace Perry Mason. I made the character a comic, a police chief. The suits at 20th [Century Fox] were worried about it, but Wally ignored them, thank god. I can't remember the name of the other movie. It was a ninety-minute. Ray Milland was in it in a minor role, and Gene Tierney a minor role. It was quite exciting to be in something that they were in. It restored my ego, so that in '70 when I'd not done comedy at all, except for two shows, maybe, and I came along with the interviews and readings for Mary Tyler Moore.

I guess I was just on the cattle list. The two producers were Allan Burns and [James L.] Jim Brooks. Grant [Tinker] had been an executive at 20th at the time I did the Jim Hutton pilot . . . I have a feeling that [Tinker] recommended that I was pretty funny in it, so he recommended me. They asked Ethel Winant, vice president in charge of talent, could I do comedy, and, amazing enough, she said, "He can do anything . . ."

So they had me in to read. I read, and I believe it was Jim Brooks sat down and said, "That's a very intelligent reading." I said, "Uh-huh, that means it wasn't funny." Says, "Why don't we have you back to read with Mary. We want you to read it wild, wiggy, wild, all out," blah, blah. I thought, "Well, I'm coming back, but I don't know what the hell they want." I started walking. I turned and I said,

"Well, listen, let me try it that way now, and if I don't do it, don't have me back." They were quite shocked at that kind of attitude, an attitude I rarely, if ever, have had since. So I read it like a meshugenah, and they laughed their asses off. They said, "Read it just like that when you come back to read with Mary." So I said, "What did I do? What was it I did? What did I say? How did I do?" I still didn't really know . . . Came back a week or two later and read with Mary, still trying to remember what I had done, and they laughed again, and they thanked me and I left. After I left, Mary turned to them and said, "Are you sure?" She certainly had her doubts. They said, "That's your Grant." Okay . . .

I loved the script. The script was funny. I just wanted to be able to be good at it, to find a way to be good at it, to be funny. I believe they had a guarantee of thirteen. So we went to work. But before we went to work, they wanted us to do that same scene to show to the advertisers, so we worked at a dreg-ish studio down in Hollywood, and the interesting story there is that Jay Sandrich was the director and I found him to be quite a pain in the ass. I thought to myself, "Well, once this show gets off and we're running, I'll make sure that they keep him away from the show. I'll see to it. I'll work at it." He directed 95 percent of the seven years. But what it taught me, having that good year, of doing the best I had earned, I came into that reading humbled, but at the same time sustained by the ego of the previous year. It was a nice combination and gave me enough confidence to act like I knew what I was doing. They later acted like they were very embarrassed at the way that scene looked, but you could look at it today and it would look very close to what we ended up doing on the show. Supposed to do promos with Mary, so I went to Chicago with Mary, and because I didn't want to wear glasses in the show, I tried memorizing all of the—each individual station's blah, blah. By the time we got to the third room, I had a headache trying to memorize, so Mary took over big time and got us through the remaining promos. Then was sent down to Atlanta to do the second half of the country with Cloris Leachman, and I was still wondering, "What am I going to do? What am I going to do?" She looked at the stuff and she said, "Oh, let's just do it our own." So we improvised our way through, with her as the catalyst, and it became a breeze.

We started rehearsals on the show. The first year was at a leaky-roofed studio down in Hollywood on McCadden, and we had a wonderful cast. As it came to the week of doing the show, they decided to tape it in front of an audience on a Tuesday night. We taped it, the audience was not receptive, and we had to shoot on the following Friday night. Mary was in tears, and as Grant left that evening, he turned to Allan and Jim and he said, "Fix it."

Source: Edward Asner. 2012. *Interview of Edward Asner*. Interviewer Jane Collings. UCLA Center for Oral History Research, Interview number 3, December 13, 2011. No pagination. Courtesy of Center for Oral History Research, Charles E. Young Research Library, UCLA.

ADVERTISING ACCOUNT EXECUTIVE

Advertising account executives managed client relationships, built advertising campaigns, designed advertisements, and sought to instill brand loyalty and convince cautious Americans to purchase a wide range of goods. The American advertising industry came of age in the 1920s and created a collective "image of a market democracy in which advertisers appealed to constituencies of consumer citizens and won election of their brands as popular products" (Marchand 1985, 64). Print advertising in magazines of the period as well as ads in the new medium of radio convinced Americans afflicted by common, benign ailments—like body odor—that their interpersonal problems could be solved if they just switched to a different brand of soap. Playing on Americans' anxieties about modern life, creative artists and writers created advertisement copy that provided ways for American consumers to adapt to modern urban life.

The Great Depression and World War II (1939–1945), however, altered the tenor of advertising as advertisers toned down their pleas to consumers to buy goods without restraint. In the years after World War II, and as the economy recovered from the Depression and war, the advertising industry blossomed. Advertisers again suggested to Americans that vigorous consumption of American products would lead to health and happiness.

In the advertising industry during the postwar years, Madison Avenue in New York City was synonymous with success—it was there that the great American advertising firms created catchy slogans and jingles that captured the attention, even if just subliminally, of American consumers. But behind these talented writers, composers, and artists were the army of advertising account executives, those men and women who serviced the accounts. Account executives combined the work of market research, accounting, and sales; unlike the "creatives" (writers, artists, photographers, and composers), account executives provided the necessary assistance that their firms needed to convince businesses (clients and prospective clients) of the value of advertising.

Account executives typically worked in an advertising firm's accounts management division, where they ensured the agency's clients were satisfied with the agency's work. To prepare a pitch for services, account executives also performed basic market research: they analyzed competitors' products, ran cost-benefit ratio calculations, and procured media space in which to advertise products. Some account executives also wrote copy (advertisement), though this was unusual; more common was the role that account executives played in connecting a client's needs to the talents of a creative worker in the agency.

New technologies—like the expansion of radio, growth of TV, and, much later, the internet—created enormous new spaces in which account executives could sell advertisements. Account executives spent a great deal of their workdays researching and contacting media outlets about advertising rates. Additionally, postwar psychological research into human motivation provided account executives with knowledge about consumer behavior that was critical to securing more clients. In the case of large clients—General Mills or Ford Motors, for instance— a number of account executives worked together to keep the client engaged with the advertising agency's work. Advertising is often described as a form of communication between consumers and manufacturers—the account executive's job was to facilitate that communication through the work of the agency.

The career of Lester Wunderman, a New York advertising executive who pioneered a form of advertising known as direct marketing, illustrates the many duties of an advertising account executive. Wunderman began his career during the Depression, operating a fledgling advertising agency with his brother, Irving. They had modest success until World War II. After the war, Wunderman went to work for the famous advertising agency Max Sackheim and Company, where, as a young account executive, he specialized in devising marketing strategies for prospective clients; among these efforts were analyzing split-run results, a kind of experimental advertising campaign using a control case (the existing advertisements) in comparison to new advertisements placed in different media. Wunderman then analyzed the results: Did elements of new advertising work better to generate sales? If so, what parts of the advertisements appealed most to consumers? Analyzing these business metrics was key to Wunderman's success as an account executive.

In 1958, the CEO of American Express approached Wunderman about company plans to create a credit card and sought his expertise in analyzing advertising costs. In his analysis of the plan, Wunderman evaluated the value of additional services that American Express could offer to business travelers; in 1950, the Diner's Club had become the first credit-issuing company to offer a membership-based multiple service credit card that allowed consumers to make purchases at any business that accepted the card, unlike gasoline credit cards that could be used only to purchase goods and services at one company.

To obtain the American Express account, Wunderman identified the market and potential consumers and hired a market research company to help him analyze competing providers' services and customers. Wunderman's research revealed that consumers were willing to pay more for membership credit services if those cards could be widely used, and he devised a strategy to promote a tiered card service that could be used at travel agencies, hotels, restaurants, car rental companies, gift shops, liquor stores, and gas stations, among other businesses. The Executive Card had no monthly credit limit and was marketed to executives at major corporations, while the basic card had a lower monthly credit limit and was widely available to credit-worthy consumers. Wunderman used insights from psychology to create an elite brand strategy for American Express, rather accidentally creating its later motto, "More services available in more places." The American Express card became, in Wunderman's words, a "prestige instrument which will appeal to the ego of the user and influence suppliers of services as well" (Wunderman 1996, 135–136). He secured the account for the Sackheim agency without having any sample advertising copy. Instead, his business acumen convinced the CEO of American Express that the idea for a multiple-service credit card was profitable. Soon thereafter, Wunderman left the Sackheim firm to open his own advertising agency—one that would become a global presence in the field.

Account executives performed the basic business research and sales functions that were needed to make the cost of advertising profitable for manufacturers and providers of goods and services. By the 1960s, account executives needed knowledge about the regulatory environment that prevented the advertising and marketing of certain products, such as alcohol, in some media. They obtained advertising space for their clients to target potential consumers: obtaining space in *Esquire* magazine, for instance, to advertise luxury men's wear. In the 1960s, Congress passed legislation requiring warning labels on cigarette packages, and in response, the Federal Trade Commission ordered media companies to stop advertising tobacco on television shows likely to be watched by children and youths; later, the government prohibited tobacco ads in all nonprint media. Account executives had to keep track of these kinds of changes that affected their industry. They also had to be conscious of and attentive to changes in American culture and how those changes, such as the women's rights movement, affected the ways that companies advertised their products and the venues in which they did so. Account executives were the unheralded workers in what many Americans saw as the glamorous industry of advertising.

Nancy Quam-Wickham

See also: *1992–2019:* Project Manager

FURTHER READING

Berger, Arthur Asa. 2015. *Ads, Fads, and Consumer Culture: Advertising's Impact on American Character and Society.* Lanham: Rowman Littlefield.

Marchand, Roland. 1985. *Advertising the American Dream: Making Way for Modernity, 1920–1940.* Oakland: University of California.

Pennock, Pamela E. 2007. *Advertising Sin and Sickness: The Politics of Alcohol and Tobacco Marketing, 1950–1990.* DeKalb: Northern Illinois University Press.

Roman, Kenneth. 2009. *The King of Madison Avenue: David Ogilvy and the Making of Modern Advertising.* London: Palgrave Macmillan.

Wunderman, Lester. 1996. *Being Direct: Making Advertising Pay.* New York: Random House.

AERONAUTICAL AND AEROSPACE ENGINEER

While aeronautical and aerospace engineers must be highly competent in physics and mathematics, not every such engineer wears a lab coat or sits in front of a computer all day. Aeronautical engineers also wear business suits and pitch airplane or missile concepts to clients, work in typical business offices, write contracts, design new aircraft and components, and create product designs based on customer feedback. They sometimes wear lab coats or mechanics' jumpers when researching new materials and construction methods or flight suits when they fly alongside test pilots who are testing the aircraft that the engineer has designed and helped build. The aeronautical engineering field requires and incorporates a variety of expertise; aptitude with aircraft and the design of propulsion systems, materials science, and fluid mechanics are each essential for an aeronautical engineer to be successful. Aeronautical engineers of the 1940s built on the work of early aviation pioneers and advanced aviation into the jet age during World War II (1939–1945). They continued refining their craft to the next revolution: computer-aided aircraft design in the mid-1990s.

Early degrees in aeronautical and aerospace engineering required the study of all different fields of engineering—mechanical, civil, electrical, and chemical—because that background provided a solid scientific foundation for everything that 1940s airplane research and construction required. Some graduate students developed side projects to test and hone their scientific endeavors and fund their education, such as putting Studebaker Motor Company automobiles into wind tunnels in attempts to streamline their form and improve the vehicle's effective power and fuel efficiency.

The Lockheed P-38 *Lightning*, which the U.S. military used in combat operations between 1942 and 1949, stood out as a masterpiece of aerodynamics, power, and design. Aeronautical engineers designed this twin-engine, twin-tailed fighter to be highly maneuverable, fly at high elevations, and accommodate machine guns in the nose of the aircraft, where pilots and their gunners could be more accurate. Working in engineering labs and wind tunnels and making mathematical calculations and blueprint plans on paper, engineers made designs to meet demands of the U.S. Army Air Forces (USAAF). Ultimately, they created several designs before creating a successful prototype. Army pilots then put the successful prototype, the YP-38, through many stress tests to determine if the aircraft was structurally sound and operated at the speeds, elevation, and maneuverability required. The P-38 represented the ultimate piston-engine fighter, capable of flying faster than contemporary aircraft, and marked the extent to which the piston engine could propel aircraft and pilot through the air. During World War II, to compete with newly developed axial-flow jet engine aircraft, the German Messerschmitt ME

262, General "Hap" Arnold, of the U.S. Army Air Forces, funded U.S. aeronautical engineering's development of a jet-powered fighter by pairing university research, civilian aircraft industry, and military procurement.

After World War II, the United States continued the development of progressively faster and higher-flying military aircraft. The newly created U.S. Air Force, as an independent military branch in 1947, kept aeronautical and aerospace engineers busy as jet aircraft and missile defense systems became pivotal technologies. Jet technology during the late 1940s and early 1950s was also important for the commercial sector, focused on the profitability of transnational and transatlantic flights.

The boom of post–World War II jet aircraft caused a split in the aeronautical engineering career between highly centralized pockets of aircraft designers for military application and more generalized engineering jobs as a part of the big-business model for mass-produced commercial aircraft. The best aeronautical engineers found themselves part of small teams, best demonstrated in Lockheed Martin's famed Skunk Works, producing radically advanced aircraft such as the 1950s U-2 *Dragon Lady,* 1960s SR-71 *Blackbird*, and the F-117 *Nighthawk* in the 1980s. At Skunk Works, engineers worked at desks to create blueprints for sophisticated military aircraft and space systems that were designated "top secret" at the time. Some engineers accompanied company executives to Washington to confer with military leaders and congressional funders; others built models to scale. On occasion, engineers and machinists constructed full-sized prototypes of safety gear (like helmets and pressurized pilot suits), missiles, aircraft, and defense systems. At the same time, Skunk Works' parent company, Lockheed, competed with other aircraft companies such as Boeing, Douglas, and Convair to produce commercial aircraft.

In the late 1940s and early 1950s, as aeronautical engineers spent more time at their desks and in the engineering laboratories, designing aircraft and testing new materials, they became distanced from the operational testing of their new designs. As a result, test pilot casualties in prototype aircraft designs rose significantly. Pilots and military officials had to emphasize to aeronautical engineers that aeronautical theory must be tempered with limitations in materials and manufacturing processes. What emerged was an increased emphasis on the need for redundancy in aircraft systems. Subsequently, hydraulically assisted controls were included in aircraft to help pilots control airplanes that began flying faster and higher and increased in both size and carrying capacity. Redundant fuel, hydraulic, and other systems also became a priority for aviation safety and were integrated into aircraft design.

After the war, the United States concentrated on transition to jet-powered aircraft as well as aerospace systems, like missile defense. The piston-engine Boeing

B-29 *Superfortress* was the most expensive American project of the war; the aircraft continued operational deployment in the Korean War (1950–1953) despite the threat of Soviet-supplied jet fighters. So Boeing continued to develop both military bombers and civilian aircraft. In 1947, Boeing introduced the B-47 *Stratojet* and, in 1952, the B-52 *Stratofortress*, a plane that is still in service today. Concurrently, engineers at Boing developed the 707, a jet-powered civilian airliner; it first flew in 1954. These engineering marvels were each responsible for great technological advances in military aircraft and further pushed new technologies toward commercial viability; the same military desires for improved range, speed, and altitude of early aircraft translated well to the development of civilian airliners.

With the increasing bureaucratization of the military-industrial complex, aeronautical engineering trended toward "decision by committee" in the 1980s; projects became too big to fail. While this developmental method reduced critical errors and increased margins of safety and profit, it tended to diminish radical and brilliant developments that the Second World War and Cold War competitions demanded from aircraft design and manufacturing. Fourth-generation fighter aircraft such as the General Dynamics F-16 *Falcon* and the McDonnell Douglas F-15 *Eagle* were evolutions rather than revolutions. The development of these platforms and, later, the Lockheed F-22 *Raptor* in the 1990s shows a more conservative approach to aeronautical design. While the technology and warfighting ability of these aircraft continue to evolve, they are more reliant on radar advancements, armaments, and network integration than record-setting speeds and altitude advantages.

The revolution of computer-aided design in aeronautical engineering was solidified in history with the design and construction of the Boeing 777 in the 1990s. This was the first modern commercial aircraft to use the twin-engine, wide-body airliner configuration. It was also the first jetliner to be completely designed by engineers and preassembled through use of computer three-dimensional modeling. Just as the problem of limitations of piston engines in the P-38 pushed aviation into the jet age and fueled revolutionary jet engine refinements at a rapid pace, the computer revolution of the '90s has pushed aircraft design into an era of ever-increasing efficiency and safety. Tomorrow's aeronautical engineers will use hypersonic theory and 3D-printing technology to build aircraft that are just as inspiring as the P-38; we will marvel at the fusion of theory, art, and industry. Radical designs are now possible based on the evolution of computers and materials; engineers will use modern technology to safely push the existing boundaries of aeronautics.

Daniel Walton

See also: Astronaut; Pilot; *1915–1945:* Mechanical Engineer

FURTHER READING

Abramovitz, Melissa, and Erika L. Shores. 2012. *Military Airplanes*. North Mankato: Capstone Press.

Anderson, John D. 2002. *The Airplane: A History of Its Technology*. Reston: American Institute of Aeronautics and Astronautics.

Kermode, Alfred Cotterill, and J. C. Haddon. 1962. *An Introduction to Aeronautical Engineering*. London: Pitman.

ANESTHESIOLOGIST

Anesthesiologists are licensed, highly specialized medical doctors who are tasked with administering incapacitating gases and intravenous drugs to patients prior to surgery, monitoring those patients' cardiovascular systems during the surgical procedure and reviving patients at the procedure's conclusion. In 1930s America, members of the medical profession took steps to recognize anesthesiology as a medical specialty, separate from surgery and other mainstream specialties, as well as distinct from auxiliary services. At this time, anesthesiology referred to the practice of medicine in which doctors, nurses, and anesthesiology technicians provide medical care for surgical patients. These professionals ensure that the patient is prepared for surgery, has been administered the drugs (in the early days, ether) to deaden their senses and make surgery painless, and help patients recover safely from the anesthetic effects of surgery. Anesthesiologists also helped patients manage postsurgical pain. The American Society of Anesthesiology was founded in 1935, while the American Association of Nurse Anesthetists was formed a few years earlier, in 1931. Previously, allied health practitioners administered ether as it was not considered a position requiring great skill. Among physicians and nurses, though, anesthesiology made great strides during this period through World War II.

At the start of World War II (1939–1945), American military facilities were seriously understaffed; the armed services sent key medical personnel to Great Britain to study the country's more modern hospital practices. There, most anesthesiologists were physicians, not allied health workers or nurses, and they managed more complex surgical procedures including the use of chloroform and other pain- and consciousness-deadening substances. Subsequently, both the U.S. Army and the U.S. Navy began intensive training programs in anesthesia procedures for doctors, nurses, medics, and hospital corpsmen in anticipation of high rates of battle casualties. In particular, military officials rightly predicted that American soldiers and sailors would suffer high rates of burns, thoracic (chest) injuries, mangled limbs from land mines, and possibly inhalation of poisonous gases. These types of injuries required more advanced surgical treatment as well as more intensive and longer periods of pain management. Medics would have to manage many of these catastrophic injuries in the field, often with only minimal equipment. Other personnel transferred these patients to field hospitals. Reflecting on the need for professionalism in treating severely injured patients, one navy manual cautioned hospital corpsmen trainees to avoid alarming patients awaiting surgery by making "careless or thoughtless remarks," even if the patient seemed unconscious. High levels of anxiety among presurgical patients often resulted in poorer overall postsurgical outcomes.

In confronting these challenges, the U.S. military medical services helped to establish anesthesiology as a valuable medical specialty in its own right. Newly trained medical anesthesiologists perfected the use of block, or localized, anesthetics that deaden the affected body part while a patient stays awake in surgery. They also developed new techniques of endotracheal intubation, or "blind" insertion of a tube into a patient's airway, either through the mouth or nose, to enable a patient to breathe during surgery or to enable the anesthesiologist to administer oxygen to a surgical patient. Wartime anesthesiologists also refined the use of intravenously (IV) administered drugs—especially pentothal—for general surgery, dangerous medicines that suppressed a patient's respiratory system, and if used improperly, result in death. Medical historians generally agree that the successes of military anesthesiology during the war led civilian surgeons and hospitals to employ significant numbers of medically trained anesthesiologists during the postwar period.

During the postwar period, anesthesiologists prepared patients for surgery; they were the physicians, nurses, and technicians who met with patients and surgeons before surgery (except for in critical emergencies), assessed a patient's overall health, recorded a medical history, and, in consultation with the surgeon, explained the procedure to a patient. For general surgery, the anesthesiologist normally ordered the administration of a mild sedative the night before the procedure to help ease patient anxiety. On the day of the surgery, anesthesiologists administered the anesthetics to the patients, either through patient inhalation (as in ether, nitrous oxide, chloroform, or other chemical agents), by blocks (using local anesthetics like Novocain for topical administration or other drugs injected directly into the spinal canal), or by IV. While nurse anesthetists commonly administered anesthesia before World War II, after the war, physician anesthesiologists were responsible for this job; nurse anesthetists and anesthesiology technicians only assisted the anesthesiologist, particularly in procedures requiring general anesthetics.

During surgery, the anesthesiologist and his or her assistants (nurses, technicians) monitored the patient's health: watching blood pressure and heartbeat on monitoring screens, checking respiration rates and blood-oxygen saturation rates, and ensuring unobstructed access to a patient's airways. The last of these duties sometimes required the worker to remove mucus, blood, and vomit from an intubation tube, for instance. At this time, physicians believed that general anesthesia produced four states of unconsciousness, with the last stage being fatal; anesthesiologists endeavored to titrate—or continuously monitor and adjust—the anesthetics in order to reach the second or third stages, where surgery was optimal, without exceeding dosages that could lead to cardiac arrest and death. Working collaboratively with other members of the surgical team, anesthesiologists also supervised blood transfusions or were required to administer more anesthetics if needed. After surgery, the anesthesiology team accompanied the patient to the recovery room, where they monitored patients as they regained consciousness.

In the postwar period, innovations in surgical treatment also drove the growth of workers in the anesthesiology field. Lengthier and more complicated surgeries—such as organ transplantations—required more-skilled anesthesiologists as, generally, the longer a patient is under, the more opportunities exist for things to go wrong. New pharmaceuticals also required more-extensive training regimes for physician anesthesiologists as these powerful sedatives worked faster but also had lower overdose thresholds. Health insurance also played a role in the growth of this field: In the postwar period, more working Americans had private health insurance than was the case before the war. In 1965, the federal government expanded health insurance for those citizens over the age of sixty-five and for the indigent and impoverished, with the passage of legislation establishing Medicare and Medicaid, respectively.

Even as more Americans had health insurance coverage, through private or public sources, medicine underwent profound technological changes. Patient-monitoring machines improved, allowing an anesthesiologist to collect multiple data at once. New surgical techniques advanced medicine in unanticipated ways, such as angioplasty, generally a minimally invasive surgical procedure in which a surgeon clears a blockage from a blood vessel feeding a patient's heart. Joint-replacement surgery using high-tech materials made it possible for geriatric patients to regain their mobility and live healthier lives. More patients being treated surgically, rather than simply medically (medical management of conditions with drugs), helped to inflate health care costs too. Paradoxically, as costs rose, insurers pushed for better care and shorter hospitalization periods for patients—leading to more opportunities for nurse anesthetists and anesthetic technicians, who, under the supervision of an anesthesiologist, often work in outpatient surgical clinics, where they are primarily responsible for patient anesthesiology in procedures like arthroscopic repair of knee joints, biopsies, cataract removals, and colonoscopies.

Nancy Quam-Wickham

See also: Radiologist and Radiology Technician; *1861–1914:* Surgeon; *1992–2019:* Emergency Medical Technician

FURTHER READING

American Association of Nurse Anesthetists. https://www.aana.com/about-us.
Anesthesia History Association. http://www.ahahq.com/.
Cole-Adams, Kate. 2017. *Anesthesia: The Gift of Oblivion and the Mystery of Consciousness.* Berkeley: Counterpoint.
Waisel, David B. 2001. "The Role of World War II and the European Theater of Operations in the Development of Anesthesiology as a Physician Specialty in the USA." *Anesthesiology* 94: 907–914.

ARCHITECT

Architecture is a field with enormous challenges and opportunities to serve a variety of clients. Generally speaking, architects are involved in the design of buildings and structures and sometimes in the construction supervision of those designs. Some architects take leadership roles; others prefer to work behind the scenes. Some prefer developing general layouts; others create interiors or design the myriad details that comprise a building. In all cases, architects and those who work with them are problem solvers.

As in any field, there are increasing levels of responsibility. A recent graduate of a college architecture program typically puts in several years as an intern under the guidance of an experienced, licensed architect. A typical day will find a young architect taking measurements and photographs of an existing site or building, laying out a bathroom's floor plan, building a scale model of a neighborhood, or delivering a set of drawings to the building department for review and approval. A more senior architect, or job captain, might assign drafting tasks to a team; review a set of drawings, marking them up to identify errors or incomplete information; or assemble specifications for different components or pieces of equipment. A project architect, another next step up the ladder, might create a master plan, which is a layout of several buildings, or perhaps meet with a professional engineer to discuss a structural system or detail. A typical day for an architectural project manager might require assembling the many specifications for materials and equipment, working on project budgets, or visiting a job site to ensure that the builder is doing the work as proposed. A firm's owner, or principal, might make a presentation to a client, consult with members of the team, or sign contracts for a new project.

Most buildings are designed using the local vernacular, or style. In Europe and the Americas, the Industrial Revolution brought about a new architecture style called modernism. By the late 1800s, concrete had been rediscovered as an inexpensive, durable, and good-looking building material, and industrial developments in glass and steel production allowed buildings to be lighter; these advances, along with the invention of the modern elevator, gave rise to the skyscraper.

After World War II, the United States scrambled to build housing for its returning war veterans, who were entitled to federal housing subsidies as a part of the G.I. Bill. Architects and builders designed and built flat-roofed, glass box office buildings and low-slung ranch-type houses by the millions. This surge in development inspired contemporary masters of architecture, such as Frank Lloyd Wright and Mies van der Rohe, whose designs were often imitated.

In the early 1960s, architect Robert Venturi designed a house for his mother in Philadelphia. Instead of following Mies van der Rohe's famous maxim "Less is more," Venturi countered with "Less is a bore." He turned his mom's small house, completed in 1964, into an homage to traditional architectural details, such as arches and gable roofs, that had been frowned upon by modern architects. He wrote a book criticizing modernism and called for architects to reconnect architecture to history, complexity, and "messy vitality." His words ignited a style called postmodernism, which helped usher in a return to heavier materials like brick and granite, usually in the form of a thin veneer. Another important architect, who preferred heavier materials like brick and concrete, was Louis Kahn. Some of his most notable buildings include the iconic Salk Institute in La Jolla, California, of 1963 and the parliament building in Bangladesh, which was completed in 1982.

Until the late 1980s, architects drew plans for buildings using pencil and pen on paper. With the rise of office and home computers in the 1990s, digital design techniques became the norm. New computing technologies led to a proliferation of more sculptural forms as well as a greater capacity to control the fabrication of building parts and to more easily resolve complex environmental, structural, or other data-driven design problems.

By the 1990s, the environmental movement had become a significant influence on architects across the globe, resulting in using sustainable design and construction strategies to conserve earth's resources for future generations. By the turn of the twenty-first century, women were entering the profession in ever greater numbers, and the Iraqi-born British architect Zaha Hadid had become one of the world's best-known architects. Increasingly, architecture had become even more of a global endeavor, and many American architects began working abroad, especially in developing Asian economies. Architectural academies sprung up to meet development needs worldwide. The English architect Norman Foster, one of the most renowned and successful architects in the world, said, "As an architect you design for the present, with an awareness of the past for a future which is essentially unknown." As in every profession, architecture has its standouts, such as those named above. But for each famous architect, thousands of others design interesting, good buildings that help their clients achieve their goals.

Ken Conzelmann and Judith Raymond

See also: Construction Worker; *1915–1945:* Draftsman; Glazier; Ironworker

FURTHER READING

Colonial Society of Massachusetts. 1979. *Architecture in Colonial Massachusetts: A Conference Held by the Colonial Society of Massachusetts, September 19 and 20, 1974*. Boston: The Society.

Cousins, Frank. 1912. *Colonial Architecture*. Garden City: Doubleday, Page & Co.

Watkin, David. 2015. *A History of Western Architecture*. London: Laurence King Publishing.

ARTIST

An artist produces paintings or drawings or practices various creative arts like sculpting, filmmaking, photography, or writing, for personal or professional benefit. In short, an artist's purpose is to create art. People who pursue a career in the arts will typically choose one of two directions: to earn an arts degree as a means of understanding the theory and practice of art or to become self-educated, relying on natural talent and dedication to become successful.

The craftsman is one of the oldest types of artist. Craftsmen work in trades that date back hundreds or thousands of years, such as glassblowing, potting, weaving, metalworking, or woodworking. In contrast, applied artists tend to specialize in a specific material, such as glass, clay, or metal, and they learn about both its capabilities and limitations (Getlein 2008). In ceramics, for example, the artist takes clay, mixes it with water, and molds it with the hands or on the potter's wheel to form a specific shape, such as a bowl or vase. The potter then fires it in a kiln to harden it, which changes its chemical composition. Similarly, the glassblower heats up sand or silica to mold it into a cup or other shape or to create stained glass, and he or she can change its shape during heating by blowing. After cooling, the glass becomes a work of art, the product of skilled hands. In earlier times, these art forms tended to have a specific use, such as for cooking or drinking; today, they can be both useful and decorative, depending on the aim of the artist or the wish of the consumer who acquires the artwork.

One example of a master craftsman was Sam Maloof (1916–2009), who designed and made wood furniture and wooden objects. The first known craftsman to receive a MacArthur fellowship, Maloof specialized in chairs, preferring to use the woods black walnut, cherry, and oak. He was born in California of Lebanese descent, and his patrons included U.S. presidents and commoners alike. In addition to being used in people's homes, his work was eventually featured in museums across the United States, including the Smithsonian American Art Museum, the

Metropolitan Museum of Art in New York, and the Los Angeles County Museum of Art (Adamson 2006).

In contrast to the applied arts, the fine arts usually have a decorative—rather than a practical—function. These art forms can include such media as painting, sculpture, illustration, or photography. The term "fine art" refers to visual art with a particular aesthetic that appeals to the eye or has some other function that gives us pleasure from viewing it (Gombrich 2000). The value given to fine art can be highly subjective and can change over time.

Many artists have studios where they work on a regular basis, experimenting with different forms or ideas and seeking patrons who can support them in their work. They are inspired by such themes as politics, religion, nature, and science. Those in the fine arts usually support themselves by taking part in exhibitions or installations in galleries, museums, art fairs, or online stores. As every type of art is different and every artist is unique, their daily habits and routines may vary greatly. All artists are dedicated to their craft and spend most of their working hours producing art on commission or for later sale or practicing and refining their skills and techniques. Most artists assume the tasks associated with running a small business too; they must budget for materials, rent, and utilities, and they must be able to manage their money—or be able to hire a bookkeeper, manager, or other financial professional to make sure that their finances are in order.

Artists who work in the fine arts typically create pieces in two- or three-dimensional forms. Two-dimensional art includes painting, drawing, prints, and photography, whereas three-dimensional includes sculpture, architecture, and concept art, or works that arise from a particular concept or idea, such a mobile hanging from a ceiling or an abstract modern piece using a variety of artifacts or objects. How the artist chooses to express him- or herself can determine whether he or she works in two- or three-dimensional art. Some of the greatest artists were masters of both forms.

The post–World War II period in North America saw the rise of abstract expressionism, and many artists were inspired by the movement. Among these were Jackson Pollock (1912–1956), who created "action paintings," similar to a dancer's movements, with dripping paint and heavy brush strokes. Dutch-born artist Willem de Kooning (1904–1997), who lived during most of his career in New York, also created abstract works filled with color and even violent imagery. As American art moved into the pop art era, such artists as Robert Rauschenberg (1925–2008), Niki de Saint Phalle (1930–2002), and Andy Warhol (1928–1987) combined different media such as oil, pencil, and photography to create an entirely new style, at times in combination with other art forms such as music and dance (Getlein and Howard 2015). These artists often drew on everyday, mass-produced objects and images as a commentary on contemporary American culture.

Another artist who has worked in multiple forms is Maya Lin (1959–), who took the advice of Los Angeles architect Frank Gehry: don't worry about the distinctions of merging sculpture and architecture and "just make the work" (Getlein 2008). She produced the Vietnam Veterans Memorial (1982) in Washington, D.C., to commemorate those who died during the Vietnam War. It serves as wall, memorial, and public art, using a pure black surface to etch in the names of the fallen soldiers. Other memorials and sculptures she has produced have continued in a creative, modernist vein.

To be educated in the field of art, many aspiring artists attend an institution, such as a university or a private school like the Otis Art Institute, the California Institute of the Arts, Pratt Institute, and the New York Institute of Art and Design. Whether at an art school or university, students take courses in the theory and practice of art to earn an MA (master of arts) or MFA (master in fine arts) degree. In this way, they learn thoroughly about their field before seeking ways to support themselves as professional artists. Many seek internships or assistant positions before applying for a full-time job in order to gain contacts and experience (Wojak and Miller 2015). If they don't wish to be solely dependent on their art, among the careers that some artists choose are teacher, museum director, curator, or art conservator.

Kenneth Marcus

See also: Singer; *1861–1914:* Painter, Commercial; Photographer; *1915–1945:* Animator; Screenwriter

FURTHER READING

Adamson, Jeremy. 2006. *The Furniture of Sam Maloof.* New York: W. W. Norton.
Artcritical: The Online Magazine of Art and Ideas. www.artcritical.com.
Getlein, Mark. 2008. *Living with Art.* 8th ed. New York: McGraw-Hill.
Getlein, Mark, and Annabel Howard. 2015. *Art Visionaries.* London: Laurence King.
Gombrich, E. H. 2000. *Art and Illusion: A Study in the Psychology of Pictorial Representation.* Princeton: Princeton University Press.
Wojak, Angie, and Stacy Miller 2015. *Starting Your Career as an Artist.* 2nd ed. New York: Allsworth Press.

ASTRONAUT

Astronauts are specifically trained by a space program to serve on the crew of a mission to space. While the aerospace field employs professionals across a great variety of fields and disciplines, fewer than 600 people have traveled into space—and of those, fewer than 350 have been American. Astronauts spend most of their working hours preparing for space missions, which are often scheduled more than a year in advance. While in space, astronauts' follow schedules that are very structured, and their days are filled by running experiments, operating the spacecraft, and performing maintenance on equipment.

Becoming an astronaut is very difficult. Only military test pilots were selected for the earliest spaceflights. For U.S. astronauts, their test-flight experiences equipped them with the skills to provide meticulous scientific feedback to scientists back at mission control while also keeping cool heads in often extreme situations.

The U.S. space agency, the National Aeronautics and Space Administration (NASA), was formed in 1958. Although the first astronauts were military test pilots, NASA itself is a civilian agency with flight control headquarters in Houston, Texas. The career of Alan Shepard, the first American astronaut, illustrates the typical background and kinds of training regimens that the first generation of American astronauts shared. Shepherd was a graduate of the U.S. Naval Academy in Annapolis, Maryland, and was a World War II veteran. He had trained as a pilot after the war; by 1950, he was a test pilot for the navy. The role of a test pilot was to evaluate new jet aircraft for possible purchase by the U.S. military; test pilots put each plane through speed and maneuverability tests: rolling, diving, and making other sharp movements to test the aircraft's limitations. If an aircraft did not respond, a test pilot had to execute an emergency ejection, called bailing out, deploying his parachute to land safely. Shepard bailed out at least once during his test pilot years.

As a naval officer, he was also sent to the Naval War College in Newport, Rhode Island, to pursue postgraduate education. After NASA was organized, Shepard was one among those test pilots chosen for astronaut screening, an intense process of physical, psychological, and skills testing. He was one of a dozen or so potential astronauts chosen for the first U.S. manned space flight, the Mercury project. Two years of intensive training followed. Shepard spent time in class, in simulators, and in rigorous psychological and physical training. Finally, on May 5, 1961, Shepard became the first American in space.

The Mercury capsule was lifted into space on a rocket, reaching a height of approximately 116 miles before plunging back to earth, where it landed in the Atlantic Ocean, in a type of flight known as a ballistic trajectory suborbital flight—essentially going up into space and back down again. The entire flight lasted about 15 minutes. After that experience, Shepard was appointed chief astronaut, the senior military officer of all astronauts. Later, Shepard went into space a second time, this time to the moon on the Apollo 14 mission in early 1971. While on the moon, using a 6-iron with just one hand, Shepard hit a golf ball into orbit. Eventually, Shepard retired from the navy with the rank of rear admiral.

Astronauts have served in a variety of different roles in addition to simply crewing their missions. The first astronauts found themselves thrust in the public spotlight as they became celebrities overnight while the Cold War between the United States and Soviet Union turned into the space race. The early classes of astronauts also found themselves in the roles of explorers and test subjects. These were the first people to experience a microgravity environment for extended periods of time; with that meant stepping into the realm of scientific uncertainty. One example of this uncertainty is the development of food for space missions. The first astronaut meals created were as simple and utilitarian as possible since scientists were not sure that the human body could even keep food down during spaceflight.

Early astronauts' roles as explorers appear most prominently with the astronauts who participated in the Apollo program. The 17 Apollo missions not only produced the twelve men to step foot on another astronomical body but also provided reminders that space exploration is a serious, life-threatening task. The Apollo program began with tragedy as the crew of Apollo 1 burned to death in a fire on the launch pad; Apollo narrowly avoided another tragedy as Apollo 13 suffered an explosion in space and had to abandon the attempted moon landing. In total, eighteen astronauts and Russian cosmonauts have died as a result of incidents during spaceflight, with an additional thirteen astronaut deaths resulting from training and testing.

In the 1960s, American media characterized these first astronauts as possessing bravery, skills, discipline, physical strength, and mental fortitude. Yet the first two decades of American spaceflight showed little in the way of diversity. Shortly after the first American astronauts were named, a private initiative was launched, intent on conducting the same physical tests on women. While the all-white and all-male NASA astronaut corps of the 1960s pushed for the moon, these first female test subjects had their testing suspended despite initially promising results. These women even appeared before a congressional committee to investigate the issue of gender discrimination, but only men were chosen to become astronauts. In 1969, Apollo 11's crew planted the U.S. flag on the moon, but NASA would wait another nine years to name a new class of astronauts. This 1978 class contained the first female and minority astronaut trainees. In 1983, Sally Ride and Guion (Guy) Bluford were named to the Space Shuttle crews, finally beginning a trend of inclusion within NASA's astronaut corps.

Modern astronauts face a more defined checklist: For commander and pilot positions, one must meet the minimum requirements of one thousand flight hours at the controls of a jet aircraft. One must also hold a bachelor's degree in one of several technical fields, like aerospace engineering, physics, mathematics, or biology and medical sciences. Mission specialist positions require less flight time but more advanced education. Doctoral degrees have become the norm for prospective astronauts, given the competitive nature of the astronaut selection process and very limited number of astronaut positions. Many astronauts with advanced graduate education earn their PhDs in scientific fields like particle physics or fluid mechanics, while some have been medical doctors and even veterinarians. After the initial voyages into space with the Mercury program, working in space as an astronaut became much less of an explorer's position and much more like that of a scientist, though not earthbound.

Work as astronauts began to evolve with the advance of manned orbital space stations, like that of Skylab (1973–1979), the Russian space station Mir (1992–2001), and the International Space Station (1998–), on which American astronauts have served and that basically serve as scientific laboratories in space. Some of the first scientific experiments on Skylab included measuring red blood cell volume of astronauts in space, examining astronauts' inner ear and balance physiology, experimenting with metals in microgravity, and X-raying the galaxy. Many early scientific studies focused on testing technologies in space. More recently, astronauts have engaged in scientific studies of how being weightless affects the physiology of exercise, detecting particle physics from deep space, and studying the lifecycle of microscopic worms in space.

The backgrounds of NASA's most recent class of astronaut candidates (2017) reflect both astronaut traditions and more recent emphasis on advanced scientific training. The twelve men and women who began their two-year training in August 2017 include two medical doctors, a faculty member at Massachusetts Institute of Technology (MIT), and several active members of the U.S. military from the air force, marines, and navy. All twelve hold at least master's degrees; many also have doctorates. To be assigned a flight role, each of these astronaut candidates must successfully graduate from NASA's intensive training regime.

Change may be on the horizon for astronauts with the recent emergence of private aerospace companies more focused on commercial spaceflight. In 2004, the first privately funded human spaceflight was successful as Mike Melvill piloted SpaceShipOne on a flight that topped the 100 km altitude requirement to be considered a spaceflight. The success of SpaceShipOne has helped cultivate more private investment in space programs with developmental projects currently including space tourism, exploratory efforts, and the facilitation of scientific missions for organizations without the means or funding to secure a more traditional ride into space. As these new projects mature, the demand for astronauts will increase as slots open up to pilot the craft, conduct experiments, and adapt and survey whatever alien environments they may encounter.

Jacob Ingram

See also: Aeronautical and Aerospace Engineer; Pilot; Scientist; *1915–1945:* Mechanical Engineer

FURTHER READING

Atkinson, Joseph D., and Jay M. Shafritz. 1985. *The Real Stuff: A History of NASA's Astronaut Recruitment Program*. New York: Praeger.

Evans, Ben. 2007. *Space Shuttle Challenger: Ten Journeys into the Unknown.* New York: Springer.

Hadfield, Chris. 2013. *An Astronaut's Guide to Life on Earth: What Going to Space Taught Me about Ingenuity, Determination, and Being Prepared for Anything*. Columbus: Little, Brown.

PRIMARY DOCUMENT

The following pages are taken from an interview with astronaut Walter M. Schirra, Jr., who was among those first seven astronauts chosen for the Mercury *program in 1959. He was interviewed by Roy Neal in 1998. In this interview, he explains how he felt about being a U.S. Navy test pilot and being ordered to Washington, D.C., to become a member of the inaugural class of NASA astronauts. He describes some of the first duties of those first astronauts, as well as the unexpected celebrity status they instantly attained.*

Neal: Somehow or another, though, you wound up being an astronaut. How did that happen?

Schirra: That is probably a scary recollection. But I can recall going to Washington, looking at three men on a stage: two engineers and a shrink. (We'd learned to say "shrink." I think he was really a psychologist) . . . These three men tried to convince me how neat it would be to get in a rocket, or a capsule on top of a rocket. I said, "No way! I'm an aviator. I'm a hotshot flyboy. I'm a test pilot."

So I'm a test pilot. And a result of that is that, I really wanted to get out of that. Then they said, "Well, don't worry. We're going to put monkeys and chimps in there first." I *really* want to get out of there. We didn't even volunteer. We were ordered to Washington. That was the time to say "No." I went back to Patuxent [River Naval Air Station, Maryland], where I was testing aircraft, and talked to my peer group. And they said, "Look, Schirra. If you want to go higher, farther, and faster, this is the one way to do it." "Okay, I'll go along for a while."

Neal: Did you ever regret that decision?

Schirra: A number of times I have regretted that, because I missed my Navy very much. I was trained to be a commanding officer, and NASA never understood what a commanding officer was. This was sort of a group of people with equal rank . . .

This was a big surprise. Seven of us sitting on a stage in Washington, D.C., with a bunch of Press corps. You don't know what those people are, I know. But they were there, interrogating us, and we all had these dumb answers. Except for [John] Herschel [Glenn, Jr.]. John had a good answer—John Glenn, of course—for almost anything. And the rest of us said, "Gee, this guy has some ideas we don't know about." And we began to realize we were becoming public features, or public individuals. It was something we were not prepared for at all . . .

I've done interviews here now enough that I know—My favorite memory, though, really, was going after that Press conference, *from* that Press conference to the Hill, and watching Senators and Representatives make absolute *idiots* of themselves in front of all these news people. We all looked at each other, "Why are they doing this?" And we visited with the Senate Majority Leader, Lyndon [B.] Johnson. Then I knew what a mogul was, what a *power* this man was! He had an office that looked like a Hollywood set. And here we are, looking around, somewhat awestricken ourselves, and our local Representative or Senator would come in and salaam practically. I said, "My gosh! we've joined a whole new world! And we haven't done a damn thing yet!"

Neal: And so it was. However, once you got into Mercury you started doing some honest engineering. So let's start with that, if we can. Let's engineer the Mercury spacecraft as you lived it.

Schirra: Well, when we joined the Space Task Group at Langley Air Force Base in Virginia, we all sat in this one big office—large, steel desk, which is the greatest threat to mankind as an officer to get a large, steel desk (you hope for a mahogany desk, not one of these big metal slabs). We sat there and said, "What are we going to do now? We've got to make this thing flyable. We're all test pilots." So we all picked various areas of concern that we felt we could individually do the best with. I got on the environmental control system, the suit system. I think Deke [Donald K. Slayton] was on the controls, the flight controls.

We all unanimously had one vote, every time. We wanted a window in front of us, a window we could look through. The initial version had a little, tiny, round window down by your right knee and a little, tiny, round window by your left shoulder, and they looked like—well, little half-moons when you tried to look through them. You couldn't see a darn thing. That's what Shepard had to fly, because we couldn't change the windows in time.

Neal: That early in the program, did you have any real objective in mind? Or were you just going to fly in space?

Schirra: We felt we would put man-in-the-loop. We wanted to replace chimpanzees. We wanted to prove we could fly the vehicle, do something that man had never done before, of course. We wanted to be sure we could do it well. We knew the tools we needed. We needed this window so we could make observations out that window to align the spacecraft with the horizon, with the star patterns, with the geographic patterns. We had to make a hand controller, with this right hand, we had to make a pitch, roll, and yaw, and no room for rudder pedals. So a whole new flight control system with our hands rotating back and forth [aircraft passing]. This is a pretty difficult task.

Neal: How would you describe the engineering in the Mercury system? Good, bad, indifferent? How would you describe it?

Schirra: I was amazed, because Mr. [Daniel S.] Goldin, the present Administrator of NASA, said something about "risky devices." I thought that was a very well-made machine, and very, very carefully designed. I took great umbrage with his saying that. I told him that, by the way, personally. It was not something necessary that could be cut out of the film. He didn't know that we had gone so far with every engineer, with every detail, to get that spacecraft exactly the way we wanted. Including the booster, here in San Diego. We came out and visited General Dynamics. We made Atlas. I'll never forget [Virgil I.] Gus Grissom saying, "Do good work." Very poor grammar, but it got the message in.

And we touched every facet of that vehicle. We went to McDonnell [Aircraft Corp.] in St. Louis, long before it was McDonnell-Douglas or now Boeing or whatever they are. The result of it was, we got to know Mr. Mac [James S. McDonnell, Jr., President of McDonnell Aircraft Corp.]. We got to know the engineers, Walter [F.] Burke, John [F.] Yardley. They were just like brothers. We worked with these men around-the-clock, visiting, living in St. Louis! And that kind of thing really made Mercury go. We knew what the spacecraft was like, every component of it. About the only thing we didn't know about was that escape hatch that I hit with my hand one time . . .

Neal: You know, a good way to describe all this might be to just take your Mercury mission and relive it. Could we do that?

Schirra: Gee. Before my time [laughs]. Well, I think probably the best part of my Mercury mission was naming it *Sigma 7*. Naming it the sum of engineering effort. Not a fancy name like *Freedom* or *Faith* or *Aurora*. Not that I didn't appreciate those names. But I wanted to prove that it was a team of people working together to make this vehicle go. That's why I talk so wildly about knowing the engineers, how they were brothers and buddies. And all of them were! And that's what I saw as the ultimate on that mission, was that [it was] an engineering test flight, where we weren't going to look around for fireflies. We weren't going to look for the lights of Perth [Australia]. We weren't going to give prayers to the peasants below. We were going to make this thing work like a vehicle, and I never gave those missions when I flew a Mach-2 fighter. I flew the damn thing until I got done! I wanted the Mercury flight the same way.

So when we got into orbit, the boost phase was quite simple, although I found out later that it was going faster than it was supposed to have, but it did stop at the right time. But once we got into orbit I realized I could take control of it, because

I said, "I do not want this to be an automatic control." What happened on John's flight and Scott's flight, as soon as they got into orbit they separated and "Ssshh!" turned it around rapidly to get the retro attitude so that Mission Control could then have reassurance that they could bring it home. I'm not up there flying for Mission Control. I'm flying for Old Natasha [points to himself]. So I separated and went off automatic and went "Pttt!" and waited about 5 minutes. It finally came around to the right attitude, which was looking the heatshield first. I'm looking aft, looking back toward where the booster was; but I never got to see it, there was so much time between the time I turned around and when the booster settled out of orbit. So I couldn't see it.

Neal: You were conserving fuel among other things with that.

Schirra: That was the whole idea, to conserve fuel. Not to criticize John and Scott, but the mission was designed to have a chimpanzee in there. They replaced the chimp. But that meant they had to have a lot of automatic maneuvers. Automatic maneuvers took a *tremendous* amount of attitude control fuel. I said, "I don't want to do that. I just want to save that." And as a result, I ended up, I think, about retrofire, about 80% of my attitude fuel was still remaining.

Neal: You were able to stay up for a full-duration mission. Yours was rather an open-ended mission, if I recall.

Schirra: It was. It could have gone on and on. Thank God I didn't, because Gordon Cooper, he used all of my talent and had to use every bit of his own to endure that long! [laughs] But the interesting part of it was, I'll never forget this part either. Gordo and I were trying to figure out how we could look at the world from orbit. We had no simulators that could do that for us. So we took an [Project] Echo balloon, 100 ft in diameter, and painted on it the geographic points that we would pass over on an orbit 32 N, 32 S, adding a little bit so we could see out to the horizon. We took a cherry picker, hoisted ourselves up a little, tiny vehicle with a window (like we had asked for), and looked at the globe at tangent as if we would be in orbit. The technique worked perfectly . . . So we looked at this large Echo balloon, with the Earth painted on it, and practiced our retrofire maneuver . . . I got back from the flight and said, "Gordo, I had a real problem. Our [balloon] Earth had no clouds on it. You've got to put clouds on that" [laughs].

From: NASA Johnson Space Center Oral History Project. www.jsc.nasa.gov/history/oral_histories/SchirraWM/WMS_12-1-98.pdf.

For interested readers, the Johnson Space Center (JSC) Oral History Collection has transcribed interviews with over nine hundred NASA employees, including astronauts, engineers, managers, mission control specialists, and others. The JSC Oral History Collection updates its online holdings at least four times per year.

https://www.jsc.nasa.gov/history/oral_histories/oral_histories.htm.

ATTORNEY

Attorneys—also called lawyers—are appointed to act for other people or entities in legal or business matters. Attorneys have had a profound impact on American history. Whether it was drafting the United States' founding documents, arguing cases in front of the Supreme Court, writing legislation, defending those accused of crimes in court, or using their knowledge of the legal system to catapult them into the political sphere, individuals with a legal education have played a significant role in shaping the United States.

The United States inherited many English customs, although the common law legal tradition may be one of the most significant. The basic difference between the common law legal tradition and its most popular counterpart, the civil law tradition, is easy to simplify: the common law tradition allows for judge-made, binding law (also called "precedent"), while the main sources of law in the civil law tradition are written, codified principles. The type of legal tradition that operated in a country typically also informed the type of legal system in that country. The type of legal system then dictated the roles of attorneys, judges, and other legal professionals.

In 1942, like now, the United States had an adversarial legal system wherein attorneys were at the core. Unlike an inquisitorial system, where judges are responsible for investigating facts and attorneys typically act more as referees in legal disputes to ensure that proceedings are fair and impartial, attorneys in the adversarial legal system were the main players. Each party, represented by either one or many lawyers, in a legal dispute had an opportunity to present its understanding of the facts and the law to the judge and jury. The person or people presenting these facts and understandings of law were typically attorneys—highly trained legal professionals who were responsible for representing their client's interests in court, negotiations, investigations, or any other proceeding where a party had an attorney.

The daily tasks of attorneys varied widely depending on which type of law they specialized in. While there were many different types of law, the main differentiation was, and remains, transactional lawyering versus litigation. While all lawyers, regardless of specialization, were still responsible for representing their client's best interests, the lawyer's specialization dictated the type of situation in which the lawyers found themselves.

Transactional lawyers mostly concerned themselves, unsurprisingly, with transactions. These transactions could arise whenever an individual or organization required legal representation, such as negotiating a contract, writing a will, purchasing a property, or ensuring that a company complied with certain tax or incorporation requirements. Unlike litigators, transactional lawyers did not participate in the famous courtroom antics depicted on television and in movies. Instead, transactional lawyers typically spent their days drafting legal documents, negotiating for their clients, and advising clients on which course of action to take. One of the most famous examples of transactional lawyers were corporate lawyers, or lawyers who represent corporations and other business organizations as a whole. These lawyers usually acted in an advisory capacity—their entire jobs were to ensure company compliance with state and federal regulations, review business agreements, and give guidance to the organization and its board of directors or officers on how to operate the legal ins and outs of the business. Rather than just a general practice, there were also highly specific areas of knowledge that transactional lawyers specialized in. For example, an attorney interested in corporate law could specialize in mergers and acquisitions, a practice dedicated to facilitating and negotiating the merger, buyout, or sale of one or more companies. On the other hand, an attorney interested in government work could go to work at a federal agency such as the U.S. Department of Defense and specialize in government contracts, the practice of negotiating, procuring, and awarding contracts to or from the government.

The transactional lawyer's more famous counterpart is the litigator. Litigators concerned themselves with litigation, or the process of beginning, continuing, or concluding a legal action. Litigators were most often the lawyers who were portrayed in movies and television shows—they were the ones who went to court to argue a case in front of a judge and jury.

A legal action arose whenever a dispute or conflict of interest occurred that couldn't be settled among the parties themselves. For instance, if a driver in an automobile did not stop at a stop sign and ran into a pedestrian but refused to pay medical bills for the pedestrian's injuries, the pedestrian could initiate a lawsuit—or sue—against the driver for money to pay his or her medical bills based on the wrongdoings of the driver. Litigators were typically categorized into two groups: criminal and civil. Regardless of specialization, all litigators spent a great deal of time doing legal research, reading cases, writing legal memoranda, and conducting counseling sessions with clients in attempts to hear their side of the story.

Criminal litigators were all either prosecutors or defense attorneys. Prosecutors worked for the state or federal governments and were tasked with enforcing the law. They ensured that, if a person or group of people committed or were accused of committing a crime, those people would be charged with the crime and face the consequences if they were found guilty by a jury. Defense attorneys then represented the people who had been accused of crimes. Contrary to popular belief, defense attorneys were not there to let a guilty person walk away without facing jail time. Instead, the main function of defense attorneys was to ensure that their clients, guilty or innocent, were given a fair trial. Certain provisions in the U.S. Constitution ensure that individuals accused of crimes have certain rights, regardless of guilt, that cannot be taken away. This is where the familiar "guilty beyond a reasonable doubt" saying comes from—prosecutors were required to prove that individuals were guilty beyond a reasonable doubt before they could be convicted of a crime, and defense attorneys were there to make sure that the prosecutors actually met that burden before their clients were subjected to imprisonment.

Civil litigators, on the other hand, typically did not deal with those accused of crimes. Depending on the situation, civil lawyers would help their clients initiate or defend lawsuits for various types of legal claims. For example, after it became widely known that asbestos, a mineral commonly used in the construction industry, caused certain types of cancer and other types of serious diseases, civil litigators helped hundreds of thousands of workers, consumers, and other individuals bring lawsuits against asbestos producers and manufacturers. The theories that acted as the basis of the lawsuit were largely that the asbestos producers and manufacturers knew that asbestos caused the diseases long before the public did yet refused to stop producing asbestos or using it in their products because their industries were so lucrative. Ultimately, the litigation surrounding asbestos led to the bankruptcy and downfall of asbestos-related industries. Now, the use of asbestos is heavily regulated by state and federal governments.

Regardless of specialization, attorneys have always acted as vast catalysts in social change. For instance, as a young civil litigator, Baltimore native Thurgood Marshall (1908–1993) argued *Brown v. Board of Education* in front of the Supreme Court. Asserting that the segregation of public schools was unconstitutional under the Fourteenth Amendment's Equal Protection Clause, Marshall, who himself was later appointed as a Justice of the Supreme Court, argued on behalf of people of color that segregation had no place in American public schools and the idea of "separate but equal" facilities was violative of the Constitution of the United States. His argument was convincing—the Court unanimously agreed with Marshall and ordered the desegregation of American public schools. There is no doubt, regardless of social issue, that attorneys will continue to lead and shape the outcome of American history.

Rosalia Quam-Wickham

See also: *1776–1860:* Judge; *1915–1945:* Stenographer

FURTHER READING

Harvard Law School. "Transactional Law." Harvard Law School. Accessed October 29, 2018. https://hls.harvard.edu/dept/opia/what-is-public-interest-law/public-interest-work-types/transactional/.

Hurst, James W. 1967. "Lawyers in American History." Institutional Repository for Marquette Law School. https://scholarship.law.marquette.edu/cgi/viewcontent.cgi?referer=https://www.google.com/&httpsredir=1&article=2502&context=mulr.

BASEBALL PLAYER

As factory and farming technology improved during the 1800s, most of the American workforce separated into two major subcultures: white-collar workers, who worked in places like offices and banks, and blue-collar workers, whose jobs required manual labor. During the second half of the nineteenth century, the average blue-collar worker's income almost doubled, and so those workers began spending increasing amounts of their hard-earned money and leisure time on sporting events like horseracing and bare-knuckle boxing. During this time, baseball also became extremely popular both to watch and to play.

Though the first mention of baseball in the United States was in 1791, the first baseball team to play under mostly modern rules was the New York Knickerbockers, founded in 1845. In 1857, sixteen other New York area clubs had formed, and they came together to create the first baseball organization The National Association of Base Ball Players. The association decided on a standardized ruleset, established a championship, and recognized the teams' players as amateur athletes.

By 1875, baseball was profitable, and almost all baseball players were being paid a salary that was as good as or better than the average blue-collar worker—but for only a few months' worth of work. The best professional players might make over four thousand dollars per season, which was fantastic money considering that a skilled laborer might only make fifteen hundred dollars per year for a sixty-hour workweek. Just like today, baseball was only played during the spring and summer months, so baseball players usually returned to the workforce and performed normal, usually blue-collar jobs during the fall and winter. This sort of seasonal double income meant that many people aspired to become professional baseball players.

Until about 1915, the lifestyle and routines of a professional baseball player remained mostly the same, though baseball's ever-increasing popularity meant that players were making more money every year. During the baseball season, teammates often shared rental apartments or homes, or sometimes they slept in small dormitories. They always traveled together for away games, often via train. During the season, players kept to a regular routine set out by the team's management: they practiced and worked out together in the morning, ate lunch, and then played a league game in the afternoon. (Until 1935, all baseball games were played during the day—and if the sun went down before one team won, the game would be scored as a tie). If the team didn't have a league game on any given day, then the team might practice again in the afternoon, or on occasion the management gave the players the rest of the day off. In the evening, management encouraged—or sometimes required—players to eat dinner together to reinforce the team's morale and then might enforce a curfew. In the early years of professional baseball, a common frustration for the team owners and managers was that their young players often stayed out very late at bars and saloons and would then be too hungover to play the next day. Curfews helped address this problem; if a player violated curfew too many times, he could be thrown off the team—no matter how talented he might be on the field.

Between the end of World War I (1914–1918) and the start of World War II (1939–1945), baseball continued to grow in popularity, and by the end of the 1930s, most professional players had stopped working offseason jobs. This is partly because almost all players were finally being paid wages that could support an average family; it's true that very few players could be considered wealthy, but most made a comfortable living. Money aside, another reason that players started focusing most of their time on baseball year round was that the league had become very competitive, and every roster was filled with very strong players; if a player didn't dedicate time and effort to his training during the offseason, he might find himself out of a job in the spring.

Just like in World War I, baseball continued during World War II. But many players—even some superstars—chose to enlist in the armed forces. The players who stayed in the United States and kept the league going became very popular. Whenever they weren't training or playing, most professional ballplayers were getting involved with both the national war effort and their local communities. Players hung around restaurants and parks to meet people, or they offered free baseball clinics. Some players even dropped by local pickup games and played baseball with regular folks.

During the second half of the twentieth century, the life of a baseball player became more and more involved and increasingly lucrative. Specialty player roles were defined and redefined across the league. Specific kinds of pitchers and hitters began being trained from very early on in their careers to excel at one small aspect of the game. Tony Gwynn was one such player, and he became legendary even though he rarely hit homeruns—his entire strategy was to do nothing more than try to hit the ball away from the defense, even if that meant hitting the ball softly. Another specialty player was Jesse Orosco, who pitched in more games than any player in history, and his only job was to strike out one or two left-handed hitters during a critical moment in a game.

In 1966, baseball players formed a union, which allowed them to bargain collectively and, among other things, join another team in the offseason if that team wanted to pay them more money. In 1980, Nolan Ryan became the first player to make a million dollars per season; less than fifteen years later, the average annual salary in Major League Baseball was even higher than Ryan's record-setting contract.

Today, many of Major League Baseball's players are millionaires. Players train year round and have access to cutting-edge training facilities, doctors, physical therapists, dieticians, and coaching personnel. Most teams even employ full-time statisticians, who analyze every aspect of every game being played at every level across the league to try to find an advantage. But perhaps what's most charming about the lives of baseball players is the ways in which they are very similar to those athletes who played the same game more than 150 years ago. They still get up early, work out, and play together on a field that looks mostly the same as it did when the game was first played. Players run many of the same drills during practice and use broadly similar strategies in games.

Ben Tyler Elliott

See also: Broadcast Journalist; *1915–1945:* Radio Announcer

FURTHER READING

Altherr, Thomas L., and Nancy L. Struna. 1997. "People of Prowess: Sport, Leisure, and Labor in Early Anglo-America." *The Journal of American History* 84, no. 2: 630.

Burns, Ken, director. 1994. *Baseball*. Arlington County: PBS Film.

Delforge, Gary D., and Robert S. Behnke. 1999. "The History and Evolution of Athletic Training Education in the United States." *Journal of Athletic Training* 34, no. 1: 53–61.

Gelzheiser, Robert P. 2006. *Labor and Capital in 19th Century Baseball*. Jefferson: McFarland & Company.

Haupert, Michael J. 2003. "The Economic History of Major League Baseball." *The Economic History Association Encyclopedia*, August 27, 2003.

Lewis, Michael. 2013. *Moneyball: The Art of Winning an Unfair Game*. New York: W. W. Norton.

"MLB's Annual Salary Leaders Since 1874." Society for American Baseball Research. Accessed November 6, 2017. http://sabr.org/research/mlbs-annual-salary-leaders-1874-2012.

Montgomery, David, and Roy Rosenzweig. 1985. "Eight Hours for What We Will: Workers and Leisure in an Industrial City, 1870–1920." *American Journal of Sociology* 90, no. 6.

Obermeyer, Jeff. 2010. "War Games: The Business of Major League Baseball during World War II." *NINE: A Journal of Baseball History and Culture* 19, no. 1: 1–27.

Tygiel, Jules. 1983. *Baseball's Great Experiment: Jackie Robinson and His Legacy*. New York: Oxford University Press.

Witnauer, William D., Richard G. Rogers, and Jarron M. Saint Onge. 2007. "Major League Baseball Career Length in the 20th Century." *Population Research and Policy Review* 26, no. 4: 371–386.

PRIMARY DOCUMENT

While Americans followed professional athletes in the major leagues (MLB), athletes on semiprofessional and local teams played for both money and honor. Outside of the big leagues, among the most prominent baseball players in the 1940s were those who played in the old Negro Leagues, professional teams whose players were barred from competing with whites in the major leagues. Jackie Robinson was the first player to integrate Major League Baseball in April 1947, when he joined the Brooklyn Dodgers. In the following interview, Neale Henderson describes his childhood interest in playing baseball professionally and his experiences playing for the Kansas City Monarchs. The last full season of Negro League baseball was in 1951.

[B]aseball was my life dream. I ate and slept baseball . . . My favorite player at that time was— You know who. You seen him in the paper here today. Babe Ruth . . . My favorite team, I always wanted to play with the [New York] Yankees. That's who I wanted to play with, until— I knew about prejudice and everything, and I thought maybe that thing would change, which it did. But you had to be strong. If you were like me, I was raised up to not be taken, let nobody rub my head, not let nobody spit on me. I couldn't take that. So I was going to be a man regardless . . .

[B]ack in the days when Jackie [Robinson] was at UCLA, I followed him in his baseball career at UCLA and wished him the best. But when he signed with the Kansas City Monarchs and he played in the Negro League, and I came two years behind him. He played shortstop and also played second base. Well, he could play any position, and he didn't know how to play first base until he got with the Brooklyn Dodgers. They pushed him over to first base . . . But I came two years behind Jackie and I came behind— Can't think of the name right now. But I came with Ernie Banks, Elston Howard, Roy Campanella was still there, and Buck O'Neil and Sherwood Brewer and the brothers, the ones that live here in L.A. . . .

They saw that Jackie Robinson could take abuse. He wouldn't fight back verbally or physically, you know. And a lot of us, just through the tone of our voice to the white man, could be abusive to him, you know. He would fear you, you know. And they really did a complex on some of us, and they know we— There was better ballplayers than Jackie Robinson, but they knew who to put there for to get us into baseball history . . .

I was happy. I said, "Oh, the ball is rolling now. Yeah, the ball is rolling now." And they picked a lot of guys from the Monarchs and everything, and I was proud of that. And I just knew that some day I might would make it to the majors . . . To play for the Yankees. But I was farmed out to a little team down in Abilene, Kansas, and that's where I met [Eldrick] Tiger Woods' dad, Earl Woods. He played for a team out on the army base there. It wasn't Jackson City. It wasn't in Kansas. What's the name of where the army base is there in Kansas? But we played them for the championship and we won. And like I was saying, I was one of the first blacks to sign for Abilene. I was down there . . . See, even though they might not jump good into the majors with the farm teams and everything, they could still play in the Negro League, which would boost them forward to the farm teams for the major leagues, which it didn't. Everything started folding up. But here's the way I looked at it. The white man was after that dollar, you know, and, see, we— Little do they know, we, the Negro League, saved a lot of ballparks here in the United States. A lot of the ballparks was going broke, and we went in there and played at the ballparks and put them back on their feet. But see, history don't tell this, but it really happened and everything. This is what I would like to go on the record, that we played a role in saving a lot of the ballparks here in the United States.

See, we used to have like the National League against the American League, just like the white team, the National League against the American League. We used to pull in eighty- to a hundred-thousand people at our World Series games and everything. They saw this, and they out for that dollar. So they said, "Well, hey, if they can pull in that kind of money, now what if we get them to playing in our league and pull in? We could make this money," you know . . .

Oh, like I said, my first night up to Kansas City, they was out on a road trip, and I arrived there late that night. The Monarchs, they came in round about one, and they woke me up, and I happened to— I thought I was going to sleep with my buddy Gene Richardson, but they put me with Elston Howard. That night, before the game and everything, they didn't have a uniform for me, so Elston Howard gave me— He happened to have an extra uniform, and Elston Howard was way bigger than me, and they made me damn near look like a clown . . . Anytime a new player come in, they tried to— I don't know what it is, but they don't seem like they try to help you. They try to hinder you and everything. But when I got out on the field, even though I had a uniform on that was dragging the wind and everything, couldn't move the way you wanted to, I performed excellent. Buck O'Neil was out there with me, and Barney Serrell was playing second base, and he really helped me out. He made me look good. After I'd throw the ball to him made on a double-play or whatever, and Buck hit one out over second base, and I went over and got it and made a perfect throw to first base, and I got a standing ovation from the crowd . . . Oh yeah. And Willie Mays and [Henry Louis] Hank Aaron and them was over in the opposite dugout, and that's the night they signed professional with Birmingham Black Baron. And Piper Davis, which was the manager for the Birmingham Black Baron, after the game and everything was over, he talked with my manager and everything, and he tried to buy me from the Monarchs . . . I had scouts to come from the Yankees and from Chicago [Cubs] and from different ones . . .

I showed aggressiveness. Like we played San Bernardino one game and Eddie Mathews hit a home run. And when he was coming around second base, I put my hand out to shake his hand and he shoved me. And I fell back and fell down, but when I came up, I decked him, see. And I got a standing ovation from the crowd and everything, you know, and everybody asked me, well, why was I being aggressive? I said, "He could have broke my leg, he could have hurt me, and I wasn't expecting on him to push me, you know, that hard and push me down and everything."

So that was one of the reasons why I probably didn't go into the majors, because they said I couldn't take it. But, hey, I could take it. But we're out here to play ball, we're not out here to clown and for somebody just to abuse me or something like that and spit on me. No . . . No matter if I didn't go into professional ball, I was going to be a man in any sport that I go in.

Source: Neale Henderson. 2006. *Baseball, Race, and Los Angeles: Interview of Neale Henderson.* Interviewed by La'Tonya Rease Miles. UCLA Center for Oral History Research. Interview date: March 21, 2004. Courtesy of Center for Oral History Research, Charles E. Young Research Library, UCLA.

BEAUTICIAN

Beauticians encompass a wide range of personal care professionals, including aestheticians, hairstylists, and cosmetologists. They provide consultation, advice, and services to customers in the area of cosmetics and the application of makeup, skin care, and care (washing, drying, cutting, coloring, and styling) of hair. At work, beauticians work at a station and typically attend to one or two customers at a time; a hairstylist, for instance, might color and wash a client's hair and then have her sit under a hair dryer while attending to another customer, who only needed her hair trimmed. While most beauticians worked in private salons, providing individual care to customers, others worked in hospitals, nursing homes, and other institutions that provided limited personal care services to patients and residents. In all cases, the work environment changed for beauticians during the last half of the twentieth century.

The post–World War II era was a golden age for small, independently owned and operated beauty shops. Located in kitchens, living rooms, and downtown business districts, beauty shops afforded an entry for female entrepreneurship. In the 1950s and 1960s, the popularity of the bouffant—a hairstyle that features puffed-out, rounded shapes—often demanded hours of labor to transform straight hair into gravity-defining updos. Similarly, people spent many hours with a straightening iron to turn highly textured curls in to a smooth, silky bob. It was common then for women to have standing, weekly appointments to get their hair washed and styled, which made the beauty shop as important as church for many women who were looking to enhance their social lives and escape from their daily routines. The hairdresser's work varied along with the styles of the era, but the industry as a whole created a place where hairstylists not only touted their skills in beauty but also created a female-dominated space where women could share their personal concerns as well as tackle larger political and community issues.

The beauty industry developed along distinct lines of race, culture, and community. African American beauty patrons, for example, were far more likely to frequent black-owned salons employing black beauticians, and these establishments have remained one of the few independently black-owned businesses. Indeed, they continue to serve as a center of political activism much like they did during the height of the civil rights movement. Regardless of race, the hairdresser is often thought of as a confidant, at times even a psychologist, who offers everything from advice to a sympathetic ear while doing hair. These intimate bonds between hairstylists and their customers have in turn created a long-lasting loyalty that has managed to transcend other changes in the industry.

Since the early 1970s, hairstyling has faced several challenges that continue to shape the stylists' contemporary work culture. Do-it-yourself products flooded drug store shelves during this period—and, more recently, have become widely available for order over the internet. While these products offered some women more opportunities to manage their time and budgets, the hidden skills of hairstyling combined with the public's typical inexperience in working with and combining chemical hair treatments have often brought beauty patrons rushing back to their hairstylists. To be sure, a more natural look altered the frequency of beauty salon visits for a new generation preferring easy-to-care for styles, but it did not eliminate the hairdresser. Emulating a California beach girl—a style made famous by actress/model Farrah Fawcett in a 1976 swimsuit poster—required frosted highlights and blown-dry layers carefully coiffed to create a sun-kissed, windswept look. While less-processed styles did contribute to a decline of many small, independently owned beauty shops, the hairstylist, much like the makeup artist, continued to find a niche in making the clientele appear "naturally" beautiful.

The 1970s also witnessed the rise of unisex styles that brought men and women into the same salon. Not only were women more likely to find male patrons sitting in the chair next to them, but the male hairstylist also became much more common. In the late twentieth century, beauticians were now more apt to be called "hairdressers" or "stylists," and the more professional image they have embraced has allowed them to distance themselves from their grandmother's "kitchen beautician." The quest for professionalism has been particularly beneficial for male hairstylists, who have become the epitome of expertise. Like with chefs, women have had a long history of cooking, but the most famous chefs have typically been men—a trend that continues today in the beauty industry.

The rise of low-budget chain salons also created competition for the independently owned beauty shop. Increasingly visible since the 1970s, these chain salons often require a faster turnover rate and less personal interaction with customers, undermining wages and job satisfaction. Such businesses tend to hire new hairstylists with less experience who often move to other locations after they develop a clientele. While there may be less control over the pace of production, corporate-owned salons are sometimes able to offer hairstylists more benefits and greater job security. In an age where nail salons, massages, waxing, and other spa treatments are seen as an escape from the stress and strains of men's and women's daily lives regardless of budget, beauty services, including hairstyling, offer various degrees of pampering despite a segmented industry.

The hairdressing industry has remained the same yet in many ways has become safer and more reliable than it was in the past. Hairstylists still stand on their feet for most of the day, and they are prone to suffer from carpal tunnel syndrome and other ailments associated with repetitive motion. The wages are better than many service occupations, but hairstylists still struggle to earn a middle-class income. The industry maintains a high level of regulation in that most states require hairstylists to have the equivalent of a high school education and become licensed only after they have been formally trained in cosmetology. Training to prevent the spread of disease is taught along with how to work with hair, nails, and other beauty processes. Cosmetology courses are offered in high schools, community colleges, and private beauty schools and average anywhere from nine months to two years in duration. Perhaps the most significant improvement has been the hair products themselves that are increasingly designed to be less harsh for the sake of customers and the environment, making the substances that stylists use day in and day out far less of a health risk. All in all, hairdressing remains a fulfilling service occupation that still offers an entrepreneurial niche and a unique relationship with a loyal clientele.

Julie Willett

See also: Fashion Designer and Model; *1776–1860:* Barber

FURTHER READING

Gill, Tiffany M. 2010. *Beauty Shop Politics: African American Women's Activism in the Beauty Industry*. Chicago: University of Illinois Press.

Peiss, Kathy Lee. 2012. *Hope in a Jar: The Making of America's Beauty Culture*. Philadelphia: University of Pennsylvania Press.

Roberts, Blain. 2014. *Pageants, Parlors, & Pretty Women: Race and Beauty in the Twentieth-Century South*. Chapel Hill: The University of North Carolina Press.

Willett, Julie A. 2000. *Permanent Waves: The Making of the American Beauty Shop*. New York: New York University Press.

BROADCAST JOURNALIST

Broadcast journalists were culturally influential figures, particularly from the 1960s through the 1980s, when a majority of Americans turned to television to get their news. Most journalists worked for for-profit television stations, serving as reporters, camera operators, newsreaders or anchors, writers, editors, directors, and producers of locally oriented news programs. Others worked for noncommercial public broadcasting outlets. The rest were employed by the major New York-based networks (ABC, CBS, and NBC), where they performed many of the same jobs on programs designed for a nationwide audience. Some journalists who distinguished themselves at local stations were able to graduate to network jobs that paid more and offered greater opportunities for exposure and influence, and a handful—Walter Cronkite, David Brinkley, Barbara Walters, and Ted Koppel, for example—were able to become widely recognized journalistic stars.

In television's early years, most journalists began their careers working for newspapers and wire services like the Associated Press, and when they moved to television, they brought with them reporting styles strongly influenced by print journalism. By the 1970s, however, increasing numbers of broadcast journalists had apprenticed in radio and television news. An example of this career trajectory is Edward R. Murrow, who graduated with a bachelor's degree in speech from Washington State College, now known as Washington State University. Historians often call Murrow the "Dean of Broadcast Journalism" because of his pioneering work in the field. He was not a news writer but instead worked for CBS in New York City during the 1930s, where he scheduled radio speakers for the network. From that position, Murrow moved to Europe to supervise radio operations at CBS there. As World War II began in the late 1930s with the German occupations of Austria and Poland, Murrow began delivering news and opinions on current events as he had been interested in politics and international affairs since his days at Washington State. During the London Blitz—the campaign of Nazi bombing of London in 1939 and 1940—Murrow reported from London, not from the comfort of a studio protected by bomb shelters but from outside, from rooftops, from the streets, where his reportage captured the sounds of the bombings and made the events come alive for listeners in Europe and the United States. Men like Murrow led the way in developing a brand of journalism that was better suited to radio and television than newspapers or magazines. These reporters incorporated sounds of events, gave thrilling accounts of events like bombings, riots, and even baseball plays, and sometimes even incorporated studio sounds into their broadcasts to enliven their reportage. By this time, too, the vast majority of journalists were college educated, and by the 1980s, many had graduated from programs specifically designed to prepare them for careers in broadcasting.

Most broadcast journalists worked on local news programs, which first appeared in the 1950s but didn't become popular with viewers until the mid-1960s and 1970s. Local news shows were overseen by producers who assigned stories to teams of reporters and camera operators. Each day, these teams would travel to the scenes of stories and provide film and narration about what had occurred. In most cases, they would report after the fact, interviewing sources and witnesses and relying on station archives for background film needed for illustrative purposes; reporters in the field sometimes wrote their own copy but often relied on information created by station-based news writers. Sometimes, however, broadcast journalists would report live as a fire, public disturbance, or hostage situation was unfolding. In these cases, viewers could witness the live event with the reporter, often sharing in the emotional impact of critical events as reporters delivered the news extemporaneously, without the help of a formal news script. Their training in fields like speech or communications prepared broadcast journalists with the tools needed to report news in radio and especially television formats; they were essentially both journalists and also media personalities. The ability of broadcast journalists to report on live events was greatly enhanced by the development of satellite technology, especially portable uplinks installed in mobile vans. Back at the news studio, the material submitted by reportorial teams was rapidly edited into short packages and then inserted into news programs. The order in which stories appeared was determined by producers, who were sensitive to the importance of stories, the mix of subjects covered, and the program's flow.

The evening news programs broadcast by local stations offered viewers a variety of information: news about crimes, fires, and natural disasters; accounts of developments in local and state politics; consumer, health, and entertainment news; investigative exposés; weather and traffic reports; and the results of local professional, collegiate, and high-school sporting events. The programs were hosted by appealing anchors, often male-female teams, and they usually featured charismatic or humorous weather and sports reporters who engaged in banter with the anchors. Producers were committed to providing viewers with "news you can use," and their anchors cultivated a down-to-earth broadcast style popular with audiences. Anchors and other on-air personalities would prepare for their programs for hours before the airing of the show. This preparation usually included some editing of news copy and reviewing information about the day's events and news to be broadcast, as well as being fitted with appropriate apparel for the camera, receiving assistance with hair and makeup, and rehearsing the show content, much as a contemporary actor or actress would do. News anchors had often worked as members of reportorial teams prior to being promoted to their anchor positions.

Although most broadcast journalists emphasized local news, when a big national or international story broke, they did their best to cover it. This was easiest for stations affiliated with a major network, which provided them with short reports that could be inserted into local broadcasts. Stations unaffiliated with a network could get national and international news from syndicators, who provided them with similar reports for a fee. Before the 1970s, these reports—or feeds—were conveyed by a coaxial cable leased from telephone companies; afterward, they were distributed via satellite.

Network news programs were produced in much the same way—with reporters and camera crews doing the reportorial legwork and writers and editors turning this material into packages for insertion into meticulously scripted thirty-minute programs presided over by anchors. Reporters, camera operators, and producers were assigned to bureaus in major cities in the United States and around the world as well as in New York, allowing the networks to cover news virtually anywhere it occurred. Teams of reporters might work long hours or around the clock to complete an important assignment. The material they produced was sent back to network headquarters via satellite, where it could be broadcast during the evening newscast or held for airing on a later date. Like the producers of local news shows, producers of network news programs extensively deliberated about the lineup of stories and kept close watch on unfolding stories to determine if their importance warranted breaking into the program with live reports. Network news shows emphasized national and international news, and during the 1960s and 1970s in particular, they were more serious in tone and in their selection of stories than local news shows. Most producers and reporters were disdainful of the human-interest features and emphasis on "news you can use" that prevailed on local news programs. But the popularity of local news eventually undermined their resistance, and beginning in the 1980s, in the face of increased competition and declining viewership, network news programs began to adopt many of the most popular features of local news stations.

Network journalists also worked on more specialized network programs. These included morning news-and-features shows like *Today* (NBC) and *Good Morning America* (ABC) and magazine-format programs like *60 Minutes* (CBS). The morning shows provided regular summaries of the latest news, delivered by anchors and reporters whose work might also appear on evening news programs, and they offered journalists an opportunity to produce longer, more detailed stories. Magazine-format programs were broadcast in the evening, when viewership was at its peak. They were hosted by top-flight network anchors and employed the most-talented and respected reporters, writers, editors, and producers. The typical magazine-format program was an hour long and included three or four stories per episode, a mix of hard-hitting investigative exposés, well-researched features, and newsmaker and celebrity interviews. Many stories took weeks, sometimes even months, to prepare, and a job at a program like *60 Minutes* represented the pinnacle of achievement for a reporter, writer, or field producer.

Charles L. Ponce de Leon

See also: *1776–1860:* Journalist; *1915–1945:* Radio Announcer

FURTHER READING

Barkin, Steven M. 2003. *American Television News: The Media Marketplace and the Public Interest*. London: Routledge.
Bliss, Edward. 1991. *Now the News: The Story of Broadcast Journalism*. New York: Columbia University Press.
Epstein, Edward J. 1973. *News from Nowhere: Television and the News*. Chicago: Ivan R. Dee.
Matusow, Barbara. 1983. *The Evening Stars: The Making of the Network News Anchor*. Boston: Houghton Mifflin.
Ponce de Leon, Charles L. 2015. *That's the Way It Is: A History of Television News in America*. Chicago: University of Chicago Press.
Postman, Neil, and Steve Powers. 1992. *How to Watch TV News*. New York: Penguin Group.

PRIMARY DOCUMENT

Journalist Stan Atkinson spent nearly fifty years on air on television stations in the western United States. Like many early broadcasters, he started his career in radio but early on made the transition to television. In this selection from his oral history, Atkinson reveals how haphazard the new industry of television was and how he got some of his first jobs.

It was . . . 1951, that I got . . . the FCC license, and went to work in Los Alamos, New Mexico. And then in '52, I went in the Army. I'd never had any dramatic training of any kind, but I became an instructor. They said, "Oh, you were a radio announcer. You'll be a good instructor." And that was before they were going to ship me to Korea.

So I thought, "Okay, fine. I'll be anything. Just don't send me to Korea." And indeed, being an instructor worked out really well. I stayed at Fort Ord and was what we called a general subjects instructor. You had to stand before three hundred rather unhappy, usually sweaty, hot, and very uncomfortably attired trainees and keep them interested with the materials that you had to give. That was my training. I had to learn to stand on my feet, to get a rap going that was interesting, and try to keep the attention of these recalcitrant Army trainees . . . I learned a lot from that experience.

So when I went to Spokane for my first job out of the Army, I ended up getting the job in the radio station. The company built a TV station. One day they came back and they said, "Hey, you're going to go to TV."

And I said, "No, I like radio. I want to stay here."

And they said, "No, you're going to TV."

And I said, "Well, I can't, because I don't have a coat and a tie."

"Go get a coat and a tie. You're going to TV." I went to the TV studio, started to work, and fell in love with it . . .

In those days, we did everything. I did a kiddie show, I did the news, I did weather, did commercials, and then in the control room ran all the equipment, the switcher, the shader, operated the audio booth, actually edited commercials in and out of movies, which was our stock-in-trade. I mean, we were an ABC station, so we had ABC network, but there wasn't that much material available even from the network in those days, so a lot of what you had was syndicated material on film, so you had to understand how to splice the commercials in and out. So we did all of that, and so you learned a lot . . .

[O]ne of the reasons I was unsure about working in television even in 1954 was there weren't any television stations. One of the reasons I was so concerned about making a personal investment in television, even in 1954, was there weren't many TV sets around . . . You began to wonder is television going to stick, is it going to work nationally. Well, of course, the technology improved, the prices came down, and everybody had a TV set. But just to give you a sense of what the world was like in 1954, vis-à-vis television, that was my mindset and I think many people that I worked with . . .

[I] left Spokane in '56 and drove south, decided I didn't like the winters anymore, and said I was going to try to get the first job I could find. Got some gas in Redding. Getting back in the car, I said, "Are they any TV stations around here?"

The guy says, "Yeah, there's one that just opened up by the junior college."

I drove up, I walked in, and they were in a total fret. They couldn't get a signal to their new transmitter up on the top of a 5,000-foot mountain, and so they were very busy. They were trying to keep the station on the air, and here this stranger was walking in. And they said, "What do you want?"

And I said, "Well, I want a job."

They said, "Huh? What do you mean, you want a job?"

I said, "Yeah, I've been working for the ABC station in Spokane for two years."

"You've been in TV for two years?" Nobody could believe it. I was hired on the spot. That was 1956, and that's the way the business was. There just weren't people around who'd had any television experience of any kind. I mean, it was still such a fledgling industry.

At Channel 7 in Redding in those days, there was really no coverage of news on the street by any of us. It was rip and read, off the wires, you know, and doing as many commercials as any of us could possibly get done, and running camera and editing syndicated films, putting commercials in them, announcing from the booth, running switcher and shader and all the equipment, as well as doing stuff on the air . . .

In 1957, got the job the first time at KCRA [in Sacramento] and came to work. Gene Kelly, who had founded the station and raised the money and put it on the air, he was a remarkable man. He was the epitome of the self-made, successful businessman, creative, entrepreneurial, and tough, tough to the core. Scared the hell out of me. If I ever saw him walking down the hallway towards me, I'd go the other way into the bathroom or something, and especially after what happened when I went on the air the first night. He came into the staff morning the next morning and said, "Who the hell hired that kid?" Here I was, I was doing eleven o'clock newscasts, and I looked like I was fifteen years old. I wore a butch haircut, flattop.

I heard about it, and I thought, "I'm going to be outta here." But, you know, something really interesting happened. All these sweet old ladies called the station that afternoon and evening and said, "Who was that sweet young man that you had doing the news last night? We so enjoyed him. We're going to watch that newscast every night. We like him so much." And I always said it was the blue-hairs who saved my career, because it was almost over that day.

Source: Stan Atkinson. 2018. *Oral Interview of Stan Atkinson.* Interviewer Steve Swatt. "Valley Broadcast Legends Oral Histories" Project. Center for Sacramento History, 2–5, passim. Courtesy of Center for Sacramento History, Valley Broadcast Legends, 2018/010/001.https://ia902808.us.archive.org/21/items/AtkinsonOralHistTranscript/2018-010-001-AtkinsonOral-2017.pdf.

COLLEGE PROFESSOR

College professors are instructors of a specific, high academic ranking who teach classes and advise undergraduate and postgraduate students at colleges and universities. The modern system of higher education is a global, multibillion-dollar industry. Since the 1970s, higher education has been influenced by the forces of free-market capitalism, often to the detriment of those institutions' instructors. There are now over a million faculty members teaching in public, nonprofit private, and for-profit private institutions. They include faculty at community colleges (the largest single group), liberal arts colleges, and universities granting MAs or PhDs and doing substantial research. These college professors teach classes, assign projects, write and administer tests, grade papers, and assist with and perform academic research. College professors of previous eras could reasonably expect to earn tenure, which is a lifelong, guaranteed work contract, after a five- or six-year probationary period "on the tenure track," but modern professors rarely achieve tenure. Instead, they are likely to be working for their entire careers on short-term contracts that last one to three semesters at the most.

At the end of World War II, two great changes in higher education simultaneously took place. One such change occurred after servicemen returned from the war as the G.I. Bill paid for them to attend college. Prior to World War II, few people pursued or received college degrees; now, most high-school graduates receive at least some college education, and most businesses prefer to hire applicants who have received a college degree or completed some educational program beyond high school. The civil rights movement further increased attendance at postsecondary institutions by demanding access for those who had previously been excluded from higher-education opportunities.

The other great change in higher education, especially for the faculty working in it, has been the transformation of the job from a permanent, full-time, living-wage career position with benefits like health insurance and pensions into a mostly insecure, low-wage, often unreliable job with few or no benefits. Many professors are paid as little as two thousand or three thousand dollars per class and have to work at multiple institutions to make around twenty-five thousand dollars per year. Ostensibly, teaching institutions often rationalize the instructors' low pay as a cost-saving strategy, but such an approach has not caused institutions to keep their tuitions low; instead, tuition costs have increased. This means that a high percentage of students have to take on loans and also work, sometimes full time, while studying. A common criticism is that, in the meantime, the salaries of administrators have skyrocketed—some administrators' compensation is comparable to that of a corporate CEO.

A college professor is responsible for planning classes, choosing books and materials, writing lectures and exercises, constructing and grading quizzes and examinations, assigning grades, counseling and advising students, and drafting letters of recommendation and referral—all while staying apprised to academic developments in his or her field of study by researching, writing, publishing, updating teaching techniques, serving on committees, and participating in institutional governance. Many teachers also lead student clubs and speak to the public through newspapers and public forums. College faculty traditionally had a widespread and varied list of tasks that were all tied to the central core goal of producing and delivering knowledge for the next generation. The core work of an academic might actually have more variety in it than any other job. A single person might in fact do most of these things in the course of a single day. This has always been the job's primary draws: the work is somewhat creative, and days are not usually boring or repetitive.

But a typical college professor's quality of life—and the educational services that he or she provides—has dropped noticeably since the academic industry began the common practice of only offering their professors short employment contracts; when professors don't know whether or not they'll receive a new contract once their current one expires, it becomes difficult for an institution to create and maintain a lasting, consistent curriculum. Also, more and more of the workload is being offloaded onto the shrinking minority of now-overworked, full-time, tenure-track faculty and an increasing number of administrators, who often become isolated and out of touch with the rest of their peers by virtue of their departments' staff constantly turning over or a particular professor needing to relocate to a new academic institution if he or she is unable to renew an expiring contract.

In response to these stressful conditions, faculty members formed unions and have attempted to reform professional associations. There are also new organizations being formed that advocate for current college faculties in their efforts to improve their working conditions. All of these organizations struggle to protect academic freedom, establish and maintain job security, and keep faculty control over the educational content. Modern faculty members are often engaged with donors, foundations, and employers that have often demonstrated a preference for higher education to evolve into direct job-training operations or corporate research institutions. Faculty organizations have taken on how the work of education should be measured and evaluated, objecting, for example, to the use of student learning objectives and the loss of government funding for higher education at all levels and subsequent replacement by many corporate and private investments.

College teaching remains a career that attracts thousands of students to postgraduate study. This is despite the job often having lower pay, less security, and stressful working conditions compared to other jobs with similar educational requirements. There remain great social attractions involved with a career spent helping students learn to think more critically. College teaching remains as a job with great deal of public prestige.

Joe Berry and Helena Worthen

See also: Economist; Librarian; Scientist; Statistician; *1992–2019:* Museum Curator

FURTHER READING

Change Panel on Academic Economics. 1976. *Colleges and Money: A Faculty Guide to Academic Economics*. New Rochelle: Change Magazine.

Shaw, Victor N. 2008. *In View of Academic Careers and Career-Making Scholars: Innovative Ideas for Institutional Reform*. Charlotte: Information Age Pub.

Vesilind, P. Aarne. 2000. *So You Want to Be a Professor?: A Handbook for Graduate Students*. Thousand Oaks: Sage Publications.

COMMUNITY ORGANIZER

Community organizers in the postwar period were both paid and unpaid workers who sought to empower local people to change the social order. Community organizers worked to address racial, ethnic, gender, and class inequities in local areas like neighborhoods, cities, and regions by changing public policies to create a more equitable and democratic society. Before the war, there had been widespread racial segregation in education, occupations, and housing in America. New Deal reforms of the 1930s, in which the federal government attempted to restructure society—such as by providing electricity to rural areas of the nation and aid for the elderly with the creation of the Social Security Administration—eliminated some of the most jarring economic inequities. Organizing and union struggles of the Great Depression had also contributed to improvements in working conditions in some industries like meatpacking, auto assembly, and coal mining. But the nation of the United States entered World War II much as a divided country.

War presented opportunities previously unknown to many Americans. The field of community organizing grew after World War II, in part because Americans of all backgrounds had participated in the fight against totalitarianism and fascism during the war. For instance, African American soldiers came home to the United States, having fought to eliminate racism in Europe, but found themselves deprived of voting rights due to Jim Crow laws in the South. Likewise, during the war, millions of women had migrated into good-paying jobs in factories, building engines, airplanes, bombs, and ships for the war effort, but found themselves pushed back toward domestic work and traditional fields of women's work, like food production and janitorial work, after the war. Social historians write of an awakening of great numbers of men and women who sought better housing, jobs, and economic and social opportunities after the war. This social awareness helped to make the field of community organizing ripe for growth.

Community organizers worked to expand the social and economic opportunities that many had found elusive. In Chicago's Back of the Yards neighborhood, for instance, successive waves of immigrants from Eastern and southern Europe had settled just south of the city's packinghouse district. In 1939, Saul Alinsky and Joseph Meegan, two pioneering community organizers, founded the Back of the Yards Neighborhood Council. There, Alinsky and Meegan worked with local groups in the neighborhood—unions, Catholic parishes, social clubs—to launch residents' campaigns to fight juvenile delinquency, demand funding for housing renewal, and lobby for community resources like parks.

As a city historically fractured by class, ethnic, racial, and religious divisions, Chicago had a long background of what might be called community works programs in which social reformers worked to improve the lives of residents. Founded in 1889, Jane Addams's Hull House provided English-language training, daycare, social activities, and other services to poor and often immigrant Chicago residents; well-educated, middle- and upper-class, mostly white, native-born women provided these social services to their clientele. This model of settlement houses dominated community works throughout the 1930s in Chicago, where one in three settlement houses in the nation could be found. The community-organizing institutions that were formed later, however, sought to empower local citizens to represent themselves with local public officials, employers, banks, and other institutions, not simply to provide necessary social services.

This focus on community empowerment differentiated modern community organizing from the work of earlier social reformers. A typical community organizer of this time had training in sociology or social work; in Chicago, he or she might have been trained in some of the tenets of the Chicago School of sociology (and social work), developed at the University of Chicago, where research into the new fields of human ecology and urban sociology posited that community change comes most often when local residents themselves assumed responsibility for their own destiny. That is, local residents could change their environments; they were not bound by them. Community organizers worked to create opportunities for local residents to solve their own local problems. This is grassroots organizing. They helped to organize voter registration drives so that residents had greater political power to wield at city hall. They offered leadership classes for residents, teaching skills such as public speaking. They helped connect different local groups with each other to mobilize for major campaigns addressing issues such as unemployment or crime. Community organizers also helped local residents create block clubs, local neighborhood improvement groups in which residents of a single block volunteered to take on community projects like clearing garbage-strewn vacant lots or demanding streetlight repairs.

The daily work of a community organizer widely varied depending on the organization for which he or she worked. In the late 1950s, community organizer Septima Poinsette Clark worked with faith-based groups to recruit African Americans in the South to become adult literacy teachers in their local communities to prepare residents to pass the literacy tests required to register to vote before 1965 (Clark 1976). A community organizer might spend days at a time on a voter registration drive, going door to door to inquire if residents were registered to vote and holding evening meetings in union halls and church basements to emphasize to local citizens how voting could help empower the community to demand change from city officials. He or she might spend afternoons directing a youth-activities program providing sports, crafts, and homework help to neighborhood children and staffed by local residents. This was the path of community organizer Leroi Archible, a resident of the Morrisania neighborhood of the Bronx, who brought together public school teachers and local residents to create neighborhood sports programs for unemployed teenagers with the goal of getting dropouts back into schools during the 1970s (Archible 2004).

Mobilizing political groups (such as a local Democratic club), religious officials (such as a group of local priests or a local ecumenical council), members of labor unions, educators, and residents was a way to create powerful coalitions for change. At other times, a community organizer would facilitate meetings between local government representatives and neighborhood groups. He or she might help residents create boycott campaigns against local businesses that did not hire neighborhood residents or help to publicize practices of absentee landlords who neglected their buildings and ignored tenants' needs. Sometimes, community organizers staffed mimeograph machines late into the night, printing brochures, leaflets, or newsletters written by representatives for distribution to the community. In the 1980s, a young Barack Obama, later to become president of the United States, worked as a community organizer for a small Chicago-based agency, the Developing Communities Project, that sought to organize African Americans on the city's South Side with the goal of improving conditions in Altgeld Gardens, a public housing complex, after the loss of manufacturing jobs had left local neighborhoods devastated and significant numbers of black residents unemployed.

The nature of community organizing is such that the work duties of a community organizer varied with the organization's focus. After the civil rights movement of the 1960s, with the Civil Rights Act (1964) and Voting Rights Act (1965), when federal laws declared illegal segregation and voting restrictions by race, many community organizations turned to collective action to achieve other forms of community empowerment and social change—for the environment, school reform, healthcare, immigrant rights, parks and recreation, and many other causes.

Nancy Quam-Wickham

See also: Social Worker

FURTHER READING

Alinsky, Saul. 1969. *Reveille for Radicals*. New York: Vintage.

Archible, Leroi. 2004. "Oral History." Bronx African American Oral History Project, Fordham University. https://fordham.bepress.com/baahp_oralhist/240/.

Barber, William J., II, and Barbara Zelter. 2014. *Forward Together: A Moral Message for the Nation*. St. Louis: Chalice Press.

Clark, Septima Poinsette. 1976. "Oral History Interview with Septima Poinsette Clark, July 30, 1976." Documenting the American South Collection, University of North Carolina. http://docsouth.unc.edu/sohp/G-0017/menu.html.

Khan, Si. 2010. *Creative Community Organizing: A Guide for Rabble-Rousers, Activists, and Quiet Lovers of Justice*. Oakland: Berrett-Koehler Publishers.

Milkman, Ruth, Joshua Bloom, and Victor Narro. 2010. *Working for Change: The L.A. Model of Organizing and Advocacy*. Ithaca: Cornell University ILR Press.

CONSTRUCTION WORKER

Construction workers include a broad category of laborers who, in earlier periods, might have been known by and identified themselves by their specific skills or trades: joiners, carpenters, masons, brick carriers, framers, electricians, plumbers, and others. These tradesmen, who were mostly male workers, worked in specific trades and were generally represented by labor unions that organized along those craft divisions within the workplace; for instance, by 1888, the United Brotherhood of Carpenters merged with the Joiners' Union to become the United Brotherhood of Carpenters and Joiners (UBCJ), an organization that still exists today. During the post–World War II period, however, Americans increasingly referred to all workers in the construction trades as "construction workers," regardless of their particular duties. There were many reasons for this transformation, particularly the decline of unionism in private industry in the 1970s. In construction trades before the 1970s, 80 percent of construction workers were union members, a rate of unionization that few other occupations could achieve.

After World War II, most regions in the United States experienced unparalleled economic growth. Arguably, the construction industry benefited most from this economic expansion. Low-interest home loans provided under the popular G.I. Bill, coupled with pent-up demand for housing, stimulated home construction across much of the nation. Other economic stimuli included expansion of the burgeoning federal interstate system and internal migration of Americans—many of whom relocated to California and other western states, where the aerospace industry provided hundreds of thousands of jobs during the Cold War. Much of the home construction occurred in suburbs, which were new communities on the periphery of older urban centers. So dominant was the construction industry that nearly one in ten American men worked as a construction worker during the period from the end of the war until the early 1960s.

The collective image of construction workers as a general category of workers, rather than as individual tradesmen who performed only the duties of their respective crafts, emerged in the postwar era. Americans viewed construction workers as "hardhats," a cultural concept epitomized by images of physically fit, (mostly) white men wearing hardhats and blue jeans and carrying tools or blueprints, whose crafts distinctions went unacknowledged. Construction workers built homes, shopping centers, roads, piers, schools, government buildings, and countless other structures. Construction workers also repaired and remodeled existing buildings, and if they worked in the field of building demolition, they also destroyed old buildings. Their individual work duties largely depended on their union membership; in all areas except the South, carpenters were generally members of the UBCJ. Skilled carpenters did not perform the work of masons (bricklayers, concrete finishers, or tile setters), nor did they work as hod carriers (general laborers who carry brick and other construction materials to skilled workers), even if that position required little skill. Specific skillsets and union divisions thus demarcated what an individual construction worker might do on any given job, or worksite.

In the case of constructing a house, construction workers might use heavy mechanized equipment to grade a building pad until it was level and had good drainage, and they might then define the boundaries of the soon-to-be-built house with site markers. Other workers might then prepare the graded building pad for concrete-pouring in preparation for on-pad (or above-grade) building foundations. Sewer, water, and gas lines would then be installed, and the structure's framing would be erected; in wood-framed buildings, construction workers measured and cut lengths of lumber to precise dimensions and then normally nailed the boards together for framing, per construction plans. Other construction workers installed electrical lines throughout the building so that every room had power. Roofers—specialized workers—covered the top of the building with sheathing (generally sheets of plywood) and underlayment (typically waterproof plastic membranes) that provided protective layers between a building's attic and the outside environment; then roofers installed shingles or other exterior roofing materials, followed by flashing and rain gutters, among other roof elements.

Construction workers often worked in either interior or exterior settings—building walls, stairs, closets, or cabinetry, so a bricklayer put up the exterior walls if the building was a brick or masonry one, while a carpenter built framing for interior walls. Drywallers hung large panels of drywall, which is a type of board typically made from plaster, wood pulp, or gypsum, to create smooth, finished interior walls. Construction workers also installed windows, doors, and chimneys or vents. Finally, the detail work of a building was finished; this normally included painting as well as flooring, electrical outlets, and plumbing fixtures like toilets, sinks, and faucets.

All construction workers used an architect's or engineer's building plan, known as blueprints—a set of documents that specified dimensions of a structure and materials to be used, including such detailed instructions as where to place fasteners and what size fasteners should be used, for instance, in the frame. Much of a construction worker's day consisted of consulting plans (or being directed by a supervisor, who consulted plans) and then measuring and preparing materials for installation. As construction workers put in place each element of a house, they had to measure dimensions, recheck plans, and then measure again before finally securing that element to the building. If a construction worker deviated from the plans, he likely had to tear down his work and redo it to conform to design specification, or spec.

Post–World War II, the ways in which new homes were built and financed transformed, which caused rapid suburban growth; builders and real estate developers implemented mass-production techniques modeled on Henry Ford's assembly line innovation, while the Federal Housing Authority (FHA) offered mortgage insurance and other financial instruments to take the risk out of building large projects. New American suburbs of the postwar era included Levittown, New York, and Lakewood, California, where real estate developers built planned communities on large tracts of what was, for most, agricultural land. In many of the nation's new suburbs, real estate developers and construction companies rationalized the process of producing a new community. Uniformity was a hallmark of postwar suburbanization. Developers offered prospective buyers only a handful of floor plans and exterior options, used prefabrication techniques (where elements of a house are built offsite at a factory and then transported for assembly), and subdivided the labor process into discrete tasks to which workers were assigned. Furthermore, developers often subcontracted the work; subcontractors were generally nonunion, often employing only semiskilled workers who knew how to do just one or two tasks in house building. As the developer Henry Levitt of Levittown once famously noted, "We are not builders . . . we are manufacturers." The cultural image of the hardhat, a generic construction worker, was based in part on reality.

Political tensions and demographic changes also affected construction workers in the postwar era. The building trades unions had a long history of discriminating against African American workers and women. In the early 1960s, as the struggle for civil rights in the South became more violent each year, leadership of several black civil rights organizations, including the National Association for the Advancement of Colored People (NAACP) and the Congress of Racial Equality (CORE), demanded equal opportunity for black workers in the building trades, particularly in northern and far western cities. In some cities, the NAACP and CORE organized mass protests to slow work on major public construction projects and demanded that black workers have access to construction work. The 1964 Civil Rights Act included a provision (Title VII) that prohibited exclusionary racial practices in unions; construction unions fought these efforts at desegregating the workforce, even as the nation's population was changing. More blue-collar workers were minorities—not just African Americans but also Latinos and women—and they demanded access to good-paying construction jobs. But a devastating economic recession in the 1970s led to a pronounced slowdown in construction—as measured by federal "new housing starts" statistics. Widespread unemployment of construction workers followed.

When a rush of new construction resumed for a time in the 1980s, builders were emboldened to hire nonunion workers, many of whom were from the same groups who had previously been excluded from union membership and jobs in the industry. In some areas, construction workers pursued contractors' licenses, allowing them access to smaller projects or to work as subcontractors on larger public projects. Technological advancements, changes in the organization of work and labor, and demographic shifts in the working-class population all transformed what it meant to be a "construction worker" by the end of the Cold War.

Nancy Quam-Wickham

See also: *1915–1946:* Ironworker

FURTHER READING

Goldberg, David A., and Trevor Griffey. 2010. *Black Power at Work: Community Control, Affirmative Action, and the Construction Industry*. Ithaca: ILR Press/Cornell University Press.

Jackson, Kenneth T. 1985. *Crabgrass Frontier: The Suburbanization of America*. New York: Oxford University Press.

Riemer, Jeffrey W. 1979. *Hard Hats: The Work World of Construction Workers*. Beverly Hills: Sage Publications.

DENTIST

Dentists are specialized, highly skilled medical workers—usually doctors—who treat conditions, ailments, and diseases that affect the gums and teeth. Their work primarily involves the cleaning, repair, and extraction of teeth and, when necessary, the installation of artificial teeth. Dentists' responsibilities also include diagnosing diseases of the mouth, interpreting X-rays and other diagnostic tests, promoting oral health, ensuring the safe administration of anesthesia or local anesthetics during dental procedures, and monitoring the development and growth of the jaws and teeth in young patients.

At the conclusion of World War II (1939–1945), the vast majority of dentists in America were white men who practiced independently in isolated, private offices, usually attached to or inside of their homes. A typical dentist had a receptionist and an assistant. Dental patients would sit in a specialized dental chair, which looked like a sophisticated barber chair with a spittoon, a cord-driven, low-speed drill, and a small white porcelain tray to hold instruments and filling materials. Dentists wore short white coats and stood while treating their patients. Dentists of the 1950s did not wear any protective gear: no mask, gloves, or eye shields. For more elaborate work like making dentures, crowns, or bridges, most dentists used the services of an outside dental technical laboratory. The dentist used dental plaster to take an impression of a patient's mouth and then sent it to the lab for fabrication of a prosthodontic device. Weeks later, the lab work returned, and the dentist made last-minute adjustments for a better fit. In the 1940s, these devices were less aesthetically pleasing and somewhat obvious to a trained eye.

Dentists worked four or five days a week, usually six to eight hours a day. They had to have expert manual dexterity and good eyesight, demonstrate a keen attention to detail, and possess the strength and patience to stand for hours each day. The assistant helped prepare impression or filling materials, handed instruments, and cleaned up after patients. Dentists could see the outcome of their work almost instantly as they restored form, function, and aesthetics to a patient's teeth and mouth. Being a dentist meant independence, a good standard of living, and high public esteem. Dentistry was considered a highly desirable profession.

The late 1940s saw the introduction of fluoride into Americans' water supplies in an effort to prevent dental decay. Fluoridated water reduced dental decay by at least 25 percent in the United States ("Community Water Fluoridation"). During the early 1950s, a new type of filling material called restorative fillings, because they restored the look of healthy teeth using bonded resins, was introduced, replacing dental cement. Resins looked more natural and adhered better to teeth. In the late 1950s, the air-driven high-speed drill was introduced; this new drill cut teeth much faster. High-speed drills required a water jet to cool the generated heat. Excess cooling water during treatment required a suction device and another set of hands to manipulate these new tools. All these inventions were added to an even more sophisticated reclining dental chair.

Also in the 1950s, sterilizing instruments became the norm. Initially, boiling water was used, and subsequently, high-pressure autoclaves provided a cleaner environment. A full range of infection-control protocols followed.

By the late 1950s, dentists began sitting while treating patients, with the dental assistant sitting across and providing "four-handed" dentistry. No longer did the assistant simply provide the dentist with basic tools and equipment during a procedure; now dental assistants were technically proficient, and most had formal postsecondary training. These well-trained dental hygienists performed some of the basic duties of general dentists, including routine cleaning and prophylactic fluoride administration. Registered dental hygienists, like dentists, had their own professional organizations and licensure requirements.

During the same decade, as more patients sought necessary treatment, many general dentists found it desirable to pursue a specialization in one of the subfields of dentistry. These specialties included periodontics (gum disease), pediatric dentistry (children's dentistry), orthodontics (straightening teeth), endodontics (root canal), prosthodontics (dentures, crown, and bridge), oral surgery (surgical extractions and soft tissue operations), and oral pathology (microscopic examination of tumors and other oral diseases).

During the decades after the 1950s, a great deal of change came to modern dentistry, redefining what it meant to practice dentistry and how a dentist approached everyday tasks. In broad terms, changes came to dentistry in the appearance and management of dental offices, the materials and tools they used, the type of treatments they offered, the specialists they consulted, and even those who practiced. New public health initiatives, expanded dental insurance coverage during the postwar era, and technological advances and societal needs transformed American dentistry.

Within both prosthodontics and general dentistry, the first titanium implants became available during the 1960s, and anchoring replacement teeth became a better treatment option. Each of these specialized subfields of dentistry experienced exponential growth during the postwar years, with formalized training programs in dental schools, new specialized professional organizations and journals, and expanded opportunities for dentists to obtain postgraduate education through new continuing education unit (CEU) credit programs. All but two U.S. states required practicing dentists to attain fifteen to twenty hours of CEU training per year to retain their professional licenses.

Historically, the vast majority of general dentists have worked in isolated, one-person dental practices, but in the second half of the twentieth century, it became more common for specialty dentists to band together to form group practices, which provided centers of specialist practice that were easier to scale. General dentists easily referred patients to specialists as the latter were often just an office away. These offices had treatment rooms called operatories and now contained additional chairs for many patients to be seated simultaneously, extra chairs for hygienists for cleaning, safer X-ray machines, a panoramic imaging device, and often an in-house technical lab to cut cost and time of delivery for work. Because of the required space, such practices were housed in commercial shopping malls or professional office buildings. With the adoption of personal computers in the 1970s and the internet in the 1990s, offices became modernized, with sophisticated accounting and efficient office management.

Andrew I. Spielman

See also: Pharmacist; Radiologist and Radiology Technician; *1776–1860:* Physician; *1861–1914:* Nurse; Surgeon

FURTHER READING

"Community Water Fluoridation." Centers for Disease Control and Prevention. Last modified November 5, 2018. https://www.cdc.gov/fluoridation/index.html.

Otto, Mary. 2017. *Teeth: The Story of Beauty, Inequality, and the Struggle for Oral Health in America.* New York: The New Press.

Taylor, James Anderson. 2012. *The History of Dentistry: A Practical Treatise for the Use of Dental Students and Practitioners.* London: Forgotten Books.

DIETITIAN

A dietitian is a specialized, certified expert on diet and nutrition. From the founding of the American Dietetic Association in 1917, dietitians have served an integral role in providing Americans with the best, most scientifically current nutritional advice and therapy. While nutrition scientists—including biochemists, molecular biologists, and physicians—are responsible for the development of the foundational, chemical science behind the understanding of nutrition, dietitians carefully tailor that knowledge to practical diets and plans that address the specific needs of clients and medical patients, many of whom rely on this guidance as an integral component of their medical treatment.

Immediately after World War II, dieticians found work in four major contexts: diet therapy, administration, teaching, and social welfare. In each of these positions, dietitians were responsible for taking national nutritional recommendations, along with specific dietary requirements for individuals or populations, and distilling them into meals. Diet therapy, the subspecialty that attracted the greatest number of dietitians, was the delivery of nutritional services to patients in hospitals. Administrative dietitians were typically charged with planning meal services for government institutions like schools or prisons. Social welfare dietitians worked to promote what is now called community nutrition, which assesses the needs of at-risk communities and helps them to obtain adequate nutrition from limited resources. Finally, teaching was an important way for dietitians to pass their knowledge along to the next generation of trainees.

Dietetics, especially in hospitals, is not simply the preparation of food. Rather, hospital dietitians work closely with doctors and nurses to design and deliver nutritional care. As an example, some patients with genetic disorders like phenylketonuria require a diet low in phenylalanine, an amino acid that occurs in many common food products such as eggs, milk, and soybeans. For a person with phenylketonuria, a dietitian provided guidance regarding what foods to avoid and which similar products might be good substitutes.

Dietitians often work with patients with diabetes, hypertension, and obesity, patients recovering from surgery who may have trouble chewing or swallowing, and patients with diseases in their digestive systems that prevent them from properly digesting certain nutrients. Matters can be further complicated when patients have more than one dietary restriction, if they have food allergies or religious restrictions against certain foods, or if they maintain a strict dietary lifestyle like vegetarianism.

In the hospital, dietitians are responsible for ensuring that patients with specific dietary requirements are adequately fed. They assure that each meal has the right number of calories and an appropriate distribution of nutrients, the food is safe from contamination and spoilage, it is served at an appropriate temperature, and the food is varied enough for the patients to eat it.

As a profession, dietetics emerged on the coattails of other fields such as home economics and nursing that were typically dominated by—and often reserved for—women. Women were drawn to dietetics not only because of the gendered expectations that the labor of food preparation and meal service was appropriate for women but also because the greatest demand for dietitians was during wartime. With many able-bodied men fighting abroad instead of participating in the workforce, the U.S. government heavily recruited women during the First and Second World Wars to fill these ancillary positions to support the war efforts.

Most military dietitians provided food service to the troops and dietetic services to military hospitals. Some were placed in charge of administering the distribution of civilian food rations too, which was key to the war effort because it assured there would be enough food for soldiers. In part due to their great success in helping the United States during the First and Second World Wars, dietitians remained important throughout the twentieth century. They continued to perform integral roles in the Korean War, the Vietnam War, and the Gulf Wars. In the Korean War, one of the major challenges that military dietitians faced was preventing food supplies from being stolen and resold on the black market. Because hospitals kept more robust food supplies than were available in the local markets, hospital pantries were in constant danger of being pilfered. Dietitians often duplicated sets of records to ensure that they had more than one copy of their inventory; thieves tried to steal paperwork along with food to cover their tracks.

The military recruitment of dietitians during WWII posed a problem: when more than a thousand dietitians—with vastly different training experiences—returned from the war and hoped to join the domestic workforce, there were not enough positions available. In peacetime, most civilian dietitians worked in hospitals in the treatment or prevention of disease, but after the war, there was a critical shortage of hospital beds throughout the United States. Congress passed the Hill-Burton Hospital Construction Act in 1946, which greatly expanded the number of American hospitals and healthcare facilities. These new hospitals created a large demand for dietitians to manage their increasingly centralized food service programs. Before the Hill-Burton Act, hospitals typically provided a fixed menu for all patients, where the food was batch-cooked and distributed throughout the hospital at regular mealtimes. This was a problem for patients who were out of their rooms for medical examinations or procedures as they did not receive fresh food. Dietitians helped hospitals to adopt the kinds of centralized kitchens that they use today, with flexible menus where food could be prepared fresh and delivered on demand to any patient at any time of day.

Dietitians also became powerful advocates for underprivileged populations. In the mid-1960s, the ADA acquired a permit to lobby in Washington, D.C., to promote its own political interests. Organized dietitians became important boosters for social programs in the 1970s that were aimed at ending hunger in America: the Food Stamp Program, school lunch and breakfast programs, childcare and summer food service for children, supplemental feeding programs for women, infants, and children (WIC), and nutrition for the elderly. Through the end of the Cold War, the dietetic profession continued to grow and diversify, adding new specialties like sports medicine, neonatal care, pediatrics, and even research.

Travis Weisse

See also: Pharmacist; *1776–1860:* Physician; *1992–2019:* Physical Therapist

FURTHER READING

Hodges, Patricia A. M. 1996. "Perspectives on History: Army Dietitians in the European, North African, and Mediterranean Theaters of Operation in World War II." *Journal of the American Dietetic Association* 96, no. 6 (June): 598–601.

Hodges, Patricia A. M., and Joan M. G. Lyon. 1996. "Perspectives on History: Army Dietetics in Southwest Asia during Operation Desert Shield/Desert Storm." *Journal of the American Dietetic Association* 96, no. 6 (June): 595–97.

Nyhart, Lynn K. 1997. "Home Economists in the Hospital, 1900–1930." In *Rethinking Home Economics: Women and the History of the Profession*, edited by Sarah Stage and Virginia V. Vincenti, 125–144. Ithaca: Cornell University Press.

Todhunter, E. Neige. 1973. "Some Aspects of the History of Dietetics." *World Review of Nutrition and Dietetics* 18: 1–46.

ECONOMIST

Economists study, design, and apply theories about economic policies, which help communities and governments understand and shape their economies. Economists study the production and consumption of goods and services; a system that permits the market to set prices and wages without external regulation or control is generally called a free market economy. The practice of American economists in the postwar years was closely tied to a strong political belief of the nation: the connection between capitalism and democracy or, more specifically, that free-market capitalism, if largely left unfettered by rules and legislation, would provide wealth, full employment, and freedom to all Americans. During the Great Depression, the theories of the great English economist John Maynard Keynes (1883–1946) and the Canadian-American economist John Kenneth Galbraith (1908–2006) agreed that global economic distress needed government intervention, at least in the United States, to help the economy recover. Yet after the Second World War (1939–1945), American economists largely worked in universities, think tanks, and corporations to demonstrate that the free market could correct itself through a series of checks like supply-demand and prices.

In the wake of World War II, both economists and the population at large were unsure whether our nation's economy would revert to Depression-era characteristics or trend upward toward full employment and a higher standard of living than had characterized the Great Depression. Since the end of World War II, American economists, unlike many of their international counterparts, have privileged mathematical modeling and theoretical advances based on mathematics over other practices used by economists (such as in Great Britain, where until the 1980s, economists had the elimination of poverty as one primary goal of economic research and practice). To develop these mathematical models, most professional economists in the United States hold graduate degrees, either an MS or a PhD, in economics. Those individuals holding BAs or MBAs in business are seldom considered or present themselves as economists, even if they have specialized in finance or other allied fields.

Most American economists utilized advanced mathematical calculations to understand the workings of a free-market economy and to make predictions that would optimize this system. The work of important economists in America demonstrates these phenomena: In the 1950s, working at the University of Chicago, economist Milton Friedman developed a theory about the problem of consumer spending. Using mathematical analysis to support a new theory, the permanent income hypothesis, Friedman argued that Americans' consumer spending is not linked to current income but to future expected income. Thus, Americans tended to continue to spend at high levels in expectation of higher incomes and thus not save money for the future. Friedman studied the monetary supply and argued that when the Federal Reserve released more money into circulation, Americans simply bought more goods. When too many consumers demanded goods that could not be produced, theorized Friedman, inflation occurred. Through mathematical analysis of complex sets of empirical data, Friedman argued that the government should not be allowed to manage monetary policy; this is a stark departure from the economic studies of Keynes and Galbraith, who believed that government management of the economy was often necessary.

While many American economists worked in higher education, others were employed in the applied economics fields. A labor economist, for example, analyzed how the demand for goods affected the labor supply while working at the U.S. Bureau of Labor Statistics, a branch of the Department of Labor. A labor economist also tracked such statistics as changes in labor force participation as more women went to work or differentials in labor union representation as union workers historically have earned more than nonunion workers in most industries. Applied economists often worked for government, but others worked for business.

Health insurance companies employed both actuaries and economists to determine trends in profitability, depending on the statistical characteristics of those insured individuals. Applied economists were also employed by businesses to determine pricing structures for key goods such as gasoline and tobacco. All of these activities provide key indicators about the health of our national economy.

The employment of economists has been steady, with about fifty thousand economists employed in the United States. The trends of employment, however, have shifted, with more economists employed in think tanks—the Brookings Institution, American Enterprise Institution, Hoover Institution—to which the federal government has awarded major grants to facilitate economic analysis of the economy. In contrast, economists have also been employed in higher-education institutions. Economists employed in these two divisions—think tanks and universities—have often produced economic models that are diametrically opposed to each other.

Nancy Quam-Wickham

See also: College Professor; Statistician; *1992–2019:* Data Analyst

FURTHER READING

Backhouse, Roger E., and Jeff Biddle, eds. 2000. *Toward a History of Applied Economics.* Durham: Duke University Press.

Fourcade, Marion. 2009. *Economists and Societies: Discipline and Profession in the United States, Britain, and France, 1890s to 1990s.* Princeton: Princeton.

Pressman, Steven. 1999. *Fifty Major Economists.* London: Routledge.

PRIMARY DOCUMENT

In this selection from his oral history, economist Robert C. Holland recalls an experience in 1964 during which the Federal Reserve considered making some significant changes in monetary policy and how those policy changes were tied to the escalation of the war in Vietnam and President Lyndon Baines Johnson's War on Poverty.

[Chairman of the U.S. Federal Reserve Bank] William McChesney Martin was absolutely gifted in his way to have [good] relationship[s], even with people with whom he disagreed. The most outstanding example of that that sticks in my mind was one that came along in the mid-60s, as the Vietnam War was getting going. Johnson was relatively new as President, with a strong desire in both, in effect, guns and butter. That is, he wanted to carry forward that Vietnam War creditably.

And he wanted that war on poverty to go. And he was pushing them both . . . And as . . . he made the decisions for internal buildup in the military power of the United States, to gear it to deal with more, if need be, in Vietnam, and of course it turned out to be needed by his standards and so forth. That decision, when it was made, was very closely held, that decision for a major escalation in the military buildup. And it could be closely held for a while, because a lot of it involved, you know, getting factories ready to do more orders and that kind of thing and so forth. Very closely-held. And the Federal Reserve was not told about it.

Martin…had become good friends with [Secretary of Defense] Bob McNamara. And McNamara, of course, was part of that buildup decision with the Pentagon. McNamara was under orders, as everybody else was in the Pentagon, not to say anything. And I remember Martin telling . . . that McNamara didn't give him a clue . . . [We] were sitting there . . . as the [military] build-up went on, there was nothing . . . We were reading the economic evidence, and the districts, and the GNP . . . you could see a strengthening economic thrust percolating through the economy . . . [W]e knew about [the tax cut of early 1964 and the high money growth of 1964]. This was more push than we could explain by either of those two. Now, we weren't into the—our econometric modeling wasn't nearly as far along then as it was later. But still, in all, what we were sensing, what we felt was more sign of economic demand in the system than those two things would explain. And I remember two different efforts to do it. I remember Martin went over to sit down and talk to McNamara about this kind of thrust, and if McNamara had any judgment he could share with him on this kind of thing. And McNamara couldn't, didn't tell him.

. . . I remember one meeting that Dan Brill and Bob Solomon and I did. We were going to label it troika at that time I think, that went over and met with Art Okun, and he had some other people with him—one or two other persons with him. George Perry, as I recall, saying, talking about, "Where's this thrust coming from? We just can't put our finger on it, and yet it seems like it's there." And they didn't know, and Art swore afterwards that he didn't know it was happening. He didn't know what was happening. He could see the numbers too. He could see the signs of that demand, but he did not know where it was coming from . . . Finally, we felt like we saw enough efforts, so we tightened money and raised the discount rate. And I don't know, at that stage—I have not much knowledge about how much the Chairman of the Federal Reserve would communicate with a President of the United States about what was going to happen. But it was clear to us that there had been—over several months, Johnson had communicated to Martin that he thought easy money was the right thing to accompany the advancement on the war on poverty, and he didn't want anything, any accidents to tighten money. He'd lose count—he just, he passed that message several different ways. And of course, you know, most Presidents feel that way most of the time. So we made that decision, and Johnson was down in Texas at the time. He was at the ranch. I believe he called and ordered Martin down, to talk to him about this. [H]e went down, met with the President, he came back, and he called the three of us in the office. We were dying to hear what had happened, both on what to do with the institution, and because you couldn't help being a little curious about it.

I remember him telling us that he got down there, and the President took him for a ride around the parts of the ranch . . . in a big convertible he had with the top down, that was apparently a reasonably thrilling ride. Not because of what the President had said, though he talked along the way, but the way he drove. But they came back, and they were walking along the banks of that little Pedernales River out in front of the ranch house. And Johnson had been asking him and working him over pretty good about what happened, and Martin had tried to explained to him why, you know. And he told us, he said finally, you know, "I looked out in the middle of that river. There was a big boulder sitting out in the middle of it, causing ripples and ripples around in the water and that kind of thing as it ran by and so forth," I guess [a] pretty . . . disturbance of the water flow there.

And he said, "Mr. President, this low discount rate and low prime rate that we've got in our financial system, given the status, the way economic developments and financial developments are going, that low rate . . . that's lower than the market calls for in order to function," he said. "That low rate was a little bit like that boulder out there in the middle of the stream. It just sat there blocking things and causing ripples and troubles and disturbances around. We needed to move that up, to get it out of the road, and let things flow." [Martin replied,] "You know, Mr. President, that's very interesting. But you know, technically, that is not quite an accurate analogy to the way the credit flows and rates would behave there." And he looked up to me with a quiet smile, and he said, "But it worked."

Source: Robert C. Holland. Interviewed by Robert Hetzel, July 13, 1994. Robert Hetzel Oral History Collection, Fraser. *Robert Hetzel Oral History Collection.* https://fraser.stlouisfed.org/archival/4927.

FASHION DESIGNER AND MODEL

Fashion designers and fashion models have different responsibilities, but they are mutually dependent, and both have the same goal: to create and sell clothing and other consumer goods that enhance a customer's body and appearance. Although Americans have been fascinated with fashion trends for centuries, the period after World War II marked the emergence of American fashion designers and models on the world stage. Prior to the war, most elite fashion designers were European or were trained in European fashion sensibilities under such giants as Paul Poiret, Jacques Doucet, or Coco Chanel, among many others. These were some of the stars of high fashion, those designers who set the standard for their times. But even before the war, American designers envisioned a new American aesthetic, one that emphasized that wearers of clothing could, in the words of historian Annemarie Strassel, "alter their embodied experience and challenge gender inequality" (Strassel 2008, 36). Fashion designers sought to create clothing that allowed women to move freely in their clothes while still looking fashionable. American fashion emphasized beauty but also utility and comfort. Fashion models, on the other hand, were those men and women who dressed in new seasons' clothing, demonstrating the look of a suit or dress on the wearer. Models appeared in designers' clothing on runways at fashion shows and in advertisements in magazines, in newspapers, and on television.

Before the war, most fashion designers on both sides of the Atlantic specialized in haute couture, or high fashion: fancy clothing so expensive that it was out of the reach of all but the wealthiest of consumers. In the years leading up to the Second World War, though, both French and American designers began to experiment with ready-wear fashion—or well-designed clothing that the middle class could afford and that might be replicated for even lower prices. More than their European counterparts, American designers were also cognizant of the business side of fashion; their collections should be marketed to a wider range of potential consumers. Some American designers, like Bonnie Cashin, created lines of "lifestyle" clothing that featured simple lines and were interchangeable with other clothing from the collection. Both women's and men's sportswear collections were also important to the business of fashion design as, after the war, economic prosperity allowed more Americans to pursue leisure activities. Other designers rejected the idea that they created "fashion" of any kind, preferring to be known as designers of specialty or utilitarian clothing—as was the case with the outdoors clothing company Patagonia.

A fashion designer creates collections or lines of clothing based on study of consumer preference, as well as their predictions about new trends in the ways that Americans will live their lives. Market researchers provided much of this information for fashion designers and clothing companies. Among such considerations would be changing labor force participation, especially among women (but also among men) in the 1960s, 1970s, and 1980s, when more women became full-time workers for longer periods of their lives, including once they became mothers. Many women workers realized that they needed interchangeable items that could be mixed and matched to produce outfit ensembles, which could fit into different sorts of workplaces—and they needed those constituent pieces at an affordable price.

Fashion designers choose color palettes and fabrics as they consider creating new collections, ordering quantities of fabrics from different textile mills. Once a designer sketched out designs for clothing in the new lines, he or she used mannequins to make prototypes and then collaborated with textile wholesalers to ensure they could source required amounts of the desired fabrics. The connection between textile companies and designers was so important that the California-based designer Adolph Schuman was employed by the U.S. government to assist with the reconstruction of French woolen mills in Normandy after World War II. Fashion is a collaborative activity. Once a designer obtained the desired fabrics, he or she worked with seamstresses to create the three-dimensional representation of the artistic design, or the prototype item or outfit. Independent fashion designers employed fashion models to wear these prototype designs at fashion industry events such as independent fashion shows and exhibitions; only the most accomplished fashion designers show their work at global Fashion Week shows in New York, Paris, London, and elsewhere.

One of a fashion designer's primary responsibilities is marketing and selling his or her products. Fashion designers work hard to get media attention about their work. Sometimes, fashion designers directly employ fashion models and photographers to take high-quality photographs of models dressed in their collection; designers then arrange for independent gallery shows and try to get media attention to have their designs featured in both popular and industry magazines and sometimes to obtain celebrity endorsement. Other designers work long hours marketing their lines to professional fashion buyers at industry shows and conventions. When a fashion buyer requests an order, the designer must then contract out the production of his or her clothing, using either domestic or, more commonly after the 1970s, international (offshore) clothing factories. When designer Georges Marciano sold twenty-four pairs of his new Guess? jeans to Bloomingdale's, he was stunned that they sold out within a day; Bloomingdale's buyers immediately placed an order for three hundred more pairs to be delivered the next week. Fashion designers contracted to provide collections for major retailers have already entered into agreements with manufacturers beforehand. The designer's success depends on a variety of business factors, not just his or her talent in artistic design of clothing: marketing of a collection, interest from fashion buyers and merchandisers, capacity of a factory to complete the order on time and under or on budget, transportation, textile availability, and consumer taste.

Fashion modeling is the work of individuals who model clothing for designers and retailers. While some of the famous models of this time were well-known names like the English model known as Twiggy or the American model Lauren Hutton, in reality, most fashion models worked long hours for relatively low pay in the retailing and media sections of the fashion business. Men, women, and children all worked as models: child models, for example, might be photographed wearing special holiday clothing; those photographs were then featured in retailer catalogs sent by mail to consumers across the nation. Modeling agents generally assisted models in obtaining contracts for photo sessions. Model agencies had booking agents who procured interviews and bookings with different designers, media outlets (like major women's fashion magazines), and photographers. Discipline was critical: models had to maintain their appearance; keep well groomed; arrive on time to interviews, shows, and sessions; and be willing to work in a variety of settings. Models might have to travel to distant locations or do photo shoots in a studio. Some fashion photographers requested certain models because of the ease of working with them. Some models became actors and actresses in television and film, went into clothing manufacturing, or became designers themselves.

Fashion designing and modeling is a serious business. Designers often had a background in art or sewing, often designing clothing for themselves before being discovered by industry professionals. Some toiled for years as buyers or merchandisers. Many attended specialized art or fashion design colleges, while others had worked their way up in theaters, from backstage laborers to costume and set designers. Models often began their careers as children or teenagers with interests first in theater and acting but then in entering the modeling industry. The shared characteristics of fashion designers and models are that most worked long hours for years, often earning only a modest income, before they became successful in their fields.

Nancy Quam-Wickham

See also: Beautician; *1776–1860:* Milliner; *1915–1945:* Garment Worker; Textile Worker

FURTHER READING

Angel, Samata. 2013. *Fashion Designer's Resource Book.* London: Bloomsbury.
Baudot, Francois. 2006. *Fashion: The Twentieth Century.* Bloomington: Universe Books.
Bullis, Douglas. 1987. *California Fashion Designers.* Layton: Peregrine Smith Books.
Strassel, Annemarie Elizabeth. 2008. *Redressing Women: Feminism in Fashion and the Creation of American Style, 1930–1960.* New Haven: Yale University Press.

FLIGHT ATTENDANT

From the 1930s through the 1960s, airlines exclusively hired white, single women who were young, slender, attractive, educated, and well-mannered to serve refreshments and provide comfort to airline travelers. Airlines provided these flight attendants—known then as stewardesses—with specialized instruction aimed at increasing their elegance and appeal. Airlines also provided their flight attendants with classy, voguish uniforms. Artists, authors, reporters, and airline marketers held flight attendants in high esteem, viewing them as cosmopolitan, globetrotting providers of refreshments and comfort who were also soothing and familiar. The combination of flight attendants' chic image and unpretentious, approachable nature made them popular icons of femininity. Flight attendants enjoyed a host of benefits, including the easy ability to travel all around the country—or, in many cases, the world. It meant a welcome escape from the confines of the earthbound jobs most young white women held in the middle decades of the twentieth century, such as secretary, nurse, and teacher.

Flight attendants had many responsibilities, not all of which involved looking after their passengers' food and beverage requests. They were also responsible for the care of unwell travelers, enforcing safety rules and regulations, and being the first responders to in-flight emergencies. Regardless of the task at hand, airlines maintained an expectation that flight attendants would present themselves as so self-assured and comfortable with their duties that it seemed as though their work took no effort at all. Airlines expected their flight attendants to stand for the duration of the flight, except for the minutes before and during takeoff and landing, but required that their appearance remained pristine. Flight attendants were forbidden from speaking sharply with passengers; they were expected to treat every passenger as if he or she were a distinguished guest in the flight attendants' personal homes. In spite of the job's strict on-duty responsibilities and expectations, flight attendants would still be forced to resign if ever they got married, and they could expect to be reprimanded and put on probation if they put on weight or failed to observe the airlines' other numerous rules. Many airlines stopped renewing employment contracts for any stewardess older than thirty-five.

Stewardesses accepted the strict rules and modest wages in exchange for all the distinctive benefits the job offered. The job attracted adventurous young women and required that they be competent and independent enough to oversee a cabin full of passengers and manage the challenges of each flight mostly on their own; pilots were their supervisors but were often preoccupied with flying the airplane. As it happened, flight attendants were willing to speak out about the downsides of their job and demand that they be respected for their hard work and skills.

The first flight attendant union appeared in the late 1940s. By the end of the 1950s, most flight attendants had unionized. Their unionization resulted in increased wages, more reasonable working conditions, and the ability to file grievances against their employing airlines should those companies try to employ unfair practices or neglect their reasonable requests. Union leaders also lobbied the federal government to issue safety licenses to flight attendants similar to those held by many other airline employees whose job responsibilities were vital to passengers' safety, such as mechanics and pilots. Flight attendants demanded to be acknowledged by the labor movement and called for the ability to manage their own union affairs, and when union activists felt unacknowledged or harassed by (often male) labor leaders, they organized protests. However, the flight attendants were unable to get safety licenses, and a fully autonomous union remained elusive. Still, their hard work and concerted effort were extraordinary when considering that 30 to 40 percent of the flight attendant workforce resigned annually—usually to get married—and unionization was broadly seen as a masculine, blue-collar goal.

Flight attendants grew to become more vocal during the women's movement and the sexual revolution during the late 1960s and through the 1970s, and they began to view their specific concerns to be exemplars of the predominant women's rights issues of the time. Growing activism was also spurred by increased strength in numbers. With the advent of larger, faster jets, flight attendants' ranks were expanding, especially with the jumbo jets that arrived in the late 1960s. The flight attendant workforce jumped from about thirty thousand in 1970 to forty thousand in 1974. The passage of Title VII of the Civil Rights Act of 1965, which forbade gender discrimination in employment, ignited a new era of feminist activism. Flight attendants were quite tired of the airlines' long-standing policy of forced resignation whenever they married or began to approach the age of forty. The flight attendants' union actions and civil suits began chipping away at the airlines' unfair policies. By the end of the 1960s, the resulting legal successes and union pressures fostered an end to the airlines' discriminatory policies and obligated airlines to greatly revise—or in many cases eliminate—their unfair practices in the 1970s.

With the sexual revolution of the 1960s came a more sexually provocative era in advertising and popular culture, and airlines joined the trend with eye-catching uniforms and cheeky advertising. Marketing teams and popular media became even more explicit in their portrayal of flight attendants as poster girls of a newer, racier era. A new group called Stewardesses for Women's Rights, along with the flight attendants' unions, began fevered protests of the exploitative ways that flight attendants had been portrayed. By the end of the 1970s, flight attendants began to actively eschew the colloquial term of "stewardess," which for decades had been associated with the vocation's lingering struggles associated with restrictive company practices, and transformed themselves into "flight attendants," with more career opportunities, strong unions, and clear recognition of the necessity and importance of the added safety that they provided to every commercial passenger flight.

The years since the feminist triumphs of the 1970s brought new challenges. Airline deregulation in 1978 shook an industry long accustomed to government control over routes and fares. The results for airline employees were job losses, pay cuts, and anti-union efforts by airline management. Service standards also changed, frustrating passengers and making cabin crews' work more difficult. More calamitous for the airline industry were the terrorist attacks of September 11, 2001, which inaugurated a new era of heightened security and fear as well as even deeper economic turmoil. Following 9/11, federal authorities determined that flight attendants should have safety licenses. In a far-reaching aviation bill passed late in 2003, Congress mandated a licensing program for flight attendants, a goal they had sought for more than half a century. Throughout those years, as more and more American women worked for wages and the service sector exploded, flight attendants both embodied and challenged stereotypes surrounding "women's work" and women's potential for militancy in the workplace.

Kathleen M. Barry

See also: Pilot; Travel Agent; *1915–1945:* Sleeping Car Porter

FURTHER READING

Aviation Education Programs. 1992. *Flight Attendants*. Washington, DC: U.S. Dept. of Transportation, Federal Aviation Administration, Office of Public Affairs, Aviation Education Program.

Lobus, Catherine Okray. 1995. *Careers As a Flight Attendant: Flight to the Future*. New York: Rosen Pub. Group.

Whitelegg, Drew. 2007. *Working the Skies: The Fast-Paced, Disorienting World of the Flight Attendant*. New York: New York University Press.

PRIMARY DOCUMENT

Like all commercial airlines, Pan American Airways provided lengthy training manuals to their flight attendants. These manuals specified attire, personal conduct, duties on board, and, as the following document shows, acceptable forms of address and conversation.

Pan American Airways: Traffic Training Section, Latin American Division

Chapter Three: "RULES OF CONVERSATION"

Stewards and Stewardesses should consider conversation as one of the best mediums of rendering Passenger Service, and It is not the Company's intention to bind them with rules and regulations to such an extent that this valuable asset will be restricted in its benefit. However, in order to present a standard policy covering rules and regulations of conversation the following are to be adhered to when talking with the public or Company Personnel.

1. USE OF TITLES

A. With other Crew Members and Company Personnel;

1. When speaking to other Crew Members or Company personnel within earshot of the Public, they should be addressed as follows:

Captain: "Captain Jones".

All other Crew Members: "Mister" or "Miss".

Company Personnel: "Mister", "Miss", or "Mrs.".

2. When speaking of other Crew Members to the passengers their titles are to be used, as follows: "The Captain" or "Captain Williamson", "The First Officer" or "Mr. Johnson", (Not "The Co-Pilot") "The Flight Engineer" or "Mr. Smith", (Not "The Mechanic") "The Radio Officer" or "Mr. Smith". (Not "The Radio Operator"), "The First Stewardess" (Not "The Sto'wardess").

3. When out of earshot of the public or passengers, the Steward/ess may address other Crew Members by their given names. However, as a matter of respect and courtesy, the Captain should always be spoken to as "Captain".

B. With the Passengers and Public:

1. The Steward/ess should as much as possible call the passenger by his/her name. The best Flight Steward/ess will acquaint him/herself as soon as possible with the names of the passengers from the ships papers or in any other way possible. Provided the passenger holds no special title, the use of Mister or Mrs./Miss is correct. In cases where the Steward/ess is not aware of the passenger's name Sir or Madam must be used. Military personnel should be referred to according to their rank. It Is advantageous for the Steward/ess to acquaint him/herself with the meanings of the different military insignia in this respect. Other titles such as Mr. Ambassador, Reverend, Your Holiness, etc. should be used where called for.

2. SUBJECTS TO BE AVOIDED IN CONVERSATION:

(a) Company affairs and policies,
(b) Religion.
(c) Politics.
(d) Risque Subjects,
(e) Race.
(f) Information pertaining to type of Cargo being carried.
(g) Information pertaining to passengers travelling incognito,
(h) Avoid Arguments.

3. MANNER OF SPEAKING

(a) Speak in a well modulated voice.
(b) Speak in the passenger's native language if possible.
(c) Present leading questions.

(d) Avoid giving flippant answers.
(e) Do not place your face too close to passenger's face.
(f) Do not talk about yourself.
(g) Stand slightly bent, as nearly as possible in front of the passenger.
(h) Avoid a kidding and over-fraternizing attitude.

4. CONVERSATION WITH REPRESENTATIVES OF THE PRESS

Flight Stewards/esses are not permitted to give any information to Representatives of the Press whatsoever. If in Miami, refer them to Public Relations. If at a down-the-line Airport, refer them to the Station Manager. If in flight, refer them to the Captain.

Source: Pan American World Airways, Inc. 1945. *Flight Service Training Manual: Traffic Training Section, Latin American Division,* 10–11. https://merrick.library.miami.edu/cdm/compoundobject/collection/asm0341/id/107231/rec/1.

FOREIGN SERVICE OFFICER

While World War II secured the United States' place as the dominant world power, in the aftermath of this devastating war, political realignments reshaped alliances across the globe. During the Cold War (1947–1991), American Foreign Service officers (FSOs) provided services to people all over the world. As employees of the U.S. Department of State, the Foreign Service officer's primary job was to represent the nation's interests. They work in offices in the United States and abroad and are generally considered part of the nation's diplomatic corps. Within the U.S. Department of State, the Foreign Service comprises a number of important positions. Among them, FSOs are the largest group and play the primary role in managing the country's day-to-day foreign relations; small numbers of FSOs also served in other departments and agencies. After passing a rigorous entry examination process and completing training, which may mandate that a candidate learn new languages, Foreign Service officers spend the majority of their career in overseas postings at embassies or consulates. They are often known as generalists, and over the course of their careers, they may work in a number of countries on a range of different issues. A posting usually lasts two to four years, with occasional shorter postings to Washington, D.C.

FSOs share a commitment to the goals of U.S. diplomacy while developing expertise in a special function. Appointed by the president and confirmed by the senate, FSOs are responsible for upholding the Constitution. As representatives of the U.S. government, FSOs convey national policy to officials and the public in their host country. Meanwhile, FSOs communicate important information and policy guidance back to the State Department in Washington, D.C. They are also responsible for a range of activity in host countries, including the protection of American citizens abroad, negotiations on a variety of issues, the execution of U.S. laws, and the presentation of American culture to local populations. In theory, FSOs inform and support the policymaking process in the United States and then advance those policies to the best of their ability overseas. In practice, the relative influence of the State Department in the policymaking process and the amount of trust, support, and reciprocity between Foreign Service and the rest of government have changed over time. In any case, they tend to be skilled in adaptation to foreign cultures, sensitivity to difference, communication, analysis, and negotiation. FSOs are placed in one of five career tracks (now known as cones), which are responsible for different diplomatic tasks. These include public diplomacy, consular affairs, political affairs, management, and economic affairs.

The specific roles of members of the diplomatic corps have evolved throughout history. During the Revolutionary War (1775–1783), the Continental Congress first began appointing diplomatic and consular officers to represent its interests abroad. From 1789, the president held the right to appoint diplomats and consuls, which the Senate then confirmed or blocked. Continuing long-standing precedents in European foreign policy, diplomatic and consular functions were separated: diplomats held a more privileged status as the official intermediaries between sovereign states, and consuls were responsible for supporting U.S. citizens abroad and advancing national commercial interests. Throughout the nineteenth century, U.S. diplomacy struggled to overcome Americans' aversion to federal spending, foreign entanglements, and the perception that diplomacy was an elitist and superfluous activity. But during its first century and a half of existence, the Foreign Service underwent reform and became a more professional—if still somewhat elitist—institution. The diplomatic and consular services were integrated through the Rogers Act of 1924, when the modern U.S. Foreign Service took shape.

The State Department remained weak during World War II (1939–1945). During the first years of the Cold War, the number of FSOs dramatically grew, although they were put under unprecedented scrutiny for alleged communist sympathies. To project American influence abroad, the number of diplomatic posts markedly increased in the second half of the twentieth century from 74 to 168; meanwhile, consular posts were reduced from 179 to 89. In these years, the number of FSOs stationed overseas fell from the historic high of 7,700 in 1950 to fewer than 6,000 for much of the 1970s and 1980s. In the aftermath of the Cold War, there was a lack of FSOs to fill positions around the world. The number would increase through hiring surges to almost 7,400 in 2000, followed by much more active promotion after the terrorist attacks of September 11, 2001, by Secretary of States Colin Powell and, later, Condoleezza Rice.

Into the late twentieth century, the Foreign Service struggled to build a more diverse diplomatic corps that would more accurately reflect the United States' racial and ethnic diversity or its female population. The Foreign Service did not hire its first female FSO, Lucile Atcherson, until 1922 or its first black FSO, Clifton R. Wharton Sr., until 1924. Officers remained predominantly male and white, and numerous FSOs who were suspected of homosexuality were fired during the 1950s. From early in the Cold War, a small group of upper-middle-class Protestant men hailing from elite schools and independent wealth dominated the Foreign Service. In 1949, the Foreign Service's first black and first female ambassadors were appointed: Edward Richard Dudley, who was stationed in Liberia, and Eugenie Moore Anderson, who was stationed in Denmark. However, only a small handful of women and nonwhite men had become FSOs by the 1950s. The Foreign Service retained its negative popular reputation as an elitist club, and public confidence in the importance of its work remained low.

Even amid the civil rights era (1954–1964), there were extraordinary impediments to women and people of color who sought entry to the Foreign Service. These discouraged many from even applying. Of those who did, very few passed the Foreign Service Exam, and once accepted, there were many impediments to an applicant's promotion. For example, until 1971, female FSOs were required to retire if they married.

In the 1960s and 1970s, these practices slowly began to change. Alongside the Women's Action Organization, which worked to support women in U.S. foreign affairs, FSO Alison Palmer was a crucial advocate for gender equity in the Foreign Service. She pursued an influential class-action antidiscrimination suit against the State Department on behalf of all female FSOs from 1976. In response to this and other pressures, a major reform, the Foreign Service Act of 1980, sought to form a diplomatic corps "truly representative of the American people throughout all levels of the Foreign Service."

Today, these processes remain slow. In 1997, Madeleine Albright became the first female secretary of state, and since 2000, two secretaries of state, Condoleezza Rice and Colin Powell, have been people of color. In the 1990s, discrimination based on sexual orientation was prohibited. Founded in 1992 and 2002, respectively, the Pickering Fellowship and Rangel Program recruit Foreign Service Officers from diverse backgrounds. Today, the Foreign Service remains about four-fifths white and two-thirds male, with very small percentages of black, Latino, and Asian diplomats.

Derek Kane O'Leary

See also: *1776–1860:* Diplomat; Intelligencer; *1992–2019:* Spy

FURTHER READING

Ambrose, Stephen E. 2011. *Rise to Globalism: American Foreign Policy since 1938*. New York: Penguin.

Borstelmann, Thomas. 2003. *The Cold War and the Color Line: American Race Relations in the Global Arena*. Cambridge: Harvard University Press.

Gaddis, John Lewis. 2001. *George F. Kennan: An American Life*. New York: W. W. Norton and Co.

Kopp, Harry W., and Charles A. Gillespie. 2011. *Career Diplomacy: Life and Work in the U.S. Foreign Service*. Second Edition. Georgetown: Georgetown University Press.

Moskin, J. Robert. 2013. *American Statecraft: The Story of the U.S. Foreign Service*. New York: St. Martin's Press.

FORESTER

Foresters in the postwar period worked for local, state, or national levels of government, private companies, or semiprivate cooperatives. Understanding the types of organizations that employed foresters gives context to the ways in which forestry was practiced. For instance, some trained foresters worked for timber companies like Weyerhaeuser, where the goal was to acquire forested lands and profitably manage them by harvesting wood to be sent to sawmills and then be used in construction, furniture, and pulp and paper industries. Alternatively, foresters employed by the government often prioritized different kinds of needs alongside profitable timber production. The Forest Reserve Act of 1891 set aside swaths of forested land for national forests. The Transfer Act of 1905 gave control of these reserves to the U.S. Forest Service (USFS). Foresters at the USFS managed national forests by considering timber sales alongside range, watershed, and wildlife and fish management priorities. In the postwar period, professional foresters came to prioritize both old and new considerations in managing national forests.

While the day-to-day tasks of foresters differ by specialty and type of employer, they spend the majority of their time outdoors. Some focus on fire control and others on watershed protection. Some do it all. For example, Forester Leland Berriman worked for the USFS from 1933 to 1965. In the Fall River District, Berriman did a "little bit" of everything, from timber sales and recreation to fire management (Berriman 2004, 5). Many foresters do a variety of activities, including but not limited to tracking timber sales, issuing grazing permits and recreational leases, designating government money for flood control, and investigating insects and diseases. Forester Earl McGowin worked for a private timber company starting in the 1920s. As a child in the 1900s and 1910s, McGowin saw his father wake up early each morning to monitor the local mill. He would also take occasional trips to wholesalers in the South, exporters in Florida, and annual meetings in New Orleans. Like his father, McGowin joined the private forest industries, in the 1920s. And like his father, he woke up early, monitored thousands of acres of timberlands, and cultivated relationships with landowners (McGowin). Another forester in the early twentieth century, Joseph McCaffrey joined the profession because of a desire to be outside. Born in Fulton, New York, in 1896, McCaffrey attended the New York State Ranger School and in 1916 began working for the Laurel River Logging Company, operating a mill in western North Carolina. Each day he oversaw the local logging operations, including operating a Clyde skidder, used to pull cut trees from the cut site to a landing, where they were loaded onto railroad cars and transported to the mill (McCaffrey 2016, 30).

The work of foresters changed during the twentieth century. Before the Second World War (1939–1945), foresters—no matter who employed them—worked to maximize and maintain long-term production of forests by predicting and accounting for future lumber demands. By determining how much timber to extract each year, foresters treated a forest like a crop rather than a mine; just like the farmer's field that lays fallow to regain fertility, forests needed time to grow. Foresters were trained in part by theories of European silviculture (the growing and cultivation of trees) and in part by American schools of forestry, which emphasized technical skills applied to local landscapes, to maximize the long-term health of forests. In this European vision, they worked to create an ideal, ordered, and productive landscape. In this context, harvesting timber was not seen as destructive but as a long-term balancing act.

During the war, unprecedented demand for wood led to increased timber production, especially in national forests. In this context, foresters rushed to embrace intensive forestry as a solution to war shortages. At the same time, foresters inventoried forested lands to determine whether or not present conditions could meet war and postwar demands.

After the war, demand continued unabated. National organizations like the Society of American Foresters, the American Forestry Congress, and the American Forestry Association, often representing profit-making companies, pushed for public aid to industry in the form of cooperative assistant programs. Foresters began assisting industrial-scale lumber companies, small woodland owners, and others by focusing, again, on maximizing harvests to meet demand. Other foresters provided technical reports on fire behavior, how-to manuals on pest control, and recommendations for small woodland owners in the form of publications known as circulars. Concurrently, many private foresters worked to reforest lands. For instance, the Weyerhaeuser Timber Company led the Tree Farm Campaign, in which foresters planted in-demand tree species. At this time, foresters looked to solve complicated problems without fully anticipating the ecological consequences of their management techniques.

The heightened demand of resources during and after World War II and the expansion of transportation systems throughout national forests made the American public aware of the importance of forests and of those who managed them. But with this awareness came scrutiny.

The rise of public activism and concern for the environment brought major changes to professional forestry in the 1960s and 1970s. New broad and powerful laws forced foresters to accommodate environmental directives. The Multiple-Sustained Yield Act of 1960 required that national forests be managed with an eye toward outdoor recreation, alongside range, timber, watershed, wildlife, and fish management priorities. The Wilderness Act of 1964 designated specific natural areas within the spaces as worth protecting. The National Environmental Policy Act of 1970 signed by President Richard Nixon required federal agencies to write environmental impact statements before undertaking activities that would significantly affect the natural environment. The Endangered Species Act of 1973 and the National Forest Management Act of 1976 required the Forest Service to maintain viable wildlife populations. Foresters now needed to consider these legal requirements in addition to their old practices. Altogether, foresters still considered national forests as sources of wood as well as sources of rangeland, watershed protection, recreational space, and habitats for wildlife.

Since the 1940s, foresters have worked to accommodate the diverse and often conflicting demands of national forests. The profession of foresters has changed and will continue to change as Americans' views of forests shift. As such, training in forestry has broadened to include coursework in ecology, biodiversity, recreation, conservation, and land and water management.

Lauren Ayers

See also: Scientist; *1861–1914:* Logger; *1915–1945:* Firefighter

FURTHER READING

Arnold, R. Keith. 2016. "An Interview with R. Keith Arnold." Transcript of oral history conducted in August 1992 by Harold Steen, Oral History Collection of the Forest History Society, Durham, North Carolina. https://foresthistory.org/wp-content/uploads/2016/12/Arnold.pdf.

Berriman, Leland. 2004. "Leland Berriman Oral History Transcript." Transcript of oral history conducted in June 2004 by John Fiske, United States Forest Service Region 5 Oral History Project, UC Berkeley. http://digitalassets.lib.berkeley.edu/roho/ucb/text/berriman_leland.pdf.

Bramwell, Lincoln. 2014. *Forest Management for All: A History of State & Private Forestry in the US Forest Service.* Durham: Forest History Society.

Drew, Harry. 1979. *Weyerhaeuser Company: A History of People, Land, and Growth—Eastern Oregon Region.* Klamath Falls: Weyerhaeuser Company.

Hays, Samuel. 2007. *Wars in the Woods: The Rise of Ecological Forestry in America*. Pittsburgh: University of Pittsburgh Press.
McCaffrey, J. E. 2016. "Go South Young Man." Transcript of oral history conducted in 1974 by Elwood R. Maunder, Oral History Collection of the Forest History Society, Durham. https://foresthistory.org/wp-content/uploads/2016/12/McCaffreyOHI.pdf.
McGowin, Earl M. 2016. "Oral History Interview with Earl M. McGowin." Transcript of oral history conducted in March 1976 by Elwood R. Maunder, Oral History Collection of the Forest History Society, Durham. https://foresthistory.org/wp-content/uploads/2016/12/McCaffreyOHI.pdf.
Steen, Harold. 2006. *The Chiefs Remember: The Forest Service, 1952–2001*. Durham: Forest History Society.

HOTELIER

Hoteliers are owners or managers of lodging establishments—hotels and motels as well as resort complexes and other businesses offering overnight accommodations. The duties of hoteliers depend on the nature of their business. Independent hoteliers are those who operate a private establishment not affiliated with a chain or franchise. These hoteliers must organize and supervise all aspects of their business, including finances, marketing and advertising, supervising other workers, and assisting with customers. Hoteliers who work for larger hotel chains or franchises operate similarly to independent hoteliers, but the chain or franchise hotelier will often have to follow branding and decorum guidelines and business practices as directed by corporate preferences and bylaws.

Americans have always patronized lodging houses, though the form has dramatically changed from earlier days. During the 1920s and 1930s and continuing well into the 1960s, many Americans favored motor hotels, or motels, while business travelers and urban dwellers patronized larger establishments in cities, the hotels, places like the Waldorf-Astoria in New York, the Sir Francis Drake in San Francisco, and the Palmer House in Chicago. While motels often provided rooms organized around a central parking area, large hotels had hundreds of rooms, bar and dining facilities, and often luxurious lobbies where patrons could rest after a day's work. In the early postwar period, motels dominated American lodging facilities: in 1964, there were over 61,000 motels (of 64,000 lodging establishments) in the United States. But also at this time, the lodging industry began a transformation, resulting in a concentration of the industry: in 1972, less than a decade later, there were fewer total establishments—approximately 58,700—but they had revenues of more than twice of 1963, and a decade later, by 1982, revenues had increased almost another threefold. Chain and franchises also grew in popularity, to almost 70 percent of all motels and hotels, over the private "mom-and-pop" business that typified earlier patterns within the lodging industry. The job of the hotelier changed along with these transformations within the industry.

Among the most important duties of an independent hotelier is supervising the large staff of cleaning and maintenance workers. Hoteliers must also supervise the hiring and training of these workers. Every morning, a hotelier surveys the daily room inventory, ensures that the cleaning staff is at work, audits front desk operations, and monitors sales staff. In large establishments, hoteliers generally have subordinates who supervise the operations of each division: sales, cleaning, maintenance, food and bar service, and customer relations. Hoteliers determine pricing schemes for different services such as room prices for different classes or hotel rooms and days of the week, determining discounts for large groups (such as tours or conventions), and working with the food services division heads to set prices for meals.

In the period before the internet, marketing skills were critical to an independent hotelier. Hoteliers entered into complex agreements with sports teams, professional organizations, craft and hobby associations, trade shows, alumni groups, and others to sell the establishment's services and guarantee full sales, or in the language of the hotelier, full occupancy rates in group sales. Hoteliers and their division subordinates created special services for frequent customers, or in the case of American Express corporate card members, for credit card holders, including guaranteed booking, precheck-in, and easy checkout services. Complementary turn-down services might be offered as well. Many hotels offered a segregated women's-only floor for single women travelers, though this was often impossible for motel owners. Independent hoteliers were responsible for all such business aspects of their hotels.

Hoteliers who are franchise owners or who work at chain hotels have higher marketing expenses in the form of fees paid to the chain or franchise for the right to a hotel's or motel's brand. Unlike independent hotels, however, large hotel chains generally have regional or district managers and other personnel who assist franchise operators and local managers with daily managerial duties. Advertising and production of merchandise and promotional materials were usually coordinated with central offices, so these hoteliers had fewer direct sales responsibilities. Hoteliers working within the franchise and chain system also received access to centralized reservation and purchasing systems, employee training manuals, and insurance coverage. The duties of hoteliers within these systems more solidly focused on customer relations: ensuring that patrons were satisfied with services received, taking complaints, and monitoring cleaning and maintenance personnel. Basic management decisions were reported to the district or regional manager, who assisted franchise owners and chain operators with their business operations.

The model of the Days Inn corporation, founded in 1970 by hotelier Cecil Day, illustrates the power of marketing to the leisure travelers who tended to patronize chain lodging establishments: offering discounts to students, sports teams, government and military personnel, "simple saver" rates for prepaid reservations, and other financial benefits. This marketing model was developed at the corporate level to target the "80% of travelers" who are price sensitive, and in fact, the corporate offices generally prohibited individual hoteliers from engaging in any marketing activities. Days Inns' corporate business philosophy was to create establishments that travelers recognized for their uniformity and reasonable rates, thus creating brand loyalty.

All hoteliers needed to be informed about local regulations, generally known as "Innkeepers Laws," at the state level, which regulated such things as check-in and check-out times, maximum daily room rates, and age of patron at check-in. Some hoteliers required young couples to present their identification or marriage certificate in efforts to regulate social mores. Other hoteliers worked in resort facilities, such as Disneyland (1955), which had their own rules and regulations regarding customer behavior.

After 1965, changes in immigration laws led to new opportunities for immigrants from India, particularly those from Gujarat state, to enter the hotelier field. Members of the largest clan from this state, typically denoted by the surname Patel, took advantage of business investment provisions within immigration law to obtain immigrant visas by purchasing distressed hotels, rehabilitating them, and operating them. Like immigrants of other eras, these Gujarati entrepreneurs were willing to work long hours at marginal profitability for a chance to become Americans. As one immigrant motel entrepreneur recalled, a motel "is easy to run. You don't need fluent English, just the will to work long hours. And, it's a business that comes with a house—you don't have to buy a separate house" (Turkel 2002, 2). By the year 2000, Indian immigrants owned nearly 50 percent of economy motels in the United States, making their story as hoteliers one of the successes of American immigrants.

Nancy Quam-Wickham

See also: Travel Agent; *1992–2019:* Housekeeper

FURTHER READING

Henkin, Shephard. 2000. *Opportunities in Hotel and Motel Management Careers.* New York: McGraw Hill.

Lundberg, Donald. E. 1989. *The Hotel and Restaurant Business.* New York: Van Nostrand Reinhold.

Okrant, Mark. 2012. *No Vacancy: The Rise, Demise, and Reprise of America's Motels.* Concord: Plaidswede.

Sharp, Isidore. 2009. *Four Seasons: The Story of a Business Philosophy.* New York: Penguin.

Turkel, Stanley. 2002. "From Rags to Riches." http://ishc.com/wp-content/uploads/From-Ragas-To-Riches-Part-I.pdf.

INDUSTRIAL HYGIENIST

Industrial hygienists are committed to protecting the health and safety of workers and the community at large by using science and engineering to evaluate, control, and prevent health and safety hazards in the workplace and also eliminate hazards that could affect the community and the environment. Industrial hygienists evaluate a wide range of hazards, including diseases, chemical exposures, physical agents (noise, temperature, and vibration), and ergonomic and repetitive motion hazards. After the scientific assessment, an industrial hygienist uses his or her "art" to recommend control measures and work practices that would eliminate or minimize the hazards that can result in injuries, illnesses, and death on the job.

In the United States, Dr. Alice Hamilton conducted the first field studies of men and women workers in factories and mines in the early 1900s that proved there was a direct correlation between workers' illnesses and their exposure to toxic chemicals and other hazards at work. In 1911, the first states passed workers compensation laws to provide financial compensation to injured and ill workers, largely due to the work that Dr. Hamilton began and championed. In 1913, New York and Ohio became the first states to establish industrial hygiene programs, and by 1948, all fifty states had government industrial hygiene programs.

In 1914, the American Public Health Association established an Occupational Health and Safety Section, which was followed by the founding of the American Conference of Governmental Industrial Hygienists in 1938 and the American Industrial Hygiene Association in 1939.

But in 1970, there were still more than thirty-five workers being killed on the job every day (fourteen thousand a year) and thousands more killed by occupational diseases every year. Thus, Congress passed the Coal Mine Safety Act and the Occupational Safety and Health Act (Timeline). This legislation, signed by the president, established the Occupational Safety and Health (OSHA) and Mine Safety and Health (MSHA) Administrations. The passage of these laws and the formation of these agencies led to the enormous expansion of the industrial hygienist profession.

Whether industrial hygienists work for private companies or government agencies, they use the same tools to identify and evaluate hazards in the workplace that can produce injuries and illnesses to workers. These include activities such as a walk-though survey to inspect each section of the workplace and the machines that are in use; using instruments to determine the concentration of chemicals and dust in the air that workers breathe; using monitors to measure the level of noise in the workplace; interviewing workers and supervisors about plant operations; reviewing written information about the chemicals in use; and the employer's safety program of regular site inspections, correction of identified hazards, and worker training.

Based on the hazard assessments, industrial hygienists provide recommendations for eliminating or controlling the hazards through engineering controls (like using less-toxic chemicals or installing ventilation and machine guards), administrative controls (like reducing the time of workers' exposure to hazards), and personal protective equipment. Industrial hygienists working for government regulatory agencies have the power to require employers to implement control measures in compliance with state and federal laws.

Industrial hygienists do their work not only in industrial workplaces like factories, oil refineries, or mines but also in hospitals and healthcare facilities, schools and universities, retail stores, transit systems and public utilities, construction sites, and farms.

Likewise, the kinds of hazards that industrial hygienists evaluate are not just industrial hazards like airborne chemicals and mineral dusts, unguarded machinery, and noise in factories and mines but also bloodborne pathogens like hepatitis and HIV/AIDS, infectious diseases like tuberculosis, indoor air-quality issues, reproductive health hazards for men and women, pesticide exposures, radiation and radon gas, ergonomic and repetitive motion hazards, and exposures to hazardous wastes.

Industrial hygienists can also conduct scientific research to provide data for new government regulations or develop new methods of detecting and preventing risks. They often conduct trainings with managers and workers about occupational hazards as well as educating the public about community health and environmental risks.

There are three phases of inspections: preparing for the site visit, conducting the workplace inspection and monitoring, and then drawing conclusions and developing recommendations and safety programs based on the industrial hygiene inspection. This means that the industrial hygienist, before arriving at the work site, will research the kinds of hazards commonly present at the specific type of workplace being visited, calibrate and charge the equipment to monitor the air and noise levels, prepare cameras and video equipment to film work processes, develop checklists for walk-through surveys and lists of documents to be reviewed or requested on site, and prepare questions for interviews with workers and supervisors.

After the onsite inspection, the industrial hygienist will analyze the results of any monitoring of airborne chemicals, temperature, and noise; review the photos and video taken on site; go over the notes of interviews; and examine the safety program documents from the workplace.

Industrial hygienists stationed at a specific facility or within a single company will continually be visiting the worksite, overseeing ongoing safety programs to evaluate hazards and control the identified hazards, and conducting training and educational activities.

Industrial hygienists can come from many backgrounds, including biologists, chemists, engineers, lab technicians, doctors, and nurses with bachelor's degrees in those fields. The standard graduate degree for industrial hygienists is a university-level master of science or master of public health. The industrial hygiene graduate program curriculum includes prerequisites and adapted courses in chemistry, biology, health physics, biostatistics, epidemiology, toxicology, use of industrial hygiene monitoring equipment and laboratory analysis, mechanical engineering for hazard controls, and hazardous waste management.

A professional certification from the American Board of Industrial Hygiene is frequently sought by practicing industrial hygienists in the United States. There are comparable professional certifications in other parts of the world, where industrial hygiene is known as "occupational hygiene" everywhere outside of the United States.

Garrett Brown

See also: Machine Operator; *1915–1945:* Cannery Worker; Garment Worker; Textile Worker; Warehouse Worker; *1992–2019:* Machinist; Package Handler; Supply Chain Logistician

FURTHER READING

Alston, Frances, Emily J. Millikin, and Willie Piispanen. 2018. *Industrial Hygiene: Improving Worker Health through an Operational Risk Approach*. Boca Raton: CRC Press.

Harris, Michael K. 2000. *Essential Resources for Industrial Hygiene: A Compendium of Current Practice Standards and Guidelines*. Fairfax, VA: AIHA.

Nims, Debra. 1999. *Basics of Industrial Hygiene*. Hoboken: John Wiley & Sons.

"Timeline of OSHA's 40 Year History." n.d. Occupational Safety and Health Administration, United States Department of Labor. https://www.osha.gov/osha40/timeline.html.

PRIMARY DOCUMENT

The following document illustrates the role of industrial hygienists in determining the cause of workplace injuries and deaths. It is a federal Occupational Health and Safety inspection report for a workplace incident at Imperial Foods, Inc., of Raleigh, North Carolina. On September 3, 1991, workers at a poultry slaughterhouse in Hamlet, North Carolina, were repairing equipment when a malfunction occurred. The OSHA industrial hygienists who investigated this incident later filed this report, which resulted 83 separate workplace safety violations and a fine of $808,150.

At approximately 8:15 a.m. on September 3, 1991, maintenance employees were attempting to repair and replace a leaking hydraulic line in the process room of the main plant. During the repair operation, the incoming hydraulic line separated from its coupling at a point approximately 60 inches above the concrete floor and began to discharge hydraulic fluid at high pressure (800 to 1,200 psi). This high pressure and subsequent flow resulted in hydraulic fluid being sprayed against the floor and onto the nearby natural gas-fueled cooker, which was fully operational. The cooker's normal operating temperature was at least 350 degrees. No lockout/tagout procedures were being followed during the repair. Fire and smoke were produced when the hydraulic fluid contacted the cooker, resulting in the rapid dispersal of combustion products throughout most of the plant. Employees #1 through #24 were killed. (Employee #25 was also killed, but should be referenced in inspection #18552208.) All other employees (#26 through #88) were hospitalized for their injuries except Employees #67, #68, #78, #79, #80, #81, #82, #84, #85, #86, #87, and #88, who were treated and released. Employee evacuation from the building was hindered by locked exterior doors and inadequate means of egress.

Source: Occupational Safety and Health Administration. 1991. Accident Report Detail 170073035, Numerous Employees Killed or Injured in Plant Fire. Event Date 9/3/1991. https://www.osha.gov/pls/imis/accidentsearch.accident_detail?id=170073035.

INTERIOR AND INDUSTRIAL DESIGNER

Industrial designers and interior designers are distinct professions with different areas of responsibility, but in many ways they developed parallel to each other and have similar systems of training and education, work environments, and professional duties. While both professions have their origins in some of the earliest civilizations, in the postwar United States, architects and interior designers complemented each other's work, while the occupation of industrial designer grew more closely from industrial production processes. In the latter case, for instance, industrial designers and engineers worked closely to create more efficient automobile designs, ones that appealed to customers' tastes while also accommodating the many engineering and operational requirements of a modern automobile. Both interior and industrial designers work to incorporate art and functionality—the basic principles of design—into their work.

Industrial and interior design includes the processes through which people manipulate their environments to achieve desired outcomes. The practice is a fundamental human activity that predates written language, agriculture, and urban settlement. Design became increasingly professionalized and specialized during the Industrial Revolution with several distinct but related fields of design emerging by the early twentieth century. Industrial design and interior design developed as two of the fields most concerned with the design of three-dimensional objects and spaces, with industrial designers primarily creating products and interior designers primarily creating and designing living and working spaces such as homes, office buildings, and the items contained within them. An interior designer, for instance, may create a medical office space that promotes calm by incorporating specific elements, such as blue and indigo spectrum colors, to reduce patient anxiety and stress.

Design sits at the intersection of art, engineering, and business. It is interdisciplinary, which means it pulls from many different fields of study. Designers determine the look of objects and spaces, but they are more than just stylists. Designers are visual thinkers, communicators, and problem solvers—most designers work out their concepts and communicate their ideas primarily through sketches and drawings. Designers work closely with their customers, be it an individual family seeking to update its furniture and home décor or engineers and managers at an industrial plant that, for example, produces plastic containers for a variety of uses. Many other fields of business are not as visually oriented, so designers must be able to translate their images into words to be able to communicate with others. Designers are also intimately engaged with the material world and must know the characteristics and properties of a wide range of natural and synthetic materials and various manufacturing processes. As designers have professionalized over this period, the language that they use to communicate their work to others—known as design discourse—has shifted as well. In the first decades of the twentieth century, industrial designers often used the language of engineering to communicate with others. Since the mid-twentieth century, however, designers have incorporated insights from psychology, sociology, ecology, ergonomics, and many other fields into their research, processes, and designs. Empathy is a key professional attribute of designers and is central to many design processes used today.

Industrial designers work with manufacturers to create the objects that populate homes, stores, and workplaces. These objects are usually mass produced by machines using industrial materials and methods rather than being unique, one-of-a-kind, handmade items. Industrial designers determine the appearance of an object, including its shape, color, and any pattern or decoration, as well as its function, the materials and manufacturing methods used to make it, and the experience of its user. In the postwar years, plastics offered industrial designers new materials to make housewares, furniture, and lightweight, portable electronics. In the 1940s, Charles Eames developed new ways to mold plywood, which led to him to create his iconic Eames chairs, which arrived on the American market in 1946. While it was possible to be an industrial designer without a specialized academic degree in the middle of the twentieth century, by the turn of the twenty-first century, a bachelor's degree in a design field—preferably industrial design—is increasingly necessary, and a master's degree is often recommended to advance into design management.

Some industrial designers work directly for the corporations that manufacture their designs, usually as part of a design department that works closely with sales and marketing, production, and other stakeholders in the company to bring profitable and useful objects to market. Other industrial designers work as outside experts for design firms and consultancies that provide design services for many different corporate clients. Some industrial designers may specialize in a specific subfield like automobile design or toy design, while others may specialize in inclusive or sustainable design methodologies or develop the expertise to focus on improving the quality of all kinds of designed objects for specific groups, such as people with arthritis. In all cases, industrial designers work with a variety of individuals across disciplines, including engineers, branding and marketing experts, graphic designers, user-experience designers, and interface designers, as well as users and manufacturers, to refine their ideas, develop their concepts, and bring their designs to market.

Interior designers are responsible for creating spaces with an emphasis on human use and experience. The activities of an interior designer can range from interior architecture, including the layout and uses of spaces and the location of walls, doors, and windows, to interior decoration, including the selection and arrangement of furniture, finishes, textiles, and decorative objects within an architectural frame. Interior designers in the 1950s and 1960s promoted the style of modernism that privileged function while rejecting useless ornamentation, widely regarded as the most important aesthetic concept of the twentieth century. The wide range of activities that fall under the category of interior design allows for a variety of entry points into the profession, and licensing requirements, if any, are determined by the individual states. Many states require interior designers to hold either an associate's or a bachelor's degree in interior design and have several years of experience working under a licensed designer, while other states have no formal education or training requirements. Interior designers work in a variety of environments, including in architectural firms, in interior design firms, and as independent creative entrepreneurs and merchants, and some interior designers specialize in a particular sector of the market, such as residential, hotel and restaurant, retail, education, or healthcare design. Many interior designers also gain access to fabrics, furnishings, and other merchandise that is not available to the general public—it is only available "to the trade"—and sell these goods to their clients at a mark-up as part of their business.

While some interior designers create spaces that are duplicated many times over—particularly in hospitality design (like hotels and restaurants)—interiors are intimately tailored to the individual needs and preferences of their intended inhabitants and are often quite personal. In addition, interior designers are also responsible for ensuring the health and safety of the people who use their spaces and must know and follow building standards and codes, including those associated with the Americans with Disabilities Act (ADA), after this act was passed in 1990. Later, sustainability became a crucial consideration for interior designers, and knowledge of green building systems such as Leadership in Energy and Environmental Design (LEED), defined in 2000, is increasingly important to advance in the field.

Designers shape environments and construct the spaces people inhabit and the objects they use every day. Designers must be creative, curious, inquisitive, and empathetic, always questioning the way things are and asking how they could be better for people. Design is a unique field in that it utilizes a powerful process to define and understand a problem, develop potential solutions to that problem, refine those solutions using collaborative research and creative exploration, and then implement that solution in the real world.

Tom Tredway

See also: Architect

FURTHER READING

Gura, Judith. 2000. "'A Woman's Place...'? Women Interior Designers Part Two: 1950–2000." In *Women Designers in the USA, 1900–2000: Diversity and Difference.* New York: Bard Graduate Center.

Kirkham, Pat, and Penny Sparke. 2000. "'A Woman's Place...'? Women Interior Designers Part One: 1900–1950." In *Women Designers in the USA, 1900–2000: Diversity and Difference.* New York: Bard Graduate Center.

Sparke, Penny. 2018. "Introduction." In *Industrial Design in the Modern Age.* New York: Rizzoli Electra.

JANITOR

Janitors are employed as caretakers to a building and are responsible for its cleaning and maintenance. Too often viewed as nonessential or expendable, janitors—also called custodians—play a significant role in most businesses and establishments. Part of the expanding service sector, janitorial service consists of a variety of tasks and is done in a variety of locations, including offices, factories, hospitals, and public and commercial buildings.

In about 1900, a janitor's official workday began at 5:00 a.m. and would end around 10:00 p.m. Most janitors had no days off and made less than twenty dollars a month, and a single complaint could result in the worker being fired. By the 1920s, conditions continued to be poor, with janitors often working over eighty hours per week. Since the 1920s, janitors have worked in many different institutional contexts. Cleaning consists of disposing of waste, dusting, washing, and sweeping and polishing floors, among other duties. Janitors are also responsible for cleaning bathrooms, kitchens, and other high-use interior spaces. Cleaning tasks are often completed with the aid of cleaning products, including ammonia, soaps, floor strippers and waxes, caustic cleaning agents, and other chemicals. Janitors use both hand-propelled tools like brooms and mops, as well as electric cleaning items like vacuums and floor buffers. They routinely lock up a building and night and reopen it in the morning. Sometimes maintenance and repair work is also part of the job, as is starting up the furnaces in schools and office buildings at the beginning of a day. Most janitors work indoors. Until recently, janitors worked relatively autonomously, ordering their tasks themselves and developing their own procedures, but this has changed significantly in recent years.

Cleaning is one of the faster-growing occupations and one of the most common for both men and women, although a larger portion of the workers are women. Many janitors today are people of color, while, historically, it was a job often done by immigrants. Cleaners are among the lowest-paid workers in the American workforce. They are often employed on a part-time, contractual, or informal basis. They often tend to be older compared with other workers. Many entered into the occupation at a young age and continue working past the customary age of retirement due to contingent and informal work arrangements. Many undocumented workers have found jobs as cleaners.

Subcontacting positions increased during the 1980s and 1990s. This occurs when instead of directly hiring people to clean a building, whereby a janitor would be considered a full employee and receive medical care, vacation, and sick leave, the employer chooses to contract a firm to do so. Today, nearly one million people are employed by janitorial service subcontractors. Despite similar skill levels as in-house workers, subcontracted workers tend to make significantly lower wages, receive fewer benefits, and have lower rates of unionization. As a result of this trend, the average wage for janitors has fallen. Subcontracted cleaners are more likely to be part time, Latino, and female than in-house workers. This has contributed to the rapid shift of the workforce from immigrants, African Americans, and whites to Latinos.

Cleaning has always been a job rife with occupational hazards. As a profession, janitors have had poorer health than other workers, including high cancer rates. Repeated movement and moderate bending can result in musculoskeletal disorders. Cleaning is the profession with the most shoulder and neck pain complaints. Due to contact with cleaning agents such as detergents and disinfectants, respiratory and dermatologic problems may arise. Cleaners also often work evening or night shifts to not interfere with activities carried out in the same spaces. There is an increased risk of violence if they are alone and in isolated areas. Cleaners in medical laboratories and hospitals particularly have the potential to come into contact with infectious diseases. Beyond the physical hazards, cleaners experience job dissatisfaction due to the monotony of the job and limited potential for promotions.

Unions have represented janitors for decades, with Service Employees' International Union (SEIU) founded by seven small janitor unions in 1921. Diversity helped build early janitors' unions. The Chicago Flat Janitors' union, today part of SEIU, had both black and white members at a time when most unions either barred African Americans or had segregated locals.

Unions have placed high priority on organizing low-wage service sector workers, including janitors, in recent decades. The Justice for Janitors campaign by SEIU is a successful bottom-up union organizing campaign conducted in multiple places around the country, characterized by a high level of participation from rank-and-file workers and public demonstrations. Started in the 1980s, Justice for Janitors has been seen as a resounding success as it helped organize new workers at a time of challenge for the labor movement. It is "hailed as one of the most innovative and comprehensive campaigns designed by an International union" (Savage 2006, 653).

However, the 1980s saw a decline in union members as subcontracting grew. Nationally, SEIU committed 30 percent of its resources to organizing, taking the lead in organizing janitors and healthcare workers. Organizing by geographic area rather than worksite and showing a commitment to representing immigrants, one of the most successful campaigns involved Local 3999 in Los Angeles. In 1987, at the start of the campaign, only 10 percent of the Los Angeles building service janitors were unionized. The number jumped to 90 percent by 1995. Many involved in the Los Angles campaign were women, immigrants, and Latinos, groups traditionally considered difficult to organize. Campaigns were sometimes met with resistance, such as when Los Angeles police attacked and arrested striking Century City janitors during a peaceful march in May 1990. The 2000 film *Bread and Roses* has helped bring the Justice for Janitors story to a wide audience. Justice for Janitors rendered an often unnoticed group of workers visible, helped diversify union membership, and improved working conditions and pay for cleaners.

Amanda Walter

See also: *1861–1914:* Waste Collector; *1992–2019:* Housekeeper

FURTHER READING

Charles, Luenda E., Dana Loomis, and Zewditu Demissie. 2009. "Occupational Hazards Experienced by Cleaning Workers and Janitors: A Review of Epidemiological Literature." *Work* 34: 105–116.

Dube, Arindrajit, and Ethan Kaplan. 2010. "Does Outsourcing Reduce Wages in the Low-Wage Service Occupations?: Evidence from Janitors and Guards." *Industrial and Labor Relations Review* 63: 287–306.

Savage, Lydia. 2006. "Justice for Janitors: Scales of Organizing and Representing Workers." *Antipode* 38, no. 3: 645–666.
Stillman, Don. 2010. *Stronger Together: The Story of SEIU*. White River Junction: Chelsea Green Publishing.
Zlolniski, Christian. 2006. *Janitors, Street Vendors and Activists: The Lives of Mexican Immigrants in Silicon Valley*. Berkley: University of California Press.

LIBRARIAN

Librarians are professionals with specialist training in literacy and information sciences who work in public and private libraries. They staff information centers, order books and magazines (among other materials), organize events such as story hours for children, sponsor reading and essay competitions, and work in other ways to promote literacy, reading, and learning. Libraries today are legally obligated by federal law to provide a physical environment for learning to everyone, regardless of race, class, or gender. One of the important duties of a librarian is to promote literacy and nurture community growth. As education professionals, librarians are acutely aware of the role of literacy in expanding opportunities for personal development and community growth. A librarian generally works in an institution, such as a library or school, in an office or public setting. They serve library patrons and also inventory collections, create bibliographies and cataloging schemes, organize library resources, bind books, and pursue professional learning in new forms of literacy education.

In the period after World War II, librarianship as a profession grew remarkably, with the labor force increasing six-fold between 1950 and 1990, as American cities and towns expanded their services to include educating their citizenry, and the federal government provided resources for rural and impoverished communities to build public libraries. Most librarians were women, giving these workers uncommon opportunities to actively better their communities. Librarians endorsed the tenet of a citizen's "right to knowledge," the idea that libraries provided resources so that patrons could learn about all sides of a controversial issue. Libraries, and the librarians who staffed them, played a central role in community development during this era. In the 1950s and early 1960s, for example, many local librarians helped to convert their institutions into civil defense centers, providing information about the dangers of exposure to radioactive fallout in the case of nuclear war; local libraries were often designated atomic shelters. At the same time, librarians helped to educate Americans about communism, as well as the dangers of both totalitarianism and the anticommunism of McCarthyism. A national Get Out the Vote campaign in 1952 emphasized the role that librarians played in voter registration and participation. Many librarians also promoted racial equality; the

Houston Public Library was among the first southern institutions to adopt integrated services in 1953.

Not all Americans, however, had access to libraries and the resources contained within them. Before 1895, public library services were sparse in southern regions and in the North, almost exclusively served white Americans. Many librarians worked in private libraries as the first public library, the Boston Free Library, opened only in 1854. The nation's first public library organized to serve African Americans, however, the Louisville (Kentucky) Western Branch Library, did not open until 1905. The first National Library Week, organized by the American Libraries Association (ALA), was held in 1958, while the ALA only began to advocate for well-equipped public school libraries in 1963. The rapid expansion of public libraries as community institutions, and of school libraries as institutions integral to equality in public education, largely occurred in the twentieth century. The role of librarians expanded with these public community libraries in the post–World War II years as public libraries began to offer a range of community resources. In turn, the work of librarians changed as well as they took on the roles of educators and activists for the public they served.

Librarians' efforts to promote both access and racial equality during the postwar era is testament to these workers' activism and efforts to improve their communities. The role of African American women librarians is central to this story. Despite "separate but equal" laws, African American librarians made many improvements for African American education in circumstances where access to materials was separate but in no way equal to that of whites. These same women greatly contributed to the eventual desegregation of libraries. African American librarians created a place where African Americans could access information, check out books, and learn to read. Financial assistance from outside the African American community, such as from the Carnegie Foundation and the Julius Rosenwald Fund, provided support to build the first libraries for people of color and created opportunities for female African American librarians. Many librarians volunteered with social and political organizations, like the Young Women's Christian Association (YWCA) and local chapters of the National Association for the Advancement of Colored People (NAACP), and, later, for voter registration and other activist causes. To improve citizens' access to libraries, some librarians organized traveling libraries, often called Bookmobiles, where they brought resources to African American patrons excluded from segregated libraries in their own communities. In 1962, Congress passed the Library Services and Construction Act, which provided funding to expand libraries into many underserved minority, rural, and working-class communities throughout the nation.

The career of librarian Eliza Atkins Gleason provides an example of the struggles of African American women librarians in a segregated society, as well as the changes their work could bring to all Americans. In 1941, Gleason became the first African American to receive her PhD in Library Science from the University of Chicago. In an era before the personal computer and the internet, information resources were found most commonly in libraries, and Gleason knew that literacy and knowledge empowered black Americans. After she received her PhD, Gleason was dedicated to developing outstanding library services and providing African Americans training in librarianship; she established the first library science department and program for African American students at the historically black institution Atlanta University in the 1940s. In 1978, she became a member of the board of the Chicago Public Library.

South Carolina public activist Ethel Martin Bolden is another example of the librarian-activist. After receiving her master's in library science from Atlanta University, she offered workshops around the nation, educating librarians on ways to improve library services in African American schools. In 1968, Bolden accepted a teacher-librarian position at Dreher High School, a newly desegregated school in Columbia, South Carolina. She was the first African American woman to lead a school library in a predominantly white school in the South. Another community activist librarian, Pura Belpré, was the first Puerto Rican-born librarian in New York City, where she organized Spanish-language book collections and children's story hours, provided space for meetings of Puerto Rican community organizations, hosted adult education classes, and organized celebrations of traditional Puerto Rican holidays in the Harlem and Bronx libraries where she worked.

The backgrounds of Gleason, Bolden, and Belpré illustrate the remarkable ways in which librarians worked to increase access and equality in public spaces. Librarians helped to educate Americans by providing information resources to patrons. In the postwar era, though, librarians did so much more as they organized voter registration drives, provided classes in citizenship for immigrants, arranged for help to obtain disaster relief funds, and strove to provide equal opportunities for all. Librarians educated their patrons about the dangers of McCarthyism and nuclear war and, during the civil rights movement, fought for the inclusion of black history books in school curricula. These pioneer female librarians labored to provide equal access to library materials and information to all Americans as they sought to eventually desegregate the libraries in which they worked.

Bree'ya Brown

See also: College Professor; Community Organizer; *1861–1914:* Teacher; *1992–2019:* Museum Curator

FURTHER READING

Battles, David M. 2009. *The History of Public Library Access for African Americans in the South, or Leaving Behind the Plow*. Lanham: The Scarecrow Press, Inc.

Gleason, Eliza Atkins. 1941. *The Southern Negro and the Public Library: A Study of the Government and Administration of Public Library Service to Negros in the South.* Chicago: The University of Chicago Press.

Gubert, Betty K. 1993. "Sadie Peterson Delaney: Pioneer Bibliotherapist." *American Libraries* 24: 2, 124–125,127,129–130.

Harris, Rachel Davis. 1917. "Work with Children at the Colored Branch of the Louisville Free Public Library." In *Library Work with Children: Reprints of Papers and Addresses*, edited by Alice I. Hazeltine, 60–66. White Plains: H. W. Wilson Co.

Speaking of History: The Words of South Carolina Librarians. School of Library Sciences Collection, University of South Carolina. http://www.libsci.sc.edu/histories/oralhistory/.

Sutton, Allison M. 2005. "Bridging the Gap in Early Library Education History for African Americans: The Negro Teacher-Librarian Training Program (1936–1939)." *The Journal of Negro Education* 74: 2, 138–150

MACHINE OPERATOR

Machine operators use machines to make or package goods. After World War II, the modern mine and mill, chemical plant, and factory all utilized an enormous number of semiskilled workers whose sole job it was to stand or sit at a machine and operate it. These operators ran machines that filled large, heavy paper bags with minerals, drilled holes in stainless-steel plates, and shaped table legs on industrial lathes. Machine operators worked in most kinds of manufacturing and were positions created by the process of industrialization. Frederick Winslow Taylor's "scientific management" and efficiency studies evaluated workers' discrete movements and led to time-motion studies that rationalized individual manufacturing processes. With these management techniques, industries divided the manufacturing process into discrete steps and trained unskilled workers to perform only one or two tasks, leading to the deskilling of work. Machines replaced some workers, but others were needed to operate these machines. By their nature, all operators worked with machines that accomplished some task, though there are great distinctions between the kinds of work—and the skills needed to operate that machine—among workers known as machine operators.

An unskilled machine operator may have to do little more than monitor a machine and remove products as they are created. Consider bagging-machine operators in mineral-mining operations. A machine operator in this environment had to attend to a bagging station, a machine that simultaneously filled four hundred-pound bags of coal dust. The machine operator securely placed the empty bags on the nozzles and then activated a switch that started the flow of coal dust into the bags. As each bag was filled, it was ejected from the filling area; as this happened, the machine operator quickly attached new bags onto each nozzle. This position required some basic skill but also attentiveness. A distracted or sleepy operator might not notice that a bag had been ejected and fail to quickly attach another to one of the nozzles, leading to overflow of the product and excess exposure to silica dust. In fact, bagging-machine operators had the highest exposure to coal dust in the entire mining industry during the 1970s and 1980s—leading to cases of silicosis, a deadly lung disease.

Other machine operators operate basic machinery requiring few skills in less-hazardous conditions. Motion-picture projectionists operated machines that projected images from film onto movie theater screens for the enjoyment of theatergoers. Sewing machine operators worked in clothing manufacturing establishments, or in sweatshops, often in immigrant neighborhoods. Some machine operators worked at industrial photo processing plants, operating the machines that processed exposed camera film, and then printed contact sheets and prints for customers. In dry cleaners, machine operators place laundered clothing on large pressing machines.

In many work environments, however, machine operators require more advanced skills: mathematical ability to adjust their machines with precision to create a new product, mechanical skills sufficient to inspect and make basic repairs to machines, and quality control skills to evaluate products as they exit the production process. In the time before computer-assisted machine operations, in the period between World War II and the widespread use of computerized production machines beginning in the 1980s, according to one observer, "A good operator could tell you whether things at his machine were in or out or control by the way it sounded or the way it vibrated when he touched it. This way, being a good machine operator was often 'art' as well as 'skill.' Operators were rightfully proud of their skills and their instincts. In those days a successful business depended on the quality of the people on the manufacturing floor. There was a great deal of pride in the work they produced as well as the skills required" (Weber 1992, 26). In metal fabrication shops, machine operators use high-speed boring and cutting tools as determined by the patternmaker or machinist. An operator in this work environment is required to use micrometers and other tools to measure the item they produce at the machine so that the product meets specifications. Operators who work on metalworking machines also have to adjust guards to prevent flying bits of metal from injuring themselves and others.

Even the most competent and skilled machine operator, however, made errors, which could lead to serious injury—especially eye injuries. Other occupational hazards also affected machine operators' health and safety. In metal fabrication shops, machine operators often developed a chronic lung disease, pneumonitis, and skin conditions caused by exposure to lubricating oils, cutting solvents, and other chemicals used in fabrication. Similarly, in automobile factories, machine operators had higher rates of lung disease due to exposure to mold and bacteria.

While machine operators of this period worked in various environments, their jobs transformed with the introduction of computerized manufacturing processes. Newer, automated machines had presets that could be entered into a machine; the computer made adjustments as necessary. In manufacturing, machine operators were increasingly assigned to positions as loaders or unloaders. While demand for machine operators is high, the duties and responsibilities of the modern machine operator is seldom characterized by a worker's "art" or "skill" but his or her ability to diligently monitor the machine's output without distraction.

Nancy Quam-Wickham

See also: *1915–1945:* Autoworker; Warehouse Worker; *1992–2019:* Machinist; Package Handler

FURTHER READING

Barkus, Philip. 1992. *How to Prepare for the Postal Distribution (Machine) Clerk Examination (Letter-Sorting Machine Operator).* New York: Barron's Educational Series.

Milking Machine Manufacturers Council (Farm Industrial Equipment Institute). 1989. *The Modern Way to Efficient Milking: A Summary of Uniform Recommendations by Milking Machine Manufacturers Concerning the Machine, the Cow and the Operator.* Chicago: Milking Machine Manufacturers Council.

Weber, Earnest G. 1992. "Computers, Metrology, and Manufacturing." *Quality* 31: 1, 26.

OCEANOGRAPHER

Some of the first oceanographers were naval officers, like Matthew Fontaine Maury, who published many books about oceanography in the mid-1800s. Although Maury is considered to be the "Father of Oceanography," modern oceanography began during the 1940s in response to submarine warfare during World War II (1939–1945). Scientists realized they could borrow technology created for national defense, such as sonar, to create more accurate maps of the ocean floor. They used magnetometers to find the metal hulls of submarines to learn about the properties of seafloor rocks. Oceanographers are scientists and engineers who study all aspects of the ocean.

Exploring the ocean is a challenging task. Getting to the ocean floor requires overcoming pressure, extreme temperature, and lack of oxygen. Oceanographers continue to partner with governments and businesses to develop technology that can bring scientists to the ocean depths or bring samples from the ocean to the surface. The resulting images, video, data, and actual samples are used to create more detailed maps of the seafloor, discover new organisms and ecosystems, and understand how the planet works. Many discoveries by oceanographers are applied to fields of energy, national defense, and space exploration.

Oceanography is a young branch of science and is interdisciplinary in nature. An oceanographer generally works in a laboratory at a university or a specialized marine science center. Some oceanographers work at universities but do most of their scientific studies on ships with scientific cruises that last a few days to a few months. There are very few vessels that are designed for oceanography, and working at sea can be challenging due to weather, so time on the water is packed with activity throughout the day and night. Crews work in shifts to make the most of the time they have.

Scientists, engineers, and mathematicians work together on problems since most oceanic research questions require people with a variety of expertise to solve them. For example, one area of interest to oceanographers is understanding the composition of the seafloor and its substrata below, which may contain untapped sources of oil, natural gas, and minerals. To study the seafloor requires a knowledge of the sea and its processes, including ocean currents. An oceanographer will work with research ship crews to be taken to the research site; an engineer to design a vehicle that can reach the seafloor and bring back data, images, and samples; a technician to capture all that data and organize it; a geologist to understand the surface and subsurface features; a biologist to understand the organisms living around the feature; and an ecologist to understand the impacts that humans are making on that environment.

After a research cruise, an oceanographer may spend months on shore in a university laboratory or office studying the data to make important discoveries about the ocean. This scientific research process is very slow and labor intensive: an oceanographer may need thousands of water-temperature readings over many years to make scientific predictions about, for instance, the role of a warming ocean in changing weather patterns. Warm currents circulating in the eastern equatorial Pacific move northward in El Niño events, sometimes leading to wetter winters along the west coast of North America. Like most forms of scientific research, oceanographers spend much of their careers working in laboratories or using computers to analyze their scientific findings and then carefully crafting essays for publication in scientific journals.

Most people who want to become oceanographers study sciences, engineering, math, or other disciplines in college; most get bachelor's degrees, while many also pursue more advanced study to obtain master's and doctoral degrees. It is most important to have a passion for the ocean, learn how to communicate with people who have different areas of expertise, and be excited about solving scientific problems that few have encountered before. Many oceanographers need to write grants and communicate their findings to the general public, so it is important to be a good communicator. Taking courses in writing and the arts can be invaluable tools for such work. Some oceanographers go to technical schools rather than traditional college, learning how to build, maintain, and pilot a remote-operated vehicle (ROV) or work in the lab processing samples. Artists and educators are often part of expeditions to communicate findings and keep the team thinking creatively about their work. Many oceanographers know how to snorkel or scuba dive so they can go to shallow locations by themselves.

In the past, an oceanographer's work was done by hand, drawing and measuring samples, cataloging them, and creating publications. Now, oceanographers develop technologies like ROVs and landers to collect images and data from the world's ocean, bringing back images and information to help scientists understand never-before-seen worlds, expanding existing knowledge about how science defines life. The amount of data collected is far greater than ever before, and technology is needed to process and organize it. Sometimes discoveries are made later when the data is sorted.

Until recently, people believed that the ocean basins were relatively flat with few features. Now that oceanographers can map the ocean floor with far greater precision, it is known that the topography is covered with mountains, valleys, trenches, and other features. Since the depths of the oceans are great, it was believed that there could be little life living in those deep regions. Yet in the 1980s, scientists discovered hydrothermal vents and organisms that live not on energy from the sun (photosynthesis) but on the chemicals that come out through the vents (chemosynthesis). In 2016, discoveries of methane seeps just off the California coast uncovered new ecosystems of organisms that consume the seeping methane.

Oceanography is changing with every new technology that helps scientists gather information and see new parts of the planet.

Stacy Sinclair

See also: Scientist

FURTHER READING

Carson, Rachel. 1991. *The Sea Around Us, Special Edition.* New York: Oxford University Press.

Earle, Sylvia A. 2010. *The World Is Blue: How Our Fate and the Ocean's Are One.* Washington, DC: National Geographic Press.

Kunzig, Robert. 2000. *Mapping the Deep: The Extraordinary Story of Ocean Science.* New York: W. W. Norton & Co.

Rozwadowski, Helen. 2005. *Fathoming the Ocean: The Discovery and Exploration of the Deep Sea.* Cambridge: Harvard University Press.

Sverdrup, Keith, and Raphael Kudela. 2013. *Investigating Oceanography.* New York: McGraw Hill.

PRIMARY DOCUMENT

In the following documents, participants describe work of scientists from Scripps Institute of Oceanography (SIO) on the Capricorn oceanographic expedition, a seven-month voyage, to the Pacific Ocean during 1952–1953. Two years earlier, SIO oceanographers on the MidPac, or mid-Pacific, expedition of 1950 had discovered the Mid-Pacific Mountains, a range of underwater mountains that extended nearly twenty-five hundred miles from the Hawaiian archipelago to Wake Island. On the way back to San Diego from that first expedition, scientists also discovered the "great cliffs of the Mendocino escarpment," as Dr. Roger Revelle, then director of the SIO at the University of California, described it. That expedition, although discovering the "great fracture zones" of the Pacific basin, did not make any hypotheses about plate tectonic theory, which was proven only during the mid-1960s. However, work on the Capricorn and later SIO expeditions did contribute to the understanding of geomagnetism, paleogeography, and other scientific knowledge upon which plate tectonics was based.

In this document, Roger Revelle recalls memorable moments from the Capricorn expedition, as recorded in 1975.

On Capricorn [1952]: Falcon Island is and was a disappearing island west of the Tonga Islands. It's an active volcano, and every now and then it explodes and piles up a huge pile of cinders several hundred feet above sea level. Then the waves come and wash it away. Most of the time it's about 20 or 30 feet below sea level. We decided . . . that we would investigate Falcon Island, more or less over the dead body of our captain. We went right to the top of this shoal, this island with a shallow bank. As I remember, when we came in to Falcon Island we were rather scared that the depth was too shallow and prepared to back up. Art Maxwell came rushing up to the bridge and said, "We're aground!" What had happened was that the wake of the ship had created an echo which was shallower than the ship itself. Actually the top of the bank was about 20 feet down. But for a moment we thought it would be the end of the expedition right there.

Walter Munk and several other people dived on Falcon Island; I remember Walter's mission in life was to measure the temperature of this submerged volcano. He stuck a thermometer into a rock and he happened to look around and there was a shark looking over his shoulder, reading the thermometer along with him. There was nothing really to do but go on reading the temperature. Eventually the shark lost interest and went away, and Walter is still here.

It was very shortly after that that Helen Raitt joined the expedition at Tonga. She had been meeting us at the different ports, and by this time we managed to see that she really belonged to the expedition and us, so she joined us there and went home the rest of the way with us. This was in some way a great first: she was the first woman, so far as I know, that ever took part in a major oceanographic expedition. She wrote a book about it; it began her long love affair with the Tonga Island, particularly the magical island of Vava'u. Actually I had asked Rachel Carson to come along on the expedition, to write a book about it, and she had planned to do so when at the last minute she couldn't do it. But Helen's book, *Exploring the Deep Pacific*, is, I think, a worthy surrogate for what Rachel Carson might have written . . .

It was on Capricorn that we explored the Tonga Trench, one of the most remarkable features of the earth. I remember very well one of the exciting parts of it was the discovery of Bob Fisher's mountain—a little mountain that rises, if you will, from 35,000 feet to about 1500 feet below the sea surface, so in some ways it is the highest mountain in the world . . .

Palmerston Island was one of the most isolated places I can possibly think of. It's in the middle of the South Pacific; ships call there on the average of once every seven or eight years. It was first found by Captain Cook in one of his expeditions in the 1760s, and he surveyed the island. He concluded that there were very strong currents around the island, two-knot currents or more, and that statement by Captain Cook has been repeated in the pilot's book ever since. If you look carefully, you read that a ship that called there in 1875 couldn't find any currents . . . We surveyed around the atoll and we found no currents. What had happened clearly was that Captain Cook in his surveys had depended on sextant sights on the atoll, and the only landmarks are palm trees and it was very easy to mistake one palm tree from another as he went around the atoll. We had the great benefit of a recording echo sound with the result that we could actually make a closure, and there were no currents at all. This for me at least was an enormous satisfaction to be able to do better than Captain Cook, the greatest explorer, greatest navigator who ever lived . . .

[W]e were right in at the beginning of one of the great ages of exploration. It's quite obvious now that the 15 or 20 years from 1948 to 1965 were one of the great ages of discovery of the earth, and the things that we found and the things that our expeditions found later . . . we've raised the basis for a scientific revolution of the most profound kind that, in some ways perhaps not as important to human beings spiritually or psychologically as the Darwinian revolution, nevertheless intellectually and in terms of a complete change of understanding at least as profound a revolution as the Darwinian revolution in its nature. We were lucky, of course. There is nothing in this world that could happen without luck. We were lucky to be at the right place at the right time. We were also lucky that we had so many people who were curious and able and interested and excited and willing to try to spend their lives in conditions that weren't often very pleasant, trying to find out what the world was all about.

Source: Roger Revelle. "Transcription of a Tape made at the 25th reunion of people who participated in Midpac (1950) and Capricorn (1952) expeditions by Scripps Institute of Oceanography." Collection 2011-49. In the SIO Oral History Collections, University of California, San Diego, 3–5, 8–11. Used by permission of Special Collections & Archives, UC San Diego. http://libraries.ucsd.edu/speccoll/siooralhistories/2011-49-revelle.pdf.

OFFICE CLERK

Clerical work encompasses a variety of positions including file clerk, typist, secretary, and bookkeeper. Prior to the late nineteenth century, clerical workers performed a wide variety of tasks. By the first decades of the twentieth century, clerical workers came to be divided into two basic groups. Lower-level employees executed a small number of routine tasks, such as retrieving files or typing letters. These clerical workers spent much of every workday completing these relatively mundane tasks as well as answering phones, taking messages, or preparing mail. They worked in numerous settings, from small single-station offices to large pools of clerical workers seated at desks in large workrooms. In the latter setting, clerks who worked as typists typed all sorts of documents (both originals and edited versions), while those who worked as stenographers transcribed notes taken in shorthand (a form of symbolic writing). Higher-level employees, such as secretaries, were responsible for a wider variety of tasks and had more opportunities for decision making on the job than lower-level employees. These clerks often combined basic bookkeeping duties with basic office management tasks, such as keeping schedules, arranging meetings, and operating other types of office machinery, like dictation and transcribing machines, adding machines, tape recorders, and the like. Many of the higher-skilled clerical workers worked in single-station offices or in suites of clerical offices or cubicles. In both cases, the work hours were generally 8:00 a.m. to 5:00 p.m., Mondays through Fridays. Many women workers sought out office clerical work because the conditions and hours of labor were often much better than factory work or other unskilled and semiskilled occupations open to women.

For much of the twentieth century, white women performed clerical work. Women of color rarely held office jobs in private industry until the 1960s due to racism, though significant numbers of women of color entered the clerical occupations in government and public employment settings after World War II, especially in the 1950s, when many public employers, such as the postal service, adopted more equitable employment policies. When women of color did enter the ranks of clerical workers, they tended to be concentrated in the lower-paid positions and in government positions, rarely seen by the public, whereas white women were much more likely to hold the higher-paid, front-office position of secretary.

Unlike household work, office work had not always been a women's job. During the first two-thirds of the nineteenth century, clerks were predominantly young men. They received better pay than workers in manufacturing, and they had opportunities for job advancement. They learned the business prior to becoming managers or owners in their own right, although many never achieved high status due to economic instability and the small number of positions available. With the Industrial Revolution, the clerical labor force expanded, as did the needs for record keeping and communications. Women got a foot in the door during the Civil War (1861–1865) as they were needed, given wartime labor shortages of men, but the typewriter, invented in the early 1870s, paved the way for clerical work to become women's domain. Typewriters, being new technology, were sex neutral, thus available as a work implement for women. Contemporary writers contended that women had a competitive advantage in the mechanized office as they were seen as tolerant of routine, careful, and dexterous. A clerical job for women paid better than most other jobs considered appropriate for women, making it coveted by the working class as a relatively high-status job. As the work became routinized and mechanical, the profession became feminized, and the chances for occupational advancement were significantly lowered.

By the late 1940s, women overwhelmingly occupied clerical jobs. The working conditions were far from ideal. Many women clerical workers expressed disappointment in the work after years of education, or, as one clerk remembered, "The eight by ten box is your reward for passing exams, doing what you were told, and trying hard to please" (Benet 1972 , 61). Clerical jobs also became increasingly factorylike. There was less flexibility in work routines and a faster pace and heavier workload. Most general secretaries and clerks worked in secretarial pools, which gave them less autonomy and greater supervision.

The 1970s was a decade of enormous growth in the number of working women. The typical working woman in the 1970s and 1980s was a clerical employee. One in three women remained in clerical jobs in 1979. Women made up 80 percent of workers in clerical occupations, 91.1 percent of bank tellers in 1976, and 99.1 percent of secretaries in 1980. Only the private household workforce, including maids, nannies, and home care attendants, had a higher percentage of women employees. Women in the clerical field encountered pay inequality, with the minority of male clerical workers, who usually held higher-status clerical jobs, receiving higher salaries. Pay inequality with men in clerical work, while notable, was only part of the issue. Due to the sex-segregated labor force, where women erroneously continued to be seen as temporary workers or secondary wage earners, the women-dominated clerical workforce, overall, earned insufficient wages to support a family.

While managers were selected for the masculine-typed qualities of aggressiveness, toughness, and practicality, women were selected for clerical jobs, particularly secretaries, due to their ability to fill the ideal of an office wife, mother, or maid. Cooperation, compliance, and even subservience were seen as desirable feminine qualities for clerical work, with men employers seeking elegant secretaries as a status symbol or motherly secretaries, who coddled and took care of the boss.

Inaccurate job descriptions, duties that had nothing to do with the job (such as having to run personal errands for a boss), and the lack of a voice in workplace decisions plagued the clerical workplace. Beginning in 1970, the median salary for clerical work was lower than every type of blue-collar work. Several common office myths also eroded the public status of women clerical workers and lowered their morale. The ideas that the job was not important and did not deserve better pay or that management took good care of its white-collar workers undermined arguments for improved conditions. These myths came to be questioned in the wake of the women's movement as women sought to change their roles as second-class citizens. Better pay and improved benefits clearly were only part of the answer for many women workers, and many issues, such as lack of respect, were not resolvable by traditional union grievance procedures.

By the early 1970s, women office workers began to organize in associations that seriously questioned the working conditions of clerical workers. The working women movement, which included women from a variety of occupations, thus emerged in independent local organizations such as 9to5 in Boston, Women Office Workers in New York City, and Women Employed in Chicago. These organizations, using tactics derived from the women's movement such as rallies and consciousness raising, addressed the needs of working women in the local environment and reinforced expectations that women workers were entitled to certain basic rights, such as respect on the job and equal pay.

Despite labor organizing among women clerical workers in the early 1900s and attempts in the 1930s, many in the clerical workforce had little contact with the labor movement in the 1970s, but that was beginning to change. Up to that point, most unions had ignored industries with a predominantly women workforce or abandoned their attempts to organize in the service and clerical sectors, believing that the women clerical workers and women in other pink-collar jobs were not interested in or capable of organizing and leading their own unions. Unions, one means of earning better wages and working conditions, began investing more in organizing clericals as a way to combat the decline in labor union membership and due to the activism of women workers. Despite the increased union organizing, the sector is largely unorganized. Although computers significantly changed the work routines of clerical workers in the 1990s and thereafter, secretary and administrative assistant continue to be the most common occupations for women in this century.

Amanda Walter

See also: *1861–1914:* Bookkeeper; *1915–1945:* Stenographer

FURTHER READING

Benét, Mary Kathleen. 1972. *The Secretarial Ghetto*. New York: McGraw-Hill.

Cobble, Dorothy Sue. 2004. *The Other Women's Movement: Workplace Justice and Social Rights in Modern America*. Princeton: Princeton University Press.

Davies, Margery. 1982. *A Woman's Place Is at the Typewriter, 1870–1930*. Philadelphia: Temple University Press.

Maclean, Nancy. 1999. "The Hidden History of Affirmative Action: Working Women's Organizations in Workplace Struggles in the 1970s and the Gender of Class." *Feminist Studies* 25: 43–78.

Moody, Kim. 2007. *US Labor in Trouble and Transition: The Failure of Reform from Above, the Promise of Revival from Below*. New York: Verso.

Rotella, Elyce. 1981. *From Home to Office: U.S. Women at Work, 1870–1930*. Ann Arbor: UMI Research Press.

Strom, Sharon Hartman. 1992. *Beyond the Typewriter: Gender, Class, and the Origins of Modern American Office Work, 1900–1930*. Chicago: University of Illinois Press.

PHARMACIST

Pharmacy is one of humankind's oldest professions, with evidence of crude pharmacology showing up in some of the earliest historical records. Pharmacists prepare and dispense prescriptions and provide expert advice to patients and other healthcare professionals concerning the safe use of chemical medicines. Historically, most pharmacists have practiced in community pharmacies, and they've been perhaps the most publicly accessible healthcare professionals. In addition to community pharmacies, contemporary pharmacists work in research and academic institutions, pharmaceutical companies, hospitals, and nursing homes. Pharmacists in the early United States were known as apothecaries, chemists, and druggists. They came to be called "pharmacists" after an 1867 resolution was adopted by the American Pharmaceutical Association (known today as the American Pharmacists Association), which was proposed by Edward Parrish.

The American pharmacist evolved as a profession immediately after World War II (1939–1945). In the postwar period, corner drugstores became a popular and venerable part of most towns and neighborhoods and were designed to encourage frequent, convenient visits. The typical corner drugstore featured a luncheonette with a soda fountain, which became a central gathering place for locals to socialize and share a snack or a meal. The typical corner drugstore was also a convenience store that featured a wide variety of products ranging from over-the-counter medications to cosmetics, personal hygiene products, newspapers, magazines, household products, toys, food, greeting cards, and local souvenirs. A pharmacy's lead pharmacist was also often the business's owner and as such was responsible for performing or overseeing all of the pharmacy's day-to-day operations.

A postwar pharmacist's typical day was similar to other workers in small retail shops and grocers. The pharmacists would often arrive at the store around an hour before opening. They would spend this time cleaning, processing any shipments that may have arrived overnight, organizing and placing products on shelves, and preparing the cash register. During the day, the pharmacist would manage any employees they had on staff and handle any customer prescriptions, run the register, and dispense soda or make malts and shakes if their pharmacy had a soda fountain. After the pharmacy closed, the pharmacist would often stay late to clean, complete paperwork, place orders for products and drugs, and prepare for the next day.

The two most popular reasons for a patient to visit a pharmacy are to treat pain or fight infection. After World War II, antibiotics and sulfa drugs became broadly available to the public, and pharmacies that carried them began to see their sale as a major profit center.

In the 1980s, lower-priced pharmacy chains, supermarkets, big-box department stores, mail-order companies, and internet pharmacies supplanted the idyllic corner drugstore of the 1940s to 1970s, though many independent pharmacies have managed to survive by remaining involved in other aspects of community life. One of these aspects involves the pharmacist's role as one of the most publicly accessible healthcare professionals. Every day, pharmacists field questions from their patients, dispense medicines, and keep an eye out for harmful interactions between drugs. Consequently, public opinion survey data has shown pharmacists to be regarded as among the most trusted professionals.

In the 1940s, a bachelor of science in pharmacy took four years to complete, and all registered pharmacists were required to hold such a degree. By 1965, pharmacy degrees took around five years. In 2000, the bachelor of science in pharmacy was replaced by the six- or seven-year doctorate of pharmacy degree, requiring a full year of clinical rotations under the direct supervision of clinical pharmacists, which typically takes place during the student's last year of study.

The development of new classes of drugs over the decades has offered relief and cures and has cemented the importance of pharmacists in the United States. Today, U.S. pharmacists dispense over 3.7 billion prescriptions per year, and about half of Americans take at least one prescription drug per month (CDC). There are nearly sixty-seven thousand pharmacies in the United States (Qato 2016).

Federal legislation has had a profound impact upon the practice of pharmacy in the United States. The 1952 Durham-Humphrey Amendment to the 1938 Federal Drug and Cosmetic Act clearly created two classes of drugs: prescription and over-the-counter. This law ushered in the era of "count and pour" pharmacy in which pharmacists primarily engaged in dispensing manufactured, pre-prepared medicines in ever-increasing volumes to a willing public while being prohibited from discussing prescriptions with patients. Pharmacists were obliged to refer patients back to their prescribing physician for drug information. The 1990 Omnibus Budget Reconciliation Act ushered in the era of pharmaceutical care in which pharmacists were encouraged to counsel patients directly about their medications and to advise them how to get the best benefit from taking them. Since 2006, with the Medicare Prescription Drug Improvement and Modernization Act of 2003, better known as Medicare Part D, pharmacists have practiced medication therapy management (MTM). MTM enhanced pharmaceutical care by calling upon pharmacists to monitor a patient's drug therapy to yield optimal health outcomes. Over the last decade, pharmacists have administered a wide variety of vaccinations in their pharmacies.

Since the 1940s, American pharmacists have come a long way in advancing their profession from the corner druggist to clinical pharmacists who have become parts of hospital healthcare, working alongside other healthcare professionals. As a result of automation, the rise of pharmacy technicians and third-party payers, and the digital revolution, pharmacists have shifted their focus from dispensing the drug product (medicine) to providing expert drug information to patients and other healthcare professionals in multiple venues. The twenty-first-century pharmacist is a clinical-level drug expert who is increasingly becoming an integral part of the modern healthcare team of professionals.

Bob Zebroski

See also: *1607–1775:* Apothecary; *1776–1860:* Physician; *1992–2019:* Epidemiologist

FURTHER READING

Bender, George A., and Robert A. Thom. 1967. *Great Moments in Pharmacy: The Stories and Paintings in the Series, a History of Pharmacy in Pictures*. Detroit: Northwood Institute Press.

Cowen, David L., and William Helfand. 1990. *Pharmacy: An Illustrated History*. New York: Harry Abrams.

"FastStats." 2017. Centers for Disease Control and Prevention. Last modified May 3. https://www.cdc.gov/nchs/fastats/drug-use-therapeutic.htm.

Qato, Dima M., Shannon Zenk, Jocelyn Wilder, Rachel Harrington, Darrell Gaskin, and G. C. Alexander. 2016. "The Availability of Pharmacies and Pharmacy Services in the United States: 2007–2015." *Value in Health* 19, no. 3: A268.
Zerbroski, Robert A. 2014. *Brief History of Pharmacy: Humanity's Search for Wellness.* New York: Routledge.

PILOT

Pilots operate the flying controls of commercial, civilian, or military aircraft. For the Allies to defeat fascism during World War II, they needed all kinds of machines: guns, mortars, cannonry, tanks, trucks, cars and jeeps, boats, and ships—and especially aircraft. The influence of the men and women who operated those military airplanes—and of World War II on the aviation industry—cannot be overstated. The U.S. government's emphasis on the "war in the skies" was critical as multiple battlefronts extended across the globe. As a consequence, aviation companies in wartime expanded enormously; large aircraft-manufacturing facilities operated by companies like Douglas Aircraft, Lockheed, and Boeing implemented assembly-line production techniques to rapidly produce aircraft, like the B-17 heavy bomber. Douglas alone produced over twenty-eight thousand aircraft during the war. In 1940, Ford Motor Company commissioned the Willow Run facility outside Detroit to build aircraft, converting the land it owned and previously used as a farm demonstration for urban youth; only after the war did the plant build automobile parts (after General Motors purchased the property). As a whole, the aircraft industry grew to become the industry that employed the most civilians during World War II. Opportunities for pilots increased accordingly with the growing aircraft production industry.

While in the military, pilots received intensive training in flight operations, and once the war ended, many pilots took their training and experiences into the civilian sector. They flew planes for airlines—an industry that expanded enormously during an extended period of postwar economic prosperity. Pilots flew experimental airplanes for corporations that built airplanes and the new jets of the postwar period, like Douglas Aircraft and North American Aviation. Pilots supplied remote indigenous communities, especially in Alaska, with mail, medicine, and other goods that could only be delivered by air or on the ground by foot, dogsled, or snowmobiles (which came into widespread use only in the 1960s and 1970s). Pilots in both the military and in civilian roles flew aircraft to rescue those in distress, as would a U.S. Coast Guard member piloting a helicopter to rescue the crew of a sinking fishing vessel. Military pilots flew planes and helicopters in every conflict in which U.S. forces were engaged, ferrying troops back and forth to combat zones, dropping bombs and missiles on enemy targets, and retrieving wounded forces and the dead. Pilots flew airplanes for research and other commercial purposes as well: to track extreme weather events like hurricanes, facilitate aerial photography for geologists and government, locate schools of tuna and other high-value fish for deep-water fishing fleets, scout by air our national forests for endangered wildlife for the Forest Service, and monitor long stretches of interstate travel for speeding and dangerous drivers. Pilots had many more roles in both military and civilian employment during the postwar years.

The duties of a pilot might vary according to his or her work role, but overall, all pilots required training in principles of aerodynamics, weather, mechanics, navigation, radar systems, radio communication, flight rules, and the structures of different aircraft. All pilots need to pass rigorous medical and vision requirements, as well as examinations that test their knowledge of the above principles and their flying abilities, which include practical demonstrations of runway takeoff and landing, control of aircraft, and emergency protocol, like handling a plane when its engine stalls. The U.S. military provided this training to its airmen and airwomen, although from 1946 to 1977, most branches of the military prohibited women from pursuing pilot training, even in support (noncombatant) roles. During the 1970s, women were admitted to the service academies, which opened the doors for them to begin pilot training at the air force, navy, and army academies. Civilian flight training schools also became popular during the war and afterward; in fact, the U.S. government's Civilian Pilot Training Program (1938–1944) trained nearly 440,000 civilian pilots for wartime military duty. After the war, experienced pilots opened specialized flight schools in local communities to train private pilots, while colleges and universities established departments and colleges of aviation that provided flight training to students in Reserve Officer Training programs and others. In the 1960s, the federal department of education and regional accreditors granted Embry-Riddle Aeronautical Institute status as a university providing training in all areas of aviation.

Despite the variation in working environments, some tasks were and are common to nearly all pilots. Whether civilian or military pilots, all pilots receive work (flight duty) orders from their supervisors; private pilots who operate their own flight services may write their own work orders. A flight order indicates type of aircraft and its individual identifying information, where a pilot is to meet an aircraft, and where they are scheduled to fly; these orders also indicate when the work is to occur and the aircraft's cargo (for commercial airline pilots, the cargo includes passengers, luggage, and mail). The flight orders will also normally provide information on support staff (navigator, co-pilots, flight attendants). The pilot must inspect the flight orders, determining flight path, or route, for the flight, although after 1958, the Federal Aviation Agency (later, Administration) developed rules for managing airspace over the United States and specified certain flight paths for commercial airlines—in response to a series of midair commercial aircraft collisions. By the late 1950s, the skies were so congested that only the federal government had the authority to police the skies across state boundary lines.

Pilots must also assess weather conditions, often by using information provided by the National Weather Service. If the flight order calls for flying through dangerous weather, pilots may alter the order and file a new flight path document, or they may simply delay takeoff. Before takeoff, pilots visually inspect their aircraft's exterior and perform extensive preflight checks of the mechanical, electrical, and hydraulic systems. Pilots supervise the loading of cargo as well—including passengers.

Before and after takeoff, pilots communicate with flight controllers at local airport air-traffic control centers; the first control centers were established in the 1930s, but they did not become universal until the 1950s. Pilots then control the aircraft's entire flight, though in emergency situations, they must follow traffic control or military orders communicated by radio. Pilots also use radar to track other aircraft in the skies, as well as radios for communicating their positions to nearby planes. Pilots are responsible for all operations of an aircraft. Most pilots spend the majority of their workdays not actually flying the aircraft but in preparatory work before the flight and in filing appropriate paperwork after the flight is complete.

Pilots' near-absolute responsibility for controlling their aircraft created labor strife within the industry, even before airline travel expanded. Pilots employed by the U.S. Postal Service (as Air Mail pilots) threatened to strike in the summer of 1919 when ordered by their supervisors to fly in inclement weather and operate planes that pilots viewed as dangerous. Eventually, the Air Mail Bureau was absorbed into the Army Air Force in the late 1920s, with most air mail letters and packages—which often required premium postage—being shipped on military flights. In 1946, however, labor relations within the commercial airline industry led to a series of strikes by the national pilots' union, the Air Line Pilots' Association (ALPA), which was organized in 1931. The key issue for many pilots was the introduction of new aircraft that required them to control pressurized aircraft that flew at higher altitudes and at greater speeds than earlier machines. Aircraft like Boeing's Stratoliner were also heavier than earlier planes, which required pilots to manage takeoffs and landings, the most dangerous parts of any flight, at greater speed. Pilots wanted companies to pay higher wages for these duties and wanted industrywide labor agreements rather than the typical contracts between a single airline company and its employee pilots.

Strikes against Transcontinental and Western Airlines (TWA) in 1946, National Airlines in 1948, American Airlines in 1954, and Southern Airways from 1960 to 1962 largely established the ALPA's rights to negotiate pay and conditions on a national basis, even if it did not achieve its goal of industrywide contracts. Throughout this period, ALPA negotiated with airlines not only on pay and conditions but also on safety issues, lobbying for the creation of the National Transportation Safety Board, demanding improvements in flight technologies and instrumentation, insisting on new technologies for collision avoidance systems, establishing minimum crew complements for each type of aircraft, and endorsing regular medical exams, including drug and alcohol testing of pilots.

The commercial airline industry experienced some economic contractions as a result of the 1973 and 1978 oil crises, but passenger demands for service remained strong. Americans were traveling longer distances and more often than they had before. After the 1978 deregulation of the airline industry, commercial air traffic grew even more, creating more opportunities for pilots. By 1990, commercial air pilots had attained status as highly trained professionals who were paid well for their work.

Nancy Quam-Wickham

See also: Aeronautical and Aerospace Engineer; Astronaut; Flight Attendant; Travel Agent

FURTHER READING

Federal Aviation Administration. "A Brief History of the FAA." Last modified January 4, 2017. https://www.faa.gov/about/history/brief_history/.

Hopkins, George E. 1971. *The Airline Pilots: A Study in Elite Organization.* Cambridge: Harvard University Press.

Hopkins, George E. 1982. *Flying the Line: The First Half Century of the Air Line Pilots Association.* Washington, DC: ALPA.

PRIMARY DOCUMENT

In this document, one of the navy's first women navigators to serve after World War II, Linda Maloney, describes her experiences assisting a navy pilot during one flight in February 1991, while on a training mission. Maloney served twenty years in the U.S. Navy, eventually earning the combat air medal for her service in Iraq.

I was flying in the EA-6A for about 6 months when on a warm February day in 1991 I was scheduled to fly an electronic attack aggressor flight with a senior pilot in the squadron. We were flying up Jacksonville, with another EA-6A. The flight would be a training exercise for the USS Forestall and its battle group, about 100 miles off the Florida coast. The pilot of my aircraft was the Mission Commander and he briefed the flight for the two EA-6A's and all the emergency procedures. The flight would take all day since we would do a couple of "runs" on the USS Forestall and then fly into an Air Force Base up near Tampa to refuel and then fly back out to conduct an afternoon mission.

We launched from NAS Key West in our vintage EA-6A and headed up the coastline to work with the carrier battle group for an electronic warfare exercise. It was a beautiful sunny February morning. It took about an hour to fly from Key West to the area east of Jacksonville, Florida where the battle group was stationed. I radioed the ship that we were ready to begin our simulated electronic and missile attacks. After several runs on the ship, about 12:30 pm, we radioed the ship we were complete and would see them later in the afternoon. We told our wingman to rendezvous and then go to a cruise position. Then we headed for Patrick Air Force Base (AFB), approximately 200 miles away. The area controller cleared us on our way at 15,000 feet.

As we started our climb, the plane acted a little sluggish. The pilot adjusted the controls. The aircraft fishtailed as though we had flown through some mild jet wash. Then the master caution light on the front display panel began flashing and the backup hydraulics light illuminated. The flight hydraulic system indicated zero pressure.

I started going through the procedures for a single hydraulic failure, instructing the pilot to secure the automatic flight control system. He pulled back the throttle to slow down from our 300 knots. We called our wingman, and discussed options, deciding that we needed to take an arrested landing over at Naval Air Station (NAS) Cecil Field.

I radioed to the Air Traffic Controller that we were declaring an emergency and needed clearance to Cecil Field for an arrested landing. He cleared us directly to NAS Cecil Field. My pilot and I quickly discussed our game plan, and then began to climb to 15,000 ft and slow to 270 kts. Neither of us expected what happened next.

The master caution light illuminated again and then the rudder-throw light came on. A quick glance showed the combined hydraulic system at zero. No sooner had I noticed the reading, the aircraft began a rapid roll to the left and the nose fell below the horizon. The pilot pulled the stick to the right and aft to no effect. He fed in full right rudder, but the airplane did not respond. The aircraft continued to roll left and descend. As we passed through 60 degrees left bank, and 20 degrees nose down, I heard the pilot say, "I don't have control. Eject!"

I grabbed the upper ejection handle and my seat exploded through the canopy glass. I recall a tremendous explosion, riding the rails of the ejection seat upward amidst the yellow confetti of my kneeboard paper. I lost consciousness and when I came to, I was hanging in my parachute descending towards the ocean. I usually would wear my contacts but that day I'd decided to wear glasses. My helmet visor had ripped off from the force of the ejection and my glasses were gone. All I could see was the ocean below me and the shoreline far in the distance.

Source: Shannon Huffman Polson. 2016. "She's Got Grit: A Conversation with Pioneer Navy Navigator Linda Maloney." The Grit Factor. https://shannon-polson.squarespace.com/grit-project-blog/grit-flygirl-linda. Used by permission of Shannon Huffman Polson. www.shannonpolson.com.

PROFESSIONAL ATHLETE, *see* BASEBALL PLAYER

RADIOLOGIST AND RADIOLOGY TECHNICIAN

Radiology technicians use X-rays and other medical imaging techniques to help radiologists diagnose patients' illnesses, like cancer, and injuries, like broken bones. Radiologists are medical doctors, and radiology technicians are auxiliary health workers; both are specialists in the field of radiology, which emerged in the twentieth century. In the later twentieth century, radiologists also used this technology to treat some patients through a practice known as interventional radiology.

Radiology had its origins in the work of the German physicist Wilhelm Conrad Röentgen (1845–1923), who discovered that X-rays, when directed through a patient's body, could produce an image of the internal structure of the body that could be captured on film. This discovery revolutionized medicine as now physicians could assess a patient's condition using scientific means—the X-ray—rather than through experienced touch (assessing a broken arm, for instance) or exploratory surgery (assessing a tumor). The field of radiology, then called röentgenology, after Röentgen, grew enormously as a result of World War I (1914–1918), when military doctors on all sides needed the accuracy provided by even rudimentary X-rays to quickly diagnose and order treatment for wounded soldiers. In the United States, radiology emerged as a separate field of medicine in the 1920s and 1930s; in 1934, the American Board of Radiology was formed and began to issue board certification to specialists in radiology.

Improvements in radiography, or the use of medical imagery, contributed to changes in the work of both radiologists and radiology technicians, leading to many new occupational opportunities for individuals trained in this science. During the post–World War II period, radiology developed into four subspecialties: diagnostic radiology, therapeutic radiology, radiation physics, and radiobiology. Radiation technicians largely participated in the first two subspecialties, while radiologists practiced in all areas. The duties of each of these occupations vary based on training requirements, practice settings (hospitals, clinics, or private offices), particular areas of interest (gastroenterology, chest and cardiovascular illnesses, orthopedics), and technology used. The commonality among all of these workers, though, is the use of X-rays, technologies employing nuclear physics, and imaging techniques to diagnose and treat patients.

Radiology technicians, now referred to as radiologic technicians, provided auxiliary health services to patients and their doctors; they operated the X-ray and other machines that provided radiologists with the images of a patient's body. By the 1950s and 1960s, radiology technicians also began to work in the new and exciting field of radiation therapy, the use of radiation to treat illnesses like cancer. Radiologists began to advocate for this new auxiliary healthcare position by the 1920s; performing the duties of this job required less professional education and could be done just was well and with less expense to patients by trained technicians.

The duties of a radiology technician included reviewing a physician's orders for diagnostic imaging or radiological treatment. For imaging services, often performed in hospitals and clinics, radiology technicians then took those physician orders and prepared the patient for imaging. They adjusted the X-ray machines to the target body part, such as the chest, and then inserted X-ray film into the device located behind or underneath the patient. The patient had to be carefully positioned to optimize the X-ray image. Radiology technicians then took the X-ray, activating the X-ray machine that released a small amount of radiation through a diffuser that prevented radiation burns while still providing adequate and uniform radiation to create a useful diagnostic image. Most often, X-ray technicians took several images, adjusting the patient to ensure that views from different perspectives were achieved, thereby making the job of reading the image results more accurate. Radiology technicians then developed the film and delivered the final images to the physician team treating the patient.

Prior to 1952, the United States had no specific training requirements for radiology technicians; many had been instructed on the duties of the job by assisting other radiology technicians, working in an X-ray film lab, or serving in the hospital corps forces during World War II (1939–1945) and the Korean War (1950–1953). The American Society of X-Ray Technicians (ASXT), a professional organization, led the effort to create uniform training standards. This national organization lobbied for a year-long postsecondary course of study that included instruction in physics, anatomy, darkroom techniques, communication with patients, and safety. The issue of safety was important, as was the lack of a standard curriculum for training radiology technicians. Positioning a patient on the X-ray table and taking multiple radiographs exposed radiologists and radiology technicians to excess radiation. By the 1940s, most radiology technician training programs and radiologists recognized the importance of protecting workers from the harmful effects of radiation. Radiology technicians began to wear lead aprons, while new imaging spaces provided a wall or cubicle that gave radiology technicians protection from radiation exposure. It was not uncommon for early practitioners of radiology and radiologic technology to develop and succumb to radiation-caused cancers.

Unlike radiation technicians, however, radiologists were trained medical doctors, with postsecondary degrees and post-training internships. Radiologists worked with other teams of healthcare professionals—emergency room physicians and nurses, orthopedic surgeons, family doctors treating individual patients, and others—to determine patient diagnostic and treatment needs. Radiologists ordered X-rays from the radiology lab staffed by X-ray technicians and then "read" the films (images) that were returned to the team. Radiologists had training in understanding how to interpret these images and assisted the treatment team in developing care plans. By the 1960s and 1970s, radiation therapists, or interventional radiologists, also participated in patient treatment as new machines allowed targeted beams of radiation to be directed at a specific cancerous tumor, for instance, to slow or stop its growth before surgery. After surgery, interventional radiologists might also use the same technology to eliminate any metastasis (or spread) of cancer cells to surrounding tissues. Radiology technicians assisted in this work as well, operating the machines as directed by interventional radiologists.

The technology of diagnostic and interventional radiology continually improved and expanded during the 1960s to 1980s, with new machines with greater capacity to detect and treat illnesses, especially cancer. Mammography, for instance, is a preventative medical procedure to screen for breast cancer. As new techniques were developed, the need for radiologists and radiologic technicians also increased exponentially. One federal study in 1968 found that barely half of all radiology technicians were certified—had received the appropriate training recommended by the ASXT (by then, the ASRT or American Society of Radiologic Technicians) and had not taken or passed any examinations that would have qualified them for the position. As a result, the ASRT lobbied Congress for laws that would regulate who could practice this occupation; because radiologists were licensed medical doctors, they were less involved in this legislative activity. The ASRT succeeded in 1981 with the passage of the Consumer Patient Radiation Health and Safety Act, which mandated formal training in accredited postsecondary institutions and certification for radiology technicians.

While the ASRT was successful in its efforts, medical doctors and nuclear physicians collaborated on developing new technologies for the field—some of which failed, despite initial promising results. Many of the techniques developed in the 1950s and 1960s are no longer in use. An example is total body opacification, a belief that the entire human body opacified after administration of intravenous iodine; proponents believed that as a result of opacification, diseased tissues looked denser and may have taken on a darker hue on diagnostic X-ray images. (Iodine was and is used to provide contrast between healthy and diseased tissues.) Despite counterclaims about the basis for the belief in opacification, many radiologists believed in its efficacy until new technologies, such as sonography (imaging by ultrasounds) and computerized tomography (known as CT scans), provided much more reliable results in the mid-1970s. These later techniques had the advantage of providing three-dimensional imagery of patients' bodies as well. Radiologists' belief in the pseudoscientific basis for opacification evaporated once these newer technologies provided better results. Radiology as a science has many similar stories of failure. Not all technologies developed in postwar America proved useful.

Radiology as practiced by radiologists and radiology technicians is now part of mainstream medicine. Its emergence as a major field of practice provided opportunities for employment for doctors and for allied healthcare professionals throughout the country. That positive outlook still exists today.

Nancy Quam-Wickham

See also: Anesthesiologist; Dentist; Veterinarian; *1992–2019:* Physical Therapist

FURTHER READING

"ASRT History." 2018. American Society of Radiologic Technologists (ASRT). Accessed August 31. https://www.asrt.org/main/about-asrt/asrt-history.

Freidson, Eliot. 1989. *Medical Work in America: Essays on Health Care*. New Haven: Yale University Press.

Garland, Joseph, and Joseph Stokes. 1962. *The Choice of a Medical Career; Essays on the Fields of Medicine*. Philadelphia: Lippincott.

Griscom, N. Thorne, and John F. O'Connor. 1995. "The Rise and Fall of a Radiologic Technique." *American Journal of Radiology* 164: 1011–1012.

REGISTRAR

Registrars are government officials who are tasked with keeping a register of eligible voters and other official records. Registrars, also known as electoral clerks, were the gatekeepers of voting registration and access to the polls. Any citizen seeking to register to vote had to go through the registrar, who verified the person's identity and eligibility. Registrars' role was especially influential on registration and elections leading up to the passage of the Voting Rights Act of 1965. Registrars were responsible for enforcing local and state voting registration laws, including those that discriminated against African Americans and other minorities and those that enforced racial segregation. Before the federal government began to get meaningfully involved after World War II (1939–1945), local registrars had wide discretion and control over voting registration and access to polling places in their communities.

Registrars were responsible for overseeing voter registration, scheduling and conducting registration sessions, providing necessary forms for citizens to fill out and return to confirm their eligibility and any special voter-accessibility needs, and processing mail-in ballots. Registrars also maintained voter registry lists, organized and prepared polling places, supervised poll workers on election day, ensured the maintenance, storage, preparation, and transportation of any voting booths and machines, and participated in absentee voting administration.

Employed at the local levels of government, registrars were responsible for keeping voter registry lists, often with some oversight by a state official. Most polling places received a list of voters so that poll workers on Election Day would be able to verify each voter's identity. Registrars organized and conducted elections, trained poll workers, supervised the polls, managed absentee voting, and counted votes. They were also responsible for maintaining voting machines as they were adopted, first as lever machines and then as computerized systems starting in the 1960s.

Registrars—particularly those in rural areas and the South—were instrumental in facilitating election fraud by routinely disqualifying African Americans. Despite the Fourteenth Amendment removing the race barrier to voting after the Civil War (1861–1865), discriminatory practices remained widespread for nearly a century. Registrars and state officials imposed residency requirements, poll taxes, literacy and morality tests, and other obstacles to prevent African Americans and other minorities from voting, often at the complete discretion of the registrar.

In 1944, the Supreme Court declared white-only primary elections to be unconstitutional, meaning that registrars could no longer legally prohibit racial minorities from voting in primary elections because of their race. As the civil rights movement began to emerge in the mid-1950s, white authorities remained reluctant to protect or assist African Americans who were dismissed or attacked when they tried to vote or register to vote. Federal authorities largely failed to enforce the exiting voter protections for minorities. When a court ordered a registrar to cease a certain discriminatory practice, the registrar would often simply switch to a different one.

The Twenty-Fourth Amendment addressed the demands of the emergent and increasingly popular civil rights movement at the federal level, abolishing the poll tax. In the same year, the Civil Rights Act of 1964 prohibited segregation in public places based on race, color, religion, sex, or national origin. The Voting Rights Act of 1965 required federal involvement in local and state elections in areas with a history of voting discrimination. The act prohibited registrars from refusing to record the vote of anyone who was qualified. It also required these areas to receive federal approval before changing their voting practices, binding registrars to those that were federally approved.

After the Voting Rights Act was enacted, the federal government objected to hundreds of discriminatory changes in voting policies submitted for approval by local and state governments. Federal oversight severely limited the wide discretion previously enjoyed by registrars, leading to marked increases in voter registration and election turnout among minorities.

Thomas Nakano

See also: Office Clerk; *1992–2019:* Campaign Manager

FURTHER READING

Hale, Kathleen, et al. 2015. *Administering Elections: How American Elections Work*. New York: Palgrave Macmillan.

Keyssar, Alexander. 2000. *The Right to Vote: The Contested History of Democracy in the United States*. New York: Basic Books.

Medvic, Stephen K. 2017. *Campaigns and Elections: Players and Processes*. New York: Routledge.

Pitts, Michael J. "Section 5 of the Voting Rights Act: A Once and Future Remedy?" *Denver University Law Review* 81.2 (2004): 225–288.

Saltman, Roy G. 2006. *The History and Politics of Voting Technology: In Quest of Integrity and Public Confidence*. New York: Palgrave Macmillan.

PRIMARY DOCUMENT

In this remarkable document, the U.S. Department of Justice outlines the extraordinary efforts that the state of Alabama, supervised by state Registrar of Voters Agnes Baggett, made to limit the franchise, restricting African Americans from registering to vote through a combination of property, literacy, and educational requirements. Agnes Baggett was named as one of the defendants, showing the power that a state-level official had over the right of all Americans to vote. The second part of this court case shows the powers that local registrars and electoral clerks had to enforce the state's agenda.

The United States of America alleges:

1. This action is brought by the Attorney General in the name and on behalf of the United States of America under 42 U.S.C. 1971 as amended, by the Civil Rights Acts of 1957, 1960, and 1964. It seeks to enjoin the use in the State of Alabama of voter registration tests which violate the Constitution and laws of the United States . . .

3. The defendant State of Alabama through its officials and agents prescribes and administers the voter registration tests and requirements in Alabama. The principal State offices and the Capital of the State are in Montgomery.

4. Agnes Baggett is the Secretary of State for the State of Alabama. In this capacity she provides to the registrars of voters of each county the forms of applications and tests to be administered in the registration of voters. She also receives reports periodically from each county regarding the registration of voters. Her office is located and she resides in Montgomery, Alabama.

5. In Alabama, registration is a prerequisite to voting in any election. Registration is permanent and in the absence of special legislation, voters are not required to reregister except when they move from one county to another.

6. Prior to November 14, 1946, the Constitution of Alabama of 1901 provided by section 181 that after January 1, 1903 persons otherwise qualified shall be qualified to register as electors if they are able to read and write any article of the Constitution of the United States or if they own 40 acres of land in Alabama, or own real or personal property in Alabama assessed for taxation at the value of $300 or more. Illiteracy was not a disqualification if the applicant for registration could meet the property qualifications. On November 14, 1946 the voters of Alabama adopted Amendment LV, commonly known as the "Boswell amendment." The property qualification alternative was abandoned and all persons seeking thereafter to register to vote were required to be able to read, write, understand and explain any article of the Constitution of the United States. After the Boswell amendment was declared unconstitutional, the voters of Alabama on December 19, 1951 adopted amendment XCI. Under section 181 of the Constitution of Alabama of 1901, Amendment XCI, citizens over the age of twenty-one years who possess the qualifications as to residence prescribed in section 178 are qualified to register as electors provided they are not disqualified under section 182, if they can read and write any article of the Constitution of the United States and if they are of good character and embrace the duties and obligations of citizenship under the Constitution of the United States and under the Constitution of Alabama. In order to aid the county registrars in determining whether applicants for registration possess the above qualifications, each applicant is to answer in writing without assistance a questionnaire prescribed by the Supreme Court of Alabama. This portion of the Constitution of Alabama has not since been further amended.

7. During the period from about January 1952 to about February 1964 the county registrars in Alabama used a four-page application form and questionnaire in the registration of voters. This form and questionnaire was prescribed by the Supreme Court of Alabama . . .

8. During the period referred to in paragraph 7 applicants for registration to vote in Alabama, except in two counties, rarely were required to demonstrate their

ability to read or write any article of the Constitution. White applicants were not required to complete the application form and questionnaire without error or omission and they were not required to fill out the application form and questionnaire without assistance. During the same period numerous Negro applicants for registration to vote in Alabama were denied registration on the ground that they made errors and/or omissions in completing the application form and questionnaire. They were denied assistance in filling out the application form and questionnaire. Negroes in the State of Alabama have been deprived of their right to vote without distinction of race pursuant to a pattern and practice of racial discrimination.

9. In the State of Alabama there are approximately 1,353,058 white persons and 431,320 Negroes of voting age. Of these, approximately 935,695 white persons (or about 69%) and about 93,737 Negroes (or about 19%) are registered to vote. In each of the 67 counties of Alabama more than 50% of the adult white persons are registered to vote. In at least 40 of these counties less than 25% of the adult Negroes are registered to vote.

10. On January 14, 1964, the Supreme Court of Alabama prescribed a new and different application form and questionnaire to be used by the boards of registrars throughout the State. This new application form and questionnaire included a page labeled "Insert Part III", which contained tests to be used as part of the questionnaire. These tests contained four questions testing the applicant's knowledge of government; four excerpts from the United States Constitution one or more of which were to be read aloud by the applicant to the registrar; and a space for the applicant to write from the dictation of a registrar several words from the Constitution. The Supreme Court's order provided for twelve of these inserts—a different one to be used each month. A total of twenty-four different questions on government and nineteen provisions of the Constitution appeared on twelve Part III inserts . . .

19. The use in Alabama of the Insert Part III tests promulgated in January 1964 and the revised Insert Part III tests promulgated in August 1964 as prerequisites to voting violates 42 U.S.C. 1971(a) and the Fifteenth Amendment to the Constitution of the United States for the following reasons:

(a) It imposes testing procedures and standards which are different from and more stringent than any testing procedures or standards which have been applied to other individuals who have been found by Alabama registrars to be qualified to vote in Alabama, in violation of 42 U.S.C. 1971(a)(2)(A).

(b) It nullifies the sixth grade presumption of literacy established by Congress in 42 U.S.C. 1971(c) by requiring a comprehension and literacy level higher than is normally attained by the completion of six grades of education, in violation of Article VI of the Constitution of the United States.

(c) It imposes an oral dictation test in violation of 42 U.S.C. 1971(a)(2)(C).

(d) It discriminated against Negro applicants and in favor of white applicants because of distinctions in the quality of educational opportunities resulting from a segregated public school system in Alabama, in violation of the Fifteenth Amendment to the Constitution of the United States.
(e) It freezes the existing racial imbalance of the voting structure in Alabama by imposing new and more stringent registration requirements and standards upon future applicants following a long period of discrimination against Negroes in the registration of voters in Alabama, in violation of the Fifteenth Amendment to the Constitution of the United States.
(f) It imposes arbitrarily difficult voter registration requirements and standards at a time when less than 20% of the adult Negroes and more than 65% of the adult white persons in Alabama are registered to vote in a state where there has been a long standing policy of racial segregation and discrimination.

Source: *United States v. Agnes Baggett*. 1965. Civil Action No. 2159-N. VR-AL-0246, 1–5, 9, 10, passim.

SALESPERSON

A salesperson engages prospective buyers, informs them about an item they are considering purchasing, and often helps to complete the purchase, sometimes facilitating payment arrangements if a consumer can't immediately afford a full purchase price—especially for such big-ticket items as automobiles or large household appliances. But a salesperson does much more than sell an item to a prospective consumer.

After World War II, the United States enjoyed a period of unprecedented economic prosperity, though the material benefits of this prosperity were not shared equally across the population. Nonetheless, Americans who had survived both the Great Depression of the 1930s and the strains and stresses of wartime generally experienced more access to more consumer goods than ever before. The salesperson was, in some ways, at the center of this new and exciting consumer lifestyle. Salespeople were frontline workers in the business and marketing enterprises: They collected information about consumer preferences, improved strategic communications between seller and buyer, and helped companies develop better products. Salespeople also had key responsibilities as employees as they had to learn product information to be able to speak knowledgably with consumers, consider the ethical implications of sales (and selling tactics and approaches), and serve as the representative of a company's products.

At their most fundamental duty, salespeople were employed to sell a product. To do so effectively, a salesperson had to understand the function and purpose of a company's product, including having a grasp of alternatives to the product. For instance, an automobile salesperson who worked for a new car dealership selling only Ford cars and trucks had to know all about those models (which changed each year), how models were improved or were different one year from the next, all of the various accessories a buyer might request, special features of a car, options for engine and interior and exterior colors, as well as how a Ford sedan, for instance, was a better car for a prospective consumer than a competing sedan. To effectively represent the company's product, both a broad understanding of the product and its alternatives (Ford and other auto manufacturer's sedans) and deep knowledge of one's particular product (Ford vehicles) was critical for success. When not engaged with a customer, salespeople often spent their work time learning more about the products they sold or in training sessions with other salespeople and managers. When a customer decided to commit to making a purchase, the salesperson is said to have "closed the deal" or made a "closing."

Salespeople have other duties during work hours. Sales has been called a "people business"—one that requires good communication skills, professional demeanor, and basic understanding of human motivation (as it relates to buying products). Salespeople had a series of steps they employed to sell a product, which varied according to the product and the sales environment. Salespeople who worked on a team that sold medical supplies regionally, for instance, engaged in prospecting: they worked closely to identify prospective clients, following leads or making telephone calls or visits to a medical center, clinic, or doctor's office. Salespeople then followed leads to make initial contacts, which in this case might be several clinics and small hospitals within a 150-mile radius. A salesperson visited those prospective customers, educated them about the company's products, and tried to persuade them to buy those products. In the postwar period, studies of exceptional salespeople revealed that talented ones were generally extroverts, competitive yet empathetic, and demonstrated a strong work ethic. In particular, they were not easily discouraged by challenges such as a skeptical potential consumer might present.

In this period of postwar American consumerism, customers were able to purchase products in different environments: retailers like groceries and department stores that sold many different brands of products, dealerships that sold products made by only one manufacturer, and even within their own homes. Door-to-door salespeople traveled throughout neighborhoods selling goods directly to consumers. The Fuller Brush Company, for instance, sold its consumer products only through a door-to-door sales model from its founding in 1906 through 1985, with the exception of the two world wars, when its products were redesigned for military use. The iconic "Fuller Brush Man" sold the Fuller products to buyers throughout the nation: A man wearing a suit and carrying a suitcase full of products rang doorbells or knocked on doors to get the attention of the resident. He then introduced the company's products, which included a variety of brushes for personal care (hairbrushes, brushes for scrubbing fingernails) and home care and cleaning (baby bottle brushes, whisk brooms, scrub brushes for cleaning floors and ovens).

The company's salesmen were expected to pitch the products by offering to demonstrate their use, so the Fuller Brush Man might scrub a kitchen floor in one home, clean bottles in another, and sweep the front porch in yet a third home, all in an effort to show customers the value of the products. The Fuller Brush Man was so recognizable to American consumers that a comedy motion picture of the same name was released in theaters in 1948. Other companies used door-to-door sales models to sell other home-based goods: cosmetics, vacuum cleaners, and health improvement items, as well as others.

Whether salespeople worked in a central or regional sales office, a retail store or dealership, or even door to door, they used the people skills and product knowledge to convince Americans to buy more and more products. Buying to buy, though, was not just an attitude; in fact, since most salespeople had quotas or sales expectations requiring them to sell a certain number of products per week or month, the salesperson's job itself depended on this practice of continual purchase of material goods (and, in some cases, services). Those salesmen employed by the Fuller Company had to walk a daily route of at least six miles, carrying their products along with them and demonstrating their use whenever a customer requested it. In addition, most salespeople worked long hours to meet their employers' expectations. A medical supplies salesperson, for instance, often had an assigned region, requiring travel and work away from one's home for days at a time.

Salespeople also provided market research to their employer, filing regular reports about consumers' product questions and noting any persistent concerns or trouble they encountered with the products they were tasked to sell. This valuable information helped manufacturers and companies make good decisions about a product's lifecycle, for instance, whether the product was going to continue to sell or whether it needed revamping or retiring. A company's marketing department depended on the information that salespeople provided it to maintain the company's sales and profitability.

The work of a salesperson—and the salesperson's stature in American culture—waxed and waned during this post–World War II era. While the "used car salesman" often evoked a negative image of an unethical salesperson in the mind of most consumers, in reality the extraordinary success of American businesses during this time depended on the hard work of the salesperson.

Nancy Quam-Wickham

See also: Advertising Account Executive; Travel Agent; *1776–1860:* Huckster; *1992–2019:* E-Commerce Specialist

FURTHER READING

Beckley, Donald K., and William Boyd Logan. 1949. *The Retail Salesperson at Work*. New York: Gregg Pub. Co.

Dawson, Roger. 2012. *Secrets of Power Persuasion for Salespeople*. Wayne: Career Press.

Spears, Timothy B. 1995. *100 Years on the Road: The Traveling Salesman in American Culture*. New Haven: Yale University Press.

SCIENTIST

Because the construction of a large base of fundamental scientific knowledge is widely considered to be a public good that leads to beneficial new products and inventions, in the post–World War II period, governments increasingly used taxpayer funds to support scientific research. Scientists are men and women who conduct basic research in laboratories, known as bench scientists. Other scientists conduct field research, like geologists, while also working in offices analyzing data collected in the field. Other scientists, like nuclear physicists and atmospheric chemists, work in specialized research facilities with sophisticated equipment, like nuclear particle accelerators, that allow them to model basic scientific processes, which they study to understand a complex world. Some scientists are leading researchers, supervising the work of bench scientists, laboratory workers, and field technicians who collect needed data. Biomedical research scientists are one such type of researcher, and their field is focused on the study of the treatment and prevention of disease and the environmental and genetic factors that affect human health.

Among all branches of scientific work, there are clear hierarchies of worker organization. Bench scientists in laboratories ran experiments, carefully collected and logged data, and at the end of an experiment, analyzed the data, often using computers. Field technicians collected specimens, cataloged, and classified them, taking careful notes about the location and characteristics of the environment in which a specimen was collected. Many bench scientists have bachelor's degrees in basic science fields, like microbiology, chemistry, and zoology, though in both lab and field, other technicians assisted bench scientists; these workers were generally students, technicians, and other workers who had been trained for particular duties, such as logging the amount of food that laboratory animals consumed during a particular experiment. Laboratory and field supervisors often had greater responsibilities and more experience; they often communicated and implemented a research scientist's experimental design, instructing and managing bench scientists and technicians in their work and reporting out to the research scientist any promising data collected during the experiment. Supervising scientists managed the entire research project in conjunction with those at the highest level of the scientific worker hierarchy: the research scientists, who often worked as professors in colleges and universities as well. Research scientists propose new hypotheses, conceptualize experiments, and, importantly, obtain the funding to support expensive research.

During the Cold War, the United States and the Soviet Union (U.S.S.R.) competed for global scientific and technological leadership. The U.S.S.R.'s 1957 launch of the world's first satellite, Sputnik, startled the United States and led the government to increase support for research in science and technology. These investments included a substantial increase in research on molecular biology, biochemistry, and nuclear physics. Among biologists and biomedical research scientists, an impetus for this allocation was the discovery of the DNA double helix in 1953, which suggested that an understanding of the molecular basis for life was within reach. New university departments were founded focused on molecular biology, and the relatively few PhDs in this field were quickly snapped up as assistant professors, even though many of them were still in their twenties.

Many research scientists during the Cold War period started as professors at universities; these institutions paid the scientists and provided laboratory spaces. However, many scientists' work required specialized equipment that was often too costly for the university to obtain. Therefore, scientists competed with one another for a limited supply of U.S. government research grants, most notably from the National Science Foundation (NSF) or the National Institute of Health (NIH). Obtaining these research funds required a lot of work and the preparation of grant applications. Researchers in some scientific fields, like physics and oceanography, found that their research activities had clear military applications and thus secured regular research funding from the Department of Defense. Geologists and nuclear physicists also obtained funding from the U.S. Department of Energy. Finally, a wide range of scientific researchers—especially in geosciences, pharmaceutical and biochemical sciences, and materials science—received funding from corporate sponsors.

A peer group of scientists evaluated each scientist's proposal and then ranked each against competing proposals. As such, all grant applicants aimed to convince their peers that the question they sought to pursue was an important one, that their strategy for addressing that question was innovative and feasible, and, if funded, they would have access to the talent, environment, equipment, and resources necessary to complete their project. Grant applications were competitive; only about 40 percent of all applications were funded. But most faculty hired by major universities received such grants within one or two years. Once a researcher secured funding from the federal government, the scientist then had to make substantial progress toward the project's research goals. This often required professors to enlist a selection of their most talented students to provide research assistance in return for mentorship. Within the biomedical sciences, for instance, the research process might take a form much like this: Inspired by the elegant simplicity of DNA as the carrier of genetic information for life, researchers sought to decipher the molecular basis for protein synthesis and gene control and many other central biological processes. A typical research project's challenge was first to identify an important question about how a cell or an organism works at a molecular level—a question that, if answered, would increase the understanding of some life process. Next, a researcher needed to create a strategy—or research plan—for solving that mystery, which involved the use of research methods that other scientists had previously developed and which could, in principle, be combined to try to address the research project's central question. Good research plans required a great deal of creativity.

Research grants are generally given to support three to five years of research, which was usually enough time for a research project to achieve significant results. One important mark of success was the acceptance a research project's results for publication in a scientific journal. In general, a researcher needs only a few publications of important findings to launch a successful researching career. In the second half of the twentieth century, a successful researcher would be expected to create a new research plan every few years to compete for follow-up research grants. A typical career as a research group leader ended with mandatory retirement at age sixty-five.

Much has changed since the end of the Cold War. The ending of mandatory retirement by Congress in 1986 led to a substantial aging of research faculty. In addition, a large increase in the number of PhDs produced in the United States each year has generated a long postdoctoral holding period that has dramatically increased the age at which a typical faculty member receives an initial government research grant. Finally, the need for most faculty members today to provide a large portion of their own salary from research grants and an increased difficulty of obtaining funding—with success rates below 20 percent—has required much more frequent writing of grant applications.

Bruce Alberts

See also: College Professor; Economist; Oceanographer; *1992–2019:* Forensic Scientist; Scientific Illustrator

FURTHER READING

Alberts, B., M. W. Kirschner, S. Tilghman, and H. Varmus. 2014. "Rescuing US Biomedical Research from Its Systemic Flaws." *Proceedings of the National Academy of Sciences* 111, no. 16: 5773–5777.

"Beyond Discovery Home." 2018. National Academy of Sciences. http://www.nasonline.org/publications/beyond-discovery.

Levitt, Michael, and Jonathan M. Levitt. 2017. "Future of Fundamental Discovery in US Biomedical Research." *Proceedings of the National Academy of Sciences* 114, no. 25: 6498–6503.

SINGER

The singer, a person who sings professionally, as an occupation is largely a twentieth-century invention as technology—primarily audio records (especially the long-playing LP) and the reproduction of sounds on radio and in motion pictures—made singing a financially viable profession. Singers provide entertainment to listeners. Some write their own songs, while others perform songs written by songwriters. In the postwar era, singers worked in many different venues: opera houses and theaters, nightclubs and lounges, concert halls and casinos, dance halls, and local community centers. Some singers performed in churches and other houses of worship. Others performed in outdoor stadiums. Singers were invited to perform at presidential inaugurations, national party conventions, and major sporting events.

Singers are those musically talented individuals who are able to use their voices as their musical instrument. They read music from a song sheet, understand notes and scales, and recognize different rhythmic structures. Singers practice their instrument—their voice—through repetitive musical exercises under the tutelage of a voice instructor in a studio, conservatory, or other practice space. Singers and voice instructors may have especially close student-teacher relationships that span decades. Voice lessons may not only focus on improving a singer's tone and pitch through musical scale and other exercises but also emphasize breathing techniques and diction (enunciation of words). Singers must also learn how to project their voices and convey emotion through their voices and bodies. Convincingly conveying emotion is part of every singer's job as music is a form of communication; songs inspire, motivate, memorialize, and calm others. Professional singers are able to communicate the emotions contained within each song to audiences. Think, for instance, of the ways that different singers have performed the "Star-Spangled Banner:" Jose Feliciano's folk version at the 1968 World Series, Jimi Hendrix's electric rock version at Woodstock in 1969, or Marvin Gaye's rhythm and blues 1983 rendition at the NBA finals. All of them evoked different reactions among listeners.

Many singers also play at least one musical instrument: piano, guitar, or one or more of any others, while some instrumentalists, like jazz trumpeter Louis Armstrong, also sang in performances. In bands, singers combine their voices with other instruments, while other singers are accompanied by backup instrumentalists. The rockabilly and rock-and-roll pioneer Elvis Presley, for instance, played guitar, though initially it was his voice that brought fame; he was accompanied by more accomplished guitarist Scotty Moore and bassist Bill Black on his first commercial recordings, made in 1954. Singers who also played instruments like guitar had not only voice lessons, normally on a weekly basis, but also practiced playing their instruments for hours each day. All professional singers, regardless of musical style, also rehearsed regularly before performances. In fact, performances represented relatively little of a working day for a singer. Not long after blues singer Janis Joplin joined the band Big Brother and the Holding Company in San Francisco in 1966, she and the band moved to a communal house in Marin County, where they practiced all day and much of every night, performing only on weekends at Bill Graham's Fillmore Theater. A singer could perform solo, be a member of a chorale, symphony, opera, or theater company, or be an employee of an entertainment venue or company. Some singers, for instance, were employed as studio musicians at production companies that made both movies and television. Others worked as regular employees in leisure venues, such as resorts in the Catskills (New York) or Poconos (Pennsylvania) or, beginning in the 1980s, on the new vacation cruise ships.

Theaters, nightclubs, and live performances provided steady work for many singers in the years before television. In the agricultural regions of south Texas and California, singer Lydia Mendoza performed in different small towns—often separated by just a few miles—in the early part of the week, Mondays through Wednesdays, then rested on Thursday, and then sang on Friday and Saturday nights in variety shows in larger movie theaters after the Spanish-language feature film. Travel was a given for singers, but as Mendoza later realized, as television became more popular, opportunities for live performances in local theaters declined; instead, she moved to Los Angeles for regular bookings at larger venues like the Million Dollar Theater. Already a star among Mexican-American audiences, in the 1950s, Mendoza recorded a number of LPs with a *conjunto norteno* band, broadening the appeal of her former work in balladry. Mendoza's career as a singer spanned more than fifty years, which she attributed to her work ethic and clean lifestyle, as well as her willingness to adapt to changing musical tastes and technological innovations.

The career arc of tenor Jacob Pincus Perelmuth, later adopting the Anglicized name Jan Peerce, also demonstrates some of the ways in which a professional singer gained fame and a solid career. A son of Russian Jewish immigrants in New York City, Perelmuth first learned to play the violin; he later took voice lessons as a teenager and then formed a band of fellow teenagers, who played dance music for neighborhood events and, later, in the Catskills. In the 1930s, Perelmuth changed his name to Peerce and found work singing in Broadway plays and on the radio program "Radio City Music Hall of the Air." Peerce also sang cantorial music, or Jewish religious songs, on another radio show. Later, the great opera singer Arturo Toscanini heard Peerce on the radio and invited him to sing with the NBC Symphony on a radio show; in 1939, Peerce was hired to sing with New York Metropolitan Opera, a role he held until 1968. Audiences across the country heard Peerce, since the Saturday matinee performances were recorded as well as broadcast nationally, on the show "Live at the Met." During his time at the Met, Peerce also toured with other groups, primarily the Bach Aria Group, and had solo performances in Europe. He served as cantor for two services at the Great Synagogue of Moscow in 1956 and 1963. Peerce also recorded opera, as well as other more popular songs, while singing on television, on radio, and in the movies. When he left the Met, he moved to musical comedy on Broadway, for which he won great acclaim as Tevye in *Fiddler on the Roof* in the 1970s.

Successful professional singers often secured the assistance of talent managers, who handled the daily business needs of performers: booked performances, arranged for studio time, negotiated with record companies, and handled travel arrangements. Particular record companies, or labels, with which a singer was under contract often set live performance schedules and determined the songs a singer could perform in concert—usually to boost record sales. Production companies, too, set schedules for singers who appeared in movies. Under contract to Paramount in the late 1950s, the singer Pearl Bailey was cast in the movie *St. Louis Blues*. At the time of filming, however, Bailey was also under contract to appear in two nightly shows at the Flamingo Hotel on the Las Vegas Strip. As Bailey recounted in her 1968 autobiography, she commuted for three weeks, satisfying the terms of her contract for both employers: "I'd do the show [in Las Vegas], leave in a car at 1:30 A.M., arrive at the studio in time to dress at 8 A.M., finish at 3 P.M., catch a plane (which most of the time was late), arrive in Vegas to bathe and get ready for two shows at eight-thirty and midnight. This went on for the entire picture" (Bailey 1968, 76). Those singers who starred in movies also had to appear in promotional events for studios.

Whether a star or a journeyman, singers worked long hours to improve their performances and perfect their musical skills. At each performance, a singer faced a new audience. Connecting to that audience powerfully and authentically through song was a great responsibility and challenge for every singer.

Nancy Quam-Wickham

See also: Actor/Actress (Film and Television); Artist

FURTHER READING

Bailey, Pearl. 1968. *The Raw Pearl.* New York: Harcourt, Brace, & World.
Broyles-Gonzalez, Yolanda. 2001. *Lydia Medoza's Life in Music.* London: Oxford.
Davis, Peter G. 1999. *The American Opera Singer.* New York: Anchor Books.
Echols, Alice. 1999. *Scars of Sweet Paradise: The Life and Times of Janis Joplin.* New York: Owl Books.

SOCIAL WORKER

A social worker is a helping professional who assists other people with securing shelter, finding job training, adjusting to life after institutional care, protecting children and the elderly from abuse and neglect, and by providing care to those who seek counseling to overcome a wide variety of health, social, and economic problems. In the mid-twentieth century, the occupation of social work in the United States grew from a small number of volunteers without educational training, who worked largely among the poor in local charities, to an organized profession of several hundred thousand well-trained members with a global reach. Throughout this period, social workers have played leadership roles in developing and implementing significant government reforms, such as Social Security, Medicare, Medicaid, and unemployment insurance. They have advocated for features of modern life we now take for granted, including playgrounds and kindergartens, public health clinics, street lighting, food and drug safety, and the civil rights of racial and ethnic minorities, women, immigrants, and persons with disabilities. They are employed in child welfare agencies, corporations, hospitals, schools, unions, and the military, among many other places. In fact, social workers are the largest source of mental health counseling in the United States and one of the fastest-growing occupations in the nation.

Social work emerged as a formal occupation in the late nineteenth century. At this time, most social workers worked in three types of organizations that responded in different ways to the increasing social problems created by rapid industrialization and urbanization and mass immigration. One was Charity Organization Societies (COS), which attempted to coordinate the haphazard distribution of poor relief. The so-called volunteer "friendly visitors" of the COS eventually became social caseworkers; they are the ancestors of today's clinical social workers (those who do mental health counseling) and case managers. A second was Settlement Houses, urban missions that delivered a wide range of "concrete" services primarily to immigrant families. Settlement workers introduced the use of groups, community organizing, and policy advocacy to the social work field. The third was local and state government agencies that protected children from abuse and operated public hospitals and mental health facilities. Social workers in these agencies helped found the fields of public management and public policy development, implementation, and evaluation. For several decades, most social workers were unpaid volunteers, largely from wealthy families. By the beginning of the twentieth century, however, social work leaders realized the nation's problems were too complex and widespread for untrained volunteers to effectively address them. They founded the first schools of social work in large cities such as Boston, New York, and Philadelphia and for years tried with some success to have social work recognized as a profession similar to law and medicine.

While social workers organized professional associations and established public and private agencies all across the United States during the 1920s, largely as a result of growing awareness of the traumas produced by World War I (1914–1918), particularly what was then called "shell shock" (today, post-traumatic stress disorder, or PTSD), the devastating consequences of the Great Depression dramatically transformed the scope of social workers' functions. President Franklin Roosevelt's New Deal agencies required thousands of new social workers to staff the agencies that administered them. Consequently, the number of social workers in the United States tripled in just a decade. In response, private, nongovernmental organizations (often called nonprofit or voluntary organizations in the United States) shifted their focus from serving low-income persons toward the provision of counseling middle-class families. During this period, many social workers were also actively involved in the creation of labor unions, community engagement, youth development, and mental health counseling.

World War II and its aftermath further expanded and revised the scope of social workers' activities. During the war and afterward, social workers organized childcare facilities for working mothers. They also found public employment with local child protection agencies, meeting with parents, teachers, neighbors, and others to intervene in cases of abuse or neglect. Some social workers visited the homes of families in crisis, evaluating the needs of children and providing education on parenting, raising healthy children, and meeting the educational needs of at-risk children, in order to keep families together. In 1954, Philadelphia social worker Margaret Moffatt Toy worked with a local community agency to organize a delivery service providing meals and companionship to homebound senior and disabled citizens; this program later spread throughout the country and is now known as Meals on Wheels. Some social workers specialized in the field of juvenile delinquency, intervening with youngsters who were incarcerated and providing afterschool activities for those children in need. Others worked as hospital social workers, helping patients and their families navigate a complex healthcare system and obtain post-hospitalization services. Others worked in offices, offering counseling, health, and mental health services to union members, military personnel, veterans, older Americans, and their families. Through the introduction of psychiatric theories, especially those of Sigmund Freud, social workers began to serve middle-class individuals and families, especially children, in clinics, schools, hospitals, and multipurpose agencies. In the 1950s, the formation of the National Association of Social Workers and the Council on Social Work Education consolidated the social work field and symbolized its growing significance in U.S. society.

The social ferment of the 1960s and early 1970s, particularly the impact of the civil rights, women's, and anti-war movements and the reforms introduced by the War on Poverty and the Great Society programs of the Kennedy and Johnson Administrations, revived the community-practice component of social work. They also expanded social work's role in such areas as services to the aged, community mental health, job training, substance abuse counseling, and domestic violence treatment and prevention. In these areas, social workers organized and staffed social service agencies, worked in hospital and jail settings to lead individual and group therapy sessions, and trained volunteers to handle calls to suicide prevention agencies. Geriatric social workers worked in offices to coordinate care for isolated elderly community residents and sometimes made home visits to consult with families about safe housing alternatives. Child and family service social workers typically spent their days reviewing cases, consulting with children and families, making home visits, and sometimes attending court hearings on the behalf of their clients. Other social workers partnered with nurses and physicians in community health departments, providing methadone treatment to individuals recovering from heroin addiction. Some social workers were employed in school settings to coordinate programs for youths. The federal government funded many of these programs; as a result, social workers, especially in the nonprofit sector, became increasingly dependent on public support. Consequently, the cuts in social spending implemented by the Reagan and Bush Administrations forced many social workers and social service agencies to defend their programs and to advocate more extensively for their clients and constituents.

As they struggled with the effects of deep funding cuts during the 1980s, social workers also confronted unprecedented social problems that challenged them to develop new knowledge and skills. These problems included increasing homelessness, the HIV/AIDS epidemic, the spread of crack cocaine, and large-scale immigration from Southeast Asia, Central America, and the Caribbean. One way in which the field of social work responded was by developing many new educational programs at the baccalaureate, master's, and doctoral levels to meet the growing demand for social work personnel. Another was to strengthen the role of research in social work as part of an emphasis on evidence-based practice. Finally, social workers expanded their traditional functions to include client advocacy and greater attention to the efficient use of resources in their agencies. The latter reflected the growing trend for managed care in such varied areas as healthcare and child welfare. As a result, social workers spend significant time each day attending meetings and consultations with other professionals, working on agency budgets, identifying and applying for funding opportunities, and meeting with government officials to secure more public funding.

Another major development among social workers during the 1980s and 1990s reflected widespread, bipartisan concerns about the nation's welfare system. Many social workers became involved at the state and local levels in a variety of experimental programs that attempted to reduce the welfare rolls by providing both "carrots" (incentives such as support services) and "sticks" (punishments such as the loss of assistance) to welfare recipients to encourage or coerce them to transition from welfare to work. These efforts culminated in a 1996 welfare reform legislation signed by President Clinton. In addition to dramatic revisions in the nation's welfare system, welfare reform also changed social workers' roles and created new problems for them to address. Social workers increasingly served as case managers in states' varying attempts to implement the provisions of welfare reform. Building on prior efforts to enhance the role of social work research, by the beginning of the twenty-first century, they focused on evaluating the effectiveness of programs' interventions with current and former welfare recipients and other populations in need, such as at-risk youth, homeless individuals, older adults, formerly incarcerated individuals, and those who abused alcohol or illegal drugs.

Michael Reisch

See also: Community Organizer; *1992–2019:* Psychologist

FURTHER READING

Beito, David T. 2000. *From Mutual Aid to the Welfare State: Fraternal Societies and Social Services, 1890–1967*. Chapel Hill: University of North Carolina Press.

Ehrenreich, John H. 1985. *The Altruistic Imagination: A History of Social Work and Social Welfare in the United States*. Ithaca: Cornell University Press.

Iglehart, Alfreda P., and Rosina M. Becerra. 2011. *Social Services and the Ethnic Community: History and Analysis*. Long Grove: Waveland Press

Lasch-Quinn, Elizabeth. 1993. *Black Neighbors: Race and the Limits of Reform in the American Settlement House Movement, 1890–1945*. Chapel Hill: University of North Carolina Press.

Lubove, Roy. 1965. *The Professional Altruist: The Emergence of Social Work as a Career, 1880–1930*. Cambridge: Harvard University Press.

Margolin, Leslie. 1997. *Under the Cover of Kindness: The Invention of Social Work*. Charlottesville: University Press of Virginia.

Morris, Andrew J. F. 2009. *The Limits of Voluntarism: Charity and Welfare from the New Deal through the Great Society*. New York: Cambridge University Press.

Morris, Robert, and Michael Freund, eds. 1966. *Trends and Issues in Jewish Social Work in the United States, 1899–1952.* Philadelphia: Jewish Publication Society of America.
Popple, Philip R. 2018. *Social Work Practice and Social Welfare Policy in the United States: A History*. New York: Oxford University Press.
Pumphrey, R., and M. Pumphrey, eds. 1961. *The Heritage of American Social Work: Readings in Its Philosophical and Institutional Development.* New York: Columbia University Press.
Reisch, Michael, and Janice Andrews. 2002. *The Road Not Taken: A History of Radical Social Work in the United States*. Philadelphia: Brunner-Routledge.
Ross, Edyth L., ed. 1978. *Black Heritage in Social Welfare, 1860–1930*. Metuchen: The Scarecrow Press.
Simon, Barbara Levy. 1994. *The Empowerment Tradition in American Social Work: A History*. New York: Columbia University Press.
Specht, Harry, and Mark E. Courtney. 1994. *Unfaithful Angels: How Social Work Abandoned Its Mission.* New York: Free Press.
Trolander, Judith Ann. 1987. *Professionalism and Social Change: From the Settlement House Movement to Neighborhood Centers, 1886 to the Present.* New York: Columbia University Press.
Wagner, David. 1990. *The Quest for a Radical Profession: Social Service Careers and Political Ideology.* New York: University Press of America.
Walkowitz, Daniel. 1999. *Working with Class: Social Workers and the Politics of Middle Class Identity.* Chapel Hill: University of North Carolina Press.
Wenocur, Stanley, and Michael Reisch. 1989. *From Charity to Enterprise: The Development of American Social Work in a Market Economy*. Urbana: University of Illinois Press.

PRIMARY DOCUMENT

In this oral history, retired social worker David Kuroda discusses his role as a social worker for the Family Division of the Los Angeles County Superior Court system. Kuroda was born in the Amache Internment Camp in Colorado during World War II, and his parents had expected him to pursue a medical degree, but Kuroda choose social work instead. After completing his MSW degree at USC in 1972, Kuroda worked in a Los Angeles area community mental health clinic, for the Psychiatric Emergency Team (PET) of the health department, and, later, supervising social work graduate students at Children's Hospital of Los Angeles. In 1981, he was recruited to start a family mediation team for divorcing couples. In the passage below, he describes the distinct role that social workers can play in the contemporary legal system.

There was great excitement because of the newness of the mediation program. It was probably one of the best times for court-based mediation programs in the country. Not only were we one of the—I think we were one of the first court programs that had mediation, we were the largest, and in those years, I think, we were the best. This is compared to all the other courts in the nation. I'd say 80% of our staff was social workers by training. What we did was resolve disputes between parents so that the courts wouldn't have to hear these cases and the parents and families could avoid the costly trials . . .

[Parents were referred to the mediation staff.] By this time, it was mandatory. It was required by state law. California had passed the first mandatory mediation law in the country. Actually, family law in California has been very, very progressive. It was ten years before then, in 1971, that California first passed the no-fault divorce law. Since that time, all the other states have followed California's example. So, ten years later, California, again, set the trend and really a better way of helping people get divorced which was good for children and families by-passing the law that required mediation before all hearings and trials . . . Mediation was different from therapy and counseling and relied heavily on skills that we learned in the School of Social Work. We look at the problem, which typically was how they were going to take care of the children after divorce. Then they were called "custody visitation disputes," and now we refer to them as "differences over parenting plans." What we would do is use our clinical skills in listening and trying to understand the reasoning behind peoples' positions and help them put aside those differences and get beyond the anger and resolve disputes and come to agreements for their own children.

The lawyers typically had people together, so we used that model a lot. We would have both parents, the father and the mother of the children, together. But occasionally, we would see people separately and individually, and over the years, the laws regarding domestic violence cases affected how we provided services also. There are some laws, now, that require individual sessions when there are concerns about domestic violence . . . Lawyers didn't do that, but the contribution that we made, that social workers made to the process, was to recognize that and to honor individual differences in perceptions and communications, so we would often have individual sessions . . .

My work changed over the years because I was interested in more than just the mediation. I became interested in working with lawyers, with the Bar Association. I became interested in more education models in doing things in the community. For example, when I was assigned to the District Court in Van Nuys, I was invited by the Bar Association to speak at one of their monthly meetings. During that meeting I realized that lawyers and our staff, our mediators, really needed to know more about each other's work. I began to express interest in doing work with the Bar Association and with lawyers. I called Hugh, our director then—and he was always encouraging of that—even though it meant I might see one less case that day. I was encouraged to go to these meetings and meet those people in the community to develop these collaborative relations. That became something that I did more and more. Eventually, I was put in charge of all the district courts, and we would put on divorce seminars that were provided as a community service. These became model programs, and we would have these all over the County, attracting as many as 700 people at one time. We got press coverage and television shows would cover these programs. What we were doing was getting the word out about the needs of children of divorce.

Source: David Kenichi Kuroda. 2003. Oral History, interviewed by Frances Loman Feldman. California Social Welfare Archives. University of Southern California, 15–19. Courtesy of USC Libraries Special Collections. https://libraries.usc.edu/sites/default/files/kuroda_david.pdf.

STATISTICIAN

Statisticians are mathematicians who deal with the collection, organization, analysis, and interpretation of data. They are responsible for far more than just data processing; many statisticians spend their days examining how experiments are designed, surveys are conducted, or data is gathered to ensure that the quality of their ultimate results remains high and that investigators, governments, or businesses are to learn something meaningful. Statisticians might suggest changing the way questions are phrased or measures are calculated, advise companies to expand how many people are surveyed, or determine whether a distinction between two results is a significant one.

Though people have been keeping numerical records for centuries, professional statisticians were rare before the 1940s. Before then, assistants and clerks performed the statisticians' role. That is, a statistician was not considered as a professional like a doctor or lawyer but more like a mechanic or a tradesperson. Two historical changes helped establish the statisticians' profession. First, statisticians in the early twentieth century developed tests and tools that enabled them to not just describe numerical data but also help them make decisions and reach conclusions with incomplete data. For example, a statistician hired at a plant nursery in 1900 might spent the first years of his career collecting daily data that described phenomena—the average height of a certain plant and variations in that average over time—but not much else would be done with those observations. By 1950, though, a similar nursery statistician had statistical models which allowed him or her to associate the heights of the plants to hypothesize about causes of that height.

Second, as electronic computers and other technologies enabled the storage of ever-increasing quantities of numbers after the 1940s, statisticians became crucial to the development and understanding of the vast amounts of data and experimental design that computer technology made available.

The largest employers of statisticians have traditionally been governments and state agencies. The English term "statistics" itself emerged from the German word *statistik* for the study of political facts and figures. The first statisticians helped kings and parliaments keep track of a nation's wealth and population. Even by the 1940s, most active statisticians in the United States worked in government operations and state-level record keeping, particularly in the Census Bureau and Bureau of Labor Statistics.

Agriculture is another important field in which statisticians have worked. It was in agriculture that the British statistician R. A. Fisher (1890–1962) first developed the technique of hypothesis testing—using observational and experimental data to test a potential explanation—that would eventually dominate the practice of statistics. George Snedecor (1881–1974), head of one of the first departments of statistics in the country, helped introduce Fisher's techniques into American agriculture.

Though there were fewer than five university departments of statistics in the 1940s, many new ones were created in the following years. University-based statisticians tended to spend their days working like mathematicians, inventing new techniques, refining mathematical theories, and teaching undergraduate and graduate students. Most statisticians, however, were involved in the application of these techniques. They often worked with private companies to analyze revenues and processes, or they worked for federal and state governments to calculate unemployment rates, population dynamics, or legislative efficacy.

Statisticians' skill of interpreting numbers meant they were soon needed in a wider and wider range of settings. In clinical medicine, for example, statisticians were not commonly used in the early 1900s. Physicians themselves observed their patients to determine which therapies were effective. Over the course of the twentieth century, however, hospital, universities, pharmaceutical companies, and federal agencies increasingly employed statisticians because their expertise was needed to find better and more reliable ways to test new drugs and treatments. Today, data are being used to inform decisions about the best cancer treatments, to entice people to click an ad on the internet, and to identify fraudulent banking transactions. Statisticians play crucial roles day to day in all these areas, helping companies, governments, and individuals make sense of the numbers around them.

Because statistics is a relatively new profession, it has been more open to people who had traditionally been denied places in universities and elite institutions. Jews, African Americans, and women, for example, held positions as statistical clerks and calculators early in the century and were able to move into positions as professional statisticians more easily than in some other areas. The first African American elected to the National Academy of Sciences was David Blackwell (1919–2010), a statistician and former chair of UC Berkeley's Statistics Department. Gertrude Cox (1900–1978) not only organized and led a new Department of Experimental Statistics at North Carolina State College in the 1940s, but she edited important journals for the American Statistical Association and assumed the presidency of the association in 1956.

Because there were few graduate degrees in statistics before the 1950s, many of the leaders in the field had learned statistics on the job, opening the ranks of the profession to those without access to higher-education degrees. As late as 1974, the president of the American Statistical Association, Jerome Cornfield, possessed only a bachelor's degree in history from New York University but had acquired his statistical knowledge and reputation while employed as a statistician for the federal government.

Statisticians increasingly find themselves in demand as industries, governments, and businesses need people able to make sense of huge quantities of data. It has been one of the fastest-growing technical professions of the last century, and based on its own data, the Bureau of Labor Statistics expects the field to continue growing over the coming years—exactly the sort of predictive ability that has made statisticians essential.

Christopher J. Phillips

See also: College Professor; Scientist; *1992–2019:* Data Analyst

FURTHER READING

American Statistical Association. n.d. "Statisticians in History." https://ww2.amstat.org/about/statisticiansinhistory.

American Statistical Association. 2018. http://www.amstat.org/.

Salsburg, David. 2001. *The Lady Tasting Tea: How Statistics Revolutionized Science in the Twentieth Century*. New York: Freeman.

Stigler, Stephen M. 2016. *The Seven Pillars of Statistical Wisdom*. Cambridge: Harvard University Press.

PRIMARY DOCUMENT

During the 1960s, The American Statistician, *the primary journal for professional statisticians, regularly published poetry, word games, and humorous stories written by statisticians for statisticians. The three poems below represent some of these contributions that the nonprofessional reader might find more accessible.*

1. DEAR STATISTICIAN

Bags of rice and tons of grain,
Counted up by your big, bright brain;
Multipliers, tabulators
Are for you the prime creators.
People walking down the streets
Make their mark on tally sheets.
Most die young and some die old—
Simple figures you behold.

Standard error and deviation
Surpass for you the state of nation.
Men and women correlating
Submit to your extrapolating.

Never mind how hot the blood runs—
Cancelled out in calculations.
On broken hearts and cries of pleasure
May statistics try no measure.
Sincerely yours,
Layle Silbert Aidenoff
112 W. 15th Stt.
New York, N.Y. 10011

Source: *The American Statistician.* 1967. Volume 21, no. 4 (October), 49. Reprinted by permission of Taylor & Francis Ltd, www.tanfonline.com.

2. Dear Sir:

In the belief that statistics can contribute to the higher art forms, I respectfully submit the following statistical limericks.

There was a statistician from Knossus,
Who had a nonnormal neurosis.
With techniques of newness,
He'd measure the skewness,
And also the data's kurtosis.

There was a biometrician named Mabel,
Who'd never look at populations unstable.
Using intricate relations,

She'd find life expectations,
From the 1x's of her life table.

There was a statistician from Needham,
Who was so bright, his clients would heed him.
Yet his embarrassed confession
Was that, in linear regression,
He'd never subtract an extra degree of freedom.

An Israeli statistician named Hare,
Had five factors he wished to compare.
Levels of each were nine, So of course his design
Was a Hebreo-Greco-Latin square.
Sincerely yours,
Joseph L. Fleiss,
Principal Biostatistician
Biometrics Research
Department of Mental Hygiene
State of New York

Source: *The American Statistician.* 1967. Volume 21, no. 4 (October), 49. Reprinted by permission of Taylor & Francis Ltd, www.tanfonline.com.

3. Opa Statistica: Simplicitas Difficultatis
When you earnestly hope
To determine the slope
Of your students' tremendous success,
Just group the raw data,
Discrete, and prorate,
'Til the histogram heightens your mess!

When you earnestly hope
To determine the scope
Of a mushrooming plague on the nerve,
Just round off and rant,
And the ogive will plant
All your density under the curve.

Some numbers befuddle
And huddle the muddle

But the clue to the answer is *zeta*;
To solve the enigma
Determine the *sigma*
By adding continuous data.

Take the normal to serve
The binomial curve;
Fit the mean to the *mu* of the bell;
You succeed or you fail
At the will of each tail
As it flails each side of the swell.

Take your "*n*," "*p*," and "*q*,"
Aid multiply through,
But shadow the whole with a surd;
Find the root of the matter;
Lift "*x*" from the batter—
Now read the significant word!

Samuel H. Plotkin
Associate Professor of Statistics
Montgomery County Community College, Pa.

Source: *The American Statistician*. 1969. Volume 23, no. 4 (October), 54. Reprinted by permission of Taylor & Francis Ltd, www.tanfonline.com.

TRAVEL AGENT

Travel agents work at agencies that make necessary arrangements for people who are traveling, especially people who are booking airline tickets and hotel rooms. The economic boom that followed World War II, along with new transportation technologies, made distant travel accessible to the average American; travel agencies and their agents facilitated this new burgeoning industry. During the postwar years, travel agents helped individuals plan vacations and other forms of travel. A significant segment of the travel industry catered to business clientele. Some travel agents worked for advocacy organizations, like the American Automobile Association, while others worked for individual resorts or hotel chains. Some specialized in planning trips to certain destinations, such as Europe or the Caribbean, while others worked for agencies that created group package deals that provided not only transportation and accommodations but also tour, educational, and recreational activities for those travelers who joined groups. Some agencies specialized in oceangoing cruises, while most worked primarily with the airline industry. Some even specialized in planning honeymoons for newlyweds. Regardless of their particular industry niche, all travel agents worked to promote travel to the burgeoning middle class, market new and exciting adventures to families, and support efforts to improve Americans' engagement with the world away from their homes. While travel agents found many opportunities in the decades immediately after the war, by the 1980s, new technological developments led to declining employment for travel agents.

Unprecedented economic prosperity after World War II provided many Americans with new wealth, which propelled many into the middle class. For the generation who had matured during the Great Depression and fought against fascism during WWII, either abroad or on the home front, these economic developments were previously inconceivable. The federal government sparked economic growth by providing veterans with a generous package of postwar social and economic benefits in the form of the Serviceman's Readjustment Act (1944), also popularly known as the G.I. Bill. This act provided honorably discharged WWII-era veterans with educational benefits (tuition and living expenses to complete high school or attend college), low-interest mortgages, and a number of other payments and benefits. Veterans flocked to colleges across the nation, pursuing higher education that most had only dreamt about before the war. Veterans with college degrees found well-paying jobs—in defense industries, business, civil service, teaching, and technology—and bought tract housing hastily constructed after the war to solve the impending national housing crisis.

For many Americans, pursuing a middle-class lifestyle included taking family vacations, while business professionals increasingly had to travel for work. At the same time, the U.S. interstate highway system developed under President Dwight D. Eisenhower's leadership, and airline travel became more accessible and affordable. While travel agents had primarily helped wealthy Americans plan international and domestic travel prior to WWII, in the postwar period, this group of professionals—travel agents—experienced enormous job growth and growing status.

Throughout this initial period, most travel agents worked for businesses as service professionals; some successful agents owned their own small businesses. In this era, airline commissions were the sources of most of travel agents' income, so most spent a majority of their workdays booking airline reservations for customers. In the immediate postwar years, travel agents had no access to automated airline reservation systems; instead, they had to contact an airline's reservation system by telephone. The first airline to implement an automated reservation system that tracked inventory (seats on flights) was American Airlines in 1948. American Airlines' Electromechanical Reservisor system required a large mainframe computer and used magnetic tape to store data; this system allowed its own employees to monitor seats on available flights.

Over the next decade, other airlines followed American Airlines' example and developed their own computerized inventory tracking systems, but none of these systems allowed travel agents to independently determine flight availability. Travel agents still had to make contact by telephone with the airlines' booking offices—an often frustrating and lengthy process. During the 1950s, some large hotel chains like Sheraton also implemented automated, computerized inventory tracking systems, but as with the airlines, their inventory control and tracking systems were for in-house use only; independent travel agents had to contact hotels' booking offices to determine availability for their customers.

Leisure customers commonly met with travel agents to make decisions about their travel plans: preferred destinations, dates, number and ages of travelers, and desired activities and accommodations. Travel agents educated customers about their options, provided promotional items in the form of glossy brochures and other materials, advised customers about special travel considerations (such as required immunizations for international travel), and educated their customers about available travel options. Knowledge about destinations, transportation, and accommodations helped travel agents sell bookings, so many travel agents subscribed to industry magazines (*Travel Agent*) or attended corporate-sponsored gatherings where they learned about new developments in tourism. Some even traveled frequently themselves as having personal experience with a particular popular destination like southern California's Disneyland Park, which opened in 1955, gave travel agents an authoritative advantage when conferring with their customers.

Travel agents who specialized in business travel might only interact with a corporate contact over the telephone; arranging travel for business clients was a more straightforward process of obtaining an executive's travel requirements and then making the bookings. Whether the travel agent's client was a business professional or a vacationer, the agent would need to book the itinerary via telephone once the customer's desired travel plans had been finalized. Payment was typically arranged after the bookings were secured.

In the 1960s and 1970s, several developments at the national level affected how travel agents conducted their work. In 1964, American Airlines introduced SABRE, a computerized airline inventory tracking system that was far more efficient than the earlier Electromechanical Reservisor. In 1970, United offered travel agents access to its own proprietary tracking system, Apollo; other airlines soon followed. While United's Apollo system allowed travel agents to see seat inventory throughout the industry, they could make automatic bookings in real time only on United flights. Later in the decade, some airlines began installing computer booking terminals in airports and airline offices, offering customers the ability to directly book their own flights.

By the late 1970s, tourism had become a major industry in the United States, generating over $100 billion in annual sales. Entrepreneurial individuals entered the industry, hoping to capture some of these profits. While the American Society of Travel Agents (ASTA) had been founded in 1931 as the nation's premier advocacy and professional organization for travel agents, the travel agency industry had little regulation; there were no national standards for training, certification, or licensure. Consumer complaints against travel agents often included horror stories of being abandoned abroad on a group tour or arriving at a distant resort only to find that the travel agent had failed to confirm the planned hotel reservations. In 1977, the increasing prevalence and severity of such issues led Congress to hold a series of formal hearings on two proposed bills that would require that all American travel agents be duly registered by the U.S. Department of Commerce. This legislation divided the travel and tourism industry; the ASTA and similar organizations, like the American Automobile Association, opposed any legislation.

While these proposed bills, 95 H.R. 9068 and 95 H.R. 6222, failed, within a decade, technological and political decisions further transformed the work of travel agents. In 1978, the U.S. government deregulated the airline industry: Commercial airlines were no longer held to federal requirements but instead could set their own routes and fares. Travel agents struggled to keep up with the changing landscape of air travel. Then the personal computer further revolutionized the field; by the mid-1980s, customers with access to their own computers could book their own tickets through TCP/IP protocols (a crude form of the modern internet), which bypassed travel agents entirely. The early 1990s saw the rise of the internet and a dramatic decline in prices for personal computers. These simultaneous developments, along with new websites that provided discount fare search capabilities, provided tourists and travelers with the ability to do the work that previously required a travel agent's assistance. Today, travel agents have rebranded themselves as "travel advisers," and they often spend far less time booking their customers' travel itineraries than did their postwar counterparts. Instead, they educate tourists about sustainable options for travel, exotic wildlife protection initiatives, and work to prevent sex tourism worldwide.

Nancy Quam-Wickham

See also: Flight Attendant; Hotelier; Pilot

FURTHER READING

Archer, Jane. 2016. *Manual of Travel Agency Practice*. London: Routledge.

Morrison, James W. 1980. *Travel Agent & Tourism: A Manual of Travel Agency Operations*. New York: Arco Pub.

Morton, Alexander C. 1982. *The Official 1982–1983 Guide to Travel Agent & Travel Careers*. Miami Springs: International Pub. Co. of America.

URBAN PLANNER

Urban planners created plans for land use and programs that develop and revitalize communities. They worked primarily in local government, nonprofit organizations like housing authorities or community development groups, or the private sector like real estate development or environmental consulting firms. Government planners typically administered state and federal housing, transportation, and environmental programs. They provided advice on cost effectiveness, feasibility, and conforming with regulations.

Much as today, urban planners have historically been responsible for administering government plans or policies regarding land use. They must gather research and process these studies, such as data from industry or market research about industrial production requirements for land, water, electricity, and other resources. Some urban planners conduct their own research using field investigations; for instance, a planner evaluating street diversions may sit at designated street corners and count vehicles passing through a neighborhood. Urban planners also collect and analyze census and demographic data. An urban planner, for example, may have to determine who might be displaced as a result of an urban renewal project and then suggest ways to accommodate the displacement of certain populations. Much of an urban planner's workday is spent locating maps, assessing community development projects, determining the feasibility of developments, and reviewing zoning laws and site plans. Urban planners also meet with developers, public officials, community members, and members of advocacy groups to discuss land use and development plans. Urban planners must also keep up with changes to zoning and building codes, regulations, and landmark legal issues. Once all of this planning work has been established, an urban planner presents projects to commissions, officials, and community members, often recommending whether proposals should be approved, denied, or modified.

A typical urban planner works full time during normal business hours, though sometimes they may work evenings and weekends if an important project has a looming deadline or if they need to attend a meeting or event. In 2016, the United States Bureau of Labor Statistics reported that only about 25 percent of urban planners worked more than forty hours per week, and about two-thirds of urban planners worked for local governments. Urban planners work throughout the country, but most work in larger metropolitan and urban areas. Urban planners generally needed at least a BA degree in planning, architecture, or public planning in the period after World War II, though by the 1970s, most entry-level urban planning jobs required at least an MA degree in planning. Some urban planners have advanced degrees in urban planning, public policy, architecture, transportation studies, or other disciplines.

In the middle of the twentieth century, planners sought to mitigate problems caused in cities with dense populations. Federal legislation, such as the Housing Act of 1949, established federal funding for mortgage assistance, urban renewal, and slum clearance. Suburban development grew rapidly after federal legislation and housing subsidies in the 1950s enabled the construction of new roads and the interstate highway system. The 1950s also saw the creation of shopping malls and shopping centers. As private developers built planned suburban communities across the country, the urban population declined. Government funds that had gone to improving inner-city neighborhoods were increasingly redirected to the new suburbs.

By the early 1960s, many planners became critical of traditional modes of planning, advocating instead that each city rebuild in ways unique to its residents. Planners involved the community in the planning process, resulting in more responsive outcomes to persistent problems. The 1960s also saw a rise in environmental planning. It culminated in 1969 when Congress passed the National Environmental Protection Act, requiring an environmental impact report for every federal or federally aided development that would affect the environment. This sweeping legislation created a great demand for planners capable of analyzing environmental, cultural, and community impacts of proposed projects.

Urban planners, particularly those in the South, were also involved in the implementation of segregationist policies through zoning, which dictated whether certain uses of land or types of buildings were prohibited or permitted, meaning that they were approved for public adoption despite their segregationist origins. Zoning policies that explicitly segregated by race survived until the late 1940s, but discriminatory policies persisted in less overt forms. For example, state and local governments sometimes used federal funding designated for new roads and highways to demolish and build over predominantly black neighborhoods. However, in the 1960s, as African Americans gained greater political and social power, planners were more inclined to adopt nondiscriminatory approaches to urban development.

Thomas Nakano

See also: Architect; *1992–2019:* Landscaper

FURTHER READING

Birch, Eugenie, and Christopher Silver. 2009. "One Hundred Years of City Planning's Enduring and Evolving Connections." *Journal of the American Planning Association* 75, no. 2: 113–22.

Bureau of Labor Statistics, U.S. Department of Labor. 2018. *Occupational Outlook Handbook.* Urban and Regional Planners. https://www.bls.gov/ooh/life-physical-and-social-science/urban-and-regional-planners.htm.

Hall, Peter. 2002. *Cities of Tomorrow: An Intellectual History of Urban Planning and Design in the Twentieth Century*. Oxford, UK: Blackwell.
Jacobs, Jane. 1961. *The Death and Life of Great American Cities*. New York: Random House.
Krueckeberg, Donald A., ed. 1983. *Introduction to Planning History in the United States*. New Brunswick: Center for Urban Policy Research.
Manning Thomas, June, and Marsha Ritzdorf, eds. 1996. *Urban Planning and the African-American Community: In the Shadows*. Thousand Oaks: Sage Publications.

VETERINARIAN

Veterinarians are medical professionals who treat diseases, disorders, and injuries in animals. Prior to 1940, veterinary medicine was fairly simple and was sometimes dubbed as "barnyard medicine." There were few veterinary textbooks or journals, and most diagnoses and treatments were anecdotal, symptomatic, and empirical. The Veterinary College of Philadelphia, founded in 1852, was the United States' first veterinary school. The University of Pennsylvania's School of Veterinary Medicine opened its doors in 1883, and its size, quality, and alumni helped establish, stabilize, and expand the veterinary profession in the United States and around the world; the School of Veterinary Medicine still operates today.

For as long as veterinarians have been around, they've spent their days advising owners about animal behavior, feeding, and breeding, and they've euthanized animals when necessary. Modern veterinarians provide specialized preventative care to keep animals healthy; they perform diagnostic tests like EKGs, X-rays, and ultrasounds, and they process animals' laboratory work.

A small animal veterinarian's typical workday often begins with evaluating all of their in-hospital animal patients and establishing a treatment plan for the day. This initial review often includes reviewing the previous day's laboratory reports and imaging data, which often arrive overnight. Then the veterinarian begins seeing the day's scheduled patients, often in visits that are fifteen to twenty minutes long. Later in the morning, the veterinarian may perform surgeries as needed—spay, neutering, and the removal of bladder stones—and will supervise dental exams and procedures. In the afternoon, a veterinarian may often eat lunch at his or her desk and catch up on paperwork or make time for emergency or unscheduled duties. Throughout the afternoon, a veterinarian usually sees patients and provides treatments. Most veterinary offices close around 5:00 or 6:00 p.m., similar to other businesses, though a veterinarian will sometimes stay late to finish paperwork or prepare for the next day. Some veterinarians take emergency calls late into the evening.

After World War II (1939–1945), the U.S. population experienced dramatic growth—a generation of children that would come to be known as the baby boomers. New houses, schools, and cities were built. The population soared, and the demand for veterinarians rose comparably. Funding for research from National Institutes of Health (NIH) and other organizations spurred both human and animal medical research, resulting in productive improvements in oncology, cardiology, imaging, and surgery.

The American Veterinary Medical Association started accrediting veterinary schools in the late 1940s. This resulted in the closure of some older archaic veterinary schools and the opening of a number of new schools. In 1950, there were 12 accredited veterinary schools in the United States; in 1970, there were 18, and in 2010, there were 30. In 1945, there were fewer than 15,000 veterinarians; now there are more than 110,000. Specialty colleges were rare prior to 1970. As they organized, they developed their own training and certification programs. Their numbers increased from 3 in 1970 to over 25 by 2000. In 1970, there were fewer than 100 specialty college diplomates; now there are over 10,000 (AVMA). Specialists are needed in academic faculty, but the vast majority of modern veterinarians work in private practice.

To become a veterinarian, a student must complete pre-veterinary courses including chemistry, biology, physics, embryology, genetics, and microbiology. Most admitted students have already earned BA or BS degrees before going to veterinary school; however, some students get accepted without a degree. In veterinary school, the first two years focus on general medical education with anatomy, biochemistry, physiology, pharmacology, histology, and pathology. Animal behavior and the techniques of animal restraint and physical examination are learned prior to the clinical rotations. In the third and fourth years of school, each student performs required clinical rotations through medicine, surgery, and pathology of all animal species, plus imaging, hematology, and clinical pathology. Some schools offer elective rotations in areas such as dermatology, dentistry, sports medicine, or cardiology.

After graduation, the majority of the students go into private practice with most in companion animal medicine and fewer in food animal or equine practice. Some veterinarians opt for nondomestic animals, pocket pets, and exotic or zoo animals. Other job opportunities are in medical research, industry, or the U.S. military. Thirty percent work in internships, and about half of those continue with residency training after an internship. Approximately 10 percent of all graduates ultimately become board certified by a specialty college. Those in practice usually work in a multi-doctor practice and often one that is owned by a much larger corporation.

A veterinarian's average number of work hours per week has always varied depending on the vet's position and responsibility, but for the first few years, a forty- to sixty-hour workweek is common. Emergency work after hours or on the weekends is sometimes performed by new graduates, but this need is filled in most communities by emergency clinics with experienced veterinarians.

In addition to family pets, many animals are trained as service animals for people with sight, hearing, or physical impairments. Others have dogs for emotional or medical needs. Military dogs are trained not just for guard work but for search and rescue or as bomb sniffers and messengers. Animal breeders work with veterinarians to maintain a strong genetic basis of the offspring by selected breeding. Veterinarians are now able to decrease the number of animals with inheritable defects such as hip dysplasia, progressive retinal atrophy, or some cancers, such as hemangiosarcoma in golden retrievers.

As a result of improved veterinary care from good science and caring veterinarians, animals are living longer and are healthier, with better nutrition and fewer communicable diseases. When a disease does strike, there is improved knowledge for diagnosis and treatment applications.

The human-animal bond has increased since the 1980s. Animals have always been important in American culture, but recent decades have seen an increase in owners who care for pets, sometimes in lieu of having children. These animal owners desire high-quality medicine for their pets—and they are willing to pay for it. In the last thirty years, veterinary specialists have begun researching, developing, and offering state-of-the-art diagnostics and therapeutics; these services are often gleaned directly from human medical research and pharmacology. The pursuit of a definitive diagnosis with evidence-based medicine became the credo, and therapies became much more specific and exacting. The downside, of course, was that these offerings tended to raise these treatments' costs to the consumer.

Veterinary medicine is supported by owners paying their own way. Pet insurance has been around since the 1980s, but fewer than 10 percent of animal owners purchase policies. Therefore, most veterinary bills today are paid for out of pocket. Many medical procedures are elective, such as cataract removal, a hip replacement, or a root canal, and therefore this sophisticated medicine can only be afforded by clients with the disposable income. For those owners who cannot afford the fees, either no treatment is done, or the animal may be euthanized.

Veterinary medicine is a wonderful, rewarding profession, and most people who choose it as a career are happy that they did. The major downside of the profession today is the large student debt loads that new graduates incur and incomes that are less than those received from other professions such as law, medicine, or dentistry.

Jerry Owens

See also: Anesthesiologist; Radiologist and Radiology Technician; *1992–2019:* Epidemiologist

FURTHER READING

Aiello, Susan E., Michael A. Moses, and Dana G. Allen. 2016. *The Merck Veterinary Manual*. Kenilworth: Merck.

American Veterinary Medical Association. http://www.avma.org.

Bellwood, Brianne, and Melissa Andrasik-Catton. 2014. *Veterinary Technician's Handbook of Laboratory Procedures*. Hoboken: Wiley-Blackwell.

Crow, Steven E., Sally O. Walshaw, and Steven E. Crow. 2006. *Manual of Clinical Procedures in the Dog, Cat, and Rabbit*. Ames: Blackwell Publishing.

PRIMARY DOCUMENT

In his oral history, Dr. William Waddell, who worked as a veterinarian providing care to large animals, describes some of his more unusual animal patients as one of the few veterinarians—and the only African American one—in Morgantown and Philippi, West Virginia, during the 1950s and early 1960s. He also notes the importance of veterinarians in promoting public health efforts; during his time in West Virginia, Dr. Waddell was in charge of rabies vaccinations for three counties. It was common for him to vaccinate over one thousand dogs a day during anti-rabies campaigns.

I used to treat animals for the zoo—not for the zoo, but for circuses that came to town. I treated gorillas. I extracted a tooth from a gorilla one time. I treated elephants, but I never did get to treat the lions and tigers, and I wasn't too crazy about treating them . . . either. But I did and I treated a bear, treated bears, and, you see, what will happen, people feed gorillas and bears candy, chewing gum, and stuff like that and over a period of years, they would get hollows and you had to extract the tooth, but we'd put them to sleep to do it, you know.

But one night I had—it wasn't a gorilla, it was a baboon. A man owned a baboon there, and these were drinking people and they would take this baboon to the bars, and everybody called themselves being nice to Lucky. And they'd give him drinks of whiskey and he'd shake their hands, clap the hands, and hug 'em, and stuff like that, you know. But one night, he came out to my hospital, and he had put a ring on his hand and they didn't know it. And this ring had worn down to the bone. And his hand was swollen up quite a bit. So, the owner brought him out there.

In the meantime, we had one or two football players. I believe one was Sam Huff, one was Joe Mahoney. It was a time when West Virginia [University] had some good football teams. They came to the clinic that night when Lucky was out there. Lucky was the guy's [baboon's] name, and we tried to work on Lucky, and Lucky wouldn't let (anybody) get near that finger.

So finally, I got some jelly beans, and I put some chloral hydrate in it and Lucky would eat the jelly beans and spit out the medicine, and then finally, I found out that I wasn't getting anyplace, so it was quite a show that night, because I had about fifty and twenty clients in my hospital, and they were watching this monkey raise—a baboon—raise a devil. He jumped on a man and bit somebody. And finally I went and got my choke collar, big choke collar, and choked him down and gave him a shot and put him asleep, and we took the ring off his finger. But it had eaten to the bone, had gone to the bone, and he had made it bad by scratching on it. But that was the most exciting thing 'cause he had everybody laughing and jumping around, everybody was afraid of him. And it took just about half [an] hour maybe to subdue him. And he's snarling at people and trying to bite them, and he's big. But once we got him straight, he was all right after that . . .

[A]nother time I went to see a cow that had rabies, and they told me that this cow had just swallowed an apple and everybody'd seen her. At least ten men sitting around on a fence said they had seen this cow that had swallowed the apple. So I told the owner, "Let's go in then and check her."

So, he said he had to go in the house for something. So, I went and checked this young bull. It wasn't a cow, it was a young bull. And he charged me, and I jumped the fence. And they were laughing there, rabble sitting on the fence started laughing then, and I began to curse them out for laughing. Number one, because the cow could have killed me. He would have killed me. He could have gored me to death, he was large enough. So then, this animal had, instead of the normal type of mooing, it had a bellow with it, and right away, when I heard that bellow, I knew that animal had rabies.

So, I told them that I'm not going in there because that animal had rabies. And I said, "The animal will die within a day or so. I don't want to shoot the animal 'cause I want to make certain when we take that head down to the capital, that it won't be any trouble, you know, find[ing] what they want." And the animal died that night, and I had the state police to take it all the way to state capital. And they came back right away that the animal had rabies. But that animal that bit this animal had, let's see, I think it attacked about eight or ten animals and dogs. So that meant that a lot of them that we gave shots to. Most of them did live. But several of them died, and (there was) no question about it. They had rabies.

But [these are] the type of things which you experience in practicing with large animals as well as small animals 'cause we had so much rabies in Philippi [West Virginia] at one time, that I am certain that thirty-one people with animals were taking the shots to keep them from coming down with it. And the cats are very vicious because they attack people in the house, and people think that they are playing, you know. But we had about eight or nine cats that attacked people, old people had to take the treatment and some were allergic to this particular treatment.

Source: Oral History Interview with Dr. William Waddell. 1988. Typescript. Center for Oral History, University of Hawaii, Manoa. Interviewed by Kathryn Waddell Takara on July 26. Honolulu, 151–152, 154–155.

1992–2019: POST–COLD WAR AND THE TWENTY-FIRST CENTURY

INTRODUCTION

In the 1990s, writer-activist Barbara Ehrenreich embarked on a research trip for her book *Nickel and Dimed: On (Not) Getting By in America* (2001), which focuses on the daily struggles of impoverished workers in contemporary America—people who live in substandard housing and barely manage to pay their bills with the low wages they earn, often taking on another part-time job (or two) to make ends meet. Over the next several months, Ehrenreich worked at a series of minimum- and low-wage jobs: as a waitress in Florida, a motel housekeeper in Maine, and a retail clerk in Minnesota, among many others. While Ehrenreich spent less than half a year on her research, the difficult circumstances she experienced and wrote about remain the standard of living for millions of Americans.

The structural transformation of the American economy coupled with previously unimaginable technological innovations—computers and the internet—have created gross economic inequities within American society. In the last quarter of a century, real household incomes have stagnated for those workers in the bottom 90 percent of all Americans, those who, in 2015, earned less than $312,000 per year—and an average of just over $34,000 per year (Institute for Policy Studies 2019). At almost no time in American history, except for a brief period in the 1920s, has the wealth gap been so great as it is in the late 2010s. Ehrenreich's subjects are the norm, not the exception among the American working class. They are the landscapers, home health aides, early childhood educators, housekeepers, and package handlers of this era.

When personal computers first became widely accessible in the late 1980s and early 1990s, labor economists understood that computers would replace human workers. Yet this is not all that computers and a wired world entail. In 2004, economists Frank Levy and Richard Munane observed that "beyond replacing humans, computers have become the infrastructure of the global economy, helping jobs move quickly to sources of cheap labor" (Levy and Munane 2004, 2). Today, one would be hard pressed to identify a single occupation in America that is unaffected by computers. Even the home health aides receive medical care instructions for patients via computers, while landscapers connect with their peers via professional networks facilitated in computer chat rooms and with customers through sites that allow consumers to search for and find services. Machinists use computer-aided design software and operate precision metal cutting tools using computers. The United States Postal Service has embraced automation and computer tracking; it now offers all customers daily electronic mail services that include computerized scans of incoming envelopes. Postal workers handle mail that is rapidly sorted by computer-driven scanning machines.

Computers and the internet make possible the rapid exchange and transfer of information, creating a knowledge economy that privileges college-educated and highly trained workers. New occupations such as IT architect, social media coordinator, and e-commerce specialist were unknown a few decades ago. Tracking commerce, transportation, people, and even diseases is made easier with use of sophisticated technologies. As Levy and Munane note, postsecondary education—college or technical and vocational training—is necessary to obtain some measure of personal success in today's globalized economy.

The bifurcation of the American workforce and attendant growing economic disparity are a result of this paradigmatic shift in these technological systems of American industry. Consumerism remains a powerful force, and while computers may connect retail stores with the sources of desired goods, low-wage workers in both locales are essential. As historian Nelson Lichtenstein writes, a factory worker in south China, Li Xiao Hong, assembles Disney-themed dolls in a darkened and solvent-smelling factory for sixty-five dollars per month, while Kelly Gray, a displaced union retail clerk in Las Vegas, now sells these dolls, as well as other goods, in a Wal-Mart "supercenter," making just 60 percent of what she earned in her previous job and with "inferior benefits" (Lichtenstein 2006, 6). In this system, low-paid American workers and their counterparts abroad are mutually dependent on each other's labor.

This is the globalized and highly technologically dependent economic world in which all Americans work in the twenty-first century. It is a world of opportunities but is also fraught with hardship and one that will not ever return to the nation-centered economy of the past.

FURTHER READING

Ehrenreich, Barbara. 2001. *Nickel and Dimed: On (Not) Getting By in America.* New York: Macmillan.

Institute for Policy Studies. 2019. "Income Inequality." https://inequality.org/facts/income-inequality/.

Levy, Frank, and Richard Munane. 2004. *The New Division of Labor: How Computers Are Creating the Next Job Market.* Princeton: Princeton University Press.

Lichtenstein, Nelson, ed. 2006. *Wal-Mart: The Face of Twenty-First-Century Capitalism.* New York: The New Press.

CAMPAIGN MANAGER

A campaign manager's role is to organize and oversee a political campaign's fundraising, polling, advertising, and voter-enthusiasm efforts. The modern political campaign as it is known today took shape during the 1930s with the introduction of political consulting firms, political polling using sound statistical forecasting methods, and professionals whose responsibilities were to curate a candidate's reputation. With the internet and social media platforms that allow users to instantaneously send and receive information, the job of the campaign manager has taken on even more dimensions. While modern campaign managers utilize many of the same types of tools as their predecessors did, their jobs on the ground are quite different. Campaign managers are those individuals who coordinate the activities needed to elect a candidate or pass an issue, such as a school funding bond or local library tax. Those at the national level typically have significant experience working on and supervising a political campaign, and these workers have both high stress and high-paying careers. At the local and regional levels, campaign managers may be salaried professionals, or they may work entirely on a voluntary basis, with similarly stressful working environments but without the compensation of their national counterparts. In both cases, however, campaign management requires excellent communication and organizational skills, a talent for fundraising, and a strong belief in the worthiness of the candidate or cause.

Campaign managers have multiple responsibilities, though in larger state and national election contests, they delegate some of these responsibilities to assistants, who may hold such titles as communications director or director of finance. In local and regional contests, campaign managers evaluate historical voting patterns using elections data obtained from local elections offices or state registrars.

In such cases, analysis typically centers on the precinct, the smallest unit of electoral measurement in most U.S. states. Campaign managers determine where voters and prospective voters will be favorable to one's cause or candidate (whether an issue or individual). They organize teams to canvass precincts within neighborhoods and cities; in local elections, a candidate often accompanies these canvassing teams at key points in the campaign, such as just before a primary or voter registration deadlines occur. Campaign managers and the candidate will have jointly created a message and theme that canvassing teams will bring to individual voters, whether at community events or during door-to-door visits. Political consultant Katherine Shaw defines theme as "the overarching issues that capture the spirit of what voters want," while the message is "a single idea used to bring that theme" to prospective voters (Shaw 2014, 47). Campaign managers stress to team members the importance of staying on message. James Carville, who was campaign manager for Bill Clinton's 1992 presidential run, reportedly coined the famous message used in that campaign, "It's the Economy, Stupid."

Campaign managers also help to create a campaign budget and coordinate fundraising activities, including ensuring that campaign donations—in-kind as well as monetary—are properly reported to government offices that enforce campaign finance laws. Significantly running afoul of campaign finance laws can spell the end of a candidate's political future, as well as lead to criminal charges, though this is uncommon today. A skilled campaign manager also coordinates with political action committees (PACs) for financial support. Campaign funds help spread the campaign message by allowing campaign managers to purchase media time (radio and television ads), create signage (lawn signs as well as banners and other materials), print and distribute campaign brochures and send out mailings, and hire additional staff. Campaign managers increasingly purchase advertisements on social media sites like Facebook and Twitter, which utilize sophisticated user-analytics software to target campaign ads to those users most likely to endorse the campaign's message and the candidate or cause. Recent investigations into social-media-targeted advertisements, however, have shown that unethical opponents, including state actors like Russia's intelligence agency (GRU), manipulate voter sentiment through these means.

A campaign manager must also know the candidate well and prepare for unexpected events that might negatively affect a campaign. In curating a candidate's reputation, campaign managers must be attentive to media coverage of the candidate and react appropriately when confronted with information that might harm a candidate's election bid, such as the rumors of adultery that led 1988 presidential candidate Gary Hart to withdraw from the Democratic primary. Dishonest representations of candidates' qualifications or character can also affect their chances for election: Melissa Howard, a candidate for state office in Florida in 2018, falsely claimed to have a college diploma, but she dropped out of the race when the institution, Miami University (Ohio), responded to media questions with a statement that Howard attended but did not graduate from that university. Campaign managers have to know the candidate as well to avoid potentially embarrassing him or her in front of potential voters and the media. Dan Pfeiffer, a member of the communications team on Barack Obama's 2008 presidential campaign, for instance, arranged for Obama to meet with NASCAR officials on a cable sports network; Obama was clearly not knowledgeable about NASCAR, or even generally interested in the sport of auto racing, so he floundered his way through the interview. Candidate Obama later approached the campaign team, demanding to know "Who thought this interview was a good idea?" Pfeiffer acknowledged his mistake (Pfeiffer 2018, 9).

Given the dramatic increase in campaign spending, campaign management has become a specialty profession in the last two decades, even at the local level. While candidates and campaigns in small towns may still recruit campaign managers from the local community, professional managers are in high demand for political campaigns of all kinds. Campaign workers often first gain experience as volunteers, and then as their organizational and communication talents become evident, they move into paid positions. Distinguishing oneself in campaign work can lead to invitations to become a campaign manager, as was the case for twenty-four-year-old Emma Brown, who managed first-time candidate Lindsey Davis Stover's unsuccessful campaign for the Democratic nomination for a seat in the House of Representatives. More seasoned campaign managers work for political consulting firms, of which there are hundreds in the contemporary United States. Some of these firms specialize in nonpartisan races, while others align with particular political parties. The largest of these firms offer full-service consulting, including PAC consulting, digital strategy services, mobile phone app development, poll taking, fundraising, mapping, developing content for text messaging and radio ads, and even providing voice actors for television commercials.

Nancy Quam-Wickham

See also: Social Media Coordinator; *1946–1991*: Community Organizer; Registrar

FURTHER READING

Jamieson, Kathleen Hall. 1996. *Packaging the Presidency: A History and Criticism of Presidential Campaign Advertising*. New York: Oxford University Press.

Pfeiffer, Dan. 2018. *Yes, We (Still) Can: Politics in the Age of Obama, Twitter, and Trump.* New York: Hachette.

Shaw, Katherine. 2014. *The Campaign Manager: Running and Winning Local Elections.* London: Routledge.

CASINO WORKER

Casino workers are employees who work in casinos, which are public buildings or rooms where gambling games are played. There are three main types of casino worker: dealers, floor workers, and service staff. Dealers deal dice at the craps table, pass out cards at the poker and blackjack tables, run roulette games, and operate a variety of other games of chance. Pit bosses work with the dealers, provide oversight of and support with gambling games, and resolve disputes. Floor workers comprise the cashiers who exchange gamblers' cash money for chips that are used for gambling and also those workers who provide refreshments to the gamblers and clean the casino. Service staff perform back-of-the-house duties, including meal preparation, shipping and receiving, and accounting.

Dice dealers work in the center area of the casino, called the pit. The game of craps has three dealers, one floor person who watches over several tables, and the pit boss, who is responsible for the area. Smaller tables for games of poker or blackjack surround the pit. These dealers are diverse in background and frequently female. Before equal opportunity employment laws, dealer positions were saved for white men. The Civil Rights Act of 1964 and the actions of local National Association for the Advancement of Colored People (NAACP) members challenged the discrimination and opened up positions for all qualified workers.

Floor workers include beverage servers, bartenders, slot attendants, and cashiers. Although men and women work as bartenders, beverage servers (formerly known as cocktail waitresses) are almost entirely women. The job of the servers is to walk through their section of the casino to take orders and provide drinks to the gambling customers. Beverage servers receive a wage, but the majority of their compensation comes from the tips they receive.

Historically, beverage servers were required to maintain weight and appearance standards, but these requirements have been challenged in courts to some success. Some casinos have been able to maintain these standards as a bona fide occupational qualification in that the job requires a certain physical appearance. Other casinos have loosened the standards. The combination of alcohol and gambling has made sexual harassment a job hazard, but casino management has increased its response to unruly customers to make the workplace safer.

Service employees comprise the third major category of casino worker. They often work in the back of the house, not on the casino floor, but their work supports the customers who gamble. These workers are employed in food preparation and serving, cleaning, and building maintenance. Service work provides opportunities for entry-level work, on-the-job training, and, in some cases, jobs for those without English proficiency. This category has the greatest diversity of race and ethnic backgrounds among its workers. For example, after World War II (1939–1945),

African Americans from southern states migrated to Las Vegas for alternatives to domestic work and field work. They filled the majority of service worker positions in Las Vegas at the time. After 1965, changes in immigration policy brought more Latinos and Asians into the entry-level positions.

Today, casino workers come from many parts of the world. The Hotel Employees and Restaurant Employees (HERE) union has made it possible for service workers to maintain a decent standard of living. In Las Vegas, where the union is strong, it enabled service workers to earn wages that can support a family, buy a house, receive medical care, and send kids to college. Not all service workers are unionized. Some casinos attempt to address workers' needs by privately providing specific benefits, thereby keeping control over the cost of benefit packages.

Casinos became major employers in the 1960s. Before then, small gambling clubs and bars often dotted the country to provide entertainment for locals. These casinos were often illicit and would take measures to conceal their games. When Nevada legalized gambling in 1931, it provided a haven for people who worked as casino dealers and operators; they could legally work their trade. The migration of casino workers to Nevada expanded in the 1950s and 1960s as local law enforcement cracked down on gambling in other parts of the United States. Nevada benefited from the revenue source that casinos provided, and lawmakers made efforts to ensure the operations of Nevada casinos could grow with funding from legitimate businesses. Nevada's Corporate Gaming Act, passed in 1969, allowed large corporations to begin running casinos. Nevada had a monopoly on legal gambling in the United States until the mid-1970s, when the voters in New Jersey approved casino gambling, which started a movement by cities and states to generate needed state income by adding casino gambling. In the 1980s, after significant negotiation between tribes and state governments, the Indian Regulatory Gaming Act allowed tribes to control casinos on their lands. Jobs in casinos have been in demand in thriving communities. Nevertheless, the work can be grueling. Major casinos are open for business all day, every day—even holidays. A casino worker may have a night shift or work weekends and holidays. Gambling tables exist in different configurations; at some low tables, dealers will sit while they run the game, but at other higher tables, dealers stand for the duration of their time at that particular table. It is not uncommon for some dealers to be on their feet for their entire shift. Breaking into a new job as a dealer can mean the employee works a different schedule every two weeks. If the employee is new and trying to get a steady job, he or she often needs to call in daily to see if he or she has work that day. On some properties, smoke can provide a health hazard for those constantly on the floor.

The casino industry shows no sign of slowing down, although the Bureau of Labor Statistics predicts a slow-paced 2 percent increase in jobs between 2016 and 2026 (Bureau of Labor Statistics 2018). According to Statista, the number of commercial casinos increased from 455 in 2005 to 524 in 2016 (Statista n.d.). The median annual pay for casino floor workers was $22,300 in May 2017, underscoring the importance of tips in the line of work. The location of a casino also influences the level of pay. During an era of declining industrial production, casinos slowly filled the void.

Joanne L. Goodwin

See also: *1946–1991:* Hotelier

FURTHER READING

Bureau of Labor Statistics. 2018. *Occupational Outlook Handbook.* Gaming Service Workers. https://www.bls.gov/ooh/personal-care-and-service/gaming-services-occupations.htm.

Chandler, Susan, and Jill B. Jones. 2011. *Casino Women: Courage in Unexpected Places.* Ithaca: Cornell University Press.

Goodwin, Joanne. 2014. *Changing the Game: Women at Work in Las Vegas, 1940–1990.* Lincoln: University of Nevada Press.

Kraft, James P. *Vegas at Odds: Labor Conflict in a Leisure Economy, 1960–1985.* Baltimore: Johns Hopkins Press.

McGinley, Ann C. 2007. "Babes and Beefcake: Exclusive Hiring Arrangements and Sexy Dress Codes." *Duke Journal of Gender Law & Policy* 14: 257.

Statista. n.d. "Number of Commercial Casinos in the United States from 2005 to 2017." https://www.statista.com/statistics/187972/number-of-us-commercial-casinos-since-2005/.

CLERGYPERSON

Clergy provide for the spiritual, social, and personal needs of faith communities, and most members of the clergy lead daily, weekly, or ceremonial religious services. Clergypersons are known by many names. In Christian religions, Catholic clergy include priests, nuns, brothers, and members of other Catholic orders; Protestants typically call their clergy "pastors," "ministers," or "reverends"; clergy in the Mormon Church are bishops. A rabbi leads members of Jewish synagogues in the practice of their faith. In the contemporary United States, an Islamic mosque leader is generally called an "imam," though other terms are used within various Islamic sects and in other parts of the world. In other religions like Buddhism and Hinduism, religious practices may involve reciting texts and praying at home or attending worship in temples led by monks, nuns, or laypeople. A chaplain is a clergyperson who serves the needs of those in the military, in police and fire departments, and in institutional settings like colleges and hospitals—regardless of doctrinal affiliation. In matters of religion, the United States has always been pluralist, as the Constitution—unique for the time of its drafting—provided no established formal national religion.

In their strictly religious duties, clergypersons lead worship services, as well as coordinate—sometimes with the assistance of laypeople—the religious practices of a congregation. Clergy set the weekly agenda for worship services, including planning liturgies (the rites of worship in which a congregation's members participate), designate scriptural readings and hymn singing among congregants, and write and deliver sermons. The sermon is a short speech focused on the teaching of a religious text, like the Torah, the Quran, or the Bible; it may or may not address contemporary controversies within society. Clergy may also lead daily or weekly prayer meetings, organize youth worship and weekly educational activities (commonly called Sunday school), and administer the sacraments in Christian communion. Normally, the day of worship is hectic for clergy; the entire day is often spent preaching and engaging with their congregation. Some religions, like Islam and Catholicism, require daily worship services, though clergy may still formally preach on only a weekly basis.

A clergyperson's work continues throughout the week, however; congregants and others often seek ministry during the week, and clergy are often called on to preside over rituals and practices, like formal professions of faith or conversion (baptism, witnessing *shahada*), rites of passage (Bar and Bat Mitzvahs), marriage ceremonies, funerals, and celebrations of special festivals in the religion's calendar.

Many clergy offer spiritual-based counseling to congregants as well; those who have been formally educated in a theological program or seminary often have specific training in individual, couples, and family psychological counseling practices. Priests receive confession, which is a formal practice among Catholics wherein the faithful confess their sins in anonymity. Clergy may visit elderly members of their congregation, as well as the sick and infirm, the hospitalized, and sometimes the imprisoned. Clergy also tend to be active in community activities, such as helping to set up food banks, leading afterschool groups, and registering voters, embodying a life of service to the larger community in ways that positively reflect on the congregation. Within the Islamic faith, imams are expected to hold positions of community leadership and to represent the faithful in all areas of society. In most congregations, another of the clergy's primary duties involves supervision of the institution's finances, including expense and donation tracking. Larger congregations and those within more established denominations may employ bookkeepers or special lay committees to do this work.

Individuals report that they became clergy for several reasons and through a variety of pathways. Many clergy people speak of a calling to serve. They generally describe this calling—a heartfelt and deeply personal sense of duty to a higher being and to live a life of service to others—as a personally and spiritually transformational experience, a sense of oneness with a deity, and of being directed by that higher being to join the clergy. Some clergy come from hereditary lines of religious leaders; such persons are often groomed to become religious leaders by being educated in faith institutions from a young age. Most religions stipulate a period of intense training to become a clergyperson, though this varies by denomination and doctrine. In many religions, formal training includes a postbaccalaureate degree program in theology or religious studies. Before a clergyperson can begin official work, many faiths require a form of ordination or consecration by a faith's religious leaders; ordination may also include a congregation's formal acceptance of its leader.

The work of clergy members has changed remarkably in the last several decades in America. Formerly, clergy affiliated with established, or mainline, Protestant denominations, as well as Catholic and Jewish religious leaders, were generally employed full time in their positions. But the practice of formal religion, especially various forms of Christianity, has declined nationwide, leading to church and parish closures even as more people train for the clergy (Pew 2017). For many clergy in contemporary America, maintaining the duties of a demanding pastoral care position, while difficult, is no longer a full-time job. While televangelists and megachurches (large congregations of several thousand members) may generate millions of dollars of revenue each year, many clergy still find money to be a matter of constant concern. Since the 1980s, the congregations have gotten older and poorer as younger generations drift away from organized religion, and existing congregations are more often filled with retirees on low or fixed incomes. Donations and operating budgets are declining, and the absolute number of Christian churches is in decline nationally. Additionally, the practice of faith has taken on different forms. The rise of Christian evangelism in the United States, wherein an expression of faith is often seen as adherence to original scripture, allows the faithful to practice without an alliance to an established denomination.

Those who adhere to a fundamental reading of scripture include not just Christians but also members of the Islamic, Jewish, Buddhist, and other faiths. There has been the most institutional innovation in Christian evangelical practice, however, as new congregations, small and large, have emerged in recent decades. This institutional splintering of Christian faiths has also contributed to the decline in the numbers of churches in more established denominations.

In many churches, clergy are now part-time workers who must take on other jobs to make ends meet. Some find work as teachers or school administrators; others work as social workers or in positions in nonprofit community agencies. Still others may drive for car-share services, work in business, do freelance work in the "gig economy," or, increasingly, are pursuing religious work as a second career after retirement from the secular economy. So widespread is this bi-vocational ministry trend, wherein clergy work more than one job, that in 2013, the *Religion News Service*, a nondenominational national publication that reports on religious matters, advised seminary students that full-time clergy positions are no longer the norm, especially among Protestant denominations (RNS, 2013). In some areas, laypersons are performing many religious duties. Wages for clergy have traditionally lagged behind many white-collar professions, even though clergy often work considerably more hours per week; this trend, however, has reversed in recent years as the average clergy person works just over half of the hours of clergy in the 1970s while wages, paradoxically, have risen as well—though wages still remain lower than those for peers in other professions. Full-time clergy made an average salary of about $47,500 in 2010, according to data from the U.S. Department of Labor.

Today, leadership initiatives for these smaller congregations include workshops on expanding membership through community outreach and honing a sense of mission, websites that educate clergy members about all manners of successful practice, and fellowship communities and mentorship programs for younger pastors. Specialized professional consulting firms advise congregations about how to meet the needs of their congregants in the most cost-effective manner. The practice of professional religious work promises to change in coming decades.

Nancy Quam-Wickham

See also: *1607–1775:* Minister; Sexton; *1776–1860:* Missionary; *1946–1991:* Community Organizer; Social Worker

FURTHER READING

"As Denominations Decline, Number of Unpaid Ministers Rise." 2013. *Religion News Service*,. September 17. https://religionnews.com/2013/09/17/denominations-decline-numbers-unpaid-ministers-rise/.

Bickers, Dennis. 2013. *The Art and Practice of Bivocational Ministry: A Pastor's Guide.* Kansas City: Beacon Hill Press.

Moore, Kathleen M. 2013. "Muslim Advocacy in America." In *Islam in the Modern World*, edited by Jeffrey T. Kenney and Ebrahim Moosa, 369–388. New York: Routledge.

"More Americans Now Say They're Spiritual but Not Religious." 2017. Pew Research Center. (September 6). http://www.pewresearch.org/fact-tank/2017/09/06/more-americans-now-say-theyre-spiritual-but-not-religious/.

Olson, Laura R., Sue E. S. Crawford, and Melissa M. Deckman 2005. *Women with a Mission: Religion, Gender, and the Politics of Women Clergy.* Tuscaloosa: University Press of Alabama.

Sparks, Paul, Tim Soerens, and Dwight J. Friesen. 2014. *The New Parish: How Neighborhood Churches Are Transforming Mission, Discipleship, and Community.* Downers Grove: IVP Books.

PRIMARY DOCUMENT

In this document, Rev. Brian Bailey discusses the challenges of being a clergyperson in modern America. Like many, he felt the calling to provide service to others at an early age. He describes the many duties of a clergyperson: mentoring others, counseling people in time of distress, attending to his congregation's social needs, preparing for weekly Bible study, and writing and delivering his sermons every Sunday. His work as a clergyperson requires him to be on call at all hours of the day and night to minister to members of his congregation while also holding down full-time employment elsewhere. His experiences are common among many clergypersons today.

The sun shines no brighter on me on any given morning than it does any other person blessed to see a new day. I gather myself and go about normal routines to get ready for a day of work. I deal with a commute like most Americans. I start my workday as a school teacher as the rest of my colleagues do each and every school day. I leave work to run a few errands before businesses close for the day. I come home to a loving wife and try to spend some quality time with her before it is time to get some rest for the upcoming day. The overarching difference between my life and most others is that I am a Christian pastor and have been a clergyman for the last 14 years of my life. I navigate the same day with an increased circumspection, introspection, and accountability to God, my family, my congregants, and each person I interact with on a daily basis.

I indeed wake up like most adults with a workday in front of me. Before I begin to face that environment, I pray over my wife and my life. I ask God to guide my actions and show his wisdom through my interactions throughout my day. That request calls me to think before any response I want to have while sitting in Los Angeles traffic or when dealing with an unruly student. In all things, I am a representative of God and am called to represent Him well as a leader He has chosen.

I am a pastor twenty-four hours a day. I am a high school history teacher between the hours of 7:55 am and 3:20 pm. In that time, I must show professionalism, tact, patience, and engage students to help them succeed academically. While I cannot legally evangelize during work hours, I do not lie about my calling to ministry when asked. Students regularly, accurately accuse me of being a pastor as my lecture style tends to mirror a sermon I preach about history between two and three times a day. I actually had a student say Amen after I made a point about gender inequality during the industrial revolution. I laughed inside. That incident revealed that I am my best self not when I separate my life into silos but allow that which defines my life to permeate all parts of it. I must practice patience with coworkers even when negative reactions are socially justified. I regularly encounter anti-Christian sentiment from coworkers who may or may not know my religious stance. However, I am called to love others not out of reciprocation or mutuality but as an overflow of God's love for me.

I clock out of my job at 3:20 pm but clocking out does not apply to the life of a pastor. On top of the constant concern for congregants and the furtherance of God's kingdom on earth, I frequently receive online messages by email or social media, text messages, and phone calls asking me to perform various rites, pray for various situations, or to give biblical advice. It is very difficult to ignore these requests. It is even more difficult to say no to them when you are compelled to be of help at all times. In a given day, I can be asked to perform a funeral, begin or continue marriage counseling, preach a sermon, pray for someone's situation, and give approval for a church program all before lunch. I may not answer the requests by the time I leave my day job but they are all on my mind while I am teaching tenth graders about the history of the world.

I tend to try to return phone calls on my drive home from work so that I can have uninterrupted time with my wife after a day of work. That plan rarely works as calls continue to come in during the evening. I am not yet blessed to minister as a pastor full time but the expectation of many is that I am available as a pastor even if I may be asleep. I thank God for the responsibility. It has caused me to learn how to prioritize and organize my time to be as effective as I can be as a husband first, pastor second, teacher third, and a regular man somewhere down that list.

I am asked often, "Why would you choose to be a pastor or go into ministry?". My response has evolved to this: I chose to accept what I know I was called to do. I am not a pastor who sought out the position. I accepted Jesus Christ as Lord and Savior as a child. I was active in church and looked up to my father who was a minister and later became a pastor himself. While I admired the man, I did not desire the title or responsibility of clergyman or pastor. I was well acquainted with the stress, anxiety, pressure and isolation of Christian leadership. I lived through the perceived neglect of a father who worked so hard for the church that he was most times too exhausted to spend time with his children. It was not until I accepted the call at 18 years of age, that I began to understand why a person would work themselves so hard for the cause of Christ.

Early on in ministry I was tasked with mentoring young children. All of them are adults now and a majority of them who began in my Sunday school class are now active members of my congregation. I mentored them as young as eleven years of age and now they are preparing to graduate from college. Others have started families of their own. Witnessing their continued growth as individuals guided by Godly principles compels me to continue in ministry. I have learned not to rely on accolades or appreciation to encourage me to continue being a pastor. Encouragement is rare and accolades are few. But growth and progress no matter how slight in the lives of the people I have been commissioned to lead sustains me. When others resist divine wisdom that would otherwise enhance their lives, I am compelled to engage them more passionately for their benefit.

There are many days I wake up, get through work, run errands, engage the congregation, kiss my wife and pass out without a pat on the back from one person. That may be an average day for me but I am still drawn to the work God has before me because I experience His encouragement in the form of affirmation from serendipitous sources. I receive His accolades through opportunities opened to me that can only be explained by His grace in my life. More than any of that, I am drawn to this work because the same work of others influenced me to come to know Jesus Christ and receive everlasting life as well as peace, joy, love, and prosperity in this life through Him. I am totally compelled to continue that work and influence others to the same abundant life that has been granted to me.

Source: Brian L. Bailey, Letter to author. June 8, 2017. Courtesy of Brian L. Bailey

COMBAT ENGINEER

Every military force needs skilled soldiers to perform five essential engineering functions: mobility, counter-mobility, survivability, construction, and topography; the first three of these functions comprise the primary activities of combat engineers, or those engineering soldiers serving in combat operations. First, because every military unit of any size must have mobility to maneuver on battlefields, combat engineers remove natural or manmade obstacles that reduce movement, including rivers that need to be bridged, explosive mines to be cleared, or enemy fortification to be breached by tunneling, battering, or scaling the walls or other barriers. Second, the counter-mobility task mirrors that of mobility in that combat engineers prepare obstacles to defend their own units by depriving enemy forces of freedom of movement. Combat engineers destroy bridges, lay mines, or construct roadblocks to stop, disrupt, direct, or delay enemy mobility. Third, when large military forces and civilian popular centers require more permanent fortifications that can withstand bombardments, undermining, and direct assaults by enemy forces, combat engineers build these hardened defenses to provide survivability.

Apart from these three activities on battlefields, combat engineers are skilled craftspeople who can design and build structures like roads, aqueducts, dams, or other structures as part of construction engineering. They also understand how topographical features may be used to help perform the other four tasks. Rivers, for example, can be used to defend friendly forces or impede enemy forces' movements. Aside from battlefield operations, rivers offer means to produce water power or hydroelectric power that help militaries and civilians alike.

Combat engineering remained relatively consistent from antiquity until the emergence of gunpowder in the 1400s, the steam engine in the 1800s, the gasoline engine in the 1900s, and information technologies in recent decades. Each of these new applications offered advantages and disadvantages. When cannons became powerful enough to bombard medieval castles to dust, fortification shifted from tall, thin walls to short, thick barriers more like trenches than walls. Schools for engineers sprang up in Western Europe to provide advanced training for officers in the tactics and techniques of siege warfare. The students learned to apply advanced geometry and physics principles to building fortifications and aligning cannons in assaults or defensive operations. This same period saw the advent of combat engineering specialists called sappers and miners among the enlisted ranks. The sappers were soldiers who dug the trenches—called saps—as part of siege operations to capture enemy fortifications, and the miner tunneled under enemy emplacements, filled the tunnels with explosives, and ignited the explosive to collapse those emplacements.

The First World War from 1914 to 1918 heralded the formal creation of combat engineering units. The Germans, French, and British militaries used variants or translations of the word "pioneer" for the American term "combat engineers." All shared similar training and performed mobility, counter-mobility, and survivability functions. These became especially critical during the bloody, endless operations in trench warfare in France. Combat engineers directed the design and construction of trenches running from the English Channel to the French border with Switzerland. They emplaced razor wire and landmines as defensive measures. When infantrymen climbed "over the top" and advanced across no-man's land to assault enemy trenches, combat engineers also accompanied them to assist in breaching those defensive measures. Tragically, because the defending soldiers enjoyed decisive advantages in firepower from machine guns and artillery, the assaulting forces could rarely overcome the defenses or win decisive victories.

During the Second World War, combat engineers expanded in their numbers, tasks, and significant contribution to military operations. In the U.S. Army, for example, some 600,000 soldiers served in the engineer branch out of a total of 8 million men and women in the army as a whole. Each of those soldiers spent several weeks in basic combat training and then several more weeks of advanced engineer training at one of two bases at Fort Leonard Wood in Missouri and Fort Belvoir in Virginia. After they graduated, the soldiers joined several hundred engineer combat battalions (with some 900 soldiers each) and accompanied American soldiers in infantry, tank, and artillery units to the front line. The combat engineers removed German and Japanese landmines, bridged rivers, and destroyed enemy gun emplacements, thus giving mobility to the other American units. When the Germans or Japanese counterattacked, the American engineers switched to defensive activities such as constructing roadblocks, laying mines, or destroying bridges as part of their counter-mobility function that limited the maneuverability of enemy units on battlefields. Combat engineering in the Korean War was very similar to that of the Second World War.

The Vietnam War marked another change in combat engineering as the U.S. military as a whole tried to fight an unconventional conflict against the enemy Viet Cong (VC) and North Vietnamese Army (NVA) insurgents. The army's engineer training shifted to emphasize ways to identify and neutralize enemy landmines and booby traps. This process started a competition between the American combat engineers and the VC and NVA: as the U.S. Army developed sensitive metal-detecting devices to find explosive landmines with metal components, the enemy insurgents shifted to mines with nonmetallic materials that evaded the metal detectors. The military faculty at the U.S. Army Engineer School at Fort Leonard Wood worked tirelessly to teach new combat engineers how to identify landmines and booby traps by sight or pattern of location, in addition to using metal detectors. The faculty at the Engineer School also compiled doctrinal manuals that provided written instruction on identifying and neutralizing those landmines and booby traps. Despite the best efforts by combat engineers, the American attempts to stop the VC and NVA insurgent tactics never fully succeeded.

Following the September 11, 2001, terrorist attacks, the U.S. military invaded Afghanistan and Iraq. After the initial military operations, conflicts in both nations devolved into unconventional insurgencies, not unlike the Vietnam War. Indeed, the insurgents and terrorists in Afghanistan and Iraq made even more effective use of what have become known as IEDs, or improvised explosive devises. These terrorists and insurgents often fabricated these from household items like pots or pans filled with unused American munitions or unexploded American bombs. Hidden on roadsides, under rubbish, or in tunnels, the IEDs inflicted grievous physical and psychological injuries on American military personnel, as well as damage to vehicles. The majority of American deaths in the Middle East occurred because of IED strikes.

The U.S. Army Corps of Engineers once again started training soldiers and officers alike in identifying and neutralizing IEDs before they could cause harm. Just as in Vietnam, however, the insurgents and terrorists shrewdly found ways to limit every American solution. If metal detectors were used, the enemy turned to nonmetallic materials and so on. As the conflict dragged on, the U.S. Army combat engineers found that the most effective ways to locate IEDs came from two unsophisticated sources: soldiers examining the nearby terrain and looking for telltale signs like disturbed soil or tripwires and soldiers with dogs specially trained to sniff out explosives patrolling the areas near roads or buildings.

The future of combat engineering will include not only the most ancient of tasks like building bridges and destroying fortifications but also the employment of advanced technologies like ground-penetrating radar, aerial drone surveillance, and satellite imagery to locate enemy positions and enable combat units to maneuver on battlefields.

David J. Ulbrich

See also: *1915–1945:* Infantryman; Mechanical Engineer

FURTHER READING

Bass, Paul W. 2016. *The History of Fort Leonard Wood*. Sikeston: Acclaim Press.

McLeod, Toby. 2001. "Fortifications and Siegecraft." In *The Oxford Companion to Military History*, edited by Richard Holmes, 308–312. New York: Oxford University Press.

Pergrin, David E., and Eric Hammel. 1989. *First Across the Rhine: The 291*st *Engineer Combat Battalion in France, Belgium, and Germany*. Pacifica: Pacifica Press.

U.S. Army. 1969. *Viet Cong Boobytraps, Mine and Mine Warfare Techniques* (Training Circular 5–31). Government Printing Office. https://archive.org/details/milmanual-tc-5-31-viet-nam-version.

U.S. Army. 2014. *Engineer Operations* (Field Manual 3–34). https://usacac.army.mil/sites/default/files/misc/doctrine/CDG/cdg_resources/manuals/fm/fm3_34.pdf.

U.S. Army Corps of Engineers History Office. 2008. *The U.S. Army Corps of Engineers: A History*. Alexandria: U.S. Army Corps of Engineers, Office of History.

COMPUTER PROGRAMMER

A computer programmer creates computer software. With the invention of the personal computer in the 1970s and 1980s and the development of the internet in the early 1990s, the occupation of computer programmer expanded enormously in both knowledge and skill requirements for successful workers. Computer programmers write and test specific software language, or code, to instruct computers to make complex business calculations, solve problems, create video games and animated movies, and create artificial intelligence (or AI), all of which allow machines themselves to make decisions, run machinery, and do all kinds of other processes that were formerly completed by hand or not done at all. Before the development of inexpensive computer hardware in the 1950s, most programmers wrote programs that served as complex sets of instructions in software languages like Fortran, for mathematical and scientific applications, or C and its subsequent revisions, C+ and C++, used in both business and scientific applications. Programming languages have syntax rules, just like all human languages around the world, which require computer programmers to learn the structure and syntax of software to write and manipulate their programs.

In many ways, the personal computer democratized computer programming as more individuals, both hobbyists and professionals, created new software running in new operating systems, such as Microsoft's DOS, or disk operating system, in which an entire computer's computational capacities are stored within a single machine on its hard drive. Previously, computer programmers wrote their instructions (programs), which were then linked and often transmitted to other larger machines to which data had been entered, either on tape or via punch cards.

While some programmers helped to create software, programmers more commonly receive instructions from senior systems designers, who identify, design, and communicate the business or engineering (or other) problem to be solved or action to be taken. For instance, a bank's system analyst or system designer will help bankers conceptualize and develop a new product or action, such as an automatic withdrawal of funds each month for customers who elect this service to pay their credit card balances. The system designer determines the options based on the bank's computer operating system as well as bank priorities and then completes a set of requirements that the bank's computer systems must respond to, such as ensuring correct account information, what to do if a customer's bank balance is insufficient, what fees are assessed if insufficient funds are encountered, when to update credit card balances, and how to determine the appropriate interest-rate discount for customers who elect this auto-pay option.

A systems designer or analyst then communicates these requirements and parameters to the programmer. In turn, a computer programmer writes the program using the appropriate software and then tests and debugs it to create a set of instructions that order the computer to automate this entire auto-pay process. A computer programmer must also maintain the software, ensuring that the bank's computers continually operate as designed while adjusting to new business demands.

An ordinary workday for a computer programmer involves writing, testing, and debugging code in an office environment, working independently but with supervision. A programmer must focus on the task at hand, always attentive to avoid errors—just as people do when they converse about important topics. Depending on the task, the computer programmer might be able to write a simple program in a few hours, or for more complex applications, a programmer (or group of programmers) might take weeks or months to complete a set of instructions. As they write code, the programmers also continually test it within a contained computer environment known as an integrated development environment (IDE). In this way, a programmer can correct an error in syntax or structure when he or she first writes the code rather than trying to find an error once a complex program has been completed but the computer does not understand the directions in the code, commonly leading to error messages. Once a programmer has written, tested, and debugged the code, he or she works with the systems designer to create an interface with the computer's operating software.

Since the 1990s, computer software developers have created code libraries that allow computer programmers to use interchangeable modules of code that are commonly used in certain applications; these lines of code ease the work of the programmer. Source code developers are specialized computer programmers who write, test, and debug these codes used by others. Additionally, web-based software languages, like hypertext markup language—or HTML—are used by both computer programmers and savvy end-users to create structures for websites. Computer programmers also work for web-hosting companies that provide "What You See Is What You Get" (WYSIWG) packages that allow users to build their own websites using common word-processing actions (write, format, cut and paste). These packages now allow even children to accomplish what a skilled programmer might have done twenty-five years ago, but even a website that a child creates is based on the sets of instructions written and tested by programmers. Other simple-to-use yet powerful software, like Microsoft's Excel, can be used by consumers (computer owners) to collect, store, and analyze significant amounts of data, eliminating the need for small business owners to contract the services of a computer programmer.

Even as software packages make the work of an earlier generation of computer programmers simpler and more accessible, new software languages today, like Python, Ruby, and others, have been created, requiring programmers to gain more education and greater skills to utilize them. Computer programmers use these newer languages to write and test code for mobile phone applications, for instance. Extensive web-based instructional manuals, textbooks, programming academies, and massively open online courses (MOOCs) have emerged to provide free information to computer programmers as well as those interested in pursuing coding skills. However, most computer programmers pursue college educations to become highly fluent in several software languages. Computer programming students also learn about basic hardware to understand the limitations of a particular computer system and thus choose the correct language for individual machines. Computer programmers may also pursue degrees in software engineering to become systems analysts and designers.

Nancy Quam-Wickham

See also: E-Commerce Specialist; Information Technology Architect

FURTHER READING

Leeds, Herbert D., and Gerald M. Weinberg. 1970. *Computer Programming Fundamentals*. New York: McGraw-Hill.

O'Regan, Gerard. 2012. *A Brief History of Computing*. London: Springer.

Wexelblat, Richard L. 2014. *History of Programming Languages*. Burlington: Elsevier Science.

CORRECTIONAL OFFICER

Correctional officers (COs) are uniformed officials responsible for the care and control of prisoners who have been convicted of crimes or are in custody pending trial, and they serve a critical—but often invisible—role in public safety. Correctional officers are employed by a state's department of corrections or by the federal government's Bureau of Prisons.

Although they vary by state, requirements and qualifications to become a correctional officer are relatively consistent. To be eligible for a CO position, individuals often must be at least eighteen or twenty-one years old, possess a high school diploma or an equivalent certification—such as a GED—have no previous felony records, pass medical and psychiatric tests, and successfully pass the department's entry-level exam. If an individual is hired, he or she will go through a training academy, which ranges in length. For example, Arizona Department of Corrections' (ADC) training academy is seven weeks, New York Department of Corrections and Community Supervision's (DOCC) and Michigan Department of Corrections' (MDOC) are eight weeks, and California Department of Corrections and Rehabilitation's (CDCR) is thirteen weeks. These academies provide training in self-defense and safety tactics, communication skills, ethics and professionalism, firearms, and a range of other topics important for the job. Once new officers complete their academy, they are often put through on-the-job training (OJT) or placed with field training officers (FTO), who put their academy education into practice with supervision and guidance.

Correctional officers are both men and women of all ages and backgrounds, but the Department of Labor reports that more than 70 percent of correctional officers in the United States are male. Depending on the department, officers usually work for twenty to twenty-five years to collect a full retirement package. According to the Bureau of Labor Statistics, the median pay for COs in the United States is forty-three thousand dollars per year, though this varies by jurisdiction.

A CO's primary role is to supervise inmates and ensure that every prisoner stays safely in custody for the duration of his or her sentence. Correctional institutions consistently state that their top priorities are safety and security. Specifically, they emphasize the safety of both staff and inmates and the security of the facility as a whole.

Correctional officers have other responsibilities while discharging their duties, some of which include providing prisoners with meals; accounting for the presence of inmates multiple times through the day (often known as count time); escorting inmates to and from classes, medical appointments, visits, and recreation; distributing needed items such as hygiene and mail; and responding to emergencies.

In addition to these and other tasks, COs work with several inmate classifications. Inmates are classified based on their criminal history, behavior, and personal characteristics and placed into custody levels. Custody level typically means the level of risk the inmate poses to staff and other inmates. Officers who work in higher custody—often known as maximum security—have more physically demanding jobs in that they do everything for the inmates.

The job of a CO can be very challenging and dangerous. They are responsible for individuals who have been convicted of crimes, who may be violent, angry, or agitated about their incarceration, and, in some cases, who have mental health diagnoses. Training prepares officers for physical violence, acts of self-harm, medical emergencies, and other events. Officers are equipped with tools to assist them, including radios, handcuffs, and oleoresin capsicum (OC) pepper spray. Although the media, television, and movies depict prison as a consistently dangerous and chaotic environment, prison riots and serious assaults are rare.

Similar to police departments, correctional departments have room for growth and promotion. Once officers complete a certain amount of time at their entry-level position, they can apply and test for promotions or new types of jobs within the department. Most states have two types of work above the basic CO level, which are generally defined as security and caseload management. The security path is based on inmate supervision and the other responsibilities detailed above. There are many opportunities to promote within the security path, including sergeant, lieutenant, captain, and higher positions. Caseload management officers are often considered counselors. These officers are most often tasked with teaching rehabilitative classes, assisting inmates with personal needs such as managing their bank accounts, and planning for release or parole, among other important responsibilities. Like the security path, there are opportunities to promote as well.

Many states have specialized units or positions within their facilities. Specialized units often include criminal investigations, crisis response teams, K-9 search dog teams, tactical support or emergency response units, and escape search teams. Other positions that are often considered part of the correctional field include juvenile or youth correctional officers and parole officers. Although both jobs are different than the standard CO, they include various levels of supervision, such as community supervision in parole, and involve different populations such as juveniles or those released from prison.

Caitlin Matekel

See also: *1861–1914:* Police Officer; Prison Guard

FURTHER READING

Conover, Ted. 2001. *Newjack: Guarding Sing*. New York: Vintage Books.

Foucault, Michael. 1977. *Discipline and Punish: The Birth of the Prison.* New York: Vintage Books.

Hassine, V. 2011. *Life without Parole: Living and Dying in Prison Today.* New York: Oxford University Press.

Maruna, S. 2001. *Making Good: How Ex-Convicts Reform and Rebuild Their Lives.* Washington, DC: American Psychological Association.

Western, B. 2018. *Homeward: Life in the Year after Prison.* New York: Russel Sage Foundation.

DATA ANALYST

Data analysts collect, process, perform statistical analyses on, and present data to discover how it can be used to answer questions, make decisions, and solve problems. Data analysts can be found in generally any field or industry, such as healthcare, higher education, agriculture, or business, as every industry collects data, whether it is from clinical trials, educational research, or market research. As a result, "data analyst" is an umbrella term, and there are many different types of data analysts, including research data analysts, quantitative analysts, operations analysts, and similar field-specific positions. There is often a good deal of job crossover with business intelligence analysts and data warehouse analysts, which can be confusing as there is generally no agreed-upon definition for many of these titles. As with all job titles, the exact job description can vary from company to company or even department to department.

In general, data analysts summarize and evaluate the meaning and implications of quantitative (numerical) and qualitative (primarily words) data that is gathered. Depending on the field and level of expertise, research data analysts clean and prune data to look for possible discrepancies and isolate errors in data recording, analyze and interpret results using standard statistical tools and techniques, pinpoint trends and relationships in complicated data sets, and provide concise data reports and clear data visualizations. Professionals may also create and maintain relational databases and data systems, design and coordinate data collection, and provide consultation and technical assistance to leadership and other stakeholders.

Data analysts most commonly work in office settings in a regular five-day work week, though some may telecommute (work from home) or work out of several business offices, depending on the situation and analysis tasks. Some may even participate in data collection: harvesting specific data (like demographic characteristics of a particular subset of customers, for instance) from larger databases developed by business intelligence firms, or they may help conduct focus groups—interview small groups of consumers about a new product or marketing campaign. Most data analysts use computers and sophisticated software in their day-to-day work. Many also use data visualization software as well to present complex patterns of numerical relationships (data) in a visual manner more accessible to the average, nontechnical person. Some data visualization techniques include creating bar graphs, bubble charts, cartograms, Veroni diagrams, and network analysis. When a data analyst embeds any of these data representations into a web-based platform, the user (a consumer, supervisor, or member of the public, for instance) can manipulate the data representation by selecting certain data sets to visualize. The United States Census Bureau maintains a website, the Data Visualization Gallery, on which the bureau's data analysts present weekly explorations of demographic (population) data drawn from the decadal census.

Most research data analysts have degrees in fields like math, statistics, computer science, or something closely related to their field or industry. A bachelor's degree is needed for most entry-level jobs, although many employers prefer a graduate degree for this position. Depending on the field, certifications are available and may be valuable to a career path. There are numerous data analytics certifications available from universities and companies (e.g., SAS and IBM).

Research data analysts work with large amounts of data, facts, and figures, so strong math and analysis skills and a keen attention to detail are important. Professionals in this field need to be able to evaluate information and form conclusions based on the data gathered. They are often called to present their findings or translate the data into an understandable document, so communication skills are also important. Research data analysts must explain results and information in formats that work for various audiences (e.g., in reports, on websites, in meetings, at conferences, and elsewhere), and almost all work with numbers as much as words, so spreadsheet (e.g., Excel) and database (e.g., ACCESS) skills are important. Research data analysts will often use specialized software applications to organize information and run statistical analyses.

While there is a lot of desk time, research data analysts often work as part of a team. Professionals need to be happy sharing information and developing theories regarding results with anyone and everyone. Curiosity and creativity are also key attributes of a good research data analyst. While it is important to have a strong grounding in statistical methods, even more critical is having the desire to find better explanations for whatever phenomena is being studied.

Today's research data analysts should be prepared for a shift toward big data analytics. While self-service business intelligence software and automation are replacing many of the regular reporting tasks that technical experts have been required to handle in the past, big data analytics are fast becoming essential in many fields and industries. Organizations are looking for data scientists and analysts with expertise in the techniques required to analyze big data. They also need big data systems architects to translate requirements into systems, data engineers to build data pipelines, developers who know their way around technologies, and systems administrators and managers to tie everything together.

Lindsey Brown

See also: *1946–1991:* Scientist

FURTHER READING

Baesens, Bart. 2014. *Analytics in a Big Data World: The Essential Guide to Data Science and Its Applications*. New York: Wiley.

Granville, Vincent. 2014. *Developing Analytic Talent: Becoming a Data Scientist.* New York: Wiley.

Guglielmi, Giorgia. 2017. "Meet the Scientist Who Turns Data into Music—and Listen to the Sound of a Neutron Star." *Science*, July 21. http://www.sciencemag.org/news/2017/07/meet-scientist-who-turns-data-music-and-listen-sound-neutron-star.

United States Census Bureau. "Data Visualization Gallery." https://www.census.gov/dataviz/.

DELIVERY DRIVER, *see* PACKAGE HANDLER

EARLY CHILDHOOD EDUCATOR

Early childhood educator is a relatively new occupational category that only recently arose in the United States. Early childhood educators care for young children, generally those between two and five years of age. As part of their work, early childhood educators provide basic instruction in social and academic skills to their young students. Beginning in the 1960s, federal and state governments began to define quality in early childhood education programs, specify required training for educators, and establish maximum teacher-student ratios. As a result, early childhood educators are not simply babysitters or nursery workers, but, instead, they must meet minimum educational and certification requirements.

Before the last decades of the twentieth century, the task of caring for young children in America had been work performed by mothers, grandmothers, and other female kin. Some specialized childcare centers, generally called day nurseries, were founded to care for children of working mothers—primarily widows—beginning in the 1850s, while the kindergarten movement of the 1870s and 1880s provided places for structured play for children ages five through eight years old, regardless of a mother's working status. During much of America's history, desperate workers who had no access to childcare for their young children had few options: leave their children with neighbors, lock them up inside and leave them alone while working outside of the home, find apprenticeship or indentures for even very young children, or temporarily leave them in orphanages.

Most mothers who had children younger than the age of six did not work outside of the home until the early 1980s. Beginning in the latter decades of the twentieth century, however, broad economic and social transformations created the need for vast numbers of workers called early childhood educators. By the 1970s and 1980s, inflation, slow economic growth, and the declining industrial base of the United States meant that the parents of young children increasingly both had to work outside the home to maintain their earlier standards of living. Most states began liberalizing divorce laws at this time as well, making it easier for couples to separate for reasons other than abandonment, infidelity, or domestic violence. Lastly, President Lyndon Johnson's War on Poverty program of the 1960s created a national initiative, Head Start, that provided young children from low-income families with free public school-readiness classes; these early public initiatives were expanded in 2001 under President George W. Bush's No Child Left Behind Act and President Barack Obama's 2013 Preschool for All Initiative. By the early 2000s, decades of research had shown that children who attended formal programs (offering a mix of basic academic instruction, social skills training, structured and unstructured play activities, and opportunities for outdoor, health, and wellness education) were far more likely to do better academically in elementary and secondary schools, were less likely to demonstrate disruptive behavioral problems and engage in delinquent and criminal activities, and, over a lifetime, earned significantly more money annually than those who did not attend formal early childhood education programs.

In the 1960s, the U.S. Congress passed the Early Childhood Education Act. For the first time, the federal government recommended basic standards for early childhood programs; since that decade, both the federal government and most states have adopted additional regulations that define "high-quality" early childhood programs, which include training and educational requirements for early childhood teachers. Only those public early childhood programs that meet federal "high-quality" requirements can receive financial support from governments. For example, all teachers in Head Start programs must have at least an associate degree, a two-year postsecondary degree offered at community colleges, in early childhood education. Many of the largest states, including Florida, Texas, California, and New York, require early childhood teacher applicants to hold at least an associate degree, though many require applicants to possess a bachelor's degree in early childhood education, child development, or another field with substantial course work in those two areas. Almost all states also require early childhood educators to obtain professional licenses or certifications, whether they work in public or private, often home-based, facilities; criminal background checks are normally required for any educator, even for aides who meet fewer formal educational requirements. For those early childhood educators who operate their own home-based businesses, there are additional licensing and state inspections required before opening a childcare facility. Finally, all applicants for certification as early childhood educators must complete additional training requirements, including classes in CPR, mandated child abuse reporting, school violence reduction, and other areas depending on state and local requirements. Despite significant educational and certification requirements, as well as the demonstrated impact that high-quality educational programs have for very young children, early childhood educators—or preschool teachers—earn some of the lowest annual wages of all American workers, with a median salary of just $28,570 in 2016, according to the U.S. Bureau of Labor Statistics (U.S. Department of Education, 2016). It is also a field dominated by women workers as over 98 percent of all preschool teachers are female.

The daily life of an early childhood educator is often a demanding one. Developmentally, young children often lack the ability to communicate well, are more likely to have difficulty regulating their emotions, and may have varying levels of fine and gross motor skills—meaning that some children may cry quickly when frustrated, while others might act out forcefully when tired or hungry. Early childhood educators have the responsibility to keep children on task, respond individually to children having difficulty, and create a safe and respectful learning environment for all. A typical day consists of greeting children as they arrive at the center, usually by 7:30 a.m. After arrival, children are encouraged to use the bathroom and wash up for breakfast (a form of education in self-care). Once children finish the morning breakfast or snack, the teacher will advise them to get ready for class activities; this consists again of a bathroom visit, including opportunities to brush their teeth and hair (more education in self-care). Research has shown that children tend to learn better when clean and groomed.

Once all students are ready for learning, the teacher may lead pupils in a brief period of physical activity, or kinesthetic learning, that provides a way for young children to focus on a task: yoga, stretching, dance, or meditation. These activities signal to children that school is formally beginning while promoting skills in listening and following directions, as well as practice in coordination and body movement. On any given day, an educator introduces various academic skills—learning days of the week, names of the month, colors, numbers, and letters—in age-appropriate ways, such as art projects (painting and playing with nontoxic modeling compounds like Play-Doh), stories, songs, and finger plays. Repetitive speaking, individually and in groups, by reciting songs, poems, and counting activities reinforces basic academics as well as helps young children expand their vocabularies.

Many teachers help students learn colors, shapes, and numbers by associating them with months. For example, January might include a focus on the color white and incorporate projects relating to snow, or students learn to associate February, the second month of the year, with the color pink and the heart shape in a nod to Valentine's Day. By mid-March, many centers have reached the one-hundredth day of the school year, and by this time, students will have learned how to count confidently to ten. Teachers might ask children to bring in one hundred items (such as Cheerios) and count them out in groups of ten, providing instruction in mathematical concepts while celebrating this important milestone of the school year. Teachers need to provide young children with hourly bathroom breaks, emphasizing handwashing for cleanliness and health promotion.

Since young children learn through play activities, teachers break up these instructional periods with free (yet carefully designed) play. Students might play house or dress-up, practice problem solving and fine motor skills with puzzles or blocks, or play hide-and-seek games or navigate easy obstacle courses created by the teacher. Riding trikes or playing with balls and other recreational equipment gives students practice in gross motor skills (or learning to control the body's large muscle groups). In many centers, students are provided with a nutritional lunch; teachers normally supervise students as they get ready for lunch, including instructing them in self-calming activities like looking at books, watching movies, or relaxing in specified quiet areas such as indoor tents. Handwashing is always emphasized. Teachers also supervise students as they eat and then clean up after eating. Bathroom visits, toothbrushing, and preparation for nap or rest time follow. Most young children benefit from quiet time during the afternoon, especially after an invigorating morning of learning and socialization. In full-day programs, youngsters spend most of the period after rest time engaging in play activities. Although childcare centers have different closing times, most expect parents to pick up their children by 5:30 p.m., thus accommodating parents' normal 8:00 a.m. to 5:00 p.m. workday.

For those early childhood educators working in home-based daycare, the workday begins earlier and extends later into the evening. Preparing food for breakfast, lunch, and snacks takes additional work; menu planning and grocery shopping often extends into a worker's weekends. Home-based workers must clean their classrooms daily. Early childhood educators create lesson plans, schedule holiday and birthday celebrations for children, and must keep up with recertification requirements. They shop for new learning tools and art supplies, maintain recreational equipment, and prepare items needed for each week's lessons. Additionally, home-based educators must run their businesses—keep attendance records, prepare billing statements, and maintain accounts of business receipts and expenditures.

Regardless of the setting, early childhood educators often find their work deeply rewarding as they watch their young students acquire the skills to succeed in school and in society. While carefully structured, one workday is never the same as another.

Cindy Roberts Yarber and Nancy Quam-Wickham

See also: *1861–1914:* Teacher; *1946–1991:* Social Worker

FURTHER READING

Gordon Biddle, Kimberly A., Ana G. Garcia-Nevarez, Wanda J. Roundtree Henderson, and Alicia Valero-Kerrick. 2013. *Early Childhood Education: Becoming a Professional.* Los Angeles: Sage.

Gramling, Michael. 2015. *The Great Disconnect in Early Childhood Education: What We Know vs. What We Do.* St. Paul: Redleaf Books.

Mooney, Carol Garehart. 2013. *Theories of Childhood: An Introduction to Dewey, Montessori, Erikson, Piaget, and Vygotsky.* Second edition. St. Paul: Redleaf Press.

Rogers, Fred. 2003. *The World According to Mr. Rogers: Important Things to Remember.* New York: Hachette Books.

E-COMMERCE SPECIALIST

"E-commerce specialist" is a catch-all category that includes several different occupations within business and digital media. In the formal economy, e-commerce specialists design websites and mobile applications to improve the shopping experiences of consumers, whether a client is buying a lipstick from an online beauty outlet, trying to e-reserve an available campsite at a state park for a holiday weekend, or evaluating a prospective college. E-commerce specialists in business also write and maintain computer code that facilitates the movement of money between the online platform and the business, such as through electronic funds transfers, or digital "wallet" transactions between individuals in peer-to-peer networks. In the informal economy, e-commerce specialists may promote particular products on television or on user-sharing video platforms, or they may serve as cultural influencers, using various social media platforms. Also falling within this broad category of e-commerce specialists are those workers who manage online reputations for both individuals and businesses. Generally, e-commerce specialists are workers well trained in media and digital design who use their skills to promote the sale of some kind of "product."

In business, digital media specialists design commercial websites to encourage shoppers to spend money on products offered for sale. These e-commerce specialists evaluate business and retailer websites, whether or not those businesses or retailers have a physical, brick-and-mortar presence in the retail world. For example, a sporting goods store might be local, specializing in regional equipment—perhaps deep-sea fishing gear and tackle along the Florida coast—or it might be national in scope, such as a large chain of retail sporting goods stores. In both cases, these firms have both brick-and-mortar stores but also offer items for sale online to customers who want particular items, or a business might be primarily online—such as Amazon—and sell sporting goods equipment through electronic means.

E-commerce specialists must design logos and create user interface experiences in an effort to create visually pleasing webpages that distinguish the business from competitors; they also create pop-up ads that market related products and incorporate links that ask customers if they would like to purchase additional items. These specialists in marketing and digital design must also ensure that customers who land on the site's pages are able to easily navigate the website; some studies have shown that customers will leave a website within a minute if they cannot easily the find the information they're seeking. The metric that describes the rate at which website visitors leave without exploring the site's content is called the bounce rate, and it costs businesses in lost revenue. E-commerce specialists incorporate website traffic monitors, like Google Analytics, into a site, which allows them to analyze data about customer behavior. This information is essential when an e-commerce specialist is trying to optimize a website's design to maximize customers' engagement and satisfaction.

E-commerce specialists in the formal economy also help businesses gain customers by helping to market the company. They write and post regular blogs about company products or services because business consulting companies have shown that frequent, readable blog posts drive customer engagement. E-commerce specialists procure advertising space on other corporate websites or, more commonly, sell advertising space on their own sites to other companies because such arrangements can provide consistent revenue; even if a customer does not ultimately purchase a product from one business's website, if that person clicks on another company's advertisement, it generates a small amount of revenue for the original website. Each click on one of these pay-per-click (PPC) advertisements might generate only a few cents—or even just fractions of a cent—in revenue, but enough clicks can become a significant source of income.

E-commerce specialists also design websites for search engine optimization (SEO) so that when potential customers use an internet search engine, the specialist's company will appear higher in the prospective customer's search results. If a company specializes in selling bandanas, for instance, website content needs to stipulate all of the colors sold, so that if wearing orange bandanas becomes a fashion craze among youths, the bandana company's page will top the list of e-retailers selling orange bandanas in the search results. SEO is very important; studies have shown that for any search engine query, the topmost search result will receive about a third of all resulting traffic, and the second search result will receive about a quarter of all traffic. Essentially, if a website is not properly optimized for SEO and appears third or lower in the search results, a prospective customer has less than a 50 percent chance of ever visiting the business's website.

E-commerce specialists in business also write code that facilitates electronic payments for goods and services between the customer and his or her bank and the business and its banks. Because customers cannot purchase items using cash, the e-commerce specialists confer with fiscal managers in the business to improve and optimize other forms of convenient payment, whether by digital wallet technologies, internet-based payment companies, or bank cards (both credit and debit). E-commerce specialists work with computer security specialists to ensure that a customer's purchase is secure.

In the informal economy, e-commerce specialists may possess a variety of subspecialties. Entrepreneurs, for instance, can open online retail stores with much less capital than a physical store requires. With some skills in digital design and communication strategies, an entrepreneur can build a low-cost website and then purchase items in large quantities at wholesale prices to sell through an online retailer, such as eBay. A customer may wish to purchase 25 pink popsicle sticks to make cake pops for a child's birthday, but most of the big retailers—both electronic and physical stores—only sell plain wooden popsicle sticks in lots of 500 or 1000. An ambitious entrepreneur might purchase 100,000 plain wooden popsicle sticks and then carefully dye them different colors using food-safe dyes and offer them for purchase in smaller lots of various sizes (perhaps 25, 50, or 100) at a price that is reasonable to the customer but still represents a significant profit for the entrepreneur. A customer would then find the reseller's website and place an order, and the reseller would ship the customer's small quantity of pink popsicle sticks. Such entrepreneurs take advantage of online retailer store technologies to manipulate, repackage, and resell items for profit. There is some risk in this kind of entrepreneurial business, however—a product presumed to be popular may not sell, an online retailer might be slow to ship goods in a timely manner, or the business may not be able to respond quickly to customer inquiries. These and many other factors may lead to negative customer reviews, which can cripple an electronic retailer's sales.

In the 2010s, many other entrepreneurs have taken on an e-commerce role in which they become cultural influencers who use social media to pitch other companies' products to their followers in exchange for a small commission on any sales that the influencer generates. Video influencers, for example, work with brands to create brand recognition and allegiance among targeted populations, like teenagers. Many influencers work directly with either businesses or marketing agencies to create instructional, product-centered videos; for example, an influencer might work with a cosmetics company to produce a video that demonstrates the process of applying a particular brand of makeup. Other times, the influencer's corporate relationships are subtler. An influencer might not ever create an instructional video but might only use a certain brand of products when producing any of his or her video content, or one company may pay him or her to avoid using a competitor's product. In any case, an influencer's revenue is based in part on his or her followers resolving to purchase a product that that influencer has a vested interest in promoting.

Influencers create video and visual content that sells an enormous number of products: video games, beauty products, alcohol, fashion clothing and shoes, snacks, and fitness equipment. So important are influencers in today's e-commerce that large marketing consulting firms, like Nielsen, and large influencer talent agencies have taken note, tracking the marketing prowess of influencers and representing them in negotiations with businesses. A 2017 *Forbes* magazine article reported that some top influencers may demand fees of $250,000 or more to market a product, while influencers with much smaller audiences of followers can make a reasonable wage based solely on their promotional content and contracts.

E-commerce specialists are a diverse group of business specialists who use digital means to promote and sell products. In our consumer society, they provide customers with ease-of-buying experiences, monitor marketing trends, and help businesses stay profitable in a highly competitive global market.

Nancy Quam-Wickham

See also: Computer Programmer; Information Technology Architect; Social Media Coordinator

FURTHER READING

Jones, Kristopher B. 2103. *Search Engine Optimization: Your Visual Blueprint for Effective Internet Marketing*. Indianapolis: Visual.

Laudon, Kenneth C., and Carol Guercio Traver. 2018. *E-Commerce: Business, Technology, Society*. Boston: Addison-Wesley.

O'Connor, Clare. 2017. "Earning Power: Here's How Much Top Influencers Can Make on Instagram and YouTube." *Forbes* (April 10). https://www.forbes.com/sites/clareoconnor/2017/04/10/earning-power-heres-how-much-top-influencers-can-make-on-instagram-and-youtube/#154b367e24db.

EMERGENCY MEDICAL TECHNICIAN

Emergency medical technicians (EMTs) and responders are entry-level workers in the emergency medical care field who are tasked with providing basic emergency medical care to patients and, often, responding to emergencies by working on ambulance crews, which are owned and operated by both public and private ambulance companies. EMTs who work in hospitals, urgent care clinics, correctional centers, and other facilities do not work in the field but instead attend to patients within an institutional setting. EMTs are licensed to provide basic emergency medical care: assess and stabilize a patient for transport, clear airways, provide cardiovascular resuscitation (CPR) if needed, control bleeding if present, and stabilize any possible broken bones. Most EMTs provide support to and comfort patients as they prepare them for transport to centers offering higher levels of care.

The occupation of EMT arose directly from the expansion of automobiles and the national highway system in post-World War II America. Before the war, many families did not own their own cars, but that changed with rising standards of living after the war. In response to consumer demand, the automobile industry designed, built, and sold cars with bigger, more powerful engines; these cars were faster than earlier models, and their owners could drive on highways and the newer multilane freeways that circumvented slower residential streets with stoplights and pedestrians. As a result, automobile accident rates dramatically increased in the 1950s and 1960s.

In 1966, President Lyndon Baines Johnson signed the Highway Traffic Safety bill, which created the National Highway Traffic Safety Administration, a federal agency devoted to making travel safer on our nation's roadways. As part of this effort, government officials advocated for a national system of training and licensure that ensured those who responded to traffic accidents were properly trained. In 1970, the National Registry of Emergency Medical Technicians formed to advance these efforts through public policy recommendations for emergency response services, a set of minimum training requirements for emergency medical technicians, and a series of licensure examinations and continuing education programs for those trained as EMTs and paramedics. Although the EMT profession was created in response to America's increasing need for quality emergency medical care in the field, EMTs and paramedics quickly began responding to many other kinds of onsite urgent patient health needs.

Although some states have their own training, examination, and licensure requirements, almost all states still require national level certification to obtain a job as an EMT or paramedic. Today, EMTs and paramedics are but two of the occupations for which the National Registry offers certification; others include emergency medical responder and advanced EMT. Worker training in each occupational category varies, as do each role's responsibilities. The most basic position is that of the emergency medical responder, followed by the EMT, and at the most skilled, the paramedic. Paramedics have to have at least a year's experience working as an EMT or other licensed position; other requirements include significantly more training in both the classroom (at an institution of postsecondary education accredited by a healthcare accreditation body) and practically, or on the job.

Many EMTs spend their workdays simply transporting patients in ambulances: taking non-ambulatory patients from hospitals at time of discharge to rehabilitation centers, nursing homes, or back to patient residences—or the reverse: taking patients from other medical facilities to receive critical care in hospitals. Many EMTs respond to routine calls for services, such as lifting a patient from the bed or bathtub, assisting police officers who are subduing a person who is agitated or delirious and might require simple medical attention, or helping to assess an inebriated person before the police can safely transport him or her to jail. Some EMTs work in hospital or other healthcare institutions, where they help the emergency medical care team stabilize the patient before further treatment. To obtain certification as an EMT, an individual must be at least eighteen years old, hold a CPR certification, have completed a basic EMT course, and have passed national examinations. Many EMTs earn their certification as part of a long-term plan to eventually become a nurse, physician, or other advanced medical care provider; the work an EMT does requires basic medical training and experience but also allows individuals the opportunity to test the waters of a healthcare career choice.

In contrast to EMTs, paramedics are more knowledgeable and experienced emergency medical care providers. Paramedics provide more advanced emergency medical care than EMTs, whose primary directive is to stabilize a patient until he or she is treated by a doctor or paramedic. Paramedics must have all the skills and training of EMTs but also be able to treat patients. Training requirements are more extensive, and, like EMTs, they must pass rigorous examinations and meet other qualifications. For instance, an EMT may help to clear a patient's airway, but a paramedic can also intubate or perform a tracheotomy if simply clearing the patient's airway is insufficient. Working in concert with a nurse practitioner or medical doctor, paramedics also administer drugs in the field, insert IVs, adjust administration of fluids (like saline drips), and administer and read electrocardiograms. In America's aging population, paramedics are less likely to respond to car accidents than to acute and chronic health crises like heart attacks and diabetic comas. Unlike a basic EMT, paramedics may treat auto accident victims, helping fire department personnel and other emergency responders cut patients out of badly damaged cars, while EMTs assist the paramedics, help state patrol officers redirect traffic, and assess the needs of people who may have witnessed a bad accident.

Because of the great variety of calls to which EMTs and paramedics respond, those individuals must be able to think quickly and critically to assess a patient's condition and formulate plans for stabilization, treatment, and transport. A dispatch of "GSW, female, forty-one years of age" means that a middle-aged woman is suffering from a gunshot wound, but the responding EMTs might not know whether they are responding to a "through and through" wound to the hand—which is rarely life threatening—or something far more injurious, like a large-caliber bullet wound to the head.

EMTs and paramedics must have good communication skills and compassionate natures to comfort patients and their families. They must also have integrity—and, in fact, criminal records, especially involving assault, sex offenses, or child or elder abuse, are grounds for the National Registry to deny an applicant's request for licensure and certification. As for employees within the healthcare system, the occupational outlook for EMTs and paramedics is positive, especially as the American population grows and ages.

Nancy Quam-Wickham

See also: *1861–1914:* Nurse; Surgeon

FURTHER READING

Morkes, Andrew, ed. 2002. *Exploring Health Care Careers: Real People Tell You What You Need to Know.* New York: Ferguson Publishing.
National Registry of Emergency Medical Technicians. https://www.nremt.org/rwd/public.
Stanfield, Peggy S., and Y. H. Hui. 1998. *Introduction to the Health Professions.* Burlington: Jones and Bartlett.

EPIDEMIOLOGIST

Epidemiologists are often called "disease detectives." Trained in medicine, science, and public health, epidemiologists examine outbreaks of diseases and medical conditions to locate their sources. Epidemiologists also examine patterns of diseases and medical conditions and their treatment to make recommendations for prevention and quality care. Not all epidemics are caused by viruses, like Zika, or bacteria, like *E. coli*. In modern America, hypertension and obesity are medical conditions that have reached epidemic proportions—nearly 40 percent of

Americans were overweight in 2015–2016, according to the Centers for Disease Control. Being overweight increases an individual's likelihood of developing other chronic diseases, like type 2 diabetes, hypertension, heart disease, and stroke. Epidemiologists use scientific practices (laboratory work), statistical methods, surveys, investigations of disease and patient behavior, socioeconomic studies, and other means to create studies of diseases to educate doctors to provide better care for their patients and to assist public health officials in implementing more effective preventative measures. Epidemiologists working at the Centers for Disease Control, a federal agency, also produce weekly informational bulletins that provide morbidity (disease) and mortality (causes of death) statistics for the nation.

Epidemiologists use a variety of tools in their work. Some perform their work in scientific laboratories, examining viruses under controlled conditions to see how they mutate over time. For some viruses, like influenza, understanding mutation—called antigenic shift—is critical so that, each year, vaccines can be modified to prevent disease. Other epidemiologists work in the field, consulting with local public health officials, patients, and healthcare professionals to understand disease outbreaks. Some epidemiologists specialize in certain diseases or conditions, while others examine causative and preventative actors for chronic diseases like type 2 diabetes. An epidemiologist uses specialized computer software, the open source *EPI-INFO* package, developed in the 1980s, to collect data about particular diseases and medical conditions. This software has functions that allow epidemiologists to create surveys for distribution to individual patients, as well as to input information from other sources, such as public health officers. Using statistical processing software, epidemiologists and statisticians then crunch the data, or direct the computer to analyze the collected data, looking for correlations among seemingly unrelated pieces of information. An epidemiologist might use this computer analysis to then investigate further which factors individual patients have in common.

Epidemiology as a field in the United States emerged largely in the twentieth century, although studies of a disease within certain populations and how to manage or prevent epidemics—such as smallpox—predated the field. Most early studies were completed by physicians observing outbreaks among their patients. The pioneering work of Alice Hamilton, a physician and medical professor at Harvard, in the areas of industrial toxicology and occupational health led epidemiologists into new fields. Hamilton's 1925 book, *Industrial Poisons in the United States,* linked occupational exposure to toxics like lead (among refinery workers and painters) to disease, both acute and chronic, among these workers. In the early twentieth century, epidemiologists also began using new statistical methods, including machine-assisted computational techniques, to process greater amounts of data, thus developing more sophisticated methods of examining information.

While workers in the 1920s may have known that exposure to ethyl lead in a gasoline refinery could induce psychosis, physicians and epidemiologists needed more than anecdotal evidence to determine the neurobiological impact of lead exposure. Once they had hard evidence of the correlation and causation of lead-induced psychosis, epidemiologists issued recommendations on exposure limits as a form of disease prevention.

Epidemiology, as a field, also benefited from advances in treatment—such as the invention of antibiotics like penicillin—and in prevention methods, like the polio vaccine. Each of these advances, however, has added complexity to epidemiological studies. For example, epidemiologists track antibiotic-resistant strains of bacteria, like the superbug MRSA.

In 1976, to celebrate Independence Day and to honor the two-hundredth birthday of the United States, hundreds of members of the American Legion gathered for their annual convention, and without warning—and in the heat of mid-July—men and women fell ill with flu-like high fevers and aching muscles, followed by dangerous upper respiratory infections. Within days, eight people had died, more than a hundred were ill, and twenty-seven more would soon be dead.

The epidemiologists of the Center for Disease Control in Atlanta, Georgia, the CDC's Epidemic Intelligence Service, sprang into action. Dr. David Fraser led the investigation. He immediately assembled his group to take blood samples from the victims and send them to the laboratories in Atlanta on an emergency basis to identify the pathogen. The epidemiology team in the laboratory in Atlanta, after lengthy research, concluded that the cause was a new bacterium, which they named Legionnella pneumophilia.

In Atlanta, the new pathogen was compared to other samples in the CDC's vast library of frozen or preserved bacteria. Soon it was recognized that the Legionnella pneumophilist microbes resembled other pathogens known to exist in freshwater lakes and ponds. The unique characteristic of these bacteria was that they were virulent but could remain dormant in puddled pools of water found sometimes in parts of hot tubs and humidifiers before becoming active by some event that stirred the water and triggered their activation. The location in this case was the ancient air-conditioning water towers on the roof of the hotel. Because the system had been in heavy operation during the extreme hot weather on that fourth of July weekend, the awakened and deadly bacteria had been activated and then floated in water droplets through the hotel's air conditioning system to sicken those unfortunate victims while they slept. The mystery was solved, and action to prevent more cases and cure the existing ones could begin.

In 1993, when a healthy twenty-four-year-old Navajo woman from Gallup, New Mexico, suddenly became feverous with a severe headache and began frantically gasping for air, her family rushed her to a nearby health clinic. Unfortunately, her acute respiratory attack was fatal; the doctors could not save her. Two days later, her boyfriend suffered the same aliment and also died. This sudden and mysterious disease caused panic in the community. Dr. Bruce Tempest, an alert physician in the Indian Health Service, suspecting a possible dangerous new epidemic, began calling other clinics on the Navajo reservation. He discovered that there had been other equally mysterious respiratory illnesses and deaths at other clinics. He quickly contacted Dr. Jim Cheek, a local epidemiologist, who in turn began examining fluids from the victims. At the same time, Dr. Cheek enlisted help from the CDC. They assembled a medical staff of epidemiologists who traveled to New Mexico and began asking questions in an urgent effort to find what was in common with all of the young victims. The CDC was able to identify the microbe as within a category known as hantaviruses. This was a new strain of hantavirus, which they named Muerto Canyon virus. Their growing suspicion was that the virus had come from an animal—rodents were the primary suspects.

When all of the data had been assembled, it was recognized that the harvest of edible seeds from the pinon pine trees had been great that year and that the mice and rat population had also increased proportionately. The conclusion of the investigation was that the deadly virus had been spread by contact with unnoticed mice droppings from infected deer mice invading dark corners of people's houses and trailers. A massive cleanup of mouse droppings from houses and reduction of the infestation of mice ended the epidemic of the Muerto Canyon virus.

Mark P. Friedlander, Jr.

See also: *1946–1991:* Scientist

FURTHER READING

Daniel, T. M. 2006. *Wade Hampton Frost, Pioneer Epidemiologist, 1880–1938: Up to the Mountain*. Rochester: University of Rochester Press.

Friedlander, Mark P. 2009. *Outbreak: Disease Detectives at Work*. Minneapolis: Twenty-First Century Books.

National Learning Corporation. 2012. *Public Health Epidemiologist: Test Preparation Study Guide: Questions & Answers*. Syosset: Author.

FORENSIC SCIENTIST

Forensic science is a discipline that relies on the natural sciences, such as biology, chemistry, physics, and medical science, to analyze physical evidence at crime scenes or in crime labs. In contrast, the discipline of forensic studies recognizes a wider, multi- and interdisciplinary approach that expands to include elements of behavioral science—like psychology—and social sciences, such as criminal justice, criminology, and law, to combine analyses from the crime scene, lab, and behavioral and sociolegal perspectives to understand and solve crimes. Today, forensic science—often shortened to forensics—refers to the application of any scientific principles, knowledge, methods, and practices to the adversary process where guilt or innocence is determined in a court of law. From a practical perspective, scientists and technicians who work inside a forensic crime lab are commonly referred to as forensic scientists, and they are a subset of the broader group of forensic workers whose work entails the collection, analysis, and processing of evidence in the investigation of a crime.

Laboratory examiners usually have a degree in natural sciences, such as biology, chemistry, physics, anthropology, or forensic science-related fields. They are civilians, wearing white lab coats and examining various types of physical evidence in different units in a crime lab. After a few years, these lab examiners may become a level I, II, or III forensic specialist and may be required to testify in court. In most jurisdictions, they are called forensic technologists or scientists.

A crime scene investigation relies on the application of forensic science to determine the details of a crime—its location(s), victims, suspects, weapons or tools involved, and timeline. Processing a crime scene is a complex procedure that comprises many technical fields and legal steps. A crime scene investigation is a technical process performed by a team of two types of personnel: crime scene investigators (CSIs), who are sworn law enforcement officers usually possessing the rank of sergeant or higher, and crime scene technicians, who are industry professionals with a college education and special training. The crime scene investigation focuses on interviews at the scene; any arrests near the scene are almost always carried out by law enforcement officers.

A criminal investigation is a broader legal process performed by pertinent police divisions, such as homicide, major crime, sex crime, auto theft, or burglary. Such investigations are focused on gathering evidence from the perspective of the perpetrator's or victim's social network. While a crime scene investigator focuses on detecting and collecting evidence around the crime scene, a criminal investigator goes beyond a crime scene. In most situations, criminal investigators usually interview victims, eyewitnesses, and people with knowledge of the crime and conduct a background check of the suspect. A criminal investigator will sometimes collect evidence from sources far from the crime scene, such as bank, cellphone, or internet service records.

A typical day for a forensic scientist doesn't always begin or end at the same time. Larger cities and forensics departments might have several forensic scientists who work on scheduled shifts and are responsible for going to new crime scenes as they occur, but smaller departments might only have a small number of forensic scientists available. In these smaller departments, a forensic scientist might be called out to a new crime scene in the middle of the night or on a scheduled day off.

After the forensic scientists have collected evidence at the crime scene, they will head back to the laboratory to process the evidence. In the laboratory, they will take and process additional samples, prepare and ship specialty samples for processing at more advanced laboratories, label and organize photographs, and write reports. It is important for a forensic scientist to be detailed, accurate, and precise when writing these reports and processing evidence; such reports are often major pieces of evidence in subsequent legal proceedings.

In recent years, law enforcement agencies have begun to fill CSI posts with civilian employees who possess advanced college degrees because crime scene processing requires high-level skills and scientific understandings of many different types of evidence. Law enforcement agencies will commonly use a mixed model, wherein an experienced, sworn law enforcement officer will lead a crime scene team comprising civilian investigatory professionals who do not perform any frontline law enforcement actions, like arresting suspects or serving warrants.

A debate exists as to whether a crime scene technician should perform basic examinations in the lab. Due to the budget constraints, some small crime labs normally allow civilian CSIs to both process crime scenes and perform some basic lab duties, such as fingerprint and basic firearms examinations. Most police departments separate the two jobs to avoid scene bias; just seeing a crime scene may influence an investigator's ability to fairly examine evidence in a laboratory. Most importantly, there is consensus that detecting, collecting, and packaging pieces of physical evidence are quite different from testing, examining, and analyzing pieces of evidence—each step in the process requires a specialized mindset and unique skills.

The field of forensic science focuses on detection, preservation, examination, and interpretation of evidence using scientific principles and methods. Forensic science plays an integral role in the criminal justice system and has many important impacts on the citizens, the community, and the social justice it serves.

John Zheng Wang

See also: *1861–1914:* Police Officer; *1946–1991:* Scientist

FURTHER READING

Gaensslen, R. E., H. A. Harris, and H. Lee. 2008. *Introduction to Forensic Science & Criminalistics*. Boston: McGraw-Hill.

Saferstein, Richard. 2014. *Criminalistics: An Introduction to Forensic Science*, 11th ed. Upper Saddle River: Prentice Hall.

Ubelaker, Douglas H. 2013. *Forensic Science: Current Issues, Future Directions*. New York: John Wiley & Sons.

PRIMARY DOCUMENT

In the document below, the Federal Bureau of Investigation lists the many items each crime scene investigator must possess to conduct an efficient investigation. The toolkit comprises many items, of which each crime scene investigator has considerable training in using.

Crime Scene Investigator/Evidence Technician.
Essential: Bindle paper. Biohazard bags. Body fluid collection kit. Camera (35 mm) with flash/film/ tripod. Casting materials. Consent/search forms. Crime scene barricade tape. Cutting instruments (knives, box cutter, scalpel, scissors). Directional marker/compass. Disinfectant. Evidence collection containers. Evidence identifiers. Evidence seals/tape. First-aid kit. Flashlight and extra batteries. High-intensity lights. Latent print kit. Magnifying glass. Measuring devices. Permanent markers. Personal protective equipment (PPE). Photographic scale (ruler). Presumptive blood test supplies. Sketch paper. Tool kit. Tweezers/forceps.

Optional: Audiotape recorder. Bloodstain pattern examination kit. Business cards. Chalk. Chemical enhancement supplies. Entomology (insect) collection kit. Extension cords. Flares. Forensic light source (alternate light source, UV lamp/ laser, goggles). Generator. Gunshot residue kit. Laser trajectory kit. Maps. Marking paint/snow wax. Metal detector. Mirror. Phone listing (important numbers). Privacy screens. Protrusion rod set. Reflective vest. Refrigeration or cooling unit. Respirators with filters. Roll of string. Rubber bands. Sexual assault evidence collection kit (victim and suspect). Shoe print lifting equipment. Templates (scene and human). Thermometer. Traffic cones. Trajectory rods. Video recorder. Wireless phone.

Crime Scene Investigator, Evidence Collection Kits:
Blood Collection: Bindle. Coin envelopes. Disposable scalpels. Distilled water. Ethanol. Evidence identifiers. Latex gloves. Photographic ruler (ABFO scales). Presumptive chemicals. Sterile gauze. Sterile swabs. Test tubes/test tube rack.

Bloodstain Pattern Documentation: ABFO scales. Calculator. Laser pointer. Permanent markers. Protractor. String. Tape.

Excavation: Cones/markers. Evidence identifiers. Metal detectors. Paintbrushes. Shovels/trowels. Sifting screens. String. Weights. Wooden/metal stakes.

Fingerprint: Black and white film. Brushes. Chemical enhancement supplies. Cyanoacrylate (super glue) wand/ packets. Flashlight. Forensic light source. Lift cards. Lift tape. Measurement scales. One-to-one camera. Powders.

Pattern Print Lifter: Chemical enhancement supplies. Electrostatic dust lifter. Gel lifter. Wide format lift tape.

Toolmarks: Casting materials.

Trace Evidence Collection: Acetate sheet protectors. Bindle paper. Clear tape/adhesive lift. Flashlight (oblique lighting). Forceps/tweezers. Glass vials. Slides and slide mailers. Trace evidence vacuum with disposable collection filters.

Trajectory: Calculator. Canned smoke. Dummy. Laser. Mirror. Protractor. String. Trajectory rods.

Source: United States Department of Justice. 1999. *Crime Scene Investigation—Guide for Law Enforcement. A Research Report.* Washington, DC: 34–36.

HOME HEALTH AIDE

Home health aides provide paraprofessional health and personal care to many Americans. Some are family members—parents, siblings, or other relatives of disabled Americans who need assistance with basic health needs. Others work for community agencies, providing care for elderly or other house-bound patients on an as-needed or regular basis. Some work regular shifts for contracting companies that provide round-the-clock health care for the ill, frail, disabled, or elderly. Others work directly for individual clients on a daily basis. All provide healthcare to those who live in their homes and cannot fully care for themselves.

Americans who need the services of home health aides may be young with exceptional medical needs that, for instance, a single parent alone cannot meet. Or they may be adults who have recently become dependent on others as a result of declining personal health: the onset of dementia, a broken hip caused by a fall, or a long battle with a chronic disease like diabetes. Home health aides perform many client-specific tasks based on the needs of an individual patient. Home health aides normally receive training from hospitals, doctors, community agencies, or formally in college coursework. Except in family placements, in most cases, home health aides are assigned to patients by case managers, or social workers trained to assess the needs of a patient and develop a care plan in conjunction with the patient, his or her family members, treating physicians, and other professionals. Many hospitals have case managers, as do many county departments of health and the national network of Area Agencies on Aging, a federal program to provide care for the elderly.

The daily duties of any individual home health aide vary based on the patient. An aide may visit with an isolated and depressed, recently retired patient who would benefit from medication checks and other services. In this case, an aide may be assigned to the patient for only a few hours each week; duties might include helping the patient prepare meals, monitor health (blood pressure checks, for instance), clean and do laundry, and ensure that the patient is taking his or her medications regularly. The visit might include accompanying the patient on a brief walk (or wheelchair ride) outside or chatting with the patient to reduce his or her social isolation. Another patient, perhaps one with dementia and other physical ailments, might need more extensive daily care for a few hours a day: helping the patient bathe and manage personal hygiene (such as shaving and dressing), assisting to orient the patient with his or her surroundings by reading the newspaper to or talking with him or her about loved ones, guiding the patient in brief therapeutic physical exercises using strength bands or beach balls, and helping the patient eat preplanned and prepared meals.

Some home health aides may perform many other duties with especially ill or frail patients on a daily basis for eight or more hours each day: managing incontinence (changing adult diapers), attending to medical devices that assist in bodily functions (cleaning tracheotomy tubes, replacing catheters, helping with colostomy bags), feeding patients special nutrition drinks, or treating bedsores and other physical problems. Aides caring for these patients may also administer medications, monitor machines, and sit with patients to provide companionship near the end of their lives.

All home health aides must document their work for the agencies that employ them; this is the case even for family members who are paid by Medicare for their care services. Some agencies utilize administrative staff to whom aides regularly report, noting changes in a patient's health, family relationships, and living situations. Among those who work with very ill or disabled patients, aides may complete a checklist of routine duties during or at the end of each shift. Accountability is important in this field as a home health aide is often the person with whom a patient has the most contact. Home health aides may also help to coordinate care with family members, as would be the case with a caregiver for a disabled child with severe cerebral palsy, blindness, and developmental delays whose parents work during the day, or an aide may provide respite care for the spouse of an elderly dementia patient; in this case, the aide attends to the patient so that family members can have time to themselves, thereby limiting the stresses of constant care for a loved one—a duty that sometimes leads to a family member's own caregiver fatigue (a stress-related illness with varying symptoms).

As family structures have changed in the last fifty years due to many factors—climbing divorce rates, increased geographic mobility, increased labor force participation among parents of young children, among others—home health aides have undertaken the responsibilities formerly assumed by family members. Policies of the federal government, under Medicare, and states have also helped to increase the demand for home health aides as they have endeavored to keep patients in their homes, a less costly alternative to nursing home placement, as part of the Home and Community-Based Services program.

Although a job with great responsibilities, working as a home health aide is a position that has historically been low paid. A 2015 study found that immigrants are twice as likely as native-born Americans to work as home health aides, while among the latter, African Americans and Hispanic Americans form a significant percentage of the workforce. Rural areas outside of America's largest cities may experience the greatest shortage of home health aides. Employment opportunities for home health care workers are predicted to increase as the nation's population ages, especially members of the Baby Boom generation born after World War II. As a result of these trends, economists predict that home health care positions will be the third-fastest-growing occupation in the country between 2015 and 2030. However, proposed changes to government policies—restricting the use of Medicaid and Medicare funding to support family caregivers—threaten this projected growth and the health of all Americans.

Nancy Quam-Wickham

See also: Physical Therapist; *1607–1775:* Midwife; *1776–1860:* Physician; *1861–1914:* Nurse; *1946–1991:* Dietitian

FURTHER READING

Partnership for a New Economy. 2015. *A Helping Hand: How Immigrants Can Fill Home Health Aide Shortages in America's Rural Communities.* http://www.newamericaneconomy.org/wp-content/uploads/2015/10/Home-Health-Aides.pdf.

Pelham, Anabel O., and Clark, William F. 1986. *Managing Home Care for the Elderly: Lessons from Community-based Agencies.* Berlin: Springer.

Rosengarten, Lucille. 2000. *Social Work in Geriatric Home Health Care: The Blending of Traditional Practice with Cooperative Strategies.* Philadelphia: Haworth Press.

HOUSEKEEPER

A housekeeper or maid is a worker, usually a woman, who is paid in cash or kind to do various types of cleaning for others. In the United States, maids who work in private homes are considered domestic workers, while those working in institutional (private and public) settings form part of a janitorial staff. In the hospitality industry, such as in hotels, maids are referred to as housekeepers, though they more formally part of the janitor workforce. As a racialized and feminized occupation, housekeepers and maids in the United States typically are poorer women who lack advanced schooling. Many scholars link the relatively low status and low pay to the reality that this type of labor is widely viewed as an extension of the unpaid work of cleaning, childcare, and specific tasks such as cooking, washing, and mending or ironing clothing that society expects women to perform in their own homes (Ehrenreich 2001). Housekeepers generally work in the households of their employers, spending the day cleaning. Some housekeepers provide child or elder care. Most work alone or in small groups for agencies, traveling from work site to work site on a daily basis. They utilize cleaning items (brooms, dusters), chemical and natural cleaning agents (cleansers, bleach, vinegar), and machines like vacuums and floor polishers.

Although Lewis Coser (1973) predicted that this job would disappear as capitalism advanced, this has not been the case. At the start of the twenty-first century, paid household work is among the fastest-growing occupations across the globe. The International Labour Organisation (ILO) reports that sixty-seven million women, men and children perform waged household chores. In parallel to global patterns, in the United States, this occupation is racialized, meaning it is shaped by ethnic or racial identity and immigration status in addition to gender and socioeconomic status. The National Domestic Workers Alliance estimates that two million residents of the United States perform some kind of paid domestic labor and maintains that the majority of workers are women who disproportionately identify as African American or immigrants. Maids typically work for middle- or upper-class households in one of two arrangements: live-in or live-out. There has been a shift away from the patronage and residential servitude that once defined employer-employee relationships, where elite households often employed multiple live-in domestic workers. Currently, although there are still women who live in their employers' homes, following the World War II era, it has been most common for women to work on an hourly, weekly, or per task basis (live-out employees), especially for middle-income households.

These patterns have historical precedence yet vary regionally. Prior to the twentieth century, African American women commonly worked as maids in the Southeastern United States, and many lived in the homes of employers in middle-class or elite households until the mid-twentieth century, when they began to migrate north (Sharpless 2013). In the Northeastern United States, through the World War I era, African American women and primarily northern European immigrants worked as domestic servants. Many of the latter were live-in workers, a situation that provided the newly arrived with room and board. This pattern parallels the migration of poorer U.S.-born women who move to urban areas in search of employment and need a place to live.

Following World War II, it has been more common for employees to work on an hourly, daily, or per task basis. Research suggests that live-out employees tend to earn a higher wage than live-in employees and have greater privacy and autonomy and more free time to spend with their own families. Nevertheless, working as a maid or housekeeper may be the best of a limited range of job options for those who do it because maids often work in the unregulated domestic sector, where they are in a vulnerable economic position and may have few if any legal recourses if they are fired. The latter is especially applicable to women who are immigrants, whose number has increased in the past last half century. Since the 1960s, women from the Caribbean have dominated work as housekeepers in New York City (Colen 1990), while record numbers of Latinas in other regions, including the American Southwest, work as housekeepers or maids (Hondagneu-Sotelo 2001; Romero 2016, [2002]). Although there is no national union of maids, and the solitary nature of working in homes may make organizing difficult, a number of regional organizations do attempt to protect home workers' rights, including helping them gain documentation or citizenship.

Even though the stereotype that many picture is of a middle-aged woman working on an hourly basis and then returning home to her family or of a teenager living with a family while providing childcare, the late twentieth century saw an increase in the number of women working for cleaning agencies. Whereas maids in these agencies may strive for a paternalism that replicates relations reported between employees and homeowner employers, maids working in institutional settings are those most likely to be unionized. The U.S. Department of Labor Bureau of Labor Statistics reports that in 2016, approximately 925,000 individuals in the United States worked commercially as maids and cleaners in the travel industry, office buildings, residential care facilities, and hospitals. The average annual income was $22,000 to $27,000, with an average wage between $10 and $11 per hour. Workers' income is often lower in right-to-work states, where unionization rates are lower.

A number of these workers are involved in the Service Employees International Union (SEIU), an umbrella group whose members have consistently engaged in labor actions including work and hunger strikes, marches, and picketing to demand better conditions. Within the United States, the West Coast-based Justice for Janitors is a labor and social movement comprised of low-paid, primarily undocumented commercial cleaners. A turning point in the quest for higher pay, increased benefits, and better working conditions occurred in June 1990, when police assaulted picketers in Century City (Los Angeles County). Images that appeared in the local media garnered public support, leading to these workers earning higher wages, and spurred janitors in other regions (Miami; Washington, D.C.; San Francisco; Houston) to demand a living wage from owners and administrators. Despite these advances, the average hourly income for maids is below fifteen dollars, and housekeepers seldom have affordable healthcare that the SEIU deems to be suitable compensation for the millions of U.S. workers in a vulnerable sector.

Jayne Howell

See also: Home Health Aide; *1946–1991:* Hotelier; Janitor

FURTHER READING

Colen, Shellee. 1990. "'Housekeeping' for the Green Card: West Indian Household Workers, the State, and Stratified Reproduction in New York." In *At Work in Homes: Household Workers in World Perspective*, edited by R. Sanjek and S. Colen, 119–145. Washington, DC: American Anthropological Association.

Ehrenreich, Barbara. 2001. *Nickle and Dimed: On (Not) Getting By in America.* New York: Henry Holt and Company, LLC.

Hondagneu-Sotelo, Pierrette. 2001. *Doméstica: Immigrant Workers Cleaning and Caring in the Shadows of Affluence.* Berkeley: University of California Press.

Romero, Mary. 2002. *Maid in the USA.* New York: Routledge.

Service Employees International Union. 2019. http://www.seiu.org/.

Sharpless, Rebecca. 2013. *Cooking in Other Women's Kitchens: Domestic Workers in the South, 1865–1960.* Chapel Hill: University of North Carolina Press.

INFORMATION TECHNOLOGY ARCHITECT

Information technology (IT) architects lead teams of software developers and business leaders in an effort to optimize business operations and improve data infrastructures. Most IT architects primarily operate as planners and project managers, but IT architects in smaller organizations may also function as developers who work directly on hardware and software development tools, such as software compilers and database management systems. IT architects usually work during regular weekday business hours in an office alongside other employees, and they are typically paid a salary rather than on an hourly basis.

In the 1950s and 1960s, when computers were being used for simple, discrete applications, it was possible for small groups of people to write the software programs for those applications that would operate on a large, centralized mainframe computer. Because each application operated independently, there was no need to coordinate the small teams that were building individual applications. But beginning in the late 1960s, it became apparent that businesses could operate much more efficiently if these individual computer programs could share data or integrate with one another.

At the same time, emerging technologies allowed multiple programs to be run simultaneously on a mainframe computer, and smaller computers and processers were developed, which allowed businesses to own and operate several computers, each potentially running different programs. To take advantage of these technologies, computers needed new ways to connect with one another and share data.

Before this need for IT architects was fully recognized, IT systems were often chaotic. In the 1970s and 1980s, many businesses began sharing data between applications by extracting data to a storage medium, such as magnetic tape or floppy disks, and then physically shuttling that data to other computers or applications that needed it. It has been reported that a single business in this era might do as many as forty-five thousand such data extracts per day. Early IT architects were often computer workers who were tasked with performing these extracts and worked on building new systems and processes that could simplify or eliminate manual data extractions.

IT architects also spend a great deal of time searching for redundancy and inefficiency in new or existing processes. When one business acquires another, there will typically be redundancies between each business's IT systems. An IT architect might examine both sets of systems and then design and execute a plan for the transition to the new, larger organization's data infrastructure.

Today, the field of IT architecture has become quite specialized; there isn't just one type of IT architect anymore. For example, enterprise architects are tasked with developing the top-level plans for how an entire enterprise, such as a corporation or nonprofit entity, will use several smaller, independent, specialized IT systems, and solutions architects develop the highest-level design concept for the system and lead a team of other architects such as business, application, and data architects to further define specific aspects of the system design so it can be implemented by developers. Business architects define the business needs for applications and data to support business goals and processes, and application architects develop a blueprint or plan for the application defining the individual pieces and how those pieces interface with each other so that individual teams can work on the individual parts. Data architects develop a blueprint of the data needs of a business enterprise or a single application, and infrastructure architects work to understand the needs or requirements for the infrastructure, such as how much processing power is required, how much data must be stored, or how reliable and available the infrastructure must be, and then identify the best commercially available products to implement. Network architects define the high-level requirements and design for these networks, such as the number of data sources and users on the network, how much bandwidth is required for the network to deliver all the data it needs to in the time required, how multiple networks are connected to each other, and how to implement security on networks so they are not vulnerable to attacks or data breaches. Backing up all of these roles, security architects work to define how to keep a business's network of computers applications and data safe from hacks and breaches.

At first, most architects worked by producing paper or word-processing documents and diagrams to define their architectural designs. Today, there are computerized tools that produce mathematically precise diagrams and designs for many aspects of IT architecture such as unified modeling language (UML) for application architecture, entity-relationship (ER) diagrams for data architecture, and business process model and notation (BMPN) for business architecture.

The education of IT architects has evolved over time. Until the 1990s, there was little formal education, and most architects learned on the job by reading and by trial and error. Beginning in the 1990s, many software and hardware vendors began offering courses in how to design systems using their products. Training and consulting companies also began offering courses. More and more IT architecture courses are now being taught in universities. More technical types of architecture, such as application, infrastructure, and network architecture, are usually taught in computer science or specialized technical programs. More business-oriented architectures such as business and data architecture are generally taught in business departments. Undergraduate courses tend to be more overview or introductory in nature. Graduate courses tend to get more into the details of any specific type of architecture.

There are also many sources of professional certification in IT architecture disciplines. For example, the Data Administration Management Association (DAMA) International offers certification for data architects. The Open Group offers certification in the Open Group Architecture Framework (TOGAF), which is an enterprise architecture framework. Many hardware and software vendors offer certification programs related to their products. Microsoft (for infrastructure and application architecture) and Cisco (for network architecture) are prime examples. These vendors often have different courses and certification examinations for architects, developers, administrators, and users.

Architects tend to be senior people in the IT or executive departments and usually rise through the ranks of IT developers and administrators to be promoted into the IT architect's role. They typically spend most of their day in meetings in an effort to understand the organization's needs, assign new tasks, troubleshoot existing issues, or plan for future projects.

Richard Howey

See also: Computer Programmer; E-Commerce Specialist; Project Manager

FURTHER READING

Carbone, Jane A. 2004. *IT Architecture Toolkit*. Upper Saddle River: Pearson Professional Education.

Inmon, William H. 2011. *Building the Data Warehouse*. Indianapolis: Wiley.
"Network Architecture." 2018. All-In-One Cross-Platform Diagram Software for Flowchart, Org Chart and Mind Map. Accessed August 10. https://www.edrawsoft.com/Network-Architecture.php.
Perks, Col, and Tony Beveridge. 2011. *Guide to Enterprise IT Architecture*. New York: Springer.

LANDSCAPER

Landscapers and groundskeepers curate and attend to plants and lawns in public and private spaces across the nation. They work for private companies, city and county parks and recreation departments, construction contractors, real estate companies, and as independent entrepreneurs. Landscapers mow lawns in suburban yards and city parks, prune bushes, weed flower beds, and plant new seedlings in gardens. They clear out undergrowth along freeways and highways, treat lawns with weed prevention chemicals, trim rose bushes to keep them healthy, and clip and shape shrubbery into hedges and topiary. They work with arborists (tree surgeons) to determine if trees are healthy. Many landscapers also build garden structures: raised beds for vegetation, trellises for vines, pathways, and other hardscape designs. Landscapers routinely repair sprinkler systems, replacing sprinkler heads or troubleshooting broken water connections.

Americans have long sought to beautify the natural environment by creating parks and gardens for their enjoyment. In the early twentieth century, *Sunset* appeared; this glossy, photo-filled magazine emphasized the splendor of the American West, as conceived by its creators, the Southern Pacific Railroad Company—which sought to increase tourism. In the postwar period, other lifestyle publications featured such suburban ideals as the green, lush, weed-free front lawn, while the environmental movement of the 1960s and 1970s led many Americans to reassess their relationship with nature. Cities and towns across the nation adopted regulations that mandated green spaces. Recreational facilities contributed to this trend too; the number of golf courses in the United States has increased by 24 percent since 1990. Office parks, strip malls, city centers, and freeways, as well as the family home, were all transformed by the work of landscapers and groundskeepers.

Landscapers typically work outside; those who live and work in snow-free areas work in gardens, parks, and yards outside year round, while those who live in colder climates may provide snow removal and other such duties during the winter. The day of a landscaper, especially those who work as independent entrepreneurs, is often monotonous. A landscape entrepreneur typically has a truck or van stocked with equipment: lawn mowers, hedge trimmers, power edgers, leaf blowers, rakes, pole saws, loppers, shovels, brooms, and pruning shears. Most use gas-powered tools, so they must also carry gasoline. They are knowledgeable about these tools, which break down and must be repaired, often on the spot, to complete a customer's regular yard care. Landscaper entrepreneurs travel from one site to another, completing care on six to ten or more yards per day. While every yard is different, the work generally involves mowing the lawn, routine weeding, trimming shrubbery, edging along pathways sidewalks, and then cleaning up before going to the next work site. It is strenuous work, and landscapers hurry to make it to their next client as wasted time means less income. Landscaper entrepreneurs complete paperwork for their businesses at least monthly to keep track of work and earnings, calculate self-employment taxes, reconcile business expenses, and generate and send out billing statements to their clients.

There are regional patterns to landscaping employment in the modern United States. Florida, California, and Texas have the most landscapers, not only because they are among the most populous states but also because of climate. Subtropical gardens, lush lawns, and large areas devoted to suburban development create work for landscapers in these states. In comparison, the next most populous state, New York, has disproportionately fewer landscapers, who are concentrated in the New York City-Long Island area. A higher proportion of New York's landscapers, however, work for companies that provide landscape and groundskeeping services, not as entrepreneurs, so they earn more than their most of their counterparts in other states. Landscapers in Washington, D.C., however, earn significantly more than those working elsewhere since most are employed by the federal government to keep important sites, like the National Mall, clean and well maintained.

Although some landscapers may have completed undergraduate degree programs in horticulture, agriculture, or even landscape architecture, there are no educational requirements to enter the field as a self-employed entrepreneur. Because of the relatively low wages, low capital entry costs (vehicle and tools), and lack of supervision, landscape entrepreneurs have little oversight. In some regions, like California, Florida, and the desert Southwest, immigrant workers have become one of the largest pools of landscape labor; in 2016 alone, the landscaping and groundskeeping industry was the largest user of the federal H-2A visa program, which allows companies to bring foreign workers into the United States on a seasonal (up to ten-month) basis. Even more immigrants work as self-employed landscape entrepreneurs. The industry trade group, the National Association of Landscape Professionals (NALP), has been among the most vocal employer groups pressing for federal immigration reform. In 2016, most immigrant landscapers entering the country as seasonal workers on H2-B visas were from Mexico, Guatemala, and Jamaica. Most landscapers work six days a week outdoors, whether in the sun or rain, doing hard work for average wages of twelve to fifteen dollars per hour.

In recent years, however, one smaller group of landscapers with horticultural and design skills has responded to urgent needs to conserve water and stop soil erosion in drought-prone urban areas like California, the Southwest, and Texas. In these areas, city governments have adopted programs to prohibit the installation of lawns in new housing and business developments and sponsor programs so that homeowners can receive payments to remove existing lawns and replace them with native or drought-resistant plants. To keep an average grass lawn green throughout the summer, it takes approximately six hundred gallons of water per week. For many communities experiencing water shortages, having a lawn of green grass is environmentally unsustainable. Both national- and state-level organizations, such as the Audubon Society and the American Public Gardens Association, have lobbied landscapers, homeowners, urban planners, and architects to practice these new conservation techniques, using water-thrifty native plants, which not only save water but also promote local biodiversity.

Nancy Quam-Wickham

See also: *1915–1945:* Farmworker; *1946–1991:* Construction Worker; Urban Planner

FURTHER READING

Boy Scouts of America. 1960. *Landscaping.* New Brunswicks: Boy Scouts of America.

Institute for Career Research. 2001. *Careers in the Landscape Nursery Business: Landscaper, Landscape Contractor: Use Your Love of Plants and Gardening to Start and Own Your Own Business.* Chicago: Institute for Career Research.

Price, Jenny. 2000. *Flight Maps: Adventures with Nature in Modern America.* New Haven: Yale University Press.

MACHINIST

A machinist is a skilled craftsperson who works with a variety of hand and machine tools to create precision metal products ready for direct sale or use in a larger assembly. Machinists have been essential workers in machine and metal production for over two centuries, since inventor David Wilkinson devised a machine to cut threads into metal rods, creating screws. In the late twentieth century, however, the work of a machinist has transformed remarkably from its early-nineteenth-century origins. Machinists work in machine shops, where they use lathes, cutting machines, grinders, calipers and other measuring devices, and other tools to shape metal (and sometimes plastic or wood) into these products. Machinists also increasingly operate and maintain robotic machining and metal production tools that create precision metal products. While some might argue that robotics have replaced the work of a machinist, in fact, it is the work of the machinist that makes it possible for robotics to mass produce precision metal parts. A machinist's job is to turn product or component drawings and designs into actual, physical objects. Machinists create all of the pieces that comprise other, larger objects so that assembly workers or craftspeople can assemble a final product. The modern machinist may then program a computer in an automated manufacturing system to recreate the prototype piece.

A machinist is one term used for workers in the material removal type of manufacturing. This type of work involves a cutter removing material from a work piece to create a more desirable shape or condition. This might be as simple as cutting a longer piece of material into shorter pieces, or it might be as complicated as taking a large piece of aluminum and making an automotive cylinder head for a race car. This process is similar to that of a sculptor who uses a chisel to carve a block of marble.

There are many types of machinists, just as there are many names that machinists are known as, but all machinists have some things in common. Most use wrenches and screwdrivers to adjust their tools, but measuring instruments are the tools that a machinist uses most often. Machinists use rulers and tape measures, but they also use precision-measuring devices that can measure far more accurately than a ruler; micrometers that can measure to one-thousandth of an inch are commonly used. Machinists are also responsible for knowing how to use and care for the measuring tools that they use.

A typical machinist is familiar with engineering drawings, which are sometimes known as blueprints. When an engineer designs a part, he or she creates a blueprint that gives all of the technical specifications of the object that will be created. The machinist must be able to read the blueprint to both create the part specified and inspect the part to ensure that it meets the required specifications.

Machinists have many different job types and responsibilities in the industry, but there are two main categories: conventional machinists and computer numerical control (CNC) machinists. Conventional machinists use hand tools and machinery that do not have computerized controls; these machinists rely more on their experience and developed skills to ensure that their work meets its requirements. Conventional machinists' equipment is typically older or less expensive than a CNC machinist's, but the conventional machinists that use this equipment are usually able to charge higher rates since their work is controlled by hand rather than by software and, as such, requires far more hands-on experience. A conventional machinist must be able to configure the equipment that he or she uses. A machinist must be able to securely hold the workpiece, and the cutter that is being used must be installed in the correct position; the machinist must then be able to manipulate the machine to create the part specified in the blueprint. After creating the part, the machinist must ensure that the part is made to specifications by comparing it to its original design.

A CNC machinist uses hand tools like a conventional machinist, but the equipment that he or she uses is sometimes driven and controlled by an onboard computer. Computer numerical control machines must be programmed, and so machine shops that use them will often have a dedicated CNC programmer, who is in charge of converting drawings and designs into instructions that the CNC computer can process. Still, a typical CNC machinist will know how to read the code to find mistakes and edit programs that contain errors in order to produce the proper precision-machined pieces. Most CNC machinists work in automated manufacturing plants that produce high volumes of machined products; using software-driven robotic production, a CNC machinist can usually produce more products at a lower cost than conventional machinists. In the twenty-first century, more machine shops are adopting robotic CNC machining as there is a shortage of skilled conventional machinists in the United States.

For many machinists, a formal training program at either a community college or a private machinist training school provides entry into the field. Unfortunately, most high schools no longer offer industrial training programs. Community college programs are less expensive than private training schools, which offer similar training at a faster, more intensive pace but at a much higher cost. Prospective machinists must be good working with their hands, have mathematical skills, and have strong spatial, problem-solving, and communication abilities. Some machinists grow into the role after first being hired by a company to perform entry-level work and then slowly picking up small, simple machinists' jobs that are delegated to them by the company's senior machinists. Often, a formal apprenticeship is the fastest, most efficient way to become a successful machinist.

Factory automation has been a part of manufacturing for over one hundred years. Robotics are increasingly part of the machinist's experiences, whether working to maintain and repair them or working with them as CNC machinists. While articulating-arm robots working like a droid on an assembly line might capture the imagination of the American public, CNC machine tools take many forms. Some look like small boxes, while others are essentially three-dimensional printers. Such CNC machine tools are the most commonly used form of robotic factory automation, available to both large manufacturing plants and smaller machine shops that specialize in creating certain products like high-precision gears and cutting tools. Automation has changed the machinist's practice, but the skills of the conventional machinist of the nineteenth century are still valued in today's workplace.

Steven Shibuya

See also: *1607–1775:* Blacksmith; *1861–1914:* Mechanic; Patternmaker; *1915–1945:* Mechanical Engineer

FURTHER READING

Overby, Alan. 2010. *CNC Machining Handbook: Building, Programming, and Implementation*. New York: McGraw-Hill Education.

Smid, Peter. 2007. *CNC Programming Handbook*, 3rd ed. Norwalk: Industrial Press, Inc.

Stephen, Krar F., Arthur Gill, and Peter Smid. 2001. *Computer Numerical Control Simplified*. Norwalk: Industrial Press, Inc.

MEDICAL ILLUSTRATOR, *see* SCIENTIFIC ILLUSTRATOR

MUSEUM CURATOR

A museum curator manages and oversees items in a museum collection. They are typically involved with selecting new items for the collection, researching objects, helping create exhibits, protecting objects from harm, and sometimes even managing the museum. Curators come from a wide variety of backgrounds and have varying levels of education and experience. A curator's role can be very specific to the size and type of organization that he or she is working for. Curators can be found in art galleries, museums, and even zoos and aquariums.

In larger museums such as the Smithsonian Institution, a curator is more likely to be a specialist in one content area. He or she may be a scholar devoted to the study of medieval art, bats in South America, or miniature trains. Curators typically hold an advanced degree such as a master's or PhD in their field of study. There is no specific degree for becoming a curator, though there are programs for a master of arts in museum studies and curatorial practice. This means one can have a degree in any subject and still become a curator, though in the special world of larger art museums, most curators will have an educational background in studio art or art history. At larger institutions, curators serve as the experts in their content areas, and a museum may have more than one curator. For example, a natural history museum may have one curator for paleontology, another for geology, another for mammals, and another for aquatic life. These curators complete significant research about objects in their museum and write scholarly content for exhibits. Those employed in larger museums are not as involved with the day-to-day running of the museum or the care of the collections.

The role of a curator at smaller museums is very different than at large museums. At smaller institutions, curators may be the only paid employee at the museum.

They may have the content knowledge about a particular collection, but they must also be concerned with the overall running of the museum. They may give tours, run the gift shop, and hold fundraising activities as well as doing their curation work. At slightly larger small museums, curators may be part of a small team and can focus more on the museum collection. Their job may change from day to day depending on the needs of the collection. They are responsible for receiving object donations, deciding which objects should be displayed and how, doing research, handling paperwork, and packing and shipping objects. They must be knowledgeable about legal issues regarding donations and the display of sensitive materials from their collections. Curators are responsible for the care of the collections and ensuring items are stored in a safe environment. This includes monitoring temperature and humidity and making sure they are correctly packaged in storage or secured on display.

Curators must also be knowable about current laws (both domestic and international) and respectful of cultural associations. For example, curators in the United States need to follow complex legal requirements for collecting, handling, and storing items, such as those specifying proper handling of Native American remains as set out in the 1990 Native American Graves Protection and Repatriation Act (NAGPRA), as well as ensuring that they do not collect or store illegal items as specified in engendered species laws and in the International Council of Museums (ICOM) inferential polices. Museums can face legal trouble if they accept items like stolen art or a feather hat made from an endangered bird into their collection. Curators should also be mindful and respectful of the cultural aspects of their collections.

Curators may also be called upon to participate in public programming activities, such as planning special events at a museum, writing exhibition manuals, and hosting educational events such as class visits to the museum. Curators must be thinking of all aspects of their collection at all times. In preparing a space for an event planned for outside, a curator must also have a rain plan in case of inclement weather on the event date. If the rain plan for the event stipulates that museum staff members bring visitors inside the museum galleries during a rainstorm, a curator would need to think about which objects are at risk to be bumped or sat on, what pests may come in with the food and drink, how increased foot traffic could cause vibrations to the ground, and what effect the temperature and humidity change could have with increased numbers of people in the room with wet shoes. All these are factors that go into collections and even planning decisions.

The responsibilities of a museum curator can be broad, and a curator will need to have a broad skillset. The most commonly required skills are to be very detail oriented, good at scholarly research, fond of writing and paperwork, and have excellent time management skills. These skills are crucial for a curator and are used every day. Curators also use design, mathematical, and construction skills while building crates or figuring out dimensions of exhibits. Objects in museums are cataloged and tracked, usually with paper files and a computer database. Curators not only research an object's history but also detail the object's condition and storage location in a database. They make sure the museum has insurance and a disaster plan in case something goes wrong, like a flood or an earthquake. A particular work week may include installing an exhibit, working with interns to complete an annual inventory, giving a lecture, coordinating the return of an object from conservation, assisting with an event planned months earlier, traveling to an offsite case-making company to investigate its products for an upcoming exhibit, packing an object to be sent on loan, and supervising staff.

Breaking into the museum field can be very difficult. Those looking to become a curator often undertake significant volunteer work while in school before looking for a curator's position. This is often accomplished by volunteering or being an intern at a local museum or zoo.

Museum curators work hard and often put in more than forty hours a week, especially as they prepare new exhibits for opening deadlines or rush to complete a major fundraising activity before its debut. As educational practitioners, they are dedicated to learning and helping other people learn through their museum; they work to help visitors make connections and relate to objects as they write item descriptions and arrange objects in ways that give meaning and context to contemporary museum visitors. Curators protect and showcase objects for visitors' knowledge and enjoyment today, as well as for future generations.

Robin Matty

See also: *1861–1914:* Teacher; *1946–1991:* College Professor; Librarian

FURTHER READING

Ambrose, Timothy, and Crispin Paine. 2018. *Museum Basics: The International Handbook*, 4th ed. New York: Routledge.

Anderson, Gail, ed. 2012. *Reinventing the Museum: The Evolving Conversation on Paradigm Shifts.* Lanham: Alta Mira Press.

Simmons, John E. 2016. *Museums: A History*. Lanham: Rowman and Littlefield.

Stevens, Greg, and Wendy Luke, eds. 2012. *A Life in Museums: Managing Your Museum Career*. Arlington: American Alliance of Museums.

Yerkovich, Sally. 2016. *A Practical Guide to Museum Ethics.* Lanham: Rowman and Littlefield.

MAID, *see* HOUSEKEEPER

MENTAL HEALTH COUNSELOR, *see* PSYCHOLOGIST

NAVIGATOR

A navigator is the person onboard a ship or other vessel responsible for choosing a safe route for the vessel and ensuring that it stays on that route. Some planes, spaceships, and satellite systems also require navigators. To fulfill this responsibility, navigators need specialized training and several years' experience on ships or training as airline pilots, astronauts, system engineers, or drone operators. Navigators use a set of special tools and must know several methods of using them in case of equipment failure. On large ships, navigators have several assistants working for them; in the navy, these workers are called quartermasters. Navigators may supervise their work but remain responsible to the captain for the ship's safe navigation. Even on the smallest vessel, though, someone must fill the role of navigator, even if on top of other duties.

The job as navigator starts long before the ship ever leaves port. When a ship navigator is informed where the vessel is going, he or she must first choose the charts—maps of the ocean—that will be needed for the voyage. These charts might be on paper or in electronic form, but either way the navigator is responsible for making sure the ship has the proper charts and that any published corrections to them have been made. Once the charts are selected and corrected, navigators choose the route. The chart gives important information about which parts of the ocean are safe for the ship to travel through and which waterways it should avoid. Unlike most road maps on land, the nautical chart includes information on the depths of the ocean and the topography of the seafloor.

To utilize this information, a navigator must know the ship's characteristics, such as its draft—how deep it sits in the water—and how easily it turns or stops. In the nineteenth century, the turning radius of a large sailing ship might be as much as twenty-five miles, though, today, a modern destroyer in the U.S. Navy might be able to turn at full speed—forty knots—in a circle as small as a few hundred yards. Among the most important duties of a navigator is collision avoidance. Knowledge of the ship's characteristics and the ocean's depth and bottom features will help a navigator avoid areas where the chart records the water as not being deep enough for the ship. The charts will also help a navigator take other restrictions into consideration, such as if there are underwater hazards that would make it dangerous to drop an anchor or if there are buoys in place to control traffic, much like street lanes and stoplights on land. As a navigator chooses a safe route, he or she and the assistants draw it in pencil on the paper chart or input it into the electronic one.

A long voyage will require several charts, usually with different scales, and a navigator must make sure the route is consistent across them to make it safe and easy to go from one to the other while the ship is moving. Whether the ship will be anchoring or mooring to a pier at the other end of the voyage, navigators will need to prepare the plans for docking. A navigator works with the other officers and crewmembers to make sure everyone understands what will be necessary when a ship is to dock or drop anchor: that any necessary gear is ready, such as the proper anchors and lengths of anchor chain, and that there are no temporary restrictions on the ship's capabilities, such as engines or rudders that are not working properly. With their input, a navigator may need to modify the chosen track. He or she will also brief the team before every departure from or entrance to a port or any other time the ship will be in restricted waters.

Navigators use two different kinds of navigation when the ship is underway. Within sight of land, he or she guides the ship through a technique known as marine piloting, which requires a highly specialized set of skills and knowledge, especially in cases of emergency, such as if a smaller vessel sails too close to a ship underway. When the ship is out of sight of land, a navigator uses open-ocean navigation. While both of these techniques share the goal of keeping the ship on track and out of danger, they use different tools and sets of skills.

When the ship is close to land, such as when it is entering or leaving a port or transiting a strait, a navigator and navigational team use the position of objects on land as well as on water to know where they are. The nautical chart contains very little information about the land, but it does include the position of landmarks that can be easily identified from the water, such as a water tower, church steeple, or other tall or unusual feature. It will also show buoys and markers in the water. As the ship moves along the coast, navigators pick appropriate landmarks from the chart and tell their assistants to monitor them. On the mark, the assistants will tell the navigator the compass bearing to each landmark. Then the navigator draws lines on the chart for each of these bearings; the spot where at least three lines overlap on the chart shows the position of the ship at that time mark, called a fix. Using this, as well as information from the fathometer, which uses a sonar ping to measure how deep the water beneath the ship is, the navigator gives the captain and pilot advice on maneuvering the ship to stay on course.

When the ship is out of sight of land, a ship's crew cannot see any landmarks, so the navigator must use other methods to determine the ship's location. Before about the mid-1990s, navigators usually used celestial navigation. For this, the navigator used a sextant to determine the position of the sun or stars in the sky; with this information, the ship's latitude and longitude could be determined—a celestial fix—but it required long tables of information and some complicated, though not difficult, mathematics. "Shooting" the sun or a star accurately while standing on the deck of a moving ship in even moderate seas also takes great skill. Since about 1994, most ships use the global positioning system (GPS) when out of sight of land. A GPS receiver onboard receives signals from a constellation of satellites in orbit around the earth and calculates the ship's latitude and longitude, which the navigator plots on the chart. Recently, many navigators have begun to worry about losing the skills needed to do celestial navigation, and they would like a backup to GPS. In 2015, the Unites States Naval Academy started teaching celestial navigation again so that future navigators in the navy will know how to do it if necessary. Courses in aeronautics at the U.S. Air Force Academy and at specialized colleges provide training for flight, space, and drone navigators.

Penelope K. Hardy

See also: *1946–1991:* Astronaut; Oceanographer; Pilot

FURTHER READING

Ackerman, James R., ed. 2006. *Cartographies of Travel and Navigation.* Chicago: University of Chicago Press.

Bartlett, Tim. 2009. *The Book of Navigation.* New York: Skyhorse Publishing.

Denny, Mark. 2012. *The Science of Navigation: Dead Reckoning to GPS.* Baltimore: Johns Hopkins University Press.

Hobbs, Richard R. 1997. *Marine Navigation Workbook: Piloting and Celestial and Electronic Navigation.* Annapolis: Naval Institute Press.

PACKAGE HANDLER

Package handlers work in warehouses and are responsible for transferring warehoused items into shipping boxes and preparing those boxes for shipment. Delivery drivers are responsible for the "last mile" of a package's transit from the seller's warehouse to a consumer's doorstep. The internet has dramatically changed how Americans shop for goods, and with that, it has transformed the traditional supply chain that takes products from producers to consumers. While warehouse workers and teamsters labored in the supply chain of the early twentieth century, package handlers and delivery drivers are their twenty-first-century counterparts. Any American who purchases items through the internet benefits from the services provided by package handlers and delivery drivers, who work for small, family-run organizations as well as large, impersonal corporations. They may be union members who earn good wages and have benefits and retirement plans, or they may work in businesses for relatively low wages. The experience that unites all package handlers and delivery drivers is that they must collect, sort, transport, and deliver items quickly.

Package handlers tend to work in large warehouse-type sorting and shipping facilities. United Parcel Service (UPS) is one such corporation, with more than five hundred facilities worldwide. When a customer or business brings a package to a UPS facility or storefront, the package begins its journey. Once the package arrives at a shipment facility, a package handler scans and sorts the packages according to destination. Packages may weigh more than seventy pounds and can be oddly shaped. Packages destined for a distant community are routed toward an airport drop and are sent to one area, while those being shipped to local destinations are sent to another conveyor belt, which is color coded by destination. Different companies demand different package handling rates, with some demanding sorting rates of nearly one thousand packages per hour, so mis-sorts are common. Any missorted package is rerouted to the sorting line. Because most deliveries are made during the day, most package handlers at UPS work during the graveyard shift, from 11:00 p.m. to morning, usually 8:00 a.m. or later. The work of most package handlers is physically difficult: lifting, moving, sorting, and placing packages of all shapes and weights on different conveyor belts or in different bins, according to destination. Some package handlers at large warehouses are pressured to speed up the pace of work so much that they are forced to skip bathroom breaks to meet their daily quota. In some cases, the buildings are so large that it is almost impossible for a worker to take a lunch break and return to his or her station in the allotted time (Jamieson 2014). Package handling is a low-wage job that requires stamina and much physical exertion.

Some package handlers prepare the preload for individual delivery trucks, moving the packages from the delivery facility to the loading docks, where the packages are organized according to delivery address or order. Most corporations use sophisticated software to determine the most efficient delivery routes, so package handlers need only to follow instructions on their computer screen or handheld device. Handlers arrange the packages by delivery order for each set of pickups as a delivery driver may make three trips to the facility a day to reload her or his truck. Package handlers use hand-trucks, or dollies, to organize packages to be placed on the delivery truck. At warehouses like Amazon's facilities, package handlers may only pull items from their storage bins and take them to a central area for transport to delivery services like UPS or the U.S. Postal Service. Handheld computer devices scan barcodes on the bins so that the inventory system of the warehouse can keep track of the stock of merchandise.

At most package delivery facilities, delivery drivers arrive in the early morning and prepare their delivery vehicles—vans, trucks, or larger vehicles—for their day's work. Delivery drivers receive their instructions and routes, or traces and tracks, from delivery supervisors and are expected to complete their routes according to the delivery instructions provided. Large delivery services count every second and every fraction of a mile as part of their profit or loss calculation, so drivers are generally committed to delivering their packages by the route provided. In reality, though, delivery drivers are permitted to make on-the-spot modifications to their routes for important reasons. For instance, an experienced package delivery driver who is familiar with the regular customers on his or her route might know that the local floral shop has more outgoing packages on Fridays than on other days, so it would be best to deliver any packages to the floral shop first so that the driver can pick up outgoing packages that can then be transferred to the "air" (airport) driver. Drivers can make individual decisions about deviating from a prescribed route, though they can also anticipate being questioned about why they made that decision once they return to the transfer facility.

A delivery driver might have an urban or a rural route; the latter may take him or her on a route that exceeds 200 miles per day, with over 60 or 70 deliveries. In an urban or suburban area, most UPS delivery drivers, for instance, deliver some 120 or more packages per day, driving over 150 miles daily. Drivers also pick up packages for delivery to both local and distant customers. At each delivery address, whether business or personal, the driver takes the package, scans it, and then delivers it—either handing it directly to a recipient or leaving the package at a convenient and secure place such as a customer's drop box near the entrance to his or her property. At a delivery address, the delivery driver normally inquires about outgoing packages; if the customer is using that company's service, he or she will give the outgoing package to the delivery driver for transport to the transshipment facility.

Delivery drivers and package handlers also form part of the chain of direct-to-consumer sales. Artisans selling table legs on an internet site such as Etsy may sell and ship directly to a consumer. Delivery drivers also deliver important legal documents from attorney's offices to courts. Some transport medical items, such as organs for transplants or fluids for testing on a stat (or emergency) basis. In 2015, about 750,000 Americans worked as delivery drivers or couriers in the United States. The sheer number of employees in this field make it an important element of the modern U.S. economy.

Nancy Quam-Wickham

See also: Postal Worker; Supply Chain Logistician; *1915–1945:* Truck Driver; Warehouse Worker

FURTHER READING

"How UPS Works." 2006. HowStuffWorks. Last modified November 1, 2006. https://money.howstuffworks.com/ups2.htm.

Jamieson, Dave. 2014. "Amazon Warehouse Workers Barely Have Time to Eat Lunch: Lawsuit." *Huffpost.* May 7, 2014. https://www.huffingtonpost.com/2014/05/07/amazon-warehouse-workers-lunch-breaks_n_5283329.html.

"The Mechanical Sorting of Postal Packages." 1903. *Scientific American* 56, no. 1443: 23120–23121.

St. James, Lorelei. *U.S. Postal Service: Information on Workforce Injuries Arising during Mail Delivery*. Washington DC: U.S. Government Accountability Office, 2013. https://www.gao.gov/assets/660/658174.pdf.

PRIMARY DOCUMENT

In the following document, U.S. Supreme Court Justice Stephen Breyer provides the majority opinion for the case Young v. United Parcel Service *(2015). In this case, UPS package handler Peggy Young sued her employer, UPS, on the basis of sex discrimination as UPS managers refused to accommodate her request for temporary assignment to light duty. Young was pregnant and had a doctor's orders to limit the weight she could lift; UPS's requirement was that all package handlers must be able to lift seventy pounds, and the company argued that her request could not be accommodated because her pregnancy did not qualify as a "disability" as defined by UPS management and the Teamsters' Union. The Supreme Court overruled a lower court's ruling in favor of UPS and directed the courts to address her claims. This document provides an intimate look at the relationships among women package handlers, unions, and employers in the workplace.*

Justice Breyer delivered the opinion of the Court.

The Pregnancy Discrimination Act makes clear that Title VII's prohibition against sex discrimination applies to discrimination based on pregnancy. It also says that employers must treat "women affected by pregnancy . . . the same for all employment-related purposes . . . as other persons not so affected but similar in their ability or in-ability to work." 42 U. S. C. 2000e(k). We must decide how this latter provision applies in the context of an employer's policy that accommodates many, but not all, workers with nonpregnancy-related disabilities . . .

Ultimately the court must determine whether the nature of the employer's policy and the way in which it burdens pregnant women shows that the employer has engaged in intentional discrimination. The Court of Appeals here affirmed a grant of summary judgment in favor of the employer. Given our view of the law, we must vacate that court's judgment.

We begin with a summary of the facts. The petitioner, Peggy Young, worked as a part-time driver for the respondent, United Parcel Service (UPS). Her responsibilities included pickup and delivery of packages that had arrived by air carrier the previous night. In 2006, after suffering several miscarriages, she became pregnant. Her doctor told her that she should not lift more than 20 pounds during the first 20 weeks of her pregnancy or more than 10 pounds thereafter . . . UPS required drivers like Young to be able to lift parcels weighing up to 70 pounds (and up to 150 pounds with assistance) . . . UPS told Young she could not work while under a lifting restriction. Young consequently stayed home without pay during most of the time she was pregnant and eventually lost her employee medical coverage.

Young subsequently brought this federal lawsuit. We focus here on her claim that UPS acted unlawfully in refusing to accommodate her pregnancy-related lifting restriction. Young said that her co-workers were willing to help her with heavy packages. She also said that UPS accommodated other drivers who were "similar in their . . . inability to work." She accordingly concluded that UPS must accommodate her as well . . . UPS responded that the "other persons" whom it had accommodated were (1) drivers who had become disabled on the job, (2) those who had lost their Department of Transportation (DOT) certifications, and (3) those who suffered from a disability covered by the Americans with Disabilities Act of 1990 (ADA), 104Stat. 327, 42 U. S. C. 12101 *et seq.* UPS said that, since Young did not fall within any of those categories, it had not discriminated against Young on the basis of pregnancy but had treated her just as it treated all "other" relevant "persons."

Title VII of the Civil Rights Act of 1964 forbids a covered employer to "discriminate against any individual with respect to . . . terms, conditions, or privileges of employment, because of such individual's . . . sex." 78Stat. 253, 42 U. S. C. 2000e 2(a)(1). In 1978, Congress enacted the Pregnancy Discrimination Act, 92Stat. 2076, which added new language to Title VII's definitions subsection. The first clause of the 1978 Act specifies that Title VII's "ter[m] 'because of sex' . . . include[s] . . . because of or on the basis of pregnancy, childbirth, or related medical conditions." 2000e(k). The second clause says that "women affected by pregnancy, childbirth, or related medical conditions shall be treated the same for all employment-related purposes . . . as other persons not so affected but similar in their ability or inability to work . . . "

In July 2007, Young filed a pregnancy discrimination charge with the Equal Employment Opportunity Commission (EEOC). In September 2008, the EEOC provided her with a right-to-sue letter. See 29 CFR 1601.28 (2014). Young then filed this complaint in Federal District Court. She argued, among other things, that she could show by direct evidence that UPS had intended to discriminate against her because of her pregnancy and that, in any event, she could establish a prima facie case of disparate treatment under the *McDonnell Douglas* framework . . .

After discovery, UPS filed a motion for summary judgment. See Fed. Rule Civ. Proc. 56(a). In reply, Young pointed to favorable facts that she believed were either undisputed or that, while disputed, she could prove. They include the following:

Young worked as a UPS driver, picking up and delivering packages carried by air . . .

Young was pregnant in the fall of 2006 . . .

Young's doctor recommended that she "not be required to lift greater than 20 pounds for the first 20 weeks of pregnancy and no greater than 10 pounds thereafter . . . "

When Young later asked UPS' Capital Division Manager to accommodate her disability, he replied that, while she was pregnant, she was "too much of a liability" and could "not come back" until she " 'was no longer pregnant.' " *Id.,* at 20.

Young remained on a leave of absence (without pay) for much of her pregnancy . . .

Young returned to work as a driver in June 2007, about two months after her baby was born . . .

As direct evidence of intentional discrimination, Young relied, in significant part, on the statement of the Capital Division Manager . . . As evidence that she had made out a prima facie case under *McDonnell Douglas*, Young relied, in significant part, on evidence showing that UPS would accommodate workers injured on the job (7), those suffering from ADA disabilities (8), and those who had lost their DOT certifications (9). That evidence, she said, showed that UPS had a light-duty-for-injury policy with respect to numerous "other persons," but not with respect to pregnant workers.

Several employees received accommodations while suffering various similar or more serious disabilities incurred on the job, [including those with 10 pound lifting limitation, a foot injury, and an arm injury] . . .

Several employees received accommodations following injury, where the record is unclear as to whether the injury was incurred on or off the job. [Including . . . recurring knee injury, an ankle injury, another knee injury, a stroke, and a leg injury] . . .

Several employees received "inside" jobs after losing their DOT certifications. [Including . . . one worker whose DOT certification suspended after conviction for driving under the influence, another who failed DOT test due to high blood pressure, and a third with a DOT certification lost due to sleep apnea diagnosis] . . .

Some employees were accommodated despite the fact that their disabilities had been incurred off the job. See [ankle injury and cancer diagnoses] . . .

According to a deposition of a UPS shop steward who had worked for UPS for roughly a decade . . . "the only light duty requested [due to physical] restrictions that became an issue" at UPS "were with women who were pregnant," *id.,* at 504 . . .

Before Congress passed the Pregnancy Discrimination Act, the EEOC issued guidance stating that "[d]isabilities caused or contributed to by pregnancy . . . are, for all job-related purposes, temporary disabilities" and that "the availability of . . . benefits and privileges . . . shall be applied to disability due to pregnancy or childbirth on the same terms and conditions as they are applied to other temporary disabilities." 29 CFR 1604.10(b) (1975). Indeed, as early as 1972, EEOC guidelines provided: "Disabilities caused or contributed to by pregnancy . . . are, for all job-related purposes, temporary disabilities and should be treated as such under any health or temporary disability insurance or sick leave plan available in connection with employment." 37 Fed. Reg. 6837 (1972) (codified in 29 CFR 1604.10(b) (1973)).

Under this interpretation of the Act, the judgment of the Fourth Circuit must be vacated. A party is entitled to summary judgment if there is "no genuine dispute as to any material fact and the movant is entitled to judgment as a matter of law." Young also introduced evidence that UPS had three separate accommodation policies (on-the-job, ADA, DOT). Taken together, Young argued, these policies significantly burdened pregnant women. See App. 504 (shop steward's testimony that "the only light duty requested [due to physical] restrictions that became an issue" at UPS "were with women who were pregnant"). The Fourth Circuit did not consider the combined effects of these policies, nor did it consider the strength of UPS' justifications for each when combined. That is, why, when the employer accommodated so many, could it not accommodate pregnant women as well?

We do not determine whether Young created a genuine issue of material fact as to whether UPS' reasons for having treated Young less favorably than it treated these other nonpregnant employees were pretextual. We leave a final determination of that question for the Fourth Circuit to make on remand, in light of the interpretation of the Pregnancy Discrimination Act that we have set out above.

* * *

For the reasons above, we vacate the judgment of the Fourth Circuit and remand the case for further proceedings consistent with this opinion.

It is so ordered.

Source: *Young v. United Parcel Service*. 2015. 575 U.S.

PHYSICAL THERAPIST

A physical therapist is a medical professional who treats patients using physical methods like massage, exercise, and heat treatment with the goal of restoring full bodily functions. Physical therapists provide treatments that focus on restoring body movements to ill and injured patients. The occupation involves many duties: examining patients, creating treatment plans, teaching, and everyday learning. Becoming a physical therapist requires many years of education, which is crucial because one learns how to expand one's thinking, understand people, challenge oneself, and enhance techniques needed in the field.

At the undergraduate level, students who want to be physical therapists must complete chemistry, biology, physics, anatomy, and physiology classes, as well as courses in biomechanics and kinesiology. In graduate classes, students learn more about the science that informs practice, as well as about types of physical therapy geared to different settings and patient needs, such as outpatient, inpatient, pediatrics, sports, geriatric, and more. However, the overall goal of each specialty is the same: to help people recover and return to the state of how they once were, if not better. But physical therapy has not always been constant; in fact, it continues to evolve in goals, knowledge, and practice.

As a profession, physical therapy did not exist until the early 1900s, primarily arising in response to the challenges of World War I and poliomyelitis. During this time, physical therapy expanded to help treat soldiers who suffered from disabling war injuries, while physical therapists also learned how to help patients suffering from polio, a disease that caused paralysis and muscle loss. Later, demand for physical therapists grew as medical doctors and other practitioners realized the value of physical therapy and exercise in disease and injury recovery and rehabilitation. The demand for more physical therapists led to the creation of the American Physical Therapy Association (APTA) in 1921. Over the years, APTA has existed as a membership organization, representing physical therapists, determining requirements for entry into the profession, and developing educational programs that encourage a healthy lifestyle. The practice of physical therapy has become more technical as medical knowledge of the human body has increased.

By the 1990s, physical therapists increasingly needed a doctoral degree (doctorate of physical therapy, or DPT) to enter the profession as physical therapists often worked independently, without supervision from doctors or nurses. In the course of a normal day, a physical therapist was now required to meet with patients, determine what the physical disabilities were, and develop a care plan to help patients recover (Woods 1994, 33). The work varied from patient to patient. One patient might have injured a knee while playing soccer; the treatment plan would involve using certain exercises to strengthen the knee's ligaments. Another patient might have cerebral palsy and need muscle flexibility exercises, which involves bending the patient's limbs. A patient with back pain might need spinal manipulation. An elderly patient recovering from a fall might need to work on his or her balance using a stepstool and a ball. The physical therapist directs all of these activities. One physical therapist worked with a patient who had a stroke after a brain tumor was surgically removed. To help him recover and regain function, the therapist used a rather simple instrument: a string and beads. The therapist had him place the beads onto the string to help his fine motor movement and help his mind concentrate on the task (Woods 1994, 34). Such ordinary objects, with the creativity of physical therapists, can be used as tools for recovery.

Before the 1990s, many different instruments and techniques were introduced into the field, and many are still used today. But, generally, work for physical therapists was less stressful than it is today. In this period, physical therapists were considered allied health professionals, and there was less emphasis on revenue and a greater emphasis on personnel and compassionate care for patients. Physical therapists often met with the patient's family members to ensure they supported the patient's recovery. After a patient's appointment, the physical therapist worked on planning more exercises beneficial to helping him or her recover; these treatment notes were often handwritten.

With the rise of computers and advancing medical knowledge in the 1990s and early 2000s, practicing physical therapists performed much of the same tasks but also had new demands put on their time. Computers allowed physical therapists to electronically store and retrieve patient documentation as well as rapidly communicate with a patient's referring doctor. Computers also helped physical therapists stay better organized with the introduction of new scheduling software. Scheduling and patient note-transcription software allowed physical therapists to speed up their work, and many took on more patients. Other technology such as exercise machines, sterilizers, and robotics improved patient care while adding to the costs of operating a physical therapy practice. With the 2010 passage of the federal Affordable Care Act, insurance companies were required to provide physical therapy as benefits, leading to even greater patient demand.

Today, some aspects of a physical therapist's job are essentially the same as they were in the late twentieth century. A physical therapist meets with patients and directs their physical recovery from illness and injury. They also develop programs that encourage healthy lifestyles and ways to prevent injury. The typical day of an outpatient physical therapist consists of seeing perhaps eight patients a day, with individual appointments lasting about forty-five to sixty minutes each. Most therapists will also have one or two new patient evaluations, about one hour long each, daily. At the end of the day, therapists have about an hour to finish paperwork, return patients' calls, call doctors, and finish what they were unable to during the day. Although the routine has been consistent, technology has changed the tools that physical therapists use. Some of these new technologies have led to remarkable patient recoveries. For instance, in 2010, a quadriplegic patient participated in an experiment with the aim of helping him move his hand again. Working with medical doctors and physical therapists, this patient was fitted with a new tool, the Neurobridge, a device implanted in the brain. The Neurobridge captures the neural impulses and then translates the signals to a special sleeve on the arm of the patient; as the patient thinks about the action of moving his hand, his hand will proceed to move ("Health Care Technology Today"). Another example of a new tool that physical therapists are working on is an advanced walker designed to help patients with Parkinson's disease walk without shaking. There are also walkers that have laser lights projected on the floor to help patients see where to plant their foot to take their next step. Thanks to rapid advancements in technology, a physical therapist can help a paralyzed person move again or a patient walk more confidently and safely.

Because medical technology changes rapidly, physical therapists usually meet once a month to learn about new equipment and techniques as part of their continuing education. States require physical therapists to stay current with the field through continuing education as a condition of maintaining a license to practice. Physical therapists must also keep up to date with legal issues, such as patient confidentiality, and with ethical and professional standards. A physical therapist must also stay in good physical condition as treating patients requires strength and agility. While physical therapists originally helped injured war veterans gain mobility and patients who were recovering from polio relearn how to walk, today, physical therapists treat patients with all kinds of diseases and injuries. There are physical therapists who specialize in treating victims of domestic violence, cardiac patients, babies in neonatal intensive care, patients in hospice, and even athletes with concussions and soldiers with traumatic brain injuries. The demand for physical therapists is expected to rapidly increase in the next decade as the roles for these professionals grow in our highly technological medical care system.

Atun Cawker

See also: Home Health Aide

FURTHER READING

Doidge, Norman. 2007. *The Brain That Changes Itself: Stories of Personal Triumph from the Frontiers of Brain Science.* New York: Penguin.

"Health Care Technology Today." 2016. *PT in Motion* 8, no. 10: 32–39.

Levine, Adele. 2014. *Run, Don't Walk: The Curious and Chaotic Life of a Physical Therapist at Walter Reed Army Medical Center.* New York: Penguin.

Woods, Ellen. 1994. "Just Another Day." *Pediatric Physical Therapy.* (March 1994): 32–38.

POSTAL WORKER

Postal workers are a diverse group of individuals who work for the United States Postal Service, including mail handlers in centralized facilities; clerks in post offices, who assist customers with their mailing needs; postal carriers, who deliver the mail to businesses and residences alike; truck and forklift drivers, who move heavy bins of mail and packages through facilities and on to their destinations; as well as operational engineers, distribution center supervisors, postal inspectors, and customer care workers. Some postal workers are janitors and maintenance staff. All postal workers contribute to the flow of mail.

Taverns served as some of the first post offices in colonial America. During the antebellum period, Americans built post offices in advance of their settlements in the West, and the United States established informal post offices throughout the world in the early nineteenth century. Wherever Americans went, the post office followed—or preceded—their arrival. As the institution that handles the exchange of written communication like letters, newspapers, magazines and books as well as packages, the post office serves a critical need in the lives of most Americans. Americans exchange letters with loved ones and other correspondents. Businesses transmit bills for service, and banks send customer statements through the mail. Direct mail marketing firms promote their products through the post. Beneficiaries receive pensions, Social Security, and other payments through the mail. Postal workers handle the mail and packages that move through these post offices.

While many Americans associate postal workers with the adage "Neither snow nor rain nor heat nor gloom of night stays these couriers from the swift completion of their appointed rounds," this saying was originally coined by an architect, William Mitchell Kendall, in 1914; there is no official motto of the United States Postal Service (USPS). Postal carriers, however, do work in all weather conditions, six days a week, with occasional duties on Sundays that sometimes include delivering mail from the post office to customers' addresses. Postal carriers—formally divided into rural carriers and city carriers—are just one of many occupations classified as postal workers.

The United States Postal Service, as it is now known, was formally established on July 1, 1971, as part of a federal government reorganization of the Post Office Department. Previously, the Continental Congress loosely organized the post office and appointed Benjamin Franklin as its postmaster general in 1775. In 1872, Congress created a formal Post Office Department, and under the Pendleton Act of 1883, postal workers were classified as members of the civil service, subject to examinations and qualifications for work rather than simply obtaining their positions by virtue of the political spoils system, which is similar to patronage.

Before the reorganization of the postal service, postal workers could enjoy stable jobs, but wages stagnated throughout the 1960s as Congress did not approve postal workers' wage increases for many years. In early 1970, militant postal workers, who were members of multiple unions based on their job classifications, called for a general strike in an effort to secure higher wages, health benefits, and better retirement. This brief strike was successful in many of the nation's largest cities, and it pushed President Richard Nixon to order Congress and his secretary of labor to approve negotiations with postal worker unions. Federal reorganization of the postal department followed.

Beginning in the 1970s, the USPS became a semiautonomous independent agency within the federal government, using private-sector management practices; because of the reorganization, postal workers gained the rights to collectively bargain with management. The rights to collective bargaining, previously denied to federal workers before reorganization, resulted in a consolidation of many smaller postal worker unions into several larger ones, the most powerful of which are the American Postal Workers Union (APWU), primarily representing some 200,000 clerks and maintenance workers, and the National Association of Letter Carriers (NALC), which represents nearly the same number of postal carriers who work as city carriers (regular full-time letter carriers) and city carrier assistants (workers who substitute for regular mail carriers on a temporary basis, though many CCAs, especially in larger metropolitan areas, work full time). A smaller union, the National Association of Rural Letter Carriers, represents about 50,000 postal carriers who deliver mail in rural areas.

While all of the major postal workers' unions have signed collective-bargaining agreements that stipulate seniority rules (and, thus, determination of order of work), wages, hours of labor, overtime payment, benefits, and sick leave procedures, the distinctions among the different unions are important to understand. Although the USPS employs over 500,000 people, employee positions are not interchangeable: a postal truck driver, for instance, cannot change his or her classification to rural letter carrier unless he or she takes additional examinations, applies for a new position within the USPS, meets seniority requirements, and successfully bids for a route assignment. That employee would then need to be retrained for this new position, even though the position is essentially the same: driving a vehicle on a prearranged route to pick up and deliver mail and packages.

Today's post office markedly differs from post offices of the past. After the strike of 1970, when more than 200,000 postal workers walked off the job, the government led efforts to modernize the postal service by implementing new machines and technologies. These upgrades led to an increase in mail delivery efficiency while dramatically affecting the daily lives of postal workers. Some of these new machine technologies include the widespread installation of optical character readers (OCR) that recognize typed addresses (1982), self-service terminals in post offices (1984), use of automatic small package sorters (1988), use of automated bar code readers in postal sorting machines (1991), deployment of robotic containerization systems (1997), and the introduction of a new intelligent mail barcode system (2006).

When a customer deposits a letter in a mail slot at the local post office, the letter makes a number of stops. First, post office clerks collect the mail into bins and separate letters and flats (magazines, classified circulars, and so forth) from packages. At the end of each day, clerks load the bins of mail into USPS trucks that transport the mail and packages to a processing and distribution center. At the center, another group of mail handlers moves the bins of mail to an automated processing machine, called the advanced facer canceller system, using both hand-pushed carts and mechanized carts and forklifts. Using OCR technologies, these machines can read both handwritten and typed addresses, take images of each item, compare those images to a national database of known addresses, and automatically cancel the stamp and print out a delivery barcode on the item; the item is then sorted into local mail using the USPS delivery point sequence, which organizes local mail into the order in which a carrier would deliver the mail on his or her route. Nonlocal mail is sent to other distribution centers across the nation and abroad. These machines can process upward of fifty thousand letters per hour; in 1960, less sophisticated machines could sort fewer than two thousand letters per hour. Packages and flats are now also processed using these computer and machine systems.

The mail handlers attend to these machines, while supervisors who specialize in human resource management oversee operations. Operational engineers also work in large mail and processing centers, helping adjust the system machines, troubleshooting computer glitches, and making repairs and improvements as needed. Today, the USPS uses more than eighty-five thousand mail-sorting and cancelation machines. Once the mail is sorted by the machine into separate slots, mail handlers take the sorted pieces of mail and place them into trays. Those trays are then delivered to delivery stations, where postal carriers pick them up at the start of their workday.

City carriers and rural carriers (and their assistants) deliver mail to customers. Each day, they report to their assigned stations, pick up the trays of mail, and proceed along a predetermined route. Each route is designed to be covered in eight hours of work, though workdays may be longer during holiday seasons and in certain weather. In cities, postal workers bid on routes; the most physically demanding routes (with lots of apartment buildings, stairs, or businesses or in neighborhoods with many unleashed dogs) tend to be assigned to new workers, who hold the lowest seniority and are less likely to receive the more favored routes as a result of bids. Even on "easy" routes, however, city carriers may walk ten miles per day, in all weather. Some rural carriers deliver mail in isolated communities and may routinely drive over one hundred miles per day. Rural carriers must navigate a low-horse-powered mail truck, known as an LLV (or in some cases, their own vehicles), across stretches of gravel roads, through snow, and in all kinds of weather. Rural carriers are often accosted by residents' dogs (as are city carriers) and also by wildlife; rural carriers on the Great Plains are routinely harassed by rafters of wild turkeys, a very territorial bird.

Whatever the position and conditions of work, postal workers all work to ensure that Americans can communicate with each other. Challenges presented by private mail services, social media use, electronic mail, web-based banking and bill payments, and other newer technologies have not led to the long-forecasted death of the USPS.

Nancy Quam-Wickham

See also: Package Handler; Supply Chain Logistician; *1915–1945:* Warehouse Worker

FURTHER READING

Trumbauer, Lisa. 2005. *What Does a Mail Carrier Do?* Berkeley Heights: Enslow Publishers.

United States Postal Service. 1993. *History of the U.S. Postal Service, 1775–1993.* Washington, DC: The United States Postal Service.

Walsh, John. 1992. *Labor Struggle in the Post Office: From Selective Lobbying to Collective Bargaining.* Armonk: M. E. Sharpe.

PRIMARY DOCUMENT

Every November, the publication of the National Association of Letter Carriers, The Postal Record, *features extraordinary work of U.S. postal workers in the annual "Heroes" section. In 2018, postal worker Peter Monteleone of New York received the 2018 Eastern Region Hero of the Year Award. The story from this publication describes why Monteleone was honored.*

"I heard two women scream," Westchester Merged, NY Branch 693 member Peter Monteleone said of delivering his route one day last October. "I haven't heard a scream like that. It was total fear. It caught me off guard."

A woman and her 12-year-old daughter had just run from their house and were standing in their driveway. The two had returned home to find a man inside. "The intruder happened to be in the daughter's bedroom and it scared the living daylights out of her," Monteleone said.

He understood the situation in part, he said, because he has two children, 10 and 12, "so I understand how scared she was. I heard fear in the screams, so that really caught me off guard. She had quite a shock when she opened her bedroom door to find that guy."

Seeing the two residents distraught, the carrier attempted to calm them. The carrier then confronted the man as he tried to leave the scene through a side door. Monteleone would not let him leave. "There were a few choice words and an ultimatum," the Cold War Navy veteran said. "I was serious. I told him that if he attempted to leave, there was going to be a confrontation."

Noticing kitchen knives protruding from the man's pants pockets, Monteleone quietly urged the woman to call police and assured her that he was not going to leave them until law enforcement got there. Police officers soon arrived and arrested the intruder, who was carrying knives, blank checks and jewelry that he had stolen.

Monteleone, who has worked for USPS for 26 years, said, "I just reacted, and it worked out. I'm sure any letter carrier would have done the same thing."

The Heroes of the Year judges disagreed—they said he had demonstrated uncommon courage and determination and named him NALC's 2018 Eastern Region Hero.

"He placed himself between a clear and present danger and risked his life," the judges said during deliberation. "It was a stand-up action."

The carrier's actions also earned him praise from his customers. "Undoubtedly, Peter's poise, courage and steadfast clear judgment helped to keep a very tense and dangerous situation from escalating into catastrophic violence, and resulted in a quick and efficient apprehension of an armed criminal," the woman's husband, John Piazza, wrote to the local post office. "My entire family owes Peter a huge debt of gratitude for his brave and conscientious actions that day."

Monteleone preferred to shift the praise to letter carriers as a whole. "We help people daily, weekly and yearly and we do more than deliver the mail," Monteleone said in accepting his award. "We look out for the communities. They become an extended part of our family, and we become an extended part of their family."

Source: *The Postal Record.* 2018. Used by permission of the National Association of Letter Carriers. November, p. 25.

PROJECT MANAGER

Project managers are professionals who are specifically trained to coordinate the operational aspects of business, educational, medical, or other types of administrative units. Such units are found in both private and nonprofit corporations and in public institutions. These administrative units may be single offices that provide a service, such as a marketing office that specializes in providing research for new products prior to their launch, or arrival in stores, or a unit may be located within an educational institution in which the project manager coordinates the work of several subordinates, who themselves manage discrete operational functions within each subunit. A bachelor's degree is normally a prerequisite for a position as a project manager; many project managers also hold master's degrees. Many employers require their project managers to pass the internationally recognized Project Management Professional (PMP) examination. Project managers are usually supervised by a program manager, a business professional with a master of business administration (MBA) who oversees the business and financial elements of a project. A program manager, for instance, will provide financial support to a project manager.

The work of a project manager is primarily operational, in which the project manager is a team leader responsible for creating and managing the scope, budget, and schedule of any particular project. The duties of a project manager are known as process improvement techniques, or a set of activities that reduce the probability of costly errors in creating a project or new service. As a business prepares a new product for market, the project manager must map the project from the very beginning. One might work with a conceptual plan in which a product (or item) is just an idea to produce a schedule for production of the item, determine resources (materials, labor, monetary investments) needed to produce the item, establish a production goal (how many individual units of the new item will be created), create a budget for production, determine quality assurance and quality control measures, and then manage the project as it moves from idea to reality. Project managers refer to the phases of their work as planning, running, executing, managing, monitoring, and closing a project. The last step refers to the postproduction assessment of the ways in which the entire project could be improved in the future.

Project managers are expected to have expert communication, planning, and time management skills. In some specific settings, project managers are required to hold specialized postgraduate certificates, in a subject such as pharmaceutical research, that prove additional training in very highly technical legal, ethical, budgetary, and managerial requirements needed to manage a particular project. In the information technology (IT) field, project managers obtain special Six Sigma certification, a training plan developed by engineers for IT projects. Many universities offer Six Sigma certification; certificate holders are even classified into black belt, green belt, and lean sensei levels. In highly complex institutions or businesses, one particular project may have multiple project managers, each responsible for just one element of the project. Employment opportunities are expanding for project managers as businesses and institutions become more specialized in the kinds of products and services they provide.

The various duties that project managers have are usually determined by the kind of "product" the unit produces. A large university's graduate school, for example, consists of programs that provide training leading to various degrees.

Many graduate schools often provide dual degrees (such as the doctorate of medicine and master of public health), as well as specialty programs, public health education programs, clinical research educational programs, and nondegree programs. In this case, the "product" that the unit produces is simply a highly trained individual (an expert) who at the end of the "project" is awarded an advanced degree in medical sciences. There are many variables in the "production process" of training these experts; one of these variables in the process is admissions. For medical professionals, even though most applicants to a medical school will be equally qualified in terms of superior academic preparation, each applicant will have different life experiences, motivations, readiness for intensive study, and reasons for pursuing a medical education. All of these factors influence the experience and success of graduate and professional students as they prepare for careers in medical sciences.

A project manager in such a university medical program's graduate admissions processes would work with a team to recruit excellent candidates. They would manage meeting schedules, candidates' hotel bookings, and itineraries for the day of their interview visit. After the admissions session is over, the project manager would invite students to revisit, which consists of scheduling more interviews as well as booking fun activities throughout the city. This is a way to impress candidates so they elect to attend that graduate program; medical programs want the very best applicants as recruiting exceptionally qualified students contributes to the program's high national and international rankings.

Once admitted students enroll in the graduate school, the project manager helps to manage new student orientation. Orientation is also a very busy season as the students must be provided with helpful instructions and advice about how to get around campus and manage their studies; the idea of new student orientation is to make the incoming class as comfortable as possible to ease their transition to demanding new academic programs that most will attend for the next several years, with some there as long as a decade or more.

Finally, the other process that this project manager would help to manage is curriculum support for students in the medical sciences graduate programs. As a curriculum supporter, this project manager would facilitate student and faculty use of the learning management system, or LMS. The LMS is an electronic space in which students and faculty communicate with one another. Students can e-mail through this portal, while faculty members can both communicate with students and deliver critical parts of the medical sciences curriculum—such things as learning materials, the course syllabus, class handouts, study guides, and grade postings. In their work in "closing the project," at the end of the course, the project manager ensures that students complete their course evaluations through the LMS. This way, each course director and members of the curriculum committee can better assess the course strengths and weaknesses. Students are able to evaluate the course organization, class expectations, and overall quality of the faculty teaching their courses. This is the final quality assurance element in the project manager's job and, like that of all project managers, assists the institution in its efforts to produce the best product with the fewest errors. Project managers must be attentive to all aspects of bringing a project to successful conclusion. It is a job that requires one to manage multiple duties at the same time.

Arjana Gjokaj

See also: Information Technology Architect; Social Media Coordinator

FURTHER READING

Harned, Brett. 2017. *Project Management for Humans: Helping People Get Things Done.* Brooklyn: Rosenfeld Media.

Lyons, Nancy, and Meghan Wilker. 2012. *Interactive Project Management: Pixels, People, and Process.* San Francisco: New Riders.

Russell, Lou. 2012. *Managing Projects: A Practical Guide for Learning Professionals.* New York: Pfeiffer.

Schmidt, Terry. 2009. *Strategic Project Management Made Simple: Practical Tools for Leaders and Teams.* Hoboken: John Wiley & Sons.

PSYCHOLOGIST

Psychologists and mental health counselors possess clinical skills to help individuals cope with challenging life events, mental health problems, and more. In the contemporary United States, the mention of psychologists and mental health counselors may bring up the image of a man sitting with a notepad while a person lies on a couch, talking about his or her problems. While this image might have fit the role of a psychologist or psychiatrist at the turn of the twentieth century, much has changed in how and where psychologists and counselors work.

In the late 1800s and early 1900s, most psychologists and counselors were actually medical doctors that had an interest or specialty in disorders of the mind, which became the field of psychiatry. They were also predominately men because many universities and schools of higher learning did not grant graduate degrees to women. This paradigm has shifted dramatically over the last century. Now, approximately 70 to 80 percent of the individuals training to become psychologists and counselors are women.

Psychologists and counselors are also no longer required to train solely as medical doctors. Becoming a mental health counselor usually requires getting a master's degree in psychology, social work, counseling, or a related field that involves both academic study and applying that knowledge through practice under supervision by licensed counselors or psychologists. Psychologists, on the other hand, are required to obtain a doctoral degree in psychology to legally call themselves psychologists and provide mental health services. Psychologists, similar to counselors, likewise spend years studying and practicing techniques under the supervision of a psychologist. However, becoming a psychologist also requires learning how to conduct scientific studies of the mind, body, and related factors, and they learn to contribute to the field of psychology through research.

Therapy, which refers to the process by which mental health concerns are rectified, is the primary work for which psychologists and counselors are known. The therapy process usually begins by meeting individuals face to face to ascertain their concerns, collect background information, and provide orientation to what therapy may look like for them. Individuals who seek services from psychologists or counselors are often referred to as "clients," and their reasons for seeking services can include a wide range of disruptions and impairments in how a person is thinking, feeling, and functioning. Some psychologists dedicate a large portion of their time solely to conducting assessments to help figure out what may be functioning incorrectly, especially if the client is having a hard time understanding what the problem may be. For example, a neuropsychologist focuses on identifying problems in thinking that may point to damage in the brain, while other psychologists assess clients' personalities to gain insight on more deeply rooted causes for disorders or what therapy approach may work best in light of different personality factors.

Once a problem or diagnosis is identified, there are many ways for psychologists and counselors to provide therapy to help clients recover their normal way of functioning, but it usually involves talking, discussing, and exploring the situation with an objective perspective. Unlike close people in the client's life, such as friends, family members, and colleagues, psychologists and counselors start with a blank slate that is free from both positive and negative attitudes about the client. This blank slate allows them to see the problem and potential solutions with more clarity and flexibility and offer the client guidance on how to best proceed. In addition, psychologists and counselors are also knowledgeable about the solutions that are supported by science and keep up to date on any new developments in the research.

However, human beings are wondrously complex creatures, so therapy can take many different forms other than just talking to a person in an office. Certain disorders, like extreme fears called phobias, may require psychologists and counselors to help clients face the feared situations, environments, or objects side by side with the client in the community. Working with children may require using toys and other props or games to engage them. In fact, there is no reason that psychologists and counselors even have to work with one person at a time. Group therapy involves anywhere from two to fifteen people meeting to discuss and explore problems, as well as solutions, under the guidance of a psychologist or counselor.

A clinical psychologist's and mental health counselor's work primarily involves individuals and groups of individuals. Psychologists and counselors can therefore be found working almost anywhere there are people. This can be a hospital with lots of other healthcare professions, a community clinic, a private office, a school, a place of business, government agencies, and even prisons and jails.

Technology has also affected the work that psychologists and counselors do, as well as where and how they do it. Computers and communication systems in the early 1990s were cumbersome and too slow to allow people the degree of connectivity that we now enjoy. There are now increasing numbers of counselors and psychologists who provide services over the internet or video conferencing software. Even more recent technological advancements have allowed the use of virtual reality hardware and software to help clients overcome disorders, while the increased availability of mobile phones has opened up the possibility of psychologists and counselors helping to develop applications and interact with clients through them.

The training that counselors and psychologists receive allows them to do a lot more than just provide therapy. Many psychologists and counselors devote their time to teaching in academic settings or helping to train individuals on the path to becoming psychologists and counselors. Since psychologists receive intensive training in psychological science, they also often conduct research, either in addition to or instead of providing clinical services. It is not uncommon to find psychologists teaching, providing therapy, and conducting research to different degrees throughout a normal week. There are even counselors and psychologists who focus on mental health policy and laws, consult with businesses or agencies to help them run more effectively, and write books for the general public that help make psychological information easier to understand.

Overall, psychologists and mental health counselors enjoy relative freedom and diversity regarding with whom they work, where they work, and how they work. With almost one out of every five adults in the United States likely to have at least one mental health disorder over the past year (Bose et al. 2016), there is always a need for well-trained, empathic mental health professionals to help people adapt, recover, and lead productive lives.

Rokas Perskaudas

See also: *1946–1991:* College Professor; Scientist; Social Worker

FURTHER READING

American Psychological Association. *Psychology Careers for High School Students of Color*. http://www.apa.org/careers/resources/guides/high-school-students.aspx.

Benjamin, L. T., Jr. 2007. *A Brief History of Modern Psychology*. Malden: Blackwell Publishing.

Bose, Jonaki, Sarra L. Hedden, Rachel N. Lipari, Eunice Park-Lee, Jeremy D. Porter, and Michael R. Pemberton. 2016. "Key Substance Use and Mental Health Indicators in the United States: Results from the 2015 National Survey on Drug Use and Health." Substance Abuse and Mental Health Services Administration (December 2016). https://www.samhsa.gov/data/sites/default/files/NSDUH-FFR1-2015/NSDUH-FFR1-2015/NSDUH-FFR1-2015.pdf.

Rogers, Carl. 1995. *On Becoming a Person: A Therapist's View of Psychotherapy*. New York: Houghton Mifflin Company.

Sacks, O. 1998. *The Man Who Mistook His Wife for a Hat*. New York: Touchstone.

SCIENTIFIC ILLUSTRATOR

A medical or scientific illustrator specializes in creating artistic renderings of medical or scientific subjects. Creating medical or scientific illustrations before the twenty-first century was the work of artists trained in both sciences and the arts. Unlike most artists, however, who generally use artistic forms and methods to interpret their subjects for the viewer, scientific and medical illustrators must render a specimen accurately, in great detail, without interpretation. At its most fundamental, medical and scientific illustration is a form of visual communication with the goal of helping to explain medical or scientific principles, phenomena, and processes. From the earliest times of drawing to the 1990s, hand-rendered illustration was the primary way in which detailed scientific and medical images were produced for the reading and viewing public.

Scientific illustration has ancient origins, with individuals who practiced anatomical dissection, observed animals or plants in the natural world, or used illustration to demonstrate the mechanical or physiological inner workings of natural phenomena. Some early anatomists created sketches of animal and human bodies in ancient Greece. Later, during the fifteenth century, for instance, Leonardo da Vinci kept journals in which he created elaborate drawings realistically representing horses and human bodies, among other subjects, while in the early nineteenth century, the naturalist John Audubon painted realistic renderings of birds and animals in the Americas to document species as well as to sell as art works.

Before the late 1990s, scientific and medical illustrators used paper and pencils, pens, colored pencils, inks, and watercolor paint to create detailed renderings of subjects that could be reproduced by photographic techniques or to illustrate specific elements of a subject that cannot be easily illustrated in other ways, such as the musculoskeletal system of the human body. These illustrators are generally called "classical" medical or scientific illustrators. A classical medical illustrator, for instance, might help a team of surgeons illustrate how a series of facial reconstruction operations would resolve deep scars and injuries for a burn patient by hand drawing the intended facial renderings of the patient after each reconstructive surgery. Classical illustration techniques used by these professionals provide greater precision and detail than is possible when using photographic or computer-generated techniques. Since the late 1990s, digital photography and computer-generated illustration has largely overtaken the field of hand rendering since it is faster to complete illustrations, requires fewer hand-rendering artistic skills as computer-drawing programs allow for digital shadowing and other such techniques, and the product is thus cheaper than hand-rendered illustrations.

A classical scientific illustrator might work in a museum, university, hospital, or even in the field. They might start their day in consultation with a supervising scientist or scientific team to determine what illustration was needed and for which purpose. Like any form of communication, the intended audience is important to scientific illustrators. For a museum exhibit about deep oceanic life, a classical scientific illustrator might be tasked with rendering drawings of a series of fish, tiny marine organisms, jellyfish, and other life forms within their natural environment, deep in the ocean where light does not permeate the water column. For a scientific paper in marine biology in a professional journal, a classical scientific illustrator might be required to detail differences between two species of newly discovered deepwater eels, focusing on the anatomical structure of the two subjects without providing an environmental setting for those life forms. In both cases, the illustrator must study the organisms in detail before beginning the hand renderings.

Then, using paper and graphite pencils, they might first sketch out the illustration on paper, sharing the works with the scientists in charge to ensure that the renderings are what is required. Once scientists approve these concept sketches, classical scientific illustrators would often then spend two or three days on each illustration, working in a studio setting to create a very precise and comprehensive representation of the specimen. Once the illustrator completes the work, the illustrations are provided to the scientists or organization that requested it, to be displayed in a museum or accompany a scientific manuscript as it is submitted to a professional journal for publication. Creating these works of art is a highly skilled activity, requiring patience, extreme attention to detail, scientific knowledge, an understanding of communication principles, knowledge of color theories, and expert artistic skills. A keen eye for detail is particularly important, notes scientific illustrator Natalia Wilkins-Tyler, who observes that "you really have to work on training your eye to draw what is actually there instead of what you see" (NHMU 2017).

With the advent of computer-assisted illustration and digital photography and digital revising and modification techniques, the work of classical scientific illustrators has changed dramatically. Some moved into the field of medical illustrating, where opportunities are often greater. Many illustrators adopted use of the new computer and digital technologies, drawing by hand only when specifically commissioned to do so. Most classical scientific illustrators argue that the classical techniques provide higher-quality illustrations, though with some journals becoming electronic only, that precision might not be necessary given that the audience consumes the images through the media of computer, tablet, or phone screens. These digital media represent images in pixel forms, in which very fine detail may not be easily represented. Many classical scientific and medical illustrators also teach art to students in schools and colleges, as well as to the large public of novice artists who enjoy painting or drawing as hobbies. Many classical illustrators teach at museums, in birding or botanical clubs, and in other venues that are centered on understanding, appreciating, and conserving the natural world.

Today, many classical scientific illustrators have joined the illustration arts movement—a form of artistic work in which classical illustrators create artistic work for sale to museums, collectors, art magazines, book authors, and for sale in galleries. There are illustration artists who specialize in plants (the botanical artists), machines including historical machinery (mechanical artists) and natural artists, whose art parallels that of classical scientific illustrators but whose works are valued for their aesthetic qualities, not their sole focus on scientific accuracy and precision.

Currently, there is an international market for such illustrations, in which a buyer in Hong Kong or Rome, for instance, might desire a highly detailed colored pen-and-ink illustration of the lifecycle of a rare species of tropical butterfly as a work of art, not a form of scientific communication. Domestic and international competition in the illustration arts has introduced many art collectors to the subtle details of classical scientific illustration. Organizations like the Guild of Natural Science Illustrators (GNSI) provide education to the public about scientific illustration, represent illustrators, give professional and career advice to artists, and advocate for scientific illustrators with publishers, museums, competition organizers, and other potential clients.

Nancy Quam-Wickham and Molly Brown

See also: Epidemiologist; *1915–1945:* Draftsman; *1946–1991:* Artist

FURTHER READING

Guild of Natural Science Illustrators. https://gnsi.org/.

Haeckel, Ernst, Olaf Briedbach, Richard Hartmann, and I. Eibel-Eibesfeldt. 2008. *Art Forms in Nature: The Prints of Ernst Haeckel.* Munich: Prestel Publishing.

Hodges, Elaine R. S. 2003. *The Guild Handbook of Scientific Illustration, 2e.* Hoboken: John Wiley Company.

Laurent, Anna. 2016. *Botanical Art from the Golden Age of Scientific Discovery.* Chicago: University of Chicago Press.

Mozdy, Michael. 2017. "The Art and Details of Scientific Illustration." Natural History Museum of Utah (blog). https://nhmu.utah.edu/blog/2017/01/29/art-and-details-scientific-illustration.

SOCIAL MEDIA COORDINATOR

Social media emerged as a professional field with the maturation of the internet and allows individuals to utilize new technologies to facilitate a variety of traditional business goals in new, innovative ways. Professional social media coordinators are employed by organizations with the common goals of marketing of a product or cause, releasing public relations information, and increasing the public's awareness of the organization. Social media may still be a fledgling profession, but it has quickly become an important aspect in any marketing or outreach campaign in American business, advocacy work, and politics.

While there are no strictly defined educational requirements for social media coordinators, undergraduate degrees in the liberal arts like history and English, as well as communications studies, marketing, and similar fields, equip job seekers with the skills to succeed in the social media world. Other useful areas of study to bolster social media expertise should include sociology and geography to better understand demographics, statistics to help identify trends in the data, and business or economics to optimize social media presence. Social media coordinators spend their workdays working with others to prioritize an organization's products or services, research possible markets, and devise communication strategies to meet the targeted audiences. They must also conscientiously monitor those social media campaigns launched by their competitors as well as their own employers. Social media coordinators write short content pieces, locate media (GIFs, videos, images), create graphs, and collect and nurture their audiences, or fans. They must be nimble in using a wide variety of tested and new technologies; many social media coordinators also have some training in web design or computer programming.

The history of social media actually predates computers, going back to the late 1800s. The 1890s brought two inventions into the world that fundamentally changed the way people communicated and obtained their information about the outside world: the radio and the telephone. Fast forwarding to the second half of the twentieth century, the computer age arrived. While the computers of the 1960s and '70s look nothing like the smartphones in our pockets today, the computer scientists of the era laid the foundation of modern social media with the earliest forms of e-mail and digital newsletters. The first social media websites sprang up before the end of the millennium, but social media did not begin receiving serious professional treatment until the Web2.0 era arrived. Web2.0 refers to the emergence of user-generated content as a primary function of the internet.

Content creators had been few and far between before Web2.0, but it became possible in the 2000s for anyone (or any organization) to maintain a presence and push content to platforms that would include Myspace, YouTube, Facebook, Twitter, Instagram, and more. While many people saw *Time* magazine's awarding its Person of the Year award in 2006 to "You" as a joke, it signaled how much cultural force was building behind Web2.0. This explosion of user-generated content laid the foundation for modern social media marketing as tags and metadata became the subjects of deep analysis.

A successful social media campaign can come in almost any form. Some of the earliest success stories have almost nothing in common besides both using online marketing efforts. Among first successes was Hotmail.com, which offered free e-mail services as early as 1996 and let customers know that it delivered a free service by including a brief text ad at the bottom of every e-mail sent from its service. A few years later, ultra-low-budget movie turned cultural phenomenon *The Blair Witch Project* (1999) set the bar for what it meant to "go viral." Those behind the film generated hype by posting "news clippings" in forums and a website that alleged to document the history of the "Blair Witch" back to 1785. The power of social media reached another level in 2008, when Barack Obama won the presidency after beginning the election as a mostly unknown candidate. Obama's 2008 campaign used over a dozen social media platforms to raise awareness among the American public and focused heavily on engagement with the followers, making him the first "digital president" in a way.

The latest adjustment that social media coordinators have had to account for is the rise of the smartphone. Global smartphone ownership has skyrocketed since 2009, and the devices themselves have seen a considerable improvement in performance and versatility. This has allowed social media campaigns to go mobile and offer location-specific content with geotags marking users present at high-demand events like conventions and festivals.

Social media has faced criticisms over time and still does today. There is a barrier to participating in the technology required to use social media platforms, lending concern that those facing conditions of poverty may not be afforded the same access to a society trending more and more digital. User-generated content going through no verification for accuracy has led to a culture wherein almost any piece of information can be dismissed as untrustworthy or the reverse: accepted as fact when there is no factual basis for the information. Passive participation and privacy have people concerned over what information about them is being collected and what it may be used for by organizations, governments, and businesses.

Today, social media coordinators face a glut of established platforms on which to maintain a presence as well as the necessity to keep an eye out for new emerging technologies that might once again redefine the field. Digital strategy has never been more important, and some businesses, like the twenty-four-hour diner Denny's, have built cult-like followings based on their presence on social media. On the other hand, social media mistakes have placed otherwise normal brand marketing efforts at the center of public scrutiny, be it one off-color tweet or an entire campaign built on questionable messaging. Social media coordinators must remain conscious of their audience and how they might not react as intended to a campaign.

Jacob Ingram

See also: Campaign Manager; E-Commerce Specialist; Information Technology Architect; Project Manager

FURTHER READING

Aker, Jennifer, and Andy Smith. 2010. *The Dragonfly Effect: Quick, Effective, and Powerful Ways to Use Social Media to Drive Social Change.* San Francisco: Jossey-Bass.

Ho, Marcus. 2014. *Social Payoff.* Singapore: Write Editions.

Safko, Lon. 2012. *The Social Media Bible: Tactics, Tools, and Strategies for Business Success.* New York: Wiley.

SOUND ENGINEER

In the world of professional audio, sound engineers place and configure microphones during studio recording sessions, monitor instrument and vocal volumes, and perform postproduction audio mixing and editing. Sound engineers are the last ones to influence the sounds that make it onto a recording. For every new album, movie, or live concert, there is at least one sound engineer working behind the scenes. Sound engineers have expertise with musical and recording equipment and have a good "ear" or feel for what the audio recording needs to sound its very best.

During the recording process, the sound engineer often runs the console, which is a large board with switches, buttons, and sliders that controls every aspect of how the performed sound is recorded to media. A sound engineer works with a producer, who operates like a film's director, providing direction and advice to the performer and the sound engineer, though sometimes, especially on smaller projects, the sound engineer will assume the producer's role.

Most sound engineers need an extensive knowledge of foundational sound recording and engineering techniques, both scientific and subjective. Just as a sound engineer must know how a sound wave will form and be conveyed, a good sound engineer will also know which sounds and styles of recording will produce the best—and most desirable—result. The best sound engineers are highly creative, and their creativity allows them to stand out from their peers. Sound engineers must also be adept problem solvers, and most are able to jury-rig custom solutions to problems in the studio.

The sound engineer's profession is creative and possesses a rich history. Every distorted guitar track on every record can in some sense be traced back to a handful of musicians in the 1940s and 1950s who began deliberately doctoring their equipment after hearing how much people loved the sounds that had been coming from overused and partly broken equipment. One of the first cases of distortion being recorded was with R&B and blues legend Ike Turner's band The Kings of Rhythm. The story goes that the guitarist's amp had been damaged on the way to the recording studio; one story says the amp fell off the trunk of the band's car when they were fixing a flat tire on the highway. After stuffing the amp full of newspaper to hold the damaged speaker cone in place, they got a fuzzier, more distorted sound from it. Producer Sam Phillips liked the sound. In spite of how much historical significance it would come to hold, Turner and the band sold the song, called "A Fool in Love," for $20 in 1951, equivalent to around $190 in the late 2010s.

The modern sound engineering industry is built up around the pursuit of particular sounds and was kick started by the digital revolution of the early 1990s and 2000s. Where artists once needed access to studio time and special equipment to produce a high-quality record, newer, smaller, more powerful equipment started to change what was possible. Production equipment like the MPC 3000 (MIDI Production Center) or a Moog synthesizer helped democratize who could produce music in newly engineered ways. Hip-hop is a model genre to hear this on display as new technological tools allowed for easier sampling and manipulation of the sound.

Modern sound engineers often study acoustics (the raw science of sound), computer engineering, physics, electronics, or a handful of engineering subfields like acoustical, broadcast, or electrical engineering. Each of these courses of study prepares an apprentice sound engineer in a slightly different way: a sound engineer's early forays into the industry might include helping a band configure and tune its instruments or providing assistance to an acoustic architect who helps design the angles of the walls and ceiling in a venue or sound space. Some of the strongest specialized sound engineering programs are located at the Ontario Institute of Audio Recording Technology in London, Canada, and Full Sail University in Winter Park, Florida.

Sound Engineering is a large field with many specialized roles; however, the expansion of technology has allowed for more people to taken on greater roles inside the recording studio. Sound engineering is a critical part of any audio production, and more recent histories of music have proven that anyone with the drive to understand what goes into the technical part of sound can succeed in this role too.

Jacob Ingram

See also: Computer Programmer; *1915–1945:* Animator; *1946–1991:* Artist; Singer

FURTHER READING

Beranek, Leo L. 2008. *Riding the Waves: A Life in Sound, Science, and Industry*. Cambridge: MIT Press.

Morton, David. 2000. *Off the Record: The Technology and Culture of Sound Recording in America*. New Brunswick: Rutgers University Press.

Self, Douglas. 2010. *Audio Engineering Explained: Professional Audio Recording*. Oxford: Focal.

SPY

Spies secretly collect and report information on the movements, plans, and activities of a competitor or enemy. The spy's profession is as old as warfare, and it has been mentioned in the earliest historical records. Over twenty-five hundred years ago, the ancient Chinese military classic *The Art of Warfare,* by Sun Tzu, famously stresses the spy's utmost importance in deciding the outcome of a war and further identifies five types of spies essential to the spy craft: local spies, which are the enemy's own countrymen who work for the opposite side; inside agents, or moles, who gradually achieve an important position within the security defenses of one group and provide information to another; double agents, who secretly change their allegiance; expendable agents, who spread disinformation; and indispensable agents, who perform clandestine operations and then return home to report their findings.

Today, spying has become an indispensable sinew of modern life. Many aspects of modern society hinge on the gathering, transmission, and control of political, economic, industrial, and military secrets, as well as private information that can be used for political influence or social control. As a result, the world's major nations are spending enormous amounts of money on spying activities—which are now collectively called intelligence. As a result, spy organizations, which often are collectively identified as the intelligence community, have grown at an unprecedented rate. China, for example, is the world's second-largest spender on military and defense, but China's annual intelligence budget is larger than any other nation's, including the United States'; China spends more on intelligence than it does on its conventional military. China's intelligence budget is primarily spent on military and industrial espionage against the West and monitoring and surveillance over its 1.4 billion citizens in an effort to maintain the Communist Party's political monopoly. The United States, on the other hand, has also dramatically increased its intelligence operations, especially after the September 11, 2001, terrorist attacks.

Modern spy craft is divided into two major categories: intelligence and counterintelligence. Intelligence spy craft is any action or technique that is used to gather and analyze information for later use by military and political decision makers. Counterintelligence is any spy craft that is used as a defense against hostile intelligence spy craft.

Broadly speaking, there are also two major divisions of intelligence methods: human intelligence and technical intelligence. Human intelligence involves human agents who are operating in the conventional, physical sense. Two types of people are usually involved in human intelligence: case officers—or handlers—and field agents. A handler will give assignments to field agents and provide them with any necessary resources, and field agents will be conducting intelligence and counterintelligence operations in the field.

Technical intelligence includes radio and audio surveillance, satellite reconnaissance, cyber penetration and counter-penetration, and coding and code breaking. The U.S. government runs the world's largest technical intelligence organization, the National Security Agency, headquartered near Baltimore, Maryland, which employs tens of thousands of the world's best computer experts, mathematicians, and cybersecurity specialists.

Because of the profession's clandestine nature and high-stake missions, spies are subject to unusually rigorous checks for loyalty and trustworthiness. All spy agencies are extremely vigilant about catching three types of traitors: double agents, moles, and defectors.

Double agents were originally loyal to the agency that recruited them but changed their minds and turned against their original agency. Among the most famous double agents in recent history are the CIA's Richard Ames, the FBI's Robert Hanssen, and the U.S. Navy's John Anthony Walker, Jr., each of whom betrayed their country by working for the Russian government. During World War II, Admiral Wilhelm Franz Canaris, the chief of Nazi Germany's military intelligence organization, the Abwehr, became a double agent for the U.S. spy agency the Office of Strategic Services (OSS), sending top-secret Nazi information to Allen Dulles, who headed OSS's office in Bern, Switzerland. Admiral Canaris's betrayal was discovered in July 1944, and he was executed in April 1945.

Moles are long-term spies who work for another country or organization. The most notorious mole in the U.S. history is Larry Wu Tai Chin, who joined the CIA in 1952 and provided secret information to the Chinese government until his suicide in 1985. The best-known mole inside the KGB was Colonel Oleg Penkovsky, who worked for the CIA during the height of the Cold War and provided vital secrets to the West about Soviet military capabilities. He was discovered and executed in 1963.

Defectors are agents who betray their country by physically fleeing to—and joining—a hostile country. The most notorious defectors are the Cambridge Five, who held some of the most senior and sensitive positions in the British intelligence but were secretly working for Moscow because they favored an ideological commitment to communism. The Cambridge Five included Donald Maclean, Guy Burgess, Kim Philby, Sir Anthony Blunt, and John Cairncross, and they were handled by KBG Case Officer Yuri Modin. When exposed, Maclean, Burgess, and Philby fled to Moscow and became defectors working for the Soviet intelligence efforts against the West.

Spies are responsible for more than just gathering and analyzing information and secrets from hostile countries. A unique, modern feature of spying also involves special operations. These activities include industrial and infrastructure sabotage, assassination, and torture. In the 1970s, the U.S. Congress banned the CIA and other U.S. intelligence agencies from conducting any assassinations overseas, but after the September 11, 2011, terrorist attacks, the CIA began operating a torture program that attempted to extract important information from captured terrorists. This stirred a passionate national debate over the ethics of such activities.

The Soviet KGB, along with Russia's current spy agency the Russian Federal Security Service (FSB), and Moscow's Foreign Intelligence Service of the Russian Federation (SVR RF) are well known for their kidnappings and assassinations of political dissidents and double agents. The latest such example occurred in England on March 4, 2018, when Russia's spies used Novichok, which is a deadly nerve agent, to attempt to assassinate a former Russian military intelligence officer and a double agent for Great Britain's MI6, Sergel Skripal, and his daughter, Yulia, in Salisbury, England.

In popular culture, spies are often glamorously portrayed. In reality, the life of a spy can be extremely stressful and dangerous. Although spy agencies sometimes publish job advertisements to recruit agents, these solicited positions are often for roles as technical specialists who provide operational assistance from a government office or military base. Most spies are recruited without open advertisements. Recruiters usually adopt discrete ways of contacting targeted candidates after a certain period of oblique observation and background evaluations of a candidate's language skills, physical attributes, performance under stressful conditions, and overall emotional strength. After being recruited, a candidate spy must submit to specialized training regimens and protocol, which can sometimes take years to complete.

Spies usually operate under two conditions: either with a cover identity inside an embassy or consulate to take advantage of those jobs' diplomatic immunity—meaning that embassy or consulate workers cannot be subject to another nation's laws for minor offenses—or as fully covert operatives who do not have diplomatic immunity. Spies operating under the latter condition are usually known as illegals. They are subject to extreme danger and severe punishment. If caught, these spies typically are at the mercy of the hostile country's legal and judicial system, which usually renders a maximum—often capital—sentence to sovereign spies who are captured while performing clandestine operations.

Any spy's most essential asset is his or her character strength. A good spy must have the moral and ethical fortitude to resist powerful temptations, including money, loneliness, ideological biases, and other behaviors that might make him or her subject to blackmail by a hostile entity. As such, counterintelligence units constantly check their agency employees' financial records and political affiliations, and they often subject their agents to random drug tests.

In the modern world, cyber espionage has far surpassed human intelligence in scale and impact. Today, a motivated person can succeed at much of what a traditional spy can accomplish—and far beyond—with little more than an internet-connected computer.

Maochun "Miles" Yu

See also: *1776–1860:* Intelligencer; *1946–1991:* Foreign Service Officer

FURTHER READING

Benson, Robert Louis. 1997. "A History of US Communications Intelligence during World War II: Policy and Administration." Series IV (World War II) 8. Washington, DC: National Security Agency Center for Cryptologic History.

Casey, William J. 1988. *The Secret War against Hitler*. Washington, DC: Regnery Gateway.

Colby, William E., and Peter Forbath. 1978. *Honorable Men: My Life in the CIA*. New York: Simon & Schuster.

Dulles, Allen. 1966. *The Secret Surrender*. New York: Harper & Row.

SUPPLY CHAIN LOGISTICIAN

Supply chain professionals, or logisticians, work in the field of supply chain logistics: the field of study and professional practice responsible for the movement of goods and services from the raw material stage to final consumer and even through the recycling and repurposing stages. This business discipline is crucial for successful commerce and has been so since humans began trading on a commercial level. Supply chain professionals work in business management fields, concentrating on the physical distribution of goods using a multimodal process that includes ships (maritime), trucks, trains, and planes. The use of these various transportation assets is referred to as intermodal freight transport. Yet supply chain professionals don't only move freight. The movement of passengers via train, bus, plane, and ship also requires professionals with an education and skillset in this field.

Supply chain professionals generally work in offices and use computers to help them track the movement of goods and people. They may be called upon to track inventory, order goods, process paperwork, create daily work logs within warehouses or transport terminals, issue billing statements, and negotiate costs for transport with shippers of all kinds. They may also analyze patterns of sales, distribution, and consumption of goods. Some logistics professionals work at freight terminals, while others work in warehouses or in factories, where they also plan production schedules based on predictions of demand for goods.

Supply chain professionals often have an undergraduate degree in business, management, or a similar field, and many also earn a specialist master's degree or an MBA. Although a degree in business is encouraged, the field consists of professionals from various areas of study and diverse backgrounds. These professionals may earn a specialized certificate and designation in logistics or supply chain management such as the Certified Supply Chain Professional or Certified Logistics, Transportation and Distribution, which are offered by the Association for Operations Management (APICS). While professionals in this field must understand the flow of goods and services in the physical sense, they must also be capable of utilizing quantitative tools such as forecasting, linear programming, and process mapping to solve logistical problems.

Studies in this field should include courses in accounting, economics, management, finance, marketing, statistics, operations management, and corporate strategy as well as classes in logistics and supply chain management. Individuals pursuing a career in this area are encouraged to take additional studies in oral and written communication, team building, problem solving, information technology, geographic information systems, and international business. Proficiency in a foreign language and exemplary spreadsheet (Excel) and database (ACCESS) skills also help create a competitive advantage. Data analysis skills are extremely important for use in forecasting customer demand and analyzing customer trends. It is a profession in demand as many businesses and even hospitals and school districts employ supply chain professionals. In 2017, the average annual wage of a supply chain manager in the United States was $79,440, according to the U.S. Bureau of Labor Statistics.

The physical workspace of supply chain professionals has changed dramatically over the past two hundred years. During the early to mid-nineteenth century, most freight in America was transported by vessel (ship) either internationally (transoceanic) or along the coast (coastwise), was loaded and unloaded by gangs of stevedores and longshoremen by hand, and was very labor intensive. Supervisors, freight brokers, and other supply chain professionals were physically stationed near the wharves close to both the freight and the ship. Business was conducted face to face on or near the dock. From the mid-nineteenth to the early twentieth century, much of the coastwise trade shifted from marine (sail then steam) to train as tracks and trains (steam then diesel) began to expand the nation westward, and thus the management of these processes became less centralized along the waterfront.

During the twentieth century, the development of truck transportation and an expanded interstate highway system spread the management function over a much wider area. With the advent of the shipping container (Malcolm McLean) in the 1950s, the intermodal (ship-truck-train) movement of goods exponentially grew. Globalization resulted in a much larger physical market and distribution network (made easier by the containerization process), and the rapid development of the computer in the late twentieth century made it easier for supply chain professionals to supervise the flow of goods from behind a computer screen far removed from the proximity of the wharf. Technology drastically changed the role and daily duties of the supply chain manager. Since supply chain management is such a broad discipline, however, jobs exist in a multitude of settings. Freight brokers, customs officials, steamship line professionals, and dispatchers often work in an office environment, relying on computers and radio frequency identification (RFID) technologies to be their eyes and ears on the dock, ship, truck, or train. Some people working in this field find themselves working on loading docks, in warehouses, in distribution centers, or in manufacturing facilities. Most of these individuals spend some of their time in an office environment and the rest on the "floor."

Globalization marches on, and America's need for foreign products will continue to grow, thus providing ample opportunities for individuals interested in getting into the field. Ports are expanding and channels deepening, thus allowing post-Panamax ships entry to both of the U.S. coasts. Distribution centers will continue to grow, and it is believed that, although modestly, U.S. manufacturing will finally start to expand, creating greater export opportunities. Successful supply chain professionals will meet this growth by providing superior service, solving logistical problems, and continually improving processes and technologies.

Paul L. Ewell

See also: Data Analyst; Package Handler; Postal Worker; Project Manager; *1915–1945:* Truck Driver; Warehouse Worker

FURTHER READING

McKeller, John M. 2014. *Supply Chain Management Demystified.* New York: McGraw-Hill Education.

Ross, David Frederick. 1997. *Competing through Supply Chain Management: Creating Market Winning Strategies through Supply Chain Partnerships.* New York: Springer.

Sarkar, Suman. 2017. *The Supply Chain Revolution: Innovative Sourcing and Logistics for a Fiercely Competitive World.* AMACON: American Manufacturing.

Bibliography

Baptist, Edward. 2014. *The Half Has Never Been Told: Slavery and the Making of American Capitalism*. New York: Basic Books.

Barrett, James R. 2017. *History from the Bottom Up and the Inside Out: Ethnicity, Race, and Identity in Working-Class History*. Durham: Duke University Press.

Bates, Beth Tompkins. 2012. *The Making of Black Detroit in the Age of Henry Ford*. Chapel Hill: University of North Carolina Press.

Bender, Daniel E. 2009. *American Abyss: Savagery and Civilization in the Age of Industry*. Ithaca: Cornell University Press.

Benson, Peter. 2012. *Tobacco Capitalism: Growers, Migrant Workers, and the Changing Face of a Global Industry*. Princeton: Princeton University Press.

Besen-Cassino, Yasemin. 2014. *Consuming Work: Youth Labor in America*. Philadelphia: Temple University Press.

Boris, Eileen. 2014. *Home to Work: Motherhood and the Politics of Industrial Homework in the United States*. Cambridge, UK: Cambridge University Press.

Boris, Eileen, and Jennifer Klein. 2012. *Caring for America: Home Health Workers in the Shadow of the Welfare State*. Oxford, UK: Oxford University Press.

Boustan, Leah Platt. 2016. *Competition in the Promised Land: Black Migrants in Northern Cities and Labor Markets*. Princeton: Princeton University Press.

Brody, David. 1970. *Steelworkers in America: The Non-union Era*. New York: HarperCollins.

Brody, David. 2005. *Labor Embattled: History, Power, Rights*. Urbana: University of Illinois Press.

Bronstein, Jamie L. 2016. *Two Nations, Indivisible: A History of Inequality in America*. Santa Barbara: Praeger.

Buhle, Paul. 1994. *Taking Care of Business: Samuel Gompers, George Meany, Lane Kirkland, and the Tragedy of American Labor*. New York: Monthly Review Press.

Chung, Sue Fawn. 2015. *Chinese in the Woods: Logging and Lumbering in the American West*. Urbana: University of Illinois Press.

Clark, Daniel. 2018. *Disruption in Detroit: Autoworkers and the Elusive Postwar Boom*. Urbana: University of Illinois Press.

Cowie, Jefferson. 2010. *Stayin' Alive: The 1970s and the Last Days of the Working Class*. New York: The New Press.

D'Antonio, Patricia. 2010. *American Nursing: A History of Knowledge, Authority, and the Meaning of Work*. Baltimore: Johns Hopkins University Press.

Dearinger, Ryan. 2015. *The Filth of Progress: Immigrants, Americans, and the Building of Canals and Railroads in the West*. Berkeley: University of California Press.

Demos, John. 1995. *The Unredeemed Captive: A Family Story from Early America*. New York: Vintage.

Dennis, Michael. 2014. *Blood on Steel: Chicago Steelworkers and the Strike of 1937*. Baltimore: Johns Hopkins University Press.

Draut, Tamara. 2016. *Sleeping Giant: How the New Working Class Will Transform America*. New York: Doubleday.

Dunbar-Ortiz, Roxanne. 2014. *An Indigenous Peoples' History of the United States*. Boston: Beacon.

Ehrenreich, Barbara. 2001. *Nickel and Dimed: On (Not) Getting By in America*. London, UK: Picador.

Faue, Elizabeth. 2013. *Rethinking the American Labor Movement*. Abington-on-Thames, UK: Routledge.

Feagin, Joe R. 2015. *How Blacks Built America: Labor, Culture, Freedom, and Democracy*. Abington-on-Thames, UK: Routledge.

Fink, Leon, Joseph Anthony McCartin, and Joan Sangster. 2014. *Workers in Hard Times: A Long View of Economic Crises*. Urbana: University of Illinois Press.

Flores, Lori. 2016. *Grounds for Dreaming: Mexican Americans, Mexican Immigrants, and the California Farmworker Movement*. New Haven: Yale University Press.

Freeman, Joshua. 2018. *Behemoth: A History of the Factory and the Making of the Modern World*. New York: W. W. Norton & Company.

Garcia, Matt. 2012. *From the Jaws of Victory: The Triumph and Tragedy of Cesar Chavez and the Farmworker Movement*. Berkeley: University of California Press.

Glass, Fred. 2016. *From Mission to Microchip: A History of the California Labor Movement*. Berkeley: University of California Press.

Glenn, Evelyn Nakano. 2010. *Forced to Care: Coercion and Caregiving in America*. Cambridge: Harvard University Press.

Glymph, Thavolia. 2009. *Out of the House of Bondage: The Transformation of the Plantation Household*. Cambridge, UK: Cambridge University Press.

Goldstein, Dana. 2015. *The Teacher Wars: A History of America's Most Embattled Profession*. Norwell: Anchor Books.

Gordon, Robert. 2016. *The Rise and Fall of American Growth. The US Standard of Living since the Civil War*. Princeton: Princeton University Press.

Gorman, Thomas. 2017. *Growing Up Working Class: Hidden Injuries and the Development of Angry White Men and Women*. New York: Palgrave Macmillan.

Gray, La Guana. 2014. *We Just Keep Running the Line: Black Southern Women and the Poultry Processing Industry*. Baton Rouge: LSU Press.

Green, Hardy. 2012. *The Company Town: The Industrial Edens and Satanic Mills That Shaped the American Economy*. New York: Basic Books.

Green, James. 1998. *The World of the Worker: Labor in Twentieth-Century America*. Urbana: University of Illinois Press.

Greenberg, Brian. 2017. *The Dawning of American Labor: The New Republic to the Industrial Age*. Hoboken: Wiley-Blackwell.

Holmes, Seth. 2013. *Broken Bodies: Migrant Farmworkers in the United States*. Berkeley: University of California Press.

Hyman, Louis. 2018. *Temp: How American Work, American Business, and the American Dream Became Temporary*. New York: Viking Press.

Innis-Jiménez, Michael. 2013. *Steel Barrio: The Great Mexican Migration to South Chicago, 1915–1940*. New York: New York University Press.

Isenberg, Nancy. 2016. *White Trash: The 400-Year Untold History of Class in America*. New York: Viking.

Johnson, Rashauna. 2016. *Slavery's Metropolis: Unfree Labor in New Orleans during the Age of Revolutions*. Cambridge, UK: Cambridge University Press.

Johnson, Walter. 2013. *River of Dark Dreams: Slavery and Empire in the Cotton Kingdom*. Cambridge: Harvard University Press.

Jones, William Powell. 2013. *The March on Washington: Jobs, Freedom, and the Forgotten History of Civil Rights*. New York: W. W. Norton & Company.

Kahan, Paul. 2014. *The Homestead Strike: Labor, Violence, and American Industry*. Abington-on-Thames, UK: Routledge.

Katz, Daniel, and Richard Greenwald. 2012. *Labor Rising: The Past and Future of Working People in America*. New York: The New Press.

Kessler, Sarah. 2018. *Gigged: The End of the Job and the Future of Work*. New York: St. Martins Press.

Kessler-Harris, Alice. 1983. *Out to Work: A History of Wage-Earning Women in the United States*. Oxford, UK: Oxford University Press.

King, Martin Luther, Jr. 2011. *"All Labor Has Dignity."* Edited by Michael K. Honey. Boston: Beacon Press.

Knight, Frederick. 2012. *Working the Diaspora: The Impact of African Labor on the Anglo-American World, 1650–1850*. New York: New York University Press.

Kraft, James. 2010. *Vegas at Odds: Labor Conflict in a Leisure Economy, 1960–1985*. Baltimore: Johns Hopkins.

Land, Stephanie. 2019. *Maid: Hard Work, Low Pay, and a Mother's Will to Survive.* New York: Hachette Books.

Lause, Mark A. 2015. *Free Labor: The Civil War and the Making of an American Working Class*. Urbana: University of Illinois Press.

LeFlouria, Talitha. 2014. *Chained in Silence: Black Women and Convict Labor in the New South*. Chapel Hill: University of North Carolina Press.

Lichtenstein, Nelson. 1995. *The Most Dangerous Man in Detroit: Walter Reuther and the Fate of American Labor.* New York: Basic Books.

Lichtenstein, Nelson. 2013. *A Contest of Ideas: Capital, Politics, and Labor*. Urbana: University of Illinois Press.

Lichtenstein, Nelson, and Elizabeth Tandy Shermer. 2012. *The Right and Labor in America: Politics, Ideology, and Imagination.* Philadelphia: University of Pennsylvania Press.

Mapes, Kathleen. 2009. *Sweet Tyranny: Migrant Labor, Industrial Agriculture, and Imperial Politics*. Urbana: University of Illinois Press.

Martin, Lou. 2014. *Smokestacks in the Hills: Rural Industrial Workers in West Virginia*. Urbana: University of Illinois Press.

Martin, Philip. 2009. *Importing Poverty? Immigration and the Changing Face of Rural America*. New Haven: Yale University Press.

Meyer, Stephen. 2016. *Manhood on the Line: Working-Class Masculinities in the American Heartland*. Urbana: University of Illinois Press.

Meyerowitz, Joanne. 1991. *Women Adrift: Independent Wage Earners in Chicago, 1880–1930.* Chicago: University of Chicago Press.

Milkman, Ruth. 2016. *On Gender, Labor, and Inequality*. Urbana: University of Illinois Press.

Mitchell, Don. 2012. *They Saved the Crops: Labor, Landscape, and the Struggle over Industrial Farming in Bracero-Era California*. Athens: University of Georgia Press.

Montgomery, David. 1989. *The Fall of the House of Labor: The Workplace, the State, and American Labor Activism, 1865–1925.* Cambridge, UK: Cambridge University Press.

Morgan, Jennifer. 2004. *Laboring Women: Reproduction and Gender in New World Slavery.* Philadelphia: University of Pennsylvania Press.

Murphy, Ryan Patrick. 2016. *Deregulating Desire: Flight Attendant Activism, Family Politics, and Workplace Justice*. Philadelphia: Temple University Press.

Orleck, Annalise. 1995. *Common Sense and a Little Fire: Women and Working-Class Politics in the United States, 1900–1965.* Chapel Hill: University of North Carolina Press.

Orozco, Cynthia E. 2009. *No Mexicans, Women, or Dogs Allowed: The Rise of the Mexican American Civil Rights Movement.* Austin: University of Texas Press.

Pacyga, Dominic. 2015. *Slaughterhouse: Chicago's Union Stock Yard and the World It Made*. Chicago: University of Chicago Press.

Perales, Monica. 2010. *Smeltertown: Making and Remembering a Southwest Border Community*. Chapel Hill: University of North Carolina Press.

Phillips, Kimberley. 2012. *War! What Is It Good For? Black Freedom Struggles and the US Military from World War II to Iraq*. Chapel Hill: University of North Carolina Press.

Rediker, Marcus. 2014. *Outlaws of the Atlantic: Sailors Pirates and Motley Crews in the Age of Sail*. Boston: Beacon Press.

Reich, Steven A. 2013. *Working People: A History of African American Workers since Emancipation*. Lanham: Rowman and Littlefield.

Reséndez, Andrés. 2016. *The Other Slavery: The Uncovered Story of Indian Enslavement in America*. Boston: Houghton Mifflin Harcourt.

Rockman, Seth. 2010. *Scraping By: Wage Labor, Slavery, and Survival in Early Baltimore*. Baltimore: Johns Hopkins University Press.

Roediger, David, and Elizabeth Esch. 2012. *The Production of Difference: Race and the Management of Labor in US History*. Oxford, UK: Oxford University Press.

Rosenbaum, Susanna. 2017. *Domestic Economies: Women, Work, and the American Dream in Los Angeles*. Durham: Duke University Press.

Rosenow, Michael K. 2015. *Death and Dying in the Working Class, 1865–1920*. Urbana: University of Illinois Press.

Rouleau, Brian. 2014. *With Sails Whitening Every Sea: Mariners and the Making of an American Maritime Empire*. Ithaca: Cornell University Press.

Ruef, Martin. 2014. *Between Slavery and Capitalism: The Legacy of Emancipation in the American South*. Princeton: Princeton University Press.

Schmidt, James D. 2010. *Industrial Violence and the Legal Origins of Child Labor*. Cambridge, UK: Cambridge University Press.

Shackel, Paul A. 2018. *Remembering Lattimer: Labor, Migration, and Race in Pennsylvania Anthracite Country*. Urbana: University of Illinois Press.

Simon, Bryant. 2017. *The Hamlet Fire: A Tragic Story of Cheap Food, Cheap Government, and Cheap Lives*. New York: The New Press.

Smith, Abbott Emerson. 2012. *Colonists in Bondage: White Servitude and Convict Labor in America, 1607–1776*. Chapel Hill: University of North Carolina Press.

Srole, Carole. 2009. *Transcribing Class and Gender: Masculinity and Femininity in Nineteenth-Century Courts and Offices*. Ann Arbor: University of Michigan Press.

Stoll, Steven. 2017. *Ramp Hollow: The Ordeal of Appalachia*. New York: Hill and Wang.

Storch, Randi. 2013. *Working Hard for the American Dream: Workers and Their Unions, World War I to the Present*. Hoboken: Wiley-Blackwell.

Terkel, Studs. 1972. *Working: People Talk About What They Do and How They Feel About What They Do.* New York: The New Press.

Tomlins, Christopher. 2010. *Freedom Bound: Law, Labor, and Civic Identity in Colonizing English America, 1580–1865.* Cambridge, UK: Cambridge University Press.

Turk, Katherine. 2016. *Equality on Trial: Gender and Rights in the Modern American Workplace.* Philadelphia: University of Pennsylvania Press.

Twarog, Emily. 2017. *Politics of the Pantry: Housewives, Food, and Consumer Protest in Twentieth-Century America.* Oxford, UK: Oxford University Press.

Ulrich, Laurel Thatcher. 1991. *A Midwife's Tale: The Life of Martha Ballard, Based on Her Diary, 1785–1812.* New York: Vintage.

Urban, Andrew. 2017. *Brokering Servitude: Migration and the Politics of Domestic Labor during the Long Nineteenth Century.* New York: New York University Press.

Vapnek, Lara. 2009. *Breadwinners: Working Women & Economic Independence, 1865–1920.* Urbana: University of Illinois Press.

Weise, Julie M. 2015. *Corazón de Dixie: Mexicanos in the US South since 1910.* Chapel Hill: University of North Carolina Press.

White, Ahmed. 2016. *The Last Great Strike: Little Steel, the CIO, and the Struggle for Labor Rights in New Deal America.* Berkeley: University of California Press.

Williams, Carol. 2012. *Indigenous Women and Work: From Labor to Activism.* Urbana: University of Illinois Press.

Woloch, Nancy. 2014. *A Class by Herself: Protective Laws for Women Workers, 1890s–1990s.* Princeton: Princeton University Press.

Zieger, Robert. 2012. *Life and Labor in the New New South.* Gainesville: University Press of Florida.

About the Editors and Contributors

EDITORS

Nancy Quam-Wickham is professor of history at California State University Long Beach, where she teaches courses in U.S., environmental, and gender history; she also served as Chairperson and as Editor of *The History Teacher* journal. She received her PhD in history at the University of California at Berkeley. She is a passionate advocate for inclusive pedagogies and the meaningful use of assessment to advance equity in higher education. She is affiliated with the National Institute for Learning Outcomes Assessment at the University of Illinois and has participated in the American Historical Association's Tuning Initiative and the Social Science Research Council's Measuring College Learning Project. She is currently a member of the national advisory board for the AHA's History Gateways Project and holds an advisor role in that project with the Gardner Institute for Excellence in Undergraduate Education. She has published many articles about the oil industry and is now working on a book, *Gastronautica: What the Whalers Ate*, which is about labor, foodways, and cultural exchanges throughout the world in the whaling industry during the nineteenth century.

Ben Tyler Elliott is a San Francisco Bay Area–based writer and editor. He has worked closely with students and faculty at Stanford University and throughout the University of California and California State University systems. His writing has appeared in *Calliope*, *The Talking Book*, and *You're Going to Die*. He holds a master's degree in English literature from San Francisco State University, where his research explored the symbiotic relationships among allegory, angst, and the subversive narrative. By day, he runs a small consulting company and edits books, articles, newsletters, advertisements, and anything else he can get his hands on. By night, he writes fiction and freelances as a graphic designer and video producer. Whenever he isn't working or buried in a book, he can likely be found riding his bicycle, baking bread, watching baseball, attending a heavy metal concert, or wallowing in Wikipedia's quieter corners. His debut novel, *Sifting Through Static*, was published in 2015.

CONTRIBUTORS

Bruce Alberts is a U.S. National Medal of Science awardee. Dr. Alberts has served as editor-in-chief of *Science* and as one of President Obama's first three U.S. Science Envoys. Alberts holds the Chancellor's Leadership Chair in Biochemistry and Biophysics for Science and Education at the University of California, San Francisco, to which he returned after serving two six-year terms as the president of the National Academy of Sciences. He coauthors the prominent *Molecular Biology of the Cell* textbook.

Marcus Anthony Allen is a lecturer in the Department of History and Political Science at North Carolina A&T State University. Dr. Allen's dissertation explores the savings accounts and economic lives of African Americans in antebellum and postbellum Baltimore. He is currently working on an article that explores the relationship between these black savers and the origins of the racial wealth gap.

Erik Altenbernd is assistant professor of history at College of the Canyons in Santa Clarita, California. Dr. Altenbernd's research focuses on arid and semiarid environments, settler colonialism, and U.S. territorial expansion during the nineteenth century. He is currently at work on a book manuscript on federal scientific exploration of the desert West as well as an article on Los Angeles and its contentious history as a desert city.

Lauren Ayers is a former Doctoral Student of American Environmental History interested in the role of government in economic development at home and abroad. She works as a freelance researcher and a conflicts analyst at a national law firm. In her spare time, she continues to work on her former dissertation topic on the history of the Forest Products Laboratory, a federally funded lab dedicated to the research and development of products from and related to forest industries.

Brian L. Bailey Sr. is a sixteen-year Christian minister and pastor of Ark Builders Christian Fellowship in Long Beach, California. Pastor Bailey graduated with a bachelor of arts in history from California State University, Long Beach, in 2015. He formerly taught World History at Alain LeRoy Locke College Preparatory Academy in Los Angeles. He currently hosts a Christian podcast, "People's Pastor Podcast."

Elsa Barraza Mendoza is a PhD Candidate in History at Georgetown University. Her dissertation focuses on the relationship between slavery and the expansion of Jesuit Higher education in the United States. Barraza-Mendoza also collaborates as the assistant curator of the Georgetown Slavery Archive, a digital repository of materials relating to the Maryland Jesuits, Georgetown University, and slavery. In this role, she identifies archival material in Jesuit and University Archives and processes it for publication online.

Kathleen M. Barry is a scholar of the twentieth-century United States, whose research has focused on women and labor. Dr. Barry is the author of *Femininity in Flight: A History of Flight Attendants* (2007). She has taught U.S. history at New York University and the University of Cambridge, where she was the Mellon Research Fellow in American history for three years. Barry is currently the assistant director of the National Fellowships Program at Johns Hopkins University.

Evan P. Bennett is associate professor of history at Florida Atlantic University. He is the author of *When Tobacco Was King: Families, Farm Labor, and Federal Policy in the Piedmont* (2014) and coeditor of *Beyond Forty Acres and a Mule: African American Landowning Families since Reconstruction* (2012). He has published a number of essays on southern agricultural history. As a scholar, he is most interested in the intersections of work and the environment in people's lives.

Joe Berry wrote the only book on organizing adjuncts. Having been active in all the major higher education unions, he has published widely on the topic of higher education as a workplace. Retired from City College of San Francisco and the University of Illinois, he teaches at Ton Duc Thang University in Vietnam. He serves on the boards of New Faculty Majority, the Coalition of Contingent Academic Labor, and the Center for the Study of Academic Labor.

Elaine G. Breslaw is a retired professor of history from Morgan State University (Baltimore) and most recently an adjunct at the University of Tennessee (Knoxville). Dr. Breslaw has published five books on early American history, including a biography of the colonial physician Dr. Alexander Hamilton of Annapolis and *Lotions, Potions, Pills, and Magic: Health Care in Early America.* She is the author of numerous articles on aspects of early American history published in a variety of historical journals.

Bree'ya Brown is a graduate student of Information Studies at the University of Texas at Austin. Brown earned her MA in history from California State University, Long Beach. Prior to joining the graduate program at UT Austin, she taught recent U.S. history undergraduate courses and was appointed the Jewish Studies Stuhlbarg Fellowship at CSULB. Her most recent research focuses on diversity in the American environmental movement. Her teaching and research focus on identity, libraries, and environmental history.

Garrett Brown, MPH, is a Certified Industrial Hygienist who worked for California's Division of Occupational Safety and Health (Cal/OSHA) for twenty years as Field Compliance Officer and then as Special Assistant to the Chief of the Division before retiring in 2014. Since 1993, Brown has been the volunteer Coordinator of the Maquiladora Health & Safety Support Network, organizing projects in Mexico, Central America, Indonesia, China, and Bangladesh.

Lindsey Brown is a Research Data Analyst in the Office of Assessment of Teaching and Learning at Washington State University, where she analyzes data from various sources and prepares visual displays of data and reports for a range of audiences, including faculty, administrators, and the public. She previously worked as an associate in research with the WSU School of Food Science, focusing on the role of functional foods in health.

Molly Brown is a teacher of botanical drawing, painter, and scientific illustrator. She founded the Bolinas School of Botanical Art, where she has been teaching for the last five years. She studied science illustration at UC Santa Cruz and illustrated for several ichthyologists at the California Academy of Sciences.

Nicholas Browning is an instructor of American history at the United States Military Academy at West Point. Major Browning's most recent research concentrates on the development of Anglo-American martial ideology during the American colonial period. He also serves as Department of History Head Academic Counselor at West Point, a role in which he leads efforts to recruit, manage, and advise the Academy's history majors.

Sean Cameron is a writer based in Los Angeles. He has published four novels and written articles for digital outlets such as the BBC. He has taught filmmaking at Orange County High School of the Arts and through nonprofit organizations.

Rosalba Campbell earned her Bachelor of Science degree with an emphasis on accountancy at California State University Long Beach in 1993. She passed all four parts of the CPA exam during her last semester. She worked as a tax auditor for the California Franchise Tax Board for six years. After a break to stay at home, she worked in public accounting and gained the experience to become a CPA. She has been working at the same firm for fourteen years.

Theresa Case has taught at UHD since 2002, after completing her PhD at the University of Texas at Austin and an editorial internship with the Texas State Historical Association. She has served as Coordinator of the History Program since 2014. While at UHD, Dr. Case has contributed to the organization of the UHD Gender Conference and the development of the university seminar courses and introductory history courses. Her research area is late-nineteenth-century and early-twentieth-century United States, especially social and cultural, history.

Atun Cawker is a fourth-year Student at California State University Long Beach. He is majoring in Kinesiology with an option in Exercise Science. He obtained his Bachelor of Science degree in May 2019 and will enter a Doctorate of Physical Therapy program in 2020. He has participated on a research project that focused on whaling in the nineteenth century and the impact it had on indigenous people. His current role is mentoring undergraduate students with their research projects.

Lindsay M. Chervinsky is a postdoctoral fellow at the Center for Presidential History at Southern Methodist University. Dr. Chervinsky wrote the first book on the extra-constitutional creation of the president's cabinet in the 1790s. She has also published several articles, book chapters, and editorials on executive political practices, the president's cabinet, and its contemporary significance.

Ken Conzelmann is assistant professor of Architectural Technology at New York City College of Technology in Brooklyn, New York. He has discovered that education and practice are distinct yet interdependent realms, which together offer a potent synergy. Ken's work explores many fronts with a particular interest in cultural context, textural conditions, and the physical/psychological dimensions of the architectural experience. His research on passive house principles has been published in several conference proceedings and most recently in the Sustainability Conference, Vancouver, January 2019. He has had the opportunity to participate in a full spectrum of work settings and genres, allowing for engagement on a wide range of projects, from urban high-rises to rural dwellings, and an award-winning entry for The High Line Design Ideas Competition.

Stephanie Cornejo is a student at California State University Long Beach majoring in journalism and minoring in philosophy. She will graduate with her BA in the fall of 2020 and is expecting to enter the journalism field. She currently has a blog wherein she focuses on modern film reviews and multimedia journalism. She is expecting to intern at CSULB's *Daily 49er* in the future.

Christy Davenport is a PhD student at Mississippi State University. She focuses on nineteenth-century U.S. Southern history, with an emphasis on the culture of enslaved individuals. She has discussed the perceptions and survival of maroon communities at several conferences and symposiums including the Southern Historical Association's annual meeting in 2018. She has also published pamphlets for Black History Month celebrations and multiple book reviews on monographs associated with American enslavement and early African American histories.

Ryan Dearinger has been a member of the History Faculty at Eastern Oregon University since 2009. Dr. Dearinger's research and teaching interests include the American West, immigration, labor and working-class history, environmental history, and violence in American history. His work has been widely published in the abovementioned fields. His book, *The Filth of Progress*, received the 2017 Best First Book Award from Phi Alpha Theta, the National History Honor Society. He has two ongoing book projects. The first is a coedited book on the nexus of labor and environmental history in the American West, and the second focuses on indigenous, immigrant, and American hop pickers in the Pacific Northwest. Dr. Dearinger serves on the Editorial Board of the *Oregon Encyclopedia* and on the Program Committee of the Pacific Northwest Labor History Association, is a contributor to Stanford University's *Chinese Railroad Workers in North America Project*, and was recently named to the Distinguished Speakers Program by the Center for Pacific Northwest Studies at Western Washington University. He is also a lead contributor to *Manifest Destiny Reconsidered*, a summer 2019 NEH Landmarks of American History & Culture workshop hosted by the University of Utah.

Melissa DeVelvis is a doctoral candidate in history at the University of South Carolina, specializing in the Civil War era, gender studies, and sensory and emotions history. She works in manuscript processing at the South Carolina Special Collections Library and is also a part-time site interpreter and guide for the Historic Columbia Foundation. Her dissertation examines gender, politics, and emotions on the eve of South Carolina's secession from the United States in 1860.

Vincent DiGirolamo is professor of history at Baruch College, CUNY. Dr. DiGirolamo is the author of *Crying the News: A History of America's Newsboys* (2019). His essays have appeared in *Labor History*, *Journal of Social History*, *Radical*

History Review, and several edited volumes, including *Cast Out: Vagrancy and Homelessness in Global and Comparative Perspective*. He received his BA from UC Berkeley, MA from UC Santa Cruz, and PhD from Princeton University.

Ina Dixon is a doctoral student in American Studies at UNC Chapel Hill and a Field Scholar with the Southern Oral History Program. Her current research explores memory, labor, and revitalization in former textile towns of the American Piedmont South.

Paul L. Ewell is professor of management and business & economics; chair of the Department of Management, Business, & Economics; and director of the MBA Program at Virginia Wesleyan University in Virginia Beach, Virginia. Dr. Ewell's teaching and research primarily focus on supply chain management and logistics in the maritime sector. Additionally, he is the executive director of the Watermen's Heritage Foundation of Virginia's Eastern Shore and director of the Eastern Shore Watermen's Museum and Research Center.

Christina Flores is a history PhD student at the University of Chicago and holds a BA in history and English from UC Berkeley. She is currently completing a dissertation entitled "*Workin' Man Blues* and *La Causa*: The Rise of Grassroots Conservatism, the UFW, and a Multiracial Religious Right in California's San Joaquin Valley, 1930–1980." Christina is a proud native of Bakersfield, California, the source of inspiration for much of her historical research.

Kate Fortmueller is assistant professor in the Department of Entertainment and Media Studies at the University of Georgia. Dr. Fortmueller's research explores historical and contemporary issues of film, television, and digital production labor. She is working on a book manuscript about actors and the growth of freelance labor in Hollywood. Her work appears in *Film History*, the *Historical Journal of Film, Radio, and Television, Journal of Film and Video,* and *Television & New Media*.

Mark P. Friedlander Jr. is a practicing attorney and author and coauthor of seven books including *Outbreak, Disease Detectives at Work*, a young adult study of epidemiology with a preface by Dr. Leonard Kirland, retired Chief of Department of Epidemiology at the Mayo Clinic; an NCSSLI Honor Book and an NCSS/CBC Notable Children's Trade Book in the Field of Social Studies; and an article, "The Role of Epidemiology in the Court," in *Minnesota Medicine*, a Minnesota Medical Association publication.

Arjana Gjokaj is a project manager at the Icahn School of Medicine at Mt. Sinai Hospital in Ossining, New York.

Joanne L. Goodwin is a professor of history at the University of Nevada, Las Vegas. Dr. Goodwin's publications include two monographs, nine articles and chapters, and one coedited encyclopedia. In addition, she has created several digital history projects focused on women's history in Nevada. She served as the Founding Director of the Women's Research Institute of Nevada at UNLV from 1999 to 2017. She currently serves as the secretary of the National Collaborative for Women's History Sites.

William Hal Gorby is a teaching assistant professor of history at West Virginia University, specializing in Appalachian history. Dr. Gorby is finishing a book on the Polish immigrants of Wheeling, West Virginia, from 1880 to 1945. His current research focuses on the role of Catholic immigrants in West Virginia's coalfields. He consulted on the research and script editing for the PBS American Experience documentary "The Mine Wars," which received an Emmy nomination for original research.

Penelope K. Hardy is assistant professor of history at the University of Wisconsin-La Crosse, where she teaches the global history of science and technology. Dr. Hardy studies the historical intersection of technology and the ocean sciences and has published on the history of oceanography, history of meteorology, and maritime history. Her current research project examines the role of research vessels in the development of oceanography as a field of interdisciplinary scientific study in the nineteenth and twentieth centuries.

Jayne Howell is professor of anthropology at California State University Long Beach. Dr. Howell has published a number of journal articles, essays, and book chapters and coedited two anthologies. Her ongoing research focuses on education and employment in Mexico, including informal sector workers such as domestic workers. She was formerly coeditor of the journal *Practicing Anthropology* and has served as president for the Society for Urban, National, Transnational/Global Anthropology.

Richard Howey has worked in information technology and data management since 1975. At Univac (now Unisys) Defense Systems, Dr. Howey developed software for real-time air-traffic control and military command and control systems. Later, he was a data warehouse/business intelligence consultant for PricewaterhouseCoopers and IBM, among others. Most recently, he worked in enterprise architecture, information architecture, data warehousing/business intelligence, and data governance at Target and UnitedHealth Group. Since retiring from his primary career, he has taught courses in information technology and management information systems at Augsburg University, Capella University, and the University of Minnesota. He is a Certified Data Management Professional (CDMP), a Certified Business Intelligence Professional (CBIP), and a Certified TOGAF 9 Enterprise Architect. His education includes a Doctorate of Business Administration from Metropolitan State University in St. Paul, Minnesota, a master's of science in management of technology from the University of Minnesota in Minneapolis, Minnesota, and a Bachelor of Science in mathematics from Lawrence Technological University in Southfield, Missouri.

Andrew T. Huse is an archivist and librarian at the University of South Florida Tampa Library's Special Collections. Huse led the research for a history of USF and wrote the centennial history of the Columbia Restaurant in Tampa. A book about the social history of Tampa is forthcoming.

Jacob Ingram studied history at California State University Long Beach and received his BA in 2014. His research interests focused on cultural intersections in the history of science and technology, with particular attention to the history of human space travel. He currently works as a web developer and is pursuing a graduate degree in Public Policy and Administration.

Erik Loomis is associate professor of history at the University of Rhode Island. His books include *Empire of Timber: Labor Unions and the Pacific Northwest Forests* (2016) and *A History of America in Ten Strikes* (2018). His essays have been published in the *New York Times*, *Washington Post*, *New Republic*, *The Nation*, *Dissent*, and many other journals. He blogs about politics and labor at the site Lawyers, Guns, and Money.

Daniel Lynch is a historian of the American West currently writing a book on masculinity, politics, and race in early Los Angeles. Dr. Lynch's work has appeared in *California History*, *The Western Historical Quarterly*, and in the companion volume to the 2015 Autry National Center exhibition, "Empire of Liberty: The Civil War and the West." Lynch has taught history at the middle school, high school, and college levels for over fifteen years and currently teaches at Marlborough School in Los Angeles.

Robert Marcell is a National Park Service historian at Homestead National Monument of America. He received his BA in history from the University of Nebraska at Omaha and his MA in the social sciences from the University of Chicago. He has written and reported on a variety of historical subjects, appeared on television and radio, and presented at national conferences and state-based conferences across the Great Plains.

Dr. Kenneth Marcus is professor of history at the University of La Verne and Chair of International Studies. He specializes in the field of Los Angeles cultural history and has published over twenty peer-reviewed journal articles, two book chapters, and three books, most recently *Schoenberg and Hollywood Modernism* (hardback 2016, paperback 2018). He teaches courses in European, American, and world history as well as history methods. He is currently working on a grant-funded project involving the use of the arts in teaching history.

Edward J. Martin is an adjunct history professor who currently teaches at Endicott College, Saint Anselm's College, and Salem State University. He has published a forthcoming peer-reviewed article in the *London Journal of Canadian Studies* and book reviews in the *Northern Mariner* and *Maine History*. Dr. Martin is currently working on a book-length monograph on privateering in New England and the Maritime provinces during the Revolutionary War and the War of 1812.

Caitlin Matekel is a doctoral student at Arizona State University in the School of Criminology and Criminal Justice. She is a student in the Center for Correctional Solutions, and her research focuses on the experiences of those living and working in prisons. She is currently working on a grant examining the effects of restrictive housing on both incarcerated individuals and corrections staff. Caitlin also teaches the Impact of Crime on Victims class and is a trained Inside-Out Prison Exchange Program instructor.

Robin Matty earned her MA in Museum Studies from the Indiana University–Purdue University Indianapolis. She has held museum positions at the Homestead National Monument and the Baltimore Museum of Industry and is now the Curator of Collections at Historic Annapolis, Inc.

Scott McClellan received his doctorate in history from the University of California, Irvine. Dr. McClellan's research interests include the intersection of business, law enforcement, and labor in urban development. He retired from law enforcement in 2014 after more than twenty-three years of service. He currently volunteers his time developing national and international standards for investigations, critical incidents, and security management.

Jennifer Metz Foster earned her BA in history at California State University, Sacramento, and her MA in history at the University of California. She has been a fellow of the Munson Institute in Maritime Studies in Mystic, Connecticut. She currently teaches in the Global Studies and Maritime Affairs program at the California State University Maritime Academy.

Dane A. Morrison is professor of Early American history at Salem State University. He is the author of *A Praying People: Massachusetts Acculturation and the Failure of the Puritan Mission, 1600–1690* and *True Yankees: The South Seas and the Discovery of American Identity* and has edited several other works on Native American and world history. He is currently at work on two book projects: *Yankees Abroad: Critical Themes in World History* and *Eastward of Good Hope: Early America in a Dangerous World.*

Loren Michael Mortimer received his PhD in history with a designated emphasis in Native American Studies at the University of California, Davis. He specializes in early American, Native American, and environmental history. His research uses digital mapping and spatial analysis of colonial maps to understand patterns of ecological and political change in Native American communities along the St. Lawrence River. Dr. Mortimer's current book project investigates the way early American environments shaped native and colonial societies from the sixteenth to the early nineteenth centuries.

W. P. Munsell holds a Professional Engineer license and is a consulting engineer and a historian of science and technology at the University of Oklahoma. He holds four patents and has lectured on design and failure analysis. His most recent paper is "Technology on Trial: The Social Framework of Safe Design," published by the American Society of Mechanical Engineers.

Thomas Nakano is a graduate of the University of California, Hastings College of the Law, where he served as senior editor for the *West-Northwest Journal of Environmental Law and Policy*.

Peter Nekola has served as assistant director of the Hermon Dunlap Smith Center for the History of Cartography, associate editor of *The History of Cartography, Volume 5: The Nineteenth Century*, and managing editor of *International Labor and Working-Class History*. Dr. Nekola is author of the forthcoming book *Mapping the Northwoods: Cartography and Geographical Knowledge in the Lake Superior Country, from Industry to Conservation* and currently serves as visiting assistant professor of philosophy at Luther College.

Tomas Nonnenmacher is the Patricia Bush Tippie Professor of Economics at Allegheny College. He and three coauthors recently published *Institutional and*

Organizational Analysis: Concepts and Applications. His other research includes the industrial organization of the telegraph industry and labor relations on Mexican haciendas during the nineteenth and early twentieth centuries.

Derek Kane O'Leary is a PhD candidate in UC Berkeley's History Department, where he studies and teaches about U.S. history and the Atlantic World. His dissertation is on the construction of archives, historical memory, and Romantic historians in the early United States. He has an MA in International Relations from the Fletcher School at Tufts University and a BA from Amherst College. He also edits the *Journal of the History of Ideas* blog.

Jerry Owens holds a Doctor of Veterinary Medicine degree, and is a board-certified Diplomate in Radiology (American College of Veterinary Radiology). Dr. Owens was in specialty referral veterinary practice in the San Francisco Bay Area from 1976 until retirement in 2015, providing services in internal medicine, radiology, radiation therapy, ultrasonography, computed tomography, and teleradiology, working with over six hundred veterinary hospitals in Northern California and Nevada. He has authored or coauthored three textbooks and more than fifteen scientific articles and presented more than one hundred lectures, seminars, short courses, and workshops to veterinarians and public groups. He currently writes articles for veterinary periodicals and is authoring three books as well as being a gentleman farmer at Madrone Farm, raising chickens, New Zealand miniature pigs, and Nigerian dwarf goats.

Anne Paulet is a professor at Humboldt State University, where she has been employed since 2000. While she has several published articles and is working on her book, her main focus is on teaching. In addition to a variety of history topic courses, she has designed a special career-preparation course for history students and a course to help students integrate into college with the right major and the skills for success. She is presently working on a complete redesign of the post–Civil War U.S. history course to center it around food and increase student interest and grades.

Matthew Pehl is associate professor of history at Augustana University in Sioux Falls, South Dakota. His book *The Making of Working-Class Religion* was published in 2016. He is currently writing about gender politics in the Midwest during the "long 1960s." In the spring of 2019, he launched a history podcast series with his students at Augustana.

Rokas Perskaudas holds an MA degree and is a doctoral candidate in clinical psychology at the Catholic University of America. He currently splits his time among clinical work at a Washington, D.C., private practice, teaching, mindfulness-based research, and interning at the Psychology Services Branch of the Federal Bureau of Prisons. Previous clinical placements have included working with veterans with severe mental illnesses at the D.C. Veterans Affairs Medical Center and at the Counseling Center at the Catholic University of America.

Christopher J. Phillips is the author of *Scouting and Scoring: How We Know What We Know about Baseball* and *The New Math: A Political History*. He is a historian of science, who has written broadly on the history of statistics, mathematics, and data. He is currently researching the history of statistics in twentieth-century medicine while teaching at Carnegie Mellon University.

Charles L. Ponce de Leon was born and raised in Palo Alto, California, and received his BA from UC Santa Barbara, where he was a college journalist and worked in community radio. He received his PhD from Rutgers University. He has taught at Princeton University and Purchase College, a branch of the State University of New York. In 2008, he moved to Long Beach State, where he is now professor of history and American Studies. Ponce de Leon is a specialist in U.S. cultural and intellectual history. His fields of expertise include mass media and the popular culture industries, American intellectual life, and modern U.S. political culture. He has written books on the origins of celebrity journalism, Elvis Presley, and the history of television news. He is currently writing a book on the rise of "hip capitalism" in the 1960s and 1970s.

Rosalia Quam-Wickham received her Juris Doctor in 2019 from The George Washington University Law School.

Judith Raymond is an architect and writer and teaches at the New York City College of Technology in Brooklyn.

Jonathan Rees is professor of history at Colorado State University–Pueblo. He is the author of several books, including *Managing the Mills: Labor Policy in the American Steel Industry During the Nonunion Era* and *Representation and Rebellion: The Rockefeller Plan at the Colorado Fuel and Iron Company, 1914–1942*. He serves as a historical advisor at the Steelworks Center of the West in Pueblo, Colorado.

Michael Reisch is distinguished professor of social justice at the University of Maryland. He has held faculty and administrative positions at five other major U.S. universities and has been a visiting professor in Europe, Asia, and Australia.

Reisch has written over thirty books and monographs and four hundred other publications and papers on poverty, the history and philosophy of social welfare, and contemporary policy issues. He has held leadership positions in national, state, and local advocacy, professional, and social justice organizations.

Vicki L. Ruiz is distinguished professor emerita of history and Chicano/Latino studies at the University of California, Irvine. An award-winning scholar and educator, she is the author of *Cannery Women, Cannery Lives*, and *From Out of the Shadows: Mexican Women in Twentieth- Century America*. A fellow of the American Academy of Arts and Sciences, she is past president of the American Historical Association and the Organization of American Historians. In 2015, President Barack Obama awarded Ruiz the National Humanities Medal.

Hanno Scheerer is administrative director of the Faculty of Languages and Literatures at Ludwig-Maximilians-Universität Munich, Germany. Dr. Scheerer's current research focuses on land speculation in the early American republic. Employing geographic information systems, he has studied the land appropriation process in Ohio's Virginia Military District. Parts of this study were published in an article in *Ohio Valley History*.

Harvey Schwartz is curator of the Oral History Collection at the International Longshore and Warehouse Union library in San Francisco. Dr. Schwartz's publications include *The March Inland: Origins of the ILWU Warehouse Division, 1934–1938*, *Solidarity Stories: An Oral History of the ILWU*, *and Building the Golden Gate Bridge: A Workers' Oral History.* He is a labor historian with an oral history specialty. His research focuses on workers along the Pacific Coast and in Canada and Hawaii.

Steven Shibuya teaches in the Metals Technology and Machining Programs at Los Angeles Trade-Tech College. He also coaches high school teams in robotic competitions in the greater Los Angeles area.

Stacy Sinclair is an environmental scientist with the Los Angeles Metropolitan Transportation Authority. Dr. Sinclair is creator of Metro's Environmental Construction Awareness Project (www.metro.net/meca) and the *Snapshots on Sustainability* blog (www.usgbc-la.org/blog) and is coauthor of *Building Healthy Communities* (2012) and *Building Resilience LA: A Primer* (2017). As a consultant, she creates interactive eLearning environments and educational games. She is an Environmental Leadership Fellow (2018) and Aspen Institute Fellow (2017). Her recent research on Aeolian transport as a mitigation strategy for sea-level rise received the Academy of Sciences Excellence Award (2017).

Robert G. Slawson, a fellow of the American College of Radiology, is a Radiation Oncologist who served in the U.S. Army for eight years and joined the faculty in the Department of Radiation Oncology at the University of Maryland. Dr. Slawson has been a volunteer at the National Museum of Civil War Medicine for the last sixteen years doing research and presentations on various aspects of Civil War medicine, including female physicians in the war as well as African American physicians who served. He has published many articles on Civil War medicine, including the book *Prologue to Change: African American Physicians in the Civil War Era.*

Nora Slonimsky is the Gardiner Assistant Professor of history at Iona College, where she also serves as director of the Institute for Thomas Paine Studies (ITPS). She received her PhD in American history in 2017 from the Graduate Center of the City University of New York (CUNY). Nora's research focuses on the intersection of intellectual property, commerce, and politics in the long eighteenth century, and she is currently working on her first book, *The Engine of Free Expression: Copyrighting the State in Early America*, which won the Society for the History of the Early American Republic (SHEAR) prize for best manuscript and was a finalist for the Zuckerman prize in American studies. This project, as well as her other research in the Digital Humanities and aspects of Copyright Studies, has been generously funded by the Huntington Library, the Library Company of Philadelphia, the New York Historical Society, and the America Antiquarian Society, among others. Nora is also a former Mellon Material Texts Fellow at the McNeil Center for Early American Studies at Penn as well as a current Advisory Council Representative and serves as the Social Media Editor for the *Journal of the Early Republic*. She teaches courses ranging from the American Revolution to copyright and innovation in U.S. history, all of which incorporate Digital Humanities.

Sean Smith teaches history at California State University, Long Beach, and courses in Digital Humanities and eSociety at the University of Arizona. He has been codirector of the Elizabeth Murray Project: A Resource Site for Early American History, has been integral to maintaining VOAHA II: The Virtual Oral/Aural History eRepository at the CSULB Library, and is now codirector of the Center for the History of Video Games and Critical Play at CSULB.

Bradley Sommer is a doctoral candidate in the Department of History at Carnegie Mellon University. He has written for the Labor and Working Class History Association (LAWCHA), *Jacobin Magazine*, and the *Journal of Northwest Ohio History*. His research focuses on class theory and consciousness; the nature of work, race, and class politics; and the Midwest. His most recent work was on the role of nonunion supporters during the 1934 Electric Auto-Lite strike in Toledo, Ohio.

Andrew I. Spielman is professor of Basic Science and Craniofacial Biology at New York University, New York. Dr. Spielman has published over seventy-five peer-reviewed articles and thirty-five chapters and has authored or edited three books. Over the past decades, his research focused on taste mechanisms and more recently on the integration of the basic sciences and clinical disciplines and the history of the NYU College of Dentistry and the digitization of its one-thousand-volume rare-book library.

Michelle Stonis is lecturer in U.S. history at California State University, Long Beach, and Glendale Community College. Her research interests include gender, social, and cultural history as well as history pedagogy. She is particularly interested in the intersections between constructs of gender, especially as communicated through religious or government propaganda, and actual behavior. Her research on missionary wives in the nineteenth-century Sandwich Islands won the 2006 Best Thesis award in the College of Liberal Arts at California State University, Long Beach. Stonis is currently working on a study of gun culture in the nineteenth-century United States.

Lisa C. Tolbert is associate professor of history at The University of North Carolina at Greensboro, where she teaches courses in American cultural history, research methods, and historical thinking pedagogy. Her current book project, *Beyond Piggly Wiggly: A Cultural History of the Self-Service Store in the Machine Age*, explores the cultural challenges of inventing the self-service store in the early twentieth century and evaluates the ways that local entrepreneurs and consumers transformed the spaces and social practices of shopping in the emerging mass market.

Sean Trainor teaches professional writing at the University of Florida. His writing has appeared in *The Atlantic, TIME, Salon, The Chronicle of Higher Education*, and elsewhere. He is currently completing a book on the history of men's grooming in the nineteenth-century United States.

Tom Tredway is assistant professor of design at California State University, Long Beach. He has authored or coauthored book chapters on fashion designer Elsa Schiaparelli, industrial designer Eva Zeisel, architect Paul Rudolph, late-twentieth-century design, and design for the social good. His most recent research focuses on tableware at Tiffany & Co. in the postwar period.

David J. Ulbrich is currently associate professor and director of the online MA in history and Military History Programs at Norwich University. Dr. Ulbrich previously served as a Civilian Historian at the U.S. Army Engineer School. He coedited

The Routledge History of Global War and Society with Matthew Muehlbauer and, more recently, coauthored *Race and Gender in Modern Western Warfare* with Bobby Wintermute.

Benjamin Van Dyk teaches U.S. history and chairs the Social Studies Department at Servite High School (Anaheim, California). He earned a BA in history from UCLA and an MA in history from CSU Long Beach with the thesis *The Whaler's Casket: Whaling and Children's Literature in Antebellum America*. He serves as an AP Reader for College Board, has served as adjunct professor for CSU Fullerton's High School Transitory Program, and was graduate intern for *The History Teacher*.

Amanda Walter is a PhD candidate of Gender, World, and Modern American History at Wayne State University. At Wayne State, she was a Thomas C. Rumble Fellow and received the Charles F. Otis and Dr. Jeffrey L. Reider Scholarship in the History of Gender and Sexuality. Her dissertation examines the impact of the U.S. working women's movement on the labor movement through a study of clerical unionism in higher education.

Daniel Walton is Instructor of Airpower at the Air Command and Staff College, Maxwell Air Force Base, Montgomery, Alabama. Prior to serving at Air University, Major Walton most recently served back-to-back overseas tours flying the C-130J Hercules in Germany and KC-135 Stratotanker in Japan. He has flown missions in support of operations in Afghanistan, Iraq, Libya, and the Horn of Africa.

John Zheng Wang is professor of forensic studies and criminal justice in the School of Criminology, Criminal Justice, and Emergency Management at California State University–Long Beach. Dr. Wang also serves as director and instructor for the Applied Forensic Science & Crime Analysis certificate program. He is also a fellow of the American Academy of Forensic Sciences and a member of International Association for Identification, ASB's Firearms & Tool-mark Consensus Body, Southern California Association of Fingerprint Officers, American Chemical Society, and the American Association for the Advancement of Science. Since 2009, he has been an Expert Instructor for California Police Command College (POST). Dr. Wang has published several books and many research articles in the fields of forensic science, criminology, and criminal justice.

Travis Weisse is a PhD candidate in the history of science, medicine, and technology at the University of Wisconsin-Madison. His dissertation focuses on the construction of dietary expertise in the mid-twentieth-century United States, with an emphasis on the diet industry. He is currently serving as the National Conference Coordinator for the Graduate Association for Food Studies.

David Welky is professor of history at the University of Central Arkansas and specializes in twentieth-century American history. Dr. Welky has written or edited thirteen books, including *Marching Across the Color Line: A. Philip Randolph and Civil Rights in the World War II Era*, *A Wretched and Precarious Situation: In Search of the Last Arctic Frontier*, and *The Thousand-Year Flood: The Ohio-Mississippi Disaster of 1937*. He has published numerous works on the history of film, mass media, and the Great Depression era.

Linda Welters is professor of textiles, fashion merchandising, and design at the University of Rhode Island. Dr. Welters specializes in the cultural history of textiles and fashion. Her research is grounded in the study of artifacts, and she employs a material culture approach in her work. Her publications include ten books and monographs, eighteen book chapters, and twenty-six peer-reviewed articles, some of which are coauthored. She is currently researching New England's homespun fabrics.

Julie Willett is associate professor of history at Texas Tech University. She has previously published *Permanent Waves: The Making of the American Beauty Shop* (2000) and edited *The American Beauty Industry Encyclopedia* (2010). She is also the coauthor of *A Theory of Humor: How Feminists, Animals, and Other Subversives Talk Truth* (2019). She is currently writing a history of masculinity and childcare.

James Wolfinger holds a joint appointment in history and education at DePaul University. Jim is the author of *Running the Rails: Capital and Labor in the Philadelphia Transit Industry* (2016) and *Philadelphia Divided: Race and Politics in the City of Brotherly Love* (2007) as well as numerous articles and reviews that have appeared in the *Journal of American History*, *American Historical Review*, *Labor*, *Journal of Urban History*, and *Pennsylvania History*. Jim is currently editing a collection on African American politics in Philadelphia for Temple University Press.

Helena Worthen published several novels and started her teaching career as a Composition Teacher, working at numerous community colleges, state universities, and private nonprofit colleges in the Bay Area. She became active in her union, studied labor education, wrote her PhD thesis on community college literacy practices, and eventually worked as a Labor Educator at the University of Illinois. She currently teaches in the Labor Relations and Trade Unions Department at Ton Duc Thang University in Ho Chi Minh City, Vietnam, but lives most of the time in California and Vermont.

Cindy Roberts Yarber obtained her BA in Foodservice Management in 1982. She managed corporate restaurants for ten years. When she was ready to start a family, she used her management degree to build a thriving preschool and daycare business for twenty-four years. She is currently retired.

Maochun "Miles" Yu is a professor of East Asia and Military/Naval History at the U.S. Naval Academy (USNA). His books include *OSS in China: Prelude to Cold War* (1997) and *The Dragon's War: Allied Operations and the Fate of China, 1937–1947* (2006). He is the recipient of USNA's Top Researcher Award, U.S. Navy Special Action Award, and U.S. Navy Meritorious Service Award. He received a doctorate in history from the University of California, Berkeley; a master's degree from Swarthmore College; and a bachelor's degree from Nankai University. He lives in Annapolis, Maryland.

Bob Zebroski is a professor of history and chair of the Liberal Arts Department at the St. Louis College of Pharmacy. Dr. Zebroski's most notable work to date is *A Brief History of Pharmacy: Humanity's Search for Wellness* (2015). His most recent work with coauthor Dr. Dennis Doyle is *Pharmacy Pioneers: The First 150 Years of St. Louis College of Pharmacy* (2019).

Index